CONTEMPORARY FAMILIES: LOOKING FORWARD, LOOKING BACK

Contemporary Families

Looking Forward, Looking Back

Edited by Alan Booth

NCFR

National Council on Family Relations

Preface

The task of preparing a comprehensive collection of essays to survey recent family research and what it means required not only the painstaking efforts of the contributing authors but also careful planning. The articles first appeared in the *Journal of Marriage and the Family*; six are from volumes 50 and 51 and the remainder comprised the November 1990 issue, a decade review of research on marriage and the family. The editorial board of *JMF* played a central role in the planning of these articles. The six essays from volumes 50 and 51 were prompted by a reader poll undertaken early in my term as editor of *JMF*. Readers gave strong support to the idea of commissioning a number of review articles on special topics. After examining the results of the poll, board members assisted in the formulation of the topics and suggested potential authors.

In planning the November 1990 decade review issue of *JMF,* board members rated potential topics for the issue and suggested additional topics as well as the names of scholars who might be invited to contribute to the collection. Their responses were summarized and presented at an editorial board meeting for further deliberation. The stimulating discussion that ensued set this gathering apart from the usual board meetings.

The authors of all 28 essays were asked to write their papers for advanced college students, researchers, and educators; to report on and analyze the best work of the last decade; to provide updates on the latest research methods; and to suggest future directions for scholarly work. Each article was to be comprehensive, interdisciplinary, forward-looking, issue-oriented, succinct, lucid, and free of jargon. With these goals in mind, we sent first drafts of each manuscript to three representative readers for comment. The authors responded with care to the critics' suggestions.

Our aim was to prepare a volume that could serve as a reference work, an advanced-level classroom text, and a guide for policy makers, administrators, and journalists who need state-of-the-art information about family research. We are indebted to the publications committee and board of directors of the National Council on Family Relations, who enthusiastically supported this project from the outset.

ALAN BOOTH, *editor*

Felix M. Berardo   *University of Florida*

Family Research in the 1980s:
Recent Trends and Future Directions

Throughout the eighties, families in the United States as well as in other parts of the world continued to modify their structures and functions to accommodate changes in the larger society and its institutions. Indeed, it is generally acknowledged that the survival of the family unit is highly dependent on its chameleonlike ability to absorb such external challenges and to adapt accordingly. It is during periods of rapid and extensive social change that this resilient character of families is particularly tested.

In the United States the consequences of meeting that challenge are reflected in widespread variations in "the" family. A recent special edition of *Newsweek* on *"The 21st Century Family"* led one author to conclude,

> The American family does not exist. Rather, we are creating many American families, of diverse styles and shapes. In unprecedented numbers, our families are unalike: We have fathers working while mothers keep house; fathers and mothers both working away from home; single parents; second marriages bringing children together from unrelated backgrounds; childless couples; unmarried couples, with or without children; gay and lesbian parents. We are living through a period of historic change in American life. [Footlick, 1990: 9]

None of this, of course, is really new to family scholars. They have been researching and chronicling the evolution of most of these family changes for decades (Berardo, 1980, 1987).

What was evident in the 1980s was a renewed and growing concern, perhaps even a greater sense of urgency, that our marriage and family institutions were being severely weakened and threatened under the press of accelerated and pervasive social change. Much of that change has been taking place within the context of altering attitudes and values; in particular, the long-recognized shifting of emphasis away from familism toward individualism. We are just beginning to acknowledge that exchanging traditional family-oriented values for independence and self-expression may exact a price (Footlick, 1990: 11). That is to say, the expanding range of alternative marriage and family forms brings with it not only new freedoms and responsibilities but also associated problems. The emerging panorama of modern marriage and family types provokes new challenges for their members and the communities in which they are embedded.

This decade review, compiled by family scholars representing a number of scientific disciplines, documents these changes and attempts to gauge their immediate consequences and long-term implications. Each selects one or more salient aspects of marriage and family living and then critically synthesizes the major research completed in that area over the past decade. The present essay presents a brief overview of their assessments. At the same time it identifies several recurrent themes and major issues that emerge in their reviews. Previous decade reviews (Berardo, 1980; Broderick, 1969) offer backgrounds and points of reference for these state-of-the-field reports. As the essays reveal, much progress in theory and research has been made over the past decade. However, it is also evident that much more remains to be done before we can approach

Department of Sociology, University of Florida, Gainesville, FL 32611.

the level of conceptual and methodological clarity essential to building a family science that can offer pragmatic options to families in the 21st century.

FAMILY THEORY

A family science capable of achieving those options must rest upon systematic conceptual thought and firm theoretical foundations. Sprey's appraisal of "mainstream theorizing" in the family field leads him to conclude that the eighties witnessed little conceptual and propositional developments beyond those achieved by the end of the seventies. However, the past decade did produce an increase in the volume and quality of theory-oriented family research.

Progress in this area will require attending to the "unfinished business" of integrating existing conceptual and theoretical schemes into broader, more flexible vocabularies and linking these with appropriate models of explanation. In this connection, Sprey suggests that mainstream family thought would benefit from the challenges posed by alternative approaches and, in particular, the hermeneutic, critical, and feminist perspectives because they contain "ideas that can improve the quality of questioning and explanation and, last but not least, the practical relevance of family scholarship." The extent to which these perspectives will advance the development of family theory in the years ahead remains to be seen.

MARITAL QUALITY

During the seventies, marital quality was one of the most widely studied topics in the field. This interest continued throughout the eighties, adding a modest increment in our understanding of the causes and consequences of marital success. Glenn notes two important methodological developments during this period: an increase in the use of large and representative samples and a rise in longitudinal studies. There was also an increase in the use of advanced statistical techniques. Indeed, several authors in this issue note similar developments in the areas they are surveying. The result is an enhanced ability to probe critical questions surrounding marriage and family life.

Investigators found additional confirmation of the familiar curvilinear relationship between family life stages and marital quality—that is, quality is higher in the preparental and postparental

stages. Considerable research also documented the decline in marital quality following the assumption of the parental role. This was especially noticeable in remarriages involving stepchildren. While cohabitation rose substantially during the past decade, the hypothesis that such activity is associated with subsequent marital success was not supported by the research.

The marital quality literature is characterized primarily by a practical orientation guided by simple propositions revolving around homogamy and marital success. Conceptual confusion and disagreement about the measurement of marital quality and marital success remains. Future progress will require shifting from an emphasis on cross-sectional data to longitudinal or retrospective studies in which marital quality and marital stability are both taken into account.

MARITAL COMMUNICATION

The 1980s witnessed a growing recognition that marital communication difficulties are among the major causes of unhappiness and instability. Hence, there was a greater focus on the causal processes involved in the connection between couple communication patterns and dimensions of the marital relationship. Researchers examined the relationship between marital satisfaction and patterns of dominance and submission, accuracy in encoding and decoding nonverbal cues, information exchange and self-disclosure, and affect.

Methodological advances occurred in the measurement of multiple communications, the refinement of coding schemes, the utilization of social interaction analysis techniques, and model-building designed to account for the relationship between marital communication and marital satisfaction. These models all emphasize that spousal behavior during marital interaction is affected by both present and past affect and cognition. As Noller and Fitzpatrick note, the eighties brought a number of attempts to describe in more detail the cognitive and affective processes that provide the context of marital communication. The continuation of this mode of inquiry in the nineties is essential if we are to gain greater comprehension of the complexities of marital interactions.

MATE SELECTION

Surveys of mate selection research in the seventies revealed a noticeable decline in dating studies, an expanded interest in the courtship process, and a resurgence of the research on love. It was projected that the eighties would move toward a greater concentration on the causes rather than the correlates of marital choice, and this occurred. Two themes characterize the research conducted over the past decade: (*a*) a concern for understanding the causes of developmental change in premarital relationships, and (*b*) an emphasis on testing theories of how relationships are established, maintained, or decline. Pursuit of these themes broadened knowledge of the processes by which close heterosexual unions come about.

The decade saw dramatic shifts toward the postponement of marriage and a substantial rise in cohabitation, as well as an increase in heterogamous unions. New evidence provided additional support for the finding that cohabitation is negatively related to marital stability and to other indicators of marital quality. Interracial marriages tripled over the decade, a trend suggesting that heterogamous patterns of mate selection will continue into the nineties.

The role of social psychological influences on mate selection was also pursued, with an emphasis on the interface between social network ties and the continuity or discontinuity of premarital relationships. Propositions from exchange theory and theories of distributive justice have dominated this area. However, research on love and romance, the nonrational elements in mate selection, also thrived during the decade. New theories were proposed and old ones were elaborated regarding the content and organization of love.

Surra notes the emergence of several new developmental models of mate selection as promising alternatives to the now familiar stage or filter models. These new models should prove useful in the decade ahead, where interest in studying the continuity and discontinuity of relationships over time is apt to be even more salient than it was in the eighties.

FEMINIST PERSPECTIVES: GENDER

The delineation of distinct feminist perspectives on marriage and the family was initiated in the seventies and gained widespread momentum in the eighties. The insistence on viewing marital and familial role definitions within wider systems of economic and political structures and ideologies has led to a reconceptualization of sex roles and

the emergence of gender as a pivotal concept. Thompson and Walker review the growing research on the complexity of gender specialization by focusing on three major domains—marriage, wage and family work, and parenthood. Within each of these, the variant experiences of men and women are stressed in relation to family life. Scholars are encouraged to conceptualize gender in terms of its relational or interactional properties rather than as an individual characteristic of males or females or an assigned or assumed role. In their view, "Gender in families includes structural constraints and opportunities, beliefs and ideology, actual arrangements and activities, meanings and experiences, diversity and change, and interaction and relation." This broader view may help to extend our understanding of the nature and persistence of gender differences and specialization in families.

The feminist view of the gendered nature of work-family linkages as historically specific social constructions, with different implications for women and men, marked a major theoretical reorientation—one that dramatically challenges traditional structures of the work-family system and the division of labor. It also centers attention on the allocation of resources, especially money, within the household in determining the status of wives and mothers. Ferree concludes that the feminist perspective on marriage and family issues can be expected to continue its challenge of earlier ideologies through its ability to reconceptualize both women's and men's roles in relation to the larger economic and political structures.

PARENT-CHILD RELATIONSHIPS AND DAY CARE

The decade witnessed efforts to better specify the factors and processes that have an impact on parent-child relationships beyond demographic indices and to examine multiple determinants of parenting. These include studies of the role that behavioral and temperamental characteristics of children play in shaping the child-parent relationship, the effect of adult psychological health and well-being on parenting, how sex-role attitudes and values influence parental behavior, the influence of the parents' own histories on their subsequent parenting, and the effects of the marital relationship on parent-child relationships.

Throughout the decade, evidence accumulated to document associations between early infant-mother attachment security and subsequent socioemotional functioning and competence. As Belsky notes, there is much support for the proposition that cooperation and compliance occur in parent-child relationships in which control is shared and the child's needs and desires are responded to and taken into consideration.

Important developments occurred in both the science and ecology of day care. Domestic changes in maternal employment patterns have greatly exacerbated the demand for alternative child-care arrangements. Research focused on identifying social structural features of care that are systemically related to daily processes within the child-care setting and to the child's tested functioning. It is important that studies analyzing the developmental outcomes of contrasting ecologies of day care be continued in order to untangle the complex and sometimes controversial issues involved.

Marital Dissolution

The significant rise in marital dissolutions gave impetus to a broad and accelerated research agenda in the 1980s that focused on the causes of divorce. White's review of this effort encompasses macro-structural approaches, life-course and demographic factors, and marital processes. Most of the findings were derived from secondary analyses of large data sets designed for other purposes. The result is that our knowledge of the demography of divorce has advanced significantly while our understanding of the social psychological factors leading to marital instability remains limited. More process research is essential if we are to grasp the complex dynamics of marital instability. The paucity of theoretical development in divorce analysis must be overcome to help us integrate and understand current findings and to give direction to future explorations.

Consequences of Divorce

Research on the causes of divorce has been accompanied by a proliferation of literature on the multiple consequences of divorce, much of it centered on adult adjustment to the health and economic aftermaths, especially for women and children, of this experience. Kitson and Morgan point up the need for instruments that better capture changes in standard of living following the complex transitions of divorce. A more multidimensional view of the consequences of divorce that takes into account the major adjustment dimensions for the participants is necessary to develop an understanding of this transition. We need to explore the role that mediation services play in relation to postdivorce accommodations.

Several legal issues were researched over the past decade. The focus of greatest attention and controversy was on the various types of joint custody. Complete evaluation of the consequences of joint custody arrangements awaits better-designed, controlled studies. While evidence is mounting that economic settlements under no-fault divorce laws are less advantageous to women, the broader impact of this legislation has yet to be gauged adequately in terms of expected benefits.

The long-term implications of divorce for adults and children demand fuller exploration. Demo and Acock's assessment of the scientific evidence concerning the impact of divorce on children points to serious inconsistencies and methodological deficiencies that future research must address. They cautiously conclude that "the pattern of empirical findings suggests that children's emotional adjustment, gender-role orientation, and antisocial behavior are affected by family structure, whereas other dimensions of well-being are unaffected." While there is some indication that many of the effects of parental divorce on children may be of a temporary nature, additional confirmation is needed.

Remarriage and Stepfamilies

In the last decade review, it was predicted that reconstituted families and the complexity of interrelationships they encompassed would emerge as a critical topic in the eighties. Indeed, the past decade has clearly been the most productive period for research on remarriage and stepfamilies. Studies of stepchildren in terms of psychological effects, cognitive effects, social attitudes and behaviors, and family relations were the major focus of this latest literature. However, nonresidential stepparent-child relationships remain underresearched, despite the fact that they appear to be significantly related to marital satisfaction. The latest studies focused on marital satisfaction, well-being in marriage, and older persons and remarriage. The latter area has basically been ignored by researchers, but as our population ages, studies of older marriages should achieve greater prominence.

The past decade brought a slight increase in efforts to test theoretical propositions and to build theory related to remarriage and stepfamilies. However, research in this area still contains a number of critical inconsistencies and methodological shortcomings. Moreover, the deficit-comparison model, which assumes greater problems among reconstituted families compared to nuclear families, has blinded researchers to the complexity of stepfamily forms. As Coleman and Ganong correctly point out, adherence to this model also leads to erroneous assumptions concerning stephouseholds and stepfamilies. Much remains to be done before we can speak with confidence about this large, diverse, and growing population.

ADOLESCENCE

The study of adolescence during the 1980s saw a shift in focus from individual development to the social context in which physical, cognitive, and emotional development takes place. There was a renewed emphasis on the family context of adolescent development and behavior, particularly parental control and support. Gecas and Seff observe that studies consistently found parental support and control to be consequential for a wide range of socialization outcomes. However, these two dimensions need further refinement and specification if we wish to achieve better comprehension of the myriad connections between family relations and adolescent self-images, sexuality (including teenage childbearing), educational and work orientations, and delinquency.

Additional investigations reflected the perennial theme of conflict and stress, value congruences between adolescents and their parents (the generational-gap theme), and the influence of the peer group in the socialization of the young (the adults-versus-youth-culture theme). Unfortunately, studies utilizing bidirectional and reciprocal models of parent-adolescent relations were comparatively scarce, as was research on fathering behavior. While the decade produced little theoretical advancement in this area, it did offer the promising momentum of the life course orientation to research, along with a growing interdisciplinary consciousness.

FAMILIES IN LATER LIFE

Research on later-life families rose sharply during the 1980s and centered around couple relations, divorce, widowhood, remarriage, childless families, sibling relations, grandparenthood, and family caregiving. Brubaker identifies numerous and interesting future research challenges for each of these areas. Given the rising population of older families, it is imperative that we continue to assess the consequences of the caregiving responsibility for familial relationships and for the larger society. Studies are needed on how caregivers and other family members interface with formal agencies to secure supports for older parents and relatives.

Brubaker concludes that the thrust of later-life family research during the 1980s was similar to that of the seventies in that the majority of studies were at the micro level, with a major emphasis on internal transactions between family members. If this assessment is correct, then a message from the last decade review bears repeating: we need to give greater attention to the macroenvironment and its impact on the older families' microenvironment—the effect of pension provisions, service programs, changes in medical care provisions, and so on. Family-bureaucratic linkages in particular offer some of the most challenging opportunities in the nineties.

A rapidly expanding literature has evolved regarding the lifelong relations between older parents and their adult children. Mancini and Blieszner examine that literature with respect to dominant themes of roles and responsibilities, parent-child involvements (including contact and exchange patterns, assistance, and support), individual well-being, relationship quality, and caregiving by adult children. The research findings repeatedly confirm a significant amount of instrumental and affective intergenerational involvement. Moreover, it is clear that the qualitative dimensions of filial responsibility—affection, for example—and not simply direct assistance, are especially meaningful to older parents. The nuances of reciprocities of exchange between generations are important to understanding the quality of adult child–older parent relations.

During the eighties researchers continued their efforts to clarify the effects of the extended empty-nest period. The consequences of "refilling the empty nest," either by adult children returning to the parental home or by middle-aged adults assuming the care of older parents—that is, multi-generational households—needs further explora-tion. Mancini and Blieszner's arguments for either reconceptualizing the concept of well-being or else "to cease correlating every family variable in sight with it" should be heeded. The related call for the future research agenda in family gerontology to move beyond the older parent-child dyad to the study of whole families is well taken. Indeed, such a thrust is essential to developing a more represen-tative picture of families in later life.

RELIGION AND THE FAMILY

For a variety of reasons, studies of the relation-ships between religion and the family have lagged behind most other areas of family scholarship. The dominant approach has been to emphasize the importance of religious belief systems in pro-viding a moral base that supports marital and family behavior. Thomas and Cornwall suggest that a more explicit conceptualization of those aspects of the belief system that influence behavior is needed—for example, in explaining the long-documented positive relationship be-tween religiosity and marital satisfaction.

They also call for a shift to analyses of the im-pact of family influences on major dimensions of religiosity. This will require greater meth-odological advances and the development of alter-native paradigms to the dominant secularization model. Scholars in the decade ahead are encour-aged to study not only how changes in religion and family are associated, but also how these two institutions are related to the economic and political realms.

BLACK FAMILIES

The 1970s witnessed some disturbing shifts in black family life, namely, dramatic increases in teenage pregnancies, out-of-wedlock births, single-parent households, and marital dissolu-tions. The 1980s saw a tremendous increase in the diversity and breadth of studies designed to assess these and other changes and relate them to current and emergent ideological perspectives on the black family. In the process, models of black family life that stressed their resilient-adaptive features gained greater prominence, although remnants of the earlier pathological-disorganiza-tion or cultural-deviant perspective are still evi-dent.

The racial comparative rationale and frame-work, in which white behaviors are designated as the standard, and which guided much of the earlier research, was increasingly called into ques-tion. The extensive review by Taylor, Chatters, Tucker, and Lewis reveals the emergence of a more sensitive and balanced depiction of black family life. They caution, however, that "to deny the existence of problems [among significant numbers of black families] or to underestimate their impact would be both naive and irresponsi-ble. Likewise, to permit their existence to dominate or restrict the research agenda and/or compromise the research process in relation to black families would be equally detrimental." It is a note of caution germane to the family science enterprise in general.

HISPANIC FAMILIES

The research perspective on Hispanic families underwent a noticeable change in the 1980s because of a growing population emanating from massive immigration, internal migration, and high fertility. The diversity of the Hispanic population gradually gained recognition. This was accom-panied by a shift from a stereotypic cultural model of family life, characterized by rigidity, authoritarianism, and a patriarchal structure, to a social adaptation perspective based on themes of family metamorphoses, resilience, flexibility, and cohesion in the face of changing social en-vironments and economic circumstances.

Gender roles in the Hispanic family continued to be a primary area of conjecture. However, the implication of the adaptive perspective is that gender role expectations can and will change as social conditions require. Hence, increasing atten-tion was turned toward improving understanding about how family relations are affected by the ac-culturation process.

Vega is led to conclude that much conjecture and recitation of old work remains. Without greater comparability of findings it is impossible to draw firm conclusions about similarities or dif-ferences among Cuban, Puerto Rican, or Mexican American families. As we commented in the pre-vious decade review, the overriding task is to de-velop theory and research capable of producing a balanced account of the strengths and weaknesses of minority families.

ADOLESCENT CHILDBEARING

Evidence accumulated over the decade provided additional documentation of the range of negative consequences of adolescent childbearing, including lower social and economic attainment of the teenage parents, and higher rates of marital dissolution, poverty, and welfare dependency. There is also much evidence that the children of adolescent parents tend to be at risk of poorer health, reduced cognitive development, lower school performance, and problem behavior.

Establishing the causes and the prevention of teenage parenthood remains high on the research agenda for the future. The influence of the family, the peer group, and cultural norms on adolescent sexual behavior require further specification. Additional work on the major determinants of contraceptive behavior is called for, given that STDs and AIDS place sexually active adolescents at risk of serious and potentially fatal health consequences. Miller and Moore observe that because many adolescent pregnancy issues are immersed in personal and cultural values, there are often conflicting views about how research and policy agendas should be pursued. Despite such differences, the scientific community must move forward to address the basic questions and critical implications raised by a growing volume of adolescent pregnancy-related behaivor.

FAMILY VIOLENCE

Family violence became an established sub-discipline during the 1980s, with an expanded literature encompassing child abuse and neglect, courtship aggression, spousal abuse, and elder abuse. Research seeking to identify the causes of violence was conducted throughout the decade but was augmented by extensive analyses of the consequences of being a victimized child or woman.

Concern for the serious social-psychological effects of child sexual abuse gave rise to considerable interest in developing prevention and intervention programs. Identifying factors that increase a child's risk for sexual abuse is of considerable importance to the implementation of such efforts. Thus, the eighties witnessed the ex-pansion of experimental field studies and clinical tests that assessed the effectiveness of intervention strategies designed to ameliorate or prevent wife and child abuse.

Gelles and Conte conclude that while the study of violence has broadened to include dimensions not recognized a decade ago, the field still needs to integrate its empirical findings into more refined and better tested theories. That conceptual task, along with the continued assessment of intervention schemes, should have high priority on the agenda for the nineties.

THE FAMILY AND HEALTH

Analyses of significant associations between marital and family relations and health were prominent over the last decade. Studies confirmed that, compared to the single, separated, divorced, or widowed, married persons generally exhibit better physical health, greater psychological well-being, and lower mortality. Socioemotional support and economic well-being explain much of the positive effects of marriage. There is now strong evidence that social support improves psychological well-being, which in turn improves physical health and survival.

The association of low socioeconomic status with poorer mental and physical health has been well documented. Ross, Mirowsky, and Goldsteen call attention to the process of structural amplification in which "low education, poverty, and low support feed on each other, magnify each other's impact *on* sickness in the family, and magnify the impact *of* sickness in the family."

A sense of control over one's own life may be one of the most important determinants of psychological and physical well-being, and one of the most important links between family status and health. Chronic economic difficulties decrease feelings of mastery, instrumentalism, and control, and increase feelings of powerlessness and a fatalistic outlook, which in turn have a negative impact on well-being and problem-solving ability. In contrast, people in higher socioeconomic positions achieve a sense of control that enhances their family problem-solving actions and their well-being. How family characteristics affect this sense of control poses important questions for future research on the impact of the family on health.

PARENTAL EMPLOYMENT AND FAMILY LIFE

Research on parental employment and family life, fueled by long-term trends of wives and mothers entering the labor force, continued to attract scientific inquiry during the 1980s. The application of microeconomic theory to this area has much potential, given its ability to integrate within a single framework the description and analysis of a variety of family-related topics. The theory has suggested a number of hypotheses, motivated the production of new data, and stimulated the application of sophisticated econometric techniques. Attempts to integrate sociological and economic ideas may provide the foundation for a more comprehensive and inter-disciplinary theory.

While traditional arguments regarding the nature of work-family conflicts are now familiar themes, investigators pursued these notions in innovative contexts during the eighties. The pressures and potential role disagreements in dual-earner and dual-career marriages came under particular scrutiny. Clearly, employed wives and mothers still bear major responsibility for housework and frequently compromise their own aspirations to accommodate family needs and husbands' careers.

Research utilizing work socialization perspectives and social stress perspectives began calling attention to the influence of varied and changing work environments on individuals' well-being and their marital and family life. Menaghan and Parcel's survey cites evidence that economic pressures profoundly affect parental feelings of mastery and self-sufficiency, heighten distress, and color the quality of marital and parent-child interactions.

In the coming decade, investigators will need to devote greater attention to the effects of varying working conditions, the sequencing of jobs, employment, and unemployment, as well as underemployment, on family outcomes. Analyses that propose and evaluate solutions to the role strains in dual-worker and single-earner families—solutions "unfettered by traditional sex role assumptions"—will be particularly important in the years ahead.

Spitze shows the direction such analyses are likely to take, in her overview of the past 15 years of a wide range of research devoted to gauging (a) the effects of women's employment on the forma-tion and dissolution of marriage, marital quality, and spouse health and well-being, (b) the division of housework and its relation to issues of power and equity, (c) issues relating to the interaction of husbands' and wives' jobs, (d) the relation between women's employment and fertility, child care, and other outcomes for children, and (e) the impact of female employment on extended family relations.

The accumulated evidence has in large part neutralized earlier views that stressed the negative consequences of women's working outside the home for husband-wife relations and for children. The rapid increase of dual-earner couples has shifted the research emphasis to the resulting accommodations in marital and family relations and responsibilities. This focus on the internal dynamics of husband-wife negotiations will no doubt continue throughout this decade.

MOTHER-ONLY FAMILIES

Among the most significant changes in the national demographic profile of families in the United States has been the proportional rise in mother-only families. As McLanahan and Booth observe, single motherhood has become increasingly commonplace over the past three decades. This has provoked considerable controversy and debate among researchers, policy makers, and the public. They examine mother-only families with respect to their economic and social well-being, their long-term consequences for children, and their role in the politics of gender, race, and social class.

Mother-only families exhibit higher levels of poverty and economic insecurity than other families. Their low income is in large part a reflection of (a) the low earning capacity of the mother, (b) the lack of child support from the nonresidential father, and (c) insufficient government subsidies. These and other conditions place children in different types of mother-only families in a disadvantaged position across a wide range of socioeconomic outcomes, and produce several negative intergenerational consequences. Research initiatives in the nineties should continue to (a) explore the internal dynamics of member relations within mother-only families, which may serve to correct negative stereotypes about their lifestyles and values, and (b) assess the possibilities for enhancing their economic well-being while at the same time reducing their economic vulnerability. The latter task will be especially difficult. As the authors note, analyses of mother-only families ''are never totally objective but are fraught with the conflicting values and biases of the different interest groups that are affected by the phenomenon.''

ECONOMIC DISTRESS AND FAMILY RELATIONS

Several contributors to this volume note that shifts in economic and family structure must be taken into account if we are fully to understand the effects of related stress among families. For the first time the decade review attempts to synthesize the empirical literature on relationships between components of economic distress and family relations. Employment instability and uncertainty, economic deprivation, and economic strain have been found to be negatively related to individual adjustment, marital and family satisfaction, and the quality of family relations.

Several problem-focused coping resources and behaviors, such as the use of social supports and monitoring expenditures, which mediate relationships between economic distress and individual or familial responses, are being identified and measured. Voydanoff suggests that future progress in this area requires expanding the traditional focus on unemployment among men to include other aspects of economic distress, especially employment uncertainty. In the decade ahead the complementary theoretical approaches evident in this area—life events, family stress, and life course analysis—will need more complete integration. This is necessary if we are to achieve clarity in our knowledge of the relations between economic distress and family life.

MARRIAGE AND FAMILY THERAPY

Data on organizational memberships, certification, and licensure indicate that in the 1980s marriage and family therapy was achieving recognition as an emerging profession. Piercy and Sprenkle review the extensive conceptual and empirical developments taking place within a wide range of marital and family therapies. The decade was characterized by efforts to (a) take into account feminist and epistemological critiques, which challenged some of the basic theoretical

tenets of the field; (b) resolve issues concerning the measurement of family health; and (c) develop greater consensus regarding family management of schizophrenia.

Significant research advances are apparent concerning the family therapy of addictive behaviors, sexual disorders, and divorce mediation. However, studies regarding the effects of treatment on children of divorce, or interventions related to single-parent or remarriage households, are largely absent. The most effective treatment variables for family violence and child sexual abuse have yet to be isolated. Research is needed on family therapy as a potential prevention and treatment of AIDS. Marriage and family relationships among aging populations constitute a new frontier for the extension and elaboration of family therapy.

Piercy and Sprenkle conclude that while the field has amassed reasonable evidence for its general efficacy, we know much less about the specificity question: what treatment works best for what problem under what set of circumstances. Pursuing the answers to that question through improved theoretical, methodological, and analytical techniques sets the stage for the research agenda of the nineties. Researchers and clinicians must cooperate in developing programs and therapies to assist families who are coping with stress at high levels in an increasingly complex world.

MARITAL AND FAMILY ENRICHMENT

The related and overlapping area of marital and family enrichment research and programs has shown noticeable progress over the past ten years. The most advanced meta-analytic study of the enrichment field was published at mid-decade, and Guerney and Maxson employ its findings throughout their review. Some theory-based measures appropriate for enrichment research emerged during this period. The eighties also produced studies utilizing better control groups and more sophisticated statistical techniques, as well as more studies employing alternate treatment comparisons and follow-up assessments.

The accumulation of evidence confirmed that enrichment programs can produce improvements in premarital, marital, and family capabilities, and these gains often are sustained over several months. An extensive research agenda for the nineties centers around the major questions of which programs work best for what populations, what makes them best, and how they—and new programs—can be made more efficient, less costly, and better known. This is a formidable task.

FAMILY POLICY

Politicization of family issues continued throughout the 1980s. This was a decade of extremes with respect to family policy in the United States, ranging from attempts to dismantle welfare programs to modest efforts at reform. Controversy centered on the efficacy of government intervention to reduce poverty and promote family well-being. The Family Support Act was passed, linking family welfare payments to job training or work obligations and strengthening child support enforcement strategies, so that families would ultimately become economically independent.

Another family policy debate arose over the question of whether government programs had improved the situation of the elderly at the expense of other groups, especially children. Issues were raised concerning the use of age-based public policies instead of a broader political economy model. The growth in the numbers of frail elderly, and the costs and stress they place on families, was increasingly recognized as problematic. The major policy question of who should bear the increasing costs of long-term care remains unsettled as we enter the nineties.

Much of the controversy surrounding family policy lies in the lack of agreement on objectives. Moreover, as Aldous and Dumon note, a major impediment to sound family policy is its emotional nature, often visible in the actions and statements of highly vocal pressure groups. Policy makers become bogged down in hotly debated ideological and morality issues with respect to such items as family planning and abortion, or child care and parental leave legislation. There is little indication that the sharp differences over the role of families and government will be resolved in favor of more rational solutions in the near future.

CONCLUSIONS

The range and breadth of family scholarship during the 1980s was impressive in terms of empirical output as well as conceptual and methodological advances. Among the major themes that characterize that literature, the dynamic role of economic variables on marriage and family life was given recurrent prominence. Analyses completed in the past decade repeatedly confirmed what history has already taught us, namely, that changing economic conditions are intimately connected to the state of family health and welfare.

Tracking the implications of the related work-family nexus comprised a second major theme. The multiple ramifications of an ongoing stream of wives and mothers into the labor force were the foci of numerous investigations. These changing employment patterns have prompted challenges to traditional sex and gender role definitions, triggered a strong and persistent wave of renegotiations within the family regarding the division of labor and other matters, and accelerated demands on other institutions to accommodate the realities and requirements of the changing role of women.

A third theme revolves around the growing recognition and acceptance of the diversity of American families and their lifestyles. As I have stated elsewhere, "the mixtures reflected in the pluralism of our society, for example, the immigrant and hyphenated ethnic family units, are real and different. The so-called homogenization of the nation's families (like the elusive melting pot notion) often turns out to be an illusion" (Berardo, 1987: 427). This diversity is reflected in studies over the past ten years of the major minority black and Hispanic populations. Researchers detected a noticeable shift from pathological-disorganization or cultural-deviant perspectives to a greater emphasis on models of minority families that stressed their resilient-adaptive features. However, this shift in orientation should not blind us to the overwhelming obstacles a majority of these families face in seeking economic independence and a healthy home environment.

We now recognize that social and technological changes influence variant family structures, relationships, and values in different ways. In this connection, the research findings forcefully remind us of a fourth major theme—that contemporary families function within the context of an increasingly complex milieu—one that exposes them to considerable conflict and stress. If they are to meet the responsibilities of transmitting basic social values while raising the young to become competent adults, they will require assistance. It is imperative in the decade ahead that scholars and practitioners alike use their expertise to sensitize the public and the policy makers to family needs. Applying updated research knowledge to the development, implementation, and refinement of human resource policies designed to meet those needs should be the overarching objective of the future.

REFERENCES

Berardo, Felix M. 1980. "Decade preview: Some trends and directions for family research and theory in the 1980s." Journal of Marriage and the Family 42: 723–728.

Berardo, Felix M. 1987. "The American family: A commentary." Journal of Family Issues 8: 426–428.

Broderick, Carlfred (ed.). 1971. A Decade of Family Research and Action: 1960–1969. Minneapolis, MN: National Council on Family Relations.

Footlick, Jerrold K. 1990. "What happened to the family?" Newsweek (special edition), Winter/Spring, pp. 8–13.

JETSE SPREY   *Case Western Reserve University*

Current Theorizing on the Family:

An Appraisal

This essay presents an appraisal of current theorizing about the institutions of marriage and the family in the United States. It aims to exemplify rather than explain or in any way treat the process exhaustively. Central to the discussion is a view of theorizing as an intentional activity that occurs within a time-bound sociocultural setting. The current and future course of mainstream family thought is evaluated and a number of rival approaches toward knowledge acquisition are recognized. It is suggested that three of these, hermeneutics, critical theorizing, and feminist thinking, must be considered both challenges and potential sources of enrichment to family scholarship.

The word *theory* comes to us from the Greek *theoria,* which means "to contemplate" and, in past times, also could stand for "looking in wonderment at a deity." Currently, deity seems to have been replaced by the computer screen, while contemplation is regimented by methodologies that aim, in varying ways, to qualify its products as "causal" and/or "scientific." Obviously, we live in a different time. What has not changed, though, is the fact that theorizing remains a human endeavor in which questions and answers are conceived within a unique and time-bound sociocultural setting. The approach taken here reflects this premise.

A representative review of recent theory-oriented work on the family would require far

Department of Sociology, Case Western Reserve University, Cleveland, OH 44106.

more than this relatively brief essay. Instead, the focus is selective and thus colored by personal views. To prevent too much idiosyncracy and arbitrariness, the discussion is anchored but not determined by several recent scholarly assessments of the field. They vary in focus and format but together raise pertinent issues and provide a bridgehead from which to venture into a still disputed and unsettled domain.

A prime source of ideas and facts is Thomas and Wilcox's recent and thorough treatment of the "rise of family theory" (1987). I adopt their notion of "mainstream" to categorize the bulk of contemporary family research and share the view that it is especially its ontological and epistemological underpinnings that are under attack by alternative strategies toward knowledge acquisition.

A second, older source is the often quoted Holman and Burr review of the growth of family theories during the seventies (1980). In addition to its specific content, I see it as representative of other stock-taking efforts (e.g., Broderick, 1971) that have become expected and recognizable "milestones" along the collective path of family theory. A third and slightly different point of reference is found in Berardo and Shehan's treatment of the linkages between family scholarship and the actual changes that occur in the institutions of marriage and the family (1984). What determines the choice of research problems is crucial to the understanding of the current status and future development of our field.

Apart from these publications, a selection of additional sources is used to illustrate rather than exhaust specific topics involving current theorizing on marriage and the family. It contains unpublished working papers, foreign inputs, monographs on substantive topics, and research articles. Their main function is to provide points of reference to the discussion.

"Mainstream" family studies, then, is the central point of reference for this essay; but I see the attention paid to hermeneutic, critical, and feminist persepectives as an essential part of the discussion. Obviously, it is not possible here to deal thoroughly with these latter realms of social thought. I will, however, identify them and attempt to assess the challenge each poses to the premises and professional values that remain associated with most current theorizing on marriage and the family.

AIMS AND PREMISES

The purpose of this essay is to explicate or to "unfold" rather than to causally explain the current state of knowledge acquisition in the domain of marital and family studies. Furthermore, it is not about theory building per se, nor is it a strictly methodological effort. It takes a look at recent trends in theory-oriented family research and contemplates its future course. Of course, the approach taken does reflect conceptual and theoretical premises which, at this point, need to be spelled out briefly.

Family theorizing is seen as a process. It is what theory-oriented family scholars actually do, and as such, its course and outcomes must be understood as a consequence and reflection of the intentions, attitudes, skills, and professional networks of those involved. At the present the term *family theory* serves as a descriptive label rather than as a genuine analytic category. It is of limited explanatory value, and its usage implies more consensus on theoretical issues than actually exists. In a similar vein, the terms *family field* and *discipline* are used here—interchangeably—to identify the professional activities of individuals who are involved in research, theorizing, or clinical work related to the social world of marriages and families. To posit the existence of a "real" family discipline makes analytical sense only if it decisively influences the individual and collective output of its membership. At this time I see no conclusive evidence of that.

The theorizing process is dealt with functionally, and as an intentional activity. So far, assess-

ments of family theory have focused almost exclusively on its linguistic products or theories. Growth is then evaluated formally, that is, on the perceived quality of the development of "metatheory and methodologies of building theory" (Holman and Burr, 1980: 735). This makes sense as long as we judge the structure and validity of theories per se; but if we also wish to comprehend their societal implications, such a basis is too narrow. It is apparent that theorizing about marriages and families is expected to do more than just satisfy our intellectual curiosity. Its relevance and credibility also depend on its potential to instigate effective social policy, improve the quality of marriages and families, and help "emancipate" those whose lives are locked into unfair or oppressive structures (cf. Burr, Herrin, Day, Beutler, and Leigh, 1987). Family theory, then, means many things to its producers and consumers. We have known this for a long time, of course (e.g., Hill, 1981), but a refusal to acknowledge the situation makes it impossible to understand the current challenges to family *theorizing* that are posed by critical theory, the hermeneutic approach, and contemporary feminist thought.

An appraisal of family theorizing obviously cannot ignore formal issues. Its theories must account for marital and familial phenomena, while its methodologies function as "theory selectors" by providing the norms to judge their relative worth (Sarkar, 1983: 1). In this essay both questioning and explanation are seen as the core of theory building. Following Elster (1983: 16–24), I categorize explanations as "causal," "functional," or "intentional." Causal statements represent "the unique mode of explanation in physics," which is "the standard instance and model of a science using causal explanation" (p. 18). Biology, in turn, "is the paradigm for functional explanation, much as physics is for causal and social science for intentional explanation" (p. 19). Finally, behavior is explained intentionally "when we are able to specify the future state it was intended to bring about." This does not mean explanation in terms of a future outcome, because "the intended future state may not come about at all" (p. 70).

These three modes of explanation are different. Intentional explanations, for example, are irrelevant to physics, questionable in biology, and well suited to social science. Needless to say, this does not mean that family scholars cannot or should not opt for causal explanations but rather that the latter's range of application is limited. Equally, the application of functional analysis to the explanation of human behavior is more problematic than to that of animals. It is wrong, therefore, to attack functional analysis as not being "causal." It isn't meant to be. Each approach pursues its own line of questioning and is not directly competitive with any of the others. What sort of explanation *is* appropriate, then, depends a good deal on what it is one wishes to explain.

Questioning, finally, can be seen to differentiate between proximate and ultimate, or final, levels of causality. The former concern the "how," the second the "why" of social phenomena. How, for example, the many forms of human marriage developed is a proximate issue, but why it came into being at all represents an ultimate one. I do not see these levels as totally distinct, but they appear sufficiently separate to warrant recognition.

MAINSTREAM THEORIZING

According to Thomas and Wilcox, family theory can be considered "an instance of mainstream sociological theory, which was in large measure shaped by a positivist heritage in Western thought" (1987: 82). This claim is not new but remains pertinent because, even at first glance, much contemporary family research indeed does reflect, self-consciously or on a taken-for-granted basis, the methodology and professional values of traditional positivist thought.[1] Contemplation, as an attribute of theorizing, has taken a back seat, while understanding remains relevant as long as what must be understood is presented in a proper propositional format.

All this need not be a fault or a liability. It merely places restrictions on theorizing in order to safeguard the presumed validity of its outcomes. Constraints notwithstanding, the volume and quality of theory-oriented family research in recent years appears to be increasing (e.g., Holman and Burr, 1980; Lavee, 1986). I see this as a result of rapid advances in research methodology. In terms of theorizing we still find little sense of direction and not much explicit consensus about priorities attached to problem formulation. Indicative of this is, among other things, the increasing "Balkanization" of our theoretical domain into a multitude of "perspectives" and "mini-

theories," each professing to deal exclusively with a relatively narrow slice of family existence. Berardo and Shehan's question, "Is current family scholarship a reflection of the changing family?" (1984: 577) seems to deserve an affirmative response.

Conceptual and Propositional Frameworks

Hill and Hansen's original identification of conceptual frameworks meant to take a "step that raises the inventory beyond simple accumulation toward real significance" (1960: 299). They accomplished this and were instrumental in establishing conceptualization—that is, the deliberate creation of coherent theoretical vocabularies—as an integral part of family scholarship.[2] More than 25 years later the demand for all-inclusive propositional inventories has abated somewhat, but systematic conceptual thought has proven to be of great value to the family field. But, as Hill himself recognized (cf. 1955), it also created new problems and certainly has shown itself to be no *substitute* for theorizing. Thomas and Wilcox trace the relatively brief but active career of such frameworks in some detail (1987: 85–88). Suffice it to note here that the genesis of not one but several perspectives seems to have peaked with the publication, in 1979, of an ambitious and comprehensive two-volume work, *Contemporary Theories about the Family* (Burr, Hill, Nye, and Reiss). Its stated purpose was "to make Volume I a volume of inductively constructed family theories, while Volume II would be a volume delineating and specifying general sociological and sociopsychological theories and applying them deductively to the family domain" (1979, Vol. 2: xi). At this writing it seems generally agreed that the project was "unsuccessful in creating general theoretical formulations" (Thomas and Wilcox, 1987: 90). Apparently, the plan "to follow Merton's procedures of codification of the middle-range theories from Volume 1 into more general theories by means of inductive processes" (p. 90) did not work. As Thomas and Wilcox write somewhat wryly,

Volume 2 makes one thing clear: The relationship between conceptual framework and theory is still ambiguous. If theory is taken to be an interrelated set of propositions, then constructing more general theory by integrating middle-range theories through the use of different theoretical perspectives did not necessarily produce theory. [1987: 89]

In retrospect, this should have been clear at the outset!

The 22 topical chapters constituting the first volume were not theoretical—even at "middle" range—and frequently only alluded to linkages between descriptive propositions and conceptual frameworks. It is thus remarkable, and indicative of the state of theorizing at that time, that anyone actually expected a final synthesis leading to "more general theories." Descriptive propositions, even if properly formulated and verified, are not prefitted building blocks that—like the compilation of a telephone directory—can be "inductively" synthesized into coherent theory. Even middle-range theorizing—a common excuse for not trying harder—can reflect different levels of questioning and explanation. Perhaps a limited measure of codification and synthesis would have been feasible, but its outcomes could hardly have been more than a series of loosely interconnected and rather vacuous generalizations. In other words, conceptual frameworks and sets of empirical propositions do not theory make. The former are a first stage of theoretical thinking, the latter an appropriate format for the organization of descriptive or theoretical statements.

This is not meant to be a critique of the volumes edited by Burr and his colleagues. Far from it. The topical chapters offered an impressive inventory of family research during the sixties and most of the seventies, while the second volume presented conceptual perspectives, most of which, so far, have remained in use. Finally, the production of this work clearly increased the extent of "organic solidarity," to use a familiar concept, among those who were, in one way or another, involved with its conception, gestation, and ultimate delivery. Its publication, then, solidified a cognitive plateau beyond which neither subsequent conceptual nor propositional efforts seem to have moved noticeably. This is not to say that nothing has happened. Some conceptual schemes continued to attract followers; others declined in popularity. Their use has been debated (e.g., Klein, 1980; Rodman, 1980), but their continuance does not seem in immediate danger. The propositional format, in its turn, has become established further and, in line with developments in research methodology, more closely linked to advanced forms of data analysis, such as causal modeling. Yet, is the news, then, that there is no further news? To answer this a brief assessment of the actual content of the mainstream is in order.

Currents in the Mainstream

As stated earlier, theory-oriented research still seems on the increase. What varies, however, is the way in which individuals integrate "theory" into their work and judge its worth relative to its research-methodological component. There seems an implicit consensus among many that research cannot be kept waiting till the problems connected with the final synthesis of conceptual frameworks, propositional inventories, and general theory are solved to everyone's satisfaction. As a matter of fact, such "finer" points may seem somewhat academic to many research-oriented authors (e.g., Walters, 1986). Yet this orientation apparently does not result in collective randomness, and it is possible to identify some currents in the mainstream.

First, there is, as mentioned, the large segment that, to varying degrees, still operates within a rather clear-cut positivist frame of reference. Here we note, among other things, the clear distinction between ideas and reality, theory and fact, subjectivity and objectivity, quantitative and qualitative analysis, and discovery versus verification. Furthermore, there is the still widespread faith in the potential of statistical and measurement techniques to "bridge" such troublesome gaps (cf. Sprey, 1987). The ultimate aim of theorizing is seen to be explanation patterned after the physical science model, which, in turn, should lead to valid prediction and, where technically feasible, control. Understandably, most published theory-oriented research in this category is straightforwardly inductive.[3]

A brief look at some recent publications may help clarify the above.[4] Waite and her colleagues, for instance, base their question about "the consequences of time spent in non-family living" for young people (1986) primarily on reported trends observed in recent census data and formulate their hypotheses mainly on those grounds. Only one brief allusion to "life course theory" is made (1986: 541). Their finding that the plans and attitudes—toward work, family size, and family roles—of young women are more affected than those of young men raises a host of further questions but does not directly feed into life-course theory or any other perspective, for that matter.

The authors of a different article propose that, because of increasing life expectancy, current cohorts can be expected to pass more time in family roles, such as parent, child, or spouse (Watkins and Menken, 1987). Aided by a simulation of demographic conditions in 1800, 1900, 1960, and 1980 they explore how much of this possibility actually has been realized and conclude that "much of the potential offered by longer life spans has not been achieved" (1987: 346). They identify this increased new time spent in conjointly existing family positions as a potential source of societal change. Again, however, it remains up to the reader to formulate direct linkages with either conceptual or theoretical perspectives. A profusion of the solid inductive research exemplified by these two papers supports my contention that its authors evaluate their work—including its theoretical component—largely on its verificational quality. Large samples or data sets, for example, are desirable ipso facto because they allow for broader generalizations. Longitudinal designs are seen to be advantageous because they allow for the discovery of social trends and, thus, add a much-needed third dimension to findings and conclusions. By definition, multivariate analyses outrank simpler statistical techniques, while precise and high-level measurement procedures are considered to be a sine qua non to valid theorizing. It is no coincidence, then, that the rejection of qualitative analysis by many mainstream scholars is based primarily on research-methodological criteria; theoretical considerations, such as the quality of questioning, have little to do with it. Finally, explanation is almost always on a proximate level. Ultimate, or final, causality is delegated to other—nonscientific—domains: "we must in our role as scientists, leave the search for ultimate reality to religion and to those philosophies of life that strive to present the total 'truth' about any subject" (Reiss, 1986: 5).

Inductive theorizing is not necessarily "middle range," for it may involve broad generalizations or complex models designed to explain a maximum amount of variance in our designated dependent variables. But through the nature of its problem formulation, it remains close to reality. It is not surprising, then, that its findings and interpretations seem to follow, rather than precede, what happens in the world of marriages and families. Predictions often extend what currently is visible into a foreseeable future. For example:

> . . . recent information for the United States on marriage, divorce, and living arrangements has been used to arrive at reasonable projections of these variables. Underlying the projections is the implicit assumption that the direction of recent changes will continue but that the rate of change will be moderated during future years. As additional relevant information is gathered through demographic methods, the projections presented here can be appropriately revised. [Glick, 1984: 24]

The intention, then, is to identify and describe trends, make sense of the past on the basis of what we know about the present and, if reasonable, project them into the future (e.g., Cherlin, 1981).

Since the main focus of this essay is on the theorizing process, the aims and expectations of those involved are of major interest. As such, it is pertinent to consider the following comment by the senior author of the most recent, and quite comprehensive, handbook on marriage and the family:

> The task of the family scholar is to continue to map families over time and to provide the kinds of information for families to control their own futures and for governmental elites to use such information in the best interest of families. [Sussman, 1987: xli]

There is a Comtean message in the above, but it is the notion of "mapping" that is essentially relevant here. Webster's Dictionary defines a map as a "plane surface representation of a region of the earth or sky." Most are purely descriptive, an exception being weather maps, which include arrows indicating the expected course of air masses and fronts. This offers, I believe, a good analogy to mainstream inductive theorizing. Its intended "maps" or inventories detail familial and marital reality and, wherever possible, include the "arrows" that depict forces that may direct its future course. However, meteorology, despite the fact that the accuracy of its weather forecasts parallels that of family "science," has a better theoretical foundation than the family field. Those arrows reflect a knowledge base that is not *on* the map, which means that faulty weather predictions are, as a rule, better explained than their counterparts in family studies.

Inventories of empirical knowledge are essential to the comprehension of the changing nature of contemporary marriage and the family. They provide a foundation for further questioning and for explanations that can be monitored and corrected, with the aid of computer technology. Augmented by feedback from exploratory research and journalistic accounts, such maps allow us to follow the course of phenomena such as divorce and remarriage, dual-earner families, fertility, marital interaction, and domestic violence, to mention just a few. Furthermore, technological devices such as the telephone (cf. Gelles, 1984) narrow the time lag between what is happening "out there" and our existing inventories. In each instance, however, the content of such scholarship remains, in Berardo and Shehan's terms, "a reflection of the major changes that it studies" (1984: 577).

Mainstream work need not be atheoretical. In fact, the line between descriptive and theory-oriented research is hard to draw. From the standpoint of this essay—theorizing as an intentional effort—research conducted to achieve conceptual quality and that designed to verify theoretical statements both are theoretical in nature. Because of the advances in the quality of statistical reasoning among family researchers, a mode of inductive theorizing—considered "causal" and patterned after the exemplar of physical science—is likely to grow in popularity in mainstream family studies. Its intentions and explanatory mode are increasingly perceived as "theoretical" (cf. Glass, Bengtson, and Dunham, 1986; Lavee, McCubbin, and Patterson, 1985), and as such, this brand of explanatory "modeling" is likely to become an important type of thinking among quantitatively oriented family scholars.

A second mainstream current encompasses theorizing of a more deliberate a priori nature. Much of this work remains in the positivist tradition, but its stated aim and design places its theoretical component on equal footing with its verificational approach. In such cases, especially in qualitative work, theoretical intent becomes an integral part of the research strategy and data analysis. They are no longer separable. In this category, some authors employ one or a combination of existing conceptual schemes; others may move directly toward the development of a theoretical or propositional structure. Because of the plethora of conceptual schemes, perspectives, and incipient theoretical orientations in current family scholarship, this category is even broader,

and harder to describe, than the previous one. With this caveat in mind, a few illustrations are presented.

Reiss's book about human sexuality, for instance, proposes a "scholarly, integrated, societal-level explanation of human sexuality" (1986: 2) and is based on "a new approach that is restricted only by the scientific principles of sociology" (p. 3). Indeed, the book offers new cross-cultural information and a tentative theory that is presented in both narrative and propositional form. But its wholistic or "societal" approach and strict adherence to positivist methodology are quite Durkheimian and solidly within the mainstream tradition.

A different "work of comparative social science" (Paige and Paige, 1981), presents an explanation of "the nature and distribution of reproductive rituals in preindustrial societies" to serve as a starting point "for the analysis of beliefs about women and reproduction in industrial societies" (p. 2). As in the previous case, the authors use cross-cultural data and propose a "new theory that interprets reproductive rituals as political tactics used to solve social dilemmas that become crucial at certain points in the human reproductive cycle" (p. 43). Their theoretical approach falls within the context of exchange theory but also contains a functional component in its search for a deeper meaning. The outcome is a challenging and informative book that demonstrates what can be accomplished within the mainstream tradition; but there is also an indication of its limitations when it comes to asking what, if anything, underlies the exchange processes that gave rise to the ritual practices and arrangements that serve to channel unresolvable conflicts of interest away from violence into competitive but peaceful rituals.

There are other examples of exploratory and confirmatory theorizing in this category. Giles-Sims's book on wife abuse (1983) is a good qualitative study that approaches its complex topic in a systems perspective. Kaufman's important study of women who return to an orthodox Jewish life (1985) combines a qualitative approach with a well-articulated feminist perspective. Molm's recent paper—one of several publications by this author on the use of power—compares "predictions from three theoretical perspectives . . . in a laboratory experiment on power" (1986: 1356). Finally, we note that theoretical orientations may be "implicit" in published work:

> . . . the selection of family outcome measures seemingly has proceeded with little theoretical guidance. Instead, researchers have appeared to proceed by focusing on those aspects of family life that would appear to have some prima facie connection to work schedules. . . . Yet, implicitly this research is based in a rudimentary conception of role theory. As Clark, Nye and Gecas write, " . . . roles compete for scarce time." [Kingston and Nock, 1985: 621]

Such "undercover" theorizing can be judged in two ways. It can be seen as indicative of an unwillingness or inability to make one's theoretical ideas explicit, but it also may reflect the premise that some concepts or ideas are so well known that they need no explication. It is, then, up to the informed reader to decide which is which.

Unfinished Business

I see the "unfinished business" within the realm of mainstream theorizing as threefold. Below I will offer a brief sketch of what seems to be involved. The first problem concerns the integration of existing conceptual schemes into broader, more flexible vocabularies. Most current approaches are not necessarily unique in the sense that their underlying theoretical and methodological assumptions contradict those of *all* others. Nor are they necessarily competitive with each other. Of the five frameworks presented in the book by Burr and his coworkers, for example, only the phenomenological one (McLain and Weigert, 1979) reflects ontological and epistemological premises that clearly differ from those that underlie the rest. To conceptualize families as "systems in conflict" (Sprey, 1969), for example, does not preclude the analysis of their negotiated order of process within a perspective of conflict *and* exchange. Moreover, both these approaches are "systemic," which, in turn, calls for the incorporation of ideas derived from systems thinking. In fact, syntheses like these are taking place—it would be remarkable if they did not—but often somewhat haphazardly. Authors tend to choose one perspective and include others implicitly through the ad hoc borrowing of concepts. Conceptual and theoretical integration, therefore, is not a new idea (e.g., Jurich, 1987; Ritzer, 1975); but so far it has not deliberately been pursued by family scholars. One reason for this may be the erroneous belief that most existing conceptual

frameworks—like Kuhn's "paradigms"—are competitive and, as such, can develop only by replacing rather than incorporating "rivals." Integration of this kind requires not only "thinking things through" but also "acting through." As long as this does not happen we will continue to find many barren islands in the mainstream.

Conceptual integration may be "horizontal" as well as "vertical," and at times must be both to be effective. If we reconsider the possible synthesis of exchange and conflict within a "realist" theoretical perspective (cf. Outhwaite, 1983; Wilson, 1983: 166–175), bargaining and negotiation can be considered "surface" phenomena and be explained within a Homans-type, individualistic exchange perspective. On the other hand, the deeper structural "contradictions" that underlie surface inequalities—what is being negotiated about—perhaps can be better understood within a conflict or structural-functional perspective. In other words, if we move to a more "layered" version of reality, it makes sense to structure our levels of questioning and explanatory modes accordingly.

The second issue concerns modes of explanation. Family scholars must deal with the selection, use, and possible combination of these in a more purposeful and articulate way. This would involve, among other things, the proper linking of explanatory levels with appropriate questioning, but also the integration of conceptual vocabularies with selected explanatory levels. For example, explanation in both symbolic interactionist and phenomenological perspectives is "intentional." But it is also apparent that a causal explanation of intentions—regardless of their outcomes—is compatible with most symbolic interactionist thought but not with that of phenomenology. In a similar vein, structuralist and macro exchange perspectives can be integrated with functional thinking. But the compatibility of functionalist reasoning with a rational-choice perspective or individualistic exchange theory is questionable. It should be added, at this point, that at least one major current perspective—the life-course framework—seems broad enough to allow for conceptual linkages with all three modes of explanation (e.g., Elder, 1975).

Finally, there is the problem of the still ambiguous relationship between conceptualization and theory building. To deal with it, family theorists must develop vital centers from which their questioning can derive its focus and direction. I mean by this "images" or "models," which describe what Polanyi called "the intimation of something hidden, which we may yet discover" (1967: 22–23). These theoretical models are idealized and abstract, and they can be constructed with ordinary language or mathematics. They are not intended to "fit" reality but rather to provide a way to think about it. They may vary a great deal in specificity, but the less specific do not determine the more specific ones because "there are many ways of filling in a highly nonspecific model to achieve a highly specific version of that model" (Giere, 1984: 12).

In theorizing about marriage and the family, such models provide a speculative and, it is hoped, imaginative starting point that will lead to the selection—or formulation—of a conceptual vocabulary, the formulation of a line of questioning, a choice of explanatory mode, and, of course, a methodology. These choices are not independent—they all reflect the ontological and epistemological premises that shape our thinking—and, therefore, can be made in any order. All this is not new, of course. All axiomatic theorizing on the family and, I assume, also most inductive efforts are guided by questions that reflect at least some image of what it is one expects to discover. Such systematic "imagining" is lacking in much mainstream family theorizing. It may be fed by many sources: tacit knowing, counterfactual reasoning, or the interpretation of descriptive information. Concepts allow us to think theoretically and propositions provide a deductive format, but neither is a substitute for the imagination that must give rise to content.

Finally, before an appraisal of what appear to be the main challenges to current family scholarship, it must be emphasized that mainstream theorizing cannot be considered to be static or unchanging. Within the mainstream tradition, family scholars are moving toward a more flexible form of logical empiricism (cf. Jurich, 1987: 1; Thomas and Wilcox, 1987: 94–95). Rigid adherence to "scientism" seems to be relaxing somewhat, while the dualistic thinking that is so characteristic of traditional positivist thought is under attack. These changes are evident and bound to continue. They are likely to improve the quality and relevance of family scholarship but are not in direct response to the challenges outlined below.

CHALLENGES TO THE MAINSTREAM

To challenge implies being critical, which, in turn, often means to judge adversely. Negative judgments, however, that do not reflect a clear alternative or a "better way" are, even when valid, not overly helpful. The three approaches identified below propose a range of alternatives to current mainstream family theorizing. But their potential to provide—singly or jointly—a clear, unambiguous alternative remains, at this writing at least, an open question. I am, therefore, not in a position to suggest or predict the *replacement* of mainstream thinking by hermeneutic, critical, or feminist orientations. Instead, I argue that each of these complex and far from homogeneous approaches contains ideas that can improve the quality of questioning and explanation and, last but not least, the practical relevance of family scholarship. In other words, the challenges posed by these ideas, ranging from the theoretical to the political, can no longer be ignored or trivialized by serious students of marriage and the family.

The methodological question implicit in mainstream family scholarship is: how "scientific" can our theorizing be? The challenges described in the following begin with a *different* question: will being "scientific"—even if feasible—lead to the best possible theoretical understanding of the social institutions of marriage and the family? To which hermeneutic, critical, and many contemporary feminist scholars respond in the negative. Their answers come from different theoretical and philosophical orientations that, regrettably, must be left largely unexplored within the limited context of this essay. Because of such differences, however, it seems appropriate to recognize each challenge, separately and in brief.

Hermeneutics

The idea of *hermeneutics* comes to family scholars from philosophy, general social theory, and methodology. No wonder that it generates not only interest but also confusion. The term traditionally refers to the art or theory of interpretation. It passed from theology into philosophical discourse and, subsequently, into the realm of "human studies," or *Geisteswissenschaften*. Its basic message is well illustrated by the following:

> Every single human expression represents something which is common to many and therefore

part of the realm of objective mind. Every word or sentence . . . [is] only understandable because the person expressing himself and the person who understands him are connected by something they have in common; the individual always experiences, thinks, acts and also understands, in this common sphere. [Wilhelm Dilthey, quoted in Outhwaite, 1985: 24]

So far, to many students of the family, hermeneutics raises primarily a research-methodological issue. It echoes Max Weber's familiar notion of *verstehen*, or interpretative understanding, as a unique tool of intentional explanation, or *Motivationsverstehen* (Weber, 1956: 4). But the thrust of hermeneutics is not just research-methodological. As one of its leading scholars puts it:

From its historical origin, the problem of hermeneutics goes beyond the limits that the concept of method sets to modern science. . . . The hermeneutic phenomenon is basically not a problem of method at all. It is not concerned with a method of understanding. . . . It is not concerned primarily with amassing ratified knowledge which satisfies the methodological ideal of science. [Gadamer, 1975: xi]

Rather, it is concerned with all "modes of experience in which a truth is communicated that cannot be verified by the methodological means proper to science" (p. xii). The assumption that hermeneutics merely offers an alternative research technique to study humans only reverses the positivist duality between "objective" and "subjective" modes of human experience. Hermeneutic thought negates that distinction.

This challenges the assumption, still widely held among family scholars, that "subjective" or "qualitative" research strategies are primarily "mental" and rely only on empathic skills—and/or proclivities—which allow researchers to "understand" the motives, feelings, and attitudes of other humans. Dilthey's earlier comment clearly stresses a shared objectivity below the "communalities" that may exist between individuals. Subjectivity, then, is not just the absence of objectivity or its logical opposite, but rather something that is deliberately added to what we experience as real. Schutz (1970) and like-minded phenomenologists, for example, insist that *"verstehen"* must be considered an essential human way of managing one's daily social life. Interpretative understanding itself, then, becomes a major focus of study rather than a mere tool of social-science research methodology.

A further hermeneutic challenge—one shared with critical and feminist thought—is its stance toward the relationship between theory and practice. One of the central premises of Gadamer's hermeneutics is that "all understanding involves not only interpretation, but also application." "Ethical know-how" in this context is seen as a type of reasoning that "involves a distinctive mediation between the universal and the particular. This mediation is not accomplished by any appeal to technical rules or method . . . or by the subsumption of a pre-given universal to a particular case" (Bernstein, 1985: 272–276). In other words, the uneasy connection between the knowledge provided by empirical research and the information needed by family practitioners (cf. Gelles, 1982) is eliminated. Instead Gadamer proposes a kind of intermediary knowledge "in which both what is universal and what is particular are *co-determined*" (Bernstein, 1985: 275). The reasoning is difficult to grasp, but the challenge is there.

At this point, the direct impact of hermeneutic thought on family theorizing seems limited to the growth of idealistic and/or phenomenologically oriented perspectives. This may occur parallel to or within the mainstream (e.g., McLain and Weigert, 1979). Indirectly—that is, outside of stated phenomenological perspectives—the increasing credibility of interpretation as a research *and* theoretical strategy is reflected in the growing acceptance of so-called qualitative research *within* the mainstream (cf. LaRossa and Wolf, 1985). I see this as testimony to the influence of hermeneutic thinking on questioning in the family field. It is becoming rather clear that many questions about the intrinsic nature of marital and familial process cannot be exhaustively answered through the use of even the most sophisticated quantitative research techniques. Since hermeneutic thought takes this for granted, I assume that its influence on family theorizing will continue to grow.

Critical Thinking

Critical social science, in the Frankfurt tradition, approaches human society not only as it exists but also in the context of what it contains in terms of its possible future. In its current manifestations it reflects the ideas of a range of thinkers, most prominently Karl Marx, Friedrich Engels, and more recently Jurgen Habermas. Marie Osmond, in a recent attempt to articulate its relevance to family theory, searches for common denominators in a "perspective termed *radical critical theory*" (1987: 103). In a relatively thorough overview she brings out the multifaceted nature of this theoretical orientation. For the purpose of this sketch, a simpler description suffices:

> As critical theory, sociology does not take the social world as given, but poses the questions: what types of social change are feasible and desirable, and how should we strive to achieve them? [Giddens, 1987: 157]

As in hermeneutics, the dualities between theory and practice, subjectivity versus objectivity, and the realms of discovery and verification are blurred, while the "counterfactual" becomes a legitimate path to the "factual" in theoretical thinking.

A hypothetical example of critical work would be research aiming to show the ideological—in the Marxian sense—quality of either rational-choice or exchange-theoretical explanations of a negotiated order in contemporary dual-career marriages. Such a study might demonstrate that these approaches leave the structural contradictions that underlie the observable order unexamined. Thinking along such lines indeed may be called "emancipatory," regardless of its political connotations. The author of an essay on the "medicalisation" of marriage in England, for example, shows that the adoption of a "medical model" in marriage counseling was instrumental in

> the creation of a particular set of problems labelled as 'marital' and the existence of a body of trained persons of professional or 'quasi-professional status who exist to 'treat' these problems, guided by a cumulative body of universalistic knowledge, the norms of affective neutrality and peer-group control and guidance. [Morgan, 1985: 37]

This leads to the conclusion that, among other things, "family therapy not only treats families; it also, and at the same time, constructs families and family problems" (p. 52). One might observe, at this point, that this sort of interpretation could equally have been formulated within a number of traditional theoretical perspectives. What makes the above approach "critical," however, is—as I understand it—its intentional expository nature and a presumed willingness of its audience to accept it as such. In this particular instance, for example, it is reasonable to assume that alternative models *could* have been developed to organize the linkages between troubled families and their social environment. This, then, might have given rise to a different form of expertise, different perceptions of what is problematic, and other patterns of dependency among families. And so forth. Critical thought, as it concerns us here, is expository thinking, always linking the actual with the possible and, as such, moving beyond the preoccupation with the observable that constrains the imagination of positivist researchers. Such work is still rare in the family field, and that which exists is likely to pursue its aims in its own way (e.g., Poster, 1978; Zaretsky, 1976).

This diffuseness of the critical challenge makes it difficult for those who find themselves at the receiving end of it to separate the message from the "noise." This problem may be aggravated by the overly adversarial tone of certain critical statements. As an example, Osmond accuses "conventional family sociology" of being "locked in a social-psychological approach" and "unaware of the crucial importance of macro-societal factors external to the family." Furthermore, its "recurrent attempts to construct theory on the basis of reviewing and summarizing research publications are sterile." Finally, family sociology is presumed to be ahistorical and noncomparative, static, conservative, and overly empiricist (1987: 119).

It is quite difficult to react to such an assault. Several of its allegations harbor important elements of truth, but the nature of their delivery tends to trivialize their collective message. Each claim addresses a reified domain of "family sociology." To make sense, such accusations must be redirected from this straw category toward the intentional actions of family scholars. Then it must be shown, rather than proclaimed, that all these people are, among other things, intentionally "ahistorical," "overly social-psychological," and "noncomparative" in their scholarship. Frankly, I do not believe this to be the case. The contributions of family historians such as Hareven (1987), MacFarlane (1986), and Segalen (1983), to mention just a few out of many, are becoming increasingly a part of mainstream family knowledge. Cross-national research (e.g., Ishii-Kuntz and Lee, 1987) is still underrepresented but, nevertheless, forms an integral part of contemporary family studies. Of course, mainstream scholarship reflects "social regulation"—all science does—and, as stressed above, remains largely within the positivist research tradi-

tion. To challenge this one must do more than accuse. What is needed is research that, through its
line of questioning, explanation, research techniques, and implications for "praxis," offers better and more relevant theorizing than is currently
the case.

Which leads to a final comment: the linkage
between critical thinking and practice. As in the
case of hermeneutic thought, the interconnection
between theorizing and its application is a
"given":

> . . . the self-foundation of sociology through the
> idea of society requires a concept of abstract
> utopia, a philosophical-historical premise. When
> its transcendentally grounded meaning finally is
> transformed into a postulate of practical reason,
> then and only then can the idea of society fulfill
> its function as a critical concept. [Schrader-
> Klebert, 1968: 116]

Critical theorizing, therefore, is not just "applied
oriented" or inclined to justify its existence by
producing socially relevant findings. Rather, it
derives its raison d'être from its conception of
such utopias. At first glance, mainstream family
scholarship seems far removed from all of this. It
is, however, closely linked to its clinical counter-
part and increasingly aware of its policy implications. I believe that among practice-oriented family scholars this may lead to a growing interest in
the ideas—alien as they may seem at times—of
their critically oriented colleagues.

Feminist Theorizing

To attempt a single definition of the "feminist approach" makes little sense at this point in time
(Osmond, 1984: 571). *Feminism*, as the term is
used here, refers, then, to what persons calling
themselves feminist write and do. What unites
them in their diversity is that all arguments, to
varying degrees, "aim to redress the absence of
women in the history of social and political
thought" (Keller, 1985: 6). Because there are so
many voices, such a range of messages, and so little space, a few categories of "redress" will
organize the discussion. They are not independent
but do furnish some insight into a complex picture.

The first category is exemplified by Walker
and Thompson's question: can one be a social
scientist and a feminist at the same time? Their
answer is affirmative, although "inherent in our

response is the recognition that not all feminist
scholars want the same things" (1984: 553). I
believe that a sizable category of contemporary
feminist family scholars share this view. Yllo, for
example, argued recently that a widely held belief
that quantitative research is "patriarchal" or
"non-feminist" and that qualitative analysis is
"feminist" is "simplistic and counter-
productive" (1986: 2). This particular approach
toward theorizing reflects the view that "sexism
and androcentrism are social biases correctable by
stricter adherence to the existing methodological
norms of scientific inquiry" (Harding, 1986:
24-25). A growing proportion of female family
professionals—because of their sensitivity to
"sexism," their resources, and research interests—are introducing this "feminist empiricism," as Harding calls it (1986: 24), into the
social world of family scholarship without seriously challenging its traditional methodology. Instead, its incorporation may help correct the one-
sided, male-oriented focus of family theorizing
(cf. Meyer and Rosenblatt, 1987), boost the status
of qualitative empirical research, and improve its
social credibility, while leaving its ontological
underpinnings largely intact.

A reader, *Rethinking the Family* (1982), edited
by Thorne and Yalom, illustrates a second type of
challenge. In her introduction Thorne argues that
such feminist "rethinking" begins with

> a challenge of three widespread assumptions: the
> ideology of the "monolithic family," beliefs that
> the family is natural or biological, and analyses
> that freeze present family ideals in a language of
> function and roles. [P. 3]

At first glance, these challenges do not seem new
or uniquely feminist. The conception of "family"
as a "universal" has been effectively challenged
by historians (cf. Anderson, 1980) and anthropologists (cf. Netting, Wilk, and Arnould, 1984),
while the presumed "immutability" of families
implicit in both the biological and functional approaches is only characteristic of "pop-socio-
biology" (cf. Sprey, 1988) and a somewhat dated
version of functionalist thought. What makes
them feminist and "critical," however, is clear in
the following:

> Our rethinking of the family necessarily extends
> beyond a close consideration of what exists to
> careful thought and imagining what might be. In
> envisioning and working to create a better world,
> we will necessarily have to transcend a separation

between private and public, or family and society. [Thorne and Yalom, 1982: 20]

The above reflects a "standpoint," that is, "a morally and scientifically preferable grounding for our interpretations and explanations of nature and social life" (Harding, 1986: 26). Its feminist critique is "grounded in the universal features of women's experience as understood from the perspective of feminism" (p. 26). It is a view, then, that is "women-centered" or "maximalist" (cf. Kaufman, 1985: 544–545) because it rejects the assumption that catching up on the role of women in the family literature and including the ideas of female scholars in the theorizing process is sufficient. To redress the one-sided nature of family thought, argue authors such as Smith (1974, 1978), Flax (1982), and Keller (1985), to mention just a few, all family issues, including the raison d'être of marriage and the family itself, must be re-understood from the standpoint of female experience. As such,

Feminism makes a unique contribution to more traditional studies of science; it encourages the use of expertise that has traditionally belonged to women—not simply as a woman's perspective but as a critical instrument for examining the roots of those dichotomies that isolate this perspective and deny its legitimacy. It seeks to enlarge our understanding of the history, philosophy, and sociology of science through the inclusion not only of women and their actual experiences but also of those domains of human experience that have been relegated to women: namely, the personal, the emotional, and the sexual. [Keller, 1985: 9]

This indeed presents a profound challenge but, as I see it, also a stimulus to theoretical thinking on the institutions of marriage and the family.

There remain two more challenges to be recognized. One is the rejection of all—but especially quantitative—research methods by some feminist scholars. Acker and her colleagues, for example, see the research process as "oppressive" and argue that "research that aims to be liberating should not in the process become only another mode of oppression" (1983: 425). This is a nearly paradoxical and, therefore, quite difficult argument to address. In fact, the authors conclude, "we have not solved the problems of doing emancipatory research" but go on to suggest that "perhaps we have made a contribution to that end" (1983: 434). Because all "influencing"—bureaucratic or otherwise—is manipula-

tory and thus "oppressive," the failure of Acker and her coworkers to solve the problem of emancipatory research does not surprise me. However, they did not fail to raise a question that, given the unique nature of the realities of marriages and families, should be of great concern to *all* students of the family.

Finally, there is the challenge that grows directly from the political nature of feminism. Its use of the term *emancipatory* means more than just the freeing of the mind. Radical and socialist feminists in particular see the traditional institutions of marriage and the family as mainstays of capitalist society, oppressive, and in need of drastic change. The following statement illustrates this:

The world around the family is not a pre-existing harsh climate against which the family offers protection and warmth. It is as if the family had drawn comfort and security into itself and left the outside world bereft. . . . It is indeed a major agency for caring, but in monopolizing care it has made it harder to undertake other forms of care. It is indeed a unit of sharing, but in demanding sharing within it has made other relations tend to become more mercenary. It is indeed a place of intimacy, but in privileging the intimacy of close kin it has made the outside world cold and friendless. . . . Caring, sharing and loving would be more widespread if the family did not claim them for its own. [Barrett and McIntosh, 1982: 80]

To gauge the impact of the range of challenges outlined in this brief section would require a major essay. Here only a comment can be made. The attack on the *institutions* of marriage and the family touches family scholarship in two ways. First, a drastic change in the patterns of reproduction and child care in our society would affect the questioning of family researchers. Second, and more relevant here, the expressed desire for drastic change and its associated anger and rejection of the status quo completely contradict an "image" of marriage and the family that still guides the theorizing of a significant and influential group of North American family scholars (cf. Burr et al., 1987).

The challenges posed by various feminist "epistemologies" are likely to have different consequences. Earlier, I suggested that "feminist empiricism" is actually entering the mainstream of family scholarship. I believe this will lead to, among other things, a significant broadening of its realm of questioning and a more balanced view of the relative status of quantitative and qualitative data analysis. The impact of the various women-centered epistemologies present in the works of feminist writers such as Smith, Harding, and Keller, may—alone or in conjunction with the impact of hermeneutic and/or critical reasoning—take considerably more time to gain a foothold among family theorists.

CONCLUSIONS

Almost eighty years ago William Graham Sumner, as the outgoing president of the American Sociological Society, devoted his presidential address to the family and social change. He concluded as follows:

> It appears that the family now depends chiefly on the virtue, good sense, conception of duty, and spirit of sacrifice of the parents. They have constantly new problems to meet. They want to do what is right and best. They do not fear change and do not shrink from it. So long as their own character is not corrupted it does not appear that there is any cause for alarm. [1909: 591]

Why does that final comment still have a ring of truth? Is it one more piece of evidence for the familiar premise that *plus ça change, plus c'est la même chose?* I doubt it. Sumner's argument rested on historical and ethnographic sources, and his conclusion reflects two fundamental attributes of social theorizing: faith and hope. *That* is what remained constant over all those years. Current mainstream theorizing, despite its statistical and methodological sophistication, still leans on these pillars: faith in its positivist premises and the hope that its myopic vision of the future will not be countermanded by sudden, drastic changes in the real world. It is with that in mind that I contemplate the possible impact on family scholarship of the approaches outlined above.

The inductive theorizing characteristic of much contemporary research on marriage and the family does, as suggested earlier, accomplish the aims of those involved in it. It also seems to satisfy the demands of a significant category of the consumers of family scholarship. So why *would* the mainstream change its course? To be effective, challenges must undermine the faith and hope on which it rests. For example, if taken seriously, the hermeneutic negation of a direct linkage between "praxis" and the outcomes of empirical research makes the numerous conferences on "how to communicate with one

another" between researchers and practitioners seem somewhat irrelevant. The denial of the dichotomy between the "objective" and the "subjective," posed by critical theory, hermeneutics, and most feminist thought, challenges the faith on which much current family scholarship is founded.

But how *effective* will such challenges be? My response, speculative as it is, has been offered throughout this essay. I would like to elaborate it somewhat further by means of a final metaphor. I see the course of family scholarship as a collective march in which tempo and order are becoming visibly institutionalized. The marchers proceed from handbook to handbook, while the trajectory in between is marked further by additional "milestones," such as decade reviews and other "state of the art" reports. Where, then, does this increasingly familiar path lead the "platoon"? After all, milestones exist to be reached and left behind. Depending on past markers for guidance may keep the marchers together but also has them walking backward into a future that derives its primary meaning from the fact that it has not yet been reached. No wonder, then, that Berardo and Shehan felt compelled to ask if the content of family scholarship is a reflection on the changing family. I answered that question in the affirmative; for mainstream marchers there is no other road to follow. Moreover, because new milestones—handbooks, for instance—take years to build, the future, when we reach it, often takes on a distinct sense of déjà vu.

Is this enough? That depends on the goals of individual family scholars, on what is seen as the interest of the field, and, lastly, upon the changing needs of all those involved in the reality of marriages and families. For those who are not completely satisfied, let me conclude with some suggestions. Looking ahead—that is, *beyond* the horizons created by our causal models and empirically verified propositions—requires two things: first, using one's imagination—for example, thinking counterfactually and in terms of the possible as well as the actual. How to accomplish this without replacing our tested knowledge about the real world with mere fantasies remains, at this writing, a question that can be answered only after we have tried. Second, our questioning must be extended, when appropriate, beyond the realm of the proximate into that of ultimate causality. Can domestic violence, for example, be condered a "normal" feature of contemporary mar-age and the family, and, if so, why? How can we ome to understand fully the odds against *any* •ng-term voluntary bonds, such as marriage, ohabitation, and friendship, in an increasingly different and changing modern world? As a nal example, does the fact that our society •produces sizable numbers of babies who seem redestined to grow up deprived of essential :sources and others who are condemned to a nort and miserable life—because they carry the .IDS virus—indicate that our social institutions f marriage and the family have somehow lost ieir way? In fact, do such statistics tell us *nything* that we should be able to comprehend as xperts in our field? These clearly are not prox-nate questions. But I suggest that if family cholars continue to delegate such issues to •hilosophy, religion, or even the realm of politics, •ur field and its professionals will lose much of **t**he credibility that was earned over the past fifty ears.

NOTES

The author thanks his colleague Sarah H. Matthews and three anonymous reviewers for their very helpful comments on an earlier draft of this essay.

1. I use the term *positivist* in a relatively broad sense in this essay. Most generally it implies that family studies, as a scholarly field, is expected to construct general, predictive, and verifiable theories about a subject matter that is, in principle, no different from that of the physical sciences.

2. Concepts, as defined here, form the theoretical vocabulary of a scholarly field. A conceptual framework, then, parallels a language.

3. As used in this essay, *induction* infers from repeated instances of some conjunction of things or events toward more general or universal occurrence. Inferences whose premises do not logically entail their conclusions are inductive.

4. All publications used as exemplars here represent high-quality work and are selected strictly for the sake of clarification.

REFERENCES

Acker, Joan, Kate Barry, and Joke Esseveld. 1983. "Objectivity and truth: Problems in doing feminist research." Women's Studies International Forum 6: 423–435.

Anderson, Michael. 1980. Approaches to the History of the Western Family: 1500–1914. London: McMillan.

Barrett, Michele, and Mary McIntosh. 1982. The Anti-social Family. London: Verso Editions.

Berardo, Felix M., and Constance L. Shehan. 1984. "Family scholarship: A Reflection on the changing family?" Journal of Family Issues 5: 577–597.

Bernstein, Richard J. 1985. "From hermeneutics to praxis." Pp. 272–296 in Robert Hollinger (ed.), Hermeneutics and Praxis. Notre Dame, IN: University of Notre Dame Press.

Broderick, Carlfred B. 1971. "Beyond the five conceptual frameworks: A decade of development in family theory." Journal of Marriage and the Family 33: 139–159.

Burr, Wesley, R., Donald A. Herrin, Randal D. Day, Ivan F. Beutler, and Geoffrey K. Leigh. 1987. "An epistemological basis for primary explanations in family science." Paper presented at the Theory and Methods Workshop of the National Council on Family Relations, Atlanta.

Burr, Wesley R., Reuben Hill, F. Ivan Nye, and Ira L. Reiss (eds.). 1979. Contemporary Theories about the Family (Vols. 1 and 2). New York: Free Press.

Cherlin, Andrew J. 1981. Marriage, Divorce, Remarriage. Cambridge, MA: Harvard University Press.

Elder, Glen H. 1975. "Age differentiation and the life course." Pp. 165–190 in Alex Inkeles, James Coleman, and Neil Smelser (eds.), Annual Review of Sociology. Palo Alto, CA: Annual Reviews.

Elster, Jon. 1983. Explaining Technical Change. New York: Cambridge University Press.

Flax, Jane. 1982. "The family in contemporary feminist thought: A critical review." Pp. 223–253 in Jean Bethke Elshtain (ed.), The Family in Political Thought. Amherst: University of Massachusetts Press.

Gadamer, Hans-George. 1975. Truth and Method. New York: Seabury Press.

Gelles, Richard J. 1982. "Applying research on family violence to clinical practice." Journal of Marriage and the Family 44: 9–20.

Gelles, Richard J. 1984. "Parental child snatching: A preliminary estimate of the national incidence." Journal of Marriage and the Family 46: 735–739.

Giddens, Anthony. 1987. Sociology (2nd ed.). New York: Harcourt Brace Jovanovich.

Giere, Ronald N. 1984. "Toward a unified theory of science." Pp. 5–31 in James T. Cushing, C. F. Delaney, and Gary M. Gutting (eds.), Science and Reality. Notre Dame, IN: University of Notre Dame Press.

Giles-Sims, Jean. 1983. Wife-Battering: A Systems Theory Approach. New York: Guilford Press.

Glass, Jennifer, Vern L. Bengtson, and Charlotte C. Dunham. 1986. "Attitude similarity in three-generation families: Socialization, status inheritance, or reciprocal influence?" American Sociological Review 51: 685–698.

Glick, Paul C. 1984. "Marriage, divorce, and living arrangements: Prospective changes." Journal of Family Issues 5: 7–26.

Harding, Sandra. 1986. The Science Question in Feminism. Ithaca, NY: Cornell University Press.

Hareven, Tamara. 1987. "Historical analysis of the family." Pp. 37–58 in Marvin B. Sussman and Suzanne K. Steinmetz (eds.), Handbook of Marriage and the Family. New York: Plenum.

Hill, Reuben. 1955. "A critique of contemporary marriage and family research." Social Forces 33: 268–277.

Hill, Reuben. 1981. "Whither family research in the 1980s: Continuities, emergents, and new horizons." Journal of Marriage and the Family 43: 255–257.

Hill, Reuben, and Donald A. Hansen. 1960. "The identification of conceptual frameworks utilized in family study." Marriage and Family Living 22: 299–311.

Holman, Thomas B., and Wesley R. Burr. 1980. "Beyond the beyond: The growth of family theories in the 1970s." Journal of Marriage and the Family 42: 729–741.

Ishii-Kuntz, Masako, and Gary R. Lee. 1987. "Status of the elderly: An extension of the theory." Journal of Marriage and the Family 49: 413–420.

Jurich, Joan. 1987. "Implications of post-positivism for the theory-method-data relationship in family studies." Paper presented at the Theory and Methods Workshop of the National Council on Family Relations, Atlanta.

Kaufman, Debra R. 1985. "Women who return to orthodox Judaism: A feminist analysis." Journal of Marriage and the Family 47: 543–551.

Keller, Evelyn F. 1985. Reflections on Gender and Science. New Haven, CT: Yale University Press.

Kingston, Paul W., and Steven L. Nock. 1985. "Consequences of the family workday." Journal of Marriage and the Family 47: 619–639.

Klein, David. 1980. "Commentary on the linkages between conceptual frameworks and theory development in sociology." Sociological Quarterly 21: 443–453.

LaRossa, Ralph, and Jane H. Wolf. 1985. "On qualitative family research." Journal of Marriage and the Family 47: 531–541.

Lavee, Yoav. 1986. "The use, non-use, and misuse of contemporary family theories in empirical research." Paper presented at the Theory and Methods Workshop of the National Council on Family Relations, Dearborn, MI.

Lavee, Yoav, Hamilton I. McCubbin, and Joan M. Patterson. 1985. "The Double ABCX model of family stress and adaptation: An empirical test by analysis of structural equations with latent variables." Journal of Marriage and the Family 47: 811–825.

MacFarlane, Alan. 1986. Marriage and Love in England: 1300–1800. New York: Basil Blackwell.

McLain, Raymond, and Andrew Weigert. 1979. "Toward a phenomenological sociology of family: A programmatic essay." Pp. 160–205 in Wesley R. Burr, Reuben Hill, F. Ivan Nye, and Ira L. Reiss (eds.), Contemporary Theories about the Family (Vol. 2). New York: Free Press.

Meyer, Cynthia J., and Paul C. Rosenblatt. 1987. "Feminist analysis of family textbooks." Journal of Family Issues 8: 247–252.

Molm, Linda D. 1986. "Gender, power, and legitimation: A test of three theories." American Journal of Sociology 91: 1356–1386.

Morgan, D. H. J. 1985. The Family, Politics and Social Theory. London: Routledge and Kegan Paul.

Netting, Robert M., Richard R. Wilk, and Eric J. Arnould. 1984. Households. Berkeley: University of California Press.

Outhwaite, William. 1983. "Toward a realist perspective." Pp. 321–329 in Gareth Morgan (ed.), Beyond Method. Beverly Hills, CA: Sage Publications.

Outhwaite, William. 1985. "Hans-Georg Gadamer." Pp. 23–39 in Quentin Skinner (ed.), The Return of Grand Theory in the Human Sciences. New York: Cambridge University Press.

Osmond, Marie. 1984. "Feminist research and scientific criteria." Journal of Family Issues 5: 571–576.

Osmond, Marie. 1987. "Radical-critical theories." Pp. 103–124 in Marvin B. Sussman and Suzanne K. Steinmetz (eds.), Handbook of Marriage and the Family. New York: Plenum.

Paige, Karen E., and Jeffery M. Paige. 1981. The Politics of Reproductive Ritual. Los Angeles: University of California Press.

Polanyi, Michael. 1967. The Tacit Dimension. New York: Doubleday.

Poster, Mark. 1978. Critical Theory and the Family. New York: Seabury Press.

Reiss, Ira L. 1986. Journey into Sexuality: An Exploratory Voyage. Englewood Cliffs, NJ: Prentice-Hall.

Ritzer, George. 1975. "Sociology: A multiple paradigm science." American Sociologist 10: 156–167.

Rodman, Hyman. 1980. "Are conceptual frameworks necessary for theory building?" Sociological Quarterly 21: 429–441.

Sarkar, Husain. 1983. A Theory of Method. Los Angeles: University of California Press.

Schrader-Klebert, Karin. 1968. "*Der Begriff der Gesellschaft als regulative Idee*" ["The concept of society as ordering idea"]. Soziale Welt 19: 97–118.

Schutz, Alfred. 1970. "The problem of rationality in the social world." Pp. 89–115 in Dorothy Emmet and Alasdair MacIntire (eds.), Sociological Theory and Philosophical Analysis. New York: Macmillan.

Segalen, Martine. 1983. Love and Power in the Peasant Family: Rural France in the Nineteenth Century. Chicago: University of Chicago Press.

Smith, Dorothy. 1974. "Women's perspective as a radical critique of sociology." Sociological Inquiry 44: 7–13.

Smith, Dorothy E. 1978. "A peculiar eclipsing: Women's exclusion from man's culture." Women's Studies International Quarterly 1: 281–295.

Sprey, Jetse. 1969. "The family as a system in conflict." Journal of Marriage and the Family 31: 699–706.

Sprey, Jetse. 1988. "Sociobiology and the study of family conflict." Pp. 137–158 in Erik E. Filsinger (ed.), Biosocial Perspectives on the Family. Beverly Hills, CA: Sage.

Sprey, Jetse. 1987. "Linking family theory and reality: A bridge that never was." Paper presented at the Theory and Methods Workshop of the National Council on Family Relations, Atlanta.

Sumner, William G. 1909. "The family and social change." American Journal of Sociology 14: 577–591.

Sussman, Marvin B. 1987. "From the catbird seat: Observations on marriage and the family." Pp. xxxi–xli in Marvin B. Sussman and Suzanne K. Steinmetz (eds.), Handbook of Marriage and the Family. New York: Plenum Press.

Thomas, Darwin L., and Jean E. Wilcox. 1987. "The rise of family theory: A historical and critical analysis." Pp. 81–102 in Marvin B. Sussman and Suzanne K. Steinmetz (eds.), Handbook of Marriage and the Family. New York: Plenum Press.

Thorne, Barrie, and Marilyn Yalom (eds.). 1982. Rethinking the Family: Some Feminist Questions. New York: Longman.

Waite, Linda J., Frances K. Goldscheider, and Christina Witsberger. 1986. "Nonfamily living and the erosion of traditional family orientations among young adults." American Sociological Review 51: 541–554.

Walker, Alexis J., and Linda Thompson. 1984. "Feminism and family studies." Journal of Family Issues 5: 545–570.

Walters, Lynda H. 1986. "Thinking theory: Some observations and questions on the integration of family theory and research." Paper presented at the Theory and Methods Workshop of the National Council on Family Relations, Dearborn, MI.

Watkins, Susan Cotts, and Jane A. Menken. 1987. "Demographic foundations of family change." American Sociological Review 52: 346–358.

Weber, Max. 1956. *Wirtschaft und Gesellschaft* [Economy and Society]. Vol. 1. Tubingen, West Germany: J. C. B. Mohr.

Wilson, John. 1983. Social Theory. Englewood Cliffs, NJ: Prentice-Hall.

Yllo, Kersti. 1986. "Political and methodological debates in wife abuse research." Paper presented at the Theory and Methods Workshop of the National Council on Family Relations, Dearborn, MI.

Zaretsky, Eli. 1976. Capitalism, the Family, and Personal Life. New York: Harper and Row.

NORVAL D. GLENN   *University of Texas at Austin*

Quantitative Research on Marital Quality in the 1980s: A Critical Review

Most of the quantitative research on marital quality in the 1980s dealt with issues emphasized in earlier research, but on the average the 1980s studies were methodologically superior to the earlier ones. Debate and discussion during the decade led to some decline in conceptual confusion, and while the research produced only a modest increment in understanding of the causes and consequences of marital success, it laid the foundation for greater progress in the years to come.

The literature on marital quality published in the United States in the 1980s is immense—far too large to be summarized and evaluated in one short review article. Moreover, it lacks unity, being divided into three or four largely distinct bodies, such as a large clinical literature that rarely cites, and is rarely cited by, the social science publications in this and related journals. Within the social science literature, reports of quantitative and qualitative research form largely separate bodies, between which citations are also relatively rare. A large and diverse feminist literature on marital quality overlaps somewhat with each of the other bodies but is to some extent separate from all of them.

A review and attempted synthesis of these different literatures would be enormously worthwhile, but my task here must be more modest. In selecting a manageable portion of the total literature for treatment, I used the focus of the

Journal of Marriage and the Family and my own areas of competence as the criteria, so that the scope of the review is quantitative "mainstream" social scientific research on marital quality.[1]

Even within this restricted scope, the review cannot cover all of the publications, and thus I concentrate on the topics to which the most attention was devoted, and within those, on the few studies that, in my judgment, made the greatest contributions, were most influential, or illustrate important points. I discuss a few "miscellaneous" studies, but only to illustrate the diversity of the literature.

I first discuss theoretical, conceptual, and methodological issues and then selectively review the research findings.

THEORETICAL AND CONCEPTUAL ISSUES

Several theoretical perspectives, the most common of which are variants of exchange theory, have been used from time to time to guide quantitative research on marital quality. However, the empirical literature on this topic has never been heavily theoretical, and there was little or no increase in emphasis on theory in the 1980s. Not much of the literature was completely atheoretical, but the rationale for the major lines of research was largely practical, with elements of theory being brought in on an incidental, ad hoc basis. Research was more often guided by simple propositions—such as that homogamy contributes to marital quality—than by systematic theory, and not infrequently it was simply guided by questions, such as, What effects do children in the home have on marital quality?

Department of Sociology, University of Texas, Austin, TX 78712.

I do not take a totally negative view of this lack of a heavy theoretical emphasis. Little is likely to be gained by straining to formulate a systematic theoretical rationale for practically motivated research, and there is a refreshing honesty in marital quality researchers' lack of theoretical pretensions. The history of science provides numerous examples of the eventual crystallization of coherent theoretical positions from post hoc explanations of findings from practically motivated research, and such inductive theory building may eventually result from the numerous speculations by researchers into marital quality during the 1980s.

Nevertheless, one can only lament the relative lack of attention paid by quantitative marital quality researchers to the theoretical literature and the theoretical insights of qualitative researchers. There were some notable theoretical treatments of marriage and of male-female relations in general in the late 1970s and early and middle 1980s, including those in Rubin, *Intimate Strangers* (1983), and Bellah, Madsen, Sullivan, Swidler, and Tipton, *Habits of the Heart* (1985), but these had had little apparent impact on quantitative research on marital quality by the end of the 1980s. Rather, research continued to be concentrated largely on issues that became salient in the 1970s or earlier, and new theoretical perspectives were rarely brought to bear on them.

In American society, in contrast to most past societies, marriage has long been considered to be primarily for the benefit of the married persons rather than of the extended family, the society, or the deity or deities. One might think that the widespread agreement, although not consensus, on the primary purpose of marriage as hedonistic might have greatly simplified the conceptualization and measurement of marital quality, but instead, the literature on marital quality has for several decades been characterized by considerable conceptual confusion and disagreement about measurement. On the one hand, some researchers have viewed marital quality as being simply a matter of how married persons feel about their marriages, and they have favored such indicators of marital quality as self-reports of marital satisfaction or happiness. On the other hand, some researchers have viewed marital quality as being a characteristic of the *relationship* between spouses instead of, or in addition to, a matter of the separate feelings of the two spouses. These

researchers have usually favored measures of marital adjustment, in which at least some of the scale items deal with such relational characteristics as communication and conflict.

At the beginning of the 1980s, the "adjustment" school was apparently dominant (Spanier and Lewis, 1980). Campbell, Converse, and Rodgers (1976) had shown that persons attach different meanings to "satisfaction" and "happiness" and that measures of marital happiness and satisfaction relate differently to the same other variables (p. 328). While this finding did not discredit the "individual feelings" school, it did indicate that the two concepts favored by that school should not be used interchangeably, as they often had been.[2] Spanier's Dyadic Adjustment Scale (Spanier, 1976), a multidimensional scale with heavy emphasis on relational elements, was introduced in the mid-1970s and by the end of the decade was probably the most widely used measure of marital quality.

In the 1980s there was some shift in emphasis toward the measurement of individual (especially global) evaluations of marriages,[3] perhaps in large measure because of the availability of some large national data sets, such as the General Social Surveys Cumulative File (Davis, 1989), on which one spouse's evaluation of the marriage is the only measure of marital quality. However, the change may have come about partly because the concept of marital adjustment and some of the most popular marital adjustment scales came under rather severe criticism (e.g., Fincham and Bradbury, 1987; Johnson, White, Edwards, and Booth, 1986; Norton, 1983; Sabatelli, 1988; Trost, 1985).

The criticisms varied considerably. Huston and Robins (1982), Norton (1983), Huston, McHale, and Crouter (1986), and Fincham and Bradbury (1987) objected to including, in the same scale, global individual evaluations of marriages and variables, such as communication and conflict, that might affect, or be affected by, the global evaluations. These authors made the cogent point that how the global evaluations relate to variables that may affect or be affected by them should be left open to empirical investigation, which tends to be inhibited by including all of the variables in the same scale. In contrast, Johnson and associates (1986) criticized the summing of subscale scores in such measures as the Spanier Dyadic Adjustment Scale on empirical rather than theoretical and conceptual grounds. On the basis of a confirmatory factor analysis of five components of what they called "marital quality" (marital happiness, interaction, disagreements, problems, and instability), they found two dimensions, with happiness and interaction in one and the other three components in the other. Since these dimensions performed quite differently over forms of marital structure such as duration and sex, the authors concluded that scales including both "are likely to yield ambiguous findings and contribute little to an understanding of marital process" (p. 31).

From the perspective of the "individual feelings" school, represented especially by Norton and by Fincham and Bradbury and to which I am sympathetic, it is indeed unwise to combine the two dimensions discovered by Johnson et al. into one scale, but for reasons in addition to the empirical one given by those authors. From this perspective, only marital happiness, strictly speaking, is an aspect of marital quality, and the other four components may affect or be affected by marital happiness. For instance, low marital happiness is likely, under certain circumstances, to contribute to marital instability (the inclination to divorce, as defined by Johnson et al.), but at any given level of the spouses' marital happiness, does it make sense to consider a marriage to be of higher quality if the spouses are disinclined to divorce because they lack desirable alternatives to the marriage? Moreover, from this perspective, it would not necessarily be wise to combine the components in the same dimension into one scale. For instance, marital happiness may affect interaction, and/or vice versa, and the fact that the two variables fell into the same dimension does not mean that nothing useful can be gained by investigating the relationship between them.

Whether or not most marital quality researchers were persuaded by the arguments against summed multidimensional measures of marital quality was not apparent as the decade ended. But since even those who made the arguments did not agree about how marital quality should be conceptualized, it seems almost certain that the conceptual debates will continue into the 1990s.

METHODOLOGICAL ISSUES

At least two important methodological developments in quantitative research on marital

quality occurred during the 1980s, namely, increases in the use of large and representative samples of respondents and in longitudinal research. Several important studies during the decade were both longitudinal and based on data from a representative national sample of married persons, thanks to a survey conducted by researchers at the University of Nebraska at Lincoln (see the publications by Alan Booth, Lynn White, and their associates in the reference list). An increase in the use of advanced statistical techniques also represents progress to the extent that the techniques were appropriately and cautiously used.

In spite of these developments, quantitative researchers on family relations in general, and on marital quality in particular, tended to lag behind other areas of social scientific research in methodological sophistication.[4] By the mid-1980s there was a fairly large and very important literature dealing with how causal analysis in the social sciences tends to fail because of unmeasured selectivity and similar influences (e.g., Achen, 1986; Duncan, 1984; Holland and Rubin, 1983; LaLonde, 1986; Lieberson, 1985; Rogosa and Willett, 1985), but by the end of the decade hardly any researchers on marital quality had begun to address and deal with even the simplest and most basic issues discussed in this literature. For instance, there apparently was widespread lack of awareness that, ideally, causal analysis with cross-sectional data should be conducted with a sample of an approximately closed population, that is, one into and out of which there is little movement, and that any correlation of the dependent variable with a tendency to move out of the population poses serious problems for causal inference. To anyone aware of this fact, it should be obvious that cross-sectional data from a sample of married persons are not, strictly speaking, appropriate for a causal analysis in which marital quality is the dependent variable. The population of married persons is not approximately closed, and the tendency to move out of it is rather highly correlated with marital quality. Since the influences that tend to lower marital quality also tend to drive persons out of the married population, the effects of those influences will tend to be underestimated, or not detected at all, in studies of persons in intact marriages.

The point is illustrated by the case of age at marriage. A very young age at marriage is almost certainly conducive to marital problems and thus to low marital quality; the probability that a marriage will end in divorce during the first few years is substantially higher if one or both of the spouses was under age 20 at the time of marriage (Bumpass and Sweet, 1972; Glick and Norton, 1977; Schoen, 1975)—so much higher that a greater tendency to resort to divorce when problems arise can hardly account for all of the difference. However, age at marriage is not positively related to measures of marital quality in most samples of married persons in which the relationship has been studied (e.g., Bahr, Chappell, and Leigh, 1983; Glenn and Weaver, 1978) and even bears a significant negative relationship in some samples. Thus if one were to estimate the effect of early marriage on marital success by using only data on intact marriages and without taking into account marriages that have ended in divorce, one would conclude (almost certainly erroneously) that early marriage does not lower the probability of marital success.

And yet as recently as the late 1980s, much research was being conducted with cross-sectional data on married persons to estimate effects on marital quality. Of course, evidence from flawed research can be of value if it is interpreted with caution and awareness of how the flaws may have affected the findings. Some authors who interpreted cross-sectional data on marital quality during the 1980s were appropriately cautious and tentative in making causal inferences, but many were not.

This issue is related to a conceptual one not discussed above, namely, the distinction between "marital quality" and "marital success." Marital quality, as I point out above, is often defined as how good the marriage is from the standpoint of the spouses at one point in time, or as a combination of the spouses' feelings and relational characteristics at one point in time.[5] Marital success, on the other hand, refers to what happens to a marriage over a period of time. A marriage that is intact and satisfactory to both spouses is successful, while one that has ended in divorce or separation or is unsatisfactory to one or both spouses is a failure.

Studies of marital quality are usually motivated by interest in marital success, but because marital quality and success are not the same, a measure of marital quality, by itself, is not a satisfactory indicator of marital success. A truly adequate study of marital success must take into account whether or not the marriage has remained intact, and if it has, how satisfactory it is to the spouses. Therefore, studies of marital quality are, by themselves, inadequate for gaining insight into the causes and consequences of marital success and failure. And studies of marital stability and instability (in the sense of whether or not the couple divorces) are also inadequate by themselves for gaining understanding of marital success (a fact now rather generally recognized), although marital stability may be of interest for reasons other than its relation to marital success. Nevertheless, research on marital quality and stability have traditionally been separate, and they remained largely so in the 1980s.

Researchers on marital quality gained considerable sensitivity to some methodological problems without becoming highly sophisticated in dealing with them, an example being in research designed to estimate the effects of heterogamy. Prior to the 1980s, most researchers interested in heterogamy effects did not recognize that they faced the "identification problem"—the same problem faced in cohort analysis and in research designed to estimate the effects of such variables as mobility (social or geographic), status inconsistency, and a lack of status integration (Blalock, 1966, 1967). The identification problem exists whenever an independent variable is a linear function of two other variables that need to be included in the analysis as independent or control variables. In such a case, one cannot simply include all three of the interrelated variables as independent variables in a regression or similar analysis. If one tries to do that and does not transform or recode the variables to break the linear dependence of each on the other two, the computer program will not run. If one recodes or transforms the variables or makes an arbitrary simplifying assumption to break the linear dependence, the computer program will run but the estimates of effects will not be meaningful.

In heterogamy effects research, the three interrelated variables are wife's characteristics, husband's characteristics, and the difference between the two. Of course, one cannot hold the first two constant while allowing the third to vary, and furthermore, if all effects are linear or largely so (as when different-signed husband-wife differences have opposite and equal effects), the effects are confounded with one another so that no statistical analysis by itself can give meaningful estimates of them. Fortunately, the predicted heterogamy effects are often curvilinear (so that opposite-signed husband-wife differences are expected to have same-signed effects), and such effects can be estimated statistically since they are reflected as an interaction between husband's and wife's characteristics. Heaton (1984) apparently based his estimate of a religious heterogamy effect on such an interaction, even though he did not discuss the identification problem and gave the false impression that one can, in a straightforward manner, control the spouses' characteristics while estimating the effect of husband-wife differences.

The fact that some researchers who investigated possible heterogamy effects on marital quality at least recognized and discussed the identification problem represents progress (e.g., Glenn, 1982; Rogler and Procidano, 1989). A number of other researchers failed to discuss the problem but conducted analyses that were apparently appropriate, since the spouses' characteristics seemed to have no effects and thus did not need to be controlled (e.g., Ortega, Whitt, and Williams, 1988; Vera, Berardo, and Berardo, 1985).

Since a thorough review and trenchant critique of scales designed to measure marital quality was recently published (Sabatelli, 1988), I need not deal at length here with measurement issues.[6] However, Sabatelli restricted his review to scales, and during the 1980s there was an increase in the use of one-item and two-to-three-item indicators of marital quality. This change, which most observers will consider regressive, was associated with one of the advancements of the decade, namely, the increase in the use of large, representative national samples. Generally speaking, the large national data sets used for marital quality research did not include multiple items designed to measure marital quality, the one major exception being the longitudinal national survey conducted by Booth and his colleagues.

One of the most widely used data sets for studies of marital quality during the past decade was the General Social Survey Cumulative File (Davis, 1989), in which the only data on marital quality are responses to the simple question, "Taking things altogether, how would you describe your marriage? Would you say that your marriage is very happy, pretty happy, or not too happy?" Although one can argue against some of

the usual reasons given for the alleged superiority of scales over one-item indicators (for instance, the greater random measurement error with one-item indicators is not a serious problem when marital quality is the dependent variable if one is not excessively concerned about maximizing explained variance), this question is deficient even in comparison to other one-item indicators. It has only three response alternatives, which precludes fine distinctions, and the responses to it are highly skewed, with up to two-thirds of the respondents saying their marriages are "very happy." So few respondents say their marriages are "not too happy" that the responses are commonly dichotomized into "very happy" versus all others. This is probably the better way to score the responses for analyses that require interval-level measurement, since the assumption that the interval between "very happy" and "pretty happy" is the same as that between "pretty happy" and "not too happy" seems untenable, but of course dichotomous measures of continuous variables are at best quite crude.

Some of the deficiencies of research on marital quality are also characteristic of family research in general and indeed of most kinds of social scientific research. For instance, in marital quality research as in social science in general, an increase in the use of longitudinal designs has been a positive development, but a widespread tendency to overestimate what can be accomplished with longitudinal research has lessened its value and led to overly confident conclusions about cause and effect.[7] (Such conclusions are more characteristic of secondary reports of research than of the reports by the persons who did the research.) For instance, longitudinal studies designed to estimate the effect of the transition to parenthood on marital quality cannot provide conclusive evidence, even if a control group of nonparents is used to help separate the effects of having a child from duration-of-marriage effects. Since the control and experimental groups cannot be randomly chosen, there are likely to be unmeasured and thus uncontrolled differences between married couples who do and do not have a child during a given period of time. For instance, the nonparents may be more individualistic, on the average, than the parents, and it is possible (indeed likely) that duration-of-marriage effects are more severely negative for highly individualistic spouses than for others. If so, the use of a control group of nonparents will lead to an underestimation of any negative effect of the transition to parenthood on marital quality. Of course, it is still better to study the transition to parenthood with longitudinal than cross-sectional data and to use a control group than not to do so, but the results of the research should be interpreted with the limitations of even the best of the feasible designs in mind.

The tendency to have too much confidence in longitudinal research is an aspect of a more general shortcoming, namely, a pervasive tendency for researchers to make stronger causal conclusions than the evidence warrants. In this respect, reports of research on marital quality during the past decade were generally superior to those in many if not most other areas of social research. Although unwarranted (untentative) conclusions about causation can be found in the 1980s marital quality literature, they are far less common there than in the literature on some other family topics or in research articles in such leading social science journals as the *American Sociological Review*, the *American Journal of Sociology*, and *Social Forces*.[8] Marital quality researchers often related their dependent variables to independent variables without making any causal inferences or arriving at even tentative causal conclusions (e.g., Holman and Jacquart, 1988; Yogev and Brett, 1985). Such conservatism may seem extreme, but it is preferable to lack of caution about making causal conclusions.

A SELECTIVE REVIEW OF FINDINGS

Marital Quality as a Dependent Variable

As in the past, the main concern of quantitative researchers who studied marital quality in the 1980s was to explain it or estimate how different influences affected it. I organize the discussion below according to the kinds of independent variables used in the research, beginning with three related ones that need to be treated together.

Family stage, presence-absence of children, and duration of marriage. Prior to 1980 at least a dozen cross-sectional studies found the now familiar curvilinear relationship between family stage and marital quality, whereby the average quality is higher in the preparental and postparental stages (see Ade-Ridder and Brubaker, 1983, for a summary of the findings). Several other studies that did not compare all of the stages found that average marital quality was higher in either the preparental or the postparental stage than in the parental ones. Research in the 1980s continued to find evidence for the curvilinear pattern (e.g., Anderson, Russell, and Schumm, 1983; Glenn, 1989a), and most of the General Social Surveys show a curvilinear relationship between family stage and reported marital happiness.[9] The relationship may not exist for all dimensions of marital quality (see Swensen, Eskew, and Kohlhepp, 1981, for evidence that different dimensions of marital quality do not bear the same relationship to family stage), but that there is, or recently has been, a curvilinear relationship between family stage and some aspects of marital quality is about as close to being certain as anything ever is in the social sciences.

The meaning of the relationship remains unclear, however. The most common interpretation is that it reflects the addition of children to the family, their maturation, and their departure, but to some degree the cross-sectional variation in marital quality by family stage must also reflect the effects of (*a*) duration of marriage, (*b*) the removal of many marriages from each marriage cohort through divorce as the cohort grows older, and (*c*) differences among different marriage cohorts. During the 1980s there was an increase in the realization that the cross-sectional relationship between family stage and marital quality confounds the effects of so many influences that studying it by itself is not very useful. Furthermore, enough research focused on specific kinds of effects, or was designed to disentangle the different kinds, that some reasonable judgments can be made about the kinds of effects reflected in different aspects of the curvilinear relationship.

The most confident judgments can be made about the reasons for the difference in indicated marital quality between the preparental and early parental stages. The difference is fairly substantial, and since it has been found by many studies conducted over a period of several decades, it cannot very well be simply a difference between marriage cohorts. Furthermore, were it not for the high divorce rate in the early years of marriage, which quickly removes many marital failures from the population of intact marriages, the difference in average quality of marriages between the preparental and early parental stages would be much greater than it is. An important longitudinal study in the mid-1980s found a substantial decline in average reported marital quality during the first year (Huston et al., 1986)—a finding that essentially removes any doubt about important negative effects on the quality of marriages in the very early stages. The extent to which these are effects of duration of marriage or the transition to parenthood is less clear.

Much research during the 1980s was devoted to effects of the transition to parenthood on marriage, and many of the studies were longitudinal, with assessments of marital quality before and after the transition.[10] The research varied considerably in sample design, measurement of marital quality, and when the measures were taken in relation to the birth of the first child, but the results were quite consistent. Most of the studies found lower average quality after the transition than before (e.g., Belsky, Lang, and Spanier, 1985; Belsky and Rovine, 1984; Belsky, Spanier, and Rovine, 1983; Cowan et al., 1985; Feldman and Nash, 1984; Goldberg, Michaels, and Lamb, 1985; Miller and Sollie, 1980; Waldron and Routh, 1981), and of those that found such a change, most found it to be greater among wives than husbands.

Such change by itself of course does not prove a negative effect of the transition to parenthood, since the transition usually occurs during the early years of marriage when marital quality is likely to decline whether the couple has a child or not. To estimate the effects of the transition, at least two studies used a control group of couples who did not have a child during the course of the study. McHale and Huston (1985) gathered data on 168 couples two months after their weddings and again about a year later. Both couples who did and did not have a child experienced a decline in marital satisfaction and feelings of love for one another, the degree of change being about the same for the two groups. However, those who had a child experienced changes in companionship and marital role patterns that the nonparents did not experience. Therefore, the study provided evidence of important effects of the transition to parenthood but also suggested that much of the change often attributed to the transition is a duration-of-marriage effect.

A second important longitudinal study with a control group of nonparents was conducted by White and Booth (1985b), who interviewed (by phone) a national sample of married persons at three-year intervals, in 1980 and 1983. Of the 220 respondents who were childless in 1980 and who met other conditions for inclusion in the study, 107 had a child by 1983, while 113 did not. Marital quality, as indicated by six measures, tended to decline from Time 1 to Time 2, but the changes were about the same for persons who did and did not become parents. Again, the evidence suggests that changes often attributed to the transition to parenthood are duration-of-marriage effects instead.[11]

Their finding of no apparent negative effect on marriage of the transition to parenthood led White and Booth to consider why several cross-sectional studies, including some reported during the 1980s (e.g., Campbell, 1981; Glenn and McLanahan, 1982), estimated that the presence of a child or children in the home lessens marital quality. They speculated that while the presence of children may not appreciably lower marital quality, it may delay the divorces of many couples with low-quality marriages and thus create an association in cross-sectional data between the presence of children and low marital quality. In a follow-up study, White, Booth, and Edwards (1986) found support for the hypothesis that children delay the divorces of dissatisfied couples, but they also found evidence that children tend to lower marital quality by lessening the level of spousal interaction, creating dissatisfaction with finances and the division of labor, and moving the division of labor in a traditional direction.[12]

Another apparent reason for the cross-sectional association of the presence of children with low marital quality is a failure of many of the studies to control precisely for duration of marriage. For instance, Glenn and McLanahan (1982), who used data from the General Social Surveys, controlled age and age at first marriage, thus in effect controlling duration of marriage for persons in their first marriages, but not doing so for those in second and subsequent marriages. Those authors found a small but statistically significant estimated negative effect of children on the marital happiness of white husbands, but Glenn (1989a), in an analysis of GSS data in which duration of marriage was precisely controlled and the use of dummy variables allowed for the nonlinear relationship between marital duration and happiness, found no apparent effect among white husbands in their first marriages.

All in all, the evidence from research during

the 1980s makes any important average effect of children on the marriages of American husbands seem doubtful, although there may typically be temporary problems of adjustment after the first child is born. In contrast, important negative effects of children on the marriages of wives are quite likely, though not conclusively proven. However, the findings of two mid-decade cross-sectional studies (Abbott and Brody, 1985; Schumm and Bugaighis, 1986) suggest that the effects may be restricted to certain kinds of wives, namely, those with two children and at least one male child (first study) and low-income mothers employed full-time (second study). Since both studies used local and possibly unrepresentative samples, not much confidence can be placed in their findings, but the possibility that only a small proportion of all wives accounts for the estimated negative effects of children is important and worthy of further study.

Not much research during the 1980s was designed to estimate duration-of-marriage effects on marital quality beyond the first few years, and in contrast to the 1970s, little attention was given to the transition to postparenthood. However, a study by Glenn (1989a) estimated that marital success, as indicated by the percentage of persons still married and who say their marriages are "very happy," goes steadily and appreciably downward in a marriage cohort for at least the first 10 years and maybe for 25 years or longer.

Premarital cohabitation. Cohabitation of unmarried men and women in the United States has increased substantially in the past few years (Glick, 1988), and advocates of the practice claim that it can serve as a trial marriage to test the couple's compatibility and the individuals' suitability for marriage. This reasoning has led to the belief that couples who cohabit before they marry should generally have better marriages than those who do not do so.

The relevant research during the 1980s failed to support the hypothesis that premarital cohabitation is associated with marital success. Three American studies found cohabitation before marriage to be negatively associated with marital quality (Booth and Johnson, 1988; DeMaris, 1984; DeMaris and Leslie, 1984; Watson, 1983), while a fourth found that association among blacks but not among whites (Crohan and Veroff, 1989). As the decade ended, evidence from American studies of cohabitation and marital stability had not yet been published, but a study with Swedish data found an association between premarital cohabitation and a tendency to divorce (Bennett, Blanc, and Bloom, 1988), while a number of studies with Canadian data estimated that prior cohabitation has either a negative effect on marital stability (Balakrishnan, Rao, Lapierre-Adamcyk, and Krotki, 1987; Burch and Madan, 1986) or no effect (Trussell and Rao, 1989; White, 1987, 1989).[13]

This evidence does not refute the view that premarital cohabitation prepares couples for marriage and prevents many marriages that would have been unsuccessful, but it does indicate that any such beneficial consequences are not strong enough to offset negative effects from the cohabitation or some characteristic or characteristics of individuals who are prone to cohabit. The cohabitation itself may often exert negative influences on the marriage that follows it, or it may often lead to the marriage of incompatible persons—for instance, if cohabiting couples experience stronger average parental pressure to marry than dating couples. On the other hand, the tendencies to cohabit before marriage and to have problems in marriage may commonly result from unconventionality and/or other characteristics of individuals. This is the explanation favored by most authors who have written on the subject, and considerable evidence tends to support it. For instance, Yamaguchi and Kandel (1985) found that drug use is associated with cohabitation, and Booth and Johnson (1988) found that controlling a number of variables indicative of personality problems and lack of commitment to marriage substantially reduced the negative relationship between premarital cohabitation and marital quality.

Booth and Johnson also reasoned that some of the negative association may have resulted from the fact that premarital cohabitors marry at a later point in their relationship than other couples, perhaps typically at a time when the quality of the relationship is already declining. (See the evidence on marital duration and quality above.) That is, the best time in the relationship of many couples who cohabit and then marry may be before they marry. Booth and Johnson rejected this explanation because they found about the same relationship between marital duration and quality among couples who did and did not cohabit before marriage, but the evidence does not prove that the explanation is not partially correct.

Marriage order. Research on remarriage increased steeply in the 1980s, and much of it dealt with marital quality. The extent of the increase in research on the quality of remarriages is shown by the publication or completion dates of the 34 studies included in a recent meta-analysis of studies on the subject (Vemer, Coleman, Ganong, and Cooper, 1989): 24 in the 1980s, 7 in the 1970s, and 3 earlier.[14]

This meta-analysis supported two conclusions, namely, (a) average marital quality is slightly greater in first marriages than in remarriages after divorce, and (b) average quality in remarriages is somewhat higher for men than for women. However, these conclusions must be viewed with caution, since the meta-analysis included studies that used both probability and nonprobability samples. Of the three 1980s studies that used large national probability samples, one found average marital quality to be lower among persons in remarriages (Glenn, 1981) while two did not (Weingarten, 1980; White and Booth, 1985a), and the latter two studies used more sophisticated measures of marital quality than the first one.

Remarriages do seem to suffer from some kind of handicap, however, since they apparently are more prone to divorce than first marriages, at least during the early years (McCarthy, 1978; White and Booth, 1985a), and since the higher mean age at which remarriages occur predicts a substantially lower divorce rate for them than for first marriages. White and Booth (1985a), who reported the best available evidence on the nature of this handicap, found that the higher divorce rate among remarriages was limited to those in which both spouses had been previously married and in which there were stepchildren in the household. Furthermore, they found that remarried persons with stepchildren reported less satisfaction with their family life, though they did not feel less positively about their marriages, than married persons with only biological children in the household. Therefore, the presence of stepchildren seems to be one important handicapping influence on remarriages—possibly the only major one. White and Booth concluded that apparently stepchildren do not affect marital quality but do lower the quality of family life and parent-child relations. If so, any effect of stepchildren on

the propensity to divorce is not through marital quality, and the overall quality of family life is an important influence on marital stability.

Miscellaneous independent variables. Outside the main areas of research, dozens of independent variables were related to marital quality in the 1980s, the few studies mentioned below being illustrative of this large and diverse body of research.

Although not a major topic of concern, the effect of wives' employment attracted some attention. For instance, Locksley (1980), who used data from a large national United States sample and 14 indicators of marital quality, found no evidence that wives' employment affects marital quality from the perspective of either wives or husbands. In contrast, Houseknecht and Macke (1981), who studied 663 women with high-level graduate degrees from the same university, found average marital adjustment to be higher among those working outside the home. However, other evidence from the study indicated that the woman's working was not as important as the husband's being supportive of her working. Overall, the results of the study suggest that the effects of work-related influences on marital quality are different for highly educated women than for others.[15]

A fair amount of research focused on the quality of the marriages of older couples. In a study related to the family stage research summarized above, Lee (1988b) investigated the hypothesis that marital satisfaction tends to rise in late-life marriages because of the diminishing demands of nonmarital roles. In a Washington State sample of older spouses, he found no evidence that nonmarital roles aside from the parental one tended to lower marital satisfaction. Rather, frequency of interaction with friends was the strongest *positive* predictor of marital satisfaction. In another study with data from the same sample, Lee (1988a) found that persons who confided in their spouses had markedly higher marital satisfaction than those who did not do so.

Some important topics received surprisingly little attention. One example of a rare study of an important topic is Bowen and Orthner's (1983) study of husband-wife differences in gender role attitudes and marital quality. In a study of 331 military couples, the authors found no consistent support for the hypothesis that low marital quality is associated with incongruent attitudes, but they did find unusually low quality in marriages in which the husband's attitudes were traditional and the wife's were modern. Another example is Yogev and Brett's (1985) study of perceptions of the division of housework and child care and marital satisfaction. The relationship differed among different kinds of spouses; husbands in dual-earner marriages and wives in single-earner marriages were most satisfied, on the average, if they perceived that their spouse did more than his or her share of the work, while other spouses were most satisfied if they perceived that each spouse did a fair share.

Marital Quality as an Independent Variable

As earlier, relatively few studies during the 1980s used marital quality as an independent variable. Among those few, the most numerous ones were designed to estimate the effect of marital quality on the global well-being of married persons.

Glenn and Weaver (1981) used data from the 1973 through 1978 General Social Surveys to estimate, with regression analysis, the effect of marital happiness on global happiness separately for white men, black men, white women, and black women, and they compared the estimated effect of marital happiness with that of satisfaction with each of seven life domains, ranging from work to health. According to the estimates, the effect of marital happiness was stronger than that of any kind of satisfaction except among black males, for whom the estimated effects of satisfaction with work and community were the strongest. For married whites working full-time (both men and women) and all married black women, the estimated effect of marital happiness was greater than the estimated combined effects of all seven kinds of satisfaction. For both whites and blacks, the estimated effects of marital happiness on global happiness were stronger for women than for men.

Several subsequent studies also found a strong relationship between measures of marital quality and global subjective well-being. For instance, Benin and Nienstedt (1985) used data from the 1978 through 1983 General Social Surveys to estimate, with log-linear analysis, the effects of job satisfaction, marital happiness, stage of the life cycle, and education on global happiness in each of four subsamples (housewives, husbands of housewives, working wives, and husbands of working wives). When the dependent variable was dichotomized "very happy" versus other responses, the estimated effect was greater in each subsample for marital happiness than for any other independent variable, but when the dependent variable was dichotomized "not too happy" versus other responses, job satisfaction was the strongest estimated determinant.

The authors of studies relating reported marital and global happiness have tended to believe that the former affects the latter without there being much effect of the latter on the former, but none of the reported data can help to establish the direction of any causal relationship. Although there are reasons to believe that having a good marriage will tend to make a person pleased with life in general, people who are generally happy, for whatever reasons, may tend to have good marriages. Furthermore, some of the relationship between reported marital and global happiness is likely to be spurious, resulting from effects on both from such variables as physical health, a socially or genetically inherited proclivity to substance abuse, and pre-adult influences on adult socioeconomic status. Or, some of the relationship between the two kinds of reported happiness may result from correlated response bias, that is, from a tendency for the same respondents to "overreport" or "underreport" positive feelings of all or most kinds. The lesson is clear: evidence relating marital quality to the quality of life in general should be interpreted with caution.

Better data and more sophisticated analyses can provide additional clues about causal relationships but not definitive evidence. Ultimately, strong conclusions about causal direction must be based on theory and knowledge about the phenomena studied from sources other than the data set at hand (side information). How side information can lead to a confident conclusion, though not certainty, about the direction of causation between marital quality and an aspect of psychological well-being is illustrated by a study reported by Brodbar-Nemzer (1986). The author found in a sample of Chicago residents that a number of marital quality variables related more strongly to self-esteem among Jews than among either Protestants or Catholics. Brodbar-Nemzer predicted this outcome on the basis of literature claiming that Jews value families more highly than

Christians do, the causal hypothesis being that marital quality affects self-esteem more strongly among Jews than Christians. One can be fairly confident that the causal hypothesis is correct, since there is no apparent reason why Jews should differ from Christians in the observed manner if self-esteem affects marital quality rather than vice versa.

CONCLUSIONS

The accomplishments reviewed above are rather modest—arguably less impressive than the accomplishments in the 1970s in the quantitative study of marital quality. The 1980s were not a decade of great breakthroughs in either methods or the application of theory in research, although methodological advances were considerably greater than theoretical ones.

As the decade ended, far too many of the quantitative studies of marital quality were still being conducted with small convenience samples, and many researchers seemed still not to recognize that little can be learned about the bases of marital success from cross-sectional studies of intact marriages. Many important questions about marital quality were not addressed in the 1980s or were the subject of very little research. For instance, no data were published from systematic studies of change in the overall level of marital quality or in duration-specific rates of marital success in the United States.[16]

On the positive side, several developments laid the foundation for greater progress in the 1990s than that which occurred in the 1980s. For instance, a few longitudinal studies of married couples were started and are continuing, much intelligent discussion of conceptual and measurement issues dispelled some of the earlier confusion, and a change began that must take place before much understanding of the bases of marital success can be gained, namely, a shift from studies of marital quality at one point in time to research in which marital quality and stability (divorce or nondivorce) are both taken into account. Such a change requires longitudinal data or retrospective data gathered from previously married as well as currently married persons, and it requires new data collection efforts as well as new strategies of analysis.

Let us proceed with the work that needs to be done.

NOTES

1. I use the term "mainstream" only with reference to the major emphases of this journal.

2. They were still quite often used interchangeably during the 1980s, especially in reviews of research findings. Authors of at least two articles used "marital satisfaction" in the titles but presented data on marital happiness in the bodies of the articles (Donohue and Ryder, 1982; Heaton, 1984). The lack of correspondence between the titles and substance of the articles is not in itself a serious deficiency, but it may have encouraged other authors to compare incomparable findings.

3. The authors of one article (Donohue and Ryder, 1982) argued against the use of global evaluations, primarily on the ground that a number of independent variables traditionally used in marital quality research do not explain much of the variance in at least one single-item global evaluation (responses to the widely used marital happiness item). However, use of explained variance as a criterion of importance has recently been attacked by several sophisticated methodologists (see especially Lieberson, 1985). The considerable random measurement error in single-item indicators limits the amount of their variance that even the most important independent variables can explain, but if researchers take this into account and do not overemphasize explained variance in their interpretation of findings, such measures may nevertheless be useful. There are of course important issues about possible systematic measurement error in such indicators, but concentrating on explained variance does not help to deal with such issues.

4. I am not referring to the fact that researchers on marital quality were slow to use such faddish techniques as general structural equation modeling and meta-analysis. Although these techniques can be useful, all too often researchers have used them to delude themselves into thinking they have achieved greater rigor than they have achieved or can achieve.

5. Spanier and Cole (1976) have argued that marital adjustment is a process rather than a condition, but it has almost always been measured at one or a few discrete points in time and treated as a condition.

6. Some of the most important 1980s publications on the measurement of marital quality include Snyder, Wills, and Keiser (1981); Roach, Frazier, and Bowden (1981); Huston and Robins (1982); Spanier and Thompson (1982); Norton (1983); Sabatelli (1984); Huston et al. (1986); Schumm et al. (1986); and Fincham and Bradbury (1987).

7. For elaboration on this and related points, see Glenn (1989b).

8. I base this statement on a recent study I did of unwarranted causal conclusions in research reports in major sociology journals.

9. I base this statement on unpublished data in my files.

10. For a good review of the studies reported before mid-decade, see Worthington and Buston (1986).

11. As I point out above, longitudinal studies such as the two described here cannot definitively separate duration-of-marriage effects from the effects of the transition to parenthood, but they provide better estimates than could be provided by analysis of cross-sectional data.

12. For an extensive review of research on the effects of children on marriage, see Belsky (1989).

13. The associations on which these estimates of effects are based may be, and indeed are likely to be, spurious.

14. In many of the studies included in this meta-analysis of "marital satisfaction," the dependent variable was not marital satisfaction but was some other aspect of marital quality such as marital adjustment or marital happiness.

15. For a review of research on this topic through a large portion of the decade, see Spitze (1988).

16. A few studies conducted during the decade dealt incidentally with changes in marital quality (e.g., Greeley, 1989; McLanahan and Adams, 1989; Veroff, Douvan, and Kulka, 1981).

References

Abbott, Douglas A., and Gene H. Brody. 1985. "The relation of child age, gender, and number of children to the marital adjustment of wives." Journal of Marriage and the Family 47: 77–84.

Achen, Christopher H. 1986. The Statistical Analysis of Quasi-Experiments. Berkeley: University of California Press.

Ade-Ridder, Linda, and Timothy H. Brubaker. 1983. "The quality of long-term marriages." Pp. 21–30 in Timothy H. Brubaker (ed.), Family Relationships in Later Life. Beverly Hills, CA: Sage Publications.

Anderson, Stephen A., Candyce S. Russell, and Walter R. Schumm. 1983. "Perceived marital quality and family life-cycle categories: A further analysis." Journal of Marriage and the Family 45: 127–139.

Bahr, Stephen J., C. Bradford Chappell, and Geoffrey K. Leigh. 1983. "Age at marriage, role enactment, role consensus, and marital satisfaction." Journal of Marriage and the Family 45: 795–803.

Balakrishnan, T. R., K. Vaninadha Rao, Evelyne Lapierre-Adamcyk, and Karol Krotki. 1987. "A hazard model analysis of the covariates of marriage dissolution in Canada." Demography 24: 395–406.

Bellah, Robert N., Richard Madsen, William N. Sullivan, Ann Swidler, and Steven N. Tipton. 1985. Habits of the Heart: Individualism and Commitment in American Life. Berkeley: University of California Press.

Belsky, Jay. 1989. "The effects of children on marriage." In Frank D. Fincham and Thomas M. Bradbury (eds.), The Psychology of Marriage: Conceptual, Empirical, and Applied Contributions. New York: Guilford Press.

Belsky, Jay, Mary E. Lang, and Michael Rovine. 1985. "Stability and change in marriage across the transition to parenthood: A second study." Journal of Marriage and the Family 47: 855–865.

Belsky, Jay, Graham Spanier, and Michael Rovine. 1983. "Stability and change in marriage across the transition to parenthood." Journal of Marriage and the Family 45: 567–577.

Belsky, Jay, and Michael Rovine. 1984. "Social-network contact, family support, and the transition to parenthood." Journal of Marriage and the Family 46: 455–462.

Benin, Mary Holland, and Barbara Cable Nienstedt. 1985. "Happiness in single- and dual-earner families: The effects of marital happiness, job satisfaction, and life cycle." Journal of Marriage and the Family 47: 975–984.

Bennett, Neil, Ann Blanc, and David Bloom. 1988. "Commitment and the modern union: Assessing the link between premarital cohabitation and subsequent marital stability." American Sociological Review 53: 997–1008.

Blalock, Hubert M., Jr. 1966. "The identification problem and theory building: The case of status inconsistency." American Sociological Review 31: 52–61.

Blalock, Hubert M., Jr. 1967. "Status inconsistency, social mobility, status integration, and structural effects." American Sociological Review 32: 790–801.

Booth, Alan, and David Johnson. 1988. "Premarital cohabitation and marital success." Journal of Family Issues 9: 255–272.

Bowen, Gary Lee, and Dennis K. Orthner. 1983. "Sex-role congruency and marital quality." Journal of Marriage and the Family 45: 223–230.

Brodbar-Nemzer, Jay Y. 1986. "Marital relationships and self-esteem: How Jewish families are different." Journal of Marriage and the Family 48: 89–98.

Bumpass, Larry L., and James A. Sweet. 1972. "Differentials in marital instability: 1970." American Sociological Review 37: 754–766.

Burch, Thomas K., and Ashok K. Madan. 1986. Union Formation and Dissolution: Results from the 1984 Family History Survey. Catalogue No. 99–963. Ottawa: Statistics Canada.

Campbell, Angus. 1981. The Sense of Well-being in America: Recent Patterns and Trends. New York: McGraw-Hill.

Campbell, Angus, Philip E. Converse, and Willard L. Rodgers. 1976. The Quality of American Life: Perceptions, Evaluations, and Satisfactions. New York: Russell Sage Foundation.

Crohan, Susan E., and Joseph Veroff. 1989. "Dimensions of marital well-being among white and black newlweds." Journal of Marriage and the Family 51: 373–383.

Cowan, Carolyn P., Philip A. Cowan, Gertrude Heming, Ellen Garrett, William S. Coyish, Harriet Curtis-Boles, and Abner J. Boles III. 1985. "Transitions to parenthood: His, hers, and theirs." Journal of Family Issues 6: 451–482.

Davis, James A. 1989. The General Social Surveys, 1972–1989: Cumulative Data File. Chicago: National Opinion Research Center.

DeMaris, Alfred. 1984. "A comparison of remarriages with first marriages on satisfaction in marriage and its relation to prior cohabitation." Family Relations 33: 443–449.

DeMaris, Alfred, and Gerald R. Leslie. 1984. "Cohabitation with the future spouse: Its influence upon marital satisfaction and communication." Journal of Marriage and the Family 46: 77–84.

Donohue, Kevin C., and Robert G. Ryder. 1982. "A methodological note on marital satisfaction and social variables." Journal of Marriage and the Family 44: 743–747.

Duncan, Otis Dudley. 1984. Notes on Social Measurement: Historical and Critical. New York: Russell Sage Foundation.

Feldman, Shirley S., and S. C. Nash. 1984. "The transition from expectancy to parenthood: Impact of the firstborn child on men and women." Sex Roles 11: 84–92.

Fincham, Frank D., and Thomas N. Bradbury. 1987. "The assessment of marital quality: A reevaluation." Journal of Marriage and the Family 49: 797–809.

Glenn, Norval D. 1981. "The well-being of persons remarried after divorce." Journal of Family Issues 2: 61–75.

Glenn, Norval D. 1982. "Interreligious marriage in the United States: Patterns and recent trends." Journal of Marriage and the Family 44: 555–566.

Glenn, Norval D. 1989a. "Duration of marriage, family composition, and marital happiness." National Journal of Sociology 3: 3–24.

Glenn, Norval D. 1989b. "Some limitations of longitudinal and cohort designs in social and behavioral research." Pp. 55–62 in Lee Sechrest, Howard Freeman, and Albert Mulley (eds.), Health Service Research Methodology: A Focus on AIDS. Rockville, MD: National Center for Health Services Research and Health Care Technology Assessment.

Glenn, Norval D., and Sara McLanahan. 1982. "Children and marital happiness: A further specification of the relationship." Journal of Marriage and the Family 44: 63–72.

Glenn, Norval D., and Charles N. Weaver. 1978. "A multivariate, multi-survey study of marital happiness." Journal of Marriage and the Family 40: 269–282.

Glenn, Norval D., and Charles N. Weaver. 1981. "The contribution of marital happiness to global happiness." Journal of Marriage and the Family 43: 161–168.

Glick, Paul C. 1988. "Fifty years of family demography: A record of social change." Journal of Marriage and the Family 50: 861–873.

Glick, Paul C., and Arthur Norton. 1977. "Marrying, divorcing, and living together in the U.S. today." Population Bulletin 32.

Goldberg, Wendy A., Gerald Y. Michaels, and Michael E. Lamb. 1985. "Husbands' and wives' patterns of adjustment to pregnancy and first parenthood." Journal of Family Issues 6: 483–504.

Greeley, Andrew. 1989. "The declining morale of women." Sociology and Social Research 73: 53–58.

Heaton, Tim B. 1984. "Religious homogamy and marital satisfaction reconsidered." Journal of Marriage and the Family 46: 729–733.

Holland, Paul W., and Donald Rubin. 1983. "On Lord's Paradox." In H. Wainer and D. Messick (eds.), Principles of Modern Psychological Measurement. Hillsdale, NJ: Lawrence Erlbaum.

Holman, Thomas B., and Mary Jacquart. 1988. "Leisure-activity patterns and marital satisfaction." Journal of Marriage and the Family 50: 69–77.

Houseknecht, Sharon K., and Anne S. Macke. 1981. "Combining marriage and career: The marital adjustment of professional women." Journal of Marriage and the Family 43: 651–661.

Huston, Ted L., Susan M. McHale, and Ann C. Crouter. 1986. "When the honeymoon is over: Changes in the marriage relationship over the first year." In Robin Gilmour and Steve Duck (eds.), The Emerging Field of Close Relationships. Hillsdale, NJ: Erlbaum.

Huston, Ted L., and Elliot Robins. 1982. "Conceptual and methodological issues in studying close relationships." Journal of Marriage and the Family 44: 901–925.

Johnson, David R., Lynn K. White, John N. Edwards, and Alan Booth. 1986. "Dimensions of marital quality: Toward methodological and conceptual refinement." Journal of Family Issues 7: 31–49.

LaLonde, Robert J. 1986. "Evaluating the econometric evaluations of training programs with experimental data." American Economic Review 76: 604–620.

Lee, Gary R. 1988a. "Marital intimacy among older persons: The spouse as confidant." Journal of Family Issues 9: 273–284.

Lee, Gary R. 1988b. "Marital satisfaction in later life: The effects of nonmarital roles." Journal of Marriage and the Family 50: 775–783.

Lieberson, Stanley. 1985. Making It Count: The Improvement of Social Research and Theory. Berkeley: University of California Press.

Locksley, Anne. 1980. "On the effects of wives' employment on marital adjustment and companionship." Journal of Marriage and the Family 42: 337–346.

McCarthy, James. 1978. "A comparison of the probability of the dissolution of first and second marriages." Demography 15: 345–360.

McHale, Susan M., and Ted L. Huston. 1985. "The effect of the transition to parenthood on the marriage relationship: A longitudinal study." Journal of Family Issues 6: 409–434.

McLanahan, Sara, and Julia Adams. 1989. "The effects of children on adults' psychological well-being: 1957–1976." Social Forces 68: 124–146.

Miller, Brent, and Donna Sollie. 1980. "Normal stresses during the transition to parenthood." Family Relations 29: 459–465.

Norton, Robert. 1983. "Measuring marital quality: A

critical look at the dependent variable." Journal of Marriage and the Family 45: 141–151.

Ortega, Suzanne T., Hugh P. Whitt, and J. Allen Williams, Jr. 1988. "Religious homogamy and marital happiness." Journal of Family Issues 9: 224–239.

Roach, Arthur J., Larry P. Frazier, and Sharon R. Bowden. 1981. "The marital satisfaction scale: Development of a measure for intervention research." Journal of Marriage and the Family 43: 537–546.

Rogler, Lloyd H., and Mary E. Procidano. 1989. "Marital heterogamy and marital quality in Puerto Rican families." Journal of Marriage and the Family 51: 363–372.

Rogosa, David, and John B. Willet. 1985. "Satisfying a simplex structure is simpler than it should be." Journal of Educational Statistics 10: 99–107.

Rubin, Lillian B. 1983. Intimate Strangers: Men and Women Together. New York: Harper and Row.

Sabatelli, Ronald M. 1984. "The Marital Comparison Level Index: A measure for assessing outcomes relative to expectations." Journal of Marriage and the Family 46: 651–662.

Sabatelli, Ronald M. 1988. "Measurement issues in marital research: A review and critique of contemporary survey instruments." Journal of Marriage and the Family 50: 891–915.

Schoen, Robert. 1975. "California divorce rates by age at first marriage and duration of first marriage." Journal of Marriage and the Family 37: 548–555.

Schumm, Walter R., and Margaret A. Bugaighis. 1986. "Marital quality over the marital career: Alternative explanations." Journal of Marriage and the Family 48: 165–168.

Schumm, Walter R., Lois A. Paff-Bergen, Ruth C. Hatch, Felix C. Obiorah, Janette M. Copeland, Lori D. Meens, and Margaret A. Bugaighis. 1986. "Concurrent and discriminant validity of the Kansas Marital Satisfaction Scale." Journal of Marriage and the Family 48: 381–387.

Snyder, Douglas K., Robert M. Wills, and Thomas W. Keiser. 1981. "Empirical validation of the Marital Satisfaction Inventory: An actuarial approach." Journal of Consulting and Clinical Psychology 49: 262–268.

Spanier, Graham B. 1976. "Measuring dyadic adjustment: New scales for assessing the quality of marriage and similar dyads." Journal of Marriage and the Family 42: 15–27.

Spanier, Graham B., and C. L. Cole. 1976. "Toward clarification and investigation of marital adjustment." International Journal of Sociology of the Family 6: 121–146.

Spanier, Graham B., and Robert Lewis. 1980. "Marital quality: A review of the seventies." Journal of Marriage and the Family 42: 825–839.

Spanier, Graham B., and Linda Thompson. 1982. "A confirmatory analysis of the Dyadic Adjustment Scale." Journal of Marriage and the Family 44: 731–738.

Spitze, Glenna. 1988. "Women's employment and family relations: A review." Journal of Marriage

and the Family 50: 595–618. [Reprinted in this volume]

Swenson, Clifford H., Ron W. Eskew, and Karen A. Kohlhepp. 1981. "Stage of family life cycle, ego development, and the marital relationship." Journal of Marriage and the Family 43: 841–853.

Trost, Jan E. 1985. "Abandon adjustment!" Journal of Marriage and the Family 47: 1072–1073.

Trussell, James, and K. Vaninadha Rao. 1989. "Premarital cohabitation and marital stability: A reassessment of the Canadian evidence." Journal of Marriage and the Family 51: 535–540.

Vemer, Elizabeth, Marilyn Coleman, Lawrence H. Ganong, and Harris Cooper. 1989. "Marital satisfaction in remarriage: A meta-analysis." Journal of Marriage and the Family 51: 713–725.

Vera, Hernan, Donna H. Berardo, and Felix M. Berardo. 1985. "Age heterogamy in marriage." Journal of Marriage and the Family 47: 553–566.

Veroff, Joseph, Elizabeth Douvan, and Richard A. Kulka. 1981. The Inner American: A Self-Portrait from 1957 to 1976. New York: Basic Books.

Waldron, Holly, and Donald K. Routh. 1981. "The effect of the first child on the marital relationship." Journal of Marriage and the Family 43: 785–788.

Watson, Roy E. L. 1983. "Premarital cohabitation vs. traditional courtship: Their effects on subsequent marital adjustment." Family Relations 32: 139–147.

Weingarten, Helen. 1980. "Remarriage and well-being: National survey evidence of social and psychological effects." Journal of Family Issues 1: 533–559.

White, James M. 1987. "Premarital cohabitation and marital stability in Canada." Journal of Marriage and the Family 49: 641–647.

White, James M. 1989. "Reply to comment by Trussell and Rao: A reanalysis of the data." Journal of Marriage and the Family 51: 540–544.

White, Lynn K., and Alan Booth. 1985a. "The quality and stability of remarriages: The role of stepchildren." American Sociological Review 50: 689–698.

White, Lynn K., and Alan Booth. 1985b. "Transition to parenthood and marital quality." Journal of Family Issues 6: 435–450.

White, Lynn K., Alan Booth, and John N. Edwards. 1986. "Children and marital happiness: Why the negative correlation?" Journal of Family Issues 7: 131–147.

Worthington, Everett L., Jr., and Beverley G. Buston. 1986. "The marriage relationship during the transition to parenthood: A review and a model." Journal of Family Issues 7: 443–473.

Yamaguchi, Kazuo, and Denise Kandel. 1985. "Dynamic relationships between premarital cohabitation and illicit drug use: An event-history analysis of role selection and role socialization." American Sociological Review 50: 530–546.

Yogev, Sara, and Jeanne Brett. 1985. "Perceptions of the division of housework and child care and marital satisfaction." Journal of Marriage and the Family 47: 609–618.

Patricia Noller   *University of Queensland, Australia*

Mary Anne Fitzpatrick   *University of Wisconsin–Madison**

Marital Communication in the Eighties

This review of the research on marital communication conducted during the past decade notes an increasing emphasis on attempting to identify factors that mediate the relation between marital communication and marital satisfaction, rather than just describing the differences between those high and low in satisfaction. Longitudinal studies that allow the development of causal models have also been important. The decade of the eighties has seen the development of sophisticated technological and statistical procedures that have enabled researchers to use multiple methods and obtain different perspectives on the same interaction. Although we know much more about marital communication and the various processes involved than we did at the beginning of the decade, much more work still needs to be done.

Moving beyond theories of social learning (e.g., Birchler, Weiss, and Vincent, 1975) and behavior exchange (e.g., Gottman et al., 1976), which provided the impetus for much of the influential descriptive research on marital satisfaction that was done in the '70s and early '80s, attempts have been made more recently to develop models that focus on the processes by which marital communication affects, or is affected by, marital satisfaction. Of particular interest are the causal mechanisms that may account for this strong relation be-

tween a couples' communication patterns and the type of marriage they have. This increased interest in causal mechanisms has expressed itself in two ways: first, by the use of longitudinal designs (Kelly, Huston, and Cate, 1985; Markman, 1981; Noller and Callan, 1989), and second, by the inclusion of cognitive processes such as attributions for marital behavior (Fincham and Bradbury, 1987, 1989; Gaelick, Bodenhausen, and Wyer, 1985; Guthrie and Noller, 1988).

METHODOLOGY IN STUDIES OF MARITAL INTERACTION

In this section, we focus on three important issues: first, the sampling of actors, behaviors, and contexts; second, data analytic techniques that are unique to studies of marital communication, such as dealing with the dependencies in the data and the extent to which each partner's behavior affects the other; and third, the issue of whose perspective should be taken into account.

Sampling

In considering research in any domain, the researcher needs to be concerned with the sampling of actors, of behaviors, and of contexts. We would argue that a lack of representativeness in any sample poses a serious threat to the ecological validity of research on marital interaction. Whereas problems in the sampling of actors are often discussed, problems in the sampling of behaviors and contexts also need to be addressed.

Sampling of actors. In the past decade, the majority of the research on marital communication

Department of Psychology, University of Queensland, St. Lucia, Queensland 4067, Australia.

*Department of Communication Arts, University of Wisconsin–Madison, Madison, WI 53706.

has used convenience sampling, which relies heavily on middle-class respondents. Given the difficulty of asking for both spouses to participate in a research project that may involve hours of commitment, nonprobability sampling will continue. Although such samples are useful for an in-depth look at satisfied and dissatisfied marital interaction patterns, care must be exercised in discussing such research when we know that individuals value communication with a spouse differently, depending on such factors as occupation, education, and social class (Krokoff, Gottman, and Roy, 1988; Rubin, 1983).

Some research (Witteman and Fitzpatrick, 1986) has also involved probability sampling where married couples are selected from a pre-existing list (e.g., marriage license records) or random digit dialing (Christensen and King, 1982). Krokoff (1987) suggests ways of improving such samples. Fitzpatrick (1988) found no differences on any demographic variable between couples who participated in a questionnaire study and those who agreed to come into a laboratory for videotaping of marital interaction.

Sampling of behaviors. In the past decade there has been a general move toward the measurement of multiple communication behaviors in the same study. Recording techniques now available make microcoding of interaction possible, and videotaping can be used to record examples of natural interaction that can be coded in great detail. The availability of recordings has also stimulated the further development of coding systems to categorize units of behavior and enable the quantification of interaction data (e.g., Floyd and Markman, 1983; Hahlweg et al., 1984; Schaap, Buunk, and Kerkstra, 1988; Ting-Toomey, 1983). Two major coding schemes have dominated the literature: the Couples' Interaction Scoring System (Notarius, Markman, and Gottman, 1983) and the Marital Interaction Scoring System (Weiss and Summers, 1983).

The level of specificity at which researchers cast their hypotheses is an issue. Coding schemes can range on a continuum from the abstract (Margolin and Basco, 1984), which require more inferences on the part of the coders (e.g., defensive behavior), to the more concrete variables such as talk-time (Fitzpatrick and Dindia, 1986), which require fewer inferences. The major coding schemes used in the area tend to be abstract systems, in which reliability among coders is more difficult to achieve. Given that researchers have often found it necessary to combine codes in order to achieve appropriate levels of reliability, Revenstorf and associates (1984) offer a methodological discussion about developing summary codes. Clear rules need to be established for combining codes into summary codes.

Validity issues are also important and validity needs to be assessed. Criterion or discriminant validity are generally at the core of marital satisfaction research and are supported if the coding scheme can differentiate among couples of various identified types or can predict behaviors or marital satisfaction later in time. The CISS system (Notarius and Markman, 1981), for example, has successfully discriminated between satisfied and dissatisfied couples.

Sampling of contexts. For the most part, the focus on setting has involved the comparison of behavior in a laboratory to that in the home. Gottman (1980), in a between-subjects design, found more negativity in home settings than in a laboratory and more pronounced differences between distressed and nondistressed couples in the former situation.

In choosing a discussion task for married couples (Jacob, Tannenbaum, and Krahn, 1987), it is important to structure the task so that certain communication behaviors, such as problem-solving (Schaap et al., 1988; Ting-Toomey, 1983), emotional expression (Guthrie and Noller, 1988), or casual interaction (Fitzpatrick, 1988; Levenson and Gottman, 1983), can be examined and to ensure that the task is salient for couples. In the '70s, marital interaction frequently was elicited by using hypothetical conflicts (e.g., Olson and Ryder, 1970), while in the '80s it was far more common to allow couples to choose marital conflict issues that were important areas of disagreement for them. Salience becomes much less of an issue when real problems are used.

Data Structures and Analyses

There are a number of problems in dealing with data taken from husbands and wives, particularly because of the dependencies in the data and the fact that the effect of within-couple correlation can bias the validity of hypothesis testing. The statistical problem can generally be handled by the

use of repeated-measures designs with sex (husband-wife) as the within-subject factor.

Some marital communication researchers interested in studying the dependencies in the data
produced by husbands and wives view the problem as more substantive than statistical. The social relations model (Kenny and LaVoie, 1984) is a
model for the analysis of social interaction data
that examines explicitly the nonindependence in
interaction. The use of this model enables the separation of actor effects (consistent behavior
across interaction partners on the part of the
target), partner effects (the extent to which the individual consistently elicits particular behavior
from a range of targets), and relationship effects
(the extent to which a pair of interactants reciprocate or compensate for one another's behavior).
Fitzpatrick and Dindia (1986; see also Dindia,
1988) used the social relations model to study the
relations between an individual's interactions with
his or her spouse and interactions with strangers.

A further important methodology that has
continued to be used in the '80s involves sequential analysis in the study of pattern in marital communication (Fitzpatrick, 1984; Margolin and
Wampold, 1981; Schaap et al., 1988; Sillars, Pike,
Redmon, and Jones, 1983; Ting-Toomey, 1983).
While many excellent studies stop short of analyzing the patterning in the communication of
spouses over time, it is important to realize that
the exclusive use of rate or frequency data may
promote inferential errors such as the pseudo-
unilaterality problem (Duncan, 1983). For example, if researchers find that dissatisfied husbands
make more justifications for their behavior than
do wives, they may conclude that justifications
are related to the marital dissatisfaction of males
(an explanation based on frequency data). An
equally plausible explanation, however, is that the
wives of dissatisfied husbands act in some way
that leads their spouses to justify their behavior
(an explanation based on sequential data).

Patterning in marital communication can be
tested by examining messages in sequence with
statistical techniques (e.g., lag sequential or time
series analysis) that measure communication
behavior while preserving the timing and sequence of events (Bakeman and Gottman, 1986;
Dumas, 1986). In fact, the combination of sequential and behavioral rate data (frequency)
seems to be a better predictor of marital satisfaction than behavioral rate data alone (Gottman,

1980; Margolin and Wampold, 1981).

A related issue involves the defining of an interaction pattern or sequence: should a sequence
be confined to the immediate contingent actions
of participants, or defined more broadly? As
Christensen (1988) asks, how is the researcher to
deal with "sequences that unfold over different
settings and time periods and have considerable
extraneous interaction in between" (p. 33)? Such
patterns cannot be detected through the coding of
relatively short segments of interaction, irrespective of how detailed that coding might be. Such
connections can only be made by the participants
themselves and hence involve self-report or insider
methodologies. Kirchler (1988, 1989) dealt with
the effects of earlier interactions by having
couples in a diary study report any earlier relationship events to which they attributed their present affect.

Perspectives on Marital Interaction

Techniques for studying marital interaction have
involved taking the perspectives of both insiders
(what spouses say about the marriage) and outsiders (e.g., the researcher) (Olson, 1977).
Whereas the outsider's perspective predominated
in observational studies in the '70s, the value of
the insider's perspective has recently regained
recognition because of the extra discrimination it
provided vis-à-vis outsider's observations when
comparing couples high and low in marital satisfaction (e.g., Jacobson and Moore, 1981; Robinson and Price, 1980). Both perspectives can involve subjective and objective types of data. (See
Noller and Guthrie, in press, for a detailed discussion of this issue.)

Subjective data from the insider's perspective
has several well-known problems: tenuous relations to behavior and interaction; social desirability concerns; memory distortions; and differential
use of scale boundaries. It is difficult for participants to report on microanalytic behaviors
and/or on streams of interaction, particularly
when their relationship is unhappy (Elwood and
Jacobson, 1982). On the other hand, for some
research questions self-reports are more useful
than observations, particularly for getting
spouses' perceptions of their typical interaction.
(See Noller and Guthrie, in press.)

Self-monitoring (e.g., Broderick and O'Leary,
1986; Margolin, 1981) and diary studies (e.g.,

Peterson, 1983) that involve objective data from the insider's perspective overcome some of the problems inherent in self-report methods because they do not rely on memory or on the subjects' mental calculations of how frequently a particular behavior occurs (see Huston and Robins, 1982), but spouses may perform more socially desirable behaviors just because they are required to record them. Objective data from the outsider's perspective also may suffer from reactivity problems (see Vincent, Friedman, Nugent, and Messerly, 1979). In addition, research from this perspective is very expensive and has been limited to small, select samples of couples. (See Noller and Guthrie, in press.)

An important change over the decade has been a move from relying on outsiders' codings of the interaction, to a greater reliance on spouses' ratings of their own affect, as well as their perceptions of their partners' affect, using stimulated recall which involves couples reviewing the videotape of their own interaction (Gaelick et al., 1985; Guthrie and Noller, 1988; Levenson and Gottman, 1983). Gottman and Levenson (1985) have shown that stimulated recall ratings are significantly related to coders' judgments of marital interaction.

MARITAL SATISFACTION AND MARITAL COMMUNICATION

An important goal of research over the past decade has been to understand the differences in communication patterns between couples in distressed and nondistressed marriages. The impetus for these investigations is a therapeutic one. The key question organizing the research is, How does the behavior of happy couples differ from that of unhappy couples? While initially a couple's ability to resolve the salient conflicts in their relationship was considered the most important aspect, the general nature of communication and the affective tone in the relationship has been the focus of attention more recently.

Many researchers have compared the communication processes of couples in happy marriages with those of couples in unhappy marriages (Christensen, 1988; Guthrie and Noller, 1988; Levenson and Gottman, 1983; Schaap et al., 1988) and find clear differences between the two groups. In addition, gender differences in communication are frequently intensified in unhappily

married couples (Gottman and Levenson, 1988).

Communication Behaviors and Patterns of Behavior

In the following sections, we will look at results from self-report studies, from self-monitoring and diary studies, and from observational studies involving both frequency data and sequential data.

Self-report studies. Examples of recent self-report studies of marital communication include those of Schaap et al. (1988) and Christensen (1988). In the study by Schaap, nondistressed couples reported more satisfaction with the social-emotional aspects of their relationship, while distressed couples reported more destructive communication behaviors and conflict avoidance. Distressed and nondistressed couples reported conflicts about the same topics, although distressed couples had more frequent conflicts and spent more time in conflict, even though they avoided conflict more. The areas of higher conflict were communication, sexuality, and dispositional characteristics of the partner.

Christensen and his colleagues (see Christensen, 1988) looked at the relation between distress and self-reported patterns of behavior used in interactions involving conflict. These researchers developed their measure from previous research on sequential patterns of communication during conflict. Noller and White (in press) provide validity data for this instrument. Eggeman and his colleagues (1985) also developed a self-report questionnaire based on interaction patterns established by Gottman (1982b).

Another communication behavior frequently studied by using self-report questionnaires is self-disclosure. Competent marital communication includes the ability to disclose or reveal private thoughts and feelings about the self to the spouse (Hendrick, 1981). Discrepancies in affective disclosure between married partners (Chelune, Waring, Vosk, Sultan, and Ogden, 1984; Davidson, Balswick, and Halverson, 1983) and the disclosure of negative rather than positive feelings to the spouses are related to dissatisfaction with the marriage.

Self-monitoring and diary studies. According to work by Jacobson and Moore (1981) in which the

Spouse Observation Checklist was used, communication problems are better predictors of daily marital satisfaction than are complaints in other areas. Recordings using the Spouse Observation Checklist are able to predict subjective marital satisfaction within couples on a day-to-day basis, although agreement between the members of a couple is not always high. Recently, Elwood and Jacobson (1988) have shown that training can increase the reliability with which couples observe their own behavior.

Dickson-Markman and Markman (1988) report a study where spouses were asked to record every interaction of more than ten minutes over a three-week period. Spouses reported an average of 1.24 interactions per day with an average duration of two hours. The most common topics of conversation were work (or school), home maintenance, other family members, other relationships, conversations with others, and food. Only a small amount of talk about the relationship occurred, generally stimulated by either an argument or by sexual intercourse. In another diary study (Kirchler, 1989), happy couples reported being together about seven hours each day compared with only five hours per day for unhappy couples. Happy couples spent more time talking, discussing personal topics, and less time in conflict than other couples.

Observational studies using frequency data. A number of negative communication behaviors, such as criticizing, complaining, and sarcastic remarks, are typical of distressed spouses (Revenstorf, Vogel, Wegener, Hahlweg, and Schindler, 1980; Ting-Toomey, 1983). Schaap et al. (1988) found that unhappy couples were more likely to command, disagree, criticize, put down, and excuse, while happy couples are more likely to agree, approve, assent, and use humor and laughter. (For more detail, see review by Weiss and Heyman, 1990.) The ratio of agreement to disagreement is also a strong predictor of marital adjustment, as are negative and positive affect (see also Noller, 1984). Although research generally focuses on communication behaviors during conflict that discriminate happy from unhappy couples, an equally important issue is the relation of various communication behaviors to the immediate outcome of the interaction as well as levels of marital satisfaction (Dillard and Fitzpatrick, 1985; Koren, Carlton, and Shaw, 1980).

It is interesting to note that in the former study, some of the communication behaviors that predict winning a conflict are strongly correlated with marital dissatisfaction. In marital as in martial experience, there are many Pyrrhic victories.

Observational studies using the sequential analysis of behavior. The use of sequential analysis has enabled us to understand more clearly the reciprocal patterns of behavior that distinguish the distressed from the nondistressed (Krokoff, Gottman, and Roy, 1988; Schaap et al., 1988; Ting-Toomey, 1983). Irrespective of the method used, the evidence continues to mount that nondistressed couples exchange more rewards and fewer punishments than do distressed couples (Margolin and Wampold, 1981). Relative to the nondistressed, distressed couples are significantly more likely to exchange negative behaviors that lead to a chain of escalating, coercive interactions (Hahlweg et al., 1984). Distressed couples are also highly reactive to immediate relational events, especially negative ones (Jacobson, Follette, and McDonald, 1982), whereas those in happy marriages are less reactive. In addition, many researchers have identified "superclasses" of interaction or long sequences that discriminate types of couples (e.g., Revenstorf et al., 1984; Schaap et al., 1988; Ting-Toomey, 1983; Williamson and Fitzpatrick, 1985).

Accuracy

Gottman and Porterfield (1981) and Noller (1984) found that husbands' encoding and decoding of messages seemed more crucial than that by wives to marital satisfaction. In addition, distressed spouses are less accurate at decoding the nonverbal communication of their partners than that of strangers (Noller, 1984). On the other hand, Gottman and Porterfield (1981) found a similar decoding deficit in husbands, but not wives. Notarius and Pellegrini (1987) suggest that the escalating negative affect in the interaction may interfere with the distressed husband's ability to decode his wife's messages. Such an interpretation fits with the findings of Gottman and Levenson of higher physiological responding in conflict situations for husbands low in marital adjustment.

A later study (Noller, 1984) involved couples rating the clarity of the messages they were encoding and the confidence with which they decoded messages from the partner. This study showed that spouses in unhappy marriages are also unaware that they misunderstand one another. These findings fit with the review of the perceptual bias literature by Sillars and Scott (1983), who suggest that because of their familiarity with one another, intimates are likely to be overconfident about their understanding of each other, particularly in intensely stressful conflict situations.

Affect

Since accuracy in both the encoding and decoding of nonverbal cues of emotion is an important discriminator between happy and unhappy couples, researchers focus on affect (e.g., Guthrie and Noller, 1988; Levenson and Gottman, 1983, 1985; Noller, 1984; Notarius and Johnson, 1982). The emotional climate of distressed marriages includes less positive affect, more negative affect, and more reciprocity of negative, but not positive, affect. These findings have been replicated in different laboratories and cultures (Cousins and Vincent, 1983; Margolin and Wampold, 1981; Noller, 1984; Notarius and Johnson, 1982; Revenstorf et al., 1980; Schaap et al., 1988; Ting-Toomey, 1983). In a study by Gaelick et al. (1985), spouses reciprocated the emotion they thought their partner was conveying and saw their partners as reciprocating their own affect; however, because spouses were less accurate in decoding their partners' expressions of love, only hostility was actually reciprocated. Thus positive-affect reciprocity seems to be hampered by problems in either the encoding or decoding of positive feelings. Noller's (1984) findings would suggest that the encoding of positive messages is more likely to be the problem, particularly for husbands.

The effects of such communicative factors are tested in longitudinal investigations that show that poor communication skills precede the onset of marital distress (Markman, 1981; Markman, Duncan, Storaasli, and Howes, 1987; Noller and Callan, 1989). Levenson and Gottman (1985) found that patterns of negative-affect reciprocity (as well as high levels of physiological arousal) predicted declines in marital satisfaction three years later. In addition, there is evidence that disagreement and anger exchanges are related to low levels of concurrent marital satisfaction but improvement in marital satisfaction in the long

term (Gottman and Krokoff, 1989). (But also, see critiques by Jacobson, 1990, and Weiss and Heyman, 1990).

Studies of marital interaction during the discussion of relationship problems tend to show sex differences, with wives being more likely to express their negative feelings directly and to be more critical (Hahlweg, Revenstorf, and Schindler, 1984). In fact, wives seem to express more negativity (Noller, 1984; Notarius and Johnson, 1982) as well as more positivity (Noller, 1984). Such findings fit with the lack of behavioral responsiveness of husbands (Gottman, 1982a; Levenson and Gottman, 1983) and their general lack of expressivity in the relationship (Balswick, 1986; Rubin, 1983).

Roberts and Krokoff (1990) found a pattern of husband withdrawal/wife hostility in dissatisfied marriages that accounted for an additional 20% of the variance in satisfaction beyond that accounted for by affective tone. According to Gottman and Levenson (1988), husbands and wives differ in their ability to function in the context of high negative affect. Men, able to play a reconciling role during low levels of marital conflict, are likely to withdraw during high conflict. This withdrawal seems to be related to the high level of physiological responding of husbands in conflict situations, particularly those in unhappy marriages. Christensen and Heavey (in press) found support for the wife demand/husband withdraw pattern but added the finding that this pattern was more likely during the discussion of an issue raised by the wife. Whereas both spouses demanded more for their own issue and withdrew more for their partner's issue, husbands, overall, withdrew more than wives.

Cognition

Differences in the coding of interaction by participants and observers, as well as between participants, have provided the impetus for work on cognition (Arias and Beach, 1987; Berley and Jacobson, 1984; Christensen and Nies, 1980; Robinson and Price, 1980). The level of agreement between spouses and observers is higher for low-affect material and when marital adjustment is high or moderate (Margolin, Hattem, John, and Yost, 1985), which suggests a role for cognitive factors or interpretations. Weiss (1984: 232) comments that, rather than use the information in the interaction as outsiders do, spouses "utilize their familiarity with each other as a data base."

Positivity and negativity. While distressed husbands give more positive impact ratings of their partners' behavior than do outsiders (Floyd and Markman, 1983; Notarius and Pellegrini, 1987), the behavior of distressed wives is more likely to be coded as negative than that of non-distressed wives, and distressed wives are more likely than other wives to reciprocate negative behavior from their partner. Wives may have more to be upset about in a marital relationship than do husbands, particularly given that distressed wives are likely to have relatively unresponsive partners (Notarius and Pellegrini, 1987). Believing that their husbands are minimizing the difficulties in the relationship, they may be acting as negatively as they can in an attempt to get through to them. Again, the ways in which spouses in unhappy marriages interpret their partners' behavior is likely to be crucial to their happiness.

Attributions. Work on attributions in marriage has revealed some clear patterns that differentiate between those with satisfying and not-so-satisfying relationships. Those low in marital adjustment tend to account for problems in their relationships in terms of causes over which they have little control (such as dispositional factors; Fincham, Bradbury, and Grych, 1989). They are also more likely to blame problems in the relationship on each other and to see both their own and their partner's problem-related behavior as global and stable (Holtzworth-Munroe and Jacobson, 1985).

A related question is how spouses understand their partners' intentions in their interactions. Guthrie and Noller (1988) had couples assess their partners' intentions during interactions involving anger, depression, and affection. Those unhappy marriages were significantly less accurate than other spouses at judging the intentions of their partners for all three situations and tended to attribute more negative intentions to their partners than did other spouses.

Marital types. Fitzpatrick (1984, 1988) has developed an empirical, polythetic classification scheme of marriage in which couples are categorized with the Relational Dimension Instrument

(RDI) according to three basic dimensions of married life: ideology, interdependence, and conflict avoidance/expressivity, which provide three basic definitions of marriage—traditional, independent, and separate.

Traditionals hold conventional values about marriage and the family, are very interdependent in the marriage, and willingly argue over serious issues. Independents are more liberal in their orientation toward marital and family values, are moderately interdependent in their marriages, and are habituated to conflict. Separates are ambivalent about their family values, not very interdependent in their marriages, and tend to avoid marital conflict. The typology moves beyond the assignment of an individual to a couple type and uses the couple as the unit of analysis: husbands and wives are compared on the three basic definitions and categorized as a pure type if they agree, and a mixed type if they disagree. An important finding is that it seems to be the couple type and not the individual assignment that regulates marital interaction.

Employing a variety of empirical methods, Fitzpatrick and her associates have extensively explored the ramifications of this system for communication in marriage. (For a summary, see Fitzpatrick, 1988). The couple types differ in terms of the strategies they use in attempting to assert control; their general persuasive styles; the nonverbal cues they use in the expression of affect and intimacy; the linguistic strategies they use in dealing with conflict; and their degree of self-disclosure (Fitzpatrick, 1988). Work with the typology has also provided evidence that the relation between marital communication and marital satisfaction may depend on a couple's beliefs about marriage (Sillars et al., 1983). For those with a strong emphasis on closeness, satisfaction was related to high levels of sharing information, while for those with more emphasis on autonomy and distance, marital satisfaction was positively related to conflict avoidance.

FUTURE DIRECTIONS

During the '80s, researchers began to realize the importance of both affective and cognitive factors that mediate the relation between marital communication and marital satisfaction. Increasingly, models emphasize the context in which the interaction takes place (Bradbury and Fincham,

1987; Cornelius, 1984; Weiss, 1984). Both spouses operate in a context that includes their cognitions about marriage in general, their beliefs about each other, and each other's intentions, as well as the affect that accompanies all of these. The uniqueness of the marital relationship precludes generalizing from interaction involving strangers. The marital context affects the accuracy with which couples understand one another and the extent to which they are likely to comply with one another's requests.

Examining a marriage in the larger social context of the family and the society requires that we consider issues such as the effects of marital interaction on family functioning and child adjustment (Howes and Markman, 1989; see Grych and Fincham, in press, for a review), social support and marital interaction (Milardo, 1983), and social class and marital communication (Rubin, 1983).

Three major themes from research in the '80s will define the research agenda in the '90s. First, consonant with trends in the study of close relationships in general (Kelley et al., 1983), there will be an increase in theoretical work on marital interaction. Although important descriptive work will continue, the search for the causal mechanisms that explain patterns of marital interaction will predominate. Toward this end, more longitudinal studies of communication and marital states need to be conducted. Our hope is that more attention will be paid to couples beyond the early stages of marriage.

Second, given the powerful differences that have been uncovered in the communication behaviors of husbands and wives, more attention needs to be paid to issues of sex and gender. Current theoretical perspectives address social psychophysiological explanations for these differences, although alternative, albeit not necessarily mutually exclusive, theoretical conceptualizations exist. For example, feminist theorists argue that differences in male and female interactional styles can be attributed to the essential differences in power relationships in society. Obviously, the variance accounted for by sex versus power must be examined. One solution to this issue was that of Kollock, Blumstein, and Schwartz (1985), who considered sex and power differences in communication in close relationships by comparing homosexual and heterosexual couples.

Third, given the weight of the evidence that marital interaction causes marital satisfaction, the work in the '90s needs to ask the prior question, What factors cause those interactional behaviors and practices in the first place? Of particular interest will be work on mental models of self and relationships as exemplified through studies using adult attachment style (Hazan and Shaver, 1987) and marital schemata (Fitzpatrick, 1990).

As we have seen, the decade is notable for the tendency to use multiple methods within large programs of research. Certainly, much of the work we review comes out of the extensive programs that have involved the use of a variety of paradigms, including both insider and outsider, subjective and objective methods. We recognize the advantages and disadvantages of each method. The message of the '80s, however, is that the greater the number of different perspectives on marital communication, the more likely we are to understand this complex process. The '90s should bring us increased understanding of the factors, both affective and cognitive, that mediate between marital communication and marital satisfaction, so that these insights may be used to help couples to improve their communication and hence gain greater satisfaction from their relationship.

NOTE

The authors thank Andy Christensen and Tom Bradbury for their helpful comments on an earlier version of this article. Requests for reprints should be sent to Patricia Noller.

REFERENCES

Arias, Ileana, and S. R. H. Beach. 1987. "The assessment of social cognition in the context of marriage." Pp. 109–137 in K. Daniel O'Leary (ed.), Assessment of Marital Discord. Hillsdale, NJ: Lawrence Erlbaum.

Bakeman, Roger, and John M. Gottman. 1986. Observing Interaction. Cambridge: Cambridge University Press.

Balswick, Jack. 1986. The Inexpressive Male. Lexington, MA: Lexington Books.

Berley, Robert A., and Neil S. Jacobson. 1984. "Causal attributions in intimate relationships: Toward a model of cognitive-behavioral marital therapy." Pp. 1–60 in P. Kendall (ed.), Advances in Cognitive-Behavioral Research and Therapy (Vol. 3). New York: Academic Press.

Birchler, Gary R., Robert L. Weiss, and John P. Vincent. 1975. "Multimethod analysis of social reinforcement exchange between maritally distressed and nondistressed spouse and stranger dyads." Journal of Personality and Social Psychology 31: 349–362.

Bradbury, Thomas N., and Frank D. Fincham. 1987. "Affect and cognition in close relationships: Towards an integrative model." Cognition and Emotion 1: 59–87.

Broderick, J. E., and Daniel O'Leary. 1986. "Contribution of affect, attitudes, and behavior to marital satisfaction." Journal of Consulting and Clinical Psychology 54: 514–577.

Chelune, Gordon, E. M. Waring, B. N. Vosk, F. E. Sultan, and J. K. Ogden. 1984. "Self-disclosure and its relationship to marital intimacy." Journal of Clinical Psychology 40: 216–219.

Christensen, Andrew. 1988. "Dysfunctional interaction patterns in couples." Pp. 31–52 in Patricia Noller and Mary Anne Fitzpatrick (eds.), Perspectives on Marital Interaction. Clevedon, England, and Philadelphia: Multilingual Matters.

Christensen, Andrew, and Christopher Heavey. In press. "Gender and social structure in the demand/withdraw pattern of marital conflict." Journal of Personality and Social Psychology.

Christensen, Andrew, and C. E. King. 1982. "Telephone survey of daily marital behavior." Behavioral Assessment 4: 327–328.

Christensen, Andrew, and D. C. Nies. 1980. "The Spouse Observation Checklist: Empirical analysis and critique." American Journal of Family Therapy 8: 69–79.

Cornelius, Randolph. 1984. "A rule-based model of adult emotional expression." In C. Malatesta and C. Izard (eds.), Emotion and Adult Development. Beverly Hills, CA: Sage.

Cousins, Peter C., and John P. Vincent. 1983. "Supportive and aversive behavior following spousal complaints." Journal of Marriage and the Family 45: 679–682.

Davidson, Bernard, J. Balswick, and C. Halverson. 1983. "Affective self-disclosure and marital adjustment: A test of equity theory." Journal of Marriage and the Family 45: 93–102.

Dickson-Markman, Fran, and Howard Markman. 1988. "The effects of others on marriage." Pp. 294–322 in Patricia Noller and Mary Anne Fitzpatrick (eds.), Perspectives on Marital Interaction. Clevedon, England, and Philadelphia: Multilingual Matters.

Dillard, James P., and Mary Anne Fitzpatrick. 1985 "Compliance gaining in marital interaction." Personality and Social Psychology Bulletin 11: 419–433.

Dindia, Kathryn. 1988. "Communication with spouses and others." Pp. 273–293 in Patricia Noller and Mary Anne Fitzpatrick (eds.), Perspectives on Marital Interaction. Clevedon, England, and Philadelphia: Multilingual Matters.

Dumas, Jean. 1986. "Controlling for autocorrelation in social interaction analysis." Psychological Bulletin 100: 125–128.

Duncan, Starkey. 1983. "Speaking turns: Studies of structure and individual differences." Pp. 149–178 in John M. Wiemann and Randall P. Harrison. Nonverbal Interaction. Beverly Hills, CA: Sage.

Eggeman, K., V. Moxley, and W. Schumm. 1985. "Assessing spouses' perceptions of Gottman's temporal form in marital conflict." Psychological Reports 57: 171–181.

Elwood, Richard W., and Neil S. Jacobson. 1982. "Spouses' agreement in reporting their behavioral interactions: A clinical replication." Journal of Consulting and Clinical Psychology 50: 783–784.

Elwood, Richard W., and Neil S. Jacobson. 1988. "The effects of observational training on spouse agreement about events in their relationship." Behavior Research and Therapy 26: 159–167.

Fincham, Frank D., and Thomas N. Bradbury. 1987. "Cognitive processes and conflict in close relationships: An attribution-efficacy model." Journal of Personality and Social Psychology 53: 1106–1118.

Fincham, Frank D., and Thomas N. Bradbury. 1989. "Cognition in marriage: A programme of research on attributions" in Daniel Perlman and Warren Jones (eds.), Advances in Personal Relationships (Vol. 2). Greenwich, CT: JAI Press.

Fincham, Frank D., Thomas N. Bradbury, and J. H. Grych. In press. "Conflict in close relationships: The role of intrapersonal phenomena." In S. Graham and V. S. Folkes (eds.), Attribution Theory: Applications to Achievement, Mental Health, and Interpersonal Conflict. Hillsdale, NJ: Erlbaum.

Fitzpatrick, Mary Anne. 1984. "A typological approach to marital interaction: Recent theory and research." Pp. 1–47 in Leonard Berkowitz (ed.), Advances in Experimental Social Psychology (Vol. 18). Orlando, FL: Academic Press.

Fitzpatrick, Mary Anne. 1988. Between Husbands and Wives. Newbury Park, CA: Sage.

Fitzpatrick, Mary Anne. 1990. "Models of marital interaction." Pp. 433–451 in H. Giles and W. P. Robinson (eds.), Handbook of Language and Social Psychology. Chichester: John Wiley and Sons.

Fitzpatrick, Mary Anne, and Kathryn Dindia. 1986. "Couples and other strangers: Talktime in spouse-stranger interaction." Communication Research 13: 625–652.

Floyd, Frank J., and Howard J. Markman. 1983. "Observational biases in spouse interaction: Toward a cognitive behavioral model of marriage." Journal of Consulting and Clinical Psychology 51: 450–457.

Gaelick, Lisa, G. Bodenhausen, and Robert S. Wyer. 1985. "Emotional communication in close relationships." Journal of Personality and Social Psychology 49: 1246–1265.

Gottman, John M. 1980. "Consistency of nonverbal affect and affect reciprocity in marital interaction." Journal of Consulting and Clinical Psychology 48: 711–717.

Gottman, John M. 1982a. "Emotional responsiveness in marital conversations." Journal of Communication 32: 108–120.

Gottman, John M. 1982b. Temporal form: "Toward a new language for describing relationships." Journal of Marriage and the Family 44: 943–962.

Gottman, John M., and Lowell J. Krokoff. 1989. "Marital interaction and satisfaction: A longitudinal view." Journal of Consulting and Clinical Psychology 57: 47–52.

Gottman, John M., and Robert S. Levenson. 1985. "A valid procedure for obtaining self-report of affect in marital interaction." Journal of Consulting and Clinical Psychology 53: 151–160.

Gottman, John M., and Robert S. Levenson. 1988. "The social psychophysiology of marriage." Pp. 182–202 in Patricia Noller and Mary Anne Fitzpatrick (eds.), Perspectives on Marital Interaction. Clevedon, England, and Philadelphia: Multilingual Matters.

Gottman, John M., C. I. Notarius, H. J. Markman, D. Banks, B. Yoppi, and M. E. Rubin. 1976. "Behavior exchange theory and marital decision making." Journal of Personality and Social Psychology 34: 14–23.

Gottman, John M., and Alan L. Porterfield. 1981. "Communicative competence in the nonverbal behavior of married couples." Journal of Marriage and the Family 43: 817–824.

Grych, John H., and Frank D. Fincham. In press. "Marital conflict and children's adjustment: A cognitive-contextual framework." Psychological Bulletin.

Guthrie, Diane M., and Patricia Noller. 1988. "Spouses' perceptions of one another in emotional situations." Pp. 153–181 in Patricia Noller and Mary Anne Fitzpatrick (eds.), Perspectives on Marital Interaction. Clevedon, England, and Philadelphia: Multilingual Matters.

Hahlweg, Kurt, L. Reisner, G. Kohli, M. Vollmer, L. Schindler, and D. Revenstorf. 1984. "Development and validity of a new system to analyze interpersonal communication: Kategoriensystem für partnerschaftliche interaktion." Pp. 182–198 in Kurt Hahlweg and Neil S. Jacobson (eds.), Marital Interaction: Analysis and Modification. New York: Guilford Press.

Hahlweg, Kurt, D. Revenstorf, and L. Schindler. 1984. "Effects of behavioural marital therapy on couples' communication and problem-solving skills." Journal of Consulting and Clinical Psychology 52: 553–566.

Hazan, Cindy, and Philip Shaver. 1987. "Romantic love conceptualized as an attachment process." Journal of Personality and Social Psychology 52: 511–524.

Hendrick, Susan S. 1981. "Self-disclosure and marital satisfaction." Journal of Personality and Social Psychology 40: 1150–1159.

Holtzworth-Munroe, Amy, and Neil S. Jacobson. 1985. "Causal attributions of married couples. When do they search for causes? What do they conclude when they do?" Journal of Personality and Social Psychology 48: 1398–1412.

Howes, P., and H. J. Markman. 1989. "Marital quality and child functioning: A longitudinal investigation." Child Development 60: 1044–1051.

Huston, Ted, and Elliot Robins. 1982. "Conceptual and methodological issues in studying close relationships." Journal of Marriage and the Family 44: 901–925.

Jacob, Theodore, D. Tennenbaum, and G. Krahn. 1987. "Factors influencing the reliability and validity of observation data." Pp. 297–328 in Theodore Jacob (ed.), Family Interaction and Psychopathology. New York: Plenum.

Jacobson, Neil S. 1990. "Contributions from psychology to an understanding of marriage." Pp. 258–275 in Frank D. Fincham and Thomas N. Bradbury (eds.), Psychology of Marriage. New York: Guilford Press.

Jacobson, Neil S., W. C. Follette, and D. W. McDonald. 1982. "Reactivity to positive and negative behavior in distressed and nondistressed couples." Journal of Consulting and Clinical Psychology 50: 706–714.

Jacobson, Neil S., and Danny Moore. 1981. "Spouses as observers of events in their relationship." Journal of Consulting and Clinical Psychology 49: 269–277.

Kelley, Harold H., E. Berscheid, A. Christensen, J. H. Harvey, T. L. Huston, G. Levinger, E. McClintock, L. A. Peplau, and D. Peterson. 1983. Close Relationships. New York: W. H. Freeman.

Kelly, Carol, Ted Huston, and Rodney Cate. 1985. "Premarital relationship correlates of the erosion of satisfaction in marriage." Journal of Social and Personal Relationships 2: 167–178.

Kenny, David A., and J. Lavoie. 1984. "The social relations model." Pp. 44–85 in Leonard Berkowitz (ed.), Advances in Experimental Psychology (Vol. 18). Orlando, FL: Academic Press.

Kirchler, Erich. 1988. "Marital happiness and interaction in everyday surroundings: A time-sample diary approach for couples." Journal of Social and Personal Relationships 5: 375–382.

Kirchler, Erich. 1989. "Everyday life experiences at home: An interaction diary approach to assess marital relationships." Journal of Family Psychology 2: 311–336.

Kollock, Peter, Philip Blumstein, and Pepper Schwartz. 1985. "Sex and power in interaction: Conversational privileges and duties." American Sociological Review 50: 34–46.

Koren, P., K. Carlton, and P. Shaw. 1980. "Marital conflict: Relations among behaviors, outcomes and distress." Journal of Consulting and Clinical Psychology 48: 460–468.

Krokoff, Lowell J. 1987. "Recruiting representative samples for marital interaction research." Journal of Social and Personal Relationships 4: 317–328.

Krokoff, Lowell J., J. M. Gottman, and A. K. Roy. 1988. "Blue-collar and white-collar marital interaction and communication orientation." Journal of Social and Personal Relationships 5: 201–221.

Levenson, Robert W., and John M. Gottman. 1983. "Marital interaction: Physiological linkage and affective exchange." Journal of Personality and Social Psychology 45: 587–597.

Levenson, Robert W., and John M. Gottman. 1985. "Physiological and affective predictors of change in relationship satisfaction." Journal of Personality and Social Psychology 49: 85–94.

Margolin, Gayla. 1981. "Behavior exchange in happy

and unhappy marriages: A family life cycle perspective." Behavioral Assessment 11: 101–118.

Margolin, Gayla, and M. A. Basco. 1984. "Family and marital interaction scoring system." Unpublished manuscript, University of Southern California.

Margolin, Gayla, D. Hattem, R. S. John, and K. Yost. 1985. "Perceptual agreement between spouses and outside observers when coding themselves and a stranger dyad." Behavioral Assessment 7: 235–247.

Margolin, Gayla, and Bruce Wampold. 1981. "Sequential analysis of conflict and accord in distressed and nondistressed marital partners." Journal of Consulting and Clinical Psychology 49: 554–567.

Markman, Howard J. 1981. "Prediction of marital distress: A five-year follow-up." Journal of Consulting and Clinical Psychology 49: 760–762.

Markman, Howard J., S. W. Duncan, R. D. Storaasli, and P. W. Howes. 1987. "The prediction and prevention of marital distress: A longitudinal investigation." Pp. 266–289 in Kurt Hahlweg and Michael J. Goldstein (eds.), Understanding Major Mental Disorder: The Contribution of Family Interaction Research. New York: Family Process Press.

Milardo, Robert M. 1983. "Social networks and pair relationships: A review of substantive and measurement issues." Sociology and Social Research 68: 1–18.

Noller, Patricia. 1984. Nonverbal Communication and Marital Interaction. Oxford: Pergamon.

Noller, Patricia, and Victor J. Callan. 1989. "Communication in the first year of marriage." Paper presented at the Australian Family Studies Conference, Ballarat, Victoria (November).

Noller, Patricia, and Diane Guthrie. In press. "Studying communication in marriage: An integration and critical evaluation." In Warren Jones and Daniel Perlman (eds.), Advances in Personal Relationships: A Research Annual (Vol. 3). London: Jessica Kingsley Publishers.

Noller, Patricia, and Angela White. In press. "The validity of the Communication Patterns Questionnaire." Psychological Assessment: A Journal of Consulting and Clinical Psychology.

Notarius, Clifford I., and Jennifer S. Johnson. 1982. "Emotional expression in husbands and wives." Journal of Marriage and the Family 45: 483–489.

Notarius, Clifford, and Howard Markman. 1981. "Couples' Interaction Scoring System." In Erik E. Filsinger and Robert Lewis (eds.), Assessing Marriage: New Behavioral Approaches. Beverly Hills, CA: Sage.

Notarius, Clifford, Howard Markman, and John M. Gottman. 1983. "Advances in the Couples' Interaction Scoring System." Pp. 117–136 in Erik E. Filsinger (ed.), Marriage and Family Assessment. Beverly Hills, CA: Sage.

Notarius, Clifford I., and David S. Pellegrini. 1987. "Differences between husbands and wives: Implications for understanding marital discord." Pp. 231–249 in Kurt Hahlweg and Michael J. Goldstein (eds.), Understanding Major Mental Disorder: The Contribution of Family Interaction Research. New York: Family Process Press.

Olson, David. 1977. "Insiders' and outsiders' views of relationships." Pp. 115–136 in George Levinger and Harold Raush (eds.), Close Relationships. Amherst: University of Massachusetts Press.

Olson, David, and Richard Ryder. 1970. "Inventory of marital conflicts (IMC): An experimental interaction procedure." Journal of Marriage and the Family 32: 443–448.

Peterson, Donald. 1983. "Conflict." Pp. 360–396 in Harold H. Kelley et al. (ed.), Close Relationships. New York: W. H. Freeman.

Revenstorf, Dirk, K. Hahlweg, L. Schindler, and B. Vogel. 1984. "Interaction analysis of marital conflict." Pp. 159–181 in Kurt Hahlweg and Neil Jacobson (eds.), Marital Interaction: Analysis and Modification. New York: Guilford Press.

Revenstorf, Dirk, B. Vogel, C. Wegener, K. Hahlweg, and L. Schindler. 1980. "Escalation phenomena in interaction sequences: An empirical comparison of distressed and nondistressed couples." Behavior Analysis and Modification 4: 97–115.

Roberts, Linda, and Lowell J. Krokoff. 1990. "A time-series analysis of withdrawal, hostility, and displeasure in satisfied and dissatisfied marriages." Journal of Marriage and the Family 52: 95–105.

Robinson, Elizabeth, and M. G. Price. 1980. "Pleasurable behavior in marital interaction: An observational study." Journal of Consulting and Clinical Psychology 48: 117–118.

Rubin, Lilian. 1983. Intimate Strangers. New York: Harper and Row.

Schaap, Cas, Bram Buunk, and Ada Kerkstra. 1988. "Marital conflict resolution." Pp. 203–244 in Patricia Noller and Mary Anne Fitzpatrick (eds.), Perspectives on Marital Interaction. Clevedon, England, and Philadelphia: Multilingual Matters.

Sillars, Alan L., G. R. Pike, K. Redmon, and T. S. Jones. 1983. "Communication and conflict in marriage: One style is not satisfying to all." Pp. 414–431 in R. Bostrom (ed.), Communication Yearbook 7. Beverly Hills, CA: Sage.

Sillars, Alan L., and Michael D. Scott. 1983. "Interpersonal perception between intimates: An integrative review." Human Communication Research 10: 153–176.

Ting-Toomey, Stella. 1983. "An analysis of verbal communication patterns in high and low marital adjustment groups." Human Communication Research 9: 306–319.

Vincent, John P., L. C. Friedman, J. Nugent, and L. Messerly. 1979. "Demand characteristics in observations of marital interaction." Journal of Consulting and Clinical Psychology 47: 557–566.

Weiss, Robert L. 1984. "Cognitive and behavioral measures of marital interaction." Pp. 232–252 in Kurt Hahlweg and Neil S. Jacobson (eds.), Marital Interaction: Analysis and Modification. New York: Guilford Press.

Weiss, Robert L., and Richard E. Heyman. 1990. "Observation in marital interaction." Pp. 87–117 in Frank D. Fincham and Thomas N. Bradbury (eds.), Psychology of Marriage. New York: Guilford Press.

Weiss, Robert L., and K. Summers. 1983. "The Marital

Interaction Coding System III." Pp. 85–115 in Erik E. Filsinger (ed.), Marriage and Family Assessment. Beverly Hills, CA: Sage.

Williamson, Robyn, and Mary Anne Fitzpatrick. 1985. "Two approaches to marital interaction: Relational control patterns in marital types." Communication Monographs 52: 236–252.

Witteman, Hal, and Mary Anne Fitzpatrick. 1986. "Compliance-gaining in marital interaction: Power bases, power processes, and outcomes." Communication Monographs 53: 130–143.

CATHERINE A. SURRA   *University of Texas at Austin*

Research and Theory on Mate Selection and

Premarital Relationships in the 1980s

This article reviews major advances in research and theory on mate selection in the 1980s. Mate selection is broadly construed to include premarital relationships generally, not just those that result in marriage. Literature relevant to four levels of causal analysis is considered: societal trends and influences on the trends, social networks and premarital relationships, the behavioral features of relationships, and individual attributions for relationship development. Research that describes and explains relationship development also is reviewed, and four models of development are derived. Throughout the review, two themes appear: developmental change and theory testing. On the basis of conclusions evident in the review, prospects for future research are forecasted.

Research and theory on mate selection has a long and venerable history in family studies, and work on the topic in the 1980s did justice to that tradition. Two themes are apparent in the research done in this decade. The first was a concern for understanding the causes of developmental change in heterosexual romantic relationships. The second was an emphasis on developing and testing theories of how premarital relationships are established, maintained, or dissolved. Throughout the review, I use the term *mate selection* loosely, for choosing a spouse is only one of the many forms that close heterosexual relationships take. As this review will demonstrate, the

Department of Human Ecology, Mary Gearing Hall, University of Texas at Austin, Austin, TX 78712.

term is outdated for describing the variety of premarital relationship experiences.

The first part of the review is organized into four sections, according to different levels of causes that affect relationships (cf. Kelley et al., 1983). More distal causes are discussed first and more proximal, later. The first section addresses societal changes in mate selection. I review findings on demographic trends and on structural and other causes of mate choice that originate in the larger societal context. The next section examines the immediate social context within which relationships develop, the social network. Next, the dyadic level of analysis, the internal workings of relationships, is considered. Then I turn to the individual level of analysis and discuss partners' subjective explanations for why their relationships change. Research reviewed in the final section is aimed explicitly at describing and explaining relationship development. There, I delineate four models of development: gradual differentiation, early determinism, incremental convergence and divergence, and progressive stages.

The literature review is by no means exhaustive. Only topics that received programmatic attention on the part of one or many researchers were included. This selection process enabled me to draw integrative conclusions but meant that some notable studies were omitted. In addition, I excluded research that inquired about individual attitudes toward mate selection or about the association between different personal characteristics that pertain to mate selection (e.g., the effect of childhood family structure on attitudes toward marriage). My reason for leaving out such work is that its relevance to what actually happens in relationships is uncertain. The review is confined to research on mate selection in the United States and to research on heterosexual relationships among the never-married, unless otherwise indicated.

THE SOCIETAL CONTEXT OF MATE SELECTION IN THE 1980s

As in past decades, much of the research on mate selection in the 1980s focused on identifying demographic trends in marital behavior. This is accomplished by employing methods that permit generalization to the population, such as drawing random samples and utilizing census data or other survey data. The aim of this research is primarily descriptive. Its contribution to theory is inductive, as investigators identify some demographic trend and then attempt to interpret why it might have occurred. Two topics predominated in the descriptive demographic research of the 1980s. The first involved the dramatic changes in individual decisions about marriage, particularly the inclinations of individuals to delay marriage and to live together in nonmarital unions. The second concerned homogamy between partners and changes in homogamy over time.

What is new in the demographic research of the 1980s is the study of the structural, cultural, and individual mechanisms that underlie marital decisions. These mechanisms include the size and composition of the population, sex ratios, endogamy norms, and individual preferences for marrying socially similar partners. Research of this sort uses survey data to test hypotheses about the forces that shape marital choice.

The Postponement of Marriage, Cohabitation, and Homogamy

One of the most striking features of mate choice in this decade has been individuals' postponement of the decision to wed. The delay of marriage is evident in changes in both the extent of marriage and the age at first marriage. Regarding the former, the proportion of men aged 20 to 24 who had not yet wed was 78% in 1988, 23% higher than it was in 1970. For women in this age group, the proportion never married increased from 36% in 1970 to 61% in 1988 (U.S. Bureau of the Census, 1988a). The increase in never-marrieds has been pervasive across age groups (Rodgers and

Thornton, 1985; Saluter, 1988). For those 25–29, the proportion never married tripled for women and nearly doubled for men between 1970 and 1988, and for the 30–34 age group, the proportions tripled for both genders (Saluter, 1988).

The median age at first marriage has been rising for about the past 30 years; however, the increase was especially rapid during the decade from 1975 to 1985 (U.S. Bureau of the Census, 1986). In 1988, the estimated median age at first marriage was 23.6 years for women, higher than any on record; for men, the comparable figure is 25.9 years, the highest since the turn of the century (U.S. Bureau of the Census, 1988a). The increase in median age has been greater for women than men (Saluter, 1988). Thus, women's age at first marriage is becoming more similar to men's.

The postponement of marriage has been more pronounced for blacks than whites. In 1988, the median age at first marriage for black women was about 3 years older than for white women (Saluter, 1988). The proportion of never-married black women in their early 20s was 75% compared with 59% for white women. For black and white men, the figures were 87% and 76%, respectively (Saluter, 1988). Similar discrepancies in the proportion never married are apparent for older blacks and whites. There is some evidence that racial differences in the propensity to wed have widened in recent decades (Saluter, 1988; Schoen and Kluegel, 1988; Rodgers and Thornton, 1985).

Age at marriage and extent of marriage are closely related. Because delaying marriage increases the chances that it will never occur, increases in age at first marriage are apt to result in increases in the proportion of young adults who never marry (U.S. Bureau of the Census, 1988a). Similarly, if people who have delayed marriage subsequently decide to wed, the median age at first marriage will continue to rise (U.S. Bureau of the Census, 1986).

Although some might argue that the postponement of marriage is indicative of a more general disinterest in close or committed relationships, research on cohabitation suggests that this is not entirely the case. Living together in nonmarital unions is a lifestyle experienced by many at some point during their lifetime and is increasingly common. According to the U.S. Bureau of the the Census (1989), in 1988, the number of unmarried-couple households was 2.6 million. Although the number increased by 63% between 1980 and 1988, the increase was much greater from 1970 to 1978 (117%) (U.S. Bureau of the Census, 1988a). The problem with these figures is that they include not only close relationships but also other living arrangements (e.g., an elderly woman with a live-in male companion). More precise figures on cohabitation between unmarried intimates are available from two recent studies. Data on the 15-year cohabitation histories of 23.5-year-olds revealed that roughly one-third had cohabited by age 23.5 and that one-third of the women and two-fifths of the men who had married by that age had earlier cohabited (Thornton, 1988). The National Survey of Families and Households provides detailed information about the cohabitation experiences of over 13,000 persons aged 19 and older (Sweet, Bumpass, and Call, 1988). These data showed that by their early 30s, almost half the population lived together at some time and that 4% of the population were currently cohabiting (Bumpass and Sweet, 1989).

The personal characteristics of cohabitors have been well documented. They were mostly young adults (68% were under 35) and never-marrieds (53%), although a sizable proportion had been divorced (34%) (U.S. Bureau of the Census, 1988b). Cohabitation rates were higher for women than men and for whites than blacks once other variables (e.g., age) were taken into account (Bumpass and Sweet, 1989; Thornton, 1988). Contrary to the stereotype of cohabitation as a college-student phenomenon, cohabitation and education were inversely related (Bumpass and Sweet, 1989), and 4 out of 10 cohabiting couples had children present (Bumpass, Sweet, and Cherlin, 1989). Cohabitors were likely to be homogamous on race, age, and education (Spanier, 1983), although married couples who previously cohabited were less homogamous than those who did not (Gwartney-Gibbs, 1986). Compared with noncohabitors, cohabitors had more liberal attitudes toward family life and were more unconventional generally (e.g., substance abuse, religiosity, division of labor) (Huston, McHale, and Crouter, 1986; Macklin, 1983; Newcomb, 1986; Tanfer, 1987).

When cohabitation is considered, the changes in marriage rates are offset to a large extent (Bumpass et al., 1989). Between 1970 and 1985, for example, the percentage of young adults who had experienced a first union (cohabitation or marriage) before age 25 dropped only six points (75%

vs. 69%) (Bumpass et al., 1989). Thus, the movement away from legal marriage has been accompanied by a movement toward nonmarital unions.

Research in this decade helped to clarify the association between cohabitation and marital outcomes. In a recent review, Macklin (1983) concluded that marital quality was similar for those who cohabited before marriage and those who did not. Research conducted since then on large, and in some cases representative, samples demonstrated that cohabitation is negatively related to marital stability, measured as dissolution as well as propensity to divorce (Booth and Johnson, 1988; Bumpass and Sweet, 1989; Newcomb, 1986), and to other indicators of marital quality (Booth and Johnson, 1988; DeMaris and Leslie, 1984). Bumpass and Sweet (1989), for instance, reported that the proportion separating or divorcing within 10 years of marriage was one-third higher for those who cohabited than for those who did not. Booth and Johnson (1988) tried to explain why cohabitation and marital stability are negatively related. They hypothesized that, compared with noncohabitors, (*a*) cohabitors' more liberal attitudes and unconventional behavior make them poorer risks for marriage and (*b*) cohabitors begin their unions earlier and, therefore, experience declines in marital quality sooner. They found support for the first hypothesis but not the second, which suggests that cohabitors enter marriage with doubts, personal traits, and inadequacies that may contribute to instability.

Cohabitation unions themselves are highly unstable and relatively short-lived, because they either result in marriage or dissolve. Among men, 40% of their cohabitation relationships dissolved within 2 years, and 23% were terminated by marriage to their partners. Among women, the comparable figures were 23% and 37%, respectively (Thornton, 1988). Cohabitation has a median duration of 1.3 years (Bumpass and Sweet, 1989).

Changes in the prevalence of cohabitation have led many to conclude that cohabitation has become an institutionalized segment of the courtship process (Gwartney-Gibbs, 1986; Spanier, 1983; Tanfer, 1987). The problem is that survey research on cohabitation gives little insight into when or how cohabitation fits into dating or courtship. Neither is survey data very informative about the dynamics of the relationship between partners, such as how committed, intimate, or companionate it is. The limited data that are available indicate that cohabition encompasses a large variety of relationship experiences (Bumpass et al., 1989; Macklin, 1983). What are needed in the future are more studies of the nature of cohabiting relationships and how cohabitation intersects with other stages and forms of dating relationships.

The formation of homogamous marriages continued to be the norm in recent years; however, on most characteristics studied, heterogamy was increasingly common. This is true for homogamy with respect to religious denomination (Glenn, 1982, 1984), race, ethnicity, (Labov and Jacobs, 1986; Schoen and Wooldredge, 1989), mother tongue (Stevens and Schoen, 1988), and education (Schoen and Wooldredge, 1989). Most marriages were characterized by constrained homogamy on age; that is, an age difference of no more than 3 or 4 years (Atkinson and Glass, 1985; Vera, Berardo, and Berardo, 1985). Findings conflict about whether and how age homogamy has changed over time (Atkinson and Glass; 1985; Labov and Jacobs, 1986; Schoen and Wooldredge, 1989). Interracial marriages were more common for nonblacks than blacks (Schoen and Wooldredge, 1989) and demonstrated a preference for black grooms (Schoen and Wooldredge, 1989). Age heterogamy was more likely among blacks (Atkinson and Glass, 1985; Vera et al., 1985). When spouses deviated from educational homogamy, females tended to marry up; this tendency recently decreased (Schoen and Wooldredge, 1989).

Structural and Nonstructural Influences on Demographic Trends

Research was devoted to two types of influences on demographic trends. The first and most investigated concerns how the structural composition of the population at large constrains mate choices. Structural research is concerned with the question, How does the availability of marriageable partners in the population affect marital choice? Marriageability of partners is defined in terms of qualities that make them desirable spouses, such as the appropriate age or economic circumstance, or whether they possess characteristics similar to one's own. Structural variables include, for example, the size the population with regard to a particular characteristic and the balance between numbers of men and women of

marriageable age (sex ratios). The second set of influences on demographic trends in mate choice concerns social and personal preferences for certain mates, such as endogamy norms. Survey researchers estimate these influences by calculating the likelihood of marriage after structural factors are taken into account.

Size, heterogeneity, and intersection of social groups. One line of research on structural influences on mate choice was stimulated by Blau's (1977) theory of how the composition and size of the population affects individuals' associations with others. Blau and colleagues (Blau, Blum, and Schwartz, 1982) argued that people distinguish others along various social characteristics, such as age or race, and that the way these characteristics are distributed within the population affects social interaction generally and outgroup marriage in particular. Blau et al. hypothesized that the size of a group possessing a certain characteristic is inversely related to the rate of marriage outside it and that the degree of heterogeneity (i.e., the number of different groups and the size distribution among them) is positively related to the degree of outmarriage. In addition, the degree of intersection among an individual's different social affiliations should be positively related to outmarriage, where intersection is measured as the average correlation between sets of social attributes, such as race and occupation (Blau, Beeker, and Fitzpatrick, 1984). Data from the 1970 census supported the hypotheses for almost all nine of the various types of intermarriage studied (e.g., race, national origin, ethnic background). Other results suggest that Blau's theory can account for changes in intermarriage over time only for racial and residential intermarriage; both cultural factors (increased acceptance of intermarriage) and structural factors (heterogeneity) are needed to explain changes in intermarriage on age and prior marital status (Labov and Jacobs, 1986).

According to Blau et al. (1982, 1984), their findings support the idea that people marry outside their social group, not because they have a preference for doing so, but because of their multiple and interwoven group affiliations. Indeed, there is some evidence that, although personal preferences affect social choice, heterogeneity influences social contacts above and beyond preferences (Blum, 1985). Apparently, heterogeneity and intersection facilitate outmarriage by providing opportunities to meet and stay in contact with dissimilar others. In this way, social structure may sometimes work against social and personal preferences for similar others. One question left unanswered by the theory is the extent to which people choose to interact with diverse groups. Longitudinal research is needed to determine how much individuals create through personal choice the social structures that subsequently constrain them.

Sex ratios and the marriage squeeze. Another concentrated effort to study social structure is research on sex ratios and the marriage squeeze. The sex ratio has been operationalized in various ways; for example, as the number of men for every 100 women in a given population (Guttentag and Secord, 1983: 14) or as the ratio of the number of unmarried men of marriageable age to unmarried women of marriageable age (Heer and Grossbard-Shectman, 1981: 53). The term "marriage squeeze" was coined by Glick and his colleagues in 1959 (Glick, 1988) to refer to the oversupply of women resulting when girls of marriageable age born during the baby boom faced a shortage of older men.

In the 1980s, research on sex ratios was stimulated, in part, by Guttentag and Secord's (1983) analysis of how imbalanced sex ratios affect family relationships. An oversupply of women should be associated with higher rates of singlehood and divorce, later age at first marriage, and a lower proportion of remarriages. The hypothesis regarding age at marriage has been confirmed (Schoen, 1983). An oversupply of women also is thought to weaken traditional roles for women (Glick, 1988; Guttentag and Secord, 1983). Under these conditions, women have difficulty finding partners so they seek careers and other sources of satisfaction, whereas men have a surplus of partners, which weakens their commitment. Heer and Grossbard-Shechtman (1981) reviewed data on the women's movement that are consistent with this view. After 1980 and through the turn of the century, it will be men who experience a marriage squeeze; as the baby boomers mature, men of marriageable age will face an undersupply of women (Glick, 1988). The hypotheses that an oversupply of men is associated with relatively high marriage rates but relatively low age at first marriage (Guttentag and

Secord, 1983) were supported in a recent study of marriage among Canadian women (Trovato, 1988).

Among black Americans, there is an undersupply of men (Guttentag and Secord, 1983). Spanier and Glick (1980) maintained that this imbalance contributes to mate selection differences between blacks and whites. They argued that, because black women are faced with a shortage of marriageable men, larger proportions of black than white women would marry down educationally, marry older or younger men, marry previously married men, or remain unmarried. Data from the June, 1975, Current Population Survey were in accord with the predictions. For blacks age 20–24 through 35–39, there was a higher percentage of never-married females than males. For whites, in contrast, never-married males outnumbered never-married females in every age group from 14 to 54. The degree of heterogamy on age, education, and marital status was greater for blacks than whites.

Schoen and Kluegel (1988) questioned whether the marriage squeeze faced by black women was responsible for observed racial differences in mate selection. They argued instead that economic factors, such as the low supply of high quality marriage partners for black women, and individual preferences and social norms, may be responsible. They used Schoen's (1981, 1986) "magnitude of marriage attraction" to estimate whether blacks' propensity to marry differed from whites', independent of the composition of the population. The magnitude of marriage attraction assesses the marriage rate between spouses with certain characteristics independent of the size of the population with that characteristic. The magnitude of marriage attraction for husbands of age x to wives of age y, for example, is the sum of two ratios: (*a*) the number of x,y marriages to the number of males of age x in the population and (*b*) the number of x,y marriages to the number of females of age y in the population. Vital statistics from North Carolina and Virginia from 1969–1971 to 1979–81 showed that the magnitude declined more for blacks than whites over the two time periods, especially for black females in the lowest and highest educational categories. Decomposition of effects due to composition of the population, the magnitude of marriage attraction, and the interaction between them showed that magnitude of attraction was more influential than composition in accounting for racial differences in marriage rates. Schoen and Kluegel concluded that structure has little impact on racial differences in mate selection and that researchers need to consider economic factors, family background, and other influences.

Other research supports the claim that influences in addition to structural ones shape marital choice. While structural variables, such as region and size of place, influenced the probability of marrying similarly for men and women, other factors, such as parental educational attainment and growing up in an intact family, affected the probability differently for the genders (Goldscheider and Waite, 1986). Likewise, both economic and compositional factors explained the romantic involvements of blacks (Tucker and Taylor, 1989).

In sum, research on sex ratios is consistent with the structuralist argument that the makeup of the population affects mate choice because it limits the field of marriageable partners. Research on racial and gender differences in mate selection, however, highlights the fact that social structure is only one of the many influences on premarital relationships; other contextual (e.g., economic) and psychological (e.g., preferences) factors also prevail. Next, I review how some demographers have estimated the impact of these nonstructural forces.

Propensity to marry and endogamy norms. In order to detect nonstructural influences by means of survey data, demographers have devised strategies to control for structural and compositional effects. These methods show promise for estimating the societal and psychological influences left over once the composition of the population is taken into account. One example, defined previously, is Schoen's measure of the magnitude of marriage attraction. Schoen and colleagues (Schoen and Kluegel, 1988) maintained that marital choices result from compositional influences as well as the propensity to marry, which derives from individual and social preferences, social norms, and the interpersonal attraction between partners. By taking into account composition, the magnitude of marriage attraction reflects the impact of this latter set of influences. Schoen's measure was used to examine how marital choices involve the exchange of resources (Schoen and Wooldredge, 1989). The hypothesis

was that deviations from homogamy reflect females' concern for socioeconomic considerations and males' for such noneconomic factors as youth. Thus, males would be likely to exchange their higher education for females' younger age, and black males would be likely to bargain their higher education for white females' race. In general, these hypotheses were confirmed. In marriages between nonblack males and black females, males marry up educationally; however, in marriages between black males and nonblack females, females marry up. These findings suggest that economic resources are exchanged for racial characteristics. Similarly, the evidence indicates that males bargain their higher education for females' youthful age. Contrary to prediction, in marriages between blacks, males marry up. Although such findings are often attributed to the bleak marriage market faced by highly educated black females, this result is independent of compositional effects, suggesting that such unions partly are a matter of choice.

Another example of how survey data can be used to estimate nonstructural influences is seen in Glenn's (1984) Index of Influences for Endogamy. Glenn correctly observed that studies of homogamy are rooted in the assumption that individuals prefer to wed others like them but that the relative numbers of people with certain characteristics have not been taken into account. As a result, the influences of endogamy and preferences probably are weaker than what the literature suggests. Glenn estimated the influence of religious endogamy using an index based on the percentage of married persons in each religious category who would be married to persons of the same religion if the religious preferences of husbands and wives were uncorrelated. The index is the difference between the expected and real percentages of religiously endogamous marriages, expressed as a proportion of the maximum possible difference between the real and expected values (Glenn, 1984: 725-726). The expected percentage would obtain if marriages were to occur randomly. The maximum possible difference is the difference between the expected percentage and 100%. Using this estimate, Glenn found that the influence of endogamy was substantially higher for Jews but about the same for Catholics and Protestants during the mid-'70s compared with 1957 (Glenn, 1982, 1984). Comparisons of older with younger persons further suggested that the strength of endogamy influences has declined substantially for Protestants, Catholics, and Jews.

The research just reviewed marks two significant advances. First, the research on structural influences allows for strong tests of theoretically important variables with the use of representative samples. As the review demonstrated, however, structural influences sometimes act in concert with other mechanisms to influence marital choice. More study is needed of the way in which composition of the population interacts with personal preferences, social norms, and economic factors. Second, the research on endogamy and on marriage attraction permits the estimation of psychological and normative influences that up to now have been hard to measure with survey data. Because these measures are what is left over after compositional effects are controlled, they are a proxy for a host of psychological and social processes involved in marital choice. Ideally, survey research in the future will combine assessment of compositonal factors with more precise measurement of individual, relational, and social influences on mate selection. The remainder of this review is devoted to studies that measure such influences directly.

SOCIAL NETWORKS AND PREMARITAL RELATIONSHIPS

Networks constitute a social structure that connects relationships to the larger society. In its simplest form, an individual's social network consists of his or her associates and the linkages among the associates. As this definition suggests, the way "linkage" is defined determines who is in the network and how the network is organized. When linkage is defined in terms of face-to-face contact, the network is made up of those with whom a person interacts, and the structure of the network is determined by who in the network interact with one another. This is called the interactive network (Milardo, 1986). The psychological network or the network of significant others is defined by those who are close or important to an individual (Milardo, 1986; Surra and Milardo, in press). Below I summarize research on networks and premarital relationships, with special attention to each type of network. Research on social networks investigated (*a*) the withdrawal from and integration with social networks that accom-

pany relationship growth and deterioration, respectively; and (*b*) the impact of social support and interference on relationship development.

The Withdrawal-Integration Hypothesis

Most of the research on networks and mate selection addressed the hypothesis of dyadic withdrawal; that is, partners withdraw from the social network as they become more involved with one another. The obverse of this hypothesis is that partners become integrated or reintegrated with their networks as they get less involved with one another. For the most part, researchers were more concerned with whether integration and withdrawal occur, and less with why they do so. There are a number of mechanisms that make withdrawal a likely occurrence, however (cf. Johnson and Leslie, 1982). Affectively, partners will withdraw because they have a limited supply of emotional energy, which is consumed primarily and increasingly by the romantic partner. Cognitively, partners retreat from others as they attempt to solidify their coupleness and form dyadic boundaries. Behaviorally, partners will withdraw from others as their romance demands more of their time and attention.

Studies of psychological and interactive networks support the withdrawal-integration hypothesis, although the phenomena may be limited to certain types of network relationships. The average number of friends in the psychological network declined as stage of dating involvement increased (Johnson and Leslie, 1982), and partners reported decreases in their participation in activities with third parties as they moved from courtship to marriage (Surra, 1985). In a longitudinal study of interactive networks, Milardo, Johnson, and Huston (1983) found that, as partners became more involved, they withdrew from close friends, intermediate friends, and acquaintances, but not from kin. As the integration hypothesis predicts, partners who regressed in involvement became more active with intermediate friends and acquaintances.

A closer look at the withdrawal-integration studies suggests that withdrawal holds only for certain third-party relationships (Surra, 1988). Daters appear to be more apt to withdraw from those to whom they are least close, but not from their close friends and kin. In fact, participation with kin and close others actually may increase as partners formalize their commitments and absorb their partners' relatives and close friends into their own networks. In results consistent with this view, Milardo and his colleagues (1983) found that the size of the kin network increased at engagement, and Parks, Stan, and Eggert (1983) reported that contact with the partners' friends and family was positively associated with romantic involvement. Thus, withdrawal may be limited to relationships with third parties that are least close, and the net change in associations may be nil or may increase as partners gain some associations and lose others.

Careful consideration of the withdrawal studies further suggests that the extent of withdrawal varies considerably across couples. Large variations in network size have been observed (Milardo et al., 1983), especially in the size of the kin network at engagement and marriage (Johnson and Leslie, 1982). Some couples apparently have more involvement with kin, whereas others have less as they become formally committed. Surra (1985) also found that some couples withdraw from their networks, but others maintain about the same level of contact from dating through early marriage. Thus, within any one sample of couples, the average level of network participation may decline with more involvement, but the average differences may result from severe withdrawal on the part of some couples and weak or nonexistent withdrawal on the part of others.

In the next decade, I expect investigators will try to pinpoint the conditions under which withdrawal occurs and to give more attention to the integration hypothesis. This will require studies of the causes of withdrawal and of developmental change, including advances and declines in dating stage over long periods of time. Attention also must be given to assessing different kinds of third-party relationships (e.g., kin, close friends, and acquaintances) and to the type of network being studied. In order to understand why withdrawal and integration differ for different couples, it is necessary to examine variations in the interconnectedness of networks, as well as variations in involvement between daters (cf. Surra, 1988).

Support and Interference from the Network

Research on support and interference from the network has focused on three questions: (*a*) do the actions and reactions of third parties affect whether dating relationships thrive; (*b*) is the Romeo and Juliet effect (Driscoll, Davis, and Lipetz, 1972) valid; that is, does opposition to a romance strengthen it; and (*c*) when in the developmental course of relationships do support and interference occur?

With regard to the first question, the evidence indicates that perceived subjective reactions of third parties are more influential than actions that are interfering or supportive. In other words, assessments of the psychological network produce much stronger results than assessments of the interactive network. Parks and colleagues (Eggert and Parks, 1987; Parks and Adelman, 1983; Parks et al., 1983) operationalized support as real or anticipated approval of the dating relationship from the network of close others. Support from one's own and the partner's network was positively associated with a composite measure of romantic involvement that included love, commitment, time spent with partner, and other variables. This was true for both college-student dating relationships (Parks et al., 1983) and for adolescent dating relationships and friendships (Eggert and Parks, 1987). In addition, support from both networks predicted relationship stability over a 3-month period and the amount of uncertainty about the dating relationship (Parks and Adelman, 1983). Johnson and Milardo (1984) likewise found that interference from members of the psychological network predicted declines in dating involvement. Leslie, Huston, and Johnson (1986) examined the association between the actions parents take to show approval or disapproval of their children's dates and the actions children take to influence their parents' opinions. Parents' and childrens' actions were increasingly common as daters became more involved, which suggests that parent-child interaction about dating is most salient once relationships become serious. Developmental change in the dating relationship was only weakly related to approval and disapproval, however. Evidently, the extent to which parents and children exchange information about dating has little impact on the development of the romance.

The second question concerned the accuracy of the Romeo and Juliet effect, or the finding that parental interference and romantic involvement are positively related (cf. Driscoll et al., 1972). Most of the evidence just reviewed runs counter to the effect, instead demonstrating a negative connection between interference or disapproval and romantic involvement. Attempts to replicate the effect found little evidence of it; it occurred only for the partner's family and for slight opposition from the family (Parks et al., 1983). Surra (1987) found that network opposition and support was especially influential for a subset of couples whose commitment developed quickly initially and then lost momentum at engagement. Thus, the Romeo and Juliet effect may operate for couples in which the partner's family members or friends oppose the association.

With regard to the third question, Johnson and Milardo (1984) hypothesized that interference and dating stage would be curvilinearly related. Interference should be greatest during mid-stages, when the romance would infringe the most on network relationships. It should be lowest during initial stages when the romance was not yet established and during engagement when opposition from the network would only alienate the committed pair. Cross-sectional comparisons supported the hypothesis for interference from parents, siblings, and friends.

In general, network interference hampers relationship progress and support promotes it, at least for some forms of interference and support. The fact that studies of psychological networks produce stronger effects than studies of interactive networks suggests that perceived interference and support may have greater impact on relationships than actions taken by network members. Thus, networks may influence relationships more passively than actively, as daters anticipate or imagine the reactions of those close to them. On the basis of qualitative analyses, Surra and Milardo (in press) devised several propositions regarding the relatively indirect influence of networks on commitment. Psychologically, networks enable partners to gather information about the other's character by means of social comparison and passive observation of the other interacting with network members. Normatively, network members resocialize partners and reinforce existing norms by taking actions that emphasize appropriate social behavior (e.g., best friends getting engaged). Future research would profit from considering the indirect as well as direct influences of networks on dyads.

Future research also should address interference and support under conditions that threaten the solidarity of network identity; for example, when dating relationships are heterogamous. Up to now, studies have been done on homogeneous college-student samples, in which network opposition is low with little variation (e.g., Parks et al., 1983). A true test of active network interference and of the Romeo and Juliet effect, in particular, requires sampling outgroup dating relationships that are likely to activate strong opposition and endogamy norms.

As in the case of social withdrawal, the study of support and interference would benefit from tests of the structure or interconnectedness of networks. Such research would be especially useful for explaining why network phenomena seem to differ so across couples. Networks that are extremely tightly knit or fully saturated would be apt to strongly oppose the formation of any new romance because it would disrupt already established relationships. Networks that are loosely knit may provide a context of great freedom for developing romances but little support for them. Networks of intermediate connectedness are likely to provide an optimum balance of structural support and freedom (cf. Milardo, 1986; Surra, 1988; Surra and Milardo, in press). The full impact of networks on mate selection will be understood when researchers begin to assess the degree of network structure and its effect on dyads.

INTERDEPENDENCE AND BEHAVIORAL FEATURES OF PREMARITAL RELATIONSHIPS

In this section, I examine research at the dyadic level of analysis that addressed behavioral or outcome interdependence. Thibaut and Kelley's (1959; Kelley and Thibaut, 1978; Kelley, 1979) theory of outcome interdependence concerns the interconnections between partners that result from the rewards and costs they derive from interaction. The theory of outcome interdependence is related to social exchange theory and to theories of distributive justice (i.e., theories about the rules that govern the distribution of rewards and costs). In this section, I review research on three topics: (*a*) outcome interdependence; (*b*) social exchange, equity, and equality; and (*c*) behavioral exchange during interaction (also, cf. Cate and Lloyd, 1988).

Outcome Interdependence

On the basis of Thibaut and Kelley's (1959;

Kelley, 1979; Kelley and Thibaut, 1978) theory of outcome interdependence, Rusbult (1980, 1983; Rusbult, Johnson, and Morrow, 1986; Rusbult, Zembrodt, and Gunn, 1982) devised an investment model of relationships. The model proposes that satisfaction and commitment have different predictors. The propositions of the model are that (*a*) satisfaction should be greater when relationships provide more rewards and fewer costs compared with what individuals feel they deserve (i.e., a person's Comparison Level, or CL); and (*b*) commitment increases as satisfaction increases, as the investment of resources increases, and as the perceived quality of alternatives declines. The latter variable refers to a person's Comparison Level for Alternatives (CLalt), or the lowest level of outcomes one will accept in light of outcomes perceived to be available elsewhere (e.g., from other relationships or being alone).

Except for the hypothesized relationships pertaining to costs, the propositions have received considerable support from both experimental and field studies of college students. Higher reward levels predicted greater satisfaction with and commitment to relationships (Rusbult, 1980, 1983; Rusbult et al., 1986). Most studies have shown that more satisfied partners reported higher levels of commitment (Michaels et al., 1986; Rusbult, 1980, 1983; Rusbult et al., 1986; Sprecher, 1988). As expected, commitment increased with investments but decreased as alternatives became more attractive (Rusbult, 1980. 1983; Rusbult et al., 1986). Compared with partners who broke up over a 7-month period, those who did not reported that rewards, satisfaction, investments, and commitment increased more; costs increased less; and alternative quality decreased more (Rusbult, 1983). Contrary to the model, costs were unrelated to satisfaction and to commitment (Rusbult, 1983), or only weakly related to commitment (Rusbult, 1980). In a study of the generalizability of the investment model to noncollege students, *higher* costs were associated with *greater* commitment for those over 35 and those who were less educated or had lower incomes (Rusbult et al., 1986). The remaining propositions held for most subgroups in the generalizability study.

Some of the investment model findings reported by Rusbult have failed to replicate. Lloyd, Cate, and Henton (1984) found that relationship stability over a 7-month period was not related to satisfaction with the relationship or

with CLalt, possibly because they controlled for length of relationship whereas other researchers typically have not. Similarly, the association between investments and commitment was nil when social support was partialed out (Sprecher, 1988). In addition, differences in results may stem from differences in the way variables of the model are measured, a matter that is discussed below. Future refinements of the investment model might attend to its sensitivity to control variables and to measurement.

Social Exchange, Equity, and Equality

A number of other researchers have tested elements of interdependence theory against theories of distributive justice. Typically, absolute levels of rewards or rewards relative to CL or CLalt are pitted against two justice rules, equity and equality. Hatfield's equity theory (Hatfield, Traupmann, Sprecher, Utne, and Hay, 1985) assumes that relationships are happier and more committed when the proportions of each partner's inputs to outcomes are equal; that is, the relationship between equity and relationship outcomes is quadratic. An equality norm holds that relationships fare best when partners receive equal outcomes.

Although equity theory has received good support from past research (see Hatfield, Utne, and Traupmann, 1979; Hatfield et al., 1985, for reviews), the studies of this decade question the validity of the theory. Recent findings invariably demonstrate that absolute reward levels predict relationship satisfaction much better than either equity or equality (Cate, Lloyd, Henton, and Larson, 1982; Cate, Lloyd, and Long, 1988; Michaels, Edwards, and Acock, 1984). Although inequity and inequality do have independent effects on satisfaction, the amount of variance each explains is small (3.9% and 8.8%, respectively, in Cate, Lloyd, et al., 1982; and 3.1% and 3.7%, respectively, in Michaels et al., 1984). Moreover, the nature of the association between equity and satisfaction is not exactly what the theory predicts. Although others have found a quadratic relationship between equity and satisfaction, Michaels et al. (1984) looked carefully at the exact shape of the relationship. They found that the lower satisfaction reported by those who are underbenefited is primarily due to their reduced levels of rewards. Those who are overbenefited, in contrast, are influenced by the countervailing effects of increased rewards and inequity. The same findings apply to those disadvantaged or advantaged by inequality.

Equity and equality do even less well at predicting changes in satisfaction, commitment, and stability. The ability to predict changes in satisfaction over a 3-month period increased for rewards but decreased for equity (Cate et al., 1988). It may be that partners closely monitor the fairness of the reward distribution early on but become less concerned with it as the relationship becomes more established. Rewards also explained relationship stability (Cate, Lloyd, and Henton, 1985; Lloyd et al., 1984), but equity and equality did not (Cate et al., 1985). Although two studies suggested that equity does influence commitment (Michaels, Edwards, and Acock, 1986; Sprecher, 1988), more careful examination indicated that the relationship probably holds only when the effects of other exchange variables, such as rewards and rewards minus CLalt, were uncontrolled. When exchange variables were partialed out, they were significant, but the effect for equity was not. Controlling for exchange variables similarly affects the association between equity and emotions (Michaels et al., 1984; Sprecher, 1986).

In addition to the social exchange principle that partners seek high rewards from their relationships, the predictions pertaining to CL and CLalt from Thibaut and Kelley's interdependence theory have received some support. CLalt was an important predictor of commitment, above and beyond other strong determinants such as rewards and satisfaction (Michaels et al., 1986). In addition, the variable "rewards minus CL" explained satisfaction better than equity or equality alone, but not as well as rewards alone (Michaels et al., 1984). Evidently, partners are more committed to relationships as long as their rewards are high and exceed those available from their best alternative relationship. They are satisfied to the extent that rewards are high and exceed their expectations for what they deserve.

Behavioral Exchange during Interaction

Further confirmation that rewards affect the quality of relationships is seen in studies of how behaviors exchanged premaritally affect subsequent satisfaction and stability. Markman (1979, 1981) studied the positivity of interaction between engaged pairs (Time 1) by using the talk table, a technique in which partners placed opposite one another rate the positivity of messages received during interaction. Subsequent satisfaction was assessed 1 year (Time 2), 2½ years (Time 3), and 5½ years (Time 4) after Time 1. The positivity of interaction predicted satisfaction at Times 3 and 4, but not at Time 2. Evidently, lower levels of rewards during interaction precede the development of marital distress. Other research suggests that the interaction patterns of distressed partners are characterized by tit-for-tat exchange of both positive and negative behaviors. Filsinger and Thoma (1988) recruited a sample of couples who were seriously considering marriage, and found that, compared with those who stayed together, those who broke up after 1½ years had higher rates of negative and positive reciprocity initially. Those who broke up after 5 years likewise had higher rates of positive reciprocity initially.

Although the findings from this decade regarding outcome interdependence, distributive justice, and social exchange seem fairly uniform across studies, several methodological concerns raise doubts about this uniformity. First, there are problems with measurement. Regarding CLalt, Johnson (1985) criticized Rusbult's (1980, 1983) work on the grounds that her measure primarily assessed alternative relationships. According to Johnson, this operationalization is not true to interdependence theory, which includes in CLalt options other than relationships and constraints to terminating the relationship. Rusbult's measure of CLalt was comparative, asking respondents to consider alternatives in light of their current relationship. This confounds the measurement of CLalt with the measurement of satisfaction, increasing the likelihood of finding significant effects for the alternatives variable (Johnson, 1985). Satisfaction also is confounded with the assessment of commitment, as the latter is partly based on one's attachment to the relationship (Johnson, 1985). Many of the criticisms of Rusbult's measures of CLalt apply to other research reviewed here (Lloyd et al., 1984; Michaels et al., 1986; Sprecher, 1988). The theorizing and measurement of CLalt is also problematic. Although authors discuss the theoretical relevance of CL (e.g., Rusbult, 1980, 1983), Michaels and colleagues (1984) were the only researchers who actually measured it.

A second limitation of these studies is that they

rely almost exclusively on college-student samples. The question is, Do college-students provide a good test of the relative utility of exchange, interdependence, and distributive justice for predicting relationship outcomes? The answer probably is, no. Older adolescents possess several characteristics that might encourage them to be more concerned about what they get out of relationships than issues of equity or equality. First, they tend to be egocentric (Sears, 1986), which may make it difficult for them to consider the partner or the partner's perspective as the theory and measurement of equity and equality demand. Second, recent cohorts of young people are thought to be especially individualistic (Dizard and Gadlin, 1984), which might induce them to seek self-gratification rather than the common good. Third, compared with older or previously married individuals, college students are only beginning their relationship careers, when simple reward values may be most salient to evaluations of relationship success. Later in dating histories, equity and equality may become more relevant. Until exchange, interdependence, and justice theories are studied with older respondents, the previously married, and those who have had multiple partners, their accuracy remains an open question.

Research in this decade has lagged far behind theoretical work on interdependence in relationships. Although inquiry has focused on *behavioral* interdependence, Kelley's theory (1979) and other theorizing (e.g., Huston and Robins, 1982) have emphasized a second level of interdependence, *dispositional*. Dispositional interdependence means that partners influence one another through the outcomes they derive from the display of interpersonal dispositions during interaction. When a partner, for example, forgoes his or her own preferred outcome to go out for the evening because the other wants to stay in, the other may conclude that the partner is loving or perhaps a martyr. Interpersonal dispositions, or subjective conditions, refer to the attitudes and beliefs partners hold about one another and about the nature of their relationship (Huston and Robins, 1982). As the example suggests, dispositional and outcome interdependence emerge from and influence one another. During this decade, two types of subjective conditions, love and commitment, have been developed theoretically (cf.

Hatfield, 1988; Kelley, 1983; Sternberg, 1986). Empirical investigation of love and commitment has focused on their subjective meaning (Fehr, 1988; Shaver, Schwartz, Kirson, and O'Connor, 1987), on how this meaning affects reactions to hypothetical relationships (Fehr, 1988), and on individual styles of loving (Davis and Latty-Mann, 1987; Hendrick and Hendrick, 1986, 1988; Hendrick, Hendrick, and Adler, 1988; Hendrick, Hendrick, Foote, and Slapion-Foote, 1984; Levy and Davis, 1988). Although this work lays a strong foundation for describing subjective conditions, it is relatively uninformative about how they operate in and affect the outcome of developing relationships. Moreover, virtually no research has been done on how behavioral and dispositional interdependence are interrelated. In the next decade, research is likely to address these deficits.

INDIVIDUAL ATTRIBUTIONS FOR CHANGES IN COMMITMENT

In this section, I examine research at the individual level of analysis; specifically, individuals' subjective explanations for why their relationships change. Much of the research on mate selection assumes that the process by which partners form a relationship or a marriage is a conscious, careful, and rational choice. Studies of homogamy, for example, often presume that similarity arises out of partners' choices, and filter theories suppose that partners actively test their compatibility on sets of characteristics ordered sequentially (e.g., Murstein's stimulus, value, and role theory, described below). The assumption that partners choose one another rationally was virtually unexamined until this decade. Partly to test the assumption and partly to discover on what bases partners do make relationship decisions, researchers in this decade began conducting studies of partners' subjective explanations for why their relationships change.

This work is rooted in attribution theory, which concerns the process by which partners search for the causes of events, the products of this causal search, and the relationship between behavior and the causal process and products. The method typically used to study attributions involves having respondents reconstruct their relationship from memory by having them plot on a graph changes in commitment, which ranges from 0% to 100%, and explain why each upturn and downturn occurred (Baxter and Bullis, 1986; Lloyd and Cate, 1985; Surra, 1987; Surra, Arizzi, and Asmussen, 1988; Surra and Huston, 1987). In order to study attributions for breakups, investigators usually have respondents answer an open-ended question about why the breakup occurred (Baxter, 1986; Cupach and Metts, 1986; Stephen, 1987a).

One goal of this research was to determine the variety of attributions partners make and the extent to which explanations are centered on compatibility and the quality of the relationship. The results have shown that attributions are much more varied and complex than theories of mate choice presume. In studies of relationships that result in marriage (Surra, 1987; Surra et al., 1988; Surra and Huston, 1987), most attributions (about 65%) are dyadic, involving interaction or beliefs about the partnership. A substantial proportion of attributions, however, concern factors that originate outside the relationship. These include references to circumstances, such as coincidence, luck, holidays, job firings, or a parent's illness, and to social networks, including the expressed and imagined opinions of others and alternative dating partners. Another 4% to 7% of partners' interferences are intrapersonal-normative, reflecting the effects of predispositions to wed and expectations for marriageable partners. Although this percentage is small, even one such attribution (e.g., "I had done everything a single person should, and was ready to get married") can drive an entire relationship. The distribution of attributions in studies of breakups shows a similar wide variety of attributions, although individual attributions to the self or the partner are more common in breakups than in the decision to wed (Baxter, 1986; Cupach and Metts, 1986; Lloyd and Cate, 1985; Stephen, 1987a).

Researchers also examined how attributions are related to the development of commitment. Theoretically, attributions that concern compatibility and the nature of the relationship should be associated with deliberate, moderate changes in commitment that reflect careful decision-making. Although theories make no predictions about the association between nondyadic attributions and commitment, it is likely that some reasons may result in quickly formed commitments (e.g., the belief that it is time to settle down), whereas others (e.g., unexpected or sudden events) may prompt turbulent changes in commitments. Re-

sults from research on the decision to wed generally are consistent with these expectations. Surra (1987) found that partners whose commitments developed moderately (mean length = 26 months) reported more attributions to the relationship itself, whereas partners whose courtships were short, fast, and smooth (mean length = 14 months) reported more intrapersonal-normative attributions (Surra, 1987; Surra et al., 1988). Courtships that accelerated and then got hung up were linked to social network attributions and long rocky courtships to circumstantial ones.

Because people differ with regard to the depth and breadth of their causal analysis, reasons for commitment should predict long-term satisfaction with and stability of relationships (Surra et al., 1988). In addition, commitments based on an examination of the quality of the relationship should have better relationship outcomes than those that result from external or other influences. Indeed, Surra et al. (1988) found that newlyweds' recollections about why they became committed were associated with their marital happiness after about 4 years of marriage. The results suggested two types of commitment processes: event-driven and relationship-driven. Commitments driven by events were associated with lower levels of marital happiness, and the attributions that predicted lower marital happiness—certain social network and dyadic attributions—usually were the same ones that were associated with large, fast changes in commitment (e.g., 70% over one month). Event-driven commitments seem to result from relatively simplistic decisions based upon salient happenings. The happenings often involve third parties or dyadic events that are apt to provide distinct information about commitment (e.g., agreement on stage of involvement). Relationship-driven commitments were associated with higher levels of subsequent marital happiness. This commitment process was tied to attributions that concern spending time together, getting to know one another, and disclosing information to one another—the kinds of inferences that typically were associated with moderate, slower changes in commitment. Relationship-driven commitments more closely match the rational choice process believed to be important for marital success. Contrary to the findings of Surra et al. (1988), Baxter and Bullis (1986) found no association between current relationship satisfaction and attributions. This discrepancy might stem from the different coding schemes used, different samples (college students in Baxter and Bullis and newly-weds in Surra et al.), or the different times at which satisfaction was assessed (concurrently in Baxter and Bullis and longitudinally in Surra et al.).

Research on attributions for relationship development offers a useful alternative to traditional approaches to the study of relationship choice. The research so far has relied on reconstructions of attributions, however, and reconstructions may be biased by the present state of the relationship or by implicit theories about relationships. Future research should attempt to replicate findings with longitudinal methods.

PROCESS AND MODELS OF PREMARITAL RELATIONSHIP DEVELOPMENT

In this section I summarize research in which the major purpose was the description and explanation of developmental change in relationships. Prior to this decade, most developmental models of mate selection were stage or filter theories (see Murstein, 1980, for a review). The 1980s were noteworthy because they produced a number of promising alternatives. Below I delineate four models of relationship development: gradual differentiation, early determinism, incremental convergence and divergence, and progressive stages. As shown in Table 1, the models are derived from the key assumptions about development made in the research reviewed. These assumptions refer to (*a*) the nature of change; that is, how change is defined and measured and whether the nature of change is the same across couples; (*b*) whether behavioral and subjective properties of relationships are developmental and emergent versus ever-present and apparent at the outset in relationships; and (*c*) the types of causes used to explain change. The purpose of outlining the models is to survey the depth, variety, and sophistication of thinking about relationship development that has emerged in the past decade.

Gradual Differentiation

The gradual-differentiation model of development assumes that relationships pass through alternating periods of growth and deterioration or stability and instability over their existence (see Table 1). Instead of discontinuous shifts from one clearly demarcated state to another, developmental change is viewed as continuous but bidirectional. In addition, developmental pathways differ across couples, although common patterns can be identified. Subjective and objective properties of relationships emerge over time, and their content and definition may vary at different points in time. Different developmental paths are thought to result from different causes, with variables from some levels of analysis more influential for some couples than others. Thus, the model presupposes that multiple causes affect development. Some causes are proximal to the pair in time and space (e.g., conflict) and others are more distal (e.g., social background).

The assumptions of gradual differentiation are illustrated by a program of research aimed at describing the development of commitment and its correlates. The method typically used involves having respondents reconstruct from memory the evolution of their relationships. Respondents are asked to plot changes in the "chance of marriage," a measure of commitment, that occurred since they first met their partners (cf. Huston, Surra, Fitzgerald, and Cate, 1981). Cate, Huston, and Nesselroade (1986) used the method to study courtship pathways in a sample of newly-wed couples. Three different shapes were found to underlie the variation in the entire sample of graphs: a slow, rocky path; a path that developed quickly at first, then lost momentum; and a path that was an intermediate ascent to asymptote. Each path was differentially associated with individual background variables and with relationship properties measured for different dating stages (e.g., casual dating, serious dating). The more spouses' graphs resembled the first path, for instance, the younger they were when they met, the lower was perceived parental eagerness for them to wed, and the more conflict and ambivalence the partners experienced. Surra (1985) built upon this study by grouping couples in another sample according to similarity in the shapes of graphs and then examining variations among the types on interdependence. Four types of courtship were identified—three that were similar to those identified by Cate and associates, and an accelerated, smooth pathway. Partners in each type differed in the extent to which they performed activities with one another and with the network. Partners in the accelerated type exhibited the expected pattern whereby they became more active with one anoth-

TABLE 1. MODELS OF THE DEVELOPMENT OF PREMARITAL RELATIONSHIPS

Characteristics of Development	Model			
	Gradual Differentiation	Early Determinism	Incremental Convergence and Divergence	Progressive Stages
Nature of change	Bidirectional oscillations between advances and regressions	Changes in states or outcomes	Changes in states or outcomes	Changes in states
	Different for different couples	Similar across couples	Similar across couples	Similar across couples
Properties of relationships	Emerging over time	Present early on	Emerging over time	Present early on and emerging over time
Causes of change	Different for different couples	Similar across couples	Similar across couples	Similar across couples
	Proximal and distal	Proximal	Proximal	Proximal and distal
	Multiple causes from different levels of analysis	Multiple causes from one (dyadic) level of analysis	Single cause from one (dyadic) level of analysis	Multiple causes from different levels of analysis
Illustrative citations	Cate et al., 1986 Huston et al., 1981 Surra, 1985	Berg and McQuinn, 1986	Stephen, 1984, 1985	Leigh et al., 1984 Murstein, 1976, 1987

er and withdrew from the network as they moved closer to marriage. Those in the accelerated-arrested type also became increasingly interdependent with one another, but they withdrew more severely from the network at engagement and remained more withdrawn during early marriage. The prolonged type was characterized by increasing interdependence between partners and withdrawal from the network, but to a lesser extent than the two accelerated types. Contrary to the remaining groups, partners in the intermediate type did not become more active with one another and did not withdraw from the network as their courtships progressed.

The research just reviewed is in accord with the gradual-differentiation model: change is bidirectional and continuous; commitment develops differently for different couples; and properties of relationships (e.g., conflict, interdependence) emerge and change over time. The findings also imply that different commitment pathways result from interacting causes from various sources, such as networks and interdependence in dyads. Research by Baxter (1984) on trajectories of premarital breakups and by Altman and associates (1981) on social penetration are other examples of work consistent with the gradual-differentiation model.

Most of the research on the gradual-differentiation model has employed retrospective

methods. The findings that developmental pathways differ across couples may be influenced by errors of memory, which may be particularly affected by the present state of the relationship. The gradual-differentiation model needs to be studied with the use of prospective designs.

Early Determinism

In the early-determinism model (see Table 1), development is conceived as a change in relationship state (e.g., together or apart) or other outcome (e.g., change in satisfaction), and these changes are assumed to describe development for all couples. Perhaps the most fundamental feature of this model is that properties of relationships that are in place early on affect the course of the relationship from then on. The focus is on proximal causes of change from the dyadic level of analysis that are influential for all couples.

Research by Berg and McQuinn (1986) is based on this model. They hypothesized that measures of general relationship properties and of social exchange taken early in relationships would discriminate stable from unstable relationships. The hypothesis is based on the argument that the future course of a relationship is set early because individuals seek information that confirms their prior experiences. Consistent with the hypothesis, the initial assessments of general properties (e.g., love, liking, and conflict) and of social exchange (e.g., CL, CLalt) distinguised those who broke up from those who stayed together after 4 months. The Time 2 assessments of some properties did predict somewhat better than initial ones, however. With respect to how the variables changed over time, in most cases, initial differences were magnified over time, which supports the idea that initial differences are simply played out as relationships evolve. Although the evidence suggested that two properties did emerge over time, the particularism and symbolism of positive resources, Berg and McQuinn (1986: 951) concluded that "the seeds of . . . increasingly obvious differences were both present and discernible at an early time. The relationships then progressed along the lines laid down by these early differences."

In accordance with early determinism, the goal of the studies just reviewed is to identify early predictors of developmental change, conceptualized as a binary change in state (e.g., together or apart) or other outcome. Multiple determinants are studied, but they come from the same level of analysis, the nature of the relationship itself, and are thought to operate similarly for different couples. Findings from the studies reviewed here, and other studies of friendship development not reviewed (Berg, 1984; Hays, 1984, 1985), generally support these assumptions, though there are properties for which the assumptions do not hold. In order to ascertain the generalizability of the model across time and people, studies of early determinism are needed in which noncollege students are followed for longer periods of time.

Incremental Convergence and Divergence

In the incremental convergence and divergence model, change is conceived as a change in state or outcome that is applicable to all couples (see Table 1). Contrary to the early-determinism model, however, relationship properties emerge with the passage of time. The primary cause of change is proximal, from the dyadic level of analysis.

These assumptions are apparent in Stephen's (1984, 1985) work on symbolic exchange, which integrates social exchange theory with symbolic interactionism. The basic premise of the theory is that the development of a relationship involves partners' constructing a shared world view, or "sets of common assumptions about the way things are" (Stephen, 1984: 396). The shared world view arises primarily out of communication (Stephen, 1985, 1987b). The degree of similarity between partners' attitudes, values, and beliefs is an indication of how symbolically interdependent partners are. Stephen emphasized that his view of similarity, in which beliefs and attitudes are changeable and similarity may increase or decrease over time, departs from filter theories described below, which view similarity as matching on static traits and characteristics.

In order to test his theory, Stephen (Stephen and Markman, 1983) developed a measure called the Relationship World Index (RWI), a *q*-sort of beliefs about intimate relationships (e.g., "A relationship requires a concentrated effort to give to the other without losing oneself in the process"). Stephen reported that findings from a cross-sectional study (1984) and a longitudinal study (1985) supported the idea that similarity between partners' RWI scores increased linearly with dating stage and that the increase resulted from communication.

As yet, there is no direct evidence that similarity on the RWI is linked to communication. The only indirect evidence is weak, from a self-report study comparing geographically separated with geographically together couples on time spent talking and RWI similarity scores (Stephen, 1986). Moreover, the longitudinal study showed a decrease in RWI similarity scores at one point, which was attributed to semester break; no test for nonlinearity was reported (Stephen, 1985). The theory of symbolic interdependence posits a much more inclusive shared reality than that encompassed by the RWI, which is limited to general relationship beliefs. Although symbolic exchange offers a promising alternative to other models of development, more careful and complete study of it is needed.

Progressive Stages

Theories that fit the progressive-stage model (see Table 1), such as Kerckhoff and Davis's filter theory, Murstein's Stimulus-Value-Role theory (SVR), and Lewis's theory of Premarital Dyadic Formation, have been popular in the mate selection literature for some time (see Murstein, 1980, for a review). In this decade, SVR has received continued attention, so I use it to illustrate the model of progressive stages. SVR theory is based on two principles: (*a*) that attraction stems from the equality of exchange of the assets and liabilities each partner possesses and (*b*) that partners whose relationships progress pass through three stages: stimulus, in which partners evaluate qualities of one another that can be observed prior to interaction (e.g., appearance, reputation); value, in which partners weigh whether they are compatible on their basic values; and role, in which partners ascertain how well they function in the roles they perform as lovers, companions, housekeepers,and the like. Thus, the nature of change is that all couples pass through defined stages in a fixed sequence. Some relationship properties are apparent early on, such as the attraction that arises out of stimulus characteristics, whereas value consensus and role fit emerge as partners acquire more detailed information about one another. The causes of developmental change are distal, located in partners' background characteristics, and proximal, arising out of interaction. Individual, dyadic, and external causes are included in the theory, though the first two levels of analysis are emphasized in the progression through stages.

Murstein has written several updates of the theory and published data in support of it (Murstein, 1976, 1987). Yet considerable controversy surrounds the theory, particularly the proposed sequence of stages and whether partners actually test their degree of fit (see Huston et al., 1981). A study of the theory in this decade stimulated more debate, as the basic premises of the theory were not supported (Leigh, Holman, and Burr, 1984). Murstein (1987) criticized the methods of the study (e.g., the way individuals were grouped into stages) and clarified that stage depends on the amount of contact partners have. The first contact is the stimulus stage, the second through seventh contacts are the value stage, and eight or more contacts are the role stage. In addition, individuals acquire information about stimulus characteristics, values, and roles continuously, but the rate of acceleration with which information is acquired defines each stage. Partners, for example, are obtaining information about values during the role stage, but to a lesser extent than they did during the values stage. (See Leigh, Holman, and Burr, 1987, for their rebuttal.) In further debate, Stephen (1987b) argued that, contrary to Murstein's claim, data on symbolic ex-

change are inconsistent with SVR theory because they demonstrate the malleability of similarity.

Murstein's (1987) restatement of SVR brings it closer to the model of incremental convergence and divergence. The fact that he stressed the continued acquisition of stimulus, value, and role information throughout the relationship makes the stages less qualitatively distinct from one another. Also, the transitions between stages are smoother and less abrupt, as they are now defined in relative terms according to how much of each type of information is accrued. The stages, now defined according to number of contacts, are still somewhat arbitrary, however (Leigh et al., 1987). Finally, the role of interaction in defining the stages is more apparent. SVR theory differs from symbolic exchange in that the latter allows for alterations in shared perceptions, proposes no fixed sequence, views similarity as negotiated rather than discovered by partners, and focuses on a single causal variable. The two theories and the models on which they are based raise some elemental questions about the nature and causes of development. In the next decade, it would be useful to see tests of the theories that are more rigorous methodologically and more complete theoretically.

CONCLUSIONS

In this review, I have summarized the major advances in research and theory on mate selection in the past decade and commented on methodological problems arising out of the match between research and theory. The themes of the past decade point the way for future work. Because legal marriage is much less a marker of permanence or of relationship progress, more attention likely will be given to continuities in features of romantic relationships and to long-term predictors of relationship quality. A few studies already addressed these topics (e.g., Filsinger and Thoma, 1988; Kelly, Huston, and Cate, 1985; Markman, 1979, 1981). As marriage becomes less prevalent, peoples' heterosexual relationships will take different shapes at different points in time, as they move in and out of marriage, friendship, romance, cohabitation, and so on. Understanding heterosexual relationships in the future will require less attention to marital choice and more to the formation and development of romantic relationships generally.

In order to accomplish this, research is likely to focus more on how basic processes operate in the context of different relationships. There are already signs of this emphasis. Models for defining relationships and their fundamental properties are available (Kelley et al., 1983), and such topics as sex, usually studied independent of relationships, are being examined within the context of relationships (e.g., Christopher and Cate, 1985). In addition, topics traditionally studied only in the context of marriage are being studied premaritally; for example, abuse in premarital relationships (Cate, Henton, Koval, Christopher, and Lloyd, 1982; DeMaris, 1987). Researchers will need to be less concerned with *premarital* relationships and young adults, and more concerned with *intermarital* relationships in other populations. Evidence of such a trend is seen in scholarship on courtship among the divorced (e.g., O'Flaherty and Workman, 1988; Rodgers and Conrad, 1986) and traditional mate selection topics in older adults (Dressel, 1980; Veevers, 1988).

With changes in marital patterns, mate selection in its broadest sense becomes more relevant to more people. As a result, its importance as a research topic will intensify over the next decade.

NOTE

The author thanks Ted Huston and three anonymous reviewers for their helpful comments on an earlier draft of this article. Requests for reprints should be addressed to Catherine A. Surra.

REFERENCES

Altman, Irwin, Anne Vinsel, and Barbara B. Brown. 1981. "Dialectic conceptions in social psychology: An application to social penetration and privacy regulation." Pp. 107-160 in Leonard Berkowitz (ed.), Advances in Experimental Social Psychology (Vol. 14). New York: Academic Press.

Atkinson, Maxine P., and Becky L. Glass. 1985. "Marital age heterogamy and homogamy, 1900 to 1980." Journal of Marriage and the Family 47: 685-691.

Baxter, Leslie A. 1984. "Trajectories of relationship disengagement." Journal of Social and Personal Relationships 1: 29-48.

Baxter, Leslie A. 1986. "Gender differences in the heterosexual relationship rules embedded in breakup accounts." Journal of Social and Personal Relationships 3: 289-306.

Baxter, Leslie, and Connie Bullis. 1986. "Turning points in developing romantic relationships." Human Communication Research 12: 469-493.

Berg, John H. 1984. "The development of friendship between roommates." Journal of Personality and Social Psychology 46: 346-356.

Berg, John H., and Ronald D. McQuinn. 1986. "Attraction and exchange in continuing and noncontinuing dating relationships." Journal of Personality and Social Psychology 50: 942-952.

Blau, Peter M. 1977. Inequality and Heterogeneity. New York: Free Press.

Blau, Peter M., Terry C. Blum, and Joseph E. Schwartz. 1982. "Heterogeneity and intermarriage." American Sociological Review 47: 45-62.

Blau, Peter M., Carolyn Beeker, and Kevin M. Fitzpatrick. 1984. "Intersecting social affiliations and intermarriage." Social Forces 62: 585-605.

Blum, Terry C. 1985. "Structural constraints on interpersonal relations: A test of Blau's macrosociological theory." American Journal of Sociology 91: 511-521.

Booth, Alan, and David Johnson. 1988. "Premarital cohabitation and marital success." Journal of Family Issues 9: 255-272.

Bumpass, Larry L., and James A. Sweet. 1989. "National estimates of cohabitation." Demography 26: 615-625.

Bumpass, Larry L., James A. Sweet, and Andrew Cherlin. 1989. The Role of Cohabitation in Declining Rates of Marriage. NSFH Working Paper No. 5. Madison: University of Wisconsin, Center for Demography and Ecology.

Cate, Rodney M., June M. Henton, James Koval, F. Scott Christopher, and Sally Lloyd. 1982. "Premarital abuse: A social psychological perspective." Journal of Family Issues 3: 79-90.

Cate, Rodney M., Ted L. Huston, and John R. Nesselroade. 1986. "Premarital relationships: Toward the identification of alternative pathways to marriage." Journal of Social and Clinical Psychology 4: 3-22.

Cate, Rodney M., Sally A. Lloyd, June M. Henton, and Jeffrey H. Larson. 1982. "Fairness and reward level as predictors of relationship satisfaction." Social Psychology Quarterly 45: 171-181.

Cate, Rodney M., Sally A. Lloyd, and June M. Henton. 1985. "The effect of equity, equality, and reward level on the stability of students' premarital relationships." Journal of Social Psychology 125: 715-721.

Cate, Rodney M., Sally A. Lloyd, and Edgar Long. 1988. "The role of rewards and fairness in developing premarital relationships." Journal of Marriage and the Family 50: 443-452.

Cate, Rodney M., and Sally A. Lloyd. 1988. "Courtship." Pp. 409-427 in Steve Duck (ed.), Handbook of Personal Relationships. London: John Wiley and Sons.

Christopher, Scott F., and Rodney M. Cate. 1985. "Premarital sexual pathways and relationship development." Journal of Social and Personal Relationships 2: 271-288.

Cupach, William R., and Sandra Metts. 1986. "Accounts of relational dissolution: A comparison of marital and non-marital relationships." Communication Monographs 53: 311–334.

Davis, Keith E., and Holly Latty-Mann. 1987. "Love styles and relationship quality: A contribution to validation." Journal of Social and Personal Relationships 4: 409–428.

DeMaris, Alfred. 1987. "The efficacy of a spouse abuse model in accounting for courtship violence." Journal of Family Issues 8: 291–305.

DeMaris, Alfred, and Gerald R. Leslie. 1984. "Cohabitation with the future spouse: Its influence upon marital satisfaction and communication." Journal of Marriage and the Family 46: 77–84.

Dizard, Jan E., and Howard Gadlin. 1984. "Family life and the marketplace: Diversity and change in the American family." Pp. 281–302 in Kenneth J. Gergen and Mary M. Gergen (eds.), Historical Social Psychology. Hillsdale, NJ: Erlbaum.

Dressel, Paula L. 1980. "Assortative mating in later life." Journal of Family Issues 1: 379–396.

Driscoll, Richard, Keith E. Davis, and Milton E. Lipetz. 1972. "Parental interference and romantic love: The Romeo and Juliet Effect." Journal of Personality and Social Psychology 24: 1–10.

Eggert, Leona L., and Malcolm R. Parks. 1987. "Communication network involvement in adolescents' friendships and romantic relationships." Pp. 283–322 in M. L. McLaughlin (ed.), Communication Yearbook (Vol. 10). Newbury Park, CA: Sage.

Fehr, Beverly. 1988. "Prototype analysis of the concepts of love and commitment." Journal of Personality and Social Psychology 55: 557–579.

Filsinger, Erik E., and Stephen J. Thoma. 1988. "Behavioral antecedents of relationship stability and adjustment: A five-year longitudinal study." Journal of Marriage and the Family 50: 785–795.

Glenn, Norval D. 1982. "Interreligious marriage in the United States: Patterns and recent trends." Journal of Marriage and the Family 44: 555–566.

Glenn, Norval D. 1984. "A note on estimating the strength of influences for religious endogamy." Journal of Marriage and the Family 46: 725–727.

Glick, Paul C. 1988. "Fifty years of family demography: A record of social change." Journal of Marriage and the Family 50: 861–873.

Goldscheider, Frances Kobrin, and Linda J. Waite. 1986. "Sex differences in the entry into marriage." American Journal of Sociology 92: 91–109.

Guttentag, Marcia, and Paul F. Secord. 1983. Too Many Women? The Sex Ratio Question. Beverly Hills, CA: Sage.

Gwartney-Gibbs, Patricia A. 1986. "The institutionalization of premarital cohabitation: Estimates from marriage license applications, 1970 and 1980." Journal of Marriage and the Family 48: 423–434.

Hatfield, Elaine. 1988. "Passionate and companionate love." Pp. 191–217 in Robert J. Sternberg and Michael L. Barnes (eds.), The Psychology of Love. New Haven: Yale University Press.

Hatfield, Elaine, Jane Traupmann, Susan Sprecher, Mary Utne, and Julia Hay. 1985. "Equity and intimate relations: Recent research." Pp. 91–140 in William Ickes (ed.), Compatible and Incompatible Relationships. New York: Springer-Verlag.

Hatfield, Elaine, Mary K. Utne, and Jane Traupmann. 1979. "Equity theory and intimate relationships." Pp. 99–131 in Robert L. Burgess and Ted L. Huston (eds.), Social Exchange in Developing Relationships. New York: Academic Press.

Hays, Robert B. 1984. "The development and maintenance of friendship." Journal of Social and Personal Relationships 1: 75–97.

Hays, Robert B. 1985. "A longitudinal study of friendship development." Journal of Personality and Social Psychology 48: 909–924.

Heer, D. M., and A. Grossbard-Shechtman. 1981. "The impact of the female marriage squeeze and the contraceptive revolution on sex roles and the women's liberation movement in the United States, 1960 to 1975." Journal of Marriage and the Family 43: 49–65.

Hendrick, Clyde, and Susan Hendrick. 1986. "A theory and method of love." Journal of Personality and Social Psychology 50: 392–402.

Hendrick, Clyde, and Susan S. Hendrick. 1988. "Lovers wear rose colored glasses." Journal of Social and Personal Relationships 5: 161–183.

Hendrick, Clyde, Susan Hendrick, Franklin H. Foote, and Michelle J. Slapion-Foote. 1984. "Do men and women love differently?" Journal of Social and Personal Relationships 1: 177–195.

Hendrick, Susan S., Clyde Hendrick, and Nancy L. Adler. 1988. "Romantic relationships: Love, satisfaction, and staying together." Journal of Personality and Social Psychology 54: 980–988.

Huston, Ted L., Susan M. McHale, and Ann C. Crouter. 1986. "When the honeymoon's over: Changes in the marriage relationship over the first year." Pp. 109–132 in Robin Gilmour and Steve Duck (eds.), The Emerging Field of Personal Relationships. Hillsdale, NJ: Erlbaum.

Huston, Ted L., and Elliot Robins. 1982. "Conceptual and methodological issues in studying close relationships." Journal of Marriage and the Family 44: 901–925.

Huston, Ted L., Catherine A. Surra, Nancy M. Fitzgerald, and Rodney M. Cate. 1981. "From courtship to marriage: Mate selection as an interpersonal process." Pp. 53–88 in Steve Duck and Robin Gilmour (eds.), Personal Relationships 2: Developing Personal Relationships. London: Academic Press.

Johnson, Michael P. 1985. "Commitment, cohesion, investment, barriers, alternatives, constraint: Why do people stay together when they don't really want to?" Paper presented at the Theory Construction and Research Methodology Workshop, National Council on Family Relations, Dallas (November).

Johnson, Michael P., and Leigh Leslie. 1982. "Couple involvement and network structure: A test of the dyadic withdrawal hypothesis." Social Psychology Quarterly 45: 34–43.

Johnson, Michael P., and Robert M. Milardo. 1984. "Network interference in pair relationships: A social psychological recasting of Slater's theory of social regression." Journal of Marriage and the Family 46: 893–899.

Kelley, Harold H. 1979. Personal Relationships: Their Structures and Processes. Hillsdale, NJ: Erlbaum.

Kelley, Harold H. 1983. "Love and commitment." Pp. 265-314 in Harold H. Kelley et al. (eds.), Close Relationships. New York: W. H. Freeman.

Kelley, Harold H., Ellen Berscheid, Andrew Christensen, John H. Harvey, Ted L. Huston, George Levinger, Evie McClintock, Letitia Anne Peplau, and Donald R. Peterson (eds.). 1983. Close Relationships. New York: W. H. Freeman.

Kelley, Harold H., and John W. Thibaut. 1978. Interpersonal Relations: A Theory of Interdependence. New York: Wiley.

Kelly, Carol, Ted L. Huston, and Rodney M. Cate. 1985. "Premarital relationship correlates of the erosion of satisfaction in marriage." Journal of Social and Personal Relationships 2: 167-178.

Labov, Teresa, and Jerry A. Jacobs. 1986. "Intermarriage in Hawaii, 1950-1983." Journal of Marriage and the Family 48: 79-88.

Leigh, Geoffrey K., Thomas B. Holman, and Wesley R. Burr. 1984. "An empirical test of sequence in Murstein's SVR Theory of mate selection." Family Relations 33: 225-231.

Leigh, Geoffrey K., Thomas B. Holman, and Wesley R. Burr. 1987. "Some confusions and exclusions of the SVR theory of dyadic pairing: A response to Murstein." Journal of Marriage and the Family 49: 933-937.

Leslie, Leigh, Ted L. Huston, and Michael P. Johnson. 1986. "Parental reactions to dating relationships: Do they make a difference?" Journal of Marriage and the Family 48: 57-66.

Levy, Marc B., and Davis, Keith E. 1988. "Lovestyles and attachment styles compared: Their relations to each other and to various relationship characteristics." Journal of Social and Personal Relationships 5: 439-471.

Lloyd, Sally A., Rodney M. Cate, and June M. Henton. 1984. "Predicting premarital relationship stability." Journal of Marriage and the Family 46: 65-70.

Lloyd, Sally A., and Rodney M. Cate. 1985. "Attributions associated with significant turning points in premarital relationship development and dissolution." Journal of Social and Personal Relationships 2: 419-436.

Macklin, Eleanor D. 1983. "Nonmarital heterosexual cohabitation: An overview." Pp. 49-74 in Eleanor D. Macklin and Roger H. Rubin (eds.), Contemporary Families and Alternative Lifestyles. Beverly Hills, CA: Sage.

Markman, Howard J. 1979. "Application of a behavioral model of marriage in predicting relationship satisfaction of couples planning marriage." Journal of Consulting and Clinical Psychology 47: 743-749.

Markman, Howard J. 1981. "Prediction of marital distress: A 5-year follow-up." Journal of Consulting and Clinical Psychology 49: 760-762.

Michaels, James W., John N. Edwards, and Alan C. Acock. 1984. "Satisfaction in intimate relationships as a function of inequality, inequity, and outcomes." Social Psychology Quarterly 47: 347-357.

Michaels, James W., John N. Edwards, and Alan C. Acock. 1986. "Social exchange and equity determinants of relationship commitment." Journal of Social and Personal Relationships 3: 161-175.

Milardo, Robert M. 1986. "Personal choice and social constraint in close relationships: Applications of network analysis." Pp. 145-166 in Valerian J. Derlega and Barbara A. Winstead (eds.), Friendship and Social Interaction. New York: Springer-Verlag.

Milardo, Robert M., Michael P. Johnson, and Ted L. Huston. 1983. "Developing close relationships: Changing patterns of interaction between pair members and social networks." Journal of Personality and Social Psychology 44: 964-976.

Murstein, Bernard I. 1976. Who Will Marry Whom: Theories and Research in Marital Choice. New York: Springer.

Murstein, Bernard I. 1980. "Mate selection in the 1970s." Journal of Marriage and the Family 42: 777-792.

Murstein, Bernard I. 1987. "A clarification and extension of the SVR theory of dyadic pairing." Journal of Marriage and the Family 49: 929-933.

Newcomb, Michael D. 1986. "Cohabitation, marriage and divorce among adolescents and young adults." Journal of Social and Personal Relationships 3: 473-494.

O'Flaherty, Kathleen M., and Laura Eells Workman. 1988. "Courtship behavior of the remarried." Journal of Marriage and the Family 50: 499-506.

Parks, Malcolm R., and Mara B. Adelman. 1983. "Communication networks and the development of romantic relationships: An expansion of uncertainty reduction theory." Human Communication Research 10: 55-79.

Parks, Malcolm R., Charlotte M. Stan, and Leona L. Eggert. 1983. "Romantic involvement and social network involvement." Social Psychology Quarterly 46: 116-131.

Rodgers, Roy H., and Linda M. Conrad. 1986. "Courtship for remarriage: Influences on family reorganization after divorce." Journal of Marriage and the Family 48: 767-775.

Rodgers, Willard L., and Arland Thornton. 1985. "Changing patterns of first marriage in the United States." Demography 22: 265-279.

Rusbult, Caryl E. 1980. "Commitment and satisfaction in romantic associations: A test of the investment model." Journal of Experimental Social Psychology 16: 172-186.

Rusbult, Caryl E. 1983. "A longitudinal test of the investment model: The development (and deterioration) of satisfaction and commitment in heterosexual involvements." Journal of Personality and Social Psychology 45: 101-117.

Rusbult, Caryl E., Dennis J. Johnson, and Gregory D. Morrow. 1986. "Predicting satisfaction and commitment in adult romantic involvements: An assessment of the generalizability of the investment model." Social Psychology Quarterly 49: 81-89.

Rusbult, Caryl E., Isabella M. Zembrodt, and Lawanna K. Gunn. 1982. "Exit, voice, loyalty, and neglect: Responses to dissatisfaction in romantic involvements." Journal of Personality and Social Psychology 43: 1230–1242.

Saluter, Arlene F. 1988. Studies in Marriage and the Family: Singleness in America. Current Population Reports, Series P-23, No. 162. Washington, DC: U.S. Government Printing Office.

Schoen, Robert. 1981. "The harmonic mean as the basis of a realistic two-sex marriage model." Demography 18: 201–216.

Schoen, Robert. 1983. "Measuring the tightness of a marriage squeeze." Demography 20: 61–78.

Schoen, Robert. 1986. "A methodological analysis of intergroup marriage." Sociological Methodology 16: 49–78.

Schoen, Robert, and James R. Kluegel. 1988. "The widening gap in black and white marriage rates: The impact of population composition and differential marriage propensities." American Sociological Review 53: 895–907.

Schoen, Robert, and John Wooldredge. 1989. "Marriage choices in North Carolina and Virginia, 1969–71 and 1979–81." Journal of Marriage and the Family 51: 465–481.

Sears, David O. 1986. "College sophomores in the laboratory: Influences of a narrow data base on social psychology's view of human nature." Journal of Personality and Social Psychology 51: 515–530.

Shaver, Phillip, Judith Schwartz, Donald Kirson, and Cary O'Connor. 1987. "Emotion knowledge: Further exploration of a prototype approach." Journal of Personality and Social Psychology 52: 1061–1086.

Spanier, Graham B. 1983. "Married and unmarried cohabitation in the United States: 1980." Journal of Marriage and the Family 45: 277–288.

Spanier, Graham B., and Paul C. Glick. 1980. "Mate selection differentials between whites and blacks in the United States." Social Forces 58: 707–725.

Sprecher, Susan. 1986. "The relation between inequity and emotions in close relationships." Social Psychology Quarterly 49: 309–321.

Sprecher, Susan. 1988. "Investment model, equity, and social support determinants of relationship commitment." Social Psychology Quarterly 51: 318–328.

Stephen, Timothy D. 1984. "A symbolic exchange framework for the development of intimate relationships." Human Relations 37: 393–408.

Stephen, Timothy D. 1985. "Fixed-sequence and circular-causal models of relationship development: Divergent views on the role of communication in intimacy." Journal of Marriage and the Family 47: 955–963.

Stephen, Timothy D. 1986. "Communication and interdependence in geographically separated relationships." Human Communication Research 13: 191–210.

Stephen, Timothy. 1987a. "Attribution and adjustment to relationship termination." Journal of Social and Personal Relationships 4: 47–61.

Stephen, Timothy. 1987b. "Taking communication seriously: A reply to Murstein." Journal of Marriage and the Family 49: 937–938.

Stephen, Timothy D., and Howard H. Markman. 1983. "Assessing the development of relationships: A new measure." Family Process 22: 15–25.

Sternberg, Robert J. 1986. "A triangular theory of love." Psychological Review 93: 119–135.

Stevens, Gillian, and Robert Schoen. 1988. "Linguistic intermarriage in the United States." Journal of Marriage and the Family 50: 267–279.

Surra, Catherine A. 1985. "Courtship types: Variations in interdependence between partners and social networks." Journal of Personality and Social Psychology 49: 357–375.

Surra, Catherine A. 1987. "Reasons for changes in commitment: Variations by courtship type." Journal of Social and Personal Relationships 4: 17–33.

Surra, Catherine A. 1988. "The influence of the interactive network on developing relationships." Pp. 48–81 in Robert M. Milardo (ed.), Families and Social Networks. National Council on Family Relations Monograph Series. Newbury Park, CA: Sage.

Surra, Catherine A., Peggy Arizzi, and Linda L. Asmussen. 1988. "The association between reasons for commitment and the development and outcome of marital relationships." Journal of Social and Personal Relationships 5: 47–63.

Surra, Catherine A., and Ted L. Huston. 1987. "Mate selection as a social transition." Pp. 88–120 in Daniel Perlman and Steve Duck (eds.), Intimate Relationships: Development, Dynamics, and Deterioration. Newbury Park, CA: Sage.

Surra, Catherine A., and Robert M. Milardo. In press. "The social psychological context of developing relationships: Interactive and psychological networks." In Warren H. Jones and Daniel Perlman (eds.), Advances in Personal Relationships (Vol. 3). London: Jessica Kingsley Publishers.

Sweet, James A., Larry L. Bumpass, and Vaughn R. A. Call. 1988. The Design and Content of the National Survey of Families and Households. NSFH Working Paper No. 1. Madison: University of Wisconsin, Center for Demography and Ecology.

Tanfer, Koray. 1987. "Patterns of premarital cohabitation among never-married women in the United States." Journal of Marriage and the Family 49: 483–495.

Thibaut, John W., and Harold H. Kelley. 1959. The Social Psychology of Groups. New York: Wiley.

Thornton, Arland. 1988. "Cohabitation and marriage in the 1980s." Demography 25: 497–508.

Trovato, Frank. 1988. "A macrosociological analysis of change in the marriage rate: Canadian women, 1921–25 to 1981–85." Journal of Marriage and the Family 50: 507–521.

Tucker, Belinda M., and Robert Joseph Taylor. 1989. "Demographic correlates of relationship status among black Americans." Journal of Marriage and the Family 51: 655–665.

U.S. Bureau of the Census. 1986. Households, Families, Marital Status, and Living Arrangements: March 1986 (Advance Report). Current Population Reports, Series P-20, No. 412. Washington, DC: Government Printing Office.

U.S. Bureau of the Census. 1988a. Households, Families, Marital Status, and Living Arrangements: March 1988 (Advance Report). Current Population Reports, Series P-20, No. 432. Washington, DC: Government Printing Office.

U.S. Bureau of the Census. 1988b. Marital Status and Living Arrangements: March 1986. Current Population Reports, Series P-20, No. 418. Washington, DC: Government Printing Office.

U.S. Bureau of the Census. 1989. Marital Status and Living Arrangements: March 1988. Current Population Reports, Series P-20, No. 433. Washington,

DC: Government Printing Office.

Veevers, Jean E. 1988. ''The 'real' marriage squeeze: Mate selection, mortality, and the marriage gradient.'' Sociological Perspectives 31: 169–189.

Vera, Herman, Donna H. Berado, and Felix M. Berado. 1985. ''Age heterogamy in marriage.'' Journal of Marriage and the Family 47: 553–566.

LINDA THOMPSON   *University of Wisconsin–Madison*

ALEXIS J. WALKER   *Oregon State University**

Gender in Families:

Women and Men in Marriage,

Work, and Parenthood

We review the research on gender by focusing on three domains of family life—marriage, work (both wage and family work), and parenthood. Regarding marriage, we consider intimacy, communication and conflict, and wife-battering. Regarding wage work, we consider women and men as providers and resistance to wives as coproviders. Regarding family work, we consider the nature of family work and resistance to sharing housework and child care. Regarding parenthood, we consider the images of motherhood and fatherhood, activities and experiences of mothering and fathering, and the gender differentiation that accompanies parenting. We offer recommendations for further research and encourage family scholars to conceptualize gender as relational or interactional rather than as an individual property or role.

In this article, we examine the way women and men organize their gender relations in families (Glenn, 1987; Thorne, 1982). Gender has no specific site or context; it infuses all of life (West and Zimmerman, 1987). We focus on three domains of family life—marriage, work (both paid

Child and Family Studies, University of Wisconsin–Madison, Madison, WI 53706.

*Human Development and Family Studies, Oregon State University, Corvallis, OR 97331.

and family work), and parenthood. We try to represent the diversity of gendered family experience by race, ethnicity, class, and age, but space and available literature prevent us from doing so as often as we would like. To narrow the scope of our review, we focus on heterosexual, married couples. What follows cannot be generalized to all women, all men, or women and men in nonmarital or same-sex unions. Although the study of gay and lesbian couples would greatly inform our understanding of gender, research on same-sex couples is spare (Blumstein and Schwartz, 1983). We are also not considering dating relationships, cohabitation, separation and divorce, or single-parent and blended families. Most painful for us is omitting kinship as a fourth domain of family life. There is simply not enough space, although we recognize that this omission is especially unfair to women and black families (Rosenthal, 1985; Wilson, 1986).

Our review is not exhaustive even within the domains of marriage, work, and parenthood. Our choices reflect our own interests and ideas about what is central to the study of gender in families. The snag in gender research is more conceptual and substantive than methodological. We chose studies, therefore, that were conceptually or substantially innovative, even provocative. We gathered research from several disciplines. Diverse methodologies are represented. Gender is more than an individual characteristic of females and males, and more than a role assumed by or assigned to women and men. Gender in families includes structural constraints and opportunities, beliefs and ideology, actual arrangements and activities, meanings and experiences, diversity and change, and interaction and relation. We wanted to convey this richness and complexity as well as to review existing work. We assume readers will not take what we say as the final word about gender in families, but will grapple with and test it.

MARRIAGE

According to Bernard (1972), there are two marriages in every marriage, and the experiences and implications of marriage differ for wife and husband. In this section, we consider the variant experiences of women and men across several domains of marriage—emotional and sexual intimacy, communication and conflict, and wife-battering.

Intimacy

Emotional intimacy. Emotional intimacy is sharing one another's innermost life; expressing and listening to each other's feelings, thoughts, desires, doubts, joys, and fears; attending to, understanding, and accepting one another's "true" self. Brown and Gary (1985: 236) reported that only about one-third of married, black women would go to their husbands first for support if they had "a serious problem, such as being depressed, nervous or anxious." Only a third of these women named their husbands as one of the three people closest to them. More men than women consider their spouses as best friends (Rubin, 1984). Among older married persons, men are more likely than women to name their spouses as confidant, and women perceive less emotional support in marriage than men (Depner and Ingersoll-Dayton, 1985; Lee, 1988). Although Lee (1988) found that personal and marital well-being among older persons is connected to confiding in one's spouse, only 39% of men and 28% of women confide in their partners. Williams (1988) found that emotional sustenance in marriage is related to enhanced well-being for both women and men but is especially important for women. Although they tend to receive less emotional sustenance from marriage than men, women's well-being seems to be tied more closely to the emotional makeup of marriage.

Research consistently has shown that wives disclose more to their partners than husbands do (Peplau and Gordon, 1985). Wives usually disclose more personal feelings and opinions, and husbands tend to give more public facts (Morton, 1978). Women usually experience and express a broader range of emotion in marriage. Women tend to express more tenderness, fear, and sadness than their partners; for many men, controlled anger is the only emotion they express (Cancian and Gordon, 1988; Peplau and Gordon, 1985; Rubin, 1984; Weiss, 1985). Rubin (1984) offered a scenario that resonated with many readers: Women tend to complain that their husbands do not care about their emotional lives and do not express their own feelings and thoughts. Women often say that they have to pull things out of their husbands and push them to open up. Men tend to respond either that they are open or that they do not understand what it is their wives want from them. Men often protest that no matter how much they talk it is never enough for their wives. The women in Rubin's study want warmth as well as openness. For instance, women are more likely than men to give their partners a spontaneous hug or kiss when something good happens (Blumstein and Schwartz, 1983). Overall, women tend to be more expressive and affectionate than men in marriage, and this difference bothers many wives.

Analyzing women's magazines from 1900 to 1979, Cancian and Gordon (1988) reported change in the emotional culture of middle-class marriage. Although love and marriage as self-sacrifice is still the main message sent to women (and only women), there is a trend toward "love as an open expression of feelings and marriage as a partnership in self-development" (Cancian and Gordon, 1988: 321). This new conception of marriage allows men to express their needs and feelings and women to express controlled anger. Cancian and Gordon concluded that, even though marriage is now a matter of emotional intimacy, women are still responsible for seeing that this ideal of a loving marriage is realized. Wives, therefore, are more likely than husbands to monitor and orchestrate intimacy (Markman, 1984), which is not an easy task if husbands are not forthcoming with feelings and thoughts (Weiss, 1985).

Cancian (1986) suggested that researchers have found women better at intimacy and love because they have used a feminized definition. Scholars and public opinion have defined intimacy as emotional warmth, expressiveness, vulnerability, and sensitivity—all ideal qualities of women, not men. The qualities of intimacy that accompany our notions about men—sex and providing practical help—are ignored. Men, more than women, base their feelings of closeness on and express their love through sex, shared activities, practical help, economic support, or just being in the other's presence (Cancian, 1986; Rubin, 1976; Rubin, 1984). Wills, Weiss, and Patterson (1974) found that husbands tend to be pleased by wives' instrumental care and help (e.g., meal preparation), and wives tend to be pleased by affectionate acts (e.g., saying, "I love you"). One husband demonstrated his affection for his wife by washing her car and was bewildered when she did not get his intended message. The authors suggested that, in marriage, partners must please each other by behaving in ways that are at odds with their gender socialization and which they would not find pleasing themselves. To understand gender and intimacy, then, we need to broaden our definition of intimacy and consider all areas of sustenance and sharing. Cancian (1986) argued that this would be fair for women as well as men, because the love expressed by women's practical family work is often ignored.

Sexual intimacy. Unfortunately, few studies focus on commonplace, marital sex, although there are notable exceptions (Greenblat, 1983; Huston, 1982). Studies of sex in marriage tend to focus on sex as dispassionate and solely genital rather than as part of intimacy (Schneider and Gould, 1987). Sensuality and emotional sexuality in marriage are uncharted territory. Since sexual intimacy may be the only recognized masculine way of expressing and eliciting love (Rubin, 1976) and we know so little about sexual intimacy, it is no wonder many conclude that men cannot love (Cancian, 1986).

Women and men tend to find sexual pleasure in different ways. In their review of the literature, Schneider and Gould (1987) reported that women often get more pleasure from kissing, holding, and touching than from intercourse. Rubin (1976) found that working-class wives typically have more trouble than their husbands engaging in alternate forms of sexual interaction, and middle-

class wives are often distressed when they do not enjoy these other forms of sex. Giving and receiving oral sex tends to be connected with husbands' sexual happiness but not with wives'; wives often are more embarrassed and inhibited about oral sex than husbands (Blumstein and Schwartz, 1983). On the basis of a review of the research, Szinovacz (1984) concluded that, when married couples disagree on sex, men's wishes and desires are more likely to prevail.

Midlife women in Rubin's (1979) study tended to describe sex as getting better with age, especially after the fear of pregnancy passes and there are no small children around. Margolin and White (1987) found, however, that changes in wives' physical attractiveness with age are associated with husbands' lessened sexual interest, happiness, and faithfulness. Changes in husbands' physical attractiveness with age do not seem to matter to their wives.

Most of the women in Rubin's (1979) study said they had faked orgasms at some time in their marriage; about half still do. Rubin suggested they do so to please their partners and because it is not important to them that orgasm occur with every sexual encounter. Most of the women also indicated that they sometimes repress their own sexual desire so as not to pressure their husbands. Blumstein and Schwartz (1983) found that initiation is still the prerogative of men. Most married women are reluctant to make sexual advances, especially if their husbands are feeling troubled, vulnerable, and insecure. Although taking the sexual lead means that men's desire is satisfied more directly than women's, they also must bear the burden of rejection, since refusal is the prerogative of women (Blumstein and Schwartz, 1983). Kaufman (1985) found that Orthodox Jewish women view *niddah* (the two-week sexual separation between wife and husband during her menstrual cycle) as good because it enhances desire, gives them time to themselves, provides them control over their sexuality, and forces husbands to talk about things and show their love in nonsexual ways. Seemingly restrictive religious law allows these women to shape sexual intimacy to be more to their liking. In general, then, men are more likely than women to orchestrate sexual intimacy in marriage, and wives often alter their own sexual desires and actions to please and protect their husbands.

Communication and Conflict

Typically, there are differences between married women and men in their expression of positive and negative messages during conversation and conflict, in their ability to send and receive messages, and in their sensitivity and responsiveness to each other's messages. Husbands tend to use more neutral messages, and wives tend to use more negative and positive messages (Noller, 1982; Notarius and Johnson, 1982). One reason so many of women's messages are positive is because they smile or laugh so often (Margolin and Wampold, 1981). The enduring smile makes it difficult for wives to express clearly neutral messages, although wives are better able to send (encode) positive and negative messages than are husbands (Noller, 1981). Noller concluded that men have an advantage in decoding their partners' messages in marriage because they are receiving more clearly sent messages. Wives often have a difficult time accurately receiving their husbands' neutral messages, but this may be because neutral messages are more difficult to decode (Noller, 1981). Husbands' capacity for sending and receiving messages is more strongly connected to marital satisfaction than is that of wives (Gottman and Porterfield, 1981; Noller, 1981). That is, husbands who are more dissatisfied with their marriage make more mistakes in both sending and receiving messages than satisfied husbands (Noller, 1981). These dissatisfied husbands do not have difficulty interpreting the messages of strangers; the dampened capacity to read cues is confined to messages from their wives (Gottman and Porterfield, 1981). In general, then, wives usually are more expressive and send clearer messages than husbands in marital communication. Since most wives are better senders, most husbands, especially the happily married, have an advantage over wives in receiving messages.

Wives typically are more sensitive and responsive to their husbands' messages during conversation and conflict than the other way around. Wives are better than husbands at predicting what their partners will say next (White, 1985). Wives tend to reciprocate their partners' positive and negative speech more than husbands do (Notarius and Johnson, 1982). Women also are much more likely than their partners to work to develop the topics raised by the other in conversation (Fishman, 1978).

Women tend to be more sensitive and responsive to what is going on in their marriages. Holtzworth-Munroe and Jacobsen (1985) suggested that wives always monitor the relationship, whereas husbands only do so when things are not proceeding smoothly. In marriages that eventually ended in separation or divorce, women usually knew the relationship was in trouble long before their partners did (Hagestad and Smyer, 1982; Rands, 1983). Pearlin and Schooler (1978) reported that ignoring the unpleasant aspects of marriage is related to reduced psychological health for wives but not for husbands. Wives tend to be more sensitive and responsive to the distressing aspects of marriage and, therefore, are more likely than their husbands to bring up and confront an issue (Blumstein and Schwartz, 1983; Huston and Ashmore, 1986; Krokoff, 1987). In most conflict, either the wife begins the conversation by stating the issues or the husband begins but leaves elaborating and guiding the disagreement to his wife (Gottman and Krokoff, 1989). Women tend to see their husbands as deciding how serious certain marital problems are but see themselves as responsible for managing conflict (Madden and Janoff-Bulman, 1981).

Lavin (1987) found that husbands tend to attribute their own positive and negative behaviors during conflict to stable, internal causes. This attribution enables them to take credit for positive behaviors and resist requests that they change negative behaviors because "it's just the way I am." Husbands typically see their wives' behavior as due to unstable, internal causes. Husbands usually give their wives little credit for positive behaviors, therefore, and push their wives to change what they see as malleable negative behaviors. Lavin suggested that this attribution pattern affords husbands the greatest sense of control over interpersonal events. On the other hand, wives tend to make the same attributions about their husbands that they make about themselves.

Although differences in how wives and husbands handle conflict are small, they have a characteristic pattern (Gottman, 1979; Kelley, 1979; Krokoff, 1987; Raush, Barry, Hertel, and Swain, 1974; Rubin, 1984): Wives often use more emotional appeals and coercion, and husbands tend to remain reasonable and calm, problem-oriented and conciliatory, and try to postpone or end the dispute. Wives, more than husbands, determine the affective atmosphere of an argument. Wives usually build a climate of agreement, or more important, escalate or deescalate the conflict with their verbal and nonverbal negativity. Husbands' messages and emotions often do not make the same critical contribution to the course of the argument as wives' messages and emotions. A rare exception is among nondistressed couples in low-conflict discussions, where husbands are more likely to be the ones who dampen negativity, but in high-conflict disputes, this again is often the responsibility of wives. In distressed couples, no one tempers negativity. Similarly, in a study of conflicts during family dinners at home, Vuchinich (1987) found that daughters and especially mothers were the most active family members in closing off conflicts. Mothers made two-thirds of the compromises while daughters made about half of the submissions.

Many of the qualities that women display in marital conversation and conflict are traceable to their subordinate position. Subordinates must be more sensitive and responsive to those in power than the reverse (Glenn, 1987). Fishman (1978) reported that the speech patterns of women in everyday conversation are more tentative than those of their partners. Raush and his colleagues (1974) suggested that women expect noncompliance during conflict and, similar to other subordinates, resort to moral persuasion, emotional appeals, and harrassment through coercion. The authors suggested that husbands can afford to be more calm, conciliatory, and chivalrous because of their greater power in marriage. Other research on marital couples demonstrated that partners in the weaker position (more typical of wives) tend to use more supplication, manipulation, and back-channel methods; and partners in the stronger position (more typical of husbands) tend to interrupt more successfully and use more bullying and autocracy (Howard, Blumstein, and Schwartz, 1986; Kollock, Blumstein, and Schwartz, 1985). Wives, then, usually have more responsibility than their husbands for monitoring the relationship, confronting disagreeable issues, setting the tone of the conversation, and moving toward resolution when conflict is high. Wives often have to fulfill that responsibility, however, from a subordinate position, which makes them appear tentative during conversation and nagging and hysterical during conflict.

Wife-battering

Women's subordination is nowhere more evident than in marital violence. The more lopsided the dependence between partners, the more the "weaker" partner must rely on the morality and sentiment of the "stronger" partner to avoid the abuse of power (Eichler, 1981). Morality and sentiment are insufficient to deter wife-battering. The most promising research regarding wife-battering considers how the broader social context of inequality is connected to the private subordination and abuse of women in marriage. Although rarely done, research on wife-battering should include race, class, and gender as part of the social context of inequality (Lockhart, 1987).

Yllo (1984) considered the status of women in various American states as the structural context for marital power and violence. She found that egalitarian marriages have the lowest rates of marital violence. The incidence of violence is high in couples when wives are dominant and even higher when husbands are dominant. A high rate of wife-battering occurs in wife-dominant marriages when such couples live in states in which the status of women is low. Yllo suggested that the exercise of power by women in such states is threatening to men. Husband assaults against wives are highest, however, in husband-dominant marriages when such couples live in states in which the status of women is high. Yllo suggested that husbands need to use more force to maintain their dominance in such states.

Researchers who have interviewed battered women (Dobash and Dobash, 1979) and men who batter (Ptacek, 1988) have reported the dynamics of male dominance through violence: husbands' violence is a deliberate attempt to control their wives. Most men who beat their wives use violence to frighten or hurt their wives, silence their wives' defiance, punish their partners for not being "good wives," or simply show their wives who is in charge (Dobash and Dobash, 1979; Ptacek, 1988). Studies of marital pairs in which wives have been battered have shown that husbands tend to view their marriages as mutually violent, whereas wives tend to view them as more husband-violent (Browning and Dutton, 1986; Edleson and Brygger, 1986). Men who batter their wives tend to treat verbal and physical combativeness as the same, discount the difference in the amount of harm that men and women can inflict, and trivialize their wives' injuries (Browning and Dutton, 1986; Ptacek, 1988). Using police and court records, historical documents, coverage in popular and clinical writings, and interviews with social service providers, Dobash and Dobash (1979) and Ptacek (1988) demonstrated that the broader culture offers husbands excuses and justifications for their violence and condones wife-battering.

Women often are in a precarious position in marriage. Many wives must bolster their marital power so as not to be easily victimized, but they must contain their power so as not to threaten and incite their husbands. Wives who are economically dependent are more vulnerable to wife-battering (Kalmuss and Straus, 1982), but employed women who are economically independent are more likely to be battered than women who are full-time homemakers (Hornung, McCullough, and Sugimoto, 1981). Hornung and colleagues found that life-threatening violence is particularly high in marriages that combine an underachieving husband with a high-achieving wife. Abused women who return to their husbands are usually unemployed and have nowhere else to go (Strube and Barbour, 1984). The precarious task for many married women in abusive relationships is to be as independent as they can without threatening the status of their husbands. Because of limited opportunities for wage work, however, many battered wives are trapped in bad marriages (Dobash and Dobash, 1979).

WORK

Work, paid and unpaid, is central to family life. Recent time studies have shown that the total number of hours women and men spend as workers (combined paid and family work) is about the same (Berk, 1985; Pleck, 1985). More than men, however, women shift their time and investment back and forth between paid and family work so that family life is sustained. Since industrialization, "work" has meant men's marketplace work. Prior to the 1940s, wage work for women was invisible: the labor force participation of working-class and minority women was ignored, while middle-class women earned money in ways that were concealed from the economy, such as taking in boarders (Bose, 1987). Currently, women are highly visible in the paid labor force: families need two incomes; the service sector pro-

vides work opportunities for women; birth rates are down; and expectations have changed (Moen, 1982). Unpaid family work remains invisible, often even to the women who do most of it (DeVault, 1987). Family work is unseen and unacknowledged because it is private, unpaid, commonplace, done by women, and mingled with love and leisure (Daniels, 1987). Here, we consider women and men as providers and family workers.

Women and Men as Providers

Below, we examine how women and men provide for their families and how they define themselves and each other as providers. Even though most women do paid work and contribute 30% of family income, the responsibility and recognition for family provision falls to men (Szinovacz, 1984), and both women and men are ambivalent about women as providers. Satisfying, well-paid marketwork is related to enhanced well-being for both women and men (Baruch and Barnett, 1986b; Coleman, Antonucci, Adelmann, and Crohan, 1987; Staines and Libby, 1986), but the meaning of paid work is often different for them. Women typically say, "Work is what I do, not what I am," while men typically offer their occupation first when asked, "Who are you?" (Rubin, 1979: 56; but see Cohen, 1987). The meaning of paid work differs for women and men because the connection between paid work and family differs by gender. Men are better able than women to keep paid work and family as separate spheres of life (Gerson, 1985; Zussman, 1987). Women, in part, shape their paid work participation in response to family needs. This is sensible, given women's family obligations and limited occupational opportunities (Gerson, 1985; Rosen, 1987; Zavella, 1987). Also, because men retain responsibility and recognition for family provision, families often give special consideration and support to men, but not to women, wage earners (Ferree, 1984). All of this results in personal, as well as structural, resistance to change in the division of paid labor by gender.

Participation in Paid Work and Its Timing

More than men, women consider family needs when they go in and out of the labor force, gauge the number of hours they work, and choose what time of day they will work. The presence of small children is closely connected with women's reduced participation in paid work (Moen, 1985). Wives who are in nonday and shift work are, in part, responding to child-care needs; husbands are more likely to be in nonday and shift work because of the nature of their jobs (Presser, 1987). In dual-earner couples, wives average 6½ hours per day in paid work, while husbands average 10½ hours per day (Berk, 1985). When there is an increase in time demands for family work, wives, but not husbands, typically respond by cutting back on time spent in paid work (Berk, 1985; Pleck, 1985). Some women find it easier to temper their husbands' opposition to their employment or to integrate paid work with family responsibilities when work is part-time; but part-time work is often exploitive, fosters women's economic dependence on husbands, and undermines personal achievement and advancement (Ferree, 1976; Giele, 1982; Pleck, 1985; Ulbrich, 1988; Zavella, 1987). Women's paid work also is connected with their husbands' ability to generate family income. Wives of professional husbands are more likely to be in intermittent part-time employment, whereas wives of nonprofessional husbands tend to have intermittent full-time employment (Moen, 1985). Moen (1985) concluded that discontinuities in employment are the rule for women.

Married women's participation in wage work is not shaped solely by family concerns, husbands' earning ability, and children's needs (Rosen, 1987). Women's participation in wage work, like men's, is shaped by the opportunities provided in the market economy. Rosen (1987) found that blue-collar women who had union, factory jobs that paid well were committed to continuous wage work regardless of their circumstances at home. Women have fewer paid work opportunities than men (Haggstrom, Kanouse, and Morrison, 1986). Job opportunities continue to be segregated by sex, and most women have access only to low-paying, no-advancement, often temporary service jobs. In Kessler-Harris's (1987) view, women are stuck: employers justify offering women bad jobs because they see women as unreliable workers who are committed first to their families and only secondarily to their jobs. Because of the scarcity of good jobs for women, however, women may as well stay secondary providers and be responsive to their families. The smaller earnings of women

compared with men are a cause, as well as a result, of women's lower participation in paid work (Ferber, 1982). In addition to sex segregation in market labor, the wage workplace is often uncongenial to the needs and nature of family life (Kessler-Harris, 1987; LaRossa, 1988; Moen, 1985; Wiess, 1985). Although this affects both women and men, it is a greater problem for women, who are more accountable than men to both market and family.

Providing for Families: Earnings and Enactment, Responsibility and Recognition

Bernard (1981) argued that male authority and masculinity are identified with success in paid work for men. As single incomes have become inadequate for most families, though, the provider role has been modified slightly to allow some provision by wives. In most families, both women and men are enacting the provider role and contributing earnings to their families, but men retain responsibility and recognition for provision (Bernard, 1981; Cazenave, 1979; Haas, 1986; Hood, 1986; Szinovacz, 1984).

Thoits (1987: 21) contended that middle- and upper-class wives and husbands will be first to change their division of labor by gender, and this change "will filter down the social ladder." This assumption has justified researchers' considerable attention to dual-career couples who represent such a small group of families. Ferree (1984; 1987) found the following flaws in the dual-career model: the model contrasts financial necessity with personal reasons for women's wage work, ignores earnings and emphasizes egalitarian attitudes, neglects family interdependence in favor of individual opportunity and achievement, and characterizes housework as onerous and wage work as fulfilling. In each case, the dual-career model either ignores or distorts working-class family life. In the next few paragraphs, we examine separately the division of paid labor by gender in working-class and middle-class families.

Working-class families. Most working-class wives do wage work for both economic and personal reasons (Ferree, 1987; Rosen, 1987). Rosen interviewed married women who have jobs in mills and factories: mostly they work for their families because they must; their families need the money.

With full-time, unionized jobs, these women contribute almost half (45%) of the family income. Their income helps their families escape poverty and get ahead. Given the scarcity of good jobs for women, however, they know they could not support themselves and their children alone, and many voice the belief that they are only a husband away from welfare. Zavella (1987) reported similar findings based on her ethnography of married Chicano women who are cannery workers.

"Having" to work does not preclude "wanting" to work (Ferree, 1984). Although their jobs are often worrisome and wearisome, most working-class women take pride in their trade, welcome contact with other people, and enjoy the recognition and respect that accompanies a paycheck (Ferree, 1984; 1987; Rosen, 1987). When they want to quit work, it is typically because their jobs are not good, not because they want to be full-time homemakers (Ferree, 1987; Rosen, 1987). When they lose their jobs, most suffer emotional and economic distress just as unemployed men do (Rosen, 1987). Most of the women still have contradictory feelings, however, about combining paid work and family: they think their jobs are good for their families but, at the same time, feel guilty about their homes and children (Ferree, 1987; Zavella, 1987). Perhaps, because of their family obligations, blue-collar women are more ambivalent than men about work layoffs (Rosen, 1987; Zavella, 1987). They worry about money, but they can accept their husbands' supporting them for awhile; men are not usually as accepting of such support. Although worried that it will last too long, most women enjoy the relief that unemployment brings from the double day of wage and family work. They like the time for themselves, their families, and their homes. Rosen's is a rare study of women's unemployment and family life. Social scientists have pursued the study of unemployment as if it were only a problem for men, although 35% of displaced workers are women (Chow and Berheide, 1988; Rosen, 1987).

Like women, most working-class men work for the sake of their families in jobs where personal and economic accomplishment are structurally limited (Ferree, 1987). Unlike women, however, they see their identity on the line with every paycheck (Rubin, 1976). Factory workers are more likely than professionals to recognize their employed wives as coproviders (Hood, 1983).

Many recognize that their wives' earnings are *essential* to their families and take some of the burden of provision off them; they feel sorry for men whose wives nag them for never making enough money (Hood, 1983). Still other blue-collar husbands like the extra money but are unhappy that their wives go out to work (Hood, 1983; Rosen, 1987; Zavella, 1987). Ferree (1984) contended that, because working-class women work out of financial necessity, their husbands see them as coproviders and see their work as an essential contribution to the whole family. In her small sample of dual-earner couples, Hood (1983) found that definition of the provider role depends on how wives' earnings are viewed. Wives' responsibility and recognition as providers only occurs when both partners admit that their family is dependent on the wife's income and the husband cannot say, "Quit if you want." Blue-collar husbands who are better earners are less accepting than poor earners of their wives' work (Rosen, 1987).

The realities of class mean that working-class families often find themselves dividing paid work by gender more equitably than middle-class families, not only in terms of earnings and enactment, but also in responsibility and recognition for family provision. Similarly, racial discrimination and oppression make coprovision essential among most black couples; depending completely on husbands for economic support often has not been an option for minority wives (Higginbotham, 1983; J. Jones, 1985). Unlike white couples who were able to push themselves into the middle class with only husbands' earnings, middle-class black couples, even in the best of economic times, have had to share family provision (Willie, 1988). Many black men believe that black women have more opportunity than they do (Cazenave, 1983), even though black women's earnings are lower than black men's and it is unclear whether black women are advantaged by education and occupational status (Collier and Williams, 1982; Secord and Ghee, 1986).

Both women and men resist seeing wives as coproviders. Most working-class wives and husbands agree that husbands are the primary providers for their families and the ones whose earnings "really support the family" (Rosen, 1987: 103). Working-class women tend to see themselves as secondary providers helping their husbands fulfill their responsibilities (Rubin,

1976; Zavella, 1987). One way couples try to maintain the image of wives as secondary providers is to use husbands' salary for essentials and wives' salary for "extras" (Hood, 1983; Rosen, 1987; Zavella, 1987). Although this is harder to do in working-class families than in middle-class families, many couples manage it. Many working-class wives realize that their husbands' pride, authority, and manhood are founded on breadwinning and willingly do whatever they can to preserve the image of their husbands as primary providers (Rosen, 1987; Rubin, 1976). Blue-collar women often see that, by placing ultimate responsibility and recognition for provision on their husbands, they bolster their husbands' willingness to perform that obligation (Rosen, 1987). In turn, many blue-collar men believe that their wives and families keep them committed to their jobs (Halle, 1987).

Middle-class families. The dual-career model would have us believe that upper-middle-class men are egalitarian. But evidence mounts that these men have the most trouble sharing family provision with their wives. Fendrich (1984) found that only for upper-middle-class husbands is wives' employment related to lower self-esteem. The more money husbands make compared with their wives, however, the better these husbands feel about themselves. The author suggested income and status competition as underlying processes. Stanley, Hunt, and Hunt (1986) found that young, highly educated, and occupationally successful fathers in dual-earner marriages are less satisfied with their work, marriages, and personal lives than similar men who are sole providers for their families. The authors suggested that these successful men feel cheated because, unlike conventional breadwinners, they have no wife at home to provide full-time service. Haas (1986) reported that employed wives whose husbands have the highest earnings are most likely to combine a belief that family provision should be a shared responsibility with a recognition that, in practice, their husbands are the primary providers. Ferree (1984) argued that, in middle-class families, the size of husbands' earnings makes wives' earnings, at best, supplemental and, at worst, unnecessary. It is easy in such families for husbands to view wives as secondary providers and to view wives' wage work as a privilege for wives rather than a contribution to the whole

family (Ferree, 1984; Hood, 1983).

Weiss's (1985, 1987) interviews with middle-aged, occupationally successful men are telling: most husbands believe that their wives work for their own benefit, not as a contribution to the family. Earnings are usually seen as a less important benefit of wives' jobs than getting them out of the house and giving them an opportunity to realize and express themselves. Husbands tend to think of themselves as unselfish for supporting their wives' need to work outside of the family. Most are proud of their wives' accomplishments but feel that wives' time on the job means that, as husbands, they have to make do with wives' diminished attention to child care and home management. Wives' paid work is typically viewed as something husbands do for their wives, not something wives do for their families. On the other hand, most husbands view their own jobs as a family responsibility. Although paid work is a source of personal challenge and achievement for these husbands, family is what makes paid work meaningful.

In many upper-middle-class marriages, wives' efforts help husbands to succeed. Wives' efforts, though, are less visible and less concretely rewarded than paid work (Mortimer, 1980). Papanek (1979) described how women support their husbands' occupational advancement through family status production—maintaining clothing, entertaining colleagues, appropriately training children, and engaging in the politics of status maintenance. As Fowlkes (1987) reported, many wives of professors and physicians keep the home quiet and running smoothly, soothe and encourage their husbands, accommodate their own careers, and move when husbands have to move. Although husbands are enthusiastic, such moves often undermine wives' participation in paid work and leave them bored, lonely, depressed, and with feelings of loss (Ammons, Nelson, and Wodarski, 1982; Morrison and Lichter, 1988). Professional husbands are more likely to see their wives' career needs, rather than their own, as a source of stress (Baruch and Barnett, 1986a).

There are husbands, of course, who make professional life possible for women. Epstein's (1987) research on lawyers revealed that many husbands of high-achieving women support their wives by taking pride in their accomplishments and not being competitive with them. When both partners are lawyers, husbands can help their wives by providing contacts, drawing their wives into male net-works, and protecting them from sexual harrass-ment at the office. The nature of support for one another's work tends to differ by gender: husbands protect and mentor their wives, while wives listen, reassure, and cater to their husbands (Epstein, 1987; Weiss, 1985, 1987).

Resistance to wives as coproviders. Regardless of class and race, many men oppose their wives' employment (Blumstein and Schwartz, 1983; Ulbrich, 1988; Ybarra, 1982; Zavella, 1987). Men who have low earnings *and* oppose their wives' employment tend to be depressed (Ulbrich, 1988). Ulbrich suggested that these men suffer a double insult to their ideal of themselves as providers. There is something about the "symbolic meaning" of wives as coproviders that is dis-tressing for many men (Kessler and McCrae, 1982; Ross, Mirowsky, and Huber, 1983; Ulbrich, 1988).

Hood (1983) argued that husbands do not want to admit dependence on their wives' earn-ings and see their wives as coproviders because they would have to do more domestic work. But research shows that domestic work does not distress husbands, and child care may actually enhance well-being for husbands in dual-earner families (Kessler and McCrae, 1982; Pleck, 1985; Ross et al., 1983). Perhaps it is not that men will have to do more family work if their wives are coproviders, but that their wives do less. Many husbands feel they have lost the services of a full-time homemaker (Weiss, 1987; Zavella, 1987). Studying unemployed wives, Ratcliff and Bogdan (1988) found that, although husbands appreciate their wives' earnings, many husbands believe that their wives' place is in the home and unemploy-ment makes their wives better homemakers: wives are there when husbands get home, meals are bet-ter, and clothes are ironed. Many out-of-work wives sense that their husbands are pleased to be the sole provider again. Two-thirds of these unemployed wives have husbands who disapprove of or are hostile toward their wage work. The struggle about whether or not wives should work outside the home is not over.

Family Work: Household Work and Child Care

No matter what technique is used to measure household division of labor, wives typically do much more than husbands (Warner, 1986). Most women and men agree that women should be responsible for family work and men should "help out" (Szinovacz, 1984). Study after study has shown that attitudes and shared norms con-tinue to define household work as "women's work," and most wives seem satisfied with the small amount of housework their husbands do (Peplau and Gordon, 1985). Most men do so little in the way of housework that Miller and Garrison (1984: 328) have called research in this area "much ado about nothing." Hartmann (1981) contended that men actually contribute more to the need for household work than they contribute to its completion.

Some scholars conclude that men are doing more housework than ever before, while others conclude that not much has changed. Pleck (1985) reported that, relative to their wives, husbands do about 30% of family work, whereas they used to do about 20%. He argued that this is a mean-ingful change because men are bucking a histori-cal trend of less household work for all family members. Coverman and Sheley (1986), on the other hand, reported that husbands' time in household work and child care did not change be-tween 1965 and 1975, even though their time in paid work declined; husbands spent their extra time in leisure. Cowan (1987) concluded that the division of household work is about the same now as it was in the nineteenth century.

Most wives do two to three times more family work than their husbands (Berk, 1985; Kamo, 1988; Warner, 1986). Berk (1985) discovered 10% of husbands who did as much family work as their wives. She characterized the circumstances of these "exceptional" men: they have many, usual-ly small, children, and their wives are employed full-time. Men in these circumstances may have little choice but to do their share (Berk, 1985; Crouter, Perry-Jenkins, Huston, and McHale, 1987; Rosen, 1987). Special structural conditions foster men's family work, while family work is a structural imperative for women (Schooler, Miller, Miller, and Richtand, 1984).

Nature of Family Work for Women and Men

For most part, the nature of women's involve-ment in family work is different from men's. Besides doing more, what women do, when they do it, the circumstances in which they do it, and how they experience family work is different from men's experience. The family work most women do is unrelenting, repetitive, and routine—cleaning, cooking, shopping, child care, laundry, and straightening up (Berk, 1985). These household tasks generally must be repeated the next day or sooner (Berheide, 1984). The family work most men do is infrequent, irregular, and non-routine—household repairs, taking out the trash, mowing the lawn, yard work, and gardening (Berk, 1985; Pleck, 1983). These tasks must be accomplished only rarely (Berk, 1985). Women do three times as many domestic tasks as men (Berk, 1985). On average, women report doing three tasks at one time (Berheide, 1984). That women do several tasks at once may explain why they find domestic work less relaxing and more stressful than men do (Shaw, 1988).

Berk and Berk (1979) contended that *when* women and men do family work is as revealing as what tasks they do. Timing is especially revealing in families with children. Parents of young children do tasks together in the morning (Berk and Berk, 1979). In the early and late evenings, there is leisure time for most husbands, who give their wives little help with family work. Husbands mostly do evening child care while their wives are doing after-dinner chores. When their wives are again available for child care, most husbands quit for the evening. In the early and late evenings, women with children typically do family work, although mothers who are full-time homemakers have more time for leisure in the late evening than mothers who are employed. Men do most of their family work on weekends, while women do family work on weekdays *and* weekends (Clarke, Allen, and Salinas, 1986; Shaw, 1988). Many husbands watch children on weekends, so that their wives can have some leisure time, but, overall, wives change their schedules to match those of their husbands rather than the reverse (Clarke et al., 1986).

Men mostly do family work in the company of others, and women mostly do household tasks without others around (Berheide, 1984; Shaw, 1988). This renders women's family work less visible and more isolating than men's. Both women and men experience boredom, fatigue, and tension when they do household work alone (Baruch and Barnett, 1986a). More than men, women see family work as "work" rather than as leisure (Shaw, 1988). Shaw (1988) found that, when

women do family work, they experience less freedom of choice and more concern about their performance than men. The conditions of family work are related to women's psychological functioning but not to men's (Schooler et al., 1984). Most men do not experience family work as a test of their worth; it is not their "real" work (Weiss, 1985).

Because family work is intermingled with love and embedded in family relations, it has complex and contradictory meanings for women (Berheide, 1984; DeVault, 1987; Ferree, 1987). Most women experience family tasks as mindless but essential work done for people they love; most women usually enjoy ministering to the needs of their loved ones and keeping the family going, even if they do not find the activities themselves enjoyable and fulfilling (Berheide, 1984; Ferree, 1987). Women's family work conditions are both good and bad (Berheide, 1984; DeVault, 1987; Ferree, 1987): they are unsupervised and rarely criticized, plan and control their own work, and have only their own standards to meet. Women's family work is also worrisome, tiresome, menial, repetitive, isolating, unfinished, inescapable, and often unappreciated. Most women both cherish and resent family work.

The family work women find most enjoyable and fulfilling, cooking and child care, are the activities men often are most willing to share; this makes men's contribution a mixed blessing for their wives (Berheide, 1984; Lein, 1984). Men may "help out" with cooking and child care, but they do not take on responsibility for the full range of activities necessary to feed a family or care for children.

Beyond cooking, the day-after-day work of feeding a family involves planning and managing meals (DeVault, 1987). Cooking and cleaning up afterward are visible work; planning and managing meals are invisible work, even to the women who do almost all of it. Women, besides worrying about nutrition, must please family members with dissimilar tastes who want varied and interesting but familiar meals. Women think about tomorrow's menu while they read the evening paper and, throughout the day, think about what they need from the store. Women also have to coordinate school and work schedules so that family members can eat together—or separately, as necessary. Then, women typically orchestrate the meal so that it is a calm and pleasant social event for everyone. They monitor children and keep them in line. Women keep the conversation going and make sure everyone gets a chance to talk (see Feiring and Lewis, 1987).

Most men's contribution to child care also is confined to certain activities. Reviewing studies of parental involvement in two-parent families, Lamb (1987) drew several conclusions: he estimated that, depending upon whether they are employed or not, mothers spend from three to five hours *actively involved* with their children for every hour that fathers spend. The nature of this engagement differs for mothers and fathers: most of the time mothers spend with their children involves the practical activities of child care—feeding, bathing, dressing, and so on. Most of fathers' time is spent playing with their children. Depending upon whether they are employed or not, mothers spend one-and-a-half to three hours *being available* if children want or need something for every hour that fathers spend. Mothers, regardless of whether they are employed, carry 90% of the burden of *responsibility* for child care: they plan, organize, delegate, supervise, and schedule. Women remain the primary caretakers. While mothers are around during almost all of the time fathers spend with their children, mothers spend a lot of time just in their children's company (Baruch and Barnett, 1986a). As with feeding the family, most men help out in the more visible, leisurely activities of child care, and most women continue to do the invisible, unwitnessed, and more drudging work.

Prevailing Explanation of the Division of Family Work

With some variation, most researchers call on a particular model to explain the division of domestic work. Kamo's (1988) model epitomizes this explanation: employed women have less time to do family work, so their husbands take up the slack and do more housework and child care. Women's employment also provides them with resources, especially earnings. Partners hold certain beliefs about whether wage and family work ought to be shared or separated by gender. Women's employment, their accrued resources, and both partners' sex-role orientations combine to shape power in marriage. It is assumed that housework is onerous and it takes power to get out of it. The more power wives have in marriage,

the more housework their husbands do. Through this process, then, women's employment enhances husbands' contribution to family work. We can place the bulk of research on the division of domestic work within this prevailing model.

Wives' employment, however, is not related to husbands' family work. Husbands whose wives work outside the home do the same number of domestic tasks and spend the same amount of time doing housework as husbands whose wives are full-time homemakers (Berk, 1985; Miller and Garrison, 1984; Pleck, 1985). High-income and white husbands are the least likely to take up the slack at home when their wives are employed (Ericksen, Yancey, and Ericksen, 1979; Miller and Garrison, 1984). If husbands respond at all to their wives' employment, it is in time spent interacting with children (Baruch and Barnett, 1986a; Crouter et al., 1987; Pleck, 1985). The evidence is mixed, however, about whether the number and ages of children induce men to do more child care (Barnett and Baruch, 1987a; Coverman and Sheley, 1986). Wives cut back on their time in housework and child care in response to their participation in wage work (Barnett and Baruch, 1987b; Berardo, Shehan, and Leslie, 1987; Berk, 1985; Kingston and Nock, 1985). Husbands in dual-earner families do relatively more family work than husbands in single-career families, not because they do more but because their employed wives do less than full-time homemakers (Berardo et al., 1987).

If it is not wives' employment itself that encourages husbands to do more family work, maybe it is the number of hours women spend in paid work or their incomes (Ferree, 1988). Most researchers have found no connection between wives' paid work time and husbands' family work time (Crouter et al., 1987; but see Ferree, 1988; Piotrkowski and Repetti, 1984; Rexroat and Shehan, 1987). There is a tendency for husbands who work longer hours at their jobs to do less family work, but this tendency is weak and erratic across studies (Barnett and Baruch, 1987a; Coverman and Sheley, 1986; Crouter et al., 1987; Kingston and Nock, 1985; Pleck, 1985; Rexroat and Shehan, 1987). There is no simple trade-off of wage and family work hours between wives and husbands, nor do partners allocate family work on the basis of time availability. Wives' earnings, personal or relative to their husbands', also are unrelated to husbands' contribution to family work (Huber and Spitze, 1983; Kamo, 1988). Consider the special case in which wives earn more than their husbands (Atkinson and Boles, 1984): most wives and husbands in this uncommon arrangement emphasize traditional wifehood. Such wives, especially younger ones, attempt to be more attractive and sexual with their husbands and report catering to their husbands' whims and salving their egos. The division of domestic labor in these families tends toward the traditional. If earnings are a source of power, these wives are not using their power to push for a fair distribution of labor at home.

In spite of all the talk about egalitarian ideology, abstract beliefs about what women and men "ought" to do are not connected with the division of family work (Crouter et al., 1987; Ferree, 1988; Pleck, 1985). In an exception, Kamo (1988) found that husbands' beliefs about women's and men's proper place in families are related to the allocation of family work. When asked about their own families, over half of wives and husbands believe that housework should be done by both partners equally, and 80% believe that child care should be shared equally (Hiller and Philliber, 1986). These expectations of equality are far from fully realized in the actual division of family work. Hiller and Philliber found that partners' beliefs about the division of family work are not good predictors of who actually does family work, but husbands' preferences count more than wives'.

Power mostly is inferred in research on domestic work; that is, husbands' participation in domestic work is seen as evidence of their wives' power. Kamo (1988) found that, although compliant partners do more household chores than noncompliant partners, partners who have more say about running the household and relationships actually do more chores. We must question the assumption that doing family work is aversive and evidence of powerlessness (Ferree, 1987).

The prevailing model does little to explain the division of domestic labor. Women's employment, time availability, resources, conscious ideology, and power do not account for why wives still do the bulk of family work. More than any other factor, gender accounts for the amount and allocation of housework and child care (Berk, 1985; Pleck, 1985). Breaking away from the prevailing model, some researchers are doing promising work connecting the scheduling and meaning of women's paid work with the allocation of family work.

The scheduling of wives' paid work hours has an impact on husbands' family work. Berk and Berk (1979) reported that, when wives work evenings, their husbands typically do after-dinner chores. Presser (1988) found that father care is more substantial when fathers work full-day shifts and mothers work nonday shifts. She speculated that nonday child care is difficult to find, and evening and night care of children is easier for fathers because children may be asleep much of the time. The imperativeness of family tasks and the timing of wives' paid work combine to compel husbands' participation (Berk, 1985; Rosen, 1987; Zavella, 1987). Few researchers have studied how the everyday structure of family life shapes the fair distribution of domestic work.

Ferree (1984) contended that, as long as a woman's paid labor is construed as a privilege for her rather than as a necessity for her family, her husband will not do more family work. Husbands who see their wives as generating secondary income do fewer household tasks than those who see their wives as coproviders or who feel their wives' income is necessary but are ambivalent about who has provider responsibility (Perry-Jenkins and Crouter, 1987). In a preliminary study, Ferree (1988) found that wives who experience themselves as family breadwinners have husbands who do more housework. Wives who define themselves as providers are more likely to judge their husbands' contributions to housework as less than fair and feel entitled to more help. Many women and men underestimate their partners' willingness to share family provision and housework (Hiller and Philliber, 1986). We will not understand the distribution of domestic work by gender until we know more about the complex meanings of paid and family work for women and men and how partners change or maintain the gendered distribution of work through their daily interactions (Berk, 1985). And we are just beginning to understand diversity by class, race, and ethnicity in the meaning and allocation of wage and family work (Baca Zinn, 1980; Broman, 1988; Ferree, 1984; Kraus and Markides, 1985; Rosen, 1987; Willie, 1988; Ybarra, 1982; Zavella, 1987).

Women's and Men's Resistance to Sharing Family Work

Do women want men to do more family work? Pleck (1985) reported a historical shift in the number of wives who want their husbands to do more family work. Although a third of the wives report that they want their husbands to do more, over half of husbands sense that their wives expect more of them (Pleck, 1985). In Berk's (1985) study, a fifth of the wives think they should be doing less housework and other family members more, and only 6% of husbands view their housework arrangements as unfair. Husbands and wives report little difference of opinion about housework, although, by both partners' account, wives are more likely than husbands to give in if there is a disagreement (Berk, 1985). The professional wives in Yogev's (1981) study are responsible for family work, but only a minority (25% of women with children, 35% without) believe their husbands are not doing enough housework, and only 13% of the mothers think their husbands do not do their share of child care. Pleck (1985) found that most mothers want their husbands simply to spend more time with children rather than to do actual child care. Mothers want their husbands to be more involved with fathering, not so mothers will have less to do, but because they believe fathers and children are good for each other. Overall, women do the lion's share of family work, and from a quarter to a third of wives complain or feel that this is unfair (Barnett and Baruch, 1987b; Rosen, 1987; Yogev, 1981). Rudd and McKenry (1986) found that employed, married mothers can feel overloaded but still see children and husbands as supportive because mothers have such low expectations for help from other family members.

The fairness of the division of domestic work has different implications for women and men. Husbands are more satisfied with their marriages and less critical of their wives if their wives do more than their "fair share" of housework and child care (Barnett and Baruch, 1987b; but see Benin and Agostinelli, 1988; Yogev and Brett, 1985). This is in line with research on equity in marriage: concerning what women and men put into and get out of marriage, husbands are more likely than wives to be overbenefited and feel satisfied with an inequitable relationship that favors them (Brockner and Adsit, 1986; Schafer

and Keith, 1981). There is little evidence, however, that husbands' participation in family work distresses men (Pleck, 1985; Ross et al., 1983). Pleck (1985) found that, among husbands, family and personal well-being are positively related to time spent in family work, but more so to time spent in paid work. Overall, research has not provided a clear connection between division of family work and husbands' personal and marital well-being (Staines and Libby, 1986).

Among wives, unlike among husbands, there is a clear and positive connection between fair division of family work and marital and personal well-being. Across studies, wives whose husbands do their share of family work typically are more satisfied with marriage than other wives (Staines and Libby, 1986), while wives who feel overworked as mothers tend to evaluate their husbands more critically (Barnett and Baruch, 1987b). Pleck (1985) concluded, however, that it is not overwork or exhaustion that is the source of discontent among wives; it is inequity. He found that, among dual-earner couples, trouble brews when wives believe that their husbands are doing too little family work and they want them to do more. This combination is associated with low personal and family well-being for wives. Employment is related to enhanced personal well-being for wives only if their husbands share family work (Kessler and McCrae, 1982; Kraus and Markides, 1985). Ross and her colleagues (1983) found that, regardless of employment, wives whose husbands share housework are less depressed than other wives. Ross and her colleagues, as well as Kessler and McCrae (1982), proposed that it is the "symbolic meaning" of husbands' willingness to share family work that is important to wives. They speculated that wives appreciate their husbands' willingness to do their fair share and that neither partner is "doing service" to the other. Rosen (1987) found that blue-collar wives see their husbands' help with family work as an expression of love and concern.

The majority of wives, then, do not fret or feel that it is unfair because they do the lion's share of family work. Under this lopsided arrangement, husbands tend to think well of their wives and marriages, although husbands do not undermine their own mental health when they do more family work. Even though they may not expect help, however, wives tend to think well of their husbands and marriages when the arrangement is not so lopsided.

The ambivalent struggle: Women's reluctance to give up family work and men's resistance to take it on. Mainardi (1978) observed that there are many strategies partners, usually husbands, use to avoid housework, such as choosing to do less frequently done tasks, "out-waiting" the partner before taking on the task, and asking many questions each time a task is engaged. Among women who get help from their husbands or children, nearly half report the help must be supervised, another responsibility for women (Berheide, 1984). Berk (1985) found that, although only 5% of wives have to supervise their husbands "every step of the way," many more wives have to tell their husbands what needs to be done. Most of the upper-middle-class men in Weiss's (1987) study want to be told when and how their help is needed, but their wives do want this responsibility. Although they want their wives to tell them what to do, these husbands want to be treated with respect when given a domestic assignment. Barrett and McIntosh (1982) argued that it is often easier for women to do household tasks themselves than to get other family members to do them.

Among families with young children, fathers in dual-earner families do more child care on their own than fathers in single-earner families (Barnett and Baruch, 1987b; Baruch and Barnett, 1986a; Crouter et al., 1987). Fathers' solo child care creates problems, however: among dual-earner families, fathers' solo child care is related strongly to diminished love for their wives and negative interaction in marriage, such as wives showing anger and impatience, criticizing, or complaining (Crouter et al., 1987). Although wives are less critical of their husbands as fathers when fathers are more involved with children, highly involved fathers tend to feel less benefited by marriage and are more critical of their wives' time spent with children, work schedule, and allocation of time (Barnett and Baruch, 1987b; Baruch and Barnett, 1986a). Crouter and her colleagues suggested that employed mothers need help with child care and press their husbands into service. The cost of this help, however, may be marital distress and waning love, at least from the husbands' point of view.

Many women find it difficult to push for a fair division of domestic work if it means fighting with loved ones (Berheide, 1984). Several studies have revealed that sharing family work is associated with greater marital conflict (Benin and Agostinelli, 1988; Hoffman, 1983; Russell and Radin, 1983). One source of marital conflict when couples share domestic work is wives' complaining about the quality of husbands' housework and child care (Lamb, Pleck, and Levine, 1986). Wives with lower standards for housework have husbands who do more housework (Ferree, 1988). Husbands may hesitate to do family work if wives criticize their efforts. But pleading ineptness or doing a task poorly is one way to avoid having to do it (Huston and Ashmore, 1986; Mainardi, 1978). When wives criticize the quality of their husbands' domestic work, they are protecting threatened territory (Boulton, 1983; Lamb et al., 1986; LaRossa and LaRossa, 1981). The home is women's dominion, and many are reluctant to relinquish or share control over the only domain in which they have power (Polatnick, 1984). Ferree (1987) suggested that men do so little family work that it is not worth it to women to jeopardize their domestic control just to get a little relief. The men in Weiss's (1985) study bemoan their powerlessness in running their homes and rearing their children. When pressed, however, most admit they want to be involved in making domestic decisions, but they do not want to be burdened with details or actual activities. They want to oversee but not do the menial and manual labor.

PARENTHOOD

Parenthood is more than the "work" of child care; it is the daily experience and the larger meaning of having children (Boulton, 1983). Mostly, in studying parenthood, researchers are concerned with the interests of children rather than the interests of parents. In this section, however, we consider how the images, activities, experiences, and implications of parenthood differ for mothers and fathers. We also consider how parenthood makes marriage more gender-specialized and traditional.

Images of Motherhood and Fatherhood

The images of motherhood and fatherhood reveal

our shared ideals, standards, beliefs, and expectations regarding women and men as parents. Both enduring and emerging images exist, much to the confusion of mothers and fathers. Several authors have described the enduring image of motherhood (Boulton, 1983; Chodorow and Contratto, 1982; Daniels and Weingarten, 1988; Glenn, 1987): Motherhood is inevitable; every woman will or should be a mother. A woman's identity is tenuous and trivial without motherhood. A woman enjoys and intuitively knows what to do for her child; she cares for her child without ambivalence or awkwardness. Motherhood is a constant and exclusive responsibility. A mother is all-giving and all-powerful. Within the "magic circle" of mother and child, the mother devotes herself to her child's needs and holds her child's fate in her hands. Amidst idealization and blame, the enduring image of motherhood is also incompatible with women's sexuality and wage work. Others have described the enduring image of fatherhood (Daniels and Weingarten, 1988; Pleck, 1987): a father is a breadwinner who does not have the ability or the desire to nurture his child day-by-day, so he funds the family but keeps his distance.

Our images of motherhood and fatherhood in black and Chicano families are exaggerated so that ideals turn into flaws. Black mothers are imagined as all-powerful matriarchs (McCray, 1980). Black fathers are, at best, aloof and, at worst, absent (McAdoo, 1988). Chicano fathers are imagined as standoffish, swaggering authoritarians (Mirande, 1988). The images are myths: black couples share childrearing no less, and perhaps more, than white couples, and black husbands are as intimately involved with their children as white husbands, although it is more difficult for them to provide for and protect their children (Allen, 1981; McAdoo, 1988; Peters, 1985).

Another enduring image of black mothers is the strong woman who does everything—nurtures as well as provides for her children (McCray, 1980). The emerging white image of "superwoman," the wage-working mother who does it all, is similar to the idealized black mother except that "superwoman" usually has a husband who is the primary provider and not expected to do much at home (Ferree, 1988). The emerging "new fatherhood" or "new parenthood," however, is an image of mothers and fathers sharing the full weight of raising their children (Bronstein, 1988; LaRossa, 1988; Pleck, 1987). "New" fathers are intimately, actively involved with their children; they are responsible and care for their children day-by-day (LaRossa, 1988). Prime-time television bolsters this image: television fathers are portrayed as more active parents than television mothers (Dail and Way, 1985). With juggled schedules and good day care in the early years, "new" mothers and fathers can have fulfilling work lives and rich and rewarding family lives (Bronstein, 1988). Both "new" parents can have it all, including a sense of fairness, respect, and cooperation with one another (Bronstein, 1988).

Activities of Mothering and Fathering

Although the enduring image of motherhood is that women should have children or else forfeit meaning in life, research has shown that women without children, whether by choice or infertility, have the same level of personal well-being as women with children (Baruch, Barnett, and Rivers, 1983; Callan, 1987; Coleman et al., 1987). Once women and men become parents, they tend to do different things with and for their children and relate to their children in different ways. We know more about the nature and activities of mothering and fathering small children than we know about older children (Bradley, 1985; Giveans and Robinson, 1985). Regardless of children's age, however, mothers typically are more invested and involved in the daily lives of their children than are fathers (Clarke-Stewart, 1978; Montemayor, 1986; Kivett, 1988). Ruddick (1982) described the activities of attentive love and mothering as preserving life, fostering growth, and molding an acceptable person. Abiding, attentive, active, hands-on parenting is seen as imperative for mothers but optional for fathers (Boulton, 1983; Daniels and Weingarten, 1988). Researchers study the circumstances and personal characteristics that encourage fathers' involvement in parenting (Barnett and Baruch, 1987a; Crouter et al., 1987; Radin, 1988), but do not give similar attention to mothers' involvement. Most mothers, fathers, and researchers continue to see fathers' contributions to parenting as "helping" but never refer to mothers' contributions in this way (LaRossa and LaRossa, 1981; Ross et al., 1983). Kranichfield (1987) argued that the bonds between mothers and their children are ignored and invisible sources of women's family power.

More than fathers, mothers provide the "continuous coverage" that babies require, and they sacrifice their free time to do so; unless relieved by their husbands, mothers must be "up" and "ready" to respond to their children's needs (LaRossa and LaRossa, 1981). Mothers tend to be the abiding presence in small children's lives: more than fathers, mothers give care, attend, respond, protect, hold, soothe, and comfort (Bronstein, 1988; L. C. Jones, 1985; LaRossa and LaRossa, 1981). Most fathers come and go: more than mothers, fathers are novel, unpredictable, physical, exciting, engaging, and preferred playmates for young children (Bronstein, 1988; Clarke-Stewart, 1978; L. C. Jones, 1985). Playing is a cleaner, freer activity than caregiving, and fathers usually do other things while they are minding their children (LaRossa and LaRossa, 1981). Fathers are rarely alone with their children, and mothers typically manage and monitor what is going on between fathers and small children (Clarke-Stewart, 1978; LaRossa and LaRossa, 1981). When both parents are present, the distinction between mothers as comfort-givers and fathers as playmates is more pronounced, but when parents share daily caregiving, the distinction fades and mothering and fathering seem much the same (Daniels and Weingarten, 1988; L. C. Jones, 1985).

Most fathers are breadwinners as well as playmates. Virtually all men believe that being a good father means first and foremost being a good provider (Cazenave, 1979; but see Cohen, 1987; Daniels and Weingarten, 1988). Fathers typically are involved in the day-to-day responsibility of providing for their children and resent any claim that they do not contribute directly to their children's welfare (Cowan et al., 1985; LaRossa and LaRossa, 1981). McKee (1982; see Cohen, 1987) urged a fuller appreciation of fathering by studying fathers in their own right rather than in comparison to mothers. She suggested more attention to fathers as providers, the nature of fathers' interest and investment in children, their sensitivity to children, and fathers' involvement in the educational, moral, decision-making, and disciplinary aspects of raising children.

As children get older, fathers tend to be more directive and instructive than are mothers (Bronstein, 1988). During adolescence, children perceive their fathers as more powerful and more autocratic than their mothers; children perceive mothers as more sympathetic and responsive (Baranowski, 1978; McDonald, 1982). Adolescent children are more likely, therefore, to come in conflict with and try to get their way with mothers than with fathers (Baranowski, 1978; Steinberg, 1987). Put simply, mothers usually are more involved with the daily lives of their adolescent children than are fathers (Montemayor, 1986). When children are adults, aged fathers tend to give advice and mothers to give emotional support (Hagestad and Kranichfeld, 1982). Even late in life, mothers usually do more for and with their children, and get more help from them in return than fathers; this is especially true of older mothers and adult daughters (Kivett, 1988).

Experiences of Mothering and Fathering

Too often researchers reduce the activities of parenting to who-does-what-how-often and reduce the experience of parenting to general satisfaction with parent-child relationships or with parenting (Boulton, 1983; LaRossa and LaRossa, 1981; McKee, 1982). We need to broaden our inquiry. If parents face both enduring and emerging images of motherhood and fatherhood and the activities of mothering and fathering differ, what are the implications for women's and men's experiences as parents?

Mothering is a complex and contradictory experience: it is frustrating, irritating, and overwhelming, but also pleasing and fulfilling (Chodorow and Contratto, 1982). Boulton (1983) interviewed 50 married mothers of small children and described how mothers experience their constant and exclusive responsibility for children. Mothers expressed two modes of experience—an immediate response to the day-to-day activities of looking after children and a larger sense of purpose in raising children.

Most mothers find looking after small children a predominantly unsettling and irritating experience. The constant vigilance and the tedium of occupying children who are unreasonable and self-centered takes its toll on mothers. Children interfere with mothers' other activities (such as housework), confine mothers to home, and require routines that help mothers feel less overwhelmed, but also more restricted. On the other hand, most mothers voice the sense of meaning, purpose, fulfillment, commitment, and value children bring to life. Mothers typically focus their hopes, dreams, and ambitions on their children and strive to give their children the things they missed when they were young. But mostly mothers' sense of purpose is founded on feeling needed by and essential to their children. It is important to mothers' sense of personal worth that children want and depend upon them in particular. About a third of mothers both enjoy and find broader meaning in mothering, another third neither enjoy nor find meaning in mothering, and the others have mixed experiences.

Boulton (1983) found that children do not necessarily bring the enjoyment or sense of purpose promised by the image of motherhood. The enduring image of motherhood as a constant and complete responsibility shapes mothering, however. Most mothers experience their responsibility for children as both frustrating and a source of meaning. More than working-class mothers, middle-class mothers seem caught between enduring and emerging images of motherhood. They experience mothering as a loss of freedom and identity even as they search for meaning in their children's need and dependency. Baruch and her colleagues (1983) studied two similar experiences of mothering in their research on midlife women. They found that mothers who tend to like and enjoy their children have a stronger sense of mastery and pleasure in life. Mothers who feel needed, special, and irreplaceable to their children and embrace the meaning children give to life report less mastery. The tension between the constant-and-complete-responsibility and the have-it-all images of motherhood creates ambivalence in mothers. Hock, Gnezda, and McBride (1984) found that most new mothers believe in the importance of exclusive maternal care, and although two-thirds plan to return to paid work before their babies' first birthday, almost three-quarters of them would prefer to stay home with their babies.

LaRossa and LaRossa (1981) reported how fathers, as well as mothers, experience the daily activities and the larger social value of parenting. More than fathers, mothers are sensitive to their babies' interpersonal abilities and get more out of the time they spend with their babies. More than mothers, fathers treasure their children but do not find much pleasure in looking after them. They commit themselves to raising children and derive

status from being fathers, but they "do time" with their children rather than enjoy them. Most men report feeling impatient and irritable with their children and inadequate as fathers (Heath, 1976). They are confused and dissatisfied with their involvement in childrearing (Heath, 1976; Weiss, 1985). Fathers who are more involved with their children feel more competent as parents (Baruch and Barnett, 1986a). Rare men who are highly involved with the daily activities of looking after their children experience the same ambivalence about parenthood that mothers have always experienced: they enjoy close, rich, fulfilling relationships with their children, but they also endure frustration, worry, boredom, testiness, and tiredness (Berheide, 1984; Lamb et al., 1986). Like mothers who are active, abiding participants in their children's lives, such fathers are sensitive to their children's cues and aware of the minute and immediate changes in their children (Daniels and Weingarten, 1988).

Overall, fathers believe that they should be directly involved in their children's lives, but most are not (Backett, 1987; LaRossa, 1988). Cohen (1987) found that many men are invested emotionally in fatherhood even though their activities do not reveal their investment. Typically, fathers feel alternately good and bad about their performance: they feel proud when they compare their fathering to their own fathers and guilty when they compare their fathering to the image of "new fatherhood" (LaRossa, 1988).

Baruch and her coauthors (1987) argued that parenting is particularly stressful for women, and parental stress undermines women's well-being more than men's. With parenthood, mothers tend to experience more change, both positive and negative, in themselves and in their lives than do fathers: mothers report more change in daily routines, moods, sense of themselves as parents, feelings of autonomy and competence, and sexuality (Cowan et al., 1985; Feldman and Nash, 1984; Harriman, 1983). Most fathers, however, are more invested and involved in paid work and marriage than they are in parenthood (Cowan et al., 1985; Harriman, 1983; Weiss, 1985). Mothers with a chronically mentally ill child report more distress than fathers (Cook, 1988), and mothers grieve more when a child dies (Littlefield and Rushton, 1986). Conflict with children, especially during adolescence, is related to lower well-being for mothers but not for fathers (Baruch et al., 1983; Silverberg and Steinberg, 1987). Perhaps because daily involvement in children's lives wanes, children are not an important source of well-being for either parent later in life (Glenn and McLanahan, 1981).

Parenting and Gendered Marital Patterns and Interaction

Researchers have devoted a lot of attention to the drop in marital satisfaction, especially among wives, when partners become parents (Staines and Libby, 1986). Among the reasons offered for such a drop, one promising culprit is the gender differentiation and specialization that accompanies parenting (Cowan et al., 1985): In what ways does parenting act as an occasion for gender specialization in marriage? How does gender specialization undermine marital happiness? And how is gender-specialized parenting sustained through marital interaction?

It is structurally difficult for women to build a strong base in both domestic and public spheres; women who lack job opportunities themselves but have husbands with good earnings tend to withdraw from the workplace when they have children (Gerson, 1985). When they become parents, women tend to stop work outside the home or cut way back on their hours, while men tend to spend more time in wage work (Cowan et al., 1985). Mothers devote more of themselves to parenting, while fathers devote themselves to providing (Cowan et al., 1985; LaRossa and LaRossa, 1981). Mothers end up doing most of the child care and housework regardless of what pattern was established or expected before children arrived (Cowan et al., 1985; LaRossa and LaRossa, 1981; Ruble, Fleming, Hackel, and Stangor, 1988).

The image of "new parenthood" provides standards that are too high for most couples. Ruble and her coauthors (1988) marveled at new mothers' high expectations for shared child care and housework. The more new mothers' expectations are violated, the more they are bothered by their husbands' lack of involvement in daily baby care and lack of understanding for the difficulty of baby care (Ruble et al., 1988). The more the division of labor changes toward the traditional with the birth of the first child, the greater the plunge in marital happiness, especially among nontraditional wives (Belsky, Lang, and Huston, 1986). Cowan and her colleagues (1985) found that conflict increases after children arrive, and disagreement over who does what domestic work is at the top of the list. Many mothers experience their husbands' new devotion to providing as pulling away from home at a time when they are needed most and promised they would be around (Cowan et al., 1985).

Unlike many working-class mothers who find security in the gender-specialized work fashioned by parenthood, most middle-class mothers believe that parenting squelched whatever marital equality they had managed before children (Boulton, 1983; see LaRossa and LaRossa, 1981): they feel a loss of status, opportunity, and freedom that most husbands do not suffer and that husbands' "help" does not mitigate. Many mothers also experience a new dependence on their husbands because, for relief, they must rely on their husbands' childminding, and mothers suspect that they have to be more deferential in return. Indeed, wives tend to give in more during disagreements after children arrive (Waldron and Routh, 1981).

Mothers' enjoyment and sense of purpose in mothering is positively related to husbands' showing respect and appreciation for them as mothers and recognizing the arduousness of mothering (Backett, 1987; Boulton, 1983). Acknowledging the "pressures" in each other's lives (i.e., not thinking the other has an easier time of it) can make the division of labor appear fair to partners, even if they are not sharing work equally and fathers remain at a distance from their children (Backett, 1987; LaRossa and LaRossa, 1981; McKee, 1982). Partners seem to collaborate to sustain the belief that fathers are intimately involved with their children and "fairly" sharing child care when mothers actually are doing the daily parenting (Backett, 1987; LaRossa and LaRossa, 1981).

Backett (1987) found that couples sustain belief in father involvement in the face of contradictory evidence in three ways: (*a*) Even if fathers are not *actively* involved with their children, they are *passively* involved because wives keep them informed, and talking about children is a major part of couple conversation. (*b*) Even if fathers do it only rarely, they willingly "help" with practical care when really needed and mind the children when wives have to get out of the house. (*c*) Fathers play with their children and claim they would do more if only they had the time. Also crucial to sustaining gender-specialized parenting is the availability of gender-specific excuses and justifications for mothers' and fathers' involvement in child care: for example, it is acceptable for fathers, but not for mothers, to say that their wage work keeps them from their children or that they are impatient or incompetent in child care (LaRossa and LaRossa, 1981). McKee (1982) cited other reasons that stand up for fathers, but not for mothers—inexperience, tiredness, clumsiness, and squeamishness. Many wives are easy on their husbands and praise, excuse, and justify their husbands' minimal involvement; other wives refuse to honor their husbands' reasons and call them to account (LaRossa and LaRossa, 1981; McKee, 1982). Through their interaction, couples construct gendered parenting.

CONCLUSIONS AND RECOMMENDATIONS

Gender specialization in families persists across the domains of marriage, work, and parenthood. Everyday and ultimate responsibility for marriage, housework, and parenthood usually remains with women; and responsibility for breadwinning usually remains with men. Most women "help" men with provision, and many men "help" women with family work and parenting, although partners collude to sustain belief that men are primary providers but parenting is shared. Partners tend to view men's minimal help with raising children as substantial, and women's substantial help with provision as minimal. A growing number of women are bothered by this lopsided arrangement, but for the most part, women and men do not consider family life unfair. Given similar circumstances and opportunities, women and men seem very much alike, but the broader context often constrains their efforts to break through the boundaries that separate them. The last decade of research has taught us that gender is more complicated than we thought.

We offer several recommendations for further research on gender in families. Research that connects the private actions, beliefs, and experiences of women and men in families with the larger context of inequality is essential. We strongly encourage research, therefore, that considers the diversity of gendered experience by race, ethnicity, and social class. Diversity across individual,

family, and historical time is also important. In addition, we suggest areas of inquiry within each domain of family life. Researchers should never assume that any domain of family life belongs exclusively to either women or men, or that women and men experience families in the same way.

1. Marriage. Researchers should attend to the full range of expressions of intimacy; the balance of emotional support and dependence between partners; sensual and emotional aspects of sexuality; responsibility for monitoring and managing relationships; attribution of responsibility and blame for marital events; the context, dynamics, and consequences of wife-battering; and all of these aspects of marriage as sources of and occasions for power.

2. Work. Researchers should attend to responsibility and recognition for paid and family work; the "symbolic" meaning of coprovision and shared family work; the connection between wage work and family life; the context of housework and child care, including the structure of the immediate situation and scheduling; sense of entitlement and attribution of fairness in regard to division of labor; the experience of housework and its alleged aversiveness; family work as a source of and an occasion for power; and how partners support and sabotage each other's involvement in wage and family work.

3. Parenthood. Researchers should attend to the enduring and emerging images of motherhood and fatherhood; the ambivalent experience of mothering and fathering; the nature of mothers' and fathers' involvement in everyday parenting activities; the context of parental involvement, including the structure of the immediate situation and scheduling; emotional investment and sense of purpose in parenthood; the influence of parenthood on parents and their gender specialization in marriage, especially when children are no longer small; parenthood as a source of and occasion for power; and how partners support and sabotage each other's involvement in parenthood.

At the top of our agenda is the conceptualization of gender. Almost unfailingly, family scholars think of gender as an individual property (sex as a variable) or as gender roles. There are many problems with both prevailing approaches

(West and Zimmerman, 1987). Briefly, gender as an individual property leads to research that emphasizes stable sex differences between women and men rather than similarities between women and men or diversity among women and among men. "Sex" or "gender" are variables with ambiguous meaning, so when differences emerge between groups of women and men, researchers fill in a meaning that suits them. "Sex" or "gender" as variables stand for something, but we are never sure what that something is. Some feminists have criticized the gender role approach because it masks power, inequality, conflict, and change (Thorne, 1982). West and Zimmerman (1987) contended that roles are learned and enacted in specific contexts, whereas women and men "do gender" all the time, in all contexts. Others have suggested that we separate gender from role, so that we can explore how gender interacts with roles such as partner, provider, homemaker, or parent, making these roles different for women and men (Ferree, 1988; Lopata, 1987).

A promising approach to gender in families is a relational or interactional approach (Backett, 1987; Berk, 1985; Flax, 1987; Gerson and Peiss, 1985; LaRossa and LaRossa, 1981; Risman and Schwartz, 1989; West and Zimmerman, 1987). Rather than an individual property or role, gender is something evoked, created, and sustained day-by-day through interaction among family members. Women and men participate together to construct the meaning of gender and distinguish themselves from each other *as* women or *as* men. As our review reveals, gender is applied to the study of women, but rarely to the study of men. On the other hand, many assume that women push for similarity between women and men and shared gender roles, while men resist change. Actually, many women want to maximize gender differences (Kaufman, 1985), and most women collaborate with men to maintain gender specialization (LaRossa and LaRossa, 1981). Using a relational approach to gender would recognize men as gendered and women as active participants in creating gender. A relational approach would help us to understand why gender difference and specialization in families are so resistant to change and how change occurs (Berk, 1985; Gerson and Peiss, 1985).

NOTE

The authors thank William Turner for helping with library work and William Aquilino for thoughtfully commenting on various versions of the article.

REFERENCES

Allen, Walter R. 1981. "Moms, dads, and boys: Race and sex differences in the socialization of male children." Pp. 99–114 in Lawrence E. Gary (ed.), Black Men. Beverly Hills, CA: Sage.

Ammons, Paul, Josie Nelson, and John Wodarski. 1982. "Surviving corporate moves: Sources of stress and adaptation among corporate executive families." Family Relations 31: 207–212.

Atkinson, Maxine, and Jacqueline Boles. 1984. "WASP (Wives As Senior Partners)." Journal of Marriage and the Family 46: 861–870.

Baca Zinn, Maxine. 1980. "Employment and education of Mexican-American women: The interplay of modernity and ethnicity in eight families." Harvard Educational Review 50: 47–62.

Backett, Kathryn. 1987. "The negotiation of fatherhood." Pp. 74–90 in Charlie Lewis and Margaret O'Brien (eds.), Reassessing Fatherhood: New Observations on Fathers and the Modern Family. London: Sage.

Baranowski, Mark D. 1978. "Adolescents' attempted influence on parental behaviors." Adolescence 13: 585–604.

Barnett, Rosalind C., and Grace K. Baruch. 1987a. "Determinants of fathers' participation in family work." Journal of Marriage and the Family 49: 29–40.

Barnett, Rosalind C., and Grace K. Baruch. 1987b. "Mother's participation in child care: Patterns and consequences." Pp. 91–108 in Faye J. Crosby (ed.), Spouse, Parent, Worker: On Gender and Multiple Roles. New Haven, CT: Yale University Press.

Barrett, Michele, and Mary McIntosh. 1982. The Anti-Social Family. London: Verso.

Baruch, Grace K., and Rosalind C. Barnett. 1986a. "Consequences of fathers' participation in family work: Parents' role strain and well-being." Journal of Personality and Social Psychology 51: 983–992.

Baruch, Grace K., and Rosalind Barnett. 1986b. "Role quality, multiple role involvement, and psychological well-being in mid-life women." Journal of Personality and Social Psychology 51: 578–585.

Baruch, Grace, Rosalind Barnett, and Caryl Rivers. 1983. Lifeprints: New Patterns of Love and Work for Today's Women. New York: New American Library.

Baruch, Grace K., Lois Biener, and Rosalind C. Barnett. 1987. "Women and gender in research on work and family stress." American Psychologist 42: 130–136.

Belsky, Jay, Mary Lang, and Ted L. Huston. 1986. "Sex typing and division of labor as determinants of marital change across the transition to parenthood." Journal of Personality and Social Psychology 50: 517–522.

Benin, Mary Holland, and Joan Agostinelli. 1988. "Husbands' and wives' satisfaction with the division of labor." Journal of Marriage and the Family 50: 349–361.

Berardo, Donna H., Constance Shehan, and Gerald R. Leslie. 1987. "A residue of tradition: Jobs, careers, and spouses' time in housework." Journal of Marriage and the Family 49: 381–390.

Berheide, Catherine W. 1984. "Women's work in the home: Seems like old times." Pp. 37–55 in Beth B. Hess and Marvin B. Sussman (eds.), Women and the Family: Two Decades of Change. New York: Haworth Press.

Berk, Richard A., and Sarah F. Berk. 1979. Labor and Leisure at Home: Content and Organization of the Household Day. Beverly Hills, CA: Sage.

Berk, Sarah F. 1985. The Gender Factory: The Apportionment of Work in American Households. New York: Plenum Press.

Bernard, Jessie. 1972. The Future of Marriage. New York: World.

Bernard, Jessie. 1981. "The good provider role: Its rise and fall." American Psychologist 36: 1–12.

Blumstein, Philip, and Pepper Schwartz. 1983. American Couples: Money, Work, Sex. New York: William Morrow.

Bose, Christine E. 1987. "Dual spheres." Pp. 267–285 in Beth B. Hess and Myra M. Ferree (eds.), Analyzing Gender: A Handbook of Social Science Research. Newbury Park, CA: Sage.

Boulton, Mary G. 1983. On Being a Mother: A Study of Women with Pre-school Children. London: Tavistock Publications.

Bradley, Robert H. 1985. "Fathers and the school-age child." Pp. 141–169 in Shirley M. H. Hanson and Frederick W. Bozett (eds.), Dimensions of Fatherhood. Beverly Hills, CA: Sage.

Brockner, Joel, and Laury Adsit. 1986. "The moderating impact of sex on the equity-satisfaction relationship: A field study." Journal of Applied Psychology 71: 585–590.

Broman, Clifford L. 1988. "Household work and family life satisfaction of blacks." Journal of Marriage and the Family 50: 743–748.

Bronstein, Phyllis. 1988. "Father-child interaction: Implications for gender role socialization." Pp. 107–124 in Phyllis Bronstein and Carolyn P. Cowan (eds.), Fatherhood Today: Men's Changing Role in the Family. New York: John Wiley and Sons.

Brown, Diane R., and Lawrence E. Gary. 1985. "Social support network differentials among married and nonmarried black females." Psychology of Women Quarterly 9: 229–241.

Browning, James, and Donald Dutton. 1986. "Assessment of wife assault with the Conflict Tactics Scale: Using couple data to quantify the differential reporting effect." Journal of Marriage and the Family 48: 375–379.

Callan, Victor J. 1987. "The personal and marital adjustment of mothers and of voluntarily and involuntarily childless wives." Journal of Marriage and the Family 49: 847–856.

Cancian, Francesca. 1986. "The feminization of love." Signs 11: 692–708.

Cancian, Francesca M., and Steven L. Gordon. 1988. "Changing emotion norms in marriage: Love and anger in U.S. women's magazines since 1900." Gender and Society 2: 308–342.

Cazenave, Noel A. 1979. "Middle-income black fathers: An analysis of the provider role." Family Coordinator 28: 583–593.

Cazenave, Noel A. 1983. "Black male–black female relationships: The perceptions of 155 middle-class black men." Family Relations 32: 341–350.

Chow, Esther N., and Catherine W. Berheide. 1988. "The interdependence of family and work: A framework for family life education, policy, and practice." Family Relations 37: 23–28.

Chodorow, Nancy, and Susan Contratto. 1982. "The fantasy of the perfect mother." Pp. 54–75 in Barrie Thorne and Marilyn Yalom (eds.), Rethinking the Family: Some Feminist Questions. New York: Longman.

Clarke, David D., Christine M. B. Allen, and Maria Salinas. 1986. "Conjoint time-budgeting: Investigating behavioral accommodation in marriage." Journal of Social and Personal Relationships 3: 53–69.

Clarke-Stewart, K. A. 1978. "And Daddy makes three: The father's impact on mother and young child." Child Development 49: 466–478.

Cohen, Theodore F. 1987. "Remaking men: Men's experiences becoming and being husbands and fathers and their implications for reconceptualizing men's lives." Journal of Family Issues 8: 57–77.

Coleman, Lerita M., Toni C. Antonucci, Pamela K. Adelmann, and Susan E. Crohan. 1987. "Social roles in the lives of middle-aged and older black women." Journal of Marriage and the Family 49: 761–771.

Collier, Betty J., and Louis Williams. 1982. "The economic status of the black male: A myth exploded." Journal of Black Studies 12: 487–498.

Cook, Judith A. 1988. "Who 'mothers' the chronically ill?" Family Relations 37: 42–49.

Coverman, Shelley, and Joseph F. Sheley. 1986. "Change in men's housework and child-care time, 1965–1975." Journal of Marriage and the Family 48: 413–422.

Cowan, Carolyn P., Philip A. Cowan, Gertrude Heming, Ellen Garrett, William S. Coysh, Harriet Curtis-Boles, and Abner J. Boles III. 1985. "Transitions to parenthood: His, hers, and theirs." Journal of Family Issues 6: 451–481.

Cowan, Ruth Schwartz. 1987. "Women's work, housework, and history: The historical roots of inequality in work-force participation." Pp. 164–177 in Naomi Gerstel and Harriet Engel Gross (eds.), Families and Work. Philadelphia: Temple University Press.

Crouter, Ann C., Maureen Perry-Jenkins, Ted L. Huston, and Susan M. McHale. 1987. "Processes underlying father involvement in dual-earner and single-earner families." Developmental Psychology 23: 431–440.

Dail, Paula W., and Wendy L. Way. 1985. "What do parents observe about parenting from prime time television?" Family Relations 34: 491–499.

Daniels, Arlene K. 1987. "Invisible work." Social Problems 34: 403–415.

Daniels, Pamela, and Kathy Weingarten. 1988. "The fatherhood click: The timing of parenthood in men's lives." Pp. 36–52 In Phyllis Bronstein and Carolyn P. Cowan (eds.), Fatherhood Today: Men's Changing Role in the Family. New York: John Wiley and Sons.

Depner, Charlene E., and Berit Ingersoll-Dayton. 1985. "Conjugal social support: Patterns in later life." Journal of Gerontology 40: 761–766.

DeVault, Marjorie L. 1987. "Doing housework: Feeding and family life." Pp. 178–191 in Naomi Gerstel and Harriet Engel Gross (eds.), Families and Work. Philadelphia: Temple University Press.

Dobash, R. Emerson, and Russell P. Dobash. 1979. Violence against Wives: A Case against the Patriarchy. New York: Free Press.

Edleson, Jeffrey L., and Mary P. Brygger. 1986. "Gender differences in reporting of battering incidents." Family Relations 35: 379–382.

Eichler, Margrit. 1981. "Power, dependency, love, and the sexual division of labour: A critique of the decision-making approach to family power and an alternative approach," with an Appendix: "On washing my dirty linen in public." Women's Studies International Quarterly 4: 201–219.

Epstein, Cynthia Fuchs. 1987. "Multiple demands and multiple roles: The conditions of successful management." Pp. 23–35 in Faye J. Crosby (ed.), Spouse, Parent, Worker: On Gender and Multiple Roles. New Haven, CT: Yale University Press.

Erickson, Julia A., William L. Yancey, and Eugene P. Ericksen. 1979. "The division of family roles." Journal of Marriage and the Family 41: 301–313.

Feiring, Candice, and Michael Lewis. 1987. "The ecology of some middle-class families at dinner." International Journal of Behavioral Development 10: 377–390.

Feldman, S. Shirley, and Sharon C. Nash. 1984. "The transition from expectancy to parenthood: Impact of the firstborn child on men and women." Sex Roles 11: 61–78.

Fendrich, Michael. 1984. "Wives' employment and husbands' distress: A meta-analysis and a replication." Journal of Marriage and the Family 46: 871–879.

Ferber, Marianne A. 1982. "Women and work: Issues of the 1980s." Signs 8: 273–295.

Ferree, Myra M. 1976. "Working-class jobs: Housework and paid work as sources of satisfaction." Social Problems 27: 431–441.

Ferree, Myra M. 1984. "The view from below: Women's employment and gender equality in working-class families." Pp. 57–75 in Beth B. Hess and Marvin B. Sussman (eds.), Women and the Family: Two Decades of Change. New York: Haworth Press.

Ferree, Myra M. 1987. "Family and job for working-class women: Gender and class systems seen from below." Pp. 289–301 in Naomi Gerstel and Harriet Engel Gross (eds.), Families and Work. Philadelphia: Temple University Press.

Ferree, Myra M. 1988. "Negotiating household roles and responsibilities: Resistance, conflict, and change." Paper presented at the annual meeting of the National Council on Family Relations, Philadelphia.

Fishman, Pamela M. 1978. "What do couples talk about when they're alone." Pp. 11–22 in Dianne Butturff and Edmond L. Epstein (eds.), Women's Language and Style. Akron, OH: University of Akron.

Flax, Jane. 1987. "Postmodernism and gender relations in feminist theory." Signs 12: 621–643.

Fowlkes, Martha R. 1987. "The myth of merit and male professional careers: The roles of wives." Pp. 347–360 in Naomi Gerstel and Harriet Engel Gross (eds.), Families and Work. Philadelphia: Temple University Press.

Gerson, Judith M., and Kathy Peiss. 1985. "Boundaries, negotiation, consciousness: Reconceptualizing gender relations." Social Problems 32: 317–331.

Gerson, Kathleen. 1985. Hard Choices: How Women Decide about Work, Career, and Motherhood. Berkeley: University of California Press.

Giele, Janet Z. 1982. "Women's work and family roles." Pp. 115–150 in Janet Z. Giele (ed.), Women in the Middle Years: Current Knowledge and Directions for Research and Policy. New York: John Wiley and Sons.

Giveans, David L., and Michael K. Robinson. 1985. "Fathers and the preschool age child." Pp. 115–140 in Shirley M. H. Hanson and Frederick W. Bozett (eds.), Dimensions of Fatherhood. Beverly Hills, CA: Sage.

Glenn, Evelyn N. 1987. "Gender and the Family." Pp. 348–360 in Beth B. Hess and Myra M. Ferree (eds.), Analyzing Gender: A Handbook of Social Science Research. Newbury Park, CA: Sage.

Glenn, Norval D., and Sara McLanahan. 1981. "The effects of offspring on the psychological well-being of older adults." Journal of Marriage and the Family 43: 409–421.

Gottman, John M. 1979. Marital Interaction: Experimental Investigations. New York: Academic Press.

Gottman, John M., and Lowell J. Krokoff. 1989. "Marital interaction and satisfaction: A longitudinal view." Journal of Consulting and Clinical Psychology 57: 1–6.

Gottman, John M., and Albert L. Porterfield. 1981. "Communicative competence in the nonverbal behavior of married couples." Journal of Marriage and the Family 43: 817–824.

Greenblat, Cathy S. 1983. "The salience of sexuality in the early years of marriage." Journal of Marriage and the Family 45: 289–299.

Haas, Linda. 1986. "Wives' orientation toward breadwinning." Journal of Family Issues 7: 358–381.

Hagestad, Gunhild D., and M. Kranichfeld. 1982. "Issues in the study of intergenerational continuity." Paper presented at the National Council on Family Relations Preconference on Theory Construction and Research Methodology, Washington, DC.

Hagestad, Gunhild D., and Michael A. Smyer. 1982. "Dissolving long-term relationships: Patterns of divorcing in middle age." Pp. 155–188 in Steve Duck (ed.), Personal Relationships. 4: Dissolving Personal Relationships. London: Academic Press.

Haggstrom, Gus W., David E. Kanouse, and Peter A. Morrison. 1986. "Accounting for the educational shortfalls of mothers." Journal of Marriage and the Family 48: 175–186.

Halle, David. 1987. "Marriage and family life of blue-collar men." Pp. 317–337 in Naomi Gerstel and Harriet Engel Gross (eds.), Families and Work. Philadelphia: Temple University Press.

Harriman, Lynda C. 1983. "Personal and marital changes accompanying parenthood." Family Relations 32: 387–394.

Hartmann, Heidi I. 1981. "The family as the locus of gender, class, and political struggle: The example of housework." Signs 6: 366–394.

Heath, D. 1976. "Competent fathers: Their personalities and marriages." Human Development 19: 26–39.

Higginbotham, Elizabeth. 1983. "Laid bare by the system: Work and survival for black and Hispanic women." Pp. 200–215 in Amy Swerdlow and Hanna Lessinger (eds.), Class, Race, and Sex: The Dynamics of Control. Boston: G. K. Hall.

Hiller, Dana V., and William W. Philliber. 1986. "The division of labor in contemporary marriage: Expectations, perceptions, and performance." Social Problems 33: 191–201.

Hock, E., M. T. Gnezda, and S. L. McBride. 1984. "Mothers of infants: Attitudes toward employment and motherhood following birth of the first child." Journal of Marriage and the Family 46: 425–431.

Hoffman, Lois W. 1983. "Increased fathering: Effects on the mother." Pp. 167–190 in Michael E. Lamb and Abraham Sagi (eds.), Fatherhood and Family Policy. Hillsdale, NJ: Lawrence Erlbaum.

Holtzworth-Munroe, Amy, and Neil S. Jacobsen. 1985. "Causal attributions of married couples: When do they search for causes? What do they conclude when they do?" Journal of Personality and Social Psychology 48: 1398–1412.

Hood, Jane C. 1983. Becoming a Two-Job Family. New York: Praeger.

Hood, Jane C. 1986. "The provider role: Its meaning and measurement." Journal of Marriage and the Family 48: 349–359.

Hornung, Carlton A., B. C. McCullough, and Taichi Sugimoto. 1981. "Status relationships in marriage: Risk factors in spouse abuse." Journal of Marriage and the Family 43: 675–692.

Howard, Judith A., Philip Blumstein, and Pepper Schwartz. 1986. "Sex, power, and influence factors in intimate relationships." Journal of Personality and Social Psychology 51: 102–109.

Huber, Joan, and Glenna Spitze. 1983. Sex Stratification: Children, Housework, and Jobs. New York: Academic Press.

Huston, Ted L. 1982. "The topography of marriage: A longitudinal study of changes in husband-wife relationships over the first year." Paper presented at the International Conference on Personal Relationships, Madison, WI.

Huston, Ted L., and Richard D. Ashmore. 1986. "Women and men in personal relationships." Pp. 167–210 in Richard D. Ashmore and Frances K. DelBoca (eds.), The Social Psychology of Female-Male Relations: A Critical Analysis of Central Concepts. New York: Academic Press.

Jones, Jacqueline. 1985. Labor of Love, Labor of Sorrow: Black Women, Work, and the Family from Slavery to the Present. New York: Vintage Books.

Jones, L. Colette. 1985. "Father-infant relationships in the first year of life." Pp. 92–114 in Shirley M. H. Hanson and Frederick W. Bozett (eds.), Dimensions of Fatherhood. Beverly Hills, CA: Sage.

Kalmuss, Debra S., and Murray A. Straus. 1982. "Wife's marital dependency and wife abuse." Journal of Marriage and the Family 44: 277–286.

Kamo, Yoshinori. 1988. "Determinants of the household division of labor: Resources, power, and ideology." Journal of Family Issues 9: 177–200.

Kaufman, Debra R. 1985. "Women who return to orthodox Judaism: A feminist analysis." Journal of Marriage and the Family 47: 543–551.

Kelley, Harold H. 1979. Personal Relationships: Their Structure and Processes. Hillsdale, NJ: Lawrence Erlbaum.

Kessler, Ronald C., and James A. McCrae, Jr. 1982. "The effect of wives' employment on the mental health of married men and women." American Sociological Review 47: 216–227.

Kessler-Harris, Alice. 1987. "The debate over equality for women in the workplace: Recognizing differences." Pp. 520–539 in Naomi Gerstel and Harriet Engel Gross (eds.), Families and Work. Philadelphia: Temple University Press.

Kingston, Paul W., and Stephen L. Nock. 1985. "Consequences of the family work day." Journal of Marriage and the Family 47: 619–629.

Kivett, Vira R. 1988. "Older rural fathers and sons: Patterns of association and helping." Family Relations 37: 62–67.

Kollock, Peter, Philip Blumstein, and Pepper Schwartz. 1985. "Sex and power in interaction: Conversational privileges and duties." American Sociological Review 50: 34–46.

Kranichfeld, Marion L. 1987. "Rethinking family power." Journal of Family Issues 8: 42–56.

Kraus, Neal, and Kyria Markides. 1985. "Employment and psychological well-being in Mexican-American women." Journal of Health and Social Behavior 26: 15–26.

Krokoff, Lowell J. 1987. "The correlates of negative affect in marriage: An exploratory study of gender differences." Journal of Family Issues 8: 111–135.

Lamb, Michael E. 1987. The Father's Role: Cross-Cultural Perspectives. Hillsdale, NJ: Lawrence Erlbaum.

Lamb, Michael E., Joseph H. Pleck, and James A. Levine. 1986. "Effects of paternal involvement on fathers and mothers." Pp. 67–83 in Robert Lewis and Marvin Sussman (eds.), Men's Changing Roles in the Family. New York: Haworth Press.

LaRossa, Ralph. 1988. "Fatherhood and social change." Family Relations 34: 451–457.

LaRossa, Ralph, and Maureen Mulligan LaRossa. 1981. Transition to Parenthood: How Infants Change Families. Beverly Hills, CA: Sage.

Lavin, Thomas J., III. 1987. "Divergence and convergence in the causal attributions of married couples." Journal of Marriage and the Family 49: 71–80.

Lee, Gary R. 1988. "Marital intimacy among older persons: The spouse as confidant." Journal of Family Issues 9: 273–284.

Lein, Laura. 1984. Families without Villains. Lexington, MA: Lexington Books.

Littlefield, Christine H., and J. P. Rushton. 1986. "When a child dies: The sociobiology of bereavement." Journal of Personality and Social Psychology 51: 797–802.

Lockhart, Lettie L. 1987. "A reexamination of the effects of race and social class on the incidence of marital violence: A search for reliable differences." Journal of Marriage and the Family 49: 603–610.

Lopata, Helen Z. 1987. "Women's family roles in life course perspective." Pp. 381–497 in Beth B. Hess and Myra M. Ferree (eds.), Analyzing Gender: A Handbook of Social Science Research. Newbury Park, CA: Sage.

Madden, Margaret E., and Ronnie Janoff-Bulman. 1981. "Blame, control, and marital satisfaction: Wives' attributions for conflict in marriage." Journal of Marriage and the Family 43: 663–674.

Mainardi, Pat. 1978. "The politics of housework." Pp. 33–38 in A. M. Jaggar and P. R. Strube (eds.), Feminist Frameworks: Alternative Theoretical Accounts of the Relations between Women and Men. New York: McGraw-Hill.

Margolin, Gayla, and Bruce E. Wampold. 1981. "Sequential analysis of conflict and accord in distressed and nondistressed marital partners." Journal of Consulting and Clinical Psychology 49: 554–567.

Margolin, Leslie, and Lynn White. 1987. "The continuing role of physical attractiveness in marriage." Journal of Marriage and the Family 49: 21–27.

Markman, Harold. 1984. "The longitudinal study of couples' interactions: Implications for understanding and predicting the development of marital distress." Pp. 253–281 in Kurt Hahlweg and Neil Jacobson (eds.), Marital Interaction: Analysis and Modification. New York: Guilford Press.

McAdoo, John L. 1988. "Changing perspectives on the role of the black father." Pp. 79–92 In Phyllis Bronstein and Carolyn P. Cowan (eds.), Fatherhood Today: Men's Changing Role in the Family. New York: John Wiley and Sons.

McCray, Carrie A. 1980. "The black woman and family roles." Pp. 67–78 in LaFrances Rodgers-Rose (ed.), The Black Woman. Beverly Hills, CA: Sage.

McDonald, Gerald W. 1982. "Parental power perceptions in the family." Youth and Society 14: 3–31.

McKee, Lorna. 1982. "Fathers' participation in infant care: A critique." Pp. 120–138 in Lorna McKee and Margaret O'Brien (eds.), The Father Figure. London: Tavistock.

Miller, Joanne, and Howard H. Garrison. 1984. "Sex roles: The division of labor at home and in the workplace." Pp. 323–348 in David H. Olson and Brent C. Miller (eds.), Family Studies Yearbook (Vol. 2). Beverly Hills, CA: Sage.

Mirande, Alfredo. 1988. "Chicano fathers: Traditional perceptions and current realities." Pp. 93–106 in Phyllis Bronstein and Carolyn P. Cowan (eds.), Fatherhood Today: Men's Changing Role in the Family. New York: John Wiley and Sons.

Moen, Phyllis. 1982. "The two-provider family: Problems and potentials." Pp. 13–43 in Michael E. Lamb (ed.), Nontraditional Families: Parenting and Child Development. Hillsdale, NJ: Lawrence Erlbaum.

Moen, Phyllis. 1985. "Continuities and discontinuities in women's labor force activity." Pp. 113–155 in Glen H. Elder, Jr. (ed.), Life Course Dynamics: Trajectories and Transitions, 1968–1980. Ithaca, NY: Cornell University Press.

Montemayor, Raymond. 1986. "Family variation in parent-adolescent storm and stress." Journal of Adolescent Research 1: 15–31.

Morrison, Donna R., and Daniel T. Lichter. 1988. "Family migration and female employment: The problem of underemployment among migrant married women." Journal of Marriage and the Family 50: 161–172.

Mortimer, Jeylan T. 1980. "Occupation-family linkages as perceived by men in the early stages of professional and managerial careers." Pp. 90–117 in Helen Z. Lopata (ed.), Research on the Interweave of Social Roles: Women and Men (Vol. 1). Greenwich, CT: JAI Press.

Morton, Teru U. 1978. "Intimacy and reciprocity of exchange: A comparison of spouses and strangers." Journal of Personality and Social Psychology 36: 72–81.

Noller, Patricia. 1981. "Gender and marital adjustment level differences in decoding messages from spouses and strangers." Journal of Personality and Social Psychology 41: 272–278.

Noller, Patricia. 1982. "Channel consistency and inconsistency in the communications of married couples." Journal of Personality and Social Psychology 43: 732–741.

Notarius, Clifford I., and Jennifer S. Johnson. 1982. "Emotional expression in husbands and wives." Journal of Marriage and the Family 44: 483–489.

Papanek, Hanna. 1979. "Family status production: The 'work' and 'non-work' of women." Signs 4: 775–781.

Pearlin, Leonard, and Carmi Schooler. 1978. "The structure of coping." Journal of Health and Social Behavior 19: 2–21.

Peplau, Letitia A., and Steven L. Gordon. 1985. "Women and men in love: Gender differences in close heterosexual relationships." Pp. 257–291 in Virginia E. O'Leary, Rhoda K. Unger, and Barbara

S. Wallston (eds.), Women, Gender, and Social Psychology. Hillsdale, NJ: Lawrence Erlbaum Associates.

Perry-Jenkins, Maureen, and Ann C. Crouter. 1987. "'Husbands' and wives concepts of the 'provider role': Implications for men's involvement in family work." Paper presented at the annual meeting of the National Council on Family Relations, Atlanta.

Peters, Marie Ferguson. 1985. "Racial socialization of young black children." Pp. 159–173 in Harriette Pipes McAdoo and John L. McAdoo (eds.), Black Children. Beverly Hills, CA: Sage.

Piotrkowski, Chaya S., and Rena L. Repetti. 1984. "Dual-earner families." Pp. 99–124 in Beth B. Hess and Marvin B. Sussman (eds.), Women and the Family: Two Decades of Change. New York: Haworth Press.

Pleck, Joseph H. 1985. Working Wives/Working Husbands. Beverly Hills, CA: Sage.

Pleck, Joseph H. 1987. "American fathering in historical perspective." Pp. 83–97 in M. S. Kimmel (ed.), Changing Men: New Directions in Research on Men and Masculinity. Beverly Hills, CA: Sage.

Polatnick, M. Rivka. 1984. "Why men don't rear children: A power analysis." Pp. 21–40 in Joyce Trebilcot (ed.), Mothering: Essays in Feminist Theory. Totowa, NJ: Rowman and Allanheld.

Presser, Harriet B. 1987. "Work shifts of full-time dual-earner couples: Patterns and contrasts by sex of spouse." Demography 24: 99–112.

Presser, Harriet B. 1988. "Shift work and child care among young dual-earner American parents." Journal of Marriage and the Family 50: 133–148.

Ptacek, James. 1988. "Why do men batter their wives?" Pp. 133–157 in Kersti Yllo and Michele Bograd (eds.), Feminist Perspectives on Wife Abuse. Newbury Park, CA: Sage.

Radin, Norma. 1988. "Primary caregiving fathers of long duration." Pp. 127–143 in Phyllis Bronstein and Carolyn P. Cowan (eds.), Fatherhood Today: Men's Changing Role in the Family. New York: John Wiley and Sons.

Rands, Marilyn. 1983. "Changes in social networks following marital separation." Paper presented at the annual meeting of the Eastern Psychological Association, Philadelphia.

Ratcliff, Kathryn S., and Janet Bogdan. 1988. "Unemployed women: When 'social support' is not supportive." Social Problems 35: 54–63.

Raush, Harold, William Barry, Richard K. Hertel, and Mary Ann Swain. 1974. Communication, Conflict, and Marriage. San Francisco: Jossey-Bass.

Rexroat, Cynthia, and Constance Shehan. 1987. "The family life cycle and spouses' time in housework." Journal of Marriage and the Family 49: 737–750.

Risman, Barbara J., and Pepper Schwartz. 1989. Gender in Intimate Relationships: A Microstructural Approach. Belmont, CA: Wadsworth.

Rosen, Ellen I. 1987. Bitter Choices: Blue-Collar Women in and out of Work. Chicago: University of Chicago Press.

Rosenthal, Carolyn. 1985. "Kinkeeping in the familial

division of labor." Journal of Marriage and the Family 47: 965–974.

Ross, Catherine E., John Mirowsky, and Joan Huber. 1983. "Dividing work, sharing work, and in-between: Marriage patterns and depression." American Sociological Review 48: 809–823.

Rubin, Lillian B. 1976. Worlds of Pain: Life in the Working-Class Family. New York: Basic Books.

Rubin, Lillian B. 1979. Women of a Certain Age: The Midlife Search for Self. New York: Harper and Row.

Rubin, Lillian B. 1984. Intimate Strangers: Men and Women Together. New York: Harper and Row.

Ruble, Diane N., Alison S. Fleming, Lisa S. Hackel, and Charles Stangor. 1988. "Changes in the marital relationship during the transition to first time motherhood: Effects of violated expectations concerning division of household labor." Journal of Personality and Social Psychology 55: 78–87.

Rudd, Nancy M., and Patrick C. McKenry. 1986. "Family influences on the job satisfaction of employed mothers." Psychology of Women Quarterly 10: 363–372.

Ruddick, Sara. 1982. "Maternal thinking." Pp. 76–94 in Barrie Thorne and Marilyn Yalom (eds.), Rethinking the Family: Some Feminist Questions. New York: Longman.

Russell, Graeme, and Norma Radin. 1983. "Increased paternal participation: The father's perspective." Pp. 139–165 in Michael E. Lamb and Abraham Sagi (eds.), Fatherhood and Family Policy. Hillsdale, NJ: Lawrence Erlbaum.

Schafer, Robert B., and Patricia M. Keith. 1981. "Equity in marital roles across the family life cycle." Journal of Marriage and the Family 43: 359–367.

Schneider, Beth E., and Meredith Gould. 1987. "Female sexuality: Looking back into the future." Pp. 120–153 in Beth B. Hess and Myra M. Ferree (eds.), Analyzing Gender: A Handbook of Social Science Research. Newbury Park, CA: Sage.

Schooler, Carmi, Joanne Miller, Karen A. Miller, and Carol N. Richtand. 1984. "Work for the household: Its nature and consequences for husbands and wives." American Journal of Sociology 90: 97–124.

Secord, Paul F., and Kenneth Ghee. 1986. "Implications of the black marriage market for marital conflict." Journal of Family Issues 7: 21–30.

Shaw, Susan M. 1988. "Gender differences in the definition and perception of household labor." Family Relations 37: 333–337.

Silverberg, Susan B., and Laurance Steinberg. 1987. "Adolescent autonomy, parent-adolescent conflict, and parental well-being." Journal of Youth and Adolescence 16: 293–312.

Staines, Graham L., and Pam L. Libby. 1986. "Men and women in role relationships." Pp. 211–258 in Richard D. Ashmore and Frances K. DelBoca (eds.), The Social Psychology of Female-Male Relations: A Critical Analysis of Central Concepts. New York: Academic Press.

Stanley, Sandra C., Janet G. Hunt, and Larry L.

Hunt. 1986. "The relative deprivation of husbands in dual-earner households." Journal of Family Issues 7: 3–20.

Steinberg, Laurence. 1987. "Impact of puberty on family relations: Effects of pubertal status and pubertal timing." Developmental Psychology 23: 451–460.

Strube, Michael J., and Linda S. Barbour. 1984. "Factors related to the decision to leave an abusive relationship." Journal of Marriage and the Family 46: 837–844.

Szinovacz, Maximiliane E. 1984. "Changing family roles and interactions." Pp. 164–201 in Beth B. Hess and Marvin B. Sussman (eds.), Women and the Family: Two Decades of Change. New York: Haworth Press.

Thoits, Peggy A. 1987. "Negotiating roles." Pp. 11–22 in Faye J. Crosby (ed.), Spouse, Parent, Worker: On Gender and Multiple Roles. New Haven, CT: Yale University Press.

Thorne, Barrie. 1982. "Feminist rethinking of the family: An overview." Pp. 1–24 in Barrie Thorne and Marilyn Yalom (eds.), Rethinking the Family: Some Feminist Questions. New York: Longman.

Ulbrich, Patricia M. 1988. "The determinants of depression in two-income marriages." Journal of Marriage and the Family 50: 121–131.

Vuchinich, Samuel. 1987. "Starting and stopping spontaneous family conflicts." Journal of Marriage and the Family 49: 591–601.

Waldron, Holly, and Donald K. Routh. 1981. "The effects of the first child on the marital relationship." Journal of Marriage and the Family 43: 785–788.

Warner, Rebecca L. 1986. "Alternative strategies for measuring household division of labor: A comparison." Journal of Family Issues 7: 179–195.

Weiss, Robert S. 1985. "Men and the family." Family Process 24: 49–58.

Weiss, Robert S. 1987. "Men and their wives' work." Pp. 109–121 in Faye J. Crosby (ed.), Spouse, Parent, Worker: On Gender and Multiple Roles. New Haven, CT: Yale University Press.

West, Candace, and Don H. Zimmerman. 1987. "Doing gender." Gender and Society 1: 125–151.

White, James M. 1985. "Perceived similarity and understanding in married couples." Journal of Social and Personal Relationships 2: 345–357.

Williams, Doris Giles. 1988. "Gender, marriage, and psychosocial well-being." Journal of Family Issues 9: 452–468.

Willie, Charles Vert. 1988. A New Look at Black Families (3rd ed.). Dix Hills, NY: General Hall.

Wills, Thomas A., Robert L. Weiss, and Gerald R. Patterson. 1974. "A behavioral analysis of the determinants of marital satisfaction." Journal of Consulting and Clinical Psychology 42: 802–811.

Wilson, Melvin. 1986. "The black extended family: An analytical consideration." Developmental Psychology 22: 246–258.

Ybarra, Lea. 1982. "When wives work: The impact on the Chicano family." Journal of Marriage and the Family 44: 169–178.

Yllo, Kersti. 1984. "The status of women, marital equality, and violence against wives: A contextual analysis." Journal of Family Issues 5: 307–320.

Yogev, Sara. 1981. "Do professional women have egalitarian marriage relationships?" Journal of Marriage and the Family 43: 865–871.

Yogev, Sara, and Jeanne Brett. 1985. "Perceptions of the division of housework and childcare and marital satisfaction." Journal of Marriage and the Family 47: 609–618.

Zavella, Patricia. 1987. Women's Work and Chicano Families. Ithaca, NY: Cornell University Press.

Zussman, Robert. 1987. "Work and family in the new middle class." Pp. 338–346 in Naomi Gerstel and Harriet Engel Gross (eds.), Families and Work. Philadelphia: Temple University Press.

MYRA MARX FERREE   *University of Connecticut*

Beyond Separate Spheres:
Feminism and Family Research

Feminist scholars continue to stress that families are neither separate from wider systems of male domination nor automatically solidary and altruistic in their own right. However, feminist explanations of how families operate and contribute to maintaining women's subordination have shifted in the past decade from those that emphasize sex roles and socialization to those that describe processes of categorization and stratification by gender. This latter approach, called gender theory, is the central concern of this review. In the first portion of the essay, the premises of sex role theory and of gender theory are described and contrasted, and the uses of gender theory for understanding a variety of family roles are outlined. In the second section, the focus shifts to the ways that families operate to construct gender through the symbolic and structural dimensions of labor, both paid and unpaid, and through the control over income within the family. Gender models move theorizing about families away from the emphasis on dichotomies such as public or private, love or money, traditional or modern, and toward recognition of the diverse and contested nature of gender conventions both today and in the past. Rather than positing two opposite, comprehensive, consistent, and exclusive "sex roles," the new feminist theory identifies a variety of actively gendered roles that link families with other social institutions, offer rewards and costs to both women and men, and are both controversial and internally contradictory.

Department of Sociology, University of Connecticut, Storrs, CT 06269-2068.

Over the past two decades, feminist scholarship has opened up many neglected topics to intensive scholarly exploration. As other essays in this issue demonstrate, feminist thinking now informs some of the best research on violence in the family, on single-parent families, on the relation between employment and family life, and on the impact of public policy on families. Because any comprehensive review of feminist influence in family studies would be too broad to be useful, this essay instead attempts to clarify recent developments in feminist theory and to use the emerging gender model to examine paid work, housework, and the control over household income in more detail.

FEMINIST THEORY

Feminist Premises

Although feminism offers an internally diverse and sometimes divisive set of theories, attention to the differences can obscure fundamental points of agreement (Jagger, 1983; Tong, 1989). Feminists agree that male dominance within families is part of a wider system of male power, is neither natural nor inevitable, and occurs at women's cost. In contrast, much conventional research on families treats them as more or less closed units that can be understood in isolation from other social institutions, such as politics or the economy. Feminism thus challenges family studies to rethink both the separateness and the solidarity of families.

By *separateness* I mean the conventional distinction between public and private, with family as the "haven in a heartless world" (Lasch, 1977), where fundamentally different social relations prevail than in the rest of society and where the "separation of spheres" allows women a distinct and complementary role. In this bifurcated view, politics and economics have only small and indirect influences on what happens within the borders of "the" family. Instrumental activity (work), being equated only with wage-earning and usually associated only with men, is rendered invisible. Within this supposedly private domain, women take center stage, appear to have unlimited power, and are held responsible for everything—the quality of the marital relationship, the mental health of children, even for preventing male violence (cf. Caplan and Hall-McCorquodale, 1985). Feminism questions every aspect of this privatized view.

By *solidarity* I mean the conventional conceptualization of "the family" as a unitary whole, a "glued-together family" (Sen, 1983), anthropomorphically treated as if it were a single actor with a single class position, standard of living, and set of interests. The myth of a unitary "family interest" permeates conventional models even in the matters of reproduction, where the differential costs to women and men should be apparent (Folbre, 1983), and of violence, where fundamental conflicts of interest by gender and generation are disregarded (cf. Breines and Gordon, 1983; Brush, 1990). Feminism also challenges this assumption of unity.

Although 1970s feminist research began to question these mainstream assumptions, new feminist scholarship in the 1980s has both sharpened its critique and developed a new approach that (*a*) defines families as fully integrated into wider systems of economic and political power and (*b*) recognizes the diverging and sometimes conflicting interests of each member (see reviews in Baca Zinn, 1990, Glenn, 1987, Osmond and Thorne, 1990, Smith, 1987b). To appreciate the significance of this new gender model requires understanding the limitations of the sex role approach that it is intended to replace.

Feminism and Sex Roles

Because sex role was a well-established concept in conventional family studies, feminist scholars in the 1960s and '70s at first adopted this term and only criticized the normative implications of its theoretical framework. By the late 1970s, however, a variety of theoretical and empirical

problems became evident. In a trenchant critique, Lopata and Thorne (1978) noted that "sex role" was being used as a catchall term for everything from structural disadvantage to implied personality traits, even though a "role" should only imply specific behavioral prescriptions toward specified others. Supposedly dichotomous, internally consistent, and complementary, "sex roles" were presumed to be internalized early in life and expressed by individuals in a variety of social settings. The absurdity of a parallel concept, "race roles," they suggested, should alert us to the invisibility of social structure in this framework.

Connell (1985) emphasized role theory's static and ahistorical tendencies. Because role theory explains conformity as the result of sanctions applied by other individuals, its central focus is on individual socialization rather than social structures. This leads into an infinite regress: actors do unto others what was done to them, ad infinitum. Thus mothers socialize daughters to subordinate behaviors because they themselves have been socialized to them, not because they perceive the danger of insubordinate behavior in a male-dominated society. This logic replaces concrete, historically specific social structures with reified, impersonal norms, or "frozen descriptions" (Connell, 1985: 263). Even feminist descriptions of "sex roles" usually assumed that expected behavior was clear, consistent, and uniform, and they neglected evidence of contradiction and struggle (Stacey and Thorne, 1985).

Throughout the 1980s sex role theory came increasingly into question. First, the emergence of "sex role" as a unitary concept was recognized as a product of specific historical circumstances. Breines (1986) analyzed how Parsons, Riesman, and other sociologists of the 1950s reacted to actual changes in gender systems, such as the increasing education and employment of middle-class women and the loss of autonomy in middle-class men's jobs, by constructing ideal types of male and female behavior. The unity of personality traits, interpersonal behavior, and occupational choice that became crystallized in the concept "sex role" expressed this new idealization and wishfully asserted the existence of "traditional" arrangements as static and uniform, rather than as diverse and contested (cf. Pleck, 1987). Nonetheless, the ideological unity of the sex role label only temporarily disguised the weak or nonexistent empirical relationships between social statuses (i.e., nonemployed, housewife, mother), observable behaviors (i.e., expressing emotion, deferring to men), personality traits (i.e., passivity, conformity), and attitudes favoring the subordination of women (i.e., devaluation, fear of change). By the mid-1980s, the implicit unity in the concept of sex role began to dissolve (Vannoy-Hiller and Philliber, 1989).

Second, the concept of "sex role" placed within individuals what increasingly has come to be seen as an ongoing interaction between actors and structures. This critique takes seriously women's own reports of identity transformation in later life, claims such as "I am not the same person I was before I got married" (Acker, 1988). Gerson (1985) shows that many women see themselves as dramatically changing direction in adulthood, some in the direction of greater emphasis on paid work, some in turning unexpectedly toward motherhood. Structural opportunity is a better predictor than socialization for such later-life orientations. The instability of the traits and preferences that supposedly link playing with dolls and trucks with nurturing children and managing corporations increasingly led psychologists to more situational explanations of behavior (see review in Deaux and Kite, 1987).

Third, the association of socialization with early learning identified families as the primary focus of women's oppression, with sex roles acquired there thought to "spill over" into the labor market or educational system. Thus families often appear to be the one residue of tradition in a modernizing and increasingly egalitarian society, in which "traditional sex roles" could be defined as increasingly dysfunctional (e.g., Friedan, 1963). However, women in the working class and subordinated racial and ethnic groups argue that the emphasis on family as the central locus of oppression for women is misplaced (Jones, 1984; Rapp, 1982; Zavella, 1987). Families are also institutions of support and resistance for women as they confront other forms of social oppression, providing a cultural grounding for self-esteem as well as networks in which concrete resources can be traded (cf. reviews by Baca Zinn, 1990; Dill, 1988; Glenn, 1987). The sex role formulation fails to place family relationships in this wider structural context in which family ties support or undercut resistance to specific social arrangements.

In sum, the concept of "sex roles," rooted in socialization, internalized in individuals, and merely echoed in and exploited by other social institutions, cannot encompass the actual variation in men's and women's lives—individually over the life course and structurally in the historical context of race and class. The role approach also obscures the dimension of power and the ongoing processes of conflict associated with change. Feminist explorations of family relationships are therefore increasingly cast in a fundamentally different theoretical context, that of gender.

The Gender Perspective

The concept of gender emerged in the 1980s as the dominant feminist model. Joan Scott, a historian, defines gender as "a constitutive element of social relationships based on perceived differences between the sexes, and . . . a primary way of signifying relationships of power" (1986: 1067). Gender theory focuses upon how specific behaviors and roles are given gendered meanings, how labor is divided to express gender difference symbolically, and how diverse social structures—rather than just families—incorporate gender values and convey gender advantages (cf. Hess, 1989). While the sex role model *assumes* a certain packaging of structures, behaviors, and attitudes, the gender model analyzes the *construction* of such packages. Consequently, the gender perspective simultaneously emphasizes the symbolic and the structural, the ideological and the material, the interactional and the institutional levels of analysis (Smith, 1987a).

This conceptualization of gender highlights the process of the social construction of maleness and femaleness as oppositional categories with unequal social value. As Rubin (1975) argued, despite their differences, women and men are more like each other than like anything else in nature, so that the construction of gender as polarized dichotomies (reason and emotion, aggressive and nurturant, etc.) requires the suppression of natural similarities for social purposes by social means (p. 179). Because the active suppression of similarity and the construction of difference requires social power, the issue of domination is central to gender theory. While the basic dynamic of sex role theory is socialization, the central processes in the gender perspective are categorization and stratification (Reskin, 1988). The fundamental question is how the illusion of a gender dichotomy is constructed and maintained in the face of between-sex similarity and within-sex difference, and the answer is found in the constant and contentious process of en-gendering behavior as separate and unequal.

The proposition that gender is continuously being constructed and used to further a variety of individual and group goals is central to what West and Zimmerman (1987) call "doing gender," those interactional processes in which individuals claim a gender identity for themselves and convey it to others. Being a man or woman socially is not a natural or inevitable outgrowth of biological features but an achievement of situated conduct. Much of the work of doing gender is taken for granted and thus made invisible, but at boundaries and points of change these gender dynamics become open to explicit negotiation (Gerson and Peiss, 1985). Social structures provide the concrete resources and constraints that shape these ongoing interactions, and all sorts of objects and relationships, not only individual people, have gender meanings.

By separating the gender given to specific roles from the gender of the individuals who occupy them, the gender perspective provides a model for an authentically structural analysis of family relationships. Looking at parenthood, for example, Risman (1987) employs a "micro-structural" model to study men who "mother," that is, exercise primary parental responsibility on a day-to-day basis, and who come to think and behave in ways similar to women who mother. Barbara Katz Rothman (1989) discusses how new reproductive technologies allow women to be "fathers" more thoroughly than ever before; in addition to using (other) women to care for their children, (female) fathers can appropriate (other) women's labor to bear children from their "seed." She suggests that women, too, as "fathers" will devalue nurturing as unskilled contractual labor worth subminimum wages and define "mothers" as fungible service providers. Nelson (1989) finds evidence for this in the depersonalized view of child care providers expressed by their women employers but also points to the workers' view that they are more "feminine and motherly" than their employers as a sign of an active contest over the gender meaning and social value of their work.

From a gender perspective, the dynamics of categorization are closely associated with processes of stratification and social control (Reskin,

1988). The power to define is itself a means of social control, and this is evident even among children. Children—no less than adults—are actively engaged in working out the meaning of gender in response to the power relationships they perceive all around them. Joffe's (1973) study of an "alternative" preschool found that children who did not know the content of mainstream culture's stereotypes still used gender to manipulate other children's behavior (e.g., claiming that "girls can't play in sandboxes" to get other children to relinquish their place). Thorne (1986a) shows how children themselves actively structure gender into group games ("girls chase boys") and express their own group membership by adopting gender symbols (like Barbie dolls) and stigmatizing cross-gendered characteristics (like long eyelashes on boys).

Bem (1983) discusses the difficulty of raising children in what she calls a "gender-schematic" society, in which all sorts of objects and behaviors are imbued with gender meaning (cf. Paoletti, 1987, on the emergence of pink and blue as gender color codes in the 1920s). Bem illustrates her point about the "unnatural" nature of children's gender categorization in the story of her son wearing a barrette to nursery school, being confronted by a classmate who insisted he had to be a girl because "only girls wear barrettes." Her son's attempted demonstration that he was a boy "because he had a penis" was rejected by the other child: "anybody can have a penis, but only girls wear barrettes" (p. 612). Adult struggles over who or what is a "real" man or woman continue this dynamic.

Because "gender is relational and not essential, creating and recreating ourselves as gendered persons involves not a little struggle and ambivalence" (cf. Hess, 1989: 26; Connell, 1985). The internal conflict over what a "real" mother or father feels and does is one manifestation of this struggle. For example, studies of postpartum depression reveal the extensive "emotional work" that must be done by new mothers to produce socially appropriate feelings and repress inappropriate ones (Taylor and McCormick, 1989). External conflict over the meaning of motherhood can be seen in the varying evaluations of Mary Beth Whitehead, a so-called surrogate mother (Harrison, 1987), and in the controversy over a corporate "mommy track" (Schwartz, 1989); both issues highlight the importance of nonfamily power structures for family identities. Within a set of structural power relationships, the processes of categorization and resistance to categorization provide a lifelong dialectic of engendering identity.

In sum, the feminist critique of a unified and internalized "sex role" has matured into an alternative theoretical standpoint that defines gender as a lifelong process of situated behavior that both reflects and reproduces a structure of differentiation and control in which men have material and ideological advantages. The power that men (and adults, whites, employers, etc.) possess gives them certain advantages in using gender to advance and defend their interests, while gender itself associates maleness with power and authority, in and out of the family.

Gender and Family

Applying a gender perspective to families advances the feminist challenge to mainstream views of separateness and solidarity. First, because the gender system is theoretically distinguished from the particular family forms of a specific historical period, "family" is no longer seen as the primary focus of all women's oppression. The diversity of family forms by race and class, and what they offer to men and women in different economic circumstances, is explicitly recognized (Baca Zinn, 1990). Gender is, with race and class, a hierarchical structure of opportunity and oppression as well as an affective structure of identity and cohesion, and families are one of many institutional settings in which these structures become lived experience. To understand the diverse ways they structure the material conditions of people's lives, families need to be studied in relation to other political and economic institutions.

Second, attention to both the structural and ideological levels of analysis requires distinguishing between *households,* which are the coresidential units in which people empirically can be found, and *family,* the ideology of relatedness that explains who should live together, share income, and perform certain common tasks (Andersen, 1990; Rapp, 1982). An important contemporary example of the significance of distinguishing between family and household is the restructuring of family obligations and household composition after divorce. The extent to which fathers define their *family* obligation of support

as ceasing when they are no longer in the same *household* as their children is a major public policy problem, as well as a source of economic crisis for women and children in mother-only households (Arendell, 1987).

Third, understanding family cohesion as a cultural prescription rather than as a natural fact helps to clarify its role in legitimating male dominance, while also recognizing that it can sometimes be invoked to mitigate or resist male power (Hartmann, 1981). The social construct "family," like gender, needs to be analyzed historically to identify whose claims it legitimates and how (Davidoff and Hall, 1987; Folbre, 1983). Families are not articulate actors and cannot make demands, but family members can and do make claims on each other, using the ideology of family to legitimate their appeals and justify self-sacrifice (Ferree, 1984; Stack, 1989). The notion of a unitary family interest represented by husbands and fathers (e.g., Geerken and Gove, 1983: 74) serves to conceal men's particular familial interests.

Fourth, this perspective assumes that gender relations are always contentious; change is actively sought and partially accomplished in all historical periods. The gender model thus acknowledges the diversity of conventional gender arrangements historically and today (Baca Zinn, 1990; Bose, 1987b; Kimmel, 1987). Unlike "traditional sex roles," gender *conventions* are not assumed to be melting away in the light of "modernity." In place of a linear, evolutionary view of "progress," the gender perspective focuses attention on the continual struggles to maintain and change gender relations (Scott, 1986). The term *convention* conceptually acknowledges more diversity than the word *tradition*: what is unconventional for a working-class women (i.e., deferring childbearing) may be quite conventional in the middle class, while paid employment for mothers of preschool children may be less conventional for middle-class than for working-class mothers.

In sum, the development of a gender perspective reveals that the experience of gender in a family context cannot be limited to behavior within a household (DiLeonardo, 1987; but see Thompson and Walker, 1989, for an excellent review of marriage, work, and parenthood as gendered activities within households). As a system of obligation to specified others, family connects economic and kinship structures within and between households. Because these obligations and connections are deeply gendered, through processes that are historically developed in each particular culture, the interaction of gender with race and class is theoretically important (Baca Zinn, 1990). The gender perspective's attention to the boundary areas and points of conflict through time also makes greater methodological demands for historical specificity (Breines, 1986; Kimmel, 1987).

Because the gender perspective emphasizes the contingent historical construction of the link between households and the economy, much feminist research in the past decade has focused on families as the structural and symbolic place where this connection is forged, contested, and transformed in gender-specific ways (Hartmann, 1981). The issue of work, both paid and unpaid, is central to this model. As Hartmann puts it, "the creation of gender can be thought of as the creation of a division of labor between the sexes, the creation of two categories of workers who need each other" (1981: 393). Indeed, Berk (1985) considers the production of gender relations as such a major element of what families create in doing housework that she entitles her book on the division of household labor *The Gender Factory*. The relationship between labor and gender is a substantial portion of what family organizes, both in and out of the household.

The feminist attempt to analyze, rather than take for granted, the gendered nature of these work-family connections has created a new view of family, in which family-and-work is a single, historically variable, gendered system (e.g., collections by Benaria and Stimpson, 1987; Gerstel and Gross, 1987; Thorne with Yalom, 1982). Such volumes discuss how the ideology of "separate spheres" has obscured the links between work and family; these authors treat both men and women as family members and workers simultaneously, and recognize the gendered meaning and structural conditions of paid and unpaid work. Three issues that were marginal to mainstream views of families—waged work, housework, and the control over household income—emerge as central for understanding the historically specific structural context in which families construct gender in their daily operations. In the second half of this essay, these three issues are examined in

greater detail for the light they can throw on the relation of gender to work-family systems as such.

WAGED WORK AND THE PROVIDER ROLE

The mainstream view of the family assumes that men have "traditionally" been the only paid workers and that they thus "provided" for their dependents. The feminist sex role model accepted the truth of this view but argued that it was unnecessary, unhealthy, and open to change. In contrast, the new gender perspective contests the reality of this version of the past and points to the damaging consequences for sociological research and for people's lives produced by this political myth.

Gendered Views of Employment

The sociological study of paid employment has tended to focus on (male) workers only in the context of the workplace and to place both women and families on the periphery (Acker, 1988; Delphy and Leonard, 1986). With regard to workplace behavior and job attitudes, the sociological models used have typically been gendered: men are explained in terms of their jobs, women in terms of their families and their "nature" (Feldberg and Glenn, 1979). Models of family functioning have also been gendered: women are assumed to be present and available to meet the needs of other family members, so that women's paid employment is considered a social problem or strain on the family and women's economic dependence unproblematic (Acker, 1988; DeVault, 1990). Men's paid employment has been taken for granted, the demands it may place on other family members normalized, and men excused from active participation when their jobs interfere (Pleck, 1977). Sociology's gendered view of families corresponds to the "domestic code" of 1950s popular culture (Breines, 1986; Moeller, 1989).

The gender perspective's demand for greater historical accuracy challenges two key elements of the male "provider" myth. First, it recognizes that women have always contributed significantly to the household economy, including through paid employment in and out of the home. Second, it brings men's work into view as part of a gendered structure of employment that has changed significantly over time.

Rethinking Women's Employment

Detailed historical studies show that economic structure and household composition interact in determining which household members go "out to work" and which contribute in other ways—by subsistence production, industrial outwork, home-based enterprises, or petty commodity trading (Bose, 1987b; Kessler-Harris, 1982; Tilly and Scott, 1978). Research on women in industrializing areas of the Third World today shows broad similarities to patterns found a century or two before in Europe and America: daughters are an important part of the labor force, mothers tend to earn money in the shadow economy where work conditions and wages are worst, and few families are able to rely on a single "breadwinner," whether male or female, until industrialization is relatively advanced and unionization widespread (Boxer and Quataert, 1987; Matthaei, 1982; Tiano, 1987).

The gender model has been able to bring women's work out of the shadows by questioning the socially constructed definition of work itself. Even "objective" census statistics conceal assumptions about work and workers that tend to undercount women's paid employment, as Bose (1987a) shows in regard to the U.S. Census at the turn of the century and today. Deacon (1985) compares the British and Australian censuses in the political goals that made them more or less willing to count women among the employed and thus choose different ways of defining "employment." Because of the politics of counting, the extent to which recent rises in the labor force participation of married women overstate the degree of real change in women's work activities is unknown. Clearly, women's economic contributions have been substantial, despite the ideology that denies them; Rainwater (1979) estimated married women's cash contributions to the household economy as 25% at the turn of the century, which is not a great deal less than the 30% married women are estimated to earn today (Spitze, 1988).

Since women have always worked, the image of women's paid employment as a "nontraditional" activity "intruding" upon their "prior" responsibilities must be revised to reflect the fact that women's "traditional" responsibilities included providing income for the family when necessary (Beechey, 1988; Kessler-Harris, 1982).

Black women and working-class immigrant women were especially likely to be economically active (Jones, 1984; Kessler-Harris, 1982). Despite Victorian fantasies about "man the hunter" and woman at the hearth, the historical reality was that households were productive units in which all members contributed, in gender- and generationally specific ways, and in which jointly produced resources were (unequally) controlled and redistributed (Boxer and Quataert, 1987; Dwyer and Bruce, 1988). A central element of the feminist research agenda is to recover a more accurate accounting of the variation in women's economic contributions across time, place, class, race, and culture.

Rethinking Men's Employment

The second challenge to the "provider" myth lies in the recognition that the social construction of men as employees, spending a significant portion of the day away from home and bringing back a wage that could support a nonemployed family, is only a phenomenon of the late industrial era. The social association of masculinity with the role of sole provider is new, not "traditional" (Bernard, 1981; Carrigan, Connell, and Lee, 1987; Pleck, 1987). For example, a single male provider role was actively constructed through Henry Ford's family wage plan (May, 1987). This benefited an elite of skilled male autoworkers only; Ford also intentionally used their families' economic dependence to make wives into his allies in imposing work discipline. In contrast, Turbin shows how the wage work of women in the collar industry and of men in the iron industry in Troy, New York, in the early 19th century allowed each to support the other's strikes and create family traditions of labor militance (1987). It was the social construction of a blue-collar "labor aristocracy" of white men with "skilled" and secure jobs that allowed the ideology of dual spheres—a male provider and a wife at home—to become a working-class ideal, even when the reality was quite different (Hareven, 1982; Parr, 1987).

At the end of the 18th century, domesticity, rather than occupational achievement, was the ideal for middle-class men. Davidoff and Hall (1987) examine English entrepreneurial families' emphasis on the home as the ideal for both sexes. Home was where male property owners could develop and exercise the new bourgeois values of citizenship, self-development, and moral responsibility. Women, men, and children of the working class were expected to labor to make such domesticity possible. However, the interaction of family and economy soon separated middle-class men from the home. Ryan (1981) describes the making of a managerial middle class in early 19th-century New York, and the ideals of motherhood and masculinity that were constructed along with it. Because education was the new means of passing on class position, mothers became charged with the responsibility for instilling certain educational values and work habits in their sons, especially competitiveness. In effect, mothers were now expected to create the "human capital" that potential employers valued. The "self-made man" thus emerged as a new cultural ideal in the 19th century, but his making has been and remains a gendered process in which mothers and wives have clearly prescribed, supporting roles (Finch, 1983; Fowlkes, 1980; Ryan, 1981).

Consequences of the Gendered Provider Role

Recognition that the equation of masculinity with the provider role is a convention of modern industrial society throws new light on contemporary family dynamics. In the first place, it focuses attention on the nature and significance of women's paid and unpaid labor in making the "self-made man" and how this varies by class and ethnicity. Daniels (1989) and Ostrander (1984) examine the role of upper-class women as volunteers in the community, whose labor helps to legitimate the family's class position as "earned." At the other end of the economic spectrum, women's invisible and unremunerated work in "family-owned" but husband-controlled enterprises provides access to the middle class; Cuban, Korean, and Vietnamese family enterprises provide contemporary examples. In many disadvantaged groups, mothers labor in domestic service and sweatshops to keep their children in school and to make upward mobility possible (Dill, 1980; Glenn, 1985). Male professional success also depends on the status-production work of wives—what Papanek (1973) called the two-person career (cf. Finch, 1983; Fowlkes, 1980). Family structure, much invoked to explain poverty, should therefore also enter into sociological explanations of prosperity.

Second, understanding how paid employment has been constructed in industrial society as a gendered (male) form of work also helps explain why women's entry into the paid labor force could not be the panacea that feminist proponents of "role expansion" once expected (Crosby, 1987). Women who enter conventionally male-defined careers do "need a wife," as the complaint goes, because the expectations built into the structure of the job and the workplace take such a full-time support system for granted. Hunt and Hunt (1982) raise the possibility that the incorporation of women into "fast-track" professional and managerial careers can only succeed when both spouses are "husbands" who put minimal investment into family life. One way for "two-husband" families to manage is to hire a "wife," typically a woman of color and/or a new immigrant (Hertz, 1986; Hochschild, 1989). However, only a small proportion of employed married women have earnings high enough to make this feasible (Benenson, 1984).

Studies of two-income families support Hunt and Hunt's contention that sharing responsibility at home is facilitated if neither spouse places highest priority on their paid work, as may be more typical in working-class households (e.g., Hochschild, 1989; Hood, 1983). However, carrying responsibility for housework does have measurable occupational costs for men and women of all classes (Coverman, 1983; Shelton and Firestone, 1989). The kernel of truth, and hence popular appeal, in advocating a "mommy track" in the corporation (Schwartz, 1989) or rejecting feminist demands for equal opportunity in favor of special protection (Hewlett, 1986) lies in recognizing the gendered nature of the occupational system; these authors plead for accommodation to it, rather than transformation.

Finally, the development of gender theory helps to explain why the link between masculinity and the provider role is significant for two-income families today. In a majority of two-earner households, wives are supplemental earners rather than "co-providers" in their own and others' eyes (Ferree, 1988; Haas, 1986; Hood, 1986; Potuchek, 1989). Nearly half of all couples (43%) think income earning should be solely the husband's responsibility (Vannoy-Hiller and Philliber, 1989: 105). Because women's full-time year-round wages are still less than two-thirds of men's, the structural opportunity for married women to earn enough to share the provider role is limited. But when only husbands are seen as providers, only husbands are treated as entitled to the support that this role presumes (Ferree, 1984). Sharing the provider role can be threatening to men who have constructed their ideal of masculinity on this economic ground (Goode, 1982; Hunt and Hunt, 1987), so that even women who are providers lack the support systems at home for this role (Parr, 1987).

The provider role is not without its costs and conflicts. Working-class men have resisted and resented the pressure from their dependents that comes with the family wage. Luxton (1980: 67) notes how "some men see their wives as constantly nagging, forcing them to work when they hate it" and taking out their anger over their work on their wives. At the same time, conventional gender ideology rationalizes the costs of exclusive devotion to paid employment as the price of achieving masculinity (Carrigan et al., 1987; Hunt and Hunt, 1987). For women, being a sole or co-provider is often experienced as a loss of "freedom of choice" and perceived as a failure of men to live up to their "proper" role. Black women lose no matter how they handle the provider role: blamed for not providing adequately for their families, and blamed for harming men by taking the best jobs they can get (Baca Zinn, 1989; Collins, 1989).

In sum, the gendering of waged work, as well as of the provider role within the household, creates obstacles to achieving equality in both domains, since both are part of a single, interlocking system. It is not confinement in the home so much as the historically constructed structural and ideological incompatibilities between home and workplace that limit women's efforts to gain equality. Rather than defining the agenda as giving women the opportunity to add more roles and enrich their lives (to the point of exhaustion), the gender perspective views both macro and micro structures of the work-family system as in need of reform (Gerstel and Gross, 1987; Moen, 1989). Thus changes in transportation systems, home design, normal work schedules, recruitment and promotion structures, and national job creation policies join traditional demands for affordable child care, more flexible work opportunities, and enforcement of equal opportunity policies for women. Because men's jobs and career paths are gendered and built upon a structure of family support that is also gendered, changes for women

necessarily also imply changes for men, and men's reactions to change should be understood in these terms (Goode, 1982; Hunt and Hunt, 1987; Weiss, 1987).

HOUSEWORK

Housework is more than the invisible and unpaid labor that makes wage work possible (e.g., Brown, 1982). It is also gendered labor, that is, a set of culturally and historically specific tasks that convey social meanings about masculinity and femininity, and therefore about power (Berk, 1985). The gender perspective leads to an examination of both the material and the ideological dimensions of this work.

The Physical Labor of Housework

The label "housework" connects extremely diverse responsibilities. The nature of the work women do for their families in industrialized countries is quite unlike the work women do in many developing nations—hauling water, producing subsistence crops, processing raw materials—yet calling this labor "housework" has enabled development "experts" to ignore the needs of women workers and exclude their home production from calculations of GNP (Ciancanelli and Berch, 1987; Tiano, 1987). Even the history of housework in this country reveals important changes in the nature of the labor women provide (Cowan, 1983; Strasser, 1982). The physical labor of housework been reduced by technology—more by such public conveniences as running water, sewer systems, and electricity than by purely domestic products (Strasser, 1982)—but it has also been increasingly concentrated in the person of an individual "housewife" (Cowan, 1983).

What is actually to be defined as housework is a methodological morass: tasks change in content and they move between paid and unpaid labor, in and out of the home, while still being seen as "housework." This confusion arises because the apparent unity in the conceptualization of housework comes from imposing culturally shared gender categories on a historically shifting domain. Among cultures and across time there is no one thing that can be consistently defined as housework. The idea of housework as a distinctive form of labor only emerges with industrialization; it is the cultural opposite of waged work, reflecting the much older idea of a gender division of labor (Deacon, 1985; Luxton, 1980). This distinction conveys value—as when the labor done by "the farmer's wife" is categorized as supposedly unproductive "housework," thus reducing her claim on family resources (Elbert, 1987; Kleinegger, 1987).

Some scholars (e.g., Glenn, 1985; Nelson, 1988; Saraceno, 1984) highlight the continuity between the work women did at home without pay and the jobs they hold in the paid labor force. Thus, nursing service was once part of housework, became a paid occupation, and is now being transferred back into the home as unpaid labor, as hospitals respond to cost-containment pressures by sending patients home "quicker and sicker" to be cared for by family members, primarily wives, daughters, and daughters-in-law (Abel, 1986; Glazer, 1988). Glenn (1985) points out how women of color who did "housework" for pay as domestic servants are now channeled into similar cleaning and service jobs outside the private household. The definition of such jobs as dirty and demeaning, but "suited" for women of color, is significant (Rollins, 1985).

Looking at paid domestic labor from the vantage point of Asian, black, and Hispanic women illuminates the race and class dimensions of the division of household labor and the struggle over housework "between women" (Glenn, 1986; Kaplan, 1987; Rollins, 1985; Romero, 1988). The invisibility of the domestic worker's own family to the woman employer, the unbounded demands on time and energy created by the absence of any contract, the rituals of subordination demanded from domestic workers, and the absence of recognition of workers' skills are common themes in these studies. Rollins (1985) makes clear that wives who "hire help" are redistributing tasks for which their husbands continue to hold them personally accountable; this makes employers less rather than more sympathetic to their employees, since they get the credit for the quantity and quality of labor extracted from "their" domestic worker.

Along with recognizing the contributions of paid domestic workers, the gender perspective also directs attention to children as workers, whether paid or unpaid (Thorne, 1986b). Although the "role-sharing" focus of feminist sex role research formerly treated children as unim-

portant and invisible, the gender model recognizes that they may do significant quantities of unpaid labor (Goldscheider and Waite, 1989). Children contribute regularly to certain chores and may do more supplemental housework when their mothers are employed than their fathers do (Berk, 1985). Goldscheider and Waite (1989) argue for a reconceptualization of the division of labor as three-cornered, since the more children do, the less fathers contribute (and vice versa). Single mothers are especially likely to rely on children's housework (Michelson, 1985), and this may pose special problems for daughters, who are often expected to do the domestic work that their mothers cannot (Kaplan, 1987). Daughters are still more likely to be given housework than sons, and among sons and daughters who do housework, daughters do more hours of work (Berk, 1985). The nature of the tasks assigned to children still reflects cultural stereotypes of gender-appropriateness (White and Brinkerhoff, 1981).

Insofar as husbands and wives divide domestic labor, the majority of the chores fall to the wives (see reviews in Berk, 1985; Spitze, 1988; and Thompson and Walker, 1989). Women do from 70% to 80% of the total housework hours and the majority of the most frequently repeated and time-consuming chores (Berk, 1985; Huber and Spitze, 1983). Single mothers suggest that losing a husband actually *decreases* time pressures in housework (Graham, 1987; Michelson, 1985: 97). Although global self-reports show some increases in men's housework in recent years (e.g., Ferree, 1990; Ross, Mirowsky, and Huber, 1983), all time-budget studies are now too dated to test this (Coleman, 1988). These clearly need replication in the next decade, both to check trends and to include new, detailed measures of children's domestic labor.

The Symbolic Meaning of Housework

The gender perspective attempts to explain why the rise in married women's paid employment has not led to large and dramatic changes in their husbands' domestic labor (Pleck, 1985). In contrast to the predictions of the resource model, "there is no simple trade-off of wage and family work hours between wives and husbands, nor do partners allocate family work based on time availability" (Thompson and Walker, 1989: 856). It is not an economic bargain, even when it is rationalized as such (Acker, 1988). At least for some households, it seems more acceptable to do without certain amounts or kinds of unpaid labor than to have it done by the person of the "wrong" gender.

Since the gender perspective highlights the significance of rigid categorization, it directs attention to variations among married couples in the extent to which men participate in housework and how tasks are divided (Ferree, 1988; Maret and Finlay, 1984). While time-budget and task-allocation measures have primarily been used to examine changes in the *mean* proportion of housework men do, little attention has been paid to changes in the *variability* in these measures. Studies of participation in gender-stereotypical household tasks tend not to report or compare the standard deviation among subgroups, although differences in the amount of variation would indicate change in the degree of gender categorization. If variation in men's participation in housework is greater when wives hold full-time jobs, this would suggest that housework is becoming a contentious, boundary-defining issue. Hood (1983) and Hochschild (1989) suggest that different meanings given to women's paid employment increase the variability among husbands in the amount of housework they do, with some reducing their "share" to sabotage their wives' attempt to gain independence, while others increase their housework to "help her out."

Although Hochschild (1989) finds considerable struggle between husbands and wives over the symbolic meaning of housework, especially when wives are employed, other studies find that both husbands and wives seem to collaborate in creating and sustaining economically irrational, gendered expectations for housework (Berk, 1985; Thompson and Walker, 1989). Housework remains a "natural" (culturally expected and legitimate) part of being a wife, part of the "project of constructing 'proper' families" (DeVault, 1990). Thus, the quality of housework can be a symbolic reaffirmation of women as "good" wives and mothers, as our culture defines these roles (Berk, 1985: 198–211). Whereas women define their responsibility as providing enough housework to satisfy their husbands, husbands are accorded the right to criticize what wives do (Berk, 1985: 206–207; DeVault, 1990).

While resource models tend to see housework as an unmitigated "bad" that anyone with power

would avoid doing (Hood, 1983), from a gender perspective, doing housework is understood as an expression of love and care, but in unequal ways for men and women. Since housework supposedly flows out of her "natural" desire to care for her family, a woman may feel guilty about every unmet "need," while a man's contributions, however small, are a favor to her (DeVault, 1990; Luxton, 1980). In this gendered context, the reduction of time that women put into housework in the past two decades could be interpreted as a significant victory. However, it is important to study differences among women in their feelings about housework and perceptions of the division of labor as fair or not (Benin and Agostinelli, 1988; Ferree, 1987). When and how do women lower their standards for housework and challenge the equation between caring and cleaning?

The gendering of housework as female means the work also symbolizes subordination and can be either resisted or embraced for that reason (Hochschild, 1989). Housework-like chores are imposed in other institutions to instill discipline and deference (e.g., KP in the army: Wittner, 1980). The power symbolism in housework and class differences in the legitimacy of male authority in the family apparently lead working-class families to understate men's actual participation in chores, and middle-class couples to exaggerate it (Ferree, 1984; Hochschild, 1989). As Hochschild's case studies illustrate, when housework carries the meaning of subordination more than the meaning of caring, both partners in middle-class couples struggle to avoid it (cf. Hood, 1983; Goldscheider and Waite, 1989).

However, it is striking how little explicit conflict there is over housework in many families (Berk, 1985: 188). Despite the fact that wives clearly do most of the housework, even when employed full-time, only a minority (36%) express a desire to have their husbands do more (Pleck, 1985) or themselves do less (21%; Berk, 1985). Komter (1989) describes this as the result of the "hidden power" of gender ideology to suppress conflict by creating resignation, fear of disturbing the relationship, and denial of one's own feelings. In her study, legitimations of the status quo in the division of housework were made by invoking supposed differences in the characters of men and women ("he's not suited for it," "she enjoys it," etc.) as normal and right, and housework as something women just "have to get used to." Recognizing this suppression of conflict as an important power dynamic should lead scholars to look not only at "adjustment" and "satisfaction" but at their personal and emotional costs; for example, who is more likely to be depressed—employed women who are angry about how little housework their husbands do or those who are resigned to it?

In sum, the gender perspective on housework challenges three basic assumptions of resource models. First, housework is not allocated efficiently to the person with the most time to do it. Although the time demands of men's paid jobs explain some variation in the extent to which they participate in housework, even women's full-time employment does not reduce their domestic obligations equivalently. Second, housework is not necessarily something that either or both partners define as a "bad" to be avoided. Although women do not seem actually to like or enjoy housework more than men do, they often accept it as an expected element of being a wife, or the "price" of domestic harmony. Third, while differences in individual resources within the family influence the allocation of housework, gender influences it more: women from outside the household are hired, daughters are given more housework than sons, and employed women reduce their own housework more easily than they seek or obtain increases in their husbands' contributions.

The gender perspective points to the symbolic construction of housework as "women's work" and as an expression of both love and subordination. This explains, as economic models fail to do, why women and men so often collaborate to maintain a system that objectively imposes unequal burdens on women. It could potentially begin to explain variation here as well, indicating ways in which the gender division of labor is *not* consistent and consensual. Conflict over housework might even be a good sign, indicating women's growing sense of entitlement to a more equal division of labor at home rather than a failure of "adjustment" to a power-imbalanced status quo.

INDIVIDUAL WAGES AND HOUSEHOLD INCOME

Since modern economic systems revolve around wages, control over a wage—in particular, the ability to command a wage adequate to meet household subsistence needs—is essential for family survival. Because wages are earned by individuals and redistributed to other family members, both within and across households (Rapp, 1982; Stack, 1974), money is a significant source of family power. However, both neoclassical and Marxist economic theorists lost interest in seeing what actually happened to money once it entered the supposedly private household (Folbre, 1988). Cracking the boundaries of the family "sphere" has meant an increased recognition of how money moves into and within households and the significance of which person(s) earns, controls, redistributes, and spends it (Bergmann, 1986). The gender perspective suggests that the actual control over money and how it is used are important dimensions of power inside the household, and that gendered family norms are essential to understanding these dynamics.

Controlling Money

Earning money is not the same thing as controlling income (Blumberg, 1988). The increase in women's earnings and the decline in married women's economic dependency over the past few decades have been impressive (Sorenson and McLanahan, 1987). But while this trend has certainly contributed to increasing women's family power (Bergmann, 1986), a woman's status in the rest of society remains crucial for her ability to control even her own income (Acker, 1988). Although it seems evident that gendered ideas about family obligation guide the sharing of individual income within and between households, surprisingly little attention has been paid to money transactions among family members. The discovery of just how much money matters is one of the most exiting frontiers in feminist family scholarship today.

In the first place, recognition of the existence of conflicts over allocation of goods within families makes the very concept of "family income" problematic. Even within the same household, family members do not necessarily share the same standard of living (Pahl, 1980). In developing nations, this can produce differential mortality and malnutrition for girls and women (Dwyer and Bruce, 1988); increasing household income exacerbates these differentials, since boys and men get more of the increase (Blumberg, 1988; Sen, 1983). Policies that raise women's income do more to improve the nutrition of children in their families than those that increase the income of male family members (Blumberg, 1988; Dwyer and Bruce, 1988).

Few studies have been done of the intrahousehold economy in highly industrialized, affluent nations, but the limited evidence indicates gender differences in allocational rules and outcomes for everything from meat at meals (Charles and Kerr, 1987) to pocket money for personal expenditure (Wilson, 1987). Jan Pahl (1980) led the way in exploring this issue when she found women whose "family incomes" dropped substantially after leaving a battering spouse were reporting that their income "really" rose. The premise that family income is shared equally among all members is clearly wrong in these families and doubtful in others; to some unknown extent, poverty among women and children is disguised by their residing in a household with a man whose "adequate" income is not being shared with them (Pahl, 1980; cf. Brannen and Wilson, 1987).

Second, household allocation systems are being studied for how they incorporate and express gender. Pahl (1983) finds that wives are most likely to have financial control at the lowest absolute income levels, where money management means "allocating shortages" and forestalling creditors; when income is high enough to allow a surplus, husbands typically control it (Brannen and Wilson, 1987; Zelizer, 1989). Not all of men's earnings go into a common pot; gender norms still demand that men have "spending money," no matter how tight things are. In addition, raises and bonuses are often seen by men as "their" money that might or might not get put into the household budget (Zelizer, 1989). All monies that enter the household are not equal, but carry normative meanings that allow them to be earmarked; thus, "women's" money often goes for child care or is labeled "pin money" and kept out of the household budget (Zelizer, 1989).

Evidence from developing countries (Dwyer and Bruce, 1988) about men's propensity to spend money on themselves and women's tendency to use their "personal" money to buy things for their children (from shoes to college) has not yet been followed up by systematic empirical research in the United States (but see Gerson and Andrews, 1990, on gender and spending on food). Even though women do the work of consumption, they do not necessarily control the priorities that guide it (Blumberg, 1988; Weinbaum and Bridges,

1976). Nonetheless, large-scale economic surveys in the United States continue to treat households as economic black boxes, forcing investigators to make unrealistic assumptions about equal distribution.

Considerably more work on what happens to women's and men's money once it enters a household is desperately needed. Social policy continues to be driven by the implausible assumptions that all family members are equally well-off, that above-poverty-line household incomes imply no below-poverty-level individuals within them, and that increasing total family income has the same effect if it derives from a rise in male or female income (Acker, 1988; Blumberg, 1988). When individual income is redistributed to family members in two or more households, as in child support payments after divorce, gross inequities appear (Arendell, 1987; Weitzman, 1985). Gender and generational inequities within one household are probably less, but we have no reason to believe they are not real and consequential.

Family Bargaining

Wage-earning is an important source of family power for contemporary women, even though such power is undercut by legal structures and social norms that give women less claim on money they earn (Blumberg and Coleman, 1989; Folbre, 1988; Weitzman, 1990). Since gendered expectations about housework and childrearing mean that the cost of "replacement" domestic services and child care will be "deducted" from women's earnings rather than men's (Brannen and Moss, 1987; Parr, 1987; Zelizer, 1989), already unequal wages are more unequal in their impact on family entitlements. When and how women use their position as income-earners to improve their position within the family are questions that are only beginning to receive the empirical investigation they deserve (e.g., Hertz, 1990; Weitzman, 1990).

The theoretical model of "new home economics" suggests that such bargaining can be understood by treating the family as a two-person firm in which market transactions occur "in an imagined way at imagined prices and imagined wages" (Sen, 1983: 17). This produces an idealized account of the good of the whole emerging from self-interested calculations in which all current social constraints are taken as givens (Acker, 1988; England, 1989). Thus, when women get less, this can be (tautologically) explained by noting that they are "worth" less outside the household; this rationalizes inequality rather than acknowledging that family members also discriminate and act unjustly.

The gender perspective suggests an alternative approach in which bargaining is seen as a process that carries gender meanings. Curtis (1986) and England (1989) point out women's economic disadvantages if they follow social rules (and value connection) but trade with partners who follow market rules (and seek only personal advantage). Although marriage norms often define social rules as applying to both husbands and wives, by gender norms, women are defined as social-rule followers and men as market-rule driven. This may now be changing, as women recognize their disadvantage under the "double standard" of exchange (Curtis, 1986) and as market models become more generally legitimate in regulating personal relationships (DiLeonardo, 1987; Hunt and Hunt, 1982).

Sen (1983) suggests a model of "cooperative conflict" in which active bargaining over the choice among a set of equally efficient cooperative arrangements takes place within changing societal parameters. In each marriage, some set of (gendered) social and market rules are chosen for a reason other than efficiency. Thus, a cooperative conflict approach tries to define the conditions under which reciprocity and altruism emerge, rather than insisting that they are always or never characteristic of families (DiLeonardo, 1987; Folbre, 1983), and suggests that conflict over the nature of the rules themselves, not merely their application, underlies marital bargaining processes. When and how spouses apply particular rules of evaluation, and what the women and men gain and lose thereby, deserves further investigation.

In sum, as Hartmann (1981) points out, the family is a locus of struggle, not of uncontested male power. The image of a unitary "family income" disguises the continued significance of money in this process. Differences in gender and generational interests within the household are important, and control over income after it enters a household still matters. The limited research to date suggests that there is an internal allocation process that produces unequal outcomes for individual family members, depending on generation and gender, and that it is conditioned by the societal allocation of power and value outside the household. Because of the gender meanings of income and bargaining, the extent to which women's income earning increases their power and decreases dependency is not directly proportional to their wage levels.

CONCLUSIONS

The new gender perspective has shifted emphasis away from socialization and toward processes of categorization and stratification. Gender models also explicitly theorize the connection between structural and ideological levels of analysis. The family, as a cultural system of obligation, a "tangle of love and domination," is distinguished from the household, a locus of labor and economic struggle. Neither families nor households can be conceptualized as separate or solidary "spheres" of distinctive relationships; both family and household are ever more firmly situated in their specific historical context, in which they take on diverse forms and significance. Race and class are understood as significant structural features underlying the diversity of family forms (Baca Zinn, 1990). Although specific family roles are gendered, the phrase "gender role" is a theoretical self-contradiction, for there is no distinct and dichotomous "role" that uniquely embodies the variety of gender norms and meanings.

Gendered kinship relationships are not just dependent variables, affected by economic structures, although they are that, too. Rather, gendered family ties exert an independent influence upon the structure of work opportunities, definitions of skill, and wages received for both women and men. Indeed, in this new view, men as family members become far more visible than ever before. Rather than insisting on a dichotomous view of families as either solidary or oppressive, the gender model suggests that family relationships may be altruistic, or self-seeking, or carry an inseparable mix of motivations; that they may be simultaneously supportive and oppressive for women in relation to diverse others; that there is not one dimension of family power, but many (Blumberg and Coleman, 1989).

Because gender theory highlights both categorization and stratification as important dynamics, analyzing struggle over gender within families requires a more political vocabulary.

Creative borrowing of ideas from studies of the workplace (e.g., "contested terrain" in Elbert, 1987) and politics (e.g., the "third dimension of power" in Komter, 1989) can help to understand gender stratification processes within the family context. In a gender model, women as individual actors, agents with interests that are distinctive and meaningful, emerge out of history's shadows. Children as actors, negotiating identities, doing work (paid and unpaid), and contending for power, can be better conceptualized in this framework as well (Thorne, 1986b). The feminist perspective redefines families as arenas of gender and generational struggles, crucibles of caring and conflict, where claims for an identity are rooted, and separateness and solidarity are continually created and contested. Using a gender perspective to shatter such artificial dichotomies as work and home, money and love, self-interest and altruism, as well as their conventional associations with masculinity and femininity, may now begin to move family studies beyond separate spheres.

NOTE

Thanks are extended to Linda Haas, Beth Hess, Mary Alice Neubeck, Marie Withers Osmond, Jane Riblett Wilkie, Maxine Baca Zinn, all the members of the Women and Work Group, and two anonymous reviewers for their many helpful suggestions, and to the National Science Foundation, Grant No. SES 88-11944, which provided some support for the preparation of this article.

REFERENCES

Abel, Emily. 1986. "Adult daughters and care for the elderly." Feminist Studies 12: 479–493.

Acker, Joan. 1988. "Class, gender, and the relations of distribution." Signs 13: 473–497.

Andersen, Margaret. 1990. "Feminism and the American family ideal." Journal of Comparative Family Studies. Forthcoming.

Arendell, Terry. 1987. "Women and the economics of divorce in the contemporary United States." Signs 13: 121–135.

Baca Zinn, Maxine. 1989. "Family, race and poverty in the eighties." Signs 14: 856–874.

Baca Zinn, Maxine. 1990. "Family, feminism and race in America." Gender and Society 4: 68–82.

Beechey, Veronica. 1988. "Rethinking the definition of work: Gender and work." In J. Jenson, E. Hagen, and C. Reddy (eds.), Feminization of the Labor Force. New York: Oxford University Press.

Bem, Sandra. 1983. "Gender-schema theory and its implications for child development." Signs 8: 598–616.

Benenson, Harold. 1984. "Women's occupational and family achievement in the U.S. class system." British Journal of Sociology 35: 19–41.

Beneria, Lourdes, and Catherine Stimpson (eds.). 1987. Women, Households, and the Economy. New Brunswick, NJ: Rutgers University Press.

Benin, Mary, and Joan Agostinelli. 1988. "Husbands' and wives' satisfaction with the division of labor." Journal of Marriage and the Family 50: 349–361.

Bergmann, Barbara. 1986. The Economic Emergence of Women. New York: Basic Books.

Berk, Sarah Fenstermaker. 1985. The Gender Factory: The Apportionment of Work in American Households. New York: Plenum.

Bernard, Jessie. 1981. "The good provider role: Its rise and fall." American Psychologist 36: 1–12.

Blumberg, Rae Lesser. 1988. "Income under female versus male control: Hypotheses from a theory of gender stratification and data from the Third World." Journal of Family Issues 9: 51–84.

Blumberg, Rae Lesser, and Marion Coleman. 1989. "A theoretical look at the gender balance of power in American couples." Journal of Family Issues 10: 225–250.

Bose, Christine. 1987a. "Devaluing women's work: The undercount of women's employment in 1900 and 1980." In C. Bose, R. Feldberg, and N. Sokoloff (eds.), Hidden Aspects of Women's Work. New York: Praeger.

Bose, Christine. 1987b. "Dual spheres." In Beth Hess and Myra Marx Ferree (eds.), Analyzing Gender. Beverly Hills, CA: Sage.

Boxer, Marilyn, and Jean Quataert. 1987. Connecting Spheres: Women in the Western World, 1500 to the Present. New York: Oxford University Press.

Brannen, Julia, and Peter Moss. 1987. "Dual earner households: Women's contributions after the birth of the first child." In Julia Brannen and Gail Wilson (eds.), Give and Take in Families: Studies in Resource Distribution. Boston: Allen and Unwin.

Brannen, Julia, and Gail Wilson (eds.). 1987. Give and Take in Families: Studies in Resource Distribution. Boston: Allen and Unwin.

Breines, Wini. 1986. "The 1950s: Gender and some social science." Sociological Inquiry 56: 69–92.

Breines, Wini, and Linda Gordon. 1983. "The new scholarship on family violence." Signs 8: 490–531.

Brown, Clair Vickery. 1982. "Home production for use in a market economy." In Barrie Thorne with Marilyn Yalom (eds.), Rethinking the Family: Some Feminist Questions. New York: Longman.

Brush, Lisa D. 1990. "Violent acts and injurious outcomes in married couples." Gender and Society 4: 56–67.

Caplan, Paula, and Ian Hall-McCorquodale. 1985. "Mother-blaming in major clinical journals." American Journal of Orthopsychiatry 55: 345–357.

Carrigan, Tim, Bob Connell, and John Lee. 1987. "Toward a new sociology of masculinity." In Harry Brod (ed.), The Making of Masculinities. Boston: Unwin Hyman.

Charles, Nicola, and Marion Kerr. 1987. "Just the way

it is: Gender and age differences in food consumption." In Julia Brannen and Gail Wilson (eds.), Give and Take in Families: Studies in Resource Distribution. Boston: Allen and Unwin.

Ciancanelli, Penelope, and Bettina Berch. 1987. "Gender and the GNP." In Beth Hess and Myra Marx Ferree (eds.), Analyzing Gender. Beverly Hills, CA: Sage.

Coleman, Marion Tolbert. 1988. "The division of household labor: Suggestions for future empirical consideration and theoretical development." Journal of Family Issues 9: 132–147.

Collins, Patricia Hill. 1989. "A comparison of two works on black family life." Signs 14: 275–284.

Connell, Robert W. 1985. "Theorizing gender." Sociology 19: 260–272.

Coverman, Shelley. 1983. "Gender, domestic labor time, and wage inequality." American Sociological Review 48: 623–637.

Cowan, Ruth Schwartz. 1983. More Work for Mother. New York: Basic Books.

Crosby, Faye (ed.). 1987. Spouse, Parent, Worker. New Haven, CT: Yale University Press.

Curtis, Richard. 1986. "Household and family in theory on inequality." American Sociological Review 51: 168–183.

Daniels, Arlene Kaplan. 1989. Invisible Careers: Women Civic Leaders. Chicago: University of Chicago Press.

Davidoff, Lenore, and Catherine Hall. 1987. Family Fortunes: Men and Women of the English Middle Class, 1780–1850. Chicago: University of Chicago Press.

Deacon, Desley. 1985. "Political arithmetic: The nineteenth century Australian census and the construction of the dependent woman." Signs 11: 27–47.

Deaux, Kay, and Mary Kite. 1987. "Thinking about gender." In Beth Hess and Myra Marx Ferree (eds.), Analyzing Gender. Beverly Hills, CA: Sage.

Delphy, Christine, and Diane Leonard. 1986. "Class analysis, gender analysis and the family." In Rosemary Crompton and Michael Mann (eds.), Gender and Stratification. New York: Basil Blackwell.

DeVault, Marjorie. 1990. "Conflict over housework: A problem that (still) has no name." In L. Kriesberg (ed.), Research in Social Movements, Conflict, and Change. Greenwich, CT: JAI Press.

DiLeonardo, Micaela. 1987. "The female world of cards and holidays: Women, families, and the work of kinship." Signs 12: 440–453.

Dill, Bonnie Thornton. 1988. "Our mothers' grief: Racial/ethnic women and the maintenance of families." Journal of Family History 13: 415–431.

Dwyer, Judith, and Daisy Bruce (eds.). 1988. A Home Divided: Women and Income in the Third World. Stanford, CA: Stanford University Press.

Elbert, Sarah. 1987. "The farmer takes a wife: Women in America's farming families." In Lourdes Beneria and Catherine Stimpson (eds.), Women, Households, and the Economy. New Brunswick, NJ: Rutgers University Press.

England, Paula. 1989. "Rational choice models and feminist critiques: Implications for sociology." American Sociologist 20: 14–28.

Feldberg, Roslyn, and Evelyn Nakano Glenn. 1979. "Male and female: Job versus gender models in the sociology of work." Social Problems 26: 5524–5538.

Ferree, Myra Marx. 1984. "The view from below: Women's employment and gender equality in working class families." In Beth Hess and Marvin Sussman (eds.), Women and the Family: Two Decades of Change. New York: Haworth Press.

Ferree, Myra Marx. 1987. "The struggles of superwoman." In C. Bose, R. Feldberg, and N. Sokoloff (eds.), Hidden Aspects of Women's Work. New York: Praeger.

Ferree, Myra Marx. 1988. "Negotiating household roles and responsibilities: Resistance, conflict, and change." Paper presented at annual meeting of the National Council on Family Relations.

Ferree, Myra Marx. 1990. "The gender division of labor in two-earner marriages: Dimensions of variability and change." Paper presented at the annual meeting of the Eastern Sociological Society.

Finch, Janet. 1983. Married to the Job: Wives' Incoporation into Men's Work. London: Allen and Unwin.

Folbre, Nancy. 1983. "Of patriarchy born: The political economy of fertility decisions." Feminist Studies 9: 261–284.

Folbre, Nancy. 1988. "The black four of hearts: Toward a new paradigm of household economics." In Judith Dwyer and Daisy Bruce, A Home Divided: Women and Income in the Third World. Stanford, CA: Stanford University Press.

Fowlkes, Martha. 1980. Behind Every Successful Man. New York: Columbia University Press.

Friedan, Betty. 1963. The Feminine Mystique. New York: Dell.

Geerken, Michael, and W. Gove. 1983. At Home and at Work. Beverly Hills, CA: Sage.

Gerson, Judith, and Margaret Andrews. 1990. "Household food budgets: Analyzing familial resources and power." Paper presented at the annual meeting of the Eastern Sociological Society.

Gerson, Judith, and Kathy Peiss. 1985. "Boundaries, negotiations, consciousness: Reconceptualizing gender relations." Social Problems 32: 317–331.

Gerson, Kathleen. 1985. Hard Choices. Berkeley: University of California Press.

Gerstel, Naomi, and Harriet Engel Gross (eds.). 1987. Families and Work. Philadelphia: Temple University Press.

Glazer, Nona. 1988. "Overlooked, overworked: Women's unpaid and paid work in the health services' 'cost crisis'." International Journal of Health Services 18: 119–137.

Glenn, Evelyn Nakano. 1985. "Racial ethnic women's labor: The intersection of race, gender, and class oppression." Review of Radical Political Economics 17: 86–109.

Glenn, Evelyn Nakano. 1986. Issei, Nisei, Warbride. Philadelphia: Temple University Press.

Glenn, Evelyn Nakano. 1987. "Gender and the family." In Beth Hess and Myra Marx Ferree (eds.),

Analyzing Gender. Beverly Hills, CA: Sage.

Goldscheider, Frances, and Linda Waite. 1989. "The domestic economy: Husbands, wives, children." Paper presented at annual meeting of the American Sociological Association.

Goode, William J. 1982. "Why men resist." In Barrie Thorne with Marilyn Yalom (eds.), Rethinking the Family: Some Feminist Questions. New York: Longman.

Graham, Hilary. 1987. "Being poor: Perceptions and strategies of lone mothers." In Julia Brannen and Gail Wilson (eds.), Give and Take in Families: Studies in Resource Distribution. Boston: Allen and Unwin.

Haas, Linda. 1986. "Wives' orientation to breadwinning." Journal of Family Issues 7: 358–381.

Hareven, Tamara. 1982. Family Time and Industrial Time. Cambridge, MA: Harvard University Press.

Harrison, Michelle. 1987. "Social construction of Mary Beth Whitehead." Gender and Society 1: 300–311.

Hartmann, Heidi. 1981. "The family as the locus of gender, class, and political struggle: The example of housework." Signs 6: 366–394.

Hertz, Rosanna. 1986. More Equal than Others. Berkeley: University of California Press.

Hertz, Rosanna. 1990. "Financial arrangements among dual-earner couples." Paper presented at the annual meeting of the American Sociological Association.

Hess, Beth B. 1989. "Beyond dichotomy: Making distinctions and recognizing differences." Presidential address at the annual meeting of the Eastern Sociological Society.

Hewlett, Sylvia. 1986. A Lesser Life. New York: Morrow.

Hochschild, Arlie, with Anne Machung. 1989. The Second Shift. New York: Viking.

Hood, Jane. 1983. Becoming a Two-Job Family. New York: Praeger.

Hood, Jane. 1986. "The provider role: Its meaning and measurement." Journal of Marriage and the Family 48: 349–359.

Huber, Joan, and Glenna Spitze. 1983. Sex Stratification: Children, Housework, Jobs. New York: Academic Press.

Hunt, Janet, and Larry Hunt. 1987. "Male resistance to role symmetry in dual-earner households." In Naomi Gerstel and Harriet Engel Gross (eds.), Families and Work. Philadelphia: Temple University Press.

Hunt, Janet, and Larry Hunt. 1982. "The dualities of careers and families: New integrations or new polarizations?" Social Problems 29: 499–510.

Jagger, Alison. 1983. Feminist Politics and Human Nature. Totowa, NJ: Rowman and Allenheld.

Joffe, Carol. 1973. "Taking young children seriously." In Norman Denzin (ed.), Children and Their Caretakers. New Brunswick, NJ: Transaction Books.

Jones, Jacqueline. 1984. Labor of Love, Labor of Sorrow: Black Women, Work, and Family from Slavery to the Present. New York: Basic Books.

Kaplan, Elaine Bell. 1987. " 'I don't do no windows': Competition between the domestic worker and the housewife." In Valerie Miner and Helen Longino (eds.), Competition: A Feminist Taboo? New York: Feminist Press.

Kessler-Harris, Alice. 1982. Out to Work: A History of Wage-Earning Women in the United States. New York: Oxford University Press.

Kimmel, Michael. 1987. "The contemporary crisis of 'masculinity' in historical perspective." In Harry Brod (ed.), The Making of Masculinities. Boston: Unwin Hyman.

Kleinegger, Christine. 1987. "Out of the barns and into the kitchens." In Barbara D. Wright et al. (eds.), Women, Work, and Technology. Ann Arbor: University of Michigan Press.

Komter, Aafke. 1989. "Hidden power in marriage." Gender and Society 3: 187–216.

Lasch, Christopher. 1977. Haven in a Heartless World. New York: Basic Books.

Lopata, Helena, and Barrie Thorne. 1978. "On the term 'sex roles'." Signs 3: 718–721.

Luxton, Meg. 1980. More than a Labour of Love: Three Generations of Women's Work in the Home. Toronto: Women's Press.

Maret, Elizabeth, and Barbara Finlay. 1984. "The distribution of household labor among women in dual earner families." Journal of Marriage and the Family 46: 357–364.

Matthaei, Julie. 1982. An Economic History of Women in America. New York: Schocken Books.

May, Martha. 1987. "The historical problem of the family wage: The Ford Motor Company and the five-dollar day." In Naomi Gerstel and Harriet Engel Gross (eds.), Families and Work. Philadelphia: Temple University Press.

Michelson, William. 1985. From Sun to Sun. Totowa, NJ: Rowman and Allenheld.

Moeller, Robert. 1989. "Reconstructing the family in reconstruction Germany: Women and social policy, 1949–55." Feminist Studies 15: 137–169.

Moen, Phyllis. 1989. Working Parents. Madison: University of Wisconsin Press.

Nelson, Margaret. 1988. "Providing family daycare: An analysis of home-based work." Social Problems 35: 78–94.

Nelson, Margaret. 1989. "Negotiating care: Relationships between family daycare providers and mothers." Feminist Studies 15: 7–34.

Osmond, Marie Withers, and Barrie Thorne. 1990. "Feminist theories: The social construction of gender in families and society." In Pauline Boss et al. (eds.), Sourcebook of Family Theories and Methods. New York: Plenum.

Ostrander, Susan. 1984. Women of the Upper Class. Philadelphia: Temple University Press.

Pahl, Jan. 1980. "Patterns of money management within marriage." Journal of Social Policy 9: 313–335.

Pahl, Jan. 1983. "The allocation of money and the structuring of inequality within marriage." Sociological Review 31: 237–262.

Paoletti, Jo. 1987. "Clothing and gender in America, 1890–1920." Signs 13: 136–143.

Papanek, Hanna. 1973. "Men, women, and work: Reflections on the two-person career." In Joan Huber (ed.), Changing Women in a Changing Society. Chicago: University of Chicago Press.

Parr, Joy. 1987. "Re-thinking work and kinship in a Canadian hosiery town, 1910–1950." Feminist Studies 13: 137–162.

Pleck, Joseph. 1977. "The work-family role system." Social Problems 24: 417–427.

Pleck, Joseph. 1985. Working Wives/Working Husbands. Beverly Hills, CA: Sage.

Pleck, Joseph. 1987. "The theory of male sex role identity: Its rise and fall, 1936 to the present." In Harry Brod (ed.), The Making of Masculinities. Boston: Allen and Unwin.

Potucheck, Jean. 1989. "Employed wives' orientation to the breadwinner role." Paper presented at the annual meeting of the American Sociological Association.

Rainwater, Lee. 1979. "Mothers' contribution to the family money economy in Europe and the United States." Journal of Family History 4: 198–211.

Rapp, Rayna. 1982. "Family and class in contemporary America." In Barrie Thorne with Marilyn Yalom (eds.), Rethinking the Family: Some Feminist Questions. New York: Longman.

Reskin, Barbara. 1988. "Bringing the men back in: Sex differentiation and the devaluation of women's work." Gender and Society 2: 58–81.

Risman, Barbara. 1987. "Intimate relationships from a micro-structural perspective: Men who mother." Gender and Society 1: 6–32.

Rollins, Judith. 1985. Between Women. Philadelphia: Temple University Press.

Romero, Mary. 1988. "Sisterhood and domestic service: Race, class, and gender in the mistress-maid relationship." Humanity and Society 12: 318–346.

Ross, Catherine, John Mirowsky, and Joan Huber. 1983. "Dividing work, sharing work, and in-between." American Sociological Review 48: 809–823.

Rothman, Barbara Katz. 1989. "Women as fathers: Motherhood and childcare under a modified patriarchy." Gender and Society 3: 89–104.

Rubin, Gayle. 1975. "The traffic in women: Notes on the 'political economy' of sex." In R. Reiter (ed.), Toward an Anthropology of Women. New York: Monthly Review Press.

Ryan, Mary. 1981. Cradle of the Middle Class: Family in Oneida County, New York, 1790–1865. New York: Cambridge University Press.

Saraceno, Chiara. 1984. "Shifts in public and private boundaries: Women as mothers and service workers in Italian daycare." Feminist Studies 10: 7–30.

Schwartz, Felice. 1989. "Management women and the new facts of life." Harvard Business Review 67: 65–76.

Scott, Joan. 1986. "Gender: A useful category of historical analysis." American Historical Review 91: 1053–1075.

Sen, Amartya. 1983. "Economics and the family." Asian Development Review 1: 14–26.

Shelton, Beth Anne, and Juanita Firestone. 1989. "Household labor time and the gender gap in earnings." Gender and Society 3: 105–112.

Smith, Dorothy. 1987a. The Everyday World as Problematic. Boston: Northeastern University Press.

Smith, Dorothy. 1987b. "Women's inequality and the family." In Naomi Gerstel and Harriet Engel Gross (eds.), Families and Work. Philadelphia: Temple University Press.

Sorenson, Annemette, and Sarah McLanahan. 1987. "Married women's economic dependency, 1940–1980." American Journal of Sociology 93: 659–687.

Spitze, Glenna. 1988. "Women's employment and family relations: A review." Journal of Marriage and the Family 50: 595–618. [Reprinted in this volume]

Stacey, Judith, and Barrie Thorne. 1985. "The missing feminist revolution in sociology." Social Problems 32: 301–316.

Stack, Carol. 1974. All Our Kin. New York: Harper and Row.

Stack, Carol. 1989. "Kinscripts." Paper delivered at the conference, Status Passages and Risks in a Life Course Perspective, University of Bremen, West Germany.

Strasser, Susan. 1982. Never Done: A History of American Housework. New York: Pantheon.

Taylor, Verta, and Kelly McCormick. 1989. "Breaking the emotional rules of motherhood: The experience of postpartum depression." Paper presented at the annual meeting of the American Sociological Association.

Thompson, Linda, and Alexis Walker. 1989. "Gender in families: Women and men in marriage, work, and parenthood." Journal of Marriage and the Family 51: 845–871. [Reprinted in this volume]

Thorne, Barrie. 1986a. "Girls and boys together . . . but mostly apart: Gender arrangements in elementary schools." In W. Hartup and Z. Rubin (eds.), Relationships and Development. Hillsdale, NJ: Erlbaum.

Thorne, Barrie. 1986b. "Re-visioning women and social change: Where are the children?" Gender and Society 1: 85–109.

Thorne, Barrie, with Marilyn Yalom (eds.). 1982. Rethinking the Family: Some Feminist Questions. New York: Longman.

Tiano, Susan. 1987. "Gender, work, and world capitalism: Third World women's role in development." In Beth Hess and Myra Marx Ferree (eds.), Analyzing Gender. Beverly Hills, CA: Sage.

Tilly, Louise, and Joan Scott. 1978. Women, Work, and Family. New York: Holt, Rinehart and Winston.

Tong, Rosemarie. 1989. Feminist Thought: A Comprehensive Introduction. San Francisco: Westview.

Turbin, Carole. 1987. "Reconceptualizing family, work, and labor organizing: Working Women in Troy, 1860–1890." In C. Bose, R. Feldberg, and N. Sokoloff (eds.), Hidden Aspects of Women's Work. New York: Praeger.

Vannoy-Hiller, Dana, and William Philliber. 1989. Equal Partners. Beverly Hills, CA: Sage.

Weinbaum, Batya, and Amy Bridges. 1976. "The other side of the paycheck: Monopoly capital and the structure of consumption." Monthly Review 28(3): 88–103.

Weiss, Robert. 1987. "Men and their wives' work." In

Faye Crosby (ed.), Spouse, Parent, Worker. New Haven, CT: Yale University Press.

Weitzman, Lenore. 1985. The Divorce Revolution. New York: Free Press.

Weitzman, Lenore. 1990. "Legal rules vs. norms of justice: The allocation of money and property in the family." Paper presented at the annual meeting of the American Sociological Association.

West, Candace, and Don Zimmerman. 1987. "Doing gender." Gender and Society 1: 125–151.

White, Lynn, and David Brinkerhoff. 1981. "The sexual division of labor: Evidence from childhood." Social Forces 60: 170–181.

Wilson, Gail. 1987. "Money: Patterns of responsibility and irresponsibility in marriage." In Julia Brannen and Gail Wilson (eds.), Give and Take in Families: Studies in Resource Distribution. Boston: Allen and Unwin.

Wittner, Judith. 1980. "Domestic labor as work discipline." In Sarah Fenstermaker Berk (ed), Women and Household Labor. Beverly Hills, CA: Sage.

Zavella, Patricia. 1987. Women's Work and Chicano Families. Ithaca, NY: Cornell University Press.

Zelizer, Viviana. 1989. "The social meaning of money: 'Special monies'." American Journal of Sociology 95: 342–377.

Jay Belsky   *Pennsylvania State University*

Parental and Nonparental Child Care and Children's Socioemotional Development: A Decade in Review

Three aspects of the burgeoning literature on parental and nonparental child care pertaining to socioemotional development during the infancy, preschool, and school-age years are reviewed. The first section deals with the determinants of parenting and considers factors and processes that influence parental behavior and parent-child interaction—specifically, child characteristics, parent characteristics, marital relations, and social support. Second, correlational research linking parent-child interaction and child development is examined, with the focus first upon emotional support, parental responsiveness, and attachment security during the first years of life, then upon the cooperation and compliance during the toddler and preschool years, and finally upon the interrelation of relationships, especially linkages between parent-child and peer relationships. Finally, six waves of research on the effects of nonparental child care are outlined, along with directions for future research. A concluding section highlights points of convergence across these three areas of inquiry.

The feverish pace at which research on parent-child relations and day care has been reported during the past decade makes it imperative that this review be selective. In addition to restricting my focus to socioemotional development in the first decade of life, I have chosen to consider three

College of Health and Human Development, Pennsylvania State University, University Park, PA 16802.

areas of research pertaining to child care—the determinants of parent-child relations, the "influence" of parent-child relations on child development, and the social and emotional functioning of children who experience extensive nonparental care during infancy and early childhood. In large measure these areas of inquiry have remained distinct. This is especially so with regard to research on parent-child relations and research on day care; only in rare instances have investigators focused upon day care and parental care within the same inquiry. Despite the relative independence of the areas of inquiry to be examined, several consistent themes emerge across these distinct literatures. These will be commented upon in the concluding section of the review.

THE DETERMINANTS OF PARENT-CHILD RELATIONS

Prior to the 1980s most efforts to explain why parents rear their children the way they do focused upon social class. Work dating back to the early 1960s generally indicated that parents, particularly mothers, with more education and income and/or whose spouses held higher-status jobs tended to be more involved; less restrictive, punishing, and controlling; and more positively affectionate and responsive toward their offspring than parents of lower socioeconomic status. The past decade's research remains consistent with this portrait (e.g., Bradley, Caldwell, and Rock, 1989; McLoyd, 1990) but has extended it via a focus upon the deleterious consequences of job and/or income loss (e.g., Elder, Liker, and Cross, 1984; Lempers, Clark-Lempers, and Simons, 1989).

The 1980s witnessed an increased attempt to move beyond "social-address" models of environmental influence to better specify an array of factors and processes that have an impact on parent-child relations and, perhaps most significantly, to examine multiple determinants of parenting. In this section, Belsky's (1984a) conceptual model of the determinants of parenting is used as a tool for reviewing the results of many divergent studies. Based upon research on the etiology of child maltreatment (Belsky, 1980), this model draws attention to characteristics of the child, the parent (ontogenic development, personality, and psychological resources) and the social context in which the parent-child relationship is embedded—specifically, marital relations, social networks, and occupational experiences. Because occupational processes, and particularly work-family relations, are the focus of another paper in this volume (Menaghan and Parcel, 1990), the past decade's research on the influence they exert on parent-child relations is not considered here.

Child Characteristics

Appreciation of the fact that reciprocal processes of influence characterize parent-child relations has perhaps been no more evident over the past decade than in the plethora of studies that document the role that the child's behavior plays in shaping parental behavior. Correlational research has focused most intensively on dynamic features of child behavior, often conceptualized under the rubric of temperament, such as negative mood, high activity level, and inclination to disobey. Much evidence indicates that children with such difficult behavioral characteristics evoke from parents "upper-limit" control, that is, behavior designed to reduce the child's aversiveness (Bell and Chapman, 1986). Perhaps the most compelling evidence of this, as well as of true child effects, comes from experimental investigations in which either child confederates are trained to act aggressive and defiant (Brunk and Henggeler, 1984) or mothers with and without conduct-disordered children are observed interacting with both types of children (Anderson, Lytton, and Romney, 1986). In each case clear evidence emerges that mothers and other adults react to disobedient, negative, and/or highly active children with negative, controlling behavior. The fact that recent work reveals that parents vary in their susceptibility to such child effects (e.g., Bugental, Blue, and Cruzcosa, 1989; Crockenberg and McCluskey, 1986) strongly suggests that characteristics of parents moderate the effect of child characteristics (Bates and Pettit, 1981).

Parent Characteristics

It seems likely that the significance of parent characteristics was not appreciated until the past decade because most investigators viewed parents as young children do, that is, as individuals without life histories that precede the role of parent and identities that exist independent of it. Research in the 1980s demonstrated rather clearly, however, that the parent-child relationship needs to be embedded in the life course of parents and considered in terms of their psychological attributes. Repeatedly it has been found that adults who are psychologically healthy and mature are more likely to provide the very kind of care that promotes healthy psychological development in their offspring. Parents who score high on measures of ego development and ego strength, for example, behave sensitively and responsively toward their infants (e.g., Cox, Owen, Lewis, and Henderson, 1989) and develop feelings of confidence and control in their role as parents (Frank, Jacobson, Hole, Justkowski, and Huyck, 1986). General feelings of self-efficacy and control are themselves positively associated with a warm, accepting, and helpful style of teaching preschoolers (Mondell and Tyler, 1981); and mothers and fathers alike who feel positively about themselves tend to communicate more effectively with their preadolescent and adolescent offspring and manage disciplinary situations well (Small, 1988). Not surprisingly, mothers who are depressed tend to be less affectionate, responsive, and spontaneous with their infants (e.g., Field et al., 1985; Fleming, Flett, Ruble, and Shaul, 1988) and to be irritable and punitive with their older children (e.g., Conger, McCarty, Yang, Lahey, and Kropp, 1984; Kochanska, Kuczynski, Rodke-Yarrow, and Welsh, 1987).

In view of the fact that many of the characteristics of parents that have been linked to their childrearing behavior are themselves thought to result from their own developmental experiences, it is also not surprising that the quality of care

124

Contemporary Families

that parents provide has been related to their experiences in their own families of origin. The most intriguing evidence to emerge in this regard over the past decade is based upon the Adult Attachment Interview developed by Mary Main to tap adults' "internal working models" or affective-cognitive representations of their own relationship histories (Main, Kaplan, and Cassidy, 1985). Parents characterized as secure need not describe only positive childhood experiences but rather must be able to speak freely and coherently about their early experiences, acknowledge and show understanding of the poor care they might have received, and value attachment relationships. Adults who speak of relationship history as unimportant and who seem to dismiss and whitewash experiences of rejection are classified as detached-dismissing, whereas with those who still seem confused about what happened to them and are still actively struggling with anger toward parents or with attempts to please them are classified as preoccupied-enmeshed. It turns out to be adults who are secure in their relationships with their own parents who are most likely to rear infants who develop secure attachments to them (Grossman, Fremmer-Bombik, Rudolph, and Grossman, 1988; Main et al., 1985) and who provide more emotional support and assistance when interacting with their young children (Crowell and Feldman, 1988; Grossmann et al., 1988).

Adults who acknowledge and seem to have worked through the difficulties of their childhood are apparently protected against inflicting them on their own children (Main and Goldwyn, 1984). This fact underscores an important point that has been documented in several studies over the past decade, namely, that past need not be prologue. Significantly, what research on nonrisk parents (Belsky, Youngblade, and Pensky, 1990), as well as those at risk because of their own abusive histories (Egeland, Jacobvitz, and Sroufe, 1988), seriously discordant families of origin (Quinton and Rutter, 1985), and teenage status (Crockenberg, 1987) reveals is that a supportive relationship with a spouse or mate functions to prevent the intergenerational transmission of negative, rejecting, and insensitive maternal care.

The Marital Relationship

Concern for the marital relationship emerged in force in the 1980s among developmentalists, part-

ly as a result of the introduction of the father to the study of child development in the 1970s (Belsky, 1981). Investigators have repeatedly found that spousal support of both the emotional (e.g., love, intimacy) and instrumental (e.g., child care tasks) variety is associated with enhanced parental performance—of mothers and fathers alike. In fact, this is true of studies of parents rearing infants (Belsky and Isabella, 1988), toddlers (Goldberg and Easterbrooks, 1984), and preschoolers (Bristol, Gallagher, and Schopler, 1988) in the United States, and also in research on mothers in Japan (Durrett, Richards, Otaki, Pennebaker, and Nyquist, 1986), Israel (Levy-Schiff and Israelashvili, 1988), and Germany (Engfer, 1988). Recent work by Cox et al. (1989) indicates that such marital influence remains even after adult psychological adjustment is controlled.

There is some indication that patterns of fathering are more systematically related to patterns of marital interaction or measures of marital adjustment/satisfaction than are patterns of mothering (e.g., Belsky, Gilstrap, and Rovine, 1984; Goldberg and Easterbrooks, 1984), perhaps because men's parental roles are less scripted by social convention. There is also evidence to suggest that while the association between marriage and parenting is positive during the infant and toddler years, thereafter the association turns negative in the case of wives, with poor marriage being associated with seemingly more positive mothering (Belsky, Youngblade, Rovine, and Volling, in press; Brody, Pillegrini, and Sigel, 1986). One explanation for such results is that women compensate for unsatisfactory marriages by becoming enmeshed in the parent-child relationship; an alternative is that they are simply compensating for the insensitive parenting of their husbands. The next decade's research should further illuminate this issue, especially the question of why compensatory maternal involvement seems to emerge after infancy and not before.

Social Network Support

It is not just relations with spouse that are systematically related to what transpires between parents and their children. Consistent with Cochran and Brassard's (1979) theorizing, mothers with more community support (Crnic, Greenberg, Rugozin, Robinson, and Basham, 1983) and less frequent negative interactions with significant others (Zarling, Hirsch, and Landry, 1988) provide more positively affectionate and sensitive care to their infants, with parallel findings emerging in studies of parents rearing preschoolers (Cotterell, 1986; Pascoe, Loda, Jeffries, and Earp, 1981; Weinraub and Wolf, 1983). Social support can also function in a stress-buffering manner, as it has been found that mothers with highly irritable infants benefit most from assistance received from friends and relatives (Crockenberg and McCluskey, 1986).

What remains unclear in the literature linking parenting with assistance received from significant others is whether support functions simply as a "third variable" because individuals capable of providing sensitive, affectionate child care are also skilled in relating to friends and relatives. That this might be the case is strongly suggested by Crittenden's (1985) study of the social network patterns of adequate, neglecting, and abusive parents and a series of studies indicating that individuals high in social support experienced positive relationships with their own parents in their families of origin and are rated by others as being particulary trustworthy and skilled in dealing with social problems (Sarason, Sarason, and Shearin, 1986).

Multiple Determinants

Although most of the decade's research pertaining to the determinants of parenting focused exclusively on a single source of influence, there is increasing recognition that parenting, like most other aspects of human functioning, is multiply determined. Multiple factors have been examined in three types of studies. One type, reflecting an *additive influence* model, relies upon simple multiple regression procedures to evaluate the amount of variance that a series of main effects account for in some index of parent-child relations (e.g., Levy-Shiff and Israelashvili, 1988). In contrast, the *cumulative risk* model is based upon the assumption that sources of influence interact and, thus, that it is multiple rather than single risks which pose threats to the integrity of the developing parent-child relationship. As an example, Belsky and Isabella (1988) found that risk of insecure infant-mother attachment relationships increased dramatically (from 17% to 62%) when two rather than just a single source of influence (of three studied: maternal personality, marital quality, and infant temperament) fell below the sample median.

More *process-oriented* studies that rely upon path-analytic strategies comprise the third approach to studying the multiple determinants of parent-child relationships. The most noteworthy of such investigations is the prospective, multigenerational inquiry of families participating in the Berkeley longitudinal study (Elder et al., 1984). Because of its emphasis upon virtually all sources of influence reviewed, it serves to tie together much of what has been discovered during the past decade regarding the determinants of parent-child relationship.

Drawing upon the reports of adults concerning their own childhood experiences in their families of origin, Elder et al. (1984) found that growing up in a home in which parents' personalities could be described as unstable, in which marital conflict was frequent, and in which parental care could be depicted as unaffectionate, controlling, and hostile led to the development of unstable personalities in the children as adults. This personal instability on the part of the Berkeley parents was itself related to tension in their own marriages, which contributed, along with personal instability, to the administration of extreme and arbitrary discipline to their children. Exposure to such care resulted in the children (now the third generation) developing behavior problems that forecasted undercontrolled behavior in adulthood. And this developmental legacy was then predictive of functioning at work and at home. More specifically, the men with undercontrolled personalities, who had displayed problems as children as a result of the poor care they received, evinced very erratic work histories and unstable marriages. The women, too, showed evidence of intergenerational deficit, participating in unaffectionate, explosive, and conflicted marriages, and being described by their own children as ill-tempered and by their husbands as explosive in childrearing. Not surprisingly, the children (fourth generation) of these parents developed undercontrolled behavioral styles, thereby recreating the behavior patterns of their own parents.

PARENTAL "INFLUENCES" ON
CHILD DEVELOPMENT

This summary of an intergenerational study of both the determinants and consequences of parent-child relations sets the stage for a more detailed examination of the past decade's research on the "influence" of parenting and parent-child relations on child development. Before we consider this work it must be noted that virtually all of this research is subject to a fundamental limitation in that it confounds genetic and environmental influences (Plomin and DeFries, 1983). Not only is the care that parents provide potentially a function of their own genetic makeup and, as a result, possibly responsible for any empirical associations between their parenting and their offspring's functioning; but genetically determined characteristics of the child may lead parents to treat children in particular ways that then come to be correlated with indices of child functioning. To the extent that this is the case, influence can be erroneously attributed to the behavior of parents when, in fact, such behavior may largely function as a "third" variable (Plomin, Loehlin, and DeFries, 1985).

The research to be reviewed is also limited by almost exclusive reliance upon linear, correlational techniques that presume that more of a good thing, such as parental warmth and responsiveness, is always in the best interests of the child. The fact that there may be a point of diminishing returns is suggested by a few studies that document nonlinear relations between indices of the parent-child relationship and child development (e.g., Roberts and Strayer, 1987). These should alert future investigators to the possibility that linear correlational methods may actually underestimate associations that exist between the independent and dependent constructs they are studying.

Most work also assumes that the influence of parent-child relations on child development is the same across children and contexts. Although there is emerging recognition that this is not likely to be the case (Bronfenbrenner, 1986), it remains true that we generally lack theory to stipulate the conditions under which, and/or the children for whom, certain family experiences should or should not be influential. As a result, the field risks being littered by reports in which sporadic and unanticipated findings are interpreted, on a post-hoc basis, as evidence of "specificity of environmental action" (Wachs and Chan, 1986). In light of this situation, I have chosen to summarize the past decade's work on parental "influence" on child development in terms of rather consistent

patterns of findings that have emerged over the past decade. In ten more years we should be in a far better position to detail the conditions under which the findings to be summarized are most and least likely to obtain. My analysis begins during infancy with a focus upon the origins and consequences of infant-mother attachment security and proceeds from there to consider research that focuses upon older childen and derives from a quite different theoretical tradition.

Emotional Support and Responsiveness: Attachment Security

Bowlby's (1969) theory of infant-parent attachment, and elaboration of it by Ainsworth (1973), Sroufe (1979), and Main (Main et al., 1985), fueled a great deal of research as well as theoretical controversy during the 1980s. In large measure the success of this research paradigm—as well as the source of debate—has derived from the laboratory procedure developed by Ainsworth to assess infant-parent attachment security. While it has been popular to argue that the "Strange Situation" procedure, which requires the infant to cope with a series of stressful events (i.e., unfamiliar room, strange adult, parental departure), is problematical because it is so artificial, a large body of data speaks to the validity of the measurement system. In so doing, it provides reasonable substantiation of several basic propositions of attachment theory.

Central to the theory is the assertion that a sensitive, responsive caregiver is critically important to the development of a secure as opposed to insecure attachment bond—a person who accepts the child's behavioral proclivities, knows her own individual attributes, and is thus capable of orchestrating harmonious interactions between self and infant. Although there are those who contend that the evidence pertaining to this proposition is weak (Lamb, Thompson, Gardner, and Charnov, 1985), because in a number of studies associations that might have been expected have not emerged, Clarke-Stewart (1988b: 51) astutely noted that we are "doomed to frustration . . . if we demand complete consistency across different studies and different measures." We should not expect exact duplication among our results, she further observed, concluding that "the problem is probably with the measures not with the hypothesis about maternal sensitivity."

Consistent with this appraisal of the literature are findings linking ratings of maternal sensitivity in the first year to security in the Strange Situation in samples of middle-class American (Ainsworth, Blehar, Waters, and Wall, 1978) and German families (Grossmann, Grossman, Spangler, Suess, and Unrner, 1985), as well as economically disadvantaged, often single-parent ones (Egeland and Farber, 1984); evidence that security is associated with prompt responsiveness to distress (Crockenberg, 1981), moderate, appropriate stimulation (Belsky et al., 1984), and interactional synchrony (Isabella, Belsky, and von Eye, 1989), as well as warmth, involvement, and responsiveness (Bates, Maslin, and Fraukel, 1985); and data showing that insecure-avoidant attachments are related to intrusive, excessively stimulating interactional styles and insecure-resistant attachments to an unresponsive, underinvolved approach to caregiving (Belsky et al., 1984; Isabella et al., Lewis and Fiering, 1989; Malatesta, Grigoryev, Lamb, Albin, and Culver, 1989; Smith and Pederson, 1988). Thus, as Clarke-Stewart (1988b: 51) observed, "there does seem to be a significant degree of predictability from parents' behavior to infants' attachment classifications."

On the basis of such findings and attachment theory it is also anticipated that secure infants should differ from their insecure counterparts as they grow up, both because of feelings about self, others, and relationships that they internalize, which affect how they relate to others and how others relate to them, and because the relationship experiences that promoted their security (or insecurity) are assumed to be maintained unless subject to serious perturbation (Sroufe, 1988). Evidence consistent with such propositions first emerged at the end of the last decade in two longitudinal investigations, one of children from economically at-risk, often single-parent families, and the other of children from middle-class households. Whereas the former indicated that 2-year-olds with secure attachment histories were more skilled in solving challenging problems, seeking maternal assistance in the face of challenges, and tolerating frustration (Matas, Arend, and Sroufe, 1978), the latter found that 3½-year-olds with secure attachment histories exhibited, in a nursery school setting, more peer leadership and less social withdrawal and hesitation, greater self-confidence and curiosity about new things, and more sympathy to the distress of others than age-

mates judged earlier to be insecure in their relationships with their mothers (Waters, Wippman, and Sroufe, 1979). Additional evidence that has accumulated over the past decade indicates that infants and toddlers with secure attachment relationships are, on average, more sociable and ready to interact with friendly, unfamiliar adults as 1-year-olds (Main and Weston, 1981) and as 3-year-olds (Lütkenhaus, Grossman, and Grossman, 1985) and with unfamiliar age-mates at 2 years of age (Pastor, 1981; Vandell, Owen, Wilson, and Henderson, 1988). Moreover, at 3 they are responded to more positively by other children with secure attachment histories (Jacobson and Wille, 1986), and at 4 and 5 years of age they are rated by teachers as more competent with peers and are more liked by preschool classmates (LaFreniere and Sroufe, 1985). These social correlates of infant-mother attachment security no doubt result from the fact that children from 3 to 6 years old with secure histories behave more confidently when challenged (Lütkenhaus et al., 1985); are more active and independent in their exploration of a new setting (Hazen and Durrett, 1982); are less emotionally dependent on teachers in the preschool classroom, yet more skilled in seeking instrumental assistance when their own resources are insufficient (Sroufe, Fox, and Pancake, 1983); and are less likely during the early elementary school years to be judged by parents and/or teachers to have serious behavior problems (Erickson, Sroufe, and Egeland, 1985); Lewis, Fiering, McGuffog, and Jaskir, 1984; Renken, Egeland, Marvinney, Mangelsdorf, and Sroufe, 1989.)

It should be noted that in some instances these relations hold principally for boys or girls or for children judged securely attached at both 12 and 18 months of age, and in others there have been failures to replicate (e.g., behavior problems; Bates et al., 1985). Nevertheless, in the main the data consistently document associations between early infant-mother attachment security and subsequent competence. While the strength of the associations has been disputed, as have the mechanisms responsible for these linkages between early relationships and later socioemotional functioning, even critics of this research acknowledge the general trend in the literature (Lamb et al., 1985). Moreover, it should not be assumed that early security derived from the infant-mother relationship functions independently of subsequent relationship experiences. Even though some have attributed such naive theorizing to attachment researchers (Lamb et al., 1985), attentive reading of Bowlby (1969), Sroufe (1988), and others clearly reveals that prediction from early relationship security to subsequent functioning is assumed to be mediated, at least in part, by the child's ongoing experiences with mother and others—even when such subsequent experiences are not directly included in research designs.

In point of fact, as research designs became more sophisticated over the decade to reflect this understanding, evidence emerged consistent with it. In particular, Erickson et al. (1985) found that secure infants who developed behavior problems during the preschool years experienced less supportive care from their mothers after infancy than did their age-mates with secure histories whose mothers continued to provide supportive care, and Lewis et al. (1984) observed that insecurely attached boys who experienced negative environmental factors during the preschool years (e.g., life stress, few friends) were more likely to develop behavior problems at age 6 than were their insecurely attached counterparts who did not experience these factors. In other words, continuity from early relationship history to subsequent socioemotional functioning was a function of social experiences that intervened between the early and later times of measurement.

It is particularly noteworthy, in view of research on the origins and consequences of attachment security, that a large number of studies that are not based upon attachment theory underscore the importance of parents' emotional support and sensitive responsiveness in promoting children's socioemotional development. Consider in this regard the cross-lag correlational findings of Malatesta et al. (1986), indicating that mothers who were more responsive to their young infants' affective expressions had infants who subsequently expressed more positive emotion (joy, interest, surprise). Particularly instructive, however, is Roberts and Strayer's (1987) discovery that preschoolers' competence appears to be undermined when parents are either very discouraging or very encouraging of the expression of negative emotion. It is these data and that cited earlier linking attachment security to intermediate rather than very high levels of responsiveness and stimulation

which suggest that researchers need to be more alert to the possibility that there can be too much of a presumed good thing in the case of parental behavior.

Most research that suggests that emotional support and responsiveness (within limits) promotes psychological well-being in the child can be faulted for its failure to consider the role of subsequent experience before explaining children's development in terms of earlier experience with parents. Particularly impressive, therefore, is evidence that high levels of observed maternal positive involvement (affectionate contact, verbal stimulation) during the first two years of life forecast low levels of mother-reported behavior problems at age 4, *even with controls for observed maternal teaching and mother-initiated social contact at age 4* (Pettit and Bates, 1989); other noteworthy data demonstrate that maternal acceptance and responsivity during the infant and toddler years predict high levels of considerateness at age 10, *even after these same dimensions of parental behavior measured at 10 years are statistically controlled* (Bradley et al., 1988). Consistent with attachment theory, both sets of findings suggest, as Bryant and Crockenberg (1980) concluded on the basis of their investigation of the origins of sharing and comforting among siblings, that "having one's own self concerns taken care of increases the possibility of expressing concern for others" (p. 541). Dubow, Huesmann, and Eron's (1987) findings that third graders who experienced rejecting, authoritatian parental care and/or who failed to identify with their parents had higher levels of depression at age 19 (girls only, Lefkowitz and Tesiny, 1984) and evinced lower levels of ego development when followed up at age 30–31 clearly suggest, like the work of Elder and associates (1984, mentioned above), that the effects of emotionally supportive and unsupportive care may extend well beyond childhood.

Cooperation and Compliance: The Social Learning Tradition

Research grounded in the tradition of social learning theory also stimulated a great deal of research on parent-child relations during the 1980s. In contrast to attachment theory's emphasis on parental sensitivity and felt security during the beginning years of life, the social learning tradition focused attention upon the way in which parental rewards and punishments influence prosocial and anti-social behavior (e.g., cooperation, aggression) during the preschool and elementary-school years. Over the past decade it has become increasingly apparent that despite the differences in emphasis of these two schools of thought, they have much in common. In fact, it is often difficult to identify distinct predictions that researchers working from the two traditions would make with regard to parental influences upon child development, though different processes might well be invoked to explain a set of findings. Whereas attachment researchers tend to interpret findings such as those discussed above in terms of children's affective-cognitive processes, specifically, their expectations regarding interpersonal relations, students of social learning are more likely to speak in terms of social skills and reinforcement contingencies.

The research of Gerald Patterson (1986) has done much to stimulate investigation of the origins of compliance and cooperation during the toddler and preschool years. The ultimate goal of much of this work is to determine whether the coercive interactional processes by which parental nattering and explosive, inconsistent discipline and 10-year-olds' noncompliant behavior are reciprocally related and predict aggression with peers, low self-esteem, and academic problems (Patterson, 1986) have their roots at much younger ages. Although longitudinal evidence to evaluate this possibility is not yet available, certainly consistent with it are the data, cited earlier, linking insecure infant-mother attachment and behavior problems among preschool and early elementary school children.

But it is not just attachment research that suggests that the seeds of compliance, cooperation, or antisocial behavior may be sown in early childhood, or at least that the very processes implicated in Patterson's work during the elementary-school years might well be operative many years earlier. Consider in this regard the results of two experiments in which mothers of preschoolers were trained to behave in a variety of ways: one study demonstrated that mothers who proactively engaged their young children in interesting materials before they started to play with off-limits objects induced more compliance subsequently than did mothers who simply reacted every time the child handled something they were not supposed to (Holden and West, 1989); and the

other showed that following the child's lead by responding to what he or she did resulted in greater compliance subsequently than did simply engaging in free play in which mother was more directive and less responsive (Parpal and Maccoby, 1985). Also noteworthy are results from several correlational studies indicating (*a*) that mothers more skilled in following their toddlers' leads in play and thus fostering more synchronous exchanges have children who are more responsive to and compliant with maternal directions (Rocissano, Slade, and Lynch, 1987); (*b*) that 10-month-olds with more responsive (boys only) and involved mothers are more compliant and cooperative at age 2 and less coercive and negatively demanding (boys only) at 3½ years of age (Martin, 1981); (*c*) that mothers who engage in direct control strategies and frequently reprimand their 1½-to-3½-year-olds are more likely to have children who directly defy them, whereas age-mates whose mothers use indirect and persuasive strategies (such as indirect commands and explanations) are more likely to negotiate with their mothers in the face of conflict (Kuczynski, Kochanska, Rodke-Yarrow, and Girniss-Brown, 1987); (*d*) that more compliant 3½-year-olds have mothers and fathers who use more indirect (e.g., questions, declaratives) and less direct control strategies (e.g., imperatives) (McLaughlin, 1983); and (*e*) that mothers who report using physical punishment with their toddlers have children who are more likely to disobey maternal directives and handle breakable household objects (Power and Chapieski, 1986). Considered together, this methodologically diverse work suggests that age-appropriate, sensitive care that fosters long-term harmony in parent-child relationships and maintains children's inherent motivation to attend to and cooperate with the desires of adults, especially parents, reduces the likelihood that the family and child processes so clearly illuminated by Patterson among 10-year-olds will arise.

The Interrelation of Relationships

The convergence of attachment theory and social learning theory is perhaps most evident in regard to the interrelation of relationships, a topic that has gained ascendance among students of social development during the past decade and stimulated renewed interest in linkages between parent-child and peer relationship systems (Parke,

MacDonald, Beitel, and Bhavnagri, 1988). Both theoretical traditions assume that harmonious family relationships ought to foster high levels of interpersonal skill, whereas conflicted parent-child exchanges ought to lay the seeds for problematical relationships with age-mates. Although it will undoubtedly turn out to be the case that relations between family and peer processes are more complicated than this (e.g., compensatory processes), a good deal of research reported in the 1980s is consistent with this general proposition. As a result, emphasis has been placed upon conceptualizing the mediating processes linking the two relationship systems.

For example, MacDonald and Parke (1984: 1273) hypothesized that in the course of father-child play "children may be learning the social communicative value of their own affective displays as well as how to use these signals to regulate the social behavior of others," when these researchers found that fathers of popular preschoolers engage in stimulating physical play with their children (especially sons) but tend not to overstimulate them to the point where the child must withdraw. Additional insight concerning mediating mechanisms derives from Pettit, Dodge, and Brown's (1988) finding that mothers' practice and endorsement of physical discipline processes predicted 4- and 5-year-olds' reliance upon aggression as a strategy for solving hypothetical conflicts between peers, which itself predicted, in a path analysis, social rejection in the peer group. These findings, of course, are consistent with Putallaz's (1987) discovery that mothers who were more positive and less disagreeable when interacting with their first grade children and who focused conversation on feelings had offspring who were more popular in their classrooms—in all likelihood because the children themselves were less disagreeable and demanding than their less popular peers.

Even though cause and effect remain difficult to disentangle in these studies linking parent-child and child-peer relationship subsystems, for reasons considered earlier (e.g., behavior genetics, child effects), it is clear that from infancy onward, affectively negative, demanding, controlling, and generally insensitive parental patterns of behavior covary with an assortment of negative developmental "outcomes," ranging from early insecurity to peer rejection and academic difficulty, whereas more positively affective, responsive

styles in which control between parent and child is shared, if not directly negotiated, are associated with a range of competencies. Despite the fact that explanations of these findings, which emphasize internal psychological processes (e.g., internal working models), are often pitted against more overtly behavioral explanations (e.g., social skills, reinforcement), it must again be noted that such accounts are by no means mutually exclusive. In the course of their experiences with their parents, children not only learn how to behave but find out more about themselves and what to expect of others. It seems rather likely that it is the interconnection of feelings about self, expectations of others, and behavioral proclivities that is responsible for the associations chronicled between parent-child relations and contemporaneous and subsequent social-emotional functioning from infancy through the school-age years—and even on into adulthood. We can expect research in the next decade to further illuminate such interconnections.

NONPARENTAL CARE

As noted in the introduction to this essay, research on the developmental consequences of day care has been conducted, in large measure, in a context independent from the study of parent-child relations. Thus, even though it is recognized that children cared for on a routine basis by persons other than their parents experience, at minimum, two rearing environments, few investigations have examined care provided both by parents and by others. This is not to say, however, that research on nonparental child care has not progressed over the past decade. In point of fact, it is possible to distinguish several waves of inquiry (Belsky, 1984b).

Wave 1: Experimental Day Care

Research in the 1970s focused principally upon children growing up in high-quality, university-based centers, established for purposes of determining whether extensive and routine nonparental care initiated in the first years of life necessarily undermined children's psychological well-being, as earlier research on institutional rearing led some to suspect it might. A comprehensive review of this first wave of inquiry revealed little cause for concern (Belsky and Steinberg, 1978). Particularly with regard to socioemotional development, defined in terms of the affective bond between child and mother, it was noted that any evidence suggesting that children with day care experience were more likely to be insecurely attached to their parents was methodologically suspect. Only in the case of social relations with nonparental adults and with age-mates did Belsky and Steinberg (1978) draw attention to evidence that raised concerns. While some studies found day-care-reared children to be more cooperative in interacting with peers, others found them to be more aggressive when interacting with other children and less compliant with adult directives. Because of the nonrepresentative nature of the care studied in the first wave of research, Belsky and Steinberg cautioned that findings could not be generalized to the kinds of care routinely available to families in communities around the nation. They noted, too, that there was simply insufficient data to draw any definitive conclusions regarding age of entry into care and extent of care (i.e., part-time vs. full-time).

Wave 2: Beyond Between-Group Comparisons

The discovery that high-quality day care need not compromise child development changed the agenda for day care research by underscoring the need to identify child care factors and processes that affected the development of day-care-reared children, particularly practices and conditions that might be subject to legislative regulation. This second wave of inquiry proved remarkably successful in identifying social structural features of care—in particular, group size, caregiver training, and caregiver-child ratios—that systematically related to day-to-day processes within the child care setting, such as the quantity and quality of time caregivers spent interacting with children and the extent of focused attention and aimless wandering that children engaged in, and also to children's tested functioning. In centers in which group size was modest (15–18 children), ratios were low (particularly in the case of infants), and specialized training of staff in child development, early childhood education, and related fields was high, caregivers tended to be more stimulating, responsive, and positively affectionate, as well as less restrictive. Children receiving such care tended to be more cooperative, more intellectually capable, and more emotionally secure (for reviews, see

Belsky, 1984b; Clarke-Stewart, 1987a; Phillips and Howes, 1987). To be noted, too, are findings indicating that more time spent interacting with peers—perhaps because this reflects less time engaged in educationally stimulating interactions with an adult caregiver—is related to less optimal social and intellectual functioning on the part of the child (Clarke-Stewart, 1987b; Phillips, McCartney, and Scarr, 1987). Also noteworthy is the fact that generally similar findings obtain when family day care homes are studied and, significantly, that high-quality care appears more likely when providers are integrated in a network that receives supervisory assistance (material and emotional) from home visitors working for a community agency (Carew, 1979; Phillips and Howes, 1987).

In sum, when group size is large, ratios are poor, and caregivers are untrained or unsupervised, individual attention to children falls victim to the exigencies of coping with an overextended set of resources. As a result, both quality of care and child well-being are compromised. Note that in large measure this conclusion is consistent with research on the determinants of parenting and the influence of parent-child relations on child development that was reviewed in the first two sections of this essay.

While staff training, group size, and even caregiver-child ratios have been implicated in studies of variation in day care quality, the field still lacks specific knowledge about the point at which group size becomes too large, training insufficient, and ratios inadequate. Resolving such issues in future work will be no easy task, not only because the effect of group size, for example, is likely to vary as a function of other parameters of care (e.g., staff training), but also because the effect of any care feature will likely be dependent upon the age of the children in question.

Wave 3: The First Year of Life

At the same time that research on day care was moving beyond comparisons of children cared for only by their parents and those cared for in high-quality, university-based centers (Wave 1) toward a focus upon variation in care quality in community arrangements (Wave 2), dramatic changes were taking place in the ecology of day care as a result of changing patterns of maternal employment. Whereas less than one-third of all mothers with an infant under one year of age were employed in 1976 (31%), by 1985 virtually one out of every two such women were working (48%) (Hofferth and Phillips, 1987). Today the rate is 51% (O'Connell and Bachu, 1987). It seems fair to characterize the 1980s, then, as the decade of infant day care.

Since 1980, a sizable number of studies have focused upon children receiving some kind of nonparental care on a routine basis in their first year—and outside the context of the university centers studied in the 1970s. Although these investigations are notably limited by the fact that most are of the between-group variety, involving comparisons of children with and without employed mothers during their first year of life, the collective results of these inquiries have drawn special attention to the utilization of extensive nonparental care for infants as we know it and have it in this country. This is because a number of studies now indicate that children in any of a variety of child care arrangements, including center care, family day care, and nanny care, for 20 or more hours per week beginning in the first year of life, are at elevated risk of being classified as insecure in their attachments to their mothers at 12 or 18 months of age and of being more disobedient and aggressive when they are from 3 to 8 years old (for reviews, see Belsky, 1988; in press; Clarke-Stewart, 1989). It remains unclear exactly why these findings linking extensive infant day care experience with attachment insecurity and subsequent aggression and noncompliance emerge—and what they mean—particularly because they have not been discerned in each and every relevant study and, when they do emerge, they do not apply to each and every child receiving nonparental care on a routine basis for 20 or more hours per week in their first year. In fact, it is just because of this clouded state of affairs, especially with respect to mechanisms of influence, that Belsky (1986, 1988, in press) could be no more precise than to conclude, upon reviewing an ever-growing body of evidence highlighting such disconcerting associations, that extensive infant day care as we know it and have it in this country is a "risk factor" with regard to the social development outcomes in question.

By drawing attention to a series of findings that had until that point remained unintegrated, yet which were rather consistent with attachment theory and evidence generated on the develop-

mental correlates of insecure attachment apart from issues of day care (see above), Belsky (1986, 1988, in press) stimulated a "firestorm" of controversy (Clarke-Stewart, 1988a, 1989; Phillips, McCartney, Scarr, and Howes, 1987; Richters and Zahn-Waxler, 1988; Thompson, 1988). Perhaps the two most significant criticisms of Belsky's risk-factor conclusion were that the research under consideration lacked information on quality of care, which Wave 2 studies revealed to be so important for understanding the effects of day care, and that the children studied were not randomly assigned to employed and nonemployed mothers or to care arrangements that varied systematically in quality. As a result, there was no way to distinguish effects of care from effects of growing up in certain types of families that relied upon early care or care of varying quality (Clarke-Stewart, 1988a; Phillips, McCartney, Scarr, and Howes, 1987). It is of interest to note that even though this same problem of selection effects plagued many Wave 2 studies of day care quality, there was little hesitation among child care advocates to embrace the findings reviewed above pertaining to conditions of quality as evidence in favor of legislative action on behalf of day care and working mothers.

Three recent studies are especially noteworthy, as they collectively forge a rapprochement between scholars who emphasize the importance of care quality (Phillips and Howes, 1987; Phillips, McCartney, Scarr, and Howes, 1987) and the need to consider age of entry into full- or near full-time care (Belsky, 1988; Vandell, in press). One is a report of children studied longitudinally at ages 2, 4, and 5, which indicates, when both quality of care and age of entry into full-time care are taken into account, that it is children for whom care of low quality is initiated *in their first year* who function more problematically than all other children (Howes, 1990). These findings are perfectly consistent with a risk-factor conceptualization, in that the probability of risk (early full-time care) being realized increases when other sources of risk exist (poor-quality care).

The other two studies are noteworthy because they provide insight into the developmental consequences of growing up in societies that do and do not have coherent child care and family policies. Whereas Vandell (in press) discovered that middle-class third graders in Dallas, Texas, whose mothers returned to work for 30 or more hours per week in their first year scored most poorly (or were among the most poorly scoring children) on evaluations of social and academic functioning made by mothers, teachers, classmates, *and* the children themselves, Andersson (1989) discerned no such deleterious correlates of first-year day care experience in his follow-up study of Swedish 8- and 9-year-olds. In all likelihood this was because mothers of the Swedish children, in marked contrast to their American counterparts, experienced *6 months of paid parental leave* before placing their children in *well-resourced infant day care centers* staffed by *well-trained* and reasonably *well-paid* caregivers. Clearly, to the extent that developmental risk is associated with extensive care initiated in the first year, it seems to be because of the conditions of employment (e.g., no parental leave) and the nature and quality of care routinely available to families in the United States today.

Wave 4: Family, Work, and Child Care Contexts

This conclusion underscores a point now recognized by virtually all students of child care: in order to appraise accurately the effects of day care on child development, the complex ecology of human development must be considered. From an empirical standpoint, this means measuring variation not only in quality of care (Wave 2) and age of entry into full-time care (Wave 3), but also family attitudes and processes, as well as parents' occupational experiences (Belsky, in press; McCartney and Galanopoulos, 1988; Menaghan and Parcel, 1989). This new research agenda represents no short order, though progress has been made in initiating it.

Two different strategies have been employed in the Wave 4 research that has already emerged. The first derives from the view that the way to assess the effects of day care, be it age of entry, quality of care, or setting, is to control statistically for potential selection factors that might affect care utilization. This approach presumes that family factors should take precedence over child care factors, thus disregarding the possibility that maternal employment and day care processes can contribute (particularly in cross-sectioned designs) to the very family processes that are presumed to predate child care utilization and are to be controlled (Vandell, in press). McCartney and her

colleagues were among the first to adopt this approach and found that the overall quality of child care centers on the island of Bermuda made a significant contribution to children's language and social development, over and above that accounted for by parental attitudes and values (McCartney, 1984; Phillips, McCartney, and Scarr, 1987).

One of the most important benefits of research using hierarchical regression procedures is the limits it reveals of most Wave 2 studies, which simply linked variation in care quality with child development, without sufficient consideration of selection effects. Not surprisingly, a good deal of evidence now shows that good and bad child care are not randomly assigned to families. Several investigations reveal that poor quality of care is associated with family stress (Howes and Olenick, 1986; Howes and Stewart, 1987), low socioeconomic status (Goelman and Pence, 1987; Kontos, 1987; Vandell et al., 1988), and childrearing values and attitudes that emphasize conformity to adult rules (Phillips, McCartney, and Scarr, 1987), though such associations are not always obtained (Peterson and Peterson, 1986). Especially noteworthy, in fact, is a recent analysis of child care arrangements of parents participating in the 1985 National Longitudinal Study of Youth, which shows that "families with more resources (higher earnings, more education, more income, intact families) do not obtain higher quality care," at least as measured by structural indicators such as group size and caregiver-child ratio (Waite, Leibowitz, and Witsberger, 1988). Whether such failure to discern associations between family characteristics and day care quality is, in some studies, simply a function of lack of sample variation or, in the case of the Waite et al. inquiry, a result of reliance upon structural indicators of quality rather than process-oriented ones (e.g., caregiver-child interaction) remains unclear at present. When associations between family characteristics and child care quality do obtain, however, they are rather consistent with the literature reviewed earlier on the determinants of parenting, which indicates that family stress and limited psychological, interpersonal, and economic resources are associated with poorer quality child care.

Although the strategy of controlling for family factors confounded with child care quality or age of entry into care provides a means of assessing the unique contribution of such child care factors, increased attention now seems to be oriented toward understanding the additive and even interactive contribution of child care and family factors—and soon, no doubt, occupational experiences as well (Clarke-Stewart, 1987a; Menaghan and Parcel, 1989). With respect to additive influences, several investigations show that prediction of children's social, cognitive, and/or language development is increased when both child care quality and family characteristics are combined (e.g., Clarke-Stewart and Gruber, 1984; Howes and Stewart, 1987; Lamb, Hwang, Broberg and Bookstein, 1988). With regard to interactive influences, recall Howes's (1990) findings concerning the consequences of poor quality care coupled with first-year entry into care. Noteworthy, too, is evidence from her research that toddlers who develop insecure attachments to both their mothers and their family day-care providers evince the least competence in their play with their peers, but that those insecurely attached to their mothers but secure in their relationships with their caregivers function more competently (Howes, Rodning, Galluzzo, and Myers, 1988).

Results such as these lead to the expectation that as Wave 4 research develops two important themes will emerge—cumulative risk and compensatory processes—both of which are consistent with evidence pertaining to the determinants of parenting. Particular factors or processes, be they family attitudes, values, or interaction patterns, or child care quality or work stress, will likely turn out to be not so important in their own right, especially if other forces of influences are controlled, as they will be in interaction with each other. Thus, when sources of risk accumulate—for example, large group size, untrained staff, authoritarian parenting, and work stress—child development is likely to be compromised. In the face of high-quality care and supportive marital relations, however, work stress will probably exert little ultimate influence. Analogously, even mediocre care is likely to pose little long-term threat to a child's well-being if the family is harmonious and nurturant and the work place is rewarding to parents. Given what we have learned about selection of care, it may be difficult, though, to find such families using such care—unless, of course, it is all that is available.

Wave 5: Distinct Ecologies

It would be erroneous to conclude, on the basis of the "waves-of-research" metaphor being used here to organize the literature on nonparental care, that one wave of research follows directly in the wake of another. Instead, what we often have are overlapping waves in different stages of development. This is particularly so with respect to Wave 5, which is perhaps the most recent to be initiated, and well before Wave 4 has reached its zenith. Wave 5 research is based upon the proposition that developmental processes of influence may actually be distinctly different in the case of children with and without extensive nonparental care experience.

The possibility that factors and processes that shape development in the case of traditionally home-reared children may function differently—and perhaps not at all—in the case of children with extensive day care experience is suggested by several recent studies of infants. In research in Israel and the United States, findings indicate that it is not attachment to mother that predicts future development, as has routinely been found under more traditional rearing conditions, but rather security of attachment to alternative caregivers (Howes, Galluzzo, Hamilton, Matheson, and Rodning, 1989; Oppenheim, Sagi, and Lamb, 1988). Such results raise the most intriguing possibility that one consequence of extensive nonparental care initiated in the first year is that the influence that parents would otherwise exert on their children is "lost" to, or at least assumed by, nonparental caregivers. Dramatically consistent with this interpretation is provocative evidence reported by Howes (1990) indicating that when children begin full-time nonparental care in their first year of life, their later development is predicted by the quality of their day care, but *not* by family factors and processes. Intriguingly, just the reverse is true of children whose full-time care began after their first year. In another recent study, Weinraub, Jaeger, and Hoffman (1988) discovered that "different variables in the family system are predictive of optimal socio-emotional outcome for children of employed and children of nonemployed mothers" and were thus led to conclude that "we may need to conceptualize maternal employment as altering not just the *levels* of important predictor variables, . . . but their *dynamic relationships* as well.'' Weinraub and associates' hesitance in embracing this far-reaching implication of their findings seems well advised, given how little Wave 5 research is currently available. Nevertheless, to the extent that different processes of development are found to characterize children growing up in contrasting ecologies, this will prove important, not simply for our understanding of the developmental effects of day care, but for general developmental and family theory as well.

CONCLUSION

Despite reservations raised by some (Clarke-Stewart, 1988b), it is this reviewer's conclusion that important progress has been made over the past decade in the study of child care. Not only are developmentalists and family researchers increasingly concerned with factors and processes that shape parent-child relations, but they are ever more cognizant of the problems associated with drawing causal inferences from much socialization research. As we have seen, the same is true of day care researchers, who only a decade ago simply did not consider selection effects.

Given this situation, we can expect to see important changes over the next decade in research on child care. With regard to the determinants of parenting, increasing emphasis will no doubt be placed upon multiple factors rather than just a single one. With respect to research on parental influences on child development, more concern will be paid to distinguishing genetic from true environmental effects and, especially, toward identifying the conditions under which certain patterns of parent-child interaction influence or fail to influence child development. It is clear that day care research in the 1990s will be different from that in the 1980s, not only because the focus will be upon multiple factors, including care quality, family characteristics, occupational conditions, and age of entry into care, but also because it will not be assumed that processes that shape child functioning are the same under different rearing conditions.

In further considering the future of research on child care, it is useful to draw attention to two themes that cut across research on the determinants of parenting, the influence of parent-child relations upon child development, and the effects of day care. The first is that quality of child care, be it provided by parents in the home or child care workers in a day care setting, is multiply determined. A corollary of this proposition is that child care quality is well buffered. Thus, even though the accumulation of economic, social, and psychological stress will undermine the quality of care that parents and child care workers provide, it is also true that single sources of vulnerability can be counterbalanced by sources of support. What would be ideal over the next decade would be to develop a more precise understanding of the trade-offs between risk and protective factors.

The second theme to emerge from the past decade's research on both parental and nonparental child care is that sensitive, responsive rearing seems to promote attachment security in the infant and toddler and cooperation, compliance, and even achievement in the older child. Conversely, inconsistent, unsupportive, and unresponsive care, particularly when it is tinged with negative affect on the part of the caregiver, fosters uncooperative and problematic behavior. While the past decade has provided reasonable correlational support for such propositions, there remains a strong need to determine more precisely the conditions under which these principles are most valid. Certainly, these relations between experience and development are not likely to be equally applicable to all children, at all ages, and in all family, child care, and community contexts. One major task of the next decade will be to make theoretically guided progress in specifying which processes hold for which children in which contexts.

The prospect of significant advances being made in child care research seems great for one important reason: that fields of inquiry that have been rather separate are becoming ever more integrated. Studies of parent-child relation will increasingly include assessments of child care and parents' occupational experiences. Similarly, studies of day care will pay even more attention to what transpires in the family. The lesson of the past decade is clearly that whatever the research focus—be it parent-child relations, day care, or maternal employment—the phenomenon must be studied in context. However difficult and challenging it is to investigate these multiple contexts, that is exactly what is required if we are to advance understanding of the determinants of parenting, the influence of parent-child relations upon child development, and the effects of day care.

NOTE

Work on this article was supported by a grant from the National Institute of Child Health and Human Development (RO1HD15496) and by a NIMH Research Scientist Development Award (KO2-MH00486).

REFERENCES

Ainsworth, Mary. 1973. "The development of infant-mother attachment." Pp. 1–94 in Betty Caldwell and Henry N. Ricciue (eds.), Review of Child Development Research (Vol. 3). Chicago: University of Chicago Press.

Ainsworth, Mary, M. Blehar, E. Waters, and S. Wall. 1978. Patterns of Attachment. Hillsdale, NJ: Erlbaum.

Anderson, Kathleen E., Hugh Lytton, and David M. Romney. 1986. "Mothers' interaction with normal and conduct-disordered boys: Who affects whom?" Developmental Psychology 22: 604–609.

Andersson, Bengt-Erik. 1989. "The importance of public day care for preschool children's later development." Child Development 60: 857–866.

Bates, Jack, and G. Pettit. 1981. "Adult individual differences as moderators of child effects." Journal of Abnormal Child Psychology 9: 329–341.

Bates, John E., Christine A. Maslin, and Karen A. Frankel. 1985. "Attachment security, mother-child interaction, and temperament as predictors of behavior-problem ratings at age three years." Growing Points of Attachment Theory and Research: Monographs of the Society for Research in Child Development 50: 167–193.

Bell, Richard Q., and Michael Chapman. 1986. "Child effects in studies using experimental or brief longitudinal approaches to socialization." Developmental Psychology 22: 595–603.

Belsky, Jay. 1980. "Child maltreatment: An ecological integration." American Psychologist 35: 320–335.

Belsky, Jay. 1981. "Early human experience: A family perspective." Developmental Psychology 17: 3–23.

Belsky, Jay. 1984a. "The determinants of parenting: A process model." Child Development 55: 83–96.

Belsky, Jay. 1984b. "Two waves of day care research: Developmental effects and conditions of quality." Pp. 1–34 in R. Ainslie (ed.), The Child and the Day Care Setting. New York: Praeger.

Belsky, Jay. 1986. "Infant day care: A cause for concern?" Zero to Three: Bulletin of the National Center for Clinical Infant Studies 6: 1–7.

Belsky, Jay. 1988. "The 'effects' of infant day care reconsidered." Early Childhood Research Quarterly 3: 235–272.

Belsky, Jay. In press. "Developmental risks associated with infant day care: Insecurity, aggression, and noncompliance?" In S. Chehrazi (ed.), Balancing Work and Parenting: Psychological and Developmental Implications of Day Care. New York: American Psychiatric Press.

Belsky, Jay, Bonnie Gilstrap, and Michael Rovine. 1984. "The Pennsylvania Infant and Family Development Project, I: Stability and change in mother-infant and father-infant interaction in a family setting at one, three, and nine months." Child Development 55: 692–705.

Belsky, Jay, and Russell Isabella. 1988. "Maternal, infant, and social contextual determinants of attachment security." Pp. 41–94 in J. Belsky and T. Nezworski (eds.), Clinical Implications of Attachment. Hillsdale, NJ: Erlbaum.

Belsky, Jay, and L. D. Steinberg. 1978. "The effects of day care: A critical review." Child Development 49: 929–949.

Belsky, Jay, Lise Youngblade, and Emily Pensky. 1990. "Childcaring history, marital quality, and maternal affect: Intergenerational transmission in a low-risk sample." Development and Psychopathology 1: 291–304.

Belsky, Jay, Lise Youngblade, Michael Rovine, and Brenda Volling. In press. "Patterns of marital change and parent-child interaction." Journal of Marriage and the Family.

Bowlby, John. 1969. Attachment and Loss (Vol. 1). Attachment. New York: Basic Books.

Bradley, Robert H., Bettye M. Caldwell, and Stephen L. Rock. 1988. "Home environment and school performance: A ten-year follow-up and examination of three models of environmental action." Child Development 59: 852–867.

Bristol, Marie M., James J. Gallagher, and Eric Schopler. 1988. "Mothers and fathers of young developmentally disabled and nondisabled boys: Adaptation and spousal support." Developmental Psychology 24: 441–451.

Brody, Gene H., Anthony D. Pillegrini, and Irving E. Sigel. 1986. "Marital quality and mother-child and father-child interactions with school-aged children." Developmental Psychology 22: 291–296.

Bronfenbrenner, Urie. 1986. "Ecology of the family as a context for human development: Research perspectives." Development Psychology 22: 723–742.

Brunk, Molly A., and Scott W. Henggeler. 1984. "Child influences on adult controls: An experimental investigation." Developmental Psychology 20: 1074–1081.

Bryant, Brenda K., and Susan B. Crockenberg. 1980. "Correlates and dimensions of prosocial behavior: A study of female siblings with their mothers." Child Development 51: 520–544.

Bugental, Daphne B., J. Blue, and M. Cruzcosa. 1989. "Perceived control over caregiving outcomes: Implications for child abuse." Developmental Psychology 25: 532–539.

Carew, Jean. 1979. "Observation study of caregivers and children in day care homes." Paper presented at the biennial meetings of the Society for Research in Child Development, San Francisco (April).

Clarke-Stewart, K. Alison. 1987a. "In search of consistencies in child care research." Pp. 105–120 in Deborah Phillips (ed.), Quality in Day Care. Washington, DC: NAEYC.

Clarke-Stewart, K. Alison. 1987b. "Predicting child development from child care forms and features: The Chicago study." Pp. 21–42 in Deborah Phillips (ed.), Quality Day Care. Washington, DC: NAEYC.

Clarke-Stewart, K. Alison. 1988a. "The 'effects' of infant child care reconsidered." Early Childhood Research Quarterly 3: 293–318.

Clarke-Stewart, K. Alison. 1988b. "Parents' effects on children's development: A decade of progress?" Journal of Applied Developmental Psychology 9: 41–84.

Clarke-Stewart, K. Alison. 1989. "Infant day care: Maligned or malignant?" American Psychologist 44: 266–273.

Clarke-Stewart, K. Alison, and C. Gruber. 1984. "Day care forms and features." Pp. 35–62 in R. C. Ainslie (ed.), Quality Variations in Day Care. New York: Praeger.

Cochran, Moncrieff M., and Jane Anthony Brassard. 1979. "Child development and personal social networks." Child Development 50: 601–616.

Conger, Rand D., John A. McCarty, Raymond K. Yang, Benjamin B. Lahey, and Joseph P. Kropp. 1984. "Perception of child, child-rearing values, and emotional distress as mediating links between environmental stressors and observed maternal behavior." Child Development 55: 2234–2247.

Cotterell, John L. 1986. "Work and community influences on the quality of child rearing." Child Development 57: 362–374.

Cox, Martha J., Margaret T. Owen, Jerry M. Lewis, and V. Henderson. 1989. "Marriage, adult adjustment, and early parenting." Child Development 60: 1015–1024.

Crittenden, Patricia M. 1985. "Social networks, quality of child rearing, and child development." Child Development 56: 1299–1313.

Crnic, Keith A., Mark T. Greenberg, Arlene S. Ragozin, Nancy M. Robinson, and Robert B. Basham. 1983. "Effects of stress and social support on mothers and premature and full-term infants." Child Development 54: 209–217.

Crockenberg, Susan B. 1981. "Infant irritability, mother responsiveness, and social support influences on the security of infant-mother attachment." Child Development 52: 857–865.

Crockenberg, Susan. 1987. "Predictors and correlates of anger toward and punitive control of toddlers by adolescent mothers." Child Development 58: 964–975.

Crockenberg, Susan, and Karen McCluskey. 1986. "Change in maternal behavior during the baby's first year of life." Child Development 57: 746–753.

Crowell, Judith A., and S. Shirley Feldman. 1988. "Mothers' internal models of relationships and children's behavioral and developmental status: A study of mother-child interaction." Child Development 59: 1273–1285.

Dubow, Eric F., L. Rowell Huesmann, and Leonard D. Eron. 1987. "Childhood correlates of adult ego development." Child Development 58: 859–869.

Durrett, Mary Ellen, Phyllis Richards, Midori Otaki, James Pennebaker, and Linda Nyquist. 1986. "Mother's involvement with infant and her perception of spousal support, Japan and America." Journal of Marriage and the Family 48: 187–194.

Egeland, Byron, and Ellen A. Farber. 1984. "Infant-mother attachment: Factors related to its development and changes over time." Child Development 55: 753–771.

Egeland, Byron, Deborah Jacobvitz, and L. Alan Sroufe. 1988. "Breaking the cycle of abuse." Child Development 59: 1080–1088.

Elder, Glen H., Jr., J. D. Liker, and C. Cross. 1984. "Parent-child behavior in the Great Depression: Life course and intergenerational influences." Pp. 109–158 in Paul B. Baltes and Orville G. Brim (eds.), Life-Span Development and Behavior (Vol. 6). Hillsdale, NJ: Erlbaum.

Engfer, Arnette. 1988. "The interrelatedness of marriage and the mother-child relationship." Pp. 104–118 in R. Hinde and J. Stevensen-Hinde (ed.), Relationships within Families. Oxford: Oxford University Press.

Erickson, Martha Farrell, L. Alan Sroufe, and Byron Egeland. 1985. "The relationship between quality of attachment and behavior problems in preschool in a high-risk sample." Pp. 147–193 in Inge Bretherton and Everett Waters (eds.), Growing Points of Attachment Theory and Research. Monographs of the Society for Research in Child Development, Serial No. 209, Nos. 1–2.

Field, Tiffany, M. D. Sandberg, R. Garcia, N. Vega-Lahr, S. Goldstein, and L. Guy. 1985. "Pregnancy problems, postpartum depression, and early mother-infant interactions." Developmental Psychology 21: 1152–1156.

Fleming, Alison S., Gordon L. Flett, Diane N. Ruble, and David L. Shaul. 1988. "Postpartum adjustment in first-time mothers: Relations between mood, maternal attitudes, and mother-infant interactions." Developmental Psychology 24: 71–81.

Frank, Susan, Stacy Jacobson, Catherine Butler Hole, Renata Justkowski, and Margaret Huyck. 1986. "Psychological predictors of parents' sense of confidence and control and self- versus child-focused gratifications." Developmental Psychology 22: 348–355.

Goelman, Hillel, and Alan Pence. 1987. "Effects of child care, family, and individual characteristics on children's language development." Pp. 89–104 in Deborah Phillips (ed.), Quality Child Care. Washington, DC: NAEYC.

Goldberg, Wendy A., and M. Ann Easterbrooks. 1984. "Role of marital quality in toddler development." Developmental Psychology 20: 504–514.

Grossman, Frances K., Ellen Golding, and William S. Pollack. 1988. "Fathers and children: Predicting the quality and quantity of fathering." Developmental Psychology 24: 82–91.

Grossmann, Karin, Elisabeth Fremmer-Bombik, Josef Rudolph, and Klaus E. Grossman. 1988. "Maternal attachment representations as related to patterns of infant-mother attachment and maternal care during the first year." Pp. 241-260 in R. Hinde and J. Stevenson-Hinde (eds.), Relationships within Families. Oxford: Oxford University Press.

Grossmann, Karin, Klaus E. Grossman, G. Spangler, G. Suess, and L. Unrner. 1985. "Maternal sensitivity and newborn orientation responses as related to quality of attachment in Northern Germany." Pp. 233-256 in Inge Bretherton and Everett Waters (eds.), Growing Points in Attachment Theory and Research. Monographs of the Society for Research in Child Development, Serial No. 209, Nos. 1-2.

Hazen, Nancy L., and Mary Ellen Durrett. 1982. "Relationship of security of attachment to exploration and cognitive mapping abilities in two-year-olds." Developmental Psychology 18: 751-759.

Hofferth, Sandra, and D. A. Phillips. 1987. "Child care in the United States, 1970 to 1995." Journal of Marriage and the Family 49: 559-571.

Holden, George W., and Meredith J. West. 1989. "Proximate regulation by mothers: A demonstration of how differing styles affect young children's behavior." Child Development 60: 64-69.

Howes, Carollee. 1990. "Can the age of entry and the quality of infant child care predict adjustment in kindergarten?" Developmental Psychology 26: 292-303.

Howes, Carollee, and M. Olenick. 1986. "Family and child care influences on children's compliance." Child Development 57: 202-216.

Howes, Carollee, D. C. Galluzzo, C. E. Hamilton, C. C. Matheson, and C. Rodning. 1989. "Social relationships with adults and peers within child care and families." Paper presented as part of an invited symposium, Society for Research in Child Development, Kansas City, MO (April).

Howes, Carollee, C. Rodning, D. C. Galluzzo, and L. Myers. 1988. "Attachment and child care: Relationships with mother and caregiver." Early Childhood Research Quarterly 3: 403-416.

Howes, Carollee, and P. Stewart. 1987. "Child's play with adults, toys, and peers: An examination of family and child care influences." Developmental Psychology 23: 423-430.

Isabella, Russell A., Jay Belsky, and Alexander von Eye. 1989. "Origins of infant-mother attachment: An examination of interactional synchrony during the infant's first year." Developmental Psychology 25: 12-21.

Jacobson, Joseph L., and Diane E. Wille. 1986. "The influence of attachment pattern on developmental changes in peer interaction from the toddler to the preschool period." Child Development 57: 338-339.

Kochanska, Grazyna, L. Kuczynski, M. Rodke-Yarrow, and J. Welsh. 1987. "Resolutions of control episodes between well and affectively ill mothers and their young children." Journal of Abnormal Child Psychology 15: 441-456.

Kontos, Susan, and Richard Fiene. 1989. "Child care quality, compliance with regulations, and children's development: The Pennsylvania Study." Pp. 361-378 in Deborah Phillips (ed.), Quality in Child Care: What Does Research Teach Us? Washington, DC: NAEYC.

Kuczynski, Leon, G. Kochanska, M. Rodke-Yarrow, and D. Girniss-Brown. 1987. "A developmental interpretation of young children's noncompliance." Developmental Psychology 23: 1-8.

LaFreniere, Peter J., and L. Alan Sroufe. 1985. "Profiles of peer competence in the preschool: Interrelations between measures, influence of social ecology, and relation to attachment history." Developmental Psychology 21: 56-69.

Lamb, Michael E., C. P. Hwang, A. Broberg, and F. Bookstein. 1988. "The effects of out of home care on the development of social competence in Sweden: A longitudinal study." Early Childhood Research Quarterly 3: 379-402.

Lamb, Michael, R. Thompson, W. Gardner, and E. Charnov. 1985. Infant-Mother Attachment. Hillsdale, NJ: Erlbaum.

Lefkowitz, Monroe M., and Edward P. Tesiny. 1984. "Rejection and depression: Prospective and contemporaneous analyses." Developmental Psychology 20: 776-785.

Lempers, Jacques D., Dania Clark-Lempers, and Ronald L. Simons. 1989. "Economic hardship, parenting, and distress in adolescence." Child Development 60: 25-39.

Levy-Shiff, Rachel, and Ruth Israelashvili. 1988. "Antecedents of fathering: Some further exploration." Developmental Psychology 24: 434-440.

Lewis, Michael, and Candace Fiering. 1989. "Infant, mother, and mother-infant interaction behavior and subsequent attachment." Child Development 60: 831-837.

Lewis, Michael, Candace Fiering, Carolyn McGuffog, and John Jaskir. 1984. "Predicting psychopathology in six-year-olds from early social relations." Child Development 55: 123-136.

Lütkenhaus, Paul, Klaus E. Grossman, and Karin Grossmann. 1985. "Infant-mother attachment at twelve months and style of interaction with a stranger at the age of three years." Child Development 56: 1538-1542.

MacDonald, Kevin, and Ross D. Parke. 1984. "Bridging the gap: Parent-child play interaction and peer interactive competence." Child Development 55: 1265-1277.

Main, Mary, and R. Goldwyn. 1984. "Prediction rejection of her infant from mother's representation of her own experience. Implications for the abused-abusing intergenerational cycle." Child Abuse and Neglect 8: 203-217.

Main, Mary, Nancy Kaplan, and Jude Cassidy. 1985. "Security in infancy, childhood, and adulthood: A move to the level of representation." Pp. 66-104 in Inge Bretherton and Everett Waters (eds.), Growing Points of Attachment Theory and Research. Monographs of the Society for Research in Child Development, Serial No. 209, Nos. 1-2.

Main, Mary, and Donna R. Weston. 1981. "The quality of the toddler's relationship to mother and to father: Related to conflict behavior and the readiness to establish new relationships." Child Development 52: 932-940.

Malatesta, Carol, C. Culver, J. Tesman, and B. Shepard. 1989. "The development of emotion expression during the first two years of life: Normative trends and patterns of individual differences." Monographs of the Society for Research in Child Development, Serial No. 219.

Malatesta, Carol Zander, Patricia Grigoryev, Catherine Lamb, Melanie Albin, and Clayton Culver. 1986. "Emotion socialization and expressive development in preterm and full-term infants." Child Development 57: 316–330.

Martin, John A. 1981. "A longitudinal study of the consequences of early mother-infant interaction: A microanalytic approach." Monographs of the Society for Research in Child Development, Serial No. 191.

Matas, Leah, Richard A. Arend, and S. Alan Sroufe. 1978. "Continuity of adaptation in the second year: The relationship between quality of attachment and later competence." Child Development 49: 547–556.

McCartney, Kathleen. 1984. "Effects of quality of day care environment on children's language development." Developmental Psychology 20: 244–260.

McCartney, Kathleen, and A. Galanopoulos. 1988. "Child care and attachment: A new frontier the second time around." American Journal of Orthopsychiatry 58: 1–21.

McLaughlin, Barry. 1983. "Child compliance to parental control techniques." Developmental Psychology 19: 667–673.

McLoyd, Vonnie. 1990. "The declining fortunes of black children: Psychological distress, parenting, and socioemotional development in the context of economic hardship." Child Development 61: 311–346.

Menaghan, Elizabeth, and Toby Parcel. 1989. "Transitions in work and family arrangements: Mothers' employment conditions, child care arrangements, and child outcomes." Unpublished manuscript, Ohio State University.

Menaghan, Elizabeth, and Toby Parcel. 1990. "Parental employment and family life: Research in the 1980s." Journal of Marriage and the Family 52: 1079–1098. [Reprinted in this volume]

Mondell, Sid, and Forrest B. Tyler. 1981. "Parental competence and styles of problem-solving/play behavior with children." Developmental Psychology 17: 73–78.

O'Connell, Martin, and Amara Bachu. 1987. Fertility of American Women: June 1986. Current Population Reports, Series P-20, No. 421. Washington, DC: U.S. Government Printing Office.

Oppenheim, David, A. Sagi, and M. Lamb. 1988. "Infant-adult attachments on the kibbutz and their relation to socioemotional development 4 years later." Developmental Psychology 24: 427–433.

Parke, Ross D., Kevin B. MacDonald, A. Beitel, and N. Bhavnagri. 1988. "The role of the family in the development of peer relationships." Pp. 17–44 In R. Peters and R. McMahan (eds.), Marriage and Families: Behavioral Treatments and Processes. New York: Brunner/Mazel.

Parpal, Mary, and Eleanor E. Maccoby. 1985. "Maternal responsiveness and subsequent child compliance." Child Development 56: 1326–1334.

Pascoe, J. M., M. Loda, U. Jeffries, and J. Earp. 1981. "The association between mothers' social support and provision of stimulation to their children." Development and Behavior Pediatrics 2: 15–19.

Pastor, Donald L. 1981. "The quality of mother-infant attachment and its relationship to toddlers' initial sociability with peers." Developmental Psychology 17: 326–335.

Patterson, Gerald R. 1986. "Performance models for antisocial boys." American Psychologist 41: 432–444.

Peterson, Carole, and Richard Peterson. 1986. "Parent-child interaction and daycare: Does quality of daycare matter?" Journal of Applied Developmental Psychology 7: 1–15.

Pettit, Gregory, and John E. Bates. 1989. "Family interaction patterns and children's behavior problems from infancy to 4 years." Developmental Psychology 25: 413–420.

Pettit, Gregory S., Kenneth A. Dodge, and Melissa M. Brown. 1988. "Early family experience, social problem solving patterns, and children's social competence." Child Development 59: 107–120.

Phillips, Deborah A., and C. Howes. 1987. "Indicators of quality in child care: Review of the research." Pp. 1–20 In D. A. Phillips (ed.), Quality in Child Care: What Does Research Tell Us? Research Monograph of the National Association for the Education of Young Children.

Phillips, Deborah A., K. McCartney, and S. Scarr. 1987. "Child care quality and children's social development." Developmental Psychology 23: 537–543.

Phillips, D., K. McCartney, S. Scarr, and C. Howes. 1987. "Selective review of infant day care research: A cause for concern." Zero to Three: Bulletin of the National Center for Clinical Infant Studies 7: 18–21.

Plomin, Robert, and J. C. DeFries. 1983. "The Colorado Adoption Project." Child Development 54: 276–289.

Plomin, Robert, John C. Loehlin, and J. C. DeFries. 1985. "Genetic and environmental components of 'environmental' influences." Developmental Psychology 21: 391–402.

Power, Thomas G., and M. Lynn Chapieski. 1986. "Childrearing and impulse control in toddlers: A naturalistic investigation." Developmental Psychology 22: 271–275.

Putallaz, Martha. 1987. "Maternal behavior and children's sociometric status." Child Development 58: 324–340.

Quinton, D., and M. Rutter. 1985. "Parenting behavior of mothers raised 'in care'." Pp. 157–201 in Arnold R. Nicol (ed.), Longitudinal Studies in Child Psychology and Psychiatry. New York: Wiley.

Renken, Bruce, B. Egeland, D. Marvinney, S. Mangelsdorf, and L. A. Sroufe. 1989. "Early childhood antecedents of aggression and passive withdrawal in early elementary school." Journal of Personality 57: 257–282.

Richters, John, and C. Zahn-Waxler. 1988. "The infant day care controversy in perspective: Current status and future directions." Early Childhood Research Quarterly 3: 319–336.

Roberts, William L., and Janet Strayer. 1987. "Parents' responses to the emotional distress of their children: Relations with children's competence." Developmental Psychology 23: 415–422.

Rocissano, Lorraine, Arietta Slade, and Victoria Lynch. 1987. "Dyadic synchrony and toddler compliance." Developmental Psychology 23: 698–704.

Sarason, Irwin, Barbara Sarason, and Edward Shearin. 1986. "Social support as an individual difference variable: Its stability, origins, and relational aspects." Journal of Personality and Social Psychology 50: 845–855.

Small, Stephen A. 1988. "Parental self-esteem and its relationship to childrearing practices, parent-adolescent interaction, and adolescent behavior." Journal of Marriage and the Family 50: 1063–1072.

Smith, Philip B., and David R. Pederson. 1988. "Maternal sensitivity and patterns of infant-mother attachment." Child Development 59: 1097–1101.

Sroufe, L. Alan. 1979. "The coherence of individual development." American Psychologist 34: 834–841.

Sroufe, L. Alan. 1988. "The role of infant-caregiver attachment in development." Pp. 18–40 in Jay Belsky and Teresa Nezworski (eds.), Clinical Implications of Attachment. Hillsdale, NJ: Erlbaum.

Sroufe, L. Alan, Nancy E. Fox, and Van R. Pancake. 1983. "Attachment and dependency in developmental perspective." Child Development 54: 1615–1627.

Thompson, Ross. 1988. "The effects of infant day care: Through the prism of attachment theory." Early Childhood Research Quarterly 3: 273–282.

Vandell, Deborah. In press. "Child care and the family: Complex contributors to child development." New Directions in Child Development.

Vandell, Deborah, Margaret T. Owen, Kathy S. Wilson, and V. Kay Henderson. 1988. "Social development in infant twins: Peer and mother-child relationships." Child Development 59: 168–169.

Wachs, Theodore D., and Alice Chan. 1986. "Specificity of environmental action as seen in environmental correlates of infants' communication performance." Child Development 57: 1464–1474.

Waite, Linda, Arleen Leibowitz, and Christina Witsberger. 1988. "What parents pay for: Quality for child care and child care costs." Unpublished manuscript, The Urban Institute, Washington, DC.

Waters, Everett, Judith Wippman, and L. Alan Sroufe. 1979. "Attachment, positive affect, and competence in the peer group: Two studies in construct validation." Child Development 50: 821–829.

Weinraub, Marsha, E. Jaeger, and Lois Hoffman. 1988. "Predicting infant outcome in families of employed and non-employed mothers." Early Childhood Research Quarterly 3: 361–378.

Weinraub, Marsha, and Barbara M. Wolf. 1983. "Effects of stress and social supports on mother-child interactions in single- and two-parent families." Child Development 54: 1297–1311.

Zarling, Cynthia, L. Hirsch, and Susan Landry. 1988. "Maternal social networks and mother-infant interactions in full-term and very low birthweight, preterm infants." Child Development 59: 178–185.

LYNN K. WHITE   *University of Nebraska–Lincoln*

Determinants of Divorce:
A Review of Research in the Eighties

This review encompasses work published in the 1980s that concerns the causes of divorce. Substantive findings are reviewed under three broad headings: macrostructure, demographics and the life course, and family process. Trends in methods, samples, and theory are also reviewed. This decade's research on divorce is characterized by bigger and better data sets, more sophisticated research techniques, and a growing body of conclusive empirical findings in the areas of demographic and life course factors. Relatively neglected areas include theory and family process. The review ends with recommendations for future research.

In a 1989 paper, Martin and Bumpass provided the startling estimate that two-thirds of all first marriages in the United States will end in divorce. We close out the decade of the eighties, then, with the realization that high rates of divorce are not a period phenomenon of the 1970s or a cohort phenomenon of the baby boom generation. Instead, high levels of divorce seem to have become a standard part of American family experience.

This review encompasses work published in the 1980s that concerns the causes of divorce. Substantive findings are covered first, followed by a review of methods and theory. The review will highlight major findings and areas of consensus rather than attempting to cover all published material.

Department of Sociology, University of Nebraska–Lincoln, Lincoln, NE 68588-0324.

A REVIEW OF SUBSTANTIVE FINDINGS

Substantive findings are reviewed under three broad headings: macrostructure, the life course and demographics, and family process.

Macrostructural Determinants of Divorce

A shift in the lifetime divorce probability from 10% to well over 50% cannot be explained at the micro level. In addition to asking why some marriages are more likely to fail than others, we also need to examine changes in the social institutions that structure individual experience. In this section, we review theory and findings regarding law, economic cycles, the family institution, sex ratios, gender roles, community integration, and cultural values.

Law. The shift from fault to no-fault divorce was one of the major legal changes during the 1980s. Although there is little evidence that the legal shift raised U.S. divorce rates (Weitzman, 1985), comparable changes in law apparently caused a temporary surge in Canada and Australia (Balakrishnan, Rao, Lapierre-Adamcyk, and Krotki, 1987). As Weitzman's influential 1985 work argues, the most significant result of no-fault divorce law may be to eliminate legal support for norms of lifetime obligation and for the expectation that individuals will be rewarded for fulfilling normative roles. Blumberg (1985), however, argues that recent court cases finding against cohabitors' claims for the rights of marriage show that there is still legal and normative support for marriage commitments.

Economic cycles. Several studies have addressed the issue of whether divorce levels change with prosperity and recession cycles. A comparison of low divorce rates during the 1930s with high rates in the 1970s lead some to conclude that depression retarded divorce and prosperity increased it (Cherlin, 1981; Glick and Lin, 1986). The most sophisticated analysis of American time series data, however, finds that the effect of prosperity is to slightly *reduce* divorce (South, 1985). South argues that, although prosperity may make divorce more feasible, this effect is outweighed by the positive effects of prosperity on personal relationships.

The family institution. The shift from preindustrial to industrial society is marked by the development of extrafamilial institutions that provide alternative sources of financial security, personal services, satisfaction, and leisure (Davis, 1985). The result is that the family and family stability are less important (Becker, 1981; Cherlin and Furstenberg, 1988; Popenoe, 1988). Among the consequences are a decrease in marriage and fertility and an increase in divorce (Espenshade, 1985). As Schoen, Urton, Woodrow, and Baj (1985: 113) put it, "Recent economic changes have undermined the social and economic forces that maintained the institution of marriage."

High divorce rates are not characteristic of all nations that have made the transition to industrialization: Japan, Italy, and Israel have much lower divorce rates than the United States. It may be that the divorce pattern of North America and Northwestern Europe is more closely related to its historically unique marriage pattern than it is to industrialization per se.

Sex ratios. One of the most innovative ideas to explain cross-cultural and historical differences in divorce rates is the sex ratio hypothesis put forth by Guttentag and Secord (1983). Their argument assumes that women are more interested in stability than men and that the relative availability of men's alternatives determines divorce rates. Specifically they argue that divorce rates will be higher when the ratio of women to men is higher. In a comparative study of 66 societies, Trent and South (1989) do find evidence that societies with a relative shortage of women have lower divorce rates.

It may be argued that Guttentag and Secord's assumption about sex differentials in commitment is more interesting than the sex ratio hypothesis itself. It is surprising that only sociobiologists have addressed this issue.

Gender roles. Gender roles are hypothesized to relate to divorce in two ways. First, when gender roles give women more economic independence of men and families, women have more freedom to divorce (Lee, 1982). Second, similarity of women's and men's roles is hypothesized to produce less marital cohesion than complementary roles do (Becker, 1981; Schoen et al., 1985). Both of these hypotheses suggest that increasing labor force participation among females is a cause of increased U.S. divorce rates.

On a macro level, evidence is largely consistent with these expectations. A positive relationship between women's labor force participation and divorce is found in time-series data in the United States (Cherlin, 1981; Cherlin and Furstenberg, 1988; South, 1985) and in cross-cultural analyses (Seccombe and Lee, 1987; Trent and South, 1989). It is not clear, however, whether the critical factor is extrafamilial involvement, economic independence, similarity of roles, or what (Seccombe and Lee, 1987).

Social integration. Harking back to Durkheim and Wirth, there is strong theoretical consensus that social integration retards divorce. The reasoning is set forth most explicitly by Glenn and Shelton (1985): Integration increases the likelihood that people will follow social norms in choosing an appropriate spouse and fulfilling their marital roles, and decreases the likelihood that they will court community stigma by divorcing. Aggregate-level studies in the United States and Canada uniformly find that community stability, as measured by social mobility, is the best predictor of aggregate divorce rates (Breault and Kposowa, 1987; Glenn and Shelton, 1985; Trovato, 1986). One exception is a finding by Wilkinson, Reynolds, Thompson, and Ostresh (1983) that *changes* in mobility rates do not explain changes in divorce rates in nonmetropolitan, Western counties.

Cultural values. Toward the end of the 1980s much attention was devoted to the decline of community and the rise of individualism. Articulated most prominently by Bellah, Madsen, Sullivan,

Swidler, and Tipton (1985), the theme has been repeated by family scholars (Popenoe, 1988). Pejorative terms such as "hedonism" (Glenn, 1987) and "narcissistic withdrawal" (Brodbar-Nemzer, 1986) are used to describe the "flight from commitment."

In a slightly different vein, Roussel and Théry (1988) have argued that formal marriage has lost its normative support: it is no longer something that one *ought* to do, but a matter of personal taste. Distinctions between marital and nonmarital childbearing, marriage and cohabitation have lost their normative force, and marriage and divorce are reduced to mere formalities.

There may be some truth to these claims. Given the substantial evidence that changes in attitudes follow rather than precede changes in behavior, however, it seems appropriate to consider these normative and attitudinal changes as dependent or intervening variables rather than explanatory factors.

The Life Course and Demographics

The decade of the eighties saw a large volume of high-quality empirical work that related divorce to various demographic and life course factors. In some areas, this work is sufficient to provide relatively conclusive answers.

Marriage order and stepchildren. Martin and Bumpass (1989) report that the divorce rate among marriages formed between 1980 and 1985 is 25% higher for second than first marriages. There is some debate, however, about why this occurs. Martin and Bumpass and Teachman (1986) both use a "kinds of people" explanation to argue that the people in remarriages carry with them the characteristics (early age at first marriage, lower education, and so on) that raised the probability of their first marriage dissolving. White and Booth (1985), on the other hand, argue that the internal dynamics of second marriages (largely because of stepchildren) are more problematic than first marriages. Considering the growing proportion of marriages that are second marriages, this area of research has drawn remarkably little empirical attention.

Parental divorce. A growing literature shows that parental divorce increases the likelihood of divorce for their children (Greenberg and Nay,

1982; McLanahan and Bumpass, 1988). No studies contradict this finding or suggest that the increased incidence of divorce has reduced the intergenerational inheritance of divorce proneness.

Cohabitation. Several studies demonstrate that premarital cohabitation is associated with higher probability of divorce (Bennett, Blanc, and Bloom, 1988; Booth and Johnson, 1988; White, 1987). The most common explanation of this finding is a "kinds of people" one: that the kinds of people who choose to flout convention by cohabiting are the same kinds of people who flout normative marital behavior, have lower commitment to marriage as an institution, and disregard the stigma of divorce.

Age at marriage. Early marriage increases the chances of divorce (cf. Balakrishnan et al., 1987; South and Spitze, 1986; Thornton and Rodgers, 1987). In fact, Martin and Bumpass (1989) conclude that age at marriage is the strongest predictor of divorce in the first 5 years of marriage. Moore and Waite (1981) find that this effect is independent of early childbearing.

Several studies show that the negative effects of youthful marriage last far into the marriage (Heaton, Albrecht, and Martin, 1985) and indeed into subsequent marriages (Martin and Bumpass, 1989; Teachman, 1986). The reasons for the consistently negative effect of youthful marriage have been largely unexplored, although Booth and Edwards (1985) suggest that poor role performance is a factor. Witt and associates (1987) find that reduced status attainment is not the intervening mechanism.

Premarital childbearing and premarital pregnancy. Several excellent studies provide unassailable documentation of the fact that premarital childbearing increases the risk of divorce in subsequent marriage but that, by itself, a premarital conception does not (Billy, Landale, and McLaughlin, 1986; Martin and Bumpass, 1989; Morgan and Rindfuss, 1984; Teachman, 1983; Wineberg, 1988). The effect of premarital birth may be stronger for white than black Americans, however, and stronger in the early years of marriage.

Fertility within marriage. Two studies using different techniques and data sets document that a *first* child reduces divorce probability to virtually

nil in the year following the birth (Waite, Haggstrom, and Kanouse, 1985; White and Booth,
1985). This preventive effect has not been observed for subsequent births (Koo and Janowitz,
1983). At older ages, children seem to slow the
pace at which dissatisfaction is translated to
divorce, but not to prevent it entirely (White,
Booth, and Edwards, 1986). Childlessness is associated with higher divorce rates (Wineberg, 1988)
and a more rapid divorce process (White et al.,
1986).

Perhaps the most interesting finding of the
decade is Morgan, Lye, and Condran's (1988)
finding that parents of sons are less likely to
divorce than parents with daughters. The authors
attribute this finding to fathers' greater involvement with sons than with daughters, a supposition
that is supported by cross-cultural evidence showing that greater father involvement in child care
reduces divorce (Seccombe and Lee, 1987).

Age and marital duration. Because age and
marital duration are strongly correlated, it is difficult to untangle the effects of the two conceptually distinct variables. Empirically, the results
are similar: divorce is less likely when respondents
and marriages are older (Fergusson, Horwood,
and Shannon, 1984; Thornton and Rodgers,
1987). How much of this effect is due to selective
attrition through divorce and how much to actual
changes in propensity to divorce with age and
duration is unclear. It is also unclear whether the
reasons for divorce change by age and duration.
Booth and associates (1986) argue that age at marriage, health, social integration, and income are
less important predictors of divorce at higher ages
and durations, but two other studies show no
significant differences in predictors of divorce
among long verus short marriages (Heaton et al.,
1985; South and Spitze, 1986).

Race. Black Americans are more likely than white
Americans to divorce, and this difference is strong
and consistent. Some analysts have attributed the
difference to different sex ratios (Guttentag and
Secord, 1983) or to different male-to-female earnings ratios (Secord and Ghee, 1986), but others
point out that marital stability among blacks is
different from that of whites in response to the
same factors (Billy et al., 1986; Teachman, 1986).
It appears that the racial differential cannot be explained by controlling socioeconomic status and

background factors such as fertility, sex ratios,
and age at marriage.

Family Process

In their 1980 Decade in Review article on the
causes of divorce, Price-Bonham and Balswick
(1980: 962) conclude, "Whereas there are
substantial empirical bases for the relationship
between demographic variables and divorce, the
interpersonal literature is limited primarily to a
theoretical and speculative format." The same
tendency exists today. Although we have made
substantial progress in the last decade, we still
know comparatively little about how divorce is
related to relationship quality, family structure,
or social-psychological factors.

Marital happiness. Although a strong link between marital happiness and divorce seems simple
and self-evident, empirical evidence is scant.
Booth and associates (1986), however, report that
individuals with low marital happiness at Time 1
are from 4 to 5 times more likely to divorce over a
3-year period than those with very high marital
happiness.

Thinking about divorce. One area that has received substantial attention during this decade is
the predivorce process. Implicit in this research is
the assumption that divorce reflects consideration
of alternatives and barriers and is far from being a
simple reflection of marital unhappiness.

Two approaches have dominated this area.
One group of researchers (cf. Kitson, Holmes,
and Sussman, 1983; Morgan, 1988) have studied
separation and divorce petitions to determine the
factors that lead to divorce as opposed to reconciliation. Their findings, consistent with exchange
theory, indicate that reconciliations are more likely when the costs of divorce are high (children are
present) and alternatives low (older, lower income, wife unemployed). Booth and his associates (Booth et al., 1983, 1985, 1986) have taken
another approach by developing a scale to measure marital instability (propensity to divorce).
Their results also show that barriers and alternatives significantly affect the probability of trans-
lating instability into divorce.

Marital interaction. Three studies demonstrate
that shared time together is associated with lower

divorce rates (Booth et al., 1985, 1986; Hill, 1988). Because of its potential to link divorce to a variety of other measures, such as female labor force participation, this variable deserves more attention.

Socioeconomic status. Individual-level studies show a clear inverse relation between income and other measures of socioeconomic status and divorce (Ferguson et al., 1984; Greenstein, 1985; Martin and Bumpass, 1989; Smith and Meitz, 1985; South and Spitze, 1986).

Women's labor force participation. On the individual level, the findings on the relation between female labor force participation and divorce are equivocal. Several studies find that female labor force participation increases divorce (Booth, Johnson, White, and Edwards, 1984; Rank, 1987; Spitze and South, 1985), but other studies, also with national samples or panel components, show that female labor force participation *reduces* marital instability (Greenstein, 1990; Smith and Meitz, 1985; South and Spitze, 1986). Greenstein (1990) and Spitze and South (1985) find that the only indicator of wife's employment to relate positively to divorce is hours employed. Greenstein, in fact, finds that divorce is *less* likely when the wife's earnings and the wife's share of all family earnings are higher. Two studies showing a negative effect of women's hours (Hill, 1988; Spitze and South, 1985) support the idea that autonomy of husbands' and wives' lives may be the critical factor.

Although there is some support here for those who would like to hope that women's status and the family are not "at odds" (Degler, 1980), most of the findings and the theorizing is on the other side. Better attention to various dimensions of women's status (wages, hours, economic and social autonomy) and to the family processes involved (quarrels over the division of labor, and so on) are necessary to resolve this issue.

Personal accounts. Existing separately and unequally from the empirical studies that use major national data sets are several studies that actually ask divorced people what caused their divorce. These studies often rely on small, geographically narrow samples drawn from court records. Whether because of their modest samples or their reliance on social-psychological factors that can-

not be tapped easily with data sets and methods normally used, there is little integration between the results of these studies and those reviewed above.

Respondents' accounts of their own divorces illuminate several factors that receive little attention in the empirical literature: alcoholism and drug abuse, infidelity, incompatibility, physical and emotional abuse, disagreements about gender roles, sexual incompatibility, and financial problems (Albrecht, Bahr, and Goodman, 1983; Bloom, Niles, and Tatcher, 1985; Cleek and Pearson, 1985; Kitson and Sussman, 1982).

Because these studies only include divorced respondents, they can tell us little about the extent to which these factors predict divorce. It is striking, however, that so few empirical studies of divorce take these individual complaints seriously and that so few of the variables studied extensively are listed by divorcing populations (Kitson and Sussman, 1982).

METHODS AND THEORY

Analytic Techniques

Analysis of divorce determinants has become vastly more sophisticated than it was a decade ago. Although some studies rely on simple OLS regression, much of the research on divorce published in this decade uses proportional-hazards modeling or probit or logit regression. These techniques are more suited to a dichotomous dependent variable, and they also provide more flexibility in dealing with complex, time-dependent processes.

In addition to moving away from simple OLS regression, many studies show an awareness of the complexity of effects by testing for various types of interactions. Several studies deal explicitly with the possibility of different effects by cohort (e.g., Martin and Bumpass, 1989; Smith and Meitz, 1985; White, 1987) or marital duration (Booth et al., 1986; Heaton et al., 1985). Tests for modifications by sex and race are commonplace.

Samples and Data Sets

In a 1983 review, Albrecht, Bahr, and Goodman concluded that divorce research relied too heavily on a few geographically limited samples and on wives' reports. Many of these criticisms are no longer valid. During the decade of the 1980s, most of the studies appearing in major journals were based on large national data sets; many reflected the growing availability of longitudinal studies (National Labor Surveys [NLS], Panel Study of Income Dynamics [PSID], and the study by Booth and associates). Although several reports rely on national fertility studies that interview women only, few findings now rely on wife-only reports.

The major flaw in our data sets is that few were designed to study divorce. With the exception of the study by Booth and associates, which interviewed a national panel with the aim of predicting divorce rates, most of the research on divorce in this decade comes from secondary analysis of economic or demographic data sets—the NLS, PSID, National Studies of Family Growth (NSFG), Current Population Surveys (CPS), or the General Social Surveys (GSS). A direct consequence of relying on secondary data sets is that we know little about family process and much about demographic factors. The longitudinal studies (PSID, NLS) contain few social variables, and they cannot be used to examine relationship quality or social-psychological factors. Cross-sectional data sets (such as the NSFG, CPS, or GSS) are even more limited in that researchers are restricted to past divorce as a measure of the dependent variable. Since information on past relationships and attitudes is seldom available or reliable, these studies are restricted to studying the effect of static variables such as age at marriage.

A major step toward surmounting the substantive restrictions imposed by inadequate data would be funding the proposed second wave of the National Study of Families and Households. If the panel component of this broadly conceived study is funded, it will help reduce the serious limitation that data availability has placed on divorce research and should enable the next Decade in Review summary to report a much-expanded variety of findings.

Theoretical Frameworks

Theory is a relatively underdeveloped area of divorce research. Generally, researchers rely more on common sense than on theoretical perspectives, and little pretense is made that theory drives empirical analysis. When theory is invoked, it is usually some form of cost/benefit theory, either in the pure economic form (Becker, 1981) or as recast into social exchange language by Levinger (1976).

Many researchers suggest that their research is grounded in life course theory (Billy et al., 1986; Heaton et al., 1985). Although more accurately termed a conceptual framework than a theory, this perspective has made two major contributions. First, it has provided a vehicle for the integration of family studies and demography, providing a rationale for including age at marriage, marriage-pregnancy sequences, and so on in family models other than as demographic control variables. Second, life course theory directs our attention to the possibility that the effect of causal factors will interact with period, cohort, and age effects. As a result of this perspective, there is a greater sense of the time-dependency of social processes.

Overall, the study of divorce has taken place outside major theoretical currents of contemporary sociology. Although feminist or conflict theories seem to be possible candidates for explaining marital conflict (over power, the division of labor, and gender roles) and its resolution, they have not been applied to studies of divorce. An underappreciated piece by Chafetz (1980) is a rare exception. She argues that one reason for increased divorce is that sociohistorical factors have undermined the use of authority (a low-conflict power strategy) and increased the frequency with which spouses engage in more costly attempts to influence and control one another.

The major sociology journals are dominated by articles concerning gender equality, postindustrialization, and the "new structuralism." An understanding of marriage and divorce must be articulated into these larger concerns on the macro level as well as into a general theory of human behavior on the micro level.

SUMMARY AND RECOMMENDATIONS

The study of divorce has improved dramatically in the decade of the eighties. We have bigger, better data sets, more appropriate analytic techniques, and therefore more conclusive empirical findings. Despite the very substantial progress we have made in the last decade, there are some areas that need to be addressed with more rigor. The following is a brief list of some major opportunities for further development.

1. More research on family process. Although there remains a need to monitor demographic and life course trends as they affect divorce, our primary need for the future is to show *how*, through what mechanisms, these variables affect divorce. For example, why are those with remarriages, low incomes, premarital births, youthful age at marriage, and so on more likely to divorce? How do these factors relate to characteristics such as adultery, alcoholism, physical and emotional abuse, and incompatibility that are recognized by participants?

2. A broader approach to marriage. In order to understand divorce, we need to understand why people get married and why they stay married. This suggests more concern with mate selection and with the gains to marriage.

   a. Mate selection. Becker has suggested that one reason that young marriages are more likely to end in divorce is that they follow a shorter search process. Although marriage among 18-year-olds would face severe hurdles in any case, Becker identifies a critical factor that goes unexamined in studies of divorce. Research on mate selection has virtually disappeared in the last decade, with the result that we have to study the dissolution of unions with little or no information about how they are formed. Our inability to link the processes that support and encourage marital formation to the processes that affect divorce is a serious limitation.

   b. Gains to marriage. Family scholars agree that marriage is a weakened institution *and* that this is unfortunate (Davis, 1985; Glenn, 1987), yet we have few systematic studies of what benefits the family and specifically marriage offer in the contemporary world. If marriage is less important for individual happiness and societal welfare (Espenshade, 1985; Glenn and Weaver, 1988), this puts a different perspective on divorce. We need more careful assessment of the gains to marriage—to both adults and their children.

3. Sex differences in the divorce process. The accounts that men and women offer for their divorces differ substantially, and we know that many of the issues that divide marriages, such as the division of labor, are gender-related. Not only should researchers recognize that divorce is a dyadic property, there is a crying need to take explicit cognizance of the fact that divorce is the outcome of interactions between *women* and *men*. Do women and men want something different from marriage? Is marriage more important to women than men? Many scholars imply that the answers are yes (Glenn, 1987; Guttentag and Secord, 1983), but we have little supportive research or theory.

4. More theoretical development. At both the macro and the micro level, we need to place divorce within broader theoretical perspectives. This effort should help us integrate and understand the findings that we already have as well as point the way toward new possibilities.

5. More cross-cultural and historical research. The macro level remains relatively neglected in divorce research. If we are to understand why two-thirds of marriages formed today are likely to end in divorce, we need research that establishes the structural conditions of high versus low divorce. This research would place the study of divorce squarely within the study of marriage and the family as institutions.

REFERENCES

Albrecht, Stan, Howard Bahr, and Kristen Goodman. 1983. Divorce and Remarriage: Problems, Adaptations, and Adjustments. Westport, CT: Greenwood Press.

Balakrishnan, T. R., K. Vaninadha Rao, Everlyne Lapierre-Adamcyk, and Karol Krotki. 1987. "A hazard model analysis of the covariates of marriage dissolution in Canada." Demography 24: 395–406.

Becker, Gary S. 1981. A Treatise on the Family. Cambridge, MA: Harvard University Press.

Bellah, Robert N., Richard Madsen, William Sullivan, Ann Swidler, and Steven Tipton. 1985. Habits of the Heart: Individualism and Commitment in American Life. Berkeley: University of California Press.

Bennett, Neil G., Ann Klimas Blanc, and David E. Bloom. 1988. "Commitment and the modern union: Assessing the link between premarital cohabitation and subsequent marital stability." American Sociological Review 53: 127–138.

Billy, John, Nancy Landale, and Steven McLaughlin. 1986. "The effect of marital status at first birth on marital dissolution among adolescent mothers." Demography 23: 329–349.

Bloom, Bernard, Robert Niles, and Anna Tatcher. 1985. "Sources of marital dissatisfaction among newly separated persons." Journal of Family Issues 6: 359–373.

Blumberg, Grace. 1985. "New model of marriage and divorce: Significant legal developments in the last decade." Pp. 349–372 in Kingsley Davis (ed.), Contemporary Marriage. New York: Russell Sage.

Booth, Alan, and John Edwards. 1985. "Age at marriage and marital instability." Journal of Marriage and the Family 47: 67–75.

Booth, Alan, and David Johnson. 1988. "Premarital cohabitation and marital success." Journal of Family Issues 9: 255–272.

Booth, Alan, David Johnson, and John Edwards. 1983. "Measuring marital instability." Journal of Marriage and the Family 45: 387–394.

Booth, Alan, David Johnson, Lynn White, and John Edwards. 1984. "Women, outside employment, and marital stability." American Journal of Sociology 90: 567–583.

Booth, Alan, David Johnson, Lynn White, and John Edwards. 1985. "Predicting divorce and permanent separation." Journal of Family Issues 6: 331–346.

Booth, Alan, David Johnson, Lynn White, and John Edwards. 1986. "Divorce and marital instability over the life course." Journal of Family Issues 7: 421–442.

Breault, K. D., and Augustine J. Kposowa. 1987. "Explaining divorce in the United States: A study of 3,111 counties, 1980." Journal of Marriage and the Family 49: 549–558.

Brodbar-Nemzer, Jay Y. 1986. "Divorce and group commitment: The case of the Jews." Journal of Marriage and the Family 48: 329–340.

Chafetz, Janet. 1980. "Conflict resolution in marriage." Journal of Family Issues 3: 397–421.

Cherlin, Andrew J. 1981. Marriage, Divorce, Remarriage. Cambridge, MA: Harvard University Press.

Cherlin, Andrew, and Frank Furstenberg. 1988. "The changing European family." Journal of Family Issues 9: 291–297.

Cleek, Margaret, and T. Pearson. 1985. "Perceived causes of divorce: An analysis of interrelationships." Journal of Marriage and the Family 47: 179–183.

Davis, Kingsley. 1985. "Introduction." In Kingsley Davis (ed.), Contemporary Marriage. New York: Russell Sage.

Degler, Carl. 1980. At Odds: Women and the Family in America from the Revolution to the Present. New York: Oxford University Press.

Espenshade, Thomas. 1985. "Marriage trends in America: Estimates, implications, and underlying causes." Population and Development Review 11: 193–245.

Fergusson, D. M., L. J. Horwood, and F. T. Shannon. 1984. "A proportional hazards model of family breakdown." Journal of Marriage and the Family 46: 539–549.

Glenn, Norval D. 1987. "Continuity versus change, sanguineness versus concern: Views of the American family in the late 1980s." Journal of Family Issues 8: 348–354.

Glenn, Norval D., and Beth Ann Shelton. 1985. "Regional differences in divorce in the United States." Journal of Marriage and the Family 47: 641–652.

Glenn, Norval D., and Charles Weaver. 1988. "The changing relationship of marital status to reported happiness." Journal of Marriage and the Family 50: 317–324.

Glick, Paul, and Sung-ling Lin. 1986. "Recent changes in divorce and remarriage." Journal of Marriage and the Family 48: 737–747.

Greenberg, Ellen F., and W. Robert Nay. 1982. "The intergenerational transmission of marital instability reconsidered." Journal of Marriage and the Family 44: 335–347.

Greenstein, Theodore N. 1985. "Occupation and divorce." Journal of Family Issues 6: 347–357.

Greenstein, Theodore N. 1990. "Marital disruption and the employment of married women." Journal of Marriage and the Family 52: 657–676.

Guttentag, Marcia, and Paul Secord. 1983. Too Many Women? The Sex Ratio Question. Beverly Hills, CA: Sage.

Heaton, Tim B., Stan L. Albrecht, and Thomas K. Martin. 1985. "The timing of divorce." Journal of Marriage and the Family 47: 631–639.

Hill, Martha. 1988. "Marital stability and spouses' shared time." Journal of Family Issues 9: 427–451.

Kitson, Gay, William Holmes, and Marvin Sussman. 1983. "Withdrawing divorce petitions." Journal of Divorce 7: 51–66.

Kitson, Gay, and Marvin Sussman. 1982. "Marital complaints, demographic characteristics, and symptoms of mental distress in divorce." Journal of Marriage and the Family 44: 87–101.

Koo, Helen, and B. Janowitz. 1983. "Interrelationships between fertility and marital dissolution." Demography 20: 129–145.

Lee, Gary. 1982. Family Structure and Interaction: A Comparative Analysis (2nd ed.). Minneapolis: University of Minnesota Press.

Levinger, George. 1976. "A social psychological perspective on marital dissolution." Journal of Social Issues 32: 21–42.

Martin, Teresa Castro, and Larry L. Bumpass. 1989. "Recent trends in marital disruption." Demography 26: 37–51.

McLanahan, Sara, and Larry Bumpass. 1988. "Intergenerational consequences of family disruption." American Journal of Sociology 94: 130–152.

Moore, Kristin, and Linda Waite. 1981. "Marital dissolution, early motherhood, and early marriage." Social Forces 60: 20–40.

Morgan, Leslie. 1988. "Outcomes of marital separation." Journal of Marriage and the Family 50: 493–498.

Morgan, S. Philip, and Ronald Rindfuss. 1984. "Marital disruption: Structural and temporal dimensions." American Journal of Sociology 90: 1055–1077.

Morgan, S. Philip, Diane Lye, and Gretchen Condran. 1988. "Sons, daughters, and the risk of marital disruption." American Journal of Sociology 94: 110–129.

Popenoe, David. 1988. Disturbing the Nest: Family Change and Decline in Modern Societies. New York: Aldine de Gruyter.

Price-Bonham, Sharon, and Jack Balswick. 1980. "The noninstitutions: Divorce, desertion, and remarriage." Journal of Marriage and the Family 42: 959–972.

Rank, Mark. 1987. "The formation and dissolution of marriages in the welfare population." Journal of Marriage and the Family 49: 15–20.

Roussel, Louis, and Irène Théry. 1988. "France: Demographic change and family policy since World War II." Journal of Family Issues 9: 336–353.

Schoen, Robert, William Urton, Karen Woodrow, and John Baj. 1985. "Marriage and divorce in twentieth century American cohorts." Demography 22: 101–114.

Seccombe, Karen, and Gary Lee. 1987. "Female status, wives' autonomy, and divorce: A cross-cultural study." Family Perspective 20: 241–249.

Secord, Paul, and Kenneth Ghee. 1986. "Implications of the black marriage market for marital conflict." Journal of Family Issues 7: 21–30.

Smith, A. Wade, and June Meitz. 1985. "Vanishing supermoms and other trends in marital dissolution, 1969–1978." Journal of Marriage and the Family 47: 53–65.

South, Scott J. 1985. "Economic conditions and the divorce rate." Journal of Marriage and the Family 47: 31–41.

South, Scott, and Glenna Spitze. 1986. "Determinants of divorce over the marital life course." American Sociological Review 51: 583–590.

Spitze, Glenna, and Scott South. 1985. "Women's employment, time expenditure, and divorce." Journal of Family Issues 6: 307–329.

Teachman, Jay D. 1983. "Early marriage, premarital fertility, and marital dissolution." Journal of Family Issues 4: 105–126.

Teachman, Jay D. 1986. "First and second marital dissolution: A decomposition exercise for whites and blacks." Sociological Quarterly 27: 571–590.

Thornton, Arland, and Willard Rodgers. 1987. "The influence of individual and historical time on marital dissolution." Demography 24: 1–22.

Trent, Katherine, and Scott South. 1989. "Structural determinants of the divorce rate: A cross-societal analysis." Journal of Marriage and the Family 51: 391–404.

Trovato, Frank. 1986. "The relationship between migration and the provincial divorce rate in Canada, 1971 and 1978: A reassessment." Journal of Marriage and Family 48: 207–216.

Waite, Linda, Gus Haggstrom, and David Kanouse. 1985. "The consequences of parenthood for the marital stability of young adults." American Sociological Review 50: 850–857.

Weitzman, Lenore. 1985. The Divorce Revolution. New York: Free Press.

White, James. 1987. "Premarital cohabitation and marital stability in Canada." Journal of Marriage and Family 49: 641–647.

White, Lynn, and Alan Booth. 1985. "The transition to parenthood and marital quality." Journal of Family Issues 6: 435–449.

White, Lynn, Alan Booth, and John Edwards. 1986. "Children and marital happiness: Why the negative relationship." Journal of Family Issues 7: 131–148.

Wilkinson, Kenneth P., Robert R. Reynolds, Jr., James G. Thompson, and Lawrence M. Ostresh. 1983. "Divorce and recent net migration into the Old West." Journal of Marriage and Family 45: 437–445.

Wineberg, Howard. 1988. "Duration between marriage and first birth and marital stability." Social Biology 35: 91–102.

Witt, David, and associates. 1987. "The consequences of early marriage and marital dissolution." Social Spectrum 7: 191–207.

GAY C. KITSON   *University of Akron*

LESLIE A. MORGAN   *University of Maryland–Baltimore County**

The Multiple Consequences of Divorce:

A Decade Review

*Considerable research attention during the 1980s
has centered on the consequences of divorce. This
selective review focuses primarily on adults, and
on areas of controversy and new emphases in
studies of divorce. A critique of methodology and
suggested directions for future research are included.*

The 1980s saw a stabilization of the precipitous increase in United States divorce rates that occurred
in the 1960s and '70s. In 1989, the rate was 4.7
divorces per 1,000 population, down from a high
of 5.3 per 1,000 in 1979 and 1981 (Glick, 1988;
National Center for Health Statistics, 1990). Projections call for between one-half and two-thirds
of recently contracted first marriages to end in
divorce eventually (Martin and Bumpass, 1989;
Norton and Moorman, 1987).[1] Since the likelihood of remarriage decreases with age, and given
the drop in the remarriage rate (Glick and Lin,
1986), more people are spending part of their lives
dealing with the multiple consequences of
divorce.

THE SCOPE OF DIVORCE ADJUSTMENT

The concept of "adjustment" is frequently used
as an organizing theme in discussions of the con-

Department of Sociology, University of Akron, Akron, OH
44325-1905.

*Department of Sociology and Anthropology, University of
Maryland–Baltimore County, Catonsville, MD 21228.

sequences of divorce, and we follow that approach. Adjustment to divorce is defined here (cf.
Kitson and Raschke, 1981) as being relatively free
of signs and symptoms of physical or mental illness; being able to function adequately in the
daily role responsibilities of home, family, work,
and leisure; and having developed an independent
identity that is not tied to the status of being married or to the ex-spouse. While this definition includes a wide range of intra- and interpersonal
dimensions, we focus on three aspects featured in
the literature—health, economic, and social adjustment among adults.[2]

Health Consequences

The separated and divorced continue, as in past
decades, to show heightened levels of mortality
and psychological and physical morbidity as compared to the married, the single and, often, the
widowed in the United States and other societies
(Bebbington, 1987; Kisker and Goldman, 1987;
Mergenhagen, Lee, and Gove, 1985; National
Center for Health Statistics, 1988; Rosengren,
Wedel, and Wilhelmsen, 1989; Smith, Mercy, and
Conn, 1988; Trovato and Lauris, 1989). The
reasons for these findings are less clear.

One problem in interpreting findings on
marital status and health is that studies are often
cross-sectional, population-based surveys including people separated and divorced for varying
lengths of time and omitting those of the divorced
group who remarried or who died. Thus, it is difficult to disentangle issues of selectivity, time

since separation, and the impact of postdivorce events. In one study based on data from a large probability sample, Menaghan (1985) found that persons who subsequently divorced were not more distressed than other married persons at a predivorce-decision interview. Four years later, however, the divorced had higher distress levels than the married, with economic problems, unavailability of confidants, and deterioration in the standard of living contributing to this distress. On the other hand, in a study of patients in a health maintenance organization, Doherty, Su, and Needle (1989) reported lower scores on psychological well-being for persons who separated within the following year compared to those who were continuously married (see also Wertlieb, Budman, Demby, and Randall, 1984). These variations in findings may be due to the differences in the timing of the preseparation interviews and differences in the rapidity with which individuals move from identification of marital problems to filing for a divorce and completing the follow-up interview (Melichar and Chiriboga, 1988). Future research is needed to explore these issues more fully.

In an attempt to specify the mechanisms that influence health status, researchers are beginning to link psychological and physiological measures that highlight the increased risk of illness because of suppressed immunological functioning in stressful conditions such as divorce (see Ader, Cohen, and Felten, 1990; Calabrese, Kling, and Gold, 1987). In a study of separated, divorced, and married women, Kielcolt-Glaser et al. (1987) found poorer immune functioning among (a) the married with poor-quality marriages and (b) the separated and divorced who had been separated shorter periods of time and who had greater attachment to their (ex-)spouses. Further exploration of such physiological links may help to explain the heightened health disturbance of the separated and divorced.

Economic Adjustment

The 1980s saw a new focus on the economic aftermath of divorce, especially among women, with economic status being viewed as an outcome rather than as a correlate of psychological adjustment. The best-known work is Weitzman's (1985) study of divorced Californians, showing dramatic decreases in standard of living for women and sizable improvements for men in the first year after divorce. Her results have been challenged by researchers reporting more modest economic changes from better, longitudinal data (Hoffman and Duncan, 1988; Morgan, in press). Reductions both in income (around 30%) and in economic well-being for women are followed by stabilization at lower income levels (Corcoran, Duncan, and Hill, 1984; Weiss, 1984). Others report falls into or near poverty; money as a source of distress; and limited potential for economic recovery, barring remarriage (Arendell, 1987; Morgan, 1989; Peterson, 1989; Pett and Vaughn-Cole, 1986). Economic consequences for women vary according to sociodemographic characteristics (Duncan and Hoffman, 1985). Similar detail is unavailable on divorced men, because their economic situations after divorce are generally presumed to be nonproblematic (Garfinkel and Oellerich, 1989).

The 1980s saw further work detailing incomplete payment and inadequate amounts of child support (Beller and Graham, 1985; Cassetty, 1983). Recent estimates, based on federally mandated formulae for determining child support in three states, suggest that fathers are able to pay over twice the amounts currently awarded in child support (Garfinkel and Oellerich, 1989) and that they spend 50% more per capita on basic expenses than do women who receive child support (Fletcher, 1989). More child support payments were awarded in 1985 (61.3%) than in 1983 (57.7%), but the percentage of persons actually receiving such payments did not differ significantly—76% in 1983 and 74% in 1985 (U.S. Bureau of the Census, 1987). Few published reports have assessed the impact of the newer federally mandated techniques to enforce payment of child support.

Labor force involvement is a key element in the gender differences in economic status after divorce. Many studies, but not all (see Weiss, 1984), report that divorcing women increase their work involvement as defined by rates of participation and hours worked (Duncan and Hoffman, 1985; Peterson, 1989). Receipt of child support does not suppress employment by divorced women, but rarely awarded alimony—14.6% were awarded it in 1985 (U.S. Bureau of the Census, 1987)—is related to lower labor force activity, probably because it is older, longer-married women with less employment experience who receive it (Beller and Graham, 1985).

Measurement of the economic status of divorced households has become more sophisticated and in some ways more objective. Researchers now commonly use income-to-needs ratios, with needs defined by the poverty level, as a standardized measure. This overcomes the difficulties of comparing families of different sizes and adjusts automatically when a family member departs at divorce (Peterson, 1989).

Social Adjustment

Relatively few studies have looked at indicators of social adjustment as dependent variables. In a 6-month preventive-intervention study whose aims were to provide social support and enhanced competencies in family, work, and leisure activities, Bloom, Hodges, Kern, and McFaddin (1985) looked at a series of social dimensions—homemaking difficulties, work functioning, loneliness, and sexual dissatisfaction—and found that those in the intervention group experienced less difficulty than those in the control group. These differential effects continued to produce measurable group differences at 30 months and at 4 years after the intervention. Kitson and Roach (1989) developed a scale assessing eight aspects of everyday life for widowed and divorced women, including work, leisure activities, and time with children. Difficulty in the performance of these social roles accounted for more of the distress experienced for the divorced than the widowed, which suggests that adjusting to changed social roles is an important aspect of adjustment to divorce.

APPROACHES TO DIVORCE ADJUSTMENT

Two theoretical approaches have guided much of the discussion of adjustment to divorce. In one perspective, difficulties in divorce adjustment are seen as the result of selection and pathology (Halem, 1980). Those who divorce are thought to be socially and psychologically unfit to pick appropriate partners, maintain relationships with them, or cope with the disruption of their relationships. The alternative approach considers divorce as a crisis, with the events preceding and following the marital breakdown creating disruption in accustomed patterns of thinking and action. It is becoming increasingly clear, however, that neither approach addresses the issues com-

pletely. It is hard to invoke pathology as *the* explanation for divorce and its sequelae when so many people are divorcing. For some, affective disorders, alcoholism, drug use, and family violence are among the reasons given for the decision to divorce, while for others, the events leading up to and after the divorce may produce these disorders (Kitson and Sussman, 1982).

Similarly, a "crisis" implies a relatively self-contained and limited period of distress. However, longitudinal research increasingly suggests more long-term difficulties in adjustment (Bloom et al., 1985; Coysh, Johnston, Tschann, Wallerstein, and Klein, 1989; Kitson with Holmes, in press; Wallerstein, 1989; Wallerstein and Blakeslee, 1989; Wallerstein and Kelly, 1980). It may be more appropriate to look at divorce as a chronic, nagging stressor, as in McCubbin and Patterson's (1982) double ABCX model, in which events pile up at the time of and after the divorce and exacerbate adjustment problems (Buehler, Hogan, Robinson, and Levy, 1985–86; Ensel, 1986; Hetherington, Stanley-Hogan, and Anderson, 1989; Tschann, Johnston, and Wallerstein, 1989). In an attempt to link the crisis and pathological models, divorce is also seen as involving a series of losses and changes. Certain individuals take longer to adjust because of their prior psychological vulnerabilities (Jacobson, 1983; Kitson with Holmes, in press).

Those taking a more clinical focus are increasingly linking developmental theory to a systems orientation, with divorce seen as an event that requires the negotiation of developmental tasks (Ahrons and Rodgers, 1987; Carter and McGoldrick, 1988; Lalande, 1990). Although this approach seems particularly suited for examining children's adjustment (Emery, 1988; Hodges, 1986; Kalter, 1990), little empirical work with adults or families has taken this tack.

Divorce as a Process

One clear change in the divorce literature is the growing recognition of the processual nature of divorce adjustment. Although we do not define divorce as a "normal" part of family life, as Price and McKenry (1989) do, it is among the most stressful events that many individuals experience. Whether the stressfulness of divorce will decrease as it becomes a more normative event is unclear. If social context is more important than individual reaction, then adjustment difficulties should decrease as divorce becomes a more common event. In a sense it should not be surprising that the consequences of divorce are problematic. Complex marital bonds must be severed—a difficult task, since the partner was generally viewed as a "good choice" initially and not all of the marriage was bad. Following divorce, there is a growing social and legal expectation that couples with children will maintain a *civil* (meaning both "civilized" and "legal") relationship until the children reach a minimum age of 18. This socially and legally mandated continuity asks a lot of people who could not tolerate living together. Thus it is not surprising that divorce is initially stressful and has continuing stressful consequences.

INDEPENDENT VARIABLES INFLUENCING ADJUSTMENT

In this section, we review findings concerning some of the influences that account for diversity in response to divorce.

Gender

The research on gender differences in divorce adjustment is curiously mixed. Epidemiological surveys indicate that separated and divorced males have higher rates of morbidity than females (Riessman and Gerstel, 1985). Social surveys generally report higher levels of distress among females, yet women also feel more positive about the experience (Bloom et al., 1985; Kitson with Holmes, in press; for an exception, see Berman and Turk, 1981). Furthermore, more variation in divorce adjustment is generally explained for women than men (Farnsworth, Pett, and Lund, 1989; Kitson with Holmes, in press; Tschann et al., 1989). On the other hand, Bloom and Caldwell (1981) found that women had higher symptom levels prior to separation, and men, higher levels early in the postseparation period. These differences in results may derive from reliance on self-report measures of psychological symptoms in social surveys, measures on which women typically score higher than men. More research has looked at women so that the models may be better specified for them. There do appear to be "his" and "her" responses to divorce, so that new research needs to include more measures appropriate to males, such as physiological func-

tioning and antisocial and acting-out behaviors.

Ethnicity

Although divorce rates vary, with blacks' rates higher than those of Hispanics, who are similar to whites (Norton and Moorman, 1987), relatively little research has looked at ethnic differences in adjustment to divorce. The lack of divorce adjustment research among blacks may be due to the heavy reliance on pathological theory in studies of black families (Fine and Schwebel, 1987), which leads to interest in the causes of divorce. Several recent studies report fewer adjustment difficulties for blacks than for whites (Gove and Shin, 1989; Kitson with Holmes, in press; Menaghan and Lieberman, 1986). Additional research is needed to attempt to replicate these findings in a large sample of socioeconomically varied blacks who divorce and to specify the reasons for such differences. There are few studies on adjustment to divorce among Hispanics, and none (of which we are aware) that compare Mexican, Puerto Rican, Cuban, and other Hispanic groups to one another or to blacks and whites. A similar statement can be made for Asian Americans, despite diversity in divorce rates by area of national origin (Laosa, 1988).

Life Cycle Issues

Although it has been hypothesized that adjustment to divorce would be more difficult in later life, research results have not been consistent. Chiriboga (1982), in a study with small numbers of older persons, found that newly divorced older persons were lower in morale and less optimistic than their younger peers, while Gove and Shin (1989) and Roach and Kitson (1989) report that younger divorced persons were more distressed than older ones. Older divorced persons report more economic distress than the married (Uhlenberg and Myers, 1981). The mixed results for gender differences among older divorcees warrant further research in this area (Farnsworth et al., 1989; Hagestad and Smyer, 1982; Hyman, 1983).

Older (ever) divorced adults may differ from their peers. They may not recover from the economic costs of earlier divorce (Fethke, 1989; Keith, 1985). Lack of contact with noncustodial fathers removes children from the social support system that is critical to the well-being of individuals in later life (Cooney and Uhlenberg, 1990). Research delineating the uniqueness of becoming or being divorced across the life cycle must disentangle the complexities of life cycle and cohort variation in the divorce experience (Chiriboga, 1982; Emery, 1988; Hennon, 1983). Further assessment of the consequences of divorce across the life course is needed, with stratified sampling to ensure enough younger and older persons for study.

Social Support and Social Networks

Social networks are disrupted by divorce as measured by loss or change of friends, disrupted socializing, and loss of contact with affinal kin (Ambert, 1988; Furstenberg and Spanier, 1984). Kin play a key role in adjustment to divorce, especially among women (Gerstel, 1988), with friends providing distinct types of social support. Relatively little attention has been paid to the potential stress produced by social networks (Milardo, 1987; Wilcox, 1981).

The separated and divorced are more likely to seek formal sources of help than are married, single, or widowed persons. In a national probability sample, Veroff, Kulka, and Douvan (1981) found that 54% of separated and divorced women and 46% of men had sought help from professionals, compared to 28% of married women and 18% of men (see also Kitson with Holmes, in press; Spanier and Thompson, 1984).

Attachment

The 1980s have seen a substantial amount of empirical research on attachment, or continued affectional bonds between ex-spouses. A number of methodologies have been used, including laboratory studies, clinicians' ratings, and self-reports of behaviors and feelings considered indicative of the concept (Berman, 1985; 1988b; Coysh et al., 1989). While some authors have focused on the presence or absence of attachment (Brown, Felton, Whiteman, and Manela, 1980; Brown and Reimer, 1984; Kitson, 1982), others, in a departure from Bowlby's delineation of the concept (1980; see also Weiss, 1982) have looked at positive and negative dimensions of attachment (Masheter, in press; Tschann et al., 1989). Attachment is associated with psychological and physiological symptoms (Kielcolt-Glaser et al., 1987),

with attachment declining as time passes from the divorce (Jacobson, 1983; Kitson, Graham, and Schmidt, 1983). In fact, there is some evidence to suggest that continuing attachment may help account for the heightened long-term psychological distress of some divorced persons (Berman, 1988a; Tschann et al., 1989; Wallerstein and Kelly, 1980).

LEGAL ISSUES

Joint Custody

The focus of greatest attention and controversy in the recent literature is joint custody (see Folberg, 1984; Kahn and Kammerman, 1988). Joint custody variously refers to legal (decision-making) responsibility, physical custody (residence) of children, or both. Joint legal custody is far more common, and few studies have examined residential joint custody (Emery, 1988). It seems difficult to maintain true joint legal custody of children when one parent has sole physical custody (Clark, Whitney, and Beck, 1988) or when parents are unable to resolve their interpersonal conflicts (Steinman, Zemmelman, and Knoblauch, 1985).

Research on joint custody has suffered from methodological limitations, such as self-selection and researchers' incorrect assumptions that court orders regarding custody are met in everyday life (Bowman and Ahrons, 1985; Clingempeel and Reppucci, 1982). Early findings are encouraging for parent and child adjustment in cases where joint custody was voluntary (Luepnitz, 1982; Steinman, 1984; Stewart, Schwebel, and Fine, 1986; Wolchik, Braver, and Sandler, 1985; for an exception, see Coysh et al., 1989).

While controversy continues regarding the appropriateness òf joint custody in cases of ongoing couple conflict, abuse, or parental disinterest or for very young children (Gardner, 1984; Johnston, Kline, and Tschann, 1989), 33 states now have joint custody laws (Freed and Walker, 1988). Complete evaluation of joint custody awaits better-designed studies with appropriate controls and adequate sample sizes.

No-Fault Divorce

The institution of no-fault divorce in nearly all states has created "divorce on demand" with wide availability for the first time in history (Glendon, 1987). Attention has focused on no-fault divorce and related changes in property settlements to gauge whether expected benefits (i.e., speedier divorce, less acrimony, more gender equity) followed adoption of no-fault laws (Welch and Price-Bonham, 1983; Wishik, 1986). Research results, somewhat contradictory across states, suggest no effect from no-fault on divorce rates, and that divorce takes less time (Bahr, 1983; McLindon, 1987), but little research is available on the level of distress or conflict in divorcing couples, which was among the major rationales for the introduction of no-fault legislation.

Because no-fault divorce neither rewards good marital behavior nor punishes violation of marital norms, economic outcomes have also changed. Economic settlements under no-fault are less advantageous to women; alimony is awarded even less often than before and for shorter durations; and assets and liabilities are divided more equally between spouses (Weitzman, 1985). Several authors have labeled this unfair, since women typically retain custody (and most of the costs) of childrearing (McLindon, 1987; Welch and Price-Bonham, 1983). Suggested remedies include pegging child support to inflation and better evaluation of the "new marital property" (pensions, professional degrees, and "good will" associated with a business) for more equitable property settlements (Wishik, 1986).

WHAT NEXT? NEW DIRECTIONS FOR THE 1990s

Methodology: Progress and Problems

The best of the research on the consequences of divorce has shown laudable improvement in methodology during the past decade, but more can be done. Many recent studies evidence good design and instrumentation but fail in sampling, or vice versa. Some central issues concerning research methodology are discussed below.

Establishing causation. Problems remain in understanding causal connections between divorce and its outcomes. First, a number of other events are related to or contingent upon the termination of marriage. Yet, divorce has often been designated as the presumptive cause for any subsequent changes, including some that may be coincidental. Second, it is difficult to rule out alternative explanations. For example, the finding

that fathers in joint custody arrangements are more active parents may be marred by self-selection (Coysh et al., 1989).

Sampling issues. Sampling in divorce studies has improved somewhat in the 1980s. A distinction still remains between studies of psychological and interpersonal adaptation, which tend to have smaller, often nonprobability samples and are designed to study divorce in detail, and studies of demographic or economic issues, which generally have larger samples and more generalizable results but less depth on divorce issues. More attention needs to be paid to developing samples that can adequately explore adjustment for adults and children (Zaslow, 1988, 1989).

Sampling procedures as a whole remain somewhat biased toward middle-class, white, and female subjects, thus leaving important gaps in our knowledge. Such gaps call for replications in more representative samples. Problems also remain in researchers' inadequate descriptions of samples (see Kitson et al., 1982).

Methodological Directions for the 1990s

Among the most beneficial and costly approaches that merit expansion are longitudinal, or panel, studies. Such studies can capture the process of divorce adjustment and can reduce the reliance on retrospective questions (Hyman, 1983). Prospective studies that begin before the divorce is filed and perhaps even before it is contemplated also control biases from selectivity into the divorced status and may show true changes in status for persons who experience divorce (Duncan and Hoffman, 1985).

Measurement issues. Greater attention needs to be paid to the quality of the instruments used to assess adjustment and the variables that influence it. Wherever possible, researchers should promote the development or use of scales rather than single items to enhance variability. Measures with poor reliability need to be weeded out or improved. Replication with poor instruments does not advance the level of knowledge in the field.

Similarly, researchers must remain alert to problems with correlations among multiple members of families sampled in a study. When multiple respondents from some families are included in research studies, such family members may be counted two or three times and the findings become biased. As a result, it is no longer a straightforward process to generalize such results to the population. While family members will differ somewhat in their responses, troubled breakups or easy ones will affect all family members in roughly the same direction (Kalter, Kloner, Schreier, and Okla, 1989).

Statistical issues. As research moves toward more sophisticated models of adjustment, reflecting the complexity of the divorce process, new statistical procedures should be considered. These include techniques such as soft modeling, or LVPS (latent variable path analysis with partial least squares estimation), that have the advantage of being able to assess latent concepts, as does LISREL, but which allow the use of categorical and interval measures and relax the assumption of the multivariate normal distribution of variables (Falk and Miller, 1990; Lohmoeller, 1989). A drawback of such techniques is that their complexity makes research results less accessible to those in clinical practice and others less schooled in such methods. Both clinical and basic researchers need to be clear in describing research techniques they have used and to present their findings in a way that makes them accessible to all professionals in the field.

Techniques are needed to analyze data collected from both (ex-)spouses or, preferably, all family members to assess the postdivorce environment globally, not just on the basis of individual perceptions (Thompson and Walker, 1982). The systems theory perspective calls for such measures, but little progress has been made in developing them. With inconsistency in sampling and research findings on many divorce topics, the wider use of meta-analysis procedures should be considered in order to draw some firmer conclusions about variable effects and to highlight the next steps in research (Glass, McGaw, and Smith, 1981).

Additional Research Needs

Cross-cultural research on divorce adjustment is sorely needed, especially in societies with differing rates of divorce and in those societies that are in transition from more traditional patrilineal cultures. Such research could clarify the relative contribution of particular social conditions versus more universal psychological reactions to the loss of a once meaningful relationship.

Much divorce research has focused on only one or the other of the dimensions of adjustment discussed above. A more multidimensional view of the consequences of divorce is an obvious next step in developing our understanding of this transition (Emery, 1988; Kitson, Babri, Roach, and Placidi, 1989).

What approach should be taken to the concept of adjustment? Should models be divorce-specific or should they clarify what makes it easier or harder for family members to cope with a variety of stressful events? Despite the overlap in concepts, the research studies in these two traditions often run parallel to one another. Each approach would be strengthened through greater attention to the other.

Johnston and Campbell (1988) and Isaacs, Montalvo, and Abelsohn (1986) talk about "difficult divorces" and high-conflict families. The proportion of divorcing couples that can be so characterized is unclear. Data on the number of these families and their characteristics based on court records are needed, as well as measures to identify such families early in the divorce process. These might include indicators of anger and intransigence. Finally, the lack of definitive research on the stigma of divorce leaves open the question of whether others actually treat the divorced differently because of their changed status or whether feelings of being stigmatized are the result of the individual's own sense of "failure" following divorce (Gerstel, 1987; Kitson with Holmes, in press).

Conclusion

Having explored some of the issues in adjustment to divorce, we are left with a question: Why is there such continuing societal concern about divorce and its consequences? A first reason is the long Judeo-Christian heritage of antipathy to divorce that colored the ability of persons to divorce either in religious or civil courts (Phillips, 1988). With the increasing focus on single-parent families and the impact of poverty on the formation of such families, there seems to be a continuing, if not growing, emphasis on the social-pathological view of divorce, despite evidence that the situation is more complex than that encompassed by this perspective. The world-wide trend toward conservatism and religious fundamentalism also fosters this approach.

Against this backdrop of social thought on the importance and literal sanctity of the family, several other factors are heightening concern about divorce today. First are the economic, social, and psychological effects of divorce on individuals and the corresponding implications for the society. The decision to divorce creates a period of dislocation and problematic functioning for many people; the length and universality of the period of disruption are still open issues. Second, divorce produces a financial and institutional burden on society's legal and human service systems. Examples of societal responses include mandatory court mediation, federal child support legislation, and pilot income support programs (Garfinkel and McClanahan, 1986).

A third concern is the long-term consequences of divorce for society. This concern was echoed in an issue on "the state of the American family" in the *Journal of Family Issues*, in which virtually all of the 19 authors worriedly discussed the impact of divorce on childrearing and the future of the family (Glenn, 1987). Why are there such concerns? Society must recreate itself each generation by producing new and appropriately socialized members, a task entrusted to families. Several troubling consequences of divorce threaten this process: (*a*) divorce generally reduces the income of the woman, who is most often the custodial parent; (*b*) the custodial parent is often overburdened and less able to attend to her children's developmental and economic needs; (*c*) there is some evidence that children of divorce are less likely to obtain the level of education they would have obtained had their parents remained married (Wallerstein and Huntington, 1983); and finally, (*d*) there is some evidence of a small intergenerational transmission of divorce; the fact that children of divorce are more likely to experience divorce themselves tends to perpetuate these concerns (Glenn and Kramer, 1987).

As divorce continues at high rates, with a few small-scale, limited exceptions (Bloom et al., 1985; Hetherington, 1989; Kitson with Holmes, in press; Wallerstein, in press; Wallerstein and Blakeslee, 1989; Wallerstein and Kelly, 1980), we still do not know what the long-term implications of divorce are for adults or children. If the goal of the society is to produce appropriately socialized

and trained individuals who, in turn, marry and reproduce, the issues discussed in this review—many of which still lack solid research evidence—raise important questions for the future.

Notes

The writing of this review was supported, in part, by Grants AG06591 and AG0495 from the National Institute on Aging.

1. Such estimates do not mean that 56% to 64% of *all* marriages end in divorce. Despite repeated discussions, understanding of this issue has not increased substantially in this decade. Divorce rates vary by the *age of marriage cohorts,* with recent cohorts predicted to have higher eventual divorce rates, on the basis of their current experience and the experiences of prior cohorts.

2. Although the divorce reviews in this issue are divided into "causes" and "consequences," authors often write about both. Citations in White's (1990) article should also be consulted. Because of space limitations, whenever possible, we have not included mutually relevant citations already mentioned in her review. Recent reviews on consequences of divorce for children (Demo and Acock, 1988; Emery, 1988; Hetherington et al., 1989) and for adults (Kitson and Raschke, 1981; Kitson et al., 1989; Morgan, in press; Price and McKenry, 1988, 1989; Raschke, 1987) supplement the topics we cover here.

References

Ader, Robert, Nicholas Cohen, and David Felten (eds.). 1990. Psychoneuroimmunology (Vol. 2). San Diego: Academic Press.

Ahrons, Constance R., and Roy H. Rodgers. 1987. Divorced Families: A Multidisciplinary Developmental View. New York: W. W. Norton.

Ambert, Anne-Marie. 1988. "Relationships with former in-laws after divorce: A research note." Journal of Marriage and the Family 50: 679–686.

Arendell, Terry J. 1987. "Women and the economics of divorce in the contemporary United States." Signs 13: 121–135.

Bahr, Stephen J. 1983. "Marital dissolution laws: Impact of recent changes for women." Journal of Family Issues 4: 455–466.

Bebbington, P. 1987. "Marital status and depression: A study of English national admission statistics." Acta Psychiatrica Scandinavia 75: 640–650.

Beller, Andrea H., and John W. Graham. 1985. "Variations in the economic well-being of divorced women and their children: The role of child support income." Pp. 471–509 in M. David and T. Smeeding (eds.), Horizontal Equity, Uncertainty, and Economic Well-Being. Chicago: University of Chicago Press.

Berman, William H. 1985. "Continued attachment after legal divorce." Journal of Family Issues 6:

375–392.

Berman, William H. 1988a. "The relationship of ex-spouse attachment to adjustment following divorce." Journal of Family Psychology 1: 312–328.

Berman, William H. 1988b. "The role of attachment in the post-divorce experience." Journal of Personality and Social Psychology 54: 496–503.

Berman, William H., and Dennis C. Turk. 1981. "Adaptation to divorce: Problems and coping strategies." Journal of Marriage and the Family 44: 179–189.

Bloom, Bernard L., and Robert A. Caldwell. 1981. "Sex differences in adjustment during the process of marital separation." Journal of Marriage and the Family 43: 693–701.

Bloom, Bernard L., William F. Hodges, Michael B. Kern, and Susan C. McFaddin. 1985. "A preventive intervention program for the newly separated: Final evaluations." American Journal of Orthopsychiatry 55: 9–26.

Bowlby, John. 1980. Loss: Sadness and Depression. Attachment and Loss (Vol. 3). New York: Basic Books.

Bowman, Madonna E., and Constance R. Ahrons. 1985. "Impact of legal custody status on fathers' parenting postdivorce." Journal of Marriage and the Family 47: 481–488.

Brown, Prudence, Barbara J. Felton, Victor Whiteman, and Roger Manela. 1980. "Attachment and distress following marital separation." Journal of Divorce 3: 303–317.

Brown, Steven D., and Dee A. Reimer. 1984. "Assessing attachment following divorce: Development and psychometric evaluation of the divorce reaction inventory." Journal of Counseling Psychology 31: 520–531.

Buehler, Cheryl A., M. Janice Hogan, Beatrice E. Robinson, and Robert J. Levy. 1985–86. "The parental divorce transition: Divorce-related stressors and well-being." Journal of Divorce 9: 61–81.

Calabrese, Joseph R., Mitchell A. Kling, and Philip W. Gold. 1987. "Alterations in immunocompetence during stress, bereavement, and depression: Focus on neuroendocrine regulation." American Journal of Psychiatry 144: 1123–1134.

Carter, Betty, and Monica McGoldrick. 1988. "Overview: The changing family life cycle: A framework for family therapy." Pp. 3–28 in Betty Carter and Monica McGoldrick (eds.), The Changing Family Life Cycle (2nd ed.). New York: Gardner Press.

Cassetty, Judith. 1983. The Parental Child-Support Obligation. Lexington, MA: Lexington Books.

Chiriboga, David A. 1982. "Adaptation to marital separation in later and earlier life." Journal of Gerontology 37: 109–114.

Clark, Susan C., Ruth A. Whitney, and James C. Beck. 1988. "Discrepancies between custodial awards and custodial practices: De jure and de facto custody." Journal of Divorce 11: 219–228.

Clingempeel, W. Glenn, and N. Dickon Reppucci. 1982. "Joint custody after divorce: Major issues and goals for research." Psychological Bulletin 91: 102–127.

Cooney, Teresa M., and Peter Uhlenberg. 1990. "The role of divorce in men's relations with their adult children after mid-life." Journal of Marriage and the Family 52: 677–688.

Corcoran, Mary, Greg J. Duncan, and Martha S. Hill. 1984. "The economic fortunes of women and children: Lessons from the Panel Study of Income Dynamics." Signs 10: 232–248.

Coysh, William S., Janet R. Johnston, Jeanne M. Tschann, Judith S. Wallerstein, and Marsha Kline. 1989. "Parental postdivorce adjustment to joint and sole physical custody families." Journal of Family Issues 10: 52–71.

Demo, David H., and Alan C. Acock. 1988. "The impact of divorce on children." Journal of Marriage and the Family 50: 619–648. [Reprinted in this volume]

Doherty, William J., Susan Su, and Richard Needle. 1989. "Marital disruption and psychological well-being: A panel study." Journal of Family Issues 10: 72–85.

Duncan, Greg J., and Saul D. Hoffman. 1985. "Economic consequences of marital instability." Pp 427–470 in M. David and T. Smeeding (eds.) Horizontal Equity, Uncertainty, and Economic Well-Being. Chicago: University of Chicago Press.

Emery, Robert E. 1988. Marriage, Divorce, and Children's Adjustment. Newbury Park, CA: Sage.

Ensel, Walter M. 1986. "Sex, marital status, and depression: The role of life events and social support." Pp. 231–247 in Nan Lin, Alfred Dean, and Walter M. Ensel (eds.), Social Support, Life Events, and Depression. Orlando, FL: Academic Press.

Falk, R. Frank, and Nancy B. Miller. 1990. "A soft models approach to family transitions." Pp. 273–301 in Phillip Cowen and E. Mavis Hetherington (eds.), Advances in Family Research (Vol. 2). Hillsdale, NJ: Lawrence Erlbaum.

Farnsworth, Judy, Marjorie A. Pett, and Dale A. Lund. 1989. "Predictors of loss-management and well-being in later life widowhood and divorce." Journal of Family Issues 10: 102–121.

Fethke, Carol C. 1989. "Life-cycle models of saving and the effect of the timing of divorce on retirement economic well-being." Journal of Gerontology: Social Sciences 44: S121–S128.

Fine, Mark A., and Andrew I. Schwebel. 1987. "An emergent explanation of different racial reactions to single parenthood." Journal of Divorce 11: 1–15.

Fletcher, Cynthia Needles. 1989. "A comparison of incomes and expenditures of male-headed households paying child support and female-headed households receiving child support." Family Relations 38: 412–417.

Folberg, Jay (ed.). 1984. Joint Custody and Shared Parenting. Washington, DC: Bureau of National Affairs.

Freed, Doris J., and Timothy B. Walker. 1988. "Family law in the fifty states: An overview." Family Law Quarterly 21: 417–573.

Furstenberg, Frank F., Jr., and Graham B. Spanier. 1984. Recycling the Family: Remarriage after Divorce. Beverly Hills, CA: Sage.

Gardner, Richard A. 1984. "Joint custody is not for everyone." Pp. 63–71 in Jay Folberg (ed.), Joint Custody and Shared Parenting. Washington, DC: Bureau of National Affairs.

Garfinkel, Irwin, and Sara S. McLanahan. 1986. Single Mothers and Their Children: A New American Dilemma. Washington, DC: Urban Institute.

Garfinkel, Irwin, and Donald Oellerich. 1989. "Noncustodial fathers' ability to pay child support." Demography 26: 219–233.

Gerstel, Naomi. 1987. "Divorce and stigma." Social Problems 34: 172–186.

Gerstel, Naomi. 1988. "Divorce and kin ties: The importance of gender." Journal of Marriage and the Family 50: 209–219.

Glass, Gene V., Barry McGaw, and Mary Lee Smith. 1981. Meta-analysis in Social Research. Beverly Hills, CA: Sage.

Glendon, Mary Ann. 1987. Abortion and Divorce in Western Law. Cambridge, MA: Harvard University Press.

Glenn, Norval (ed.). 1987. "The state of the American family." Journal of Family Issues 8: 347–476.

Glenn, Norval D., and Kathryn B. Kramer. 1987. "The marriages and divorces of the children of divorce." Journal of Marriage and the Family 49: 811–825.

Glick, Paul C. 1988. "The role of divorce in the changing family structure: Trends and variations." Pp. 3–34 in Sharlene A. Wolchik and Paul Karoly (eds.), Children of Divorce: Empirical Perspectives on Divorce. New York: Gardner.

Glick, Paul C., and Sung-ling Lin. 1986. "Recent changes in divorce and remarriage." Journal of Marriage and the Family 48: 737–748.

Gove, Walter R., and Hee-choon Shin. 1989. 'The psychological well-being of divorced and widowed men and women: An empirical analysis." Journal of Family Issues 10: 122–144.

Hagestad, Gunhild O., and Michael A. Smyer. 1982. "Dissolving long term relationships: Patterns of divorcing in middle age." Pp. 155–188 in Steve Duck (ed.), Personal Relationships. 4: Dissolving Personal Relationships. New York: Academic Press.

Halem, Lynne C. 1980. Divorce Reform: Changing Legal and Social Perspectives. New York: Free Press.

Hennon, Charles B. 1983. "Divorce and the elderly: A neglected area of research." Pp. 149–172 in Timothy H. Brubaker (ed.), Family Relations in Later Life. Beverly Hills, CA: Sage.

Hetherington, E. Mavis. 1989. "Coping with family transitions: Winners, losers, and survivors." Child Development 60: 1–14.

Hetherington, E. Mavis, Margaret Stanley-Hogan, and Edward R. Anderson. 1989. "Marital transitions: A child's perspective." American Psychologist 44: 303–312.

Hodges, William F. 1986. Interventions for Children of Divorce: Custody, Access, and Psychotherapy. New York: John Wiley.

Hoffman, Saul D., and Greg J. Duncan. 1988. "What *are* the economic consequences of divorce?" Demography 25: 641–645.

Hyman, Herbert H. 1983. Of Time and Widowhood. Durham, NC: Duke University Press.

Isaacs, Marla Beth, Braulio Montalvo, and David Abelsohn. 1986. The Difficult Divorce: Therapy for Children and Families. New York: Basic Books.

Jacobson, Gerald F. 1983. The Multiple Crises of Marital Separation and Divorce. New York: Grune and Stratton.

Johnston, Janet R., and Linda E. G. Campbell. 1988. Impasses of Divorce: The Dynamics and Resolution of Family Conflict. New York: Free Press.

Johnston, Janet R., Marsha Kline, and Jeanne M. Tschann. 1989. "Ongoing postdivorce conflict: Effects on children of joint custody and frequent access." American Journal of Orthopsychiatry 59: 576–592.

Kahn, Alfred J., and Sheila B. Kammerman (eds.). 1988. Child Support: From Debt Collection to Social Policy. Newbury Park, CA: Sage.

Kalter, Neil. 1990. Growing Up with Divorce: Helping Your Child Avoid Immediate and Later Emotional Problems. New York: Free Press.

Kalter, Neil, Amy Kloner, Shelly Schreier, and Katherine Okla. 1989. "Predictor's of children's postdivorce adjustment." American Journal of Orthopsychiatry 59: 605–618.

Keith, Pat M. 1985. "Financial well-being of older divorced/separated men and women: Findings from a panel study." Journal of Divorce 9: 61–72.

Kielcolt-Glaser, Janice K., Laura D. Fisher, Paula Ogrocki, Julie C. Stout, Carl E. Speicher, and Ronald Glaser. 1987. "Marital quality, marital disruption, and immune function." Psychosomatic Medicine 49: 13–34.

Kisker, Ellen Eliason, and Noreen Goldman. 1987. "Perils of single life and benefits of marriage." Social Biology 34: 135–152.

Kitson, Gay C. 1982. "Attachment to the spouse in divorce: A scale and its application." Journal of Marriage and the Family 44: 379–393.

Kitson, Gay C., Karen Benson Babri, Mary Joan Roach, and Kathleen S. Placidi. 1989. "Adjustment to widowhood and divorce: A review." Journal of Family Issues 10: 5–32.

Kitson, Gay C., Antonnette V. Graham, and David D. Schmidt. 1983. "Troubled marriages and divorce: A prospective suburban study." Journal of Family Practice 17: 249–258.

Kitson, Gay C., with William Holmes. In press. Portrait of Divorce. New York: Guilford Press.

Kitson, Gay C., and Helen J. Raschke. 1981. "Divorce research: What we know; what we need to know." Journal of Divorce 4: 1–37.

Kitson, Gay C., and Mary Joan Roach. 1989. "Independence and social and psychological adjustment in widowhood and divorce." Pp. 167–183 in Dale A. Lund (ed.), Older Bereaved Spouses: Research with Practical Implications. New York: Hemisphere Press.

Kitson, Gay C., and Marvin B. Sussman. 1982. "Marital complaints, demographic characteristics, and symptoms of mental distress in divorce." Journal of Marriage and the Family 44: 87–101.

Kitson, Gay C., Marvin B. Sussman, Gwendolyn K. Williams, Randi B. Zeehandelaar, Barbara K. Shickmanter, and Jeanne L. Steinberger. 1982. "Sampling issues in family research." Journal of Marriage and the Family 44: 965–981.

Lalande, Vivian. 1990. "Divorce theory: An overview with future directions for research and theory." Unpublished manuscript.

Laosa, Luis M. 1988. "Ethnicity and single parenting in the United States." Pp. 23–47 in E. Mavis Hetherington and Josephine D. Arasteh (eds.), Impact of Divorce, Single Parenting, and Stepparenting on Children. Hillsdale, NJ: Lawrence Erlbaum.

Lohmoeller, Jan-Bernd. 1989. Latent Variable Path Modeling with Partial Least Squares. New York: Springer-Verlag.

Luepnitz, Deborah A. 1982. Child Custody. Lexington, MA: Lexington Books.

Martin, Teresa Castro, and Larry L. Bumpass. 1989. "Recent trends in marital disruption." Demography 26: 37–51.

Masheter, Carol. In press. "Postdivorce relationships between ex-spouses: The roles of attachment and interpersonal conflict." Journal of Marriage and the Family.

McCubbin, Hamilton, and Joan Patterson. 1982. "Family adaptation to crisis." Pp. 26–47 in Hamilton McCubbin, A. Elizabeth Cauble, and Joan Patterson (eds.), Family Stress, Coping, and Social Support. Springfield, IL: Charles C Thomas.

McLindon, James B. 1987. "Separate but unequal: The economic disaster of divorce for women and children." Family Law Quarterly 21: 351–409.

Melichar, Joseph F., and David A. Chiriboga. 1988. "Significance of time in adjustment to marital separation." American Journal of Orthopsychiatry 58: 221–227.

Menaghan, Elizabeth G. 1985. "Depressive affect and subsequent divorce." Journal of Family Issues 6: 295–306.

Menaghan, Elizabeth G., and Morton A. Lieberman. 1986. "Changes in depression following divorce: A panel study." Journal of Marriage and the Family 48: 319–328.

Mergenhagen, Paula M., Barrett A. Lee, and Walter R. Gove. 1985. "Til death do us part: Recent changes in the relationship between marital status and mortality." Sociology and Social Research 70: 53–56.

Milardo, Robert M. 1987. "Changes in social networks of women and men following divorce: A review." Journal of Family Issues 8: 78–96.

Morgan, Leslie A. In press. After Marriage Ends: Economic Consequences for Mid-life Women. Newbury Park, CA: Sage.

Morgan, Leslie A. 1989. "Economic well-being following marital termination: A comparison of widowed and divorced women." Journal of Family Issues 10: 86–101.

National Center for Health Statistics. 1988. "Current estimates from the National Health Interview Survey: United States, 1987." C. A. Schoenborn and M. Marano. Vital and Health Statistics 10, No. 166,

DHHS Pub. No. (PHS) 88–1594. Public Health Service. Washington, DC: U.S. Government Printing Office.

National Center for Health Statistics. 1990. "Births, marriages, divorces, and deaths for 1989." Monthly Vital Statistics Report 38, No. 12, DHHS Pub. No. (PHS) 90–1120. Hyattsville, MD: Public Health Service.

Norton, Arthur J., and Jeanne E. Moorman. 1987. "Current trends in American marriage and divorce." Journal of Marriage and the Family 49: 3–14.

Peterson, Richard R. 1989. Women, Work, and Divorce. Albany, NY: SUNY Press.

Pett, Marjorie A., and Beth Vaughn-Cole. 1986. "The impact of income issues and social status on postdivorce adjustment of custodial parents." Family Relations 35: 103–111.

Phillips, Roderick. 1988. Putting Asunder: A History of Divorce in Western Society. Cambridge: Cambridge University Press.

Price, Sharon J., and Patrick C. McKenry. 1988. Divorce. Newbury Park, CA: Sage.

Price, Sharon J., and Patrick C. McKenry. 1989. "Current trends and issues in divorce: An agenda for family scientists in the 1990s." Family Science Review 2: 219–236.

Raschke, Helen J. 1987. "Divorce." Pp. 597–624 in Marvin B. Sussman and Suzanne K. Steinmetz (eds.), Handbook of Marriage and the Family. New York: Plenum.

Riessman, Catherine Kohler, and Naomi Gerstel. 1985. "Marital dissolution and health: Do males or females have greater risk?" Social Science and Medicine 20: 627–635.

Roach, Mary Joan, and Gay C. Kitson. 1989. "Impact of forewarning on adjustment to widowhood and divorce." Pp. 185–200 in Dale A. Lund (ed.), Older Bereaved Spouses: Research with Practical Applications. New York: Hemisphere.

Rosengren, Annika, Hans Wedel, and Lars Wilhelmsen. 1989. "Marital status and mortality in middle-aged Swedish men." American Journal of Epidemiology 129: 54–64.

Smith, Jack C., James A. Mercy, and Judith M. Conn. 1988. "Marital status and the risk of suicide." American Journal of Public Health 78: 78–80.

Spanier, Graham B., and Linda Thompson. 1984. Parting: The Aftermath of Separation and Divorce. Beverly Hills, CA: Sage.

Steinman, Susan. 1984. "Joint custody: What we know, what we have yet to learn, and the judicial and legislative implications." Pp. 111–127 in Jay Folberg (ed.), Joint Custody and Shared Parenting. Washington, DC: Bureau of National Affairs.

Steinman, Susan B., Steven E. Zemmelman, and Thomas M. Knoblauch. 1985. "A study of parents who sought joint custody following divorce: Who reaches agreement and sustains joint custody and who returns to court." Journal of the American Academy of Child Psychiatry 24: 554–562.

Stewart, James R., Andrew I. Schwebel, and Mark A. Fine. 1986. "The impact of custodial arrangements on the adjustment of recently divorced fathers.'' Journal of Divorce 9: 55–65.

Thompson, Linda, and Alexis J. Walker. 1982. "The dyad as the unit of analysis: Conceptual and methodological issues.'' Journal of Marriage and the Family 44: 889–900.

Trovato, Frank, and Gloria Lauris. 1989. "Marital status and mortality in Canada: 1951–81.'' Journal of Marriage and the Family 51: 907–922.

Tschann, Jeanne M., Janet R. Johnston, and Judith S. Wallerstein. 1989. "Resources, stresses, and attachment as predictors of adult adjustment after divorce: A longitudinal study.'' Journal of Marriage and the Family 51: 1033–1046.

Uhlenberg, Peter, and Mary Anne P. Myers. 1981. "Divorce and the elderly.'' Gerontologist 21: 276–281.

U.S. Bureau of the Census. 1987. "Child support and alimony: 1985.'' (Advance data from March–April 1986.) Current Population Reports, Series P-23, No. 152. Washington, DC: Government Printing Office.

Veroff, Joseph, Richard A. Kulka, and Elizabeth Douvan. 1981. Mental Health in America: Patterns of Help-Seeking from 1957 to 1976. New York: Basic Books.

Wallerstein, Judith S. 1989. "Daughters of divorce: Report from a ten-year follow-up.'' American Journal of Orthopsychiatry 59: 593–604.

Wallerstein, Judith S., and Sandra Blakeslee. 1989. Second Chances: Men, Women, and Children a Decade after Divorce. New York: Ticknor and Fields.

Wallerstein, Judith S., and Dorothy S. Huntington. 1983. "Bread and roses: Nonfinancial issues related to fathers' economic support of their children following divorce.'' Pp. 135–155 in Judith Cassetty (ed.), The Parental Child-Support Obligation: Research, Practice, and Social Policy. Lexington, MA: Lexington Books.

Wallerstein, Judith S., and Joan B. Kelly. 1980. Surviving the Breakup: How Children and Parents Cope with Divorce. New York: Basic Books.

Weiss, Robert S. 1982. "Attachment in adult life.'' Pp. 171–184 in Colin Murray Parkes and Joan Stevenson-Hinde (eds.), The Place of Attachment in Human Behavior. New York: Basic Books.

Weiss, Robert S. 1984. "The impact of marital dissolution on income and consumption in single-parent households.'' Journal of Marriage and the Family 46: 115–127.

Weitzman, Lenore J. 1985. The Divorce Revolution: The Unexpected Social and Economic Consequences for Women and Children in America. New York: Free Press.

Welch, Charles E., and Sharon Price-Bonham. 1983. "A decade of no-fault divorce revisited: California, Georgia, and Washington.'' Journal of Marriage and the Family 46: 115–127.

Wertlieb, Donald, Simon Budman, Annette Demby, and Mary Randall. 1984. "Marital separation and health: Stress and intervention.'' Journal of Human Stress 10: 18–26.

White, Lynn K. 1990. "Determinants of divorce: A review of research in the eighties.'' Journal of Marriage and the Family 52: 904–912. [Reprinted in this volume]

Wilcox, Brian L. 1981. "Social support in adjusting to marital disruption: A network analysis.'' Pp. 97–115 in Benjamin H. Gottlieb (ed.), Social Networks and Social Support. Beverly Hills, CA: Sage.

Wishik, Heather Rush. 1986. "The economics of divorce: An exploratory study.'' Family Law Quarterly 20: 79–105.

Wolchik, Sharlene A., Sanford L. Braver, and Irwin N. Sandler. 1985. "Maternal versus joint custody: Children's postseparation experiences and adjustment.'' Journal of Clinical and Child Psychology 14: 5–10.

Zaslow, Martha J. 1988. "Sex differences in children's response to parental divorce: 1. Research methodology and post divorce family forms.'' American Journal of Orthopsychiatry 58: 355–378.

Zaslow, Martha J. 1989. "Sex differences in children's response to parental divorce: 2. Samples, variables, ages, and sources.'' American Journal of Orthopsychiatry 59: 118–141.

DAVID H. DEMO   *Virginia Polytechnic Institute and State University*

ALAN C. ACOCK   *Louisiana State University*

The Impact of Divorce on Children

With the acceleration of the divorce rate from the mid-1960s to the early 1980s, the number of non-traditional families (such as single-parent families and reconstituted families) have increased relative to intact, first-time nuclear families. This article reviews empirical evidence addressing the relationship between divorce, family composition, and children's well-being. Although not entirely consistent, the pattern of empirical findings suggests that children's emotional adjustment, gender-role orientation, and antisocial behavior are affected by family structure, whereas other dimensions of well-being are unaffected. But the review indicates that these findings should be interpreted with caution because of the methodological deficiencies of many of the studies on which these findings are based. Several variables, including the level of family conflict, may be central variables mediating the effect of family structure on children.

High divorce rates in the United States over the past 20 years have resulted in numerous changes in American family life, with perhaps the most important consequences bearing on children whose families were disrupted. In 1970, 12% of American families with children under age 18 were headed by single parents. By 1984, one-fourth of American families and nearly 60% of

black families were headed by single parents (see Table 1). Millions of other children live in two-parent but reconstituted families, separated from at least one biological parent. In fact, Furstenberg, Nord, Peterson, and Zill's recent analysis (1983) indicates that less than two-thirds of American children live with both biological parents.

A number of studies use recent social and demographic trends to predict children's future living arrangements, and while these predictions vary, the consensus is that most youth will spend some time prior to age 18 in a single-parent household (Bumpass, 1984, 1985; Furstenberg et al., 1983; Hofferth, 1985, 1986; Norton and Glick, 1986). Hofferth (1985) suggests that the percentage of black youth who will live with one parent for some period of time prior to age 18 may be as high as 94%, while for white children the corresponding figure is 70%. Norton and Glick's (1986) analysis yields a lower estimate but still projects that 60% of American children will live in a single-parent family before reaching age 18.

These trends in family composition have major implications for the life course of children and their well-being. The purpose of this article is to review and assess recent empirical evidence on the impact of divorce on children, concentrating on studies of nonclinical populations published in the last decade. We also direct attention to a number of important theoretical and methodological considerations in the study of family structure and youthful well-being. We begin by briefly describing some of the theoretical propositions and assumptions that guide research in this area.

Department of Sociology, Virginia Tech, Blacksburg, VA 24061.

*Department of Sociology and Center for Life Cycle and Population Studies, Louisiana State University, Baton Rouge, LA 70803.

TABLE 1. NUMBER AND PERCENTAGE OF FAMILIES WITH CHILDREN UNDER AGE 18, 1970–1984 (IN THOUSANDS)

Families	1970 Total[a]	1980 Total[a]	1984 Total[a]	1984 Whites	1984 Blacks
Total, children under 18	29,631	32,150	33,246	27,508	4,744
Two-parent	25,823	25,231	24,701	21,978	1,934
One-parent	3,808	6,920	8,544	5,529	2,809
Mother-headed	3,415	6,230	7,599	4,766	2,652
Never-married	248	1,063	2,102	729	1,332
Spouse absent	1,377	1,743	1,762	1,120	597
Separated	962	1,483	1,505	929	544
Other	415	260	257	191	53
Divorced	1,109	2,721	3,174	2,516	593
Widowed	682	703	561	401	128
Father-headed	393	692	945	763	157
Never-married	22	63	166	109	52
Spouse absent	247[a]	181	187	139	39
Divorced	na	340	496	445	44
Widowed	124	107	97	69	23

	1970 Total %	1980 Total %	1984 Total %	1984 White %	1984 Black %
Two-parent	87.1	78.5	74.3	79.9	40.8
One-parent	12.9	21.5	25.7	20.1	59.2
Mother-headed	11.5	19.4	22.9	17.3	55.9
Never-married	0.8	3.3	6.3	2.7	28.1
Spouse absent	4.6	5.4	5.3	4.1	12.6
Separated	3.2	4.6	4.5	3.4	11.5
Other	1.4	0.8	0.8	0.7	1.1
Divorced	3.7	8.5	9.5	9.1	12.5
Widowed	2.3	2.2	1.7	1.5	2.7
Father-headed	1.3	2.2	2.8	2.8	3.3
Never-married	0.1	0.2	0.5	0.4	1.1
Spouse absent	0.8	0.6	0.6	0.5	0.8
Divorced	na	1.1	1.5	1.6	0.9
Widowed	0.4	0.3	0.3	0.3	0.5

Source: U.S. Bureau of the Census, Population Reports, Series P-20, No. 138.
[a]Totals include other races not shown separately in the table.
[b]The 1970 figure includes families headed by divorced men.

THEORETICAL UNDERPINNINGS

Consistent with the Freudian assumption that a two-parent group constitutes the minimal unit for appropriate sex-typed identification (Freud, 1925/1961), anthropologists, sociologists, and social psychologists have long maintained the necessity of such a group for normal child development. Representative of structural-functional theorizing, Parsons and Bales (1955: 16–17) argued that one of the basic functions of the family is to serve as a stable, organically integrated "factory" in which human personalities are formed.

Similarly, social learning theory emphasizes the importance of role models, focusing on parents as the initial and primary reinforcers of child behavior (Bandura and Walters, 1963). Much of the research adopting this perspective centers on parent-child similarities, analyzing the transmission of response patterns and the in-

hibitory or disinhibitory effect of parental models. The presence of the same-sex parent is assumed to be crucial in order for the child to learn appropriate sex-typed behavior. This assumption is shared by developmental and symbolic interactionist theories, various cognitive approaches to socialization, and confluence theory, as well as anthropological theories (Edwards, 1987).

It logically follows that departures from the nuclear family norm are problematic for the child's development, especially for adolescents, inasmuch as this represents a crucial stage in the developmental process. Accordingly, a large body of research literature deals with father absence, the effects of institutionalization, and a host of "deficiencies" in maturation, such as those having to do with cognitive development, achievement, moral learning, and conformity. This focus has pointed to the crucial importance of both parents' presence but also has suggested that certain causes for parental absence may accentuate any negative effects. Lynn, for example, asserts (1974: 279):

> The research on the relationship between father absence and the general level of the child's adjustment reveals that the loss of a father for any reason is associated with poor adjustment, but that absence because of separation, divorce, or desertion may have especially adverse effects.

Some researchers suggest even more dire outcomes whenever parental separation, divorce, or desertion occur. Among these are vulnerability to acute psychiatric disturbances, the child's aversion to marriage, and proneness to divorce once they do marry (Anthony, 1974). In sum, two general propositions are suggested:

1. Children reared in households where the two biological parents are not present will exhibit lower levels of well-being than their counterparts in intact nuclear families.
2. The adverse effects on youthful well-being will be especially acute when the cause of parental absence is marital separation, divorce, or desertion.

Divorce and Family Structure

In examining research that addresses these two propositions, it is important to distinguish between studies investigating the effects of family structure and those investigating the effects of divorce. Most studies compare intact units and single-parent families, guided by the assumption that the latter family structure is precipitated by divorce. Of course, this is not always the case. Single-parent families consist of those with parents who have never married, those formed by the permanent separation of parents, and those precipitated by the death of a parent. Simple comparisons between one- and two-parent families are also suspect in that *two*-parent families are not monolithic. First-time or nondivorced units differ from divorced, remarried units in which stepparents are involved. In addition, little recognition has been given to the fact that families of different types may exhibit varying levels of instability or conflict, a potentially confounding variable in establishing the effects of family structure. In short, most investigations of the linkage between family structure and youthful well-being have failed to recognize the complexity of present-day families.

While family composition is a critical consideration in assessing the impact of divorce on children, we must also examine the unique events, disruptions, and transitions characterizing the divorce process that are not experienced by children and other members of nondivorced families. In particular, there are significant *changes* in family composition, parent-child interaction, discipline, and socioeconomic circumstances, as well as the emotional reactions that parents and children have to divorce. These events are accompanied by changes in extrafamilial relations and social networks, often as a result of stigma attached to divorced parents and their children. Although stepfamilies are beyond the scope of this review, researchers must also distinguish the consequences of divorce from those of remarriage and subsequent changes in family composition (see Ganong and Coleman, 1984, for a review of the emerging literature on reconstituted families and their impact on children).

Bearing in mind these conceptual distinctions, we now move to a systematic review of recent evidence on the impact of divorce on children and adolesecents.

EXISTING RESEARCH

A substantial amount of research has examined the effects of family structure on children's social and psychological well-being. Many studies document negative consequences for children whose parents divorce and for those living in single-parent families. But most studies have been concerned with limited dimensions of a quite complex problem. Specifically, the research to date has typically (a) examined the effects of divorce or father absence on children, ignoring the effects on adolescents; (b) examined only selected dimensions of children's well-being; (c) compared intact units and single-parent families but not recognized important variations (e.g., levels of marital instability and conflict) within these structures; and (d) relied on cross-sectional designs to assess developmental processes.

Social and psychological well-being includes aspects of personal adjustment, self-concept, interpersonal relationships, antisocial behavior, and cognitive functioning. It should be noted that some of these variables (e.g., personal adjustment) have been the subject of voluminous research, while others (e.g., interpersonal relations) have received relatively little attention. In Tables 2 to 6 we outline selected studies published since 1975 that were designed to compare the well-being of children and adolescents living in intact families and families disrupted by divorce.[1]

Personal Adjustment

Personal adjustment is operationalized in various ways by different investigators but includes such variables as self-control, leadership, responsibility, independence, achievement orientation, aggressiveness, and gender-role orientation (see Table 2). As we see when examining the 16 studies outlined in Table 2, there are also wide variations in sample size and composition. But the overall pattern of empirical findings suggests temporary deleterious effects of parental divorce on children's adjustment, with these effects most common among young children (Desimone-Luis, O'Mahoney, and Hunt, 1979; Hetherington, Cox, and Cox, 1979; Kurdek, Blisk, and Siesky, 1981; Wallerstein and Kelly, 1975, 1980a).[2] Kurdek and Siesky (1980b, c) suggest that older children adjust more readily because they are more likely to discuss the situation with friends (many of whom have had similar experiences), to understand that they are not personally responsible, to recognize the finality of the situation, to appreciate both parents for their positive qualities, and to recognize beneficial consequences such as the end of parental fighting and improved relations with parents.

On the basis of her review of research conducted between 1970 and 1980, Cashion (1984: 483) concludes: "The evidence is overwhelming that after the initial trauma of divorce, the children are as emotionally well-adjusted in these [female-headed] families as in two-parent families." Investigations of long-term effects (Acock and Kiecolt, 1988; Kulka and Weingarten, 1979) suggest that, when socioeconomic status is controlled, adolescents who have experienced a parental divorce or separation have only slightly lower levels of adult adjustment.

In two other studies Kinard and Reinherz (1984, 1986) observed elementary school children in three different family situations (never-disrupted; disrupted prior to starting school; and recently disrupted) and found that children in recently disrupted families suffered pronounced

and multidimensional effects: problems in attentiveness at school, lowered academic achievement, withdrawal, dependency, and hostility. While their findings are not definitive, Kinard and Reinherz speculate that either "the effects of parental divorce on children diminish over time; or that the impact of marital disruption is less severe for preschool-age children than for school-age children" (1986: 291). Children's age at the time of disruption may also mediate the impact of these events on other dimensions of their well-being (e.g., self-esteem or gender-role orientation) and thus will be discussed in greater detail below (also, see Rohrlich, Ranier, Berg-Cross, and Berg-Cross, 1977, for a clinical perspective on the impact of divorce on children of different ages). But two variables that critically affect children's adjustment to divorce are marital discord and children's gender.

Marital discord. A significant pattern in the empirical literature is that personal adjustment, like other dimensions of well-being, is not related to family structure but is adversely affected by parental discord (Ellison, 1983; Rosen, 1979). Kurdek and Siesky's (1980b) extensive data on children who had experienced their parents' divorce indicated that, although learning of the divorce and adjusting to the loss of the non-custodial parent were painful, children indicated that these adjustments were preferable to living in conflict. Many studies report that children's adjustment to divorce is facilitated under conditions of low parental conflict—both prior to *and* subsequent to the divorce (Guidubaldi, Cleminshaw, Perry, Nastasi, and Lightel, 1986; Jacobson, 1978; Lowenstein and Koopman, 1978; Porter and O'Leary, 1980; Raschke and Raschke, 1979; Rosen, 1979).

Children's gender. Children's gender may be especially important in mediating the effects of family disruption, as most of the evidence suggests that adjustment problems are more severe and last for longer periods of time among boys (Hess and Camara, 1979; Hetherington, 1979; Hetherington, Cox, and Cox, 1978, 1979, 1982; Wallerstein, 1984; Wallerstein and Kelly, 1980b).[3] Guidubaldi and Perry (1985) found, controlling for social class, that boys in divorced families manifested significantly more maladaptive symptoms and behavior problems than boys in intact

TABLE 2. SUMMARY OF RECENT STUDIES ON EFFECTS OF DIVORCE ON
PERSONAL ADJUSTMENT OF CHILDREN AND ADOLESCENTS

Study	Description of Sample	Family Structure of Respondents	Socioeconomic Background	Dependent Measures	Major Findings
Grossman et al. (1980)	294 white male and female college students	262 students from intact families; 24 with history of parental divorce and remarriage; 8 from divorced, nonremarried families	Middle class	EI-ISB, LLCS, LWRISB	Individuals (especially males) whose parents had divorced had higher ego-identity achievement scores than individuals in intact families.
Guidubaldi and Perry (1985)	365 boys and 334 girls in grades 1, 3, and 5 (T1); grades 2, 3, 5, and 7 at follow-up (T2) (National Association of School Psychologists –Kent State University data)	341 children with divorced parents and 358 from intact families	SES (defined separately by family income and by educational and occupational classifications) was examined and was instituted as a control in the analyses, but no breakdown by SES was given.	HESB, PAR, locus of control, optimism-pessimism, VTQ, Achenbach Parent and Teacher Rating Scales	At Time 2 (mean of 6.4 years post-divorce) and controlling for SES, boys in divorced families had a greater frequency of maladaptive symptoms, inappropriate behavior, and unhappiness. Among girls, the only significant difference was that girls in divorced families had higher internal locus of control.
Hainline and Feig (1978)	36 female college students aged 17–23 (mean age = 18.5); 80% white, 20% black	12 women whose fathers had died (6 before age 5, 6 between ages 5–11); 12 women whose parents had divorced (6 before ages 5, 6 between ages 5–11); 12 women from intact families	Lower-middle and middle class	BSRI, RRLS, RSRT, RIAS, BSF, RLCS, BMFS	Women whose fathers were absent were virtually indistinguishable from those with fathers present. Early father absence was associated with external locus of control.
Hess and Camara (1979)	32 white boys and girls aged 9–11	16 children in intact families; 16 children in recently divorced families	All children had 2 working parents, each of whom had at least 2 years of college education.	Stress, as measured by parents' ratings on a behavior checklist	Children in divorced families experienced greater stress, as did those who had poor relationships with their parents.
Hetherington, Cox, and Cox (1979)	48 white boys and 48 white girls; mean age = 3.9 at T1 and 5.8 at T2	24 boys and 24 girls from divorced, mother-custody families; 24 boys and 24 girls from nondivorced families	Middle class	Observational measures of children's free play and social interaction; teacher ratings of behavior; peer nomination measures	Play patterns of boys and girls from divorced families were less socially and cognitively mature immediately following divorce; for boys immature play continued into second year post-divorce. Children in divorced families were also less happy and more anxious, with these effects again lasting longer for boys.

(Continued on next page)

TABLE 2. SUMMARY OF RECENT STUDIES ON EFFECTS OF DIVORCE ON PERSONAL ADJUSTMENT OF CHILDREN AND ADOLESCENTS—Continued

Study	Description of Sample	Family Structure of Respondents	Socioeconomic Background	Dependent Measures	Major Findings
Kalter et al. (1984)	48 white boys and girls in 3rd and 5th grade	Evenly divided between intact and divorced families	Middle and upper-middle class	Nowicki-Strickland Locus of Control Scale	Children in divorced families had higher internal locus of control.
Kalter et al. (1985)	84 female college students aged 17–22	42 women with divorced parents; 42 with intact home	Middle- and upper-middle class students at a "highly selective, expensive college"	TAT measuring perceptions of masculinity-femininity; questionnaire measuring life satisfaction	No significant differences in life satisfaction or in satisfaction with dating. However, women in divorced families were more likely to hold negative views of both men and women.
Kinard and Reinherz (1984)	202 boys and 192 girls in 3rd grade; 99% white	38 children in early (preschool) disrupted families; 36 in recently disrupted families; 320 in never-disrupted families	Predominantly working class (Classes III and IV on Hollingshead Index)	CAAP, PBQ, SBCL	Children in recently disrupted families had significantly more problems with attention at school, withdrawal, and dependency. No differences on anxiety.
Kurdek and Siesky (1980a)	48 boys and 64 girls in grades 3–8	56 children in intact families; 56 children in divorced families	Middle class, as measured by Hollingshead's Index	Modified version of BSRI	Children in divorced families were significantly more androgynous than children in intact families, who tended to be traditionally sex-typed.
Oshman and Manosevitz (1976)	125 male college students (mean age = 19.8)	39 with biological fathers present; 47 fatherless; 39 with step-fathers	3 groups were matched on parental education and family income (presumably middle class).	EIS	Males with fathers (and stepfathers) present scored significantly higher on psychosocial development than males in fatherless families.
Parish et al. (1980)	158 female and 68 male college students	Intact and fatherless families	No information given	Rokesch Values Survey	Individuals from intact and fatherless families were similar on most values, but individuals in divorced families were more likely to value self-respect, mature love, and being polite.
Rosen (1979)	117 white males and females aged 9–28	92 individuals whose parents had divorced and 25 whose families were intact	Middle class	TAT, ISB, and an in-depth clinical interview	No differences between intact and divorced group. Poor adjustment was associated with parental conflict preceding and during the divorce.

(Continued on next page)

TABLE 2. SUMMARY OF RECENT STUDIES ON EFFECTS OF DIVORCE ON
PERSONAL ADJUSTMENT OF CHILDREN AND ADOLESCENTS—Continued

Study	Description of Sample	Family Structure of Respondents	Socioeconomic Background	Dependent Measures	Major Findings
Santrock (1975)	120 boys in 5th and 6th grade	60 boys in intact families; 20 in early-divorced (boys younger than age 6) families; 20 in late-divorced (boys between 6–10) families; 20 in father-deceased (boys between 6–10) families	Predominantly lower class. Father-present and father-absent groups were matched on SES, race, school, and other background characteristics.	A variety of behavioral measures, including Kohlberg measures of moral judgment, plus teacher ratings of social conscience (e.g., self-discipline, trust)	Controlling for relevant variables, there were no differences on behavioral measures of moral development, but teachers judged father-absent boys to have lower levels of social conscience.
Santrock and Warshak (1979)	33 boys and 27 girls aged 6–11	20 children in father-custody families; 20 in mother-custody families; 20 in intact families	Groups were matched on SES, family size, and sibling status.	A variety of projective, self-report, and observational measures, including the ABIC	Overall, there was no main effect for family structure, but children living with opposite-sex parents were not as well adjusted.
Wyman et al. (1985)	268 children in grades 4–6	98 children with divorced parents; 170 from intact families	Divorce sample "comparable to the intact sample in sociodemographic background"	STAIC A-Trait Scale used to measure trait anxiety	Children in divorced group had significantly higher anxiety.
Young and Parish (1977)	98 female college students aged 17–22	16 daughters of unmarried widows; 12 of remarried widows; 17 of unmarried divorcees; 26 of remarried divorcees; 27 with father present	Middle class	MFF, ACL, SII	Daughters who had lost their fathers (due to divorce or death) and whose mothers had not remarried were more insecure than daughters in father-present families. No differences on impulsivity-reflexivity.

Note: ABIC = Adaptive Behavior Inventory for Children; ACL = Adjective Check List; BMFS = Broverman Masculinity-Femininity Scale; BSF = Bendig Short Form of the Manifest Anxiety Scale; BSRI = Bem Sex Role Inventory; CAAP = Child and Adolescent Adjustment Profile; EI-ISB = Marcia Ego-Identity Incomplete Sentence Blank; EIS = Ego Identity Scale; HESB = Hahnemann Elementary School Behavior Rating Scales; ISB = Incomplete Sentence Blank; LLCS = Levenson's Locus of Control Scale; LWRISB = Loevinger, Wessler, and Redmore Incomplete Sentence Blank; MFF = Matching Familiar Figures Test; PAR = Sells and Roff Peer Acceptance-Rejection Rating; PBQ = Preschool Behavior Questionnaire; RIAS = Rubin's Intercourse Acceptability Scale; RLCS = Rotter Locus of Control Scale; RRLS = Rubin's Romantic Love Scale; RSRT = Rubin's Sex Role Traditionalism Scale; SBCL = Simmons Behavior Checklist; SII = Security-Insecurity Inventory; STAIC A-Trait Scale = State Trait Anxiety Inventory for Children; TAT = Thematic Apperception Test; VTQ = Vineland Teacher Questionnaire.

families. Girls differed only on the dimension of locus of control; girls in divorced households scored significantly higher than their counterparts in intact households.

One explanation for boys' greater difficulties in adjusting to parental divorce is that typical postdivorce living arrangements are quite different for them than for girls. While custodial mothers provide girls with same-sex role models, most boys have to adjust to living without same-sex parents. In examining boys and girls living in intact families and in different custodial arrangements, Santrock and Warshak (1979) found that few effects could be attributed to family structure per se, but that children living with opposite-six parents (mother-custody boys and father-custody girls) were not as well adjusted on measures of competent social behavior. While father custody is rare, this study illustrates the importance of examining variations in postdivorce family structures (and specifically the combination of parent's gender and child's gender) for estimating the effects of divorce on children.

Along related lines, a number of researchers have examined gender-role orientation and, specifically, the relation of father absence to boys' personality development. Most of the evidence indicates that boys without adult male role models demonstrate more feminine behavior (Biller, 1976; Herzog and Sudia, 1973; Lamb, 1977a), except in lower-class families (Biller, 1981b). A variety of studies have shown that fathers influence children's gender role development to be more traditional because, compared to mothers, they more routinely differentiate between masculine and feminine behaviors and encourage greater conformity to conventional gender roles (Biller, 1981a; Biller and Davids, 1973; Bronfenbrenner, 1961; Heilbrun, 1965; Lamb, 1977b; Noller, 1978). Lamb (1977a) argues that because gender identity is usually developed by age 3 and because family influences are central to this process, the effects of father absence on gender-appropriate behavior may be most pronounced among boys who are very young (ages 5 and under) at the time of family disruption. Beyond early childhood, gender roles are largely established and children experience increasingly diverse extrafamilial social contexts and relationships that bear on their development.[4] But it should be reiterated that these effects have been attributed to father absence and thus would be expected to occur among boys in all female-headed families, not simply those that have experienced divorce.

The claim has also been made that boys' adjustment problems are often compounded by custodial mothers' denigrating the masculinity of absent fathers, an occurrence that is particularly likely in black matriarchal families (Biller and Davids, 1973). The assumption here is that boys are trying to be masculine without the benefit of the same-sex role model and that the absent role model is portrayed as undesirable. However, most of the research on boys' adjustment fails to consider the quality or quantity of father-child contact or the availability of alternative male role models (e.g., foster father, grandfather, big brother, other male relatives, coach, friend, etc.), which makes it difficult to assess the impact of changing family structure on boys' behavior. There are also limitations imposed by conceptualizing and measuring masculinity-femininity as a bipolar construct (Bem, 1974; Constantinople, 1973; Worell, 1978), and there is evidence that boys and girls in father-absent families are better described as androgynous (Kurdek and Siesky, 1980a).

Positive outcomes of divorce. While much of the literature on divorce and children seems ideologically driven and biased toward emphasizing negative effects on children (Edwards, 1987; Raschke and Raschke, 1979), the tendency of children in single-parent families to display more androgynous behavior may be interpreted as a beneficial effect. Because of father absence, children in female-headed families are not pressured as strongly as their counterparts in two-parent families to conform to traditional gender roles. These children frequently assume a variety of domestic responsibilities to compensate for the absent parent (Weiss, 1979), thereby broadening their skills and competencies and their definitions of gender-appropriate behavior. Divorced parents also must broaden their behavioral patterns to meet increased parenting responsibilities, thereby providing more androgynous role models. Kurdek and Siesky (1980a: 250) give the illustration that custodial mothers often "find themselves needing to acquire and demonstrate a greater degree of dominance, assertiveness, and independence while custodial fathers may find themselves in situations eliciting high degrees of warmth, nurturance, and tenderness."

Aside from becoming more androgynous, adolescents living in single-parent families are characterized by greater maturity, feelings of efficacy, and an internal locus of control (Guidubaldi and Perry, 1985; Kalter, Alpern, Spence, and Plunkett, 1984; Wallerstein and Kelly, 1974; Weiss, 1979). For adolescent girls this maturity stems partly from the status and responsibilities they acquire in peer and confidant relationships with custodial mothers.[5]

Finally, the relationship between family structure and personal adjustment (and other dimensions of well-being) must be viewed as reciprocal. The child's psychological state prior to changes in family structure is an important element in the child's ability to adjust to new situations and relationships. There is evidence (Kurdek et al., 1981) that children and adolescents with an internal locus of control and a high level of interpersonal reasoning adjust more easily to their parents' divorce and that children's divorce adjustment is related to their more global personal adjustment.

Self-Concept

In Table 3 we summarize studies examining the impact of divorce on children's self-concept. A series of studies by Parish and his collaborators indicates that children in divorced, non-remarried families have lower self-esteem than children in intact families (Parish and Dostal, 1980; Parish and Taylor, 1979; Young and Parish, 1977). Measuring children's self-evaluations in 1979 and again in 1982, Parish and Wigle (1985) demonstrated that children whose family structure was intact throughout the study had the highest self-evaluations, while those whose parents divorced in the intervening years experienced declining self-evaluations, and those whose parents were divorced throughout the 3-year period apparently adjusted to their new situations and reported higher self-evaluations than they had previously. As is the case for most research on children of divorce, however, the studies conducted by Parish and his associates did not investigate pre- or postdivorce levels of family conflict.

Marital discord. The bulk of evidence summarized in Table 3 is consistent with the findings on personal adjustment; that is, family structure is unrelated to children's self-esteem (Feldman and

Feldman, 1975; Kinard and Reinherz, 1984; Parish, 1981; Parish, Dostal, and Parish, 1981), but parental discord is negatively related (Amato, 1986; Berg and Kelly, 1979; Cooper, Holman, and Braithwaite, 1983; Long, 1986; Raschke and Raschke, 1979; Slater and Haber, 1984). Because this conclusion is based on diverse samples of boys and girls of different ages in different living arrangements, the failure to obtain effects of family structure suggests either that family composition really does not matter for children's self-concept or that family structure alone is an insufficient index of familial relations. Further, these studies suggest that divorce per se does not adversely affect children's self-concept. Cashion's (1984) review of the literature indicates that children living in single-parent families suffer no losses to self-esteem, except in situations where the child's family situation is stigmatized (Rosenberg, 1979). Cautioning that considerably more research is needed before firm conclusions can be drawn, Long (1986: 26) suggests that future work investigate "Hetherington's (1979) idea that a stable home in which parents are divorced is better for a child than is a 'conflict-ridden' home where both parents are present."

Although countless studies have examined global self-esteem, two critical limitations characterize this body of research: (*a*) nearly all of these studies are cross-sectional, which restricts the assessment of developmental change and stability in self-concept; and (*b*) little is known about the various dimensions of self-concept (e.g., self-efficacy, nonevaluative self-descriptions) other than overall self-esteem. It is necessary, therefore, to examine different dimensions of self-concept as they change over time and as they relate to different structures and patterns of family interaction.

Cognitive Functioning

Most of the research relating cognitive functioning to family structure (summarized in Table 4) has assessed cognitive performance by using standardized intelligence and academic achievement tests or scholastic grade-point averages. Many of these studies find that family conflict and disruption are associated with inhibited cognitive functioning (Blanchard and Biller, 1971; Feldman and Feldman, 1975; Hess and Camara, 1979; Kinard and Reinherz, 1986; Kurdek, 1981; Radin, 1981).

TABLE 3. SUMMARY OF RECENT STUDIES ON EFFECTS OF DIVORCE ON SELF-CONCEPT OF CHILDREN AND ADOLESCENTS

Study	Description of Sample	Family Structure of Respondents	Socioeconomic Background	Dependent Measures	Major Findings
Berg and Kelly (1979)	57 boys and girls aged 9–15	19 children in "intact-accepted" families; 19 in "intact-rejected" families; 19 whose parents had divorced	No information given	PHCSC	Children in intact but conflict-ridden families had significantly lower self-esteem than those in other 2 groups.
Cooper et al. (1983)	258 boys and 209 girls aged 9–12	Two-parent cohesive families; one-parent cohesive families; isolated child families; divided families; parent-coalition families	40% professional or managerial; 33% clerical, sales, and skilled occupations; 27% unskilled and semiskilled occupations.	CSEI; PHCSC	Children reporting little family support, whether in one- or two-parent families, had lowest self-esteem.
Kalter et al. (1985)[a]	(1) 40 girls in 3rd and 6th grade	14 girls with divorced parents, 26 living with both natural parents	All middle class	PCS	Among 3rd graders, girls in divorced families had significantly lower perceived competence. No significant differences among 6th graders.
	(2) 522 girls aged 11–18 (1972 National Survey of Youth)	62 girls with divorced parents, 460 girls from intact households	Divorced group "represented significantly lower SES households"	Self-esteem	No significant differences.
	(3) 84 female college students aged 17–22	42 women with divorced parents, 42 with intact home	Middle- and upper-middle class students at a "highly selective, expensive college"	Self-esteem	No significant differences.
Kanoy et al. (1984)	153 white children aged 3–21	45 mothers and their 74 children from divorced families, and 44 mothers and their 79 children from intact families	Predivorce annual family income of $12,000–$40,000	Self-concept Referents Test (children 3–7); Bills Index of Adjustment and Values (children 10–21)	In divorced families, mothers' present adjustment predicted children's self-concept. In intact families, mothers' past adjustment predicted children's self-concept.
Kinard and Reinherz (1984)	202 boys and 192 girls in 3rd grade; 99% white	38 children in early (preschool) disrupted families; 36 in recently disrupted families; 320 in never-disrupted families	Predominantly working class (Classes III and IV on Hollingshead Index)	PHCSC	No significant differences.

(Continued on next page)

TABLE 3. SUMMARY OF RECENT STUDIES ON EFFECTS OF DIVORCE ON SELF-CONCEPT OF CHILDREN AND ADOLESCENTS—Continued

Study	Description of Sample	Family Structure of Respondents	Socioeconomic Background	Dependent Measures	Major Findings
Long (1986)	199 predominantly white female college freshmen (mean age = 17.7)	150 with intact families; 21 in reconstituted families; 26 in single-parent families; 2 in other arrangements	Predominantly middle class	RSE	Daughter's self-esteem significantly related to parental happiness (even with family structure controlled) but not to family structure (even with parental happiness controlled).
Parish (1981)	1,409 male and female college students	Intact; divorced non-remarried; divorced remarried; death non-remarried; death remarried families	No information given	PAIC	No significant differences by type of family structure.
Parish et al. (1981)	284 male and female children in grades 5–8	Two family types (intact or divorced) and two family dispositions (happy or unhappy)	No information given	PAIC	No main effects for family type, but children from happy families had significantly higher self-concepts. Females from happy, intact families had significantly higher self-concepts and males from unhappy, divorced families had significantly lower self-concepts.
Parish and Dostal (1980)	738 boys and girls aged 11–14	Intact; divorced and remarried; divorced and non-remarried	No information given	PAIC	Children from intact families had significantly higher self-evaluations than children in divorced, non-remarried families.
Parish and Taylor (1979)	406 boys and girls in grades 3–8	347 from intact families; 44 from divorced, female-headed families; 15 from reconstituted families	No information given	PAIC	Children whose parents had divorced and whose mothers had not remarried had significantly lower self-concepts than children in intact families.

(Continued on next page)

TABLE 3. SUMMARY OF RECENT STUDIES ON EFFECTS OF DIVORCE ON SELF-CONCEPT OF CHILDREN AND ADOLESCENTS—Continued

Study	Description of Sample	Family Structure of Respondents	Socioeconomic Background	Dependent Measures	Major Findings
Parish and Wigle (1985)	120 public school students	4 groups of 30 children each, defined by their family structure at 2 points in time (1979 and 1982): intact-intact; divorced-divorced; intact-divorced; and a control group	No information given	PAIC	Children in intact-Intact group had highest self-evaluations at both measurement points (T1 and T2). Children whose parents divorced between T1 and T2 experienced a significant decline in self-evaluations, while self-evaluations of children in divorce-divorce group significantly increased by T2.
Raschke and Raschke (1979)	289 black and white boys and girls in grades 3, 6, and 8	70% living with both parents (including re-constituted); 26% with mother only; 4% with neither parent	Unknown, but assumed to be mixed, and skewed toward lower SES	PHCSC	No significant differences by family structure, but significantly lower self-concepts among children reporting high family conflict.
Wyman et al. (1985)	268 children in grades 4-6	98 children with divorced parents, 170 from intact families	Divorce sample "comparable to the intact sample in sociodemographic background"	PCS	No significant differences in perceived social competence, physical competence, or general self-esteem. Divorced group had significantly lower perceived cognitive competence.
Young and Parish (1977)	98 female college students aged 17-22	16 daughters of un-married widows; 12 of remarried widows; 17 of unmarried divorcees; 26 of remarried divorcees; 27 with father present	Middle class	ACL	Daughters who had lost their fathers (due to divorce or death) and whose mothers had not remarried had significantly more negative self-evaluations.

Note: ACL = Adjective Check List; CSEI = Coopersmith Self-Esteem Inventory; PAIC = Personal Attribute Inventory for Children; PCS = Perceived Competence Scale for Children; PHCSC = Piers-Harris Children's Self-Concept Scale; RSE = Rosenberg Self-Esteem Scale.
[a]Three separate studies, using three different samples, are presented in Kalter et al. (1985).

Two important reviews of research on children in fatherless families produce different conclusions: Herzog and Sudia (1973) conclude that children's school achievement is not affected by father absence, but Shinn (1978) concludes that father absence has a number of detrimental effects on children's intellectual performance. Basing her conclusions on 30 studies that met reasonable methodological criteria, Shinn reports that "financial hardship, high levels of anxiety, and in particular, low levels of parent-child interaction are important causes of poor performance among children in single-parent families" (1978: 316). In this section we summarize the differential effects of family disruption on academic performance by gender and social class and offer some insights as to the mechanisms by which these effects occur.

Children's gender. Some studies suggest that negative effects of family disruption on academic performance are stronger for boys than for girls (Chapman, 1977; Werner and Smith, 1982), but most of the evidence suggests similar effects by gender (Hess and Camara, 1979; Kinard and Reinherz, 1986; Shinn, 1978). While females traditionally outscore males on standardized tests of verbal skills and males outperform females on mathematical skills, males who have experienced family disruption generally score higher on verbal aptitude (Radin, 1981). Thus, the absence of a father may result in a "feminine" orientation toward education (Fowler and Richards, 1978; Herzog and Sudia, 1973). But an important and unresolved question is whether this pattern results from boys acquiring greater verbal skills in mother-headed families or from deficiencies in mathematical skills attributable to father absence. The latter explanation is supported by evidence showing that father-absent girls are disadvantaged in mathematics (Radin, 1981).

Children's race. There is a limited amount of evidence that father absence is more harmful to the intelligence and academic achievement of black children (Sciara, 1975), especially black males (Biller and Davids, 1973), but most studies show academic achievement among black children to be unaffected by family structure (Hunt and Hunt, 1975, 1977; Shinn, 1978; Solomon, Hirsch, Scheinfeld, and Jackson, 1972). Svanum, Bringle, and McLaughlin (1982) found, controlling for social class, that there are no significant effects of

father absence on cognitive performance for white or black children. Again, these investigations focus on family composition and demonstrate that the effects of family structure on academic performance do not vary as much by race as by social class, but race differences in the impact of divorce remain largely unexplored. As Table 4 illustrates, we did not find any studies that compared white and black populations of children in divorced and nondivorced families.

Family socioeconomic status. A review by Hetherington, Camara, and Featherman (1983) underscores the importance of social class as a mediating variable. They note small differences favoring children in two-parent families on standardized tests of intelligence and academic achievement that decrease when socioeconomic circumstances are controlled. Differences remain, however, on measures of school performance (e.g., grade-point average), with children in one-parent families at a disadvantage. In a study of predominantly white working-class children, Kinard and Reinherz (1986) investigated the impact of marital disruption on specific dimensions of school performance. Fourth-graders whose families were recently disrupted (i.e., children whose parents divorced since the children entered school) had lower scores on language aptitude and a composite measure of academic achievement than children in never-disrupted families or families in which disruption had occurred several years earlier. But no group differences were detected in mathematics achievement. When maternal education was controlled, there were no differences in reading achievement. In fact, maternal education had a stronger effect on school performance than did marital disruption. Differences in teacher assessments of productivity disappeared when gender and maternal education were controlled (Kinard and Reinherz, 1984).

These findings direct attention to a major methodological problem indicated in earlier reviews (Herzog and Sudia, 1973; Shinn, 1978), namely, inadequate attention to the role of social class in moderating the effects of family disruption on children's academic performance. When social class is controlled, children in female-headed families fare no worse than children from two-parent families on measures of intelligence (Bachman, 1970; Kopf, 1970), academic achievement (Shinn, 1978; Svanum et al., 1982), and

TABLE 4. SUMMARY OF RECENT STUDIES OF EFFECTS OF DIVORCE ON COGNITIVE FUNCTIONING OF CHILDREN AND ADOLESCENTS

Study	Description of Sample	Family Structure of Respondents	Socioeconomic Background	Dependent Measures	Major Findings
Chapman (1977)	96 white college students aged 17–23 (mean = 18.9)	16 males and 16 females in each of 3 groups: father-absent, stepfather present, and intact	No information given	Field dependence measured by Form A of EFT; SAT	Intact family males were more field independent and had significantly higher SAT verbal and total scores than males in other 2 groups. Intact family females had lower SAT verbal scores than the other 2 groups.
Hess and Camara (1979)	32 white boys and girls aged 9–11	16 children in intact families; 16 children in recently divorced families	All children had 2 working parents, each of whom had at least 2 years of college education	Work effectiveness at school as measured by school records and teacher ratings	Children in divorced families were less productive in schoolwork. Present child relationships were also significantly related to children's schoolwork.
Kalter et al. (1985)[a]	(1) 40 girls in 3rd and 6th grade	14 girls with divorced parents, 26 living with both natural parents	All middle class	SAT	No significant differences.
	(2) 84 female college students aged 17–22	42 women with divorced parents, 42 with intact home	Middle- and upper-class students at a "highly selective, expensive college"	GPA	No significant differences.
Kinard and Reinherz (1984)	202 boys and 192 girls in 3rd grade; 99% white	38 children in early (preschool) disrupted families; 36 in recently disrupted families; 320 in never-disrupted families	Predominantly working class (Classes III and IV on Hollingshead Index)	CAAP	Controlling for gender and maternal education, there were no differences in students' productivity by family type.
Kinard and Reinherz (1986)	78 girls and 72 boys in 4th grade; 99% white	87 children in never-disrupted families; 33 in early (preschool) disrupted families; 30 in recently disrupted families	Working class (majority in Classes III and IV on the Hollingshead Index)	PSS, CAAP, SFTAA, CAT-70, parent and teacher ratings of academic achievement	Children in recently disrupted families had significantly lower scores on language, total achievement, and productivity. No group differences in mathematics achievement or in reading achievement with maternal education controlled.
Svanum et al. (1982)	Representative national sample of 6,109 male and female children aged 6–11 (National Health Examination Survey, Cycle II)	5,493 children in intact families; 616 children in father-absent families	Representative sample; SES (defined in terms of family income and householder education) used as control variable	Vocabulary and block design subtests of WISC; arithmetic and reading subtests of WRAT	Controlling for SES, no significant effects of father absence for white or black children.

Note: CAAP = Child and Adolescent Adjustment Profile; CAT-70 = California Achievement Test-70; EFT = Embedded Figures Test; GPA = Grade Point Average; PSS = Preschool Screening System; SAT = Stanford Achievement Test; SFTAA = Short Form Test of Academic Aptitude; WISC = Wechsler Intelligence Scale for Children; WRAT = Wechsler Reading Achievement Test.
[a] Three separate studies, using three different samples, are presented in Kalter et al. (1985). All three studies are described in Table 3.

educational attainment (Bachman, O'Malley, and Johnston, 1978).[6] Further, Svanum et al. (1982: 143) point out that there are many considerations in deciding whether to control for SES in examinations of cognitive performance. While much of the observed variance in cognitive performance may be attributable to SES, "the role that SES assumes in the underlying processes of father absence and cognitive development is unclear at this stage of research." In order to disentangle the intricate effects of family structure and SES on children's cognitive performance, family researchers need to examine the socioeconomic history of intact families and those in which disruption occurs, to examine the economic resources available to children at various stages of cognitive development, and to assess changes in economic resources and family relationships that accompany marital disruption.

Family processes. In recent years important insights have been gained into the specific processes by which marital disruption may affect children's school performance. First, family disruption alters daily routines and work schedules and imposes additional demands on adults and children living in single-parent families (Amato, 1987; Furstenberg and Nord, 1985; Hetherington et al., 1983; Weiss, 1979). Most adolescents must assume extra domestic and child care responsibilities, and financial conditions require some to work part-time. These burdens result in greater absenteeism, tardiness, and truancy among children in single-parent households (Hetherington et al., 1983). Second, children in recently disrupted families are prone to experience emotional and behavioral problems such as aggression, distractibility, dependency, anxiety, and withdrawal (Hess and Camara, 1979; Kinard and Reinherz, 1984), factors that may help to explain problems in school conduct and the propensity of teachers to label and stereotype children from broken families (Hess and Camara, 1979; Hetherington et al., 1979, 1983). Third, emotional problems may interfere with study patterns, while demanding schedules reduce the time available for single parents to help with homework. In support of the latter point, Furstenberg and Nord (1985) examined parent-child interaction patterns in different family types and found few differences in time spent together in social and recreational ac-

tivities, but found that resident parents in reconstituted and single-parent families were much less likely than parents in intact families to help with homework. In sum, a variety of personal, family, and school processes operate to the detriment of academic performance among children of divorce.

Interpersonal Relationships

Compared to the large bodies of research on personal adjustment, self-concept, and cognitive functioning, relatively few studies have examined interpersonal relations among children and adolescents in different family structures (see Table 5). Generally, investigations have focused on peer relations among children and dating patterns among adolescents.

Peer relations. Studies of preschool children (Hetherington et al., 1979) and preadolescents (Santrock, 1975; Wyman, Cowen, Hightower, and Pedro-Carroll, 1985) suggest that children in disrupted families are less sociable: they have fewer close friends, spend less time with friends, and participate in fewer shared activities. Stolberg and Anker (1983) observe that children in families disrupted by divorce exhibit psychopathology in interpersonal relations, often behaving in unusual and inappropriate ways. Other studies suggest that the effects are temporary. Kinard and Reinherz (1984) found no differences in peer relations among children in intact and disrupted families, but those in recently disrupted families displayed greater hostility. Kurdek et al. (1981) conducted a two-year follow-up of children whose parents had divorced and showed that relationships with peers improved after the divorce and that personal adjustment was facilitated by opportunities to discuss experiences with peers, some of whom had similar experiences. However, Guidubaldi and Perry (1985) observed a much different pattern: among boys, those from divorced families had greater contact with friends, and among girls there were no differences by family structure.

Dating patterns. Hetherington (1972) reported that adolescent girls whose fathers were absent prior to age 5 had difficulties in heterosexual relations, but Hainline and Feig's (1978) analyses of

TABLE 5. SUMMARY OF RECENT STUDIES ON EFFECTS OF DIVORCE ON INTERPERSONAL RELATIONSHIPS OF CHILDREN AND ADOLESCENTS

Study	Description of Sample	Family Structure of Respondents	Socioeconomic Background	Dependent Measures	Major Findings
Booth et al. (1984)	2,538 male and female college students	1,945 students from intact families; 365 with divorced or permanently separated parents; 228 whose parents' marriage was broken by death	19% from blue-collar homes; the remainder presumably from middle- and upper-middle-class background	Level and quality of dating activity	Level of dating activity was slightly higher among students with divorced parents. Quality of courtship relations was affected (negatively) only when postdivorce conflict occurred and parent-child relations deteriorated.
Guidubaldi and Perry (1985)	365 boys and 334 girls in grades 1, 3, and 5 (T1); grades 2, 3, 5, and 7 at follow-up (T2) (National Association of School Psychologists–Kent State University data)	341 children with divorced parents and 358 from intact families	SES (defined separately by family income and by educational and occupational classifications) was examined and was instituted as a control in the analyses, but no breakdown by SES was given.	Child interview used to measure friendships and other variables[a]	Boys from divorced families had greater contact with friends than boys in intact families. No differences among girls.
Hess and Camara (1979)	32 white boys and girls aged 9–11	16 children in intact families; 16 children in recently divorced families	All children had 2 working parents, each of whom had at least 2 years of college education.	Social relations with peers (e.g., peer acceptance, friendships, sociability)	No significant difference by family type, but social relations were significantly better among children who had good relationships with their fathers.
Hetherington, Cox, and Cox (1979)	48 white boys and 48 white girls; mean age = 3.9 at T1 and 5.8 at T2	24 boys and 24 girls from divorced, mother-custody families; 24 boys and 24 girls from non-divorced families	Middle class	Observational measures of children's free play and social interaction; teacher ratings of behavior; peer nomination measures; sociometric measure of popularity	Both boys and girls in divorced families exhibited immature, ineffective, and negative social behaviors but these behaviors did not last long for girls. Boys in divorced families remained unpopular two years postdivorce.

(Continued on next page)

TABLE 5. SUMMARY OF RECENT STUDIES ON EFFECTS OF DIVORCE ON
INTERPERSONAL RELATIONSHIPS OF CHILDREN AND ADOLESCENTS—Continued

Study	Description of Sample	Family Structure of Respondents	Socioeconomic Background	Dependent Measures	Major Findings
Kalter et al. (1985)	84 female college students aged 17–22	42 women with divorced parents, 42 with intact homes	middle- and upper-middle-class students at a "highly selective," expensive college"	Dating and sexual behavior	No significant differences, but women in divorced group began dating slightly later. Both groups socially active.
Kinard and Reinherz (1984)	202 boys and 192 girls in 3rd grade; 99% white	38 children in early (preschool) disrupted families; 36 in recently disrupted families; 320 in never-disrupted families	Predominantly working class (Classes III and IV on Hollingshead Index)	CAAP	No significant differences by family structure
Santrock (1975)	120 boys in 5th and 6th grade	60 boys in intact families; 20 in early-divorced (boys younger than age 6) families; 20 in late-divorced (boys between 6–10) families; 20 in father-deceased (boys between 6–10) families	Predominantly lower class. Father-present and father-absent groups were matched on SES, race, school, and other background characteristics.	Teacher ratings of sociability (e.g., adapts to new situations, social participation)	Father-absent boys were rated as significantly less sociable.
Stolberg and Anker (1983)	42 males and 37 females aged 6–16	39 children with divorced parents; 40 children in intact families	Two groups were matched on predivorce annual per capita income.	3 social competence scales from CBCL	Children in divorce group were significantly less prosocial in school-related behaviors.
Wyman et al. (1985)	286 children in grades 4–6	98 children with divorced parents, 170 from intact families	Divorce sample "comparable to the intact sample in sociodemographic background"	Parent questionnaire measuring children's sources of social support	Children of divorced parents had fewer close friends, spent less time with friends, and participated in fewer activities.

Note: CAAP = Child and Adolescent Adjustment Profile; CBCL = Achenbach Child Behavior Checklist.
[a]See Table 2 for more details on other dimensions of this study.

female college students indicated that early and later father-absent women could not be distinguished on measures of romanticism and heterosexual attitudes.

An examination of dating and sexual behavior among female college students found that women with divorced parents began dating slightly later than those in intact families, but women in both groups were socially active (Kalter, Riemer, Brickman, and Chen, 1985). Booth, Brinkerhoff, and White (1984) reported that, compared to college students with intact families, those whose parents were divorced or permanently separated exhibited higher levels of dating activity, and this activity increased further if parental or parent-child conflict persisted during and after the divorce. Gender did not mediate the effects of divorce on courtship, nor did the age at which parental divorce occurred. Regarding adolescent sexual behavior, the findings consistently demonstrate that males and females not living with both biological parents initiate coitus earlier than their counterparts in intact families (Hogan and Kitagawa, 1985; Newcomer and Udry, 1987). But Newcomer and Udry propose that, because parental marital status is also associated with a broad range of deviant behaviors, these effects may stem from general loss of parental control rather than simply loss of control over sexual behavior. Studies of antisocial behavior support this interpretation.

Antisocial Behavior

Many studies over the years have linked juvenile delinquency, deviancy, and antisocial behavior to children living in broken homes (Bandura and Walters, 1959; Glueck and Glueck, 1962; Hoffman, 1971; McCord, McCord, and Thurber, 1962; Santrock, 1975; Stolberg and Anker, 1983; Tooley, 1976; Tuckman and Regan, 1966). Unfortunately, these studies either relied on clinical samples or failed to control for social class and other factors related to delinquency. However, as shown in Table 6, a number of studies involving large representative samples and controlling for social class provide similar findings (Dornbusch, Carlsmith, Bushwall, Ritter, Leiderman, Hastorf, and Gross, 1985; Kalter et al., 1985; Peterson and Zill, 1986; Rickel and Langner, 1985). Kalter et al. (1985) studied 522 teenage girls and found that girls in divorced families committed more delin-

quent acts (e.g., drug use, larceny, skipping school) than their counterparts in intact families. Dornbusch et al. (1985) examined a representative national sample of male and female youth aged 12-17 and found that adolescents in mother-only households were more likely than their counterparts in intact families to engage in deviant acts, partly because of their tendency to make decisions independent of parental input. The presence of an additional adult (a grandparent, an uncle, a lover, a friend) in mother-only households increased control over adolescent behavior and lowered rates of deviant behavior, which suggests that "there are functional equivalents of two-parent families—nontraditional groupings that can do the job of parenting" (1985: 340). Peterson and Zill (1986) examined children of virtually the same ages (12-16) and found a higher incidence of behavior problems among children who had experienced marital disruption.

A tentative conclusion based on the evidence reviewed here is that antisocial behavior is less likely to occur in families where two adults are present, whether as biological parents, stepparents, or some combination of biological parents and other adults. Short-term increases in antisocial behavior may occur during periods of disruption, however, as children adjust to restructured relationships and parents struggle to maintain consistency in disciplining (Rickel and Langner, 1985). It is reasonable to expect that an important variable in predicting antisocial behavior is the level of family conflict, but most research has failed to examine the nature and quality of familial relationships in intact and other family structures. Peterson and Zill (1986) demonstrated that, when social class was controlled, behavior problems were as likely to occur among adolescents living in intact families characterized by persistent conflict as among those living in disrupted families. A related and often overlooked concern in tracing the effects of family structure on children's well-being is the quality of parent-child relationships experienced by children in different living arrangements. Peterson and Zill found that "poor parent-child relationships lead to more negative child behavior, yet maintaining good relationships with parents can go some way in reducing the effects of conflict and disruption" (1986: 306). Hess and Camara's (1979) analyses of a much smaller sample yielded a similar conclusion: aggressive

TABLE 6. SUMMARY OF RECENT STUDIES ON EFFECTS OF DIVORCE ON
ANTISOCIAL BEHAVIOR OF CHILDREN AND ADOLESCENTS

Study	Description of Sample	Family Structure of Respondents	Socioeconomic Background	Dependent Measures	Major Findings
Dornbusch et al. (1985)	Representative national sample of 6,710 adolescents aged 12–17 (National Health Examination Survey, Cycle III)	Primarily analyses of mother-only families and intact families	Defined separately by family income (high, middle, and low for the period 1966–1970) and father's education	Contact with the law, arrests, running away, cigarette smoking, truancy, school discipline	Youth in mother-only households were more likely to make decisions without direct parental input and more likely to exhibit deviant behavior. Results held with family income and parental education controlled.
Hess and Camara (1979)	32 white boys and girls aged 9–11	16 children in intact families; 16 children in recently divorced families	All children had 2 working parents, each of whom had at least 2 years of college education	Aggression, as reported by parents	Nonsignificant difference by family type. Parental harmony and parent-child relationships were significantly related to aggressive behavior.
Kalter et al. (1985)	522 girls aged 11–18 (1972 National Survey of Youth)	62 girls with divorced parents; 460 girls from intact households	Divorced group "represented significantly lower SES households"	Delinquent behavior	Girls in divorced families committed more delinquent acts (e.g., drug use, larceny, skipping school).
Kinard and Reinherz (1984)	202 boys and 192 girls in 3rd grade; 99% white	38 children in early (preschool) disrupted families; 36 in recently disrupted families; 320 in never-disrupted families	Predominantly working class (Classes III and IV on Hollingshead Index)	CAAP	Children in recently disrupted families displayed greatest hostility; those in never-disrupted families, least hostility.
Peterson and Zill (1986)	Representative national sample of 1,423 boys and girls aged 12–16 (National Survey of Children)	Children living with both biological (or adoptive) parents; those living with biological mothers but not fathers; and those living with biological fathers but not mothers	Nationally representative SES composition	3 subscales of Achenbach and Edelbrock index measuring depressed/withdrawn behavior; antisocial behavior; and impulsive/hyperactive behavior; plus 2 measures of school behavior problems	Both overcontrolled and undercontrolled behavior were more common in children who experienced marital disruption. Persistent marital conflict in intact families was strongly related to antisocial behavior.

(Continued on next page)

TABLE 6. SUMMARY OF RECENT STUDIES ON EFFECTS OF DIVORCE ON
ANTISOCIAL BEHAVIOR OF CHILDREN AND ADOLESCENTS—Continued

Study	Description of Sample	Family Structure of Respondents	Socioeconomic Background	Dependent Measures	Major Findings
Rickel and Langner (1985)	Representative, ethnically diverse sample of 1,034 families (T1) with children aged 6–18; 732 families at T2 (5–6 years later)	Children living with natural father, no father, or surrogate father; 25–50% had experienced marital disruption	Trichotomized into upper, middle, and low SES based on employment status, occupation, family income, and rent	Isolation; conflict with parents/siblings/friends; delinquency; as reported by mothers	At both Time 1 and Time 2, children with natural fathers exhibited the least delinquency, and children with surrogate fathers had the most disordered behavior. These findings persisted with ethnicity and social class controlled.
Santrock (1975)	120 boys in 5th and 6th grade	60 boys in intact families; 20 in early-divorced (boys younger than age 6) families; 20 in late-divorced (boys between 6–10) families; 20 in father-deceased (boys between 6–10) families	Predominantly lower class. Father-present and father-absent groups were matched on SES, race, school, and other background characteristics.	A variety of behavioral measures plus teacher ratings of social deviation (e.g., getting into trouble, stealing, cheating).	Controlling for relevant variables, there were no differences on behavioral measures, but teachers rated father-absent boys to be more socially deviant.
Stolberg and Anker (1983)	42 males and 37 females aged 6–16	39 children with divorced parents; 40 children in intact families	Two groups were matched on pre-divorce annual per capita income	9 behavior problem scales from CBCL	Children in divorce group who experienced considerable change displayed greatest behavior pathology: depression, social withdrawal, aggressiveness, and delinquency.

Note: CAAP = Child and Adolescent Adjustment Profile; CBCL = Achenbach Child Behavior Checklist.

behavior in children was unrelated to family type but was more common in situations characterized by infrequent or low-quality parent-child interaction and parental discord.

Summary of Empirical Evidence

The empirical evidence on children of divorce, although inconsistent in places, is punctuated by a number of consistent findings. Research on personal adjustment suggests that young children, particularly boys, suffer temporary deleterious effects when their parents divorce, while adolescents are not as much affected by family structure as by parental discord. Adolescents living in single-parent families also acquire certain strengths, notably a sense of responsibility, as a consequence of altered family routines. Likewise, the evidence on self-concept indicates that family structure is unrelated but parental discord is negatively related to children's self-esteem. We cannot be certain of the degree to which family structure influences children's academic performance (or other aspects of cognitive functioning) because the effects of race and social class have not been controlled. But the available body of research demonstrates that children in single-parent families are slightly disadvantaged in school performance. The evidence on interpersonal relationships is sparse but suggests that children in disrupted families experience problems in peer relations, while adolescents in such families tend to be more active in dating and sexual relations. Research on antisocial behavior consistently illustrates that adolescents in mother-only households and in conflict-ridden families are more prone to commit delinquent acts.

LIMITATIONS OF PRIOR RESEARCH

In this section we discuss some of the principal limitations of research assessing the impact of divorce on children. In most cases we do not cite individual studies because many of the problems pertain to virtually all of the extant research. However, the reader should consider these problems in evaluating the findings of particular studies.

Nonrepresentative Samples

Sampling is a virtually universal dilemma for researchers. There are excellent national surveys that analyze demographic variables but largely ignore social psychological issues such as personal adjustment or self-concept. Alternatively, there are excellent studies that incorporate these social psychological factors but are based on convenience samples.

Among the most problematic nonrepresentative samples are those that rely on clinical populations. While these studies are crucial to our understanding of children and adolescents who are most severely influenced by divorce, they tell us little or nothing about the typical experience following divorce. Since most children whose parents divorce do not receive professional help, such studies can be very misleading about the consequences of divorce for the majority of youth.

While nonrepresentative samples have shortcomings, national surveys typically involve reanalysis of data collected for other purposes and for which the effects of divorce are not a central concern. Because these surveys are not designed to investigate the consequences of divorce, many theoretically important variables are either excluded or poorly operationalized and important control variables are often absent.

What Family Structures Are Being Compared?

Generally, investigations of family structure rely on classification schemes, such as father absence, in which the types derive from different events. For example, many military families are classified as father-absent, but the absence is temporary, the father's income is available to the family, and no social stigma is attached. Alternatively, a single-parent household may consist of a 25-year-old never-married woman and her five children. Other families are father-absent as the result of death, permanent separation, or divorce. A central problem in identifying the effects of family structure is that all of these families are frequently classified as one monolithic family form called "father-absent." One investigation involved five types of black family structures (male-headed, parent-incarcerated, separated, divorced, and widowed) and found that these arrangements varied in role structure, family cohesiveness, and parent-child relationships (Savage, Adair, and Friedman, 1978). For example, separated parents spent considerably less time with their children than parents in other family structures, and women with incarcerated husbands were most inclined to use corporal punishment on their children. Until family researchers distinguish father-absent families in terms of the cause and length of father absence, the quality of mother-child interaction, and the availability of other male role models, the conclusions drawn must be viewed with skepticism.

Failure to Control for Income or Social Class

Perhaps the most significant limitation of research linking family structure and children's well-being, as Tables 2–6 reveal, is a failure to examine the moderating or mediating effects of income or social class. With very few exceptions, the studies rely on samples of children in one socioeconomic category, usually the middle class, for whom the economic consequences of divorce are dissimilar to those of children in lower socioeconomic categories. As a result, it is impossible to distinguish the effects of divorce and family structure from those of socioeconomic conditions. In explaining academic achievement, for example, the classic study by Coleman et al. (1966) demonstrated that income is more important than family structure (see also Herzog and Sudia, 1973; Rainwater and Yancey, 1967). Thus, effects that appear to be caused by divorce may actually be the result of inadequate income—the loss of the father being relatively less critical than the loss of his financial contribution.

Economic factors are important considerations in explicating causal processes for several reasons (see Greenberg and Wolf, 1982; Hill and Duncan, 1987; Kinard and Reinherz, 1984; McLanahan, 1985). First, low-income, single-parent mothers are more likely to work and, as a result, may provide inadequate supervision (Colletta, 1979). Children's behavioral problems associated with "mother-absence" (Hill, Augustyniak, and Ponza, 1986) may therefore be attributable to low income and the need for maternal employment rather than being the result of single-parent family structure per se. Second, the effects of marital disruption on children may be indirect, operating through the economic and emotional impact of divorce on custodial mothers (Longfellow, 1979; Shinn, 1978). As mothers adjust to divorce, single-parenthood, and lower economic status, their anxiety and emotional distress may induce anxiety and stress in children, which in turn may hinder children's academic performance (Kinard

and Reinherz, 1986). Failure to examine socioeconomic variation in single-parent families thus obscures the specific processes through which marital disruption affects children. Third, children in single-parent households are more likely to assume adult roles at an early age—for example, working full-time and being responsible for younger siblings, responsibilities that require many adolescents to leave school (Kelly and Wallerstein, 1979; Weiss, 1979). The effects (both positive and negative) of these accelerated life course transitions are consequences of economic deprivation.

Other issues related to income and social class need to be considered. First, it is not clear whether the effect is due to inadequate family income or loss of family income. Single-parent families precipitated by divorce may be poor as a result of a sudden loss of income. Dramatic changes in lifestyle, financial instability, and loss of status may affect children indirectly through custodial parents' loss of control and altered childrearing practices. Increased labor force participation or increased transfer payments may help, but the net effect is still a dramatic loss of income (Cherlin, 1981; Hoffman, 1977; Weitzman, 1985).

While many families lose a stable middle-class environment and encounter stigmatization and financial instability, other families experience relatively minor changes. Santrock and Warshak (1979) report that postdivorce income losses were severe for mother-custody families but not for father-custody families. Further, the source of income is an important consideration, in that welfare dollars may stigmatize the poor and child support payments are unreliable (Bould, 1977).

The generally negative effects of divorce on family income must also be distinguished from the effects of divorce on female labor force participation and single mothers' personal income. Using the National Longitudinal Survey to trace the marital and work careers of women over a 10-year period, Porter (1984) found that divorced, never-remarried women earned more than the continuously married or the currently married (also see Corcoran, 1979). The long-term positive effect of divorce on the earning power of women needs to be recognized and may explain why most of the adverse effects of divorce diminish over time. Employed single mothers may provide stronger role models than dependent mothers in intact families, fostering egalitarian sex role attitudes among both women and men whose parents divorced (Kiecolt and Acock, 1988).

Ecological Fallacy

A common error in social research is termed the "ecological fallacy," occurring when relationships examined at the aggregate level are assumed to apply at the individual level. Herzog and Sudia (1973), for example, report several studies that correlate the proportion of single-parent households with the incidence of delinquency and other behavior problems in census tracts. But even substantial correlations tell us *nothing* about whether the delinquents come from two-parent or single-parent families. Rather than providing information on family structure, such correlations may indicate the aggregate effects of poverty, discrimination, inadequate education, and lack of opportunity.

Failure to Examine Contextual Factors

A number of contextual factors that distinguish the living conditions of children in intact and disrupted families may be linked to behavioral differences between the two groups. Glenn and Supancic (1984) note that divorced persons participate less in church activities than married persons. While parents' religious orientations are individual-level factors, involvement in church activities provides a contextual variable. If children living in single-parent households are systematically less likely to be exposed to other children who are active in a church, this may have a substantial impact on their adjustment. Evidence supporting this kind of contextual effect is provided by Coleman, Hoffer, and Kilgore (1982). They found that, although children from single-parent households were much more likely than those from two-parent families to drop out of public schools, there was no difference in Catholic schools—a result that illustrates a contextual effect involving norms and social networks operating in the Catholic community.

Another contextual variable is urban residence. Single-parent households are far more common in urban areas. Urban areas provide a different environment for children than do suburbs, rural areas, or small towns. The quality of the educational system and the exposure to deviant subcultures are two correlates of residential

patterns that may affect children who live in a female-headed household. Contextual factors have an important influence on all children, regardless of family structure, adequacy of parenting, or income. Other contextual factors that influence children include the number of fatherless children in their school, neighborhood SES, presence of a gang subculture, presence of peer groups using drugs (Blechman, Berberian, and Thompson, 1977), and the geographic mobility of peers. Research has yet to disentangle such contextual factors from the direct effect of family structure. Contextual factors may prove as important as the immediate family history of the child.

Lack of Longitudinal Designs

Among the hundreds of studies on children of divorce, there are only a pair of widely cited longitudinal studies (Hetherington et al., 1978, 1979; Wallerstein and Kelly, 1980b), and even these studies have serious methodological limitations (Blechman, 1982; Cherlin, 1981). Yet adjustment to changes in family structure is a developmental process. Retrospective data are rarely used, so typical cross-sectional comparisons of children living in disrupted families with children in intact families provide very little, if any, information on the socioeconomic history of these families, level of family conflict, parent-child relations, and so on. If, for example, children from single-parent households were formerly in two-parent households that were poor and conflict-ridden, any problems the children now have may be scars from long ago rather than a direct consequence of the divorce. A partial solution is to collect retrospective information on numerous theoretically relevant dimensions of family life prior to the divorce (and to collect the same retrospective information on intact families). Unfortunately, most of the extant studies rely on cross-sectional information, and family researchers must therefore be cautious in interpreting results.

Conclusions

There is reason to question the validity of the family composition hypothesis. Theoretically, it has been assumed that the nuclear family is the norm and, by implication, that any departure from it is deviant and therefore deleterious to hose involved. Even if this were the case, no heoretical perspective recognizes that these effects may be short-lived or otherwise mitigated by compensatory mechanisms and alternative role models. In the absence of a parent, it is possible that developmental needs are met by other actors.

It is simplistic and inaccurate to think of divorce as having uniform consequences for children. The consequences of divorce vary along different dimensions of well-being, characteristics of children (e.g., predivorce adjustment, age at the time of disruption) and characteristics of families (e.g., socioeconomic history, pre- and postdivorce level of conflict, parent-child relationships, and maternal employment). Most of the evidence reviewed here suggests that some sociodemographic characteristics of children, such as race and gender, are not as important as characteristics of families in mediating the effects of divorce. Many studies report boys to be at a greater disadvantage, but these differences usually disappear when other relevant variables are controlled. At present, there are too few methodologically adequate studies comparing white and black children to conclude that one group is more damaged by family disruption than the other.

Characteristics of families, on the other hand, are critical to youthful well-being. Family conflict contributes to many problems in social development, emotional stability, and cognitive skills (Edwards, 1987; Kurdek, 1981), and these effects continue long after the divorce is finalized. Slater and Haber (1984) report that ongoing high levels of conflict, whether in intact or divorced homes, produce lower self-esteem, increased anxiety, and a loss of self-control. Conflict also reduces the child's attraction to the parents (White, Brinkerhoff, and Booth, 1985). Rosen (1979) concludes that parental separation is more beneficial for children than continued conflict, and Blechman (1982) proposes that parent absence is not the key to adjustment problems but simply a surrogate for more fundamental causes, including family conflict and a hostile family environment. Such conflict and hostility may account for adolescent adjustment problems whether the family in question goes through divorce or remains intact (Hoffman, 1971). The level of conflict is thus an important dimension of family interaction that can precipitate changes in family

structure and affect children's well-being.

Maternal employment is another variable mediating the consequences of divorce for children. Divorced women often find the dual responsibilities of provider and parent to be stressful (Brofenbrenner, 1976). But studies indicate that women who work prior to the divorce do not find continued employment problematic (Kinard and Reinherz, 1984); the problem occurs for women who enter the labor force after the divorce and who view the loss of time with their children as another detriment to the children that is caused by the divorce (Kinard and Reinherz, 1984). As a practical matter, the alternative to employment for single-parent mothers is likely to be poverty or, at best, economic dependency. The effects of maternal employment on children's well-being need to be compared to the effects of nonemployment and consequent poverty.

Other bases of social support for single-parent mothers and their children must also be examined. The presence of strong social networks may ease the parents' and, presumably, the child's adjustment after a divorce (Milardo, 1987; Savage et al., 1978). However, women who are poor, have many children, and must work long hours are likely to have limited social networks and few friends. Typically, the single mother and her children are also isolated from her ex-husband's family (Anspach, 1976). By reuniting with her family of origin, the mother may be isolated from her community and new social experiences for herself and her children (McLanahan, Wedemeyer, and Adelberg, 1981). Kinship ties are usually strained, as both biological parents and parents-in-law are more critical of the divorce than friends are (Spanier and Thompson, 1984). Little has been done to relate these considerations about kinship relations and social networks of divorced women to the well-being of children and adolescents. We believe that these social relations are important, but empirical verification is needed.

Methodologically, research in support of the family composition hypothesis has been flawed in a number of respects (Blechman, 1982). As described above, most studies (*a*) rely on simplistic classifications of family structure; (*b*) overlook potentially confounding factors such as income and social class; (*c*) use nonrepresentative samples; (*d*) examine limited dimensions of social and psychological well-being; (*e*) fail to assess possible beneficial effects deriving from different family structures; and (*f*) rely on nonlongitudinal designs to detect developmental processes.[7]

In order to address the deficiencies of previous research, future studies must compare the four most prevalent family structures: (*a*) intact nuclear families with parents in their first marriage; (*b*) reconstituted families where one biological and one stepparent are present; (*c*) single-parent families consisting of a divorced or separated mother and child; and (*d*) mother-child units where the parent has never been married. Important variations *within* these structures must also be examined—for example, mother-custody and father-custody families. Our review suggests that researchers need to explore the effects of factors that may intervene between family structure and youthful well-being—factors mediating the impact of changing family forms. Social class, marital quality, parent-child relations, and contextual factors are important considerations in tracing the effects of family structure on children's social and psychological well-being. Not least, longitudinal designs should be employed, allowing estimation of the duration of any detected adverse effects. To the extent that we lack systematic evidence of this kind, the processes through which divorce and family structure affect children's well-being remain largely unknown.

Notes

An earlier version of this article was presented at the annual meetings of the Southern Sociological Society, Atlanta, April 1987. The authors express their appreciation to John N. Edwards for sharing many valuable insights related to the focus of this review. They also thank him and K. Jill Kiecolt for critical and constructive suggestions on an earlier draft, Theodore D. Fuller for demographic consultation, Sampson Lee Blair for assistance in assembling the vast literature reviewed here, and the anonymous reviewers for their thorough comments and useful ideas.

1. In cases where a study involves measures of multiple dimensions of well-being, the study is listed in each corresponding table. Not included in the tables are studies of clinical populations (e.g., Jacobson, 1978; Wallerstein, 1984; Wallerstein and Kelly, 1975, 1980a, 1980b), studies that do not involve comparisons of children in disrupted families with children in intact families, and studies examining aspects of divorce other than children's well-being (e.g., analyses of demographic trends and examinations of adult children of divorce).

2. Other studies focusing on the timing of divorce provide evidence that children's adjustment is unaffected by the length of time since marital disruption (Hodges, Wechsler, and Ballantine, 1979; Kalter and Rembar, 1981; Santrock, 1975).

3. Other studies, several using predominantly white samples (e.g., Kinard and Reinherz, 1984), and one involving a predominantly black sample (Kellem, Ensminger, and Turner, 1977) report no gender differences in adjustment.

4. Another study presents evidence that male gender role development is unaffected by the timing of father absence and by the availability of male siblings and father substitutes, but father absence is associated nevertheless with "less appropriate" gender role orientation (Drake and McDougall, 1977).

5. This is not to say that such responsibilities and status have uniformly positive effects. Weiss (1979) contends that these arrangements may have benefits for older children but may lead to excessive self-reliance among younger children. Even for adolescents, however, the nature of confidant relations is important in that discussions of adult issues (e.g., mother's sex life, work stress) may be deleterious. There is also the risk of losing this status when the mother remarries, thus creating further problems.

6. Featherman and Hauser (1978) obtained different results in controlling for social class and race. They found that American males born between 1907 and 1951 who lived in one-parent families completed approximately three-fourths of a year less schooling than their counterparts who lived with both parents. The same pattern held for Canadian males and females.

7. The recent National Survey of Families and Households contains extensive data on diverse family structures and child outcomes. Five groups were oversampled: single-parent families, families with stepchildren, cohabiting couples, recently married couples, and minorities. Detailed information on life history and family relations was collected, and a 5-year follow-up is planned. Documentation is available through the Center for Demography and Ecology, University of Wisconsin–Madison.

References

Acock, Alan C., and K. Jill Kiecolt. 1988. "Is it family structure or socioeconomic status: Effects of family structure during adolescence on adult adjustment." Paper presented at the annual meetings of the American Sociological Association, Atlanta.

Amato, Paul R. 1986. "Marital conflict, the parent-child relationship, and child self-esteem." Family Relations 35: 403–410.

Amato, Paul R. 1987. "Family processes in one-parent, stepparent, and intact families: The child's point of view." Journal of Marriage and the Family 49: 327–337.

Anspach, Donald F. 1976. "Kinship and divorce." Journal of Marriage and the Family 38: 323–330.

Anthony, E. James. 1974. "Children at risk from divorce: A review." In E. James Anthony (ed.), The Child in His Family: Children at Psychiatric Risk (Vol. 3). New York: John Wiley and Sons.

Bachman, Jerald G. 1970. Youth in Transition, Vol. 2: The Impact of Family Background and Intelligence on Tenth Grade Boys. Ann Arbor, MI: Survey Research Center, Institute for Social Research.

Bachman, Jerald G., Patrick M. O'Malley, and Jerome J. Johnston. 1978. Youth in Transition, Vol. 6: Adolescence to Adulthood: A Study of Change and Stability in the Lives of Young Men. Ann Arbor, MI: Survey Research Center, Institute for Social Research.

Bandura, Albert, and Richard H. Walters. 1959. Adolescent Aggression. New York: Ronald Press.

Bandura, Albert, and Richard H. Walters. 1963. Social Learning and Personality Development. New York: Holt, Rinehart and Winston.

Bem, Sandra L. 1974. "The measurement of psychological androgyny." Journal of Consulting and Clinical Psychology 42: 155–162.

Berg, Berthold, and Robert Kelly. 1979. "The measured self-esteem of children from broken, rejected, and accepted families." Journal of Divorce 2: 363–369.

Biller, Henry B. 1976. "The father and personality development: Paternal deprivation and sex-role development." Pp. 89–156 in Michael E. Lamb (ed.), The Role of the Father in Child Development. New York: Wiley.

Biller, Henry B. 1981a. "The father and sex role development." Pp. 319–358 in Michael E. Lamb (ed.), The Role of the Father in Child Development (2nd ed.). New York: Wiley.

Biller, Henry B. 1981b. "Father absence, divorce, and personality development." Pp. 489–552 in Michael E. Lamb (ed.), The Role of the Father in Child Development (2nd ed.). New York: Wiley.

Biller, Henry B., and Anthony Davids. 1973. "Parent-child relations, personality development, and psychopathology." Pp. 48–77 in Anthony Davids (ed.) Issues in Abnormal Child Psychology. Monterey, CA: Wadsworth.

Blanchard, Robert W., and Henry B. Biller. 1971. "Father availability and academic performance among third-grade boys." Developmental Psychology 4: 301–305.

Blechman, Elaine A. 1982. "Are children with one parent at psychological risk? A methodological review." Journal of Marriage and the Family 44: 179–195.

Blechman, Elaine A., Rosalie M. Berberian, and W. Douglas Thompson. 1977. "How well does number of parents explain unique variance in self-reported

drug use?" Journal of Consulting and Clinical Psychology 45: 1182–1183.

Booth, Alan, David B. Brinkerhoff, and Lynn K. White. 1984. "The impact of parental divorce on courtship." Journal of Marriage and the Family 46: 85–94.

Bould, Sally. 1977. "Female-headed families: Personal fate control and provider role." Journal of Marriage and the Family 39: 339–349.

Bronfenbrenner, Urie. 1961. "The changing American child: A speculative analysis." Journal of Social Issues 17: 6–18.

Bronfenbrenner, Urie. 1976. "Who cares for America's children?" Pp. 3–32 in Victor C. Vaugh and T. Berry Brazelton (eds.), The Family—Can It Be Saved? Chicago: Yearbook Medical Publishers.

Bumpass, Larry L. 1984. "Children and marital disruption: A replication and update." Demography 21: 71–82.

Bumpass, Larry L. 1985. "Bigger isn't necessarily better: A comment on Hofferth's 'Updating children's life course.'" Journal of Marriage and the Family 47: 797–798.

Cashion, Barbara G. 1984. "Female-headed families: Effects on children and clinical implications." Pp. 481–489 in David H. Olson and Brent C. Miller (eds.), Family Studies Review Yearbook. Beverly Hills, CA: Sage.

Chapman, Michael. 1977. "Father absence, stepfathers, and the cognitive performance of college students." Child Development 48: 1155–1158.

Cherlin, Andrew J. 1981. Marriage, Divorce, Remarriage. Cambridge, MA: Harvard University Press.

Coleman, James S., et al. 1966. Equality of Educational Opportunity. Washington, DC: U.S. Government Printing Office.

Coleman, James S., Thomas Hoffer, and Sally Kilgore. 1982. High School Achievement. New York: Basic Books.

Colletta, Nancy D. 1979. "The impact of divorce: Father absence or poverty?" Journal of Divorce 3: 27–35.

Constantinople, Anne. 1973. "Masculinity-femininity: An exception to a famous dictum?" Psychological Bulletin 80: 389–407.

Cooper, Judith E., Jacqueline Holman, and Valerie A. Braithwaite. 1983. "Self-esteem and family cohesion: The child's perspective and adjustment." Journal of Marriage and the Family 45: 153–159.

Corcoran, Martha. 1979. "The economic consequences of marital dissolution for women in the middle years." Sex Roles 5: 343–353.

DeSimone-Luis, Judith, Katherine O'Mahoney, and Dennis Hunt. 1979. "Children of separation and divorce: Factors influencing adjustment." Journal of Divorce 3: 37–42.

Dornbusch, Sanford M., J. Merrill Carlsmith, Steven J. Bushwall, Philip L. Ritter, Herbert Leiderman, Albert H. Hastorf, and Ruth T. Gross. 1985. "Single parents, extended households, and the control of adolescents." Child Development 56: 326–341.

Drake, Charles T., and Daniel McDougall. 1977. "Effects of the absence of a father and other male models on the development of boys' sex roles.'' Developmental Psychology 13: 537–538.

Edwards, John N. 1987. ''Changing family structure and youthful well-being: Assessing the future.'' Journal of Family Issues 8: 355–372.

Ellison, Edythe S. 1983. ''Issues concerning parental harmony and children's psychosocial adjustment.'' American Journal of Orthopsychiatry 53: 73–80.

Featherman, David L., and Robert M. Hauser. 1978. Opportunity and Change. New York: Academic.

Feldman, Harold, and Margaret Feldman. 1975. ''The effects of father absence on adolescents.'' Family Perspective 10: 3–16.

Fowler, Patrick D., and Herbert C. Richards. 1978. ''Father absence, educational preparedness, and academic achievement: A test of the confluence model.'' Journal of Educational Psychology 70: 595–601.

Freud, Sigmund. 1961. ''Some psychical consequences of the anatomical distinction between the sexes.'' In J. Strachey (ed. and trans.), The Standard Edition of the Complete Psychological Works of Sigmund Freud (Vol. 19, 1923–1925). London: Hogarth Press. (Original work published 1925)

Furstenberg, Frank F., Jr., and Christine Winquist Nord. 1985. ''Parenting apart: Patterns of child-rearing after marital disruption.'' Journal of Marriage and the Family 47: 893–904.

Furstenberg, Frank F., Jr., Christine Winquist Nord, James L. Peterson, and Nicholas Zill. 1983. ''The life course of children of divorce: Marital disruption and parental contact.'' American Sociological Review 48: 656–668.

Ganong, Lawrence H., and Marilyn Coleman. 1984. ''The effects of remarriage on children: A review of the empirical literature.'' Family Relations 33: 389–406.

Glenn, Norval, and Michael Supancic. 1984. ''The social and demographic correlates of divorce and separation in the United States: An update and reconsideration.'' Journal of Marriage and the Family 46: 563–576.

Glueck, Sheldon, and Eleanor Glueck. 1962. Family Environment and Delinquency. Boston: Houghton Mifflin.

Greenberg, David, and Douglas Wolf. 1982. ''The economic consequences of experiencing parental marital disruption.'' Child and Youth Services Review 4: 141–162.

Grossman, Sharyn M., Judy Ann Shea, and Gerald P. Adams. 1980. ''Effects of parental divorce during early childhood on ego development and identity formation of college students.'' Journal of Divorce 3: 263–272.

Guidubaldi, John, Helen K. Cleminshaw, Joseph D. Perry, Bonnie K. Nastasi, and Jeanine Lightel. 1986. ''The role of selected family environment factors in children's post-divorce adjustment.'' Family Relations 35: 141–151.

Guidubaldi, John, and Joseph D. Perry. 1985. ''Divorce and mental health sequelae for children: A two-year follow-up of a nationwide sample.'' Jour-

nal of the American Academy of Child Psychiatry 24: 531–537.

Hainline, Louise, and Ellen Feig. 1978. ''The correlates of childhood father absence in college-aged women.'' Child Development 49: 37–42.

Heilbrun, A. B. 1965. ''An empirical test of the modeling theory of sex-role learning.'' Child Development 36: 789–799.

Herzog, Elizabeth, and Cecilia E. Sudia. 1973. ''Children in fatherless families.'' Pp. 141–232 in B. M. Caldwell and N. H. Riccuiti (eds.), Review of Child Development Research (Vol. 3). Chicago: University of Chicago Press.

Hess, Robert D., and Kathleen A. Camara. 1979. ''Post-divorce family relationships as mediating factors in the consequences of divorce for children.'' Journal of Social Issues 35: 79–96.

Hetherington, E. Mavis. 1972. ''Effects of father absence on personality development in adolescent daughters.'' Developmental Psychology 7: 313–326.

Hetherington, E. Mavis. 1979. ''Divorce: A child's perspective.'' American Psychologist 34: 851–858.

Hetherington, E. Mavis, Kathleen A. Camara, and David L. Featherman. 1983. ''Achievement and intellectual functioning of children in one-parent households.'' Pp. 205–284 in Janet T. Spence (ed.), Achievement and Achievement Motives: Psychological and Sociological Approaches. San Francisco: Freeman.

Hetherington, E. Mavis, Martha Cox, and Roger Cox. 1978. ''The aftermath of divorce.'' In J. H. Stevens, Jr., and M. Mathews (eds.), Mother-Child, Father-Child Relations. Washington, DC: National Association for the Education of Young Children.

Hetherington, E. Mavis, Martha Cox, and Roger Cox. 1979. ''Play and social interaction in children following divorce.'' Journal of Social Issues 35: 26–49.

Hetherington, E. Mavis, Martha Cox, and Roger Cox. 1982. ''Effects of divorce on parents and young children.'' In M. Lamb (ed.), Nontraditional Families: Parenting and Child Development. Hillsdale, NJ: Erlbaum.

Hill, Martha S., Sue Augustyniak, and Michael Ponza. 1986. ''Adolescent years with parents divorced or separated: Effects on the social and economic attainments of children as adults.'' Paper presented at the meetings of the Population Association of America, Detroit.

Hill, Martha S., and Greg J. Duncan. 1987. ''Parental family income and the socioeconomic attainment of children.'' Social Science Research 16: 39–73.

Hodges, William F., Ralph C. Wechsler, and Constance Ballantine. 1979. ''Divorce and the preschool child: Cumulative stress.'' Journal of Divorce 3: 55–67.

Hofferth, Sandra L. 1985. ''Updating children's life course.'' Journal of Marriage and the Family 47: 93–115.

Hofferth, Sandra L. 1986. ''Response to a comment by Bumpass on 'Updating children's life course.' '' Journal of Marriage and the Family 48: 680–682.

Hoffman, Martin L. 1971. ''Father absence and conscience development." Developmental Psychology 4: 400–406.

Hoffman, Saul. 1977. "Marital instability and the economic status of women." Demography 14: 67–76.

Hogan, Dennis P., and Evelyn M. Kitagawa. 1985. "The impact of social status, family structure, and neighborhood on the fertility of black adolescents." American Journal of Sociology 90: 825–855.

Hunt, Janet G., and Larry L. Hunt. 1977. "Race, daughters, and father-loss: Does absence make the girl grow stronger?" Social Problems 25: 90–102.

Hunt, Larry L., and Janet G. Hunt. 1975. "Race and the father-son connection: The conditional relevance of father absence for the orientations and identities of adolescent boys." Social Problems 23: 35–52.

Jacobson, Doris S. 1978. "The impact of marital separation/divorce on children: II. Interparent hostility and child adjustment." Journal of Divorce 2: 3–19.

Kalter, Neil, Dana Alpern, Rebecca Spence, and James W. Plunkett. 1984. "Locus of control in children of divorce." Journal of Personality Assessment 48: 410–414.

Kalter, Neil, and James Rembar. 1981. "The significance of a child's age at the time of parental divorce." American Journal of Orthopsychiatry 51: 85–100.

Kalter, Neil, Barbara Riemer, Arthur Brickman, and Jade Woo Chen. 1985. "Implications of parental divorce for female development." Journal of the American Academy of Child Psychiatry 24: 538–544.

Kanoy, Korrel W., Jo Lynn Cunningham, Priscilla White, and Suzanne J. Adams. 1984. "Is family structure that critical? Family relationships of children with divorced and married parents." Journal of Divorce 8: 97–105.

Kellem, Sheppard, Margaret E. Ensminger, and R. Jay Turner. 1977. "Family structure and the mental health of children." Archives of General Psychiatry 34: 1012–1022.

Kelly, Joan B., and Judith Wallerstein. 1979. "Children of divorce." National Elementary Principal 59: 51–58.

Kiecolt, K. Jill, and Alan C. Acock. 1988. "The long-term effects of family structure on gender-role attitudes." Journal of Marriage and the Family 50: 709–717.

Kinard, E. Milling, and Helen Reinherz. 1984. "Marital disruption: Effects of behavioral and emotional functioning in children." Journal of Family Issues 5: 90–115.

Kinard, E. Milling, and Helen Reinherz. 1986. "Effects of marital disruption on children's school aptitude and achievement." Journal of Marriage and the Family 48: 285–293.

Kopf, Kathryn E. 1970. "Family variables and school adjustment of eighth grade father-absent boys." Family Coordinator 19: 145–151.

Kulka, Richard A., and Helen Weingarten. 1979. "The long-term effects of parental divorce in childhood on adult adjustment." Journal of Social Issues 35: 50–78.

Kurdek, Lawrence A. 1981. "An integrative perspective on children's divorce adjustment." American Psychologist 36: 856–866.

Kurdek, Lawrence A., Darlene Blisk, and Albert E. Siesky, Jr. 1981. "Correlates of children's long-term adjustment to their parents' divorce." Developmental Psychology 17: 565–579.

Kurdek, Lawrence A., and Albert E. Siesky, Jr. 1980a. "Sex role self-concepts of single divorced parents and their children." Journal of Divorce 3: 249–261.

Kurdek, Lawrence A., and Albert E. Siesky, Jr. 1980b. "Children's perceptions of their parents' divorce." Journal of Divorce 3: 339–378.

Kurdek, Lawrence A., and Albert E. Siesky, Jr. 1980c. "Effects of divorce on children: The relationship between parent and child perspectives." Journal of Divorce 4: 85–99.

Lamb, Michael E. 1977a. "The effects of divorce on children's personality development." Journal of Divorce 1: 163–174.

Lamb, Michael E. 1977b. "The development of mother- and father-infant attachments in the second year of life." Developmental Psychology 13: 637–648.

Long, Barbara H. 1986. "Parental discord vs. family structure: Effects of divorce on the self-esteem of daughters." Journal of Youth and Adolescence 15: 19–27.

Longfellow, Cynthia. 1979. "Divorce in context: Its impact on children." Pp. 287–306 in George K. Levinger and Oliver C. Moles (eds.), Divorce and Separation: Context, Causes, and Consequences. New York: Basic Books.

Lowenstein, Joyce S., and Elizabeth J. Koopman. 1978. "A comparison of the self-esteem between boys living with single-parent mothers and single-parent fathers." Journal of Divorce 2: 195–208.

Lynn, David B. 1974. The Father: His Role in Child Development. Monterey, CA: Brooks/Cole.

McCord, Joan, William McCord, and Emily Thurber. 1962. "Some effects of parental absence on male children." Journal of Abnormal and Social Psychology 64: 361–369.

McLanahan, Sara S. 1985. "Family structure and the reproduction of poverty." American Journal of Sociology 90: 873–901.

McLanahan, Sara S., Nancy V. Wedemeyer, and Tina Adelberg. 1981. "Network structure, social support, and psychological well-being in the single-parent family." Journal of Marriage and the Family 43: 601–612.

Milardo, Robert M. 1987. "Changes in social networks of women and men following divorce: A review." Journal of Family Issues 8: 78–96.

Newcomer, Susan, and J. Richard Udry. 1987. "Parental marital status effects on adolescent sexual behavior." Journal of Marriage and the family 49: 235–240.

Noller, Patricia. 1978. "Sex differences in the socialization of affectionate expression." Developmental Psychology 14: 317–319.

Norton, Arthur J., and Paul C. Glick. 1986. "One parent families: A social and economic profile." Family Relations 35: 9–17.

Oshman, Harvey P., and Martin Manosevitz. 1976. "Father absence: Effects of stepfathers upon psychosocial development in males." Developmental Psychology 12: 479–480.

Parish, Thomas S. 1981. "The impact of divorce on the family." Adolescence 16 (63): 577–580.

Parish, Thomas S., and Judy W. Dostal. 1980. "Evaluations of self and parent figures by children from intact, divorced, and reconstituted families." Journal of Youth and Adolescence 9: 347–351.

Parish, Thomas S., Judy W. Dostal, and Joycelyn G. Parish. 1981. "Evaluations of self and parents as a function of intactness of family and family happiness." Adolescence 16 (61): 203–210.

Parish, Thomas S., and James C. Taylor. 1979. "The impact of divorce and subsequent father absence on children's and adolescents' self-concepts." Journal of Youth and Adolescence 8: 427–432.

Parish, Thomas S., and Stanley E. Wigle. 1985. "A longitudinal study of the impact of parental divorce on adolescents' evaluations of self and parents." Adolescence 20: 239–244.

Parsons, Talcott, and Robert F. Bales. 1955. Family Socialization and Interaction Process. Glencoe: Free Press.

Peterson, James L., and Nicholas Zill. 1986. "Marital disruption, parent-child relationships, and behavior problems in children." Journal of Marriage and the Family 48: 295–307.

Porter, Beatrice, and K. Daniel O'Leary. 1980. "Marital discord and childhood behavior problems." Journal of Abnormal Child Psychology 8: 287–295.

Porter, Karen. 1984. The Scheduling of Life Course Events, Economic Adaptations, and Marital History: An Analysis of Economic Survival after Separation and Divorce among a Cohort of Midlife Women. Unpublished PhD dissertation, Syracuse University.

Radin, Norma. 1981. "The role of the father in cognitive, academic, and intellectual development." Pp. 379–427 in Michael E. Lamb (ed.), The Role of the Father in Child Development (2nd ed.). New York: Wiley.

Rainwater, Lee, and William L. Yancey. 1967. The Moynihan Report and the Politics of Controversy. Cambridge, MA: MIT Press.

Raschke, Helen J., and Vernon J. Raschke. 1979. "Family conflict and the children's self-concepts." Journal of Marriage and the Family 41: 367–374.

Rickel, Annette U., and Thomas S. Langner. 1985. "Short-term and long-term effects of marital disruption on children." American Journal of Community Psychology 13: 599–611.

Rohrlich, John A., Ruth Ranier, Linda Berg-Cross, and Gary Berg-Cross. 1977. "The effects of divorce: A research review with a developmental perspective." Journal of Clinical Child Psychology 6: 15–20.

Rosen, Rhona. 1979. "Some crucial issues concerning children of divorce." Journal of Divorce 3: 19–25.

Rosenberg, Morris. 1979. Conceiving the Self. New York: Basic Books.

Santrock, John W. 1975. "Father absence, perceived maternal behavior, and moral development in boys." Child Development 46: 753–757.

Santrock, John W., and Richard A. Warshak. 1979. "Father custody and social development in boys and girls." Journal of Social Issues 35: 112–125.

Savage, James E., Jr., Alvis V. Adair, and Philip Friedman 1978. "Community-social variables related to black parent-absent families." Journal of Marriage and the Family 40: 779–785.

Sciara, Frank J. 1975. "Effects of father absence on the educational achievement of urban black children." Child Study Journal 5: 45–55.

Shinn, Marybeth. 1978. "Father absence and children's cognitive development." Psychological Bulletin 85: 295–324.

Slater, Elisa J., and Joel D. Haber. 1984. "Adolescent adjustment following divorce as a function of familial conflict." Journal of Consulting and Clinical Psychology 52: 920–921.

Solomon, Daniel, Jay G. Hirsch, Daniel R. Scheinfeld, and John C. Jackson. 1972. "Family characteristics and elementary school achievement in an urban ghetto." Journal of Consulting and Clinical Psychology 39: 462–466.

Spanier, Graham B., and Linda Thompson. 1984. Parting: The Aftermath of Separation and Divorce. Beverly Hills, CA: Sage.

Stolberg, Arnold L., and James M. Anker. 1983. "Cognitive and behavioral changes in children resulting from parental divorce and consequent environmental changes." Journal of Divorce 7: 23–41.

Svanum, Soren, Robert G. Bringle, and Joan E. McLaughlin. 1982. "Father absence and cognitive performance in a large sample of six- to eleven-year-old children." Child Development 53: 136–143.

Tooley, Kay. 1976. "Antisocial behavior and social alienation post divorce: The 'man of the house' and his mother." American Journal of Orthopsychiatry 46: 33–42.

Tuckman, J., and R. A. Regan. 1966. "Intactness of the home and behavioral problems in children." Journal of Child Psychology and Psychiatry 7: 225–233.

Wallerstein, Judith S. 1984. "Children of divorce: Preliminary report of a ten-year follow-up of young children." American Journal of Orthopsychiatry 54: 444–458.

Wallerstein, Judith S., and Joan B. Kelly. 1974. "The effects of parental divorce: The adolescent experience." In E. James Anthony and Cyrille Koupernik (eds.), The Child in His Family, (Vol. 3). New York: Wiley.

Wallerstein, Judith S., and Joan B. Kelly. 1975. "The effects of parental divorce. The experiences of the preschool child." Journal of the American Academy of Child Psychiatry 14: 600–616.

Wallerstein, Judith S., and Joan B. Kelly. 1980a. "Children and divorce: A review." Social Work 24: 468–475.

Wallerstein, Judith S., and Joan B. Kelly. 1980b. Surviving the Breakup: How Children and Parents Cope with Divorce. Basic Books: New York.

Weiss, Robert S. 1979. "Growing up a little faster: The experience of growing up in a single-parent household." Journal of Social Issues 35: 97–111.

Weitzman, Lenore. 1985. The Divorce Revolution: The

Unexpected Social and Economic Consequences for Women and Children in America. New York: Free Press.

Werner, Emmy E., and Ruth S. Smith. 1982. Vulnerable but Not Invincible: A Study of Resilient Children. New York: McGraw-Hill.

White, Lynn K., David B. Brinkerhoff, and Alan Booth. 1985. "The effect of marital disruption on child's attachment to parents." Journal of Family Issues 6: 5–22.

Worell, J. 1978. "Sex roles and psychological well-being: Perspectives on methodology." Journal of Consulting and Clinical Psychology 46: 777–791.

Wyman, Peter A., Emory L. Cowen, A. Dirk Hightower, and JoAnne L. Pedro-Carroll. 1985. "Perceived competence, self-esteem, and anxiety in latency-aged children of divorce." Journal of Clinical Child Psychology 14: 20–26.

Young, Earl R., and Thomas S. Parish. 1977. "Impact of father absence during childhood on the psychological adjustment of college females." Sex Roles 3: 217–227.

Marilyn Coleman and Lawrence H. Ganong*
University of Missouri–Columbia

Remarriage and Stepfamily Research in the 1980s: Increased Interest in an Old Family Form

Nearly all the existing empirical work on step-families has been published in the last decade. This review first describes the demographic context for this work and then surveys research on stepchildren, remarriage, and stepfamily functioning. Problems in the extant research are identified, and attention is given to areas that need to be explored in the future. Explicit and implicit theories that guided remarriage and stepfamily research in the '80s receive special emphasis. The review closes with suggestions regarding the direction of future theory in these areas of research.

Prior to 1980, only a handful of studies on remarriage and stepfamilies appeared in print (Espinoza and Newman, 1979). Today this body of research contains well over 200 published empirical works. The past decade clearly has been the most productive period for research on remarriage and stepfamilies. The quality and complexity of the studies advanced concomitantly with the quantitative increase.

The reason for the increase in empirical investigations of remarriage and stepfamily dynamics is not because either phenomenon is new; stepfamilies have existed through the ages.

However, until the early 1970s, remarriage typically followed the death of a spouse. Currently, the majority are preceded by divorce. If well over one-half of today's young persons in the United States become stepsons or stepdaughters by the year 2000, as has been predicted (Glick, 1989), the increased attention by researchers is justified.

We begin this review by summarizing some of the demographic literature. Research on stepchildren, remarriage, and stepfamily functioning is examined in separate sections. A critique of the research methodology follows, and we conclude by proposing new directions for research and by suggesting areas of study for the next decade.

The volume of research on remarriage and stepfamilies in this decade dictated that we be selective in choosing studies to review and issues to discuss. Some issues (e.g., extended kin, stepsiblings) were omitted because research in those areas was extremely limited. Many good studies were excluded for lack of space. We tried to select only well-designed research, but some investigations were included because they represented unique methods or points of view.

THE DEMOGRAPHIC CONTEXT

The demographic literature published during the past decade primarily reports data collected in the '70s or early '80s. The 1990 Census will assess stepfamily households for the first time; data previously had to be inferred from special surveys

Department of Human Department and Family Studies, 28 Stanley Hall, University of Missouri–Columbia, Columbia, MO 65211.

*School of Nursing, University of Missouri–Columbia, Columbia, MO 65211.

(e.g., Current Population Survey).

The United States has the highest remarriage rate in the world; over 40% of marriages are remarriages for one or both partners. We not only remarry at a high rate, we remarry relatively soon after divorce. In 1975, the median interval between divorce and remarriage was only 3 years (Glick, 1980). About two-thirds of recent remarriages were preceded by cohabitation (Bumpass and Sweet, 1989), which means the median interval between divorce and the establishment of a new relationship is even less than 3 years.

Remarriage rates vary by race. Blacks remarry more slowly than whites (Glick, 1984); remarriage occurs within 5 years of divorce for 42% of black women and 55% of white women (Duncan and Hoffman, 1985). Hispanics are less likely to remarry than either blacks or whites (Cherlin and McCarthy, 1985).

Age and children are factors in remarriage rates of women but not men (Glick, 1980). Younger women remarry more quickly than older women (Spanier and Glick, 1980). Women divorced after 40 have little likelihood of remarrying, although the remarriage rate of widowed persons at older ages is increasing. Childless women, divorced prior to age 25, have higher remarriage rates than women with children. However, childless women older than 35 have a lower remarriage rate than those who have children (Koo and Suchindran, 1980).

Income is also related to the probability of remarriage. The more money a divorced male has, the more likely he is to remarry, but there is an inverse relationship between income and remarriage for women (Glick, 1980). Among black and white women, those most likely to remarry are less educated, more often from the West, less apt to have experienced a stable parental marriage, and less likely to be Catholic (Teachman, 1986). Remarriage for women appears more likely when they have been raised or live in a culture more tolerant of divorce and remarriage. It would also seem that a desire for improving financial security serves as an impetus to remarry, especially for slightly older women with children.

According to Glick (1989), 2.3 million households contained stepchildren in 1980; 2.15 million were stepfather households, 338,000 were stepmother households, and 150,000 were households with children from the previous marriages of both spouses, as well as at least one mutual child. This study underestimated the number of stepfamily households, however, because remarriages formed following the death of a spouse were excluded from the sample. Because the sample was of stephouseholds rather than stepfamily systems (i.e., nonresidential stepchildren were not included), the number of stepfamilies was greatly underestimated. From 1980 to 1987 the percentage of remarried families with children decreased slightly. This change may be related to an increase in cohabitation following divorce (Bumpass and Sweet, 1989).

It has been estimated that in 1990, 69% of children in the United States were living with both parents (compared to 85% in 1970 and 76% in 1981). About 59% of those born in the early 1980s can expect to live with only one parent for at least a year, and 35% can expect to live with a stepparent before age 18 (Glick, 1989). To put this in perspective, however, it should be noted that the risk of experiencing marital disruption by age 16 has remained stable throughout this century (Sweetser, 1985).

Giving birth in remarriage is a common phenomenon; approximately 54.3% of women are expected to have a child after remarrying (Wineberg, 1990). Twenty-five percent of preschool-age stepchildren gain a half sibling in the first 18 months following remarriage (58% if their mother is under 25), and one-sixth of children 10–13 years of age gain a half sibling (Bumpass, 1984b).

Of recent interest has been the incidence of redivorce, especially when children are involved. About half the children whose parents divorce and remarry will experience a second parental divorce (Bumpass, 1984a).

There are fewer known predictors of second divorce than first divorce, especially for black women (Teachman, 1986). However, men with postgraduate training are less likely to redivorce, and women with some college have a higher probability of redivorce than either high school graduates or college graduates (Glick, 1984). According to Teachman (1986), remarriages are more stable than first marriages for blacks, although the overall divorce rates are higher for blacks than whites in both first and subsequent marriages. Marital stability increases with the number of the husband's children in the household, especially if it is the wife's first marriage (Aguirre and Parr, 1982).

In summary, remarriage is common in American society, and some of the social predictors of remarriage are well known. We do not, however, have an accurate estimation of the number of stepfamilies or stepchildren. Most data were collected on households rather than families; consequently, nonresidential steprelationships are not included in estimates. Demographic calculations based on courthouse records of remarriages exclude cohabiting couples who have formed de facto stepfamilies. Prior to this decade, Cherlin (1978) called for researchers to establish the basic demographic facts about stepfamily complexity. Progress was made in the 1980s, but the picture is still incomplete.

Research on Stepchildren

Most research on stepchildren in the '80s can be categorized into two general paradigms. The most prevalent approach has been to view stepfamilies and steprelationships from a problem-oriented perspective. Researchers using the second approach, rather than framing stepfamilies as problematic, attempted to describe and understand the dynamics of steprelationships without a priori assumptions of negative outcomes. This category might be termed the normative, or adaptive, view. Note that these perspectives do not encompass all of the hypotheses examined in the decade, but they do represent the major conceptual frames. Note also that some research contained elements of both paradigms.

These two general paradigms were characterized by different methodological approaches. Studies in the problem-oriented category were typically "between family structure" designs: examinations of differences between stepchildren and children from other family structures, particularly nuclear families. Studies from a normative-adaptive perspective typically were "within family structure" designs with samples often consisting of stepfamily members only.

The Problem-Oriented Perspective

There are several approaches to framing research questions from a problem-oriented perspective: the deficit-comparison approach, the stress hypothesis, the socialization hypothesis, the additional-adult hypothesis, the biological-discrimination hypothesis, and the incomplete-

institution hypothesis. The research designs of these approaches are similar, although important conceptual distinctions should be noted.

The deficit-comparison approach. In this perspective the assumption is that stepchildren will be deficient compared to children in nuclear families (Ganong and Coleman, 1984). We have argued that this approach has been primarily influenced by clinical writings, but it may also be that it simply reflects societal attitudes toward stepfamilies. The deficit-comparison approach dominated the study of stepchildren prior to the 1980s and was the most common approach in the first half of the decade.

Deficit-comparison research typically focused on psychological outcome variables such as self-esteem. The most frequent design was a cross-sectional comparison of stepchildren to children in other family structures. These studies tended to treat stepfamilies as uniform structures, ignoring variations such as the child's age at remarriage, years in the stepfamily, number of siblings and stepsiblings, and contact with the nonresidential parent. Process variables (e.g., quality of parent's remarriage, the closeness of step relationships) and other potentially important mediating variables were frequently ignored. Deficit-comparison studies seldom yielded fruitful insights, basically because the simplistic designs employed did not allow researchers to rule out the possibility that results were due to unmeasured variables related to family structural variations or family processes.

The stress hypothesis. The hypothesis that family transitions such as divorce, remarriage, and redivorce are stressful experiences, negatively affecting the psychological and social development of children, is based primarily on stress theory, although family systems theory and family development concepts are also evident in these studies. Multiple transitions (i.e., serial remarriages) are hypothesized to be especially stressful, since they expose children to impaired financial well-being (during the single-parent phase) as well as recurrent experiences of interparental conflict, attachment disruption, and periods of diminished parenting (Brody, Neubaum, and Forehand, 1988). Common outcome variables found in this body of literature were self-esteem, behavioral problems, and cognitive functioning. Children's relationships with other family members, particularly with parents and stepparents, were also a focus of interest.

Self-esteem. Overall, it can be concluded that stepchildren's self-esteem is similar to that of other children (Bray, 1988). Drawing conclusions regarding the effects of stressful family *transitions* on self-esteem is impeded, however, because most designs were cross-sectional.

Problem behavior. Although differences were seldom large, stepchildren were consistently reported to have more internalizing behavior problems (e.g., depression, anxiety) and more externalizing behavior problems (e.g., fighting, poor peer relations, school-related problems such as absences and expulsions) than children in nuclear families (Bray, 1988; Ferri, 1984; Zill, 1988). Few differences were found between stepchildren and children in single-parent families (Zill, 1988), although adolescent stepchildren reportedly used alcohol more (Burnside, Baer, McLaughlin, and Pokorny, 1986).

These studies often compared ratings of behavior problems of children from different family forms. Ratings were typically obtained from only one person, usually a parent, stepparent, or teacher. Raters in every study knew the children's family structure prior to evaluating their behavior, which raises the question of whether results were influenced by expectations related to the effects of divorce and remarriage on children or reflected actual differences in children's behavior.

These investigations were often similar in design to the deficit-comparison studies, although some researchers attempted to account for stepfamily complexity (e.g., length of time in the stepfamily, type of stepfamily household, child age) through sample selection criteria (Bray, 1988) or by statistically controlling for such variables (Clingempeel and Segal, 1986; Coleman and Ganong, 1987b). The designs were often inadequate to assess transition effects.

The few longitudinal studies (Baydar, 1988; Hetherington, Cox, and Cox, 1985) yielded contradictory results. Because they differed greatly on sample characteristics (e.g., the age of children) and measurement of behavior problems, determining the validity of the stress hypothesis from them is impossible. Before conclusions can be drawn about the effects of stressful family

transitions on child behavior, additional longitudinal research is needed.

Cognitive functioning. In general, stepchildren were similar to children in single-parent households in that academic performance was slightly lower than for children in nuclear families (Zill, 1988). However, a British study found that educational achievement was not lower for stepchildren when the effect of social class was controlled (Ferri, 1984). On measures of intelligence, few differences were found between stepchildren and others (Bray, 1988). Diverse samples and varied measures of academic performance and intelligence were employed in this limited group of studies.

Parent-child relationships. The most frequently used design was a comparison of stepparent-child relationships to parent-child relationships in nuclear families on variables such as levels of support and punishment (Amato, 1987; Ganong and Coleman, 1987) and conflict (Ferri, 1984). In general, these studies did not report that parents and children in stepfamily households related differently than parents and children in nuclear families. However, most of these cross-sectional studies examined family structure differences rather than the effects of stressful family transitions on parent-child relationships.

The socialization hypothesis. This perspective postulates that childhood family experiences provide the foundation for an individual's values, attitudes, and behaviors. The theoretical roots of the socialization hypothesis lie in both psychoanalytic and social learning theories. Parents are seen as important role models and valued sources of reinforcement. Marital disruptions and family reorganizations limit children's exposure to role models, and contact with important reinforcers are diminished or terminated. This is believed to result in incomplete or inadequate socialization.

A related hypothesis, the *additional-adult hypothesis,* suggests that adding another adult (i.e., the stepparent) in a single-parent household provides more control over children. It might also be called the "substitute parent" hypothesis, because there is an assumption that the stepparent takes over childrearing responsibilities once held by the nonresidential biological parent.

The socialization perspective has been employed often in studies of the effects of father absence or parental divorce on children (Demo and Acock, 1988). It has been used less often in the study of stepchildren, perhaps because it is harder to predict the effects of parental remarriage on children from this perspective. For example, following parental remarriage, children are exposed to an additional role model who has control of at least some valued reinforcers. However, numerous factors (e.g., degree of the child's identification with the stepparent, the extent to which the stepparent provides reinforcers, the availability to the child of reinforcers outside the stepfamily, and the extent to which the stepparent attempts to socialize the child) can influence the stepparent's impact.

The socialization and added-adult hypotheses have been mainly used to study stepchildren's attitudes and behaviors related to parenthood, marriage, and divorce. Parental remarriage does not seem to affect attitudes toward marriage (Coleman and Ganong, 1984; Kinnaird and Gerrard, 1986) or courtship (Booth, Brinkerhoff, and White, 1984), but stepchildren were more positive toward divorce than those from nuclear or single-parent households (Coleman and Ganong, 1984; Kinnaird and Gerrard, 1986).

Research findings on *behaviors* were mixed. Some support was found for the added-adult hypothesis. For example, McLanahan and Bumpass (1988) reported that, although living with only one parent at age 14 was predictive of having a premarital birth, parental remarriage was not. Living with a stepparent was also not related to adolescent marriage or divorce and remarriage later in life. Newcomer and Udry (1987), in a two-year study of junior high students, reported that, although marital disruption was related to premarital coitus, adolescents in stable remarried families had rates of intercourse similar to those in stable nuclear families. After controlling for several family background variables, Booth and associates (1984) found college-age stepchildren no more likely than those in nuclear families to have had premarital sexual intercourse.

On the other hand, Steinberg (1987) concluded that the "additional-adult" hypothesis was not valid if the added adult was a stepparent. He found preadolescent and adolescent stepchildren, similar to children in single-parent households, more prone to peer influence and more willing to engage in antisocial behavior than those living with both parents. Michael and Tuma (1985)

found living with a stepparent at age 14 predictive of marrying at younger ages for whites and younger parenthood for all but black males. Kinnaird and Gerrard (1986) reported that female college students whose parents had divorced and remarried were more likely to have premarital intercourse than females whose parents were still married.

The biological-discrimination hypothesis. Based on an evolutionary model of social behavior sometimes known as sociobiology, this model postulates that motivational and emotional aspects of parenthood are lacking for stepparents because of the absence of genetic ties (Flinn, 1988). Research from this perspective indicates that stepfathers interact less positively with their stepchildren than their own children (Flinn, 1988). They are also more likely than biological parents to neglect (Wilson, Daly, and Weghorst, 1980) and to inflict physical and sexual abuse on their stepchildren (Lightcap, Kurland, and Burgess, 1982). Research from this view is not without methodological flaws, however (see Giles-Sims and Finkelhor, 1984, for a critique and review of this literature).

The incomplete-institution hypothesis. According to this hypothesis, remarriages and stepfamilies are under stress because they lack guidelines for role performance, institutionalized procedures for dealing with problems, and social support (Cherlin, 1978). This hypothesis received support from studies of stepparent role ambiguity. It appears that no consensus exists regarding the proper role of stepparents (Bray, 1988; Furstenberg and Spanier, 1984; Kurdek and Sinclair, 1986). For example, although stepparents were as likely to feel like a friend as a parent to their stepchild (Furstenberg and Spanier, 1984), both remarried adults (Bray, 1988) and stepchildren (Kurdek and Sinclair, 1986) were more accepting of stepparents assuming a childrearing role than nuclear family members believed was appropriate. In fact, Giles-Sims (1984) found that half of her remarried respondents expected parents and stepparents to share equally in raising children, although only about one-third actually shared childrearing decisions. This disparity between expectations and behavior may indicate role ambiguity. There is some evidence that role ambiguity affects the quality of stepparent-child relations. One way to handle this ambiguity is to treat stepparents as emotional replacements for absent parents. White, Brinkerhoff, and Booth (1985) found that children were emotionally attached to their stepfathers or their fathers, but not to both. When nonresidential parents continue to play a part in children's lives, the uncertainty of having more than two "parent" figures may lead to stress and conflict in relationships.

The Normative-Adaptive Perspective

In the second half of the decade, an increasing number of researchers called for an abandonment of the problem-oriented perspective, particularly the deficit-comparison approach that crudely grouped stepchildren into one category without regard to stepfamily complexity. The adaptive perspective considers divorce and remarriage as normative lifestyle choices that are firmly established in society, rather than as social problems or pathological behaviors. Researchers taking this view generally studied stepfamily processes, using a nuclear family comparison group only for the purpose of examining interactive effects (e.g., if boys in stepfather families were more attached to their mothers than were girls, a comparison group from nuclear families would be needed to see if this difference was true for children in general, or if it was related to stepfamily living). This research has predominantly focused on describing and understanding stepfamily relationships. Family systems theory, family development, and social exchange models served as the primary theoretical underpinnings.

Parent-child relationships. Parent-child relationships following remarriage received less attention than stepparent-child dyads. Of particular interest was emotional closeness between parents and children (Brand and Clingempeel, 1987; Ganong and Coleman, 1987; Hobart, 1987). Drawing conclusions about parent-child relationships following parental remarriage is difficult, however, partly because of the variety of dependent variables assessed and the wide age range of children sampled.

The remarriage of either parent reduces contact between nonresidential parents and children (Furstenberg and Nord, 1985), although mothers are more likely to maintain contact with nonresidential children than fathers (Seltzer and Bianchi,

1988). Limited information exists regarding correlates of parent-child contact following remarriage or changes in contact over time. Cross-sectional data typically indicated that contact decreases as time passes, although Furstenberg and Spanier (1984) found that it increases after remarriage for some families. The effects of different custody arrangements on the parenting behaviors of residential parents and nonresidential parents were not assessed.

Most studies found children unharmed by reduced ties to an absent parent (Clingempeel and Segal, 1986; Furstenberg and Nord, 1985; Kurdek and Sinclair, 1986), although in one study contact with a nonresidential mother was positively related to fewer behavior problems (Zill, 1988). Few emotional and psychological differences were found between children in stepmother and stepfather households (Clingempeel and Segal, 1986; Coleman and Ganong, 1987b; Ferri, 1984; Zill, 1988). There is some evidence that these findings are influenced by who is reporting the behavior (i.e., child, parent, or stepparent), the behavior being assessed (Baydar, 1988), and the sex of the respondent (Bray, 1988; Coleman and Ganong, 1987b).

Stepparent-child relationships. Emotional bonds between stepparents and stepchildren were generally found to be less close than parent-child ties (Ganong and Coleman, 1987) and somewhat more likely to be characterized by conflict (Ferri, 1984). Crosbie-Burnett (1984) argued that the stepparent-child dyad has a greater impact than other relationships on family functioning and well-being, since it has the greatest potential to be stressful. Some stepparent-child relationships are quite positive, however (Hobart, 1987). In fact, it appears that the stepparent becomes a substitute for the nonresidential biological parent for many children, particularly when there is little contact with the parent (Furstenberg and Nord, 1985; Seltzer and Bianchi, 1988).

The normative-adaptive research sheds some light on predictors of the quality of stepparent-child relationships. Stepfathers were more likely than stepmothers to have good relationships with children (Ambert, 1986; Hobart, 1987), perhaps because stepmothers play a larger role in the raising of stepchildren (Ahrons and Wallisch, 1987). Research on whether stepsons or stepdaughters relate better to stepparents yielded contradictory findings (Amato, 1987; Bray, 1988; Hobart, 1987). Generally, when both adults brought children into the stepfamily, stepparent-child relations were more distant (Brand and Clingempeel, 1987; White et al., 1985). However, residential stepparent-child relationships were closer than nonresidential ones (Ambert, 1986). The quality of stepparent-child relationships was not affected by reproduction in remarriage (Ahrons and Wallisch, 1987; Ganong and Coleman, 1988; White et al., 1985). Satisfaction with remarriage and low remarital conflict, however, had a positive relationship with the quality of the stepparent-child relationship (Coleman and Ganong, 1987b; Guisinger, Cowan, and Schuldberg, 1989; Orleans, Palisi, and Caddell, 1989). It is unclear what happens to the relationship with stepparents over time. There is some evidence that stepparent-child relations get worse (Guisinger et al., 1989; Hetherington et al., 1985); women may become less optimistic about stepmothering over time and may develop less positive attitudes toward their stepchildren (Guisinger et al., 1989).

RESEARCH ON REMARRIAGE

Remarriage received less attention from researchers in the 1980s than research on stepchildren did. The focus of this section is on three general areas: marital satisfaction, well-being in remarriage, and older persons and remarriage.

Marital Satisfaction

Much of the remarital satisfaction and remarital quality literature was atheoretical, but three hypotheses were proposed in this decade. The predisposition hypothesis suggested that remarriages are more fragile because they comprise people who are predisposed to see divorce as a solution to marital unhappiness (Furstenberg and Spanier, 1984). The incomplete-institution hypothesis suggested that remarriages are less satisfying because there are fewer norms to guide behavior (Clingempeel, 1981; White and Booth, 1985). The psychopathology hypothesis proposed that divorced and remarried persons are more likely to have psychological and behavioral problems, such as alcoholism and personality disorders, that reduce the quality and stability of remarriages (Brody et al., 1988). The first two hypotheses have received some empirical support,

but the last one has not yet been examined empirically.

A meta-analysis of remarital satisfaction studies published prior to 1987 found that the magnitudes of differences between first marriages and remarriages, remarried men and women, stepmothers and stepfathers, those with and without residential stepchildren, and households where only one adult was a stepparent compared to households where both adults were stepparents were generally small and of little practical meaning. Readers should consult Vemer, Coleman, Ganong, and Cooper (1989) for a thorough critique and discussion of the research on remarital quality.

A variety of marital satisfaction and marital quality measurements were employed in these studies, with the Dyadic Adjustment Scale, the Locke-Wallace, and single-item questions (e.g., "How satisfied are you with your marriage?") being used most often. Observations of the marital behavior of remarried couples were reported in only two studies (Clingempeel, 1981; Clingempeel and Brand, 1985).

Most often investigated were differences between people in first marriages and remarriages, but a variety of other variables were also examined: gender, social support, child's age, and quasi-kin relations. Although controls were often not used, race, education, family income, length of marriage, presence and number of children living in the home, and women's employment status were each included in at least one investigation. Samples were most often whites only, although some researchers statistically controlled for race (Nock, 1981; White and Booth, 1985).

The number of remarried couples in samples ranged from 25 (Nock, 1981) to 209 (Kurdek, 1989). More recent studies had larger samples and were developed explicitly to test hypotheses about remarriage (Ganong and Coleman, 1988; Hobart and Brown, 1988; Kurdek, 1989). Previously, studies with large samples relied on secondary data sets that contained few items related to remarriage (Weingarten, 1980).

The correlates of satisfaction with remarriage were minimally explored, and drawing conclusions is hindered because few researchers examined the same variables. Social support was the only variable found to be related to remarriage satisfaction in more than one study. In general, individual characteristics correlated with relationship quality more than demographic factors did (Kurdek, 1989).

Remarriage satisfaction, similar to satisfaction in first marriages, appears to decrease over time (Guisinger et al., 1989). In fact, few differences seem to exist between marital satisfaction in remarriage and first marriages. Additional studies are probably not needed. However, studies that examine well-functioning and poorly functioning families and use designs similar to the one employed by Anderson and White (1986) in their study of 63 functional and dysfunctional first-married and remarried family triads could provide important information. As expected, Anderson and White found that marital adjustment was better in functional than dysfunctional families. A less-expected finding was that marital adjustment in stepfamilies was greater than that in nuclear families. In fact, marital adjustment in dysfunctional stepfamilies did not differ from that of functional nuclear families. These findings indicate that in stepfamilies the marital relationship and family functioning may be less related than in nuclear families, and they emphasize the need for a better understanding of how these processes differ. Unfortunately, the Anderson and White (1986) study had some design problems. For example, the nuclear family couples had been married longer than the remarried couples (several cross-sectional studies have reported that marital satisfaction diminishes over time), and the number of families in each category was small. A more tightly controlled study comparing functional and dysfunctional nuclear and stepfamilies could serve as a prototype for future research.

Remarriage and Well-being

The well-being construct was defined in a variety of ways in these studies (e.g., adjustment, satisfaction with life, happiness, self-esteem, physical health, substance abuse and other symptoms of stress), and thus it is difficult to compare studies and draw conclusions. Samples varied; some consisted of women only, others underrepresented women, still others did not indicate the sex of the respondents. The major independent variable employed was marital status and the primary question appeared to be whether people were better off married or not.

The well-being of remarried people did not differ from that of the first-married in these studies,

nor did they evaluate their lives differently than the first-married (Nock, 1981) or differ in self-confidence, feelings of vulnerability (Mitchell, 1983), or adjustment (Weingarten, 1980). Although remarried individuals were no more satisfied with life than divorced persons, they were happier (Weingarten, 1985), and Mitchell (1983) found their overall well-being to exceed that of the divorced. Two studies reported that remarried individuals were more likely to report symptoms (poor health, substance abuse) than divorced or first-married persons (Mitchell, 1983; Weingarten, 1980), which is perhaps evidence of perceived stress related to remarriage. Changes in well-being did not occur over time (Spanier and Furstenberg, 1982).

Within-group designs were more often used in recent studies of self-esteem and well-being in remarriage. Guisinger and associates (1989) found that, after three years of remarriage, lower self-esteem in stepmothers correlated with the number of stepsons and that women tended to feel better about themselves when they had stepdaughters.

There is some evidence that well-being for remarried persons is a bipolar construct; remarriage may enhance well-being for some and reduce it for others (Spanier and Furstenberg, 1982). Efforts need to be expanded in exploring this bipolar effect within remarriage. Because of within-sample variability, more studies comparing the global well-being of first-married and remarried individuals will not prove fruitful.

Remarriage among Older Adults

Remarriage among older adults was basically ignored by researchers. A longitudinal study by Burks, Lund, Gregg, and Bluhm (1988) found that remarried widows displayed less stress, greater self-esteem, more life satisfaction, better feelings about their friendships, and more positive levels of grief resolution than did those who remained single. Since these differences were manifested after the remarriage, they did not appear to be linked to differences within individuals. Bulcroft, Bulcroft, Hatch, and Borgatta (1989), using subsamples from the longitudinal Social Security Administration's Retirement History Study, found that persons with more education and good health were more likely to remarry; subsequently, remarriage was related to life satisfaction and happiness. Remarried widows also had "fewer concerns" than unremarried widows (Gentry and Shulman, 1988), although remarried widows did report concerns specifically related to the remarriage.

In spite of generally positive outcomes, few older persons remarry. Moss and Moss (1980) reported that for those who become widowed at 65 or over, less than 25% of the men and 1% of the women will remarry. Our culture creates obstacles to remarriage for older bereaved persons, including age-graded societal expectations for behavior following bereavement and public policies that tie the widow to the deceased spouse (e.g., pensions, tax waivers). Clearly, as our population ages, remarriage of older persons is an area deserving further study.

STEPFAMILY FUNCTIONING

Compared to the amount of research on remarriage and stepchildren, relatively few investigations focused on the entire stepfamily unit. Prior to this decade, however, *no* studies on stepfamily functioning had included data from multiple family members or had observed whole families interacting.

Research in the '80s was characterized by nonrandom volunteer samples, the use of self-report questionnaires, a focus on "target" children, and nuclear family comparison groups. A few researchers observed families in "lab" settings (Santrock, Warshak, Lindbergh, and Meadows, 1982), some studies were longitudinal (Ahrons and Wallisch, 1987; Bray, 1988; Hetherington et al., 1985), and some were normative-adaptive designs that examined different types of stepfamilies (Clingempeel and Segal, 1986; Ganong and Coleman, 1988).

On widely used family assessment instruments, stepfamilies were reported to be less cohesive and slightly less effective than nuclear families at problem-solving and communicating (Bray, 1988; Peek, Bell, Waldren, and Sorell, 1988). Stepfamily means were within the "functional," nonclinical range on these instruments, however, which suggests that patterns of effective stepfamily functioning may differ from those of nuclear families (Anderson and White, 1986; Coleman and Ganong, 1987b; Orleans, Polisi, and Caddell, 1989). More investigations of stepfamilies from a normative-adaptive perspective are needed to examine how functional stepfamilies differ from other family forms.

Future research on stepfamily functioning could benefit from recent theory-building efforts. Among these are clinically derived models of stepfamily development (for example, Papernow, 1984); a propositional theory combining aspects of systems, family stress, and family development theories (Rodgers and Conrad, 1986); a grounded theory of stepfamily types (Gross, 1987); and a proposed framework for understanding conflict and violence in stepfamilies (Kalmuss and Seltzer, 1989). None of these frameworks have been tested.

Social Influences on Stepfamily Functioning

Few researchers have examined extrafamilial influences on stepfamily functioning. Social support (Kurdek, 1989) and beliefs about steprelationships (Bray, 1988; Kurdek and Sinclair, 1986) were studied, but interactions between stepfamilies and other social institutions such as schools, the courts, and religious institutions have been ignored.

Cultural stereotypes of stepparents and stepchildren have been studied, however (see Ganong, Coleman, and Mapes, 1990, for a review of these studies). Stereotypes of stepfamily members were consistently found to be less positive than stereotypes of nuclear family members. Little is known about the effects these stereotypes have on self-perceptions and expectations held by stepfamily members, or on behavior directed to stepfamilies by others. The relative salience of stepfamily stereotypes in relation to other personal stereotypes such as race and sex, and the content of such stereotypes, is also unknown.

PROBLEMS IN REMARRIAGE AND STEPFAMILY RESEARCH

In an earlier review we described research on stepchildren as being plagued with inconsistencies and methodological problems, including use of a deficit-comparison model, limited conceptualizations of family structural variables, failure to account for stepfamily complexity, small and/or nonrandom samples, reliance on self-report questionnaires, and the use of data gathered from only one family member (Ganong and Coleman, 1984). The research on remarriage and stepfamilies still contains a number of critical problems.

Implicit Nuclear Family Ideology

Although studies overtly based on the deficit-comparison model are becoming less common, the nuclear family is still the implicit norm for evaluating stepfamilies. As a result of adherence to this nuclear family ideology, (*a*) inadequate attention was given to the structural complexity and diversity of stepfamilies; (*b*) positive outcome variables were ignored in favor of a focus on problems; (*c*) the functionality of stepfamilies was based on nuclear family norms, obscuring the possibility of differences in functioning between steprelationships and biological relationships; and (*d*) erroneous assumptions about the equivalence of stephouseholds and stepfamilies are made. These problems will be briefly discussed below.

Ignoring stepfamily complexity. The deficit-comparison approach has blinded many researchers to the enormous complexity of stepfamily forms. Consequently, researchers often ignore differences and group all stepfamily types together in comparison to other family structures, or they control for structural complexity through study design or statistical procedures.

When different stepfamily configurations are combined, important information is lost. Researchers may find that stepfamilies differ as a group from nuclear families but do not learn if the dependent variables are related to such structural characteristics as different custody patterns, sex of stepparent or sex of child variations, cause of prior marriage dissolutions, or reproduction in the remarriage. No information is gained about such process variables as role performance of stepmothers compared to stepfathers or the levels of marital conflict in different types of households.

The elimination of low-incidence stepfamily types has resulted in an abundance of studies of stepfather households formed after divorce. Little is known about stepmother households, households where both adults are stepparents, postbereavement families, nonresidential stephouseholds, or de facto (i.e., cohabiting) stepfamilies.

Statistically controlling for the effects of variables such as length of marriage, age at remarriage, and number of previous marriages obscures regularly occurring differences between stepfamily types that may be helpful in understanding stepfamily processes in different types of households. For example, structural differences (e.g., stepmothers are generally younger than stepfathers at time of marriage) or sociopsychological differences (e.g., families where fathers have custody often differ from mother-custody families) between stepfamily types may influence outcome variables. Such effects are masked when statistical controls are applied. Rather than treating the variations in stepfamilies as a study design problem, researchers should focus on what these differences can tell us about stepfamily functioning.

Ignoring stepfamily complexity can result in other problems for researchers. Sometimes stepfamilies and nuclear families are matched on variables that, as a result of the nonequivalence of the two family forms, unavoidably create other dissimilarities. For example, matching families on age of children means that they necessarily will be dissimilar on another variable, length of marriage.

Focus on problems. Because investigators consistently have focused on stepfamily problems rather than strengths, there is a lack of research examining processes in stepfamilies. For example, repeated studies comparing self-esteem and problem behaviors of stepchildren to children in other families have provided little insight into factors contributing to positive self-esteem in stepchildren. Similarly, comparing marital satisfaction in first-married and remarried couples has told us little about why some remarriages are more satisfying than others. In spite of the focus on problems, few studies have investigated stepfamily problems identified by clinicians (Ganong and Coleman, 1986).

Nuclear family norms applied to stepfamilies. Applying nuclear family models to stepfamilies and using instruments normed on nuclear families is questionable. As previously noted, there is no evidence that behavior identified as optimal functioning in nuclear families is the same behavior seen as optimal functioning in stepfamilies. Furthermore, comparing nuclear families and stepfamilies on variables such as cohesion does not clarify the level of cohesion that is functional for stepfamilies. Comparing stepparent-child to parent-child relationships on emotional closeness also makes little sense; there may be fundamental differences in how these two types of relationships *should* function.

Stephouseholds and stepfamilies. For most nuclear families with children younger than 18, the household unit and family unit are equivalent. The implicit adherence to a nuclear family model leads to the erroneous assumption that stephouseholds and stepfamilies are also the same. A stepfamily *household* is one in which at least one adult is a stepparent to a child residing with them. A *stepfamily* is a broader group that may contain members who do not reside full-time in the household but who are nonetheless significant family members (Ahrons and Wallisch, 1987). It is likely, especially for children, that stephouseholds and stepfamilies are different psychologically, emotionally, and physically (Gross, 1987). It is naive to assume that children having little or no contact with nonresidential parents after divorce, or whose parents died, are psychologically detached from and unaffected by those parents. The percentage of stepchildren residing at least part-time in more than one household will likely increase as laws favoring joint custody increase. For many stepfamilies, focusing only on the household results in a loss of information and misleading conclusions.

The confusion between households and families relates to a broader confusion in stepfamily terminology. For example, there is no widely agreed upon label to differentiate between first remarriages and subsequent remarriages, and few researchers distinguish between them (Brody et al., 1988, refers to people who marry more than twice as serial remarriers). Terms such as "blended" are used sometimes to refer to all stepfamilies and other times to identify only those households in which both adults bring children from previous marriages.

Increasingly, researchers use more detailed classifications of stepfamilies and more explicit terminology. However, considering the number of permutations possible and the difficulties in obtaining stepfamily samples, it is not surprising that analyses by type of stepfamily have been slow in emerging.

Remarriage as a Static Event

A common perspective of researchers has been to treat remarriage and the beginning of stepfamily life as an easily identified static event, rather than a process that may have begun with previous marriage and family experiences. Remarriage is a legal marker rather than a physical or experiential one. Longitudinal studies provide increasing evidence that stepfamilies cannot be understood without careful consideration of family members' experiences preceding the remarriage. Cross-sectional studies present distorted pictures of adjustment over time.

Sampling Problems

With the exception of demographic studies, the research on remarriage, stepchildren, and stepfamilies has largely sampled white, middle-class individuals who reside in stepfather households. The majority of investigators collected data from individual respondents in relatively small nonrandom samples. One reason for this is that procuring a sample is difficult. Remarried couples and stepfamilies are an exceptionally mobile population. Studies using marriage license records to identify remarriages report locating addresses for less than 40% (Clingempeel, 1981; Ganong and Coleman, 1988). The longer the interval between remarriage and data collection, the more difficult couples are to find. This mobility is even more problematic for longitudinal investigations. Spanier and Furstenberg (1982) easily located only half of their sample two years after the initial data collection.

Attempts to obtain random samples from sources other than marriage license records generally have failed also. Hobart and Brown (1988), using random telephoning, found only two people out of 70 willing to supply names of remarried families. Researchers typically resort to snowball sampling, but even then a high percentage of the families contacted refuse to participate partly because of negative stereotyping of stepfamilies and stepfamily members (Coleman and Ganong, 1987a).

For studies with random sampling approaches, response rates were so low it is questionable how "random" final samples actually were. For example, Kurdek (1989) reported that, of the 18% who agreed to participate, only 38% actually completed mailed questionnaires. Unfortunately, most investigators did not report response rates.

Some samples were large, statistically representative national samples (e.g., Furstenberg and Nord, 1985, in the U.S.; Ferri, 1984, in the U.K.). However, these samples can be problematic as well. There is a truncation of experience imposed by cross-sectional designs (McLanahan and Bumpass, 1988), and panel studies of large national data sets seldom provide information on exact dates of status changes. It is also possible that disrupted families are more likely to be lost from panel studies than stable families. Dysfunctional families are less likely to be included in studies because they are difficult to locate and less willing to participate.

Sample description continues to be a problem with this body of literature. Conventions for reporting sampling methods and sample descriptions are needed. At a minimum, stepfamily type (i.e., stepmother, stepfather, or complex), and the age, sex, and number of residential and nonresidential stepchildren should be reported. The unit (household or family) should be clearly identified, as well as the precursor to remarriage (e.g., death, divorce). Length of time together as a family, race, and social class should also be reported.

Reactivity of Measures and Methods

Given what is known regarding how stereotypes about stepfamilies alter perceiver's evaluations of stepparents and stepchildren (Coleman and Ganong, 1987a), the reactivity of study methods to potential researcher biases is of concern. Double-blind studies are needed in which children or families are observed by coders who are unaware of their family structure.

In spite of the dramatic increase in stepfamily research in the latter half of the '80s, our knowledge of stepfamilies remains limited. We hope that the exciting work of the last decade will stimulate both broader and more in-depth studies of remarriage and stepfamilies, using a greater variety of research designs and theoretical approaches than were employed in the '80s.

REMARRIAGE AND STEPFAMILY RESEARCH IN THE 1990s

Understudied Areas

Several areas needing more study were mentioned earlier in this review. A more complete understanding of the demographic characteristics of stepfamilies is essential. Studies of well-functioning stepfamilies and research focused on positive outcome variables for individuals and for interpersonal relationships in stepfamilies are needed. The effects of the broader social environment on stepfamilies, including the interdependencies of stepfamilies and other social institutions (e.g., schools, the courts, religious institutions) and the effects of mass media, public policy, and cultural stereotyping on remarriage and stepfamily behaviors need to be investigated. The adjustment of children and adults following redivorce and multiple remarriages is an important area only recently defined as a concern. As our population ages it will be increasingly important to examine remarriage among older adults and the effects these marriages have on various family subsystems. Certain stephousehold variations, such as stepmother households and remarriages with nonresidential children only, have been underresearched, and too little attention has been paid to social class as a mediating variable.

Relationships within stepfamilies, such as interdependencies of subsystems within the stepfamily, stepsibling relations, extended kinship ties, and examinations of gender differences in the adjustment of children and adults have been only minimally addressed. Issues related to custody need to be explored in view of the increases in joint custody and the prevalence of changes in physical and legal custody related to remarriage.

In addition to the moderating variables previously mentioned, there are several more that deserve attention in the next decade. In general, research on stepchildren has not adequately considered developmental issues and influences. Cognitive and personality variables and the role of individual family members' characteristics in mediating the quality of interpersonal and individual outcomes have been only superficially investigated in children and ignored in adults. Race as a mediator has also been relatively ignored. Research on black stepfamilies, considering the lower redivorce rate of blacks and their greater experience with permeable family boundaries and extended kin, could provide insight into issues that would be of value to all stepfamilies. Finally, little attention has been given to the financial aspects of stepfamilies. Clinicians report that financial issues are a primary source of stress in stepfamilies, yet researchers have seldom addressed this area (Coleman and Ganong, 1989).

Research Methods in the '90s

A number of research methods and study designs have been underutilized by remarriage and step-family researchers. Gains in understanding will be accelerated if investigators can move beyond the problem-oriented, between–family type, cross-sectional design that has become the "standard" approach. Research in remarriage and stepfamily dynamics in the '90s should include longitudinal stepfamily studies that begin prior to remarriage, preferably prior to separation and divorce, that allow us to investigate how people adjust to transitions and how social networks, boundaries, and roles shift to accommodate new experiences. Cross-sectional studies should be carefully designed to take into account the complex array of stepfamily characteristics. Well-defined sample criteria, appropriately selected comparison groups, and cautious and controlled generalizations must be features of these investigations. These studies should have multitrait, multilevel (individual, dyad, family), multimethod designs; there have been several such investigations in recent years, but more studies of this type are needed. The development of instruments specifically for assessing stepfamily dynamics and the development of norms for stepfamilies on well-known family instruments are needed also.

Given the complexity of stepfamilies, valuable contributions could be made by descriptive qualitative studies and detailed, in-depth studies using reliable self-report and observational measures. Single-case designs, borrowing the well-established methods developed by psychologists and educators for the intensive examination of single subjects over time, could be used to study remarried couples, entire stepfamilies, or individual stepfamily members.

There has been a dearth of intervention studies. Such research, employing either single-case designs or methods appropriate for larger samples, could be part of theory-testing or model-building efforts. Multidisciplinary collaboration would enhance these projects. We have written about the ongoing need for more discourse and cooperation between stepfamily clinicians and researchers (Ganong and Coleman, 1986), but there is also a need for researchers from different disciplines (e.g., family studies, psychology, sociology, anthropology, economics, law, public policy, journalism) to share, and perhaps to integrate, their perspectives, expertise, and methodology in the study of remarriage and stepfamilies.

Theory in the '90s

Researchers should be more explicit in identifying the conceptual frameworks or theories that guide their thinking. This would facilitate more studies in which alternative hypotheses are examined and the abandonment of less fruitful ways of thinking about and studying remarriages and stepfamilies. Greater use of theoretical approaches might also help clarify the contradictory findings so abundant in stepfamily research. Thinking more explicitly about their theoretical assumptions and perspectives will help researchers address shortcomings in the extant body of research.

Empirical examination of most, if not all, the models of remarriage and stepfamilies developed in the past decade will likely occur in the '90s. The development of new models is also needed, particularly inductive theory-building efforts, grounded theories, and other approaches that allow stepfamily members to instruct and inform researchers on important issues. This last point should not be overlooked; it represents at least one way in which researchers can produce work that may have valid meaning from the perspective of stepfamily members themselves, rather than just conducting studies of stepfamilies from the prevailing cultural, disciplinary, and personal biases of the researchers.

REFERENCES

Aguirre, B. E., and W. C. Parr. 1982. "Husbands' marriage order and the stability of first and second marriages of white and black women." Journal of Marriage and the Family 44: 605–620.

Ahrons, Constance, and L. Wallisch. 1987. "Parenting in the binuclear family: Relationships between biological and stepparents." Pp. 225–256 in Kay Pasley and M. Ihinger-Tallman (eds.), Remarriage and Stepparenting: Current Research and Theory. New York: Guilford.

Amato, Paul. 1987. "Family processes in one-parent, stepparent, and intact families: The child's point of view." Journal of Marriage and the Family 49: 327–337.

Ambert, Anne-Marie. 1986. "Being a stepparent: Live-in and visiting stepchildren." Journal of Marriage and the Family 48: 795–804.

Anderson, Judith, and G. White. 1986. "An empirical investigation of interactive and relationship patterns in functional and dysfunctional nuclear families and stepfamilies." Family Process 25: 407–422.

Baydar, Nazli. 1988. "Effects of parental separation and reentry into union on the emotional well-being of children." Journal of Marriage and the Family 50: 967–981.

Booth, Alan, D. Brinkerhoff, and L. White. 1984. "The impact of parental divorce on courtship." Journal of Marriage and the Family 46: 85–94.

Brand, Eulalee, and G. Clingempeel. 1987. "The interdependence of marital and stepparent-stepchild relationships and children's psychological adjustment: Research findings and clinical implications." Family Relations 36: 140–145.

Bray, James. 1988. "Children's development during early remarriage." Pp. 279-298 in Mavis Hetherington and J. Arasteh (eds.), Impact of Divorce, Single Parenting and Stepparenting on Children. Hillsdale, NJ: Lawrence Erlbaum.

Brody, Gene, E. Neubaum, and R. Forehand. 1988. "Serial marriage: A heuristic analysis of an emerging family form." Psychological Bulletin 103: 211–222.

Bulcroft, Kris, R. Bulcroft, L. Hatch, and E. Borgatta. 1989. "Antecedents and consequences of remarriage in later life." Research on Aging 11: 82–106.

Bumpass, Larry. 1984a. "Children and marital disruption: A replication and update." Demography 21: 71–82.

Bumpass, Larry. 1984b. "Some characteristics of children's second families." American Journal of Sociology 90: 608–623.

Bumpass, Larry, and J. Sweet. 1989. "National estimates of cohabitation: Cohort levels and union stability." NSFH Working Paper No. 2, Center for Demography and Ecology, University of Wisconsin, Madison.

Burks, Valorie, D. Lund, C. Gregg, and H. Bluhm. 1988. "Bereavement and remarriage for older adults." Death Studies 12: 51–60.

Burnside, Mary, P. Baer, R. McLaughlin, and A. Pokorny. 1986. "Alcohol use by adolescents in disrupted families." Alcoholism: Clinical and Experimental Research 10: 274–278.

Cherlin, Andrew. 1978. "Remarriage as an incomplete institution." American Journal of Sociology 86: 634–650.

Cherlin, Andrew, and J. McCarthy. 1985. "Remarried couple households: Data from the June 1980 Current Population Survey." Journal of Marriage and the Family 47: 23–30.

Clingempeel, Glenn. 1981. "Quasi-kin relationships and marital quality." Journal of Personality and Social Psychology 41: 890–901.

Clingempeel, Glenn, and E. Brand. 1985. "Quasi-kin relationships, structural complexity, and marital quality in stepfamilies: A replication, extension, and clinical implications." Family Relations 34: 401–409.

Clingempeel, Glenn, and S. Segal. 1986. "Stepparent-stepchild relationships and the psychological adjustment of children in stepmother and stepfather families." Child Development 57: 474–484.

Coleman, Marilyn, and L. Ganong. 1984. "Effect of family structure on family attitudes and expectations." Family Relations 33: 425–432.

Coleman, Marilyn, and L. Ganong. 1987a. "The cultural stereotyping of stepfamilies." Pp. 19–41 in Kay Pasley and M. Ihinger-Tallman (eds.), Remarriage and Stepparenting: Current Research and Theory. New York: Guilford.

Coleman, Marilyn, and L. Ganong. 1987b. "Marital conflict in stepfamilies: Effects on children." Youth and Society 19: 151–172.

Coleman, Marilyn, and Lawrence Ganong. 1989. "Financial management in stepfamilies." Lifestyles: Family and Economic Issues 10: 217–232.

Crosbie-Burnett, Margaret. 1984. "The centrality of the step relationship: A challenge to family theory and practice." Family Relations 33: 459–464.

Demo, David, and A. Acock. 1988. "The impact of divorce on children." Journal of Marriage and the Family 50: 619–648. [Reprinted in this volume]

Duncan, Greg J., and S. Hoffman. 1985. "A reconsideration of the economic consequences of marital dissolution." Demography 22: 485–497.

Espinoza, Renato, and Y. Newman. 1979. Stepparenting. DHEW Publication No. 48–579. Rockville, MD: U.S. Dept. of Health, Education, and Welfare.

Ferri, Elsa. 1984. Stepchildren: A National Study. Atlantic Highlands, NJ: Humanities.

Flinn, Mark. 1988. "Step- and genetic parent/offspring relationships in a Caribbean village." Ethology and Sociobiology 9: 335–369.

Furstenberg, Frank F., Jr., and C. Nord. 1985. "Parenting apart: Patterns of childrearing after marital disruption." Journal of Marriage and the Family 47: 893–904.

Furstenberg, Frank F., Jr., and G. Spanier. 1984. Recycling the Family: Remarriage after Divorce. Beverly Hills, CA: Sage.

Ganong, Lawrence, and M. Coleman. 1984. "Effects of remarriage on children: A review of the empirical literature." Family Relations 33: 389–406.

Ganong, Lawrence, and M. Coleman. 1986. "A comparison of clinical and empirical literature on children in stepfamilies." Journal of Marriage and the Family 48: 309–318.

Ganong, Lawrence, and M. Coleman. 1987. "Stepchildren's perceptions of their parents." Journal of Genetic Psychology 148: 5–17.

Ganong, Lawrence, and M. Coleman. 1988. "Do mutual children cement bonds in stepfamilies?" Journal of Marriage and the Family 50: 687–698.

Ganong, Lawrence, M. Coleman, and D. Mapes. 1990. "A meta-analytic review of family structure stereotypes." Journal of Marriage and the Family 52: 287–297.

Gentry, Margaret, and A. Shulman. 1988. "Remarriage as a coping response for widowhood." Psychology and Aging 3: 191–196.

Giles-Sims, Jean. 1984. "The stepparent role: Expectations, behavior, sanctions." Journal of Family

Issues 5: 116–130.

Giles-Sims, Jean, and D. Finkelhor. 1984. "Child abuse in stepfamilies." Family Relations 33: 407–414.

Glick, Paul. 1980. "Remarriage: Some recent changes and variations." Journal of Family Issues 1: 455–478.

Glick, Paul. 1984. "Marriage, divorce and living arrangements: Prospective changes." Journal of Family Issues 5: 7–26.

Glick, Paul. 1989. "Remarried families, stepfamilies, and stepchildren: A brief demographic analysis." Family Relations 38: 24–27.

Gross, P. E. 1987. "Defining post-divorce remarriage families: A typology based on the subjective perceptions of children." Journal of Divorce 10: 205–217.

Guisinger, Shan, P. Cowan, and D. Schuldberg. 1989. "Changing parent and spouse relations in the first years of remarriage of divorced fathers." Journal of Marriage and the Family 51: 445–456.

Hetherington, Mavis, M. Cox, and R. Cox. 1985. "Long-term effects of divorce and remarriage on the adjustment of children." Journal of the American Academy of Child Psychiatry 24: 518–530.

Hobart, Charles W. 1987. "Parent-child relations in remarried families." Journal of Family Issues 8: 259–277.

Hobart, Charles, and D. Brown. 1988. "Effects of prior marriage children on adjustment in remarriage: A Canadian study." Journal of Comparative Family Studies 19: 382–396.

Kalmus, Debra, and J. Seltzer. 1989. "A framework for studying family socialization over the life cycle." Journal of Family Issues 10: 339–358.

Kinnaird, Keri, and M. Gerrard. 1986. "Premarital sexual behavior and attitudes toward marriage and divorce among young women as a function of their mother's marital status." Journal of Marriage and the family 48: 757–765.

Koo, H. P., and C. M. Suchindran. 1980. Effects of children on women's remarriage prospects. Journal of Family Issues 1: 497–515.

Kurdek, Lawrence. 1989. "Relationship quality of newly married husbands and wives: Marital history, stepchildren, and individual difference predictors." Journal of Marriage and the Family 51: 1053–1064.

Kurdek, Lawrence, and R. Sinclair. 1986. "Adolescent's views on issues related to divorce." Journal of Adolescent Research 1: 373–387.

Lightcap, Jay, J. Kurland, and R. Burgess. 1982. "Child abuse: A test of some predictions from evolutionary theory." Ethology and Sociobiology 3: 61–67.

McLanahan, Sara, and L. Bumpass. 1988. "Intergenerational consequences of family disruption." American Journal of Sociology 94: 130–152.

Michael, Robert, and N. Tuma. 1985. "Entry into marriage and parenthood by young men and women: The influence of family background." Demography 22: 515–544.

Mitchell, K. 1983. "The price tag of responsibility: A comparison of divorced and remarried mothers. Journal of Divorce 6: 33–424.

Moss, Miriam, and S. Moss. 1980. "The image of the deceased spouse in remarriage of elderly widow(ers)." Journal of Gerontological Social Work 3: 59–70.

Newcomer, Susan, and R. Udry. 1987. "Parental marital status effects on adolescent social behavior." Journal of Marriage and the Family 49: 235–240.

Nock, Steven. 1981. "Family life-cycle transitions: Longitudinal effects on family members." Journal of Marriage and the Family 43: 703–713.

Orleans, Myron, B. Palisi, and D. Caddell. 1989. "Marriage adjustment and satisfaction of stepfathers: Their feelings and perceptions of decision making and stepchildren relations." Family Relations 38: 371–377.

Papernow, Patricia. 1984. "The stepfamily cycle: An experimental model of stepfamily development." Family Relations 33: 355–364.

Peek, Charles, N. Bell, T. Waldren, and G. Sorell. 1988. "Patterns of functioning in families of remarried and first-married couples." Journal of Marriage and the Family 50: 699–708.

Rodgers, Roy, and L. Conrad. 1986. "Courtship for remarriage: Influences on family reorganization after divorce." Journal of Marriage and the Family 48: 767–775.

Santrock, John, R. Warshak, C. Lindbergh, and L. Meadows. 1982. "Children and parents' observed social behavior in stepfather families." Child Development 53: 472–480.

Seltzer, Judith, and S. Bianchi. 1988. "Children's contact with absent parents." Journal of Marriage and the Family 50: 663–677.

Spanier, Graham, and F. Furstenberg. 1982. "Remarriage after divorce: A longitudinal analysis of well-being." Journal of Marriage and the Family 44: 709–720.

Spanier, Graham, and P. Glick. 1980. "Paths to remarriage." Journal of Divorce 3: 283–298.

Steinberg, Laurence. 1987. "Single parents, stepparents, and the susceptibility of adolescents to antisocial peer pressure." Child Development 58: 269–275.

Sweetser, Dorrian. 1985. "Broken homes: Stable risk, changing reasons, changing forms." Journal of Marriage and the Family 47: 709–715.

Teachman, Jay. 1986. "First and second marital dissolution: A decomposition exercise for whites and blacks." Sociological Quarterly 27: 571–590.

Vemer, Elizabeth, M. Coleman, L. Ganong, and H. Cooper. 1989. Marital satisfaction in remarriage: A meta-analysis." Journal of Marriage and the Family 51: 713–725.

Weingarten, Helen R. 1980. "Remarriage and well-being: National survey evidence of social and psychological effects." Journal of Family Issues 1: 533–559.

Weingarten, Helen R. 1985. "Marital status and well-being: A national study comparing first-married, currently divorced, and remarried adults." Journal of Marriage and the Family 47: 653–662.

White, Lynn K., and A. Booth. 1985. "The quality and

stability of remarriages: The role of stepchildren.'' American Sociological Review 50: 689–698.

White, Lynn K., D. Brinkerhoff, and A. Booth. 1985. "The effect of marital disruption on child's attachment to parents." Journal of Family Issues 6: 5–22.

Wilson, Margo, M. Daly, and S. Weghorst. 1980. "Household composition and the risk of child abuse and neglect." Journal of Biosocial Science 12: 526–536.

Wineberg, Howard. 1990. "Childbearing after remarriage." Journal of Marriage and the Family 52: 31–38.

Zill, Nicholas. 1988. "Behavior, achievement, and health problems among children in stepfamilies: Findings from a national survey of child health." Pp. 325–368 in E. Mavis Hetherington and J. D. Arasteh (eds.), Impact of Divorce, Single Parenting, and Stepparenting. Hillsdale, NJ: Lawrence Erlbaum.

Viktor Gecas *Washington State University*

Monica A. Seff *University of Texas, Arlington**

Families and Adolescents:

A Review of the 1980s

Research on adolescents and families in the 1980s shows considerable continuity with the themes and topics found in past decades. This review is largely organized around some of these perennial topics: the relative influence of parents and peers; the degree of "storm and stress" during adolescence; the "generation gap" and intergenerational continuity; the effects of parental behavior; self and identity issues; and life course considerations. The most noticeable change has been a shift in focus from individual development to the social contexts within which individuals develop, such as family, school, work, and historical period. Some of the deficiencies and neglected aspects of the adolescence research of previous decades are also evident (if somewhat less so) in the 1980s. Still relatively rare are studies of reciprocal influences, longitudinal studies, information from parents and children, and analyses of same-sex and cross-sex parent-adolescent relations, although arguments for the importance of these kinds of research are increasingly evident in the literature of the past decade.

The study of adolescence in the 1980s is characterized by a substantial increase in research activity

Department of Sociology, Washington State University, Pullman, WA 99164-4006.

*Department of Sociology, Anthropology, and Social Work, University of Texas, Arlington, Box 19599, Arlington, TX 76019.

and by a shift in focus from individual development to the social contexts within which adolescent development occurs. Historically, the study of adolescence has been dominated by psychologists, whose natural focus is the individual. This emphasis has not disappeared in the 1980s. Investigators who follow the theoretical leads of Piaget, Kohlberg, and Erikson continue to assess the cognitive functioning, moral development, ego identity, and developmental tasks of adolescents. In fact, this work is among the most theoretically guided reseach on adolescence.

But it is also clear that much of the focus has shifted to the social contexts within which the physical, cognitive, and emotional development of adolescents takes place. Dornbusch (1989) and Steinberg (1987), in their recent assessments of adolescence research, come to the same conclusion. Particularly important for our review is the renewed emphasis on the *family* context of adolescence. Steinberg (1987) observes that the family context was prominent in research of the 1960s, received less emphasis in the 1970s, and regained attention in the 1980s.

Some of this shift in orientation is due to the increasing interest of sociologists in studying adolescence from a life course perspective (e.g., Dornbusch, 1989; Elder, 1980, 1985; Elder, Liker, and Cross, 1984; Furstenberg, Brooks-Gunn, and Morgan, 1987; Furstenberg, Nord, Peterson, and Zill, 1983; Mortimer and Kumka, 1982; Mortimer, Lorence, and Kumka, 1986; Simmons and Blyth, 1987). But much of this reorientation also reflects an increasing "sociological consciousness" among psychologists studying adolescence (e.g., Bronfenbrenner, 1979; Greenberger and Steinberg, 1986). Bronfenbrenner's (1979, 1986) ecological perspective has been particularly influential in expanding the focus of developmental psychologists beyond the individual and the dyad. Historians have also contributed to the view of adolescence in a broader sociohistorical context (see Juster and Vinovskis, 1987; Modell, 1989).

The focus of our review is on adolescents within the context of family relations. To some extent other social contexts (e.g., school, peers, work) are considered as they overlap with the family relations of adolescents. We will also touch on the more general topic of parent-child relations, since adolescence is an ambiguous category.[1] What we exclude is most of the research on the cognitive development of adolescence, except as this is treated in the context of family relations. Also, we do not discuss mate selection, dating, and premarital sexuality, since these are covered in other articles in this special issue. Within this delimitation of our topic, we highlight the more careful, thorough, and insightful work of the past decade. We have organized our review around topics we consider important to the area of families and adolescents. Some of these topics reflect perennial issues associated with parents and adolescents, others are evolving continuities from past decades, and some are more recent themes.[2]

Parent-Adolescent Relations: Storm and Stress?

One of the perennial issues in the adolescence literature is the extent to which this is a time of conflict and stress in the relations between adolescents and their parents. The prevailing view for much of this century (at least in contemporary Western societies) is that adolescence is indeed marked by greater turmoil than the preceding and the subsequent stages of life. G. Stanley Hall (1904), who launched the study of adolescence in psychology, described the adolescent years as a period of "storm and stress," of passion and rebellion against adult authority. Erikson's (1959) influential characterization of adolescence as a time of identity crisis further accentuated the conflict-and-stress theme of this period, as has much of the work from the psychoanalytic orientation (e.g., Blos, 1962; Anna Freud, 1958).

Sociologists have emphasized the rapidity of social change in contemporary, industrial societies, creating environments that, in combination with the psychological and cognitive changes that occur during adolescence, make this a difficult time for adolescents and their families (Clausen, 1986; Rice, 1975; Simmons and Blyth, 1987; and for a classic statement of this position, see Davis, 1940).

Much of the research of the past decade has challenged this view of adolescence as a time of "storm and stress" (Conger, 1981; Dusek and Flaherty, 1981; Offer, Ostrov, and Howard, 1981; Offer, Ostrov, Howard, and Atkinson, 1988; O'Malley and Bachman, 1983; Steinberg and Silverberg, 1986). This research suggests that for most young people, adolescence is not a particularly turbulent time; that relations with parents reflect more harmony than conflict; that self-esteem does not decline; and that most identify with and like their parents. Offer et al. (1988) even found this to hold across cultures. In a study of 6,000 adolescents in ten countries (Japan, Israel, Hungary, West Germany, Italy, Australia, Turkey, Bangladesh, Taiwan, and the U.S.), most of these adolescents were found to have favorable attitudes toward their families, favorable attitudes toward themselves, and high interest in work and occupational goals. Similarly, Steinberg, Elmen, and Mounts (1989) found that about 75% of adolescents feel close to and identify with their parents, and less than 10% report a deterioration in their family relationships. Studies reporting increased conflict between adolescents and parents indicate that the conflicts are usually over minor issues of appearance and taste and not about major values (Csikszentmihalyi and Larson, 1984; Montemayor, 1984; Silverberg and Steinberg, 1987). Several recent reviews of adolescence research conclude that the view of adolescence as a time of stress and conflict is untenable, that it is a misperception of adolescents and their family relations based largely on psychoanalytic and clinical perspectives (see Dornbusch, 1989; Steinberg, 1987). We think this conclusion is only partly correct. It may indeed be true that the earlier research on adolescence exaggerated the conflict associated with this stage (especially research from a psychodynamic perspective); however, we should be wary of now exaggerating the degree of harmony during adolescence.

Perceptions of harmony or conflict during

adolescence may for the most part reflect historical changes in society. In an interesting study of adolescents' orientation to parents in the past three decades, Sebald (1986) found a curvilinear pattern. With samples of high school students taken in 1963, 1976, and 1982, Sebald found adolescents' orientation to parents (on indicators of parental identification, closeness, and influence) to be highest in the 1963 sample, to decline substantially in the 1970s, and to increase again in the 1980s. He explains this curvilinear pattern in terms of the social change occurring in American society during these decades—the relative conservatism of the early 1960s and 1980s, compared to the volatile 1970s (e.g., the counterculture movement, the Vietnam War, civil disruptions). This pattern of findings and Sebald's explanation are congruent with Kingsley Davis's (1940) earlier speculations concerning the relevance of social change for parent-youth conflict. This study also underscores the importance of the historical context in examining the relationship between parents and adolescents, a theme that we will return to in the section on life course analyses.

While there may be doubt about the extent to which adolescence is stressful for youth, there seems to be less doubt that it is a stressful time for the *parents* of adolescents (Montemayor, 1983; Pasley and Gecas, 1984; Small, Cornelius, and Eastman, 1983). Pasley and Gecas (1984) found that parents overwhelmingly perceived adolescence as the most difficult stage of parenting: 62% of mothers and 64% of fathers. The main reasons parents gave for the difficulties associated with this stage were "loss of control over the adolescent" and "fear for the adolescent's safety because of his/her increased independence." Also frequently mentioned were aggravation and annoyance with the adolescent's behavior. Small and associates (1983) found parental stress to be particularly acute during early adolescence. They also found that issues of adolescents' autonomy (e.g., pushing for more freedom than parents were willing to grant), failure to adhere to parental advice, and deviant behavior to be the main reasons for parental stress. Not surprisingly, research on marital satisfaction (e.g., Rollins and Feldman, 1970) and life satisfaction (e.g., Hoffman and Manis, 1978) indicates that the lowest levels of satisfaction are reported by parents of adolescents. Umberson (1989) found this to be true, particularly for fathers. For the parents of

adolescents, therefore, adolescence may indeed be a time of storm and stress, at least in modern times.

VALUE CONGRUENCE, DISCREPANCY, AND TRANSMISSION

Value congruence between adolescents and their parents is a central topic in the adolescence literature because it is used as an indicator of the "generation gap," intergenerational continuity, and the effectiveness of adolescent socialization.[3] The 1980s research suggests a high level of congruence, at least with regard to certain values and when based on the adolescents' perceptions (Bachman, Johnston, and O'Malley, 1987; Smith, 1981; Youniss and Smollar, 1985; also see reviews by Dornbusch, 1989; and Smith, 1983). Congruence is particularly high on values dealing with educational goals, career issues, and major life concerns. Bachman and associates (1987), in extensive surveys of high school seniors, found that adolescents perceived their parents and themselves as agreeing on the value of education (87%), important values in life (72%), religious beliefs (69%), and to a lesser extent political beliefs (52%). There was less perceived congruence on how youth should spend their money (44%) and on what is permissible on a date (46%). Reed, McBrown, Lindekugel, Roberts, and Tureck (1986) found high levels of perceived value similarity between adolescents and parents on a wide range of deviant behaviors.

It is tempting to conclude on the basis of these findings that the generation gap has diminished in the 1980s. But a few cautions are in order. Adolescents' *perceptions* of congruence are not the same as *actual* similarities between parents' and adolescents' values. The few studies that have compared reports of values, attitudes, or behaviors from parents and their adolescents have found little congruence (see Demo, Small, and Savin-Williams, 1987; Gecas and Schwalbe, 1986; Jessop, 1981; Whitbeck and Gecas, 1988). Yet, perceptions of greater congruence than may actually exist are interesting in their own right. They suggest that adolescents see more similarities than differences between the generations, which may reflect the more conservative cultural climate of the 1980s. By contrast, Acock and Bengtson's (1980) analysis of data collected in the early seventies on actual and perceived values of parents and adolescents found that the youth attributed greater value *dissimilarity* than actually existed between themselves and their parents. These findings suggested to Acock and Bengtson that the generation gap is greater in the minds of adolescents than in the actual attitudes and opinions of the two generations. They interpreted these findings in developmental and attributional terms, suggesting that parents and youth have different "generational stakes" that affect the direction of their misattributions of each other's values: "for youth, the 'stake' is more toward maximizing a sense of separate identity; for parents, the investment pays off in maximizing continuity" (1980: 512). To this we would add a historical interpretation: the 1970s were more turbulent than the 1980s, favoring an accentuation of generational differences.

Value congruence between parents and offspring does not necessarily imply value transmission. Congruence may be due to exposure to similar sociohistorical circumstances, or simply to coincidence, rather than to socialization processes (see McBroom, Reed, Bums, Hargraves, and Trankel, 1985). Some of the work in the past decade has dealt with value transmission and suggests several key mechanisms in this process: (*a*) child's perceptions of mother's and father's values, and (*b*) childrearing practices (Kohn, 1983; Smith, 1983). It is safe to say that the latter, and to a lesser extent the former, are central to *most* socialization models, not just those dealing with value transmission (a point we'll come back to later).

Research supports these conceptual links in value transmission. Acock and Bengtson (1980) found that parents' values had little direct effect on youth's orientations except as the values were perceived by the youth. Others have also found accuracy of perceptions to be important in value transmission (e.g., Smith, 1981; Whitbeck and Gecas, 1988). Kohn, Slomczynski, and Schoenbach (1986) provide an extensive analysis of value transmission in a comparative study of the United States and Poland. For the U.S. sample, they found that parents' values have a significant effect on children's (adolescents') values; that the effect of mothers' values is entirely indirect, through children's perceptions of mothers' values; and that the effect of fathers' values is only partly through children's perceptions of these values (the direct effect, they propose, is

due to fathers' values affecting the family environment in such a way as to affect children's values of self-direction). Also, these relationships are partly reciprocal; children's values affect mothers' values but not fathers' values. For the Polish sample, the mother is the key parent in value transmission. Her values strongly influence her children's values; the father's values seem to be irrelevant to children's values (which suggests that Polish mothers are much more central in child socialization than fathers). The Kohn et al. (1986) study, extensive though it is, does not tell us which childrearing or parent-child processes are responsible for the effects of parents' values on children's values. Of the childrearing or parental behavior variables, types of parental support and control that are conducive to increasing the child's identification with the parent have been found to affect the child's values (Mortimer and Kumka, 1982; Whitbeck and Gecas, 1988), as well as a wide range of other socialization outcomes, which we consider below.

PARENTS AND PEERS

In much of the earlier literature on families and adolescence, peer groups were viewed as the enemy, competing with parents for the socialization of youth and hindering successful transitions to adulthood. The idea of a "youth culture," with values, norms, and tastes distinct from and often in opposition to those of the dominant culture, has tended to polarize parents and peers as agents of socialization. Coleman's (1961) influential research on high schools as arenas of socialization, and Bronfenbrenner's (1970) analysis of age segregation and its consequences for the development of a separate youth culture, helped to crystallize the polarized view. This position was not without controversy among sociologists and psychologists even then, when a strong case could be made in the '60s and '70s for the "generation gap" and the alienation of youth from adult society. As Coleman and Husen (1985: 19–20) observe, this controversy focused on an important socialization question: "To what extent in modern society are adults the agents of socialization for adolescents . . . and to what extent are their friends and peers the agents of socialization? On the one side are those who contend that the youth culture is exceedingly important, and that the directions in which this culture focuses the attention of youth can seriously impede . . . the process of transition to adulthood. On the other side are those who see the youth culture as merely an epiphenomenon, and as closely derivative from, and reflecting the values of, the adult culture."

In the 1980s, the pendulum has swung toward the nonpolarized view. There is greater emphasis on harmony rather than conflict in parent-adolescent relations, and continuity rather than discontinuity in values and norms between the generations (see Dornbusch, 1989). The polarized view, while less evident, has certainly not disappeared in the 1980s (see Schwartz, 1987, for an interesting ethnographic study of six midwestern communities and the adolescent subcultures within them). Furthermore, even though the adults-versus-youth-culture theme is muted in the 1980s, the influence of peers is still generally perceived to be negative; it is thought to be associated with deviance, delinquency, and various forms of harmful, wasteful, or irresponsible behavior. Much of the research of the decade, comparing the relative influence of parents and peers, finds that parents have a greater influence on adolescents than do peers (Davies and Kandel, 1981; Kandel, 1985; Loy and Norland, 1981; Reed et al., 1986; Smith, 1985; Tedin, 1980). In particular, parental influence is found to be stronger on adolescents' educational goals and future plans, whereas peer influence is greater on styles of appearance, taste, and recreational behavior. This differential influence may also occur through different processes. Biddle, Bank, and Marlin (1980) suggest that parents influence adolescents' behavior primarily by establishing normative standards, and peers through modeling of behavior.

It should be noted that most of the research on parent-peer influences is based on middle-class samples. There are reasons to suspect that peers have a stronger influence on adolescents in the lower class—factors such as a greater proportion of single-parent families, less parental supervision, less of an economic stake in the family of orientation, and greater prevalence of gangs.

What worries parents is the belief that peers are more likely to provide models of negative or detrimental behavior than of positive or "approved" behavior. But is peer influence always negative? Do peers serve any positive functions for adolescent socialization? Though it was certainly not a conspicuous theme in the '80s, or in

earlier decades, a few have commented on the positive consequences of peer interactions (Fine, 1981, 1987; Gecas, 1981; Youniss, 1980). Several features of peer relations, which are distinct from features characteristic of family relations, have important socialization and developmental consequences: peer groups are *voluntary* associations of status *equals* and are based on *friendship* bonds (Gecas, 1981). In observational studies of preadolescent and early adolescent boys, Fine (1981, 1987) observes that friendships are especially appropriate for the mastering of self-presentation and impression-management skills, since inadequate displays will usually be ignored or corrected without severe loss of face. Friendships, characterized by mutual trust and tolerance, are important for exploring the boundaries of the self. A wider latitude of behavior is allowed (and even encouraged), since friends, unlike parents, are not explicitly responsible for changing or shaping the adolescent's behavior. Youniss (1980), building on Piaget's and Sullivan's developmental theories, argues that higher levels of cognitive and moral understanding can only develop within the context of relationships based on status equality. Mutual understanding, role-taking, and empathy—important to the development of self in relation to others—develop best in the context of peer relations. It should also be noted that peer groups are the context within which intimate relations with the same and the opposite sex form, providing the basis for intimacy in adulthood.

Occupational and Educational Aspirations

Two predominant lines of research are evident in the family-adolescent literature dealing with adolescents' occupational and educational aspirations. The first line of research gives primary consideration to the family's location in the broader social structure. Adolescents' educational and occupational aspirations and attainment are viewed as outcomes of parents' socioeconomic status. This emphasis is apparent in the sociological research, reflecting sociologists' natural tendency to focus on class subcultures, social structural influences, and transmission of inequality, as well as change and stability in society. These studies tend to be large-scale, often longitudinal, highly quantitative, investigations of (mostly) fathers' influence on (almost exclusively) sons' status attainment (see Alwin and Thornton, 1984; Featherman, 1980, 1981; Mortimer et al., 1986; Sewell and Hauser, 1980; Sewell, Hauser, and Wolf, 1980). The questions addressed in these investigations include, Does the family exert its influence on children by providing (or not providing) advantages such as access to better schools and social contacts, as well as economic resources? Further, does the family's socioeconomic status affect children's self-conceptions (i.e., self-esteem and self-competence), psychological orientations, and values? While it is impossible to summarize here this extensive literature, in general, family background variables such as race, parents' education, and family size affect children's economic successes. Much of this research builds on Blau and Duncan's (1967) stratification model, which posits that fathers' occupation and education, as well as family size to a lesser extent, influence sons' aspirations and educational attainment. Subsequent research has included the influence of significant others and paternal support as key mediating variables in the status attainment process (e.g., Mortimer et al., 1986; see Sewell and Hauser, 1980, for a review).

A related line of research focuses on the structural features of the family, including family configuration (e.g., family size, birth order, and sibling spacing) as well as the effects of single parenthood, on children's outcomes. Much of this work attempts to distinguish the effects of poverty associated with single-parent families from the effects of single parents per se (see Demo and Acock, 1988; Duncan and Rogers, 1988; Furstenberg et al., 1983; McLanahan and Booth, 1989; W. Wilson, 1987; Wilson and Aponti, 1985; for reviews of this literature). The conclusion seems to be that it is probably the effects of poverty, more than family structure, that detrimentally affect children.

The second line of research focuses much more on the socialization techniques that parents employ (e.g., Clark, 1983; MacLeod, 1987; Steinitz and Solomon, 1986). An interesting example is Clark's (1983) ethnographic study of 10 black families with adolescent children. Clark compared the parenting styles of 5 families with high-achieving adolescents and 5 families with low-achieving adolescents, all living in the same low-income neighborhood. Clark (1983: 129) concludes that it is the quality of family relationships, and neither the presence or absence of the father

in the home nor social class, that determines academic achievement. Perhaps structural characteristics are downplayed too much by Clark. The structure-versus-culture debate is tiresome—both affect children's outcomes, and clearly, some social structural conditions make it difficult for parents to provide the kind of emotional support needed for adolescents to survive and thrive in tough environments.

One trend in the literature is an emphasis on daughters' career and marriage goals. Much of the literature attempts to assess parents' sex role attitudes, differential expectations for sons and daughters, and daughters' aspirations (e.g., Peters, 1984; Peterson, Rollins, Thomas, and Heaps, 1982; Thornton, Alwin, and Camburn, 1983). For example, Marjoribanks (1987), studying parental supportiveness and the aspirations of adolescents, found that parents affect daughters' educational aspirations and sons' educational as well as occupational aspirations. Peters (1984) found that parents are more accepting of daughters' lack of summer employment than they are of sons' unemployment. Peterson et al. (1982), using a simulation game, found that parents, especially fathers, showed a preference for sons' career goals. Additionally, fathers tended to prefer homemaking for daughters more than daughters chose this goal for themselves. Expectations for children, as Elder (1980) has demonstrated, are affected by social structural and economic variables. Galambos and Silbereisen (1987), examining the relationship between income change, parents' outlook on life, and the extent to which adolescents expect to attain job success, found that fathers' pessimism was highly related to daughters' lower expectations of occupational success. The authors suggest that the vulnerability of daughters to fathers' pessimism, and the lack of such a relationship for boys, indicates that girls are under pressure to conform to a sex role that provides for limited career opportunities and deemphasizes achievement.

PARENTAL BEHAVIOR AND
ADOLESCENT SOCIALIZATION

By adolescence, much of the groundwork of parental socialization has been laid. The history of parent-child interactions and childrearing techniques carries into adolescence, affecting the nature of parent-adolescent interactions. In some ways, adolescence is a time of testing the effectiveness of childhood socialization. Therefore, in assessing the effects of parental behavior on adolescents, this carryover process is quite important.

Research in the 1980s on the consequences of parental behavior for adolescents shows considerable continuity with the research of previous decades: the focus, for the most part, is still on the generic dimensions of parental support and control. For the past three decades, research has found parental support and control to be consequential for a wide range of socialization outcomes for children and adolescents (there are a number of good reviews and critiques of this literature: Maccoby and Martin, 1983; Peterson and Rollins, 1987; Rollins and Thomas, 1979; Smith, 1983; Thomas, Gecas, Weigert, and Rooney, 1974).[4]

Parental support is one of the most robust variables in the socialization literature. It is positively related to cognitive development, conformity to adult standards, moral behavior, internal locus of control, self-esteem, instrumental competence, and academic achievement of children and adolescents. Rollins and Thomas (1979) subsume many of these positive socialization outcomes under the general label "social competence." After reviewing the extensive empirical research on parental support, they conclude with this general proposition: "the greater the amount of parental support, the greater the amount of children's social competence" (1979: 334). The converse of this proposition also seems to be true: lack of parental support is associated with negative socialization outcomes for children and adolescents, such as low self-esteem, delinquency, deviance, drug abuse, and various other problem behaviors (Peterson and Rollins, 1987; Simons and Miller, 1987). Support is usually treated as unidimensional, although recently several components have been identified and differentiated in terms of their effects: general support, physical affection, companionship, and sustained contact (Barber and Thomas, 1986; Peterson, Rollins, Thomas, and Ellis, 1980). Barber and Thomas (1986) found these components to vary by sex of parent and child: both parents were found to express more companionship to the same-sex child; physical affection, sustained contact, and general support had differential effects on sons' and daughters' self-esteem, depending on sex of parent. Although it is useful to make

such refinements of the concept of parental support, it is not *essential*, since the components do not differ in the valence of their effects, even though they may differ in the magnitude of effects.

The same cannot be said of parental control. The control dimension is more complicated than support, and it is essential to distinguish between different styles of control because they frequently have *opposite* socialization consequences. An important distinction is between "authoritarian" and "authoritative" control (Baumrind, 1978) or "coercion" and "induction" (Rollins and Thomas, 1979). Authoritarian or coercive control (i.e., control based on force, threat, or physical punishment) is associated with negative or unfavorable socialization outcomes, whereas authoritative or inductive control (i.e., control based on reason and explanation) has positive outcomes. Failure to distinguish between these qualitatively different styles of control has contributed to much of the inconsistency and confusion in the research on the effects of parental control (see Rollins and Thomas, 1979; Peterson and Rollins, 1987).

Other components of parental control have also been identified and found to be important, such as degree of protectiveness, supervision, surveillance and monitoring, strictness, clarity of rules, and bases of power assertions (Maccoby and Martin, 1983; Smith, 1983; Peterson and Rollins, 1987). The concept of parental power has considerable potential, even though it hasn't received much attention in the 1980s. McDonald (1980, 1982) found support for a social power theory of parental identification; that is, adolescents were more likely to identify with the parent they perceived to be more powerful. However, Acock and Yang (1984), testing McDonald's theory, found power variables to be only modest predictors of sons' and daughters' identification with parents. They found stronger support for a sex-role identification process, with the strongest child-parent identification along same-sex lines. Social power, however, may still have important consequences for other socialization outcomes. Smith (1983) has utilized the social power distinctions developed by French and Raven (1959) to argue that parental influence on adolescents increases when legitimate, referent, or expert power is utilized, and decreases when parents exercise reward or coercive power.

Continued refinement and specification of

parental control is needed, particularly in parent-adolescent relations. Much of the conflict and stress of parent-adolescent interactions revolves around the issue of parental control, since adolescents typically seek greater freedom from parental constraints and parents typically seek to retain some control over their offspring.

The most powerful models of parental influence on adolescents, as well as children, are still those that combine the dimensions of support and control (Maccoby and Martin, 1983; Peterson and Rollins, 1987; Rollins and Thomas, 1979; Thomas et al., 1974). Parents are most effective as agents of socialization when they express a high level of support and exercise inductive control. Under these conditions, children are most likely to identify with their parents (Peterson, Rollins, and Thomas, 1985), internalize parental values and expectations, and become receptive participants in their own socialization.

Conversely, problems in parental control and support are associated with adolescent deviance and delinquency. Several large-scale investigations have found laxness of parental supervision to be associated with juvenile crime and delinquency (Hirschi, 1989; H. Wilson, 1980, 1987). Especially among economically disadvantaged families living in high crime areas, parental control and supervision appear to be an effective protective buffer against delinquency.

Much of the literature that deals specifically with substance abuse, as opposed to delinquency in general, tends to focus on the effects of parental support (Barnes, Farrell, and Cairns, 1986; Barnes and Windle, 1987; Grube, Morgan, and Seff, 1989; Norem-Hebeisen, Johnson, Anderson, and Johnson, 1984). Barnes et al. (1986) found that parental support was negatively related to problem behaviors such as using marijuana, drinking alcohol, and smoking cigarettes. Parental support was also indirectly related to substance use via parent versus peer orientation—increases in parental support were associated with increases in using parents as a reference group. It seems that drug use is one of those arenas in which parents and peers are likely to be pitted against each other. Barnes et al. (1987) found that primary reliance on peers as a reference group was associated with increases in drug use. Similarly, Norem-Hebeisen et al. (1984) found that the number of friends using drugs as well as the quality of relationships with parents were associated

with adolescent drug use.

There is some evidence that sex of parent and sex of adolescent matter in parent-adolescent relations, but research on how gender affects these interactions is surprisingly sparse (Dornbusch, 1989; Steinberg, 1987). At adolescence, there is greater responsibility for socialization along same-sex lines. Also, the intensity of the mother-daughter relationship is greatest, and the father-daughter relationship is least intense (Steinberg, 1987). The consequences of parental support seem to be strongest along same-sex lines. Hill and Atkinson (1988) found that maternal support had a stronger (negative) effect on the delinquency of female adolescents, and paternal support had a stronger (negative) effect on male adolescents' delinquency. With regard to parental control, Steinberg et al. (1989) found the negative consequences (e.g., poor school performance) of excessive permissiveness among adolescents to be greater for males, whereas the effects of excessive control were greater for females. These findings may reflect the tendency in our culture to be more protective of females and more permissive of males. In line with this view, Baumrind (1980) suggests that a "harsher," more challenging socialization environment is more conducive to the development of social competence and academic achievement for girls. This may only be true for middle-class girls—Clark (1983) suggests the social environment for lower-class girls is harsh enough.

A perennial problem plaguing research on the consequences of parental behavior on children is determining the direction of influence. Since parents are typically viewed as agents of socialization and children as objects of socialization within family relations, the direction of influence is assumed to flow mainly from parent to child. However, since most studies on these topics are cross-sectional in design, the case for parental influence on adolescent development and behavior is suspect. Furthermore, over the past several decades, the thinking with regard to socialization process has shifted from unidirectional to bidirectional and reciprocal models (Gecas, 1981; Maccoby and Martin, 1983; Peterson and Rollins, 1987). Children have increasingly come to be viewed as actively affecting the nature and outcomes of parent-child relations. For example, in considering the positive relationship between parental support and child's social competence, it can be argued that the child's desirable behavior is as likely to be the "cause" of parental support as it is to be its consequence. But despite pleas for the utilization of reciprocal models in research on parent-adolescent relations, or at least longitudinal designs that would provide greater confidence in causal claims, this type of research is still rare. Walters and Walters's (1980) conclusion, in their decade review of the 1970s, that reciprocity has become a dominant theme in the literature on parent-child relations, is true at the conceptual level but not at the empirical level. With a few notable exceptions (such as Kohn et al., 1986, discussed above), empirical work on reciprocal effects is largely limited to the least reciprocal period of parent-offspring relations, the period of infancy (Maccoby and Martin, 1983; Peterson and Rollins, 1987).

Self and Identity in Adolescence

Adolescence has long been considered a time when self-concept concerns increase in prominence. Physiological changes and changes in social circumstances (e.g., high school) contribute to the increase in self-awareness and concern about how one is viewed by others (Harter, 1983). Erikson's (1968) discussion of adolescence as a time of "identity crisis" highlights these self-concept concerns.

Adolescent self-concept has continued to be an active topic of research in the '80s. Most of this research has focused on self-esteem, the evaluative aspect of self-concept (which constitutes the bulk of all research on self-concept), and has reinforced what we have known about the family antecedents of adolescent self-esteem: parental support and encouragement, responsiveness, and use of inductive control are positively related to the adolescent's self-esteem and other aspects of the adolescent's self-image (Bohrnstedt and Fisher, 1986; Demo et al., 1987; Felson and Zielinski, 1989; Gecas and Schwalbe, 1986; Hoelter and Harper, 1987; Openshaw and Thomas, 1986; Openshaw, Thomas, and Rollins, 1983; Robertson and Simons, 1989).

These relationships, however, are much stronger for the adolescent's *perceptions* of parental behavior and his/her self-esteem and self-efficacy than for actual parental behavior or parental reports of their behavior (Gecas and

Schwalbe, 1986). Furthermore, Gecas and Schwalbe (1986) and Demo et al. (1987) found that there isn't much overlap between parental reports of this behavior and the adolescent's perceptions of this behavior. When we interpret these findings from a symbolic interactionist perspective, these studies suggest that adolescents' self-conceptions are more responsive to their own interpretations of family "realities" than to the realities of other family members. This is a central tenet of the "looking-glass self," or the reflected-appraisals process in self-concept formation, upon which much of the research on adolescent self-concept is based (Gecas, 1982; Rosenberg, 1979).[5]

As in other aspects of parent-adolescent relations, we would expect a high level of reciprocity and mutual influence. Felson and Zielinski (1989) found children's perceptions of parental support to affect children's self-esteem but that children's self-esteem also affected their perceptions of parental support. In a rare attempt to actually assess reciprocity in the self-esteem of adolescents *and* their parents, Demo et al. (1987) found that adolescents affect parents' self-esteem through supportive behavior and communication and their own self-esteem is affected through parental support and communication. For parents and adolescents, perceptual variables have stronger effects on self-esteem than do behavioral reports.

Another important aspect of parent-adolescent relations is captured in Rosenberg's (1985; Rosenberg and McCullough, 1981) concept of "mattering." Mattering refers to the feeling that we matter to others, that we make a difference in their lives. It is expressed in the feeling of being a significant other to someone, being important to another, and knowing that they depend on us. In several large-scale studies of adolescents, Rosenberg (1985) found adolescents' feelings of mattering to their parents to be significantly associated with self-esteem (as well as a number of other psychological variables, including depression, anxiety, and somatic symptoms).

The concept of identity has received much less empirical attention in the adolescence literature than has self-esteem. Identity refers to the substantive aspects of the self-concept—that is, who one is (see Baumeister, 1986, for an interesting historical analysis of identity). Several lines of theory and research claim identity as a central concept. The most visible derives from

Erikson's (1959, 1968) theoretical formulations about the development of "ego-identity." Adolescence is described as the period within which the establishment of a sense of identity is the central task. Marcia (1966, 1980) extended Erikson's formulation by specifying several phases of this identity-work that adolescents experience: identity diffusion, achievement, moratorium, and foreclosure. Much of the developmental research of the past decade has utilized these categories and has examined the family conditions and parental behaviors associated with one or another of these phases (e.g., Adams and Fitch, 1982; Campbell, Adams, and Dobson, 1984; Grotevant and Cooper, 1986; Hauser, Powers, Noam, and Bowlds, 1987). The clear impression one gets from this research is that good family relations (e.g., those high in parental support, communication, involvement, and inductive control) facilitate the development of ego identity in adolescence.

Within sociology, work on adolescent identity is most closely associated with "labeling theory." This work has focused on how deviant labels or identities come to be established, such as "delinquent," "drug addict," "troublemaker," and so on. Very little of this line of research has dealt with family relations, at least in the '80s. Another body of literature focusing on identity is the extensive literature on sex-role or gender identities. Most of this research does deal with family relations and the socialization processes involved in the development of gender identities. However, its focus is largely on children, not adolescents (for extensive reviews, see Huston, 1983; and Losh-Hesselbart, 1987). By contrast, "general" identity theory in sociology (e.g., Stryker, 1980) focuses mostly on adults and not children or adolescents.

Lastly, we consider adolescent self-concept with regard to stability and change in self-orientations. The evidence suggests that global self-esteem does not decline much during adolescence (Dusek and Flaherty, 1981; O'Malley and Bachman, 1983), except under certain disruptive conditions, such as the transition to junior high school, examined by Simmons and Blyth (1987, discussed below); and Rosenberg (1985). However, the content of self-conceptions seems to change during adolescence. Rosenberg (1986) presents some of the most cogent and interesting analyses of the decade regarding these changes.

Utilizing data from several large studies, Rosenberg observes that there is a gradual shift from defining the self in terms of objective features (such as appearance, possessions, and location of residence) to internal psychological states and characteristics (such as what one thinks, feels, believes, personal qualities, etc.). Rosenberg relates these changes in self-orientation to changes in cognitive development from childhood to adolescence. In childhood, the individual functions much like a "radical behaviorist" in making self-assessments; during adolescence the individual functions like a "clinician." Other changes observed by Rosenberg are the greater tendencies of adolescents to conceptualize the self in terms of interpersonal sentiments, in abstract rather than concrete terms, and on the basis of autonomous judgments resting on logic and the evaluation of evidence.

Rosenberg also makes some interesting observations on sex differences in adolescent self-concepts. There is little consistent difference in the global self-esteem of boys and girls. However, girls' self-concepts are found to be more volatile (less stable) than boys', particularly during early adolescence but to some extent throughout adolescence (a pattern also found by Simmons and Blyth, 1987). Also, girls were found to be significantly more negative than boys in assessing their physical appearance. Rosenberg found girls (especially white girls), compared to boys, to be less satisfied with their appearance and attractiveness. These findings are congruent with Simmons and Blyth's (1987) observation that the transition to junior high school is more difficult for girls than boys, and is especially difficult for early-maturing girls.

FAMILIES AND ADOLESCENCE IN THE LIFE COURSE

The life course perspective considers adolescence in developmental, contextual, and sometimes historical terms. Some of its practitioners also consider how individual developments and transitions are embedded in the life trajectories of other family members (Elder, Downey, and Cross, 1986; Furstenberg et al., 1987). The life course orientation has been gaining momentum in the past few decades and is perhaps the most promising development in the study of adolescence. But it is also one of the most difficult to pursue empirically because it requires longitudinal research designs.

Elder's work (1980, 1985, 1986; Elder, Caspi, and Van Nguyen, 1986; Elder, Liker, and Cross, 1984; Elder, Van Nguyen, and Caspi, 1985) continues to be central to this orientation. In fact, since the mid-1970s he has been one of its major architects. Throughout the decade he has continued analyses of the Oakland and Berkeley longitudinal data sets, upon which his landmark study, *Children of the Great Depression* (Elder, 1974), was based. A central theme in much of Elder's work is that the same historical events (e.g., the Great Depression, World War II) can have very different consequences, depending on the age and sex of those experiencing these events. For example, Elder found that the Depression experience was ultimately beneficial for the boys in the older cohort (the Oakland sample, born 1920–21) and detrimental for the boys in the youngest cohort (the Berkeley sample, born 1928–29) much later in their families' lives and occupations (Liker and Elder, 1983). The older cohort, who were adolescents for most of the Depression years, were better able to help their families and themselves during these times of economic crisis than were the younger boys. Similarly, the wartime (WWII) experiences were quite different for the Oakland and the Berkeley cohorts, beneficial for the former and detrimental for the latter. During WWII, nearly all of the Oakland boys were soldiers, thereby gaining independence from their families and a wide range of experiences. Also, the educational and vocational benefits of military service had beneficial long-term consequences. By contrast, the homefront experiences of the Berkeley cohort involved continued dependence on their families during stressful times (Elder, 1986).

Elder found some interesting gender differences as well. The Oakland girls, in contrast to the boys, did not fare well. They were pressed into greater role-responsibilities at home when mothers sought work outside. They felt deprived, self-conscious about their shabby appearance, and they tended to marry at earlier ages. By contrast, the girls of the younger cohort did not have these added responsibilities, nor the pressures of dating under adverse circumstances. They tended to develop strong bonds with their mothers (Elder, Caspi and Van Nguyen, 1986; Elder, Downey, and Cross, 1986). The work of Elder

and his colleagues continues to show us how biography and history intersect.

Most of the other work of the decade has been on a smaller temporal scale. Much of it has focused on transitions, such as the transition to adolescence and high school, the transition out of adolescence, and off-time transitions. The extensive research of Simmons and her colleagues (Blyth, Simmons, and Carlton-Ford, 1983; Simmons and Blyth, 1987; Simmons, Blyth, and McKinney, 1983; Simmons, Blyth, Van Cleave, and Bush, 1979) on moving into adolescence has shown how rate of maturation interacts with social context (transition to junior high school versus high school) to affect adolescents' self-image as well as other psychological and behavioral outcomes. Simmons and her colleagues found the transition into adolescence to be less difficult for children who go directly from elementary school to high school than for those children who attend junior high school. The transition from the relatively protected environment of the elementary school to the more impersonal environment of the junior and senior high schools is handled better by the older adolescents. The children moving into junior high school must cope not only with a new organizational setting and new pressures (such as dating) but also with the onset of puberty. The junior high transition is particularly stressful for girls, especially for those who mature early. These girls had the lowest self-esteem and other problems with self-image. They were also more likely to do poorly in school, to have more behavior problems at school and at home, and to drop out of school by the 10th grade. Early-maturing boys, by contrast, had more positive self-esteem and were more satisfied with their appearance (Blyth et al., 1983). In earlier research, Clausen (1975) found early maturation of adolescent boys to be particularly valued by lower-class boys.

For many middle and late adolescents, the workplace (in the form of part-time employment) emerges as an important context affecting both school activities and family life. Greenberger and Steinberg (1986) found, somewhat surprisingly, that teenage employment has more negative than positive consequences. Among other things, they found that part-time employment (*a*) erodes parental authority, since working adolescents are less economically dependent on the parents; (*b*) interferes with school work; (*c*) is associated with higher rates of alcohol and drug use, since adolescents have more money to spend; and (*d*) may foster the development of negative attitudes toward work itself, given the high-stress, low-pay jobs that most teenagers have (e.g., in fast-food restaurants). Greenberger and Steinberg's conclusions contrast quite sharply with the prevailing view of the 1970s, extolling the virtues of youth employment (see O'Malley et al., 1977). To the extent that part-time employment diverts adolescents from long-term goals, the consequences may indeed be negative and serious. We still need research on long-term effects to make this assessment.

The transition out of adolescence has its own set of problems and concerns, such as occupational considerations, marriage, continuing education, and parenthood. Mortimer, Lorence, and Kumka (1986) have done a detailed and sophisticated analysis of factors affecting the transition to adulthood for a sample of upper-middle-class men. The study is based on a sample of 700 men who entered the University of Michigan in 1962 and were interviewed again 10 years after college graduation. One of the strongest findings for this advantaged group of men was that their relationship with their fathers (e.g., perceived paternal support) had a strong effect on their occupational attainment. This effect was mediated largely through their development of self-competence and work values. Other factors were also found to affect occupational attainment, but for all of these advantaged men the transition to adulthood was relatively smooth.

The transition to adulthood may be more problematic for those lower in the stratification system. Coleman and Husen (1985) identify the shrinking job market in most Western democracies as a serious problem for youth. Youth unemployment, they maintain, has become a matter of serious concern, leaving a large number of young people in a stage of "redundancy" (1985: 8). Without steady, secure, and meaningful employment the transition to adulthood is problematic. This circumstance is, of course, particularly severe for the lowest social class strata. William Wilson (1987), in his analysis of economically depressed areas of Chicago, has dramatically and poignantly shown how the loss of jobs has created a large pool of unemployed and "unmarriageable" men, which contributes to the substantial increase of single-parent (mother-children) families and welfare dependency. A major contribution of Wilson's analysis is the demonstration of how changes in the economic system (e.g., the decline of heavy industry in the U.S. and the jobs associated with it) have ramifications for family structure, childrearing, intergenerational relations, and the transition from adolescence to adulthood.

Transition to adulthood is especially difficult for the underclass if it occurs "off-time." Furstenberg et al. (1987) and Burton (1985) examine the personal and intergenerational consequences of adolescent childbearing. Burton's (1985) study of 41 three-generation black families in Los Angeles examines the reverberations of teenage pregnancy on the entire lineage system. Almost all of the adolescent mothers expected their own mother (child's grandmother) to play a major role in the care of their child. However, most (83%) of these grandmothers refused to assume an active grandparent role. It conflicted with their own life plans and developmental agendas. The off-time event (i.e., early pregnancy and parenthood) not only interrupted the young mother's developmental tasks (e.g., schooling, being an adolescent in the "moratorium" identity stage) but also resulted in an off-time transition for their mothers.

Furstenberg and associates' (1987; Brooks-Gunn and Furstenberg, 1986) ambitious longitudinal study of adolescent mothers is based on 300 Baltimore women, first interviewed in the mid-1960s, shortly after they became pregnant, and 17 years later. Furstenberg et al. found adolescent motherhood to be a long-term handicap. However, they also found that not all of these women were doomed to a life of poverty and disadvantage. The major escape routes to a better life were (*a*) education—those who finished high school were better off; (*b*) restricting further childbearing—no more children within five years of the first; and (*c*) a stable marriage. The most interesting findings from the follow-up study are the consequences for the children of these mothers. Furstenberg et al. found that the children of teenage parents showed more symptoms of maladjustment (e.g., behavioral problems, withdrawal) than did the children whose mothers were older when they first became pregnant. Furstenberg et al. provide one of the few studies showing a connection between mothers' life courses and the lives of their children.[6]

CONCLUSION

Reflecting on the work of the 1980s, we notice considerable continuity with the themes of earlier decades. The mainstay topics are well represented: the relative influence of parents and peers; the degree of "storm and stress" during adolescence; the "generation gap" and intergenerational continuity; the effects of parental behavior; factors associated with "successful" socialization and those associated with deviance and problem behaviors. These are not very different from the concerns most parents of adolescents have: to prepare adolescents successfully for adulthood, avoiding some of the major problems and pitfalls along the way.

The past decade has not seen much theoretical development in the study of adolescence. Much of the research is atheoretical—descriptive or exploratory studies focused on some perceived problem of adolescent development, behavior, or relations with parents, guided largely by the findings of previous research. Little of it is involved in theory testing in any rigorous sense, that is, testing hypotheses derived from a clearly articulated theory (for an exception see Tallman et al., 1983, who develop and test hypotheses about family interaction and adolescent decision-making grounded in social exchange theory).

Most of the work, however, is loosely connected with one or another of the major theoretical perspectives associated with sociology and psychology. These perspectives tend to be used as guides to the study of some phenomenon, providing concepts and suggesting possible relationships and explanations. In this sense, we are likely to see the utilization of symbolic interactionism in studies dealing with self-concept, role relationships, reference groups (e.g., parents versus peers), and some aspects of socialization (e.g., development of values, beliefs, meanings). Learning theory in some form (especially "social learning theory") is also frequently utilized in studies of socialization and parental influence (e.g., modeling, vicarious learning). Conflict theories and exchange theories are less visible but occasionally appear in studies of parental power and parent-adolescent conflict. Developmental theories (usually of the Erikson or Kohlberg varieties) are most likely found in studies of the life course. Rarely is the aim to test, extend, or modify these theories in adolescence research.

Rather, they serve as general guides for what to study and how to study it.

Although the 1980s may not have produced much that is new regarding theory, the decade has seen a shift in orientation or point of view in the study of adolescence to a greater emphasis on social context and intercontext connections: between family and school and work, between generations, and between historical periods. There is also a more interdisciplinary consciousness reflected in the increased interest in the interactions of physiological, cognitive, and social processes in adolescence. These are trends that we hope will continue.

In their 1970s decade review of parent-child relationships, Walters and Walters (1980) identified a number of emerging themes: greater concern with reciprocal relationships; second-order effects; multiple influences; information from mothers, fathers, and children in families; and greater attention to the father-child bond. These are worthy directions of development, but they have been slow to emerge in the study of parent-adolescent relationships. Our hope is that they will be more evident in the 1990s.

NOTES

Work on this article was supported in part by Project 0700, Department of Rural Sociology, Agricultural Research Center, Washington State University.

1. There is no clear demarcation of this segment of the life course. Typically, it is associated with the "teenage" years, or with the period of life between childhood and maturity. There seems to be greater consensus with regard to the beginning of adolescence as the onset of puberty than with specifying its upper limit, which is more a matter of what society defines as "adulthood" (see Clausen, 1986). For that matter, the emergence of adolescence as a life stage category is considered a relatively recent historical phenomenon, closely associated with the institution of formal education in this country (Coleman and Husen, 1985). This connection with formal schooling has contributed to the ambiguity regarding the upper limit of adolescence, since the average length of formal schooling has been increasing, from high school to college and beyond. For most of the research that we review here, however, "adolescence" largely corresponds to the "teenage" years.

2. To get an overview of the substantive research on families and adolescents, we relied on Sociological Abstracts, various inventories (e.g., Inventory of Marriage and Family Literature, 1979–1986), references gathered from various books and review

chapters on adolescents, and systematic examinations of the following journals: *Youth and Society, Journal of Adolescent Research, Child Development, Journal of Adolescence, Journal of Marriage and the Family,* and *Journal of Youth and Adolescence.*

3. The term *values* has rather broad connotations here, reflecting the way it is used in the literature reviewed. It is used to refer not only to "values" per se (i.e., conceptions of the desirable) but also to such related terms as "attitudes" (e.g., toward marijuana use), "orientations" (e.g., toward educational attainment) and even "goals" (e.g., a college degree).

4. Parental support and control have appeared under various other labels as well. Some of the labels used to designate support are warmth, affection, nurturance, and acceptance. *Support* in its various forms indicates the degree of positive affect expressed by the parent toward the child. *Control* refers to the degree and manner in which parents attempt to place constraints on the child's behavior. Other labels used for this dimension are punishment, coercion, discipline, restrictiveness, power assertion, permissiveness, and induction (see Rollins and Thomas, 1979, and Peterson and Rollins, 1987, for more extensive discussions).

5. Along with reflected appraisals (i.e., how we think others see us), two other processes are important to self-evaluations: social comparisons and self-attributions (see Rosenberg, 1979, and Gecas, 1982, for discussions of these processes). Within the family research reviewed here, the latter two processes are rarely considered.

6. The kinds of methods used in studies of adolescence in the past decade span the gamut from ethnographies, archival studies, structured diaries, and longitudinal survey data, to data gathered from games and simulations. But for the most part, studies are based on cross-sectional structured interviews or questionnaires. There are few examples of laboratory or natural observation studies.

References

Acock, Alan C., and Vern L. Bengtson. 1980. "Socialization and attribution processes: Actual versus perceived similarities among parents and youth." Journal of Marriage and the Family 42: 501–515.

Acock, Alan C., and Wen Shan Yang. 1984. "Parental power and adolescents' parental identification." Journal of Marriage and the Family 46: 487–495.

Adams, Gerald R., and Steven A. Fitch. 1982. "Ego stage and identity status development: A cross-sequential analysis." Journal of Social Psychology 43: 574–583.

Alwin, Duane F., and Arland Thornton. 1984. "Family origins and the schooling process: Early versus late influence of parental characteristics." American Sociological Review 49: 784–802.

Bachman, Jerald G., Lloyd D. Johnston, and Patrick M. O'Malley. 1987. Monitoring the Future: Questionnaire Responses from the Nation's High School Seniors, 1986. Ann Arbor: University of Michigan, Institute for Social Research.

Barber, Brian K., and Darwin L. Thomas. 1986. "Dimensions of fathers' and mothers' supportive behavior: The case for physical affection." Journal of Marriage and the Family 48: 783–794.

Barnes, Grace M., Michael P. Farrell, and Allen Cairns. 1986. "Parental socialization factors and adolescent drinking behaviors." Journal of Marriage and the Family 48: 27–36.

Barnes, Grace M., and Michael Windle. 1987. "Family factors in adolescents' alcohol and drug abuse." Pediatrician 14: 13–18.

Baumeister, Roy F. 1986. Identity: Cultural Change and the Struggle for Self (Chapters 5 and 9). New York: Oxford University Press.

Baumrind, Diana. 1978. "Parental disciplinary patterns and social competence in children." Youth and Society 9: 239–276.

Baumrind, Diana. 1980. "New directions in socialization research." American Psychologist 35: 639–652.

Biddle, Bruce J., Barbara J. Bank, and Marjorie M. Marlin. 1980. "Parental and peer influence on adolescents." Social Forces 56: 1057–1079.

Blau, Peter M., and Otis D. Duncan. 1967. The American Occupational Structure. New York: Wiley.

Blos, Peter. 1962. On Adolescence: A Psychoanalytic Interpretation. New York: Free Press of Glencoe.

Blyth, Dale A., Roberta G. Simmons, and S. Carlton-Ford. 1983. "The adjustment of early adolescents to school transitions." Journal of Early Adolescence 3: 105–120.

Bohrnstedt, George W., and Gene A. Fisher. 1986. "The effects of recalled childhood and adolescent relationships compared to current role performances on young adults' affective functioning." Social Psychology Quarterly 49: 19–32.

Bronfenbrenner, Urie. 1970. Two Worlds of Childhood: U.S. and U.S.S.R. New York: Russell Sage Foundation.

Bronfenbrenner, Urie. 1979. The Ecology of Human Development: Experiments by Nature and Design. Cambridge, MA: Harvard University Press.

Bronfenbrenner, Urie. 1986. "Ecology of the family as a context for human development." Developmental Psychology 22: 723–742.

Brooks-Gunn, Jeanne, and Frank F. Furstenberg, Jr. 1986. "The children of adolescent mothers: Physical, academic and psychological outcomes." Developmental Review 6: 224–251.

Burton, Linda. 1985. Early and On-Time Grandmotherhood in Multigeneration Black Families. Unpublished PhD dissertation, University of Southern California.

Campbell, E., Gerald R. Adams, and W. R. Dobson. 1984. "Familial correlates of identity formation in late adolescence." Journal of Youth and Adolescence 13: 509–525.

Clark, Reginald M. 1983. Family Life and School Achievement: Why Poor Black Children Succeed or Fail. Chicago: University of Chicago Press.

Clausen, John A. 1975. "The social meaning of differential physical and sexual maturation." In S. E.

Dragastin and G. Elder (eds.), Adolescence in the Life Cycle. New York: Wiley.

Clausen, John A. 1986. The Life Course: A Sociological Perspective. Englewood Cliffs, NJ: Prentice-Hall.

Coleman, James S. 1961. The Adolescent Society. New York: Free Press.

Coleman, James S., and Torsten Husen. 1985. Becoming Adult in a Changing Society. Paris, France: Centre for Educational Research and Innovation.

Conger, John Janeway. 1981. "Freedom and commitment: Families, youth and social change." American Psychologist 36: 1475–1484.

Csikszentmihalyi, Mihaly, and Reed Larson. 1984. Being Adolescent. New York: Basic Books.

Davies, Mark, and Denise B. Kandel. 1981. "Parental and peer influences on adolescents' education plans: Some further evidence." American Journal of Sociology 87: 363–387.

Davis, Kingsley. 1940. "The sociology of parent-youth conflict." American Sociological Review 5: 523–535.

Demo, David H., and Alan C. Acock. 1988. "The impact of divorce on children." Journal of Marriage and the Family 50: 619–648. [Reprinted in this volume]

Demo, David H., Stephen A. Small, and Ritch C. Savin-Williams. 1987. "Family relations and the self-esteem of adolescents and their parents." Journal of Marriage and the Family 49: 705–716.

Dornbusch, Sanford. 1989. "The sociology of adolescence." Annual Review of Sociology 15: 233–259.

Duncan, Greg J., and Willard L. Rogers. 1988. Longitudinal aspects of childhood poverty." Journal of Marriage and the Family 50: 1007–1022.

Dusek, Jerome B., and John F. Flaherty. 1981. The Development of the Self-Concept during the Adolescent Years. Monograph of the Society for Research in Child Development 46: 1–67.

Elder, Glen H., Jr. 1974. Children of the Great Depression. Chicago: University of Chicago Press.

Elder, Glen H., Jr. 1980. "Adolescence in historical perspective." Pp. 3–46 in J. Adelson (ed.), Handbook of Adolescent Psychology. New York: Wiley.

Elder, Glen H., Jr. (ed.). 1985. Life Course Dynamics: Trajectories and Transitions, 1968–1980. Ithaca, NY: Cornell University Press.

Elder, Glen H., Jr. 1986. "Military timing and turning points in men's lives." Developmental Psychology 22: 233–245.

Elder, Glen H., Jr., A. Caspi, and T. Van Nguyen. 1986. "Resourceful and vulnerable children: Family influences in stressful times." In R. K. Silbereisen, K. Eyferth, and G. Rudinger (eds.), Development as Action in Context: Problem Behavior and Normal Youth Development. New York: Springer-Verlag.

Elder, Glen H., Jr., G. Downey, and C. E. Cross. 1986. "Family ties and life chances: Hard times and hard choices in women's lives since the Great Depression." In N. Datan, A. L. Greene, and H. W. Reese (eds.), Life-Span Developmental Psychology: Intergenerational Relations. Hillsdale, NJ: Erlbaum.

Elder, Glen H., Jr., J. K. Liker, and C. E. Cross.

1984. "Parent-child behavior in the Great Depression: Life course and intergenerational influences." Pp. 109–158 in P. B. Baltes and O. G. Brim, Jr. (eds.), Life-Span Development and Behavior (Vol. 6). Hillsdale, NJ: Erlbaum.

Elder, Glen H., Jr., T. Van Nguyen, and A. Caspi. 1985. "Linking family hardship to children's lives." Child Development 56: 361–375.

Erikson, Erik H. 1959. Identity and the Life Cycle. New York: International Universities.

Erikson, Erik H. 1968. Identity, Youth, and Crisis. New York: Norton.

Featherman, David L. 1980. "Schooling and occupational careers: Constancy and change in worldly success." Pp. 675–738 in O. G. Brim, Jr., and J. Kagan (eds.), Constancy and Change in Human Development. Cambridge, MA: Harvard University Press.

Featherman, David L. 1981. "Social stratification and mobility: Two decades of cumulative social science." American Behavior Science 24: 364–385.

Felson, Richard B., and Mary A. Zielinski. 1989. "Children's self-esteem and parental support." Journal of Marriage and the Family 51: 727–736.

Fine, Gary Alan. 1981. "Friends, impression management, and preadolescent behavior." Pp. 257–272 in Gregory Stone and Harvey Farberman (eds.), Social Psychology through Symbolic Interaction. New York: Wiley.

Fine, Gary Alan. 1987. With the Boys: Little League Baseball and Preadolescent Culture. Chicago: University of Chicago Press.

French, J. R. P., Jr., and B. Raven. 1959. "The bases of social power." Pp. 150–165 in D. Cartwright (ed.), Studies in Social Power. Ann Arbor: Research Center for Group Dynamics, Institute for Social Research, University of Michigan.

Freud, Anna. 1958. "Adolescence." Psychoanalytic Study of the Child 13: 255–278.

Furstenberg, Frank F., Jr., Jeanne Brooks-Gunn, and S. Philip Morgan. 1987. Adolescent Mothers in Later Life. New York: Cambridge University Press.

Furstenberg, Frank F., Jr., C. W. Nord, J. L. Peterson, and N. Zill. 1983. "The life course of children of divorce: Marital disruption and parental conflict." American Sociological Review 48: 656–668.

Galambos, Nancy L., and Rainer K. Silbereisen. 1987. "Income change, parental life outlook, and adolescent expectations for job success." Journal of Marriage and the Family 49: 141–149.

Gecas, Viktor. 1981. "Contexts of socialization." Pp. 165–199 in M. Rosenberg and R. H. Turner (eds.), Social Psychology: Sociological Perspectives. New York: Basic Books.

Gecas, Viktor. 1982. "The self-concept." Annual Review of Sociology 8: 1–33.

Gecas, Viktor, and Michael L. Schwalbe. 1986. "Parental behavior and adolescent self-esteem." Journal of Marriage and the Family 48: 37–46.

Greenberger, Ellen, and Laurence Steinberg. 1986. When Teenagers Work: The Psychological and Social Costs of Adolescent Employment. New York: Basic Books.

Grotevant, Harold D., and Catherine R. Cooper.

1986. "Individuation in family relationships." Human Development 29: 82–100.

Grube, Joel W., Mark Morgan, and Monica Seff. 1989. "Drinking beliefs and behaviors among Irish adolescents." International Journal of Addictions 24: 101–112.

Hall, G. Stanley. 1904. Adolescence: Its Psychology and Its Relation to Physiology, Anthropology, Sociology, Sex, Crime, Religion, and Education. New York: D. Appleton.

Harter, Susan. 1983. "Developmental perspectives on the self-system." Pp. 273–385 in E. M. Hetherington (ed.), Handbook of Child Psychology: Socialization, Personality, and Social Development. New York: Wiley.

Hauser, Stuart T., Sally I. Powers, Gil Noam, and Mary Kay Bowlds. 1987. "Family interiors of adolescent ego development trajectories." Family Perspective 21: 263–282.

Hill, Gary D., and Maxine P. Atkinson. 1988. "Gender, familial control, and delinquency." Criminology 26: 127–149.

Hirschi, Travis. 1989. "Family structure and crime." Paper presented at the Social Costs of Family Breakdown Conference sponsored by the Rockford Institute Center on the Family in America, Rockford, Illinois.

Hoelter, Jon, and Lynn Harper. 1987. "Structural and interpersonal family influences on adolescent self-conception." Journal of Marriage and the Family 49: 129–140.

Hoffman, L. W., and J. B. Manis. 1978. "Influences of children on marital interaction and parental satisfactions and dissatisfactions." Pp. 164–214 in R. M. Lerner and G. B. Spanier (eds.), Child Influences on Marital and Family Interaction: A Life-Span Perspective. New York: Academic Press.

Huston, Aletha C. 1983. "Sex-typing." Pp. 387–467 in Paul H. Mussen (ed.), Handbook of Child Psychology (Vol. 4). New York: Wiley and Sons.

Inventory of Marriage and Family Literature, 1979–1986. St. Paul: University of Minnesota.

Jessop, Dorothy Jones. 1981. "Family relationships as viewed by parents and adolescents: A specification." Journal of Marriage and the Family 43: 95–107.

Juster, Susan M., and Maris A. Vinovskis. 1987. "Changing perspectives on the American family in the past." Annual Review of Sociology 13: 193–216.

Kandel, Denise B. 1985. "On processes of peer influences in adolescent drug use: A developmental perspective." Advances in Alcohol and Substance Abuse 4: 139–163.

Kohn, Melvin L. 1983. "On the transmission of values in the family: A preliminary formulation." Pp. 1–12 in A. C. Kerckhoff (ed.), Research in Sociology of Education and Socialization (Vol. 4). Greenwich, CT: JAI Press.

Kohn, Melvin L., Kazimierz M. Slomczynski, and Carrie Schoenbach. 1986. "Social stratification and the transmission of values in the family: A cross-national assessment." Sociological Forum 1: 73–103.

Liker, Jeffrey K., and Glen H. Elder, Jr. 1983. "Economic hardships and marital relations in the 1930s." American Sociological Review 48: 343–359.

Losh-Hesselbart, Susan. 1987. "Development of gender roles." Pp. 535–563 in M. B. Sussman and S. K. Steinmetz (eds.), Handbook of Marriage and the Family. New York: Plenum Press.

Loy, Pamela, and Stephen Norland. 1981. "Parent and peer influence on adolescents' gender expectations." Youth and Society 13: 175–187.

Maccoby, Eleanor E., and J. A. Martin. 1983. "Socialization in the context of the family: Parent-child interaction." Pp. 1–101 in P. H. Mussen (ed.), Handbook of Child Psychology (Vol. 4). New York: Wiley.

MacLeod, Jay. 1987. Ain't No Makin' It: Leveled Aspirations in a Low-Income Neighborhood. Boulder, CO: Westview Press.

Marcia, James E. 1966. "Development and evaluation of ego identity status." Journal of Personality and Social Psychology 3: 551–558.

Marcia, James E. 1980. "Identity in adolescence." Pp. 159–187 in J. Adelson (ed.), Handbook of Adolescent Psychology. New York: John Wiley and Sons.

Marjoribanks, Kevin. 1987. "Gender/social class, family environments and adolescents' aspirations." Australian Journal of Education 31: 43–54.

McBroom, William H., Fred W. Reed, Clarence E. Burns, J. Lee Hargraves, and Mary A. Trankel. 1985. "Intergenerational transmission of values: A data-based reassessment." Social Psychology Quarterly 48: 150–163.

McDonald, Gerald W. 1980. "Parental power and adolescents' parental identification: A re-examination." Journal of Marriage and the Family 42: 289–296.

McDonald, Gerald W. 1982. "Parental power perceptions in the family: The influence of adolescent characteristics." Youth and Society 14: 3–32.

McLanahan, Sara, and Karen Booth. 1989. "Mother-only families: Problems, prospects, and politics." Journal of Marriage and the Family 51: 557–580. [Reprinted in this volume]

Modell, John. 1989. Into One's Own: From Youth to Adulthood in the United States, 1920–1975. Berkeley: University of California Press.

Montemayor, Raymond. 1983. "Parents and adolescents in conflict: All families some of the time and some families most of the time." Journal of Early Adolescence 3: 83–103.

Montemayor, Raymond. 1984. "Maternal employment and adolescents' relations with parents, siblings, and peers." Journal of Youth and Adolescence 13: 543–557.

Mortimer, Jeylan T., and Donald S. Kumka. 1982. "A further examination of the 'occupational linkage hypothesis'." Sociological Quarterly 23: 3–16.

Mortimer, Jeylan T., Jon Lorence, and Donald S. Kumka. 1986. Work, Family, and Personality: Transitions to Adulthood. New Jersey: Ablex.

Norem-Hebeisen, Ardyth, David W. Johnson, Douglas Anderson, and Roger Johnson. 1984. "Predictors and concomitants of changes in drug use patterns among teenagers." Journal of Social Psychology 124: 43–50.

Offer, Daniel, Eric Ostrov, and Kenneth I. Howard. 1981. The Adolescent: A Psychological Self-Portrait. New York: Basic Books.

Offer, Daniel, Eric Ostrov, Kenneth I. Howard, and Robert Atkinson. 1988. The Teenage World. Adolescents' Self-Image in Ten Countries. New York: Plenum.

O'Malley, Patrick et al., 1977. Five Years Beyond High School. Causes and Consequences of Educational Attainment. Final Report. National Institute of Education, Washington, DC.

O'Malley, Patrick, and Jerald Bachman. 1983. "Self-esteem: Change and stability between ages 13 and 23." Developmental Psychology 19: 257–268.

Openshaw, D. Kim, and Darwin L. Thomas. 1986. "The adolescent self and the family." Pp. 104–129 in G. K. Leigh and G. W. Peterson (eds.), Adolescents in Families. Cincinnati: South-Western.

Openshaw, D. Kim, Darwin L. Thomas, and Boyd C. Rollins. 1983. "Socialization and adolescent self-esteem: Symbolic interaction and social learning explanations." Adolescence 18: 317–329.

Pasley, Kay, and Viktor Gecas. 1984. "Stresses and satisfactions of the parental role." Personnel and Guidance Journal 2: 400–404.

Peters, John F. 1984. "Youth, family, and employment." Adolescence 22: 465–473.

Peterson, Gary W., and Boyd C. Rollins. 1987. "Parent-child socialization: A review of research and applications of symbolic interaction concepts." Pp. 471–507 in M. B. Sussman and S. K. Steinmetz (eds.), Handbook of Marriage and the Family. New York: Plenum Press.

Peterson, Gary W., Boyd C. Rollins, and Darwin L. Thomas. 1985. "Parental influence and adolescent conformity: Compliance and internalization." Youth and Society 16: 397–420.

Peterson, Gary W., Boyd C. Rollins, Darwin L. Thomas, and G. H. Ellis. 1980. "Multiple dimensions of parental control and support." Paper presented at the annual meeting of the National Council on Family Relations, Portland, Oregon.

Peterson, Gary W., Boyd C. Rollins, Darwin L. Thomas, and L. Kay Heaps. 1982. "Social placement of adolescents: Sex-role influences on family decisions regarding the careers of youth." Journal of Marriage and the Family 44: 647–658.

Reed, Fred W., William H. McBroom, Dale M. Lindekugel, Virginia Roberts, and Anastasia M. Tureck. 1986. "Perceived value similarity in the transition to adulthood: A study with parents and peers." Youth and Society 17: 267–285.

Rice, F. Philip. 1975. The Adolescent: Development, Relationships, and Culture. Boston: Allyn and Bacon.

Robertson, Joan F., and Ronald L. Simons. 1989. "Family factors, self-esteem, and adolescent depression." Journal of Marriage and the Family 51: 125–138.

Rollins, Boyd C., and Harold Feldman. 1970. "Marital satisfaction over the family life cycle." Journal of Marriage and the Family 32: 20–28.

Rollins, Boyd C., and Darwin L. Thomas. 1979.

"Parental support, power, and control techniques in the socialization of children." Pp. 317–364 in W. R. Burr, R. Hill, F. I. Nye, and I. L. Reiss (eds.), Contemporary Theories about the Family (Vol. 1). New York: Free Press.

Rosenberg, Morris. 1979. Conceiving the Self. New York: Basic Books.

Rosenberg, Morris. 1985. "Self-concept and psychological well-being in adolescence." In R. Leahy (ed.), The Development of the Self. New York: Academic Press.

Rosenberg, Morris. 1986. "Self-concept from middle childhood through adolescence." Pp. 107–136 in J. Suls and A. Greenwald (eds.), Psychological Perspectives on the Self (Vol. 3). Hillsdale, NJ: Lawrence Erlbaum.

Rosenberg, Morris, and Claire B. McCullough. 1981. "Mattering: Inferred significance and mental health among adolescents." Research in Community and Mental Health 2: 163–182.

Schwartz, Gary. 1987. Beyond Conformity or Rebellion: Youth and Authority in America. Chicago: University of Chicago Press.

Sebald, Hans. 1986. "Adolescents' shifting orientation toward parents and peers: A curvilinear trend over recent decades." Journal of Marriage and the Family 48: 5–13.

Sewell, William H., and Robert M. Hauser. 1980. "The Wisconsin longitudinal study of social and psychological factors in aspirations and achievements." Research in Sociology of Education and Socialization 1: 59–99.

Sewell, William H., Robert M. Hauser, and Wendy C. Wolf. 1980. "Sex, schooling, and occupational status." American Journal of Sociology 86: 551–583.

Silverberg, Susan B., and Laurence Steinberg. 1987. "Adolescent autonomy, parent-adolescent conflict, and parental well-being." Journal of Youth and Adolescence 16: 293–312.

Simmons, Roberta G., and Dale A. Blyth. 1987. Moving into Adolescence: The Impact of Pubertal Change and School Context. New York: Aldine DeGruyter.

Simmons, Roberta G., Dale A. Blyth, and K. L. McKinney. 1983. "The social and psychological effects of puberty on white females." In J. Brooks-Gunn and A. Petersen (eds.), Girls at Puberty: Biological and Psychosocial Perspectives. New York: Plenum.

Simmons, Roberta G., Dale A. Blyth, Edward F. Van Cleave, and Diane M. Bush. 1979. "Entry into early adolescence: The impact of school structure, puberty, and early dating on self-esteem." American Sociological Review 44: 948–967.

Simons, Ronald L., and Martin G. Miller. 1987. "Adolescent depression: Assessing the impact of negative cognitions and socio-environmental problems." Social Work 32: 326–330.

Small, Stephen A., Steven Cornelius, and Gay Eastman. 1983. "Parenting adolescent children: A period of adult storm and stress?" Paper presented at the annual meeting of the American Psychological

Association, Anaheim, CA.

Smith, David M. 1985. "Perceived peer and parental influences on youths' social world." Youth and Society 17: 131–156.

Smith, Thomas Ewin. 1981. "Adolescent agreement with perceived maternal and paternal educational goals." Journal of Marriage and the Family 43: 85–93.

Smith, Thomas Ewin. 1983. "Parental influence: A review of the evidence of influence and a theoretical model of the parental influence process." Research in Sociology of Education and Socialization 4: 13–46.

Steinberg, Laurence. 1987. "Recent research on the family at adolescence: The extent and nature of sex differences." Journal of Youth and Adolescence 16: 191–197.

Steinberg, Laurence, J. D. Elmen, and N. Mounts. 1989. "Authoritative parenting, psychosocial maturity, and academic success among adolescents." Child Development 60: 1424–1436.

Steinberg, Laurence, and Susan Silverberg. 1986. "The vicissitudes of autonomy in early adolescence." Child Development 57: 841–851.

Steinitz, Victoria A., and Ellen R. Solomon. 1986. Starting Out: Class and Community in the Lives of Working-Class Youth. Philadelphia: Temple University Press.

Stryker, Sheldon. 1980. Symbolic Interactionism: A Social Structural Version. Menlo Park, CA: Benjamin/Cummings.

Tallman, Irving, Ramona Marotz-Baden, and Pablo Pindas. 1983. Adolescent Socialization in Cross-Cultural Perspective. New York: Academic Press.

Tedin, Kent L. 1980. "Assessing peer and parent influence on adolescent political attitudes."

American Journal of Political Science 24: 136–154.

Thomas, Darwin L., Viktor Gecas, Andrew Weigert, and Elizabeth Rooney. 1974. Family Socialization and the Adolescent. Lexington, MA: D. C. Heath.

Thornton, Arland, Duane F. Alwin, and Donald Camburn. 1983. "Causes and consequences of sex-role attitudes and attitude change." American Sociological Review 48: 211–227.

Umberson, Debra. 1989. "Relationships with children: Explaining parents' psychological well-being." Journal of Marriage and the Family 51: 999–1012.

Walters, James, and Lynda H. Walters. 1980. "Parent-child relationships: A review, 1970–1979." Journal of Marriage and the Family 42: 807–824.

Whitbeck, Les B., and Viktor Gecas. 1988. "Value attribution and transmission between parents and children." Journal of Marriage and the Family 50: 829–840.

Wilson, Harriett. 1980. "Parental supervision: A neglected aspect of delinquency." British Journal of Criminology 20: 203–235.

Wilson, Harriett. 1987. "Parental supervision re-examined." British Journal of Criminology 27: 275–301.

Wilson, William Julius. 1987. The Truly Disadvantaged: The Inner City, the Underclass, and Public Policy. Chicago: University of Chicago Press.

Wilson, William Julius, and Robert Aponte. 1985. "Urban poverty." Annual Review of Sociology 11: 231–258.

Youniss, James. 1980. Parents and Peers in Social Development: A Sullivan-Piaget Perspective. Chicago: University of Chicago Press.

Youniss, James, and Jacqueline Smollar. 1985. Adolescent Relations with Mothers, Fathers, and Friends. Chicago: University of Chicago Press.

Timothy H. Brubaker   *Miami University*

Families in Later Life:
A Burgeoning Research Area

Research focusing on families who are beyond the child-rearing years and have begun to launch their children is reviewed. These later-life families are characterized by continuity and change as they experience marriage, divorce, widowhood, remarriage, childlessness, grandparenthood, sibling relationships, and family caregiving. Challenges and suggestions for future research focusing on middle-aged and older persons' family relationships are presented.

During the 1980s, family scholars and social gerontologists dramatically increased their attention to families in later life. In a listing of the major studies that focused on later-life families in the 1960s, Troll (1971) identified a total of 16. Streib and Beck (1980) commented on the increased number of studies focusing on older-family patterns during the next decade, but the 1980s brought an explosion of research on the later portions of the life cycle. Research on later-life families appears in all of the major scholarly journals in family studies (e.g., *Journal of Marriage and the Family, Family Relations, Journal of Gerontology, The Gerontologist, Journal of Family Issues*) as well as other journals published in the fields of sociology, psychology, social work, home economics, economics, and political science. Many of these journals have published special issues or collections on this topic. The

Family and Child Studies Center, Miami University, Oxford, OH 45056. (This document is #5–90 of the Family and Child Studies Center manuscript series, Miami University, Oxford, OH 45056.)

voluminous publications that appeared during the 1980s suggest that the study of later-life families has come into vogue. With the increased number of families entering the later years and the aging of the baby boom generation, it is likely that this interest will continue in the future.

This review synthesizes research of the 1980s on the family patterns of middle-aged and older persons. After two background issues (definition of later-life families and the status of the elderly) are discussed, the following topics are addressed: couple relationships, divorce, widowhood, remarriage, childless families, grandparenthood, sibling relationships, and family caregiving. Since Mancini and Blieszner (1989) recently reviewed research on relationships between adult children and older parents, and other reviews (Bengtson, 1989; Bengtson, Cutler, Mangen, and Marshall, 1985) have been published on intergenerational relationships, these topics will not be considered here. Directions for research in the 1990s conclude this review.

BACKGROUND ISSUES

Later-life families can be examined from the perspective of family development. The definition presented herein is premised on the assumption that families experience new challenges associated with the middle and later years (T. Brubaker, 1986). The structure of the family (e.g., cultural and ethnic background, social class) and interactional characteristics (e.g., patterns and perceptions of interaction, feelings of obligation and affection) influence familial strategies for dealing with these challenges. Thus, a brief discussion of family structure and the status of older persons is included.

Definition of Later-Life Families

Middle-aged and older persons are members of later-life families. From the developmental framework, later-life families have been defined as "families who are beyond the child-rearing years and have begun to launch their children" (Brubaker, 1983: 9). Attention within the nuclear family is directed toward the contraction of the family unit and focuses on the maintenance of relationships with the remaining members of the nuclear unit as well as the establishment and maintenance of ties with independent offspring. As children mature and become relatively independent, both two-parent and one-parent families experience the changing demands of contraction during the later years. Although some adult children may return to the nuclear family (Suitor and Pillemer, 1987, 1988), most establish independent relationships. When this occurs, middle-aged and older parents begin to reorganize their lives. For childless individuals, the later years begin as plans for and the anticipation of retirement becomes a crucial consideration for major decisions within the family. In most instances, later-life families differ from younger families because they have a lengthy family history, or track record (Brubaker, 1983, 1985a). The importance of family history in the study of later-life families is increasingly noted. For example, family history provides an understanding of the way in which such families assign meaning to everyday events (Gubrium, 1988) as well as the responsibilities shared by caregiving daughters and sons (Matthews and Rosner, 1988). The historical perspective of family interactions provides an understanding of the continuity of later-life families while they are challenged by developmental changes. Consequently, it is not surprising that this unique characteristic of later-life families has been identified as crucial in understanding family caregiving during the later years (Brubaker and Brubaker, 1989).

Family relationships are important ingredients in the lives of older persons, and to fully define later-life families, several key factors (e.g., expectations and satisfactions with family, overall morale, health, and changing family responsibilities) must be considered. Seelbach and Hansen

(1980) examined older persons' expectations associated with their family relationships. Generally, there is satisfaction with family relationships in later life, and the elderly do not feel neglected or abandoned by their relatives. In a study of elderly women (Hildreth, Van Laanen, Kelley, and Durant, 1980), enjoyment with family relationships was evident. Nontask activities such as sharing conversation with a relative were the most enjoyable family activities. Aldous (1987) reported that intergenerational relationships were vibrant, voluntary, affectional, and consensual for a sample of 124 couples in their early and mid-60s. Intergenerational exchanges reflected a pattern of using "surplus resources to alleviate deficits in the other generation's living economy" (Aldous, 1987: 231). There is no doubt that family interactions, especially the interpersonal liasons, are meaningful to men and women in their later years. For many individuals, the family is a vital, contributing support group that provides enjoyment and support to older family members during favorable and unfavorable circumstances. The ways in which family members contribute to the lives of middle-aged and older people vary depending on the family situation.

While individuals are generally satisfied with their family relationships in later life, the contribution of these relationships to individual morale is less clear. Research suggests that kinship interaction has little or no effect on an older person's feelings of well-being or morale (Lee and Ellithorpe, 1982; Lee and Ihinger-Tallman, 1980). Mutual assistance may characterize the older parent–adult child relationship, but the ability to provide assistance has little effect on older persons' morale (Lee and Ellithorpe, 1982). Stoller (1985) noted that the inability to reciprocate when receiving assistance had a negative effect on the morale of older persons. Family relationships (i.e., adult children, siblings, grandchildren) are important to older persons, but feelings of morale or well-being may be derived from factors independent of kinship interaction (e.g., interaction with friends or neighbors, health).

Health is a primary predictor of the well-being of older parents (Quinn, 1983). The more health difficulties experienced in later life, the more likely morale will be negatively affected. Health also affects family members' interactions with one another. Another study (Hennon and Burton, 1986) reported that older persons' feelings of satisfaction with their financial situations are related to their health. As changes in health inhibit the daily activities of older family members, other, more healthy family members are expected to provide assistance while still maintaining the independence of the less healthy (Mutran and Reitzes, 1984; Quinn, 1983). Thus, health is a salient variable in the study of family patterns in later life.

During the middle and later years, family roles and responsibilities are characterized by continuity and change. As children become independent, spouses retire, social networks differ, and health changes, individuals and their families reorganize their roles and responsibilities. For many older families, there is a lengthy family history from which the usual later-life changes are viewed. Nonetheless, the changes experienced in the later years can result in challenges for older persons (Blieszner and Mancini, 1987). Although older parents in the Blieszner and Mancini (1987) study had been engaged in the parenting role for many years, they expressed ambiguity about their role in the later years. Discussion with their children regarding future caregiving expectations and division of property upon death was desired, but most were uncertain about how to address these topics with their children. The older parents' expectations for their children centered around affection, respect, responsibility, assistance, and open communication, and they wanted their relationships with their children to be characterized by sharing, warmth, affection, and avoidance of direct interference in each others' lives. As individuals mature and experience changes in their familial, social, economic, and health situations, the family becomes increasingly important for many. But the interpersonal relationships change as the situations change and the later-life family patterns are marked by continuity as well as innovation.

Family Structure and Status of the Elderly

To understand the relationships of families in later life, a societal perspective identifying the interrelationships between the economy, family, and individual needs to be recognized. During the 1980s several studies examined family structure and the status of the elderly. Industrialization and modernization within societies are often identified as characteristics associated with relatively low status of the elderly. Decline of extended-family structure and the predominance of the nuclear family unit may result in a lowering of the status of the elderly. Balkwell and Balswick (1981) examined the issue of economic development, family structure, and the status of the elderly in preindustrial societies. Their findings suggested that elderly are most advantaged in agricultural societies because they are afforded opportunities to participate in useful activities and become sources of information. Family structure (i.e., independent nuclear, independent polygamous, stem, small extended, or large extended) did not clearly explain the status of the elderly. With the exception of the transfer of family wealth, family variables contributed little to the status of the elderly. Similarly, Lee (1984) and Ishii-Kuntz and Lee (1987) observed that elderly persons enjoyed the highest status in the agricultural technologies and lower status in exploitative (hunting, gathering, fishing) societies. Lee also noted that family structure had some influence on the status of the elderly. Both men and women experienced higher status in small extended (stem or lineal) family systems, although this may be confounded with residence. For example, status is highest in patrilocal family systems, higher in unilocal, and lowest in neolocal. Lee (1984: 273) commented that status is derived from seniority when kin groups are "localized, internally integrated and organized according to hierarchical principles with centralized authority."

Emphasis on conformity to parental value is also related to higher status for elderly persons (Ishii-Kuntz and Lee, 1978). Societies in which the socialization process emphasizes self-reliance of offspring over conformity to parents' system of values place a lower value on the elderly. Modern industrial societies encourage the independence of the younger generations, and consequently, it is not surprising that older persons receive less status than in agricultural societies in which conformity to the senior generation is reinforced. Ishii-Kuntz and Lee (1987) found a correlation between ancestor worship and the status of the elderly, but the relationship was correlated with other familial factors. For example, societies that practiced ancestor worship also emphasized conformity to parental values and placed a higher value on older persons. These data indicate that family structure and other family factors may be related to the status societies assign to older members.

Analyses of social structure, economic development, family structure, and other familial factors of various societies provide insight into the relative status of older persons. Later-life families enjoy varying positions within a kinship network as a result of the status held by their older members. Differences between exploitative, agrarian, and industrial societies define the context in which contemporary family patterns in later life may be understood. Continued analyses of economic and kinship structures on a societal level are needed to further clarify the influence of family structural variables on the status of older family members.

The Married Couple Relationship

Most married older couples have a relationship that has endured, and their experiences in later life can be intimately shared with a marital partner. The experiences of children leaving home, retirement, traveling, and other leisure activities may be enhanced if they are shared with a spouse. Changes related to health problems and decreased mobility can also be shared. In the middle and later years, marriage "for better or worse" has meaning because individuals experience positive, enjoyable situations as well as negative, difficult changes. For most married middle-aged and elderly persons, spouses provide extraordinary companionship and support throughout the later years. There is a continuity in the marital experiences that can be seen by examining the family history, or track record (Brubaker, 1985a). In the later years, those who have vital, rewarding relationships will most generally experience continued positive interactions within the marriage, while those who have difficult, unsatisfying relationships will most likely experience continued negative marital interactions.

The later years provide an opportunity for change in a couple's relationship because they may no longer be employed and can focus on their relationship more fully. Keith, Dobson, Goudy, and Powers (1981) noted that the structure of employment influenced involvement in the household tasks of middle-aged and older men. Further, it was reported that involvement in masculine household tasks was positively related to feelings of well-being, while involvement in feminine tasks had little impact on well-being. For traditionally oriented marriages, husband's retirement provides time to share in activities around the house. Keating and Cole's (1980) study of 400 retired teachers and their wives and Szinovacz's (1980) analysis of retired women and their spouses found that husbands did not increase their participation in household activities. Rather, they continued the patterns (many of which were traditionally divided) they had established before retirement. Brubaker and Hennon (1982) found little change in the division of household tasks in a sample of women in dual-earner and dual-retired families. Although the dual-earner and dual-retired women expected to share household tasks after retirement, few of the dual-retired reported changes in previous traditional household tasks. One study (Dobson, 1983) noted some sharing of less traditional divisions of household tasks in elderly marriages. In analysis of data from a sample of couples married 50 years or more, Brubaker (1985b; Ade-Ridder and Brubaker, 1988; Brubaker and Ade-Ridder, 1988; Brubaker and Kinsel, 1985) found some sharing of activities even though the couples supported a traditional division of household tasks. For the most part, middle-aged and older couples continue to follow household division-of-labor patterns established earlier in their marriages even though they expect to share more after they retire.

Retirement may not result in the redistribution of household tasks but can influence the older couple's marital relationship. During the middle years, marital satisfaction appears to be lower than during the earlier years of marriage (Anderson, Russell, and Schumm, 1983; Rhyne, 1981; Schumm and Bugaighis, 1986; Swenson, Eskew, and Kohlhepp, 1981). Some research (Anderson et al., 1983; Johnson, White, Edwards, and Booth, 1986), suggested that marital satisfaction increases in the later years. One study (Gilford, 1984) concluded that older couples may experience a "honeymoon" phase after retirement because they are no longer encumbered by the demands of work and can spend time with one another. However, a recent study (Lee and Shehan, 1989) found no relationship between retirement and marital satisfaction. Ade-Ridder and Brubaker (1983) hypothesized that an older couple's marital satisfaction may be related to the support each spouse receives from the other after retirement. It has also been suggested (Brubaker, 1985a) that different types of retirement and the timing of retirement ("traditional—single retiree," "dissynchronized—husband initially," "dissynchronized—wife initially," "synchronized") may affect marital relationships in later life. Lee and Shehan's (1989) study of marital satisfaction and retirement suggests that an employed wife with a retired husband experiences lower marital satisfaction than a wife in a dual-retired situation or in a relationship where she has retired first. Szinovacz (1980) noted that women experience more difficulty with retirement than men and the retirement of a wife is a couple event to which both the husband and wife must adjust. Another change after retirement relates to the way in which older couples spend money. Two studies (Chen and Chu, 1982; McConnel and Deljavan, 1983) suggest that retired couples spend more on food, utilities, medical and personal care, and gifts and contributions than middle-aged, nonretired couples. While retirement is a life event that creates some changes in middle-aged and older couples' lives, the research indicates that couples who provide support to one another seem to have developed a continuity that helps them adjust to the retirement changes.

Compared to retirement, changes in the health situation of older persons may be more influential on the marital satisfaction and interactions between marital partners (Keating and Cole, 1980). A number of studies (Johnson, 1983; Johnson and Catalano, 1983; Stone, Cafferata, and Sangl, 1987) indicate that spouses, both husbands and wives, become the primary caregiver when necessary. The support provided by spouses affects interactions within the marriage as well as with individuals outside of the marriage. Johnson (1985) examined elderly couples in which either the husband or wife was recuperating from a hospital stay. The couples reported high marital adjustment and dealt positively with the demands of providing care for their ill spouse. The caregiving spouses were prepared to provide care for a long period of time. While gender made little difference in the couple relationship, husbands reported less stress and more help from other relatives than did wives when caring for their spouses. Other studies (E. Brubaker, 1986; Fitting, Rabins, Lucas, and Eastham, 1986; Zarit, Todd, and Zarit, 1986) also suggest that caregiving wives may experience more depression and feelings of burden than husbands. Married couples share the problems associated with health difficulties, and even though feelings of stress and burden are evident, their marital adjustment scores are high (Johnson, 1985).

Research challenge: As middle-aged couples enter retirement, the distribution of household tasks may differ because there may be greater awareness of an egalitarian division of household tasks. The interrelationship between work and family life in retirement needs further examination. Do "single-retiree" differ from "dual-retiree" marriages (e.g., differing divisions of household tasks, decision making, satisfaction)? How does the timing of the husband's and wife's retirement influence the marital relationship? Further explorations of middle-aged and older couples need to address the positive as well as the negative aspects of the marital relationship. For example, does retirement exacerbate the positive and negative characteristics? What are the positive and negative consequences of spousal caregiving in later life?

DIVORCE

Although a sizable number of middle-aged and older persons are divorced, little research has focused on divorce in later life. Berardo (1983) suggested that adjustments are often required following divorce during the middle years because of the loss of finances and social contacts with friends and relatives. For elderly persons, divorce may change the social support networks. How do divorced elderly compare to married older persons in the areas of finances, health, and feelings of satisfaction? Hennon (1983) and Uhlenberg and Meyers (1981) suggested that divorced or separated older persons feel disadvantaged and dissatisfied with their financial situation. Indeed, Weiss's (1984) study of the economic situation of single-parent households after divorce found that divorced persons' income declined substantially and did not rise over a 5-year period even though married persons' income evidenced increases during the same 5-year period. However, in a study of unmarried (e.g., divorced, widowed, never-married) older persons, Keith (1986b, 1989) found differences between the financial situations of divorced men and women. Divorced men had higher incomes than never-married and widowed, while widowed women reported higher incomes than divorced women. Divorced persons experience financial changes that may continue to limit their lifestyles throughout the middle and later years.

Since patterns of social interaction may be

altered by divorce and limited contacts may result in social isolation during the latter portions of life, it might be expected that the older divorced persons are isolated. Indeed, Keith (1986a, 1989), using longitudinal data to examine unmarried older persons' social contacts with family and friends, found that 36% of the divorced unmarried had not maintained contacts with friends, while 22% of the never-married had no contact with these persons. While the social contacts of the divorced elderly may be limited, there appear to be differences between men and women. Divorced men seem to be more isolated from family and friends, and divorced women are more likely to continue family contacts. Friends do not compensate for the lost family interaction experienced by older, divorced men (Keith, 1986a, 1989).

In another study, Chiriboga (1982) examined the social and psychological adaptations to marital separations of 310 persons aged 20–70 years (25% were 50 or older). Older separated men and women were less happy and had more negative social and emotional experiences (e.g., difficulties with social contacts and feelings of personal discomfort, pessimistic views of past and future, and feelings of long-term dissatisfaction) than younger persons. For many elderly, divorce marks the termination of many years of marriage. Hagestad and Smyer (1982) noted that an "orderly divorce" requires the termination of an emotional bond, the establishment of a new identity, and the development of daily routines that exclude the former spouse. Data from a sample of 43 divorced men and 50 divorced women aged 41–61 years indicated that the majority had orderly divorces and that women recognized problems with their marriages and initiated the transition to an orderly divorce earlier than did men. Two other studies (Hennon, 1983; Kitson, Lopata, Holmes, and Meyering, 1980) compared the living situations of widows and divorced persons. Kitson et al. reported that the divorced experienced limited social interactions and felt discrimination and alienation because they were divorced. Hennon noted that divorced elderly persons had lower incomes and were less likely to help their children financially than were older widowed persons.

Divorce of adult children may create short-term and long-term changes in the social support networks of the middle-aged and elderly (Berardo, 1983; Smyer and Hofland, 1982). Changes related to a child's divorce may influence an older person's receipt of support or the need for older persons to do more for their offspring. For example, limited financial resources may inhibit previously established helping patterns within the family. Or, older persons may provide more support for their divorced adult children. Also, interactions between the generations (e.g., grandparent, adult child, and grandchild) may be altered. Johnson's (1988b) data indicated that the oldest generation (grandparents) provide economic assistance, advice, baby-sitting, and other supports to ease the strains created by the divorce of their adult child.

Research challenge: While some research has been directed toward divorce and family relationships in later life, this is an area in which many issues have not been addressed. First, the divorced elderly differ in the time and number of divorces they have experienced (Brubaker, 1985a). They may be "career divorced" because they divorced during their early or middle years and never remarried or they may have divorced in their later years (the "newly divorced") or, alternatively, they may have been married and divorced a number of times during their lifetime ("serial divorce"). Little is known about the differences between the lifestyles of the different types of divorced older persons. Second, differences between men and women have been identified, but additional exploration is needed. Specifically, how do men and women with similar situations compare on social and psychological factors? Do the differing patterns of social interaction translate into a more frequent use of formal support services by older divorced men? A third area for research focuses on the effects divorce might have on the extended family network. When older parents learn about the divorce of their adult children (Matthews and Sprey, 1984), they are often concerned about the possible repercussions within the social support network (e.g., children, grandchildren). Or, the separation or divorce of a middle-aged child (Glick and Lin, 1986) may necessitate the establishment of an intergenerational household for at least a short time.

WIDOWHOOD

The later years are marked by an increased probability of experiencing the death of a spouse, especially for women. During the 1960s and '70s (Streib and Beck, 1980; Troll, 1971) the study of widowhood produced many descriptions of the adjustments associated with the death of a spouse. Research during the 1980s continued to describe the experiences of the widowed and substantially increased the number of inferential analyses that provided additional understanding about a traumatic family event. Since widowhood is characterized by a change in the family structure, research has focused on changes in the financial situation, physical and emotional health, and social support networks during the time immediately following, as well as several years after, the loss of a spouse. Also, differences between widows and widowers have been examined.

Similar to research in the previous 20 years, several studies (Hyman, 1983; Smith and Zick, 1986; Zick and Smith, 1986, 1988) suggested that becoming widowed is related to a substantial decline in income and, for many, may indicate financial hardship. However, more recent research reveals the complexity of change in the financial situation of the widowed. Morgan's (1981) analysis of the 3-year incomes from a sample of middle-aged widows reported that the average widow's income did not decrease substantially for 2 years following the death of her spouse. Morgan concluded that widowhood is more prevalent in poorer families and, over time, widows do not necessarily experience a decrease in income. Three other longitudinal analyses (Smith and Zick, 1986; Zick and Smith, 1986, 1988) based on data from the Panel Study of Income Dynamics found that age and work experience may mediate the financial situation of the widowed. While widowed experience financial difficulties, the younger (aged 50 years or less) as well as those who had a history of work experience evidenced less financial decline. Widowers were as likely to experience poverty as widows (Smith and Zick, 1986), even though the widowers experienced little significant drop during the first year (Zick and Smith, 1986). Zick and Smith (1988) found that the economic situation of continuously married individuals changed little over a 6-year period, but continuously widowed persons experienced an initial decline, which was followed by a leveling off in economic well-being. The decline in the economic situation of widowed middle-aged and elderly persons substantially changes

with remarriage for both men and women (Zick and Smith, 1988). Comparisons of the financial situations of continuously widowed and recently remarried widowed persons indicated that the remarried widowed had a better financial situation than the continuously widowed, even before they remarried. This suggests that those with more financial resources are more likely to remarry. Generally, the studies of the economic well-being of widows suggested that decline is initially experienced by both men and women. Over time, the financial situations level off or improve, especially for the middle-aged and those who remarry. In terms of the change in financial well-being, few differences are apparent between widows and widowers.

Physical and emotional health may be affected by the loss of a spouse. One longitudinal study (Fenwick and Barresi, 1981) found that widowed persons perceived more health difficulties over 14 months, even though they experienced fewer days in bed than individuals who did not lose a spouse. Three other panel studies (Ferraro, 1985; Ferraro, Mutran, and Barresi, 1984; Vachon et al., 1982) indicated that recently widowed persons perceived their health as declining more dramatically than those who had been widowed more than 4 years. Recently widowed men and women evidenced symptoms (sadness, tearfulness, dissatisfaction with self, insomnia, appetite loss, and weight loss) characteristic of depression (Breckenridge, Gallagher, Thompson, and Peterson, 1986; Feinson, 1986). The widows' perceptions of their physical and emotional health seemed to be negatively influenced by the loss of a spouse for the short term but, as time progressed, negative effects lessened.

Social support derived from relationships (personal relationships were classified as primary, and segmented or less personal were referred to as secondary) may be an important resource, and possibly a buffer, for middle-aged and older persons who experience widowhood (Longino and Lipman, 1981; Thoits, 1982). Using 1969 and 1975 data from the Longitudinal Retirement History Study, Morgan (1984) examined interaction patterns of individuals before and after they became widowed. Both widows and widowers experienced continued social contact, even when the size of the social network decreased. In fact, an increase was observed for widows. Two other studies (Anderson, 1984; Kohen, 1983) of the social supports of married and widowed persons found that the widowed elderly had patterns of more frequent social contact than their married counterparts. Generally, Kohen (1983) concluded that patterns of interaction established by married couples continue into widowhood. For example, married women were more likely to talk to close friends and relatives than were married men. Also, they turned to their children in times of crisis more frequently than did the men. Similarly, widows were more likely to talk to close friends and relatives and turn to their children in times of crisis than were widowers. Anderson (1984) reported that widows increased their contact with kin, especially sisters and other extended relatives. O'Bryant (1988) noted that sisters, especially unmarried sisters, were helpful to widows' adjustment. Further, support provided by siblings contributed positively to the childless widows' psychological well-being, but for parental widows with children living nearby, siblings' assistance had a negative effect. Since interactions with children were not affected by widowhood (Anderson, 1984), the increased social contact identified in the research may reveal a more vibrant social network for widows.

On the whole, the widowed have more social contacts than the married in the middle and later years, but is a vital social network related to the widow's emotional well-being? Gallagher, Thompson, and Peterson (1982) suggested that the adequacy of the social network can minimize the negative emotional burden of becoming widowed. Social contacts with friends, as well as good health and participation in recreation, were associated with widows' and widowers' feelings of well-being (Arens, 1982). Bankoff's (1983) study of Caucasian women who were widowed 18 months or less (the crisis-loss-phase group) and of those widowed 19–35 months (transition-phase group) identified the complexities of the relationship between social support and well-being. The impact of social support depended on the length of time a person has been widowed, the type of support, and who is providing support. For example, Bankoff reported that overall social support had no effect on the psychological well-being for the crisis-loss group. However, for the transition group, a modest positive relationship was found. Only emotional support was important to the recent widows, while intimacy, contact, and emotional support were crucial for those who had been widowed longer. For the crisis-loss group,

parents and other widowed persons were the most effective providers of support, even though children provided the most frequent support. In addition to parents and widowed friends, the transition group identified neighbors, children, and married friends as providers of support that is related to increased feelings of well-being. These findings suggested that length of time a middle-aged or elderly person has been widowed influences the effect of social support on well-being as well as the type and source of supports that are effective.

The issue of gender differences during widowhood has received attention during the 1980s. Stroebe and Stroebe (1982) reviewed research on health differences and concluded that differences between widows and widowers were infrequent, and when there was discrepancy, the men were most likely to be disadvantaged. In a study of older, rural widows and widowers (Scott and Kivett, 1985), morale was not affected by gender. Rather, morale was related to the widowed men and women's assessments of their financial and health situations. With the exception of financial status, Arens (1982) reported few differences between widows' and widowers' assessments of well-being. Feinson's (1986) analysis of emotional difficulties revealed few differences between widows and widowers. There is some evidence (Kohen, 1983) that widows may have an advantage in the development of informal social supports outside the family. With the exception of children, widowers are more likely than widows to rely on family in times of crisis. While there may be some differences between widows and widowers, the research during this decade suggests that the differences are minimal. Generally, the longitudinal studies indicate that men and women experience similar physical and emotional difficulties initially and, with time, seem to cope with the loss of a spouse. The death of a spouse changes the structure of the family for both men and women, and consequently, both establish new lifestyles based on their past patterns of interaction. For both, their financial situation is related to their feelings of well-being.

Research challenge: The economic status of middle-aged and older widowed individuals needs continued exploration. What is the importance of the differences between men and women, age, and work experience in the adjustment of widowed persons? Adjustment to widowhood over time needs additional examination. What factors are associated with the length of time spent in the crisis-loss phase before they move to the transitional phase? Is the widow's length of adjustment time influenced by the length of time the couple was married? Does the type of marital relationship (e.g., traditional, egalitarian) before the death of a spouse affect the survivor's adjustment patterns? While there seems to be more similarity than difference between widowed men and women, continued examination of gender is warranted. Since differences between the recently widowed and long-term widowed have been identified, the use of longitudinal data is appropriate when examining widowhood.

Remarriage

Remarriage is less likely as a person ages (Koo and Suchindran, 1980; Teachman and Heckert, 1985), but a small portion of middle-aged and older individuals date and remarry after divorce or the death of a spouse. Older persons' dating and remarriage patterns have been the focus of two studies. Bulcroft and O'Conner (1986) focused on the importance of dating in a qualitative study of 35 persons aged 60 years and older who had been dating. These older persons defined dating as a monogamous heterosexual relationship that tends to lead to a long-term intimate relationship. Dating was important to them, and they dated because they wanted to find a mate or companionship. Women, more often than men, noted increased prestige and enhanced identity as a result of dating, while men were more likely to focus on the need for intimacy and self-disclosure. Generally, Bulcroft and O'Conner noted that dating is a "hedge against loneliness" in the later years.

Dressel's (1980) study of endogamy and homogamy in later life examined marriage license applications of a group of younger persons (males aged 20–26 years and females aged 18–24 years) and older persons (aged 65 years and older). The findings suggested varying patterns of homogamy in the mate selection of older persons. For example, older persons were less homogamous than younger persons on age and previous marital status. Racially, both younger and older persons were highly endogamous. In terms of residential propinquity the younger and older samples evidenced few differences. One surprising finding was that an equal percentage (25%) of the younger and older persons recorded the same address prior to marriage. Differences in age and marital-status homogamy are most likely related to differing male and female longevity patterns and older persons' varied marital experiences.

After remarriage, issues of adjustment become important. For widowed elderly, Moss and Moss (1980) noted that the deceased spouses may influence adjustment in the newly formed marriage. The elderly widow, according to Moss and Moss, views the new marriage through the "prism of the first marriage." For both the divorced and the widowed, former intimate relationships may be important in the adjustment to a new marital relationship. However, little is known about the complexities of remarriage in the middle or later years. These studies suggest that dating and remarriage are important aspects of later life for a few, and additional research is needed.

Research challenge: Education, income, and number of children have been related to remarriage patterns (Glick, 1980); however, these variables have not been examined in terms of the remarriage rates of older persons. Nor have racial differences in remarriage rates been analyzed. Data are needed to identify the influence adult children have on the dating and mate selection of middle-aged and older persons. After remarriage, what factors affect the couple's adjustment to the new relationship? There is no doubt that the dating and remarriage patterns of middle-aged and older persons are areas in which research is needed.

Childless Families in Later Life

The vital relationships older people have with their adult children and the importance of adult children's contributions to the well-being of older persons are well documented (Mancini, 1989; Mancini and Blieszner, 1989). Indeed, it has been suggested (Glenn and McLanahan, 1981) that the benefits of parenthood may be the most rewarding in the middle and later years because parental responsibilities are lessened and children often hinder the development of social isolation during the later years. The potential for rewards and companionship in the middle and later years has been noted as a reason for having children (Glenn and McLanahan, 1981). However, a substantial number of middle-aged and older persons do not have children. The childless include married couples who either voluntarily or involuntarily have not had children, divorced or widowed persons who have not had children, persons who have never married and have had no children, and a small portion of older individuals whose children have preceded them in death. Who provides support to the childless elderly? On whom do the childless elderly depend when they need the types of assistance children provide to their older parents? Within the past 10 years, a limited number of studies have focused on the childless elderly, and most have compared their life situations to those of similarly aged parents.

Analysis of data based on face-to-face interviews with approximately 1,500 persons (pooled from the 1973–1978 General Social Surveys) addressed the influence of children on the psychological well-being of middle-aged and older persons (Glenn and McLanahan, 1981). The findings provide no support for the contention that middle-aged and older parents are happier and more satisfied than their childless counterparts. Children had a negative effect on dimensions of satisfaction for black men and highly educated white men. Lee (1988) noted that older parents had slightly lower marital satisfaction than the childless elderly. These data suggest that the rewards associated with parenthood in the middle and later years may be overstated and younger persons should not base a decision to have children on the anticipation that offspring will contribute positively to their satisfaction during their middle and later years.

Several studies (Bachrach, 1980; Beckman and Houser, 1982; Singh and Williams, 1981) indicate that childless elderly persons may have fewer social contacts, may be less satisfied, and are more likely to live alone, when compared to elderly parents. To illustrate, Bachrach's examination of data from a national probability sample of 2,797 individuals aged 65 years and older found that generally the childless were more likely to live alone and less likely to have had social contact in the past 2 days. The childless older person's health and social class were identified as important contributing factors to social isolation. Bachrach's analysis noted that working-class childless elderly persons who were in poor health were most likely to be socially isolated, while those who were

employed in nonmanual jobs and in good health had social contacts.

In a study of 103 childless persons and 438 parents aged 72 years or older, living in small Midwestern towns, Keith (1983) found few differences between the childless and parental elderly. While these childless older people had fewer face-to-face family contacts, an equal percentage (35%) of the parental and childless respondents noted that they were lonely. For these older persons, children did not assure greater life satisfaction or more accepting attitudes toward death. Another study (Kivett and Lerner, 1980) of rural childless and parental elderly found the childless to have fewer social contacts, but they were not any more lonely or less likely to have a confidant than the parental group. On the basis of these studies of rural elderly persons, the childless and parental elderly may have developed different, but rewarding, lifestyles.

Similarly, a study (Rempel, 1985) of 338 elderly selected from a Canadian national probability sample of persons aged 18 years and older revealed few differences between the childless and parental older persons and unique benefits for both. Elderly parents had a larger network of friends and reported more general life satisfaction, while the childless were more financially secure and in better health. Although they may be more socially isolated, childless elderly persons have developed lifestyles that include benefits that, on average, maximize the advantages and minimize the disadvantages of not having children.

Among the childless elderly, there are some differences between the married and unmarried. In an urban setting, Johnson and Catalano (1981) found that the childless elderly developed active social networks with friends and neighbors, while the married persons' interaction patterns were centered around the spouses. As health needs increased, the married and childless elderly relied on spouses and the unmarried turned to siblings, nieces, and nephews. More of the unmarried and childless elderly (44% versus 17%) were institutionalized. Although unmarried, childless older persons have developed informal support networks, marriage provides a spouse on whom childless older persons can rely. The married childless used formal support services less frequently (Johnson and Catalano, 1981) and developed more limited social contacts.

Research in the 1980s does not necessarily support the pronatal assertion that children benefit parents during the last half of life. The lifestyles established by childless older persons differ from those of older parents, but for the most part, the childless enter the later years with well-established patterns of dealing with change. While they may be more socially isolated, their financial and health situations are better and they are not more lonely than elderly parents. Declining health may be the only situation in which childlessness is detrimental. This may be especially acute for the unmarried childless elderly. While siblings provide assistance to unmarried and childless elderly persons in white and black families (Johnson and Catalano, 1981; Scott, 1983; Taylor, Chatters, and Mays, 1988), seldom does the amount or frequency of support compare to a spouse's care.

Research challenge: Although the differences between childless and parental families appear to be minimal in later life and benefits have been identified for both lifestyles, research during the 1980s identified age, marital status, and health conditions as crucial variables in the study of childlessness. Research is needed to address a number of remaining questions. For example, as childless men and women age and health problems become more evident, does the tendency to be socially isolated become more crucial? While the data suggest that there may be differences between married and unmarried childless persons, little is known about the differences between married and previously married (e.g., widowed, divorced), childless, middle-aged and older persons. Also, are there differences between childless men and women? Further research is needed to define the types of support that could buffer the childless elderly's social isolation and their entrance into institutions. Inquiry into the social isolation of childless older persons is needed. On the one hand, few social contacts may not be a problem because the childless elderly may enjoy the limited contacts and the freedom to choose persons with whom they interact. But, as their health declines, their ability to choose social intimates may become more difficult and they may become increasingly more isolated. What support is needed to enable the childless unmarried, older persons to remain in the community? What needs do siblings, friends, neighbors, nieces, and nephews have as they care for the childless elderly? How

unhealthy childless be identified before they need institutional support?

GRANDPARENTHOOD

Grandparenthood is frequently experienced by middle-aged and older adults and usually begins sometime from the third to the fifth decade of life. Shanas (1980) estimated that nearly 75% of older persons are grandparents and nearly 50% experience great-grandparenthood. More recently, Hagestad (1988) reported data from a study in the eastern part of the United States in which 77% of the persons aged 65 years or more were grandparents and 51% were great-grandparents. The age of grandparents varies considerably. For example, the median age of grandmothers in one study of black grandmothers was 32 years (Burton and Bengtson, 1985), and the median age for the great-grandmothers was 56 years. In another study of college students, their mothers, and grandmothers, most of the grandmothers were 60 years of age and older (Thompson and Walker, 1987).

The transition into and timing of grandparenthood have received attention from researchers during the 1980s. Unlike role transitions that are selected voluntarily, becoming a grandparent is beyond the control of the older generation (Sprey and Matthews, 1982); whenever their child becomes a parent, the older generation experiences grandparenthood. Sprey and Matthews (1982) suggested that the transition into grandparenthood begins when an adult child marries and the birth of the grandchild reinforces bonds within the extended family network. Research by Fisher (1981) suggested that the transition into parenthood strengthens the relationship between daughters and their mothers because they share the activities and concerns about parenting. However, the transition into parenthood may be influenced by the age of the older generation when they initially become grandparents. The Burton and Bengtson (1985) and Hagestad and Burton (1986) studies of black grandmothers suggest that women who became grandmothers at an early age (25–38 years) experienced more discomfort with the role of grandparenting than those who became grandmothers at a more expected or "on time" age (42–57 years). The discomfort was associated with becoming a member of the "older" generation.

In many family networks, grandparents represent stability and continuity in family rituals and values (Bengtson and Robertson, 1985; Hagestad, 1985; Troll, 1983; Wentowski, 1985). In addition, they frequently assist their adult children's parenting activities by providing emotional support, encouragement, help with day-to-day parental needs such as baby-sitting, and help in time of emergencies or crises, including illness or divorce (Bengtson and Robertson, 1985; Cherlin and Furstenberg, 1986; Johnson, 1988a, 1988b; Presser, 1989). While the role of grandparent is ambiguous (Fisher, 1983; Sprey and Matthews, 1982) and contemporary grandparents have been defined as "pioneers" (Shanas, 1980), several reviews (Barranti, 1985; Bengtson and Robertson, 1985; Gutmann, 1987; Sprey and Matthews, 1982) of grandparenting research indicate that grandmothers and grandfathers are integral members of active extended family relationships, both in traditional and nontraditional settings. Their concerns for family legacy, maintenance of family patterns, and encouragement of the continuation of family rituals has earned them the label of "family watchdogs" (Troll, 1983). Two studies (Doka and Mertz, 1988; Wentowski, 1985) indicate that there is similarity between grandparenthood and great-grandparenthood. The great-grandmothers regarded their role as similar to being a grandmother, and they emphasized the emotional and symbolic aspects rather than the social and instrumental factors. Often, grandparenthood provides middle-aged and older adults with the possibility of having a meaningful role, becoming valued family elders, and feeling immortal within the family as well as a chance to relive life and indulge grandchildren (Kivnick, 1982, 1983).

As Kivnick (1982) noted, grandparenting can be an experience characterized by happiness and fulfillment or, if the grandparent is unrecognized, it can result in disillusionment and disappointment. Although the styles and types of grandparenting relationships vary, generally both grandparents and grandchildren value the relationships they have with one another (Baranowski, 1982; Hartshorne and Manaster, 1982; Kivnick, 1982; Sprey and Matthews, 1982). Also, there may be gender differences in grandparenting. The grandparent role may be more salient to women than men during the middle and later years (Hagestad, 1985). Thomas (1986b) reported

that grandmothers were more satisfied with grandparenting, but the magnitude of the gender difference is not large. In another study (Thomas, 1986a), grandfathers felt more responsibility for caretaking and offering child-rearing advice and less satisfaction with grandparenting than did grandmothers. One study (Kivett, 1985b) suggested that grandfathers viewed the grandparenting role as unimportant but, at the same time, expected grandchildren to provide assistance in times of need. Continued attention to gender differences in grandparenting need to consider middle-aged and older men and women's definitions of nurturing and expressiveness.

The relationship between the adult parents and grandparents may mediate the relationship between the grandchildren and grandparents, even though the older generation may not be cognizant of their adult child's mediation effects (Kivnick, 1983; Sprey and Matthews, 1982). In a study of 99 rural and urban grandfathers (Kivett, 1985b), it was reported that 7 out of 10 grandfathers had the most contact with a grandchild who was the son or daughter of the adult child with whom the grandfather also had the most contact. Sprey and Matthews (1982) noted that the mediating effects of parents may be related to the age of the grandchild. While younger grandchildren are dependent on their parents for transportation and contact with their grandparents, older grandchildren can interact independently with their grandparents and modify the mediating role of parents. Dellman-Jenkins, Papalia, and Lopez (1987) reported that the onset of adolescence may have resulted in positive changes in relationships a sample of working-class adolescents had with their grandparents. However, in another study by Matthews and Sprey (1985), college-aged grandchildren's feelings of closeness were related to their perceptions of their parents' relationship to their grandparents. Thompson and Walker (1987) examined the mediating effects of mothers on the relationships of college-aged women. These data suggest that grandmothers' feelings for their granddaughters are indistinguishable from their feelings for their daughters. Rather, grandmothers' feelings are related to a global feeling about the family, and they feel emotionally close to their daughters and granddaughters because they are members of the family. Granddaughters' feelings of closeness were based on direct contact with their grandmothers, feelings mediated by their mothers, and feelings for their own mothers that overflowed to their grandmothers.

Research on divorce and grandparenting (Fisher, 1983; Matthews and Sprey, 1984) indicated that the parental generation may mediate the relationship between grandchildren and grandparents. For example, maternal grandparents may be able to continue relationships with grandchildren because mothers receive custody more frequently than fathers. Also, if the divorced mother and grandchild live in close proximity, grandparents are able to continue their relationship more easily. In a study of 80 grandmothers whose adult children were separated or divorced, Gladstone (1988) found that increased contact between grandparents and grandchildren was related to geographical proximity and custody. Johnson and Barer (1987) reported that nearly one-half of the grandparents had an expanded kin network after the divorce of their child. Paternal grandmothers' network was increased by the continued contact with their former daughters-in-law and the addition of new relatives as a result of their sons' remarriages. These studies suggested that the interrelationship between the generations is complex and the mediating role of parents is not unilateral. Mediation effects may be obvious in the grandchild generation, especially when the grandchildren are younger or the parents are divorced. However, for the most part, grandparents develop ties to grandchildren without parental influence.

The frequency of remarriage provides the possibility of stepgrandparenting. It is estimated that there were 9.75 million children under 18 years of age in remarried families, 8.78 million were in stepfamilies, and 5.85 million were stepchildren (Glick, 1989). Many of these stepchildren have the possibility of being involved in a relationship with a stepgrandparent. The age of the child when the stepfamily was formed has been related to the formation of a relationship between the stepgrandchild and stepgrandparent. The younger the child at the remarriage, the more likely a relationship will develop (Cherlin and Furstenberg, 1986). In a study that compared the grandparent and stepgrandparent relationships of college students (Sanders and Trygstad, 1989), persons who became stepchildren at age 10 years or less were more likely to define the stepgrandparent relationship as important than those who became stepchildren after age 10. In comparisons of

grandchildrens' view of their grandparents and stepgrandchildrens' view of their stepgrandparents, the Sanders and Trygstad data indicated that grandchildren viewed their relationships with grandparents as more important and stronger and that they expected more from their grandparents.

Research challenge: Research has provided a description of the grandparent role, with primary emphasis on grandmothers. The differences between grandfathers' and grandmothers' perceptions of grandparenting need to be clarified. Since many families include four and five generations and most of the research has focused on three-generation family networks, little is known about great-grandparents and their contributions to the family. While stepgrandparenting has received some attention during this decade, more research is needed to understand further the dynamics of this frequent family role. With the exception of Burton, few have examined grandparenthood in ethnic minority families. Future research needs to examine the role of grandparenting in black, Hispanic, Asian, and other minority families.

SIBLING RELATIONSHIPS

A unique family relationship is represented in the study of the sibling relationships of older adults. Siblings represent a continuity in family history that is uncommon to most other family relationships and, in some families, may represent the only surviving dyadic relationship from the family of origin. Toward the latter stages of the family life cycle, as Cicirelli (1985b: 184) noted, "the individual's family of procreation expands while the family of origin gradually disintegrates as its members die. Only fragments of the original nuclear family system remain, in the form of sibling dyadic relationships." The shared family history provides a foundation for interaction that enables validation of an older person's reminiscences of family events throughout life (Bedford, 1989c; Goetting, 1986). Discussion of family experiences in earlier years is characteristic of adult sibling interactions (Cicirelli, 1985a; Ross and Milgram, 1982), and the validation of positive experiences in previous family interactions may be related to positive feelings about the family in later life (Gold, 1989; Ross and Milgram, 1982).

In addition to the validation of earlier family experiences, Goetting (1986) noted that older adult relationships with siblings provide companionship and emotional support, the possibility of resolving sibling rivalries, and the provision of consultative or material aid and support to meet challenges in later life. Since this may be the longest, most durable, and egalitarian family relationship (Cicirelli, 1980, 1982), the saliency and continuity of this family relationship should not be overlooked. While frequency of contact and feelings of closeness remained consistent over time, siblings thought about each other more often and deepened their approval and acceptance of one another (Gold, 1989). At the same time, they reduced feelings of resentment and envy (Gold, 1989).

Research (Cicirelli, 1980, 1982; Scott, 1983) indicates that most older adults have at least one living sibling, and when compared to younger cohorts, adult siblings report feelings of increased closeness and companionship (Goetting, 1986). For example, in a sample of rural elders, more than 70% had at least one living brother or sister, and of these, nearly 70% resided in the same or adjacent county (McGee, 1985). Similarly, O'Bryant (1988) reported that nearly 85% of a sample of urban, Midwestern widows had at least one living sibling and nearly 50% had a living sibling in the same city. Many elders have contact with their siblings on a weekly or monthly basis. Seventeen percent of Cicirelli's (1980) sample of urban older persons visited weekly with a sibling and another one-third visited at least once a month. In Scott's (1983) sample of urban elders living in the Southwest, approximately one-half reported telephone contact on a weekly basis. Cicirelli (1985b) noted that siblings who visit are likely to have frequent telephone contact.

Most studies reported frequent contact with siblings who live in close proximity. For example, Kivett (1985a) found that nearly 90% of a sample of rural-transitional older men and women had the most contact with their sibling who lived the closest to them. In Scott's (1983) study, siblings who had the most frequent contact lived within 31 to 60 minutes of each other. Likewise, Cicirelli (1980) found that more than one-quarter had the most frequent contact with the sibling who lived in the same city and more than 50% had the most frequent contact with those who lived within 100 miles of each other. The data clearly demonstrate that most older adults have living siblings with whom they have frequent contact, but the frequency of contact is premised on living in close proximity to one another.

Feelings of closeness between siblings have been identified in various studies. For example, Scott (1983) reported that older men and women felt "very close" to their siblings, while Cicirelli (1980, 1982) noted that more than 50% felt "extremely close" and another 30% felt "close" to at least one living sibling. Cicirelli (1985b) also reported that there is a high degree of compatibility between siblings in the middle and later years of the life span (i.e., siblings gained satisfaction from their relationships with one another, they took an interest in one another, and they felt that they could discuss intimate topics with each other, even though many did not discuss important decisions with siblings). Ross and Milgram (1982) noted that older persons identified siblings as confidants more frequently than younger persons did. Further, they noted that feelings of closeness appeared to be established in the younger years and few developed close feelings after adulthood. These studies suggest that the childhood shared by siblings provides bonds that continue into the middle and later years of life.

While siblings are valued by middle-aged and older people, their influence on life satisfaction or morale is unclear but appears to be gender related. For instance, Lee and Ihinger-Tallman's (1980) analysis of 870 persons aged 60 years and over revealed that neither the presence of nor interaction with siblings had an influence on emotional well-being. But McGee (1985) found that the availability of a sister had a positive effect on rural, older women's life satisfaction scores, while there was no appreciable effect of the availability of a sibling on men's life satisfaction scores. McGloshen and O'Bryant's (1988) study of older, recent widows suggested that the presence of siblings contributed positively to the widows' well-being scores. There is no doubt that siblings are valued by older persons, but their impact on overall life satisfaction differs by gender and may be minimal.

Differing sibling relationships are apparent when gender is examined. With the exception of Scott's (1983) study, in which the impact of the type of sibling relationship (sister-sister, brother-brother, or brother-sister) did not differ, several studies (Cicirelli, 1980; McGee, 1985; O'Bryant, 1988) indicated that the sister-sister relationship is the most potent of sibling relationships, followed by the sister-brother and brother-brother relationship. Although the sister-sister relationship may be characterized by competition, sisters have developed supportive relationships with one another. Similarly, research (Chatters, Taylor, and Jackson, 1986) on the informal support networks of black older persons indicates that sisters were utilized more frequently than brothers. Overall, it appears that older women are more effective in sibling relationships than men (McGee, 1985; O'Bryant, 1988). Bedford's (1989a; 1989b) studies of sibling relationships indicate that women, compared to men, are more aware of and agree more about their underlying feelings toward their sisters. While there is consistency in the way women perceive their sisters, they evidence more themes of conflict with their sisters than men do with their brothers (Bedford, 1989a; 1989b). These studies suggest that the gender of the siblings may be a distinguishing factor in the study of sibling relationships in later life.

Siblings' contribution to the caregiving of older adults, especially unmarried persons, has been recognized for many years (Troll, 1971). While siblings helped older adults with situations such as transportation, decision making, illness, minor household repairs, financial support, shopping, and adjustments to widowhood, they provided less assistance in each of these areas than did children (Cicirelli, 1982; McGloshen and O'Bryant, 1988; O'Bryant, 1988; Ross and Milgram, 1982; Scott, 1983). Kivett (1985a) examined the provision of care and closeness within the consanguineous kinship line (e.g, adult children and their children, siblings and their children, and cousins) and found that siblings and siblings-in-law provided assistance in amounts similar to the help from grandchildren. For childless older persons, assistance from siblings becomes more frequent and essential (Scott, 1983). Research on black families suggests that siblings' contributions may exceed the assistance provided by siblings in white families. For example, Taylor, Chatters, and Mays (1988; Chatters, Taylor, and Jackson, 1985; Chatters, Taylor, and Neighbors, 1989) found that middle-aged and older black men and women often utilized siblings for emergency assistance. Also, for both blacks and whites, Suggs (1989) reported that mutual helping behaviors and residential propinquity were predictors of sibling association. It is clear that siblings are a part of a kinship support system throughout the life span.

Research challenge: Little is known about the sibling relationships in minority families. Data have been collected from rural and urban samples with little attention to minority and ethnic differences. Since there is some indication (Gibson, 1982) that middle-aged and older blacks utilize a larger family support network (including siblings) than do whites, future research on the sibling relationship in middle-aged and older families needs to examine the possibility of cultural differences in patterns of interaction, influence, and assistance. The companionship and competition aspects of the sibling relationship need additional exploration (Goetting, 1986; McGee, 1985). Does competition between sisters contribute to or result from companionship? Another avenue for research relates to the dynamics of the sibling relationship within the consanguineous kinship system as the family adjusts to changes during the latter portions of the life cycle (Brubaker, 1985a). For example, how do siblings deal with the death of a sibling or sibling-in-law? Sibling relationships of middle-aged and older adults provide a fertile field for research in the 1990s.

FAMILY CAREGIVING IN LATER LIFE

Research during the 1970s described ways in which family members provided care for dependent elders. During the 1980s, research on family caregiving increased in quantity and frequently appeared in family and gerontology journals as well as in books. Many families who have an older member with health difficulties provide extraordinary care (Brody, 1981; Cicirelli, 1981, 1983; Horowitz, 1985a; Seelbach, 1984; Stephens and Christianson, 1985; Stolar, Hill, and Tomblin, 1986), and many are reluctant to utilize extrafamilial assistance (Doty, Liu, and Wiener, 1985). Gender has been identified as differentiating variable in several studies (Brody, 1981; Cantor, 1983; Horowitz, 1985b; Sheehan and Nuttall, 1988; Stoller, 1983). Women family members (e.g., wives, daughters, daughters-in-law) provide most of the care, and they make numerous sacrifices in the process. On the basis of data from the 1982 National Long Term Care Study, it was reported that 72% of the primary, informal caregivers of the frail elderly were female (Stone, Cafferata, and Sangl, 1987; see also, American Association of Retired Persons, 1988). Wives (23%) provided care to husbands and adult daughters (29%) assisted parents, while fewer husbands (13%) cared for wives and still fewer sons (9%) helped parents (Stone, Cafferata, and Sangl, 1987). Although women were more likely to provide care for dependent elderly family members, a portion of the care was provided by males (American Association of Retired Persons, 1988; Horowitz, 1985a, 1985b; Miller, 1987; Patterson, 1987; Smallegan, 1985; Stoller, 1983; Stone, Cafferata, and Sangl, 1987).

With the exception of age (husbands tended to be older), fewer differences between husband and wife caregivers (both are as likely to quit paid employment, both have similar assistance patterns) have been identified. However, there may be some differences in the way in which husbands and wives assess the impact of caregiving on their lives and marriage. As noted earlier, Fitting and associates (1986) found that younger wives were more depressed about their caregiving responsibilities. More wives reported a deterioration in their marital relationship, while one-quarter of the husbands noted that their marital relationships improved after they started to provide care. Another study (Zarit et al., 1986) suggested that caregiving wives experienced more subjective burden when initially interviewed than did caregiving husbands. Men seemed to approach the daily activities of caregiving in an instrumental, detached manner, whereas wives initially had difficulty distancing themselves emotionally from the caregiving tasks. When reinterviewed 2 years later, the wives were more stoic about the demands of caregiving, and their feelings of subjective burden had lessened to resemble the feelings of burden expressed by the caregiving husbands. These studies suggest that husbands and wives provide care to dependent spouses but there may be differences in the ways in which they define the caregiving tasks.

When an adult child is the primary caregiver, it is more likely to be a daughter than a son. Indeed, early in the 1980s, Brody (1981) characterized adult children as "women in the middle" when describing the assistance patterns of daughters. With regard to primary caregiving by adult children, daughters continue to be "in the middle" and sons appear to be "on the periphery." Studies have noted that employment may be related to level of involvement in the care of the elderly family member, but nonetheless, employed daughters are still more likely to provide assistance (Brody and Schoonover, 1986; Matthews, Werkner, and Delaney, 1989; Stoller, 1983). Stoller's (1983) analysis of the assistance provided by employed sons and daughters indicated that employment did not affect the amount of care daughters provided, but for sons, working reduced their amount of help. Brody and Schoonover (1986) and Matthews, Werkner, and Delaney (1989) examined the assistance of employed and unemployed caregiving daughters. Both studies found that unemployed daughters provided more personal and tangible services (e.g., transportation, daytime emergencies, cooking) than employed daughters, but employed daughters contributed in meaningful ways. For example, the employed daughters provided care during the evenings or weekends. Matthews and Rosner's (1988) qualitative study of the caregiving contributions of adult daughters and sons indicated that daughters provided more of the routine and backup care, while sons provided assistance in specific or narrowly defined situations. Contributions of caregiving daughters and sons need to be examined within the context of each family (Matthews et al., 1989). Adult children are aware of the resources, abilities, and inclinations of one another, and the provision of care to a dependent parent emerges from the unique ways in which each can contribute. While adult children may have feelings of inequity, the research indicates that most families coalesce to provide the necessary assistance.

Many adult children who provide the primary care for an older parent are married. Kleban, Brody, Schoonover, and Hoffman (1989) examined the consequences of such caregiving from the vantage of the female caregivers and their husbands. The findings suggested that the burden felt by married daughters who are caregivers is also shared by their spouses. The sons-in-law noted that they felt the strain of caregiving, even though their wives were the ones who had the primary responsibilities for providing the care. These caregiving wives and husbands stated that their schedules (daily and occasional, such as vacations) were affected and their family and personal time was hampered by the demands of caregiving. Even though the men reported that they argued about the care of their wife's parent, they did not feel that their marriage was negatively affected. However, the wives tended to feel that their marital relationships were detrimentally affected by the caregiving situation. This study further underscores the need to explore the caregiving relationship from the perspectives of the caregiver and the caregiver's family of procreation.

Research challenge: The caregiving situation needs to be examined within the context of the unique family situation as well as the family relationships of the caregiver (e.g., spouse, offspring). The family history, types of dependencies, individual responsibilities, and other contextual variables call for further exploration (Brubaker and Brubaker, 1989). During the 1980s, women seemed to provide most of the primary care of the frail elderly and men were more involved on a secondary level. Are women the primary caregivers or is this an artifact of the research methodologies most frequently used? Will the apparent differences between women's and men's contributions to caregiving disappear as more "egalitarian" daughters and sons provide care for dependent parents? Attention to the context within which families establish caregiving routines should provide more information about the positive and negative aspects associated with caregiving.

DIRECTIONS FOR FUTURE RESEARCH

Although research on families in later life burgeoned during the past decade, future research should consider several key issues. The 1990s represent the decade in which the baby boomers and their parents become members of their own later-life families. Giordano (1988) predicted that the future middle-aged and older persons will place a high value on family and other interpersonal relationships. It was also suggested (Giordano, 1988) that self-improvement through health enhancement, education and counseling programs, and community services and resources will be valued and the future elderly will have higher expectations for family caregiving than the elderly on which present data are based. In many ways, forthcoming middle-aged and elderly will be more socially active and demand more from family members and society. Bengtson (1989) recently commented that cohort, maturation, period, and lineage may explain differences between generations. As the baby boomers move into the latter stages of life, these factors cannot be overlooked. Consequently, future analyses will need to examine cohort differences to predict accurately the lifestyles and needs of future later-life families. Since there is a large body of research on which to build future analyses, the use of complementary or consistent measures will enhance the development of new information and analyses for cohort differences. The following are some key issues relevant to the development of research in the next decade.

1. The need to ground research in theory and develop theoretical approaches to the study of later-life families: Research on families in later life needs to be better grounded in theory. During the 1970s and 1980s, research has provided a description (though limited primarily to white, middle-class families) of the familial relationships of later-life families. However, few attempts have been made to explain these relationships (exceptions include Lee, 1985; Mutran and Reitzes, 1984; Stoller, 1985). Using theory to develop research questions and hypotheses may provide more explanation of family patterns in later life. Also, the development of theory about specific aspects of later-life families (e.g., caregiving, sibling interactions, intergenerational relationships) will undoubtedly provide a better understanding of such families.

2. The need to continue the use of longitudinal designs: The 1980s marked the analyses of a number of longitudinal data sets that have provided some information about family patterns in later life. For the next decade, the continued use of longitudinal data sets is encouraged. While the large survey data sets provide information about the family patterns of large groups of middle-aged and older persons, there is a need to develop longitudinal data sets focusing on the dynamics of family interaction and the interdependencies between generations within families. Gathering data when children begin to leave home, through the retirement years, and into old age from the same sample would be useful to explore the continuity in family relationships that seems evident from the cross-sectional studies presently available. Shorter-term longitudinal studies are also needed. For example, gathering data about the caregiver career of a spouse who becomes the primary

caregiver for a number of years would be useful. Longitudinal research has become more prevalent in the 1980s, and the hope is that this trend will continue in the next 10 years.

3. The need for qualitative analyses of family patterns in later life: There is a need to examine families in their own contexts as they deal with the issues related to later life. For example, survey data provide information about marital satisfaction during retirement, but there is limited information on how families make decisions related to retirement. What trade-offs are discussed when a couple is deciding whether to retire early? Qualitative designs that seek to capture the dynamics of families in their own settings can provide a more complete picture of later-life families. In the area of family caregiving, Gubrium (1988) and Matthews and Rosner (1988) provide two examples of the fruitfulness of the qualitative approach. To fully understand the strengths and strains experienced by families in later life, additional qualitative studies are warranted.

4. The need to explore ethnic and minority differences: Although Streib and Beck (1980) identified the possibility of the use of imaginative studies focusing on ethnic groups who were seldom explored during the 1980s, little research on ethnic minority families was realized during this decade. During the 1990s, research on the later-life family patterns of ethnic minority families is needed. Most later-life family research is based on samples of middle-aged and older white persons. Few studies have focused on the differences between white and minority families, and still fewer have examined differences between minority groups. Minority elderly are a growing population who require descriptive as well as analytic study. Often research on minority families in later life is reported as part of a study that had some minority individuals in the sample. There is a need to develop extensive, in-depth studies focusing primarily on the families of minority middle-aged and elderly persons.

5. The need to examine gender differences: Differential experiences by men and women in the middle and later years need continued exploration. As future cohorts enter mid-life and later years, research is needed to determine if more egalitarian divisions of labor are developed. Are there differences in the way in which men and women participate in family caregiving for dependent family members? Does retirement differen-

tially affect men's and women's family relationships? Do childless men deal with adjustments to later life differently than childless women? There are a number of issues in which gender differences need to be examined. Thus, gender will continue to be a crucial variable in research during the 1990s.

6. The need to further explore the interface between individuals, families, and bureaucracies: As individuals and families address issues related to later life, the influence of bureaucracies will continue to be important. For example, changes in the Social Security System affect the timing of retirement, available financial resources, and other issues relevant to later-life families. Similarly, pension and annuity programs, health care policies, and the tax system (e.g., IRAs) represent bureaucratic structures that have an impact on older families in their everyday lives. In many instances, a triadic relationship exists between an older person, the family, and the bureaucracy that includes structural and social-psychological aspects (Brubaker, 1987). Research is necessary to identify the impact that changes in these bureaucracies have on middle-aged and older families. Also, structural and social-psychological aspects of the triadic relationships need additional discussion.

7. The need to continue to address issues related to health and caregiving: Research on families in later life will need to continue to consider health as a salient variable. As individuals age and increasingly lead healthy lives into their seventh decade, the possibilities of health difficulties increase. Family relationships (including spouse, children, and grandchildren) are structurally and emotionally affected by changes in health. As families mobilize to provide care for their dependent elderly members, their relationships may become stronger or experience stress. Although numerous research studies have addressed the issue of family caregiving during the 1980s, continued attention to health and family caregiving is expected in the next decade.

References

Ade-Ridder, Linda, and Timothy H. Brubaker. 1983. "The quality of long-term marriages." Pp. 21–30 in Timothy H. Brubaker (ed.), Family Relationships in Later Life. Beverly Hills, CA: Sage.

Ade-Ridder, Linda, and Timothy H. Brubaker. 1988. "Expected and reported division of responsibility of household tasks among older wives in two residential settings." Journal of Consumer Studies and Home Economics 12: 59–70.

Aldous, Joan. 1987. "New views on the family life of the elderly and the near-elderly." Journal of Marriage and the Family 49: 227–234.

American Association of Retired Persons. 1988 (October). National Survey of Caregivers: Summary of Findings. Washington, DC: American Association of Retired Persons.

Anderson, Stephen A., Candyce S. Russell, and Walter R. Schumm. 1983. "Perceived marital quality and family life-cycle categories: A further analysis." Journal of Marriage and the Family 45: 127–139.

Anderson, Trudy B. 1984. "Widowhood as a life transition: Its impact on kinship ties." Journal of Marriage and the Family 46: 105–114.

Arens, Diana Antos. 1982. "Widowhood and well-being: An examination of sex-differences within a causal model." International Journal of Aging and Human Development 15: 27–40.

Bachrach, Christine A. 1980. "Childlessness and social isolation among the elderly." Journal of Marriage and the Family 42: 627–637.

Balkwell, Carolyn, and Jack Balswick. 1981. "Subsistence economy, family structure, and the status of the elderly." Journal of Marriage and the Family 43: 423–429.

Bankoff, Elizabeth A. 1983. "Social support and adaptation to widowhood." Journal of Marriage and the Family 45: 827–839.

Baranowski, Mark D. 1982. "Grandparent-adolescent relations: Beyond the nuclear family." Adolescence 17: 575–584.

Barranti, Chrystal C. R. 1985. "The grandparent/grandchild relationship: Family resource in an era of voluntary bonds." Family Relations 34: 343–352.

Beckman, Linda J., and Betsy B. Houser. 1982. "The consequences of childlessness on the social-psychological well-being of older women." Journal of Gerontology 37: 243–250.

Bedford, Victoria H. 1989a. "Ambivalence in adult sibling relationships." Journal of Family Issues 10: 211–224.

Bedford, Victoria H. 1989b. "A comparison of thematic appreciation of sibling affiliation, conflict, and separation at two periods of adulthood." International Journal of Aging and Human Development 28: 53–66.

Bedford, Victoria H. 1989c. "Understanding the value of siblings in old age: A proposed model." American Behavioral Scientist 33: 33–44.

Bengtson, Vern L. 1989. "The problem of generations: Age group contrasts, continuities, and social change." Pp. 25–54 in Vern L. Bengtson (ed.), The Course of Later Life: Research and Reflections. New York: Springer.

Bengtson, Vern L., Neal E. Cutler, David J. Mangen, and Victor W. Marshall. 1985. "Generations, cohorts, and relations between age groups." Pp. 304–338 in Robert H. Binstock and Ethel Shanas (eds.), Handbook of Aging and the Social Sciences. New York: Van Nostrand Reinhold.

Bengtson, Vern L., and Joan F. Robertson (eds.). 1985. Grandparenthood. Beverly Hills, CA: Sage.

Berardo, Donna Hodgkins. 1983. "Divorce and remarriage at middle age and beyond." Annals of the American Academy of Political and Social Sciences 464: 132–140.

Blieszner, Rosemary, and Jay A. Mancini. 1987. "Enduring ties: Older adults' parental role and responsibilities." Family Relations 36: 176–180.

Breckenridge, James N., Dolores Gallagher, Larry W. Thompson, and James Peterson. 1986. "Characteristic depressive symptoms of bereaved elders." Journal of Gerontology 41: 163–168.

Brody, Elaine M. 1981. "Women in the middle and family help to older people." Gerontologist 25: 19–29.

Brody, Elaine M., and Claire B. Schoonover. 1986. "Patterns of parent-care when adult daughters work and when they do not." Gerontologist 26: 372–381.

Brubaker, Ellie B. 1986. "Caring for a dependent spouse." American Behavioral Scientist 29: 485–496.

Brubaker, Timothy H. (ed.). 1983. Family Relationships in Later Life. Beverly Hills, CA: Sage.

Brubaker, Timothy H. 1985a. Later Life Families. Beverly Hills, CA: Sage.

Brubaker, Timothy H. 1985b. "Responsibility for household tasks: A look at golden anniversary couples aged 75 years and older." Pp. 27–36 in Warren Peterson and Jill Quadagno (eds.), Social Bonds in Later Life. Beverly Hills, CA: Sage.

Brubaker, Timothy H. 1986. "Developmental tasks in later life." American Behavioral Scientist 29: 381–388.

Brubaker, Timothy H. (ed.). 1987. Aging, Health and Family: Long-Term Care. Newbury Park, CA: Sage.

Brubaker, Timothy H., and Linda Ade-Ridder. 1986. "Husbands' responsibility for household tasks in older marriages: Does living situation make a difference?" Pp. 85–96 in Robert A. Lewis and Robert E. Salt (eds.), Men in Families. Beverly Hills, CA: Sage.

Brubaker, Timothy H., and Ellie Brubaker. 1989. "Toward a theory of family caregiving: Dependencies, responsibility and utilization of services." Pp. 245–257 in Jay A. Mancini (ed.), Aging Parents and Adult Children. Lexington, MA: D. C. Heath, Lexington Books.

Brubaker, Timothy H., and Charles B. Hennon. 1982. "Responsibility for household tasks: Comparing dual-earner and dual-retired marriages." Pp. 205–219 in Maximilliane E. Szinovacz (ed.), Women's Retirement: Policy Implications of Recent Research. Beverly Hills, CA: Sage.

Brubaker, Timothy H., and Beth I. Kinsel. 1985. "Who is responsible for household tasks in long term marriages of 'young-old' elderly?" Lifestyles: A Journal of Changing Patterns 7: 238–247.

Bulcroft, Kris, and Margaret O'Conner. 1986. "The importance of dating relationships on quality of life of older persons." Family Relations 35: 397–401.

Burton, Linda M., and Vern L. Bengtson. 1985. "Black

grandmothers: Issues of timing and continuity of roles." Pp. 61–80 in Vern L. Bengtson and Joan F. Robertson (eds.), Grandparenthood. Beverly Hills, CA: Sage.

Cantor, Marjorie H. 1983. "Strain among caregivers: A study of experiences in the United States." Gerontologist 23: 23–43.

Chatters, Linda M., Robert J. Taylor, and J. S. Jackson. 1985. "Size and composition of the informal helper networks of elderly blacks." Journal of Gerontology 40: 605–614.

Chatters, Linda M., Robert J. Taylor, and J. S Jackson. 1986. "Aged blacks' choices for an informal helper network." Journal of Gerontology 41: 94–100.

Chatters, Linda M., Robert J. Taylor, and Harold W. Neighbors. 1989. "Size of informal helper network mobilized during a serious personal problem among black Americans." Journal of Marriage and the Family 51: 667–676.

Chen, Yung-Ping, and Kwang-Wen Chu. 1982. "Household expenditure patterns: The effect of age of family head." Journal of Family Issues 3: 233–255.

Cherlin, Andrew J., and Frank F. Furstenberg. 1986. The New American Grandparent: A Place in the Family, a Life Apart. New York: Basic Books.

Chiriboga, David A. 1982. "Adaptation to marital separation in later and earlier life." Journal of Gerontology 37: 109–114.

Cicirelli, Victor G. 1980. "Sibling relationships in adulthood: A life span perspective." Pp. 455–462 in Leonard W. Poon (ed.), Aging in the 1980's. Washington, DC: American Psychological Association.

Cicirelli, Victor G. 1981. Helping Elderly Parents: Roles of Adult Children. Boston: Auburn House.

Cicirelli, Victor G. 1982. "Sibling influence throughout the lifespan." Pp. 267–284 in Michael E. Lamb and Brian Sutton-Smith (eds.), Sibling Relationships: Their Nature and Significance across the Lifespan. Hillsdale, NJ: Lawrence Erlbaum Associates.

Cicirelli, Victor G. 1983. "Adult children and their elderly parents." Pp. 31–46 in Timothy H. Brubaker (ed.), Family Relationships in Later Life. Beverly Hills, CA: Sage.

Cicirelli, Victor G. 1985a. "The role of siblings as family caregivers." Pp. 93–107 in William J. Sauer and Raymond T. Coward (eds.), Social Support Networks and the Care of the Elderly. New York: Springer.

Cicirelli, Victor G. 1985b. "Sibling relationships throughout the life cycle." Pp. 177–214 in Luciano L'Abate (ed.), The Handbook of Family Psychology and Therapy. Homewood, IL: Dorsey Press.

Dellman-Jenkins, Mary, Diane Papalia, and Martha Lopez. 1987. "Teenagers' reported interaction with grandparents: Exploring the extent of alienation." Lifestyles: A Journal of Changing Patterns 3 and 4: 35–46.

Dobson, Cynthia. 1983. "Sex-role and marital role expectations." Pp. 109–126 in Timothy H. Brubaker (ed.), Family Relationships in Later Life. Beverly Hills, CA: Sage.

Doka, Kenneth J., and Mary Ellen Mertz. 1988. "The meaning and significance of great-grandparenthood." Gerontologist 28: 192–197.

Doty, Pamela, Korbin Lui, and Joshua Wiener. 1985. "An overview of long-term care." Health Care Financing Review 6: 69–78.

Dressel, Paula L. 1980. "Assortive mating in later life: Some initial considerations." Journal of Family Issues 1: 379–396.

Feinson, Marjorie Chary. 1986. "Aging widows and widowers: Are there mental health differences?" International Journal of Aging and Human Development 23: 241–255.

Fenwick, Rudy, and Charles M. Barresi. 1981. "Health consequences of marital-status change among the elderly: A comparison of cross-sectional and longitudinal analyses." Journal of Health and Social Behavior 22: 106–116.

Ferraro, Kenneth F. 1985. "The effect of widowhood on the health status of older persons." International Journal of Aging and Human Development 21: 9–25.

Ferraro, Kenneth F., Elizabeth Mutran, and Charles M. Barresi. 1984. "Widowhood, health, and friendship support in later life." Journal of Health and Social Behavior 25: 245–259.

Fisher, Lucy R. 1981. "Transitions in the mother-daughter relationship." Journal of Marriage and the Family 43: 613–622.

Fisher, Lucy R. 1983. "Transition into grandmotherhood." International Journal of Aging and Human Development 16: 67–78.

Fitting, Melinda, Peter Rabins, M. Jane Lucas, and James Eastham. 1986. "Caregivers for demented patients: A comparison of husbands and wives." Gerontologist 26: 248–252.

Gallagher, Dolores E., Larry W. Thompson, and James A. Peterson. 1982. "Psychosocial factors affecting adaptation to bereavement in the elderly." International Journal of Aging and Human Development 14: 79–95.

Gibson, Rose C. 1982. "Blacks at middle and later life: Resources and coping." Annals of the American Academy of Political and Social Sciences 464: 79–90.

Gilford, Rosalie. 1984. "Contrasts in marital satisfaction throughout old age: An exchange theory analysis." Journal of Gerontology 39: 325–333.

Giordano, Jeffrey A. 1988. "Parents of the baby boomers: A new generation of young-old." Family Relations 37: 411–414.

Gladstone, James W. 1988. "Perceived changes in grandmother-grandchild relations following a child's separation or divorce." Gerontologist 28: 66–72.

Glenn, Norval, and Sara McLanahan. 1981. "The effects of offspring on the psychological well-being of older adults." Journal of Marriage and the Family 43: 409–421.

Glick, Paul C. 1980. "Remarriage: Some recent changes and variations." Journal of Family Issues 1: 455–478.

Glick, Paul C. 1989. "Remarried families, stepfamilies,

and stepchildren: A brief demographic profile." *Family Relations* 38: 24–27.

Glick, Paul C., and Sung-ling Lin. 1986. "More young adults are living with their parents: Who are they?" *Journal of Marriage and the Family* 48: 107–112.

Goetting, Ann. 1986. "The developmental tasks of siblingship over the life cycle." *Journal of Marriage and the Family* 48: 703–714.

Gold, Deborah T. 1989. "Generational solidarity: Conceptual antecedents and consequences." *American Behavioral Scientist* 33: 19–32.

Gubrium, Jaber F. 1988. "Family responsibility and caregiving in the qualitative analysis of the Alzheimer's disease experience." *Journal of Marriage and the Family* 50: 197–207.

Gutmann, David. 1987. *Reclaimed Powers: Toward a New Psychology of Men and Women in Later Life.* New York: Basic Books.

Hagestad, Gunhild O. 1985. "Continuity and connectedness." Pp. 31–48 in Vern L. Bengtson and Joan F. Robertson (eds.), *Grandparenthood.* Beverly Hills, CA: Sage.

Hagestad, Gunhild O. 1988. "Demographic change and the life course: Some emerging trends in the family realm." *Family Relations* 37: 405–410.

Hagestad, Gunhild O., and Linda Burton. 1986. "Grandparenthood, life context, and family development." *American Behavioral Scientist* 29: 471–484.

Hagestad, Gunhild O., and M. Smyer. 1982. "Dissolving long-term relationships: Patterns of divorcing in middle age." Pp. 155–188 in S. Duck (ed.), *Personal Relationships 4: Dissolving Personal Relationships.* New York: Academic Press.

Hartshorne, Timothy S., and Guy J. Manaster. 1982. "The relationship with grandparents: Contact, importance, role conceptions." *International Journal of Aging and Human Development* 15: 233–245.

Hennon, Charles B. 1983. "Divorce and the elderly: A neglected area of research." Pp. 149–172 in Timothy H. Brubaker (ed.), *Family Relationships in Later Life.* Beverly Hills, CA: Sage.

Hennon, Charles B., and John R. Burton. 1986. "Financial satisfaction as a developmental task among the elderly." *American Behavioral Scientist* 29: 439–452.

Hildreth, Gladys J., Gana Van Laanen, Eleanor Kelley, and Thomas Durant. 1980. "Participation in and enjoyment of family maintenance activities by elderly women." *Family Relations* 29: 386–390.

Horowitz, Amy. 1985a. "Family caregiving to the frail elderly." Pp. 194–246 in Carl Eisdorfer (ed.), *Annual Review of Gerontology and Geriatrics* (Vol. 5). New York: Springer.

Horowitz, Amy. 1985b. "Sons and daughters as caregivers to older parents." *Gerontologist* 18: 301–306.

Hyman, Herbert H. 1983. *Of Time and Widowhood.* Durham, NC: Duke University Press.

Ishii-Kuntz, Masako, and Gary R. Lee. 1987. "Status of the elderly: An extension of the theory." *Journal of Marriage and the Family* 49: 413–420.

Johnson, Colleen L. 1983. "Dyadic family relationships and family supports: An analysis of the family

caregiver." *Gerontologist* 23: 377–383.

Johnson, Colleen L. 1988a. "Active and latent functions of grandparenting during the divorce process." *Gerontologist* 28: 185–191.

Johnson, Colleen L. 1988b. "Postdivorce reorganization of relationships between divorcing children and their parents." *Journal of Marriage and the Family* 50: 221–231.

Johnson, Colleen L. 1985. "The impact of illness on late-life marriages." *Journal of Marriage and the Family* 47: 165–172.

Johnson, Colleen L., and Barbara M. Barer. 1987. "Marital stability and the changing kinship networks of grandparents." *Gerontologist* 27: 330–335.

Johnson, Colleen L., and Donald J. Catalano. 1981. "Childless elderly and their family supports." *Gerontologist* 21: 610–618.

Johnson, Colleen L., and Donald J. Catalano. 1983. "A longitudinal study of family supports to impaired elderly." *Gerontologist* 23: 612–618.

Johnson, David R., Lynn K. White, John N. Edwards, and Alan Booth. 1986. "Dimensions of marital quality: Toward methodological and conceptual refinement." *Journal of Family Issues* 7: 31–49.

Keating, Norah, and Priscilla Cole. 1980. "What do I do with him 24 hours a day." *Gerontologist* 20: 84–89.

Keith, Pat M. 1983. "A comparison of the resources of parents and childless men and women in very old age." *Family Relations* 32: 403–409.

Keith, Pat M. 1986a. "Isolation of the unmarried in later life." *Family Relations* 35: 389–395.

Keith, Pat M. 1986b. "The social context and resources of the unmarried in old age." *International Journal of Aging and Human Development* 23: 81–96.

Keith, Pat M. 1989. *The Unmarried in Later Life.* New York: Praeger.

Keith, Pat M., Cynthia D. Dobson, Willis J. Goudy, and Edward A. Powers. 1981. "Older men: Occupation, employment status, household involvement and well-being." *Journal of Family Issues* 2: 336–349.

Kitson, Gay, Helena Lopata, William Holmes, and Suzanne Meyering. 1980. "Divorcees and widows: Similarities and differences." *American Journal of Orthopsychiatry* 50: 291–301.

Kivett, Vira R. 1985a. "Consanguinity and kin level: Their relative importance to the helping network of older adults." *Journal of Gerontology* 40: 228–234.

Kivett, Vira R. 1985b. "Grandfathers and grandchildren: Patterns of association, helping, and psychological closeness." *Family Relations* 34: 565–571.

Kivett, Vira R., and R. Max Lerner. 1980. "Perspectives on the childless rural elderly: A comparative analysis." *Gerontologist* 20: 708–716.

Kivnick, Helen Q. 1982. "Grandparenthood: An overview of meaning and mental health." *Gerontologist* 22: 59–66.

Kivnick, Helen Q. 1983. "Dimensions of grandparenthood meaning: Deductive conceptualization and empirical derivation." *Journal of Personality and Social Psychology* 44: 1056–1068.

Kleban, Morton H., Elaine M. Brody, Claire B. Shoonover, and Christine Hoffman. 1989. "Family help to the elderly: Perceptions of sons-in-law regarding parent care." Journal of Marriage and the Family 51: 303–312.

Kohen, Janet A. 1983. "Old but not alone: Informal social supports among the elderly by marital status and sex." Gerontologist 23: 57–63.

Koo, Helen P., and C. M. Suchindran. 1980. "Effects of children on women's remarriage prospects." Journal of Family Issues 1: 497–515.

Lee, Gary R. 1984 "Status of the elderly: Economic and familial antecedents." Journal of Marriage and the Family 46: 267–275.

Lee, Gary R. 1985. "Theoretical perspectives on social networks." Pp. 21–37 in William J. Sauer and Raymond T. Coward (eds.), Social Support Networks and the Care of the Elderly. New York: Springer.

Lee, Gary R. 1988. "Marital satisfaction in later life: The effects of nonmarital roles." Journal of Marriage and the Family 50: 775–783.

Lee, Gary R., and Eugene Ellithorpe. 1982. "Intergenerational exchange and subjective well-being among the elderly." Journal of Marriage and the Family 44: 217–224.

Lee, Gary R., and Marilyn Ihinger-Tallman. 1980. "Sibling interaction and morale: The effects of family relations on older persons." Research on Aging 2: 367–391.

Lee, Gary R., and Constance L. Shehan. 1989. "Retirement and marital satisfaction." Journal of Gerontology 44: S226–S230.

Longino, Charles F., and Aaron Lipman. 1981. "Married and spouseless men and women in planned retirement communities: Support network differentials." Journal of Marriage and the Family 43: 169–177.

Mancini, Jay A. 1989. Aging Parents and Adult Children. Lexington, MA: Lexington Books.

Mancini, Jay A., and Rosemary Blieszner. 1989. "Aging parents and adult children: Research themes in intergenerational relationships." Journal of Marriage and the Family 51: 275–290. [Reprinted in this volume]

Matthews, Sarah H., and Tena Tarler Rosner. 1988. "Shared filial responsibility: The family as the primary caregiver." Journal of Marriage and the Family 50: 185–195.

Matthews, Sarah H., and Jetse Sprey. 1984. "The impact of divorce on grandparenthood: An exploratory study." Gerontologist 24: 41–47.

Matthews, Sarah H., and Jetse Sprey. 1985. "Adolescents' relationship with grandparents: An empirical contribution to conceptual clarification." Journal of Gerontology 40: 621–626.

Matthews, Sarah H., Janet E. Werkner, and Paula J. Delaney. 1989. "Relative contributions of help by employed and nonemployed sisters to their elderly parents." Journal of Gerontology 44: S36–S44.

McConnel, Charles E., and Firooz Deljavan. 1983. "Consumption patterns of the retired household." Journal of Gerontology 38: 480–490.

McGee, Jerrie L. 1985. "The effects of siblings on the life satisfaction of the rural elderly." Journal of Marriage and the Family 47: 85–91.

McGloshen, Thomas H., and Shirley L. O'Bryant. 1988. "The psychological well-being of older, recent widows." Psychology of Women Quarterly 12: 99–116.

Miller, Baila. 1987. "Gender and control among spouses of the cognitively impaired: A research note." Gerontologist 27: 447–453.

Morgan, Leslie A. 1981. "Economic changes at midlife widowhood: A longitudinal analysis." Journal of Marriage and the Family 43: 899–912.

Morgan, Leslie A. 1984. "Changes in family interaction following widowhood." Journal of Marriage and the Family 46: 323–331.

Moss, Miriam S., and Sidney Z. Moss. 1980. "The image of the deceased spouse in remarriage of elderly widow(er)s." Journal of Gerontological Social Work 3: 59–70.

Mutran, Elizabeth, and Donald D. Reitzes. 1984. "Intergenerational support activities and well-being among elderly: A convergence of exchange and symbolic interaction perspectives." American Sociological Review 49: 117–130.

O'Bryant, Shirley L. 1988. "Sibling support and older widows' well-being." Journal of Marriage and the Family 50: 173–183.

Patterson, Shirley L. 1987. "Older rural natural helpers: Gender and site differences in the helping process." Gerontologist 27: 639–644.

Presser, Harriet R. 1989. "Some economic complexities of child care provided by grandmothers." Journal of Marriage and the Family 51: 581–591.

Quinn, William H. 1983. "Personal and family adjustment in later life." Journal of Marriage and the Family 45: 57–73.

Rempel, Judith. 1985. "Childless elderly: What are they missing?" Journal of Marriage and the Family 47: 343–348.

Rhyne, Darla. 1981. "Bases of marital satisfaction among men and women." Journal of Marriage and the Family 43: 941–955.

Ross, Helgola G., and Joel I. Milgram. 1982. "Important variables in adult sibling relationships: A qualitative analysis." Pp. 225–266 in Michael E. Lamb and Brian Sutton-Smith (eds.), Sibling Relationships: Their Nature and Significance across the Lifespan. Hillsdale, NJ: Lawrence Erlbaum Associates.

Sanders, Gregory F., and Debra W. Trygstad. 1989. "Stepgrandparents and grandparents: The view from young adults." Family Relations 38: 71–75.

Schumm, Walter R., and Margaret A. Bugaighis. 1986. "Marital quality over the marital career: Alternative explanations." Journal of Marriage and the Family 48: 165–168.

Scott, Jean Pearson. 1983. "Siblings and other kin." Pp. 47–62 in Timothy H. Brubaker (ed.), Family Relationships in Later Life. Beverly Hills, CA: Sage.

Scott, Jean Pearson, and Vira R. Kivett. 1985. "Differences in the morale of older, rural widows and widowers." International Journal of Aging and Human Development 21: 121–135.

Seelbach, Wayne C. 1984. "Filial responsibility and the care of aging family members." Pp. 92–105 in William H. Quinn and George A. Hughston (eds.), Independent Aging. Rockville, MD: Aspen Publications.

Seelbach, Wayne C., and Charles J. Hansen. 1980. "Satisfaction with family relations among the elderly." Family Relations 29: 91–96.

Shanas, Ethel. 1980. "Older people and their families: The new pioneers." Journal of Marriage and the Family 42: 9–15.

Sheehan, Nancy, and Paul Nuttall. 1988. "Conflict, emotion, and personal strain among family caregivers." Family Relations 37: 92–98.

Singh, B. Krishna, and J. Sherwood Williams. 1981. "Childlessness and family satisfaction." Research on Aging 3: 218–227.

Smallegan, M. 1985. "There was nothing else to do: Needs for care before nursing home admission." Gerontologist 25: 364–369.

Smith, Ken R., and Cathleen D. Zick. 1986. "The incidence of poverty among the recently widowed: Mediating factors in the life course." Journal of Marriage and the Family 48: 619–630.

Smyer, Michael A., and Brian F. Hofland. 1982. "Divorce and family support in later life: Emerging concerns." Journal of Family Issues 3: 61–77.

Sprey, Jetse, and Sarah H. Matthews. 1982. "Contemporary grandparenthood: A systemic transition." Annals of the American Academy of the Political and Social Sciences 464: 91–103.

Stephens, Susan A., and Jon B. Christianson. 1985. Informal Care of the Elderly. Lexington, MA: Lexington Books.

Stolar, E., M. A. Hill, and A. Tomblin. 1986. "Family disengagement—Myth or reality: A follow-up study after geriatric assessment." Canadian Journal of Aging 5: 113–124.

Stoller, Eleanor Palo. 1983. "Parental caregiving by adult children." Journal of Marriage and the Family 45: 851–858.

Stoller, Eleanor Palo. 1985. "Exchange patterns in the informal support networks of the elderly: The impact of reciprocity on morale." Journal of Marriage and the Family 47: 335–342.

Stone, Robyn, Gail Lee Cafferata, and Judith Sangl. 1987. "Caregivers of the frail elderly: A national profile." Gerontologist 27: 616–626.

Streib, Gordon F., and Rubye Wilkerson Beck. 1980. "Older families: A decade review." Journal of Marriage and the Family 42: 937–956.

Stroebe, Margaret S., and Wolfgang Stroebe. 1982. "Who suffers more? Sex differences in health risks of the widowed." Psychological Bulletin 93: 279–301.

Suggs, Patricia K. 1989. "Predictors of association among older siblings: A black/white comparison." American Behavioral Scientist 33: 70–80.

Suitor, Jill J., and Karl Pillemer. 1987. "The presence of adult children: A source of stress for elderly couples' marriages." Journal of Marriage and the Family 49: 717–723.

Suitor, Jill J., and Karl Pillemer. 1988. "Explaining intergenerational conflict when adult children and elderly parents live together." Journal of Marriage and the Family 50: 1037–1047.

Swenson, Clifford H., Ron W. Eskew, and Karen A. Kohlhepp. 1981. "Stage of family life cycle, ego development and the marriage relationship." Journal of Marriage and the Family 43: 841–853.

Szinovacz, Maximilliane E. 1980. "Female retirement: Effects on spousal roles and marital adjustment." Journal of Family Issues 1: 423–440.

Taylor, Robert J., Linda M. Chatters, and Vickie M. Mays. 1988. "Parents, children, siblings, in-laws, and non-kin as sources of emergency assistance to black Americans." Family Relations 37: 298–304.

Teachman, Jay D., and Alex Heckert. 1985. "The impact of age and children on remarriage." Journal of Family Issues 6: 185–203.

Thoits, Peggy A. 1982. "Conceptual, methodological, and theoretical problems in studying social support as a buffer against life stress." Journal of Health and Social Behavior 23: 145–159.

Thomas, Jeanne L. 1986a. "Age and sex differences in perceptions of grandparenting." Journal of Gerontology 41: 417–423.

Thomas, Jeanne L. 1986b. "Gender differences in satisfaction with grandparenting." Psychology and Aging 1: 215–219.

Thompson, Linda, and Alexis J. Walker. 1987. "Mothers as mediators of intimacy between grandmothers and their young adult granddaughters." Family Relations 36: 72–77.

Troll, Lillian E. 1971. "The family of later life: A decade review." Journal of Marriage and the Family 33: 263–290.

Troll, Lillian E. 1983. "Grandparents: The family watchdogs." Pp. 63–74 in Timothy H. Brubaker (ed.), Family Relationships in Later Life. Beverly Hills, CA: Sage.

Uhlenberg, Peter, and Mary Anne P. Myers. 1981. "Divorce and the elderly." Gerontologist 21: 276–282.

Vachon, Mary L. S., Joy Rodgers, W. Alan Lyall, Wilhelm J. Lancee, Adrienne R. Sheldon, and Stanley J. J. Freeman. 1982. "Predictors and correlates of adaptation to conjugal bereavement." American Journal of Psychiatry 139: 998–1002.

Weiss, Robert S. 1984. "The impact of marital dissolution on income and consumption in single-parent households." Journal of Marriage and the Family 46: 115–127.

Wentowski, Gloria J. 1985. "Older women's perceptions of great-grandmotherhood: A research note." Gerontologist 25: 593–596.

Zarit, Stephen, P. Todd, and J. Zarit. 1986. "Subjective burden of husbands and wives as caregivers: A longitudinal study." Gerontologist 26: 260–266.

Zick, Cathleen D., and Ken R. Smith. 1986. "Immediate and delayed effects of widowhood on poverty: Patterns from the 1970s." Gerontologist 26: 669–675.

Zick, Cathleen D., and Ken R. Smith. 1988. "Recent widowhood, remarriage, and changes in economic well-being." Journal of Marriage and the Family 50: 233–244.

Jay A. Mancini and Rosemary Blieszner
Virginia Polytechnic Institute and State University

Aging Parents and Adult Children:
Research Themes in Intergenerational Relations

Dominant themes representing the relationships of older parents and their adult children are discussed. These pertain to roles and responsibilities, parent-child interaction (contact patterns, exchange, assistance, and support), individual well-being, relationship quality, and caregiving by adult children. These are discussed within the context of societal age structure changes. Speculation on the future of research on aged parents and adult children focuses on the application of theory, the need for studies on conflict, the role that qualitative inquiry could play, alternative approaches to family companionship, and investigations on socialization in adulthood.

Research on older people and their families has often been driven by concern over whether the aged and their kin are alienated, wonder about the contribution that family life makes to the mental health of the elderly, debate over who will care for the frail elderly, interest in the changing age structure of the society, and the nature of changing family patterns. Because the literature is most rich with regard to older parents and their adult children, that relationship will be our sole focus. We will organize the literature around specific themes and suggest where theory and new empirical work ought to be directed. These themes were chosen because of the preponderance of recent work involving them and because of their

Department of Family and Child Development, College of Human Resources, Virginia Polytechnic Institute and State University, Blacksburg, VA 24061-0416.

significance for understanding the parent-child relationship: population trends, roles and responsibilities, interaction patterns, relationships and individual well-being, and care provided by adult children.

POPULATION TRENDS

Pifer and Bronte (1986: 3) suggested that the current "demographic revolution" will have an impact rivaling that of "the conquest and subsequent closing of the frontier, the successive waves of European immigration, the development of our great cities, the post–World War II baby boom, the civil rights and women's movements, the massive influx of women into the paid labor force, the revolution in sexual mores, and the decay of many of our large urban centers."

The aging of our society is occurring at an exceedingly rapid pace, as evidenced by the fact that over the past 80 or so years average life expectancy in the United States increased from 47 to 75 years. In 1900 fewer than one in eight Americans was 55 years of age or older, and only one in 25 was 65 years old and beyond. But in the mid-1980s about 29% were 55 and older and about one in nine was at least 65 years of age (U.S. Senate Special Committee on Aging, 1985–86). For children born during 1980 more than three of four will reach the age of 65 (Riley and Riley, 1986). Siegel and Taeuber (1986) reported that in 1900 life expectancy at 65 years of age was 11.9 more years, and in 1980 it had risen to 16.4 years. Much of the graying of America is a women's phenomenon (Markson, 1983). In 1980 about 55% of the population 40 years of age and older were women, and about 60% of people 60 and over were women. In 1984, among people 65 to 69 years old, there were 81 men for every 100 women, and for those in the age range of 70 to 74 years there were 72 men for every 100 women.

Information on population aging suggests that the rate of age structure change is rapid, the rate of aging in the older segment of the population is more rapid than that of the general population, the baby boom cohort will graphically change and increase the median age of the population, the proportion of those older to those younger has shifted from the young being dominant toward a case where there will be equal proportions, life expectancy in general and at older ages has increased, and women on the average now outlive and will continue to outlive men.

Several important implications of these data are suggested by Riley and Riley (1986: 55): the opportunity for amassing social and psychological experience is increased, the opportunity for making a greater number of changes in one's life is increased (as examples, the changing of careers, of marriage partners, or of educational plans), and in general there are opportunities to "exercise new and expanded options." Pertinent to our inquiry are the implications for the relationships between older parents and their adult children. In terms of the above analysis by Riley and Riley, there will be increased opportunities for a continuation of the parent-child relationship, increased opportunities for parents and children to experience the outcomes of frailty of those parents, and expanded opportunities for the continued development of one of life's longer-standing relationships.

ROLES AND RESPONSIBILITIES

What do elderly parents expect of their adult children and what is the content of their respective roles? What changes in their interaction patterns might we expect to attend the societal changes noted above? In this section we take a look at research on the expectations that older adults and their grown children hold for their relationship and the roles that they play in each others' lives.

Expectations of Elderly Parents and Adult Children

Seelbach and his colleagues conducted a series of studies on the filial responsibility expectations of older adult parents (Hanson, Sauer, and Seelbach, 1983; Seelbach, 1977, 1978, 1981, and 1984; Seelbach and Sauer, 1977). They investigated the extent to which parents expect their children to assist them in times of need, correlates of such expectations for filial responsibility, and predictors of the actual types and amounts of assistance that adult children provide. The areas of responsibility examined in these studies involved children living near or sharing their home with their parents, frequency of contact, and provision of various forms of emergency assistance.

The results of these studies revealed no racial differences in types of expectations or in level of support provided. There were gender differences, with females more likely than males to endorse living with their children if they did not wish to live alone or if they were unable to care for themselves. Parents who received high levels of filial support from their children were likely to be female, not married, of low income, and in poor health.

Interestingly, this program of research found that holding expectations of high filial responsibility was inversely related to older parents' morale. The authors suggested that this finding may be due to discrepancies between parents' and children's views of appropriate levels of filial responsibility or failure of the offspring to live up to parental expectations.

Blieszner and Mancini (1987) reported a study in which older parents generally failed to endorse the filial responsibility items used in the research by Seelbach et al. mentioned above. Instead, this group of respondents held expectations for more abstract demonstrations of filial responsibility, such as affection, thoughtfulness, and open communication. They expressed concern about how to negotiate the desired level of noninterfering closeness with their children and how to discuss their wishes with respect to issues such as care in a future medical emergency, long-term care preferences, funeral arrangements, and disposition of their property after death. These findings suggest that well-educated, healthy, resourceful elderly parents are comfortable with routine interactions with their children and do not expect direct assistance except for the most extreme circumstances.

Brody and her colleagues have pursued investigations of filial responsibility from the perspective of multiple generations of women (Brody, Johnsen, and Fulcomer, 1984; Brody, Johnsen, Fulcomer, and Lang, 1983). They were especially interested in determining whether women's changing roles in the family and work force had any effect on attitudes about and preferences for parental caregiving by children. They found that each successively younger generation had more egalitarian attitudes about the appropriateness of both sons and daughters providing parental care than the previous one, although members of all three generations favored sharing this task between the genders. The highest endorsement of the use of formal services for elderly parents came from the oldest generation of women, and the lowest from the youngest generation, but all respondents believed that children should be available to help parents when needed. This help should be facilitated by adjustment of family schedules and assistance with health care costs if necessary, but respondents were not in favor of family caregivers adjusting their work schedules or sharing households with their parents.

Content of Adult Child and
Aged Parent Roles

The parent-child bond can endure for many decades, with both partners moving through adulthood and into old age over the duration of the relationship. Although in contemporary society there is flexibility in the ways that parents of minors accomplish childrearing, there is social and legal consensus concerning the roles of parent and child: parents are to provide affection, physical sustenance, socialization, and recreation; children are to respect and obey their parents, do well in school, and attain social skills. No such clear-cut role parameters exist for the period when both child and parent are adults, but certainly there is widespread recognition that the relationship changes.

A major change occurs when all of the children have left home and the parents experience the "empty nest" period. This stage is a 20th-century phenomenon, because in earlier times parents continued to have children later in life than now, thus extending the childrearing and launching phases of family life into old age (Borland, 1982). Glick (1977) estimated that the empty-nest period has increased from 2 to an average of 13 years during this century.

Research during the 1970s attempted to clarify the effects of the empty nest on parents. One hypothesis was that diminishment of this major role leads to identity crisis and depression, especially for women whose primary focus has been on child care. The opposite perspective suggested that decline in childrearing responsibilities frees parents to pursue their own interests more fully. Although evidence has been garnered to support both positions, most recent studies have demonstrated that the transition to the empty nest is not necessarily or usually traumatic for women (e.g., Borland, 1982; Harkins, 1978). At the same time, at least a few reports suggested that fathers may be affected more negatively by this change in parenting than stereotyped views of the remote, uninvolved father would suggest (Back, 1971; Lewis, Freneau, and Roberts, 1979).

A recent trend that has caught the attention of family gerontologists is the return of adult children to the parental home (Mancini and Blieszner, 1985; Shehan, Berardo, and Berardo, 1984.) Census data revealed a decline in the rates of intergenerational doubling-up from the 1940s to the 1970s but a sharp increase thereafter (Shehan et al., 1984). Preliminary reports from the popular press and an exploratory study (Clemens and Axelson, 1985) have indicated financial and emotional reasons for this situation: high unemployment rates and other economic problems contribute to the need to economize by sharing a household, and high divorce rates along with other personal problems lead adult children to seek social support, assistance with child care, and other forms of aid from their parents via co-residence.

The benefits of multigenerational households have been noted (Shehan et al., 1984) and can include increased intergenerational understanding and mutual assistance. The list of potential problems, however, is much longer. At the top of it is the disruption of the parents' plans and activities because of having additional people in the household. Also critical are the problems associated with this "nonnormative" situation, such as lack of role clarity and failure to accomplish a normative transition, and those associated with crowding, lifestyle differences, increased household tasks and expenses, and the like (Clemens and Axelson, 1985; Shehan et al., 1984). Suitor and Pillemer (1987) analyzed the effects of parent-child co-residence on the elderly parents' marital relationship. Although they found that the mere presence of adult children in the household was not related to the amount of parental conflict, it was the case that conflict between the parents and children was associated with marital conflict between the parents. Even though the parent-child relationship may not have much impact on older adults' overall psychological well-being (discussed below), it does have the potential of affecting the quality of family life. Additional research on the ''refilling'' of the empty nest is needed, particularly to determine whether this is a transitory phenomenon rooted in current socioeconomic circumstances or whether it represents a new aspect of parenting and attitude toward family support for which future generations of older parents should be prepared.

The empty nest can also be refilled if the middle-aged individual assumes the care of an older parent. In this situation, discussed in greater detail below, the opportunities for personal fulfillment that many parents anticipate with the emancipation of their children are lost (Tobin and Kulys, 1980).

Another line of research on parent-child roles when both are adults has focused on older adults' subjective perceptions of the role (Blieszner and Mancini, 1987). Three-fourths of the parents in this exploratory study stated that they still had a parenting role, but three-fourths also said that they do not need the role at this time in their lives. They enjoyed the feeling of being needed and loved by their children, and they were flattered when their children asked them for advice. They mentioned that parenthood continued to add interest to life, but they did not rely on their children as major sources of identity or activity. As they reflected on changes in the parenting role over time, they stated that direct caretaking and influence had diminished, and they viewed their children more as friends now than as subordinates. Love, interest in their children's activities and welfare, and exchanges of assistance and advice endured, but for these parents, responsibility for their children clearly was less intense in old age. Their perceptions of the role of parent in old age reflected the ''friend'' relationship between parents and children described by English (1979) in her essay on responsibilities of aged parents and adult children for each other.

A case study analysis by Fischer (1985) presents a different picture of parent and child roles in later life and shows how crisis affects their enactment. The cases involved families in which the parents were experiencing a medical crisis and children were planning to care for them. The children viewed themselves as having a more protective relationship with their parents than ever before, and some explicitly declared that a role reversal had taken place in the relationship. The role reversal centered on the child's assumption that he or she could now make better decisions about the parent's care than the parent could. Parents in the sample, however, did not acknowledge that any such shift in responsibilities had taken place, and children expressed frustration about this perceptual difference in the nature of the roles. The parents had to trade decision-making for the nurturance they needed, while the children had to assume the burdens of caregiving along with their worry about the parents' future well-being.

The following section explores the character of parent-child interaction patterns in more detail. Included are discussions of both the frequency and quality of their joint activity.

PARENT-CHILD INTERACTION

Frequency of Contact

One of the first questions that social scientists asked with regard to the relationship that older people have with their children involved the extent to which they saw each other, spoke on the phone, and corresponded. This interest was related to general sociological concern about what was happening to the American family as a result of societal and technological change.

Cohler (1983) and Hagestad (1987b) have discussed the roots of this interest. Cohler (1983: 33) stated, ''It is part of the American romance with the rural past to believe that urbanization resulted in the destruction of the tightly knit extended family.'' He expanded his argument by saying that scientists such as Wirth, Park, and Burgess believed that the diversity of urban life necessarily weakened primary relationship cohesion and that the accompanying social and geographic mobility was not compatible with extended family relationships. Theorists assumed that a necessary artifact of industrialization and urbanization was a decrease in the importance of kin. They wondered whether or not, or to what degree, older people were alienated from their families (Shanas, 1979). In her discussion of the alienation hypothesis, Shanas (1979: 6) noted its components: "Because of the geographic mobility of the population of the U.S. most old people who have children live at great distances from their children; Because of the alienation of old people from their children, most older parents rarely see their children; Because of the predominance of the nuclear family in the U.S. most old people rarely see their siblings or other relatives; and, Because of the existence and availability of large human service bureaucracies, families are no longer important as a source of care for older people." A review of research studies of the 1960s showed that many studies were designed to find out if older people were alienated, and concluded that they were not (Troll, 1971). Unfortunately, research continues to pursue this line of work, even though the question has long been answered.

Troll, Miller, and Atchley (1979) indicated that about three-fourths of older parents have face-to-face contact with a child on a weekly or semiweekly basis, and when face-to-face contact is not possible, they rely upon other methods of staying in touch. Even in cases where geographical distance is considerable, families and their elders stay in contact (Dewit, Wister, and Burch, 1988). Local, regional, and national surveys of older parents also have shown that a vast majority are in regular face-to-face contact with their children (Louis Harris and Associates, 1975; Shanas et al., 1968). A survey of adult children in the U.S. Midwest found that almost 70% saw an older parent on a weekly basis (Cicirelli, 1981). Recent research on a sample of older parents in the southeastern United States found that almost one-half saw a child at least several times a month for task accomplishment reasons, and about two-thirds saw a child at least several times a month for companionship purposes (Mancini and Blieszner, 1986).

Exchange, Assistance, and Support

A related aspect of spending time in one another's presence pertains to the nature of support in the relationship, that is, the nature of instrumental and emotional exchange and reciprocity. This question was also asked some years ago, but it would seem that the intricacies of interdepend-

ence have yet to be captured. It has been assumed that what one generation does for another is a behavioral indicator of concern, respect, caring, and the quality of family life. The exchange domain has been carved in two, that considered practical and that considered emotional. Among the aspects of assistance and support that have been included in surveys are caring for someone during illness; giving money; providing gifts other than money; running errands; preparing meals; taking care of children; giving advice on home management; cleaning house and making repairs; giving advice on jobs, business matters, and expensive purchases; helping with transportation; counseling about life problems; and giving emotional support and affection (Lee and Ellithorpe, 1982; Mancini and Blieszner, 1986; Louis Harris and Associates, 1975). Studies of exchange, assistance, and support conducted over the past 25 years showed a large amount of intergenerational involvement, both instrumental and affective. Not only are parents and their children in frequent contact, but also the practical things they do for each other are considerable.

Reciprocity in these relationships has come to be seen as important for understanding relationship quality. It is known that older parents continue to provide support of various kinds to their adult children and are not only the recipients of support (Morgan, 1982; Troll, Miller, and Atchley, 1979); the provision of support by parents appears to be an enduring aspect of their role (Morgan, 1982). Cheal (1983) noted that even with regard to economic assistance to others, older people feel substantial obligation. On average, older parents are more likely to give help to their children rather than to receive help from their children (Riley and Foner, 1968). What seems to impinge on the degree to which parents provide support is a change in health or in economic status (Atchley and Miller, 1980; Mutran and Reitzes, 1984; Seelbach, 1978; Shanas et al., 1968). Atchley and Miller (1980) said that neither the parent nor the child generation should be considered exclusively as a giver or as a receiver of aid when all types of support are considered, and that several patterns of aid exist: a direct flow of aid from the old to the young, flow of aid from the middle generation to their parents and to their own children, and a true reciprocal flow among all generations in the family. Zopf (1986) asserted that the durability of family relations in part stems from the functions that the family fulfills for an older person and, similarly, the inputs that the older person has into the family. Kivett (1985) showed that if support is forthcoming at all, the sources are likely to be children and children-in-law.

A social support system, according to Cantor (1980) addresses three needs that older people have: for socialization, for accomplishing everyday life tasks, and for personal assistance in difficult times. Social support has its formal and its informal components, and what we have been discussing falls into the informal realm. The literature shows that adult children address those needs pertaining to everyday life tasks and support during difficult times. What is far less clear is the socialization function that families represent.

Parents and children engage in mutually supportive exchange patterns. Their contact is frequent and within that contact time they exchange a variety of personal services. In a way the existence of these exchanges represents the well-being of a family. Research, however, often has contrasted these exchanges, and the contact parameters in which they occur, with measures of the older parents' personal well-being.

RELATIONSHIPS AND INDIVIDUAL WELL-BEING

A substantial portion of the literature on how parents and their children relate in adulthood has been concerned with the impact that the relationship has on the well-being of the parent. It is not surprising that family variables have been contrasted with well-being, since the preponderance of social gerontological research has been focused on life satisfaction, morale, happiness, and psychological well-being (Adams, 1971; Larson, 1978). Since the 1940s social gerontology researchers have been investigating the correlates of this construct.

With well-being established as the bottom-line variable of choice, it wasn't long before social scientists were asking questions of the family's contribution to it. The assumption was that there ought to be some relationship between aspects of family life and life satisfaction, and that a variety of socially and psychologically oriented variables each had a contribution to make to life satisfaction.

Contact with Children

Contact patterns were chosen as indicating something important about the parent-child relationship; by inference, how often the generations spent their time together and by what means they communicated with each other would make a statement about the quality of family life. In addition, how a person felt about her or his family would have an impact on personal well-being. Numerous researchers sought to extend the alienation hypothesis (Shanas, 1979) one step further. This search led them to examine the enrichment hypothesis (Mancini, 1980), which supposed that because families were in regular contact there was a necessary connection between such contact and well-being. In short, it was assumed that the greater the contact and interaction, the greater the sense of well-being experienced by the older parent. At this stage of the research little regard was given to what actually happened during contact with one's adult children, that is, whether the interaction was friendly or hostile, or whether it was by choice or mostly because of feelings of duty (Bengtson and DeTerre, 1980). It was as if all it took to make an older parent content with life was to be in contact with a child. Was it assumed that the needs of a parent were so simple, or that their lives were so deficient that simple contact would wend its way into a person's overall feelings about life? The studies that examined simple frequency of contact consistently found no relationship between it and well-being; it did not matter whether the contact was face-to-face, over the telephone, or by letter. One of the earlier reports on the relationship between family contact and well-being was by Edwards and Klemmack (1973). The family area, as represented by visiting relatives and visiting children, was the only major domain in the study that did not relate to well-being (the other domains were socioeconomic status, background characteristics such as age, formal participation, informal nonfamilial participation, and health). Research since that time has also failed to find an important relationship between simple contact and well-being (Dowd and LaRossa, 1982; Lee, 1979; Mancini, 1979).

There appears to be a conceptual gap in the expected connection between one's well-being and the extent of contact with adult children. Although an extensive analysis of well-being measures is beyond the scope of this review, it is instructive to examine briefly their content. Items that typically are found in these measures include: "I sometimes worry so much that I can't sleep" (Lawton, 1975); "The things I do are as interesting to me as they ever were" (Neugarten, Havighurst, and Tobin, 1961); and "During the past few weeks did you ever feel upset because someone criticized you?" (Bradburn, 1969). A question that has rarely been asked in the studies that have sought to connect family variables with well-being measures has to do with the logic behind expecting there to be a systematic relationship. For example, why should the frequency with which a parent and child spend time together relate to the degree to which a parent is upset because he or she has been criticized? Parent-child contact items ought not to relate to well-being as it has been conceptualized and measured. On the other hand, intergenerational contact is more likely to relate to one's feelings about the well-being of the relationship.

The Provision and Receipt of Support

Indicators of instrumental and emotional support have also been contrasted with psychological well-being. This line of research is not surprising, since it was known that various sorts of exchanges with kin were economically important for older people. It was assumed that since contact did not correlate with well-being of older parents, it may be that voluntary exchanges really represented intergenerational cohesion. Lee and Ellithorpe (1982) expected that an older parent's well-being would relate positively to providing aid to adult children and would relate negatively to receiving aid from them. They found little support for either hypothesis. They did find that among fathers, aid received related negatively to well-being, but the correlation was modest.

Mutran and Reitzes (1984) examined intergenerational support and well-being via symbolic interaction and social exchange perspectives. Their causal model was tested separately for the married and the widowed; for the married there was no relationship between well-being and the exchange variables (the reception of aid and the provision of aid), but for those who were widowed they found that the help they received from children reduced negative feelings and that giving help increased negative feelings. Mancini and Blieszner

(1986) contrasted the amount of emotional and instrumental support exchanged between parents and children with three dimensions of well-being. Although these exchanges were unrelated to the older parents' loneliness and feelings about their own aging, there was a relationship with level of personal agitation. Greater amounts of instrumental and emotional support covaried with greater agitation, though the relationship was modest.

Stoller (1985) examined how reciprocity in exchange patterns influences well-being. About one-third of the parents in her sample reported reciprocity in exchanges with their children. She found that the receipt of help was related to depression-like symptoms, but that the provision of help to children was more strongly related to well-being. Stoller concluded that "the inability to reciprocate rather than the need for assistance undermines the morale of the older person" (p. 341). Even though correlating well-being with aspects of exchange, assistance, and support is less superficial than the single focus on contact, the logic behind expecting a significant association is flawed. In comparison to the data on contact patterns, however, assistance and support are more relevant for personal well-being.

Relationship Quality

Though too much of the research has concerned itself only with parent-child contact patterns, several studies have examined how relationship quality covaries with well-being. These studies have looked into communication patterns, the amount of affection and interpersonal conflict, and so on. As expected, these variables were relatively more important for the well-being of the older parent than the contact variables. As examples, the older parent's feeling of competence in the parenting role was positively related to her or his well-being (Mancini, 1979), as were communication (Quinn, 1983) and feelings of affection (Mancini and Blieszner, 1986; Quinn, 1983). Extant findings suggest that examining these aspects of relationships is far more rewarding than studying frequency of contact. Moreover, relationship quality variables are aspects of satisfaction, and as such, they ought to be associated with well-being.

CARE PROVIDED BY ADULT CHILDREN

When parents are healthy and living independently, interactions with their children take on a friendly, supportive character. As indicated above, adult children and aged parents participate in an ongoing give-and-take, depending on the needs and resources of each generation and their geographic location with respect to each other. When parents become widowed, develop frail physical health, and/or suffer from conditions affecting their cognitive functioning, however, the parent-child interaction pattern often changes. Many adult children in contemporary society are providing direct care to their needy parents; Brody (1985) wondered if parent caring is so widespread as to be considered a normative life event of adult children.

Structural Variables That Affect Caregiving

The data on who cares for elderly parents are not definitive. It is usually thought that one child is tasked as the primary caregiver (Horowitz, 1985). Steinmetz (1982) suggested that families use a variety of methods to identify the child who will provide care to the needy parent. Sometimes there is someone who possesses nursing skills, sometimes a child assumes the caregiving role in hopes of obtaining parental love, and sometimes the unmarried or childless or unemployed sibling is delegated to be the caregiver by the others. Most studies find that the vast majority of caregiving children are daughters (Brody, 1981; Stoller, 1983). Matthews (1987), however, has demonstrated that we may need to rethink what we know about children as caregivers. In her studies (Matthews and Rosner, 1988) it has been shown that most children in the family participate in caregiving in some fashion and that there are several styles of participation (routine, backup, circumscribed, sporadic, and dissociation).

A number of conditions affect the ability and willingness of adult children to provide care to their parents. Kivett and Atkinson (1984) found that parents of only children were less likely than others to receive assistance, and the effects of income, geographical proximity, gender, and parents' health on children's helping behavior varied according to the number of children in the family. Stoller and Cicirelli are among the researchers who have examined the connection between the child's marital status and parental caregiving. Married children provide less help to parents than single ones, presumably because of other demands on their time (Stoller, 1983). On the other hand, children with disrupted marriages—the divorced, widowed, or remarried—assisted significantly less than those in intact marriages (Cicirelli, 1983, 1984). Finally, participation of the caregiver in the work force will affect the amount of time available for helping parents. Brody and Schoonover (1986) investigated types and amounts of assistance given by working versus nonworking daughters of disabled elderly widows. Although the amounts of help with tasks such as shopping, transportation, housekeeping, money management, and emotional support did not differ between the two groups of daughters, those who were employed provided less personal care and cooking than the nonworking daughters. Families of employed caregivers tended to use paid helpers for these personal care and meal tasks. Stoller (1983) compared help provided by working daughters with that of working sons. She discovered that employment reduced the assistance that sons provided to parents, but it made no difference in the amount of help that daughters gave.

Affection and Caregiving

The character of the relationship that parents and children had earlier in life is likely to affect that of the later years. With respect to parental caregiving, Hess and Waring (1978) pointed out that researchers should not assume that previous conflicts will automatically be resolved just because the parents are aged and in need of assistance. Nonetheless, Horowitz and Shindelman (1983) reported that children who did not feel a great amount of affection for their parents still were able to provide the needed assistance. Care given in the context of positive affect, though, was perceived as less stressful than care given under other circumstances. The following section elaborates further on the difficulties of caring for dependent parents.

The Stresses and Burdens of Caregiving

Providing care to a disabled parent has a profound impact on the primary caregiver and her or his family. Daily routines are disrupted and caregivers are confined to home (Chenoweth and Spencer, 1986; Robinson and Thurnher, 1979), caregivers experience physical and emotional strain (George and Gwyther, 1986; Snyder and Keefe, 1985), and parent-child conflict and negative affect may increase (Johnson and Catalano, 1983; Poulshock and Deimling, 1984). Parents who are cognitively impaired, cannot accomplish basic daily tasks of self-care, have poor social functioning, and/or engage in disruptive behavior are the most difficult to care for (Deimling and Bass, 1986). On the other hand, caregiving children are not necessarily burdened by the parents' degree of impairment per se but rather by the nature of the caregiving tasks they must perform. Caregivers perceive tasks that involve personal care and bodily contact as more burdensome than impersonal assistance such as shopping and housecleaning (Montgomery, Gonyea, and Hooyman, 1985). Similarly, tasks that restrict caregivers' time or geographic location are harder to cope with than others (Montgomery et al., 1985).

The nature of the parent-child bond and the degree of involvement of other family members also affect the caregiver's experience of strain in the helping situation. Cantor (1983) found that the closer the emotional bond between the child and parent, the more stressful the caregiving role. Zarit, Reever, and Bach-Peterson (1980) highlighted the importance of total family support in easing the caregiver's burden. When other relatives visited the frail parent frequently, caregivers reported lower feelings of burden than in the cases where such support was not forthcoming.

Adults are living longer, and some will experience many years of poor health and dependence on younger family members. The research cited here points out the problems associated with this situation. In contrast, it is also important for investigators to determine whether there are any benefits to caring for an aged parent. It is only with a complete picture of the positive as well as negative aspects of caregiving that adequate social policies and assistance programs can be developed for this new family responsibility.

FUTURE INQUIRY: RESEARCH AND THEORY

There is no lack of opinion about where researchers ought to be directing their energies. In recent years Bengtson and DeTerre (1980), Blieszner (1986), Hagestad (1987b), Mancini (1980, 1984b), Ragan (1979), Streib and Beck (1980), Troll (1971), and Troll, Miller, and Atchley (1979) analyzed research deficits in the family gerontology field and suggested new avenues of research. Most of those reviews, however, were not directed especially at the older parent–adult child relationship.

Given the speed with which research has changed over the past 30 years, it is sometimes difficult to believe that researchers pay much attention to what their peers suggest about future investigations. A clear example can be seen between the two family gerontology reviews published in *Journal of Marriage and the Family*, one on the decade of the 1960s (Troll, 1971) and the other on the period of 1970–1979 (Streib and Beck, 1980). We noticed that Streib and Beck's estimate of deficits and their recommendations for future work are similar to what Troll had to say approximately 10 years earlier. Nevertheless we provide here our own recommendations of the most fruitful research opportunities in the aging parent–adult child area. We will draw on the reviews listed above, on other papers published recently whose scope is more narrow than the above general reviews, and on our own speculations.

Before discussing suggestions for studies of specific content areas, we offer some observations concerning research methods. First, there still is insufficient longitudinal research to enable us to understand the true developmental aspects of aging parent–adult child relationships. Few researchers are employing designs that bridge cross-sectional and longitudinal approaches. Sequential designs (Baltes, Reese, and Nesselroade, 1977) that combine a series of cross-sectional and longitudinal studies into one research effort take only a little longer than simple longitudinal studies to complete, yet they afford more chance of disentangling relationship change due to aging of the partners from that associated with generational changes or time of measurement.

Second, relatively little research appears to be guided a priori by theories or conceptual frameworks. Most of the work is concerned with addressing a defined problem. Although research driven by problem solving is not without merit, when it is devoid of a theoretical context the understanding of the larger picture is stunted. The result is an unlinked series of descriptive studies, with little possibility of establishing causal associations among variables or predicting future outcomes (Baltes et al., 1977). Moreover, interventions that are not based on theory and explanatory research are apt to be misguided at best and ineffective or harmful at worst. In our perusal of the literature cited herein, we noted very few instances where established social and behavioral science theory directed the research. And when a theory was used to generate the research questions and method, it was likely to be a brand of social exchange. Although a social exchange approach is appropriate in some instances, it is shortsighted to assume that social exchange theory can sufficiently explain the multiple facets of a relationship. As a case in point, a recent report from Mutran and Reitzes (1984) showed the merits of combining social exchange and symbolic interaction perspectives for understanding parent-child relationships and the well-being of older parents.

We also believe that theory development is a legitimate end in and of itself, and need not be directed by a particular research interest or by available funding. The family social science field has struggled with theories of the family for practically 30 years, endeavoring to explicate both general and particularistic models. Considering family life and aging would appear to be an important vehicle for general theorizing about the family and a forum where such theorizing could be applied to other areas in the family realm. If one considers the principal issues in the aging family, the following come to mind: multiple generations; individual and relationship development; power and control; socialization; emotional and practical support; decision making; gender; and communication. Each of these is not only relevant for family gerontology but equally significant for a general understanding of the family. An approach that is based on the concept of family solidarity is one example of both cumulative theoretical work and a more generally applicable framework (Bengtson, Olander, and Haddad, 1976; Bengtson and Shrader, 1982; Mangen, Bengtson, and Landry, 1988). The key terms of this family solidarity framework are associational, consensual, and affectional solidarity; exchange of services; functional solidarity; norms of family solidarity; and intergenerational family structure. This approach serves as one of the few ongoing ef-

forts at theory development in family gerontology.

Over the years a common lament of family gerontology critics has been the underrepresentation of qualitative dimensions of relationships in research endeavors. In some respects this may not be a great problem because many social-psychological studies have been conducted, and they tend to focus on the microanalytical level of analysis. But we have noted the tendency to take a quantitative approach to studying qualitative aspects of a relationship. There are many dimensions pertaining to relationship quality that can be tapped by the structured researcher-driven method, but on the other hand, a person's innermost feelings about another may be quite different from the revelations that a quantitative approach will permit. Family relationships are complex, so it is desirable that qualitative approaches should see more play. A focus on the respondents' own words, unique experiences, and personal interpretation of relationship matters could greatly enhance our understanding of family gerontology. In the research that we reviewed there were relatively few examples of such qualitative research; rather, the structured social survey was the dominant method. An example to support this position is Mangen and McChesney's (1985) recent suggestion that the study of family solidarity would be improved by greater use of qualitative methods, the results of which could be verified by quantitative means. The generation of grounded theory and the clarification of conceptual ambiguities are among the merits of qualitative approaches. Gubrium (1988) demonstrates that qualitative approaches are particularly sensitive to family dynamics and to the diversity of family experiences. Though we do not suggest leaving quantification aside, we do believe that it ought to be integrated with methods that provide the respondents with greater opportunities to reflect their lives from their personal perspectives.

As a bridge between our discussion of general research needs and particular content areas, let us consider the investigation of conflict. Marshall and Bengtson (1983) stated that one should never take family solidarity as a given when considering intergenerational relationships. Yet few researchers have looked at the negative aspects of the older parent–adult child relationship. Most discussions of intergenerational conflict are not data-based but rather are grounded in informal therapeutic observations (Steinman, 1979). Even under conditions of the best rapport, it is difficult to get an older parent to display the underside of his or her relationship with a child. Though the association between social desirability and talking about one's family has not been explored adequately, we would guess that selective reporting is widespread. In fact, it has been shown that older people tend to describe their relationships with their children more favorably than the children describe their relationships with their parents (Hagestad, 1987b). Thus the literature on older parents and their adult children paints a picture wherein cohesion is pervasive and conflict practically is nonexistent. A qualitative approach, employed clumsily, will be no better at eliciting talk on conflict than traditional surveys. But well-crafted personal interviews built on rapport, in-depth interviews, multiple data collection points, participant observations, or perhaps even document analyses may be able to capture more effectively some of the negative aspects of the parent-child relationship in late life.

We would like researchers and synthesizers of that research to spend less time and space on the "myth of abandonment" or "alienation hypothesis." The case appears to be closed. Most older people are as integrated in their family system as they desire to be. There always will be some older parents who are neglected, abandoned, and alienated, but they are the outliers. The only condition under which we can see research focusing on alienation would be to do in-depth study of those parents who are apart from their family and who do not desire it that way. Oddly enough, research so far has not taken that road.

Also, it is past time either to reconceptualize well-being or to cease correlating every family variable in sight with it. As we discussed earlier, the manner in which well-being is measured may not be logically compatible with the variables presumed to influence it. One artifact of the way in which the well-being issue has been approached by family researchers is that the role that the family plays in aging has been underestimated. Social scientists have been mistaken in thinking that well-being is the pivotal bottom-line variable. If a satisfaction-oriented dependent variable must be used, then it ought to be relationship satisfaction (and beyond that, researchers ought to delineate the particular satisfactions rather than employing

some global assessment). We suspect that this recommendation will be taken lightly in a field that has had its problems with assessing the quality of married life. The literature that we have cited here, as well as that mentioned in other papers, shows that family variables are often unrelated to measures of well-being. Current measures of well-being were designed to be sensitive to conditions of health and wealth, and for the most part, other variables of social life will not correlate with those measures.

Some years ago Gelfand, Olsen, and Block (1978) discussed families in which there is more than one older generation. One of several important points made in that article was that both older cohorts are experiencing change, so that the younger of the older generations may be ill-equipped to provide much support when the older generation is in need. Variation in the "tracks" that the respective older generations are on, at least at face value, is an important consideration in understanding (and researching) relationship quality. Yet research has not juxtaposed older parents and their aging children with regard to developmental needs and abilities or in terms of crises in their lives. Attention should be given to examining parents and their children in a concomitant fashion, so that their respective life phases and experiences can be placed side by side.

The heterogeneity of the parent-child relationship category is considerable and causes great difficulty for conducting research and for making general statements about aging parents and adult children. For example, if we account for age differences between the generations, respective health levels, geographic proximity, family size, respective marital statuses, and their shared and unique life experiences, it represents an overwhelming array of conditions under which the relationship is experienced. Yet research designs should be sensitive to these variegations typically found in parent-child relationships.

Our focus has been on the older parent-child *dyad* rather than on the older *family*. There is an important conceptual distinction between the two foci, with the latter potentially encompassing a collection of dyads, triads, and even larger interpersonal groups. While difficult to conceptualize and to research, the study of whole families ought to be included on family gerontology's future research agenda. Dyadic studies can be misleading in that they typically do not account for the influence of other family members. Studies of larger family groups should provide a more representative picture of phenomena such as solidarity, cohesion, and quality of family life.

We would like to draw attention to a suggestion offered by Hagestad (1987b) involving the incorporation of theories and methods from child development when one is studying parent-child relationships in old age. She asserts that in order for the gerontological approach to parents and their children to have greater merit, it should be linked with studies conducted at earlier life cycle phases. Examples of concepts that can be studied in multiple generations of parent-child pairs are support and strain between middle-aged parents and their children as well as between middle-aged persons and their parents, sources of emotional security and attachment between parents and children of all ages, and reciprocal socialization in the parent and child roles across all stages of the life span (Hagestad, 1987a).

We were struck by the paucity of research that qualifies as replication and extension of earlier work. In many respects what we know is known from a single study, rather than from a collection of studies on the same or similar domain. This is not the case with regard to parent-child contact and psychological well-being but is more so in the areas of affection, conflict, and communication.

The use of discretionary time within a family context continues to be a potentially fruitful area of future research. We suggested already that conventional studies of contact between aged parents and their adult children are incompatible with the needs of the family gerontology field. We also recognize, however, that time and its parameters that govern our days should be accounted for in studies of aging. Our own approach has been to examine time with regard to activity, competence, preference, and time itself (Mancini, 1984a). We recommend examining what older people do, what they prefer to do, how they understand the nature of time, and their feelings of well-being associated with time use. There is still a tendency in studies of older people to look only at one form of social time use, participation in clubs and associations, and to ask perfunctory questions on in-person, telephone, and correspondence contact with children. Researchers rarely ask if the time spent with an adult child is by choice or obligation, or if time was spent because a task had to be accomplished or because the principals were de-

siring companionship. Nor do they ask about the meaningfulness of the activity. Whether one is young, in mid-life, or chronologically old, life is lived within the parameters of time.

One approach, based in symbolic interaction theory, is to examine in detail the meanings attached to spending time with family (Mancini, 1984a; Mancini and Orthner, 1982; Orthner and Mancini, 1980). Relevant concepts from the approach include communication, reciprocal feedback, defining situations, role patterning, and significant others. Thus far the conditions under which older parents and their children spend time together has been mostly left open to speculation; likewise the outcomes of time spent have been limited to studies of global, individual well-being, and we see these as inadequate.

Studies of the affective aspects of the parent-child relationship are still quite rudimentary (Hagestad, 1987a), even though several elegant models have been developed and tested (Mutran and Reitzes, 1984; Quinn, 1983). The incorporation of better-defined theory would be helpful for this area of research. For example, the notion of attachment (Antonucci, 1976; Troll and Smith, 1976) could be more completely applied to older parent-child pairs. Similarly, the concept of the functional specificity of relationships (Weiss, 1969) also could be applied; our own work has demonstrated the promise of this approach (Blieszner and Mancini, 1985; Mancini, 1984a; Mancini and Simon, 1984). The framework proposed by Weiss (1969) examines relationships with regard to intimacy, social integration, opportunity for nurturant behavior, reassurance of self-worth, assistance, and guidance. This functional specificity approach enables researchers to examine a broad range of relationship dimensions across a variety of relationships, both kin and non-kin. The functional specificity framework also addresses the need to increase our knowledge about the roles and functions of the informal support network (Ward, 1985).

A great deal of the recent research on parent-child relationships has focused on questions related to caregiving and care receiving, a trend consistent with family gerontology's tendency to respond to personal and social problems. At the same time that we laud this work, we wish to caution researchers against focusing too heavily on relationships in which the parent is seriously ill. The study of relationships between normally aging parents and their children has not reached its zenith; witness the many reviews that have argued for continued, better research on normative family dynamics (Bengtson and DeTerre, 1980; Blieszner, 1986; Hagestad, 1987b; Mancini, 1984a; Troll, 1971).

A few years ago Riley (1983) discussed the contemporary family as a "matrix of latent relationships." She suggested that family relationships continually change, that family members have partial control of that change, and that family members' lives are interdependent. We cannot do justice here to the approach outlined by Riley, but her suggestions have an important implication for future research: the family must be analyzed as a system of interdependent lives, and socialization must be recognized as a reciprocal, lifelong process (also see Hagestad, 1987a, for a discussion of adult socialization). Mutual influence in family groups has never received a great deal of attention, especially compared to those areas dealing with marital quality, premarital sexual permissiveness, or dating and courtship. The approach to socialization in the family has tended to be truncated and not extended into the adult years. Interdependence is a reality throughout the family cycle, and not just something that emerges late in life; it could even be argued that in the family, interdependence is as viable a term as dependence and independence.

CONCLUSIONS

We have examined domains that pertain to the relationships of older parents and their adult children. We sought to provide a sense of where the research has been over the years, but spent more of our review efforts on current studies. Several areas of research have been studied by too many investigators for too many years. There should be no doubt by now about whether older people are alienated from their families. Nor should there be a necessary assumption about how families promote the well-being of their older members; by now we clearly know that our measures of the well-being construct are not especially sensitive to family relationship variables. By now we also should be convinced that older people and their children are characterized by patterns of reciprocal support.

Even though over the past 30 years a sizable number of social scientists have investigated aspects of the older parent–adult child relationship, several critical deficits remain. One is that the ebb and flow in these relationships has yet to be captured. A second is that too few studies rely on established theory in social and behavioral science. Third, a cumulative knowledge base has been slow in developing. A fourth gap is that the interpersonal, social-psychological aspects of these relationships have not been adequately connected with the social and societal context in which they function. A fifth deficit is that a developmental approach has been missing, so that it is difficult to know the life cycle of a relationship and to understand how it has changed and how it has remained stable.

We are reminded of what Shanas (1980: 14) said with regard to older families: "Old people and their families are the new pioneers of our era. They have ventured into uncharted areas of human relationships, and developed systems of exchange and interaction without help or guidance from the so-called helping agencies in our industrial society." The study of aging parents and adult children remains a potentially rewarding area of investigation. This relationship is unique because it has a long history, it begins by virtue of obligation but is sustained by both obligation and choice, it experiences a definite shift in power and status, and it is expected to endure and to be intrinsically rewarding for both generations. In many respects we must agree with Kaplan (1975: 385), who long ago said that "we have only begun our knowledge search on the family in aging."

REFERENCES

Adams, David L. 1971. "Correlates of satisfaction among the elderly." Gerontologist 11: 64–68.

Antonucci, Toni C. 1976. "Attachment: A life-span concept." Human Development 19: 135–142.

Atchley, Robert C., and Sheila J. Miller. 1980. "Older people and their families." Pp. 337–369 in Carl Eisdorfer (ed.), Annual Review of Gerontology and Geriatrics, Vol. 1. New York: Springer.

Back, Kurt. W. 1971. "Transition to aging and the self-image." Aging and Human Development 2: 296–304.

Baltes, Paul B., Hayne W. Reese, and John R. Nesselroade. 1977. Life-Span Developmental Psychology: Introduction to Research Methods. Monterey, CA: Brooks/Cole.

Bengtson, Vern L., and Edythe DeTerre. 1980. "Aging and family relations." Marriage and Family Review 3: 51–76.

Bengtson, Vern L., E. B. Olander, and A. A. Haddad. 1976. "The generation gap and aging family members: Toward a conceptual model." Pp. 237–263 in Jaber F. Gubrium (ed.), Time, Roles, and Self in Old Age. New York: Human Sciences Press.

Bengtson, Vern L., and S. S. Schrader. 1982. "Parent-child relations." Pp. 115–186 in David J. Mangen and W. A. Peterson (eds.), Research Instruments in Social Gerontology. Minneapolis: University of Minnesota Press.

Blieszner, Rosemary. 1986. "Trends in family gerontology research." Family Relations 35: 555–562.

Blieszner, Rosemary, and Jay A. Mancini. 1985. "The Social Provisions Scale: Concept and measurement." Paper presented at the 38th Annual Scientific Meeting of the Gerontological Society of America, New Orleans (November).

Blieszner, Rosemary, and Jay A. Mancini. 1987. "Enduring ties: Older adults' parental role and responsibilities." Family Relations 36: 176–180.

Borland, Delores C. 1982. "A cohort analysis approach to the empty-nest syndrome among three ethnic groups of women: A theoretical position." Journal of Marriage and the Family 44: 117–129.

Bradburn, Norman. 1969. The Structure of Psychological Well-being. Chicago: Aldine.

Brody, Elaine M. 1981. " 'Women in the middle' and family help to older people." Gerontologist 21: 471–480.

Brody, Elaine M. 1985. "Parent care as a normative stress." Gerontologist 25: 19–29.

Brody, Elaine M., Pauline T. Johnsen, and Mark C. Fulcomer. 1984. "What should adult children do for elderly parents? Opinions and preferences of three generations of women." Journal of Gerontology 39: 736–746.

Brody, Elaine M., Pauline T. Johnsen, Mark C. Fulcomer, and Abigail M. Lang. 1983. "Women's changing roles and help to elderly parents: Attitudes of three generations of women." Journal of Gerontology 38: 597–607.

Brody, Elaine M., and Claire B. Schoonover. 1986. "Patterns of parent-care when adult children work and when they do not." Gerontologist 26: 372–381.

Cantor, Marjorie H. 1980. "The informal support system: Its relevance in the lives of the elderly." Pp. 131–144 in Edgar F. Borgatta and Neil G. McCluskey (eds.), Aging and Society: Current Research and Policy Perspectives. Beverly Hills, CA: Sage.

Cantor, Marjorie H. 1983. "Strain among caregivers: A study of experience in the United States." Gerontologist 23: 597–604.

Cheal, David J. 1983. "Intergenerational family transfers." Journal of Marriage and the Family 45: 805–813.

Chenoweth, Barbara, and Beth Spencer. 1986. "Dementia: The experience of family caregivers." Gerontologist 26: 267–272.

Cicirelli, Victor G. 1981. Helping Elderly Parents: The Role of Adult Children. Boston: Auburn House.

Cicirelli, Victor G. 1983. "A comparison of helping behavior to elderly parents of adult children with intact and disrupted marriages." Gerontologist 23: 619–625.

Cicirelli, Victor G. 1984. "Marital disruption and adult children's perception of their siblings' help to elderly parents." Family Relations 33: 613–621.

Clemens, Audra W., and Leland J. Axelson. 1985. "The not-so-empty-nest: The return of the fledgling adult." Family Relations 34: 259–264.

Cohler, Bertram J. 1983. "Autonomy and interdependence in the family of adulthood: A psychological perspective." Gerontologist 23: 33–39.

Deimling, Gary T., and David M. Bass. 1986. "Symptoms of mental impairment among elderly adults and their effects on family caregivers." Journal of Gerontology 41: 778–784.

Dewit, David J., Andrew V. Wister, and Thomas K. Burch. 1988. "Physical distance and social contact between elders and their adult children." Research on Aging 10: 56–80.

Dowd, James J., and Ralph LaRossa. 1982. "Primary group contact and elderly morale: An exchange/power analysis." Sociology and Social Research 66: 184–197.

Edwards, John N., and David L. Klemmack. 1973. "Correlates of life satisfaction: A re-examination." Journal of Gerontology 28: 497–502.

English, Jane. 1979. "What do grown children owe their parents?" Pp. 351–356 in Onora O'Neill and William Ruddick (eds.), Having Children: Philosophical and Legal Reflections on Parenthood. New York: Oxford University Press.

Fischer, Lucy R. 1985. "Elderly parents and the caregiving role: An asymmetrical transition." Pp. 105–114 in Warren A. Peterson and Jill Quadagno (eds.), Social Bonds in Later Life. Beverly Hills, CA: Sage.

Gelfand, Donald E., Jody K. Olsen, and Marilyn R. Block. 1978. "Two generations of elderly in the changing American family: Implications for family services." Family Coordinator 27: 395–403.

George, Linda K., and Lisa P. Gwyther. 1986. "Caregiver well-being: A multidimensional examination of family caregivers of demented adults." Gerontologist 26: 253–259.

Glick, Paul C. 1977. "Updating the life cycle of the family." Journal of Marriage and the Family 39: 5–13.

Gubrium, Jaber F. 1988. "Family responsibility and caregiving in the qualitative analysis of the Alzheimer's disease experience." Journal of Marriage and the Family 50: 197–207.

Hagestad, Gunhild O. 1987a. "Families in an aging society." Zeitschrift Für Sozialisationsforschung und Erziehungssoziologie (ZSE) 2: 148–160.

Hagestad, Gunhild O. 1987b. "Parent-child relations in later life: Trends and gaps in past research." Pp. 405–433 in Jane B. Lancaster, Jeanne Altmann,

Alice S. Rossi, and Lonnie R. Sherrod (eds.), Parenting across the Lifespan: Biosocial Dimensions. New York: Aldine de Gruyter.

Hanson, Sandra L., William J. Sauer, and Wayne C. Seelbach. 1983. "Racial and cohort variations in filial responsibility norms." Gerontologist 23: 626–631.

Harkins, Elizabeth B. 1978. "Effects of empty nest transition on self-report of psychological and physical well-being." Journal of Marriage and the Family 40: 549–556.

Harris, Louis, and Associates. 1975. The Myth and Reality of Aging in America. Washington, DC: National Council on the Aging.

Hess, Beth B., and Joan M. Waring. 1978. "Parent and child in later life: Rethinking the relationship." Pp. 241–273 in Richard M. Lerner and Graham B. Spanier (eds.), Child Influences on Marital and Family Interaction: A Life-Span Perspective. New York: Academic Press.

Horowitz, Amy. 1985. "Family caregiving to the frail elderly." Annual Review of Gerontology and Geriatrics 6: 194–246.

Horowitz, Amy, and Lois W. Shindelman. 1983. "Reciprocity and affection: Past influences on current caregiving." Journal of Gerontological Social Work 5: 5–20.

Johnson, Colleen L., and Donald J. Catalano. 1983. "A longitudinal study of family supports to impaired elderly." Gerontologist 23: 612–618.

Kaplan, Jerome. 1975. "The family in aging." Gerontologist 15: 385.

Kivett, Vira R. 1985. "Consanguinity and kin level: Their relative importance to the network of older adults." Journal of Gerontology 40: 228–234.

Kivett, Vira R., and Maxine P. Atkinson. 1984. "Filial expectations, association, and helping as a function of number of children among older rural-transition parents." Journal of Gerontology 39: 499–503.

Larson, Reed. 1978. "Thirty years of research on the subjective well-being of older Americans." Journal of Gerontology 33: 109–125.

Lawton, M. Powell. 1975. "The Philadelphia Geriatric Center Morale Scale: A revision." Journal of Gerontology 30: 85–89.

Lee, Gary R. 1979. "Children and the elderly: Interaction and morale." Research on Aging 1: 335–360.

Lee, Gary R., and Eugene Ellithorpe. 1982. "Intergenerational exchange and subjective well-being among the elderly." Journal of Marriage and the Family 44: 217–224.

Lewis, Robert A., Phillip J. Freneau, and Craig L. Roberts. 1979. "Fathers and the postparental transition." Family Coordinator 28: 514–520.

Mancini, Jay A. 1979. "Family relationships and morale among people 65 years of age and older." American Journal of Orthopsychiatry 49: 292–300.

Mancini, Jay A. 1980. "Strengthening the family life of older adults: Myth-conceptions and investigative needs." Pp. 333–343 in Nick Stinnett, Barbara Chesser, John DeFrain, and Patricia Knaub (eds.), Family Strengths: Positive Models for Family Life. Lincoln: University of Nebraska Press.

Mancini, Jay A. 1984a. "Leisure lifestyles and family dynamics in old age." Pp. 58–71 in William H. Quinn and George A. Hughston (eds.), Independent Aging: Family and Social Systems Perspectives. Rockville, MD: Aspen.

Mancini, Jay A. 1984b. "Research on family life in old age: Exploring the frontiers." Pp. 265–284 in William H. Quinn and George A. Hughston (eds.), Independent Aging: Family and Social Systems Perspectives. Rockville, MD: Aspen.

Mancini, Jay A., and Rosemary Blieszner. 1985. "Return of middle aged children to the parental home." Medical Aspects of Human Sexuality 19(4): 192–194.

Mancini, Jay A., and Rosemary Blieszner. 1986. "Successful aging and close relationships with children." Paper presented at the 39th Annual Scientific Meeting of the Gerontological Society of America, Chicago (November).

Mancini, Jay A., and Dennis K. Orthner. 1982. "Leisure time, activities, preferences, and competence: Implications for the morale of older adults." Journal of Applied Gerontology 1: 95–103.

Mancini, Jay A., and Joyce Simon. 1984. "Older adults' expectations of support from family and friends." Journal of Applied Gerontology 3: 150–160.

Mangen, David J., and Kay Y. McChesney. 1985. "Intergenerational cohesion: A comparison of linear and nonlinear analytical approaches." Research on Aging 7: 121–136.

Mangen, David J., Vern L. Bengtson, and P. H. Landry (eds.). 1988. Measurement of Intergenerational Relations. Newbury Park, CA: Sage.

Markson, Elizabeth W. (ed.). 1983. Older Women. Lexington, MA: Lexington Books/D.C. Heath.

Marshall, Victor W., and Vern L. Bengtson. 1983. "Generations: Conflict and cooperation." Pp. 298–310 in Manfred Bergener, Ursula Lehr, Erich Lang, and Reinhard Schmitz-Scherzer (eds.), Aging in the Eighties and Beyond. New York: Springer.

Matthews, Sarah H. 1987. "Provision of care to old parents: Division of responsibility among adult children." Research on Aging 6: 45–60.

Matthews, Sarah H., and Tena T. Rosner. 1988. "Shared filial responsibility: The family as the primary caregiver." Journal of Marriage and the Family 50: 185–195.

Montgomery, Rhonda J. V., Judith G. Gonyea, and Nancy R. Hooyman. 1985. "Caregiving and the experience of subjective and objective burden." Family Relations 34: 19–26.

Morgan, Leslie A. 1982. "Social roles in later life." Pp. 55–79 in Carl Eisdorfer (ed.), Annual Review of Gerontology and Geriatrics, Vol. 3. New York: Springer.

Mutran, Elizabeth, and Donald C. Reitzes. 1984. "Intergenerational support activities and well-being among the elderly: A convergence of exchange and symbolic interaction perspectives." American Sociological Review 49: 117–130.

Neugarten, Bernice L., Robert J. Havighurst, and Sheldon S. Tobin. 1961. "The measurement of life satisfaction." Journal of Gerontology 16: 134–143.

Orthner, Dennis K., and Jay A. Mancini. 1980. "Leisure behavior and group dynamics: The case of the family." Pp. 307–328 in Seppo Iso-Ahola (ed.), Social Psychological Perspectives on Leisure and Recreation. Springfield, IL: Charles C Thomas.

Pifer, Alan, and Lydia Bronte (eds.). 1986. Our Aging Society: Paradox and Promise. New York: W. W. Norton.

Poulshock, S. Walter, and Gary T. Deimling. 1984. "Families caring for elders in residence: Issues in the measurement of burden." Journal of Gerontology 39: 230–239.

Quinn, William H. 1983. "Personal and family adjustment in later life." Journal of Marriage and the Family 45: 57–73.

Ragan, Pauline K. (ed.). 1979. Aging Parents. Los Angeles: University of Southern California Press.

Riley, Matilda W. 1983. "The family in an aging society: A matrix of latent relationships." Journal of Family Issues 4: 439–454.

Riley, Matilda W., and Anne Foner. 1968. Aging and Society (Vol. 1). An Inventory of Research Findings. New York: Russell Sage Foundation.

Riley, Matilda W., and John W. Riley. 1986. "Longevity and social structure: The potential of the added years." Pp. 53–77 in Alan Pifer and Lydia Bronte (eds.), Our Aging Society: Paradox and Promise. New York: W. W. Norton.

Robinson, Betsy, and Majda Thurnher. 1979. "Taking care of parents: A family-cycle transition." Gerontologist 19: 586–593.

Seelbach, Wayne C. 1977. "Gender differences in expectations for filial responsibility." Gerontologist 17: 421–425.

Seelbach, Wayne C. 1978. "Correlates of aged parents' filial responsibility expectations and realizations." Family Coordinator 27: 341–350.

Seelbach, Wayne C. 1981. "Filial responsibility among aged parents: A racial comparison." Journal of Minority Aging 5: 286–292.

Seelbach, Wayne C. 1984. "Filial responsibility and the care of aging family members." Pp. 92–109 in William H. Quinn and George A. Hughston (eds.), Independent Aging: Family and Social System Perspectives. Rockville, MD: Aspen.

Seelbach, Wayne C., and William J. Sauer. 1977. "Filial responsibility expectations and morale among aged parents." Gerontologist 17: 492–499.

Shanas, Ethel. 1979. "Social myth as hypothesis: The case of the family relations of old people." Gerontologist 19: 3–9.

Shanas, Ethel. 1980. "Older people and their families: The new pioneers." Journal of Marriage and the Family 42: 9–15.

Shanas, Ethel, P. Townsend, D. Wedderburn, H. Friis, P. Milhoj, and J. Stehouwer. 1968. Old People in Three Industrial Societies. New York: Atherton Press.

Shehan, Constance L., Donna H. Berardo, and Felix M. Berardo. 1984. "The empty nest is filling again:

Implications for parent-child relations." Parenting Studies 1: 67–73.

Siegel, Jacob S., and Cynthia M. Taeuber. 1986. "Demographic dimensions of an aging population." Pp. 79–110 in Alan Pifer and Lydia Bronte (eds.), Our Aging Society. New York: Norton.

Snyder, Barbara, and Kathy Keefe. 1985. "The unmet needs of family caregivers for frail and disabled adults." Social Work in Health Care 10: 1–14.

Steinman, Lynne A. 1979. "Reactivated conflicts with aging parents." Pp. 126–143 in Pauline K. Ragan (ed.), Aging Parents. Los Angeles: University of Southern California Press.

Steinmetz, Suzanne K. 1982. "Family care of elders: Myths and realities." Pp. 213–233 in Nick Stinnett, John DeFrain, Kay King, Herbert Lingren, George Rowe, Sally Van Zandt, and Rosanne Williams (eds.), Family Strengths 4: Positive Support Systems. Lincoln: University of Nebraska Press.

Stoller, Eleanor P. 1983. "Parental caregiving by adult children." Journal of Marriage and the Family 45: 851–858.

Stoller, Eleanor P. 1985. "Exchange patterns in the informal support networks of the elderly: The impact of reciprocity on morale." Journal of Marriage and the Family 47: 335–342.

Streib, Gordon F., and Rubye W. Beck. 1980. "Older families: A decade review." Journal of Marriage and the Family 42: 937–956.

Suitor, J. Jill, and Karl Pillemer. 1987. "The presence of adult children: A source of stress for elderly couples' marriages?" Journal of Marriage and the Family 49: 717–725.

Tobin, Sheldon S., and Regina Kulys. 1980. "The family and services." Pp. 370–399 in Carl Eisdorfer (ed.), Annual Review of Gerontology and Geriatrics, Vol. 1. New York: Springer.

Troll, Lillian E. 1971. "The family of later life: A decade review." Journal of Marriage and the Family 33: 187–241.

Troll, Lillian E., Sheila J. Miller, and Robert J. Atchley. 1979. Families in Later Life. Belmont, CA: Wadsworth.

Troll, Lillian E., and Jean Smith. 1976. "Attachment through the life span: Some questions about dyadic bonds among adults." Human Development 19: 156–170.

U.S. Senate Special Committee on Aging. 1985–1986. Aging America: Trends and Projections. Washington, DC: American Association of Retired Persons.

Ward, R. A. 1985. "Informal networks and well-being in later life: A research agenda." Gerontologist 25: 55–81.

Weiss, Robert S. 1969. "The fund of sociability." Trans-Action/Society 6: 36–43.

Zarit, Steven H., Karen E. Reever, and Julie Bach-Peterson. 1980. "Relatives of the impaired elderly: Correlates of feelings of burden." Gerontologist 20: 649–655.

Zopf, Paul E. 1986. America's Older Population. Houston: Cap and Gown Press.

Darwin L. Thomas and Marie Cornwall*
Brigham Young University

Religion and Family in the 1980s:

Discovery and Development

Journals in the fields of family, religion, sociology, psychology, and therapy were searched for articles examining both religion and the family. The interface between religion and family is being addressed by social scientists studying the family who also have an interest in religion, and by some social scientists studying religion who also have an interest in family. Few articles examine the interrelations among multiple dimensions of each institution. This review reveals a pressing need for more serious theoretical and conceptual work that incorporates multidimensional approaches and is specifically designed to illuminate the interrelationships between religion and the family.

The study of religion and the family is the focus of increasing attention in the social sciences. The following events of the past decade demonstrate this new interest: (*a*) a 1981 seminar at the University of Notre Dame resulted in a book edited by D'Antonio and Aldous (1983); (*b*) the "Middletown Studies" treated family (Caplow, 1982) and religion (Caplow, Bahr, and Chadwick, 1983), respectively; (*c*) the National Council on Family Relations established a section on religion (Thomas and Sommerfeldt, 1984); (*d*) a 1984 conference at Brigham Young University on religion and family resulted in both a section on religion in

the *Journal of Marriage and the Family*, May 1985, and a subsequent book (Thomas, 1988b); and (*e*) a review chapter on religion (Marciano, 1987) was included in the second *Handbook of Marriage and the Family*. These activities are especially noteworthy in contrast with the lack of attention to religion and family in earlier decades. The earlier *Handbook of Marriage and the Family* (New York: Plenum Press, 1964) included no extensive discussion of religion. The topic of religion was almost completely ignored in the two volumes on *Contemporary Theories about the Family* (New York: Free Press, 1979). No *JMF* decade review of articles published in the '60s and '70s focused on religion. Religion was not included as a special topic in any of the 18 special issues of the *Journal of Marriage and the Family* published from 1960 to 1979.[1]

In our assessment of research in the eighties, we begin with an overview of journals publishing articles on religion and the family. Next we consider studies with religion and family as independent and dependent variables, and follow with a review of more extensive efforts to model religion and family influences on each other. We end with suggestions for future research and theory.

Overview of Research in the Eighties

Representative journals in the areas of family (5), religion (4), sociology (5), psychology (4), and therapy (3) were searched for articles treating religion and the family. Knowledgeable informants in each area were consulted for suggestions on the most likely journals to analyze. In addition, a journal was included if it published a

Department of Sociology and Center for Studies of the Family, Brigham Young University, Provo, UT 84602.

*Department of Sociology and Women's Research Institute, Brigham Young University, Provo, UT 84602.

special issue on religion and family during the decade. If a key word on the topic of religion or family appeared in either the title or abstract, a search was made to see if the other dimension was represented in a table or figure. If both dimensions appeared, the article was included.

This procedure produced 427 articles. Since only representative journals in each of the five areas were searched, this is not a comprehensive list of all the pertinent research published in the decade, but we think we have located most of the relevant literature.

Journal Articles

Table 1 presents the number of articles on religion and family that were published in each journal during the decade. Seventy-eight percent of the articles appear in family or religion journals; 31% were found in the *Journal of Marriage and the Family.* Two religion journals (the *Journal for the Scientific Study of Religion* and *Review of Religious Research*) account for 85 (20%) of the articles. Only 2% of the articles appear in psychology and therapy journals.

The trends across the decade show the greatest increase in research in the religion and family journals (56% and 57%, respectively, in the last five years). The three journals with the greatest in-

crease for any journal having at least 10 articles are *Review of Religious Research* (62%), *Journal of Marriage and the Family* (60%), and *American Sociological Review* (59%). Overall, 55% of articles were published during the last half of the decade.

The institutional support and funding of research further illuminates the views of social scientists and of the larger society on this type of research. While almost half the articles did not report a funding source, 30% reported government funding and 16% reported university funding. University support is probably underestimated, since most of the studies that do not specify funding were probably supported by academic departments and colleges. Furthermore, government support is probably responsible for more than 30%. Much of the research coming from universities represents secondary analysis of data originally gathered with government support.

Only 2% of the studies were supported and/or funded by religious organizations. At mid-decade, some observers saw the "outpouring of research" sponsored by the churches as contributing "significantly to the religious literature in the social sciences" (Thomas and Henry, 1985: 371). The research published in the eighties does not support such a conclusion. A more complete

TABLE 1. NUMBER OF ARTICLES ON RELIGION AND FAMILY FOUND IN
EACH OF 17 REPRESENTATIVE JOURNALS

Journal	1980–1984	1985–1989	Total
Family			
Journal of Marriage and the Family	52	79	131
Family Perspective	22	9	31
Journal of Family Issues	9	10	19
Family Science Review	0	9	9
Family Relations	2	2	4
Religion			
Journal for the Scientific Study of Religion	22	26	48
Review of Religious Research	14	23	37
Journal of Psychology and Theology	14	13	27
Sociological Analysis	10	14	24
Sociology			
Demography	17	16	33
American Sociological Review	9	13	22
Social Forces	8	9	17
American Journal of Sociology	8	3	11
Sociology and Social Review	1	3	4
Family therapy			
Family Process	2	1	3
American Journal of Family Therapy	1	2	3
Psychology			
Journal of Social Psychology		4	4

analysis of relevant publication, including books, might reveal a different picture, but this seems unlikely because most large research projects that are reported in books also spawn journal articles.

Substantive Focus

A summary of the substantive focus of religion and family research is provided in Table 2. Family is more likely to be the dependent variable than is religion, and family relations is the most common area of study—although only 46% of the research in this area was published after 1984. When religion is the dependent variable, religiosity (belief, practice, commitment, etc.) is by far the most common focus of attention. Furthermore, this is an area of increasing emphasis, with 64% of

studies published after 1984. Also of interest is the large number of studies in which neither family nor religion is the dependent variable, but rather the research examines the impact of family and religion on well-being, socioeconomic characteristics, or suicide. The increase in such articles (62% since 1984) suggests a trend toward examining the additive and/or interactive effects of family and religion on other variables.

The dominance of research in which family is the dependent variable is more likely a function of a general approach in the social sciences than an ontological position that the social order is characterized by religion's impact on the family and not vice versa. Social scientists generally treat religion as a social institution and then ask what are the consequences of participation in that in-

TABLE 2. NUMBER OF JOURNAL ARTICLES BY FAMILY AND RELIGION AS DEPENDENT VARIABLES ACROSS MOST FREQUENTLY STUDIED AREAS

Dependent Variable	1980–1984	1985–1989	Total[a]
Family			
Family relations			
Family problems	15	11	26
Sex roles	12	9	21
Parent-child relations	10	9	19
Premarital and extramarital sex	5	11	16
Family strengths	8	3	11
Conjugal relations			
Marital quality, violence, conflict	18	15	33
Marital stability	15	18	33
Family structure, marriage	4	11	15
Childbearing			
Fertility	18	18	36
Childbirth, spacing, conception	6	10	16
Abortion	5	7	12
Contraception	3	7	10
Religion			
Religiosity	14	24	38
New religious movements	4	5	9
Intergenerational religious values	4	4	8
Apostasy, switching	2	6	8
Missionaries and clergy	3	2	5
Religious homogamy	3	2	5
Other variables	8	7	15
Miscellaneous			
Variables not religion or family			
Well-being	7	9	16
Socioeconomic characteristics	4	8	12
Substance abuse	4	7	11
Suicide	1	7	8
Other variables	9	10	19
Nonempirical essays			
General nonempirical	13	10	23
Specific religious groups	7	9	16
Therapy with religious clients	1	6	7

Note: For a copy of the key words used in this category system, and a bibliography of the 427 articles, contact the authors.
[a]Totals in this table will not sum to 427 because some articles have multiple dependent variables and are counted twice.

stitution for family life. One looks almost in vain for research that treats religious orientations, attitudes, and behaviors as dependent variables and explains variation in them according to involvement in the family as a social institution. As Thornton's (1985) analysis of the reciprocal effects of religion and family indicates, we need more and better research on the effects of family upon religious variables. With respect to the Catholic family, for example, D'Antonio (1985) argues that dominant family attitudes and values will continue to affect the functioning of the religious institution. He predicts that if the religious institution continues to ignore contemporary family patterns, the result will be the decline in the moral authority of the institutional church.

CONCEPTUAL AND METHODOLOGICAL ISSUES

The research we reviewed often lacks creativity both in concept and method. The multidimensional nature of religiosity, for example, is rarely considered, particularly in studies where religiosity is the independent variable. It is generally measured by affiliation or frequency of church attendance. While methodological limitations sometimes flow from general research constraints, they also result from not giving careful attention to how the connection between religion and family is or ought to be conceptualized. It is clear from our review that while religious and family variables are included in the research effort, they are frequently of secondary importance. For example, religious preference or church attendance may be "thrown in" to the analysis simply because the research has shown that one cannot ignore the impact of religion. But there is little discussion at the theoretical level that might suggest why these variables are important.

Fortunately, several writers in the past decade have published important theoretical pieces (D'Antonio, Newman, and Wright, 1982; Thomas, 1988a; Thornton, 1985) that may influence future research. D'Antonio suggested that religions and families reinforce one another in two ways: through social support and social control. The social support dimension emphasizes that religion supports family life through norms that encourage love, family solidarity, and marital satisfaction; the social control dimension emphasizes

the impact of religion as constraining behavior—for example, by sanctioning deviance.

While we agree that this is a useful starting point, it produces fuzzy theoretical explanations. For example, it is clear from our review that the distinction between social control and social support is as much determined by how the dependent variable is conceptualized as with what the impact of religion is theorized to be. The hypothesized relationship between church attendance and *attitudes and feelings* is assumed to emphasize normative or supportive aspects of religion, while the hypothesized relationship between church attendance and *behaviors*, particularly deviant behaviors, is assumed to emphasize the social control aspects of religion. The measurement of religious variables is the same in both studies; only the theory differs. Better theoretical work needs to be done.

D'Antonio and his associates concluded in 1982 that research conducted through 1980 focused disproportionately on the social control aspects of religion. Our review suggests that the most dominant perspective emphasizes the normative or supportive aspects of religion. Religion provides a belief system that produces a moral base, encourages family behavior, and discourages antifamily behavior. For example, Heaton (1986) examines the influence of religion on the fertility of Mormons, suggesting that "religious involvement creates a context, not only for indoctrination into a particular theology, but also for socialization regarding normative expectations" (p. 249). And Thornton and Camburn (1989) suggest that "because religious values are the source of moral proscriptions for many individuals, the teachings of the churches are likely to play a role in the formation of individual attitudes, values, and decisions" (p. 642).

In order to fully understand the normative aspect of religion, however, we must conceptualize and measure the implicit intervening variable(s). Such a perspective would follow a Weberian tradition of identifying a particular belief system (e.g., the Protestant ethic) that affects behavior and shapes family, economic, and political systems. Researchers could profitably pay attention to the particular values and attitudes that are being shaped and which, in turn, influence behavior. For example, Jelen (1984) found that reasons for opposing abortion differ by religious preference and frequency of church attendance. Catholics and frequent church attenders oppose abortion on "right to life" grounds. Fundamentalists and infrequent church attenders oppose abortion because they believe it contributes to sexual promiscuity.

In much of the research, religion's impact is conceptualized in terms of social control. Of particular note is the research on adolescent deviant behavior. The basic premise (Hirschi, 1969) is that youth who make attachments to the conventional order (e.g., religion, schools, family) are less likely to engage in deviant behavior. Church attendance and importance of religion (salience) are used as indicators of attachment. Sexual activity is the dependent variable in a study by Udry (1988) and drug use is the dependent variable in a study by McIntosh, Fitch, Wilson, and Nyberg (1981). The latter authors state that the relevant concept is "commitment to religion," not simply attendance or belief. They hypothesize differences in drug use by religious group, since some religions "directly and vociferously" inveigh against deviant behavior (p. 57). The findings suggest that youth who report that religion is important to them and who attend church frequently also report less soft drug use, regardless of the religion or denomination, with one exception—soft drug use is even lower among Baptist youth who attend church regularly. Udry reports that religiosity is a deterrent to sexual activity for adolescent girls but not for adolescent boys. Thus, both studies conclude, religion functions as a mechanism of social control.

Many questions remain, however. What does attachment to social institutions mean? One approach is to ask how individuals develop a personal religious identity, a highly salient and directive sense of self that is defined by group membership, such as Catholic, Mormon, or Jew. Furthermore, how do families foster religious identities, and how do families influence attachment to a peer group that helps sustain this personal identity (see Cornwall, 1989)? Or how does religion foster attachment to parents and channel young people into religious peer groups? And finally, does religion operate as a social control mechanism because of group sanctions (fear of punishment) or through socialization processes (the social support functions) that create in the individual a high level of personal commitment to the norms of the religious group? How religion functions as social support and social control is as important a question as whether or not it does.

Another promising direction in the literature is the study of religious socialization as it relates to family life. Religiosity is almost always the dependent variable when research focuses on religious socialization, and it is typically treated multidimensionally (Cornwall, 1988; Hoge, Petrillo, and Smith, 1982). But the degree to which individuals are socialized into a religious tradition may also be highly predictive of family behavior. The reciprocal effects between religion and family need more study, with efforts on conceptualizing and measuring the group characteristics of religions and families, not just individual characteristics.

Studying religious socialization requires that we give attention to religion as a cultural system (Geertz, 1968). Berger (1967) speaks of a religious world view as a plausibility structure, a subjective reality maintained by conversation with significant others, and Greeley (1982) and Fowler (1981) point to the role of religious stories in creating meaning.

Heaton's (1986) study of Mormon fertility provides a useful example of research that examines the impact of being socialized into a specific religious group. He uses three measures of socialization: whether or not both parents were active participants in the Mormon Church during the individual's adolescence (age 16), the size of the family of orientation, and age at baptism.[2] Each variable is an indicator of a slightly different aspect of socialization: parental participation, modeling behavior, and length of socialization period. Heaton found that coming from a large family and from a family with two participating Mormon parents each has a positive influence on fertility. Age at baptism has no effect. In the ideal study, socialization effects would be more fully modeled as the extent to which individuals have adopted a particular world view. Heaton's attempt to measure the impact of socialization marks an important step forward in the way religious effects are conceptualized.

In studies of faith development where religiosity or the transmission of religious values is the major focus, family factors become the independent variables. It is apparent from the research that the acquisition of religious beliefs and values has as much or more to do with what goes on within the family than what goes on at church

(Cornwall, 1989).

Unfortunately, it is the macrosociological approach that is most lacking in the studies we reviewed. Research on religion and family has been neglected particularly in the areas of secularization, social integration, and church growth and decline.

Secularization

The secularization debate continues among sociologists who study religion. Within that debate are a few studies that focus on linkages between the family and religion over time. Thornton points out the reciprocal effects of religion and family (1985), and later suggests that trends in family attitudes parallel trends in religious change (1989). According to secularization theories, religious institutions and symbols have become differentiated over time. Religious institutions therefore have less control or influence over political and economic institutions. However, since both religion and family have been relegated to the private sphere (Berger, 1967), the connection between religion and family remains strong. In order to test this theory, Heaton and Cornwall (1989) examined religious group differences in the family and the economic behavior of women. They found that religious group differences in the economic status of women declined between 1971 and 1981 but that changes in the variability of family behavior across groups were less dramatic. Thus, religion influences economic behavior less than it does family behavior. These studies suggest the need for further discussion about how changes in religious and family institutions are associated, and how both of these are related to educational, economic, political, and other institutions.

Social Integration

Durkheim emphasized that religion promotes shared values, interaction, and strong social bonds, and in doing so protects individuals from anomie and suicide. This tradition is reflected in several studies that examine religious and family integration, individualism, religious involvement, and group commitment (Brodbar-Nemzer, 1986; Stack, 1985). These studies suggest that religion is an important social resource that provides community, bonding, and social integration and encourages individuals to emphasize group commitments over individual desires.

Studies of Church Growth and Decline

Much of the research we reviewed seems to emphasize the impact of religion on family life. Despite some theoretical insights that suggest that families have an impact on religion, there is very little research that attempts to measure that impact. The literature on church growth and decline reveals attempts to understand the factors that influence the success or failure of particular Protestant congregations. It is a debate that questions whether congregational success is a function of local community factors (middle-class neighborhoods, single-family homes, the absence of minorities), or institutional factors (overall satisfaction of laity with church worship and program, congregational harmony, theological conservatism). Taking an organizational approach to the study of religion, we might want to ask whether some religious institutions serve families more effectively and whether this more effective service is associated with growth. Research has already demonstrated that youthful congregations are more likely to grow, but it is not known why some congregations are more able to attract younger people (McKinney and Hoge, 1983). Perhaps the congregations that offer family services are more likely to attract baby boomers who are returning to religion as they take on family responsibilities (Briggs, 1990).

Measurement Issues

The research under review gives only perfunctory attention to the variability across dimensions of religiosity. This variability can be illustrated by the following U.S. data: 91% report a religious affiliation, 75% maintain the religious affiliation of their youth, 43% report a "strong" religious preference, 36% report attending church at least weekly with an average of 26 weeks each year, 56% report daily prayer with an average of 6.5 times a week, 71% believe in life after death, and 82% report feeling at least somewhat close to God (data from the General Social Survey, 1983–1987).

Social scientists have developed a number of multidimensional models of religiosity that could easily be incorporated into family research (Roof, 1979). The challenge of conceptualizing and measuring religiosity is that religion is a cultural system and religious groups express religious meaning through words and phrases that convey different meanings to different groups. Furthermore, each religious group has its own behavioral expectations. We were surprised at the number of studies that included measures of religiosity (church attendance, belief, etc.) but did not include religious affiliation. Careful measurement requires attention to the nuances of different belief systems in order to explain variation in their impact on family life.

MODELING FAMILY AND RELIGION INFLUENCES

While most of the research published in the decade tends to analyze the religion and family variables in bivariate relationships, there are some studies that have moved beyond the bivariate analysis to multivariate formulations. In some areas these replicated bivariate relationships cry out for more extensive analysis in an effort to gain a better understanding of the social-psychological realities of religion and family life. One of the first such areas to emerge in the 1980s was the relationship between religiosity and marital quality.

As Schumm, Bollman, and Jurich (1982) note, research in the area of the family had for decades documented the fact that people who were more highly involved in religious activities also reported that their marriages were generally more satisfying than did people not involved in religious institutions. This relationship tended to be ignored in discussions about family life, or, at best, was seen as a spurious artifact. The explanation proffered was that religiously oriented people would be likely to score high on social desirability measures or other indices of acquiescence response bias and therefore say that their marriage was more satisfying.

Schumm's research was the first to test the above explanation and he finds no support for the "marital conventionalization" argument. Filsinger and Wilson (1984) next addressed the issue. In their first study of 208 Protestant couples, they found that religiosity was more predictive of marital adjustment than were socioeconomic or family developmental characteristics, even when social desirability was controlled. They extended their analysis further in their second study (Wilson and Filsinger, 1986) where they analyzed multiple dimensions of both religiosity and dyadic relationships. Their finding replicates the first study in that religiosity is more strongly related to

marital satisfaction when social desirability is controlled. Most of the dimensions of religiosity are related to satisfying dyadic relationships, with the consequential dimension being the least predictive.

In related research, Heaton (1984) showed that religiously homogamous marriages are more satisfying, but when he controlled for religious attendance, the homogamy effects became nonsignificant. He thus concluded that something about religious involvement is related to higher marital satisfaction, since that relationship held when he introduced other control variables, such as conflict over children.

The above research argues that it is time for the social scientists to ask more systematically what it is about religion that contributes to marital satisfaction, rather than treating it as a spurious relationship. Multivariate models will have to be developed where multiple dimensions of both family and religion are measured in an effort to assess how these variables may be related.

The 1982 study by Hoge and associates is important in that they attempted to look at value transmission from parents to adolescents and used multiple measures of religiosity as well as of values. As this research replicated previous work showing that relationships tend to be relatively weak between parental values and children's values, Hoge et al. argued that future research should pay more attention to other factors than those they investigated in this study. Whatever form the "more elaborate paradigm" (page 579) takes, with respect to value transmission from parents to adolescents, the paradigm would have to include, along with religion and family, at least some dimensions of the peer world.

Cornwall (1988) conceptualized and measured multiple dimensions of family and religiosity, linking them in a structural-equation model and attempting to account for variation in adult dimensions of religiosity, according to self-reported influences in home, church, and peer worlds during the adolescent years. This research is important because it shows that what the family was doing during the adolescent years by way of "home religious observance" (family prayer, scripture study, etc.) has only a weak direct effect upon adult commitment to the church. However, it has an important set of indirect effects through the peer world.

Cornwall's research argues for the relevance of

the channeling hypothesis. The patterns in these multivariate analyses support the conclusion that the religious socialization practices in the home channel children into religious educational settings, which in turn influence the type and number of friends they have. It is the network among friends in the peer world that has the strongest direct effect upon adult church commitment.

Additional research employing structural-equation modeling gives insight into how multiple dimensions of both religion and family variables influence each other. Research reported by Thomas (1988a) attempts to explain variation in adult well-being according to the multiple influences of home and religion variables. The religion and family variables account for 57% of the variance in adult well-being operationalized as satisfaction with life and lack of depression.

This research shows that with respect to adult well-being, both the marital dimension and parental dimension in the family need to be conceptualized as distinct variables, having differential effects upon adult well-being. Being satisfied with the parental role has an impact on adult well-being, independent of what is happening in the marital domain. In addition, the research underscores the importance of religion's multiple dimensions. With respect to understanding adult well-being, "personal spiritual devotion" is the single most important variable in the model. Not only does it have a strong and consistent direct effect upon adult well-being, but it also has an impact upon both marital and parental satisfaction, which in turn influence adult well-being.

One additional surprise from this research is the importance of the family-of-orientation variable "closeness to parents." While the direct effect on adult well-being is significant, though small, "closeness to parents" has a significant indirect effect on adult well-being through various family and religion variables. When both direct and indirect effects on adult well-being are computed, personal spiritual devotion is the strongest (.46), followed by parental satisfaction (.34), followed by closeness to parents (.32). These findings call attention to the importance of the parent-child relationships in understanding adult well-being among Mormons. Is the importance of parent-child relations seen in this model idiosyncratic to Mormons, or would it be true of any familistic religion? Comparative research is needed to answer such questions.

From Here to Where?

Some trends observed during the decade portend a bright future for religion and family research. The movement toward multivariate analyses of religion and family variables reveals both methodological and conceptual development. Across the journals analyzed in this review, there is a broadening rather than a declining interest in religion and family.

Research and theory committed to understanding questions about multiple institutional interface, social change, socialization practices, religious identity formation, and spiritual influences in human lives cannot continue to rely on cross-sectional data, survey research, census data, and the operationalization of religion as affiliation and/or attendance. This area of inquiry calls for more research that is longitudinal and that utilizes both qualitative and quantitative designs focusing on the social psychological reality of simultaneous membership in multiple social institutions, which themselves are changing over time.

The best research and theory of the future will be that which attempts to chart institutional and individual change by analyzing direct, indirect, and reciprocal causal relations. In the ideal research, other institutional networks such as work and education would be combined with religion and family to see how an individual's involvement in and commitment to various social institutions change over time. Such research calls for a broad-based social support network over an extended period.

Given that there are no national institutes of family and religion, and few universities able and/or willing to fund such expensive long-term research in this area, it may be left for religious organizations to pick up the ball and generate long-term programs of research.

In our view, research of the future designed to answer questions about the interrelations between religion and family will have to address questions about the meaning of the human condition. Such an approach cannot ignore issues regarding the purposes of life, humankind's relationship to the divine, or the whys of births, deaths, and other intimate family and religious experiences. Perhaps then we will begin to understand the place of family and religion in our rapidly changing world.

NOTES

The authors express their appreciation to the Center for Studies of the Family and the Women's Research Institute at Brigham Young University for support of this research; to Jackie DeGaston, Karen Frazier, Greg Mueller, and Zhang Zie for library research; and to Larry Young, Boyd Rollins, and two anonymous reviewers for suggestions on earlier versions of this article.

1. The source materials used for this analysis are the decade review publications of the *Journal of Marriage and the Family* in 1970, 1971, and 1980. See especially the articles by Jewson (1970, 1980) where she presents information on publication by NCFR for each decade.

2. Latter-Day Saints baptize their children at age eight. Those who are converted at a later date will have experienced socializing influences over a shorter period of time.

REFERENCES

Berger, Peter. 1967. The Sacred Canopy. Garden City, NY: Anchor Books.

Briggs, Kenneth A. 1990. "Baby boomers: Boom or bust for the churches?" Progressions 2(1): 4–7.

Brodbar-Nemzer, Jay Y. 1986. "Divorce and group commitment: The case of the Jews." Journal of Marriage and the Family 48: 329–340.

Caplow, Theodore. 1982. Middletown Families: Fifty Years of Change and Continuity. Minneapolis: University of Minnesota Press.

Caplow, Theodore, Howard M. Bahr, and Bruce A. Chadwick. 1983. All Faithful People: Change and Continuity in Middletown's Religion. Minneapolis: University of Minnesota Press.

Cornwall, Marie. 1988. "The influence of three agents of religious socialization: Family, church, and peers." Pp. 207–231 in D. L. Thomas (ed.), The Religion and Family Connection: Social Science Perspectives. Provo, UT: Religious Studies Center, Brigham Young University.

Cornwall, Marie. 1989. "The determinants of religious behavior: A theoretical model and empirical test." Social Forces 68: 572–592.

D'Antonio, William V. 1985. "The American Catholic family: Signs of cohesion and polarization." Journal of Marriage and the Family 47: 395–405.

D'Antonio, William V., and Joan Aldous (eds.). 1983. Families and Religions: Conflict and Change in Modern Society. Beverly Hills, CA: Sage.

D'Antonio, William V., William M. Newman, and Stuart A. Wright. 1982. "Religion and family life: How social scientists view the relationship." Journal for the Scientific Study of Religion 21: 218–225.

Filsinger, Erik E., and Margaret R. Wilson. 1984. "Religiosity, socioeconomic rewards, and family development: Predictors of marital adjustment." Journal of Marriage and the Family 46: 663–670.

Fowler, James. 1981. Stages of Faith: The Psychology of Human Development and the Quest for Meaning. San Francisco: Harper and Row.

Geertz, Clifford. 1968. "Religion as a cultural system." In D. Cutler (ed.), Religious Situation 1968. Boston: Beacon.

Greeley, Andrew. 1982. Religion: A Secular Theory. New York: Free Press.

Heaton, Tim B. 1984. "Religious homogamy and marital satisfaction reconsidered." Journal of Marriage and the Family 46: 729–733.

Heaton, Tim B. 1986. "How does religion influence fertility?" The case of Mormons." Journal for the Scientific Study of Religion 25: 248–258.

Heaton, Tim B., and Marie Cornwall. 1989. "Religious group variation in the socioeconomic status and family behavior of women." Journal for the Scientific Study of Religion 28: 283–299.

Hirschi, Travis. 1969. Causes of Delinquency. Berkeley: University of California Press.

Hoge, Dean R., Gregory H. Petrillo, and Ella I. Smith. 1982. "Transmission of religious and social values from parents to teenage children." Journal of Marriage and the Family 44: 569–580.

Jelen, Ted G. 1984. "Respect for life, sexual morality, and opposition to abortion." Review of Religious Research 25: 220–231.

Marciano, Teresa Donati. 1987. "Families and religions." Pp. 285–316 in M. B. Sussman and S. K. Steinmetz (eds.), Handbook of Marriage and the Family. New York: Plenum Press.

McIntosh, William Alex, Starla D. Fitch, J. Branton Wilson, and Kenneth L. Nyberg. 1981. "The effect of mainstream religious social controls on adolescent drug use in rural areas." Review of Religious Research 23: 54–75.

McKinney, William, and Dean R. Hoge. 1983. "Community and congregational factors in the growth and decline of Protestant churches." Journal for the Scientific Study of Religion 22: 51–66.

Roof, Wade Clark. 1979. "Concepts and indicators of religious commitment: A critical review." In Robert Wuthnow (ed.), The Religious Dimension: New Directions in Quantitative Research. New York: Academic Press.

Schumm, Walter R., Stephan R. Bollman, and Anthony P. Jurich. 1982. "The 'marital conventionalization' argument: Implication for the study of religiosity and marital satisfaction." Journal of Psychology and Theology 10: 236–241.

Stack, Steven. 1985. "The effect of domestic/religious individualism on suicide, 1954–1978." Journal of Marriage and the Family 47: 431–447.

Thomas, Darwin L. 1988a. "Future prospects for religion and family studies: The Mormon case." Pp. 357–382 in D. L. Thomas (ed.), The Religion and Family Connection: Social Science Perspectives. Provo, UT: Religious Studies Center, Brigham Young University.

Thomas, Darwin L. 1988b. The Religion and Family Connection: Social Science Perspectives. Provo, UT: Religious Studies Center, Brigham Young University.

Thomas, Darwin L., and Gwendolyn C. Henry. 1985. "The religion and family connection: Increasing dialogue in the social sciences." Journal of Marriage and the Family 47: 369–379.

Thomas, Darwin L., and Vern Sommerfeldt. 1984. "Religion, family, and the social sciences: A time for dialogue." Family Perspective 18: 117–125.

Thornton, Arland. 1985. "Reciprocal influences of family and religion in a changing world." Journal of Marriage and the Family 47: 381–394.

Thornton, Arland. 1989. "Changing attitudes toward family issues in the United States." Journal of Marriage and the Family 51: 873–893.

Thornton, Arland, and Donald Camburn. 1989. "Religious participation and adolescent sexual behavior and attitudes." Journal of Marriage and the Family 51: 641–653.

Udry, J. Richard. 1988. "Biological predispositions and social control in adolescent sexual behavior." American Sociological Review 53: 709–722.

Wilson, Margaret R., and Erik E. Filsinger. 1986. Religiosity and marital adjustment: Multidimensional interrelationships." Journal of Marriage and the Family 48: 147–151.

ROBERT JOSEPH TAYLOR   *University of Michigan*

LINDA M. CHATTERS   *University of Michigan**

M. BELINDA TUCKER   *University of California, Los Angeles***

EDITH LEWIS   *University of Michigan****

Developments in Research on Black Families:

A Decade Review

The literature on black families from the past decade is reviewed. An overview of topics and issues of importance to black families considers (a) black families in relation to their age, gender, and family roles, (b) substantive issues of relevance to black American families, including social support and psychological well-being, and (c) an examination of recent demographic trends in black family structure. The conclusion provides comments on research on black families and recommendations for future efforts.

The past ten years have witnessed a tremendous increase in the diversity and breadth of research on the family lives of black Americans. Despite this impressive growth, significant limitations persist in the dissemination of these efforts and their integration into the corpus of family life litera-

School of Social Work and Institute for Social Research, University of Michigan, Ann Arbor, MI 48109–1285.

*School of Public Health and Institute for Social Research, University of Michigan, Ann Arbor, MI 48109–2029.

**Center for Afro-American Studies, University of California, Los Angeles, 160 Haines Hall, 405 Hilgard Avenue, Los Angeles, CA 90024–1545.

***School of Social Work, University of Michigan, Ann Arbor, MI 48109–1285.

ture. It is frequently the case that books investigating black family issues are not well publicized and, as a consequence, remain relatively obscure. Other works that employ predominantly black samples fail to use the term *black* (or other racial designations) in their title (e.g., Furstenberg, Brooks-Gunn, and Morgan, 1987; Thompson and Ensminger, 1989), thus making it difficult to locate these materials. Similarly, it is not uncommon that research on black families is overlooked in major reviews of family life research.

As with all social science, research and writing on black families transpires within a larger social and political context that influences the nature and direction of inquiry, as well as the interpretation and application of findings. The area of black family studies has been particularly sensitive to the impact of various competing paradigms or orientations that have served both to identify significant areas of inquiry and to frame the nature and scope of debate on issues of black family life (Allen, 1981; Farley and Allen, 1987). Although extant models of black family life emphasize their resilient-adaptive features (Farley and Allen, 1987), remnants of the pathological-disorganization or cultural deviant perspective on black families are evident in several current writings (e.g., Anderson, 1989; Schoen and Kluegel, 1988), as are frameworks that place inordinate emphasis on the social problems facing black Americans (e.g., Jaynes and Williams, 1989, chap. 10). These works stand in contrast to emerging research that (*a*) employs resilient-adaptive perspectives on black families, (*b*) examines a broad range of topics and their interrelationships, and (*c*) illuminates the diversity of family life among black Americans (Hill et al., 1990).

The scope of research and writing dictates a selective approach to reviewing literature on black families. In an attempt to address the breadth of concerns in a fairly comprehensive manner, several priorities have been adopted in providing an overview of topics and issues of importance to black families. First, this article almost exclusively relies on material that has been published since the last decade review (Staples and Mirande, 1980), and priority is given to more recent research. Second, topics such as family violence and family policy, which are examined in other articles in this volume, are not discussed here. The organizational structure of the review is as follows: the first section considers black families in relation to their age, gender, and family roles; the second focuses on substantive issues of relevance to black American families, including social support and psychological well-being; and the third section examines recent demographic trends in black family structure. The conclusion provides final comments on research on black families and recommendations for future efforts.

LIFE COURSE ISSUES

This section of the literature review addresses distinct family issues related to life course position. Research reviewed in this section examines black children and racial socialization, the period of adolescence, gender and role behavior among black couples, role strain among black women, the salience of the provider role among black men, and informal support networks of elderly black adults.

Black Children

One of the most researched areas addressing children in black families is that of racial socialization (Spencer, Brookins, and Allen, 1985). Black parents, like all parents, play a pivotal and crucial role in instructing their children on how to participate successfully as

citizens in the wider society. The general goals of the socialization process are to provide children with an understanding of roles, statuses, and prescribed behaviors within society and an appreciation of their position within the social structure (Thornton, Chatters, Taylor, and Allen, 1990). For the most part, parental socialization values mirror those of the wider community and society, and in turn, societal agents (e.g., schools, religious institutions) reinforce the socialization themes that are expressed in the family context. However, for black parents, racial prejudice and discrimination are important intervening factors in this process. For black Americans, socialization occurs within a broader social environment that is frequently incompatible with realizing a positive self and group identity.

In the 1980s, there was much speculation about the manner in which parents and the family environment functioned as a buffer between the child and this hostile social climate (Jackson, McCullough, and Gurin, 1988; Peters and Massey, 1983). During this period, several studies examined family socialization techniques (Bowman and Howard, 1985; Peters, 1985; Spencer, 1983) as intermediaries between the child and the immediate context. The process of explicit racial socialization is clearly a distinctive childrearing activity that black parents engage in as an attempt to prepare their children for the realities of being black in America. However, recent studies suggest that close to a third of black parents do not report conveying racial socialization messages to their children (Bowman and Howard, 1985; Thornton et al., 1990). Among those who do, the family sometimes provides specific socialization messages stressing a proactive orientation toward existing social inequalities (Bowman and Howard, 1985; Peters, 1985). For some black parents, issues of race are a central concern in raising their children. Their efforts involve explicit preparation for their unique situation and experiences as black Americans (Peters, 1985) or an attempt to forewarn their children concerning the nature of the broader social environment (Harrison, 1985).

Bowman and Howard (1985) and Thornton et al. (1990) identified various structural factors that were significantly correlated with whether or not parents imparted racial socialization messages to their children. Differential patterns of socialization emerged, particularly with regard to sex of the child and of the parent. Black male adolescents were more likely to be cautioned about racial barriers, whereas young women were more likely to be socialized with reference to issues of racial pride (Bowman and Howard, 1985). Reflecting differences for men and women (Thornton et al., 1990), fathers who were older and who lived in the Northeast (versus the South) were more likely to impart race-related socialization strategies to their children, while being widowed or never married decreased the probability of this practice. Mothers who resided in neighborhoods in which the racial composition reflected roughly equal numbers of blacks and whites were more likely to socialize their children racially than were mothers who lived in all-black areas. Mothers who had never been married were less likely, while highly educated, older women were more likely to familiarize their children with racial realities. Among the many unexplored topics in the area of racial socialization, there remains scant information concerning the conflict between the socialization messages of the family and society and the manner in which these differences are resolved.

Adolescence

Historically, literature on the nature of adolescence has had as its primary focus the variety of challenges and problems that face this group, and the general depiction of adolescence is that it is a developmental period characterized by conflict and transition. What is unique to the study of black adolescents is the extent to which being black and adolescent has come to be viewed as synonymous with a variety of social problems. Even a cursory examination of the statistics on physical and mental health, educational attainment, teenage pregnancy and parenting, crime (as perpetrator and victim), substance abuse, and job and employment patterns attests to the fact that these problems are both numerous and significant.

What is not evident in the literature on this group is an appreciation for the diversity of black youth as individuals who come from different family, neighborhood, and community settings and socioeconomic backgrounds (Jones, 1989). Black youth are monolithically portrayed as urban, low-income, plagued by a multitude of problems, and lacking in the resources and/or motivation to effect change in their lives. Further, by restricting the scope of research on black adolescents to social problems and/or "problem youth," we have learned relatively little about issues of motivation, personality and psychological development, cognitive and moral development, identity and self-esteem, attitude formation, family relationships with parents and siblings, family socialization issues—in short, issues for which there exists an established and burgeoning literature regarding white youth.

Married Couples

A collection of research findings suggest that gender distinctions in the provider and homemaker roles are not as rigid in black families as they are in white families (Beckett and Smith, 1981; Ericksen, Yancey, and Ericksen, 1979). Black women have historically had higher levels of participation in the paid labor force than white women, and black men are more likely than white men to endorse the view that women should be employed (Huber and Spitze, 1981). The involvement of black women in the provider role may reflect a wider acceptance of women's labor force participation among blacks generally and/or reflect an economic necessity in relation to the precarious and uncertain conditions that characterize the employment and earning patterns of black men within particular segments of the labor market. With regard to the homemaker role, black husbands are more likely than their white counterparts to share housework and child care (Ericksen et al., 1979). Greater levels of egalitarianism in the division of household labor among black couples is maintained when the analysis controls for wife's employment status, relative earning power, and sex-role attitudes (Ross, 1987). Despite the fact that black households are more egalitarian, gender differences in contributions to household work indicate that black women still perform the majority of the traditional chores of cooking, cleaning, and laundry, and are more likely than black men to feel overworked (Broman, 1988a).

Black Women

As noted in other sections of this review, the status and position of black women in relation to general issues such as psychological well-being (Brown and Gary, 1985, 1987), informal support networks (H. McAdoo, 1980) and extended-family households (Beck and Beck, 1989) is well represented in the literature. One of the more interesting areas of research among this group addresses the correlates and consequences of role strain. Thompson and Ensminger (1989) argue that among poor, black women, long-term single parenting represents a chronic stressor. Two studies examined the correlates of role strain within the areas of parenting, economic concerns, and household maintenance among black mothers (Lewis, 1988, 1989). With regard to the parental role, black mothers who had a current partner, fewer children in the household, and extended kin who lived some distance away but not out of state were less likely to report strain in this area. Black mothers who indicated that they had someone to help with child care were less likely to report role strain in the area of household maintenance. Women who had a current partner, earned higher incomes, and were older were less likely to report experiencing economic role strain. An examination of the multiple roles of middle-aged and elderly black women found that traditional social roles of parent and spouse did not significantly affect their psychological and physical health (Coleman, Antonucci, Adelmann, and Crohan, 1987).

Black Men

In contrast to the volume of work focused on the position of black women, the role of black men in families is one of the most conspicuously neglected areas of family research. The absence of a reliable knowledge base on the role of black men in families has resulted in a portrayal of black men as peripheral to family and as performing poorly in the family roles of spouse and father (Allen, 1981; J. McAdoo, 1981). A few studies have investigated the saliency of the provider role and perceptions of role performance among black men. Cazenave found that the role of economic provider was a frequently cited familial role among both middle-income black fathers (1979) and blue-collar black men (1984). Among middle-income black fathers, the goal of exceeding the socioeconomic status of their own fathers (who had low incomes and irregular employment) was central to their self-perceptions of being better providers for their families (Cazenave, 1979). Other research (Taylor, Leashore, and Toliver, 1988) found that personal income and age were positively associated with the likelihood that black men perceived themselves as being good providers for their families. Provider role strain, however, was found to affect life happiness adversely among a sample of married black fathers (Bowman, 1985). The centrality and significance of the provider role for this group is supported by the findings that having a higher personal income is associated with the probability of being married among black men (Tucker and Taylor, 1989) and satisfaction with family life among black husbands (Ball and Robbins, 1986a).

Research efforts examining the affective roles and functions of men in black families are exceedingly rare. Limited work among lower-middle to middle-class families suggests that black men are highly involved in the parental and childrearing role (J. McAdoo, 1981) and are successful in that capacity, as evidenced by their producing children who are well adjusted and positively motivated on several indicators (Allen, 1981). In addition, research indicates that both black fathers and mothers are involved in the racial socialization of children (Thornton et al., 1990).

Black Elderly

A vast majority of research on the family life of elderly blacks has addressed their informal social support networks. An analysis of the correlates of support from extended family (Taylor, 1985) found that for those elderly persons with children, gender, income, education, region, and familial interaction were all significant predictors of the frequency of support. Among the childless elderly, however, having an available pool of relatives was of singular importance. Gibson and Jackson (1987) found that the support resources of older black adults were tailored to their individual needs, specifically in relation to age and physical and functional health status. Family members figured prominently in the support networks of the elderly. Adverse changes in the economic viability of black families are viewed as potentially jeopardizing these support resources.

Two sets of analyses found that sociodemographic and family factors influenced the size and composition of informal helper networks of elderly blacks (Chatters, Taylor, and Jackson, 1985, 1986). Marital status was particularly important, with married older blacks having larger helper networks consisting of immediate family. Unmarried elderly persons had smaller networks that comprised a wide variety of individuals. The significance of region for the size and composition of the helper network was particularly intriguing and suggested that Southern residents had larger networks that were more likely to include a diverse group of helpers (see Taylor, 1988a, for a review of this literature).

SUBSTANTIVE ISSUES

This section of the literature review examines research and writings on extended-family household arrangements, intergenerational relations, informal social support networks, social support and psychological well-being, and family therapy.

Extended-Family Households

Existing research has consistently documented that blacks are more likely to reside in extended-family households than are whites (Angel and Tienda, 1982; Beck and Beck, 1989; Farley and Allen, 1987; Hofferth, 1984; Tienda and Angel, 1982). A longitudinal analysis of the incidence of extended-family households among middle-aged women (Beck and Beck, 1989) revealed that 6 out of 10 black women experienced some form of household extension during the period from 1969 to 1984. Racial comparisons revealed that the higher proportion of extended households among black women was primarily due to the presence of grandchildren residing within their households (Beck and Beck, 1989).

Racial differences in household composition are sustained even in the presence of controls for socioeconomic status. Farley and Allen (1987) found that, when they controlled for income, extended living arrangements were twice as common among black compared to white households. In contrast, marital status emerges as an important predictor of household extension. Research suggests that both blacks and whites who are not married have a higher probability of residing in an extended household (Beck and Beck, 1989; Farley and Allen, 1987).

Extended-family arrangements are recognized to have important economic benefits and are viewed as an effective mechanism for pooling limited economic resources. The practice of "doubling up" in extended households has an important bearing on the economic welfare of the family and, in comparison to direct cash transfers, is generally a less expensive method of providing for needy relatives. Angel and Tienda's (1982) research on sources of household income suggests that among blacks, the relative contributions of a wife, adult children, and non-nuclear relatives constitute a greater portion of the total household income than is the case among whites. Because of the generally lower earnings of black heads of households, supplemental income from family members was required to achieve a desired standard of living or, in many cases, simply to meet daily needs.

Other supportive benefits have been examined in relation to extended-family household arrangements, and in particular, the presence of non-nuclear adults within the household has been associated with the reallocation of employment and domestic responsibilities. Research suggests that another adult in the household (who assists with child care and other household duties) may help alleviate the burden associated with caring for an impaired family member or provide the opportunity for a single parent with a young child to pursue educational goals and obtain employment outside the home (Hogan, Hao, and Parish, 1990).

Intergenerational Relations

The majority of recent research on intergenerational relationships within the black population has been concerned with the exchange of assistance across generations. In particular, several studies have examined the role that adult children play in the support networks of elderly black adults and the assistance that black grandmothers provide to children and grandchildren. Elderly black adults who had children had a greater likelihood of receiving support from extended-family members (Taylor, 1985, 1986) and church members (Taylor and Chatters, 1986a). Similarly, elderly black adults who were parents had a larger helper network (Chatters et al., 1985) and utilized more informal helpers in response to a serious personal problem (Chatters, Taylor, and Neighbors, 1989). Adult children, daughters in particular, were selected most frequently by older black adults as the person who would help them if they were sick (Chatters et al., 1986). In contrast, childless elderly persons were more likely to rely upon brothers, sisters, and friends (Chatters et al., 1986). Despite these substitutions, childless elderly adults were still at a distinct disadvantage with regard to the size of their informal helper networks. An investigation of the use of informal helpers during an emergency demonstrated that the parent-child bond is important across the life course. Younger adults tended to rely heavily on their parents, older adults relied on their adult children, and middle-aged black adults tended to depend on both their parents and children (Taylor, Chatters, and Mays, 1988).

Racial comparisons of the grandparent role reveal that, in comparison to whites, black grandparents take a more active part in the parenting of grandchildren (Cherlin and Furstenberg, 1986). The greater involvement of black grandparents may be due to several circumstances. First, the greater probability of blacks residing with grandchildren and in three-generation households (Beck and Beck, 1989) provides increased opportunities for involvement in active grandparenting (Hogan et al., 1990). Second, a higher incidence of marital (i.e., separation, divorce), employment (i.e., layoffs, unemployment) and health (i.e., morbidity and mortality) events among blacks (Cherlin and Furstenberg, 1986) may have important consequences for both household arrangements and family child-care responsibilities. Finally, it may be the case that there are explicit cultural norms in support of extended-family relations in operation among black Americans (Sudarkasa, 1981).

Research indicates that mothers of black teenage parents play a prominent role in the lives of their children and grandchildren. The assistance that adolescent mothers receive from their extended family generally and their own mothers in particular has a positive impact on their educational and economic achievement and parenting skills and their children's development (Brooks-Gunn and Furstenberg, 1986; Stevens, 1984, 1988; M. Wilson, 1989).

Recent and accelerating changes in family structure (e.g., increase in nonmarital childbearing, shortened length of time in marriage) among blacks may have important consequences for intergenerational relationships (Burton and Dilworth-Anderson, in press). Burton and Bengtson (1985) investigated the role perceptions and concerns of women who experienced, in a normative sense, early (median age 32 years) vs. on-time (median age 46 years) entry into the grandmother role. The pattern of early grandmotherhood tended to result from two generations of teenage pregnancy: their own and their daughter's. "Early" grandmothers expressed significant discomfort in their role as a result of the inordinate caretaker burdens and childrearing responsibilities for both their adolescent child and grandchild and the role incongruency arising from being young and a grandmother.

Informal Social Support

Extended family networks. During the past decade, one of the most significant areas of research in the black family literature has concerned the role and functioning of the extended family in informal support networks. Indeed, much of the research focusing on intergenerational relationships and the family lives of elderly black adults has addressed questions that pertain, either directly or indirectly, to informal support networks. Several recent literature reviews that are concerned with extended-family networks in relation to childhood development (M. Wilson, 1986, 1989) and aging black adults (Taylor, 1988a) attest to the significance of this substantive area.

Taylor (1986) found that both family and demographic factors were important predictors of receiving support from extended-family members among black Americans. With regard to family variables, having an available pool of relatives, frequent interaction with family members, and close familial relationships were predictors for receiving support from extended family. A recent study examined the level of familial involvement among two groups of black adults who reported that they did not receive assistance from their extended families (Taylor, 1990). Multivariate analyses contrasting individuals who had never received assistance (support-deficients) with those who reported that they had never needed assistance (self-reliants) indicated that self-reliants reported significantly higher levels of familial involvement. Dressler, Hoeppner, and Pitts's (1985) examination of household structure in a black community found evidence of diverse household forms that varied on the basis of gender of household head and level of integration in extended networks, and that were related to one another through mutual interaction and support exchange. Collectively, these findings underscore the importance and pervasiveness of extended-family members in the support networks of black Americans.

Two studies investigated the use of informal helpers specifically in relation to a serious personal problem that the respondent had experienced (Chatters et al., 1989; Neighbors and Jackson, 1984). Neighbors and Jackson's (1984) investigation of informal and professional help utilization revealed that 8 out of 10 respondents enlisted informal help solely or in conjunction with professional assistance. Chatters et al. (1989) found that being female, having higher income, and maintaining greater levels of contact with family were all predictive of larger informal helper networks. Significant differences by problem type indicated that respondents with interpersonal, economic, and emotional problems utilized smaller networks than persons who indicated that they had a physical health problem.

Friendship and church support networks. Emergent research has investigated the role of friends and church members in the informal support networks of black Americans. Several studies have indicated that friends, neighbors, coworkers, and in-laws are important sources of assistance for black Americans (Brown and Gary, 1987; Chatters et al., 1986, 1989; Dressler, 1985; Ellison, 1990; Jackson and Berg-Cross, 1988; H. McAdoo, 1980; Malson, 1983; Oliver, 1988; Taylor, Chatters, and Mays, 1988; Ulbrich and Warheit, 1989). However, it is generally agreed that kin are more prevalent in informal networks than non-kin (Chatters et al., 1986, 1989). An analysis of the use of kin and non-kin during an emergency revealed that older blacks were more likely than younger blacks to use non-kin (Taylor, Chatters, and Mays, 1988). Among elderly black adults, those who indicated that they were not affectively close to their families, and the childless elderly, had a higher probability of having helper networks comprised of friends (Chatters et al., 1986).

Marital status has shown a significant predictive relationship with the composition of support networks. Unmarried elderly black adults apparently compensated for the absence of a spouse by using other relatives and non-kin in their informal helper networks (Chatters et al., 1985, 1986). In comparison to married respondents, divorced elderly blacks were more likely to use friends and

neighbors as helpers, widowed persons were more likely to utilize friends, and the never-married were more likely to select neighbors (Chatters et al., 1986).

The past few years have witnessed an emergence of interest in the area of religion and families, and specifically, the role and functions of religious institutions as a surrogate for the family. The majority of this research has addressed these issues among black Americans. This area of work is particularly relevant for this racial group because blacks consistently display higher levels of religiosity than whites (see Taylor, 1988b), and religious participation has been found to buffer psychological distress among blacks (Brown and Gary, 1987). Church members have been found to be a critical source of support among blacks. Dressler (1985) found that church members were important sources of assistance in coping with stress associated with racism, marital difficulties, and psychological problems. In an investigation of church support networks, church attendance, church membership, and subjective religiosity were positively related to the receipt of support from church members, whereas being Catholic (as opposed to Baptist), divorced (as opposed to married), older, and female were negatively associated (Taylor and Chatters, 1988). Similarly, research among elderly blacks notes the importance of church attendance as a predictor of both the frequency and the amount of support received from church members (Taylor and Chatters, 1986a). Taylor and Chatters (1986b) examined concomitant support to elderly blacks from family, friends, and church members. Observed patterns of support revealed that if elderly blacks received help from church members, it was likely that family and friends were also part of the network. An examination of the types of support provided indicated that church members provided advice and encouragement, help during sickness, and prayer (Taylor and Chatters, 1986b).

Psychological Well-being

A long tradition of work has explored the nature and correlates (i.e., family and marital life influences) of subjective well-being (SWB) among the general population. However, relatively few investigations have explored SWB and its correlates among black adults (Chatters, 1988).

Marital status was not significantly associated with psychological distress (i.e., reports of significant personal problems) among a national sample of black Americans (Neighbors, 1986) or an urban sample of black women (Brown and Gary, 1985). Among black women with school-age children, however, those who lived with a spouse or another adult had lower levels of psychological distress than those who were the only adult in the household (Thompson and Ensminger, 1989).

With regard to the impact of marital status on reports of life satisfaction, happiness, and other indicators of psychological well-being, married blacks generally express higher levels of well-being than their unmarried counterparts (Broman, 1988b; Jackson, Chatters, and Neighbors, 1986; Zollar and Williams, 1987). Broman (1988b) found that separated and divorced statuses were both negatively associated with life satisfaction, and further, being divorced was negatively related to family life satisfaction. Among black adults who were 55 years and older, persons who were widowed and separated had lower levels of happiness as compared to married individuals (Chatters, 1988). Marital status, however, was not significantly related to self-esteem or perceived control among middle-aged and older black women (Coleman et al., 1987). Further, Ball and Robbins (1986b) found that while marital status was not related to reports of life satisfaction among women, for men being married was associated with generally lower levels of satisfaction (see Chatters and Jackson, 1989, for a comprehensive review of subjective well-being research among black adults).

Although the diverse effects of parental status on psychological well-being have been routinely investigated among whites, these issues remain a neglected research area among blacks. Preliminary evidence suggests that while being a parent is associated with lower levels of happiness and satisfaction and higher levels of anxiety among whites (McLanahan and Adams, 1987), it is unrelated to SWB among blacks. Parental status was unrelated to (a) both life satisfaction and family life satisfaction (Broman, 1988b) and (b) self-esteem and perceived control among middle-aged and older black women (Coleman et al., 1987). In addition, black parents with children residing in the home had lower levels of psychological distress than their childless counterparts (Reskin and Coverman, 1985).

Social Support and Psychological Well-being

A growing collection of research findings suggests a connection between involvement in extended-family support networks and mental health and psychological well-being. Black adults with supportive family and friendship relations were found to have heightened self-esteem and personal efficacy (Hughes and Demo, 1989). Similarly, reported satisfaction with social support from family and friends significantly reduced psychological distress among both employed and unemployed black women (Brown and Gary, 1988). Among blacks who were experiencing an economic crisis (Neighbors and LaVeist, 1989), those who received financial assistance reported lower levels of psychological distress; the primary sources of financial aid were family and friends. The literature is somewhat equivocal concerning the effects of gender on social support and the relationship between structural characteristics of support networks and well-being. With regard to gender differences, Brown and Gary (1987) found that perceived support from family buffered psychological distress, but only among women. In contrast, Dressler (1985) found that this relationship existed solely among men. In several studies, structural aspects of supportive networks, such as frequency of contact between network members (Thomas, Milburn, Brown, and Gary, 1988), number of extended kin (Dressler, 1985), and proximity of relatives (Warheit, Vega, Shimizu, and Meinhardt, 1982) failed to influence psychological distress. Brown and Gary (1987), however, found that the number of proximate relatives reduced distress among black women. Antonucci and Jackson's work (1989) on older black adults suggests that the potential for feelings of dependency and exploitation in support relationships are diminished when social exchange are governed by normative rules and expectations regarding reciprocity. The notion of reciprocity is a useful framework for examining supportive behaviors across the life course as well as how involvement in supportive behaviors may be related to positive individual outcomes (e.g., personal competency, perceptions of control, successful adaptation to aging).

Family Therapy

The decade of the 1980s has focused specific attention on the role of ethnicity and race in family intervention. The family therapy literature among black Americans reflects the renewed interest in the impact of race and culture. An edited volume addressing social work practice among black American famlies (Logan, Freeman, and McRoy, 1990) critiques past perspectives on and orientations toward the family (particularly with regard to issues of diversity in family forms). Further, this work attempts to develop a framework for practice that is grounded in current literature on the black family and addresses the culturally specific needs of black families. Robinson's recent work (1989) suggests that race has a definite and significant impact on the clinical treatment of black families. She presents a framework and a specific treatment strategy for working with black clients, incorporating issues of (*a*) the racial identity congruence of the client, (*b*) the implications of race in the presenting problem, and (*c*) the racial awareness of the clinician. Wilson (1986) suggests that intervention approaches within black extended families should recognize the validity of extended-family forms, clarify the role relationships among family members and generational patterns of influence, and assess members' resources in developing and realizing the goals of family therapy. Barbarin's (1983) work proposes a model of coping among black families and elaborates classes of variables specific to black Americans that may affect the process of adaptation (i.e., appraisal, behavioral strategies, and access to coping resources and support). These and other recent efforts reflect an attempt to (*a*) acknowledge the cultural distinctiveness of black families, (*b*) make explicit the broader social context and its impact on the presentation of problems and the therapeutic relationship, and (*c*) propose specific therapy and intervention approaches that are appropriate for black clients and families. Finally, Boyd-Franklin's (1989) critique of various models of family therapy underscores the importance of identifying the historical, social, and political variables that have an impact on family process and outcome.

DEMOGRAPHIC TRENDS IN FAMILY STRUCTURE

In the past three decades, American families have experienced a number of substantial demographic changes. These demographic trends include declining rates of marriage, later ages at first marriage, higher divorce rates, an increase in female-headed households, a higher proportion of births to unmarried mothers, larger percentages of children living in female-headed families, and a higher percentage of children living in poverty (Jaynes and Williams, 1989; W. Wilson, 1987). Although these changes have been experienced by both blacks and whites, black families have disproportionately suffered their impact. This section of the review examines these demographic trends in black family structure. In particular, this section presents research investigating fertility patterns, well-being of black children, teenage pregnancy, adolescent mothers and fathers, single-parent families, demographic constraints on marriage among blacks, interracial marriage, and the black underclass.

Fertility

One of the major trends in fertility over the past few decades among both blacks and whites is the increase in the percentage of unmarried women who give birth (Farley and Allen, 1987; Garfinkel and McLanahan, 1986; Jaynes and Williams, 1989). In 1960, the proportion of out-of-wedlock births among blacks was 22%. By 1984, almost 6 of 10 black babies were born to unmarried mothers, whereas among whites, 1 birth in 8 occurred to an unmarried woman (Farley and Allen, 1987; Jaynes and Williams, 1989). This increase in the percentage of out-of-wedlock births among blacks was due to two demographic changes (Farley and Allen, 1987; Jaynes and Williams, 1989). First, the age at which black women marry has risen and the overall length of time they are married has shortened. Consequently, among black women the length of time in which a non-marital pregnancy can occur has increased, while the period of marital childbearing has shortened. Second, there has been a greater decline in the fertility rate of married black women than of unmarried black women. This difference in fertility rates results in an increase in the percentage of total births to unmarried black women. Therefore, it is erroneous to interpret the increase in the percentage of births to unmarried black women as a rise in their birth rate. In reality, the birth rates of unmarried black women actually declined during the seventies and early eighties (Farley and Allen, 1987, Table 4.1).

Children's Well-being

Three aspects of black children's well-being are addressed: living arrangements, foster care, and childhood poverty.

Living arrangements of children. The increasing number of female-headed families has important implications for the living arrangements of black children. In 1985, half (51%) of all black children (persons under age 18) lived with their mothers but not with their fathers (Jaynes and Williams, 1989). The incidence of single-father families among blacks is very low; only 2% of black children lived in these households in 1980 (Sweet and Bumpass, 1987). In addition, it has been projected (Bumpass, 1984) that 86% of all black children are likely to spend some time in single-parent households.

Foster care. In addition to the high proportion of children residing in female-headed household, black children are more likely than whites or Hispanics to reside with neither biological parent. Although the practice of informal adoption among black extended families absorbs many children, a disproportionate number of black children live in institutions, in group homes, and with foster families. Research on foster care is limited by a lack of high-quality national data and the failure of many states and communities to keep relatively current and reliable information. Available research, however, has noted several consistent findings (Jenkins and Diamond, 1985; Morisey, 1990). First, black children have a higher likelihood of being placed in foster care because of neglect (e.g., leaving children without adequate supervision, inadequate housing, nutrition). Second, it has been estimated that black children are three times more likely to be in foster care than white children. Last, black children remain in foster care for longer periods of time and, consequently, are more likely to undergo multiple placements. Because of the developmental risks associated with long-term residence in the foster care system, this is a high-risk group that deserves serious attention from both researchers and policymakers (see NBCDI, 1989, for a more detailed examination of black children in foster care).

Childhood poverty. In the last two decades, the rate of poverty among black children has increased dramatically, and in 1986, close to half of all black children lived in poverty (Zill and Rogers, 1988). The high incidence of poverty among black children is partially due to the lower earnings of black men relative to white men, higher rates of female-headed households among blacks, and a decline in the real value of government cash transfers directed at children. Within the larger group of individuals and families in poverty, there are those for whom poverty status may be of a temporary nature. Consequently, researchers delineate between those individuals who have temporary "spells" of poverty in contrast to persons and families who are persistently poor (Bane and Ellwood, 1986).

Research on the duration of poverty status suggests that while long-term poverty is a rare occurrence for whites, it is much more common among the black population (Ellwood, 1988). Duncan and Rodgers (1988) investigated the length of childhood poverty during a 15-year period, using data from the Panel Study of Income Dynamics. Fewer than one in seven black children lived comfortably above the poverty line during the entire 15-year period. Further, almost a quarter of black children were poor for 10 of those 15 years. Blacks accounted for almost 90% of the children who were poor during at least 10 out of 15 years. Length of poverty was longer for black children who lived in families in which the household head was disabled and for those who resided with a single parent. Living in poverty places a large proportion of black children in jeopardy for serious health problems, low educational achievement, and minimal labor market participation (Jaynes and Williams, 1989).

Zill and Rogers (1988), argue that two recent changes in black American families are beneficial for children's well-being: a reduction in the proportion of families that have large numbers of children and an increase in the educational level of parents. Although a black child is presently more likely to live in a single-parent family than a comparable child was in the '60s and '70s, the child's mother has a higher probability of having completed high school or attended college.

Teenage Pregnancy

Although adolescent pregnancy affects every

racial and income group, it has a disproportionate impact on black teenagers. Estimates for 1984 indicate that 41% of black females and 19% of white females became pregnant by the age of 18 (Furstenberg, Brooks-Gunn, and Chase-Lansdale, 1989). Two demographic patterns in the last 25 years help explain the rate of pregnancy and nonmarital births among black teenagers: relatively high rates of sexual activity among teenagers and a decreasing incidence of marriage among blacks generally and among younger blacks in particular.

With regard to sexual activity, data from the National Longitudinal Study of Youth (NLSY) reveal that young unmarried black females (ages 15 to 19) were more likely to have engaged in sexual intercourse than their white counterparts. In 1982, 53% of black females in this age group had engaged in sexual activity, as compared to 40% of white females (Hayes, 1987). It is important to note that although a higher percentage of young black females engage in sex, they have intercourse less frequently than their white counterparts (Zelnik, 1983). NLSY data also reveal large gender differences in the age of initiation of sexual activity among blacks. Among black males, 42.4% of those who were 15 and 85.6% of those who were 18 years of age indicated that they were sexually active. The corresponding percentages among black females were 9.7% and 59.4%, respectively (Hayes, 1987).

Because of the inconsistent use of contraceptives, a substantial number of sexually active black and white teenagers eventually become pregnant (Hayes, 1987). Black teenagers are less likely to use a contraceptive method than are white teens (Hayes, 1987; Moore, Simms, and Betsey, 1986; Zelnik and Shah, 1983), but these differences are substantially reduced when age of sexual initiation is controlled (Zelnik, Kantner, and Ford, 1981). Among teenagers who use some form of contraception, however, black females are more likely to use oral contraceptives and white females are more likely to use withdrawal (Moore et al., 1986).

A nonmarital pregnancy can result in one of several outcomes, including abortion, adoption, and childbearing outside of marriage. Black teenagers are less likely to terminate a pregnancy by abortion than are white teenagers (Farley and Allen, 1987; Hayes, 1987). Since black teenagers

had a higher incidence of unintended pregnancy, however, their abortion rate in 1981 was twice as high as the rate for white girls aged 15 to 19: 68.9 per 1,000 women compared with 35.8 per 1,000 (Hayes, 1987). With regard to adoption, available data indicate that despite the high levels of unintended pregnancy, 9 out of 10 black and white teenagers kept and raised their children (Bachrach, 1986; Hayes, 1987).

Black adolescents are more likely to give birth outside of marriage than white adolescents. In 1984, the rate of nonmarital childbearing among persons 15–19 years old was 87 per 1,000 unmarried black women compared to 19 per 1,000 white women. Between 1970 and 1984, however, the rate of nonmarital childbearing decreased by 10% among blacks, whereas among whites it increased by 74% (Farley and Allen, 1987; Hayes, 1987). Consistent with the fertility data presented earlier, the declining rates of marriage among blacks have contributed to the high rate of nonmarital childbearing among black adolescents. In 1960, almost a third of black women 18–19 years old were married, whereas in 1984 less than 3% were married. Consequently, by the mid-1980s, almost all children born to adolescent mothers were out of wedlock (Furstenberg et al., 1987). For a more thorough examination of adolescent pregnancy and sexual behavior, refer to the work of Furstenberg et al. (1987), Furstenberg et al. (1989), Hayes (1987), Hofferth and Hayes (1987), and Moore et al. (1986).

Adolescent Mothers

In the past decade researchers have investigated several consequences of adolescent pregnancy for the mother. In particular, research has examined issues such as family structure, family size, educational achievement, and labor force participation. Early marriage is strongly associated with early childbearing and there is a high incidence of divorce among persons who marry at young ages (Hayes, 1987; Sweet and Bumpass, 1987). Furstenberg and colleagues' (1987) 17-year follow-up of a sample of adolescent mothers (mostly black) found that among those who had married early, approximately two of three of their marriages had been dissolved. With regard to family size, the adolescent mothers in this study tended not to have a large number of children.

About a fifth never had a second child (20.8%), two-fifths had one additional birth (41.3%), and one-fourth had two more children (26.0%).

The interruption of school with a birth generally decreases the educational attainment of young girls. This decrease in educational attainment, however, is smaller for black adolescents than for their white counterparts. Furstenberg et al. (1987) found that many of the adolescent mothers in their sample resumed their education after the birth of the first child. Most of the educational attainment following the birth of a child took place 6 or more years later. The educational attainment of this group, however, was still significantly lower than that of comparably aged black women who postponed childbearing.

Early childbearing has important implications for eventual labor force participation and economic attainment. In comparison to mothers who have children later in life, early childbearers have a lower likelihood of finding stable employment and a greater tendency to go on welfare (Furstenberg et al., 1989). These differences are more notable at younger ages, but many early childbearers recover from these interruptions later in life (Furstenberg et al., 1989). For instance, the rate of welfare use among the respondents in the Furstenberg et al. (1987) sample decreased substantially as the women reached middle age. Racial variations in the labor force participation of black and white early childbearers indicate that black mothers accumulate more work experience than their white counterparts, and the difference in work experience between early and late childbearers is smaller among blacks (Hayes, 1987; Hofferth and Hayes, 1987).

Adolescent Fathers

Research on adolescent pregnancy and parenting demonstrates the relative scarcity of work examining the role of adolescent fathers (Hendricks and Montgomery, 1983). This absence of information hampers a comprehensive understanding of teenage pregnancy and parenting (Lerman, 1986; Marsiglio, 1989; Parke and Neville, 1987). Methodological critiques of this literature (Parke and Neville, 1987: 146) include issues of sampling (e.g., determining appropriate age ranges, use of volunteer samples, samples from clinic or service agency–based populations), method (e.g., reliance on self-report and proxy questionnaires vs.

other methods), and design (e.g., inclusion of appropriate comparison groups, use of longitudinal data). Reservations in the use of volunteer samples reflect the concern that such samples are biased toward adolescent males who are more accepting of parental responsibilities. This concern is particularly crucial if attitudes about early childbearing vary for distinct subgroups of the population (i.e., higher acceptance of early childbearing and out-of-wedlock births among black Americans) (e.g., Marsiglio, 1987).

The emergent literature on black adolescent fathers suggests a greater appreciation for the diversity of this population group in relation to the developmental aspects of adolescence (Parke and Neville, 1987) and their individual enactment of the fatherhood role. Black adolescent fathers have distinctly different patterns of fatherhood experiences (i.e., age at paternity, timing of fatherhood in relation to work and educational experiences, number of children, length of fatherhood experience, relationship with child's mother, marital experience). A study of attitudes among unwed black adolescent fathers (Hendricks and Montgomery, 1983) suggests that parenthood was desirable, and in retrospect, fathers indicated being prepared for that role. In an earlier investigation (Hendricks, Howard, and Caesar, 1981), black adolescent fathers were less sanguine and reported problems in interpersonal relationships and in social and economic areas (i.e., educational and occupational).

Marsiglio's (1987) examination of initial living arrangements, marital experiences, and educational outcomes for adolescent fathers found that young black men were more likely than Hispanics or whites to have had a nonmarital first birth and were least likely to live with that child. However, in comparison to other adolescent fathers, blacks were more likely to complete high school. Adolescent fathers have a higher probability of living apart from their partner and/or child than do nonadolescent fathers (Danziger and Nichols-Casebolt, 1988), and this is particularly the case among black adolescent fathers (Lerman, 1986; Marsiglio, 1987). However, a recent report among a sample of teenage-mother families (Danziger and Radin, 1990) suggests that father's absence from the home does not necessarily reflect noninvolvement in parenting; minority fathers were more likely to be involved than were white fathers. Separate analyses for minority teen-mother families (predominately black) indicated that fathers were more likely to be involved if they were younger (roughly 6 out of 10 minority fathers were under 21 years of age), if they had been employed in the last year, and if their child was younger.

Female-Headed Households

As compared to whites, black families are considerably less likely to be headed by a married couple and more likely to be headed by single females. In 1980, one in four black households was headed by a single female (27.2%). In the past 20 years there has been a significant increase in the proportion of female-headed households among both blacks and whites. Among blacks the increase in female-headed households is due primarily to a decreasing propensity to marry among young black men and women. This declining likelihood of marriage is strongly linked to the high levels of unemployment and low earnings of young black men (Wilson and Neckerman, 1986).

Black female-headed families are one of the most impoverished groups in America. Among black Americans, 53% of female-headed families were in poverty, as compared to 15% of male-headed families (Farley and Allen, 1987). Similarly, in 1985, black female-headed families were twice as likely to have incomes at the poverty level than were white female-headed families (Jaynes and Williams, 1989). Jaynes and Williams (1989: 525) and McLanahan and Booth (1989) have identified several mechanisms that explain the disproportionate degree of poverty of black female-headed families. First, many black families rely on the income of two employed adults to remain out of poverty. Simply because of its reliance on a sole wage earner, a single-parent family has a higher likelihood of being poor. Second, because black women have lower incomes than black men (Farley and Allen, 1987), among single-parent families, those with a female head are more likely to be poor than those with male head. Third, young black women who form single-parent households generally come from poor households and often lack the skills to generate high earnings. Fourth, because of the scarcity of inexpensive child care and lack of health insurance associated with lower-status occupations, many black single mothers of young children cannot earn enough from employment to

justify working outside the home. Fifth, Aid to Families with Dependent Children (AFDC, or welfare) and food stamps accounted for 28% of the income for black female-headed households (Garfinkle and McLanahan, 1986, Table 2); AFDC benefits are recognized to be woefully inadequate. Sixth, child support and alimony payments to single mothers are meager, accounting for only 3.5% of the income of black single mothers (McLanahan and Booth, 1989). Finally, the birth of a child may disrupt the educational or job experiences of the mother and reduce future earning potential.

Several studies have suggested that there are important intergenerational consequences with regard to the subsequent socioeconomic and marital status of children who live with mother-only families as compared with two-parent families. These studies indicate that among black children, those who live with their mothers only generally do less well on several social indicators than those who live with two parents. There is some evidence to suggest that black children who reside with one parent are less likely to be in school at the age of 17 and less likely to graduate from high school (McLanahan, 1985). Daughters of black single mothers were found to be at a higher risk of establishing a female-headed household at the age of 16 than were daughters of two-parent black households (McLanahan, 1988). This risk was increased if the marital disruption of the parents occurred when the child was older (15–16) as opposed to younger (12 or less). Controlling for income reduced but did not eliminate the risk of a daughter establishing a single-parent household (McLanahan, 1988). In another analysis (McLanahan and Bumpass, 1988), black daughters who spent part of their childhood in a single-parent family because of marital disruption (i.e., divorce, separation) or because the parent never married were 36% more likely to have a teenage birth, 52% more likely to have a premarital birth, and 32% more likely to have a marital disruption. The effects of residing in a single-parent family on these various outcomes were much more pronounced among whites than blacks. In addition, Hogan and Kitagawa (1985) found that black adolescent girls from single-parent families were more likely to be sexually active and to have premarital births than adolescents from two-parent households. It is important to note that this collection of findings is not definitive (Jaynes and Williams, 1989), and it remains to be seen whether some other variables are more important than family structure in determining the future socioeconomic and marital status of black children.

Garfinkle and McLanahan (1986) argue that the negative intergenerational consequences of residing in single-parent families may be attributed to economic deprivation, maternal employment, and the absence of a residential father. Since black female-headed families have such a high incidence of poverty, it is not surprising that their offspring fare worse in adulthood than children from two-parent families. It is also important to note that extended-family involvement may help mitigate some of the differences between being raised in single versus two-parent households.

Constraints on Marriage

Rapidly changing marriage patterns among African Americans has spawned a renewed focus on the determinants of marriage behavior. The long-established pre-1950 pattern of blacks marrying earlier than whites has been replaced by an increasingly divergent pattern of blacks marrying later than whites (Cherlin, 1981). Between 1975 and 1985, the proportion of black women who had ever married declined sharply from nearly 80% to 65% (compared to an 89% to 82% drop among whites) (Norton and Moorman, 1987). Also, the percentage of black women who were divorced increased from 22% to 31% (compared to 18% to 27% among whites) (Norton and Moorman, 1987).

The decline in expectation of marriage for black women has been particularly striking. When Rodgers and Thornton (1985) used annual synthetic cohorts to estimate proportions of groups expected to marry by age 44, they found that between 1970 and 1979, the proportions had declined to approximately 90% for white men and women, as well as black men. However, the proportion of black women expected to marry declined from the already low figure of 86% to 76%, meaning that by 1980, one-quarter of the existing population of black women were not expected to have married by their 44th birthday. Projecting proportions of later cohorts likely to every marry (by projecting cumulative marriage probabilities), Rodgers and Thornton (1985)

estimated that close to 90% of white males and females and 86% of black males born in 1954 will have married by their 45th birthday; but only 70% of black females born in 1954 are expected to marry. In contrast, 94% of black women born in the 1930s eventually married.

Among the consequences of these trends are an increase in the number of female-headed households, an increased burden of childrearing for women, and an increase in the percentage of women and children living in households with incomes below the poverty level. Concerns about the societal consequences of having large numbers of young males unattached to the traditional socializing structures have also been raised (Rossi, 1984).

Theories of causation. Significant changes in the distribution between the sexes have been posited as a possible factor in these shifts in marital patterns in the general population. Known as "marriage squeeze" among demographers, it is hypothesized that a decrease in the availability of marriage partners for female members of the "baby boom" has led to delays in marriage and lower marriage rates, particularly for women (Glick, 1981; Rodgers and Thornton, 1985; Schoen, 1983). This shortage of partners is the result of the ever-increasing cohort sizes that characterized the post–World War II baby-boom years, coupled with the tendency of women to marry men who are two to three years older. Baby-boom women were therefore seeking husbands from older and numerically smaller cohorts. Although the marriage squeeze phenomenon affected blacks as well as whites, it also served to exacerbate the impact of the long-standing black male shortage that is due primarily to differential mortality rates. The black sex ratio has been steadily decreasing since the 1920s, and some have suggested that this prolonged shortage of men has led to a broadening of mate selection standards among black women. Spanier and Glick (1980) found that black women compared to white women were more likely to marry men who were previously married, less educated, and older.

Guttentag and Secord (1983) have argued that imbalanced sex ratios (i.e., the number of men per 100 women) have had major societal consequences. Male shortages, in particular, have been accompanied by higher rates of singlehood, divorce, out-of-wedlock births, adultery, and transient relationships; less commitment among men to relationships; lower societal value on marriage and the family; and a rise in feminism. Guttentag and Secord (1983) have asserted that the extended male shortage in the black American population is a major contributor to marital decline among blacks and an increasing out-of-wedlock birth rate. There is some empirical support for these theories. Tucker's (1987) analysis of sex ratios for five ethnic groups (including blacks) found fairly substantial associations between sex ratio and percentage divorced and separated, percentage of single women aged 25–34 (peak marriage ages), and percentage of households with female heads and no husbands. Using international data, South (1986) found female shortage to be associated with lower female marriage and fertility rates, higher age at marriage among women, and higher female literacy, divorce, and crime involvement (South and Messner, 1987). U.S. sex ratio studies have typically relied on census data, which are biased by an undercount of black men. Even when corrected for coverage errors, the black ratio remains about five points below that of whites, and therefore, in the view of Guttentag and Secord (1983), still likely to have significant effects on social structure. Yet, Tucker and Mitchell-Kernan (in press) argue that sex ratio is only one component of the constraints on mate availability that have resulted in declining marriage among blacks. That is, numerical availability is further qualified by an individual's *potential* for relationship formation, which is shaped by willingness or ability to enter into relationships with the opposite sex (e.g., heterosexual, noninstitutionalization), attractiveness (how one measures up on the basis of specific sociocultural preferences—e.g., economic status, physical features); and eligibility (whether one fits the socioculturally prescribed definitions of eligibility—e.g., same race). Although there is little research that explores how these three factors might differentially affect black marriage behavior, sociologists and economists have been particularly concerned about the relationship between the economic condition of black males and black family structure. William Wilson (Wilson, 1987; Wilson and Neckerman, 1986) and Darity and Myers (1986–87) have argued that the increasing economic marginality of black males makes them less attractive as potential husbands, since they are constrained in the ability to perform the

provider role in marriage. Views of the economic incentive associated with marriage may undergo change when the societal inclination for women to marry men of higher (or at least equal) socioeconomic status is coupled with the substantial joblessness, underemployment, and decreasing educational attainment that are disproportionately characteristic of major segments of the black male population. These factors reduce the likelihood that marriage will occur, as well as undermine the stability of existing partnerships. There is some support for these economic arguments. Testa, Astone, Krogh, and Neckerman (1989) found that employed fathers in inner-city Chicago were twice as likely as nonemployed fathers to marry the mother of their first child. Also, Tucker and Taylor (1989) found that, among men, personal income was positively associated with the probability of marriage but unrelated to the probability of being involved in a nonmarital romantic relationship.

Interracial Marriage

Overall, interracial marriage involving black Americans remains relatively rare. In 1988, only 4.6% of black males' marriages and 2.1% of black females' marriages included partners of other races. Yet these figures can overshadow significant geographic differences in outmarriage behavior (Tucker and Mitchell-Kernan, 1990). According to the 1980 Census, intermarriage rates among blacks ranged from a low of .6% among black females in the South to 12.3% among black males in the West (U.S. Bureau of the Census, 1985). Furthermore, as Tucker and Mitchell-Kernan (1990) point out, there is evidence of a rather dramatic rise in outmarriage in Western states. One out of every six black men in the West who married for the first time between 1970 and 1980 (i.e., more recent marriages) married women of another race.

Overall, as well as by region, intermarriage for black females remains about one-quarter the male level. Lieberson and Waters (1988) used 1980 Census data to calculate odds ratios representing the tendency to marry in one's ethnic group versus marrying out of one's ethnic group (i.e., percentage in/percentage out) and have determined that black women have the highest overall odds of any ethnic group in the United States of marrying another black when they marry for the first time:

32,998 (as compared to 3,468 for Puerto Rican women; 743 for Mexican women; and 16 for American Indian women). However, the odds of black women under 25 years of age marrying a black man drops to 8,602 (in contrast to a ratio of 115,660 for black women aged 55 to 64 years). Therefore, although blacks still remain relatively unlikely to marry persons of other races, the likelihood of interracial marriage among younger blacks had increased substantially by 1980. Intercensal estimates from the Current Population Surveys indicate that the level of interracial marriage among blacks increased 1.1 percentage points for males as well as females between 1981 and 1988. It seems likely that interracial marriage rates will continue to rise for black Americans.

Tucker and Mitchell-Kernan (1990) examined the structural factors that are associated with black interracial marriage, using 1980 census data for Los Angeles County (where black interracial marriage rates are relatively high). They found that the predictors of interracial marriage were virtually identical for black men and black women: interracially married blacks compared to those who married within the race tended to be younger, were more likely to have been married previously, and had greater spousal age differences (both younger and older). Additionally, interracial marriage seemed to be associated with living away from your place of birth, coupled with having been raised in a more racially tolerant region of the country. These findings suggested that social control (from the community of origin) still strongly supports black marriage within the race. Schoen and Wooldredge (1989), examining marriage choices in North Carolina and Virginia, found a greater likelihood of intermarriage among more highly educated black men.

The rate of interracial marriage has implications for mate availability, particularly in the West, where outmarriage among black men is relatively high and quite different from the black female outmarriage rate. Moreover, marriage squeeze in the general population may account for an increased tendency for white women to consider black men as mates (Guttentag and Secord, 1983). Further declines in the marital expectations for black women will occur should black men define their pool of eligible mates as including nonblacks, while black women limit their mate choices to those of the same race.

Black Underclass

During the past decade, a significant body of research has addressed the development of a black underclass. Much of this work, as it relates to family issues, investigates topics that have been previously discussed in this review (e.g., the increase in female-headed households, poverty and family structure). However, a remaining issue germane to our review of research on black families is the increasing economic marginality of black men. Recent research efforts have examined the growing economic marginality of black men in relation to the underclass. Black men have a higher likelihood than white males of being unemployed and working part-time (Farley and Allen, 1987; Jaynes and Williams, 1989). Black men are disproportionately employed in low-wage jobs, unprotected by seniority, and work in industries that are particularly sensitive to business downturns (Jaynes and Williams, 1989).

As noted previously in this review, the declining economic status of black men has important ramifications for family structure. The precarious economic situation of black men is a major predictor of the decreasing rates of black marriage (W. Wilson, 1987; Wilson and Neckerman, 1986). Additionally, the decreasing rate of marriage among blacks is an important contributing factor in the substantial increases in both nonmarital births and female-headed households (Farley and Allen, 1987). Collectively, these findings reinforce the argument that black family structure and the economic situations of black men and women are inextricably linked (see Danziger and Weinberg, 1986; Ellwood, 1988; Glasgow, 1981; and W. Wilson, 1987, 1989, for detailed discussions of underclass issues).

CONCLUSION

Although the scope of this review makes it difficult to propose specific recommendations for research, it is useful to summarize four general trends in research on black families and to suggest how they might influence future research directions. First, there was phenomenal growth in this area, reflected in both the quantity and quality of efforts to examine the nature of black family life, as well as the manner in which black families were regarded in the social scientific community. The increase in volume of research encouraged replication, debate, synthesis, and the generation of new efforts. Further, black family researchers acknowledged the value orientations that framed their work, as well as the political ramifications of research (Dilworth-Anderson, Johnson, and Barton, in press; Fine, Schwebel, and James-Myers, 1987).

Second, investigations of black families during this decade demonstrated greater conceptual, methodological, and analytic sophistication. Conceptually, research displayed a greater appreciation for the relationships between macro-level and micro-level influences in relation to black family phenomena (e.g., Staples, 1985). With regard to sample selection, design, and analytic frameworks, important improvements were made, including the availability of nationally representative samples of black respondents, the development of adequate samples of blacks within comparative studies, the use of nonclinical groups of respondents, greater efforts to recruit and utilize groups that are difficult to locate, and the development of appropriate comparative frameworks (i.e., black to white and within-black contrasts).

Third, as a result of the first two trends, a more balanced depiction of black family life emerged. Research increasingly reflected an appreciation for variability in the status of black families overall, as well as within particular social strata. As a result, a more precise understanding emerged concerning the operation of relevant causative factors for particular family phenomena and the specific consequences for individual families. Finally, related to the recognition of diversity in black family status and form, the past decade saw the establishment of black families within the legitimate body of family research. It can be argued that with few exceptions, the raison d'etre of research on black families was not to explore basic questions of family functioning, but to explain black families in comparison to white, middle-class families.

The racial comparative rationale and framework that guided this research was increasingly called into question by numerous researchers (many of whom identified this problem prior to the 1980s). Central among their criticisms is that the exercise of simple racial comparisons in which white behaviors are designated as the standard or baseline invariably indicates the presence of deficiencies in blacks. Further, black behaviors have

no inherent significance other than the extent to which they differ from that of whites. Rather than advancing the legitimate task of generating knowledge concerning commonalities across racial groups, the simple and routine application of comparative frameworks ultimately denies the significance of differences for informing the scientific enterprise and ignores the mechanisms through which observed disparities are manifested. A comprehensive understanding of the impact of race on any phenomena is fundamentally incompatible with such an orientation and framework for research.

At this point, we consider some implications of these general trends for the current state of research on black families. First, continuing research on black families must consider the impact and interrelationships among factors that operate at varying levels (i.e., micro- versus macro-level) and potentially manifest themselves through diverse behaviors and phenomena. For example, additional work is needed to examine the linkages between changes in family structure (e.g., nonmarital adolescent births) and alterations in family relationships and functioning (e.g., changes in the grandparent role) or household structure (e.g., multigeneration household arrangements). Second, it is clear that research on black families must occur within expanded disciplinary frameworks. The use of an interdisciplinary approach is an important corrective to viewing black family phenomena in isolation and separate from other perspectives. For example, in research on black adolescence, it may be productive to team a professional in the area of child welfare and social policy with a researcher whose areas of expertise include human development. The dual concentration on issue of both applied and basic research will bring a clearer and more comprehensive focus to the examination of black adolescence. This expanded perspective will provide important information about black adolescence as a developmental stage (i.e., by identifying commonalities across youth), the varied ways that being young and black relate to one's position within the social structure (i.e., by distinguishing experiences unique to black youth), and the relationship between social location and developmental phenomena.

Finally, the tendency to view black families as a collection of the problems and challenges they face has diverted attention from important and basic issues of family function, structure, and relationships and restricted the research focus to that of "problem black families." This caution is particularly relevant for current considerations of the black underclass, whose position and status in society are especially urgent and compelling. Among both lay and scientific communities, there exists a real concern for the serious difficulties and problems that face significant numbers of black families. Certainly, to deny the existence of these problems or to underestimate their impact would be both naive and irresponsible. Likewise, to permit their existence to dominate or restrict the research agenda and/or compromise the research process in relation to black families would be equally detrimental. As students of African American families we would do well to remember that our attempts to understand and address phemonena (including those identified as social problems) that are of relevance to black families requires the application of our best scientific efforts to specify their character and identify causes and consequences and the exercise of the scientific method in the most precise and scrupulous manner possible.

NOTE

The authors acknowledge the assistance of Cheryl Burns and Rukmalie Jayakody for bibliographic search and acquisition. They are deeply indebted to Harold W. Neighbors, Sandra K. Danziger, James S. Jackson, and Michael C. Thornton for comments on earlier drafts of the manuscript. This work was supported in part by FIRST Awards to the first and second authors from the National Institute of Aging (Nos. R29 AG 06856 and R29 AG 07179), and a Research Scientist Development Award to the third author from the National Institute on Mental Health (No. K01 MH00681). Address correspondence to Robert J. Taylor, School of Social Work, University of Michigan, Ann Arbor, MI 48109.

REFERENCES

Allen, Walter R. 1981. "Moms, dads, and boys: Race and sex differences in the socialization of male children." Pp. 99–114 in Lawrence E. Gary (ed.), Black Men. Beverly Hills, CA: Sage.

Anderson, Elijah. 1989. "Sex codes and family life among poor inner-city youths." Annals of the American Academy of Political and Social Science 501: 59–78.

Angel, Ronald, and Marta Tienda. 1982. "Determinants of extended household structure: Cultural pattern or economic model?" American Journal of Sociology 87: 1360–1383.

Antonucci, Toni, and James Jackson. 1989. "Successful aging and life course reciprocity." Pp. 83–95 in A. M. Warnes (ed.), Human Aging. London: Hoder and Stoughton.

Bachrach, Christine A. 1986. "Adoption plans, adopted children, and adoptive mothers." Journal of Marriage and the Family 48: 243–253.

Ball, Richard E., and Lynn Robbins. 1986a. "Black husbands' satisfaction with their family life." Journal of Marriage and the Family 48: 849–855.

Ball, Richard E., and Lynn Robbins. 1986b. "Marital status and life satisfaction among black Americans." Journal of Marriage and the Family 48: 389–394.

Bane, Mary Jo, and David T. Ellwood. 1986. "Slipping into and out of poverty: The dynamics of spells." Journal of Human Resources 21: 1–23.

Barbarin, Oscar A. 1983. "Coping with ecological transition by black families: A psychological model." Journal of Community Psychology 11: 308–322.

Beck, Ruby W., and Scott H. Beck. 1989. "The incidence of extended households among middle-aged black and white women: Estimates from a 5-year panel study." Journal of Family Issues 10: 147–168.

Beckett, Joyce O., and Audrey D. Smith. 1981. "Work and family roles: Egalitarian marriage in black and white families." Social Service Review 55: 314–326.

Bowman, Philip. 1985. "Black fathers and the provider role: Role strain, informal coping resources and life happiness." Pp. 9–19 in A. W. Boykin (ed.), Empirical Research in Black Psychology. Rockville, MD: NIMH.

Bowman, Philip, and Cleopatra Howard. 1985. "Race-related socialization, motivation, and academic achievement: A study of black youth in three-generation families." Journal of the American Academy of Child Psychiatry 24: 134–141.

Boyd-Franklin, Nancy. 1989. Black Families in Therapy: A Multisystem Approach. New York: Guilford.

Broman, Clifford L. 1988a. "Household work and family life satisfaction of blacks." Journal of Marriage and the Family 50: 743–748.

Broman, Clifford L. 1988b. "Satisfaction among blacks: The significance of marriage and parenthood." Journal of Marriage and the Family 50: 45–51.

Brooks-Gunn, Jeanne, and Frank F. Furstenberg. 1986. "The children of adolescent mothers: Physical, academic, and psychological outcomes." Developmental Review 6: 224–251.

Brown, Diane R., and Lawrence E. Gary. 1985. "Social support network differentials among married and non-married black females." Psychology of Women Quarterly 9: 229–241.

Brown, Diane R., and Lawrence E. Gary. 1987. "Stressful life events, social support networks, and physical and mental health of urban black adults." Journal of Human Stress 13: 165–174.

Brown, Diane R., and Lawrence E. Gary. 1988. "Unemployment and psychological distress among black American women." Sociological Focus 21: 209–220.

Bumpass, Larry L. 1984. "Children and marital disruption: A replication and update." Demography 21: 71–81.

Burton, Linda M., and Vern L. Bengtson. 1985. "Black grandmothers: Issues of timing and continuity of roles." Pp. 61–77 in Vern L. Bengtson and Joan F. Robertson (eds.), Grandparenthood. Beverly Hills, CA: Sage.

Burton, Linda M., and Peggye Dilworth-Anderson. In press. "The intergenerational family roles of aged black Americans." Marriage and Family Review.

Cazenave, Noel A. 1979. "Middle-income black fathers: An analysis of the provider role." Family Coordinator 28: 583–593.

Cazenave, Noel A. 1984. "Race, socioeconomic status, and age: The social context of American masculinity." Sex Roles 11: 639–656.

Chatters, Linda M. 1988. "Subjective well-being evaluations among older black Americans." Psychology and Aging 3: 184–190.

Chatters, Linda M., and James S. Jackson. 1989. "Quality of life and subjective well-being among black adults." Pp. 191–214 in R. L. Jones (eds.), Adult development and aging. Berkeley, CA: Cobb and Henry Publications.

Chatters, Linda M., Robert J. Taylor, and James S. Jackson. 1985. "Size and composition of the informal helper network of elderly blacks." Journal of Gerontology 40: 605–614.

Chatters, Linda M., Robert J. Taylor, and James S. Jackson. 1986. "Aged blacks' choices for an informal helper network." Journal of Gerontology 41: 94–100.

Chatters, Linda M., Robert J. Taylor, and Harold W. Neighbors. 1989. "Size of the informal helper network mobilized in response to serious personal problems." Journal of Marriage and the Family 51: 667–676.

Cherlin, Andrew J. 1981. Marriage, Divorce, Remarriage. Cambridge, MA: Harvard University Press.

Cherlin, Andrew J., and Frank F. Furstenberg, Jr. 1986. The New American Grandparent: A Place in the Family, a Life Apart. New York: Basic Books.

Coleman, Lerita M., Tony C. Antonucci, Pamela K. Adelman, and Susan E. Crohan. 1987. "Social roles in the lives of middle-aged and older black women." Journal of Marriage and the Family 49: 761–771.

Danziger, Sandra K., and Ann Nichols-Casebolt. 1988. "Teen parents and child support: Eligibility, participation, and payment." Journal of Social Service Research 11: 1–20.

Danziger, Sandra K., and Norma Radin. 1990. "Absent does not equal uninvolved: Predictors of fathering in teen mother families." Journal of Marriage and the Family 52: 636–642.

Danziger, Sheldon H., and Daniel H. Weinberg (eds.). 1986. Fighting Poverty: What Works and What Doesn't. Cambridge, MA: Harvard University Press.

Darity, William, and Samuel L. Myers. 1986–87. "Public policy trends and the fate of the black family." Humboldt Journal of Social Relations 14: 134–164.

Dilworth-Anderson, Peggye, Leanor Boulin Johnson, and Linda M. Burton. In press. "Reframing theories for understanding race, ethnicity, and families." In Pauline Boss, William Doherty, Ralph La Ross, Walter Schumm, and Suzanne Steinmetz (eds.), Sourcebook of Family Theories and Methods: A Contextual Approach. New York: Plenum Press.

Dressler, William W. 1985. "Extended family relationships, social support, and mental health in a Southern black community." Journal of Health and Social Behavior 26: 39–48.

Dressler, William, Susan Haworth Hoeppner, and Barbara J. Pitts. 1985. "Household structure in a Southern black community." American Anthropologist 87: 853–862.

Duncan, Greg J., and Willard L. Rodgers. 1988. "Longitudinal aspects of childhood poverty." Journal of Marriage and the Family 50: 1007–1021.

Ellison, Christopher G. 1990. "Family ties, friendships, and subjective well-being among black Americans." Journal of Marriage and the Family 52: 298–310.

Ellwood, David T. 1988. Poor Support. New York: Basic Books.

Ericksen, Julia A., William L. Yancey, and Eugene P. Ericksen. 1979. "The division of family roles." Journal of Marriage and the Family 41: 301–313.

Farley, Reynolds, and Walter R. Allen. 1987. The Color Line and the Quality of Life in America. New York: Russell Sage Foundation.

Fine, Mark, Andrew I. Schwebel, and Linda James-Myers. 1987. "Family stability in black families: Values underlying three different perspectives." Journal of Comparative Family Studies 18: 1–23.

Furstenberg, Frank F., Jr., Jeanne Brooks-Gunn, and Lindsay Chase-Lansdale. 1989. "Teenaged pregnancy and childbearing." American Psychologist 44: 313–320.

Furstenberg, Frank F., J. Brooks-Gunn, and S. Philip Morgan. 1987. Adolescent Mothers in Later Life. New York: Cambridge University Press.

Garfinkel, Irwin, and Sara S. McLanahan. 1986. Single Mothers and Their Children: A New American Dilemma. Washington, DC: Urban Institute Press.

Gibson, Rose C., and James S. Jackson. 1987. "The health, physical functioning, and informal supports of the black elderly." Milbank Quarterly 65: 421–454.

Glasgow, Douglas. 1981. The Black Underclass. New York: Vintage Books.

Glick, Paul C. 1981. "A demographic picture of black families." Pp. 106–126 in Harriette P. MacAdoo (ed.), Black Families. Beverly Hills, CA: Sage.

Guttentag, Marcia, and Paul F. Secord. 1983. Too Many Women: The Sex Ratio Question. Beverly Hills, CA: Sage.

Harrison, Algea. 1985. "The black family's socializing environment." Pp. 174–193 in Harriette P. McAdoo and John L. McAdoo (eds.), Black Children. Beverly Hills, CA: Sage.

Hayes, C. D. (ed.). 1987. Risking the Future: Adolescent Sexuality, Pregnancy, and Childbearing (Vol. 1). Washington, DC: National Academy Press.

Hendricks, Leo E., Cleopatra Howard, and Patricia Ceasar. 1981. "Help-seeking behavior among select populations of unmarried adolescent fathers: Implications for human service agencies." American Journal of Public Health 71: 733–735.

Hendricks, Leo E., and Teresa Montgomery. 1983. "A limited population of unmarried adolescent fathers: A preliminary report of their views on fatherhood and the relationship with the mothers of their children." Adolescence 18: 201–210.

Hill, Robert B., Andrew Billingsley, Eleanor Ingram, Michelene R. Malson, Roger H. Rubin, Carol B. Stack, James B. Stewart, and James E. Teele. 1989. Research on African-American Families: A Holistic Perspective. Boston: William Monroe Trotter Institute.

Hofferth, Sandra L. 1984. "Kin networks, race, and family structure." Journal of Marriage and the Family 46: 791–806.

Hofferth, Sandra L., and C. D. Hayes (eds.). 1987. Risking the Future: Adolescent Sexuality, Pregnancy, and Childbearing (Vol. 2). Working Papers and Statistical Reports. Washington, DC: National Academy Press.

Hogan, Dennis P., Ling-Xin Hao, and William L. Parish. 1990. "Race, kin networks, and assistance to mother-headed families." Social Forces 68: 797–812.

Hogan, Dennis P., and Evelyn M. Kitagawa. 1985. "The impact of social status, family structure, and neighborhood on the fertility of black adolescents." American Journal of Sociology 90: 825–855.

Huber, Joan, and Glenna Spitze. 1981. "Wives' employment, household behaviors, and sex-role attitudes." Social Forces 60: 150–169.

Hughes, Michael, and David H. Demo. 1989. "Self-perceptions of black Americans: Self-esteem and personal efficacy." American Journal of Sociology 95: 132–159.

Jackson, Jacqueline, and Linda Berg-Cross. 1988. "Extending the extended family: The mother-in-law and daughter-in-law relationship of black women." Family Relations 37: 293–297.

Jackson, James S., Linda M. Chatters, and Harold Neighbors. 1986. "The subjective life quality of black Americans." Pp. 193–213 in F. M. Andrews (ed.), Research on the Quality of Life. Ann Arbor: Institute for Social Research, University of Michigan.

Jackson, James, Wayne McCullough, and Gerald Gurin. 1988. "Family, socialization environment, and identity development in black Americans." Pp. 242–256 in H. McAdoo (ed.), Black Families (2nd ed.). Beverly Hills, CA: Sage.

Jaynes, Gerald David, and Robin M. Williams, Jr. (eds.). 1989. A Common Destiny: Blacks and American Society. Washington, DC: National Academy Press.

Jenkins, Shirley, and Beverly Diamond. 1985. "Ethnicity and foster care: Census data as predictors of

placement variables." American Journal of Orthopsychiatry 55: 267–276.

Jones, Reginald L. (ed.). 1989. Black Adolescents. Berkeley, CA: Cobb and Henry Publishers.

Lerman, Robert I. 1986. "Who are the young absent fathers?" Youth and Society 18: 3–27.

Lewis, Edith A. 1988. "Role strengths and strains of African-American mothers." Journal of Primary Prevention 9: 77–91.

Lewis, Edith A. 1989. "Role strain in black women: The efficacy of support networks." Journal of Black Studies 20: 155–169.

Lieberson, Stanley, and Mary C. Waters. 1988. From Many Strands: Ethnic and Racial Groups in Contemporary America. New York: Russell Sage Foundation.

Logan, Sadye M. L., Edith M. Freeman, and Ruth G. McRoy. 1990. Social Work Practice with Black Families. White Plains, NY: Longman.

Malson, Michelene. 1983. "The social-support systems of black families." Marriage and Family Review 5: 37–57.

Marsiglio, William. 1987. "Adolescent fathers in the United States: Their initial living arrangements, marital experience, and educational outcomes." Family Planning Perspectives 19: 240–251.

Marsiglio, William. 1989. "Adolescent males' pregnancy resolution preferences and family formation intentions: Does family background make a difference for blacks and whites?" Journal of Adolesent Research 4: 214–237.

McAdoo, Harriette. 1980. "Black mothers and the extended family support networks." Pp. 125–144 in L. F. Rodgers-Rose (ed.), The Black Woman. Beverly Hills, CA: Sage.

McAdoo, John L. 1981. "Black father and child interactions." Pp. 115–130 in Lawrence E. Gary (ed.), Black Men. Beverly Hills, CA: Sage.

McLanahan, Sara S. 1985. "Family structure and the reproduction of poverty." American Journal of Sociology 90: 873–901.

McLanahan, Sara S. 1988. "Family structure and dependency: Early transitions to female household headship." Demography 25: 1–16.

McLanahan, Sara, and Julia Adams. 1987. "Parenthood and psychological well-being." Annual Review of Sociology 13: 237–257.

McLanahan, Sara S., and Karen Booth. 1989. "Mother-only families: Problems, prospects, and politics." Journal of Marriage and the Family 51: 557–580.

McLanahan, Sara S., and Larry Bumpass. 1988. "Intergenerational consequences of family disruption." American Journal of Sociology 94: 130–152.

Moore, Kristin A., Margaret C. Simms, and Charles L. Betsey. 1986. Choice and Circumstance: Racial Differences in Adolescent Sexuality and Fertility. New Brunswick, NJ: Transaction Books.

Morisey, Patricia G. 1990. "Black children in foster care." Pp. 133–147 in Sadye M. L. Logan, Edith M. Freeman, and Ruth G. McRoy (eds.), Social Work Practice with Black Families. New York: Longman.

National Black Child Development Institute. 1989. Who Will Care When Parents Can't? A Study of

Black Children in Foster Care. Washington, DC: National Black Child Development Institute.

Neighbors, Harold W. 1986. "Socioeconomic status and psychologic distress in adult blacks." American Journal of Epidemiology 124: 779–793.

Neighbors, Harold W., and James S. Jackson. 1984. "The use of informal and formal help: Four patterns of illness behavior in the black community." American Journal of Community Psychology 12: 629–644.

Neighbors, Harold W., and Thomas A. LeVeist. 1989. "Socioeconomic status and psychological distress: The impact of financial aid on economic problem severity." Journal of Primary Prevention 10: 149–165.

Norton, Arthur J., and Jeanne E. Moorman. 1987. "Current trends in marriage and divorce among American women." Journal of Marriage and the Family 49: 3–14.

Oliver, Melvin L. 1988. "The urban black community as network: Towards a social network perspective." Sociological Quarterly 29: 623–645.

Parke, Ross D., and Brian Neville. 1987. "Teenage fatherhood." In Sandra L. Hofferth and C. D. Hayes (eds.), Risking the Future: Adolescent Sexuality, Pregnancy, and Childbearing (Vol. 2). Washington, DC: National Academy Press.

Peters, Marie. 1985. "Racial socialization of young black children." Pp. 159–173 in H. McAdoo and J. McAdoo (eds.), Black Children. Beverly Hills, CA: Sage.

Peters, Marie, and G. Massey. 1983. "Chronic vs. mundane stress in family stress theories: The case of black families in white America." Marriage and Family Review 6: 193–218.

Reskin, Barbara F., and Shelly Coverman. 1985. "Sex and race in the detriments of psychophysical distress: A reappraisal of the sex role hypothesis." Social Forces 63: 1038–1059.

Robinson, Jeanne B. 1989. "Clinical treatment of black families: Issues and strategies." Social Work 34: 323–329.

Rodgers, William L., and Arland Thornton. 1985. "Changing patterns of first marriage in the United States." Demography 22: 265–279.

Ross, Catherine E. 1987. "The division of labor at home." Social Forces 65: 816–833.

Rossi, Alice S. 1984. "Gender and parenthood." "American Sociological Review 49: 1–10.

Schoen, Robert. 1983. "Measuring the tightness of the marriage squeeze." Demography 20: 61–78.

Schoen, Robert, and James R. Kluegel. 1988. "The widening gap in black and white marriage rates: The impact of population composition and differential marriage propensities." American Sociological Review 53: 895–907.

Schoen, Robert, and John Wooldredge. 1989. "Marriage choices in North Carolina and Virginia, 1969–71 and 1979–81." Journal of Marriage and the Family 51: 465–481.

South, Scott J. 1986. "Sex ratios, economic power, and women's roles: A theoretical extension and empirical test." Journal of Marriage and the Family 50: 19–31.

South, Scott J., and S. F. Messner. 1987. "The sex ratio and women's involvement in crime: A cross-national analysis." Sociological Quarterly 28: 171–188.

Spanier, Graham B., and Paul C. Glick. 1980. "Mate selection differentials between whites and blacks in the United States." Social Forces 58: 707–725.

Spencer, Margaret. 1983. "Children's cultural values and parental child-rearing strategies." Developmental Reviews 3: 351–370.

Spencer, Margaret, Geraldine Kearse Brookins, and Walter Rechard Allen. 1985. Beginnings: The Social and Affective Development of Black Children. Hillsdale, NJ: Lawrence Erlbaum Associates.

Staples, Robert. 1985. "Changes in black family structure: The conflict between family ideology and structural conditions." Journal of Marriage and the Family 47: 1005–1014.

Staples, Robert, and Alfredo Mirande. 1980. "Racial and cultural variations among American families: A decennial review of the literature on minority families." Journal of Marriage and the Family 42: 157–173.

Stevens, Joseph H., Jr. 1984. "Black grandmothers' and black adolescent mothers' knowledge about parenting." Developmental Psychology 20: 1017–1025.

Stevens, Joseph H., Jr. 1988. "Social support, locus of control, and parenting in three low-income groups of mothers: Black teenagers, black adults, and white adults." Child Development 59: 635–642.

Sudarkasa, Niara. 1981. "Interpreting the African heritage in Afro-American family organizations." Pp. 37–53 in Harriette P. McAdoo (ed.), Black Families. Beverly Hills, CA: Sage.

Sweet, James A., and Larry L. Bumpass. 1987. American Families and Households. New York: Russell Sage Foundation.

Taylor, Robert J. 1985. "The extended family as a source of support for elderly blacks." Gerontologist 26: 630–636.

Taylor, Robert J. 1986. "Receipt of support from family among black Americans: Demographic and familial differences." Journal of Marriage and the Family 48: 67–77.

Taylor, Robert J. 1988a. "Aging and supportive relationships among black Americans." Pp. 259–281 in James Jackson (ed.), The Black American Elderly: Research on Physical Health. New York: Springer.

Taylor, Robert J. 1988b. "Structural determinants of religious participation among Black Americans." Review of Religious Research 30: 114–125.

Taylor, Robert J. 1990. "Need for support and family involvement among black Americans." Journal of Marriage and the Family 52: 584–590.

Taylor, Robert J., and Linda M. Chatters. 1986a. "Church-based informal support among elderly blacks." Gerontologist 26: 637–642.

Taylor, Robert J., and Linda M. Chatters. 1986b.

"Patterns of informal support to elderly black adults: Family, friends, and church members." Social Work 31: 432–438.

Taylor, Robert J., and Linda M. Chatters. 1988. "Church members as a source of informal social support." Review of Religious Research 30: 193–203.

Taylor, Robert J., Linda M. Chatters, and Vickie Mays. 1988. "Parents, children, siblings, in-laws, and non-kin sources of emergency assistance to black Americans." Family Relations 37: 298–304.

Taylor, Robert J., Bogart Leashore, and Susan Toliver. 1988. "An assessment of the provider role as perceived by black males." Family Relations 37: 426–431.

Testa, Mark, N. M. Astone, Marilyn Krogh, and Kathryn Neckerman. 1989. "Employment and marriage among inner-city fathers." Annals of the American Academy of Political and Social Science 501: 79–91.

Thomas, Veronica, Norweeta G. Milburn, Diane R. Brown, and Lawrence E. Gary. 1988. "Social support and depressive symptoms among blacks." Journal of Black Psychology 14: 35–45.

Thompson, Maxine S., and Margaret E. Ensminger. 1989. "Psychological well-being among mothers with school-age children: Evolving family structures." Social Forces 67: 715–730.

Thornton, Michael, Linda M. Chatters, Robert J. Taylor, and Walter R. Allen. 1990. "Sociodemographic and environmental influences on racial socialization by black parents." Child Development 61: 401–409.

Tienda, Marta, and Ronald Angel. 1982. "Headship and household composition among blacks, Hispanics, and other whites." Social Forces 61: 508–531.

Tucker, M. Belinda. 1987. "The black male shortage in Los Angeles." Sociology and Social Research 71: 221–227.

Tucker, M. Belinda, and Claudia Mitchell-Kernan. In press. "Sex ratio imbalance and Afro-Americans: Conceptual and methodological issues." In Reginald Jones (ed.), Advances in Black Psychology. Berkeley, CA: Cobb and Henry.

Tucker, M. Belinda, and Claudia Mitchell-Kernan. 1990. "New trends in black American interracial marriage: The social structural context." Journal of Marriage and the Family 52: 209–218.

Tucker, Belinda, and Robert J. Taylor. 1989. "Demographic correlates of relationship status among black Americans." Journal of Marriage and the Family 51: 655–665.

U.S. Bureau of the Census. 1985. 1980 Census of the Population, Subject Reports: Marital Characteristics. Washington, DC: Government Printing Office.

Warheit, George, William Vega, D. Shimizu, and Kenneth Meinhardt. 1982. "Interpersonal coping networks and mental health problems among four race-ethnic groups." Journal of Community Psychology 10: 312–324.

Wilson, Melvin N. 1986. "The black extended family: An analytical consideration." Developmental Psychology 22: 246–259.

Wilson, Melvin N. 1989. "Child development in the context of the black extended family." American Psychologist 44: 380–385.

Wilson, William Julius. 1987. The Truly Disadvantaged. Chicago: University of Chicago Press.

Wilson, William Julius (ed.). 1989. "The ghetto underclass: Social science perspectives." Annals of the American Academy of Political and Social Science 501: 8–192.

Wilson, William Julius, and Kathryn J. Neckerman. 1986. "Poverty and family structure: The widening gap between evidence and public policy issues." Pp. 232–259 in Sheldon H. Danziger and Daniel H. Weinberg (eds.), Fighting Poverty: What Works and What Doesn't. Cambridge, MA: Harvard University Press.

Ulbrich, Patricia M., and George J. Warheit. 1989. "Social support, stress, and psychological distress among older black and white adults." Journal of Aging and Health 1: 286–305.

Zelnik, Melvin. 1983. "Sexual activity among adolescents: Perspectives of a decade." In Elizabeth McAnarney (ed.), Premature Adolescent Pregnancy and Parenthood. New York: Grune and Stratton.

Zelnik, Melvin, John Kantner, and Kathleen Ford. 1981. Sex and Pregnancy in Adolescence. Beverly Hills, CA: Sage.

Zelnik, Melvin, and Farida K. Shah. 1983. "First intercourse among young Americans." Family Planning Perspectives 15: 64–72.

Zill, Nicholas, and Carolyn C. Rogers. 1988. "Recent trends in the well-being of children in the United States and their implications for public policy." Pp. 31–98 in Andrew J. Cherlin (ed.), The Changing American Family and Public Policy. Washington, DC: Urban Institute Press.

Zollar, Ann Creighton, and J. Sherwood Williams. 1987. "The contribution of marriage to the life satisfaction of black adults." Journal of Marriage and the Family 49: 87–92.

WILLIAM A. VEGA   *University of California, Berkeley*

Hispanic Families in the 1980s:
A Decade of Research

A selective literature review covering the period of 1980 until early 1990 suggests certain changes within the knowledge base about Hispanic families in the continental United States. While the long-standing interest in cultural patterning of gender roles and family process continues, a "social adaptation" approach is evident in the demographic and migration research literature. The focus of this approach is on formative effects of environment on family structure, and the role played by family networks in facilitating international immigration and socioeconomic incorporation. The research of the 1980s also underscores gender role flexibility, which has accompanied the movement of women into the labor force, as well as effects of acculturation in multigenerational Hispanic populations. Despite an increase in empirical research, there remains much conjecture about family socialization patterns and differences in attitudes and values across cultures. The available evidence favors an interpretation that Hispanic families are increasingly vulnerable to marital disruption, but that familism—defined as either face-to-face interaction or supporting behaviors—remains a more typical feature of Hispanic families than of non-Hispanic white families. It is also evident that different Hispanic ethnic groups have had dissimilar experiences in family viability, and comparative research is needed to clarify contributory factors.

Department of Social and Administrative Health Sciences, School of Public Health, Warren Hall, University of California, Berkeley, CA 94720.

This review considers research on the Hispanic family in the United States that has appeared in print during the 1980s. The scope of the review includes studies in articles and books on families of Mexican, Puerto Rican, and Cuban origin. The coverage is selective and limited primarily to those studies that represent original research or contribute new theory to the arena of Hispanic family research. Other literature reviews that have appeared during this time period are not covered, except in instances when they involve a new synthesis of theory or information.

A change of research perspectives occurred in the 1980s, owing in great part to the social events and conditions experienced during this decade. Massive immigration and internal migration have had far-reaching consequences for family formation and structure among Hispanics. However, this situation is not unprecedented. Rather, it represents the latest chapter of cyclical trends in American ethnic history (Muller and Espenshade, 1985). In this regard, contemporary research perspectives may aid us in demythologizing the Hispanic family in the past, present, and future. They may also help us to understand better how families change in response to new and challenging social situations and cultural influences.

Since the contemporary research literature derives its discourse and imagery from the research of the past, it is not possible to partition this review completely from the abiding theoretical questions that have occupied students of the Hispanic family for decades. Current research is driven by these enigmas. For example, the long-standing debate about whether depictions of traditional family values, behaviors, and structure are either accurate or relevant has not diminished, despite persistent attempts to put it aside (Staples and Mirande, 1980). Similarly, the ramifications of multigeneration acculturation on family functioning are not well understood, despite numerous attempts to conceptualize the process. It is clear that, while we understand more, we still don't have enough of the right kind of information to adequately explain the complexity and volatility of Hispanic families. In the 1980s, empirical research with an emphasis on "social adaptation" has become the alternative to earlier simplistic formulations of Hispanic families and reflects the most prominent social facts about Hispanic society in the past decades, including migration, immigration, acculturation, socioeconomic incorporation, minority group status, and the entry of women into the labor force. This review critically summarizes what has been learned in the past decade and points out deficiencies in theory and analytical perspectives. It also outlines new directions for future research.

THE STATUS OF THE HISPANIC POPULATION

The dramatic changes that have occurred during the 1980s place Hispanics into a demographic trajectory wherein they can be expected to become the largest ethnic minority group in the continental United States shortly after the turn of the century. Of course, the Hispanic population is not unitary, but is composed of numerous Spanish-speaking ethnic groups whose cultural origins are rich and diverse. Overall, between 1980 and 1988, there was an increase of 34.4% in the size of the Hispanic population (U.S. Bureau of the Census, 1988). This represented a total population in 1988 of 19,431,000. Most of this increase was fueled by immigration from Mexico. Indeed, the Mexican-descent population increased by 39.9% between 1980 and 1988 to a total of 12,110,000. The traditional Southwestern enclaves of Mexican descent have now been transcended, making way for Mexican Americans to become a national minority group. Puerto Ricans, Cubans, and other Latin Americans each increased by proportions of at least 25% during the same period of time. However, Cubans and Puerto Ricans remained essentially regional populations. The states of California, Texas, New York, and Florida contain almost three-quarters of the Hispanic population in the continental United States.

The proportion of Hispanic families below the poverty level has increased slightly to a 1987 level of 25.8% compared to a non-Hispanic level of 9.7% in that same year. Furthermore, Hispanic fertility was 29% higher than non-Hispanic white fertility in 1980 (Bean and Tienda, 1987), a discrepancy that is primarily attributable to women of Mexican origin because they have the highest fertility levels and they are the largest Hispanic ethnic group. On the other hand, Cuban women had fertility rates slightly below those of non-Hispanic white women (Perez, 1986). Mainland Puerto Ricans have high fertility rates, are most likely to have female-headed households with children, and have the lowest family income (Moore and Pachon, 1985: 62).

Some important conclusions are reached by Bean and Tienda (1987) in their monumental review of 1980 census data. Among the most pertinent is their challenge to the long-held supposition that Hispanic families are more stable than non-Hispanic white families. They report negligible variations in rates of marital disruption between non-Hispanic whites, Mexican Americans, and Cuban Americans, but Puerto Rican rates that are much higher than those of the other groups. Although other investigators (Frisbee, Opitz, and Kelly, 1985) had reported lower divorce rates for Mexican Americans, Bean and Tienda point out that when separation is included in marital disruption, such differences disappear. Further, Angel and Tienda (1982) report that nonnuclear family members are more likely to contribute to household income in Hispanic households precisely because there is a higher percentage of female-headed households in Mexican (19.9%) and Puerto Rican (38.6%) than in non-Hispanic white households (14.1%). Therefore, having other adults living in the household or contributing to its maintenance may be indicating an erosion of Hispanic family strengths, even though traditional cultural expectations may be motivating this supportive behavior.

The census data suggest two important trends for Hispanics between the 1960 and 1980 census: (a) the average size of Hispanic households is decreasing, and (b) marital disruption is increasing. Frisbee (1986) points out that Mexican American and Cuban American marital stability is inversely related to educational attainment, but among Puerto Ricans, educational attainment increases marital stability. Moreover, the lifetime fertility of Hispanic-origin women varies strongly with educational attainment. As noted by Bean and Tienda (1987), "If lower education tends generally to make for higher fertility, and if the Spanish origin women are relatively more concentrated in the lower educational categories, it is not difficult to see why higher fertility persists within many of the groups" (p. 224).

In summary, we have the profile of a Hispanic population that is increasing at a much faster rate than the non-Hispanic population but continues to experience substandard levels of educational attainment and family income. It is likely that the continental Hispanic population will continue these demographic trends (Bean, Schmandt, and Weintraub, 1989; Hayes-Batista, Schink, and Chapa, 1988). The primary contributory factor to population growth will be immigration. Despite the passage of the Immigration Reform and Control Act of 1986, it is unlikely that either legal or undocumented immigration will be markedly curtailed. Moreover, there is some evidence that undocumented immigrants form Mexico are more likely to arrive with the anticipation of becoming permanent residents, and an increase of women and families is noticeable in a migratory stream that was formerly dominated by men (Passel and Woodrow, 1984).

FAMILY STRUCTURE AND SOCIOECONOMIC CONDITIONS

The morphological characteristics of the Hispanic family are increasingly understood to be a response to socioeconomic conditions. Griswold del Castillo (1984) notes that while the extended family was an "ideal type" in the second half of the 19th century, Mexican Americans were no more likely than non-Hispanics to have extended families. Furthermore, the vicissitudes of life on the frontier rendered families highly susceptible to disruption and reformulation. This required great resourcefulness on the part of both men and women, and gender roles were not highly differentiated. Indeed, by 1870 in Los Angeles, almost 38% of Mexican-descent families were headed by females, with similar proportions found in San Antonio and Santa Fe (p. 32). Griswold del Castillo concludes, "The Mexican American family has had to be flexible, pluralistic, and adaptive to survive" (p. 132).

The parallels between this historical situation and the current research on the Hispanic family are illuminating. Portes and Bach (1985) note that 75% of Cubans and 50% of Mexican Americans reported some or a great deal of help from relatives during their first three years of postimmigration residence. The use of families for migration and adaptation has been assessed in two important studies, which conclude that binational, intercommunity linkages are sustained through resilient family network ties (Alvarez, 1987; Massey, Alarcon, Durand, and Gonzalez, 1987).

Chavez, in two articles (1985 and 1988), traces the ties between family structure and legal residence. In one study (1985) he contrasts undocumented and documented Mexicans on direction of family extension and finds that 76.6% of undocumented families are extended laterally, which indicates a predominance of households where "the additional relative is of the same kinship generation, for example, a brother, sister, cousin" (p. 323). Among legal immigrants, less than half were in lateral extension, and in contrast, 30.6% were up-extended—that is, residing in a household that included a mother, father, aunt, or uncle. Among the undocumented, only 5.3% were up-extended. Among legal residents there is a tendency for families to reunify as members are brought in from Mexico or these households expand because of marriage and childbearing.

Among undocumented immigrants the process is more complex, because some migrants choose to go home, usually after one year. Others stay, which is indicated by the dramatic increase from 22% to 42.4% in simple family households among those migrants staying longer than one year. Simple family households are defined as conjugal units and any of their children. This indicates a rapid rate of family formation even among the undocumented group (see also Browning and de la Garza, 1986). This profile of flexibility in family formation resonates with the historical evidence cited previously. Both illustrate the requirement for adaptive capacities within Hispanic families in dealing with the exigencies of economic marginality, labor market pressures, and physical relocation. Moreover, as noted by Chavez in another article (1988), undocumented migrants "living in households comprised of families more often viewed their employment as permanent than did their single counterparts" (p. 102). This tendency was true of even recent arrivals. Naturally, as the family has offspring who are native-born U.S. citizens, the long-stay perspective is reinforced and the family becomes "binationalized."

Muschkin and Myers (1989) report that recent migrants from Puerto Rico have an overrepresentation of disrupted families, and cohabitation seems more common for second-generation families (p. 500). On the other hand, families on the island are more likely to be intact (Bird and Canino, 1982). This difference has preoccupied some researchers who believe that such variations "point to the need to explore the variations in ecological settings and the different locales of challenge in which Puerto Ricans (single and families) strive to make the most of difficult economic and social circumstances" (Pelto, Roman, and Liriano, 1982: 43). In fact, these authors report finding a variety of "household structures, extra-household ties, and general patterns of helpful exchange" (p. 54); and they add that similar findings would probably be common if research designs were sensitive to their identification. Disrupted families that are headed by females are seen as an outcome of highly stressful environments where unemployment is common. Nevertheless, it would be enlightening to study variations in family stability across Hispanic ethnic groups within the same social ecology.

CULTURAL MAINTENANCE AND FAMILY FUNCTIONING

Changing cultures is an adaptive process, and acculturation is also idiosyncratic, producing distinctive levels of change in individual family members (Vega, Hough, and Romero, 1983). For example, cultural values and behaviors as well as ethnic identification may differ intergenerationally (Keefe and Padilla, 1987; Szapocznik and Hernandez, 1988). Historically, immigrants have represented a bulwark of resistance to acculturation, and it has been expected that their family processes would deviate most markedly from "American" families. However, it is not accurate to juxtapose Latin American ethnic cultures with American culture as if they are truly discrete or static. Culture change is a worldwide phenomenon, and wide intracultural variations can be expected in all complex Western societies, including those in Latin America. It remains an empirical question whether specific cultural differences between Hispanics and non-Hispanics are responsible for systematic variations in familism, gender roles, or family process. Much of the literature of the 1980s, especially the literature about Mexican Americans, is devoted to exploring these interrelated issues.

Familism and Social Support

The belief that Hispanics are more family-oriented than Anglos has been a consistent theme in the social science literature for decades. In fact, this line of reasoning has been a cornerstone of the extended traditional family stereotype and is linked to many of the pejorative images that have beset discussions of the Hispanic family. Because this stereotype has been so controversial and the empirical evidence so inconsistent, contemporary researchers have continued their quest for conceptual precision and empirical evidence that could clarify this issue (Alvirez, Bean, and Williams, 1981). As noted by Zinn (1982–83: 225), "The literature on familism among Chicanos reflects a mixed bag of assumptions, approaches, findings, and interpretations."

In a reflective article culminating extensive field research, Keefe (1984: 65) notes that despite the adaptive requirements of acculturation and urbanization, Mexican Americans are still credited with enjoying large extended-family networks and that this perception is "somehow related to real behavior patterns (authors see values variously as cause, effect or reinforcing agent)." From her own research, Keefe describes differences in family network and support patterns between Mexican Americans and non-Hispanics. One of the most noteworthy variations is the tendency for Mexican Americans to participate in relatively large kin networks and to engage in high rates of visiting and exchange. This pattern was true for immigrant and non-immigrant Mexican Americans. On the other hand, non-Hispanics maintained ties with fewer kin, and often these relationships were long-distance contact situations. Corresponding differences were found in the greater willingness of Mexican Americans to agree that the family should be the resource for dealing with problems. However, both ethnic groups strongly valued kin relationships and acknowledged that there are disadvantages to maintaining strong ties (Keefe, 1984: 67). The difference seems to lie in the geographic propinquity of Hispanic extended kin networks, which facilitates visiting and exchange behaviors, whereas non-Hispanics are more readily satisfied with long-distance relationships while restricting intimate contact to the nuclear family. The Mexican American family, then, is more multiplex, since it is more likely to be available and used to meet instrumental and affective needs. In this sense, it should be considered more extended.

Confirmatory empirical findings sustain much of what Keefe has elaborated. Mindel (1980) concludes that non-Hispanics migrate away from kin networks and Hispanics migrate toward them. He attributes these differences to cultural traditions, in that "close kinship ties are not merely a convenient form of aid but a well-known, enjoyable, and expected set of practices and attitudes" (p. 32). However, he somewhat qualifies the "family-as-resource" perspective by stating that kin networks are more likely to meet social-emotional needs than instrumental ones. Three separate empirical studies have also reported the tendency for Mexican American immigrants to have smaller social networks available than second-generation offspring have, and to rely on family more exclusively for emotional nurturance and problem solving (Golding and Burnam, 1990; Griffith and Villavicencio, 1985; Vega and Kolody, 1985). However, the second generation has broader social networks available because these consist of multigeneration kin and friend contacts.

Griffith and Villavicencio (1985) report that education and income were the best predictors of "more available support and more contact with network members." This finding is provocative, because it throws into question the appropriateness of comparing Hispanic and non-Hispanic patterns of familism without appropriate controls for socioeconomic differences across groups. There are no studies comparing patterns of middle-class Hispanics and non-Hispanics, which would be illuminating for predicting the future of Hispanic familism. There is also no consensus about the context of extended-family support. The historical case has been made for kinship networks as exchange systems for people who are economically marginal, but recent writings have been more likely to confirm emotional support as the main outcome of familism (Valle and Bensussen, 1985).

Markides, Hoppe, Martin, and Timbers (1983), in their three-generation study, concluded that older Mexican Americans and non-Hispanics had good relationships with family members. However, the Mexican American elderly were more likely to expect more from their children and not receive it. It may be that the acculturation process has created distinctive intergenerational expectations. However, in a later article, Markides, Boldt, and Ray (1986) reconfirmed the familistic orientation of Mexican Americans by noting that the family is the dominant source of advice and help in all generations.

These findings underscore the complexity of linking affiliational patterns with their underlying motives. The reasons why family members prefer contact with each other can have multiple and simultaneous rationales, and these are difficult to capture in descriptive studies using a limited theoretical framework. Similarly, relationships between expressed values and actual behaviors cannot be precisely understood without taking heed of how interpersonal transactions occur in the process of daily living. Some familial interactions may be instrumental, others may be symbolic, while others may be inescapable. Given the tendency for Mexican Americans to lean toward socially desirable answers, great care must be taken in the design of research in order to determine what people really mean, not just what they are saying, and whether their behaviors are consistent with normative expressions.

Gender Roles

Gender roles in the Hispanic family continue to be a primary area of conjecture and research in the 1980s. Paul Kutsche (1983) provides a detailed ethnographic description of Hispanic families in northern New Mexico that is a "throwback" to the traditional ethnographic literature. He describes the patriarchal model as follows: "The double standard of responsible adult behavior is quietly rampant in New Mexico, so a man who keeps his family well and is directly known to other men to indulge himself away from home is tacitly admired" (p. 154). On the other hand, "the wife owes her husband absolute sexual fidelity and, like Caesar's wife, also the appearance of it" (p. 159). Nevertheless, despite this type of gender stereotyping, Kutsche notes that strict gender roles deviate from the traditional division of labor when men are away working for extended periods. Under these circumstances, "either sex will do any job without hesitation" (p. 154). He also notes that childrearing is a joint parental obligation.

It is very common in the contemporary literature, as it was in the past, to find descriptions of the Hispanic family that contain references to continuity in traditional cultural expectations as well as evidence of female role transformations that openly challenge male dominance or a notion of a culturally ordained division of labor (Gonzalez, 1982; Zinn, 1982). For example, in a historical review, Zinn (1980) found that availability of employment was the most important determinant of whether Mexican American women worked or not. Similar findings have been reported for Puerto Rican women in New York (Moore and Pachon, 1985: 104). In describing gender roles in Puerto Rico, Bird and Canino (1982) restate the familiar "machismo" cultural motif. Nevertheless, family decision-making is described as either a joint process of both parents or primarily the job of the mother. As implied by Ybarra (1982a), an understanding of flexibility in gender roles within the Hispanic family has been obfuscated by the reliance on monocausal explanations (e.g., machismo) "for all changes that occur within the family structure" (p. 42). The result, she states, is the tendency for the Hispanic family to be studied in "a vacuum," while the social context of behavior and gender roles is ignored. The implication is that Hispanic families are adaptive, and gender role expectations will change as social conditions require. In Ybarra's empirical study of gender roles among Mexican Americans, she found a range "from a patriarchal (role-segregated) structure to an egalitarian (or joint-role) structure, with many combinations of these two polar opposites evident" (Ybarra, 1982b: 172).

In a rare example of a comparative ethnographic study, Kelly and Garcia (1989) contrast the experience of Cuban women in Miami and immigrant Mexican women in Los Angeles. These authors conclude that despite similar gender role expectations about female employment in both groups, their outcomes differed as a result of economic and political conditions in the two study sites. Immigrant Mexican women in Los Angeles find themselves in a process of "proletarianization," where their labor is required for family survival, whereas many Cuban women left the labor force when short-term goals of improving living standards were attained. In many ways, women entering the labor force remains a culturally anomalous behavior, requiring constant negotiation, conflict, and justification. Indeed, these authors conclude that Hispanic women attain greater personal autonomy via external employment. However, when this occurs in the context of socioeconomic marginality, employment is often a sign of family vulnerability.

Employment may also be a marker of individual vulnerability for married working women. Canino and associates (1987) find much higher depressive symptom levels among married women than among married men who are working fulltime in Puerto Rico, and as a consequence, these investigators conclude, "Employment status does represent a different social role for married men and women" (p. 455).

Family Process

Within the contemporary literature, attention has increasingly turned toward improving our understanding about how family process characteristics of Hispanic families are being affected by living in a multicultural environment. Martinez (1986) offers a theoretical model for conceptualizing family socialization that is based on two fundamental statements. First, "individuals are members of multiple social groups" (p. 266), and therefore, they can be aware of and even participate in multiple social systems simultaneously. This predisposes them to be opportunistic and adaptable. Second, "membership in social systems is further assumed to be progressive, and in this sense the model is developmental" (p. 266). That is, the individual is a member of a family, that family lives in a community, and this has implications for social affiliations of all types. Therefore, membership will radiate to multiple groups and institutions whereby the individual is shaped by these experiences and is influenced by the broader social environment as well. This framework stresses the "interconnective relationships of the individual, the family and society." Regrettably, this type of model does little to identify which extrafamilial factors will provoke specific types of family changes.

Starting from similar theoretical premises and writing about the Cuban family, other researchers (Szapocznik and Hernandez, 1988) report from clinical and empirical studies that, typically, adult immigrants acculturate at a rate that is much slower than that of their children, a difference that leads to profound intergenerational conflicts. In turn, these conflicts are aggravated by parental efforts to gain control over their children. Eventually children can move even farther in the direction of rejecting parental expectations. In short, dramatic differences in cultural orientation exacerbate normal intergenerational strains to produce unique parenting problems and family vulnerability among Cuban Hispanics. Evidently, the process could be generalizable to other Hispanic ethnic groups as well.

Among the relatively few comparative studies about Hispanic family process, most have focused on family dynamics and marital experience. For example, family cohesion and adaptability were compared among a sample of non-Hispanics and Mexican Americans by using the Family Adaptability and Cohesion Scale (Vega et al., 1986). Overall, families in both samples functioned well and had similar family process characteristics, on the basis of the circumplex model of Olson, Russell, and Sprenkle (1980). However, the characteristics of low-acculturation Mexican American families differed from both high-acculturation Mexican American and non-Hispanic white families. For example, low-acculturation parents were more likely to be low in stress and to be satisfied with family life and spouse personality during the stage of raising preadolescent children, which was the focus of this study.

In quite a different type of empirical research, the sources of marital strain among Mexican American women were compared to those for non-Hispanic women (Vega, Kolody, and Valle, 1988). The sources of marital strain were found to be very similar in both cultural groups. However, the less acculturated Mexican Americans, most of whom were low-income housewives, were more likely to experience marital strain based on nonreciprocity of spouse but were less likely to experience frustrations about spouse's ability to provide adequately for them. Nonreciprocity involves circumstances where the spouse insists on having his own way and will not give in to his wife's wishes. However, this study restricted the selection of marital strain items only to those used in a previous study with a non-Hispanic community sample.

Another comparative study of family roles found few differences in perceptions about siblings' and parents' roles between Mexican American and non-Hispanic children. An important aspect of this study is that it controlled for the socioeconomic status of the families. Birth-order dynamics were similar for all children except the last-born, which suggests that the values operating in family dynamics, and especially in the socialization of children, differed little in both ethnic groups (Jaramillo and Zapata, 1987). These authors conclude that their findings further disconfirm the idea that Hispanic families are categorically discrete from non-Hispanic families.

DISCUSSION AND CONCLUSION

Despite the passage of time, the shortage of empirical studies on the Hispanic family noted by Ramirez and Arce in their highly cited literature review (1981) continues to persist. Notwithstanding several important demographic studies, the need for new empirical research is most evident in the case of the Cuban American family. However, even within the expansive literature on Mexican Americans, there remains much conjecture and recitation of old work, with few new hard facts on which to base a viable resynthesis of heuristic models. Most of the studies reported in the literature must be considered "exploratory or first-level research" (Rothman, Gant, and Hnat, 1985: 211), lacking comprehensive theoretical grounding for a continuing program of investigation. Given the noncomparability of most contemporary findings about the Hispanic family, and the lack of a consistent conceptual grounding, it is difficult to develop hypotheses about cultural similarities or differences in family process that may exist among Cubans, Puerto Ricans, or Mexican Americans. Several recommendations that could help in overcoming this impasse are summarized below.

1. Historical, ethnographic, and empirical studies are needed that investigate the relationship of family characteristics to social and economic incorporation. Complementary studies using a common theoretical framework would be most enlightening, especially comparative studies, which permit using ethnographic and historical information to design empirical field studies, as well

as to interpret the results of those studies (Alvarez, 1987).

2. Researchers should be circumspect about overgeneralizing from idiosyncratic samples, and replications (or partial replications) of carefully done research using common instrumentation and designs would help establish convergent validity and reliability in Hispanic family research.

3. Since virtually all empirical research is currently limited to cross-sectional studies, it is very difficult to assess dynamic family processes. Developmental theoretical models and prospective multivariate designs are needed to establish causal links between designated independent variables (e.g., SES, labor markets effects, cultural factors) and predicted changes in family relations, structure, or processes.

4. Care should be taken not to confuse assenting statements in interviews about family values and normative expectations with actual behavior. Values can be countervailing. Values can be retained that are conflicting or that neutralize actual behavior. For example, see the account by Weeks and Cuellar (1981) about the Hispanic elderly in their field study who believed they should be able to count on family ties for support but failed to seek such assistance because of the more closely held value of self-reliance, which inhibits help-seeking from family members.

5. Specific ethnic group membership and the intergenerational and acculturation characteristics of samples should be measured and reported in all types of research. These are potentially confounding factors that can seriously limit the generalizability or interpretation of empirical studies (Trevino, 1988).

6. Systematic ethnographic studies are needed regarding language and the role it plays in preserving family practices, familism, intergenerational cohesion, and ethnic identity (Moore and Pachon, 1985; Portes and Rumbaut, 1990).

7. More attention should be paid to current developments in non-Hispanic theory and research, such as the work reported in this volume. The Hispanic family research literature reflects isolation and will benefit from the introduction of new perspectives and analytical paradigms. In conducting this review, it was apparent to me that a great deal of exciting family research is appearing in books about migration and adaptation rather than within journals about family process.

8. Hispanic family research should encompass the study of the rapidly increasing population of Central and South Americans in the United States (Suarez-Orozco, 1989) and the implications of settlement patterns for intermarriage and cultural dissemination between members of different Hispanic ethnic groups (for an excellent recent example of appropriate procedures, see Jiobu, 1988).

9. Family strengths and the role of culture in sustaining these should be studied with empirical methods rather than by conjecture.

An important limitation of this review is the exclusion of the literature on fertility regulation and family planning, which may be an increasingly important area of research in the 1990s. Nonetheless, despite a moderate yield of new studies in the last decade, there is an encouraging movement toward social-environmental conceptual frameworks that transcend the long-debated limitations of emic cultural models of family life among Hispanics. This trend has facilitated a wideranging discourse regarding antecedent and contemporary processes that have contributed to the social adaptation of Hispanic families in American culture. It has also opened the path for more sophisticated study designs and methodological procedures.

REFERENCES

Alvarez, Robert. 1987. Families: Migration and Adaptation in Baja and Alta California from 1800 to 1975. Berkeley: University of California Press.

Alvirez, David, Frank Bean, and David Williams. 1981. "The Mexican American family." In C. H. Mindel and R. W. Habenstein (eds.), Ethnic Families in America. New York: Elsevier Press.

Angel, Ronald, and Marta Tienda. 1982. "Determinants of extended household structure: Cultural pattern or economic need?" American Journal of Sociology 6: 1360–1383.

Bean, Frank, Jurgen Schmandt, and Sidney Weintraub. 1989. Mexican and Central American Population and U.S. Immigration Policy. Austin: University of Texas Press.

Bean, Frank, and Marta Tienda. 1987. The Hispanic Population of the United States. New York: Russell Sage Foundation.

Bird, Hector, and Glorisa Canino. 1982. "The Puerto Rican family: Cultural factors and family intervention strategies." Journal of the American Academy of Psychoanalysis 10: 257–268.

Browning, Harley L., and Rodolfo O. de la Garza. 1986. Mexican Immigrants and Mexican Americans. Austin, TX: Center for Mexican American Studies.

Canino, Glorisa J., Martiza Rubio-Stipec, Patrick Shrout, Milagros Bravo, Robert Stolberg, and Hector R. Bird. 1987. "Sex differences and depression in Puerto Rico." Psychology of Women Quarterly 4: 443–459.

Chavez, Leo. 1985. "Households, migration, and labor market participation: The adaptation of Mexicans to life in the United States." Urban Anthropology 14: 301–346.

Chavez, Leo. 1988. "Settlers and sojourners: The case of Mexicans in the United States." Human Organization 47: 95–108.

Frisbie, W. Parker. 1986. "Variation in patterns of marital instability among Hispanics." Journal of Marriage and the Family 48: 99–106.

Frisbie, W. Parker, Wolfgang Opitz, and William R. Kelly. 1985. "Marital instability trends among Mexican Americans as compared to blacks and Anglos: New evidence." Social Science Quarterly 66: 587–601.

Golding, Jacqueline, and Audrey Burnam. 1990. "Stress and social support as predictors of depressive symptoms in Mexican Americans and non-Hispanic whites." Journal of Social and Clinical Psychology 9: 268–286.

Gonzalez, Alex. 1982. "Sex roles of the traditional Mexican family." Journal of Cross-Cultural Psychology 13: 330–339.

Griffith, James, and Sandra Villavicencio. 1985. "Relationships among acculturation, sociodemographic characteristics, and social supports in Mexican American adults." Hispanic Journal of Behavioral Sciences 7: 75–92.

Griswold del Castillo, Richard. 1984. La Familia. Notre Dame, IN: University of Notre Dame Press.

Hayes-Bautista, David E., Werner O. Schink, and Jorge Chapa. 1988. The Burden of Support. Stanford, CA: Stanford University Press.

Jaramillo, Patricio, and Jessie T. Zapata. 1987. "Roles and alliances within Mexican-American and Anglo Families." Journal of Marriage and The Family 49: 727–735.

Jiobu, Robert. 1988. Ethnicity and Assimilation. Albany, NY: SUNY Press.

Keefe, Susan. 1984. "Real and ideal extended familism among Mexican Americans and Anglo Americans: On the meaning of 'close' family ties." Human Organization 43: 65–70.

Keefe, Susan E., and Amado M. Padilla. 1987. Chicano Ethnicity. Albuquerque: University of New Mexico Press.

Kelly, Patricia F., and Anna Garcia. 1989. "Power surrendered, power restored: The politics of home and work among Hispanic women in Southern California and Southern Florida." In L. Tilly and P. Guerin (eds.), Women and Politics in America. New York: Russell Sage Foundation.

Kutsche, Paul. 1983. "Household and family in Hispanic Northern New Mexico." Journal of Comparative Family Studies 14: 151–165.

Markides, Kyriakos S., Joanne S. Boldt, and Laura A. Ray. 1986. "Sources of helping and intergenerational solidarity: A three generations study of Mexican Americans." Journal of Gerontology 41: 506–511.

Markides, Kyriakos S., Sue K. Hoppe, Harry W. Martin, and Dianne M. Timbers. 1983. "Sample representativeness in a three-generation study of Mexican Americans." Journal of Marriage and the Family 45: 911–916.

Martinez, Marco A. 1986. "Family socialization among Mexican Americans." Human Development 29: 264–279.

Massey, Douglas, Rafael Alarcon, Jorge Durand, and Umberto Gonzalez. 1987. Return to Aztlan. Berkeley: University of California Press.

Mindel, Charles H. 1980. "Extended familism among urban Mexican Americans, Anglos, and blacks." Hispanic Journal of Behavioral Sciences 2: 21–34.

Moore, Joan, and Harry Pachon. 1985. Hispanics in the United States. Englewood Cliffs, NJ: Prentice-Hall.

Muller, Thomas, and Thomas J. Espenshade. 1985. The Fourth Wave. Washington, DC: Urban Institute Press.

Muschkin, Clara, and George C. Myers. 1989. "Migration and household family structure: Puerto Ricans in the United States." International Migration Review 23: 495–501.

Olson, David H., Candyce S. Russell, and Douglas H. Sprenkle. 1980. "Circumplex Model of Marital and Family Systems: II. Empirical studies and clinical intervention." In J. P. Vincent (ed.), Advances in Family Intervention, Assessment, and Theory (Vol. 1). Greenwich, CT: JAI Press.

Passel, J. S., and K. A. Woodrow. 1984. "Geographic distribution of undocumented aliens counted in the 1980 census by state." International Migration Review 18: 642–671.

Pelto, Pertti, Maria Roman, and Nelson Liriano. 1982. "Family structures in an urban Puerto Rican community." Urban Anthropology 11: 39–58.

Perez, Lisandro. 1986. "Immigrant economic adjustment and family organization: The Cuban success story reexamined." International Migration Review 20: 4–20.

Portes, Alejandro, and Robert L. Bach. 1985. Latin Journey. Berkeley: University of California Press.

Portes, Alejandro, and Ruben G. Rumbaut. 1990. Immigrant America: A Portrait. Berkeley: University of California Press.

Ramirez, Oscar, and Carlos Arce. 1981. "The contemporary Chicano family: An empirically based review." In A. Barron (ed.), Explorations in Chicano Psychology. New York: Prager.

Rothman, Jack, Larry Gant, and Stephen A. Hnat. 1985. "Mexican American family culture." Social Service Review 59: 197–215.

Staples, Robert, and Alfredo Mirande. 1980. "Racial and cultural variations among American families: A decennial review of the literature on minority families." Journal of Marriage and the Family 42: 887–903.

Suarez-Orozco, Marcelo. 1989. Central American Refugees and United States High School: A Psychosocial Study of Motivation and Achievement. Stanford,

CA: Stanford University Press.

Szapocznik, Jose, and Roberto Hernandez. 1988. "The Cuban American family." In C. H. Mindel, R. W. Habenstein, and R. Wright (eds.), Ethnic Families in America. New York: Elsevier Press.

Trevino, Fernando. "Uniform minimum data sets: In search of demographic comparability." American Journal of Public Health 78: 126–127.

U.S. Bureau of the Census. 1988. Population Characteristics. Current Population Reports, Series P-20, No. 438. Washington, DC: Government Printing Office.

Valle, Ramon, and Gloria Bensussen. 1985. "Hispanic social networks, social support, and mental health." In William A. Vega and Manuel Miranda (eds.), Stress and Hispanic Mental Health. DHHS Pub. No. 85-1410. Rockville, MD: NIMH.

Vega, William A., Richard Hough, and Annelisa Romero. 1983. "Family life patterns of Mexican Americans." In G. J. Powell (eds.), The Psychosocial Development of Minority Group Children. New York: Brunner/Mazel.

Vega, William A., and Bohdan Kolody. 1985. "The meaning of social support and the mediation of stress across cultures." In William A. Vega and Manuel Miranda (eds.), Stress and Hispanic Mental Health. DHHS Pub. No. 85-1410. Rockville, MD: NIMH.

Vega, William A., Bohdan Kolody, and Ray Valle. 1988. "Marital strain, coping, and depression among Mexican-American Women." Journal of Marriage and the Family 50: 391–403.

Vega, William A., Thomas Patterson, James Sallis, Philip Nader, Catherine Atkins, and Ian Abramson. 1986. "Cohesion and adaptability in Mexican-American and Anglo families." Journal of Marriage and the Family 48: 857–867.

Weeks, John R., and Jose Cuellar. 1981. "The role of family members in the helping networks of older people." Gerontology 21: 388–394.

Ybarra, Lea. 1982a. "Marital decision-making and the role of machismo in the Chicano family." De Colores 6: 32–47.

Ybarra, Lea. 1982b. "When wives work: The impact on the Chicano family." Journal of Marriage and the Family 44: 169–178.

Zinn, Maxine B. 1980. "Employment and education of Mexican American women." Harvard Educational Review 50: 47–62.

Zinn, Maxine B. 1982. "Chicano men and masculinity." Journal of Ethnic Studies 10: 29–44.

Zinn, Maxine B. 1982/3. "Familism among Chicanos: A theoretical review." Humboldt Journal of Social Relations 10: 224–238.

BRENT C. MILLER   *Utah State University*

KRISTIN A. MOORE   *Child Trends, Inc.* *

Adolescent Sexual Behavior, Pregnancy, and Parenting: Research through the 1980s

As the 1990s begin, research and policy interest in adolescent sexual behavior, pregnancy, and parenting continues at a high level, both because these behaviors are critical in the process of family formation and because their precocious timing often makes them problematic for the individual and for society. Research from the 1980s is summarized on the topics of adolescent sexual activity, contraception, abortion, marriage, adoption, and childrearing. Research about the antecedents of adolescent sexual and contraceptive behavior is emphasized because they are the key risk factors in adolescent pregnancy. Advances in data and methods are discussed, and research gaps are highlighted.

Sexual intercourse, pregnancy, and parenthood are usually valued aspects of individual development, family formation, and societal well-being. However, the precocious timing of these life experiences often makes them individually and socially problematic. The early onset of sexual activity is related to less effective contraceptive use, to unintended pregnancy, and to becoming a parent "too soon."[1] In this review we summarize research from the 1980s regarding adolescent

_____

Department of Family and Human Development, Utah State University, Logan, UT 84322-2905.

*Child Trends, Inc., 2100 M Street, N.W., Suite 610, Washington, DC 20037.

fertility-related behavior among persons aged 19 or younger in the United States.[2] Sexual activity among teens is discussed first, followed by sections on contraception, abortion, marriage, adoption, and childrearing. The article ends with a summary of advances in theory, data, and methods that have emerged during the decade of the 1980s.

SEXUAL INTERCOURSE

The Sequential Nature of Adolescent Sexual Behavior

Researchers have documented a normative developmental pattern in the sequence of adolescent heterosexual behaviors. Couples usually embrace and kiss first, move on to fondling and petting next, and subsequently engage in more intimate behaviors that include sexual intercourse (McCabe and Collins, 1984). The most sophisticated analysis of the sequence of heterosexual behaviors among younger adolescents used both cross-sectional scalogram analysis techniques and longitudinal linking of individual sexual behavior separated by two years (Smith and Udry, 1985). Among white adolescents who were ages 12–15 at the first round, strong evidence was found for a developmental sequence from necking, feeling breasts through clothing, feeling breasts directly, feeling sex organs directly, feeling penis directly, to intercourse. However, the percentage of black adolescents who indicated that they had had intercourse was greater than the percentage who reported any of the unclothed petting behaviors. Apparently, white and black adolescents have somewhat different normative expectations regarding intercourse, with whites typically engaging in a longer and more predictable sequence of behaviors prior to having intercourse.

Incidence of and Transition to Sexual Intercourse

During the 1980s there was a continued increase in the incidence of sexual intercourse among teens, though the magnitude and consistency of the changes were weaker during the 1980s than the 1970s. Data from the 1988 National Survey of Family Growth indicate that by age 15, approximately one-quarter of females have had sex; by age 19, four out of five females have had sexual intercourse (London, Masher, Pratt, and Williams, 1989; Pratt, 1990). Data from the 1988 National Survey of Young Men indicate that a third of teen males have had sex by age 15, as have 86% by age 19 (Sonenstein, Pleck, and Ku, 1989).

Even by the late 1980s, relatively little had been learned about the context of first sexual intercourse, despite the significance of the event both to the individual and to society. What is known, moreover, continues to be more descriptive than explanatory. The partners of young women who first have sex during their teen years average about three years older than they are, while teen males' first partners average less than a year older. It is uncommon, however, for first partners to be substantially older; only 9% of young women and 3% of young men reported their first partner to be 23 or older (Zelnik and Shah, 1983). In addition, most partners of young women, especially white teens, are persons they are dating or going steady with. Though the relationships between males and their first partner tend to be characterized by less commitment, males and females are similar in reporting that their first sexual experience was unplanned or "just happened" (Harris and Associates, 1986).

Other analyses indicate that for a substantial minority of young people, the initiation of sex is not voluntary (Moore, Nord, and Peterson, 1989). Among youth aged 18–22 interviewed in the 1987 wave of the National Survey of Children, 6.3% of white females, 3.2% of black females,

0.4% of white males, and 1.4% of black males reported that they had been raped or forced to have sex by age 15. Nonvoluntary sex accounted for a large proportion of all sexual exposure before the age of 14 among females. For example, among white females, the proportion sexually experienced was 2.3% if only voluntary sex was considered but 6.9% if both voluntary and nonvoluntary sex were considered. Among black females, the comparable proportions were 6.2% and 9.0%. A history of sexual abuse seems to be quite high among teenage young women receiving child welfare services or in foster care (Polit, Morton, and White, 1989), teenage mothers (Gershenson et al., 1989), and young women whose parents drank or used drugs (Moore et al., 1989). Further work is needed to clarify the circumstances under which sex is initiated and continued, and the implications for adolescent pregnancy, sexually transmitted diseases, and HIV infection.

Frequency of Intercourse and Number of Partners

To understand the risks posed by adolescent sexual intercourse, it is important to know how often adolescents have intercourse and with how many different partners. Few teens have sex only once (Moore and Peterson, 1989, Sonenstein et al., 1989). More than two-thirds have sex again within six months of first intercourse. Even among youth who experienced forced sex, virtually all initiated voluntary sex during their teen years (Moore et al., 1989). Nevertheless, the frequency of sexual intercourse among unmarried teenagers is considerably lower than among married teens. Vinovskis (1988) concluded that never-married teenagers are about one-fourth as sexually active as their married counterparts.

Among youth in their late teens, Moore and Peterson (1989) found that the majority had had zero or just one partner in the previous year. However, 4% of white females, 6% of black females, 11% of white males, and 23% of black males reported six or more partners.

Antecedents of Adolescent Sexual Intercourse

Biological antecedents. There is substantial evidence that precocious pubertal development is associated with early initiation of sexual activity.

This finding appears to hold net of other factors and also with various measures of sexual activity, from masturbation to intercourse (Morris, Mallin, and Udry, 1982; Zabin, Smith, Hirsch, and Hardy, 1986). There is still debate, though, about whether heterosexual interaction is influenced more by an individual's level of sexual maturation or by chronological age. Dornbusch and associates (1981) found that individual levels of sexual maturation added little to explained variance in dating behavior after age was taken into account. Thus, he concluded that social pressures to date, not maturation, determined the onset of dating in adolescence. Other research (Zabin et al., 1986) suggests, however, that early pubertal development applies a downward pressure on the age of sexual debut. As age of puberty increases, the cultural influence of social norms becomes stronger relative to the individual levels of development. Udry and associates (1985) report strong evidence for the hormonal basis of sexual motivation and behavior in adolescent males. In models of sexual intercourse that included age, pubertal development (Tanner Scale), and hormonal levels (obtained from blood samples), only the hormonal influence retained its effect. In a parallel study of females, Udry, Talbert, and Morris (1986) found strong hormonal effects on motivation but weak effects on sexual behavior, and concluded that intercourse behavior of females is influenced to a greater extent by social controls. Further research by Udry (1988) revealed interactions between hormonal and sociological variables, but hormone level remained the only strong predictor of the timing of the transition to coitus among males:

> The initiation of sexual behavior, including coitus, of early adolescent males is strongly differentiated by the effects of male hormones (androgens), but the effects of social controls, if they exist, are so uniform that they do not have explanatory power in microanalysis. Sexual motivation and noncoital sexual behavior of early adolescent white females are substantially influenced by androgens, but their coital behavior is primarily differentiated by social control processes, not hormones. [Udry and Billy, 1987].

Although there appears to be a strong relationship between hormone levels, pubertal development, and sexual activity, hormone levels cannot account for societal increases in early sexual intercourse. Also, there appear to be gender and racial differences in the ways that biological and social factors influence sexual behavior, with social psychological factors often playing an important role.

Psychosocial antecedents. Adolescents' cognitive and emotional development often lag behind their biological development. Teens who are physically capable of sexual and reproductive behavior may lack the cognitive and behavioral skills necessary to choose a responsible course of action and understand its long-term consequences and implications. Zabin, Hirsch, Smith, and Hardy (1984) reported that the majority of urban adolescents in their survey held values and attitudes consistent with responsible sexual conduct, but 83% of sexually experienced teens cited a best age for first intercourse that was older than the age at which they began having sex.

Several personality measures have been found to be associated with early onset of sexual intercourse. Adolescents generally seem to have a feeling of invulnerability and tend not to associate consequences with actions. Infallibility is a common belief among adolescents which makes them more prone to risk-taking behaviors (Chilman, 1983). In their 10-year longitudinal study, Donovan and Jessor (1985) found that adolescents who experienced sexual intercourse sooner placed a higher value on and expectation for independence and a lower value on and expectation for academic achievement; they were more socially critical, more tolerant of deviance, and less religious. In another longitudinal study (Vernon, Green, and Frothingham, 1983), levels of self-esteem did not differentiate those who became pregnant from those who did not. But Miller, Christensen, and Olson (1987) found self-esteem to be positively related to sexual intercourse experience among adolescents who believed that premarital sex was usually or always right, and negatively related to sexual intercourse among those who believed it was wrong. How self-esteem influences sexual behavior, or sexual behavior influences self-esteem, appears to depend on the normative context.

Adolescent sexual involvement and pregnancy are related to other problem behaviors. Studies of males who have become teen fathers suggest that a high percentage of them have conduct disorders and have engaged in criminal activity (Elster, Lamb, Peters, Kahn, and Tavare, 1987). Among both males and females, delinquent behavior, smoking, drinking alcohol, using drugs, and early onset of sexual intercourse tend to occur among the same teenagers (Donovan and Jessor, 1985; Mott and Haurin, 1988) and may constitute a "syndrome" of problem behavior (Donovan and Jessor, 1985; Elliot and Morse, 1989; Rodgers and Rowe, 1990).

Family antecedents. Many aspects of the family could affect adolescent sexual behavior, including parents' characteristics; family structure or configuration, family relationships, and interactions; and attitudes, values, and norms of family members (Miller and Jorgensen, 1988). One parental characteristic associated with adolescents' sexual behavior is the mother's adolescent sexual experience. The earlier the mother's first sexual experience and first birth, the earlier the daughter's sexual experience, an association that could be due to common biological or social factors (Newcomer and Udry, 1984). Adolescents with older sexually active siblings are also more likely to begin sexual activity at an earlier age (Hogan and Kitagawa, 1985).

The more years of education completed by parents, the less likely their teens are to be sexually active (Forste and Heaton, 1988; Zelnik, Kantner, and Ford, 1981). This may be explained by the finding that parents with more education tend to set more goals and put a higher value on achievement and work; and low educational goals and poor educational achievement are associated with greater sexual activity among both adolescent boys and girls (Miller and Sneesby, 1988). Teens who score high on intelligence tests, who are academically motivated, and who do well in school are less likely to initiate sexual activity at a young age (Hayes, 1987; Hofferth, 1987b).

Several studies have shown that adolescents—daughters in particular—from single-parent families are more likely to begin sexual intercourse at younger ages than their peers from two-parent families (see Forste and Heaton, 1988; Hayes, 1987; Miller and Bingham, 1989; Newcomer and Udry, 1987). The sexual activity of children in remarried or "blended" families is usually in between the levels found in stable two-parent and single-parent families (Thornton and Camburn, 1987). Rodgers (1983) reported that, in addition to living with a single parent, having older brothers predicted early adolescent sexual intercourse. Miller and Bingham (1989) did not

observe the older brother effect but did replicate the effect of parents' marital status on sexual intercourse experience. Several reasons have been suggested for the higher rates of sexual activity among teenagers in single-parent households. There is less parental supervision in single-parent homes (Dornbusch et al., 1985), both because there are fewer parents and because single mothers are more likely to work full-time than are mothers in two-parent households. Also, among single parents who are dating, their own sexual behavior may have a role-model effect. Adolescents and parents who have experienced divorce also have more permissive attitudes about sexual intercourse outside of marriage (Thornton and Camburn, 1987).

A number of studies have focused on sexual socialization and communication within the family, but results have been inconsistent. For example, some find more communication associated with a lower probability of adolescent sex or greater use of birth control (Fox and Inazu, 1980; Furstenberg, Moore, and Peterson, 1985). However, another study (Kahn, Smith, and Roberts, 1984) indicates that, while increased communication with the mother was associated with a lower likelihood of sex, boys who discussed a larger number of sexual topics with their fathers were more likely to have had premarital intercourse. Miller, McCoy, Olson, and Wallace (1986) reported a curvilinear association between parental supervision and adolescent sexual behavior, such that the lowest levels of attitudinal permissiveness and sexual activity were found among teens whose parents were moderately strict, with higher levels among teens who perceived their parents as very strict and the highest levels among teens wose parents were the least strict. On the other hand, a prospective study did not identify communication as a predictor of sexual initiation (Newcomer and Udry, 1985). Moore, Simms, and Betsey (1986) found parent-teen communication to have no overall association with whether youth had sex; however, when the nationally representative sample was partitioned according to the parents' values, daughters of traditional parents who had communicated about sex were found less likely to have had sex than daughters of more liberal parents or daughters of consevative parents who had not communicated about sex. Similar interaction effects have been reported by Fisher (1989), Miller, Dyk, and Norton (1990), and

Weinstein and Thornton (1989).

Positive affect between parent and child increase the probability that family values will be transmitted successfully (Weinstein and Thornton, 1989), whether parental values are liberal or conservative. Adolescent girls whose parents exert greater supervision of their dating report less sexual activity (Miller, McCoy, and Olson, 1986) and are less likely to become pregnant (Hogan and Kitagawa, 1985). Also, Baker, Thalberg, and Morrison (1988) reported that parental norms accounted for 5% of the variance in whether adolescents had experienced intercourse. Fathers' approval of the child's sexual activity accounted for the greatest proportion of the variance, which indicates a need to examine the influence not only of father presence or absence but of paternal values and communication.

Several explanations may account for these mixed family findings. Samples differ greatly, as do measures; some studies rely on adolescent reports of parent attitudes, while others have data from one or both parents as well as youth; some studies employ cross-sectional data, while others measure both attitudes and behavior over time. Future studies should obtain prospective data from both parents and from children on attitudes, communication, and parent-child closeness.

Peer influences. Peer group influence can affect behaviors, as has been demonstrated in studies of delinquency, drug abuse, smoking, and many other behaviors of teenagers (Yamaguchi and Kandell, 1987). High peer involvement tends to work against and sometimes overrides the effects of parental involvement. Among youth from 12 to 17 years old in a recent Harris Poll (1986), social pressure was identified by 73% of girls and 50% of boys as a reason why adolescents do not wait until they are older to have sexual intercourse. Newcomer, Gilbert, and Udry (1980) have argued that sexual behavior and attitudes are more closely related to what adolescents *perceive* as the behavior and values of their peers rather than what peers really do. Billy and Udry (1985) attempted to test more adequately the peer influence hypothesis through longitudinal peer network studies in which actual friendship matches could be made. They reported that the sexual behavior of white girls was influenced by the behavior of their best male and female friends; that is, girls who were virgins when the study

began were more likely to have intercourse between waves of the survey if they had sexually experienced friends. In contrast, white males appeared to pick their friends on the basis of prior sexual activity, rather than be influenced by friends' behavior. Blacks appeared neither to be influenced by friends' sexual behavior nor to pick their friends on that basis (Billy, Rodgers, and Udry, 1984; Billy and Udry, 1985). Using the same unique data on actual rather than perceived responses of siblings and peers, Rodgers and Rowe (1990) found that both best friends' and siblings' sexual and other mildly deviant behaviors predicted these behaviors among young adolescents.

Compared to their peers who have not had intercourse, teenage girls who are sexually active appear to be more susceptible to pressure from their male partners (Cvetkovich, Grote, Lieberman, and Miller, 1978). Early and steady dating are strongly related to permissive attitudes and to early and later sexual behavior among both males and females (Miller, McCoy, and Olson, 1986; Thornton, 1990). Sexual activity is high for girls who lack effective communication skills and perceive the expectation of sexual activity from their partner (Jorgensen, King, and Torrey, 1980).

Sociocultural antecedents. Adolescent sexual behavior is strongly influenced by cultural norms. Visually apparent changes in secondary sexual characteristics are signals to the individual and to others of the adolescent's sexual potential, but sociocultural factors determine how that potential will be expressed (Chilman, 1983). It has been argued (DeLamater, 1981) that social institutions, especially the family and religion, control sexuality in three ways. First, these institutions provide a specific perspective on the meaning of sexuality that defines the norms for individual conduct. Second, persons in institutional roles use these norms about the meaning of sexual behavior as the basis for informal controls. Third, formal rules often constrain sexual behavior through fear of institutional sanctions.

Religion has been found to be strongly related to adolescent sexual intercourse. The tendency to be devout and observant of religious custom and teaching is more important than any specific affiliation. Young women aged 15–19 who said religion was important to them and who attended church more frequently were less likely to report having had sexual intercourse (Forste and Heaton, 1988). Several studies (Miller and Olson, 1988; Thornton and Camburn, 1987) have found that adolescents who were members of churches that teach sexual abstinence before marriage were significantly less likely to have had sexual intercourse, compared to those affiliated with other denominations. However, the highest level of premarital intercourse occurs among those with no religious affiliation. The most recent and sophisticated study of religion and adolescent sexual behavior (Thornton and Camburn, 1989) shows that the effects operate in both directions; more religious adolescents are less likely to engage in sexual intercourse, and adolescents who become sexually active at young ages have a tendency to become less religious.

Living in poverty is associated with both early sexual activity and early pregnancy. As socioeconomic status decreases, rates of sexual activity and early pregnancy rise (Hogan and Kitagawa, 1985; Moore et al., 1986). This effect may operate through a perceived lack of options and desirable alternatives for the future. It may also operate through community norms and supervision practices. One study has linked social and economic variation among neighborhoods with levels of sexual activity among black female teens (Hogan and Kitagawa, 1985).

Race is one of the most powerful factors differentiating early from later initiators of sexual activity. There are large black-white differences in sexual activity in the raw data, and these differences do not disappear when controls for other factors, including poverty status, are introduced. There is some evidence for mediating differences in attitudes of blacks and whites. Blacks appear to be more tolerant of sexual activity outside marriage, rate marriage as less important than do whites, and perceive a greater tolerance in their neighborhood for an out-of-wedlock birth (Moore and Peterson, 1989; Moore et al., 1986). Furstenberg, Morgan, Moore, and Peterson (1987) tested three explanations for racial differences in the prevalence and timing of adolescent sexual behavior. The results offered limited support for a demographic-composition argument and stronger support for a contextual-subgroup argument. For example, blacks in a predominantly black school were much more likely to report ever having intercourse than were blacks in racially integrated schools. The relative influences of individual, family, and community-level factors represent a promising area for further research.

CONTRACEPTION AND PREGNANCY

Few teenagers report wanting to become pregnant when they begin having sex. However, among youth aged 17 or younger when they first had sex, more than 1 in 10 whites and 1 in 5 blacks reported that they either didn't think about pregnancy or they didn't care whether a pregnancy occurred (Moore and Peterson, 1989). Despite the preference of most adolescents to avoid pregnancy, teens in the United States have a higher rate of pregnancy than in any other industrialized democracy (Jones et al., 1985). In addition, rates of pregnancy, after rising in the 1970s, have remained high through 1985, the last year for which data are available. As shown in Table 1, 9.9% of all females aged 15–19 were estimated to become pregnant in 1974. By 1980, the proportion had risen to 11.1%, and it has remained near that level during the 1980s.

Since levels of sexual activity in most other Westernized countries are comparable to levels in the United States (Jones et al., 1985), the reason for the relatively high pregnancy rates among American youth seems to be less adequate contraception. Researchers have repeatedly found that U.S. teens are slow to adopt contraception. About two-thirds of never-married teens exposed to the risk of unintended pregnancy report currently using a method (primarily the pill), but only about half of females aged 15–19 in 1982 reported using some method of contraception at first intercourse (Bachrach and Mosher, 1984).

TABLE 1. AMONG ALL FEMALES AGED 15–19, THE PERCENTAGE EACH YEAR WHO BECAME PREGNANT, HAD A LEGAL ABORTION, OR GAVE BIRTH

Behavior	1974	1976	1978	1980	1982	1984	1985
Became pregnant	9.9%	10.1%	10.5%	11.1%	11.0%	10.9%	11.0%
Had a legal abortion	2.7	3.4	4.0	4.3	4.3	4.3	4.4
Gave birth	5.8	5.3	5.2	5.3	5.3	5.1	5.1

Among women aged 15–24 making their first family planning visit to a doctor or clinic in 1982, only 17% came before having intercourse. Another 10% made their initial visit the same month. For the remaining 73%, the median delay between first intercourse and first visit was 23 months (Mosher and Horn, 1989). Of course, many of these young women used nonmedical methods of contraception in the interim, at least some of the time. Unfortunately, the risk of pregnancy for nonmedical methods is very high. Only 10–20% of sexually active teens do not use contaception of any kind (Moore and Peterson, 1989; Sonenstein et al., 1989). The pill is the primary and most effective method used by sexually active teenagers (Hayes, 1987; Jones and Forrest, 1989); but it is expensive, involves contact with the medical establishment, and is believed by many teens to be harmful. Even among pill users, 18% of nonwhite and 9% of white teen users experience pregnancy in the first 12 months of use (Jones and Forrest, 1989). High as these proportions are, they are considerably lower than those found for nonusers (Koenig and Zelnik, 1982).

Recent data suggest that an increase in condom use occurred in the second half of the 1980s. Sonenstein and colleagues (1989) compared data for males aged 17–19 interviewed in 1979 with data for comparable males in 1988. They reported that condom use more than doubled—from 20% to 54% at first intercourse and from 21% to 58% at most recent sex. Still, 4 in 10 unmarried males aged 17–19 in 1988 used no method or only an ineffective method at first intercourse, as did 2 in 10 at most recent intercourse.

Why are American teenagers so slow to initiate contraception and relatively ineffective in its use? To answer these questions, it is necessary to consider what it means for teenagers to use contraception (Byrne and Fisher, 1983; Hofferth, 1987a; Nathanson and Becker, 1983; Whitley and Schofield, 1986). At the most basic level, the adolescent has to recognize that he or she is or will be sexually active. The young person also has to understand that sexual intercourse leads to pregnancy and that methods of birth control can prevent pregnancy. The possibility that pregnancy could happen has to be personalized, and the adolescent has to feel that pregnancy would be a negative occurrence. In addition, the social, economic, and psychic costs of obtaining and using a method of birth control must be weighed against the perceived risks and costs of pregnancy. The use of contraception may need to be negotiated with the partner. Moreover, this calculation must be repeated regularly, since most birth control methods require action on a daily basis or with every act of sex.

The complexity of this process provides a partial explanation for both the poor contraceptive behavior of adolescents and the inadequacy of existing research. Some studies have focused on the use of contraception at first intercourse; others have examined most recent sex; others have tried to summarize usage into global categories of accuracy or consistency such as *always, sometimes,* and *never.* A critical task for future research will be to find better ways to measure and explain contraceptive use.

Antecedents of Contraceptive Use

Psychosocial antecedents. Among the most crucial predictors of contraceptive use are the ability to recognize oneself as sexually active without guilt and the capacity to take action based on that recognition (Gerrard, 1987; Gruber and Chambers, 1987; Holmbeck, Gasiewski, and Crossman, 1989; Whitley and Schofield, 1986; Winter, 1988). These abilities develop with cognitive and psychological maturity, increasing with age as youth recognize that to be sexually active is more normative for older than for younger teens (Cvetkovich and Grote, 1981; Winter, 1988). In addition, older teens have more information about birth control, including where to obtain a method, are more likely to plan their first intercourse, are less likely to fear having their parents informed, and are more likely to have access to money and transportation so that they can obtain contraception. For all of these reasons, one of the strongest and most consistent predictors of contraceptive use is the age of the adolescent (Brooks-Gunn and Furstenberg, 1989; Hofferth, 1987a; Moore and Peterson, 1989; Zabin and Clark, 1981). Part of the reason for the higher contraceptive use of white teens is their older age at initiation. In their late teens, blacks are about as likely to use birth control as whites (Hofferth, 1987a; Moore and Peterson, 1989; Sonenstein et al., 1989). Another explanation for racial differences in contraceptive use is that unplanned pregnancy is viewed as a more negative consequence by white than nonwhite adolescents (Swenson, Erickson, Ehlinger, Carlson, and Swaney, 1989).

As teens become more sexually experienced, they tend to become more consistent contraceptors (Hofferth, 1987a). In part this is a reflection of the declining embarrassment of obtaining and using contraception. Adolescent males report considerable embarrassment over buying condoms, discussing it with their partner, putting it on, and possibly losing their erection (Sonenstein et al., 1989). Females might feel even greater embarrassment about seeking contraceptives, given that they usually must go to a doctor or clinic (Cvetkovich and Grote, 1981). Teens in stable relationships are more likely to use contraception, though we lack specific understanding of these partner influences (Hofferth, 1987a).

There is an association between high educational expectations, school success, opportunities, and contraceptive use (Moore et al., 1986; Swenson et al., 1989). It is clear that adolescents who have high educational expectations and school success are more likely to use contraception effectively (Hayes, 1987). This is generally regarded as a reflection of higher motivation to prevent pregnancy among teens who are better students, but it may also reflect a less adequate understanding about the use and effects of birth control and a lower capacity among less able teens to manage the rather demanding tasks of obtaining and using contraception. Philliber, Namerow, Kaye, and Kunkes (1983) found that those who used effective contraception at last intercourse were higher in their assessment of the risk of pregnancy, lower on perceived advantages and higher on perceived disadvantages of pregnancy, unlikely to abort in the event of pregnancy, and low in their assessment of the disadvantages of birth control.

Since sexual activity is more common among adolescents who are disadvantaged and who have academic problems and low educational expectations, their poorer contraceptive use makes pregnancy a relatively more likely occurrence. One of the thorniest research and policy questions with regard to adolescent pregnancy is to discover the predictors of consistent contraceptive use among youth who do *not* have high aspirations or high expectations for their present or future.

Family factors. The role of the family can range from being a source of information regarding birth control, including being a companion at the first family planning visit and paying the costs, to opposing the use of contraception as part of family opposition to early sexual activity. Adolescent contraceptive use can range from rebellion against parental authority to responsible behavior that conforms to family norms (Nathanson and Becker, 1986). Adolescents whose parents accept or approve of teenage sexuality are more likely to use contraceptives (Baker, Thalberg, and Morrison, 1988). In general, parental communication about contraception and support for contraceptive use seems to increase its use (Hayes, 1987). For example, in a test of Fishbein's model, Jorgensen and Sonstegard (1984) found that sexually active females were more likely to use contraception consistently if they felt their parents supported this decision and they were motivated to comply with their parents. Parents whose marriages are disrupted or who never married have been found to be more likely to discuss sex, pregnancy, and birth control than parents in intact marriages (Moore and Peterson, 1989).

Peers. The role of peers in the initiation and maintenance of contraceptive use is assumed to be important, but relatively little is known about this topic. Although parents and relatives are the leading source of referral (51%) for young women who go to private doctors for family planning services, friends are the leading referral source (44%) for young women who attend clinics (Mosher and Horn, 1989). Partners are rarely a source of referral, but peers and partners seem to be involved when parents are not. Perhaps peer support is a fallback strategy when parental disapproval precludes their involvement in contraceptive seeking (Nathanson and Becker, 1986). The role of parents, peers, and sexual partners ranks high among topics for further research on adolescent contraceptive use.

Sociocultural antecedents. The availability of family planning services for sexually active teens has been shown to reduce the incidence of childbearing (Anderson and Cope, 1987; Hayes, 1987); but nonuse and inadequate use among teens provide substantial room for more efficient policies and programs. Use of birth control increases dramatically after age 20, remaining relatively constant from age 25 to the end of the reproductive years (Westoff, 1988). With current technology, Westoff (1988) estimates that universal use among teenagers would reduce their unintended pregnancy rate by 35% among whites and 63% among blacks. However, sex education programs as currently constituted do not seem to have much effect on behavior (Dawson, 1986; Hayes, 1987; Marsiglio and Mott, 1986). The mass media in their varied forms rarely mention contraception, though a study of a direct mail campaign to adolescent males showed a slight increase in ordering condoms by mail (Kirby, Harvey, Claussenius, and Novar, 1989). Confidentiality, convenience, and low cost draw teenagers who seek birth control to clinics; however, as noted above, most arrive only after substantial delay. Several clinic studies have examined counseling and service strategies to improve contraceptive use, but only modest results have been reported to date (e.g., Namerow, Weatherby, and Williams-Kaye, 1989). Interestingly, while religious young women are more likely to postpone sexual activity, they are less likely to use a medical method of contraception if they do have sex (Studer and Thornton, 1987). There is great need for studies of how, where, and when which types of education or services will encourage teenagers—both male and female—to initiate contraception simultaneously with sexual debut and to use contraception consistently and correctly thereafter.

PREGNANCY RESOLUTION

Major changes have occurred in the disposition of teenage pregnancies in the past two decades. The proportion of all pregnancies to teens aged 15–19 ending in abortion has risen from 29% in 1974 to 42% in 1985 (Moore, 1989). During the same time marriage has declined precipitously among teens who carry their pregnancies to term. The proportion of births to teens that occur inside marriage has fallen from 70% in 1970 to 51% in 1980 and 36% in 1987.

Once an adolescent becomes pregnant, she (and often her parents and/or partner) faces several options. She could have an abortion. If she is unmarried, she could marry the father if he is available and willing to marry or she could (at least theoretically) marry someone else. Alternatively, she could have the baby and either relinquish it for adoption or raise it herself, with or without the assistance of her family, the father, and/or his family. Research describing this decision-making process and identifying the determinants of resolution choices is in short supply. Recent studies on adolescent responses to hypothetical unplanned pregnancies have produced insights into the pregnancy resolution preferences and intentions of adolescent males and females by race (Marsiglio, 1989; Marsiglio and Menaghan, 1990), and have suggested the relative influence on pregnancy resolution decisions of the adolescents' close friends and parents (Brazzell and Acock, 1988).

There are formidable obstacles to implementing a sampling plan that would actually allow researchers to study adolescent pregnancy resolution in progress over time. Because adolescents tend to underreport pregnancies ending in abortion and adoption, studies using data from nationally representative samples of teens may produce biased results. Studies that use clinic populations, on the other hand, tend to have smaller samples and, depending on the type of agency, may under- or overrepresent teens who make certain types of decisions. Despite these problems, the studies completed to date tend to be fairly consistent in terms of the factors leading to each of the outcomes described below.

Abortion

Among pregnant teens, the decision to obtain an abortion is more frequently made by teens who are enrolled in school, who have never dropped out, who are doing well in school, and who have higher educational aspirations (Carlson, Kaiser, Yeaworth, and Carlson, 1984; Eisen, Zellman, Leibowitz, Chow, and Evans, 1983; Henshaw and Silverman, 1988; Leibowitz, Eisen, and Chow, 1986; Yamaguchi and Kandell, 1987). In addition, teens who use illicit drugs are more likely to ob-

TABLE 2. THE PROPORTION OF BIRTHS OCCURRING OUTSIDE OF MARRIAGE, TO MOTHERS UNDER AGE 20

	1970	1980	1981	1982	1983	1984	1985	1986	1987
Percentage Nonmarital	30%	48%	50%	51%	54%	56%	59%	61%	64%

tain abortions (Yamaguchi and Kandell, 1987), while fundamentalist and highly religious teens are less likely to abort (Henshaw and Silverman, 1988). Once pregnant, black and white teens are equally likely to resort to abortion; the higher abortion rates among blacks are due to their higher pregnancy rates (Henshaw and Van Vort, 1989). Young women with liberal attitudes concerning abortion are, not surprisingly, more likely to intend abortion should they experience an unplanned pregnancy (Brazzell and Acock, 1988), to choose abortion in the event of a premarital pregnancy (Eisen et al., 1983), and six months after abortion to be satisfied with their decision (Eisen and Zellman, 1984).

Significant others have important influences on the decision to abort. Unmarried teens who marry during pregnancy are less likely to seek abortion, while teens receiving support for abortion from their boyfriend are more likely to elect abortion (Eisen et al., 1983). Support for abortion from family members, particularly the teen's own mother and sister, and from close friends are also important influences (Brazzell and Acock, 1988; Eisen et al., 1983).

Although it is clear that legalization and accessibility increase the likelihood that an adolescent will terminate a pregnancy by abortion (Nathanson and Kim, 1989), the impact of other public policies (such as welfare benefit levels) is not clear (Moore, 1988b). There is, however, substantial state and regional variation in the incidence of abortion, with rates being from two to four times higher in California (79 abortions per 1,000 females aged 15–19 in 1985) than in some midwestern and southern states (Henshaw and Van Vort, 1989). The economic, social, and policy factors that result in such large differences within the United States merit further research (Moore, 1988b).

Marriage

Among white females under age 20, about half of all births occur outside of marriage, compared with 18% in 1970. More than 90% of births among black teens are outside of marriage, compared with two-thirds in 1970 (Moore, 1988a; National Center for Health Statistics, 1989).

The decision to have the baby outside of marriage is affected by support for this decision from the mother and from the partner (Ortiz and Nuttall, 1987). Being willing to consider having a

child out-of-wedlock has also been found to predict becoming an unmarried mother, particularly among blacks (Abrahamse, Morrison, and Waite, 1988; Hanson, Myers, and Ginsburg, 1987).

The availability of welfare benefits to unmarried mothers is associated with the probability of a nonmarital birth (Leiboweitz et al., 1986; Plotnick, 1988), but the evidence concerning policy and contextual variables is scant. As with abortion, the incidence of nonmarital childbearing varies substantially across states, at least among whites. The proportion of all births to white teenagers that occur outside marriage ranges from about one-third in Alabama, Georgia, and Hawaii to nearly three-quarters in Massachusetts, Rhode Island, and Minnesota. Among blacks (in states with at least 100 births to black teens), the proportion of teen births that occur outside of marriage always exceeds 81% (Moore, 1989).

Given pregnancy, black women are substantially less likely to marry than are white women (Cutright and Smith, 1988; Nathanson and Kim, 1989). These differential marriage patterns reflect in part the lower availability of employed, marriageable men in the black community (Moore et al., 1986; Wilson, 1984). For example, among fathes of babies born to Baltimore mothers under age 18, Hardy, Duggan, Masnyk, and Pearson (1989) found that 19% of the white fathers but 40% of the black fathers were neither in school nor working. Blacks' lesser propensity to marry also seems to reflect differing attitudes about family and marriage; blacks are more accepting of nonmarital childbearing (Abrahamse et al., 1988; Moore et al., 1986).

Teenage mothers who marry receive substantially less assistance from family (Cramer, 1989b). On the other hand, those mothers who marry and remain married are more likely to escape poverty (Cramer, 1989b; Furstenberg, Brooks-Gunn, and Morgan, 1987). This may reflect a selection process whereby marriages occur among those couples most likely to be economically self-sufficient. The poor economic circumstances of young and minority fathers is likely to influence young mothers to postpone marriage. Certainly, young black mothers are more likely to remain with their parents than are white or Hispanic mothers (Cramer, 1989a; Testa, 1987; Upchurch, 1988).

Evidence suggests that teenage fathers had

lower educational expectations than nonfathers, were more likely to have dropped out of school even before the birth, and were both more likely to complete a GED and substantially less likely to complete high school than nonfathers (Marsiglio, 1987). Marsiglio found that white teen fathers were more likely to live with or marry the mother if they had lived with two parents at age 14, been raised Catholic, and lived in a rural area. Older teens were more likely to cohabit with their partner, while men with a diploma were slightly more likely to marry. No factor was identified that was related to the probability of cohabitation or marriage among black teens. Most reseach on teenage parents has focused on the mother. There is a need for additional studies of fathers and decision-making processes among couples.

Adoption

The incidence of adoption dropped sharply about the time abortion became legal. Data from surveys in 1971, 1976, and 1982 indicate that the proportion of babies born to white unwed teenagers and relinquished for adoption fell from 18% in the 1971 survey to 7% in 1976 and 1982. Among blacks, the proportion fell from 2% to under 1% (Bachrach, 1986). The propensity to relinquish now seems to have stabilized. With increasing numbers of babies born outside of marriage, the number of babies available for adoption may actually have increased recently, though not to the pre-1973 level (Bachrach, Maza, Mosher, and Ventura, 1988).

Research on the determinants of adoption is very limited and fraught with methodological problems. Resnick's (1984) review notes the importance of mothers to teenagers who relinquish and the higher social status of their families (see also Bachrach, 1986; McLaughlin, Manninen, and Winges, 1988). Teens who relinquish tend to have less influence from their male partners, and tend to have more education and to be in school more often than unmarried mothers who keep and raise their baby themselves. Results from a recent study of placers and parents among whites in Minnesota (Resnick, Blum, Smith, Bose, and Toogood, 1989) also indicate that those who relinquish are from more well-to-do families, have higher educational aspirations, and more often live with two parents. A large majority among both those who placed and those who kept their

children had friends and relatives who became pregnant as adolescents; but those who relinquished were more likely to have an adopted family member. Placers and parents had adopted friends, but placers more often had a positive view of how well their friends' adoptions had worked out.

McLaughlin and associates (1988) conducted retrospective interviews with women who parented or relinquished a child for adoption. Relinquishers who had not yet begun their last year of high school at delivery were more likely to complete further education than comparable childrearers; but no educational differences were found if the mothers were high school seniors. Relinquishers were more likely to obtain vocational training and to be working 6 and 12 months after the birth; but relinquishers and childrearers were equally satisfied with their decision. Both groups of young mothers were somewhat disadvantaged relative to nonmothers. McLaughlin and associates are now conducting a prospective study of adolescent mothers who relinquish or parent their offspring. Although such studies are difficult to conduct for ethical and practical reasons, there is a need for better understanding of the consequences of adoption.

ADOLESCENTS AS PARENTS

Parenthood

Relatively few adolescent mothers live alone with their child. Most white and Hispanic children born to mothers aged 14–19 initially live with the mother and her partner, but a substantial minority also live with other relatives. The vast majority of babies born to black teen mothers live with their mother and her relatives (Cramer, 1989a; Moore and Peterson, 1989). The proportion of adolescent mothers living with relatives declines rapidly over time among whites and more slowly among Hispanics and blacks. When their babies were age 3, 15% of white, 54% of black, and 21% of Hispanic mothers lived with relatives, while 71% of white, 20% of black, and 57% of Hispanic mothers lived with a spouse or partner. Six percent of white, 3% of black, and 11% of Hispanic mothers lived with both spouse and relatives (Cramer, 1989a).

An analysis of young, single black mothers found similar patterns; 56% shared a household with other adult kin (45% with their mother), while another 19% had mothers in the same neighborhood. Thirty-one percent of young, single white mothers lived with adult kin (23% with their mother); and another 27% had mothers who lived in the neighborhood (Hogan, Hao, and Parish, 1990). Teen mothers, especially those who did not marry, were very likely to receive help and tangible assistance from their families. For example, a grandparent provided child care to 48% of young, single black mothers and 44% of comparable white mothers (Hogan et al., 1990). Overall, young black mothers were found to have greater access to kin than comparable young white mothers, because of their greater likelihood of residing with kin and use of free child care, but not because of greater financial support from kin. However, almost a third of young, single black mothers and nearly half of young, single white mothers were not involved in a support network, defined as coresidence, receipt of half or more of income from someone other than the husband, or unpaid child care (Hogan et al., 1990).

Although teen mothers are very likely to receive welfare assistance during their child's early years (Adams, 1987), receiving substantial financial assistance both from relatives and from public programs tends to be uncommon (Cramer, 1989b). Also, receiving both financial assistance and child care from relatives is uncommon. Families tend to provide one or another type of assistance, with young white mothers more likely to receive financial assistance and black mothers more likely to live with kin. Also, mothers with just one child are more likely to get family assistance and those with two or more children are more likely to get public assistance. Similarly, Testa (1987), in a study of teen mothers on welfare in Illinois, found that the first pregnancy precipitated leaving home among whites and Hispanics; black mothers were not highly likely to leave until the birth of the second child.

Adolescent Parenting

There is a strong consensus in the developmental literature that children's emotional and cognitive development are enhanced by actively involved, nurturing, and verbally responsive parenting. In studies prior to and beginning the decade of the 1980s, adolescent mothers (and sometimes fathers) compared with older parents were re-ported to be less aware of and knowledgeable about infants' and children's developmental milestones, less sensitive to infant signals and needs, less aware of how to stimulate children's development, less inclined to spontaneous play, and less likely to spend time looking at and talking to their infants, while being more ambivalent toward motherhood and more prone to use physical punishment. A broad review of these studies, however, ends with the statement that "much of our 'knowledge' of childrearing skills of teenage mothers is based on myth rather than empirical fact. . . . Poor social-economic status, family support systems, marital stability, nutrition, and prenatal care may be far more important determinants of development for these children than the age of their mothers" (Roosa, Fitzgerald, and Carlson, 1982: 15).

By the mid-1980s it had become more evident that when adolescents are compared with older mothers, age of parent is almost unavoidably confounded with other variables, especially education and economic resources. Relatedly, investigators began to point out the diversity among teenage mothers, the competency of some teen mothers, and that there are teenage mothers who probably cannot be differentiated from older mothers except by their age at first birth (Roosa and Vaughan, 1984). Diversity in parenting behavior and multiple trajectories in the life courses of adolescent mothers are central themes reported in the long-term longitudinal follow-up of adolescent mothers who are now in mid-life (Furstenberg, Brooks-Gunn, and Morgan, 1987).

While less adequate parenting among adolescents appears to be due more to social and economic deficits than to age per se, the consequences for infants and children born to adolescents remain problematic. There is much consistency, for example, in recent studies showing that adolescents have lower scores on the HOME (Home Observation for Measurement of the Environment) Scale than do older mothers (Coll, Hoffman, and Oh, 1987; King and Fullard, 1982; Luster and Rhoades, 1989; Schilmoeller and Barnowski, 1985). Similarly, detailed behavior observations of teen and adult mother-infant interaction (Culp, Culp, Osofsky, and Osofsky, 1989) continue to repeat and refine earlier findings that adolescent mothers have a lower frequency and quality of vocalization, are less expressive, exhibit poorer quality of play and less reciprocity, and have less positive attitudes toward their infants than older mothers. Young mothers are also more likely to feel sad and blue, to feel tense and edgy, to worry about money, to lose control of their feelings, and to feel that they would not want to have children again (Moore, 1986). They are less likely to be positive about their child and about being a parent than women who became mothers in their early twenties (Moore and Peterson, 1989).

Less positive assessments of their infants is highlighted in two recent studies of adolescent mothers' perceptions. Benn and Saltz (1989) and Zeanah and associates (1987) report that the majority (63% and 67% in the studies, respectively) of infant temperament profiles completed by adolescent mothers describe their infants as "moderately difficult or difficult." These adolescent mothers' perceptions of infant temperament are in sharp contrast to the more usual 10% to 28% perceived to be "difficult" by older mothers (Carey and McDevitt, 1978). However, independent grandmothers' perceptions of the same infants rated them as much less difficult than perceived by the adolescent mothers (Benn and Saltz, 1989). This is important because evidence in the temperament literature indicates that children whose mothers perceive them as difficult are at much higher risk for later behavioral problems, even when the parents' perceptions of their child are not consistent with independent ratings by others (Bates, Maslin, and Frankel, 1985; Chess and Thomas, 1984).

Adolescent Parents and Child Abuse

During the 1980s, a link between adolescent parenthood and child abuse was suggested because, like some adolescent mothers, abusive mothers have been described as having unrealistic expectations of the child's development, being unaware of the child's needs, and having a strong belief in the value of physical punishment (Bolton, 1980). However, for the most part, the evidence (Altmeier, O'Connor, Vietze, Sandler, and Sherrod, 1984; Bolton, Laner, and Kane, 1980; Miller, 1984) does not support the hypothesis that infants of adolescent mothers are at higher *immediate* risk for child abuse and neglect than are infants of older mothers.

Some evidence is accumulating, however, for a *delayed* effect of an early birth on child abuse and

neglect. Creighton (1985) found motherhood prior to age 20 to be significantly overrepresented among 5,000 families reported for both abuse and neglect in England; during the late 1970s and early 1980s, 35% of the mothers of abused children and 30% of the mothers of neglected children were less than age 20 at their first birth, compared to 10.7% of mothers in the comparison population. Zuravin (1988) examined the number of births since the first teen birth, the mother's educational attainment, and her employment history to determine their mediating effect on reported child abuse and neglect. The number of live births was the most important chronic stressor that mediated the relationship between age at first birth and child abuse and neglect in this population of low-income, single-parent mothers. Excess fertility could have a delayed negative effect on maternal behavior for these women, as it would mean having to divide already limited material and emotional resources even further, decrease the chance of marrying and obtaining social support from a spouse, and lessen the ability of other formal and informal sources of support to provide adequate help with the children. Some evidence (Testa, 1987) suggests that subsequent births have a tendency to push adolescent mothers out of their parental home, further distancing them from an important source of social and material support (Cramer, 1989b).

ADVANCES IN THEORY, DATA, AND METHODS

Theoretical Advances

Many initial studies of adolescent childbearing were descriptive rather than theoretical. More recent studies have drawn on a number of theories developed in other areas (Miller and Fox, 1987), including problem behavior theory (Donovan and Jessor, 1985), social control theory (Hirschi, 1969), social learning theory (Bandura and Walters, 1963), the Health Belief Model (Eisen, Zellman, and McAlister, 1985), and developmental perspectives (Miller and Simon, 1980). Recent studies of genetic and hormonal influences have suggested the potential of a biosocial model (Smith, 1989) of adolescent sexual behavior. In addition, a number of researchers have taken a perspective in which teenagers are presumed to follow a more or less rational process of assessing costs versus benefits in their sexual and fertility behavior (Moore and Burt, 1982). Most recently an "opportunity cost" approach has received attention. According to this perspective, many disadvantaged and minority teenagers perceive that they have few occupational or economic opportunities and, therefore, that the occurrence of an early or out-of-wedlock birth will have little real impact on their future prospects (Hayes, 1987; Moore et al., 1986). None of these perspectives has been thoroughly researched; it is nevertheless clear that no one model will fully explain adolescent sexual, contraceptive, pregnancy, and parenting behavior.

Data

Data to address issues of adolescent fertility have become more generally available over the past decade, and most major data bases are now routinely archived in the Data Archive on Adolescent Pregnancy and Pregnancy Prevention.[3] Topics covered in the surveys of females aged 15–19, directed by John Kantner and Melvin Zelnik in 1971, 1976, and 1979, have been incorporated into the National Survey of Family Growth. The NSFG is fielded periodically by the federal government (in 1982 and 1988, and again in 1992) and includes both ever-married and never-married women aged 15 through 44. Extensive contextual variables, ranging from proximate neighborhood features to state and regional characteristics, have recently been developed and individually linked to existing NSFG survey data.[4]

Data on males have continued to be less available, but the 1979 survey of males aged 17–21 conducted by Kantner and Zelnik was replicated and expanded by Freya Sonenstein and Joseph Pleck in 1988. In addition, data on both males and females are available in the third wave of the National Survey of Children conducted in 1987 (Moore and Peterson, 1989) and in the National Longitudinal Survey of Youth (NLSY), initiated in 1979 and continued through the 1980s. Furthermore, the children of females in the NLSY have been assessed, thus providing a unique opportunity for studying the outcomes of children born to young parents.

Concern over the spread of AIDS has clarified how little is really known about the circumstances under which sex actually takes place. Little is known about teens under age 15 (the youngest age for respondents in most fertility surveys), the characteristics of sexual partners, and the situational nature of preventive behaviors. The need for data on specific episodes of sex and the factors leading to the use of a prophylactic at a given episode has become clear to the research community, although there are political and social obstacles to the collection of such data.[5]

Statistical Methods

During the past several decades, the types of statistical approaches used to study adolescent fertility have changed radically. Initial studies of adolescent parenthood generally used bivariate analysis, including perhaps one or two control variables. A second generation of studies have used multivariate analysis to control numerous confounding variables. Nevertheless, researchers who conduct multivariate studies generally recognize that potentially important variables are still unmeasured or inadequately measured, particularly intellectual ability, peer influences, partner variables, motivation, family values, and parental communication and supervision, as well as neighborhood and community influences.

In the next generation of studies, researchers need to examine some of these influences that have not yet been explored, and assess interaction among variables, such as an interaction between ability and job opportunities. Further, in forthcoming studies they need to take advantage of new methods such as event history methods to model the timing of events, endogenous switching regression models that permit control for multivariate influences and also take account of sample selectivity and sample censoring, and proportional-hazards life table methods that correct for truncation bias and allow for the analysis of several covariates simultaneously.

DISCUSSION

The fact that U.S. adolescents are subtantially more likely to experience pregnancy than their counterparts in other Western democracies indicates a continuing need for basic and applied research on early sexual activity, contraceptive use, pregnancy, and parenthood. Yet, because these adolescent issues are immersed in personal and cultural values, there are conflicting views about how research and policy agendas should be pursued. As stated by the specially convened panel of the National Research Council, "Some view the problem as early, nonmarital sexual activity: if teenagers were not engaging in sexual intercourse, they would not become pregnant. . . . Others, however, argue that changing patterns of teenage sexual behavior are the inevitable consequences of broader social trends . . . [and] believe that public programs should help teenagers guard against unintended pregnancy. . . . Still others believe that abortion is the problem. . . . Still others view the most compelling problem as neither early sexual activity nor abortion, but as teenage childbearing" (Hayes, 1987: 16–18). The recognition of values associated with adolescent fertility-related behavior is an important reality for those who study these phenomena.

During the 1980s there was a marked shift in both policy and scholarly orientations regarding adolescent pregnancy. The Office of Adolescent Pregnancy Programs (OAPP) was established in 1978 under the Department of Health and Human Services to administer care service programs for pregnant and parenting teens; but in 1981 the Title XX Adolescent Family Life Act replaced that legislation and the postponement of sexual activity became emphasized while care service programs were continued. Since 1986, AFL programs have operated under a continuing resolution, and the appropriate focus of governmental policy has been a matter of ongoing debate.

Interplay between the social-behavioral sciences and policy-making in the area of adolescent fertility-related behavior is likely to continue. From the standpoint of data, theory, and methods, however, researchers are in a better position at the beginning of the 1990s than ever before to address the critical basic questions that have so far remained unanswered.

NOTES

Appreciation is expressed to Patricia A. H. Dyk and anonymous reviewers for their help in refining this article. The production assistance of Margaret Daly is gratefully acknowledged. Correspondence and requests for reprints may be sent to either author.

1. Several excellent summaries of these issues appeared in the late 1980s. See Brooks-Gunn and Furstenberg (1989), Furstenberg, Brooks-Gunn, and Chase-Lansdale (1989), Hayes (1987), and Hofferth and Hayes (1987).

2. Space limitations preclude coverage of other relevant issues. See Jones et al. (1985), United Nations

(1988), and Rodman and Trost (1986) for international perspectives. See Card (1989), Hofferth (1989), Zabin and Hirsch (1987), and Weatherly, Perlman, Levine, and Klerman (1986) for examples and evaluations of recent adolescent prevention and intervention programs. A discussion of the consequences of early childbearing appears in a longer version of this paper, which can be obtained from either author (see also Hayes, 1987).

3. The Data Archive on Adolescent Pregnancy and Pregnancy Prevention is operated by Sociometrics Corporation, 170 State Street, Suite 260, Los Altos, CA 94022-2812, (415) 949-3282.

4. This work was done by John O. G. Billy, Battelle Human Affairs Research Centers, Seattle, WA 98105.

5. A major data collection effort is under development at the University of North Carolina to study the behaviors that put adolescents at risk of AIDS, other STDs, and pregnancy. This would be a nationally representative, longitudinal survey of approximately 20,000 adolescent males and females in grades 7 through 11 from a sample of 200 schools; it would include considerable information about peer networks as a context that affects adolescent behaviors.

REFERENCES

Abrahamse, Allan F., P. A. Morrison, and L. J. Waite. 1988. "Teenagers willing to consider single parenthood: Who is at greater risk?" Family Planning Perspectives 20: 13–18.

Adams, Gina C. 1987. "The dynamics of welfare recipiency among adolescent mothers." Memorandum of March 17, Human Resources and Community Development Division, Congressional Budget Office, Washington, DC.

Altmeier, William A., S. O'Connor, P. Vietze, H. Sandler, and K. Sherrod. 1984." Prediction of child abuse: A prospective study of feasibility." Child Abuse and Neglect 21: 393–400.

Anderson, John E., and L. G. Cope. 1987. "The impact of family planning program activity on fertility." Family Planning Perspectives 19: 152–157.

Bachrach, Christine A. 1986. "Adoption plans, adopted children, and adoptive mothers." Journal of Marriage and the Family 48: 243–253.

Bachrach, Christine A., P. Maza, W. Mosher, and S. Ventura. 1988. "The adoption squeeze: Demographic trends affecting adoption." Working paper, National Center for Health Statistics, Hyattsville, MD.

Bachrach, Christine A., and W. Mosher. 1984. "Use of contraception in the United States, 1982." Advance Data from Vital and Health Statistics 102.

Baker, Sharon A., S. P. Thalberg, and D. M. Morrison. 1988. "Parents' behavioral norms as predictors of adolescent sexual activity and contraceptive use." Adolescence 23: 265–282.

Bandura, Albert, and R. H. Walters. 1963. Social

Learning and Personality Development. New York: Holt.

Bates, John E., C. A. Maslin, and K. A. Frankel. 1985. "Attachment security, mother-child interaction, and temperament as predictors of behavior problem rating at age three years." In I. Bretherton and E. Waters (eds.), Growing Points of Attachment Theory and Research. Monographs of the Society for Research in Child Development 50: 167–193.

Benn, Rita, and E. Saltz. 1989. "The effects of grandmother support on teen parenting and infant attachment patterns within the family." Paper presented at the meeting of the Society for Research in Child Development, Kansas City, MO.

Billy, John O. G., J. L. Rodgers, and J. R. Udry. 1984. "Adolescent sexual behavior and friendship choice." Social Forces 62: 653–678.

Billy, John O. G., and J. R. Udry. 1985. "The influence of male and female best friends on adolescent sexual behavior." Adolescence 20: 21–32.

Bolton, Frank G., Jr. 1980. The Pregnant Adolescent: Problems of Premature Parenthood. Beverly Hills, CA: Sage.

Bolton, Frank, Jr., R. H. Laner, and S. P. Kane. 1980. "Child maltreatment risk among adolescent mothers: A study of reported cases." American Journal of Orthopsychiatry 50: 489–504.

Brazzell, Jan F., and A. C. Acock. 1988. "Influence of attitudes, significant others, and aspirations on how adolescents intend to resolve a premarital pregnancy." Journal of Marriage and the Family 50: 413–425.

Brooks-Gunn, Jeanne, and F. F. Furstenberg. 1989. "Adolescent sexual behavior." American Psychologist 44: 249–257.

Byrne, Donn, and W. A. Fisher. 1983. Adolescents, Sex, and Contraception. Hillsdale, NJ: Erlbaum.

Card, Josephina J. (ed.). 1989. Evaluating Programs Aimed at Preventing Teenage Pregnancies. Palo Alto, CA: Sociometrics Corporation.

Carey, William B., and S. C. McDevitt. 1978. "Revision of the infant temperament questionnaire." Pediatrics 61: 735–739.

Carlson, Mary L., K. Laux Kaiser, R. C. Yeaworth, and R. E. Carlson. 1984. "An exploratory study of life-change events, social support, and pregnancy decisions in adolescents." Adolescence 19: 765–780.

Chess, Stella, and A. Thomas. 1984. Origins and Evolutions of Behavior Disorders: From Infancy to Early Adult Life. New York: Brunner/Mazel.

Chilman, Catherine S. 1983. Adolescent Sexuality in a Changing American Society: Social and Psychological Perspectives for the Human Services Professions. New York: Wiley and Sons.

Coll, Cynthia T. G., J. Hoffman, and W. Oh. 1987. "The social ecology and early parenting of Caucasian adolescent mothers." Child Development 58: 955–963.

Cramer, James C. 1989a. "Early childbearing and family structure." Paper presented to the Graduate Group in Demography, University of California, Berkeley.

Cramer, James C. 1989b. "Patterns of poverty and financial assistance among premature mothers." Paper presented at the annual meetings of the Population Association of America, Baltimore, MD (March 31).

Creighton, S. 1985. "Epidemiological study of abused children and their families in the United Kingdom between 1977 and 1982." Child Abuse and Neglect 9: 441–448.

Culp, Rex E., A. M. Culp, J. D. Osofsky, and H. J. Osofsky. 1989. "Adolescent and older mothers: Comparison of their interaction with their six-month-old infants." Paper presented at the meeting of the Society for Research in Child Development, Kansas City, MO.

Cutright, Phillips, and H. L. Smith. 1988. "Intermediate determinants of racial differences in 1980 U.S. nonmarital fertility areas." Family Planning Perspectives 20: 119–123.

Cvetkovich, George, and B. Grote. 1981. "Psychosocial maturity and teenage contraceptive use: An investigation of decision making and communication skills." Population and Environment 4: 211–225.

Cvetkovich, George, B. Grote, E. J. Lieberman, and W. Miller. 1978. "Sex role development and teenage fertility-related behavior." Adolescence 13: 231–236.

Dawson, Deborah Anne. 1986. "The effects of sex education on adolescent behavior." Family Planning Perspectives 18: 162–184.

DeLamater, John. 1981. "The social control of sexuality." Annual Review of Sociology 7: 263–290.

Donovan, John E., and R. Jessor. 1985. "Structure of problem behavior in adolescence and young adulthood." Journal of Consulting and Clinical Psychology 53: 890–904.

Dornbusch, Sanford M., J. M. Carlsmith, S. J. Bushwall, P. L. Ritter, H. Leiderman, A. H. Hastorf, and R. T. Gross. 1985. "Single parents, extended households, and the control of adolescents." Child Development 56: 326–341.

Dornbusch, Sanford M., J. M. Carlsmith, R. T. Gross, J. A. Martin, D. Jennings, A. Rosenberg, and P. Duke. 1981. "Sexual development, age and dating: A comparison of biological and social influences upon one set of behaviors." Child Development 52: 179–185.

Eisen, Marvin, and G. L. Zellman. 1984. "Factors predicting pregnancy resolution decision satisfaction of unmarried adolescents." Journal of Genetic Psychology 145: 231–239.

Eisen, Marvin, G. L. Zellman, A. Leibowitz, W. K. Chow, and J. R. Evans. 1983. "Factors discriminating pregnancy resolution decisions of unmarried adolescents." Genetic Psychology Monographs 103: 69–95.

Eisen, Marvin, G. M. Zellman, and A. McAlister. 1985. "A health belief model approach to adolescents' fertility control: Some pilot program findings." Health Education Quarterly 12: 185–216.

Elliott, Delbert S., and B. J. Morse. 1989. "Delinquency and drug use as risk factors in teenage sexual activity." Youth and Society 21: 32–60.

Elster, Arthur B., M. Lamb, L. Peters, J. Kahn, and J. Tavare. 1987. "Judicial involvement and conduct problems of fathers of infants born to adolescent mothers." Pediatrics 79: 230–234.

Fisher, Terri D. 1989. "Family sexual communication and adolescent sexual behavior." Journal of Marriage and the Family 51: 637–639.

Forste, Renata T., and T. B. Heaton. 1988. "Initiation of sexual activity among female adolescents." Youth and Society 19: 250–268.

Fox, Greer L., and J. K. Inazu. 1980. "Patterns and outcomes of mother-daughter communication about sexuality." Journal of Social Issues 36: 7–29.

Furstenberg, Frank F., J. Brooks-Gunn, and L. Chase-Lansdale. 1989. "Teenage pregnancy and childbearing." American Psychologist 44: 313–320.

Furstenberg, Frank F., J. Brooks-Gunn, and S. P. Morgan. 1987. Adolescent Mothers in Later Life. Cambridge: Cambridge University Press.

Furstenberg, Frank F., Jr., K. A. Moore, and J. L. Peterson. 1985. "Sex education and sexual experience among adolescents." American Journal of Public Health 75: 1331–1332.

Furstenberg, Frank F., Jr., S. P. Morgan, K. A. Moore, and J. L. Peterson. 1987. "Race differences in the timing of first intercourse." American Sociological Review 52: 511–518.

Gerrard, Meg. 1987. "Sex, sex guilt, and contraceptive use revisited: The 1980's." Journal of Personality and Social Psychology 52: 975–980.

Gershenson, Harold, J. Musick, H. Ruch-Ross, V. Magee, K. Rubino, and D. Rosenberg. 1989. "The prevalence of coercive sexual experience among teenage mothers." Journal of Interpersonal Violence 4: 204–219.

Gruber, Enid, and C. V. Chambers. 1987. "Cognitive development and adolescent contraception: Integrating theory and practice." Adolescence 22: 661–670.

Hanson, Sandra L., D. E. Myers, and A. L. Ginsburg. 1987. "The role of responsibility and knowledge in reducing teenage out-of-wedlock childbearing." Journal of Marriage and the Family 49: 241–256.

Hardy, Janet B., A. K. Duggan, K. Masnyk, and C. Pearson. 1989. "Fathers of children born to young urban mothers." Family Planning Perspectives 21: 159–163.

Harris, Louis, and Associates. 1986. American Teens Speak: Sex, Myths, TV, and Birth Control. New York: Louis Harris and Associates.

Hayes, Cheryl (ed.). 1987. Risking the Future: Adolescent Sexuality, Pregnancy, and Childbearing (Vol. 1). Washington, DC: National Academy Press.

Henshaw, Stanley K., and J. Silverman. 1988. "The characteristics and prior contraceptive use of U.S. abortion patients." Family Planning Perspectives 20: 158–168.

Henshaw, Stanley K., and J. Van Vort. 1989. "Teenage abortion, birth, and pregnancy statistics: An update." Family Planning Perspectives 21: 85–88.

Hirschi, T. 1969. Causes of Delinquency. Berkeley: University of California Press.

Hofferth, Sandra L. 1989. "Programs for high risk adolescents: What works?" Evaluation and Program Planning 20: 1–34.

Hofferth, Sandra L. 1987a. "Contraceptive decision-making among adolescents." Pp. 56–77 in Sandra L. Hofferth and Cheryl D. Hayes (eds.), Risking the Future: Adolescent Sexuality, Pregnancy, and Childbearing (Vol. 2). Washington, DC: National Academy Press.

Hofferth, Sandra L. 1987b. "Factors affecting initiation of sexual intercourse." Pp. 7–35 in Sandra L. Hofferth and Cheryl D. Hayes (eds.), Risking the Future: Adolescent Sexuality, Pregnancy, and Childbearing (Vol. 2). Washington, DC: National Academy Press.

Hofferth, Sandra L., and C. D. Hayes (eds.). 1987. Risking the Future: Adolescent Sexuality, Pregnancy, and Childbearing (Vol. 2). Working Papers and Statistical Appendixes. Washington, DC: National Academy Press.

Hogan, Dennis P., L. Hao, and W. L. Parish. 1990. "Race, kin networks, and assistance to mother-headed families." Social Forces 68: 797–812.

Hogan, Dennis, and E. Kitagawa. 1985. "The impact of social status, family structure, and neighborhood on the fertility of black adolescents." American Journal of Sociology 90: 825–836.

Holmbeck, Grayson N., E. Gasiewski, and R. Crossman. 1989. "Cognitive development, egocentrism, and adolescent contraceptive knowledge, attitudes, and behavior." Paper presented at the meeting of the Society for Research in Child Development, Kansas City, MO.

Jones, Elise, and J. Forrest. 1989. "Contraceptive failure in the United States: Revised estimates from the 1982 National Survey of Family Growth." Family Planning Perspectives 21: 103–109.

Jones, Elise, J. Forrest, N. Goldman, S. Henshaw, R. Lincoln, J. Rosoff, C. Westoff, and D. Wulf. 1985. "Teenage pregnancy in developed countries: Determinants and policy implications." Family Planning Perspectives 17: 53–63.

Jorgensen, Stephen R., S. L. King, and B. A. Torrey. 1980. "Dyadic and social network influences on adolescent exposure to pregnancy risk." Journal of Marriage and the Family 42: 141–155.

Jorgensen, Stephen R., and J. S. Sonstegard. 1984. "Predicting adolescent sexual and contraceptive behavior: An application and test of the Fishbein model." Journal of Marriage and the Family 46: 43–55.

Kahn, Joan R., K. W. Smith, and E. J. Roberts. 1984. "Family communication and adolescent sexual behavior." Unpublished manuscript, American Institutes for Research, Cambridge, MA.

King, Timothy, and W. Fullard. 1982. "Teenage mothers and their infants: New findings on the home environment." Journal of Adolescence 5: 333–346.

Kirby, Douglas, P. D. Harvey, D. Claussenius, and M. Novar. 1989. "A direct mailing to teenage males about condom use: Its impact on knowledge, attitudes, and sexual behavior." Family Planning Perspectives 21: 12–18.

Koenig, Michael A., and M. Zelnik. 1982. "The risk of

premarital first pregnancy among metropolitan-area teenagers: 1976–1979." Family Planning Perspectives 14: 239–247.

Leibowitz, Arleen, M. Eisen, and W. K. Chow. 1986. "An economic model of teenage pregnancy decision-making." Demography 23: 67–77.

London, Kathryn, W. Mosher, W. Pratt, and L. Williams. 1989. "Preliminary findings from the NSFG, Cycle IV." Paper presented at the annual meeting of the Population Association of America, Baltimore, MD.

Luster, Tom, and K. Rhoades. 1989. "The relation between child-rearing beliefs and the home environment in a sample of adolescent mothers." Family Relations 38: 317–322.

Marsiglio, William. 1987. "Adolescent fathers in the United States: Their initial living arrangements, marital experience, and educational outcomes." Family Planning Perspectives 19: 240–252.

Marsiglio, William. 1989. "Adolescent males' pregnancy resolution preferences and family formation intentions: Does family background make a difference for blacks and whites?" Journal of Adolescent Research 4: 214–237.

Marsiglio, William, and E. G. Menaghan. 1990. "Pregnancy resolution and family formation: Understanding gender differences in adolescents' preferences and beliefs." Journal of Family Issues 11: in press.

Marsiglio, William, and F. L. Mott. 1986. "The impact of sex education on sexual activity, contraceptive use, and premarital pregnancy among American teenagers." Family Planning Perspectives 18: 151–161.

McCabe, Marita P., and J. K. Collins. 1984. "Measurement of depth of desired and experienced sexual involvement at different stages of dating." Journal of Sex Research 20: 377–390.

McLaughlin, Steven D., D. L. Manninen, and L. D. Winges. 1988. "Do adolescents who relinquish their children fare better or worse than those who raise them? Family Planning Perspectives 20: 25–32.

Miller, Brent C., and C. R. Bingham. 1989. "Family configuration in relation to the sexual behavior of female adolescents." Journal of Marriage and the Family 51: 499–506.

Miller, Brent C., R. Christensen, and T. D. Olson. 1987. "Self-esteem in relation to adolescent sexual attitudes and behavior." Youth and Society 18: 93–111.

Miller, Brent C., P. A. H. Dyk, and M. Norton. 1990. "Parental values, parent-child communication, and adolescent sexual behavior." Under review.

Miller, Brent C., and G. L. Fox. 1987. "Theories of adolescent heterosexual behavior." Journal of Adolescent Research 2: 269–282.

Miller, Brent C., and S. R. Jorgensen. 1988. "Adolescent fertility-related behavior and its family linkages." In D. Klein and J. Aldous (eds.), Social Stress and Family Development. New York: Guilford Press.

Miller, Brent C., J. K. McCoy, and T. D. Olson. 1986. "Dating age and stage as correlates of adolescent sexual attitudes and behavior." Journal of Adolescent Research 1: 361–371.

Miller, Brent C., J. K. McCoy, T. D. Olson, and C. M. Wallace. 1986. "Parental discipline and control attempts in relation to adolescent sexual attitudes and behavior." Journal of Marriage and the Family 48: 503–512.

Miller, Brent C., and T. D. Olson. 1988. "Sexual attitudes and behavior of high school students in relation to background and contextual factors." Journal of Sex Research 24: 194–200.

Miller, Brent C., and K. R. Sneesby. 1988. "Educational correlates of adolescents' sexual attitudes and behavior." Journal of Youth and Adolescence 17: 521–530.

Miller, Patricia Y., and W. Simon. 1980. "The development of sexuality in adolescence." Pp. 383–407 in J. Adelson (ed.), Handbook of Adolescent Psychology. New York: Wiley.

Miller, Shelby H. 1984. "The relationship between adolescent childbearing and child maltreatment." Child Welfare 63: 553–557.

Moore, Kristin A. 1986. Children of Teen Parents: Heterogeneity of Outcomes. Final report to the National Institutes of Child Health and Human Development. Grant R01-HD-18427. Washington, DC: Child Trends, Inc.

Moore, Kristin A. 1988a. Facts at a Glance. Washington, DC: Child Trends, Inc.

Moore, Kristin A. 1988b. "Policy-relevant research on teenage chlidbearing: Potential topics." Family Perspectives 22: 189–209.

Moore, Kristin A. 1989. Facts at a Glance. Washington, DC: Child Trends, Inc.

Moore, Kristin A., and M. R. Burt. 1982. Private Crisis, Public Cost. Washington, DC: Urban Institute Press.

Moore, Kristin, C. W. Nord, and J. Peterson. 1989. "Nonvoluntary sexual activity among adolescents." Family Planning Perspectives 21: 110–114.

Moore, Kristin, and J. Peterson. 1989. The Consequences of Teenage Pregnancy: Final Report. Washington, DC: Child Trends, Inc.

Moore, Kristin, M. C. Simms, and C. L. Betsey. 1986. Choice and Circumstance. New Brunswick, NJ: Transaction Books.

Morris, Naomi M., K. Mallin, and J. R. Udry. 1982. "Pubertal development and current sexual intercourse among teenagers." Paper presented at the annual meeting of the American Public Health Association.

Mosher, William D., and M. C. Horn. 1989. "First family planning visits by young women." Family Planning Perspectives 21: 33–40.

Mott, Frank L., and R. J. Haurin. 1988. "Linkages between sexual activity and alcohol and drug use among American adolescents." Family Planning Perspectives 20: 129–136.

Namerow, Pearila B., N. Weatherby, and J. Williams-Kaye. 1989. "The effectiveness of contingency-planned counseling." Family Planning Perspectives 21: 115–119.

Nathanson, Constance A., and M. H. Becker. 1983. "Contraceptive behavior among unmarried young women: A theoretical framework for research." Population and Environment 6: 39–59.

Nathanson, Constance A., and M. H. Becker. 1986. "Family and peer influence on obtaining a method of contraception." Journal of Marriage and the Family 48: 513–525.

Nathanson, Constance A., and Y. J. Kim. 1989. "Components of change in adolescent fertility, 1971–1979." Demography 26: 85–98.

National Center for Health Statistics. 1989. "Advance report of final natality statistics, 1987." Monthly Vital Statistics Report, U.S. Department of Health and Human Services.

Newcomer, Susan F., M. Gilbert, and J. Richard Udry. 1980. "Perceived and actual same sex peer behavior as determinants of adolescent sexual behavior." Paper presented at the annual meeting of the American Psychological Association.

Newcomer, Susan F., and J. R. Udry. 1984. "Mothers' influence on the sexual behavior of their teenage children." Journal of Marriage and the Family 46: 477–485.

Newcomer, Susan F., and J. R. Udry. 1985. "Parent-child communication and adolescent sexual behavior." Family Planning Perspectives 17: 169–174.

Newcomer, Susan F., and J. R. Udry. 1987. "Parental marital status effects on adolescent sexual behavior." Journal of Marriage and the Family 49: 235–240.

Ortiz, Carmen G., and E. Vazquez Nuttall. 1987. "Adolescent pregnancy: Effects of family support, education, and religion on the decision to carry or terminate among Puerto Rican teenagers." Adolescence 22: 897–917.

Philliber, Susan G., P. B. Namerow, J. W. Kaye, and C. H. Kunkes. 1983. Pregnancy Risk Taking among Adolescents. New York: Columbia University Press.

Plotnick, Robert D. 1988. "Determinants of teenage out-of-wedlock childbearing." Paper presented at the annual meetings of the Population Association of America, New Orleans, LA.

Polit, Denise, T. Morton, and C. White. 1989. "Sex, contraception, and pregnancy among adolescents in foster care." Family Planning Perspectives 21: 203–208.

Pratt, William F. 1990. "Premarital sexual behavior, multiple sexual partners, and marital experience." Paper presented at the annual meetings of the Population Association of America, Toronto.

Resnick, Michael D. 1984. "Studying adolescent mothers' decision making about adoption and parenting." Social Work 29: 5–10.

Resnick, Michael, R. Blum, M. Smith, J. Bose, and R. Toogood. 1989. "Characteristics of adolescents who parent or place for adoption." Under review.

Rodgers, Joseph L. 1983. "Family configuration and adolescent sexual behavior." Population and Environment 6: 73–83.

Rodgers, Joseph L., and D. C. Rowe. 1990. "Adolescent sexuality and mildly deviant behavior: Sibling and friendship effects." Journal of Family Issues, in press.

Rodman, Hyman, and J. Trost (eds.). 1986. The Adolescent Dilemma: International Perspectives on the Family Planning Right of Minors. New York: Praeger.

Roosa, Mark W., H. Fitzgerald, and N. A. Carlson. 1982. "Teenage parenting and child development: A literature review." Infant Mental Health Journal 3: 4–18.

Roosa, Mark W., and L. Vaughan. 1984. "A comparison of teenage and older mothers with preschool age children." Family Relations 33: 259–265.

Schilmoeller, Gary L., and M. D. Barnowski. 1985. "Childrearing of firstborns by adolescent and older mothers." Adolescence 20: 805–822.

Smith, Edward A. 1989. "A biosocial model of adolescent sexual behavior." Pp. 143–167 in Gerald R. Adams, R. Montemayor, and T. Gullotta (eds.), Biology of Adolescent Behavior and Development. Newbury Park, CA: Sage.

Smith, Edward A., and J. R. Udry. 1985. "Coital and non-coital sexual behaviors of white and black adolescents." American Journal of Public Health 75: 1200–1203.

Sonenstein, Freya L., J. H. Pleck, and L. C. Ku. 1989. "Sexual activity, condom use, and AIDS awareness among adolescent males." Family Planning Perspectives 21: 152–158.

Studer, Marlena, and A. Thornton. 1987. "Adolescent religiosity and contraceptive usage." Journal of Marriage and the Family 49: 117–128.

Swenson, Ingrid, D. Erickson, E. Ehlinger, G. Carlson, and S. Swaney. 1989. "Fertility, menstrual characteristics, and contraceptive practices among white, black, and SE Asian refugee adolescents." Adolescence 24: 647–654.

Testa, Mark F. 1987. "The social support of adolescent mothers: Pregnancy, school completion, and remaining in the parental home." Findings from the Adolescent Family Life Survey, funded by Grant APR 000909-02-0, Office of Adolescent Pregnancy Programs, U.S. Dept. of Health and Human Services.

Thornton, Arland D. 1990. "The courtship process and adolescent sexuality." Journal of Family Issues, in press.

Thornton, Arland D., and D. Camburn. 1987. "The influence of the family on premarital sexual attitudes and behavior." Demography 24: 323–340.

Thornton, Arland D., and D. Camburn. 1989. "Religious participation and adolescent sexual behavior." Journal of Marriage and the Family 51: 641–653.

Udry, J. Richard. 1988. "Biological predispositions and social control in adolescent sexual behavior." American Sociological Review 53: 709–722.

Udry, J. Richard, and J. O. G. Billy. 1987. "Initiation of coitus in early adolescence." American Sociological Review 52: 841–855.

Udry, J. Richard, J. O. G. Billy, Naomi M. Morris, T. R. Groff, and M. H. Raj. 1985. "Serum androgenic hormones motivate sexual behavior in adolescent human males." Fertility and Sterility 43: 90–94.

Udry, J. Richard, L. Talbert, and N. M. Morris. 1986. "Biosocial foundations for adolescent female sexuality." Demography 23: 217–230.

United Nations. 1988. Adolescent Reproductive Behavior (Vol. 1). Evidence from Developed Countries. New York: United Nations.

Upchurch, Dawn. 1988. The Effects of Early Child-bearing on High School Completion among Recent Cohorts of American Women. PhD dissertation, Johns Hopkins University.

Vernon, Mary, J. A. Green, and T. E. Frothingham. 1983. "Teenage pregnancy: A prospective study of self-esteem and sociodemographic factors." Pediatrics 72: 632–635.

Vinovskis, Maris A. 1988. An "Epidemic" of Teenage Pregnancy? New York: Oxford University Press.

Weatherly, Richard A., S. B. Perlman, M. H. Levine, and L. V. Klerman. 1986. "Comprehensive programs for pregnant teenagers and teenage parents: How successful have they been?" Family Planning Perspectives 18: 73–78.

Weinstein, Maxine, and A. L. Thornton. 1989. "Mother-child relations and adolescent sexual attitudes and behavior." Demography 26: 563–577.

Westoff, Charles. 1988. "Contraceptive paths toward the reduction of unintended pregnancy and abortion." Family Planning Perspectives 20: 4–12.

Whitley, Bernard E., Jr., and J. W. Schofield. 1986. "A meta-analysis on adolescent contraceptive use." Population and Environment 8: 173–203.

Wilson, William J. 1984. The Truly Disadvantaged. Chicago: University of Chicago Press.

Winter, Laraine. 1988. "The role of sexual self-concept in the use of contraceptives." Family Planning Perspectives 20: 123–127.

Yamaguchi, Kazuo, and D. Kandell. 1987. "Drug use and other determinants of premarital pregnancy and its outcome: A dynamic analysis of competing life events." Journal of Marriage and the Family 49: 257–270.

Zabin, Laurie S., and S. D. Clark, Jr. 1981. "Why they delay: A study of teenage family planning clinic patients." Family Planning Perspectives 13: 205–217.

Zabin, Laurie S., and M. B. Hirsch. 1987. Evaluation of Pregnancy Prevention Programs in the School Context. Lexington, MA: Lexington Books.

Zabin, Laurie S., M. B. Hirsch, E. A. Smith, and J. B. Hardy. 1984. "Adolescent sexual attitudes and behavior: Are they consistent?" Family Planning Perspectives 16: 181–185.

Zabin, Laurie S., E. A. Smith, M. B. Hirsch, and J. B. Hardy. 1986. "Ages of physical maturation and first intercourse in black teenage males and females." Demography 23: 595–605.

Zeanah, Charles H., M. A. Keener, T. Anders, and B. S. Vieria-Baker. 1987. "Adolescent mothers' perceptions of their infants before and after birth." American Journal of Orthopsychiatry 57: 351–360.

Zelnik, Melvin, J. F. Kantner, and K. Ford. 1981. Sex and Pregnancy in Adolescence. Beverly Hills, CA: Sage.

Zelnik, Melvin, and F. K. Shah. 1983. "First intercourse among young Americans." Family Planning Perspectives 15: 64–70.

Zuravin, Susan. 1988. "Child maltreatment and teenage first births: A relationship mediated by chronic sociodemographic stress?" American Journal of Orthopsychiatry 58: 91–102.

Richard J. Gelles   *University of Rhode Island*

Jon R. Conte   *University of Washington**

Domestic Violence and Sexual Abuse of Children:

A Review of Research in the Eighties

This article reviews research on family violence and sexual abuse of children in the 1980s. The first section focuses on research on changing rates of family violence, the intergenerational transmission of violence, the effects of violence on children and women, and assessments of the effectiveness of intervention strategies. The second section reviews the issue of the sexual abuse of children and examines the issues of defining sexual abuse, its prevalence, research on sexual offenders and risk factors, the impact of sexual abuse, and studies of the effectiveness of prevention efforts.

The expansion of research on the topic of domestic violence in the last decade has been substantial, perhaps greater than in any other substantive area in the social sciences. In addition to work on child and wife abuse, a substantial body of research developed on the topics of violence toward parents, especially elderly parents, courtship violence, and sexual abuse. The substantive focus of the study of family violence and sexual abuse also expanded in the 1980s. Research was less heavily weighted toward measuring the extent of family violence but more concerned with assessing the changing rates of violence and abuse in the home. The investigation

Department of Sociology and Anthropology, University of Rhode Island, Kingston, RI 02881.

*School of Social Work, University of Washington, Seattle, WA 98195.

of factors related to violence continued but was augmented by extensive examination of the consequences of abuse to children and women. There were some advances in theory testing and building, especially feminist theory (see, for example, Yllo and Bograd, 1988). Investigators also examined the effectiveness of treatment programs in reducing the incidence of family violence.

The heterogeneity of research on family violence and the space limitations for this article preclude a comprehensive review of all forms of domestic violence and all the relevant issues. As a result, we will not touch on the topics of courtship violence, elder abuse, or husband abuse, nor will we provide updates of research on factors that are associated with violence between family members. Comprehensive and recent reviews of these topics have been published elsewhere.[1]

The organizing principal for this review is twofold. In the first section we concentrate on selected issues in the study of family violence that have been the subject of controversy and concern, and for which there are data that meet normal standards of scientific evidence (i.e., the research is. not entirely based on small, nongeneralizable clinical samples; comparison or control groups have been employed; and multivariate analysis has been used to rule out spurious relations and to explain and specify relationships). The topics include research on changing rates of family violence, the intergenerational transmission of violence, the effects of violence on children and women, and assessments of the effectiveness of intervention strategies. The second section reviews the issue of the sexual abuse of children. This topic drew the greatest increase in attention and research in the last decade. Our review examines the basic issues of defining sexual abuse, its prevalence, research on sexual offenders and risk factors, the impact of sexual abuse, and studies of the effectiveness of prevention efforts.

CHANGING RATES OF DOMESTIC VIOLENCE

Child Abuse

Since the early 1960s there has been a widespread belief that the rates of child abuse have been increasing. Data collected by the American Association for Protecting Children (1989) support this belief. For all forms of maltreatment, there has been a 225% increase in reporting between 1976 and 1987.[2]

The National Center on Child Abuse and Neglect has conducted two national surveys of the incidence of reported child abuse and neglect (Burgdorf, 1980; National Center on Child Abuse and Neglect, 1988). The most recent survey reported that countable cases of child maltreatment increased 66% over the number of cases found in 1980. Stated in terms of incidence, there were 9.8 cases of maltreatment per 1,000 children in the population in 1980 and 16.3 cases of maltreatment per 1,000 children in the population in 1986. Increases in the incidence of physical and sexual abuse were significant, with physical abuse increasing by 58% and sexual abuse more than tripling between 1980 and 1986. Straus and Gelles (1986), however, found that parent self-reports of very severe violence toward children had *declined* 47% between 1975 and 1985 from 36 per 1,000 to 19 per 1,000 children (from 3 to 17 years old and living with both parents).

The three major data sources on the changing rate of child abuse yield contradictory results. Noting the contradictory findings, the National Center on Child Abuse and Neglect (1988) stated that the decline in the rate of violence toward children reported by Straus and Gelles could be a function of parents becoming less candid because of the unacceptability of admitting to abusive behavior. Straus and Gelles (1986) recognized that changing attitudes about child abuse could be a plausible explanation for their findings. They also noted, however, that the declining rate of child abuse is consistent with the changing character and structure of the American family, the improving economy, increased publicity about child abuse, and the rapid expansion of treatment and prevention programs for child abuse.

It is simply not possible to resolve the contradictory findings at this point. It is axiomatic that the resolution can only be found in further research and analysis of the data on incidence as well as the methodological issues regarding such research.

Marital Violence

There are no appropriate national official report data on marital violence that can be used to examine changing rates. Straus and Gelles (1986) report that the self-reports of the rate of wife abuse declined 21.8% from 1975 to 1985. This decline, while substantively large, is not statistically significant.

The rate of abusive violence toward husbands remained essentially unchanged in the general population (Straus and Gelles, 1986). The topic of violence and abuse of husbands remained controversial in the 1980s (see, for example, McNeeley and Robinson-Simpson, 1987; and letters to the editor in *Social Work* 33: 189–191, 1988). As a result of the controversy and the attendant name-calling (including threats of physical harm—see Straus, 1990: 11–14), most scholars hesitate to publish articles on battered husbands and very little new empirical research on the topic was published in the 1980s.

THE INTERGENERATIONAL TRANSMISSION OF VIOLENCE

Violence toward Children

The notion that abused children grow up to be abusing parents and violent adults has been widely expressed in the child abuse and family violence literature (Gelles, 1980). When data were presented, they often consisted of case studies or clinical data without appropriate comparison groups or adequate measurement techniques.

Kaufman and Zigler (1987) reviewed the empirical literature that tested the hypothesis of intergenerational transmission of violence. Reviewing the self-report studies that examined the cycle-of-violence hypothesis, Kaufman and Zigler found that the rate of intergenerational transmission ranged from 18% to 70%. They concluded that the best estimate of the rate of intergenerational transmission appears to be 30% (plus or minus 5%). While a rate of 30% intergenerational transmission represents quite a bit less than the majority of abused children, it is considerably higher than the abuse rate of between 2% and 4% that has been found for children in the general population (Straus and Gelles, 1986).

Three recent studies provide data on the intergenerational transmission of abuse. Egeland and his colleagues (Egeland, Jacobvitz, and Papatola, 1987; Egeland, Jacobvitz, and Sroufe, 1988) have conducted a prospective study of the phenomenon by following a sample of 160 high-risk, low-income mothers. Seventy percent of the parents who were identified independently as having experienced child abuse were observed to maltreat or provide borderline care. Egeland, Jacobvitz, and Sroufe (1988) found that those mothers who were able to break the cycle of violence were significantly more likely to have received emotional support from a nonabusive adult during childhood; to have participated in therapy during any period in their lives; and to have a nonabusive, stable, emotionally supportive, and satisfying relationship with a mate.

A second study, conducted by Herrenkohl, Herrenkohl, and Toedler (1983), found that 47% of the parents who were abused as children abused their own children. This proportion is significantly higher than the percentage for the non-abused parents.

A third study of the cycle of violence changes the focus from whether abused children become abusive adults to whether being an abused child increases one's risk for delinquency, adult criminal behavior, and violent criminal behavior. Widom (1989) notes that the child abuse literature claims not only that abuse leads to abuse but that abuse leads to delinquency, violent behavior, and aggressive behavior in children. She identified a large sample of validated cases of child abuse and neglect from approximately 20 years ago, established a control group of nonabused children, and assessed official arrest records to establish occurrences of delinquency, criminal behavior, and violent criminal behavior. Widom reports that abused and neglected children have a higher likelihood of arrest for delinquency, adult criminality, and violent criminal behavior than the matched controls.

Marital Violence

Marital violence has also been a focus for those who test the intergenerational-transmission hypothesis. Kalmuss (1984) analyzed data from the First National Family Violence Survey and found that observing hitting between one's parents is more strongly related to involvement in severe marital aggression than is being hit as a teenager by one's parents. Malone, Tyree, and O'Leary (1989) report that experience with aggression influences the present aggression differently for men and women. Women's aggression toward their spouses was correlated with observation of parental aggression and the hitting of siblings. For men, experiencing parental aggression was correlated with aggression toward wives at 6 months of marriage, but there was no significant association at 18 months of marriage.

Evidence from studies of parental and marital violence indicate that while experiencing violence in one's family of origin is often correlated with later violent behavior, such experience is not the sole determining factor. Moreover, the process by which violence is transferred from one generation to the next is more complex than simple modeling of behavior. When the cycle of violence occurs, it is likely the result of a complex set of social and psychological processes.

OTHER EFFECTS OF VIOLENCE AND MALTREATMENT

Violence toward Children

Abused children have frequently been described as having a number of cognitive, emotional, and social difficulties. Most of our knowledge is based on retrospective studies, so it is not clear whether these deficits were present prior to maltreatment and were causal, or are a consequence of maltreatment.

Emery (1989), reviewing studies of the effects of child abuse, notes that no single behavioral or emotional reaction has been found to characterize all abused children. He lists the following difficulties that have been observed in empirical research: increased aggression, troubled peer relationships, impaired social cognition, lack of empathy, depression, and lower performance on cognitive tasks. However, Emery (1989) cautions that being a victim of violence may not be the principal factor responsible for the many difficulties that abused children may experience. Other aspects of the child's environment that accompany abuse may be more psychologially damaging.

Some research indicates that children who experience the more severe forms of maltreatment suffer more significant intellectual deficits (Dietrich, Starr, and Weisfield, 1983); however, other studies fail to confirm this finding (Starr, 1982; Starr, Dietrich, Fishoff, Ceresnie, and Zweier, 1984). Other studies find various social and emotional deficits, including communication problems, poor performance in school, and learning disabilities (Starr, 1988).

Youngblade and Belsky (1989) provide an exhaustive review of the data on the social and emotional consequences of child maltreatment. They review research for the developmental stages of infancy and toddlerhood, preschool and elementary years, and adolescence. Among the findings were that maltreated toddlers were more aggressive, less prosocial, and more disturbed in their responses to others' distress than children who have not been maltreated. They note that there is a general consensus that maltreatment is associated with elevated rates of insecure infant-mother attachments. Maltreated children were found to exhibit more anger and conflict with their family and were found to be more aggressive with their peers than nonmaltreated children. Maltreated children were also found to exhibit more internalizing and externalizing behavior than nonmaltreated children (Youngblade and Belsky, 1989).

Starr (1988) concludes his review of the consequences of maltreatment by noting that the picture that emerges is of verbal and physical aggression as a response to violent behavior. However, he cautions that there is no typical maltreated child nor a typical maltreating adult. Furthermore, most studies of the consequences of abuse have significant methodological deficiencies (Aber and Cichetti, 1984).

The Effects of Violence toward Women

Descriptive and clinical accounts of wife abuse consistently report a high incidence of depression and anxiety among samples of battered women (Christopoulus et al., 1987; Hilberman, 1980; Schechter, 1983). The evidence that is offered has

been largely clinical and descriptive in nature. Gelles and Harrop's (1989) examination of the data from the Second National Family Violence Survey confirms the findings from clinical and descriptive research. Women who reported experiencing violence and abuse also reported higher levels of moderate and severe psychological distress. Multivariate analysis indicated that violence made an independent and nonspurious contribution to the psychological distress experienced by women (Gelles and Harrop, 1989).

ASSESSING THE EFFECTIVENESS OF INTERVENTION STRATEGIES

Intervention into Child Maltreatment

There are only a handful of evaluations of prevention and treatment programs for violence toward children. Olds, Henderson, Tatelbaum, and Chamberlin (1986) used a randomized clinical trial to evaluate the effectiveness of a family support program during pregnancy and the first two years after birth for low-income, unmarried, teenage, first-time mothers. Of those children of unmarried teenage mothers who were provided with the full complement of home visits by a nurse during the mother's pregnancy and for the first two years after birth, 4% had confirmed cases of child abuse and neglect reported to the state child protection agency, in contrast to 19% of the comparison groups that had cases of maltreatment reported. Olds and his colleagues caution that the findings may be the result of systematic reporting bias. The nurse-visited women may have been less likely to be reported for maltreatment by friends and neighbors.

Daro and Cohn (1988) review four major evaluations of child maltreatment programs: (*a*) Berkeley Planning Associates' evaluation of 11 federally funded programs; (*b*) Abt Associates' evaluation of 20 demonstration and treatment programs funded by the National Center on Child Abuse and Neglect; (*c*) E. H. White's evaluation of 29 service improvement grants funded by the National Center on Child Abuse and Neglect; and (*d*) Berkeley Planning Associates' evaluation of 19 clinical demonstration projects funded by the National Center on Child Abuse and Neglect.[3] The Abt Associates' study noted that there was no noticeable correlation between a given set of services and positive client outcomes. In fact, the more services a family received, the worse the family got. Both evalutions by the Berkeley Planning Associates reported that lay counseling, group counseling, and parent education classes resulted in more positive treatment outcomes. Assessing the effectiveness of length of treatment for abusive adults, the Berkeley Planning Associates noted that the optimal treatment period appeared to be between 7 and 18 months.

The Berkeley Planning Associates and Abt Associates assessed the likelihood of further maltreatment among the participants in the federally funded demonstration projects. Overall, reincidence occurred among 30% to 47% of the cases evaluated by Berkeley Planning and Abt Associates. Daro and Cohn (1988) note that, at least on the basis of the evaluation of the demonstration projects, existing treatment programs have not been terribly effective in protecting children from further harm. Those projects that were successful in reducing recidivism accomplished this by separating children from abusive parents, either by placing them in foster homes or requiring the maltreating adult to move out of the house.

Intervention into Marital Violence

The best-known assessment of intervention into marital violence is the Minneapolis Police Experiment (Sherman and Berk, 1984). This study called for the police to assign incidents of misdemeanor family assaults randomly to one of three experimental conditions: arrest, separation, or advice/mediation. Those households receiving the arrest intervention had the lowest rate of recidivism (10%) and those who were separated had the highest (24%).

There were a number of internal and external validity problems with the Minneapolis Police Experiment (Berk and Sherman, 1988). The National Institute of Justice is currently sponsoring six replications of the Minneapolis Police Experiment. The results from the first replication cast some doubt on the optimistic conclusions that arrest deters domestic violence. Dunford, Huizinga, and Elliot replicated the Minneapolis Police Experiment in Omaha, Nebraska (1989), and attempted to correct for the threats to the internal validity of the Minneapolis study. The major finding was that, contrary to the evidence from Minneapolis, arresting subjects had no more effect in deterring future arrests or complaints of violence than did separation or counseling. Dunford, Huizinga, and Elliot (1989) expanded the Minneapolis design to include an experimental trial of issuing arrest warrants in cases when suspected abusive men were not present when the police arrived. The researchers found that those men who had warrants issued against them scored lower on prevalence and frequency of repeated offences.

Survey research results suggest that the threat of arrest would indeed reduce the risk of domestic violence. Williams and Hawkins (1989) report that arrest appears to be meaningful to men in terms of the indirect cost it poses to them in their social environment. The personal humiliation of arrest appears to be the central factor in the meaning of arrest for wife assault and the possible deterrent effect of arrest (Williams and Hawkins, 1989).

Thus, arrest itself may not deter violent men, especially if the arrest does not result in any indirect costs. On the other hand, the threat of arrest, both in the form of warrants issued against violent men and the awareness of the existence of mandatory or presumptory arrest policies, may indeed function as a deterrent. Perhaps as a result of this, and because arrest did not increase the risk of violence, Dunford, Huizinga, and Elliot (1989) conclude their report by urging that mandatory arrest policies continue to be followed and adopted.

Other assessments of intervention strategies designed to prevent and treat violence between spouses include assessments of shelters and counseling programs. Berk, Newton, and Berk (1986) obtained face-to-face interviews with 155 wife-battery victims in a two-wave panel study. Overall, the investigators found no significant main effect of shelter stays for victims of spousal violence. They did find that the effects of shelters seem to depend on the attributes of the victims. When a victim is actively engaged in taking control of her life, a shelter stay can dramatically reduce the likelihood of new violence. For other victims, a shelter stay may have no impact, while for still others it may actually lead to an escalation of violence when they return home.

Other studies of shelters tend to focus on whether battered women return to their partners. Giles-Sims (1983) and Turner and Shapiro (1986) report that between one-third and two-thirds of women return to their partners.

Researchers have also evaluated group programs developed for violent men. Dutton (1986) reports that 50 men enrolled in a court-mandated program and followed for up to three years had recidivism rates as low as 4%. Neidig and Freidman (1984) followed men enrolled in a quasimandatory military group program. Four months after the program, the rate of recurrent violence was 13%. Gondolf (1987) reports that among men who completed voluntary programs, from two-thirds to three-quarters were nonviolent. Results of assessments of men's groups must be read cautiously because such groups tend to have low recruitment rates and high attrition rates (Pirog-Good and Stets, 1986). The more optimistic findings typically apply only to those men who complete counseling programs. Social and psychological factors are clearly related to both the propensity to complete a counseling program and the risk of violent behavior.

Lastly, investigators have examined the benefits of conjoint family counseling for cases of family violence. Critics have argued that conjoint counseling places women at risk of violence, but Geller (1982) has advocated such counseling and reports success rates in excess of 90% for couples staying in treatment for a 2-year period.

SEXUAL ABUSE OF CHILDREN

Among the most dramatic changes taking place over the past decade has been the increased attention to sexual abuse of children. Over the decade, research has tended to address the concerns of professionals working in the community with cases of child sexual abuse. For example, there has been research interest in how common is sexual use of children by adults and what are the effects of sexual abuse in childhood. A great amount of literature deals with the men who violate the taboo of having sex with children. Concern for the serious social-psychological effects of sexual abuse has given rise to considerable interest in developing programs to help children prevent or escape the experience of sexual abuse.

The Nature and Definition of Sexual Abuse

Sexual use of younger persons by older persons involves a wide range of specific behaviors. A popular definition of sexual abuse is *forced,*

tricked, or coerced sexual behavior between a young person and an older person. Many current definitions of sexual abuse include the element of an age difference of at least five years between victim and offender. Elements of *force, manipulation, or coercion* are also predominant characteristics. As Finkelhor (1979) argued, children are assumed to be incapable of consenting to sex with an adult because they lack the power to decline involvement and often do not know to what they are consenting. The elements defining *sexual abuse* are intended to exclude consensual sexual exploration or experimentation, without coercion, between age-mates. The sexual behaviors most often reported in the literature include (*a*) direct contact by one body to another as in fondling, (*b*) penetration of the child's body by nonsexual objects or the offender's sexual organs, and (*c*) noncontact behaviors, such as voyeurism or pornography.

Estimates of the Extent of the Problem

Different rates of specific sexual behavior (e.g., vaginal intercourse vs. fondling) are found in different studies. Studies of child victims and adult sexual offenders may yield different rates for the same type of behaviors. Researchers have often tended to use different definitions or criteria for sexual behaviors, and self-report data from sexual offenders are generally regarded as unreliable (Quinsey, 1984).

In a comprehensive and thoughtful review of studies on the incidence and prevalence of child sexual abuse, Peters, Wyatt, and Finkelhor (1986) report that estimates of the prevalence range from 6% to 62% for females and from 3% to 31% for males. As they point out, this variation may be accounted for by a number of methodological factors, such as differences in definitions of abuse, sample characteristics, interview format (e.g., in-person vs. phone interview), and number of questions used to elicit information about abuse experience. Whatever the number, it is clear that sexual abuse is a problem that affects large numbers of children. The only question is how large that number is in a particular community.

Research on Sexual Offenders

Over much of the decade, two distinct literatures (for reviews, see, e.g., Conte, 1985a; Conte, 1986;

Quinsey, 1984) have developed, one dealing with incest (especially abuse of daughter by father or stepfather) and the other dealing with pedophilia.

The belief that incest or "family sexual abuse" is a fundamentally different kind of clinical problem than pedophilia is at the basis for current policy that advocates the treatment of incestuous fathers and stepfathers in community settings. At the center of this belief are ideas that incest is the sexual expression of nonsexual needs (e.g., the need to feel important and powerful) and that therefore the clinical focus should be on the nonsexual aspects of the problem. Also important is the belief that through incestuous behavior, such fathers and stepfathers give expression to a problem that has its origins and ongoing psychological processes within the family, and they therefore have no need to express the problem outside of the family by having sex with nonrelated children.

Research on sex offenders continues to be based on these core tenets; however, recent data tend to raise questions about the validity of characteristics once believed to differentiate various types of sexual offenders. For example, Abel, Becker, Cunningham-Rathner, Mittelman, and Rouleau (1988) indicate that 49% of the incestuous fathers and stepfathers who were referred for outpatient treatment at their clinics also abused children outside of the family, and 18% of these men were raping adult women at the same time that they were sexually abusing their own children. Indeed, these data suggest that many offenders are polyperverse, with considerable overlap between types of victims.

There has been a great deal of research on the characteristics of sexual offenders; but current research has failed to identify characteristics, especially demographic, social, or psychological, that discriminate between sexual offenders and normal persons (Quinsey, 1984).

For some time, many professionals have believed that sexual abuse of children is not really a sexual problem but, rather, the sexual expression of nonsexual problems, such as depression, lowered self-esteem, and feelings of inadequacy. The development of laboratory assessment of sexual arousal has generated considerable questions about this notion. Such assessments involve the direct measuring of penile erections to various kinds of sexual stimuli (e.g., 5-year-old boys vs.

24-year-old females), usually consisting of either slides or verbal descriptions of sexual acts (see Earls and Marshall, 1983; Laws and Osborn, 1983).

Although some research indicates that child molesters are different from normal persons in their response to children (see, e.g., Quinsey and Chaplin, 1988) or that child molesters who inflict gratuitous violence can be discriminated from relatively less violent offenders by their arousal to verbal descriptions of sex and violence against children (Avery-Clarke and Laws, 1984), there has been little empirical evaluation of the sexual arousal of incest offenders. In an early study, Quinsey, Chaplin, and Carrigan (1979) evaluated nine incestuous and seven nonincestuous child molesters and found that the incestuous (father or stepfather) offenders exhibited more appropriate (i.e., adult) sexual arousal than did the nonincestuous child molesters. Abel, Becker, Murphy, and Flanagan (1981) developed a pedophile index that was calculated by dividing the percent of arousal to children by the percent of arousal to adults, and found that incest offenders were more aroused to children than to adults. Laboratory assessment of sexual arousal is a promising area of research but one with much work yet to be done. Many adults simply do not respond to any sexual stimuli in the lab (see, e.g., Marshall, Barbaree, and Christopher, 1986, where 22% of child molesters and 34% of incest offenders failed to respond). Studies differ on whether subjects can control their arousal in the lab when instructed to do so (Laws and Rubin, 1962; Quinsey and Bergersen, 1976). As Marshall and associates (1986) have observed, studies often include natural fathers, stepfathers, and adoptive fathers in the same category of *incest* offenders, thereby making interpretation of results difficult (e.g., by masking results associated with one subtype of offender).

Whether sexual abuse of children is, at least in part, a sexual problem has significant implications for the nature of treatment that is likely to be effective in treating adult offenders. To the extent that the problem involves sexual arousal to children, therapy directed toward dealing with other psychological processes (e.g., self-esteem) whose relevance to sexual abuse has not yet been demonstrated—such therapy is not likely to be of much use to the client.

Risk Factors

One of the key questions raised in discussions about sexual abuse is whether all children are at risk for sexual abuse or whether some children, because of some specific characteristic (e.g., age or poverty status), are at greater risk than others. If risk factors could be identified, greater precision could be applied in directing prevention where it is most needed. In their review of studies on prevention, Finkelhor and Baron (1986) conclude that it is currently not clear what factors increase children's risk for sexual abuse. It appears that girls are at greater risk, although boys are also victimized. Girls are more likely to be victimized if they have sometime been separated from their mothers (e.g., if they ever lived away from mother or if the mother was ill or disabled) or if they report poor relationships with their mothers. As the authors note, these factors may be consequences of sexual abuse as much as risk factors. The data point to the importance of mothers in protecting children from sexually aggressive men.

The Impact of Sexual Abuse

Among the issues surrounding the sexual abuse of children, the greatest attention has been addressed to the effect of sexual victimization experiences on children. In fact, it was in the late 1890s that Freud first postulated a connection between "hysterical" illness in 18 of his adult patients and their reports of childhood sexual experiences with adults (Masson, 1984). Books and articles on the impact of abuse have been published periodically since that time (see reviews by Browne and Finkelhor, 1986; Conte, 1985b). Until recently, much of this literature consisted of anecdotal reports of work with relatively small clinic samples. Most of the published literature has been based on samples of unknown representativeness and usually small in size, consisting of subjects who were identified because they had some mental health problem; most of these studies also lack measurement or group comparisons.

Notwithstanding these limitations, clinical observations of sexually abused children indicate a variety of behavioral and emotional problems, including depression, guilt, learning difficulties, sexual promiscuity, runaway behavior, somatic complaints, and sudden changes in behavior (Bur-

gess, Groth, and McCauseland, 1981); hysterical seizures (Goodwin, Simms, and Bergman, 1979; Gross, 1979); phobias, nightmares, and compulsive rituals (Weiss, Rogers, Darwin, and Dutton, 1955); and self-destructive or suicidal behavior (Carroll, Schaffer, Spensley, and Abramowitz, 1980; de Young, 1982; Yorukoglu and Kempe, 1966).

Recent research, on the other hand, has employed more specific measures of psychological functioning and some form of control group. These studies, in turn, have helped reveal differences in psychological functioning between children who have been sexually abused and those who have not. For example, in the Tufts New England Medical Center study, Gomes-Schwartz, Horowitz, and Sauzier (1985) compared 156 sexually abused children to the norms provided with the *Louisville Behavior Checklist* (LBC). Results indicated that sexually abused children were generally rated more pathological than the normative group but less pathological than children receiving mental health services.

Conte and Schuerman (1987) and Conte, Berliner, and Schuerman (1990) compared a sample of 369 sexual abuse victims aged 4 to 17 years old with a community comparison group of 318 children who had not been abused. On a 110-item behavior checklist (Child Behavior Profile, CBP) completed by parents, sexually abused children were found to display significantly higher scores (reflecting dysfunction) on 12 dimensions: concentration problems, aggressive, withdrawn, somatic complaints, character personality style (e.g., nice or pleasant disposition, too anxious to please), antisocial behavior, nervous/emotional, depression, behavioral regression, body image/self-esteem problems, fear, and symptoms of post-traumatic stress. (See also Friedrich, 1988; Gale, Thompson, Moran, and Sack, 1988.) Rimsza, Berg, and Locke (1988) examined 368 children and adolescents receiving medical evaluations in Maricopa County, Arizona. Seventy-two sexually abused children were compared to a matched control group of children who were general clinic patients. Sexually abused children were more likely to report symptoms of muscle tension, gastrointestinal and genitourinary difficulties, emotional reactions, runaway behavior, and other behavior problems. Differences for school problems and early pregnancy, however, were not significant.

Kolko, Moser, and Weldy (1988) report the results of a study on sexually ($n = 29$) and physically ($n = 52$) abused children in psychiatric hospitalization. Children were assessed on a 26-item Sexual Abuse Symptom Checklist (SASC) assessing child functioning in four domains (home routines/relationships, behavioral and affective reactions, physical/sexual behavior, and school behavior). The SASC was administered to the child's parent or guardian by the unit nurse practitioner. Factor analysis of the SASC identified six factors: sexual activity, fear/mistrust, unhappiness/escape, conduct problems, school apathy/neglect, and withdrawal/poor appetite. Sexually abused hospitalized children were found to exhibit significantly more sexual activity, fear/mistrust, and withdrawal/poor appetite.

Specific differences in the functioning of sexually abused children have been observed in the research, and it is clear that such children display a variety of negative social, emotional, and physical sequelae in comparison with children who are not known to have been abused and those who are identified as having psycho-social problems (e.g., those who seek outpatient mental health treatment). It is unclear, however, the extent to which differences associated with sexually abused children are specific to sexual abuse per se or to childhood trauma in general. The work of Gale, Thompson, Moran, and Sack (1988) and Kolko and associates (1988) establishes a direction for future research that is likely to deal with the question of whether there are effects specific to sexual abuse or to trauma or emotional abuse in general.

Investigators in the future are likely to try to address several methodological issues to increase the generalizability of findings and their applied significance. For example, researchers to date have employed various measures of psychosocial functioning (i.e., effects) and different comparison groups. Thus, making comparisons across studies has been quite difficult. Further, as Berliner and Wheeler (1987) note, much of the existing research has been atheoretical or has lacked a conceptualization of effects or a diagnostic relevance that is likely to be helpful in treatment. The listings of symptoms or aspects of child functioning that may be affected by abuse is not helpful to the clinician unless such groupings lead to implications for treatment. Another problem is that groupings of symptoms vary considerably in

terms of how behaviorally specific they are. Some describe quite broad aspects of functioning in abstract terms (e.g., "externalizing behavior" or "behavioral regression"). Others describe relatively circumscribed or more limited clusters of behavior (e.g., "fearfulness of abuse stimuli").

Prevention of Sexual Abuse

Interest in designing programs to help children escape or prevent being abused began early in the decade. By the end of the decade, prevention programs had been developed for every conceivable audiovisual technology (e.g., film, video, audiotape, filmstrip) and format (e.g., story books, coloring books, songs, plays, board games). These programs and materials are based on a set of core assumptions: that many children do not know what sexual abuse is, that sexual touch need not be tolerated, that adults want to know about sexual touching by older persons, and that it is possible to tell about sexual abuse in order to have it cease. Children can be taught knowledge (e.g., the difference between a safe and unsafe touch, and who to tell about abuse) and skills (e.g., how to say "No" assertively to unwanted touch) that will be useful in preventing or escaping the experience of abuse (for reviews, see Conte and Fogarty, 1990; Kolko, 1988).

There are differences among these programs and materials in terms of the range of material presented, the time it takes to deliver the message to the child, the concepts or words used to describe the concepts, the location in which the material is presented (e.g., home or school), the format of presentation (e.g., video, instruction by adult trainers, printed matter), the degree to which the child interacts with the materials (e.g., reads a book, listens and asks questions of an instructor, observes a model demonstrating a prevention behavior and then role-plays the skills), and occupation of the trainer.

The 1980s have witnessed a number of efforts to evaluate prevention programs and materials. Most of these projects have employed some means of assessing knowledge gains, usually by asking children questions such as "What is sexual abuse?" or "What should a child do if touched inappropriately?" Many assessments include questions about strangers, secrets, social supports, and body ownership. Knowledge gains have been found in evaluations of several different programs that use a variety of training formats (Binder and McNiel, 1987; Conte, Rosen, Saperstein, and Shermack, 1985; Downer, 1984; Garbarino, 1987; Harvey, Forehand, Brown, Holmes, 1988; Plummer, 1984; Ray and Dietzel, 1984; Wolfe, MacPherson, Blount, and Wolfe, 1986; Wurtele, Kast, Miller-Perrin, and Kondrick, 1989; Wurtele and Miller-Perrin, 1987). A few studies include a follow-up assessment to look at "long-term" knowledge retention. (See Harvey et al., 1988; Ray and Dietzel, 1984; Wurtele, Marrs, and Miller-Perrin, 1987).

Prevention programs often teach children to follow three strategies in a "dangerous" or sexually abusive situation. Children are taught to say "No," get away from the assailant or dangerous situation, and report the incident to a trusted adult. Many evaluations have assessed the learning of these skills with multiple-choice, true/false, or yes/no questions such as "If an older child touched your private parts, would you tell?" (Binder and McNiel, 1987; Conte et al., 1985; Plummer, 1984; Wolfe, MacPherson, Blount, and Wolfe, 1986). Another method of assessing the ability of children to learn behavioral rules and skills has involved presenting scenarios including appropriate and inappropriate touch and asking the child what should be done in such a situation (see, e.g., Harvey et al., 1988; Kenning, Gallmeier, Jackson, and Plemons, 1987; Kolko, Moser, Litz, and Hughes, 1987; Wurtele and Miller-Perrin, 1987).

Assessments of this kind have the advantage of requiring a child to apply prevention knowledge to novel situations, not just to recite the rules. As is typical of all analogue measures, it is not clear the extent to which the responses of children to these "What if?" scenes accurately describe what in fact they would do when faced with such a situation in real life.

There has been some effort to develop behavioral-skills measures that more closely approximate real-life situations. Some researchers have created "stranger abduction situations," where a child is approached by a research confederate, unknown to the child, and the child's help is solicited (Fryer, Kraizer, and Miyoshi, 1987; Miltenberger and Thiesse-Duffy, 1988). In a sample of 44 children in kindergarten through second grade, children who had been exposed to a prevention program were more likely to refuse to help the unknown confederate than were those in a control

group. However, 22% of the experiment children still failed the test at posttest. Although these findings are encouraging, considerations arise in the use of such procedures because of the possibility of desensitizing children to abduction situations, and incomplete debriefing (Conte, 1987). These measures also do not assess responses to approaches by nonstrangers, who make up the majority of offenders.

Recent research has examined the most effective way to teach prevention skills (see, e.g., Chadwick, 1988; Ray and Dietzel, 1984; Wurtele, Marrs, and Miller-Perrin, 1987; Wurtele et al., 1989). For example, children in a "Participant Modeling" prevention program, which incorporated role-play, modeling, and rehearsal, scored significantly higher on an analogue measure of prevention skills than did children in a "symbolic modeling" program, which taught the same skills, but the child watched the experimenter model on a video (Wurtele, Marrs, and Miller-Perrin, 1987). (See also Blumberg, Chadwick, Forgarty, Speth, and Chadwick, 1988, and Miltenberger and Thiesse-Duffy, 1988.)

From almost the initial effort to train children to prevent their own sexual victimization, some have raised concern that such programs may be harmful to children. Researchers have attempted to address this concern by evaluating immediate behavioral changes or increases in fear and anxiety. Using these outcomes to measure effects, evaluations have generally found positive results (Binder and McNiel, 1987; Kenning et al., 1987; Miltenberger and Thiesse-Duffy, 1988; Wolfe et al., 1986; Wurtele and Miller-Perrin, 1987). Binder and McNiel (1987) found no significant increases in behavior problems recorded by parents' ratings after prevention programs in a sample of children 5 through 12 years old, but they did find a decrease in 3 of 18 problem behaviors. Similarly, no significant increases in children's anxiety problem behaviors were found after the implementation of prevention training (Kenning et al., 1987). In another study, no increases in the child's fear, as reported by the child and parent, were found (Wurtele and Miller-Perrin, 1987).

Miltenberger and Thiesse-Duffy (1988) found no new behavioral problems, nightmares, or other lasting emotional reactions after prevention training, according to parent reports, but nearly a third of the children were "a little more scared" and over two-thirds were more cautious. Similarly, in an evaluation of the *Spiderman* comic on sexual abuse prevention, Garbarino (1987) found that a sizable minority of children of both sexes and in each of three grades reported that the comic worried or scared them (from 17% to 50%). The reason given most often was that they realized "it" might happen to them. Increased awareness, if not accompanied with unmanageable anxiety, may be a desirable result of prevention efforts.

LOOKING AHEAD

As we look ahead, many of the recommendations and suggestions we made in the last decade review of family violence research still apply. While the study of family violence has broadened to include examinations of violence and victimization not recognized ten years ago, the empirical findings that have been generated still need to be integrated into more refined and better tested of theories of family violence. Longitudinal designs, such as the one used by Egeland and his colleagues, are still the exception in the field. With the increased concern with assessing the effects of violence and sexual victimization, longitudinal designs are imperative.

While clinical and official report data remain staple sources in family violence and sexual abuse research, the use of larger, nonclinical samples has expanded. In some cases, employing such samples has resulted in the discrediting of entrenched stereotypes about the patterns of family violence (see, for example, Pillemer and Finkelhor's finding that abused elderly persons are more likely to be victimized by their spouses than their children, 1988).

Researchers are likely to increase their efforts to study phenomena across types of interpersonal violence, addressing such issues as how many battered women are subjected to other forms of violence, how many sexually abused children are also physically abused, and whether offenders of one type of violence engage in others as well. We are also likely to see increased effort to understand the effects of various types of violence and to learn if the type of violence is associated with specific types of effects (e.g., whether the effects of sexual abuse in childhood are different from effects of physical abuse).

Studies of the outcomes of social intervention (e.g., arrest of offenders, changes in legislation) and treatment outcome studies are likely to ex-

pand greatly over the next decade. Such research will become increasingly clear as the field moves from awareness of how large the problem of violence is, to what can effectively be done to reduce the occurrence and consequences of abuse.

NOTES

This article is part of the Family Violence Research Program at the University of Rhode Island. A complete list of books and articles is available upon request. This research was funded by a grant from the National Institute of Mental Health, MH 40027.

1. An expanded version of this review is available from the first author. The major review articles and books published in the 1980s on family violence are Ohlin and Tonry (1989), Steinmetz (1987), and Van Hasselt, Morrison, Bellack, and Hersen (1988). For a complete review of the methodological and design issues in the study of family violence, see Gelles (1990) and Weiss (1989). Research on courtship violence is reviewed in Pirog-Good and Strets (1989). Research on elder abuse is reviewed in Pillemer and Suitor (1988).

2. The report does not include a breakdown for types of maltreatment.

3. For complete references for the four evaluations, see Daro and Cohn, 1988.

REFERENCES

Abel, Gene G., Judith Becker, Jerry Cunningham-Rathner, Mary Mittleman, and Joanne L. Rouleau. 1988. "Multiple paraphiliac diagnoses among sex offenders." Bulletin of the American Academy of Psychiatry and the Law 16: 153–168.

Abel, Gene G., Judith Becker, W. Murphy, and B. Flanagan. 1981. "Identifying dangerous child molesters." In Richard B. Stuart (ed.), Violent Behavior: Social Learning Approaches to Prediction, Management, and Treatment. New York: Brunner/Mazel.

Aber, J. Lawrence, and Dante Cicchetti. 1984. "The socio-emotional development of the maltreated child: An empirical and theoretical analysis." Pp. 147–205 in H. Fitzgerald, B. Lester, and M. Yogman (eds.), Theory and Research in Behavioral Pediatrics (Vol. 2). New York: Plenum.

American Association for Protecting Children. 1989. Highlights of Official Child Neglect and Abuse Reporting, 1987. Denver: American Humane Association.

Avery-Clark, Constance A., and D. R. Laws. 1984. "Differential erection response patterns of sexual child abusers to stimuli describing activities with children." Behavior Therapy 15: 71–83.

Berk, Richard A., Phyllis Newton, and Sara F. Berk. 1986. "What a difference a day makes: An empirical study of the impact of shelters for battered women." Journal of Marriage and the Family 48: 481–490.

Berk, Richard A., and Lawrence W. Sherman. 1988. "Police responses to family violence incidents: An analysis of an experimental design with incomplete randomization." Journal of the American Statistical Association 83: 70–76.

Berliner, Lucy, and J. R. Wheeler. 1987. "Treating the effects of sexual abuse on children." Journal of Interpersonal Violence 2: 415–434.

Binder, Renee L., and Dale E. McNiel. 1987. "Evaluation of a school-based sexual abuse prevention program: Cognitive and emotional effects." Child Abuse and Neglect 11: 497–506.

Blumberg, Elaine, Michelle W. Chadwick, Linda A. Fogarty, Timothy Speth, and David Chadwick. 1988. "The good touch/bad touch component of a sexual abuse prevention program: Unanticipated positive consequences." Unpublished manuscript.

Browne, Angela, and David Finkelhor. 1986. "Initial and long-term effects: A review of the research." Pp. 143–179 in David Finkelhor (ed.), A Sourcebook on Child Sexual Abuse. Beverly Hills, CA: Sage.

Burgdorf, Kenneth. 1980. Recognition and Reporting of Child Maltreatment. Rockville, MD: Westat.

Burgess, Ann W., A. Nicholas Groth, and M. Mc-Causeland. 1981. "Child sex initiation rings." American Journal of Psychiatry 51: 110–119.

Carroll, J., C. Schaffer, J. Spensley, and S. I. Abramowitz. 1980. "Family experience of self-mutilating patients." American Journal of Psychiatry 137: 852–853.

Chadwick, Michelle W. 1988. A Comparison of Two Approaches to Child Sexual Abuse Prevention Training. Unpublished doctoral dissertation, University of California, Irvine.

Christopoulos, Christina, Deborah A. Cohn, Daniel S. Shaw, Susan Joyce, Jean Sullivan-Hanson, Sherry P. Kraft, and Robert Emery. 1987. "Children of abused women: Adjustment at time of shelter residence." Journal of Marriage and the Family 49: 611–619.

Conte, Jon R. 1985a. "Clinical dimensions of adult sexual use of children." Behavioral Sciences and the Law 3: 341–354.

Conte, Jon R. 1985b. "The effects of sexual abuse on children: A critique and suggestions for future research." Victimology 10: 110–130.

Conte, Jon R. 1986. "Child sexual abuse and the family: A critical analysis." Journal of Psychotherapy and the Family 2: 113–126.

Conte, Jon R. 1987. "Ethical issues in evaluation of prevention programs." Child Abuse and Neglect 11: 171–172.

Conte, Jon R., Lucy Berliner, and John Schuerman. 1990. "The follow-up results of sexual abuse." (Under review)

Conte, Jon R., and Linda Fogarty. 1990. "Sexual abuse prevention programs for children." Education and Urban Society 22: 270–284.

Conte, Jon R., Carole Rosen, Leslee Saperstein, and Roberta Shermack. 1985. "An evaluation of a program to prevent the sexual victimization of young children." Child Abuse and Neglect 9: 319–328.

Conte, Jon R., and John R. Schuerman. 1987. "Factors associated with an increased impact of child sexual abuse." Child Abuse and Neglect 11: 201–211.

Daro, Deborah, and Anne H. Cohn. 1988. "Child maltreatment evaluations efforts: What have we learned?" Pp. 275–287 in Gerald T. Hotaling, David Finkelhor, John T. Kirkpatrick, and Murray A. Straus (eds.), Coping with Family Violence: Research and Policy Perspectives. Newbury Park, CA: Sage.

de Young, Mary. 1982. "Self-injurious behavior in incest victims: A research note." Child Welfare 61: 577–584.

Dietrich, J. N., Raymond H. Starr, Jr., and G. E. Weisfield. 1983. "Infant maltreatment: Caretaker-infant interaction and developmental consequences at different levels of parenting failure." Pediatrics 72: 532–540.

Downer, A. 1984. "Evaluation of *Talking about Touching.*" Available from author, c/o Committee for Children, Seattle, Washington.

Dunford, Frank W., David Huizinga, and Delbert S. Elliot. 1989. The Omaha Domestic Violence Police Experiment: Final Report to the National Institute of Justice and the City of Omaha. Boulder, Colorado (mimeographed).

Dutton, Donald G. 1986. "The outcome of court-mandated treatment for wife assault: A quasi-experimental evaluation." Violence and Victims 1: 163–176.

Earls, C., and W. L. Marshall. 1983. "The current state of technology in the laboratory assessment of sexual arousal patterns." In J. G. Greer and I. R. Stuart (eds.), The Sexual Aggressor: Current Perspectives on Treatment. New York: Reinhold.

Egeland, Byron, Deborah Jacobvitz, and Kathleen Papatola. 1987. "Intergenerational continuity of abuse." Pp. 255–276 in Richard J. Gelles and Jane B. Lancaster (eds.), Child Abuse and Neglect: Biosocial Dimensions. Hawthorne, NY: Aldine de Gruyter.

Egeland, Byron, Deborah Jacobvitz, and L. Alan Sroufe. 1988. "Breaking the cycle of abuse." Child Development 59: 1080–1088.

Emery, Robert E. 1989. "Family violence." American Psychologist 44: 321–328.

Finkelhor, David. 1979. Sexually Victimized Children. New York: Free Press.

Finkelhor, David, and Larry Baron. 1986. "High risk children." Pp. 60–88 in David Finkelhor (ed.), A Sourcebook on Child Sexual Abuse. Beverly Hills, CA: Sage.

Friedrich, W. N. 1988. "Behavior problems in sexually abused children: An adaptional perspective." Pp. 171–191 in Gail E. Wyatt and Gloria J. Powell (eds.), Lasting Effects of Child Sexual Abuse. Newbury Park, CA: Sage.

Fryer, George E., Sherryl K. Kraizer, and Thomas Miyoshi. 1987. "Measuring actual reduction of risk to child abuse: A new approach." Child Abuse and Neglect 11: 173–179.

Gale, John, Robert J. Thompson, Thomas Moran, and William H. Sack. 1988. "Sexual abuse in young children: Its clinical presentations and characteristic patterns.'' Child Abuse and Neglect 12: 163–170.

Garbarino, James. 1987. ''Children's response to a sexual abuse prevention program: A study of the *Spiderman* comic.'' Child Abuse and Neglect 11: 143–148.

Geller, Janet. 1982. ''Conjoint therapy: Staff training and treatment of the abuser and abused.'' Pp. 198–215 in M. Roy (ed.), The Abusive Partner: An Analysis of Domestic Beating. New York: Van Nostrand Reinhold.

Gelles, Richard J. 1980. ''Violence in the family: A review of research in the seventies.'' Journal of Marriage and the Family 42: 873–885.

Gelles, Richard J. 1990. ''Methodological issues in the study of family violence.'' Pp. 49–74 in Gerald R. Patterson (ed.), Depression and Aggression in Family Interaction. Hillsdale, NJ: Lawrence Erlbaum Associates.

Gelles, Richard J., and John W. Harrop. 1989. ''Violence, battering, and psychological distress among women.'' Journal of Interpersonal Violence 4: 400–420.

Giles-Sims, Jean. 1983. Wife-Beating: A Systems Theory Approach. New York: Guilford.

Gomes-Schwartz, Beverly, Jonathan M. Horowitz, and Maria Sauzier. 1985. ''Severity of emotional distress among sexually abused preschool, school-age, and adolescent children.'' Hospital and Community Psychiatry 36: 503–512.

Gondolf, Edward W. 1987. ''Evaluating progress for men who batter: Problems and prospects.'' Journal of Family Violence 2: 95–108.

Goodwin, J., M. Simms, and R. Bergman, 1979. ''Hysterical seizures: A sequel to incest.'' American Journal of Orthopsychiatry 49: 698–703.

Gross, M. 1979. ''Incestuous rape: A cause for hysterical seizures in four adolescent girls.'' American Journal of Orthopsychiatry 49: 704–708.

Harvey, Pam, Rex Forehand, Carvin Brown, and Thomas Holmes. 1988. ''The prevention of sexual abuse: Examination of a program with kindergarten-age children.'' Behavior Therapy 19: 429–435.

Herrenkohl, Ellen C., Roy C. Herrenkohl, and Lori J. Toedler. 1983. ''Perspectives on the intergenerational transmission of abuse.'' Pp. 305–316 in David Finkelhor, Richard J. Gelles, Gerald Hotaling, and Murray A. Straus (eds.), The Dark Side of Families: Current Family Violence Research. Newbury Park, CA: Sage.

Hilberman, Elaine. 1980. ''Overview: 'The wife-beater's wife' reconsidered.'' American Journal of Psychiatry 137: 1336–1346.

Kalmuss, Debra. 1984. ''The intergenerational transmission of marital aggression.'' Journal of Marriage and the Family 46: 11–19.

Kaufman, Joan, and Edward Zigler. 1987. ''Do abused children become abusive parents?'' American Journal of Orthopsychiatry 57: 186–192.

Kenning, M., T. Gallmeier, T. L. Jackson, and S. Plemons. 1987. ''Evaluation of child sexual abuse prevention programs: A summary of two studies.''

Paper presented at the National Conference on Family Violence, Durham, NH.

Kolko, David J. 1988. ''Educational programs to promote awareness and prevention of child sexual victimization: A review and methodological critique.'' Clinical Psychology Review 8: 195–209.

Kolko, David J., Joanne T. Moser, John Litz, and Judith Hughes. 1987. ''Promoting awareness and prevention of child sexual victimization using the red flag/green flag program: An evaluation with follow-up.'' Journal of Family Violence 2: 11–35.

Kolko, David J., Joanne T. Moser, and S. R. Weldy. 1988. ''Behavioral/emotional indicators of sexual abuse in child psychiatric inpatients: A controlled comparison with physical abuse.'' Child Abuse and Neglect 12: 529–541.

Laws, D. R., and C. A. Osborn, 1983. ''How to build and operate a behavioral laboratory to evaluate and treat sexual deviance.'' In J. G. Greer and I. R. Stuart (eds.), The Sexual Aggressor: Current Perspectives on Treatment. New York: Reinhold.

Laws, D. R., and M. B. Rubin. 1962. ''Instructional control of an autonomic sexual response.'' Journal of Applied Behavioral Analysis 2: 95–99.

Malone, Jean, Andrea Tyree, and K. Daniel O'Leary. 1989. ''Generalization and containment: Different effects of past aggression for wives and husbands.'' Journal of Marriage and the Family 51: 687–697.

Marshall, W. L., H. E. Barbaree, and D. Christopher. 1986. ''Sexual offenders against female children: Sexual preferences for age of victims and type of behaviour.'' Canadian Journal of Behavioral Science 18: 424–439.

Masson, J. Moussaieff. 1984. The Assault on the Truth: Freud's Suppression of the Seduction Theory. New York: Farrar, Strauss, and Giroux.

McNeely, R. L., and Gloria Robinson-Simpson. 1987. ''The truth about domestic violence: A falsely framed issue.'' Social Work 32: 485–490.

Miltenberger, Raymond G., and Ellyn Thiesse-Duffy. 1988. ''Evaluation of home-based programs for teaching personal safety skills to children.'' Journal of Applied Behavior Analysis 21: 81–87.

National Center on Child Abuse and Neglect. 1988. Study Findings: Study of National Incidence and Prevalence of Child Abuse and Neglect, 1988. Washington, DC: U.S. Department of Health and Human Services.

Neidig, Peter H., and D. H. Friedman. 1984. Spouse Abuse: A Treatment Program for Couples. Champaign, IL: Research Press.

Ohlin, Lloyd, and Michael Tonry (ed.). 1989. Family Violence. Chicago: University of Chicago Press.

Olds, David L., Charles R. Henderson, Jr., R. Tatelbaum, and R. Chamberlin. 1986. ''Preventing child abuse and neglect: A randomized trial of nurse home visitation.'' Pediatrics 77: 65–78.

Peters, Stephanie D., Gail E. Wyatt, and David Finkelhor. 1986. ''Prevalence.'' Pp. 15–59 in David Finkelhor (ed.), A Sourcebook on Child Sexual Abuse. Beverly Hills, CA: Sage.

Pillemer, Karl, and David Finkelhor. 1988. ''The prevalence of elder abuse: A random sample survey." Gerontologist 28: 51–57.

Pillemer, Karl, and J. Jill Suitor. 1988. "Elder abuse." Pp. 247–270 in Vincent B. Van Hasselt, Randall L. Morrison, Alan S. Bellack, and Michel Hersen (eds.), Handbook of Family Violence. New York: Plenum.

Pirog-Good, Maureen A., and Jan Stets. 1986. Programs for abusers: Who drops out and what can be done." Response 9: 17–19.

Pirog-Good, Maureen A., and Jan Stets (eds.) 1989. Violence in Dating Relationships: Emerging Social Issues. New York: Praeger.

Plummer, C. 1984. "Research on prevention: What school programs teach children." Paper presented at the Third National Conference on Sexual Victimization of Children, Washington, DC (April 26–28).

Quinsey, Vernon L. 1984. "Sexual aggression: Studies of offenders against women." In D. Weisstub (ed.), Law and Mental Health: International Perspectives. New York: Pergamon Press.

Quinsey, Vernon L., and S. G. Bergersen. 1976. "Instructional control of penile circumference in assessments of sexual preference." Behavior Therapy 7: 489–493.

Quinsey, Vernon L., and Terry C. Chaplin. 1988. "Penile responses of child molesters and normals to descriptions of encounters with children involving sex and violence." Journal of Interpersonal Violence 3: 259–274.

Quinsey, Vernon L., Terry C. Chaplin, and Wayne F. Carrigan. 1979. "Sexual preferences among incestuous and nonincestuous child molesters." Behavior Therapy 10: 562–565.

Ray, J., and M. Dietzel. 1984. "Teaching child sexual abuse prevention." Unpublished manuscript.

Rimsza, Mary E., Robert A. Berg, and Catherine Locke. 1988. "Sexual abuse: Somatic and emotional reactions." Child Abuse and Neglect 12: 201–208.

Schechter, Susan. 1983. Women and Male Violence. Boston: South End Press.

Sherman, Lawrence W., and Richard A. Berk. 1984. "The specific deterrent effects of arrest for domestic assault." American Sociological Review 49: 261–272.

Starr, Raymond H., Jr. 1982. "A research based approach to the prediction of child abuse." Pp. 105–142 in Raymond H. Starr, Jr., Child Abuse Prediction: Policy Implications. Cambridge, MA: Ballinger.

Starr, Raymond H., Jr. 1988. "Physical abuse of children." Pp. 119–155 in Vincent B. Van Hasselt, Randall L. Morrison, Alan S. Bellack, and Michel Hersen (eds.), Handbook of Family Violence. New York: Plenum.

Starr, Raymond H., Jr., K. N. Dietrich, Joseph Fishoff, Steven J. Cerensnie, and D. Zweier. 1984. "The contribution of handicapping conditions to child abuse." Topics in Early Childhood Special Education 4: 55–69.

Steinmetz, Suzanne K. 1987. "Family violence: Past, present, and future." Pp. 725–765 in Marvin B. Sussman and Suzanne K. Steinmetz (eds.), Hand-

book of Marriage and the Family. New York: Plenum Press.

Straus, Murry A. 1990. "The national family violence surveys." Pp. 3–16 in Murray Straus and Richard J. Gelles (eds.), Physical Violence in American Families: Risk Factors and Adaptations in 8,145 Families. New Brunswick, NJ: Transaction Books.

Straus, Murray A., and Richard J. Gelles. 1986. "Societal change and change in family violence from 1975 to 1985 as revealed in two national surveys." Journal of Marriage and the Family 48: 465–479.

Turner, S. F., and C. H. Shapiro. 1986. "Battered women: Mourning the death of a relationship." Social Work 31: 372–376.

Van Hasselt, Vincent B., Randall L. Morrison, Alan S. Bellack, and Michel Hersen (eds.). 1988. Handbook of Family Violence. New York: Plenum.

Weis, Joseph G. 1989. "Family violence research methodology and design." Pp. 117–162 in Lloyd Ohlin and Michael Tonry (eds.), Family Violence. Chicago: University of Chicago Press.

Weiss, J., E. Rogers, M. R. Darwin, and C. E. Dutton. 1955. "A study of girl sex victims." Psychiatric Quarterly 29: 1–27.

Widom, Cathy S. 1989. "The cycle of violence." Science 244 (April 14): 160–166.

Williams, Kirk R., and Richard Hawkins. 1989. "The meaning of arrest for wife assault." Criminology 27: 163–181.

Wolfe, David A., Tracy MacPherson, Ronald L. Blount, and Vicky V. Wolfe. 1986. "Evaluation of a brief intervention for educating school children in awareness of physical and sexual abuse." Child Abuse and Neglect 10: 85–92.

Wurtele, Sandy K., L. C. Kast, Cindy L. Miller-Perrin, and P. A. Kondrick. 1989. "Comparison of programs for teaching personal safety skills to preschoolers." Journal of Consulting and Clinical Psychology 57: 505–511.

Wurtele, Sandy K., Scott R. Marrs, and Cindy L. Miller-Perrin. 1987. "Practice makes perfect? The role of participant modeling in sexual abuse prevention programs." Journal of Consulting and Clinical Psychology 55: 599–602.

Wurtele, Sandy K., and Cindy L. Miller-Perrin. 1987. "An evaluation of side effects associated with participation in a child sexual abuse prevention program." Journal of School Health 57: 228–231.

Yllo, Kersti, and Michele Bograd (eds.). 1988. Feminist Perspectives on Wife Abuse. Newbury Park, CA: Sage.

Yorukoglu, A. and J. P. Kempe. 1966. "Children not severely damaged by incest with a parent." Journal of the American Academy of Child Psychiatry 55: 111–124.

Youngblade, Lisa M., and Jay Belsky. 1989. "The social and emotional consequences of child maltreatment." In R. Ammerman and Michel Hersen (eds.), Children at Risk: An Evaluation of Factors Contributing to Child Abuse and Neglect. New York: Plenum.

CATHERINE E. ROSS, JOHN MIROWSKY, AND KAREN GOLDSTEEN
University of Illinois at Champaign-Urbana

The Impact of the Family on Health:
The Decade in Review

How does the family affect the health of its adult members? It is in the family that the macro-level social and economic order affects individual physical and emotional well-being. This review presents a general model of understanding family and health that describes patterns of well-being, and then asks, "what explains these patterns?" Explanations are found in causal chains, conditional effects, and "structural amplification." The review summarizes and synthesizes ideas and findings about four factors: marriage and parenthood (which define the family), and the wife's or mother's employment and the family's social status (which connect it to the larger social order). Overall, the married are in better health than the nonmarried, but parents are not better off than nonparents. Women's employment and high family socioeconomic status tend to be associated with good physical and psychological health. Under what circumstances are these basic patterns found, and what explains these patterns—what links structure to individual health? Economic well-being and social support are considered as the basic explanations. Concluding comments point to the need for more studies of the impact of family on the sense of control, which could be an important link to health.

How does a family promote or hinder the well-being of its individual adult members? A family is more than just a collection of people who might expose each other to infections and pollutants. A family is an economic unit bound together by emotional ties. The larger social structure impinges on individuals through the family (Ross and Huber, 1985). Does the family nurture health by cushioning against an impersonal and sometimes threatening social order, and by encouraging responsible and temperate behavior? Or does it erode health with an unceasing flow of demands?

To answer these questions, we begin by defining *family* and *health*. Next we describe a general mode of understanding family and health—a format evolved from research of the past decade. Then we detail the ideas and findings about two pairs of factors: marriage and parenthood (which define the family), and the wife's or mother's employment and the family's social status (which connect it to the larger social order). Finally, we discuss the need for more studies of the impact of family on the sense of control, which could be an important link to health.

What is a family? The U.S. Bureau of the Census defines a *family* as two or more individuals related by blood, marriage, or adoption who reside in the same household (Cherlin, 1981). This definition, which combines household and kin, is appropriate for a study of the American family today, because of the low degree to which kin outside the household rely upon each other. The Census Bureau definition encompasses a great variety of family household structures, including married adults with or without children, single-parent families headed by either a woman or a man, families with three or more generations in the household, and stepfamilies, to name a few. Nearly 80% of all American families are formed

Department of Sociology, 326 Lincoln Hall, University of Illinois, 702 South Wright Street, Urbana, IL 61801.

341

around married couples, and the rest are mostly mothers and their children (Cherlin, 1981; U.S. Bureau of the Census, 1989).

The World Health Organization defines *health* as a state of physical and mental well-being, not simply the absence of disease. This broad definition of health focuses on the physical and emotional quality of people's lives, more than on rates of diagnosed illness. Well-being varies along a continuum (Mirowsky and Ross, 1989). At one extreme, people feel tired, sick, and run-down. They are physically unable to climb stairs or walk, have many short-term illnesses like colds or the flu, have ongoing problems like arthritis that interfere with activity, or feel depressed, anxious, and demoralized. At the other extreme, people feel healthy and energetic, rarely spend a day sick in bed, and feel happy and hopeful about the future. Most people fall somewhere between these two extremes. People who qualify for medical or psychiatric diagnoses tend toward the sick end of the continuum, whereas those who do not qualify for diagnoses tend toward the health end. Nevertheless, people who qualify for diagnoses differ considerably among themselves in their degree of sickness or health, as do people not qualified for diagnoses.

Physical and mental health correlate highly (Aneshensel et al., 1984; Bruce and Leaf, 1989; Mechanic and Hansell, 1987; Verbrugge, 1986). They share common causes, they affect each other, and signs of one often are signs of the other.

Physical well-being consists of feeling fit and able, unrestricted by discomfort or disability. Physical distress includes feeling unhealthy, tired, run-down, having no energy, having headaches and stomach aches, feeling faint, having trouble breathing, being in pain, having difficulty with activities such as walking, lifting, carrying, bending, and so on, feeling unable to get out of bed, and being disabled by acute and chronic health problems (Verbrugge, 1983; Waldron and Jacobs, 1988). Physical distress is indicated by self-reported symptoms, poor health, dysfunction, and sick days, but not necessarily by the number of visits to the doctor. Although feeling sick increases the likelihood of visiting the doctor, other factors such as income, insurance, time, and inclination make doctor visits a problematic measure of health.

Emotional well-being consists of feeling happy, hopeful, and energetic, with a zest for life. Psychological distress includes moods of depression or anxiety, and physiological symptoms associated with these moods (Mirowsky and Ross, 1989; Pearlin, Lieberman, Menaghan, and Mullan, 1981). Depression and anxiety correlate highly with each other and afflict everyone to some degree from time to time. They correlate with other affective problems such as anger; with cognitive problems such as paranoia; and with substance abuse such as heavy drinking (Mirowsky and Ross, 1989). (Heavy drinking decreases depression in the short run but increases it in the long run; Aneshensel and Huba, 1983; Parker, Parker, Harford, and Farmer, 1987). Depression consists of feeling sad, demoralized, lonely, hopeless, and worthless; wishing you were dead; having trouble concentrating; having trouble sleeping; not feeling like eating; crying; and feeling run-down and unable to get going. Anxiety consists of being tense, restless, worried, irritable, afraid, and having "fight or flight" symptoms such as acid stomach, sweaty palms, and cold sweats, as well as your heart beating hard and fast, shortness of breath, or feeling hot all over when not exercising or working hard. (Notice that one of the ways physical and mental health correlate is through psychophysiological symptoms of depression and anxiety.)

It is important to distinguish well-being from certain things that may affect it but are not one and the same thing. In particular, satisfaction with one's lot does not necessarily indicate well-being. Satisfaction implies a convergence of aspiration and achievement that reflects resignation as much as it does accomplishment. Whereas distress often results from deprivation, dissatisfaction results from deprivation *relative to one's expectations.* Although the two often go together, sometimes they diverge in meaningful ways. For example, among people with the same family income, higher levels of education *reduce* satisfaction but *increase* psychological well-being (Mirowsky and Ross, 1989).

The sense of control over one's own life also is not the same as well-being. Well-being is feeling pleasant rather than unpleasant, good rather than bad, up rather than down. The sense of mastery, efficacy, and control is a belief rather than a feeling. People respond emotionally to their perceptions of themselves, but the perceptions and the emotions are distinct. For example, it is one thing to consider oneself attractive and another to feel happy because of the belief, the consequences of the belief, or the consequences of the reality the belief presents.

A GENERAL MODEL OF FAMILY AND HEALTH

Structural Analysis: A Mode of Understanding

How can we describe and talk about the ways that health or sickness depend on family arrangements and situations? Obviously, health and sickness occur within the family. We want to know how the family itself generates health and sickness, or alters the impact of things that generate it. The family exists within a social context and is itself a social context. Patterns of physical and mental health, things that explain the patterns, and things that modify them all flow from the "structural arrangements in which individuals are embedded" (Pearlin, 1989: 241). Pearlin and his colleagues laid the foundation for a decade of research on social structure and well-being that focuses on durable, structured experiences that people have as they engage in their various social roles, such as economic, occupational, family, and parental roles (Pearlin et al., 1981). The research of the 1980s produced a general format for thinking about and studying how such durable, structured experiences generate and regulate variations in well-being.

The paradigm, which we call structural analysis, searches for two types of patterns. In *causal chains*, intermediate links explain patterns of well-being. Causal-chain models divide the overall correlation between family and health into component links that explain the correlation. In *conditional effects* (or interactions), one element of the social context modifies the impact of another on well-being. Conditional-effect models specify the conditions that increase, decrease, eliminate, or reverse a correlation between family and health. Both causal chains and conditional effects provide means of explaining why and how family affects well-being (Wheaton, 1985). When causal chains and conditional effects combine, they produce what we call *structural amplification,* in which an aspect of social structure erodes the barriers that would otherwise reduce its correlation with well-being.

In the sections that follow we examine research of the past decade for patterns and explanations of the association between family and health. We begin each section by describing the pattern of well-being related to one of four aspects of family: marriage, parenthood, the wife's employment, and the family's social and economic status. Next we ask, What explains the pattern? To answer, we look for links in the causal chain, conditional effects, and their combination in structural amplification.

MARRIAGE

Patterns

Marriage is associated with physical health, psychological well-being, and low mortality. Compared to people who are divorced, separated, single, or widowed, the married have better overall well-being. This overall positive effect is strong and consistent. Compared to married people, the nonmarried have higher levels of depression, anxiety, and other forms of psychological distress (Bowling, 1987; Gore and Mangione, 1983; Gove, Hughes, and Style, 1983; Mirowsky and Ross, 1989), they have more physical health problems as indicated by acute conditions, chronic conditions, days of disability, and self-reported health (Anson, 1989; Berk and Taylor, 1984; Riessman and Gerstel, 1985; Tcheng-Laroche and Prince, 1983). The nonmarried have higher rates of mortality than the married: about 50% higher among women and 250% higher among men (Berkman and Breslow, 1983; Litwack and Messeri, 1989). Compared to married people, the divorced and widowed have higher death rates from coronary heart disease, stroke, pneumonia, many kinds of cancer, cirrhosis of the liver, automobile accidents, homicide, and suicide, all of which are leading causes of death (Berkman and Breslow, 1983; Kaprio, Koskenvuo, and Rita, 1987; Tcheng-Laroche and Prince, 1983). The ratio of nonmarried to married mortality is particularly high for causes of death that have a large behavioral component, such as lung cancer and cirrhosis, or that kill young and middle-aged adults, such as suicide and accidents (Litwack and Messeri, 1989; Smith, Mercy, and Conn, 1988). The highest mortality ratios are among persons from 35 to 44 years old (Litwack and Messeri, 1989). Widows have higher levels of depression and anxiety and higher death rates

344

than the married (Bowling, 1987; Helsing, Moysen, and Comstock, 1981). Death rates are greatest immediately after the death of one's spouse (Kaprio et al., 1987) but remain elevated until the widowed remarry (Bowling, 1987; Helsing et al., 1981).

Some researchers claim that selection of the healthy into marriage accounts for the association of marriage and health, but the evidence cited is equivocal. For example, Brown and Giesy (1986) find that people with spinal cord injuries are less likely to be married. They interpret this as the consequence of selection, arguing that people with severe health problems have difficulty finding and keeping marriage partners. It is just as likely that marriage protects against spinal cord injuries, because married people engage in fewer risky activities than unmarried people. Although there may be some selection effect keeping or taking the unhealthy out of marriage, the protective effects of marriage on health probably account for more of the association.

Although marriage generally protects and improves health, it protects men's well-being more than women's. Marriage protects men from death more than it does women (Helsing et al., 1981; Litwack and Messeri, 1989), it protects men's physical health more than it does women's (Bird and Fremont, 1989), and it protects men's psychological well-being more than it does women's (Gove, 1984) (although there is some counter evidence that men's advantage over women in mental health is as large or larger among the single, divorced, and widowed; Fox, 1980). The protective effect of marriage may be declining somewhat. In terms of reported happiness, the positive effects of marriage have declined slightly between 1972 and 1986, especially for women (Glenn and Weaver, 1988), and recent studies show a weaker association between marriage and well-being than did earlier studies (Haring-Hidore, Stock, Okum, and Witter, 1985). Nonetheless, marital happiness is still the largest contributor to overall happiness (Glenn and Weaver, 1988). For men and women, now as before, marriage is associated with physical and psychological well-being.

Explanations

The literature focuses on three explanations of why marriage protects well-being: living with

someone rather than alone, emotional support, and economic well-being. Of the three, emotional support and economic well-being explain much, but not all, of the positive effect of marriage on health.

Living with someone. At first researchers thought the simple presence of another adult in the household might explain why marriage improves well-being. Since unmarried people often live alone but married people almost always live together (often with children), this might explain why unmarried people are more distressed. A person who lives alone may be isolated from an important network of social and economic ties: the privileges and obligations centered on the home and family. These ties may help create a stabilizing sense of security, belonging, and direction. Without them a person may feel lonely, adrift, and unprotected. To test this theory, Hughes and Gove (1981) subdivided three types of unmarried people (never married, divorced or separated, and widowed) according to whether they lived alone or with another adult. Contrary to what Hughes and Gove expected, they found that unmarried people who live alone are no more distressed than those who live with other adults. The big difference is between married people and others, not between people who live alone and others. The unmarried, living alone or with others, are significantly more distressed than the married. The mere presence or absence of another adult in the household does not explain the patterns of marriage and well-being.

Social support. Social support is the commitment, caring, advice, and aid provided in personal relationships. It has several dimensions, including emotional and instrumental support. Marriage typically provides social support of all forms—particularly the emotional element (Gerstel, Reissman, and Rosenfield, 1985; Ross and Mirowsky, 1989). Emotional support is the sense of being cared about, loved, esteemed, and valued as a person, and having someone who cares about you and your problems. Married people are more likely to report that they have someone they can turn to for support and understanding when things get rough, and that they have a confidant they can really talk to. Emotional support decreases depression, anxiety, sickness, and mortality (Blazer, 1982; Gerstel et al., 1985; Hanson, Isacsson, Janzon, and Lindell, 1989; House, Robbins, and Metzner, 1982; Pearlin et al., 1981; Turner and Noh, 1983).

On the other hand, when a spouse expects more than he or she is willing to give back, acts like the only important person in the family, and cannot be counted on for esteem and advice, men and women feel demoralized, tense, worried, neglected, unhappy, and frustrated. Marriages characterized by an unequal division of decision-making power are associated with high levels of depression on the part of both spouses, as compared to marriages characterized by equity (Mirowsky, 1985). It is not enough just to have someone around. It is better to live alone than in a marriage characterized by a lack of consideration, caring, esteem, and equity. Gove, Hughes, and Style (1983) show that the emotional benefits of marriage depend on the quality of the marriage. The 62% of married people who report being very happy with the marriage are less distressed than unmarrieds. The 34% who only say they are pretty happy with the marriage are no less distressed than the unmarrieds. The 4% who say they are not too happy or not at all happy with the marriage are *more* distressed than unmarrieds of all types (Gove et al., 1983).

Support from one's spouse may improve physical health several ways: by improving emotional health, by reducing risky behavior, by aiding early detection and treatment, and by helping recovery. The first impact is through the direct effect of psychological well-being on physical well-being. Social support, especially emotional support, decreases depression, anxiety, and other psychological problems (Cohen and Syme, 1985; Kaplan, Robbins, and Martin, 1983; Kessler and McLeod, 1985; LaRocco, House, and French, 1980; Mirowsky and Ross, 1989; Wheaton, 1985). Over time, psychological well-being improves subsequent physical well-being (Aneshensel et al., 1984; Mechanic and Hansell, 1987). A 15-month follow-up of people aged 50 and over finds that the severely depressed are four times more likely to die than others, with adjustment for history of hypertension, heart attack, stroke, cancer, or limitation of physical functioning (Bruce and Leaf, 1989). By protecting and improving psychological well-being, social support also improves physical health and survival. The second way support from one's spouse improves physical health is by encouraging and reinforcing protective

behaviors. Marriage provides a stable, coherent, regulated environment (Hughes and Gove, 1981; Umberson, 1987). Compared to single, divorced, and widowed people, the married experience more social control and regulation of behavior (Anson, 1989; Umberson, 1987). For the most part, married people live a healthier lifestyle than the single, divorced, or widowed. Married people are more likely to quit smoking, to eat diets low in cholesterol and high in fruits and vegetables, and to eat balanced meals (Hayes and Ross, 1987; Umberson, 1987; Venters, 1986). Married people are less likely to drink heavily, to get into fights, to drive too fast, and to take risks that increase the likelihood of accidents and injuries (Umberson, 1987; Venters, 1986). Wives, in particular, often discourage smoking, drug use, or heavy drinking in the house, cook low-cholesterol meals and keep fattening food out of the house, and schedule checkups. The fact that women generally have a healthier lifestyle than men may explain why marriage improves men's health behaviors (Umberson, 1987) and survival (Litwack and Messeri, 1989) more than women's.

The effects of marriage on a healthy lifestyle are generally positive but not completely consistent. A few healthy behaviors are not increased by marriage. Married people are more likely to be overweight, and they are less likely to engage in physical activity and exercise than the nonmarried (Hayes and Ross, 1986; Ross and Mirowsky, 1983; Venters, 1986).

On the whole, marriage produces a net improvement in avoiding the onset of disease, which is called primary prevention. There is little argument over the benefits of primary preventive behavior (Abbott, Yin, Reed, and Yano, 1986; Graham and Mettlin, 1979; Hovell, 1982; Lipid Research Clinics Program, 1984; Magnus, Matroos, and Strackee, 1979; Multiple Risk Factor Intervention Trial Research Group, 1982; Paffenbarger, Hyde, Wing, and Steinmetz, 1984; Sagan, 1987; Stamler, 1981; Surgeon General, 1982). *Quitting smoking* (or never smoking) decreases the risk of lung cancer, emphysema, stroke, coronary heart disease, and respiratory infections, including pneumonia. A balanced *diet* low in calories and cholesterol and high in fruits and vegetables decreases the risk of coronary heart disease, adult-onset diabetes, atherosclerosis, high blood pressure, and colon cancer. *Driving safely* and not drinking and driving decreases the risk of car accidents. *Avoiding heavy drinking* decreases the risk of cirrhosis of the liver, accidents, and injuries, and even suicide and homicide. All of these primary preventive behaviors are more common among the married and decrease the risk of leading causes of death in the United States: heart disease, cancer, stroke, accidents, emphysema, pneumonia and influenza, diabetes, suicide, cirrhosis of the liver, atherosclerosis, kidney disease, and homicide (Litwack and Messeri, 1989; National Center for Health Statistics, 1989).

A third way marriage may improve health, in theory, is by helping to catch and treat disease early, which is called secondary prevention. Married people are more likely to see the doctor for checkups, screening, and other early detection than the nonmarried with the same symptoms, functioning, and general level of health (Berkman and Breslow, 1983; Neale, Tilley, and Vernon, 1986). Yet, the benefits to overall health of uncovering and treating disease early are uncertain. Yearly checkups appear to have no effect on maintaining health (Sagan, 1987). Screening tests such as X rays and mammography entail some risk with the exposure to small amounts of radiation (Bailar and Smith, 1986). The risks and side effects of treatment often outweigh the benefits for low-level disease, which often gets better, or no worse, if left untreated. False alarms lead to treatments that carry risks to survival, such as septicemia or drug reactions, without providing counterbalancing benefits (Sagan, 1987).

Cancer statistics provide an example of the questionable benefits of finding and treating diseases before symptoms appear. Cancer is the second leading cause of death. Despite trends toward much earlier detection and treatment, cancer deaths in the United States have been stable or increasing over the past 40 years (NCHS, 1989). According to Bailar and Smith (1986) and Cairns (1985), early detection and treatment of cancer is largely ineffective. (Hodgkin's disease [1% of cancer deaths] and leukemia [4%] are exceptions.) For lung cancer (30% of cancer deaths) and breast cancer (10%), screening creates an illusion of improved survival because many of the small cancers detected by X ray would not be fatal even if untreated (Bailar and Smith, 1986). Also, X rays, breast examinations, and mammograms detect cancers at an early stage. The earlier cancers are detected, the longer the average time between detection and death, which gives a false impression of longer survival (Sackett, Haynes, and Tugwell, 1985). Neale, Tilley, and Vernon (1986) find that married women seek treatment sooner than do widows after noticing symptoms like a lump or change in the breast. When adjustments are made for age, SES, and stage of the disease at diagnosis, the length of time between noticing symptoms and seeking treatment does *not* affect 10-year survival. However, married women *do* live longer than widowed women with breast cancer detected at the same stage. Thus, the salutary effect of marriage on subsequent length of survival is not explained by finding the cancer at an earlier stage.

A fourth way that support from one's spouse may improve physical health is by aiding recovery. Intimacy between partners, as opposed to marital conflict, promotes emotional recovery from myocardial infarction (Waltz, Badura, Pfaff, and Schott, 1988). High levels of emotional support from one's husband reduces depression and anxiety among women with breast cancer (Neuling and Winefield, 1988). Low levels of family conflict are associated with better control of diabetes (Edelstein and Linn, 1985).

In summary, marriage has large, significant, consistent, positive effects on physical health by increasing social support. The effect of social support on health appears to be mediated by improved psychological well-being, healthier life style, and better recovery, more than by earlier detection and treatment of disease.

Economic well-being. Married people have higher household incomes than the nonmarried. In a representative sample of Illinois residents interviewed in 1985, married people had average household incomes of about $33,500. Nonmarried females had average household incomes of $21,500, and nonmarried males, $28,600 (Ross, 1989). Roughly speaking, being married increases the average household income of women by $12,000; for men the amount is about $7,000. The economic benefits of marriage hold for both women and men, even with adjustment for age, minority status, employment status, and education (Ross, 1989), although the economic benefits of marriage (and losses of nonmarriage) are greater for women than for men (Bianchi and Spain, 1986; Cherlin, 1981). Household income drops precipitously after divorce and remains close to the new low for as much as five years, especially for women (Weiss, 1984). Economic well-being, in turn, has a large effect on health and mental health (Kessler, 1982; Kessler and Cleary, 1980; Pearlin et al., 1981: Ross and Huber, 1985).

The two main health benefits of marriage—social support and economic well-being—may weigh differently for men and women. Gerstel, Riessman, and Rosenfield (1985) looked at the ways in which divorce increases the psychological distress of men and women. They found that, when divorced, women suffered more of a loss of household income than did men, whereas men suffered more of a loss of social support than did women. Both men and women gain economic well-being and emotional support from marriage, but marriage may be more of an economic benefit to women and an emotional-support benefit to men.

Unexplained effects. Social support and economic well-being explain some of the effect of marriage on depression, but not all. At the same levels of emotional support and family income, the married still have significantly lower levels of depression than the nonmarried (Ross and Mirowsky, 1989). The question of why married people have higher levels of physical and psychological well-being than the unmarried is still not completely answered empirically.

One possibility is that nonmarried people have less protective forms of social support, as well as less social support overall. People who live alone get a higher proportion of their social support outside the household than do people who live with others (Alwin, Converse, and Martin, 1985). Almost all people who live alone are unmarried (although not all people who are unmarried live alone). Having the providers of one's social support in the household may be more comforting and protective, perhaps simply because of greater availability.

Even though the nonmarried have a larger number of supportive relationships of other kinds, those relationships typically do not provide as much *emotional* support as a good marriage. Among the elderly, the married get most of their support in close personal relationships, whereas the nonmarried get a larger proportion of their support from agencies or people not personally close (Longino and Lipman, 1981). The less personal relationships specialize more in instrumental support, whereas the personal ones provide more

emotional support. The latter is more important to health and mental health (Kessler and McLeod, 1985).

PARENTHOOD

Patterns

People have strong beliefs about the positive effects of having and rearing children. Without children, women especially are said to feel empty, lonely, and demoralized. Although the strict sanctions against staying childless have abated somewhat, norms about the desirability of having children are still strong. The strength of these norms is seen partly in the fact that over 90% of all married people eventually have children. In 1980, only 7% of ever-married women reached age 44 without having any children (Bianchi and Spain, 1986). Nonetheless, a number of theorists and researchers challenge the view that children increase well-being. They argue the opposite, that children decrease the physical and psychological well-being of parents, especially mothers.

Emotional well-being. Children do not generally improve the psychological well-being of parents (Cleary and Mechanic, 1983; Gore and Mangione, 1983; Kessler and McRae, 1982; Lovell-Troy, 1983; McLanahan and Adams, 1987; Ross, Mirowsky, and Huber, 1983). People with children at home do not have higher levels of well-being than nonparents. In some instances, parents—especially mothers—are more psychologically distressed than nonparents, but in most, the effect of children on mothers' well-being is insignificant or inconsistent. Children at home either increase psychological distress or have an insignificant effect. In general, they do not decrease distress.

The studies that find a positive impact of children on well-being tend to look at the total number of children, not the number living at home (Aneshensel, Frerichs, and Clark, 1981; Kandel, Davies, and Raveis, 1985). Kandel and her colleagues, for instance, find that positive effects of children (if any) on the health and well-being of their parents appear only after the children leave home. Children at home increase depression, but parents whose children have left home are less depressed and in better health than the childless of the same age (Kandel et al., 1985), probably because of emotional support from adult children. However, elderly parents are not happier than the elderly who are childless (Glenn and McLanahan, 1981; Rempel, 1985), and giving or receiving aid from children does not affect the morale of the elderly (Lee and Ellithorpe, 1982). Overall, the evidence shows that children at home either decrease psychological well-being or have no impact on it. The positive effects of children may appear after they leave home, although studies that measure well-being as happiness find no evidence for any positive effects.

Physical well-being. Children at home have small, inconsistent, or insignificant effects on parents' physical health, too. Verbrugge (1983) looked at physical health in a comprehensive way, measuring self-reported health, number of chronic problems in the past year, number of days of restricted activity in the past year, job limitations, and a number of health measures taken from daily diaries, including physical feeling, number of health problems, and so on. In no case does the presence of children in the home significantly affect health, although the trends tend to be positive. Some researchers find that the presence of children, many children, and preschool children are associated with worse health for women (Gove, 1984), while others find insignificant effects of the number of children and the number of hours spent in child care on self-reported health (Bird and Fremont, 1989). Children at home do not significantly improve health. Marriage clearly improves health, but parenthood does not.

Explanations

Why would children at home decrease well-being, especially psychological well-being? Children tend to be valued and loved (although the disturbing facts about the prevalence of child abuse undermine our myths somewhat). How could children be loved and still increase distress levels, especially among mothers? Two explanations stand out: children increase economic hardships on families, and children decrease the amount of emotional support that spouses receive from each other. Economic well-being and social support reduce the detrimental impact of children on the health and well-being of parents, but children deplete those very resources (providing an example of structural amplification).

Economic well-being. Children increase economic strains on the family. At the same level of family income, a family with children feels more economic pressure than one without children (Ross and Huber, 1985). Each dollar must go farther—must buy more food, clothes, and medical care. Children often mean that the current house or apartment is too small. People in crowded housing conditions feel more harassed by their children (Goldsteen and Ross, 1989; Gove, Hughes, and Galle, 1979). Young children increase the pressures to acquire more living space, which requires larger rent or mortgage payments. However, the presence of young children often means the mother does not work outside the home. She may quit her job while the children are young, thus magnifying the family's economic hardship. If she continues her employment, family funds often are needed for day care. Economic hardship increases depression among both men and women. The chronic strain of struggling to pay the bills and to feed and clothe the children takes its toll, making parents feel run-down, hopeless, and worried (Pearlin et al., 1981; Ross and Huber, 1985).

Children are most detrimental to the health and well-being of single and divorced mothers (Alwin, Converse, and Martin, 1985; Aneshenshel et al., 1981; Kandel et al., 1985; McLanahan and Adams, 1987), in large part because of greater economic hardships (Moen, 1983). Nonmarried mothers and their children are the new poor in the United States. In 1980, 18% of all births were out of wedlock; and another 43% of all children born in wedlock in 1980 will experience parental separation before they are 16 years old (Preston, 1984). By 1982, 23% of all children under age 14 were living in poverty—most in female-headed households (Preston, 1984). *If* these mothers can find work, it tends to be poorly paid, and they must struggle to find and pay for child care. Both the children and their mothers are in extremely disadvantaged positions. For the mothers this disadvantage often has psychological consequences of depression and anxiety.

Social support. Children decrease the quality of the marriage and the amount of support the spouses get from each other. Emotional support and satisfaction with marriage decrease with the birth of the first child and do not return to preparenthood levels until all the children have left home. Both husbands and wives are most satisfied with their marriage when there are no children at home, either because they are childless or because the children have left home. As the number of children, especially young children, increases, satisfaction decreases (Pleck, 1983; Veroff, Douvan, and Kulka, 1981). Parents of preschool-age children report the lowest levels of support from spouses; people whose children have left home, and the childless, report the highest levels of marital support. Both voluntarily and involuntarily childless women report more support from husbands than do women with children (Callan, 1987). The involuntarily childless report the most loving marital relationships. The voluntary childless report the most time spent with husbands, exchange of ideas, and consensus with husbands (Callan, 1987). Richman, Raskin, and Gaines (1989) find that both spouses feel a decrease in mutual support following childbirth. Husbands and wives spend less time together when they have young children, and the time they do spend together is often focused on the child. Husbands feel they are getting less emotional support from their wives, whose energies now go into caring for the child. And wives, too, feel they get less support from husbands, who often distance themselves (sometimes literally) from the difficult care of young children. Women, especially those in the working class, report that their husbands are less likely to be confidants—to be there to talk to when needed—after the birth of the first child. In sum, couples with children, especially young children, report less support from and satisfaction with marriage.

Children tend to keep unhappily married couples together. Couples dissatisfied with their marriage are less likely to get divorced if they have young children, especially first children. Dissatisfied couples with no children or grown children are more likely to separate and divorce (Goetting, 1986; White and Booth, 1985; White, Booth, and Edwards, 1986). Thus, married couples without children are more satisfied than those with children partly because the dissatisfied without children get divorced.

Employed and unemployed mothers. For women, the relationship between parenthood and health may depend on employment status, child care arrangements, and the husband's participation in child care. Women with young children are less

likely to be employed than those with older children and the childless. Research indicates that children create more burden for women who are exclusively housewives than for employed women (providing another example of structural amplification). Children put strain on these mothers, apart from the quality of the marriage. Young children put constant demands on mothers who are home all day with the children. Young children separate mothers from other adults and make them feel they are stuck in the house, at the same time decreasing their privacy and time alone (Gove, 1984; Gove and Peterson, 1980). Housewives who are not employed are much more likely to feel that others are making demands on them than are employed mothers or fathers. Housewives feel more burdened by their children—feel their children are making too many demands, get in their way, are too noisy, and interfere with their privacy; and wish they could get away from their children—than do employed mothers (Goldsteen and Ross, 1989). In turn, mothers who feel burdened by their children have low levels of psychological well-being compared to mothers who feel fewer demands (Umberson, 1989).

Kotler and Wingard (1989) found an increased risk of mortality among mothers who are exclusively housewives, but no increased risk among working mothers. Employed mothers report better health than nonemployed mothers on a number of measures, including self-rated health, chronic conditions, and days of restricted activity (Verbrugge, 1983).

Cleary and Mechanic (1983) make the opposite argument, that children distress employed women more than housewives because of role strain. Many employed wives are largely responsible for child care. Role overload results from the sheer amount of effort it takes to perform in both arenas, and role conflict results from trying to meet the expectations of people who do not take each other into account (i.e., one's boss and one's children).

Employment may improve a mother's well-being under some conditions but degrade it under others. What are the conditions? Ross and Mirowsky (1988) concluded that the effect of children on a married woman's depression depends on her employment, child care arrangements, and husband's participation in child care. Two conditions are associated with the lowest levels of depression among women:

employment and no children, or employment coupled with either easy and available child care for the children while the parents are at work or with the husband's shared participation in child care. Staying at home with children is associated with higher levels of depression than these alternatives. The most stressful situation occurs if a wife is employed, has young children, has difficulty arranging child care, and gets no help from her husband with child care. These mothers are twice as depressed as employed mothers who have no difficulty arranging child care and whose husbands share the child care responsibilities with them. Thus, children seem to have very different effects on employed mothers, depending on the availability and affordability of child care and the husbands' participation in child care.

External support. Support from people in the household other than the husband also can reduce the burden of children (Goldsteen and Ross, 1989). However, help with child care by neighbors and relatives outside the household carries costs as well as benefits. Receiving support in the form of aid incurs the costs of mutual obligation (Belle, 1982: Rook, 1984). When friends and neighbors provide child care, mothers apparently have *specific* obligations to provide child care in return, which increases their sense of burden (Goldsteen and Ross, 1989). In a study of low-income women, Belle and her colleagues found that involvement with neighbors in caring for children is a strategy of desperation, not choice. It helps with basic survival but does not imply emotional support. When relatives in the area provide child care, mothers have more *diffuse* obligations that impinge on their ability to be by themselves when they want to be (Goldsteen and Ross, 1989). For women who can afford it, paying for formal child care service carries fewer emotional costs than using informal exchange networks. Paid employment sometimes frees women from demanding and restricting networks of reciprocity (Belle, 1982). People who can afford to pay for services such as child care do not need to rely on networks for aid. Instead, they benefit from intimacy, caring, and trust, without incurring burdensome obligations.

Summary

Overall, children at home decrease adult well-being. However, in the best circumstances children do not decrease well-being and may improve it. These circumstances include (*a*) enough family income so that there are no felt economic hardships, (*b*) the mother's paid employment, (*c*) available and affordable child care services, and (*d*) support from husbands, or other relatives in the household, in the shape of emotional support and shared participation in child care. The combination of children and these circumstances is uncommon, however, because children increase economic hardship, make it more difficult for women to be employed, and strain marital relationships. The result is a classic example of structural amplification. Children at home decrease health and well-being by eroding the very things that are necessary to cope successfully with children—economic well-being and supportive relationships.

WOMEN'S EMPLOYMENT

Patterns

For most Americans, employment improves physical and psychological well-being. Few ever questioned that this is true for men, and evidence continues to accumulate that unemployment is detrimental to men's health (Kessler, House, and Turner, 1987). However, it was not until the 1970s that Gove and his colleagues claimed similar benefits of employment for women. Most research finds that employed women have less depression, anxiety, and other forms of psychological distress than do housewives (Gore and Mangione, 1983; Gove, 1984; Gove and Peterson, 1980; Hall, Williams, and Greenberg, 1985; Kessler and McRae, 1982; Rosenfield, 1980; Ross, Mirowsky, and Ulbrich, 1983).

Employed women are physically healthier than nonemployed women (Lewin-Epstein, 1986; Marcus, Seeman, and Telesky, 1983; Nathanson, 1980; Verbrugge, 1983; Waldron and Jacobs, 1988; Woods and Hulka, 1979). Among women, the employed report the best physical health, housewives report lower health, and the unemployed report the worst health (Brenner and Levi, 1987; Jennings, Mazaik, and McKinlay, 1984). Death rates of women in the labor force are substantially lower than those of housewives (Passannante and Nathanson, 1985).

Interestingly, before current results were available, many speculations were pessimistic about the impact of women's employment on their health (Mortimer and Sorensen, 1984). Many thought employment would expose women to the stress and hazards of work, and thus worsen health. Accumulating evidence shows the opposite to be true. This trend is most striking in the literature on employment and pregnancy. Early work warned against possible adverse effects of employment on pregnancy. Research evidence accumulated since 1970 shows a positive association between employment and good perinatal outcomes (Saurel-Cubizolles and Kaminski, 1986).

The benefits of a wife's employment to her husband's well-being is less clear than the benefits to her own. Some studies find that the wife's employment increases her husband's psychological distress by reducing his power in the family and thus threatening his self-esteem (especially if they hold traditional sex-role attitudes), by reducing the wife's attention to him or by increasing his housework load (Kessler and McRae, 1982; Rosenfield, 1980). Others find that the wife's employment decreases her husband's psychological distress by improving or maintaining the standard of living (Ross and Huber, 1985; Ross, Mirowsky, and Ulbrich, 1983). Some find no effect (Roberts and O'Keefe, 1981). A meta-analysis by Fendrich (1984) concludes that the wife's employment generally does not increase her husband's distress. Although there is less research concerning the effect of a woman's employment on her husband's well-being than on her own, the evidence is beginning to show that it is not as detrimental as first believed.

Selection versus causation. The association of women's employment with good physical and mental health could be causal, because something about employment improves health, or it could be selective, because healthy women work outside the home whereas unhealthy women do not. Waldron and her colleagues originally thought most of the effect was due to selection. Their latest work, with better health measures, shows a large causal effect. Waldron and Jacobs (1988) used longitudinal data of a national sample of women interviewed in 1977 and again in 1982. They used a more reliable and valid health measure than was available in earlier studies. The measure assesses physical difficulties with a number of activities including walking, using stairs, standing for long periods, kneeling, lifting,

using hands and fingers, seeing, hearing, and so on; it assesses activity limitations due to poor health, such as using public transportation, personal care, and so on; and it assesses psychosomatic symptoms, including pain, tiring easily, low energy, weakness, aches, swelling, feeling sick, dizziness, and so on. Waldron and Jacobs (1988) find that participation in the labor force improves health on these dimensions over time. The association is not simply due to selection of healthier women into the labor force. Follow-up studies of mortality support the causal interpretation (Passannante and Nathanson, 1985).

Explanations

Economic well-being. Women's employment decreases economic hardship, thereby improving the psychological well-being of the family members. Employed wives provide about 31% of the family income (U.S. Bureau of the Census, 1986). Ross and Huber (1985) looked at wives' earnings ranging from 0 (not working for pay) to over $30,000. The more a wife earns, the higher the family income, which decreases her and her husband's perception of economic hardship, which decreases their levels of depression. The wife's earnings decrease her husband's depression almost as much as hers. Thus, Ross and Huber show that a wife's employment and earnings benefit both spouses' mental health by decreasing economic strain on the family. For nonmarried women, economic well-being accounts for even more of the beneficial effect of employment (Waldron and Jacobs, 1988). About half of employed women are not married. A nonmarried woman's earnings typically constitute her total family income (U.S. Department of Labor, 1986). Waldron and Jacobs speculate that the woman's employment is more beneficial, the more critical her earnings to her family's economic well-being. Thus, employment is more beneficial to the health of nonmarried women, black women, and women in blue-collar jobs than to married women, white women, and women in white-collar jobs (Passannante and Nathanson, 1985; Waldron and Jacobs, 1988).

Social support. The second way employment improves a wife's mental health is by increasing support from her husband in doing the household chores. A wife's employment, and higher earnings

if she is employed, increase the likelihood and extent of her husband's sharing housework and
child care (Ross, Mirowsky, and Huber, 1983;
Saenz, Goudy, and Lorenz, 1989). Although only
about 20% of the husbands of employed wives
share the housework and child care *equally* with
their wives, this is almost triple the 7% that do so
if their wives are not employed (Ross, Mirowsky,
and Huber, 1983). The more a wife earns compared to her husband, the greater his share of the
housework and child care (Maret and Finlay,
1984; Ross, Mirowsky, and Huber, 1983). The
more husbands share the household work, the
lower their wives' depression (Kessler and McRae,
1982; Ross, Mirowsky, and Huber, 1983; Saenz et
al., 1989). The husband's help with cleaning,
cooking, dish washing, shopping, and caring for
children significantly decreases a wife's depression and improves her self-rated health (Bird and
Fremont, 1989; Ross, Mirowsky, and Huber,
1983; Saenz et al., 1989). The extra housework
and child care done by husbands of employed
women does not increase the husbands' distress
(Kessler and McRae, 1982; Ross, Mirowsky, and
Huber, 1983). There is no evidence that a move
toward 50:50 division of housework and child
care worsens a husband's mental health.

The effect of a wife's employment on the
quality of the marriage, spouse support and communication, and marital satisfaction may be
changing. Early studies found that wives' employment decreased marital satisfaction (Gove and
Peterson, 1980). Studies of more traditional
families, such as Mexican Americans, found that
when a wife is employed, both she and her husband are less satisfied with the marriage, possibly
because the wife resents the fact that the husband
does not share the housework and child care, and
because her work overload leaves less time for
companionship (Ross, Mirowsky, and Ulbrich,
1983; Saenz et al., 1989; White, 1983). Reduced
marital satisfaction increases psychological
distress. It appears that wives' employment
reduces marital satisfaction only under the following conditions: the family is a traditional one in
which the husband and wife believe the wife's
place is in the home, but she needs to work for
economic reasons, and she retains full responsibility for the home. This would explain why older
studies and studies of Hispanics find a negative
relationship between wives' employment and
marital satisfaction, whereas more recent studies

and studies of less traditional families do not
(Houseknecht and Macke, 1981; Ladewig and
White, 1984; Locksley, 1980; Spitze, 1988). It is
the inequality in total work load that creates
marital tension and dissatisfaction.

Summary

The woman's employment decreases economic
strains on the family, which is unambiguously
good. However, in a large minority of families
(39%), the wife is employed but she and her husband prefer that she not work. In a large majority
of families in which the wife is employed, her husband does not share the housework and child care
equally (80%) (Ross, Mirowsky, and Huber,
1983). Such conditions reduce, and sometimes
reverse, the beneficial impact of the wife's
employment. Her employment improves well-
being most when her earnings are high enough to
clearly improve the family's economic well-being,
she and her husband prefer her employment, and
he shares the household tasks. In the ideal healthy
marriage (which is rare—less than one in five hun-
dred), the husband and wife both earn good pay,
both contribute about the same amount to the
total family income, and both share the housework and child care equally.

FAMILY SOCIOECONOMIC STATUS

Patterns

The association of socioeconomic status with
mental and physical health appears consistently in
the literature. Socioeconomic status, as indicated
by education, income, and occupation, is associated with decreased depression, anxiety, physiological malaise, and other forms of psychological
distress and demoralization, and with less
schizophrenia (Kessler, 1982: Kessler and Cleary,
1980; Kohn, Naoi, Schoenbach, Schooler, and
Slomczynski, 1990; Pearlin et al., 1981; Ross and
Huber, 1985; Ross and Mirowsky, 1989). Longitudinal analysis supports a causal interpretation:
differences in the demands and resources of
various socioeconomic positions produce differences in psychological well-being and distress
(Pearlin et al., 1981). Link and his colleagues
show that occupation has a large causal effect on
depression and schizophrenia; it is not simply that
people with psychological problems are selected

into low-level occupations (Link, Dohrenwend, and Skodol, 1986).

The same pattern exists for physical health. As Syme and Berkman say, "a vast body of evidence has shown consistently that those in the lower classes have higher mortality, morbidity, and disability rates" (1986: 28). Low socioeconomic status is associated with high rates of infectious and parasitic diseases, infant mortality, many chronic noninfectious diseases, disability, self-reported poor health, lower life expectancy, and higher death rates from all causes (Gortmaker, 1979; Hayes and Ross, 1986; Leigh, 1983; Litwack and Messeri, 1989; Syme and Berkman, 1986). People in the lower social classes are more likely to get sick and less likely to survive if sick. (Of course these general patterns are not always true of every disease.)

Education is the aspect of social status most important to health. Education produces and protects physical health in many ways. It shapes knowledge and behavior, determines the kind of job a person can get, and strongly affects the amount a person earns. The well-educated are more likely than the poorly educated to quit smoking, exercise, and avoid obesity (Hayes and Ross, 1986; Leigh, 1983; Syme and Berkman, 1986), and they score higher on an index of overall health practices that includes exercising, not smoking, not being overweight, not drinking heavily, and so on (Berkman and Breslow, 1983). Low education often leads to working at hazardous, risky, and physically noxious jobs characterized by noise, heat, fumes, cold, humidity, physical dangers, exposure to carcinogens, and so on (Leigh, 1983; Link, Dohrenwend, and Skodol, 1986), in addition to working at jobs that do not pay well. The effects of education on behavior and exposure, more than on access to medical care, explain the beneficial impact of education on health (Syme and Berkman, 1986).

The poorly educated who work at low-status, poorly paid, hazardous jobs are also the ones most at risk of losing their jobs in an economic downturn (Elder and Liker, 1982). On the aggregate level, the unemployment rate is associated with morbidity and mortality, including heart disease mortality, infant mortality, and suicide (Bunn, 1979; Marshall and Hodge, 1981). Studies that follow individuals are more direct tests of the effect of unemployment on health. Most find that the people who are unemployed have worse physical and mental health than the employed (Frese and Mohr, 1987; Kasl and Cobb, 1982; Linn, Sandifer, and Stein, 1985; Pearlin et al., 1981). Kessler, House, and Turner (1987) find that the unemployed have worse self-reported health and higher levels of somatization, anxiety, and depression, none of which can be explained by selection of sicker people out of the work force.

When other aspects of status are held constant, education is the single most important aspect of status for women's well-being, whereas personal earnings are the most important for men's (Ross and Huber, 1985). Kessler (1982) and Kessler and McRae (1982) find that, for women, employed or not, education has the largest net effect on distress. Occupation has the smallest. In an analysis of eight surveys, Kessler (1982) finds that personal earnings have the largest net effect on men's distress. Family income and education have smaller net effects and occupation has none. Of course, net effects are somewhat mythical, given that education leads to a better job with higher pay, a spouse who has a better job with higher pay, and thus higher family income.

Explanations

Why is low socioeconomic status associated with poor mental and physical health? We focus on economic hardship and social support as two basic explanations. Then we introduce perceived control over life as an important explanatory mechanism on which more research is needed.

Economic hardship. Economic hardship explains much of the effect on depression of low family income and loss of family income (due to being laid off, fired, or downgraded) (Pearlin et al., 1981; Ross and Huber, 1985). A family is an economic unit bound by emotional ties. It is in the household that the larger social and economic order impinges on individuals, exposing them to varying degrees of hardship, frustration, and struggle. The struggle to pay the bills and to feed and clothe the family on an inadequate income takes its toll in feeling run-down, tired, and having no energy, feeling that everything is an effort, that the future is hopeless, that you can't shake the blues, that nagging worries make for restless sleep, and that there isn't much to enjoy in life. When life is a constant struggle to get by, when it is never taken for granted that there will be enough money for food, clothes, and shelter, people often feel worn down and hopeless, and they are susceptible to disease (Pearlin et al., 1981; Ross and Huber, 1985). Low generalized resistance increases the risk of infectious disease and of chronic diseases such as cancer (Syme and Berkman, 1986).

Low family income is obviously the major cause of economic hardship, but the translation is not one-to-one. At the same income levels, those who are poorly educated feel greater hardship than the well-educated (Ross and Huber, 1985). Not only are low levels of education associated with low incomes, but lack of education makes it more difficult to cope with an inadequate income. Ross and Huber (1985) find a synergistic effect of poverty and lack of education on economic hardship, each making the effect of the other worse. A poorly educated person needs more money to fend off economic hardship than does a well-educated person. Education provides skills, information, a sense of mastery, and well-educated friends that help a person deal with the stresses of life, including a low income. People who have not finished high school or have barely finished high school are doubly disadvantaged because their low education translates into low earnings and it increases the difficulties of coping with low earnings.

Economic hardship affects women more than men (Ross and Huber, 1985). Women and their children in female-headed households are the new poor in the United States (Moen, 1983; Preston, 1984). Even in the intact families, the wives often are more acutely aware of economic strains. Usually it is the wife's responsibility to do the shopping, make sure there is food on the table, take the children to the doctor, and pay the bills (Huber and Spitze, 1983). This arrangement is especially prevalent in working-class families, where there is just enough money to get by, but the budget must be juggled to pay the bills and still have enough money for food.

Social support. Low socioeconomic status is associated with lower levels of social support (Mitchell and Moos, 1984; Ross and Mirowsky, 1989). Middle-class women consider their husbands confidants more frequently than do working-class women. The poorly educated mobilize social support less effectively than the well-educated (Eckenrode, 1983), and generally are less likely to agree that "I have someone I can turn to for support and understanding when things get rough" (Ross and Mirowsky, 1989). The unemployment and economic hardship associated with low status decrease the sense of having a supportive and confiding spouse (Gore and Mangione, 1983; House, 1981).

The strain that low status puts on social support represents a particularly destructive instance of structural amplification. Social support reduces the distress associated with unemployment, but unemployment erodes social support (Gore and Mangione, 1983; House, 1981; Pearlin et al., 1981). Atkinson, Liem, and Liem (1986) find that long-term unemployment of both white- and blue-collar workers reduces the perceived quality of marital support and of the spouse's role performance, and increases the number of arguments between the partners. The impact of unemployment on social support magnifies the negative effects of unemployment on health. The strain of unemployment is reduced in couples who manage to maintain a high level of mutual support. Under the circumstances, few can.

Many people buckle under the strain of providing social support, particularly in difficult circumstances. Spouses of chronic pain patients have an elevated incidence of pain problems (Schaffer, Donlon, and Bittle, 1980) and depression (Shanfield, Heiman, Cope, and Jones, 1979). Noh and Turner (1987) report substantial psychological costs for families of ex-hospitalized psychiatric patients. Low socioeconomic status increases the likelihood of disability and disease, which in turn exacts a toll on the physical and mental health of the spouse. Low education, poverty, and low support feed each other, magnify each other's impact *on* sickness in the family, and magnify the impact *of* sickness in the family.

DIRECTIONS FOR RESEARCH

The Sense of Control

Not everyone in difficult circumstances breaks under the pressure. Some manage to gain control of their situation, using whatever resources are available. However difficult the circumstances, the spouses and parents who fare the best take an attentive, active, instrumental approach to solving family problems (Pearlin et al., 1981; Ross and

Mirowsky, 1989). Such an approach improves well-being and health directly (Rodin, 1986) and also indirectly by improving family welfare over the long run (Kessler and Cleary, 1980; Kohn and Schooler, 1982). Many studies explore the ways that low status or old age reduce instrumentalism and the sense of control, and thereby produce distress or disease (e.g., Krause, 1986; Pearlin et al., 1981; Rodin, 1986; Ross and Mirowsky, 1989). Only a few explore the ways that marital, parental, and work roles combine to shape the sense of responsibility and control.

Beliefs about personal control appear under a number of other names, including the sense of personal efficacy (Downey and Moen, 1987; Kohn and Schooler, 1982), self-efficacy (Gecas, 1989), self-directedness (Kohn and Schooler, 1982), mastery (Pearlin et al., 1981), helplessness (Elder and Liker, 1982; Garber and Seligman, 1980), fatalism versus instrumentalism (Wheaton, 1980, 1983), and powerlessness (Mirowsky and Ross, 1983; Seeman, 1983).

Consequences of the Sense of Control

The sense of not being in control of one's own life can diminish the will and motivation to actively solve problems. Attempts to solve problems seem pointless: "What's the use?" The result is less success in solving problems and adapting (Wheaton, 1980, 1983). The reactive, passive person fails to prevent, prepare for, and limit the consequences of problems. In contrast, instrumental people search the environment for potentially distressing events and conditions, take preventive steps, and accumulate resources or develop skills and habits that will reduce the impact of unavoidable problems. For example, Seeman and Seeman (1983) find that people with a high sense of control know about health, initiate preventive behaviors, quit smoking on their own, avoid dependence on doctors, and feel healthy more than those with a low sense of control. When undesired events and situations occur, the instrumental person is better prepared and less threatened. Thus, the instrumentalist is constantly getting ahead of problems, whereas the fatalist is constantly falling behind.

In the long run, the sense of control can lead to a change in status that further reinforces a high or low sense of control. People who feel responsible and instrumental improve their conditions with

time, which reinforces the sense of control in the long run (Downey and Moen, 1987; Kohn and Schooler, 1982; Pearlin et al., 1981). Unfortunately, the long-run feedback works both ways. People who feel powerless and fatalistic, or who are cognitively rigid, can wind up in tedious jobs that do not pay well, and sometimes lose their jobs. Little success over long periods discourages and demoralizes people, reinforcing the sense of powerlessness and fatalism.

Work, Family, and the Sense of Control

How does family shape a persons' sense of control? Research is just beginning to provide an answer. Sometimes dependency or family obligations erode the sense of control. People whose mothers were overprotective have a lower sense of control than other adults, and are more depressed as a consequence (Richman and Flaherty, 1986). Employed mothers with most of the responsibility for housework and child care have a low sense of control that reflects their role overload (Rosenfield, 1989). However, people who meet the demands of family roles successfully can benefit in the long run. Middle-class women who saved their families from economic ruin during the Great Depression by taking jobs are more instrumental 40 years later than those who did not take jobs (Elder and Liker, 1982). The sense of control may prove to be a major link between family and health (Sagan, 1987).

REFERENCES

Abbott, Robert D., Yin Yin, Dwayne M. Reed, Katsuhilo Yano. 1986. "Risk of stroke in male cigarette smokers." New England Journal of Medicine 315: 717–720.

Alwin, Duane F., Philip E. Converse, and Steven S. Martin. 1985. "Living arrangements and social integration." Journal of Marriage and the Family 47: 319–334.

Aneshensel, Carol S., Ralph R. Frerichs, and Virginia A. Clark. 1981. "Family roles and sex differences in depression." Journal of Health and Social Behavior 22: 379–393.

Aneshensel, Carol S., Ralph R. Frerichs, and George J. Huba. 1984. "Depression and physical illness: A multiwave, nonrecursive causal model." Journal of Health and Social Behavior 25: 350–371.

Aneshensel, Carol S., and George J. Huba. 1983. "Depression, alcohol use and smoking over one year: A four-wave longitudinal causal model." Journal of Abnormal Psychology 92: 134–150.

Anson, Ofra. 1989. "Marital status and women's health revisited: The importance of a proximate adult." Journal of Marriage and the Family 51: 185–194.

Atkinson, Thomas, Ramsay Liem, and Joan H. Liem. 1986. "The social costs of unemployment: Implications for social support." Journal of Health and Social Behavior 27: 317–331.

Bailar, John C., and Elaine M. Smith. 1986. "Progress against cancer?" New England Journal of Medicine 314: 1226–1232.

Belle, Deborah. 1982. Lives in Stress: Women and Depression. Beverly Hills, CA: Sage.

Berk, Marc L., and Amy K. Taylor. 1984. "Women and divorce: Health insurance coverage, utilization, and health care expenditures." American Journal of Public Health 74: 1276–1278.

Berkman, Lisa F., and Lester Breslow. 1983. Health and Ways of Living: The Alameda County Study. New York: Oxford University Press.

Bianchi, Suzanne M., and Daphne Spain. 1986. American Women in Transition. New York: Russell Sage Foundation.

Bird, Chloe, and Allen Fremont. 1989. "Gender, social roles, and health." Paper presented at the annual meeting of the American Sociological Association, San Francisco.

Blazer, Dan G. 1982. "Social support and mortality in an elderly community population." American Journal of Epidemiology 115: 684–694.

Bowling, Ann. 1987. "Mortality after bereavement: A review of the literature on survival periods and factors affecting survival." Social Science and Medicine 24: 117–124.

Brenner, Sten-Olof, and Lennart Levi. 1987. "Long-term unemployment among women in Sweden." Social Science and Medicine 25: 153–161.

Brown, Julia S., and Barbara Giesy. 1986. "Marital status of persons with spinal cord injury." Social Science and Medicine 23: 313–322.

Bruce, Martha Livingston, and Philip J. Leaf. 1989. "Psychiatric disorders and 15-month mortality in a community sample of older adults." American Journal of Public Health 79: 727–730.

Bunn, A. R. 1979. "Ischaemic heart disease mortality and the business cycle in Australia." American Journal of Public Health 69: 772–781.

Cairns, John. 1985. "The treatment of diseases and the war against cancer." Scientific American 253(3): 51–59.

Callan, Victor J. 1987. "The personal and marital adjustment of mothers and of voluntarily and involuntarily childless wives." Journal of Marriage and the Family 49: 847–856.

Cherlin, Andrew J. 1981. Marriage, Divorce, Remarriage. Cambridge, MA: Harvard University Press.

Cleary, Paul D., and David Mechanic. 1983. "Sex differences in psychological distress among married people." Journal of Health and Social Behavior 24: 111–121.

Cohen, Sheldon, and S. Leonard Syme. 1985. Social Support and Health. Orlando, FL: Academic Press.

Downey, Geraldine, and Phyllis Moen. 1987. "Personal efficacy, income, and family transitions: A longitudinal study of women heading households." Journal of Health and Social Behavior 28: 320–333.

Eckenrode, John. 1983. "The mobilization of social supports: Some individual constraints." American Journal of Community Psychology 11: 509–528.

Edelstein, Jacqueline, and Margaret W. Linn. 1985. "The influence of the family on control of diabetes." Social Science and Medicine 21: 541–544.

Elder, Glen H., and Jeffrey K. Liker. 1982. "Hard times in women's lives: Historical influences across forty years." American Journal of Sociology 88: 241–269.

Fendrich, Michael. 1984. "Wives' employment and husbands' distress: A meta-analysis and a replication." Journal of Marriage and the Family 46: 871–879.

Fox, John W. 1980. "Gove's specific sex-role theory of mental illness." Journal of Health and Social Behavior 21: 260–267.

Frese, Michael, and Gisela Mohr. 1987. "Prolonged unemployment and depression in older workers: A longitudinal study of intervening variables." Social Science and Medicine 25: 173–178.

Garber, Judy, and Martin E. P. Seligman. 1980. Human Helplessness: Theory and Applications. New York: Academic Press.

Gecas, Viktor. 1989. "The social psychology of self-efficacy." Annual Review of Sociology 15: 291–316.

Gerstel, Naomi, Catherine Kohler Riessman, and Sarah Rosenfield. 1985. "Explaining the symptomatology of separated and divorced women and men: The role of material conditions and social networks." Social Forces 64: 84–101.

Glenn, Norval D., and Sara McLanahan. 1981. "The effects of offspring on the psychological well-being of older adults." Journal of Marriage and the Family 43: 409–421.

Glenn, Norval D., and Charles N. Weaver. 1988. "The changing relationship of marital status to reported happiness." Journal of Marriage and the Family 50: 317–324.

Goetting, Ann. 1986. "Parental satisfaction: A review of the research." Journal of Family Issues 7: 83–109.

Goldsteen, Karen, and Catherine E. Ross. 1989. "The perceived burden of children." Journal of Family Issues 10: 504–526.

Gore, Susan, and Thomas W. Mangione. 1983. "Social roles, sex roles, and psychological distress." Journal of Health and Social Behavior 24: 300–312.

Gortmaker, Steven L. 1979. "Poverty and infant mortality in the United States." American Sociological Review 44: 280–297.

Gove, Walter R. 1984. "Gender differences in mental and physical illness: The effects of fixed roles and nurturant roles." Social Science and Medicine 19: 77–84.

Gove, Walter R., Michael Hughes, and Omer R. Galle. 1979. "Overcrowding in the home: An empirical investigation of its possible consequences." American Sociological Review 44: 59–80.

Gove, Walter R., Michael M. Hughes, and Carolyn B. Style. 1983. "Does marriage have positive effects on

the psychological well-being of the individual?''
Journal of Health and Social Behavior 24: 122–131.

Gove, Walter R., and Claire Peterson. 1980. "An update of the literature on personal and marital adjustment: The effect of children and the employment of wives." Marriage and Family Review 3(3/4): 63–96.

Graham, Saxon, and Curtis Mettlin. 1979. "Diet and colon cancer." American Journal of Epidemiology 109: 1–20.

Hall, Lynne A., Carolyn A. Williams, and Raymond S. Greenberg. 1985. "Supports, stressors, and depressive symptoms in low income mothers." American Journal of Public Health 75: 518–522.

Hanson, Bertil S., Sven-Olof Isacsson, Lars Janzon, and Sven-Eric Lindell. 1989. "Social network and social support influence mortality in elderly men." American Journal of Epidemiology 130: 100–111.

Haring-Hidore, Marilyn, William A. Stock, Morris A. Okum, and Robert A. Witter. 1985. "Marital status and subjective well-being: A research synthesis." Journal of Marriage and the Family 47: 947–953.

Hayes, Diane, and Catherine E. Ross. 1986. "Body and mind: The effect of exercise, overweight, and physical health on psychological well-being." Journal of Health and Social Behavior 27: 387–400.

Hayes, Diane, and Catherine E. Ross. 1987. "Concern with appearance, health beliefs, and eating habits." Journal of Health and Social Behavior 28: 120–130.

Helsing, K. J., S. Moysen, and George W. Comstock. 1981. "Factors associated with mortality after widowhood." American Journal of Public Health 71: 802–809.

House, James A. 1981. Work Stress and Social Support. Reading, MA: Addison-Wesley.

House, James S., Cynthia A. Robbins, and Helen L. Metzner. 1982. "The association of social relationships and activities with mortality: Prospective evidence from the Tecumseh Community Health Study." American Journal of Epidemiology 116: 123–140.

Houseknecht, Sharon K., and Anne S. Macke. 1981. "Combining marriage and career: The marital adjustment of professional women." Journal of Marriage and the Family 43: 651–661.

Hovell, Melbourne F. 1982. "The experimental evidence for weight-loss treatment of essential hypertension." American Journal of Public Health 72: 359–368.

Huber, Joan, and Glenna Spitze. 1983. Sex Stratification: Children, Housework, and Jobs. New York: Academic Press.

Hughes, Michael M., and Walter R. Gove. 1981. "Living alone, social integration, and mental health." American Journal of Sociology 87: 48–74.

Jennings, Susan, Cheryl Mazaik, and Sonja McKinlay. 1984. "Women and work: An investigation of the association between health and employment status in middle-aged women." Social Science and Medicine 19: 423–431.

Kandel, Denise B., Mark Davies, and Victoria H. Raveis. 1985. "The stressfulness of daily social roles for women: Marital, occupational, and household roles." Journal of Health and Social Behavior 26: 64–78.

Kaplan, Howard B., Cynthia Robbins, and Steven S. Martin. 1983. "Antecedents of psychological distress in young adults: Self-rejection, deprivation of social support, and life events." Journal of Health and Social Behavior 24: 230–244.

Kaprio, Jaakko, Markku Koskenvuo, and Heli Rita. 1987. "Mortality after bereavement: A prospective study of 95,647 widowed persons." American Journal of Public Health 77: 283–287.

Kasl, Stanislav V., and Sidney Cobb. 1982. "Variability of stress effects among men experiencing job loss." Pp. 445–465 in Leo Goldberger and Shlomo Breznitz (eds.), Handbook of Stress. New York: Free Press.

Kessler, Ronald C. 1982. "A disaggregation of the relationship between socioeconomic status and psychological distress." American Sociological Review 47: 752–764.

Kessler, Ronald C., and Paul D. Cleary. 1980. "Social class and psychological distress." American Sociological Review 45: 463–478.

Kessler, Ronald C., James S. House, and J. Blake Turner. 1987. "Unemployment and health in a community sample." Journal of Health and Social Behavior 28: 51–59.

Kessler, Ronald C., and Jane D. McLeod. 1985. "Social support and mental health in community samples." Pp. 219–240 in Sheldon Cohen and S. Leonard Syme (eds.), Social Support and Health. New York: Academic Press.

Kessler, Ronald C., and James A. McRae. 1982. "The effect of wives' employment on the mental health of married men and women." American Sociological Review 47: 216–227.

Kohn, Melvin, Atsuhi Naoi, Carrie Schoenbach, Carmi Schooler, and Kazimeierz M. Slomczynski. 1990. "Position in the class structure and psychological functioning in the United States, Japan, and Poland." American Journal of Sociology 95: 964–1008.

Kohn, Melvin, and Carmi Schooler. 1982. "Job conditions and personality: A longitudinal assessment of their reciprocal effects." American Journal of Sociology 87: 1257–1286.

Kotler, Pamela, and Deborah Lee Wingard. 1989. "The effect of occupational, marital, and parental roles on mortality: The Alameda County Study." American Journal of Public Health 79: 607–612.

Krause, Neal. 1986. "Stress and coping: Reconceptualizing the role of locus of control beliefs." Journal of Gerontology 41: 617–622.

Ladewig, Becky Heath, and Priscilla N. White. 1984. "Dual earner marriage: The family social environment and dyadic adjustment." Journal of Family Issues 5: 343–362.

LaRocco, James M., James S. House, and John R. P. French. 1980. "Social support occupational stress, and health." Journal of Health and Social Behavior 3: 202–218.

Lee, Gary R., and Eugene Ellithorpe. 1982. "Intergenerational exchange and subjective well-being among the elderly." Journal of Marriage and the Family 44: 217–224.

Leigh, J. Paul. 1983. "Direct and indirect effects of education on health." Social Science and Medicine 17: 227–234.

Lewin-Epstein, Noah. 1986. "Employment and ill-health among women in Israel." Social Science and Medicine 23: 1171–1179.

Link, Bruce G., Bruce P. Dohrenwend, and Andrew E. Skodol. 1986. "Socio-economic status and schizophrenia: Noisome occupational characteristics as a risk factor." American Sociological Review 51: 242–258.

Linn, Margaret W., Richard Sandifer, and Shayna Stein. 1985. "Effects of unemployment on mental and physical health." American Journal of Public Health 75: 502–506.

Lipid Research Clinics Program. 1984. "The Lipid Research Clinics Coronary Primary Prevention Trial results: The relationship of reduction in incidence of coronary heart disease to cholesterol lowering." Journal of the American Medical Association 251: 365–374.

Litwack, Eugene, and Peter Messeri. 1989. "Organizational theory, social supports, and mortality rates: A theoretical convergence." American Sociological Review 54: 49–66.

Locksley, Anne. 1980. "On the effects of wives' employment on marital adjustment and companionship." Journal of Marriage and the Family 42: 337–346.

Longino, Charles F., Jr., and Aaron Lipman. 1981. "Married and spouseless men and women in planned retirement communities: Support network differentials." Journal of Marriage and the Family 43: 169–177.

Lovell-Troy, Lawrence. 1983. "Anomia among employed wives and housewives: An exploratory analysis." Journal of Marriage and the Family 45: 301–310.

Magnus, K., A. Matroos, and J. Strackee. 1979. "Walking, cycling, or gardening, with or without seasonal interruptions, in relation to acute coronary events." American Journal of Epidemiology 110: 724–733.

Marcus, Alfred C., Teresa E. Seeman, and Carol W. Telesky. 1983. "Sex differences in reports of illness and disability: A further test of the fixed role hypothesis." Social Science and Medicine 17: 993–1002.

Maret, Elizabeth, and Barbara Finlay. 1984. "The distribution of household labor among women in dual-earner families." Journal of Marriage and the Family 46: 357–364.

Marshall, J. R., and R. W. Hodge. 1981. "Durkheim and Pierce on suicide and economic change." Social Science Research 10: 101–114.

McLanahan, Sara, and Julia Adams. 1987. "Parenthood and psychological well-being." Pp. 237–257 in W. Richard Scott and James F. Short (eds.), Annual Review of Sociology (Vol. 13). Palo Alto, CA: Annual Reviews.

Mechanic, David, and Stephen Hansell. 1987. "Ado-

lescent competence, psychological well-being, and self-assessed physical health." Journal of Health and Social Behavior 28: 364–374.

Mirowsky, John. 1985. "Depression and marital power: An equity model." American Journal of Sociology 91: 557–592.

Mirowsky, John, and Catherine E. Ross. 1983. "Paranoia and the structure of powerlessness." American Sociological Review 48: 228–239.

Mirowsky, John, and Catherine E. Ross. 1989. "Social Causes of Psychological Distress. New York: Aldine-de Gruyter.

Mitchell, Roger E., and Rudolf H. Moos. 1984. "Deficiencies in social support among depressed patients: Antecedents or consequences of stress?" Journal of Health and Social Behavior 25: 438–452.

Moen, Phyllis. 1983. "Unemployment, public policy, and families: Forecasts for the 1980s." Journal of Marriage and the Family 45: 751–760.

Mortimer, Jeylan, and Glorian Sorensen. 1984. "Men, women, work, and family." In Kathryn M. Borman, Daisy Quarm, and Sarah Gideonse (eds.), Women in the Workplace: Effects on Families. Norwood, NJ: Ablex.

Multiple Risk Factor Intervention Trial Research Group. 1982. "Multiple Risk Factor Intervention Trial: Risk factor changes and mortality results." Journal of the American Medical Association 248: 1465–1477.

Nathanson, Constance A. 1980. "Social roles and health status among women: The significance of employment." Social Science and Medicine 14A: 463–471.

National Center for Health Statistics. 1989. Advance Report of Final Mortality Statistics, 1987. Monthly Vital Statistics Report 38(5). National Center for Health Statistics. Hyattsville, MD: Public Health Service.

Neale, Anne Victoria, Barbara C. Tilley, and Sally W. Vernon. 1986. "Marital status, delay in seeking treatment, and survival from breast cancer." Social Science and Medicine 23: 305–312.

Neuling, Sandra J., and Helen R. Winefield. 1988. "Social support and recovery after surgery for breast cancer: Frequency and correlates of supportive behaviours by family, friends, and surgeon." Social Science and Medicine 27: 385–392.

Noh, Samuel, and R. Jay Turner. 1987. "Living with psychiatric patients: Implications for the mental health of family members." Social Science and Medicine 25: 263–271.

Paffenberger, Ralph S., Robert T. Hyde, Alvin L. Wing, and Charles H. Steinmetz. 1984. "A natural history of athleticism and cardiovascular health." Journal of the American Medical Association 252: 491–495.

Parker, Douglas A., Elizabeth S. Parker, Thomas C. Harford, and Gail C. Farmer. 1987. "Alcohol use and depression symptoms among employed men and women." American Journal of Public Health 77: 704–707.

Passannante, Marian R., and Constance A. Nathanson. 1985. "Female labor force participation and female mortality in Wisconsin, 1974–1978." *Social Science and Medicine* 21: 655–665.

Pearlin, Leonard I. 1989. "The sociological study of stress." *Journal of Health and Social Behavior* 30: 241–256.

Pearlin, Leonard I., Morton A. Lieberman, Elizabeth G. Menaghan, and Joseph T. Mullan. 1981. "The stress process." *Journal of Health and Social Behavior* 22: 337–356.

Pleck, Joseph. 1983. "Husbands' paid work and family roles: Current research issues." Pp. 251–333 in Helena Lopata and Joseph Pleck (eds.), Research in the Interweave of Social Roles (Vol. 3). Families and Jobs. Greenwich, CT: JAI.

Preston, Samuel H. 1984. "Children and the elderly in the United States." *Scientific American* 251: 44–49.

Rempel, Judith. 1985. "Childless elderly: What are they missing?" *Journal of Marriage and the Family* 47: 343–348.

Richman, Judith A., and Joseph A. Flaherty. 1986. "Childhood relationships, adult coping resources, and depression." *Social Science and Medicine* 23: 709–716.

Richman, Judith A., Valerie Raskin, and Cheryl Gaines. 1989. "The benefits of caring: Gender, social support, and postpartum depression." Paper presented at the annual meeting of the American Sociological Association, San Francisco (August).

Riessman, Catherine Kohler, and Naomi Gerstel. 1985. "Marital dissolution and health: Do males or females have greater risk?" *Social Science and Medicine* 20: 627–635.

Roberts, Robert E., and Stephen J. O'Keefe. 1981. "Sex differences in depression reexamined." *Journal of Health and Social Behavior* 22: 394–400.

Rodin, Judith. 1986. "Aging and health: Effects of the sense of control." *Science* 233 (September 19): 1271–1276.

Rook, Karen S. 1984. "The negative side of social interaction: Impact on psychological well-being." *Journal of Personality and Social Psychology* 46: 1097–1108.

Rosenfield, Sarah. 1980. "Sex differences in depression: Do women always have higher rates?" *Journal of Health and Social Behavior* 21: 33–42.

Rosenfield, Sarah. 1989. "The effects of women's employment: Personal control and sex differences in mental health." *Journal of Health and Social Behavior* 30: 77–91.

Ross, Catherine E. 1989. "The intersection of work and family: The sense of control and well-being of women and men." Paper presented at the Family Structure and Health Conference, San Francisco (August).

Ross, Catherine E., and Joan Huber. 1985. "Hardship and depression." *Journal of Health and Social Behavior* 26: 312–327.

Ross, Catherine E., and John Mirowsky. 1983. "The social epidemiology of overweight: A substantive and methodological investigation." *Journal of Health and Social Behavior* 24: 288–298.

Ross, Catherine E., and John Mirowsky. 1988. "Child care and emotional adjustment to wives' employment." *Journal of Health and Social Behavior* 29: 127–138.

Ross, Catherine E., and John Mirowsky. 1989. "Explaining the social patterns of depression: Control and problem solving—or support and talking." *Journal of Health and Social Behavior* 30: 206–219.

Ross, Catherine E., John Mirowsky, and Joan Huber. 1983. "Dividing work, sharing work, and in-between: Marriage patterns and depression." *American Sociological Review* 48: 809–823.

Ross, Catherine E., John Mirowsky, and Patricia Ulbrich. 1983. "Distress and the traditional female role: A comparison of Mexicans and Anglos." *American Journal of Sociology* 89: 670–682.

Sackett, David L., R. Brian Haynes, and Peter Tugwell. 1985. Clinical Epidemiology: A Basic Science for Clinical Medicine. Boston: Little, Brown and Company.

Saenz, Rogelia, Willis J. Goudy, and Frederick O. Lorenz. 1989. "The effects of employment and marital relations on depression among Mexican American women." *Journal of Marriage and the Family* 51: 239–251.

Sagan, Leonard A. 1987. The Health of Nations: True Causes of Sickness and Well-being. New York: Basic Books.

Saurel-Cubizolles, M. M., and M. Kaminski. 1986. "Work in pregnancy: Its evolving relationship with perinatal outcome." *Social Science and Medicine* 22: 431–442.

Schaffer, Charles B., Patrick T. Donlon, and Robert M. Bittle. 1980. "Chronic pain and depression: A clinical and family history survey." *American Journal of Psychiatry* 137: 118–120.

Seeman, Melvin. 1983. "Alienation motifs in contemporary theorizing: The hidden continuity of classic themes." *Social Psychology Quarterly* 46: 171–184.

Seeman, Melvin, and Teresa E. Seeman. 1983. "Health behavior and personal autonomy: A longitudinal study of the sense of control in illness." *Journal of Health and Social Behavior* 24: 144–159.

Shanfield, Stephen B., Elliott M. Heiman, D. Nathan Cope, and John R. Jones. 1979. "Pain and the marital relationship: Psychiatric distress." *Pain* 7: 343–351.

Smith, Jack C., James A. Mercy, and Judith Conn. 1988. "Marital status and the risk of suicide." *American Journal of Public Health* 78: 78–80.

Spitze, Glenna. 1988. "Women's employment and family relations: A review." *Journal of Marriage and the Family* 50: 595–618. [Reprinted in this volume]

Stamler, Jeremiah. 1981. "Primary prevention of coronary heart disease." *American Journal of Cardiology* 47: 722–735.

Surgeon General. 1982. The Health Consequences of Smoking. Rockville, MD: Public Health Service.

Syme, Leonard S., and Lisa F. Berkman. 1986. "Social class, susceptibility, and sickness." Pp. 28–34 in Peter Conrad and Rochelle Kern (eds.), The Sociology of Health and Illness (2nd ed.). New

York: St. Martin's Press.

Tcheng-Laroche, Francoise, and Raymond Prince. 1983. "Separated and divorced women compared with married controls: Selected life satisfaction, stress, and health indices from a community survey." Social Science and Medicine 17: 95–105.

Turner, R. Jay, and Samuel Noh. 1983. "Class and psychological vulnerability among women: The significance of social support and personal control." Journal of Health and Social Behavior 24: 2–15.

U.S. Bureau of the Census. 1986. Earnings in 1983 of Married-Couple Families by Characteristics of Husband and Wife. Current Populations Reports, Series P-60, No. 153 (March). Washington, DC: Government Printing Office.

U.S. Bureau of the Census. 1989. Household and Family Characteristics: March 1988. Current Population Reports, Series P-20, No. 437 (May). Washington, DC: Government Printing Office.

U.S. Department of Labor. 1986. Employment and Earnings Characteristics of Families. Washington, DC: Government Printing Office.

Umberson, Debra. 1987. "Family status and health behaviors: Social control as a dimension of social integration." Journal of Health and Social Behavior 28: 306–319.

Umberson, Debra. 1989. "Relationships with children: Explaining parents' psychological well-being." Journal of Marriage and the Family 51: 999–1012.

Venters, Maurine H. 1986. "Family life and cardiovascular risk: Implications for the prevention of chronic disease." Social Science and Medicine 22: 1067–1074.

Verbrugge, Lois M. 1983. "Multiple roles and physical health of women and men." Journal of Health and Social Behavior 24: 16–30.

Verbrugge, Lois M. 1986. "From sneezes to adieux: Stage of health for American men and women." Social Science and Medicine 22: 1195–1212.

Veroff, Joseph, Elizabeth Douvan, and Richard Kulka. 1981. The Inner American: A Self-Portrait from 1957 to 1976. New York: Basic Books.

Waldron, Ingrid, and Jerry A. Jacobs. 1988. "Effects of labor free participation on women's health: New evidence from a longitudinal study." Journal of Occupational Medicine 30: 977–983.

Waltz, Millard, Bernhard Badura, Holgar Pfaff, and Thomas Schott. 1988. "Marriage and the psychological consequences of a heart attack: A longitudinal study of adaptation to chronic illness after 3 years." Social Science and Medicine 27: 149–158.

Weiss, Robert S. 1984. "The impact of marital dissolution on income and consumption in single-parent households." Journal of Marriage and the Family 46: 115–127.

Wheaton, Blair. 1980. "The sociogenesis of psychological disorder: An attributional theory." Journal of Health and Social Behavior 21: 100–124.

Wheaton, Blair. 1983. "Stress, personal coping resources, and psychiatric symptoms: An investigation of interactive models." Journal of Health and Social Behavior 24: 208–229.

Wheaton, Blair. 1985. "Models for the stress-buffering functions of coping resources." Journal of Health and Social Behavior 26: 352–364.

White, Lynn K. 1983. "Determinants of spousal interaction: Marital structure or marital happiness." Journal of Marriage and the Family 45: 511–519.

White, Lynn K., and Alan Booth. 1985. "The transition to parenthood and marital quality." Journal of Family Issues 6: 435–449.

White, Lynn K., Alan Booth, and John N. Edwards. 1986. "Children and marital happiness: Why the negative correlation?" Journal of Family Issues 7: 131–147.

Woods, N. F., and Barbara S. Hulka. 1979. "Symptom reports and illness behavior among employed women and homemakers." Journal of Community Health 5: 36–45.

Elizabeth G. Menaghan and Toby L. Parcel
Ohio State University

Parental Employment and Family Life:
Research in the 1980s

This review examines recent research regarding how parents' employment experiences affect their own well-being, their marital relationships, and the interaction patterns in their families, with consequences for children. It emphasizes the contributions of several major theoretical approaches: the new home economics; work-family role conflict perspectives; and the work socialization and work stressor explanations of effects of variations in occupational conditions. Future research goals include increased interdisciplinary attention to theory; continued longitudinal investigation of employment, occupational conditions, and family life; more study of single-parent-earner families; and greater development and evaluation of workplace and governmental policies aimed at reducing work-family strains.

The intimate, daily interactions of family life are readily affected by the economic activities, paid and unpaid, of family members. Even in cross section, the connections between employment and family life are complex; the picture becomes still more complex when we consider expectable and unanticipated changes that occur in both occupational and family spheres over the life course. These considerations suggest the daunting immensity of research on relationships between employment and family life, and the tantalizing incompleteness of cross-sectional "snapshot" pictures of apparent linkages. Nevertheless, the 1980s have seen some progress in our concep-

Department of Sociology, Ohio State University, Columbus, OH 43210-1353.

tualization of those relationships and in testing the adequacy of our explanations for observed patterns. In this review, we have chosen to focus on a portion of that story, one characterized by extensive controversy and some cumulation of knowledge in the decade of the 1980s. We emphasize research examining how and under what conditions parents' employment experiences can be expected to affect their own well-being, their marital relationships, the interaction patterns in their families, and the development of their children. We focus on employment in industrialized countries, particularly the United States, and emphasize several major theoretical approaches: the new home economic approach stimulated by Becker; the work-family role conflict approach exemplified by Pleck, Voydanoff, and others; the work socialization framework emphasized by Mortimer, Kohn, and others; and the work stressor models exemplified by Bolger and Repetti.

In doing so, we reluctantly neglect several related topics and refer the reader to useful recent reviews (many in this volume): the growing literature on unpaid domestic labor and its relationship to paid employment (see Thompson and Walker, 1989, and Ferree, 1990); the linkages between characteristics of paid employment and the type and quality of supplemental child care that parents arrange (see Belsky, 1990; Hofferth and Phillips, 1987; and Presser, 1988); the antecedents and consequences of children's and adolescents' paid and unpaid labor (see Greenberger, 1984, as well as Gecas and Seff, 1990); the impact of aging parents' needs on middle-aged adults' (especially women's) occupational commitments (see Mancini and Blieszner, 1989); the linkages between anticipated and actual employment experiences and fertility (see Spitze, 1988); and the associations between married adults' employment experience and their propensity to divorce (see White, 1990). Other general reviews on work and family relations include Piotrkowski, Rapoport, and Rapoport (1987), Voydanoff (1987), and Huber (1988).

To set the research to be reviewed in context, we first provide a brief sketch of two sets of broader social changes: changes in men's and women's employment opportunities, constraints, and experiences since 1940, and changes in marriage and childbearing that have been occurring over the same period.

SOCIAL CHANGES IN OCCUPATIONAL AND FAMILY PATTERNS

Economic and Occupational Changes

Cyert and Mowery (1987, chap. 3) summarize changes in both the structure and functioning of the U.S. economy since the 1960s. Annual average growth rates of real earnings declined during this period. The rate of growth in labor productivity also declined, dropping to less than one percent between 1973 and 1986. The character of available employment was also changing. Manufacturing employment accounted for a declining proportion of total private nonagricultural employment. Most jobs added to the economy were concentrated in four industry groups: wholesale and retail trade; transportation and utilities; finance, insurance, and real estate; and services. While some have argued that many of the jobs created in the 1980s paid less than the manufacturing jobs that were lost and less than those created in earlier decades, others argue that this view is inconsistent with the substantial growth in professional, technical, and managerial positions during the 1970s and early '80s.

Cyert and Mowery (1987) note that unemployment grew after 1973 relative to levels of the 1950s and 1960s because of the 1974–75 and 1981–82 recessions, because of the lack of long-term economic expansions (until the late 1980s), and until the mid 1970s, because of entrance into the labor force of the huge baby boom cohort. By the 1980s, high unemployment rates were due to permanent job losses in manufacturing, mining, and construction. This structural unemployment reflects a mismatch between worker skills or worker locations and job availability. Blue-collar workers

account for a disproportionate share of this form of unemployment.

During this time period, men's rates of labor force participation declined while women's increased. Men's declines were steeper for black than for white men, with Hispanic men more likely to be in the labor force than white or black men (Blau and Ferber, 1986: 71). Among white men, declines were due primarily to lower age of retirement, while among minorities, the discouraged-worker effect (the unemployed dropping out of the labor force after an unsuccessful period of job search) of prime-working-age males played a greater role (Blau and Ferber, 1986: 106–108); unsuccessful job searches could reflect the decreased demand for lesser-skilled labor (see also Wilson, 1987, regarding the diminished opportunities for urban minority men). Rates of female participation became more similar for blacks and whites as white women's rates increased and black women's dropped; Hispanic women's rates remained still lower.

The large increases in women's labor force participation (from 27.9% in 1940 to 53.7% in 1984; Blau and Ferber, 1986: 69) reflected a series of changes in the age, marital status, and child care responsibilities of working women. Prior to 1940, the typical employed woman was young and single. Between 1940 and 1960, older married women entered the labor force, while rates of participation for young women did not increase sharply until after 1960. By 1970, employment had become the modal status among mothers of school-aged children. The most striking recent change is in the greater employment of mothers of babies and preschoolers (Hoffman, 1989): rates of participation for married women with children under six had risen to 54% by 1986 (U.S. Bureau of the Census, 1987). Women are now more firmly attached to the labor market, as indicated by reduced turnover and by higher proportions of women working full-time, the full year round, as opposed to part-time and/or part-year. Despite this convergence over time, the temporal patterns of women's employment still differ from the employment of men: somewhat more is part-time and/or part-year, and it is more often interrupted by demands to care for ill, aged, or young family members (U.S. Bureau of the Census, 1987). For these reasons, the percentage of women with some labor force experience is higher than any cross-sectional estimate.

The financial rewards from employment are

still lower for women than men. While rates of women's labor force participation increased, the earnings ratio improved only slightly. O'Neill (1985: 50) documents that full-time women workers earned from about 60% to 64% of what male full-time workers earned, with only minor fluctuations in this percentage between 1950 and 1980. By 1984 among full-time workers 21 to 64 years of age, women earned 70% of what men earned. The overall earnings ratio masks wide variations by occupation in the ratio of female to male earnings; for example, it is 81% for computer programmers and 69% among janitors, but only 55% among sales supervisors, 61% among managers, and 63% among lawyers (U.S. Bureau of the Census, 1987).

A number of observers suggest that the sluggish rate of change in the aggregate earnings ratio is in part a function of continued occupational sex segregation. Evidence is more ambiguous regarding whether the types of jobs women occupied by the 1980s were noticeably different from those they held in earlier decades. England (1981) argues that 1960 levels of occupational sex segregation were little different from those prevailing in 1920; the drop in segregation during the 1940s was reversed by increases in the 1950s. However, Beller (1984) argues that declines in occupational sex segregation resumed in the 1960s and accelerated in the 1970s, and under several sets of assumptions, predicts small to modest declines in these rates through the 1980s (Beller and Han, 1984). Another contribution to a decline of occupational sex segregation came from a reduction in the prevalence of sex-segregated occupations—for example, fewer household maids and servants, fewer telephone operators (due to technological change), and fewer sewers and stitchers, the latter decline partly a function of the exportation of capital from the United States. As of 1986, the percentage female had risen to 6.0 among engineers, 17.6 among physicians, and 18.1 among lawyers (U.S. Bureau of Labor Statistics, 1987). Still, in 1986, occupations such as registered nurses, elementary school teachers, cashiers, secretaries, bookkeepers, and waiters and waitresses remained at least 85% female (U.S. Bureau of Labor Statistics, 1987).

Bielby and Baron (1984) argue that estimates of sex segregation at the level of occupations may be too optimistic, since analyses of *job* segregation—that is, at a lower level of aggregation,

within occupations—suggest continued high levels of segregation. Reskin and Roos (1990) also suggest that significant resegregation occurs in the workplace—for example, more women entering medicine but clustering into a small number of specialties such as pediatrics and obstetrics. Jacobs (1989) echoes this more conservative estimate of change with the argument that while increased numbers of women enter male-dominated occupations, they also leave at high rates, thus creating a "revolving door" through which women pass, with a given group only temporarily occupying positions in male-dominated occupations. Still, it seems likely that some real declines in segregation have occurred, thus moving employed men and women somewhat closer to each other in the working conditions they experience.

These phenomena are interrelated. The transformation from a manufacturing to a service-based economy created large numbers of the types of jobs for which employers have traditionally hired women. At the same time, these jobs were often, although not always, remunerated more modestly than the manufacturing jobs that were disappearing. Declining productivity meant that in order to maintain standards of living or to get ahead, families needed two earners where in the sixties the same standard of living could be attained with only one. Changes in ideology probably both reinforced and motivated these changes, thus prompting more women with young children to enter the labor force.

Changes in Family Patterns

In the last 150 years or so, the normative American ideal for childrearing families has been a married couple with complementary roles; the husband has an occupation outside the household, which provides for the family's economic needs, while the wife has primary responsibility for the household, children, and the emotional well-being of all (see Bernard, 1981). This male family-wage-earner model is adequate only when the wages of husband-fathers are sufficient to support an unemployed woman and some unspecified number of nonearning children. For families with low-wage or intermittently unemployed husbands, this ideal was out of reach even before the structural changes in the economy summarized above. But these changes in the types of employment available prompted many families to increase their number of earners; some have argued that the influx of wives and mothers into the labor force became essential to avoid real declines in family income. Sorensen and McLanahan (1987) document that, as a result, married women's economic dependency on their husbands declined substantially between 1940 and 1980. The major determinant of decreased dependency among younger wives is increased hours of work; continuing gender differences in wage levels, however, meant that women needed to work more hours to contribute the same amount of income to their families.

While multiple earners were becoming more necessary, however, simultaneous changes in family composition made the option of multiple earners available to a smaller proportion of family households with children. Rising nonmarital fertility and high rates of marital disruption during the 1960s and 1970s left many families with a single adult member (Hernandez and Myers, 1988). By 1985, over 20% of family households with children under 18 were headed by an unmarried mother or father. While such parents did not have to negotiate with an employed spouse regarding schedules or priorities, neither did they have the income, assistance, or emotional support that a spouse might provide.

All single-parent families were increasingly disadvantaged economically; but given the continued earnings gap between men and women, single-mother families were particularly hurt: in 1987, 7.6% of married-parent families, but 47.8% of single-mother families, were below the poverty line. For women, even full-time, full-year employment did not guarantee remaining above the poverty line: 1.8% of such married-couple families, but 9.3% of single-mother families, were still in poverty (U.S. Bureau of the Census, 1989).

Such cross-sectional data understate the movement among family types and the associated changes in family income that have become increasingly common. As McLanahan and Booth (1989) have noted, the high poverty rates of unmarried mothers highlight the economic vulnerability and relatively low individual earning capacity of all women. High rates of marital disruption underscore this vulnerability: marital disruption means sharp declines in mothers' but not fathers' standards of living, especially for mothers not in the labor force.

EMPLOYMENT AND FAMILY LIFE: THE NEW HOME ECONOMICS

One of the most significant theoretical developments in the area of work and family in the 1980s comes from economics. Gary Becker's (1981) *A Treatise on the Family* extended conventional microeconomic theory to the family, an area of scholarly inquiry previously outside the scope of economics. A significant strength of the theory is its ability to integrate within a single framework the description and analysis of a variety of topics within the realm of family—for example, fertility, marriage, and the allocation of time—as well as extrafamilial (but family-related) topics such as education, health, bequests, and the distribution of income (Ben-Porath, 1982). Becker's analyses bear on our concern with the effects of parental employment on family life in two ways. First, they help to explain decisions regarding the extent and nature of female labor force participation, a major factor in influencing family economic status, division of household labor, and attendant interactional outcomes. Second, they alert us to concepts and formulations utilized with varying degrees of success in economics, and thus provide a foundation for interdisciplinary inquiry regarding employment and family welfare.

Most relevant to our discussion are Becker's hypotheses regarding sex role differentiation within nuclear families and the relative allocation of husbands' and wives' efforts to market and nonmarket activities (see Blau, 1987, for a useful summary). Briefly, Becker argues that households derive utility from commodities that are produced with some combination of market goods and nonmarket time. Since small children are time-intensive commodities, and the substitution of market goods (e.g., day care centers) may be of questionable quality and difficult to arrange, mothers will reduce labor force participation in order to devote time to this form of production within the home. According to Becker, it is most efficient, and provides greater utility for the family as a whole, to have mothers rather than fathers make these choices, since existing labor market discrimination and mothers' lower levels of human capital investment result in their obtaining lower returns to their investments than men will obtain. However, these choices do not necessarily maximize a woman's *individual* utility, since the choices have long-run negative implications for the accumulation of labor force experience and likely smaller total investments in human capital that are useful in market exchange. Married women therefore become more dependent on their husbands, with reduced bargaining power in the household. If the marriage does not endure, such choices may have additional negative economic consequences. The theory has suggested a number of testable hypotheses and motivated both new data production as well as the application of sophisticated econometric techniques to those data (Ben-Porath, 1982).

A number of sociologists have taken issue with elements of the theory. Berk (1985) responds to "the new home economics" by arguing that in addition to the household being a "factory" that combines time and resources to produce able workers and socialized children, it also produces gendered relations. Gender intervenes directly in the household division of labor via the enactment of gender ideals, gendered patterns of dominance and submission, and norms that regulate the allocation of whole sets of household tasks. These norms influence the allocation of spouses' time to family and market work (Berk, 1985: 205–206). Household members take into account what "should" be happening when they allocate time and tasks in home production, and thus it is the complex interweaving of these agendas that determines the disproportionate share of household work that women perform. Change in these arrangements is likely to come from the conflict between the demands for market work and established patterns of home production; for example, her analysis of a national sample of 335 urban husband-wife households suggests that husbands of employed wives with preschool children did more than other husbands.

Geerken and Gove (1983) combine elements of Becker's utility model of family time allocation with aspects of functionalism from sociology to construct a theory that attempts to explain the labor-leisure-home work choices of contemporary married-couple families, and they study the implications of these choices for marital viability. While endorsing the underlying assumptions of the Becker model, they argue that such choices will also be a function of the number and ages of children in the home, and that actual choices may be interactive with characteristics of household members. Similar to Berk (1985), they believe that cultural expectations regarding appropriate roles

of household members must be treated as one possible determinant of choice, in contrast to pure economic theory that relegates such notions to the residual category of "tastes." Their analysis of a 1974–75 national sample of survey respondents suggests that husbands' wages, wives' wages, and demand for child care in the home importantly influence whether the wife engages in market work; wife's sex role attitudes have some impact as well. For families of lower socioeconomic status, the choice between market and home work is particularly problematic, since avoiding market work reduces the potential for family income, while suitability of child care becomes an issue if market work is chosen. They find that while wives spend the most time on housework, husbands take somewhat more of the responsibility in households with working wives and educated husbands. There is a lag in the role allocation between the market and the home: women have moved into the work force, but husbands have not picked up much of the slack at home.

Bielby and Bielby (1988) challenge Becker's assertion that married women invest less effort in market work than men. Using the 1973 and 1977 Quality of Employment Surveys, they find that women report slightly greater work effort than men—that is, they score higher on an index where they report having jobs requiring hard work, requiring substantial physical or mental effort, and involving substantial effort beyond job requirements. Women allocate more effort than men with comparable family situations, household responsibilities, market human capital, and job rewards. Women with preschool-age children exert effort comparable to that of men with no preschool children. Having a spouse specializing in nonmarket work increases work effort. Bielby and Bielby (1988) provide additional analysis in attempts to rule out the possibility that sex differences in the perception of work effort account for the findings, and find that the original inferences are maintained. They note that in experimental settings women tend to underestimate their work effort. These findings suggest that women generate the energy they need to combine work and family roles.

Huber and Spitze (1983) also take issue with Becker while simultaneously developing their own theory of sex stratification. They argue that sex stratification is a function of the intersection of subsistence technology and childrearing: women's status in horticultural societies was greater relative to men's than in other societies because both women and men produced food. In contrast, in agricultural societies men monopolized the plow, thus increasing the value of the land and increasing the importance of monogamy so as to assure that the land was inherited only by their own children; these factors reduced women's status. In industrial societies, women's status rises as a function of increased labor force participation and production of income, facilitated by their rising educational attainments and decreased fertility. Arguing that women's labor force participation is the most important variable affecting sex role attitudes and behaviors, Huber and Spitze (1983) use survey data to assess its impact on a variety of attitudes. Wife's employment affects the perception of household division of labor—the longer she is employed, the less housework both husbands and wives perceive her to do; length of employment is also associated with more frequent thoughts of divorce among wives, and higher husbands' perceptions of their wives' power. Contrary to arguments by Becker, the wife-husband wage ratio showed no effects on division of labor and thoughts of divorce. Although Huber and Spitze (1983) do not claim that their evidence counters Becker's theory directly, they find more support for their own predictions than for Becker's. They expect substantial change in the household division of labor over the next few decades, through mechanisms such as men taking on a greater share of the burden of household work and certain activities now performed in the home being contracted out.

Other economic concepts have influenced sociological thinking on work and families. England and Farkas (1986) use the notion of the implicit contract to explain behavior both in the labor market and in the household. Just as working arrangements are often only partly defined formally, the remainder of job requirements and employer expectations being implicit in the relationship, so too are agreements regarding division of labor and familial expectations within the home. Similarly, just as workers take jobs after a labor market search, so does household formation follow a period of searching for suitable partners. England and Farkas (1986) argue for the importance of work and family arrangements as mutual determinants of each other, with the likelihood of change being motivated by changes at the macro level of the economy. They see increased demand for jobs traditionally occupied by females as motivating increased female labor force participation, thus prompting changes in role differentiation in the home, increased divorce, and later age at marriage. Other researchers also question economic models of family formation (Oppenheimer, 1988) and women's time allocation between work and family (Gwartney-Gibbs, 1988).

In summary, scholars from several disciplines have reacted to Becker's microeconomic analysis of the family with arguments and evidence regarding components missing from the theory. They question assumptions on which the theory is built and, by attempting to integrate sociological and economic ideas, provide a foundation for developing a more comprehensive theory.

EMPLOYMENT, WORK-FAMILY CONFLICT, AND PARENTAL WELL-BEING

Parental employment affects family life in part through its impact on the psychological well-being of workers, and much 1980s research has examined such effects. Most early research on the impact of employment on adult well-being was guided by sex-differentiated expectations regarding work-family conflict, evaluating the potentially negative effects of unemployment for men but of employment for women. However, studies of the impact of employment on adult well-being generally report positive effects for both men and women (for a recent example and summary of earlier studies, see Rosenfield, 1989, or Repetti, Matthews, and Waldron, 1989). Earned income also enhances self-esteem and a sense of mastery, which in turn increase overall well-being (Mirowsky and Ross, 1986; Pearlin, Lieberman, Menaghan, and Mullan, 1981).

However, the strength of these effects varies depending on other roles held, with positive effects particularly strong for those with clear "breadwinning" responsibilities, such as married men and unmarried women with minor children at home (Menaghan, 1989b). Studies of men's, particularly married fathers', *unemployment* document powerful negative effects on individual well-being (Kessler, House, and Turner, 1987) and on the quality of participation in family life (Elder, 1974; Elder, Liker, and Cross, 1984; Elder, Van Nguyen, and Caspi, 1985; see also McLoyd's 1989 review).

Most attention continues to be focused on employment status effects for married women, particularly married mothers. The responsibility of these women to be "breadwinners" or even "coproviders" (Thompson and Walker, 1989) is more ambiguous, and conflict with other family responsibilities may be more likely. The employment status per se of *married* mothers with young children, like that of married mothers of school-age children, has not proved to be a particularly powerful predictor of individual well-being (Hoffman, 1989). Research has identified two variables that appear to be important in moderating and qualifying any effects of married mothers' employment: the extent of husbands' participation in family tasks, and the match between wives' employment status and their own as well as their husbands' preferences.

The positive effects of husbands' participation in household work are not limited to *employed* wives. Ross, Mirowsky, and Huber (1983; see also Ross and Mirowsky, 1988) found that both employed and nonemployed wives were less distressed when their husbands did an equal share of the household work. But sharing was rare: they note that household work was shared equally among only 20% of the dual-earner couples and 7% of the male-earner/female-homemaker couples. Other studies also show relatively little male participation in child care and housework (see Ferree, 1990; Pleck, 1983; and Thompson and Walker, 1989), although the trend has been toward some relative increase.

Pleck (1985) argues that values have shifted in favor of greater husband involvement in the home for all husbands; he uses data from two national studies of husband-wife time allocation to show increases in husbands' actual involvement over time, particularly in direct child care, even for husbands whose wives do not work outside the home. Women have decreased the time they are spending in home work, and combined, these two trends produce a movement toward greater equality. However, husbands still contribute far less than wives, and controlling for their work hours does not explain the differential. Thornton's (1989) analysis of survey data from 1976 to 1985 also suggests a strong and continuing trend toward greater support of women's employment and men's household participation. However, his data suggest that male attitudes remain less egalitarian than women's: for example, in 1985,

64% of women but only 32% of men disagreed with a statement that it is usually better for all involved if the man is the achiever outside the home and the woman takes care of the home and family; and men were more likely than women to view women's working as causing preschool children to suffer and as taking something away from a woman's relationship with her husband.

Ross, Mirowsky, and Huber (1983; see also Mirowsky and Ross, 1986) provide evidence for the importance of congruence between preference and behavior in understanding employment effects on psychological distress among married women. Employment was associated with lower distress when it matched individual preferences. Wives' distress was least when they were employed and preferred to be so; of the two possible mismatches, wives' distress was highest when they were not employed but wished they were.

Such studies suggest that changes in employment that increase congruence between behavior and preference would be positive; however, Wethington and Kessler (1989) found that the effect of changes in wives' employment status over time did not vary with previously expressed preferences; for all wives, movement from homemaking to full-time or close to full-time employment had positive effects, while the reverse movement had negative impact. Smaller changes—from full-time to high part-time, or from homemaking to low part-time (10–19 hours) employment—had insignificant effects. Wethington and Kessler note that wives who became employed but for relatively few hours retained major responsibility for household work and child care and received little assistance from husbands or from paid helpers. As just noted, low spouse participation in household work is generally associated with greater distress for wives.

Spouses' Employment Status and Individual Well-Being among Married Couples

Relatively little work has explored the impact of men's employment status on their wives' well-being (but see Penkower, Bromet, and Dew, 1988); the general assumption is that spousal employment benefits wives. However, a series of studies has explored the potential *negative* impact of wives' employment on their husbands' emotional well-being (see, for example, Kessler and McRae, 1981, 1982; Rosenfield, 1980; Ross,

Mirowsky, and Huber, 1983; Staines, Pottick, and Fudge, 1986; Stanley, Hunt, and Hunt, 1986). These findings present a complex picture but tend to show small negative net effects. Husbands' interpretation of wives' employment for their own sense of adequacy as a breadwinner is important: Staines and associates (1986) find that when sense of breadwinner adequacy is controlled, the negative effects of wives' employment on husbands' job satisfaction and life satisfaction are no longer significant. Congruence between preference and reality also plays a role: Ross, Mirowsky, and Huber (1983) found that a husband's distress was highest when his wife was employed but he preferred that she were not. Given the larger economic changes noted earlier, many wives have entered the labor force and/or increased their work hours (despite their own and/or their husbands' preferences) to compensate for a loss in husbands' earning power (McLanahan and Glass, 1985). Thus, negative "effects" of wives' employment on husbands' emotional well-being may be confounded by effects of concurrent negative changes in their husbands' employment prospects.

It may be argued that wives' employment has more negative effects on husbands to the extent that they take on more of the household work; but neither Ross, Mirowsky, and Huber (1983), Ross and Mirowsky (1988), Kessler and McRae (1982), nor Staines, Pottick, and Fudge (1986) found that husbands were negatively affected by greater household participation. Other research suggests negative effects under some circumstances. In a sample of 40 largely blue-collar married couples with a baby or toddler, fathers with employed wives reported significantly more solo child care activity, as well as more arguments with and complaints from their wives, than did fathers with homemaking wives (Crouter, Perry-Jenkins, Huston, and McHale, 1987). These two variables were independent for male-earner/homemaker couples but strongly and *positively* related for male-earner/female-earner couples: the husbands who took more child care responsibility reported that their working wives complained more. Crouter and associates speculate that working wives may use negative tactics to "pressure" their husbands to do more. They note that such patterns may emerge only for some married employed parents—those whose dual-earner life-style does not match their own values, hopes, and expecta-

tions for married life (p. 439). Ross, Mirowsky, and Huber (1983) agree, arguing that as preferences catch up to the likely reality of dual-earner couples, the low depression levels of dual-earner husbands and wives who prefer that situation will become more common. In contrast, Stanley, Hunt, and Hunt (1986) find that the psychological costs of wife employment for husband-fathers are highest for better-educated men with higher-status occupations. Such men may benefit most in terms of occupational success from supportive, backstage wifely activities; the disadvantages of having an otherwise employed wife are real and unlikely to be erased by changes in individual attitudes.

Work-Family Role Conflict among Couples

Much of the rationale for expecting negative effects of wives' employment on both wives' and husbands' emotional well-being has emphasized the potential for extensive role conflict and role overload that wives' employment may bring. While traditional arguments regarding the nature of conflict between work and family roles are now familiar themes, sociologists pursued these notions in innovative contexts during the 1980s. Adopting a broader definition of "family," Blumstein and Schwartz (1983) interviewed heterosexual and homosexual couples to study the dynamics of paired relationships and to study whether such dynamics vary depending on the sex composition of the relationships. Blumstein and Schwartz found that work creates conflict for couples as well as personal fulfillment. Among heterosexual couples, many husbands do not want their wives to work, and argue that the needs of children as well as their own needs should come first. Wives are more likely to desire employment outside the home. When wives do work, they exercise greater power within their relationships, although there is also more conflict regarding how the children are being raised. Wives still bear the lion's share of the responsibility for the housework, and among couples where the husband does more housework, there is more conflict. Women do more housework than men in cohabiting relationships as well. Among same-sex couples, the great majority believe both partners should work. They also find that most couples have at least one partner who is relationship centered; when this is lacking, possibly because of work involvement, satisfaction with the relationship declines, as does commitment.

Pleck (1984) has identified two mechanisms that buffer work-family conflict. The first is sex segregation in both the occupational sphere and the home sphere, such that changes in work roles for women do not occur at the expense of men (although the reverse may not be true). The second is asymmetrical effects of work and family roles, with family being allowed to intrude into work life for women, and work being allowed to intrude into family for men (but see Bolger, DeLongis, Kessler, and Wethington, 1989).

Among married and unmarried parents, the form that work-family conflict may take is likely to vary by social class and the number of employed adults in the family. Mortimer and London (1984) distinguish several possibilities, thus setting the notion of role strain in broader perspective. For example, while the most important stress on a single-parent, female-headed household is economic, this source of stress is less important in a professional-managerial, single-provider, married-couple family. However, that family is more likely to be challenged by male work absorption that precludes desired family involvement. The alienating nature of work for blue-collar men, as well as financial pressures and lack of opportunities for upward mobility, leave little energy for constructive family involvement. Such conditions promote harsher discipline and greater physical punishment for children; wives are isolated from men's work roles. Dual-provider families face role overload. In blue-collar families, women remain responsible for almost all domestic tasks, although having parents work different shifts helps some. Potentially conflicting demands from two careers, in combination with heavy demands for childrearing, create pressures in dual-career families that lead to unhappy compromises and exhaustion.

Studies documenting the existence and consequences of role conflict have focused on both higher and lower socioeconomic status contexts. Fowlkes (1980) richly documents how the professional achievements of married men are "propped up" by the roles that their wives play as mothers, by their wives directly working on instrumental tasks related to their careers, and by wives creating the home and psychological environments that allow for their husbands' sustained attention to professional work; it is not surprising

that Stanley et al. (1986) find such men relatively most deprived by an employed wife. Although the time of academic men is somewhat more flexible than the time of physicians, thus allowing somewhat more participation in family life, in each arrangement the responsibility for fulfilling all but the professional functions remains with the wives. For both groups, husbands' dedication to their professions often dictates a very lonely existence for wives, who complain that even when their husbands are present in the home, they are psychologically absent.

Hertz (1986) interviewed dual-career couples employed in corporate settings. The financial rewards that accompany those positions provide a buffer against some of the stresses inherent in the demands of two high-level careers, a marriage and possibly children. However, these couples still confront the same types of difficulties that all two-earner households face: negotiating roles and a division of labor, setting of priorities for careers and families, and obtaining household assistance to realize role and priority decisions. The confrontation between traditional expectations of one or both spouses, and the demands of high-level careers, particularly for women, result in some of the same choices that dual-earner couples face: women frequently slow down their career advancement to accommodate the needs of children, although at a more comfortable financial level than many families experience.

Studies of families of modest financial means provide compatible findings. Cornfield, Filho, and Chun (1990) study households where one adult is a union member. They argue that women's participation in unions is more constrained than men's by household responsibilities, although they report a positive relationship between number of children and women's participation. In addition, men are more likely to participate if they hold ideologies supporting participation, while women are driven more by economic interests. Similarly, Roby and Uttal (1988) conducted semistructured interviews with 124 union stewards. Women stewards are less likely to be living with a spouse and children than are men stewards. Men place the union above family, while women have the reverse priorities. Women stewards do more housework than men stewards. Rosenfeld (1985) finds similar forms of conflict and adaptation in farm households.

Hochschild (1989) observed couples in dual-earner households over an eight-year period to study "the second shift," the extra month of labor per year needed to maintain the household. On this shift, division of labor is handled according to the couples' "gender strategies," those mechanisms used to accomplish needed work, given their cultural beliefs regarding gender norms. She analyzes the relative gains and costs of their strategies, richly chronicling role overload, rationalizations that less housework and child care are needed, and the timing and extent of cutting back at work, at home, or both. A particular strength is the longitudinal nature of her work, thus portraying the long-term implications of varying gender strategies and how partners renegotiate relationships over time.

An additional source of evidence of conflict between work roles and traditional family roles is the literature on the effect of adult marital and parental status on occupational attainment. Several studies suggest that while marriage may enhance men's occupation progress, delay or avoidance of marriage (and if divorced, delay or avoidance of remarriage) is more beneficial for women. Houseknecht, Vaughan, and Stratham (1987) find that among women enrolling in graduate schools, there is a positive relationship between duration of single time and educational progress, and remaining single until graduate work was completed facilitated occupational attainments.

Peterson (1989) also suggests that, over time, unmarried women fare better than their married counterparts. Using the Mature Women's sample from the National Longitudinal Survey, he argues that although the economic well-being of women drops immediately after divorce, they recover at least some of their economic standing over time. This is because they immediately increase the quantity of their labor devoted to market work; over time they experience a rise in wage rates relative to women who remain married. He speculates that women who have been divorced for a long period of time appear to employers to be "dependable," potentially promotable workers, in much the same way as do men. This is in contrast to married women, who appear "undependable," and even potentially to never-married women, who may be perceived as likely to marry and become "undependable."

Mutchler (1987) finds that women, and in particular women with children, are more likely than

men to suffer from economic underemployment (e.g., no full-time work available or poverty-level earnings despite full-time employment). Single mothers are most likely to be underemployed, as compared to childless single women or wives with children. Family status appears to affect the probability of underemployment, independent of race, sex, education, age, and occupation. Women who are not parents have underemployment profiles similar to those of men; thus for women, the critical variable is parental status. Single-parent status predicts underemployment for men as well. However, women are ten times more likely to be in this status than men—10% versus 1%.

Some research has evaluated possible solutions to the role strains of dual-earner families. Presser (1987) has argued that some couples work nonday shifts and/or stagger their hours in an attempt to manage role overload; other workers follow such work schedules by necessity. Staines and Pleck (1983) find that an irregular pattern of working days adversely affects family life in terms of family adjustment, time spent on family activities, and perceptions of interference between work and family. Husbands are more likely to have irregular working hours than are wives. Personal control over the hours of work, more common in higher-status occupations, has a moderating effect on the negative impact of erratic work schedules. Higher number of hours worked and shift work are associated with increased family conflict, thus suggesting that the shift-work pattern studied by Presser is not a cost-free option for families.

Other suggested solutions for work-family conflict emphasize some alteration in wives' activities. Moen and Dempster-McClain (1987) use the 1977 Quality of Employment Survey to study 224 dual-earner married couples with children under 13 years of age. Their findings, consistent with theories of role strain, show that married mothers working full-time prefer to work fewer hours; perceived role strain is related to preference for reducing hours of work. Implementing this preference, however, may also increase financial pressures on the family. A common suggestion is for women to sequence work and family roles as a mechanism for reducing role strain. Daniels and Weingarten (1984) describe the perceptions of women who schedule work and family differently across the life cycle—early marriage, later work; early career, later family; and so on—although they do not offer specific prescriptions.

These "solutions" generally remain at the individual level, with parents, especially mothers, expected to find idiosyncratic resolutions to work-family conflict. Even at that level, they are unsatisfying: they generally do not consider possible changes in men's occupational participation. Nor do they take seriously the critical economic contribution that increasing numbers of young mothers make to their families. An emerging and increasingly important area of research considers the effects of workplace policies and other institutional arrangements on work-family conflict (see Bohen and Viveros-Long, 1981; Fernandez, 1986; Greenberger, Goldberg, Hamill, O'Neil, and Payne, 1989; Moen, 1989). Zigler and Frank (1988) comprehensively document the need for parental leaves to care for infants, while Moen (1989) studies the extent to which the work-family policies in Sweden have eased the burdens of working parents. Greenberger and associates (forthcoming) find that both informal support and formal workplace policies and benefits that are "family-responsive" reduce feelings of strain and increase organizational commitment for both fathers and mothers. On the basis of survey data from blue- and white-collar corporate employees in the United States, Fernandez (1986) calls for corporations to adopt policies of enlightened self-interest that recognize that employees have important parental roles as well as work roles; Kamerman and Kahn (1987) provide compatible arguments. Bohen and Viveros-Long (1981) demonstrate the limited effects of somewhat greater work schedule flexibility in reducing work-family conflict for working parents, particularly working mothers, and discuss the more comprehensive changes in gendered expectations in both workplaces and families that are needed.

VARIATIONS IN OCCUPATIONAL CONDITIONS

As labor force participation rates of married women with children of all ages have increased over the last several decades, and as women's rates have converged with men's, some of the most interesting research in this decade has taken the fact of employment for granted and investigated the effects of *variations in employment experiences* on adult well-being and family lives. Two theoretical frameworks guide much of this research. Work socialization perspectives draw attention to the cumulative impact of enduring job conditions on cognitive functioning and attitudes about self and society. Socialization theorists argue that adults generalize attitudes and values as well as ways of thinking from work to other settings, and form judgments about themselves, other people, and orientations toward life in general in accord with processes of learning, generalization, and attribution (Mortimer and Borman, 1988). Partially overlapping with this line of research are studies reflecting a social-stress perspective that analyze both short- and long-term emotional effects of job stressors. These studies emphasize the mismatch between situation demands and individual capacities or resources. Demands that exceed individual capacities have been discussed in terms of role overload and overstimulation, while demands that are below individual capacities have been discussed in terms of role underload and understimulation. Work stress research has focused much more on burdensome demands than on insufficient opportunities (see Menaghan, 1990).

Work Socialization

Research in the work socialization tradition has particularly emphasized the substantive complexity and opportunities for self-direction that jobs may provide. Attention to substantive complexity is based on broader arguments regarding the positive impact of complex, demanding environments wherever they are encountered—on the job, at home, or at school. As Schooler (1987: 24-25) conceptualizes these, an environment is more complex "the more diverse the stimuli, the greater the number of decisions required, the greater the number of considerations to be taken into account in making these decisions, and the more ill-defined and apparently contradictory the contingencies." To the degree that such an environment rewards cognitive effort, "individuals should be motivated to develop their intellectual capacities and to generalize the resulting cognitive processes to other situations" (pp. 24-25). Schooler summarizes a range of evidence from studies of adult jobs as well as studies of children at home and at school, of the elderly, and of other species as supporting the general argument (see also Mortimer, Lorence, and Kumka, 1986).

Evidence is generally consistent with these

theoretical arguments. A series of studies has established that the conditions of work that are more common in less-valued, lower-paying jobs—low autonomy, heavy supervision, routinization, and little demand or opportunity for substantively complex work—negatively affect adults' intellectual flexibility (Kohn and Schooler, 1983) and shape more socially conservative and guarded orientations to society. They are also associated with lower self-esteem, self-efficacy, and personal control (Gecas and Seff, 1989; Mortimer and Borman, 1988; Spenner and Otto, 1985). The same general pattern holds for men and women, in Poland and Japan as well as in the United States (Kohn, Naoi, Schoenbach, Schooler, and Slomczynski, 1990; Miller, Slomczynski, and Kohn, 1985; Naoi and Schooler, 1985; Schooler and Naoi, 1988; Slomczynski, Miller, and Kohn, 1981). Much of this work has been summarized by O'Brien (1986) and by Spenner (1988).

The negative effects of the lack of substantively complex work are not exclusively cognitive: low substantive complexity has been associated with increased alcohol use among employed men and with greater emotional distress among employed women (Hibbard and Pope, 1987; Lennon, 1987; but see Mensch and Kandel, 1988). Other studies support this pattern, using occupational prestige or status scores (Repetti and Crosby, 1984; Saenz, Goudy, and Lorenz, 1989).

Changes in job conditions toward greater self-directedness and complexity have implications for spousal and parent-child interaction as well. In an exploratory study of workers in a "participatory" milieu involving greater teamwork and more complex and diversified tasks, Crouter (1984) reports that such work activities "carry over" into more problem-solving efforts with spouses and children, as well as greater sense of control and competence. However, some women workers reported a negative effect on spousal interaction, with their greater self-confidence and assertiveness reported as irritating or threatening their husbands. No husbands describe such effects, perhaps because the direction of change was already consistent with normatively accepted male dominance and activity. More substantively complex job conditions have been linked to valuing more self-directed qualities in one's children and so encouraging them to be more autonomous and intellectually flexible (see Gottfried and Gottfried,

1988; Piotrkowski and Katz, 1982; Schooler, 1987). Mothers in jobs involving more substantively complex work provide more cognitive stimulation and affective warmth to their young children; and such better home environments are associated, as expected, with better verbal development (Menaghan and Parcel, in press; Parcel and Menaghan, 1990).

Work Stress, Emotional Distress, and Family Interaction

While work socialization frameworks have emphasized the self-directedness of job content, other research has focused on the stressful potential of job conditions. Work by Karasek and others (Haynes and Feinleib, 1980; House, Strecher, Metzner, and Robbins, 1986; Karasek, 1979; Karasek, Baker, Marxer, Ahlbom, and Theorell, 1981) suggests that the combination of high job demands but low decision latitude, which was more characteristic of women's jobs than of men's jobs, is associated with greater mental and physical distress. Menaghan and Merves (1984) link greater distress with a set of occupational conditions—depersonalization, noxious job conditions, poor current earnings and few opportunities for advancement, and time pressures. Miller, Schooler, Kohn, and Miller (1979) also note that job pressures and long work hours are associated with more anxiety and distress (see also Voydanoff and Donnelly, 1989).

Other studies have emphasized the quality of interpersonal relations with job supervisors and coworkers. Hibbard and Pope (1987) found that feeling socially supported at work was associated with better physical and mental health. Low social support at work had particularly negative effects for nonmarried mothers. Among women working as clerical workers, job social climate, supervisor support, and job satisfaction affected psychological distress (Repetti, 1988). The effects of job conditions were stronger for women who were more job-involved. Among the married women, the negative effects of poor social climate on the job, low supervisor support, and low job satisfaction were stronger among those who also reported *more* inequality relative to their husbands in time spent on household work and care of children.

Occupations also vary enormously in wage levels and other benefits; these variations have multiple consequences. Economic pressures affect parental feelings of mastery, self-efficacy, and distress for both men and women (Andrisani, 1978; Downey and Moen, 1987; Duncan and Liker, 1983; Duncan and Morgan, 1981; Menaghan, 1989a; Pearlin et al., 1981), and heightened parental distress affects parent-child interaction (Conger, McCarty, Yang, Lahey, and Kropp, 1984; Moen, Kain, and Elder, 1983; Piotrkowski, Rapaport, and Rapaport, 1987; Siegal, 1984; Voydanoff, 1987). Siegal (1985) draws attention to the likelihood that economic deprivation negatively affects *the child's* perception of his or her parents, which in turn shapes child behavior toward adults (in addition to the more commonly discussed impact on parents' behavior toward children). Siegal distinguishes the effects of decline in socioeconomic well-being brought on by job loss or layoff from effects due to chronically low family income. He argues that economic deprivation is particularly likely to hurt father-son relations as fathers lose stature in the family relative to mothers (see also Elder, 1974). Thus, as Voydanoff (1990, this volume; see also Ellwood, 1988) develops more fully, both unstable employment and low-wage employment are associated with insufficient economic resources and less optimal home environments.

Low-wage jobs may also be associated with longer work hours: more hours in one or more poorly paid positions may be needed to obtain the same annual earnings that might be obtained in fewer hours in better-paid positions. However, the relations between wage levels and job hours are complex. While workers in low-paying jobs may work longer hours to increase earnings, many high-wage occupations also demand extensive time commitments. Some recent work suggests that paternal job conditions affect fathers' involvement with their children in somewhat offsetting ways. For example, Grossman, Pollack, and Golding (1988) find that fathers who were more satisfied and involved in their own work spent *less* time with their children than did less work-satisfied fathers; but their interaction was rated as more sensitive and more supportive of children's autonomy and affiliation. Research is needed to evaluate both the positive impact of satisfying work conditions on the quality of interaction and the potential limits to those effects that derive from the likelihood that more satisfying work will be accompanied by longer work hours and less available family time. More generally, Nock and

Kingston (1988) suggest that work hours affect fathers' time with children more than mothers', while Hill (1988) argues that greater wives' employment may result in less time in shared leisure activities for couples. Increased work hours of both mothers and fathers create real time constraints and real conflicts, but time allocation, and negotiations about appropriate time usage, may also come to represent contending views regarding investments and priorities. Moen and Howery (1988) provide a more general discussion of the significance of time for families.

Some methodologically innovative studies have examined daily variations in job stress and emotional response. Repetti (1989) studied 33 air traffic controllers and 27 of their wives who completed daily surveys on three consecutive days. When spouses were supportive following high-workload days, workload appeared to reduce overall social and emotional responsiveness, including decreases in aggressive behavior. She speculates that social withdrawal may help promote recovery from negative work experiences.

Bolger, DeLongis, Kessler, and Wethington (1989) use daily diaries from both husbands and wives for a six-week period to examine how stressful work experiences (overloads and arguments with supervisors, coworkers, or subordinates at work) predict feelings of overload, arguments with spouse, or other arguments. They conclude that there is less "contagion" from work to home than one might expect. Like Repetti, they find that overload at work was likely to be followed by a reduction of home involvement; both home work load and occurrence of arguments were lower. When their spouse experienced work overload, respondents' workload at home increased while their spouse's home workload decreased, which suggests that spouses were shouldering more of the work for a weary spouse. This effect was stronger for wives than for husbands, so that husbands were more likely to gain some breathing space at home after a bad day at work.

Interpersonal conflicts clearly showed a spillover from work to home, with arguments at work likely to be followed by spousal arguments at home that evening. In additional analysis of the same data set, interpersonal conflicts, both at work and at home, emerged as a potent source of daily fluctuations in emotional distress and depressed mood (Bolger, DeLongis, Kessler, and

Schilling, 1989). Such analysis of the "micro-structure" of linkages between employment, marital, and parental role experiences provide an important testing ground for theoretical arguments regarding social stress and role conflict.

As mothers' labor force participation has become more expectable, a new stream of research has begun to examine how father-child interaction has changed. There is disagreement regarding how much change has actually occurred. Furstenberg (1988) argues that the changes have been relatively small. Fathers may interact more with their children, but they are still unlikely to orchestrate the child's activities: "fathers are still pinch hitters or part-time players rather than regulars" (1988: 209). The picture is similar but more bleak after divorce or separation; even when fathers stay in touch, their role is recreational rather than instrumental. Hoffman (1989) suggests that employed mothers' efforts to "catch up" on missed interaction with the children actually makes their husbands' time with children less than it would be in households with a nonemployed mother; but neither Lamb, Hwang, Broberg, Bookstein, Hult, and Frodi (1988) nor Crouter et al. (1987) find this in empirical studies.

Other studies emphasize many fathers' new role as primary or solo caregivers. Presser (1987) documents the increasing proportion of married, two-job couples who take turns being solo caregivers for their children. She views the phenomenon of married parents' working different shifts as in part a dual-earner household response to difficulties in finding adequate care for children, as well as a reflection of the increased number of service-sector jobs that are available to young adults. Service-sector jobs, like many blue-collar jobs, frequently include schedules that are beyond the "9 to 5" window assumed by most organized child care settings; thus, workers in such jobs must rely disproportionately on informal arrangements among adult family members and with other relatives or neighbors.

To some extent, such parents may function as sequential single parents and thus resemble single parents more than their married counterparts. For both mothers and fathers, the quality of care they can provide will vary with the resources they command and the stressors they face. This is readily apparent from the examinations of the quality of the increased father-child contact that is prompted by disruptions in men's employment:

fathers without jobs are described as irritable, hostile, and explosive; likely to be punitive and arbitrary to their children; and irritated by increased interaction with them (see McLoyd, 1989). For both parents, unsupported, unrelieved care of several young children would be expected to be of lower quality, given poor ratios of caregivers to children and reliance on a single caregiver (Bradley and Caldwell, 1984; Howes, 1988; Howes and Stewart, 1987). Such interaction may have net negative effects on children, since low-quality interaction with socializing adults and unstable, unpredictable social contexts compromise children's attachments and sense of security, and have negative effects on learning (Crouter, Belsky, and Spanier, 1984; Estrada, Arsenio, Hess, and Holloway, 1987; Howes, 1988).

Furstenberg (1988) concludes that the effect of increasing paternal involvement in child care appears to depend on many other factors, including fathers' skill, mothers' attitudes, and their ability to cooperate with one another. Active father participation does have broader potential benefits for family functioning by reducing the feelings of role strain experienced by working mothers, which may help marital well-being and mother-child interaction. More pessimistically, Hoffman (1983) speculates that men's invasion of women's traditional arena of power and competence can bring conflict; and if the marriage ends, active and competent fathers may fight mothers for custody.

CONCLUSIONS

We see several promising directions for theory and research on work and family in the 1990s. First, we are encouraged to see the number of researchers who are actively engaged in considering the strengths and weaknesses of "the new home economics." We anticipate that additional such investigations will provide findings that are needed to refine the existing theory or possibly formulate a better one. The challenge will be to construct a parsimonious theory that incorporates needed sociological insights, particularly those regarding values and norms. Family scholars are also bringing new insights derived from neoclassical economics more generally to studies of family formation and structure, both as topics in their own right and as features that shape interaction within households.

Second, we encourage researchers to move beyond analyses of cross-sectional employment status contrasts and devote more attention to *variations* in working conditions in a given job and to the effects of employment sequences. We have drawn particular attention to studies of the changing occupational structure and of the differential allocation of men and women to occupations. Because women and men still tend to be employed in sex-segregated jobs and occupations, being employed tends to imply gender-differentiated work conditions. By taking such gender-differentiated work experiences into account, future research can better disentangle the effects of gender differences in job conditions from the impact of gender differences in household tasks in explaining individual well-being and family interaction. Dimensions of working conditions such as substantive complexity, wage levels, total work time, and the scheduling of work require additional investigation as to effects on family life. In addition, we need to know more about the effects of *underemployment* on family life, aside from economic implications. There has been more attention to the effects of such dimensions on adult outcomes than on children, a deficit that we should work to correct.

To an even greater extent we are in the infancy stage of considering how the *sequencing* of jobs, unemployment, and periods out of the labor force combine in careers to affect both adults and children. Literature on careers has been proliferating, with a number of differing models and frameworks being used as guidance. Ahead lies the task of distilling which aspects of career sequences are most critical to influencing family outcomes. In addition to considering long-term career trajectories, more research is needed to examine the daily sequences of stressors and pleasures that constitute work and family life. Studies that examine multiple time-points from the perspectives of multiple family members have enormous potential in this regard.

Work in the 1980s has well established the existence of role strain in dual-earner households across socioeconomic levels and across household types. Research in the 1990s should be specifically directed to assess solutions to role strain. We hope at least some effort will be directed to the study of solutions unfettered by traditional sex role assumptions. For example, while we have reviewed work suggesting that some dual-earner mothers

prefer reduced working hours, there is a relative paucity of research suggesting how fathers might make accommodations in work and family roles to reduce role strain in the household. Past research has viewed maternal employment as a problem, since questions are immediately raised regarding what arrangements are made to *substitute* for direct maternal care, the quality of those arrangements, and so on. Employment is viewed as competing with children and family for mothers' time, energy, and commitment. For men, *nonemployment* or *unemployment* is seen as the problem. The continued nonparallel nature of the research on employment status variations is striking. We need more systematic information regarding the possibility that husband's work involvement may *increase* problems in marital and family adjustment. We also need more systematic attention to the ways in which maternal *non*employment or underemployment may be detrimental to a variety of family-related outcomes, both economic and social. Particularly important in the search for solutions to role strain is research that goes beyond individual efforts and examines the effectiveness of various workplace and govermental policies on family interaction and welfare.

Certainly the preoccupation with married parents as the primary focus of several research agendas needs to be changed. Research must acknowledge that single parents are likely to be caring for a substantial proportion of children in the next decade and that the particular problems of financial pressure and role strain they experience are important to consider. Here, too, research that proposes and evaluates structural solutions to the strains of single-parent-earner families will be particularly important. In addition, we gain from studying work-family issues in households other than those of married couples. Blumstein and Schwartz's (1983) work notwithstanding, we need more systematic attention to work-family issues in cohabiting and same-sex households. Such work yields additional information in its own right, and it also provides an important vehicle toward exploring the external validity of conclusions derived from more conventionally formulated investigations. We hope this review will contribute to this research agenda by providing a summary of past accomplishments and by charting promising directions for future work.

NOTE

Preparation of this article was supported in part by Grants R01 HD23467 and R01 HD 26047 from the National Institutes of Child Health and Human Development. The authors thank Stacy Rogers and Martha Brown for their research assistance. They also appreciate helpful comments on earlier drafts from Joan Huber, Randall Olsen, Glenna Spitze, and the anonymous reviewers.

REFERENCES

Andrisani, Paul J. 1978. Work Attitudes and Labor Market Experience. New York: Praeger.

Becker, Gary S. 1981. A Treatise on the Family. Cambridge, MA: Harvard University Press.

Beller, Andrea. 1984. "Trends in occupational segregation by sex and race, 1960–1981." Pp. 11–26 in Barbara F. Reskin (ed.), Sex Segregation in the Workplace: Trends, Explanations, and Remedies. Washington, DC: National Academy Press.

Beller, Andrea, and Kee-ok Kim Han. 1984. "Occupational sex segregation prospects for the 1980s." Pp. 91–114 in Barbara F. Reskin (ed.), Sex Segregation in the Workplace: Trends, Explanations, and Remedies. Washington, DC: National Academy Press.

Belsky, Jay. 1990. "Parental and nonparental child care and children's socioemotional development: A decade in review." Journal of Marriage and the Family 52: 885–903. [Reprinted in this volume]

Ben-Porath, Yoram. 1982. "Economics and the family—match or mismatch? A review of Becker's A Treatise on the Family." Journal of Economic Literature 20: 52–64.

Berk, Sarah Fenstermaker. 1985. The Gender Factory: The Apportionment of Work in American Households. New York: Plenum Press.

Bernard, Jessie. 1981. "The good-provider role: Its rise and fall." American Psychologist 36: 1–12.

Bielby, Denise D., and William T. Bielby. 1988. "She works hard for the money: Household responsibilities and the allocation of work effort." American Journal of Sociology 93: 1031–1059.

Bielby, William T., and James N. Baron. 1984. "A woman's place is with other women: Sex segregation within organizations." Pp. 27–55 in Barbara F. Reskin (ed.), Sex Segregation in the Workplace. Washington, DC: National Academy Press.

Blau, Francine D. 1987. "Gender." Pp. 492–497 in John Eatwell, Murray Milgate, and Peter Newman (eds.), The New Palgrave: A Dictionary of Economics (Vol. 2). London: Macmillan Press.

Blau, Francine D., and Marianne A. Ferber. 1986. The Economics of Women, Men and Work. Englewood Cliffs, NJ: Prentice-Hall.

Blumstein, Philip, and Pepper Schwartz. 1983. American Couples: Money, Work, and Sex. New York: William Morrow.

Bohen, Halcey, and Anamaria M. Viveros-Long. 1981. Balancing Jobs and Family Life: Do Flexible Schedules Help? Philadelphia: Temple University Press.

Bolger, Niall, Anita DeLongis, Ronald C. Kessler, and E. A. Schilling. 1989. "The effects of daily stress on negative mood." Journal of Personality and Social Psychology 57: 808–818.

Bolger, Niall, Anita DeLongis, Ronald C. Kessler, and Elaine Wethington. 1989. "The contagion of stress across multiple roles." Journal of Marriage and the Family 51: 175–183.

Bradley, Robert H., and Bettye M. Caldwell. 1984. "The relation of infants' home environments to achievement test performance in first grade: A follow-up study." Child Development 55: 803–809.

Conger, Rand D., J. A. McCarty, R. K. Yang, B. B. Lahey, and J. P. Kropp. 1984. "Perceptions of child, child-rearing values, and emotional distress as mediating links between environmental stressors and observed maternal behavior." Child Development 55: 2234–2247.

Cornfield, Daniel B., Hilguias B. Cavalcanti Filho, and Bang Jee Chun. 1990. "Household, work, and labor activism: Gender differences in the determinants of union membership participation." Work and Occupations 17: 131–151.

Crouter, Ann C. 1984. "Participative work as an influence on human development." Journal of Applied Developmental Psychology 5: 71–90.

Crouter, Ann C., Jay Belsky, and Graham B. Spanier. 1984. "The family context of child development: Divorce and maternal employment." Pp. 201–238 in Annals of Child Development (Vol. 1). Greenwich, CT: JAI Press.

Crouter, Ann C., Maureen Perry-Jenkins, Ted L. Huston, and Susan M. McHale. 1987. "Processes underlying father involvement in dual-earner and single-earner families." Developmental Psychology 23: 431–440.

Cyert, Richard M., and David C. Mowery (eds.). 1987. Technology and Employment: Innovation and Growth in the U.S. Economy. Washington, DC: National Academy Press.

Daniels, Pamela, and Kathy Weingarten. 1984. "Mother's hours: The timing of parenthood and women's work." Pp. 209–231 in Patricia Voydanoff (ed.), Work and Family: Changing Roles of Men and Women. Palo Alto, CA; Mayfield.

Downey, Geraldine, and Phyllis Moen. 1987. "Personal efficacy, income, and family transitions: A longitudinal study of women heading households." Journal of Health and Social Behavior 28: 320–333.

Duncan, Greg J., and Jeffrey K. Liker. 1983. "Disentangling the efficacy-earnings relationship among white men." Pp. 218–248 in Greg J. Duncan and James N. Morgan (eds.), Five Thousand Families: Patterns of Economic Progress (Vol. 10). Ann Arbor: University of Michigan, Institute for Social Research.

Duncan, Greg J., and James W. Morgan. 1981. "Sense of efficacy and subsequent change in earnings: A replication." Journal of Human Resources 16: 649–657.

Elder, Glen H., Jr. 1974. Children of the Great Depression. Chicago: University of Chicago Press.

Elder, Glen H., Jr., Jeffery K. Liker, and Catherine E. Cross. 1984. "Parent-child behavior in the Great

Depression: Life course and intergenerational influences." Pp. 109–158 in P. B. Baltes and O. G. Brim, Jr. (eds.), Life-Span Development and Behavior (Vol. 6). New York: Academic Press.

Elder, Glen H., Jr., Tri Van Nguyen, and Avshalam Caspi. 1985. "Linking family hardship to children's lives." Child Development 56: 361–375.

Ellwood, David T. 1988. Poor Support: Poverty in the American Family. New York: Basic Books.

England, Paula. 1981. "Assessing trends in occupational sex segregation, 1900–1976." Pp. 273–295 in Ivar Berg (ed.), Sociological Perspectives on Labor Markets. New York: Academic Press.

England, Paula, and George Farkas. 1986. Households, Employment, and Gender: A Social, Economic, and Demographic View. New York: Aldine.

Estrada, Peggy, William F. Arsenio, Robert D. Hess, and Susan D. Holloway. 1987. "Affective quality of the mother-child relationship: Longitudinal consequences for children's school-relevant cognitive functioning." Developmental Psychology 23: 210–215.

Fernandez, John P. 1986. Child Care and Corporate Productivity: Resolving Family/Work Conflicts. Lexington, MA: Lexington.

Ferree, Myra Marx. 1990. "Beyond separate spheres: Feminism and family research." Journal of Marriage and the Family 52: 866–884. [Reprinted in this volume]

Fowlkes, Martha R. 1980. Behind Every Successful Man: Wives of Medicine and Academe. New York: Columbia University Press.

Furstenberg, Jr., Frank F. 1988. "Good dads, bad dads: Two faces of fatherhood." In Andrew J. Cherlin (ed.), The Changing American Family and Public Policy. Washington, DC: Urban Institute Press.

Gecas, Viktor, and Monica A. Seff. 1989. "Social class, occupational conditions, and self-esteem." Sociological Perspectives 32: 353–364.

Gecas, Viktor, and Monica A. Seff. 1990. "Families and adolescents: A Review of the 1980s." Journal of Marriage and the Family 52: 941–958. [Reprinted in this volume]

Geerken, Michael, and Walter R. Gove. 1983. At Home and At Work: The Family's Allocation of Labor. Beverly Hills, CA: Sage.

Gottfried, Adele E., and Allen W. Gottfried. 1988. Maternal Employment and Children's Development. New York: Plenum Press.

Greenberger, Ellen. 1984. "Children, families, and work." In N. D. Reppucci, L. A. Weithorn, E. P. Mulvey, and J. Monahan (eds.), Mental Health, Law, and Children. Beverly Hills, CA: Sage.

Greenberger, Ellen, Wendy A. Goldberg, Sharon Hamill, Robin O'Neil, and Constance K. Payne. 1989. "Contributions of a supportive work environment to parents' well-being and orientation to work." American Journal of Community Psychology 17: 755–783.

Grossman, Frances K., William S. Pollack, and Ellen Golding. 1988. "Fathers and children: Predicting the quality and quantity of fathering." Developmental Psychology 24: 82–91.

Gwartney-Gibbs, Patricia A. 1988. "Women's work experience and the 'rusty skills' hypothesis." Pp. 169–188 in Barbara A. Gutek, Ann H. Stromberg, and Lauri Larwood (eds.), Women and Work: An Annual Review. Beverly Hills, CA: Sage.

Haynes, Suzanne G., and Manning Feinleib. 1980. "Women, work, and coronary heart disease: Prospective findings from the Framingham study." American Journal of Public Health 70: 133–141.

Hernandez, Donald J., and David E. Myers. 1988. "Family composition, parents' work, and the need for child care among preschool children." Paper presented at the annual meeting of the Population Association of America, New Orleans (April 21–23).

Hertz, Rosanna. 1986. More Equal than Others: Women and Men in Dual-Career Marriages. Berkeley: University of California Press.

Hibbard, Judith H., and Clyde R. Pope. 1987. "Employment characteristics and health status among men and women." Women and Health 12: 85–102.

Hill, Martha S. 1988. "Marital stability and spouses' shared time." Journal of Family Issues 9: 427–451.

Hochschild, Arlie. 1989. The Second Shift. New York: Viking.

Hofferth, Sandra L., and Deborah A. Phillips. 1987. "Child care in the United States, 1970 to 1995." Journal of Marriage and the Family 49: 559–571.

Hoffman, Lois W. 1983. "Increasing fathering: Effects on the mother." Pp. 167–190 in Michael E. Lamb and Abraham Sagi (eds.), Fatherhood and Family Policy. Hillsdale, NJ: Lawrence Erlbaum Associates.

Hoffman, Lois W. 1989. "Effects of maternal employment in the two-parent family." American Psychologist 44: 283–292.

House, James S., Victor Strecher, Helen L. Metzner, and Cynthia A. Robbins. 1986. "Occupational stress and health among men and women in the Tecumseh community health study." Journal of Health and Social Behavior 27: 62–77.

Houseknecht, Sharon K., Suzanne Vaughan, and Anne Statham. 1987. "The impact of singlehood on the career patterns of professional women." Journal of Marriage and the Family 49: 353–366.

Howes, Carolee. 1988. "Relations between early child care and schooling." Developmental Psychology 24: 53–57.

Howes, Carolee, and Phyllis Stewart. 1987. "Child's play with adults, toys, peers: An examination of family and child-care influences." Developmental Psychology 23: 423–430.

Huber, Joan. 1988. "A theory of family, economy, and gender." Journal of Family Issues 9: 9–26.

Huber, Joan, and Glenna Spitze. 1983. Sex Stratification: Children, Housework and Jobs. New York: Academic Press.

Jacobs, Jerry. 1989. Revolving Doors: Sex Segregation and Women's Careers. Stanford, CA: Stanford University Press.

Kamerman, Sheila B., and Alfred J. Kahn. 1987. The Responsive Workplace: Employers and a Changing Labor Force. New York: Columbia University Press.

Karasek, Robert A. 1979. "Job demands, job decision

latitude, and mental strain: Implications for job redesign." Administrative Science Quarterly 24: 285–308.

Karasek, Robert A., Dean Baker, Frank Marxer, Anders Ahlbom, and Tores Theorell. 1981. "Job decision latitude, job demands, and cardiovascular disease: A prospective study of Swedish men." American Journal of Public Health 71: 694–705.

Kessler, Ronald C., James H. House, and J. Blake Turner. 1987. "Unemployment and health in a community sample." Journal of Health and Social Behavior 28: 51–59.

Kessler, Ronald C., and James A. McRae, Jr. 1981. "Trends in the relationship between sex and psychological distress: 1957–1976." American Sociological Review 47: 216–227.

Kessler, Ronald C., and James A. McRae, Jr. 1982. "The effect of wives' employment on the mental health of married men and women." American Sociological Review 47: 216–227.

Kohn, Melvin L., and Carmi Schooler (eds.), with the collaboration of J. Miller, K. A. Miller, C. Schoenbach, and R. Schoenberg. 1983. Work and Personality. Norwood, NJ: Ablex.

Kohn, Melvin L., Atsushi Naoi, Carrie Schoenbach, Carmi Schooler, and Kazimierz M. Slomczynski. 1990. "Position in the class structure and psychological functioning in the United States, Japan, and Poland." American Journal of Sociology 95: 964–1008.

Lamb, Michael E., Carl-Philip Hwang, Anders Broberg, Fred L. Bookstein, Gunilla Hult, and Majt Frodi. 1988. "The determinants of paternal involvement in primiparous Swedish families." International Journal of Behavioral Development 11: 433–449.

Lennon, Mary Clare. 1987. "Sex differences in distress: The impact of gender and work roles." Journal of Health and Social Behavior 28: 290–305.

Mancini, Jay A., and Rosemary Blieszner. 1989. "Aging parents and adult children: Research themes in intergenerational relations." Journal of Marriage and the Family 51: 275–290. [Reprinted in this volume]

McLanahan, Sara, and Karen Booth. 1989. "Mother-only families: Problems, prospects, and politics." Journal of Marriage and the Family 51: 557–580. [Reprinted in this volume]

McLanahan, Sara S., and Jennifer L. Glass. 1985. "A note on the trend in sex differences in psychological distress." Journal of Health and Social Behavior 26: 328–336.

McLoyd, Vonnie C. 1989. "Socialization and development in a changing economy." American Psychologist 44: 293–302.

Menaghan, Elizabeth G. 1989a. "Psychological well-being among parents and nonparents: The importance of normative expectedness." Journal of Family Issues 10: 547–565.

Menaghan, Elizabeth G. 1989b. "Role changes and psychological well-being: Variations in effects by gender and role repertoire." Social Forces 67: 693–714.

Menaghan, Elizabeth G. 1990. "Social stress and individual distress." Pp. 235–272 in James Greenley (ed.), Research in Community and Mental Health (Vol. 6). Greenwich, CT: JAI Press.

Menaghan, Elizabeth G., and Esther S. Merves. 1984. "Coping with occupational problems: The limits of individual efforts." Journal of Health and Social Behavior 25: 406–423.

Menaghan, Elizabeth G., and Toby L. Parcel. In press. "Determining children's home environments: The impact of maternal characteristics and current occupational and family experiences." Journal of Marriage and the Family.

Mensch, Barbara S., and Denise B. Kandel. 1988. "Do job conditions influence the use of drugs?" Journal of Health and Social Behavior 29: 169–184.

Miller, Joanne, Carmi Schooler, Melvin L. Kohn, and Karen A. Miller. 1979. "Women and work: The psychological effects of occupational conditions." American Journal of Sociology 85: 66–94.

Miller, Joanne, Kazimierz M. Slomczynski, and Melvin L. Kohn. 1985. "Continuity of learning-generalization: The effect of job on men's intellective process in the United States and Poland." American Journal of Sociology 91: 593–615.

Mirowsky, John, and Catherine E. Ross. 1986. "Social patterns of distress." Annual Review of Sociology 12: 23–45.

Moen, Phyllis. 1989. Working Parents: Transformations in Gender Roles and Public Policies in Sweden. Madison: University of Wisconsin Press.

Moen, Phyllis, and Donna Dempster-McClain. 1987. "Employed parents: Role strain, work time, and preferences for working less." Journal of Marriage and the Family 49: 579–590.

Moen, Phyllis, and Carla B. Howery. 1988. "The significance of time in the study of families under stress." In David Klein and Joan Aldous (eds.), Social Stress and Family Development. New York: Guilford.

Moen, Phyllis, Edward L. Kain, and Glen H. Elder, Jr. 1983. "Economic conditions and family life: Contemporary and historical perspectives." Pp. 213–259 in Richard R. Nelson and Felicity Skidmore (eds.), American Families and the Economy: The High Costs of Living. Washington, DC: National Academy Press.

Mortimer, Jeylan T., and Kathryn M. Borman (eds.). 1988. Work Experience and Psychological Development throughout the Life Span. Boulder, CO: Westview.

Mortimer, Jeylan T., and Jane London. 1984. "The varying linkages of work and family." Pp. 20–35 in Patricia Voydanoff (ed.), Work and Family: Changing Roles of Men and Women. Palo Alto, CA: Mayfield.

Mortimer, Jeylan T., Jon Lorence, and Donald S. Kumka. 1986. Work, Family, and Personality: Transition to Adulthood. Norwood, NJ: Ablex.

Mutchler, Jan E. 1987. "Gender differences in the effects of family status on underemployment." International Journal of Sociology and Social Policy 7: 5–18.

Naoi, Atsushi, and Carmi Schooler. 1985. "Occupational conditions and psychological functioning in

Japan." American Journal of Sociology 90: 729–752.

Nock, Steven L., and Paul W. Kingston. 1988. "Time with children: The impact of couples' work-time commitments." Social Forces 67: 59–85.

O'Brien, George E. 1986. Psychology of Work and Unemployment. New York: John Wiley.

O'Neill, June. 1985. "Role differentiation and the gender gap in wage rates." Pp. 50–75 in Laurie Larwood, Ann H. Stromberg, and Barbara A. Gutek (eds.), Women and Work: An Annual Review. Beverly Hills, CA: Sage.

Oppenheimer, Valerie Kincade. 1988. "A theory of marriage timing." American Journal of Sociology 94: 563–591.

Parcel, Toby L., and Elizabeth G. Menaghan. 1990. "Maternal working conditions and child verbal facility: Studying the intergenerational transmission of inequality from mothers to young children." Social Psychology Quarterly 53: 132–147.

Pearlin, Leonard I., Morton A. Lieberman, Elizabeth G. Menaghan, and Joseph T. Mullan. 1981. "The stress process." Journal of Health and Social Behavior 22: 337–356.

Penkower, Lili, Evelyn J. Bromet, and Mary Amanda Dew. 1988. "Husbands' layoff and wives' mental health." Archives of General Psychiatry 45: 994–1000.

Peterson, Richard R. 1989. Women, Work, and Divorce. Albany: State University of New York Press.

Piotrokowski, Chaya S., and Mitchell H. Katz. 1982. "Indirect socialization of children: The effects of mothers' jobs on academic behaviors." Child Development 53: 409–415.

Piotrokowski, Chaya S., Robert N. Rapoport, and Rhona Rapoport. 1987. "Families and work." Pp. 251–283 in Marvin B. Sussman, and Suzanne K. Steinmetz (eds.), Handbook of Marriage and the Family. New York: Plenum.

Pleck, Joseph H. 1983. "Husbands' paid work and family roles: Current research issues." Pp. 251–333 in H. Lopata and J. H. Pleck (eds.), Research in the Interweave of Social Roles (Vol. 3): Families and Jobs. Greenwich, CT: JAI Press.

Pleck, Joseph H. 1984. "The work-family role system." Pp. 8–19 in Patricia Voydanoff (ed.), Work and Family: Changing Roles of Men and Women. Palo Alto, CA: Mayfield.

Pleck, Joseph H. 1985. Working Wives/Working Husbands. Beverly Hills, CA: Sage.

Presser, Harriet B. 1987. "Work shifts of full-time dual-career couples: Patterns and contrasts by sex of spouse." Demography 24: 99–112.

Presser, Harriet B. 1988. "Shift work and child care among dual-earner American parents." Journal of Marriage and the Family 50: 133–148.

Repetti, Rena L. 1988. "Family and occupational roles and women's mental health." Pp. 97–129 in R. M. Schwartz (ed.), Women at Work. Los Angeles: UCLA Institute of Industrial Relations.

Repetti, Rena L. 1989. "The effects of daily workload on subsequent behavior during marital interaction: The roles of social withdrawal and spouse support." Journal of Personality and Social Psychology 57: 651–659.

Repetti, Rena L., and Faye Crosby. 1984. "Gender and depression: Exploring the adult-role explanation." Journal of Social and Clinical Psychology 2: 57–70.

Repetti, Rena L., Karen A. Matthews, and Ingrid Waldron. 1989. "Effects of paid employment on women's mental and physical health." American Psychologist 44: 1394–1401.

Reskin, Barbara, and Patricia Roos. 1990. Job Queues, Gender Queues: Explaining Women's Inroads into Male Occupations. Philadelphia: Temple University Press.

Roby, Pamela, and Lynet Uttal. 1988. "Trade union stewards: Handling union, family, and employment responsibilities." Pp. 215–248 in Barbara A. Gutek, Ann H. Stromberg, and Laurie Larwood (eds.), Women and Work: An Annual Review (Vol. 3). Beverly Hills, CA: Sage.

Rosenfeld, Rachel Ann. 1985. Farm Women: Work, Farm, and Family in the United States. Chapel Hill: University of North Carolina Press.

Rosenfield, Sarah. 1980. "Sex differences in depression: Do women always have higher rates?" Journal of Health and Social Behavior 21: 33–42.

Rosenfield, Sarah. 1989. "The effects of women's employment: Personal control and sex differences in mental health." Journal of Health and Social Behavior 30: 77–91.

Ross, Catherine E., and John Mirowsky. 1988. "Child care and emotional adjustment to wives' employment." Journal of Health and Social Behavior 29: 127–138.

Ross, Catherine E., John Mirowsky, and Joan Huber. 1983. "Dividing work, sharing work, and in-between: Marriage patterns and depression." American Sociological Review 48: 809–823.

Saenz, Rogelio, Willis J. Goudy, and Frederick O. Lorenz. 1989. "The effects of employment and marital relations on depression among Mexican American women." Journal of Marriage and the Family 51: 239–251.

Schooler, Carmi. 1987. "Psychological effects of complex environments during the life span: A review and theory." Pp. 24–49 in Carmi Schooler and K. Warner Schaie (eds.), Cognitive Functioning and Social Structure over the Life Course. Norwood, NJ: Ablex.

Schooler, Carmi, and Atsushi Naoi. 1988. "The psychological effects of traditional and of economically peripheral job settings in Japan." American Journal of Sociology 94: 335–355.

Siegal, Michael. 1984. "Economic deprivation and the quality of parent-child relations: A trickle-down framework." Journal of Applied Developmental Psychology 5: 127–144.

Siegal, Michael. 1985. Children, Parenthood, and Social Welfare in the Context of Developmental Psychology. Oxford, England: Clarendon.

Slomczynski, Kazimierz M., Joanne Miller, and Melvin L. Kohn. 1981. "Stratification, work and values: A Polish–United States comparison." American

Sociological Review 46: 720–744.

Sorensen, Annemette, and Sara McLanahan. 1987. "Married women's economic dependency, 1940–1980." American Journal of Sociology 93: 659–687.

Spenner, Kenneth I. 1988. "Social stratification, work, and personality." Annual Review of Sociology 14: 69–97.

Spenner, Kenneth I., and Luther B. Otto. 1985. "Work and self-concept: Selection and socialization in the early career." Pp. 197–235 in A. C. Kerckhoff (ed.), Research in Sociology of Education and Socialization (Vol. 5). Greenwich, CT: JAI Press.

Spitze, Glenna. 1988. "Women's employment and family relations: A review." Journal of Marriage and the Family 50: 595–618. [Reprinted in this volume]

Staines, Graham L., and Joseph H. Pleck. 1983. "The impact of work schedules on the family." Ann Arbor: University of Michigan, Institute for Social Research, Survey Research Center.

Staines, Graham L., Kathleen J. Pottick, and Deborah S. Fudge. 1986. "Wives' employment and husbands' attitudes toward work and life." Journal of Applied Psychology 71: 118–128.

Stanley, Sandra C., Janet G. Hunt, and Larry L. Hunt. 1986. "The relative deprivation of husbands in dual-earner households." Journal of Family Issues 7: 3–20.

Thompson, Linda, and Alexis J. Walker. 1989. "Gender in families: Women and men in marriage, work, and parenthood." Journal of Marriage and the Family 51: 845–871. [Reprinted in this volume]

Thornton, Arland. 1989. "Changing attitudes toward family issues in the United States." Journal of Marriage and the Family 51: 873–893.

U.S. Bureau of the Census. 1987. Statistical Abstract of the United States: 1986 (107th ed.). Washington, DC: Government Printing Office.

U.S. Bureau of the Census. 1987. Male-Female Differences in Work Experiences, Occupation, and Earnings: 1984. Current Population Reports, Series P-70, No. 10. Washington, DC: Government Printing Office.

U.S. Bureau of the Census. 1989. Poverty in the United States, 1987. Current Population Reports, Series P-60, No. 163. Washington, DC: Government Printing Office.

U.S. Bureau of Labor Statistics. 1987. Employment and Earnings. Vol. 34(1). Washington, DC: Government Printing Office.

Voydanoff, Patricia. 1987. Work and Family Life. Beverly Hills, CA: Sage.

Voydanoff, Patricia. 1990. "Economic stress and family relations: A review of the eighties." Journal of Marriage and the Family 52: 1099–1115. [Reprinted in this volume]

Voydanoff, Patricia, and Brenda W. Donnelly. 1989. "Economic distress and mental health: The role of family coping resources and behaviors." Lifestyles: Family and Economic Issues 10: 139–162.

Wethington, Elaine, and Ronald C. Kessler. 1989. "Employment, parental responsibility, and psychological distress: A longitudinal study of married women." Journal of Family Issues 10: 527–546.

White, Lynn. 1990. "Causes of marital instability: A review of research in the eighties." Journal of Marriage and the Family 52: 904–912. [Reprinted in this volume]

Wilson, William Julius. 1987. The Truly Disadvantaged: The Inner City, the Underclass, and Public Policy. Chicago: University of Chicago Press.

Zigler, Edward F., and Meryl Frank (eds.). 1988. The Parental Leave Crisis: Toward a National Policy. New Haven, CT: Yale University Press.

GLENNA SPITZE   *State University of New York at Albany*

Women's Employment and Family Relations:

A Review

*Research concerning effects of women's employ-
ment on families is reviewed for the past decade.
Researchers have changed an earlier assumption
of negative effects on marriages and children, but
they still tend to focus solely on differences by
employment status rather than on consequences
of various aspects of women's employment experience. They also tend to neglect minority,
working-class, and single-parent families. This
review begins with a discussion of effects of
women's employment on the formation and
dissolution of marital unions, on marital quality,
and on spouse health and well-being. Research on
the division of housework and its relation to
power and equity is treated next; then several
issues relating to the interaction of husbands' and
wives' jobs are reviewed. Effects on fertility and
outcomes for children are considered, followed by
a brief section on relations with extended family
members. The review concludes with suggestions
regarding future trends and research directions.*

The past 15 years have been a time of rapid
development in research on how women's paid
employment affects their family relations. Early
research (see reviews in Hoffman and Nye, 1974)
tended to view women's employment as having
monolithic, mostly negative, effects. Nonemployed wives were viewed as the norm. It was
assumed that paid employment had a variety of
consequences, such as harming marital relations
or children's development. *Employed* women,

Department of Sociology, SUNY Albany, Albany, NY 12222.

like *unemployed* men, were expected to cause
family problems (Mortimer and Sorensen, 1984).
More recent research views women's employment
more positively, and with a degree of complexity
approaching men's employment. There is still,
however, a tendency to look for consequences
without regard to the process involved or to the
variety of employment experiences.

This review focuses on consequences, rather
than determinants, of women's employment for
families. However, we should keep in mind that
during this century employed women have come
to resemble closely the general female population.
While in 1900 the typical employed woman was
young and single, today the majority of married
women and of mothers of preschool children are
in the labor force (Spitze, 1987). Employed
women are still, however, somewhat more highly
educated and younger, and if married, they have
husbands with lower incomes than those of men
married to full-time homemakers (Waite, 1981).

Most of the work reviewed here has appeared
since 1975. Earlier research was more sparse and
also tended to rely on overly simple approaches,
such as bivariate tabular presentation. Therefore,
this selection does not appear to be overly restrictive. A more serious limitation is that the review
focuses primarily on the United States. Certainly,
this is where most of the extant empirical studies
of the family have been conducted, but we should
not assume that they can be generalized, even to
all industrialized countries. The existing literature
also imposes constraints. Except for a few studies
of minority and working-class families within the
United States (e.g., Ferree, 1976, 1984; Harrison
and Minor, 1984; McAdoo, 1981; Staples and

Mirande, 1980; Ybarra, 1982), most research views the middle-class white family as the norm. Finally, researchers also tend to focus on husband-wife families and to ignore employment consequences for single parents.

This review is organized as follows. First is a discussion of the effect of women's employment on the formation and dissolution of marital unions. The second section treats marital quality and other aspects of health and well-being. The third examines the division of household labor and its relation to issues of power and equity, and the fourth deals with several issues relating to the interaction of wives' and husbands' jobs. The fifth section considers issues relating to children—the relation between women's employment and fertility, child care, and outcomes such as children's attitudes and achievements—followed by a brief discussion of relations with family members beyond the nuclear family, including living arrangements, contact and assistance patterns with extended family members, and how such persons are affected by women's employment. The review concludes with suggestions regarding the future direction of these consequences and identifies some issues for further research.

Although all the issues discussed here have a multitude of policy implications, specific policies relating to women's employment and families are not examined in this review because of space limitations. (For such discussions see Bose and Spitze, 1987; Gerstel and Gross, 1987; Harkess, 1987; Moore, Spain, and Bianchi, 1984; Waite, 1981; Wilkie, 1987). The review is also limited to the current historical period. (For a longer-term perspective, see Davis, 1984; Ferber and Birnbaum, 1982: Fox and Hesse-Biber, 1984; Gerstel and Gross, 1987; Huber and Spitze, 1983).

MARITAL FORMATION AND DISSOLUTION

Theoretical Perspectives on Marriage and Divorce

In current perspectives on marriage and divorce, the assumption is that individuals assess rationally, or are influenced by, the availability of potential partners, the feasibility or opportunity to form or dissolve a union, and the motivation or desirability of doing so (Becker, 1981; Huber and Spitze, 1988; Schoen and Urton, 1979). Women's

employment could affect the formation and dissolution of unions through the latter two processes. It could decrease women's *motivation* to marry by providing alternative sources of fulfillment and financial support. It also might increase their *opportunity* to marry by increasing their economic ability to set up a household (a "dowry effect": Hofferth and Moore, 1979) and to meet potential partners. The latter process would be similar for men, but the former might not; men's desire to marry either could increase with women's employment as women earn more, or it could decrease as the expected gain in household labor decreases.

Effects on divorce would likely be more consistently positive. A wife's employment could increase the *opportunity* for divorce at a given level of marital dissatisfaction for either spouse by increasing the wife's financial independence. Employment might also affect women's *desire* for divorce by exposing women to alternative marital partners or sources of fulfillment. On the other hand, it could affect the desire of husbands *or* wives for divorce by affecting the quality of their marriage in either direction.

Marriage

Women's employment, particularly in high-status occupations, affects their timing and slightly decreases their ultimate probability of marriage, whether because of their own preferences or the preferences of potential husbands for "non-threatening" mates (Mueller and Campbell, 1977; Preston and Richards, 1975; but see White, 1981). Although several researchers have argued that high-status women choose not to marry, rather than being rejected (e.g., Havens, 1973), none actually demonstrates the process of choice that creates these patterns. Further, it is likely that employment leads to postponement rather than ultimate rejection of marriage (see Schoen and Urton, 1979).

Women's future work plans decrease marriage probabilities over the short term (Goldscheider and Waite, 1986; Waite and Spitze, 1981), more consistently for whites than blacks (Cherlin, 1980), but current employment increases or has no effect on marriage. Studies of remarriage also show inconsistent links with employment (Hannan, Tuma, and Groeneveld, 1977; Hofferth and Moore, 1979; Mott and Moore, 1983). None of these studies directly measures "opportunity" and "motivation" effects. Rather, a net positive or negative effect is assumed to be indicative of the predominance of one process over the other. Goldscheider and Waite's results, however, show that similar economic forces influence both sexes.

Divorce

A number of sociologists and economists have linked the aggregate-level rise in female labor force participation and rising divorce rates, although some (e.g., Michael, 1977; Schoen and Urton, 1979) view female employment as leading to increased divorce, while others (e.g., Davis, 1984; Johnson and Skinner, 1985) view female employment as rising in *response* to women's perception of increased divorce risk.

At the individual level, employment status, hours worked, weeks worked, and work experience have all been linked to marital dissolution (Cherlin, 1979b; Mott and Moore, 1979; Spitze and South, 1985), although more consistently for older than younger women, and more for whites than blacks. Wife's employment in a nontraditional job has been linked to divorce (Philliber and Hiller, 1983). Results are inconsistent for wife's earnings and for the ratio between husbands' and wives' earnings (D'Amico, 1983; Hill, 1984; Moore and Waite, 1981; Spitze and South, 1985). Wife's *potential* wages and wage ratio have had consistently positive effects on dissolution (Cherlin, 1979b; D'Amico, 1983; Hannan et al., 1977; Mott and Moore, 1979). These effects do not always hold for subsamples of black women (Hannan et al., 1977; Mott and Moore, 1979), whether because of sample size or black women's history of higher employment levels and black men's attitudes toward their wives' employment.

For the most part, this research has investigated static measures of employment (but see South and Spitze, 1986). Shifts in employment status, particularly into employment, could precipitate changes in family organization that create marital strains (Welch and Booth, 1977). However, such changes could also be a response to perceived divorce risk, part of a long-range plan to end a marriage (Greene and Quester, 1982; Johnson and Skinner, 1985). Future research should focus on employment histories and the long-term effects of unstable employment (Kitson, Babri, and Roach, 1985).

This assessment would suggest the necessity of looking at the entire process leading up to marital dissolution. Several studies have done so. Udry (1981) measured both spouses' *perceptions of alternatives to the current marriage* and found wife's income unrelated to perceptions of either spouse, although the *ratio* between wife's and husband's income increased wife's perceptions of economic alternatives and decreased those of husbands. In two related studies, the extent of wife's previous work increased both spouses' *thoughts of divorce* (Huber and Spitze, 1980), as did her current employment unless family income was high (Booth and White, 1980).

Booth, Johnson, White, and Edwards (1984) constructed a scale of *marital stability*, including a variety of thoughts and behaviors that might precede divorce. Wife's income increased levels of marital instability directly as well as affecting the equality of the division of household labor, but her hours of work also affected instability indirectly through spouse interaction and the division of labor. Among the unstable, those who were divorced three years later had the highest wife incomes, and those who were still "unstable" but remained married had the lowest (Booth, Johnson, White, and Edwards, 1985). Levinger (1979) studied a group of the "unstable" by investigating the fate of applications for divorce. Wife's income increased the probability that both the separated and the nonseparated would actually divorce, although it did not increase the probability of a separation. Similarly, "battered women" are less likely to leave their spouse if they are not employed and feel economically dependent (Strube and Barbour, 1983).

This section has focused on the probability of marital dissolution and not its consequences. However, given the highly negative economic consequences of divorce for women and their children (Weitzman, 1985), we should not lose sight of consequences of employment for those women who *do* divorce. The plight of the older "displaced homemaker" has been much publicized, although not alleviated. They are the extreme group with little or no lifetime employment experience. But we know little about how employment patterns of other women affect the economic consequences of divorce or marital settlements, an area undergoing major legal changes at the present time.

MARITAL QUALITY AND SPOUSES' WELL-BEING

Marital Satisfaction

The previous section leaves unclear the process through which wife's employment leads to higher divorce levels. Is it due to higher levels of marital dissatisfaction or simply a lower threshold of satisfaction at which divorce is considered? Research linking wife's employment to marital satisfaction should help to clarify this question.

A number of theoretical perspectives have been invoked to predict *how* wives' employment might affect marital quality. The earliest perspective (Parsons, 1942), suggested that a wife's employment in a job of equal or higher status than the husband's could create *status competition* that would harm a marriage. Wives would remain nonemployed or employed in low-level occupations so as to prevent dysfunctional competition between couples. This is echoed by the economic view of marriage, that spouses derive the most benefits when they have *complementary*, rather than parallel, roles (Becker, 1981; Hiller and Philliber, 1982; Richardson, 1979). Here, however, the emphasis is on concrete work-related benefits, rather than the more amorphous social status.

On the other hand, Oppenheimer (1977) argues that wives can contribute to family status positively *or* negatively, through *status compatibility, maintenance, and enhancement* (see also Hornung and McCullough, 1981; Mueller, Parcel, and Pampel, 1979.) A wife whose job is not "compatible" with her husband's may create problems if hers is much higher in status but also may threaten family status if it is too low. The *role homophily* perspective also emphasizes positive effects (Simpson and England, 1981), suggesting that wives and husbands who are in similar structural positions have a "common framework" that promotes happiness and marital solidarity. They would understand and sympathize with each other's daily problems and would be more likely to have similar roles within the home as well.

The consequences of wives' employment may depend not only on wives' and husbands' employment situations but on how much they each contribute at home. The *equity perspective* suggests that individuals evaluate the overall division of labor, in and out of the home, and are happiest when things seem fair to both (Mueller et al., 1979; Yogev and Brett, 1985). In contrast, the *bargaining* or *social exchange* perspective predicts that individuals are happier the more work the other spouse does and the lower one's own share of work (Yogev and Brett, 1985).

Early literature seemed to indicate that employed wives and their husbands experienced lower-quality marriages (see reviews in Glenn and Weaver, 1978; Gove and Peterson, 1980; Houseknecht and Macke, 1981; Nye, 1974). Summarizing literature through the early 1970s, Nye (1974) concluded that these effects were diminishing over time and were primarily for lower-class wives, who presumably were more likely to be working out of "necessity," thus threatening the male provider role.

Currently, for the most part, this is no longer a major issue. While a few studies with small, specialized samples continue to find negative effects of wife's employment or work commitment (Burke and Weir, 1976; Ladewig and McGee, 1986), recent studies based on large national samples have reported no effects of wife's employment, occupational commitment, or higher occupational status on the reported marital satisfaction of either husband or wife (Booth, 1979; Glenn and Weaver, 1978; Houseknecht and Macke, 1981; Ladewig and White, 1984; Locksley, 1980; Richardson, 1979; Wright, 1978).

Wife's employment may improve marital relations or solidarity by providing spouses with similar experiences and concerns. Simpson and England (1981) found mostly positive effects of wife's employment and employment characteristics for both spouses' marital satisfaction, but effects were more positive for husbands during the parental stage and nonexistent for wives with preschool children. They speculated that such wives were particularly overloaded with work, while husbands benefited from the wife's earnings without having to share much of that burden. Wives who are dependent (because of non- or low levels of employment and presence of young children) are more likely to be physically abused by husbands (Kalmuss and Straus, 1982). Surely this is an indicator of low marital quality.

One might speculate that wife's employment would reduce marital happiness (and thus increase divorce) by decreasing couple interaction. While Hill (1984) does link interaction time to divorce, Kingston and Nock (1987) find only small differences between dual- and single-earner couples in time spent together. Further, it is not clear whether marital happiness or interaction time is causally prior (Kingston and Nock, 1987; White, 1983).

In summary, any effect of wife's employment on marital happiness seems to have changed from a negative to a null or perhaps even positive one, and any negative effects are now likely to be due to specific aspects of her employment, such as long hours or dissatisfaction with her job. Unresolved issues in this area include causal ordering and social selection. Women who are employed may be those who are otherwise more (or less) prone to having happy marriages, such that the null effect may result from two opposing effects. Some might seek employment because of an unhappy marriage. As Ferber and Birnbaum (1982) point out, if women dissatisfied with their marriage are more likely to enter the labor force, one might find a negative relation even if employment actually *increases* the marital satisfaction of these particular women. Most important, in order to determine the actual process through which employment influences marital satisfaction and dissolution, longitudinal data, including changes in employment and marital status and multiple measures of marital quality, will be needed.

Life Satisfaction and Health

Women's employment might also affect their own or husbands' general life satisfaction and mental or physical health. Preconceptions regarding effects on women vary: some researchers have assumed that employment is preferable to housework because of alienating aspects of the housewife role, while others have expected role overload and scheduling conflicts to cause employed women stress. For husbands, expectations were more uniformly negative: that wives' employment would increase their levels of stress and unhappiness.

For women, the few differences found in overall levels of life satisfaction and mental health favor the employed (Freudiger, 1983; Gove and Peterson, 1980; Wright, 1978). Ferree (1976) reported working-class housewives less satisfied than employed counterparts, and Gove and Geerken (1977) found fewer psychiatric symptoms among employed women than among housewives. However, there may be an initial adjustment period after a move in or out of employment that increases women's stress levels (Welch and Booth,

1977). Physical health was better among employed women as well (Verbrugge and Madens, 1985; also see Krause and Markides, 1987), although Reskin and Coverman (1985) found an interaction with family income. They speculated that nonemployed women in high-income households can afford to pay for services that enable them to pursue nonhousehold activities, thus negating the isolating aspects of the housewife role.

The key factor, however, appears to be employment preferences. Wives are least depressed when their employment status is consistent with their own and their husbands' preferences and most depressed when they are not employed but would prefer to be (Benin and Neinstedt, 1985; Ross, Mirowsky, and Huber, 1983). New mothers who stay home but were highly involved in paid work before the birth are more irritable, depressed, and lower in self-esteem (Pistrang, 1984).

Although employment is often measured dichotomously, the circumstances of the job are important as well. Job conditions affect women's mental functioning, including such factors as anxiety and fatalism (Miller, Schooler, Kohn, and Miller, 1979). Employment decreases women's depression only if they experience high levels of job satisfaction (Kessler and McRae, 1982). Working women's life satisfaction is increased by their own occupational prestige and decreased by their husband's, perhaps signaling dual-career conflicts (Freudiger, 1983). Two other studies found little effect of other aspects of *spouse* employment, such as income or hours worked, on depression, although the respondents' *own* job characteristics were important (Keith and Schafer, 1983; Schoenbach, 1985).

Some researchers have analyzed housework as a job with working conditions parallel to those of work for pay. Oakley (1974), a pioneer in the study of housework, found the majority of full-time homemakers dissatisfied with their jobs, with specific negative aspects including some of the tasks themselves (e.g., ironing), monotony, fragmentation, and excessive pace. The most valued job condition was autonomy. Schooler, Miller, and Richtand (1984) measured various dimensions of working conditions for paid jobs and housework for a sample of married men and women. Although they did not compare employed and nonemployed women, other comparisons suggested that housework was viewed as more routinized, heavier, and dirtier, and involved more contact with things and less with people, than paid work. In general, satisfaction with work seems to be slightly higher among employed women than among full-time homemakers (Wright, 1978).

Hofferth and Moore (1979) offer interesting speculations about the possible long-term consequences of women's employment for their own and other family members' physical health and longevity. Employed wives may have less time available to provide physical care (although more money to pay for it). Another area ripe for future research is the potential indirect effects of differences in employed and nonemployed women's social networks (Wellman, 1985). Since women tend to manage their families' social lives and kin contacts, women's ties may have implications for the whole family.

While early researchers were looking for negative consequences for husbands of employed women, there are also reasons to expect positive ones, since such husbands have less pressure to support the family and more freedom to change jobs or go to school (although perhaps with more geographical constraints), and may have more interesting companions (Moore et al., 1984). In examining both psychological and medical indicators of husbands' mental health, Booth (1979) concluded that there were few significant effects and those were positive. In contrast, Kessler and McRae (1982) find higher depression among husbands of employed wives. However, this is mitigated if he shares in child care responsibilities, which perhaps indicates that he has nontraditional sex-role attitudes and is not bothered by sharing the breadwinner role (see also Pleck, 1985). Husbands are most depressed when their wives work against husbands' opposition (Ross et al., 1983). Sharing housework does not affect husbands' depression (and, incidentally, decreases wives'), perhaps because only those husbands who are willing and have nontraditional attitudes do so (Kessler and McRae, 1982; Ross et al., 1983). Specific aspects of wives' employment, such as occupational status, also may affect husbands, but results are not consistent (Fendrich, 1984; Keith and Schaefer, 1983; Schoenbach, 1985).

In summary, the small differences in psychological functioning for women and their husbands seem to favor employed women over full-time homemakers. However, a key issue appears to be how the family work is divided and how equitable that division is perceived to be. As Pleck (1985) puts it, there seems to be an inequity effect rather than an exhaustion effect. This leads us to the issue of how, indeed, household labor is divided in various kinds of households.

HOUSEHOLD LABOR AND POWER RELATIONS

Housework

Studies of household labor have collected two major types of data: time budgets (Walker and Woods, 1976) and survey items on the distribution of responsibility of labor overall or on individual tasks. Most available data are from the 1970s or before; the most recent are for 1981–82 (Juster and Stafford, 1985). Coverman and Sheley (1986) find no change in adjusted hours between 1965 and 1975, but Juster (1985) reports slight increases in men's housework time and decreases in women's between 1975–76 and 1981–82. Most studies, particularly time budget ones that require extensive respondent cooperation, are of white middle-class respondents, and many have small sample sizes (but see Ericksen, Yancey, and Ericksen, 1979). A few studies present data from outside the United States, such as Sweden (Hass, 1981), Holland (Tavecchio, Ijzendoorn, Goossens, and Vergeer, 1984), Austria (Szinovacz, 1977), Israel (Shamir, 1986) and Canada (Meissner, Humphreys, Meis, and Scheu, 1975). Robinson, Converse, and Szalai (1972) present time budget data for a large number of industrialized countries by gender, employment, and marital status, although not by work status of men's wives.

Husbands of employed women spend little or no more time in housework than husbands of nonemployed women (Ferber, 1982; Fox and Nickols, 1983; Walker and Woods, 1976). This results in a longer total work week (Blau and Ferber, 1986; Meissner et al., 1975; but see Pleck, 1985) and less leisure (Newland, 1980) for employed women than men. Pleck (1979), however, argues that this may be changing, and cites 1977 data showing that husbands of employed wives spend 1.8 more hours per week in housework and 2.7 more hours in child care than other husbands (see also Pleck, 1985).

Findings based on survey items on the distribution of labor generally suggest that wives' employment (Ericksen et al., 1979; Hoffman and Nye, 1974; Huber and Spitze, 1981; Miller and Garrison, 1982; Ross, 1987) and hours worked (Barnett and Baruch, 1987; Nichols and Metzen, 1982; Spitze, 1986a) do lead to greater participation of husbands in housework. This has been explained with reference to the issue of relative versus absolute time inputs: employed women cut corners and do less housework, thus increasing their husbands' *relative* contribution (Pleck, 1977). Researchers have also made the distinction between participation in household tasks and responsibility for them (Berk, 1985). The latter seems to change most slowly; in a study of 160 white middle-class families, 150 husbands were responsible for *none* of the "feminine home chores" studied (Barnett and Baruch, 1987).

A number of research hypotheses have been generated to interpret the effects of independent variables on the division of household labor, several relating to women's employment. First, the *economic hypothesis* suggests that relative productive capacity in the labor market and in the home affects relative time devoted to both (e.g., Farkas, 1976; see Blau and Ferber, 1986). Empirically, the division of household labor does not seem to relate to relative wages or incomes (Farkas, 1976; Huber and Spitze, 1983), although it does relate to the difference between spouse earnings (Ross, 1987).

Second, the *relative resource hypothesis* assumes that those with greater power and resources (sometimes measured in earnings, sometimes in education or occupational prestige) will use that power to avoid housework. Relative share of housework has been linked to wife's professional occupation and to husbands' and wives' earnings (Berk and Berk, 1978; Ericksen et al., 1979; Maret and Finlay, 1984). However, Berardo, Shehan, and Leslie (1987) find no difference in the division of labor between "dual-earner" and "dual-career" couples.

Third, the *time availability hypothesis* assumes that people will do housework in proportion to their free time after market hours are subtracted. This would seem to be a variation on the economic perspective, but it assumes that decisions about market work are temporally prior to those regarding home work. While housework appears to relate to wife's work hours, it does not consistently relate to husband's hours (Barnett and Baruch, 1987; Clark, Nye, and Gecas, 1978; but see Haas,

1981, for Sweden), which suggests the lack of symmetry discussed by Berk (1985; see Pleck, 1977).

Haas (1981) emphasizes the potential importance of perceived *responsibility* for breadwinning, rather than actual work hours. Israeli husbands do not take on significantly more housework when they are unemployed (Shamir, 1986), thus contradicting the time availability hypothesis; presumably they retain the *responsibility* for breadwinning even when unemployed. Wife's employment may be viewed as a privilege or a necessity, a contribution to the family or a cost (Ferree, 1984). Whether or not the family makes adjustments to reduce any resulting overload will depend on how it views her labor.

Other possibly important factors are the presence or attitudes of extended family members. Szinovacz (1977) reports that wife's employment did not increase husband's contribution when other relatives were available to help. Moore and Hofferth (1979) speculate that attitudes of relatives toward a woman's employment may influence how the family itself adjusts.

Thus, there seems to be some level of disagreement as to how a wife's employment influences the division of household labor. Husbands appear to increase family time when wives are employed, but mainly through an increase in child care (Pleck, 1985). Wives appear to spend fewer hours in housework when they are employed, but there is some disagreement as to how their total workloads compare to their husbands'. Perhaps the one area of agreement is that these patterns were in a transitional phase, even in the 1970s when most of these data were collected, and that women's and men's time use patterns are converging, albeit slowly.

Marital Power

Many researchers and theorists have assumed a link between family power and the division of household labor—that those who have less power will perform household services for those who have more. Family power research has a long tradition. While it may not be viewed as quite the "bottomless swamp" it was termed in 1957 (see Hoffman and Nye, 1974), periodic reviews of the subject point to problems of conceptualization and methodology (e.g., McDonald, 1980; Safilios-Rothschild, 1970). Most research, however, continues to measure family power in terms of husband-wife decision-making. The predominant finding in this tradition is that wives who are employed wield more power relative to their husbands, at least in decisions about money matters (Ferber, 1982; McDonald, 1980; Rank, 1982; Ybarra, 1982). Ferber (1982) suggests that women enjoy this increased decision-making power, and this explains why they continue to prefer their own outside employment more than men do, even when it creates a work overload for them. When the alternative to paid employment is work that is widely recognized as more productive, as occurs on family farms, outside employment may yield women no more (Lyson, 1985) or even less (Rosenfeld, 1986) decision-making at home.

In predicting the distribution of family power, the major theoretical focus has been on resources, which may include earnings as well as education or occupational status. Resources may be viewed as operating within the household, such that the relevant factor is the comparison between husbands' and wives' resource levels, or externally, such that absolute levels of resources give each spouse a value outside the marriage and thus bargaining power within it. Rank (1982) argues that there is more support for the external than the internal model, that is, for the importance of absolute rather than relative resources.

Some have pointed out that one cannot view resources in a vacuum, whether one is focusing on their value internally or externally. Rodman's (1972) theory of resources in cultural context suggests that the same level of resources may have different consequences, depending on the values regarding family power under which they operate. Cooney, Rogler, Hurrell, and Ortiz (1982) test this theory for different generations of Puerto Rican families, finding wife's employment not significant for any generation but the operation of other variables to differ by cohort. As Ferree (1984) points out, the impact of women's employment on relative power in the household may depend on how they choose to activate their potential power and whether they view female power as legitimate. Gillespie (1971) emphasizes structural constraints on women's power in all societies, placing limits on the power they can derive within an individual bargaining situation. Among cross-sex and same-sex dyads, only lesbian couples do not allow earnings differences to determine relative power (Blumstein and Schwartz, 1983;

Wilkie, 1987; see Huber and Spitze, 1988, for more discussion of nonmarital dyads.)

New Focus on Equity

Mirowsky (1985) argues for the need to integrate prior research on marital power, equity, and depression. His data are most consistent with his "proportional equity" hypothesis, which states that husbands and wives use standards of fairness to evaluate their situations. Neither is happiest with the highest levels of power, but their equity points differ, and the gap between their optimum equity points differs across couples. Husbands' equity points are influenced by their earnings, such that their point of least depression increases with their income. Wives' equity points vary with their sex role attitudes, such that their depression is minimized with more power, the less traditional their attitudes. The greatest gap occurs when his earnings are high and her attitudes nontraditional, which occurs in high-SES groups. This, Mirowsky argues, limits the depression-inhibiting benefit of SES.

Clearly, behavior often lags far behind general norms (McDonald, 1980). There is almost universal agreement that when both spouses work full-time they should share housework equally (Huber and Spitze, 1983). However, few couples do so, and it would appear that some wives prefer it that way, believing in traditional modes of dividing labor or in an equity norm that gives a higher-earning husband a break at home (Petersen and Maynard, 1981). Most studies find little disagreement among couples as to whether the division of labor is fair. Majorities of both husbands and wives like the way things are (Berk, 1985; Hill and Scanzoni, 1982; Pleck, 1985; Yogev, 1981), increasingly with life cycle stage (Schafer and Keith, 1981), whether because of age or cohort differences. A positive relation between the amount of difference of opinion and the husband's contribution, however, suggests either that these families are in transitional periods or that wives who want a more equal division must face conflict (Berk, 1985).

Thus, the interesting issue here seems to be why more wives are not dissatisfied, even when they have relatively high levels of resources (e.g., Yogev, 1981) and presumably the potential to demand more participation by the husband. Pleck (1985) suggests several explanations, including cultural beliefs about housework responsibility, wives' fears that more demands will create conflict, and their views of husband's competency levels in housework.

Working wives absorb most of the tensions caused by work-family conflict but do not experience higher stress levels than housewives (Scanzoni and Fox, 1980). Apparently, such women are experiencing their situation in relation to the alternative of not being employed, rather than of being employed with an egalitarian division of household labor. The link between the division of household labor and marital instability (Booth et al., 1984; Huber and Spitze, 1980) may be expected to become stronger in the future as more people define this as a legitimate issue for dissatisfaction and more women come to believe that a husband who divides labor equitably is truly a possible alternative. The relations among power, housework, and equity norms will continue to be a ripe area for investigation for some time to come.

COMBINED EFFECTS OF HUSBANDS' AND WIVES' EMPLOYMENT

Most studies examining the consequences of wives' employment for families have taken husbands' employment as a given and have not looked at ways in which wives' and husbands' work interacts. There are several research areas, however, in which their interaction is the primary focus.

Family Standard of Living

Among husband-wife families, employed wives provide 31% of family earnings; when both spouses work full-time year-round, they contribute 39% (U.S. Bureau of the Census, 1986). Employed wives also help to keep such families out of poverty (Blau and Ferber, 1986). Further, about half of employed women are not married and are usually the sole support of themselves and any children (U.S. Department of Labor, 1986). Clearly, employed wives and mothers have a major impact on family income levels. They often raise their family income to the level of their "life-cycle reference group," (Strober, 1977), thus serving as an alternative to husband occupational mobility or providing a way of dealing with

unusually high expenses associated with "life-cycle squeezes" (Oppenheimer, 1977). But how does this income translate into differences in family standard of living?

Economists have investigated consumption differences between one- and two-earner families. Traditional assumptions would lead them to expect wives' income to be considered "extra," not part of permanent income, and thus to be saved or spent on consumer durables, an alternative form of savings. An alternative view suggests that this income is not differentiated from the husband's, and thus the expenditure patterns of one- and two-earner households are expected to be similar, when family income is controlled (Ferber and Birnbaum, 1982). However, two-earner families should have more employment-related expenses and also might feel less need to save as a hedge against loss of husband's income (Strober, 1977).

Evidence suggests that, with family income controlled, two-earner couples spend slightly more on consumption of nondurable items, including employment-related expenses and time-saving goods and services, save less, and spend little or no more on durable items (Ferber and Birnbaum, 1982; Lazear and Michael, 1980; Strober, 1977; Strober and Weinberg, 1980; Vickery, 1979; Weinberg and Winer, 1983). One study found differences in expenditures on food away from home and on child care but none on domestic services, clothing care, and personal care (Bellante and Foster, 1984). The authors cautioned that controls for other demographic variables are important, and without them effects of other variables may be attributed to wife's employment.

Since nonemployed women produce time-intensive services at home (see Bivens and Volker, 1986) and do not have job-related expenses, Lazear and Michael (1980) calculate that a two-earner family would need 30% more income to maintain the same standard of living as a one-earner family. Since the average difference in "real income" is actually 20% they conclude that two-earner families have a lower standard of living. These results are admittedly based on a small sample of families with particular characteristics (e.g., no children), and the studies cited above rely on relatively old data. They also analyze current income only and do not discuss possible effects of wives' current work experience on future earnings and thus future family living standards.

Location

Locational issues arise when a member of a dual-earner couple has a job opportunity in another geographical area. Alternative responses include a family move, an individual move, and rejection of the offer. An individual move may be part of a commuter marriage strategy or a marital separation leading to divorce. Although commuter marriages are still relatively rare, they are increasing in frequency and several recent studies have focused on convenience samples of such couples (Gerstel, 1978; Gerstel and Gross, 1984; Gross, 1980).

The economic theory of migration has been extended to incorporate the issue of dual earners (DaVanzo, 1977; Mincer, 1978). Each member of a dual-earner couple is assumed to decide what location would maximize his or her utility. They then pool information and choose the location that will maximize total family utility. It is assumed that this will usually be the current one, since it will occur infrequently that both could increase utility in the same new location or that one's gains would more than offset the other's losses (Becker, 1981; Mincer, 1978). A person who moves or stays because of a spouse's opportunities, contrary to his or her own optimal economic choice, is called "tied." Given current market opportunities and traditional practice, a tied mover is most likely to be a wife and a tied stayer a husband. As men's and women's market positions approach equality, family migration for dual-earner couples is expected to decrease (Becker, 1981; Mincer, 1978). The moves that do occur may be to large metropolitan areas (Marwell, Rosenfeld, and Spilerman, 1979).

Empirical results (see excellent review in Markham, 1987) suggest that dual-earner families migrate slightly less than single-earner ones, but effects are small and age patterns are not consistent (Bartel, 1979; Lichter, 1982; Sandell, 1977). Effects of wife's wages, earnings, and earnings share are similarly inconsistent, perhaps in part because of model specification (Bartel, 1979; DaVanzo, 1977; Lichter, 1982; Spitze, 1984; 1986b). The job prospects of highly educated women have a similarly weak effect on their families' mobility decisions (Duncan and Perrucci, 1976; Ferber and Huber, 1979), although higher income appears to increase their influence (Bird and Bird, 1985). It may be a long time before married-couple families will commonly move long-distance in response to a wife's job

situation, but migration levels and the ability of corporations to assume that employees will relocate readily will probably decrease in the meantime.

Scheduling

During the 1980s several researchers have begun to focus on issues related to scheduling of work among dual-earner couples. This is a welcome trend, since the implication is that many consequences arise not from women's employment alone but from its interaction with men's. Some researchers have taken scheduling as the dependent variable, attempting to explain when couples, for example, will have "off-scheduling" of hours relative to each other (when only one is at work). Others have taken scheduling as the independent variable, looking at consequences relating to family functioning and well-being.

Recent work (Presser, 1984, 1986, 1987; Presser and Cain, 1983) using Current Population Survey data has focused on shift work—on whether one or both members of couples work nonday shifts. Among fully employed couples, in one-quarter at least one spouse works a nonday shift, including 20% of husbands and 12% of wives. This varies by occupation and industry; men's jobs are more likely to involve nonday work, mainly in blue-collar occupations. The wife's work shift is found to depend on the husband's, but not vice versa. If the couple have children, one-third have at least one spouse working a nonday shift, and one-tenth have no overlap in working hours, perhaps a choice by the couple to allow sharing of child care. Presser urges future data collection on both shift and child care arrangements, and asks important questions about the consequences of such arrangements on both quality of care and marital relationships (1986; 1988).

Staines and Pleck (1983; Pleck and Staines, 1985) have analyzed Quality of Employment Survey data for 1977 on dual-earner couples, focusing in particular on whether the husband's work schedule intrudes on the family organization of household work and well-being more than the wife's. They find approximately equal numbers of significant effects, but more for husbands' weekend work and for wives' total work hours. They speculate that weekend work interferes with the "catching up" husbands may do on weekends. Their hypothesis that husbands' schedules would affect wives more than vice versa was not supported.

Nock and Kingston (1984; Kingston and Nock, 1985) have defined three dimensions of the "family work day" and tested for consequences in a variety of areas of family functioning. Data from a national survey showed dual-earner couples to have an average *total* work day (husband's plus wife's work hours) of 16.7 hours, an average workday length of 10.3 hours, and average "off-scheduling" of 4.7 hours. More off-scheduling occurred when children under six were present, a finding consistent with Presser's results. In general, there were no "dramatic" effects: the researchers concluded that most scheduling issues were dealt with nondisruptively. However, there were clear gender differences in consequences of schedules, particularly the length of the work day. The longer the day (implying more time with only one spouse at work), the more time women spent on chores and the more interference they reported with the family. With longer work days, husbands reported *more* satisfaction with family, perhaps, as the authors speculated, because the wife was doing more of the chores. Thus, the lack of disruption noted above is probably managed in large part by the wife. Voydanoff and Kelly (1984) also report women experiencing more time problems than men.

The issue of work scheduling is a fruitful new area for research, with a variety of possible consequences yet to be investigated. Further primary data collection would be ideal, since most studies thus far have been limited in scope because of the lack of key variables.

Family Social Status

Oppenheimer (1977) shows that wives are most likely to be in the labor force when they are in a position to improve family status, and wives' earnings often provide a "functional income substitute for upward occupational mobility" of the husband. Contrary to Parsons, there is no evidence of a reservoir of women who dropped out of particular occupations because of status competition with husbands, although those who entered occupations or became divorced as a result of such competition would not be detectable. Hout's (1982) analysis of the relation between husband and wife occupations also supports Oppenheimer's contentions.

A number of empirical studies have investigated whether and to what extent employed women contribute to family status. Several vignette studies (Nock and Rossi, 1978, 1979; Rossi, Sampson, Bose, Jasso, and Passel, 1974) suggested that raters do take wives' education and occupations into account, although less than those of husbands. Rossi et al. (1974) also showed that a tendency to take wife's occupation into account more is related to respondents' sex-role attitudes but not to standard demographic characteristics.

Several other studies examined class identification of both husbands and wives. Ritter and Hargens (1975) concluded that wives take their own occupation into account as much as that of husbands, while Felson and Knoke (1974) found no effect of wife's occupation on her class identification. Later studies failed to replicate the Felson-Knoke result for wives, finding that wife's occupation affects her class identification both directly and through increasing family income (Hiller and Philliber, 1978).

In contrast, husbands are not affected by wives' characteristics or family income when their own characteristics are controlled (Philliber and Hiller, 1978; Van Velsor and Beeghley, 1979). This suggests, since wives do take them into account, that wives and husbands may not share the same class identification. In Hiller and Philliber's (1986) study of married couples, approximately 75% of individuals identify as middle class, thus placing an upper limit on the possible number of disagreements between couples. However, among couples in which one member identifies as working class, about half of spouses do not. Wife's occupation becomes less influential on husbands' class identification the more she exceeds him. The authors view the results as only suggestive and needing replication.

The studies described in this section suggest that, while the husband's job is still viewed as primary to the family, the wife's contribution is increasingly a factor in how families view themselves and make decisions. Future research on families and work will be most useful if parallel aspects of husbands' and wives' jobs are examined in conjunction with each other. Further, in each of the areas examined, research on single-parent families has been neglected (Voydanoff, 1987). We have much to learn about how such families, whether headed by men or more commonly by women, make decisions about family spending, location, and scheduling, and how they define their status.

EFFECTS RELATING TO CHILDREN

Fertility

A clear relation exists between female employment and fertility in industrialized societies. Recently, the causal ordering of this relationship has been much debated. Lehrer and Nerlove (1986) discuss four possible models: employment affecting fertility; fertility affecting employment; reciprocal causation; and spurious relation due to other factors. Economists seem to favor the latter, focusing on variables such as female wages, husbands' income, and unmeasured tastes that may be captured by variables like wife's education.

Employment *plans* affect expected fertility more than the reverse (Waite and Stolzenberg, 1976), increasingly with the age of the woman (Stolzenberg and Waite, 1977). However, an analysis of *behavior* (Smith-Lovin and Tickamyer, 1978) suggested that the causal ordering was from fertility to employment. Using a sequential model by parity, Hout (1978) came up with similar results and concluded that, in the short run, fertility is the causal agent, while in the long run, employment is. Cramer (1980) criticized the past use of simultaneous equation models on a number of methodological grounds and suggested that there is potential in dynamic models, although they are not without their own problems. White and Kim (1987) also used this approach and came up with some unexpected findings (e.g., high education and job satisfaction encourage childless wives to have a first child) but also pointed out that such a model can capture timing rather than long-term effects.

Clearly, availability of child care affects women's employment: approximately one out of six nonemployed women would look for employment if high-quality, affordable child care were available (O'Connell and Bloom, 1987; Powers and Salvo, 1982). Availability also may mediate between employment and fertility (e.g., Stolzenberg and Waite, 1984), although as Lehrer and Nerlove point out, employment rates may affect availability of child care as well as vice versa, and exogenous factors such as women's market wages

may affect both. The high percentage of employed couples using informal child care arrangements complicates the attempt to measure its impact.

A related issue is the presence of other relatives in the household, which may attenuate the relationship between fertility and women's employment (Weller, 1977) because they might provide child care. Those who rely on a relative for child care are more likely to plan future fertility, perhaps because such care is more convenient and cheaper (Lehrer and Kawasaki, 1985). Black mothers are less constrained by fertility in employment decisions, perhaps because of availability of informal child care but also because of the less reliable income streams and more favorable attitudes of black husbands regarding wives' employment (Lehrer and Nerlove, 1986).

Early studies showing that highly educated women were *more* constrained in employment by the presence of young children were interpreted to mean that these women considered their high-quality inputs to childrearing to be difficult to replace with market alternatives (Hill and Stafford, 1974; Leibowitz, 1975). However, more recent studies suggest that this pattern has reversed (Hill and Stafford, 1980). This may be because educated women have changed their minds about the quality of child care available, or because they in fact do spend as much time with children as other mothers, at the expense of their own sleep and leisure (Hill and Stafford, 1980).

Changes over time in this relationship (Lehrer and Nerlove, 1986; Waite, 1976; Weller, 1977) suggest that children are becoming less of an employment constraint. As popular attitudes increasingly support the employment of young mothers, any negative relationship will possibly depend more on the actual experiences of couples in juggling child care and jobs. Citing Bulatao's (1981) study on the perceived costs of childbearing, White and Kim (1987) suggest that a rewarding career is not seen as competing with child care until *after* the first birth. This harks back to Stolzenberg and Waite's (1977) "learning hypothesis" that women learn with age the extent of incompatibility between the two commitments.

Of course, any impact of employment on fertility also would assume fertility that was largely planned and "rational" (White and Kim, 1987). To the extent that it is not, as is true of much of out-of-wedlock childbearing in this country today, any effect would likely be from fertility to employment.

Child Care

When a nonemployed woman has young or school-age children, she usually provides most of their care, with the exception of the time they spend with the father or other relatives during nonwork hours and perhaps part-time nursery school programs. When a mother is employed, she or the couple must arrange for child care (unless self-care is feasible: Cain and Hofferth, 1987). Its source and quality is likely to affect any ultimate consequences for children, yet these factors are seldom taken into account in research on those consequences.

In 1982, 9% of employed women were able to care for their preschool child while at work (O'Connell and Bloom, 1987). There are no comparable figures for fathers; presumably that situation is too rare to document (Presser, 1988). There is probably a lot of variation in the quality of such experiences, since the child may in fact receive little attention from the mother. A second arrangement involves scheduling the parents' work so that fathers and mothers can share child care responsibilities at different hours. Approximately one-sixth of full-time employed mothers of preschool children, and one-fifth of part-timers, work nonday shifts, and when they are married, fathers are the primary caregivers for children during mothers' work hours (Presser, 1986, 1988).

Among the larger group of working parents using other forms of child care, alternatives include formal group care, care by relatives (the most common form) and care by babysitters in the child's or the babysitter's home. About half of all care to children of employed mothers is provided by nonrelatives and one-third by relatives, the majority of them grandparents (Presser, 1986). Care by relatives tends to be used by those with less education, women who work fewer hours, those with more or younger children, nonwhites, and Catholics, in contrast to care by nonrelatives, whether in a center or not (Lehrer and Kawasaki, 1985; O'Connell and Bloom, 1987; Wilkie, 1987). Over time the use of formal care has increased (Hofferth and Phillips, 1987; Lehrer and Kawasaki, 1985). Child care arrangements also fluctuate much, because of dissatisfaction as well

as the aging of children (Leibowitz, Waite, and Witsberger, 1988), with changes from relatives to group care most frequent (Floge, 1985). The frequent use of multiple arrangements, while seemingly complicating parental schedules, allows more flexibility when one form of care fails and may be the key to allowing parents to continue working.

During nonwork hours, one might expect husbands of employed wives to provide more child care help, just as one would expect them to do more housework; on the other hand, one could expect fathers to interact more with children after work when the mother has been with them all day (Hoffman, 1987). In fact, several studies have documented only slight (if any) differences between the child care time of the two groups, with fathers spending surprisingly little time with children under either circumstance (Barnett and Baruch, 1987; Ericksen et al., 1979; Miller and Garrison, 1982; Tavecchio et al., 1984). Coverman and Sheley (1986) reported men's child care time by wife's employment, adjusted for other demographic factors, ranging from 25 to 26 minutes per day.

Most research on child care either focuses on married couples or does not specify the mother's marital status. An exception is a study by Johnson (1983), which focuses on how divorced mothers with child custody handle conflicts between family and work, such as children's doctor appointments and school activities. Her findings are not surprising: the degree of conflict depends on factors such as employer flexibility, help from others, and age of the child. However, she suggests that divorced women may choose jobs that allow such flexibility at the cost of low income. When unmarried mothers work nonday shifts, child care is sometimes provided by grandmothers but a large proportion is provided by babysitters, thus increasing the financial stress associated with single parenthood (Presser, 1986).

Consequences for Children

It is for children that the most negative consequences of maternal employment have been expected. However, countless studies and a number of literature reviews have concluded that "existing research has not demonstrated that mothers' employment *per se* has consistent direct effects, either positive or negative, on children's development and educational outcomes'' (Bianchi and Spain, 1986; Hayes and Kamerman, 1983; see also Kamerman and Hayes, 1982). This is not surprising, when one considers the multitude of situations being grouped into one category of ''mother's employment.'' As Moore et al. (1984: 89) put it, ''It is significant how few negative effects have been documented, given the diligence with which they have been pursued.''

There are a number of mechanisms through which one might expect an effect of a mother's employment status on children's development, although most studies of consequences do not consider possible intervening factors. Hoffman (1974) emphasizes possible psychological processes, including role modeling, the mother's emotional state, childrearing practices and extent of supervision, and possible feelings of deprivation experienced by the child. (See also an excellent review in Hoffman, 1987.) From a more sociological point of view, an employed mother is likely to have a higher family income, more liberal sex-role attitudes, and less discretionary time than her nonemployed counterparts. An employed mother, particularly one who is career-oriented, might be older as well, and thus more mature but possibly less amenable to the unpredictability involved in parenthood (Baldwin and Nord, 1984).

Daughters of employed mothers are likely to be independent (Hoffman, 1974) and to plan future employment (Bloom-Feshbach, Bloom-Feshbach, and Heller, 1982; Moore et al., 1984). Both sons and daughters of employed mothers hold more egalitarian sex-role attitudes (Mortimer and Sorensen, 1984; Wilkie, 1987; but see Powell and Steelman, 1982) and view women (and their own mothers) as more competent (Bloom-Feshbach et al., 1982; Moore and Hofferth, 1979). Most researchers of role modeling and attitude change expect, and thus are not surprised to find, more effects on daughters than sons, on the traditional assumption that mothers act as role models for daughters only. Extensions of the status attainment model for women show the importance of both mothers' employment status and occupation in predicting outcomes for daughters (Rosenfeld, 1978; Stevens and Boyd, 1980).

There is no consistent evidence of deprivation felt by children of employed mothers (Hoffman, 1974). Although such women spend less time with their children, the gap is least among the more educated, who spend time with their children at the expense of sleep and leisure (Hill and Stafford, 1980; Hoffman, 1987). Hoffman (1987) asks interesting questions (mostly unanswerable) about how interaction with children differs from that in the rosy past. She speculates that time spent in employment by women today may substitute for time previously spent in housework and care of more children (see also Ferber and Birnbaum, 1982).

Evidence on the relationship between wife's employment and the amount of supervision and independence training of children is mixed (Hoffman, 1974). However, a recent trend toward taking the child's point of view may yield other conclusions (Bloom-Feshbach et al., 1982). Trimberger and MacLean's (1982) exploratory study suggested that children's negative feelings about mothers' employment varied by age, gender, and whether they stayed alone after school. They speculated that girls, who have more negative feelings, may end up doing more extra chores. Others have documented differences in children's household work by mothers' employment (Hoffman, 1987; White and Brinkerhoff, 1981). More research is needed on the extent of supervision and self-care of children of employed women (Cain and Hofferth, 1987; Hoffman, 1987).

A number of variables may moderate any impact on children, including class and race of parents, sex and personality characteristics of children (Macke and Morgan, 1978; Moore and Hofferth, 1979; Moore et al., 1984; Wilkie, 1987), and occupational status and employment preferences of the mother (Acock, Barker, and Bengtson, 1982; Macke and Morgan, 1978). Working-class sons of employed mothers may devalue their fathers as inadequate breadwinners, while middle-class husbands of employed women may be seen as more nurturant (Hoffman, 1974).

Several studies show positive effects on academic achievement of girls but negative ones for middle-class boys (Hoffman, 1974). In response to a recent, highly publicized study that seemed to show consistently negative, albeit small, effects of mothers' employment on white children's achievement (Milne, Myers, Rosenthal, and Ginsburg, 1986), Heyns and Catsambis (1986) carefully reanalyzed the data. They showed that the negative effects could be isolated to those white middle-class children in two-parent families whose mothers worked full-time before the child entered school. Even these effects lost significance with controls. Other analyses suggested that sporadic employment rather than consistent full-time employment had more negative effects.

Again, there is little research on the effects of mothers' employment on children of single parents (Garfinkel and McLanahan, 1986; Gove and Peterson, 1980; Milne et al., 1986), perhaps because such parents are assumed to "have to work." There is also a neglect of specific aspects of fathers' employment and how they affect children (Bianchi and Spain, 1986; Heyns, 1982). We need research that focuses on characteristics of both fathers and caretakers (Moore and Hofferth, 1979), in order to move away from the traditional notion that child care is solely the mother's responsibility.

In this highly charged ideological area, we also need to think more about methodological issues (Heyns, 1982; Heyns and Catsambis, 1986). Studies of the effects of mothers' employment on children's adjustment and achievement need to take account of factors that may be causing both, and to consider ways in which women's employment decisions may be *affected by* how well their children are doing. We need longitudinal studies of mothers' employment over time, including outcome measures for all children in a family. And, as Heyns emphasizes, cross-sectional data cannot tell us much about the long-term impact of structural change on *all* families and children.

EFFECTS RELATING TO THE EXTENDED FAMILY

Middle-aged women bear the major responsibility for providing services to aging parents and adult children. Male children are expected to provide financial advice and perhaps aid, but not physical care or household help. Thus, as women's role expands into paid employment, there are bound to be conflicting pressures (Hess and Waring, 1978; Huber and Spitze, 1988; Treas, 1977). Middle-aged women are caught between needs of parents with increasing life expectancy and children who remain dependent for increasing amounts of time or need extra help during marital disruptions (Hagestad, Smyer, and Stierman, 1984). It is unclear whether these stresses are dealt with by decreasing paid work to provide more parental care, increasing employment and using the money to purchase services for parents and children (Soldo, n.d.; Treas, 1977), or increasingly sharing time-intensive labor with husbands (Brody, 1979).

It is also not known how women's employment among adult children or aging parents influences the use of extended-family living arrangements. Soldo's analysis (n.d.) suggests that female employment decreases a family's willingness or ability to provide home rather that institutional care. Cherlin (1979a) relates economic resources to the probability of young couples living with extended kin, finding those worse off more likely to move in with parents and those better off more likely to take in siblings or other kin. More research is needed, using longitudinal data, to determine how changes in extended-family living arrangements relate to female employment in either adult generation.

Few empirical studies have examined patterns of services provided to parents by employed and nonemployed adult female children, and none has examined how changes in female employment over time affect exchange. Similar questions are raised by Brody, Johnsen, and Fulcomer's (1984) study of norms held by three generations of women. Most people did not favor adult children adjusting their work schedules to help elderly parents, but oldest respondents were favorable more often. Daughters, especially if unmarried, were expected to make hypothetical adjustments more often than sons. Whether such adjustments are, in fact, made over time is an open question.

Empirical results on actual assistance patterns are mixed. In a study of "middle-generation" women, Lang and Brody (1983) found that more aid was given by women who were not employed, unmarried, and living in a household with the parent, and to older parents. Brody and Schoonover (1986) also report differences by employment status of daughters who were primary caregivers to elderly widowed women, and Matthews and Werkner (1985) found nonemployed sisters helping parents in poor health more than did their employed sisters. However, Cicirelli (1981) found no impact of women's employment on helping behavior, and Stoller (1983) reports that employment status limits sons' but not daughters' helping behavior. While her data set is larger and more representative than others, employment status is measured as a dichotomy, and it is unclear whether women's hours of work might influence or be influenced by demands of parents. She speculates that women absorb the excess time by increasing length of total work weeks, as they do for housework.

Employment among female adult children may not only decrease their availability to provide time-intensive services to parents, it also may increase the daughters' need for services. In particular, their child care needs may increase, and the interplay between female employment in the adult child and grandparent generation and the age gaps between all three generations may affect whether it is forthcoming (Baldwin and Nord, 1984). Very little data are available on such aid, and none describes the actual time of such services provided from the grandparents' point of view (see Hess and Waring, 1978; Moore et al., 1984).

FUTURE DIRECTIONS

Although the major increase in female employment will probably be completed before the year 2000, the consequences of the increase will continue for some time after that (Davis, 1984). Some have argued (e.g., Hunt and Hunt, 1982) that families will increasingly be divided into career-centered childless couples and family-centered units, since our society has failed to follow the lead of many European ones in facilitating the combination of work and childrearing (Bianchi and Spain, 1986). They argue that dual-career wives have extricated themselves from the constraints of home by getting domestic help, but without challenging the male role. In contrast, Moore and Hofferth (1979) argue optimistically that childrearing offers many pleasures not available through work and will never be entirely forsaken by career women.

I have not devoted much discussion to the notion of "dual-career" couples because I believe the concept of dual *earners* is much more useful. In an insightful critique of "the dual-career family concept," Benenson (1984; see also Ferree, 1987) points out how rare that phenomenon is, according to usual definitions, and argues that it is unlikely to become much more common. Further, such couples do not typically behave in an egalitarian manner, as they have been expected to by optimistic researchers. Thus, I would urge researchers to steer away from this and other similarly problematic typologies, looking instead at effects across the entire range of variation observable in job characteristics of husbands and wives.

Future research on women's employment and family relations needs to move in several directions. First, it should view women's employment as a complex phenomenon with many characteristics such as hours, scheduling, and job satisfaction, each dimension having possible consequences. At the same time, we need to examine parallel consequences of men's employment (see Nieva, 1985; Mortimer and Sorensen, 1984) and interactions between men's and women's situations, for families and for children, and to move away from taking men's employment as a given.

We also need longitudinal research in which we look at duration, timing, and long-term effects. Some consequences that have been documented in cross-sectional studies may disappear or reverse if the same persons are studied over a longer time period (Hoffman, 1987). Further, effects of women's employment have probably changed historically as the context for that employment has changed and it has become more commonplace.

We must also keep in mind the issue of selectivity, or possible unmeasured differences between those who choose to work for pay and to go into certain jobs, as we investigate implications for mental health, marital quality, divorce risk, children's development, and so on. As employed women become the majority, those who choose *not* to work for pay—that is, those who "resist employment" (Hoffman, 1987)—become the deviant group and may differ from employed women in ways that have a wide variety of consequences.

Although there has been some convergence in race and class differences in women's employment in recent years, researchers must work to be more sensitive to the diversity among families and how women's employment may have different meanings and effects across groups. Researchers need to go beyond both the restriction of their samples to white middle-class families and using the white middle class as the norm for comparison in the study of other groups.

One thread running through this review has been that consequences of women's employment (e.g., for mental health, marital satisfaction, children's well-being) are favorable when women's employment status is consistent with their (and their husbands') preferences about it. In other words, women who are employed and who want to be employed are happiest. This seems somewhat obvious, although it is an improvement on earlier research that simply expected negative results under all conditions. However, an emphasis on attitudes also has underlying implications. It is based on the assumption that women *should* have a choice about whether or not to contribute to family economic support. This is certainly consistent with public opinion. Only 12% of respondents to a recent national survey thought a mother with schoolage children *should* work for pay (Huber and Spitze, 1983). Even for a married woman with *no* children, less than one-third of both men and women thought she *should* be employed. While such a choice for women and not for men is usually in the context of major housework responsibilities and thus may seem reasonable, it also tends to perpetuate those inequalities within the household. Research cited above suggests that the perceived *responsibility* for breadwinning affects the internal organization of the household, even when women are employed. This may be the aspect of women's employment most resistant to change.

Thus, rather than focusing on the consequences of a conjunction between behavior and attitudes, those who are interested in moving toward gender equality might better investigate the conditions under which women's employment can occur with positive outcomes for women and their families (Moore et al., 1984). This is particularly true for the increasing proportion of families headed by single parents (Garfinkel and McLanahan, 1986; Nieva, 1985). Past research, in looking for negative outcomes, has had the consequence of either raising women's guilt about working at all or sometimes allowing them a sigh of relief that they are not irreparably damaging their children and marriage while performing their juggling act. Research that focuses on facilitating conditions can help us to design policies that will take the burden for that juggling act out of the individual households and allow the responsibility for raising healthy children to be shared by all members of the society.

NOTE

I am grateful to Marianne Ferber, Joan Huber, Scott South, Linda Waite, and three anonymous reviewers for helpful comments on an earlier version of this article. I especially wish to thank Hazel Taylor Spitze for her comments on the paper and for her helpful support while I was writing it.

REFERENCES

Acock, Alan C., Deborah Barker, and Vern L. Bengston. 1982. "Mother's employment and parent youth similarity." Journal of Marriage and the Family 44: 441–458.

Baldwin, Wendy H., and Christine Windquist Nord. 1984. "Delayed childbearing in the U.S.: Facts and fictions." Population Bulletin 39(4): 1–42.

Barnett, Rosalind, C., and Grace K. Baruch. 1987. "Determinants of fathers' participation in family work." Journal of Marriage and the Family 49: 29–40.

Bartel, Ann P. 1979. "The migration decision: What role does job mobility play?" American Economic Review 69: 775–786.

Becker, Gary S. 1981. A Treatise on the Family: Cambridge: MA: Harvard University Press.

Bellante, Don, and Ann C. Foster. 1984. "Working wives and expenditure on services." Journal of Consumer Research 11: 700–707.

Benenson, Harold. 1984. "Women's occupational and family achievement in the U.S. class system: A critique of the dual-career family analysis." British Journal of Sociology 35: 19–41.

Benin, Mary Holland, and Barbara Cable Nienstedt. 1985. "Happiness in single and dual-earner families: The effects of marital happiness, job satisfaction, and life cycle." Journal of Marriage and the Family 47: 975–984.

Berardo, Donna Hodgkins, Constance L. Shehan, Gerald R. Leslie. 1987. "A residue of tradition: Jobs, careers, and spouses' time in housework." Journal of Marriage and the Family 49: 381–390.

Berk, Sarah Fenstermaker. 1985. The Gender Factory. New York: Plenum.

Berk, Richard A., and Sarah Fenstermaker Berk. 1978. "A simultaneous equation model for the division of household labor." Sociological Methodology and Research 6: 431–468.

Bianchi, Suzanne M., and Daphne Spain. 1986. American Women in Transition. New York: Russell Sage Foundation.

Bird, Gerald A., and Gloria W. Bird. 1985. "Determinants of mobility in two-earner families: Does the wife's income count?" Journal of Marriage and the Family 47: 753–758.

Bivens, Gordon E., and Carol B. Volker. 1986. "A value-added approach to household production: The special case of meal preparation." Journal of Consumer Research 13: 272–279.

Blau, Francine D., and Marianne A. Ferber. 1986. The Economics of Women, Men, and Work. Englewood Cliffs, NJ: Prentice-Hall.

Bloom-Feshbach, Sally, Jonathan Bloom-Feshbach, Kirby A. Heller. 1982. "Work, family, and children's perceptions of the world." In Sheila B. Kamerman and Cheryl S. Hayes (eds.), Families That Work: Children in a Changing World. Washington, DC: National Academy Press.

Blumstein, Philip, and Pepper Schwartz. 1983. American Couples: Money, Work, Sex. New York: Pocket Books.

Booth, Alan. 1979. "Does wives' employment cause stress for husbands?" Family Coordinator 28: 445–450.

Booth, Alan, David R. Johnson, Lynn White, and John N. Edwards. 1984. "Women, outside employment, and marital instability." American Journal of Sociology 90: 567–583.

Booth, Alan, David R. Johnson, Lynn K. White, John N. Edwards. 1985. "Predicting divorce and permanent separation." Journal of Family Issues 6: 331–346.

Booth, Alan, and Lynn White. 1980. "Thinking about divorce." Journal of Marriage and the Family 42: 605–616.

Bose, Christine, and Glenna Spitze (eds.). 1987. Ingredients for Women's Employment Policy. Albany: SUNY Press.

Brody, Elaine M. 1979. "Women's changing roles and care of the aging family." In Aging: Agenda for the Eighties. Washington, DC: Government Research Corporation.

Brody, Elaine M., Pauline T. Johnsen, and Mark C. Fulcomer. 1984. "What should adult children do for elderly parents? Opinions and preferences of three generations of women." Journal of Gerontology 39: 736–746.

Brody, Elaine M., and Claire B. Schoonover. 1986. "Patterns of parent-care when adult daughters work and when they do not." Gerontologist 26: 372–381.

Bulatao, Rodolfo. 1981. "Values and disvalues of children in successive childbearing decisions." Demography 18: 1–26.

Burke, Ronald J., and Tamara Weir. 1976. "Relationship of wives' employment status to husband, wife, and pair satisfaction and performance." Journal of Marriage and the Family 38: 278–287.

Cain, Virginia S., and Sandra L. Hofferth. 1987. "Parental choice of self-care for school-age children." Paper presented at the meetings of the Population Association of America, Chicago (May).

Cherlin, Andrew. 1979a. "Extended family households in the early years of marriage." Paper presented at the meetings of the Population Association of America.

Cherlin, Andrew. 1979b. "Work life and marital dissolution." Pp. 151–166 in George Levinger and Oliver C. Moles (eds.), Divorce and Separation. New York: Basic Books.

Cherlin, Andrew. 1980. "Postponing marriage: The influence of schooling, working, and work plans for young women." Journal of Marriage and the Family 42: 355–366.

Cicirelli, Victor G. 1981. Helping Elderly Parents: The Role of Adult Children. Boston: Auburn House.

Clark, Robert A., F. Ivan Nye, and Viktor Gecas. 1978. "Husbands' work involvement and marital role performance." Journal of Marriage and the Family 40: 9–21.

Cooney, Rosemary, Lloyd H. Rogler, Rose Marie Hurrell, and Vilma Ortiz. 1982. "Decision making in intergenerational Puerto Rican families." Journal of Marriage and the Family 44: 621–632.

Coverman, Shelley, and Joseph F. Sheley. 1986. "Change in men's housework and child-care time, 1965–1975." Journal of Marriage and the Family 48: 413–422.

Cramer, James C. 1980. "Fertility and female employment: Problems of causal direction." American Sociological Review 45: 167–190.

D'Amico, Ronald. 1983. "Status maintenance or status competition? Wife's relative wages as a determinants of labor supply and marital instability." Social Forces 61: 1186–1205.

DaVanzo, Julie. 1977. Why Families Move. Monograph 48, Employment and Training Administration R and D, U.S. Department of Labor.

Davis, Kingsley. 1984. "Wives and work: The sex role revolution and its consequences." Population and Development Review 10: 397–417.

Duncan, R. Paul, and Carolyn Cummings Perrucci. 1976. "Dual occupation families and migration." American Sociological Review 41: 252–261.

Ericksen, Julia A., William L. Yancey, and Eugene P. Ericksen. 1979. "The division of family roles." Journal of Marriage and the Family 41: 301–314.

Farkas, George. 1976. "Education, wage rates, and the division of labor between husband and wife." Journal of Marriage and the Family 38: 473–483.

Felson, Marcus, and David Knoke. 1974. "Social status and the married woman." Journal of Marriage and the Family 36: 116–121.

Fendrich, Michael. 1984. "Wives' employment and husbands' distress: A meta analysis and a replication." Journal of Marriage and the Family 46: 871–879.

Ferber, Marianne. 1982. "Labor market participation of young married women: Causes and effects." Journal of Marriage and the Family 44: 457–468.

Ferber, Marianne A., and Bonnie Birnbaum. 1982. "The impact of mother's work on the family as an economic system." In Sheila B. Kamerman and Cheryl S. Hayes (eds.), Families That Work: Children in a Changing World. Washington, DC: National Academy Press.

Ferber, Marianne, and Joan Huber. 1979. "Husbands, wives, and careers." Journal of Marriage and the Family 41: 315–326.

Ferree, M. M. 1976. "Working class jobs, housework, and paid work as sources of satisfaction." Social Problems 22: 431–441.

Ferree, M. M. 1984. "The view from below: Women's employment and gender equality in working class families." In Beth B. Hess and Marvin B. Sussman (eds.), Women and the Family: Two Decades of Change. New York: Haworth Press.

Ferree, M. M. 1987. "Family and job for working-class women: Gender and class systems seen from below." In Naomi Gerstel and Harriet Engel Gross (eds.), Families and Work. Philadelphia: Temple Press.

Floge, Liliane. 1985. "The dynamics of child care use and some implications for women's employment." Journal of Marriage and the Family 47: 143–154.

Fox, Karen D., and Sharon Y. Nickols. 1983. "The time crunch: Wife's employment and family work." Journal of Family Issues 4: 61–82.

Fox, Mary Frank, and Sharlene Hesse-Biber. 1984. Women at Work. Mountain View, CA: Mayfield.

Freudiger, Patricia. 1983. "Life satisfaction among three categories of married women." Journal of Marriage and the Family 45: 213–219.

Garfinkel, Irwin, and Sara S. McLanahan. 1986. Single Mothers and Their Children. Washington, DC: Urban Institute Press.

Gerstel, Naomi R. 1978. "Commuter marriage: Constraints on spouses." Paper presented at the annual meeting of the American Sociological Association, San Francisco.

Gerstel, Naomi, and Harriet Gross. 1984. Commuter Marriage: A Study of Work and Family. New York: Guilford Press.

Gerstel, Naomi, and Harriet Gross (eds.). 1987. Families and Work. Philadelphia: Temple University Press.

Gillespie, Dair. 1971. "Who has the power? The marital struggle." Journal of Marriage and the Family 33: 445–458.

Glenn, Norval D., and Charles N. Weaver. 1978. "A multivariate, multisurvey study of marital happiness." Journal of Marriage and the Family 40: 269–282.

Goldscheider, Frances Kobrin, and Linda J. Waite. 1986. "Sex differences in the entry into marriage." American Journal of Sociology 92: 91–109.

Gove, Walter R., and Michael Geerken. 1977. "The effect of children and employment on the mental health of married men and women." Social Forces 56: 66–76.

Gove, Walter R., and Claire Peterson. 1980. "An update of the literature on personal and marital adjustment: The effect of children and the employment of wives." Marriage and Family Review 3: 63–96.

Greene, William H., and Aline O. Quester. 1982. "Divorce risk and wives' labor supply behavior." Social Science Quarterly 63: 16–27.

Gross, H. 1980. "Couples who live apart: Two types." Journal of Marriage and the Family 42: 567–576.

Haas, Linda. 1981. "Domestic role sharing in Sweden." Journal of Marriage and the Family 43: 957–967.

Hagestad, Gunhild O., Michael A. Smyer, and Karen Stierman. 1984. "The impact of divorce in middle age." Pp. 247–262 in R. S. Cohen, B. J. Cohler, and S. H. Weissman (eds.), Parenthood: A Psychodynamic Perspective. New York: Guilford Press.

Hannan, Michael T., Nancy Brandon Tuma, Lyle P. Groeneveld. 1977. "Income and marital events: Evidence from an income-maintenance experiment." American Journal of Sociology 82: 1186–1211.

Harkess, Shirley. 1987. "Directions for the future." In Ann Helton Stromberg and Shirley Harkess (eds.), Women Working (2nd ed.). Mountain View, CA: Mayfield.

Harrison, Algea Othella, and Joanne Holbert Minor. 1984. "Interrole conflict, coping strategies, and satisfaction among black working wives." Pp. 251–260 in Patricia Voydanoff (ed.) Work and Family: Changing Roles of Men and Women. Mountain View, CA: Mayfield.

Havens, Elizabeth M. 1973. "Women, work, and wedlock: A note on female marital patterns in the United States." American Journal of Sociology 78: 213–219.

Hayes, Cheryl D., and Sheila B. Kamerman (eds.). 1983. Children of Working Parents: Experiences and Outcomes. Washington, DC: National Academy Press.

Hess, Beth B., and Joan M. Waring. 1978. "Parent and child in later life: Rethinking the relationship." In R. M. Lerner and G. B. Spanier (eds.), Child Influences on Marital and Family Interaction: A Life-Span Perspective. New York: Academic Press.

Heyns, Barbara. 1982. "The influence of parents' work on children's school achievement." In Sheila B. Kamerman and Cheryl S. Hayes (eds.), Families That Work: Children in a Changing World. Washington, DC: National Academy Press.

Heyns, Barbara, and Sophia Catsambis. 1986. "Mother's employment and children's achievement: A critique." Sociology of Education 59: 140–151.

Hill, C. Russell, and Frank Stafford. 1974. "Allocation of time to preschool children and educational opportunity." Journal of Human Resources 9: 323–341.

Hill, C. Russell, and Frank Stafford. 1980. "Parental care of children: Time diary estimates of quantity, predictability, and variety." Journal of Human Resources 15: 219–239.

Hill, Martha S. 1984. "Marital instability: The effects of spouses' time together." Paper presented at the meetings of the Population Association of America (May).

Hill, Wayne, and John Scanzoni. 1982. "An approach for assessing marital decision-making processes." Journal of Marriage and the Family 44: 927–942.

Hiller, Dana V., and William W. Philliber. 1978. "The derivation of status benefits from occupational attainments of working wives." Journal of Marriage and the Family 40: 63–70.

Hiller, Dana V., and William W. Philliber. 1982. "Predicting marital and career success among dual worker couples." Journal of Marriage and the Family 44: 53–62.

Hiller, Dana V., and William W. Philliber. 1986. "Determinants of social class identification for dual earner couples." Journal of Marriage and the Family 48: 583–588.

Hofferth, Sandra L., and Kristin A. Moore. 1979. "Women's employment and marriage." In Ralph E. Smith (ed.), Subtle Revolution. Washington, DC: Urban Institute.

Hofferth, Sandra L., and Deborah A. Phillips. 1987. "Child care in the United States, 1970 to 1995." Journal of Marriage and the Family 49: 559–572.

Hoffman, Lois Wladis. 1974. "Effects on child." In Lois Wladis Hoffman and F. Ivan Nye (eds.), Working Mothers. San Francisco: Jossey-Bass.

Hoffman, Lois Wladis. 1987. "The effects on children of maternal and paternal employment." In Naomi Gerstel and Harriet Gross (eds.), Families and Work. Philadelphia: Temple University Press.

Hoffman, Lois Wladis, and F. Ivan Nye (eds.). 1974. Working Mothers. San Francisco: Jossey-Bass.

Hornung, Carl A., and B. Clair McCullough. 1981. "Status relationships in dual-employment marriages: Consequences for psychological well-being." Journal of Marriage and the Family 43: 125–141.

Houseknecht, Sharon K., and Anne S. Macke. 1981. "Combining marriage and career: The marital adjustment of professional women." Journal of Marriage and the Family 43: 651–661.

Hout, Michael. 1978. "The determinants of marital fertility in the United States, 1968–1970: Inferences from a dynamic model." Demography 15: 139–159.

Hout, Michael. 1982. "The association between husbands' and wives' occupations in two-earner families." American Journal of Sociology 88: 397–409.

Huber, Joan, and Glenna Spitze. 1980. "Considering divorce: An expansion of Becker's theory of marital instability." American Journal of Sociology 86: 75–89.

Huber, Joan, and Glenna Spitze. 1981. "Wives' employment, household behaviors, and sex-role attitudes." Social Forces 60: 150–169.

Huber, Joan, and Glenna Spitze. 1983. Sex Stratification: Children, Housework, and Jobs. New York: Academic Press.

Huber, Joan, and Glenna Spitze. 1988. "Trends in family sociology." In Neil J. Smelser (ed.), Handbook of Sociology. Beverly Hills, CA: Sage.

Hunt, Janet G., and Larry L. Hunt. 1982. "The dualities of careers and families: New integrations or new polarizations?" Social Problems 29: 499–510.

Johnson, Phyllis J. 1983. "Divorced mothers' management of responsibilities: Conflicts between employment and child care." Journal of Family Issue 4: 83–104.

Johnson, William R., and Jonathan Skinner. 1985. "Labor supply and marital separation." Paper presented at the Economic Demography Workshop, Population Association of America (March).

Juster, F. Thomas. 1985. "A note on recent changes in time use." In F. Thomas Juster and Frank P. Stafford (eds.), Time, Goods, and Well-being. Ann Arbor: University of Michigan, Institute for Social Research.

Juster, F. Thomas, and Frank P. Stafford (eds.). 1985. Time, Goods, and Well-Being. Ann Arbor: University of Michigan, Institute for Social Research.

Kalmuss, Debra S., and Murray A. Straus. 1982. "Wife's marital dependency and wife abuse." Journal of Marriage and the Family 44: 277–286.

Kamerman, Sheila B., and Cheryl S. Hayes (eds.). 1982. Families That Work: Children in a Changing World. Washington, DC: National Academy Press.

Keith, Pat M., and Robert B. Schafer. 1983. "Employment characteristics of both spouses and depression in two-job families." Journal of Marriage and the Family 45: 877–884.

Kessler, Ronald C., and James A. McRae, Jr. 1982. "The effect of wives' employment on the mental health of married men and women." American Sociological Review 47: 216–227.

Kingston, Paul William, and Steven L. Nock. 1985. "Consequences of the family work day." Journal of Marriage and the Family 47: 619–630.

Kingston, Paul William, and Steven L. Nock. 1987. "Time together among dual earner couples." American Sociological Review 52: 391–400.

Kitson, Gay C., Karen Benson Babri, and Mary Joan Roach. 1985. "Who divorces and why: A review." Journal of Family Issues 6: 255–294.

Krause, Neal, and Kyria S. Markides. 1987. "Gender roles, illness, and illness behavior in a Mexican American population." Social Science Quarterly 68: 102–121.

Ladewig, Becky Heath, and Gail W. McGee. 1986. "Occupational commitment, a supportive family environment, and marital adjustment: Development and estimation of a model." Journal of Marriage and the Family 48: 821–829.

Ladewig, Becky Heath, and Priscilla N. White. 1984. "Dual earner marriage: The family social environment and dyadic adjustment." Journal of Family Issues 5: 343–362.

Lang, Abigail M., and Elaine M. Brody. 1983. "Characteristics of middle-aged daughters and help to their elderly mothers." Journal of Marriage and the Family 45: 193–202.

Lazear, E. P., and R. T. Michael. 1980. "Real income equivalence among one-earner and two-earner families." American Economic Review 70: 201–208.

Lehrer, E., and S. Kawasaki. 1985. "Child care arrangements and fertility: An analysis of two-earner households." Demography 22: 499–513.

Lehrer, Evelyn, and Marc Nerlove. 1986. "Female labor force behavior and fertility in the United States." Annual Review of Sociology 12: 181–204.

Leibowitz, Arleen. 1975. "Education and the allocation of women's time." In F. Thomas Juster (ed.), Education, Income, and Human Behavior. New York: McGraw-Hill.

Leibowitz, Arleen, Linda J. Waite, and Christina J. Witsberger. 1988. "Child care for preschoolers: Differences by child's age." Demography 25: 205–220.

Levinger, George. 1979. "Marital cohesiveness at the brink: The fate of applications for divorce." Pp. 137–150 in George Levinger and Oliver C. Moles (eds.), Divorce and Separation. New York: Basic Books.

Lichter, Daniel T. 1982. "The migration of dual worker families: Does the wife's job matter?" Social Science Quarterly 63: 48–57.

Locksley, Anne. 1980. "On the effects of wives' employment on marital adjustment and companionship." Journal of Marriage and the Family 42: 337–346.

Lyson, Thomas A. 1985. "Husband and wife work roles and the organization and operation of family farms." Journal of Marriage and the Family 47: 759–764.

McAdoo, Harriette Pipes. 1981. Black Families. Beverly Hills, CA: Sage.

McDonald, Gerald W. 1980. "Family power: The assessment of a decade of theory and research, 1970–1979." Journal of Marriage and the Family

42: 841–854.

Macke, Anne, and William R. Morgan. 1978. "Maternal employment, race, and work orientation of high school girls." Social Forces 57: 187–204.

Maret, Elizabeth, and Barbara Finlay. 1984. "The distribution of household labor among women in dual-earner families." Journal of Marriage and the Family 46: 357–364.

Markham, William T. 1987. "Sex, relocation, and occupational advancement: The 'real cruncher' for women." Pp. 207–232 in Ann H. Stromberg, Laurie Larwood, and Barbara A. Gutek (eds.), Women and Work (Vol. 2). Beverly Hills, CA: Sage.

Marwell, Gerald, Rachel Rosenfeld, and Seymour Spilerman. 1979. "Geographic constraints on women's careers in academia." Science 205: 1225–1231.

Matthews, Sarah H., and Janet E. Werkner. 1985. "Employed and nonemployed sisters' relative contributions of help to their elderly parents." Paper presented at the meeting of the Gerontological Society of America (New Orleans).

Meissner, Martin, Elizabeth W. Humphreys, Scott M. Meis, and William J. Scheu. 1975. "No exit for wives: Sexual division of labor and the cumulation of household demands." Canadian Review of Sociology and Anthropology 12: 424–439.

Michael, Robert T. 1977. "Why has the U.S. divorce rate doubled within the decade?" Working Paper No. 202, National Bureau of Economic Research.

Miller, Joanne, and Howard H. Garrison. 1982. "Sex roles: The division of labor at home and in the workplace." Annual Review of Sociology 8: 237–262.

Miller, Joanne, Carmi Schooler, Melvin L. Kohn, and Karen A. Miller. 1979. "Women and work: The psychological effects of occupational conditions." American Journal of Sociology 85: 66–94.

Milne, Ann M., David E. Myers, Alvin S. Rosenthal, and Alan Ginsburg. 1986. "Single parents, working mothers, and the educational achievement of school children." Sociology of Education 59: 125–139.

Mincer, Jacob. 1978. "Family migration decisions." Journal of Political Economy 86: 749–773.

Mirowsky, John. 1985. "Depression and marital power: An equity model." American Journal of Sociology 91: 557–592.

Moore, Kristin, and Sandra Hofferth. 1979. "Women and their children." In Ralph E. Smith (ed.), The Subtle Revolution: Women at Work. Washington, DC: Urban Institute.

Moore, Kristin, Daphne Spain, and Suzanne M. Bianchi. 1984. "The working wife and mother." Marriage and Family Review 7: 77–98.

Moore, Kristin A., and Linda J. Waite. 1981. "Marital dissolution, early motherhood, and early marriage." Social Forces 60: 20–40.

Mortimer, Jeylan, and Glorian Sorensen. 1984. "Men, women, work, and family." In Kathryn M. Borman, Daisy Quarm, and Sarah Gideonse (eds.), Women in the Workplace: Effects on Families. Norwood, NJ: Ablex.

Mott, Frank L., and Sylvia F. Moore. 1979. "The causes of marital disruption among young American women: An interdisciplinary perspective." Journal of Marriage and the Family 41: 355–365.

Mott, Frank L., and Sylvia F. Moore. 1983. "The tempo of remarriage among young American women." Journal of Marriage and the Family 45: 427–435.

Mueller, Charles W., and Blair G. Campbell. 1977. "Female occupational achievement and marital status: A research note." Journal of Marriage and the Family 39: 587–593.

Mueller, Charles W., Toby L. Parcel, and Fred C. Pampel. 1979. "The effect of marital dyad status inconsistency on women's support for equal rights." Journal of Marriage and the Family 41: 779–792.

Newland, Kathleen. 1980. "Women, men, and the division of labor." Worldwatch Paper 37. Washington, DC: Worldwatch Institute.

Nickols, Sharon Y., and Edward Metzen. 1982. "Impact of wife's employment upon husband's housework." Journal of Family Issues 3: 199–216.

Nieva, Veronica F. 1985. "Work and family linkages." In Laurie Larwood, Ann H. Stromberg, and Barbara A. Gutek (eds.) Women and Work (Vol. 1). Beverly Hills, CA: Sage.

Nock, Steven L., and Paul W. Kingston. 1984. "The family work day." Journal of Marriage and the Family 46: 333–343.

Nock, Steven L., and Peter H. Rossi. 1978. "Ascription versus achievement in the attribution of family social status." American Journal of Sociology 84: 565–590.

Nock, Steven L., and Peter H. Rossi. 1979. "Household types and social standing." Social Forces 57: 1325–1345.

Nye, F. Ivan. 1974. "Husband-wife relationship." In Lois Wladis Hoffman and F. Ivan Nye (eds.), Working Mothers. San Francisco: Jossey-Bass.

Oakley, Ann. 1974. The Sociology of Housework. New York: Pantheon.

O'Connell, Martin, and David E. Bloom. 1987. Juggling Jobs and Babies: America's Child Care Challenge. Population Trends and Public Policy, No. 12. Washington, DC: Population Reference Bureau.

Oppenheimer, Valerie. 1977. "The sociology of women's economic role in the family." American Sociological Review 42: 387–405.

Parsons, Talcott. 1942. "Age and sex in the social structure of the United States." American Sociological Review 7: 604–616.

Petersen, Larry R., and Judy L. Maynard. 1981. "Income, equity, and wives' housekeeping role expectations." Pacific Sociological Review 24: 87–105.

Philliber, William W., and Dana V. Hiller. 1978. "The implication of wife's occupational attainment for husband's class identification." Sociological Quarterly 19: 450–458.

Philliber, William W., and Dana V. Hiller. 1983. "Relative occupational attainment of spouses and later changes in marriage and wife's work experience." Journal of Marriage and the Family 45: 161–170.

Pistrang, Nancy. 1984. "Women's work involvement and experience of new motherhood." Journal of Marriage and the Family 46: 433–448.

Pleck, Joseph H. 1977. "The work-family role system." Social Problems 24: 417–427.

Pleck, Joseph H. 1979. "Men's family work: Three perspectives and some new data." Family Coordinator 28: 481–488.

Pleck, Joseph H. 1985. Working Wives/Working Husbands. Beverly Hills, CA: Sage.

Pleck, Joseph H., and Graham L. Staines. 1985. "Work schedules and family life in two-earner couples." Journal of Family Issues 6: 61–82.

Powell, Brian, and Lala Carr Steelman. 1982. "Testing an undertested comparison: Maternal effects on sons' and daughters' attitudes toward women in the labor force." Journal of Marriage and the Family 44: 349–358.

Powers, Mary G., and Joseph J. Salvo. 1982. "Fertility and child care arrangements as mechanisms of status articulation." Journal of Marriage and the Family 44: 21–34.

Presser, Harriet B. 1984. "Job characteristics of spouses and their work shifts." Demography 21: 575–570.

Presser, Harriet B. 1986. "Shift work among American women and child care." Journal of Marriage and the Family 48: 551–562.

Presser, Harriet B. 1987. Work shifts of full time dual-earner couples: Patterns and contrasts by sex of spouse." Demography 24: 99–112.

Presser, Harriet B. 1988. "Shift work and child care among young dual-earner American parents." Journal of Marriage and the Family 50: 133–148.

Presser, Harriet B., and Virginia S. Cain. 1983. "Shift work among dual earner couples with children." Science 219 (18 February): 876–879.

Preston, Samuel H., and Alan Thomas Richards. 1975. "The influence of women's work opportunities on marriage rates." Demography 12: 209–222.

Rank, Mary R. 1982. "Determinants of conjugal influence in wives' employment decision making." Journal of Marriage and the Family 44: 591–604.

Reskin, Barbara F., and Shelley Coverman. 1985. "Sex and race in the determinants of psychosocial distress: A reappraisal of the sex-role hypothesis." Social Forces 63: 1038–1059.

Richardson, John G. 1979. "Wife occupational superiority and marital troubles: An examination of the hypothesis." Journal of Marriage and the Family 41: 63–72.

Ritter, K., and L. Hargens. 1975. "Occupational positions and class identification of married working women: A test of the asymmetry hypothesis." American Journal of Sociology 80: 934–948.

Robinson, J. P., P. Converse, and A. Szalai. 1972. "Everyday life in twelve countries." In A. Szalai et al. (eds.), The Use of Time. The Hague: Mouton.

Rodman, H. 1972. "Marital power and the theory of resources in cultural context." Journal of Comparative Family Studies 3: 50–69.

Rosenfeld, Rachel A. 1978. "Women's intergenerational occupational mobility." American Sociological Review 43: 36–46.

Rosenfeld, Rachel A. 1986. "U.S. farm women: Their participation in farm work and decision making." Work and Occupations 13: 179–202.

Ross, Catherine E. 1987. "The division of labor at home." Social Forces 65: 816–833.

Ross, Catherine E., John Mirowsky, and Joan Huber. 1983. "Dividing work, sharing work, and in-between: Marriage patterns and depression." American Sociological Review 48: 809–823.

Rossi, Peter H., William A. Sampson, Christine E. Bose, Guillermina Jasso, and Jeff Passel. 1974. "Measuring household social standing." Social Science Research 3: 169–190.

Safilios-Rothschild, Constantina. 1970. "The study of family power structure: A review, 1960–1969." Journal of Marriage and the Family 31: 290–301.

Sandell, Steven H. 1977. "Women and the economics of family migration." Review of Economics and Statistics 59: 406–414.

Scanzoni, John, and G. L. Fox. 1980. "Sex roles, family, and society: The seventies and beyond." Journal of Marriage and the Family 42: 743–756.

Schafer, Robert B., and Patricia M. Keith. 1981. "Equity in marital roles across the family life cycle." Journal of Marriage and the Family 2: 359–367.

Schoen, Robert, and William L. Urton. 1979. "A theoretical perspective on cohort marriage and divorce in twentieth century Sweden." Journal of Marriage and the Family 41: 409–416.

Schoenbach, Carrie. 1985. "Effects of husband's and wife's social status on psychological functioning." Journal of Marriage and the Family 47: 597–608.

Schooler, Carmi, Joanne Miller, Karen A. Miller, and Carol N. Richtand. 1984. "Work for the household: Its nature and consequences for husband and wives." American Journal of Sociology 90: 97–124.

Shamir, Boas. 1986. "Unemployment and the household division of labor." Journal of Marriage and the Family 48: 195–206.

Simpson, Ida Harper, and Paula England. 1981. "Conjugal work roles and marital solidarity." Journal of Family Issues 2: 180–204.

Smith-Lovin, Lynn, and Ann R. Tickamyer. 1978. "Nonrecursive models of labor force participation, fertility behavior, and sex role attitudes." American Sociological Review 43: 541–557.

Soldo, Beth. n.d. Family Caregiving to the Elderly. Final report to Administration on Aging, Grant No. 90-AR-2124.

South, Scott J., and Glenna Spitze. 1986. "Determinants of divorce over the marital life course." American Sociological Review 51: 583–590.

Spitze, Glenna. 1984. "Black family migration and wives' employment." Journal of Marriage and the Family 46: 781–790.

Spitze, Glenna. 1986a. "The division of task responsibility in U.S. households: longitudinal adjustments to change." Social Forces 64: 689–701.

Spitze, Glenna. 1986b. "Family migration largely unresponsive to wife's employment." Sociology and Social Research 70: 231–234.

Spitze, Glenna. 1987. "The data on women's labor force participation." In Ann Stromberg and Shirley Harkess (eds.), Women Working (2nd ed.). Palo Alto: Mayfield.

Spitze, Glenna, and Scott J. South. 1985. "Women's

employment, time expenditure, and divorce." Journal of Family Issues 6: 307–329.

Staines, Graham L., and Joseph H. Pleck. 1983. The Impact of Work Schedules on the Family. Ann Arbor: University of Michigan, Survey Research Center.

Staples, Robert, and Alfredo Mirande. 1980. "Racial and cultural variations among American families." Journal of Marriage and the Family 42: 887–904.

Stevens, Gillian, and Monica Boyd. 1980. "The importance of mother: Labor force participation and intergenerational mobility of women." Social Forces 59: 186–199.

Stoller, Eleanor Palo. 1983. "Parental caregiving by adult children." Journal of Marriage and the Family 45: 851–858.

Stolzenberg, Ross M., and Linda J. Waite. 1977. "Age and the relationships between young women's plans for childbearing and employment." American Sociological Review 42: 769–783.

Stolzenberg, Ross M., and Linda J. Waite. 1984. "Local labor markets, children, and labor force participation of wives." Demography 21: 157–170.

Strober, Myra H. 1977. "Wives' labor force behavior and family consumption patterns." American Economic Review 67: 410–417.

Strober, M. H., and C. B. Weinberg. 1980. "Strategies used by working and nonworking wives to reduce time pressures." Journal of Consumer Research 6: 338–348.

Strube, Michael J., and Linda S. Barbour. 1983. "The decision to leave an abusive relationship: Economic dependence and psychological commitment." Journal of Marriage and the Family 45: 785–794.

Szinovacz, Maximiliane E. 1977. "Role allocation, family structure, and female employment." Journal of Marriage and the Family 39: 781–791.

Tavecchio, Louis W. C., Marinus H. Van Ijzendoorn, Frits A. Goossens, and Maria M. Vergeer. 1984. "The division of labor in Dutch families with preschool children." Journal of Marriage and the Family 46: 231–242.

Treas, Judith. 1977. "Family support systems for the aged: Some social and demographic considerations." Gerontologist 17: 486–491.

Trimberger, Rosemary, and Michael J. MacLean. 1982. "Maternal employment: The child's perspective." Journal of Marriage and the Family 44: 469–476.

Udry, J. Richard. 1981. "Marital alternatives and marital disruption." Journal of Marriage and the Family 43: 889–897.

U.S. Bureau of the Census. 1986. Earnings in 1983 of Married-Couple Families, by Characteristics of Husband and Wife. Current Population Reports, Series P-60, No. 153 (March).

U.S. Department of Labor. 1986. Employment and Earnings Characteristics of Families. Washington, DC: Government Printing Office.

Van Velsor, Ellen, and Leonard Beeghley. 1979. "The process of class identification among employed married women: A replication and reanalysis." Journal of Marriage and the Family 41: 771–778.

Verbrugge, Lois M., and Jennifer H. Madens. 1985. "Women's roles and health." American Demographics 7: 36–39.

Vickery, Clair. 1979. "Women's economic contribution to the family." In Ralph E. Smith (ed.), The Subtle Revolution. Washington, DC: Urban Institute.

Voydanoff, Patricia. 1987. Work and Family Life. Beverly Hills, CA: Sage.

Voydanoff, Patricia, and Robert F. Kelly. 1984. "Determinants of work-related family problems among employed parents." Journal of Marriage and the Family 46: 881–892.

Waite, Linda J. 1976. "Working wives: 1940–1960." American Sociological Review 41: 65–79.

Waite, Linda J. 1981. "U.S. women at work." Population Bulletin 36(2): 1–43.

Waite, Linda J. and Glenna D. Spitze. 1981. "Young women's transition to marriage." Demography 18: 681–694.

Waite, Linda J., and Ross M. Stolzenberg. 1976. "Intended childbearing and labor force participation of young women: Insights from nonrecursive models." American Sociological Review 41: 235–252.

Walker, K., and M. Woods. 1976. Time Use: A Measure of Household Production of Goods and Services. Washington, DC: American Home Economics Association.

Weinberg, Charles B., and Russell S. Winer. 1983. "Working wives and major family expenditures: Replication and extension." Journal of Consumer Research 10: 259–263.

Weitzman, Lenore J. 1985. The Divorce Revolution. New York: Free Press.

Welch, Susan and Alan Booth. 1977. "The effect of employment on the health of married women with children." Sex Roles 3: 385–397.

Weller, Robert H. 1977. "Wife's employment and cumulative family size in the United States, 1970 and 1960." Demography 14: 43–65.

Wellman, Barry. 1985. "Domestic work, paid work, and net work." In Steve Duck and Daniel Perlman (eds.), Understanding Personal Relationships. London: Sage.

White, Lynn K. 1981. "A note on racial differences in the effect of female economic opportunity on marriage rates." Demography 18: 349–354.

White, Lynn K. 1983. "Determinants of spousal interaction: Marital structure or marital happiness." Journal of Marriage and the Family 45: 511–520.

White, Lynn K., and David B. Brinkerhoff. 1981. "Children's work in the family: Its significance and meaning." Journal of Marriage and the Family 43: 789–800.

White, Lynn K., and Hyunju Kim. 1987. "The family building process: Childbearing choices by parity." Journal of Marriage and the Family 49: 271–279.

Wilkie, Jane Riblett. 1987. "Marriage, family life, and women's employment." In Ann Helton Stromberg and Shirley Harkess (eds.), Women Working (2nd ed.). Mountain View, CA: Mayfield.

Wright, James D. 1978. "Are working women really more satisfied? Evidence from several national surveys." Journal of Marriage and the Family 40: 301–313.

Ybarra, Lea. 1982. "When wives work: The impact on the Chicano family." Journal of Marriage and the Family 44: 169–178.

Yogev, Sara. 1981. "Do professional women have egalitarian marital relationships?" Journal of Marriage and the Family 43: 865–871.

Yogev, Sara, and Jeanne Brett. 1985. "Perceptions of the division of housework and child care and marital satisfaction." Journal of Marriage and the Family 47: 609–618.

Sara McLanahan and Karen Booth   *University of Wisconsin–Madison*

Mother-Only Families:
Problems, Prospects, and Politics

This essay examines three aspects of mother-only families: their economic and social well-being, their consequences for children, and their role in the politics of gender, race, and social class. We conclude that economic insecurity is high in mother-only families because of the low earning capacity of single mothers, the lack of child support from nonresidential parents, and meager public benefits. We also find evidence of negative intergenerational consequences. Children in mother-only families are more likely to be poor in adulthood than children who live with both parents. They are also more likely to become single parents themselves. Economic deprivation, parental practices, and neighborhood conditions all contribute to lower socioeconomic mobility. Finally, we argue that the mother-only family has become a touchstone for a much broader set of struggles around changes in women's roles, the relationship between the state and the family, and class and racial inequality.

Mother-only families have become increasingly common during the past three decades.[1] Whereas in 1960 only about 9% of families with children in the United States were headed by nonmarried women, by 1985 the number was over 20% (U.S. Bureau of the Census, 1960, 1961, 1988). If present trends continue, nearly half of all children born since 1975 will live in a mother-only family at some point before reaching age 18 (Bumpass, 1984). Given the importance of the family as a

social institution, and given the high rates of poverty in families headed by single mothers, it is not surprising that researchers as well as policy makers have responded to recent changes in family structure with interest and concern. Some view the mother-only family as an indicator of social disorganization, signaling the "demise of the family." Others regard it as an alternative family form consistent with the emerging economic independence of women.[2] However one views the change, the mother-only family has become a common phenomenon that promises to alter the social and economic context of family life for future generations of Americans.[3]

This essay examines three aspects of mother-only families: their economic and social well-being, their long-term consequences for children, and their role in the politics of gender, race, and social class. In the first section we focus on poverty and economic insecurity and compare the status of mother-only families to that of other demographic groups. We also compare parent-child relationships in mother-only and two-parent families and the degree to which families are socially integrated into their communities.

Understanding the consequences of single motherhood for children is a central issue in evaluating the change in family structure. Whereas a decade ago the prevailing view was that single motherhood had no harmful effects on children, recent research is less optimistic with respect to the long-term outlook. In the second section we review studies on the intergenerational consequences of family disruption and discuss different theories of why children from disrupted or never-married families have lower socioeconomic

Department of Sociology and Institute for Research on Poverty, University of Wisconsin–Madison, Madison, WI 53706–1393.

attainment when they grow up than children from two-parent families.

The growth of mother-only families has stimulated much debate between liberals and conservatives, as well as among feminist activists, over the problems of these families and what should be done to reduce their poverty and economic insecurity. The debate is essentially political in that it involves arguments about the legitimacy of particular family forms and the redistribution of limited economic resources. In the last section we examine this debate and show how single motherhood has become a touchstone for a much broader set of struggles around changes in women's roles, the relationship between the state and the family, and class and racial inequality.

ECONOMIC AND SOCIAL WELL-BEING OF MOTHER-ONLY FAMILIES

Mother-only families and two-parent families differ in a number of important respects, including economic well-being, levels of stress and social integration, and parent-child relations.

Poverty and Economic Insecurity

Perhaps the most striking difference between the two family forms is disparity in economic well-being. Roughly one of two single mothers is living below the poverty line, as compared with one in ten married couples with children (Garfinkel and McLanahan, 1986). See Figure 1.

Between 1967 and 1985, mother-only families were the poorest of three major demographic groups, and their relative position actually declined via-à-vis the elderly.[4] Note that the poverty rate of mother-only families was about the same in 1985 as it was in 1967, having fallen during the seventies, risen sharply in the early eighties, and fallen again after 1983.

Although many single mothers who live below the poverty line were poor prior to becoming single mothers, a sizable majority became poor at the time of marital disruption.[5] Duncan and Hoff-

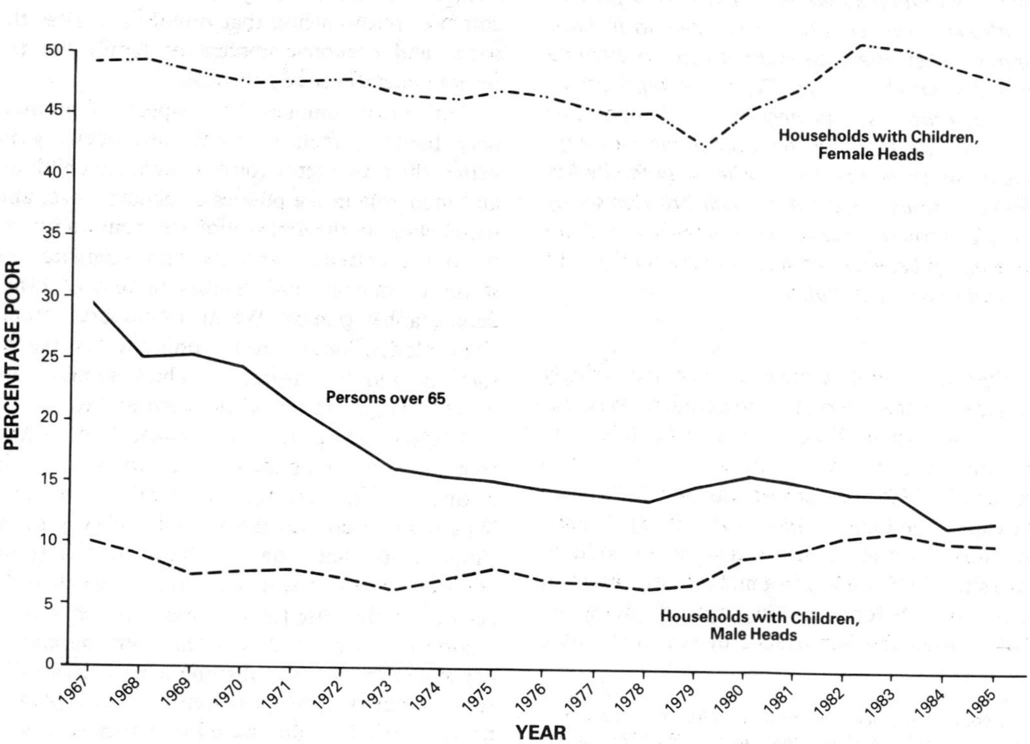

FIGURE 1. POVERTY RATES FOR MOTHER-ONLY FAMILIES, THE AGED, AND TWO-PARENT FAMILIES, 1967–85

man (1985) estimate that the income of single mothers and their children one year after divorce is only 67% of their predivorce income, whereas the income of divorced men is about 90% of predivorce income (see also David and Flory, 1988; Weitzman, 1985).[6]

Why are mother-only families more likely to be poor than two-parent families? In their analysis of different sources of income in mother-only and two-parent families, Garfinkel and McLanahan (1986) conclude that the proximate determinants of low income in mother-only families are (*a*) the low earning capacity of the mother, (*b*) the lack of child support from the nonresidential father, and (*c*) the meager benefits provided by the state (see Table 1).

Low earning capacity. The earnings of the household head constitute the major source of income for mother-only families as well as two-parent families. Thus, a mother's earning capacity is the single most important factor in determining her family's economic status. Unfortunately, single mothers earn, on average, only about one-third as much as married fathers, partly because they have a lower hourly wage and partly because they work fewer hours (Garfinkel and McLanahan, 1986).

The low earning capacity of single mothers is related to the more general problem of women's low wage rates. Women who work full-time, year-round earn only about 60% as much as full-time male workers, and the wage gap has not changed very much during the past 30 years, despite women's increased participation in the labor force.[7] Inequality in wage rates is usually attributed to one of two factors: differences in human capital (women workers earn less because

they have less education, training, and job experience) or market discrimination (employers, workers, and/or consumers prefer male workers over females and therefore the former are paid more). (For more detailed discussions of discrimination and the gender wage gap, see Bergmann, 1986; Blau, 1984; Cain, 1986; Reskin, 1984; and Reskin and Hartmann, 1986.) Differences in human capital are clearly important in accounting for the earnings difference between women and men, but the most detailed empirical studies indicate that they account for less than half of the gender wage gap (Corcoran and Duncan, 1979). This suggests that a large portion of the earnings gap may be due to sex discrimination in the labor market.

Given their lower wage rates, single mothers would be expected to earn less than male heads of households even if they worked full-time, all year. Most single mothers, however, do not work full-time. Between 30% and 40% of single mothers report no earnings at all during any given year, and among those who do work outside the home, many work less than full-time (Garfinkel and McLanahan, 1986). Aside from low wages, a major barrier to employment for most mothers is child care. Whereas in two-parent families the second parent can provide child care or share its cost, the single mother has no such support. Thus she is doubly disadvantaged with respect to earning capacity; her wage rate is lower than that of the highest earner in a two-parent family, and her child care costs are higher.

Lack of child support. A second source of income in the mother-only family is child support from the nonresidential father. According to Table 1, child support and alimony payments account for

TABLE 1. AVERAGE INCOME RECEIPTS (IN DOLLARS) OF TWO-PARENT AND MOTHER-ONLY FAMILIES BY RACE, 1982

Average Receipts	Whites		Blacks	
	Two-Parent Families	Mother-Only Families	Two-Parent Families	Mother-Only Families
Total cash income[a]	30,814	12,628	23,915	9,128
Earned income of family head	21,932	7,666	13,508	5,365
Earnings of other family members	6,377	928	8,096	837
Alimony and child support	227	1,246	253	322
Social Security, pensions, and other unearned income	2,171	1,782	1,720	907
Public assistance and food stamps	174	1,399	1,838	2,573

Source: Garfinkel and McLanahan (1986: 18–21).
[a]Sum of all categories except food stamps.

about 10% of the income of white single mothers and for about 3.5% of the income of black single mothers. While we would expect the contribution of nonresidential fathers to be lower than that of fathers in two-parent families, these figures suggest that the current contribution is grossly inadequate.

National data on child support awards indicate that in 1983 only about 58% of single mothers with children under 21 years old had a child support award. Of these, only 50% received full payment, 26% received partial payment, and 24% received no payment at all (Garfinkel and McLanahan, 1986). Even when nonresidential fathers pay support, the amount is generally low, and the value declines over time since awards are rarely indexed to the cost of living.

Determinations of what share of the cost of raising a child should be borne by the nonresidential parent depend on value judgments. Some argue that child support should depend on the "needs of the child" and the father's obligation should vary according to the mother's earnings. Others believe that child support should depend on the earnings of the nonresidential parent and that he (she) should share a proportion of his (her) income with the child regardless of absolute income level. (See Cassetty, 1983, for a discussion of different approaches to setting child support awards.) Still others argue that many nonresidential parents cannot afford to pay additional child support and requiring them to do so would push these parents and their new families into poverty (Brenner, 1987; Sarvasy and Van Allen, 1984). While the latter argument is undoubtedly true for some families at the bottom end of the income distribution, the evidence suggests that it does not hold for the majority of cases (David and Flory, 1988; Duncan and Hoffman, 1985; Garfinkel and Oellerich, 1989; Weitzman, 1985).

Meager public benefits. A final source of income for mother-only families is public transfers. The two major programs in this domain are Aid to Families with Dependent Children (AFDC) and Survivors Insurance (SI). In 1983, these two programs accounted for between 15% and 25% of the income of white and black mother-only families, respectively. Welfare, as AFDC is usually called, is available to poor single mothers and the average benefit is quite low. Survivors Insurance is provided only to widowed mothers and

is much more generous. Since only a small proportion of single mothers are widows, AFDC is the only government program that is potentially available to the majority of mother-only families.[8]

The AFDC program has many serious problems that contribute to its failure to reduce the economic insecurity of mother-only families. First and most important, AFDC is available only to poor families and does nothing to help families who experience economic hardship but do not meet the income test for welfare. Next, because the AFDC benefit is not indexed to inflation, its value falls in real terms every year if states fail to enact increases in benefits. Moreover, the fact that eligibility for AFDC also entitles mother-only families to Medicaid constitutes a serious disincentive to becoming independent of welfare because the kinds of jobs available to women receiving welfare do not usually carry health insurance. Finally, by drastically reducing benefits as earnings increase, welfare programs carry with them a high tax rate, which discourages employment. The choice faced by poor single mothers is not an attractive one: become dependent on welfare or work full-time to achieve, at best, a marginally better economic position and risk losing valuable in-kind benefits such as Medicaid and public housing.

Stress, Social Support, and Psychological Distress

Poverty and economic instability are not the only sources of strain in mother-only families. In addition to income loss, divorced mothers and their children undergo many other changes, some of which involve the loss of social status as well as social support.[9] Changes in residence are perhaps the most common form of instability in newly formed mother-only families. One study found that about 38% of divorced mothers experienced a residential move during the first year after a divorce. Subsequent household moves dropped off rapidly to about 20% a year on average, still about one-third higher than the residential mobility rates of two-parent families (McLanahan, 1983). Changes in residence not only require adjustment to new neighborhoods and living conditions, they also may mean the loss of important social networks. For children, a new residence often means starting a new school and making new friends.

Changes in employment are also common

following marital disruption. In an effort to recoup some of their lost income, many divorced and separated mothers enter the labor force for the first time or increase their working hours. Duncan and Hoffman (1985) found that the proportion of mothers who worked 1,000 or more hours per year increased from 51% to 73% after divorce. When a mother makes a substantial change in her working habits, that in itself is stressful for her as well as for her children. If the children are young, child care arrangements must be made, and both mother and child are likely to experience anxiety about the new situation.

Income insecurity and changes in work patterns indicate that single mothers experience a good deal of stress in their daily lives, whereas residential mobility suggests they may experience a lack of social integration and support from neighbors and friends. Some also argue that single mothers, and especially young black mothers, are concentrated in disadvantaged neighborhoods that are characterized by high rates of crime and poverty, low rates of employment, and poor educational facilities (Wilson, 1987). All of these factors make the job of being a single parent more difficult and may ultimately affect parenting practices and parent-child relationships.

Do single mothers lack social support and are they more likely to live in communities with limited resources? The social support literature indicates that these mothers, on average, are not isolated from their friends and kin, at least with respect to the amount of social contact they have (Alwin, Converse, and Martin, 1985). Alwin and his colleagues do find, however, that never-married and divorced mothers have less contact with neighbors than married mothers, which may be related to their higher rates of residential mobility.

Researchers have also shown that single mothers are reasonably successful at building support networks for coping with material as well as emotional stress (Leslie and Grady, 1985; McLanahan, Wedemeyer, and Adelberg, 1981; Tietjen, 1985). These studies are based on small convenience samples and therefore the results may not apply to the population in general. Nonetheless, the patterns are interesting and provide a number of useful hypotheses. In her well-known ethnographic study of social support among poor black families, Stack (1974) found that single mothers living in urban areas were in-

tegrated into complex and resilient networks of kin and friends and that such networks were governed by strong values of cooperation and economic reciprocity. Stack did not compare mother-only families with two-parent families, and therefore her findings do not tell us whether single mothers are more or less socially integrated than married mothers. Moreover, Stack's work, while highlighting the strength of poor families, does not indicate that network supports are sufficient to overcome the problems of unstable employment and poverty. Rather, it documents how poor mothers struggle to survive in neighborhoods with relatively few resources and institutional supports.

Not all researchers are as optimistic about single mothers' access to social support. Several have noted the necessity of distinguishing between the quality of social contacts and the quantity, the former being significantly more important as a determinant of well-being than the latter (House and Kahn, 1985; Milardo, 1987). Interactions with kin may be especially problematic for single mothers (Belle, 1982; Colletta, 1979; Milardo, 1987). Kin networks appear to be helpful in providing material support, but they are also more likely to interfere with mothers' parenting styles. Friendship networks appear to provide more emotional support, especially in instances where the mother is trying to change her predivorce identity and establish a new career (McLanahan et al., 1981; Tietjen, 1985). Overall, Milardo (1987) argues that support from friends tends to be outweighed by interference from kin, so that support for single mothers is negative, on average.

Are single mothers more likely to live in disadvantaged neighborhoods that are socially, and perhaps culturally, isolated from mainstream society? McLanahan and Garfinkel (1989) argue that most single mothers do not live in such communities, although their exposure is somewhat higher than that of married mothers. Using information from the 1970 and 1980 census tracts of the 100 largest central cities, they found that less than 5% of white mother-only families were living in urban areas in which over 20% of the population was poor, and less than 1% were living in areas where over 40% of the inhabitants were poor. Not surprisingly, the estimates for blacks are much higher, though again, the majority of single mothers do not live in poverty neighborhoods. About 35% of black single mothers were living in areas where 20% of the inhabitants were poor and about 10% were living in areas where 40% were poor.

Whereas single mothers appear to have reasonable access to social support, they are notably disadvantaged with respect to psychological resources, as documented by studies of depression and psychological well-being. Single mothers report more worries and are less satisfied with their lives than married mothers and women without children (McLanahan and Adams, 1987). Single mothers also use more community mental health services than married mothers (Guttentag, Salassin, and Belle, 1981).

The higher levels of psychological distress among single mothers are due in part to their gender. On average, women report more anxiety and more depression than men, although the gender gap in mental health has been declining over the past several decades (Kessler and McRae, 1981; McLanahan and Glass, 1985). Higher levels of distress are also associated with parental status. Women with children at home, and especially employed women with young children, report higher levels of anxiety than childless women or mothers who are not working outside the home (McLanahan and Adams, 1989). Finally, marital status is a strong predictor of depression, with formerly married women reporting higher levels of depression than married women (Gove, 1972). In short, single mothers face a threefold disadvantage: they are women, they are mothers, and most are formerly married.

The Socialization Process in Mother-Only Families

Given the economic and social conditions described above, one might expect the socialization process in mother-only families to differ in important ways from that in the typical two-parent family. Three factors seem crucial for understanding this process: parental values and expectations, children's attachment to parents, and parents' ability to influence their children's decisions and behavior.

Parental values and expectations. There are several reasons for expecting the values and expectations of single mothers to differ from those of mothers or parents in two-parent families. Because of income insecurity and limited resources,

single mothers may have lower educational aspirations for their children than married mothers. Conversely, because of their own experience as breadwinners, they may place a greater emphasis on children's attainment or a higher value on independence and nontraditional gender roles.

The empirical research provides no strong evidence that single mothers have lower educational expectations for their children than married mothers. In fact, at least one national study indicates that daughters in mother-only families are more likely to report that their mothers want them to attend college than are daughters in two-parent families, once income is taken into account (McLanahan, Astone, and Marks, 1988). With respect to independence and nontraditional roles, it appears that single mothers are more liberal than married mothers. Thornton, Alwin, and Camburn (1983) found that employed mothers were more likely to believe that women should engage in work and other activities outside the home, contribute to family income, and participate in family decision making than nonemployed mothers. Since divorced mothers are more likely to work outside the home, these results suggest an indirect link between divorce and nontraditional values. Waite and Goldscheider (1986) also found that living independently of men leads women to have more "liberal" attitudes about women's work and family roles.

While single mothers differ from married mothers in their views about independence and gender roles, the long-term implications of these differences are not clear. Growing up in an environment where women's economic independence is valued should raise daughters' aspirations and enhance socioeconomic attainment. Valuing nontraditional gender roles, however, may increase the likelihood that daughters will become single mothers themselves, for two reasons: nontraditional roles may be associated with more permissive attitudes about sexuality, which would increase the risk of early pregnancy, or nontraditional roles may be associated with greater acceptance of single motherhood, given a pregnancy.[10]

At least two studies provide some evidence on this issue. Data from the High School and Beyond survey show that black adolescents from mother-only families and black, white, and Hispanic adolescents from remarried families are more likely to consider having a child out of wedlock than adolescents from two-parent families (McLanahan et al., 1988). In addition, Thornton and Camburn (1987) report that divorced mothers, especially those who have remarried, hold less restrictive attitudes about premarital sex than continuously married mothers. They also find that mothers' attitudes are associated with sons' and daughters' attitudes and behavior. Adolescents whose mothers remarry perceive their mothers to be less opposed to premarital sex and less restrictive than other adolescents. Adolescent children of remarried mothers are also more sexually active. Thornton and Camburn argue that a mother's divorce and subsequent dating increases the visibility of her sexuality, which has a "disinhibiting" effect on children's attitudes and behavior. Both studies suggest that children in remarried families are even less traditional with regard to gender roles and attitudes toward sexuality than children in mother-only families.

Children's attachment to parents. Developmental theorists argue that divorce interrupts primary bonds between parents and children and may interfere with children's normal development and socialization (Hess and Camara, 1979; Rutter, 1980). The time fathers spend with their children, for example, is greatly reduced after divorce. In a study based on the National Survey of Children, Furstenberg, Morgan, and Allison (1986) found that less than half of the children with divorced parents in their sample (ages 11 to 16) had seen their fathers during the past year (see also Furstenberg and Nord, 1985). The fact that contact with the father is reduced suggests that the affective bond between fathers and children may be weakened. Indeed, at least two large studies have found that children from divorced, mother-only families feel less close to their fathers than children from two-parent families. White, Brinkerhoff, and Booth (1985) found that about 17% of college students from divorced families reported having close ties with their fathers as compared with 38% of children from two-parent families. Furstenberg et al. (1986) reached similar conclusions in their study.

Not all researchers agree about the value of a good relationship with the nonresidential father. While some studies have shown that a good father-child relationship enhances the child's well-being after divorce (Hess and Camara, 1979),

Furstenberg and his colleagues (1986) note that neither contact nor reports of closeness are related to children's well-being, as measured by an index of academic ability, problem or deviant behavior, and psychological distress. These results, which are based on a nationally representative sample of children, conflict with our basic ideas about the value of parent-child relations and suggest that more research is needed on the effects of the relationship between the child and the nonresidential parent.[11]

The mother-child relationship is also altered by divorce, although in different ways. Whereas most studies report no difference in mother-attachment among children in mother-only and two-parent families (White et al., 1985), there is some evidence that the relationship with the mother becomes closer and/or less hierarchical after a divorce (Weiss, 1979). Again, there is disagreement over the value of a nonhierarchical relationship with the parent. Weiss (1979) speaks favorably about the greater equality in mother-only families, whereas others argue that such relationships may oversensitize children to the feelings of adults and interfere with psychological development (Hess and Camara, 1979). These results are based on small, nonrepresentative samples and need to be replicated on larger samples where other factors are controlled.

Finally, parental conflict may also undermine children's attachment to parents. Indeed, many studies have suggested that it is conflict rather than living in a mother-only family which leads to family disruption and long-term negative consequences for children. This issue is discussed in more detail in the next section.

Parental involvement and supervision. Two final questions of considerable importance in assessing parent-child relations are whether the single mother spends sufficient time with her children and whether she exercises adequate supervision and control over their activities. Hetherington, Cox, and Cox (1978) have shown that during the first year after divorce single mothers are much less consistent in their discipline patterns and household routines are more erratic. The attribute disorganization to the stress associated with divorce, as opposed to single parenting in general, and note that most of the problems subside by 18 months after divorce.

Others have simply looked at the association between single parenting and parent-child relations, without considering time since marital disruption as a factor. The latter indicate that parental involvement and supervision in mother-only families is somewhat lower than in two-parent families. McLanahan et al. (1988), for example, found that adolescents in mother-only families report receiving less help with homework and with planning their high school curriculum than adolescents living with both parents. They also found that parents are less likely to monitor adolescents' social activities (see also Abrahamse, Morrison, and Waite, 1987). In a similar vein, Dornbusch et al. (1985) and Steinberg (1987) found that single mothers have less input into children's decisions than married parents, and adolescents in mother-only families are more susceptible to peer pressure than children in two-parent families.[12]

Interestingly, in the Dornbusch study the presence of adult relatives, but not stepfathers, strengthened single mothers' influence relative to that of children's peers. It is not clear, however, whether such adults provided "back-up" support for the mothers or whether they supervised the children directly. It makes sense that grandmothers would have a more positive influence on mother's parenting than stepfathers, since the former are usually in the household to help with the children whereas the latter may compete with children for the mother's time. (See Kellam, Ensminger, and Turner, 1977, for additional information on the benefits of having grandmothers in the household.)

THE REPRODUCTION OF POVERTY

Much of the present concern about mother-only families arises from the fear that such families may be harmful to children. In this section we present a brief overview of the empirical research on the consequences of growing up in a mother-only family and the changing orientations among researchers on this topic during the past three decades. Following the discussion of empirical research, we explore several different explanations for why children from mother-only families are less successful in school and more likely to become single parents themselves than children who grow up in two-parent families.

A Brief Summary of Empirical Research

The literature on the intergenerational consequences of marital dissolution and nonmarriage has undergone several transformations during the past three decades. During the 1950s and 1960s, the prevailing view was that divorce and nonmarital births were indicative of pathology (individual pathology and/or couple pathology) and that children of such unions were likely to exhibit pathological behaviors as well.[13] Much of the research at this time was based on highly selective samples, such as children in treatment for psychological disorders or wards of the criminal justice system. Thus it is not surprising that personal failure rather than social factors are used to explain the differences associated with family structure. In the early 1970s, the ideology began to change, as evidenced by Herzog and Sudia's (1973) review of the research on children in "fatherless families." These authors challenged earlier interpretations and showed that existing studies of mother-only families contained serious methodological flaws. In particular, they argued that many of the differences between mother-only and two-parent families could be explained by differences in family socioeconomic status.

The Herzog and Sudia review offered a new perspective on single motherhood and, together with a changed political climate in which black families and nonmarried mothers of all races were viewed more positively, stimulated new studies that focused on the "strengths" of mother-only families, that is, the ways in which single mothers cope successfully with poverty and stress. Despite Herzog and Sudia's assertion that father absence *did* have some negative consequences for children, their methodological critique was taken by many as evidence that differences between one- and two-parent families were minimal or due entirely to income differences.

Since the late seventies researchers have moved beyond simplistic pathological and idealizing perspectives. More recent reviews of the literature have emphasized both that children in such families are disadvantaged and that these disadvantages are outcomes of interactions among a variety of factors. Moreover, reviewers have noted that while family socioeconomic status is a major predictor of children's attainment, it cannot account for all of the problems associated with parental divorce and growing up in a mother-only family (Hetherington, Camara, and Feather-man, 1983; Shinn, 1978).[14]

Both Shinn and Hetherington et al. focused their reviews on cognitive development in young and school-age children. They found that children from mother-only families did less well on standardized tests than children from two-parent families, but the differences were minimal. The greatest difference in academic achievement was found in teacher evaluations, such as grade point average and reports of behavioral problems in school and with peers, which tended to be more negative for boys from one-parent families than for boys from two-parent families. Absences from school were also higher for children in one-parent families and were related to teachers' perceptions and evaluations.[15]

Hetherington and her colleagues also found evidence of a gender difference in the effect of single motherhood on academic achievement, boys being slightly more disadvantaged than girls. Living with a same-sex parent was advantageous for academic achievement compared to living with an opposite-sex parent. While girls in mother-only families have fewer initial problems of adjustment in response to parents' divorce, they are more likely to become depressed during adolescence (Wallerstein, 1986). Moreover, mother's remarriage has a more negative effect on daughters than on sons, increasing both aggression and depression.

Since the early 1980s, new studies have appeared that are consistent with the conclusions reached by Shinn and Hetherington et al. and at the same time extend previous research in several ways. First, these studies are based on large, nationally representative surveys, many of which have longitudinal designs. Second, they examine the long-term consequences of family disruption and single motherhood by following children from different family types through late adolescence and into adulthood. Finally, researchers have replicated the results of these studies with more than one data set, using similar measures of family structure and similar indicators of offspring behavior and attainment.[16]

The new research indicates that children who grow up in mother-only families are disadvantaged not only during childhood or immediately after parents' marital disruption, but during adolescence and young adulthood as well. Moreover, the negative consequences associated with family structure extend across a wide range of socioeconomic outcomes. Children from mother-only families obtain fewer years of education and are more likely to drop out of high school than offspring from two-parent families (Krein and Beller, 1988; McLanahan, 1985; McLanahan and Bumpass, 1988; McLanahan et al., 1988; Shaw, 1982). They have lower earnings in young adulthood and are more likely to be poor (Corcoran, Laren, and Solon, 1987; Hill, Augustyniak, and Ponza, 1987). The daughters of single mothers are more likely to receive welfare when they become adults than daughters from two-parent families (Antel, 1988; Gottschalk, 1988; McLanahan, 1988).

Children from mother-only families are also disadvantaged with respect to family formation and deviant behavior. They are more likely to marry early and have children early, both in and out of wedlock (Abrahamse et al., 1987; Hogan and Kitagawa, 1985; McLanahan and Bumpass, 1988; McLanahan et al., 1988; see Michael and Tuma, 1985, for different results). Those who marry are more likely to divorce (McLanahan and Bumpass, 1988). In short, children who grow up in mother-only families are at greater risk of becoming single mothers themselves, either through divorce or nonmarital childbearing. Finally, offspring from mother-only families are more likely to commit delinquent acts and to engage in drug and alcohol use than offspring from two-parent families (Matsueda and Heimer, 1987; Mott and Haurin, 1987).

In addition to documenting a wide range of negative outcomes among children from mother-only families, these studies contain several other findings. First, income appears to account for some, but not all, of the lower attainment of offspring from mother-only families. Second, the effects of single motherhood are somewhat different across different types of mother-only families. Offspring of widowed mothers do better, on average, than offspring of divorced and separated mothers, at least in some surveys and on some indicators. Third, the effects of single motherhood are consistent across a large number of racial and ethnic groups, including blacks, whites, Mexican Americans, Puerto Ricans, Native Americans, and Asians. Fourth, family disruptions occurring in adolescence are just as upsetting in terms of their consequences as disruptions occurring in early childhood. Finally, remarriage does *not* appear to mitigate the consequences of family disruption; if anything, it may increase the risk that a daughter will leave school early and become a teen mother.

Theories of Intergenerational Consequences

Nearly all of the research on the effects of single motherhood is descriptive and there is no universally accepted theory to explain why children from mother-only families have lower academic achievement or start their families earlier than children from two-parent families. Nevertheless, most researchers who study the phenomenon ultimately employ a particular perspective or theoretical orientation to make sense out of the relationships observed in the empirical studies. The literature on intergenerational consequences contains at least three such perspectives, which are not mutually exclusive but which reflect different disciplines and traditions. These include the "economic-deprivation argument," which attributes the disadvantage associated with the mother-only family to lack of parental investment; the "socialization argument," which claims that negative outcomes are due to dysfunctional parental values and parent-child relationships; and the "neighborhood argument," which posits that outcomes are due to structural or neighborhood characteristics such as social isolation and a lack of community resources. To some degree, these perspectives correspond to the areas described in the previous section on material and social conditions.

The economic-deprivation argument. Many researchers believe that the negative association between single motherhood and offspring attainment is due to low parental income. Single mothers have less time and less money to invest in their children, which affects both children's personal characteristics as well as how they view the parental household (Becker, 1981; Krein and Beller, 1986; Michael and Tuma, 1985). Family income is related to the quality of children's schools and to participation in extracurricular activities, including summer travel and camps, all of which are positively related to school achievement (Heyns, 1985).

Economic necessity may also promote the premature assumption of adult responsibilities by encouraging adolescents to leave school early in order to earn money for their families or to care

for younger siblings (Elder, 1974). This does not mean that early departures from school are necessarily due to poor performance or negative behavior in general. On the contrary, children who leave school prematurely to fulfill adult roles may be highly responsible. Their responsibilities, however, are directed toward family survival rather than individual achievement. Finally, adolescents from low-income families have fewer economic opportunities and may see marriage and parenthood as a means of escaping hardship and establishing an adult identity (Rubin, 1976). Thus, because of their economic position, we would expect children of single mothers to leave school sooner and to marry and/or have children earlier than offspring from two-parent families.

The economic-deprivation argument, as presented above, does not distinguish between low income as a cause and as a consequence of divorce. As noted earlier, divorced mothers, on average, experience a 33% loss in income during the first year after divorce, which means that for many mother-only families, low income is a consequence of a change in family structure. It is also true, however, that a considerable proportion of single mothers, especially never-married black mothers, are poor prior to becoming household heads, in which case low income is exogenous to family structure.

To what extent does income account for the differences in education and family formation behavior that are observed between offspring from mother-only and two-parent families? With respect to high school graduation, McLanahan (1985) found that income accounted for about 40% to 50% of the difference in high school dropout rates of children from mother-only and two-parent families, but that family differences existed, even after income was controlled. These findings have been replicated with several longitudinal surveys, including the Panel Study of Income Dynamics, the National Longitudinal Survey of Youth, and the High School and Beyond Survey (Krein and Beller, 1988; McLanahan and Bumpass, 1988; McLanahan et al., 1988).

Income is also important in explaining the association between family structure and the family formation behavior of offspring, although again it does not account for all of the correlation (Abrahamse et al., 1987; Hogan, 1985; Hogan and Kitagawa, 1985; McLanahan, 1988; McLanahan and Bumpass, 1988). In their comparison of three longitudinal surveys, McLanahan and her colleagues (1988) found that family income accounted for between 13% and 50% of the intergenerational relationship between growing up in a mother-only family and becoming a single mother in adulthood, depending on which survey was used and whether one looked at whites, blacks, or Hispanics.

The socialization argument. This argument emphasizes parental values and childrearing practices as the major factors accounting for differences in offspring behavior and attainment. Many of these family characteristics were discussed in the first section under the headings of stress, parental involvement, and parent-child relations. Socialization theorists argue variously that single mothers are more accepting of divorce and out-of-wedlock birth and therefore their offspring are more likely to become single parents themselves. They claim that single mothers have less influence over their children's behavior because of a lack of parental attachment, parental involvement, and supervision. Finally, some argue that single mothers are under considerable stress, which affects parent-child relations and parental control, at least for the first 18 months after a divorce.

The research on intergenerational consequences provides some support for the socialization hypothesis, as was noted in the previous section. With respect to parental values, we know that single mothers and their daughters are more accepting of premarital sex and divorce (Thornton and Camburn, 1983) and that single motherhood is associated with less parental involvement in school work, less supervision, and less parental influence (Dornbusch et al., 1985; Hogan and Kitagawa, 1985; Matsueda and Heimer, 1987; McLanahan et al., 1988; Steinberg, 1987).

The critical question, however, is whether differences in socialization beliefs and practices account for differences in the attainment of children; here the answer is more complicated. If we ask whether socialization is related to child outcomes, the answer is clearly yes (Abrahamse et al., 1987; Hogan and Kitagawa, 1985: Matsueda and Heimer, 1987; McLanahan et al., 1988). If we ask whether differences in socialization "account for" differences in the family structure effect, the answer is less clear. On the one hand, researchers have shown that lack of monitoring and poor

supervision are related to high school dropout and early family formation (Astone, 1989; Abrahamse, 1987). Moreover, Astone has shown that differences in socialization practices can account for some of the difference in dropout rates between adolescents in intact and nonintact families. On the other hand, these analyses do not tell us whether changes in family structure cause changes in socialization or the extent to which both are a function of economic insecurity. Additional research is needed to determine the interrelationship between socialization practices, economic status, and family disruption.

As was the case with the economic-deprivation hypothesis, some analysts argue that differences in values and socialization practices are not endogenous to divorce. Rather, they claim that such differences exist prior to parents' divorce or mothers' out-of-wedlock births. The most impressive evidence to date in support of the selection hypothesis comes from studies that distinguish between happily and unhappily married couples or between low- and high-conflict families (Block, Block, and Gjerde, 1986; Chess, Thomas, Mittelman, Korn, and Cohen, 1984; Emery, 1982; Peterson and Zill, 1986; Raschke and Raschke, 1979). These studies, which focus on outcomes for children still living at home, indicate that offspring from mother-only families are no different from offspring in unhappy or high-conflict families. This finding suggests that it is family conflict rather than divorce that is the determining factor in children's behavior. The conflict studies are based primarily on small, nonrepresentative samples and have not been replicated with larger data bases. Moreover, not all studies are consistent with this interpretation. Hetherington's work in particular shows that parental behavior and childrearing practices are less stable and consistent after divorce.

Although the selection argument is a sensible alternative, it is not an easy hypothesis to test. First, a well-designed study requires longitudinal data so that children and parents can be observed both before and after divorce. The predivorce period must be early enough so as not to be contaminated by the anticipation of a divorce. Second, the data base must be rich enough to allow the researcher to control for the critical pre- and postdivorce measures. Finally, even if one were to determine that an event such as marital disruption was associated with a change in offspring's behavior, such as dropping out of school or becoming pregnant, it is always possible that the association is due to a third, unobserved variable that is correlated with both family change and offspring behavior as opposed to parents' marital disruption itself.

The neighborhood argument. The neighborhood argument states that mother-only families are more likely to live in economically and socially isolated neighborhoods, which, in turn, lower the opportunity for economic mobility and raise the likelihood that offspring will quit school and/or become teen parents. This argument, best and most recently articulated by Wilson (1987), incorporates elements of both the economic-deprivation and socialization perspectives and raises the debate over family structure to a macro level of analysis. Whereas those who adhere to the economic-deprivation argument generally emphasize supply-side factors, such as household resources and parental investment, neighborhood theorists stress the demand side of the labor market, especially the extent to which residential location is related to the availability of jobs. According to this view, children from mother-only families have less access to jobs and therefore less incentive to invest in education or other human capital activities. Similarly, whereas socialization theorists focus primarily on parent-child relations and communication and control within the family, neighborhood analysts stress the importance of community attitudes, local networks, and peer-group activities. The latter argue that mother-only families are isolated in "underclass" neighborhoods with high levels of poverty and disorganization, which, in turn, reduce parental control and increase the likelihood that offspring will be exposed to antisocial activities.

The neighborhood hypothesis is distinct from previous arguments primarily in its emphasis on how social structure *constrains* family behavior. According to this view, economic incentives and social norms within ghettos discourage socioeconomic attainment and encourage early family formation. As was the case with the previous two hypotheses, the neighborhood effect can be viewed as a cause or a consequence of family disruption or nonmarital births. In the version set forth by Wilson, school dropout and single motherhood across generations are treated as

consequences of the lack of jobs for men. Another version suggests that single mothers are less able than married parents to cope with life in ghetto neighborhoods, where community controls are weaker and peer activities more dangerous (Sampson, 1987). Sampson's study suggests the existence of an interaction effect between single motherhood and neighborhood conditions.

Several researchers have found some support for the neighborhood argument. In their Chicago study, Hogan and Kitagawa (1985) were able to classify respondents according to census tract characteristics such as medium income, percentage poor, juvenile crime rates, marriage, and fertility rates. They found that neighborhood quality has a significant effect on early pregnancy and is strongly related to parental supervision. More recently, several researchers have shown that residential location is related to children's socioeconomic attainment (Corcoran et al., 1987; Sandefur, McLanahan, and Wojtkiewicz, 1989).

As in the case of the socialization variables, the relative power of neighborhood characteristics versus family income and socialization practices in accounting for the differences between children from mother-only and two-parent families is not known. What is clear, however, is that neighborhood quality has an independent effect on children's attainment, even after family income is controlled. A major limitation of the neighborhood hypothesis is that it applies to a relatively small proportion of all mother-only families. Whereas neighborhoods may be important in explaining variation in the behavior and attainment of black adolescents, they cannot account for differences among most whites. As noted above, less than 1% of white mother-only families live in highly concentrated poverty areas (McLanahan and Garfinkel, 1989).

Finally, the availability of social support might also be viewed as a neighborhood characteristic in that it measures whether an individual or a family is socially isolated and whether they receive informal social support of some kind. As noted, single mothers do not appear to differ from married parents with respect to contact with friends and relatives, except in one instance: they are less likely to know their neighbors. It is also possible that the quality of social exchange may be lower in mother-only families, especially poor families, which may affect mothers' ability to monitor and influence their children's behavior. Thus far, no one has examined the association between mothers' informal support or contact with friends and neighbors on the one hand and offspring behavior on the other.

THE POLITICS OF SINGLE MOTHERHOOD

The growth of mother-only families and the feminization of poverty have stimulated considerable discussion among researchers and policy makers during the past decade. Single motherhood is a highly politicized subject that involves conflicting values and competing gender, class, and race interests. First and foremost, single mothers are women, and therefore their prevalence and material condition have relevance for debates over inequality between men and women. The poverty of single mothers highlights the economic vulnerability that is inherent in women's role as mothers and calls attention to the relatively low earning capacity and disproportionate responsibility for children that is shared by all women.

Single mothers are also disproportionately poor; hence their condition is relevant to debates over inequality across social classes. Although many of these women were poor prior to becoming heads of household and although a substantial number of poor women and children live in two-parent families, the plight of mother-only families has attracted the nation's attention and raised questions about the fairness and efficiency of our social programs and income transfer system. How can a society with such a high standard of living account for the fact that about 20% of its children are living below the poverty line (U.S. Bureau of the Census, 1987)? For policy makers and analysts who support greater equality across classes, the mother-only family has become a rallying point around which to push for income redistribution.

Finally, a large number of single mothers are black, which means that discussions of the trends in family disruption and nonmarriage are inevitably linked to discussions of racial inequality and discrimination. The politics of single motherhood are perhaps nowhere more evident than in the debate over the black mother-only family, which dates back to the 1960s and the publication of the Moynihan Report (Moynihan, 1965). At that time single mothers were cited as evidence of a growing pathology in the black family and as a critical link in the intergenerational transmission of poverty. This characterization of the black family was widely criticized by many black scholars and liberal politicians for being implicitly racist and for "blaming the victim." (For a discussion of this debate, see Rainwater and Yancy, 1967.) More recently, some of these issues have reemerged in response to Wilson's research on the urban underclass (1987). Now, as then, the political and intellectual dilemma is how to develop an analysis that stresses the economic and social disadvantages faced by poor single mothers without reenforcing negative stereotypes about their lifestyles and values.

In sum, analyses of the growth and economic conditions of mother-only families are never totally objective but are fraught with the conflicting values and biases of the different interest groups that are affected by the phenomenon. To illustrate this point and help clarify the major political actors and their positions, the final section of the essay focuses on two questions that are central to the debate over single motherhood: (*a*) do mother-only families represent a "problem," and if so, what is the nature of the "problem"—is it prevalence or is it poverty? and (*b*) what kinds of social policies should be developed to deal with the poverty and income insecurity of mother-only families?

Mother-Only Families:
Social Problem or Not?

A major question debated by academicians and activists is whether the growth of mother-only families is a sign of social progress or decline. The position taken by analysts on this issue is shaped by their values regarding women's traditional family roles and whether they view single motherhood as a cause or consequence of economic insecurity. Those who view the traditional two-parent family as a primary source of gender inequality and women's oppression tend to see the growth of mother-only families as a gain for women. Those who view single motherhood as a consequence of economic deprivation and male joblessness tend to see it as a sign of declining opportunity for poor minority families.

Most mainstream feminists argue that the growth of mother-only families is a sign of forward movement in the struggle for women's equality (Bergmann, 1986; Hartmann, 1985).[17] They note that the increase in the demand for women workers and rising wage rates after World War II drew an ever greater proportion of women into the paid labor force, which, in turn, expanded women's roles and made it easier for them to support themselves outside of marriage. As a consequence, women today marry less often, divorce more, and form mother-only families at a faster rate than they did in the past.[18]

Wilson (1987) offers a very different perspective on the growth of mother-only families. He argues that the rise in nonmarriage and marital disruption is due to a decline in the ability of poor black men to support their families or at least to make a substantial economic contribution to the household. According to Wilson, the increase in male unemployment and joblessness between 1960 and 1980 was greatest in the North Central and Northeast regions of the country, areas that also showed the greatest increase in the number of mother-only families. Declines in employment during the 1970s were due to a loss of low-skilled jobs in the central northern cities where blacks are highly concentrated. Jobs for unskilled workers in cities such as New York, Philadelphia, and Baltimore declined by more than 30% during the 1970s, whereas jobs for skilled workers increased from 21% to 38%. The shift to higher-paying jobs in the central cities worked to the disadvantage of black men, who were least likely to have a college education. Wilson's theory stresses the constraints on men associated with the growth of mother-only families—as opposed to the increased options for women—and therefore he sees the current trend as indicative of social dislocation rather than progress.

The disparity between Wilson's position and that of many feminists is noteworthy inasmuch as both groups are concerned with poverty and inequality and both are viewed as spokespersons for the interests of minorities and disadvantaged persons. And yet there is considerable disagreement and some animosity between the two camps, at least on the issue of single motherhood. On the one hand, Wilson has been accused of framing his analysis exclusively around the interests of poor minority men. For example, his emphasis on men's unemployment and his use of single motherhood as an indicator of social dislocation has angered many feminists and led them to accuse him of being antifeminist. On the other hand, the liberal-feminist position has been accused of being oriented exclusively around the interests of white middle-class women and of ignoring the problems that poor minority women share with poor minority men (Brenner, 1987; Malvaux, 1985).

To some extent the conflict between Wilson and the liberal-feminists is due to the fact that the two groups are looking at different parts of the gender earnings ratio (women's earnings to men's earnings) and at different ends of the income distribution. Liberal-feminists focus on increases in women's earnings (the numerator of the ratio) and at the middle to upper end of the income distribution, whereas Wilson and his colleagues are looking at declines in men's earnings (the denominator of the earnings ratio) at the bottom of the income distribution. Since Wilson is concerned primarily with poor black families living in urban ghettos, the more relevant factor for him is the decline in male earnings, which has occurred at the bottom end of the distribution. Conversely, the liberal-feminist argument is most convincing when applied to middle-class women who are economically independent. Although women's earnings and access to income have increased at both ends of the distribution, it is hard to argue that the "independence" of poor minority mothers is a sign of progress for women or their children. By the same token, male joblessness cannot fully account for the decline in marriage and rise in single motherhood among middle-class women.

The conflict between Wilson and the socialist-feminists is somewhat different, since both focus on the bottom end of the income distribution. Here the disagreement is over traditional gender roles and women's economic independence. In Wilson's view the solution to the poverty and economic insecurity of mother-only families is to increase employment opportunities for minority men so that they can marry and support their families. The socialist-feminist solution is to increase employment opportunities for poor minority women as well, and in doing so to provide them with the ability to choose whether they will marry or live independently (Sarvasy and Van Allen, 1984).

Finally, conservative analysts such as Gilder (1981) and Murray (1984) offer a somewhat different interpretation of the recent trend in marital disruption and nonmarriage. They agree with liberal-feminists that the growth in mother-only families is related to the increase in women's earnings and income. But they disagree strongly with the claim that women's economic independence is a sign of social progress. Gilder sees the traditional two-parent family as the primary civilizing influence on men, and therefore he views women's employment and the subsequent decline in the nuclear family as disasters for society. Murray is equally pessimistic, although he blames the welfare system instead of women's employment for both the increase in mother-only families and joblessness among young black men. According to Murray, mother-only families have grown because it makes more "economic sense" for a young couple to establish separate households and live on welfare than to marry and support their family by working. Both authors blame women's economic independence for the increases in marital disruption and for increases in male irresponsibility toward family and children, and both view a return to the traditional two-parent family form as the best solution to poverty.

While appealing to conservatives, Murray's argument is inconsistent with empirical research on the relationship between rising welfare benefits and increases in divorce and nonmarital births. Using information from the best studies on the topic, Garfinkel and McLanahan (1986) estimate that the increase in welfare benefits accounted for 9% to 14% of the overall growth in mother-only families between 1960 and 1975, and for possibly 30% of the growth at the bottom of the income distribution. Gilder's assessment of women's employment as the key mechanism behind the increase in mother-only families is more scientifically accurate than Murray's, but his characterization of nonmarried men as "uncivilized" is highly ideological and his values regarding traditional gender roles are out of line with those of mainstream society.

How Should We Deal with the Poverty and Income Insecurity of Single Mothers?

In our earlier discussion of poverty and income instability we pointed to three distinct sources of income available to mother-only families: mother's earning, income support paid by noncustodial parents, and government subsidies. Changes in economic well-being can be achieved by changing any one of these sources, and not surprisingly, the current policy debate over how to aid mother-only families involves all three. Policies aimed at increasing women's earnings include affirmative ac-

tion and job integration, equal pay for equal work, and comparable worth. Affirmative action and job integration are designed to redistribute jobs between men and women and between whites and blacks, and in particular, to increase the numbers of women and of blacks of both sexes in higher-paying jobs. Comparable worth is designed to increase wages and earnings in jobs held primarily by women, and pay equity is oriented toward equalizing wages of men and women in similar jobs. Child support policies include proposals to increase the proportion of single mothers with awards, to standardize the amount of the award, to improve collections, and to guarantee a minimum child support benefit. Policies that increase government benefits to single mothers include child care subsidies and certain types of work-welfare programs. Although all of these proposals are designed to reduce the economic vulnerability of women in general, they are especially important for improving the status of single mothers.[19]

Programs designed to increase women's earnings and to increase the child support paid by nonresidential fathers are generally viewed as "private" solutions to the problem of income insecurity. Such solutions are not financed directly by the state and their primary goal is to redistribute income and economic opportunities between men and women, as opposed to across classes. These distinctions are not absolute. For example, the government is responsible for enforcing affirmative action and child support payments, and it may become involved in financing specific elements of different programs, such as guaranteeing a minimum child support benefit and implementing comparable worth in the public sector. Moreover, depending upon how private employers finance pay equity proposals, the latter may have redistributive consequences across households. Nevertheless, as compared with proposals that increase public benefits directly, this set of policies is relatively private and aimed at reducing gender inequality. (See Starr, 1988, for a more complete discussion of the public-private distinction.)

The proposals outlined above have been criticized from both the political left and right. Conservatives object to pay equity and child support on grounds that they promote women's economic independence and thereby threaten the traditional two-parent family (Gilder, 1981).

Socialists and some liberals argue, on the other hand, that such policies do not go far enough in reducing class and racial inequities and in changing the gender division of labor. With respect to employment opportunity proposals, Brenner (1987) argues that comparable worth does not help minority women, whose main problems are lack of education and low job skills. Moreover, she notes that comparable worth, as currently proposed is conservative because it does not challenge the use of market criteria for job evaluation. Several socialist-feminists point out that unless comparable worth is accompanied by enforcement of affirmative action policies, minority women will not necessarily benefit from a new wage structure (Malvaux, 1985; Sarvasy and Van Allen, 1984).[20]

With respect to child support, critics have complained that increasing child support payments may simply serve to redistribute income from poor families to the rich. They argue that collecting child support is an attempt by the state to reduce welfare costs and will have no net benefits for the economic well-being of poor single mothers on welfare (Glass, 1987). Glass's argument assumes that the income collected from nonresidential fathers will be used to save welfare dollars instead of increasing the total benefits of single mothers, but this remains to be seen. Current policy allows welfare mothers to disregard the first $50 per month of child support in calculating their welfare benefit.

Several feminists also criticize proponents of child support reform for trying to privatize the costs of child care rather than increasing the state's role in reproducing the labor force (Sarvasy and Van Allen, 1984). Other critics note that child support reform ignores the problems of poor minority men and will simply push more of them and their new families into poverty (Brenner, 1987; Brown, 1980; Malvaux, 1985). These analysts focus almost exclusively on the effect of child support at the bottom end of the income distribution and ignore the impact on single mothers who are not dependent on welfare.

Finally, some feminists object to child support on the grounds that it reinforces women's traditional dependence on men and increases fathers' control over children against mothers' wishes (Brush, 1988; Sarvasy and Van Allen, 1984). If required to pay support, nonresidential fathers will undoubtedly demand more time with and more control over their children. Hence, while child support redistributes income from fathers to mothers, parental power may go in the opposite direction.[21]

A second set of proposals for increasing the economic well-being of mother-only families can be characterized as "public" solutions, inasmuch as they are designed to shift a larger share of the cost of raising children onto government, which, in turn, pays for such programs through general revenues. Since higher-income families pay a greater share of the cost of public programs, the programs have the effect of redistributing economic resources across classes. Such programs include federally subsidized child care and certain types of work-welfare programs, such as education and training, employment placement, and wage subsidies. (See Gueron, 1986, for a description of work-welfare programs.)[22]

As was the case for "private solutions," public programs also have their critics. Not surprisingly, conservatives object to socializing child care for two reasons. First, it is expensive, and second, it is viewed as encouraging employment among wives and mothers, which, as noted above, is believed to undermine the traditional two-parent family. Gilder argues that it is unfair to tax families in which the wife is a full-time homemaker to pay for the child care costs of families in which the wife works outside the home. This argument ignores the fact that families with employed wives are currently subsidizing the social security pensions of families with full-time homemakers.

Critics from the left also have concerns about the consequences of greater public involvement in providing economic support to single mothers. A primary objection of many socialist-feminists is that public programs will merely shift women's economic dependency from husbands and fathers to the state, creating what they term a "state patriarchy" (Barrett, 1983; Brown, 1980; Eisenstein, 1983; McIntosh, 1978; Wilson, 1977). The current debate over the role of the state vis-à-vis single mothers is reminiscent of an earlier exchange involving the welfare state and the poor, which took place in the late sixties and early seventies. At that time, critics argued that the primary function of the capitalist state was one of social control and that welfare programs were designed to regulate labor rather than alleviate economic insecurity (Piven and Cloward, 1971). Today, many socialist-feminists make a similar argument with respect to the intentions and consequences of government. Not all agree, however. In her discussion of family violence, Gordon (1986) shows how the state can serve as a resource for single mothers as well as a mechanism of control. Similarly, Piven states that "the main opportunities for women to exercise power today inhere precisely in their 'dependent' relationships with the state" (1985: 266).[23]

SUMMARY AND CONCLUSIONS

The mother-only family has over the past three decades emerged as a major family form. This change has implications not only for the women who are at risk of becoming single mothers, but also for the men who are at risk of becoming non-residential fathers and whose sons and daughters may grow up in a mother-only family.

At present, we know a good deal about the economic aspects of these families. We know that single mothers have higher poverty rates than other families and that a substantial portion of their poverty is a consequence of marital disruption. We know that single mothers bear most of the economic costs of their children, even though their earning capacity is limited by lack of work experience, sex discrimination in the labor market, and the high cost of child care. We know that, on average, children who grow up in mother-only families are less likely to complete high school and more likely to be poor as adults than children who grow up with both natural parents. Moreover, we know that a significant part of children's lower attainment is due to economic deprivation in the family of origin.

Answers to other important questions are less clear. For example, we need to know more about parenting practices and parent-child relationships in mother-only and two-parent families—whether they differ and whether differences are related to child outcomes. Do single mothers have different values and expectations for their children and are they less able to control adolescent offspring than married mothers? Does contact with the non-custodial parent and/or the presence of a grand-mother in the household reduce the likelihood of dropping out of school? Does social support from friends and relatives or being part of a well-integrated and economically stable community mitigate the negative outcomes associated with single motherhood? There are sound theoretical

reasons for believing that each of these factors affects offspring's behavior, but the empirical evidence is inconclusive.

Most important, we need to know whether differences in parenting styles and parent-child relations are a consequence of marital disruption (or nonmarriage) or whether they reflect preexisting conditions among couples who divorce or never marry in the first place. A plausible explanation for why children from mother-only families do less well as adults than children from two-parent families is that "troubled couples" are more likely to break up and to have "troubled children" than "happy couples"; if this is true, children from such unions would have done poorly regardless of whether their parents stayed married or lived apart. A major challenge to researchers during the next decade is to try and sort out how much of the lower attainment of children is due to family disruption and nonmarriage and how much is due to selectivity into the single-mother status.

Is single motherhood a problem in and of itself, or do single mothers merely have more problems than married parents do? This question has stimulated considerable debate during the past decade. The answer, however, is not simple, and depends on whose point of view is taken and what part of the income distribution is considered. On the one hand, the mother-only family is more economically viable and more socially acceptable in the 1980s than it was in the 1950s, which represents an increase in women's opportunities, both economically and socially. From many women's point of view, single motherhood is not a problem in and of itself. On the other hand, if Wilson is correct, many single mothers, and especially young black mothers, no longer have the option to marry because the fathers of their children are unemployed and cannot support, or contribute to the support of, their families. For these women, most of whom depend on welfare and live below the poverty line, single motherhood is an indicator of a problem, although it is not *the* problem.

Single motherhood may also *be* a problem. The evidence on the intergenerational consequences of family disruption overwhelmingly suggests that children who grow up with both parents are better off as adults than children who live apart from one parent. The critical question is whether these children would have done better had their parents stayed together. If the answer is yes, then the increase in mother-only families is a problem from the point of view of children and from the point of view of society, which has an interest in the well-being of all children. If the answer is no, or if the children in these families would have been worse off, the increase in single motherhood is a neutral phenomenon, or a sign of progress for both women and children. As noted above, the answer to this question is unknown, and therefore the social costs and benefits of single motherhood cannot be determined.

Finally, what should be done to reduce poverty and income insecurity in mother-only families? Should we move in the direction of private solutions, such as increased child support and employment opportunities? Or should the state provide support directly, in the form of children's allowances, subsidized child care, or a minimum child support benefit? It would appear that we need a mix of public and private programs. From the point of view of political feasibility, it is unreasonable to expect taxpayers to increase public subsidies for single mothers unless parents themselves are contributing their fair share. Thus, the implementation of a publicly guaranteed child support minimum benefit is likely to be accompanied by a strengthening of the private child support system. Similarly, support for subsidized child care is most likely to be linked to programs that promote mothers' employment, especially mothers currently on welfare.

Will enforcing child support obligations reinforce women's traditional dependence on men and/or push low-income minority fathers (and their new families) into poverty? Will increasing public sector benefits create new dependencies on the state? The best way to protect poor fathers from economic hardship is to make child support obligations a percentage of current income. Then if the father is poor or if he is unemployed, his obligation will also be low. Another way is to designate a minimum income that is not subject to the child support tax. Both solutions are preferable to exempting all fathers from child support on the grounds that it may impoverish a few.

The best way to minimize single mothers' dependency is to (*a*) redistribute their sources of support across a broader array of institutions, including the family, the market, and the state; and (*b*) extend support to a wider population. Dependency itself is not the problem, but rather the loss of power and the feeling of helplessness that often accompanies it. Distributing support

across multiple institutions minimizes the degree of dependence on any one person or organization. It is one thing to depend on the ex-spouse or the state for 90% of one's income; it is another to be 20% dependent on each of these institutions and to be 60% dependent on a paid job. Extending support to a broader population would mean making programs such as child support, child care, and pay equity available to all women (as opposed to those who are poor). Universal programs have the virtue of building a strong political constituency, which in turn makes them less vulnerable to cutbacks and discretionary practices. Public education is a case in point. Nearly all families are dependent on the state for primary and secondary education, and yet this form of dependency is not viewed as oppressive. Rather, state-supported schools are seen as a public entitlement.

Ultimately, a full solution to the problems faced by mother-only families will necessitate a reorganization of the sexual division of labor, which at present places a disproportionate share of child care responsibilities on women and in doing so restricts their earning capacity and economic independence. In the meantime, achieving the goal of economic security for single mothers will require the coming together of different interest groups in support of multiple policies aimed at solving the problems of both middle-class and poor mother-only families.

NOTES

This research was supported in part by the National Institute of Child Health and Human Development, Grant HD 19375, and by the Russell Sage Foundation. Any opinions expressed are solely those of the authors. They are grateful to Ann Orloff, Irwin Garfinkel, Lisa Brush, Larry Steinberg, Duane Alwin, Kristen Moore, and several anonymous reviewers for their helpful comments on an earlier draft and to Elizabeth Evanson at the Institute for Research on Poverty, University of Wisconsin–Madison, for editorial assistance.

1. In this paper, we use the term "mother-only family" to refer to families headed by nonmarried mothers with a least one child under age 18 living in the household. This includes families headed by formerly married mothers who are currently widowed, separated, or divorced as well as families headed by never-married mothers. We also use the term "single mother" to refer to all nonmarried mothers with dependent children, except when significant differences with regard to marital status

are discussed. The latter violates the demographers' convention of reserving "single" for never-married persons. However, the broader usage is now common in the literature on family structure and provides a convenient way of talking about the aggregate category of nonmarried mothers.

2. For people who adhered to the former perspective, the traditional two-parent family is the only valid family form; other forms are considered to be dysfunctional and aberrant.

3. The present review focuses primarily on mother-only families as opposed to all one-parent families. Although interest in father-only families has been growing, the number of such families is still small—less than 10% of all one-parent families. Moreover, father-only families are a highly select group for whom most of our information is based on small convenience samples. For these reasons we decided to focus on mother-only families. Readers interested in father-only families are referred to Grief (1985a, 1985b), Pichitino (1983), Risman (1986), and Smith and Smith (1981).

4. Poverty rates are based on the official government definition of poverty. The rates presented in Figure 1 take into account the assistance provided by the major government income support programs, such as AFDC, Social Security, and Disability Insurance. They do not include the value of in-kind benefits such as food stamps and Medicaid. If the latter were included, poverty rates would be lower, but the overall pattern would remain the same.

5. This differs considerably by race. Bane (1986) has shown that about 75% of poor white single mothers become poor at the time of becoming single parents, whereas only about 33% of poor black single mothers are cases of "new poverty."

6. For a discussion of the debate over the relative income loss of divorced men and women, see Hoffman and Duncan (1988).

7. There are, however, some indications that the wage gap has decreased since 1980 for women aged 25 to 34 (Bianchi and Spain, 1986).

8. Kamerman and Kahn (1978, 1988) note that the United States is virtually unique in relying so heavily upon welfare to aid mother-only families. We also provide less child care and health care than most other industrialized countries.

9. In the empirical literature, social support is defined as material assistance, advice, and emotional nurturance (Cobb, 1976; Weiss, 1969). It is measured variously as contact with friends and relatives, exchange of services and emotional support among friends and relatives, the potential for support, and satisfaction with support (House and Kahn, 1985; House, Umberson, and Landis, 1988; Menaghan, 1983).

10. Liberal attitudes toward sex roles may also reduce the likelihood of early parenthood by promoting use of effective contraception.

11. The level of father contact is very low in this survey, which may account for the lack of a positive association between father contact and child well-being.

12. With respect to the general issue of control, Morgan, Alwin, and Griffin (1979) found that white single mothers were more likely to value conformity in their children, as opposed to self-direction. Alwin (1988) has replicated these results in a study based on the Detroit Area Survey; he interprets the emphasis on conformity as indicating that single mothers experience less control over their children and therefore value it more highly.

13. Herzog and Sudia (1973) briefly summarize this perspective.

14. Other reviews of the literature on the intergenerational consequences of divorce include Blechman (1982), Cashion (1982), Chase-Lansdale and Hetherington (1988), Demo and Acock (1988), Emery (1982), Goetting (1981), Hetherington (1980), Hetherington and Camara (1988), Wallerstein and Kelly (1979), and Zaslow (1987).

15. Much of the literature on cognitive development and other outcomes among younger children either focused on the effects of parental divorce on children or combined all mother-only families into a single category. Consequently, there was very little treatment of never-married, widowed, or separated mothers or discussion of how the children of these women might differ from those in divorced families. Furthermore, researchers tended to include stepfamilies in comparison groups of nondivorced families. Several reviews (Chase-Lansdale and Hetherington, 1989; Hetherington and Camara, 1988; Hetherington et al., 1983; Zaslow, 1987) have criticized this tendency, citing evidence of differences in family processes between stepfamilies and traditional two-parent families.

16. The major longitudinal data sets include the Panel Study of Income Dynamics (PSID), the National Longitudinal Survey Youth Cohort (NLSY), and the High School and Beyond survey (HSB).

17. Not all feminists adhere to this line of argument, which can be broadly characterized as a liberal-feminist perspective. For many socialist-feminists, the existence and growth of mother-only families is a more ambiguous sign. Sarvasy and Van Allen (1984), for example, note that unmarried mothers, especially those who were poor before becoming mothers, are not necessarily more autonomous than married women because they remain constrained by their role as unpaid domestic laborers and by sexual (and racial) stratification in the labor market, which assigns to them underpaid jobs. Only when these constraints are removed and the state takes a much larger responsibility for caretaking can single mothers be truly independent. For middle-class women, more likely to be able to earn a living wage and to be able to afford to pass on some of their domestic labor to poorer women—maids and day-care workers—heading a family alone may well be a

move toward independence. These feminist theorists criticize liberal-feminists for failing to note class and racial differences among single mothers and for idealizing these women's apparent "independence." Other feminists argue that even middle-class women have lost rather than gained from their new independence. Hewlett (1986), for example, argues that, in the absence of social policies and institutions that support women's dual roles as child care providers and breadwinners, the struggle for independence and equality has been a disaster for a majority of women.

18. These writers often ignore the potential costs to children of women's growing independence. Stacey (1986) notes in her review of "pro-family feminism" that the notion of a conflict of interest between mothers and children is a difficult issue for most feminists. And yet the potential for such a conflict is consistent with the general movement toward treating women as individuals distinct from their parental and spousal roles. See Degler (1980), Gordon (1986), Rossi (1977), and Thorne (1982), for additional discussions of the possible conflict between mothers and children.

19. For a discussion of affirmative action and job integration policies, see Bergmann (1986) and O'Farrell and Harlan (1984). For a discussion of comparable worth, see Aldrich and Buchele (1986), Hartmann (1985), and Remick (1984). For a discussion of child support, see Garfinkel and McLanahan (1986). For a discussion of child care, see Zigler and Gordon (1982).

20. For a response to socialist-feminist criticisms of comparable worth, see Hartmann (1985).

21. Sarvasy and Van Allen (1984) note that child support policies that force women to identify fathers do not promote women's autonomy and can result in increasing men's access not only to children but to women, many of whom may then be subject to abuse from their former partners.

22. Recent proposals for welfare reform contain numerous elements that are designed to increase the earnings of single mothers and to reduce their dependence on welfare. Depending on how the new work-welfare programs are implemented, they may either increase or reduce the overall public subsidy to poor single mothers. If work-welfare programs are simply used to replace welfare with work, as many critics fear, then the public subsidy will decline and single mothers will be worse off. If, however, government money is used to educate, train, and provide jobs to poor single mothers, and if welfare savings are used to finance child care, medical care, and a guaranteed child support benefit, then the public subsidy will increase and single mothers will be better off. For a discussion of work-welfare programs see *Focus*, newsletter of the Institute for Research on Poverty, "Special Issue on Welfare Reform," 11:2 (Spring, 1988).

23. Piven's argument represents a change in her earlier position; she was a leading proponent of the "welfare as social control" argument (see Piven and Cloward, 1971).

REFERENCES

Abrahamse, Allen F., Peter A. Morrison, and Linda J. Waite. 1987. "Single teenage mothers: Spotting susceptible adolescents in advance." Paper presented at the annual meetings of the Population Association of America, Chicago.

Aldrich, Mark, and Robert Buchele. 1986. Economics of Comparable Worth. Cambridge, MA: Ballinger.

Alwin, Duane F. 1988. Personal communication.

Alwin, Duane F., Philip E. Converse, and Steven S. Martin. 1985. "Living arrangements and social integration." Journal of Marriage and the Family 47: 319-334.

Antel, John J. 1988. "The inter-generational transfer of welfare dependency." Unpublished manuscript, University of Houston.

Astone, Nan. 1989. "The effect of family structure on school completion." Paper presented at the annual meeting of the Population Association of America, Baltimore (March).

Bane, Mary Jo. 1986. "Household composition and poverty." Pp. 109-231 in Sheldon H. Danziger and Daniel H. Weinberg (eds.), Fighting Poverty: What Works and What Doesn't. Cambridge, MA: Harvard University Press.

Barrett, Nancy B. 1983. "The welfare system as state paternalism." Paper presented at the Conference on Women and Structural Transformation, Institute for Research on Women, Rutgers University (November).

Becker, Gary S. 1981. A Treatise on the Family. Cambridge, MA: Harvard University Press.

Belle, Deborah. 1982. "Social ties and social support." Pp. 133-144 in Deborah Belle (ed.), Lives in Stress, Women and Depression. Beverly Hills, CA: Sage Publications.

Bergmann, Barbara. 1986. The Economic Emergence of Women. New York: Basic Books.

Bianchi, Suzanne M., and Daphne Spain. 1986. American Women in Transition. New York: Russell Sage Foundation.

Blau, Francine D. 1984. "Occupational segregation and labor market discrimination." Pp. 117-143 in Barbara F. Reskin (ed.), Sex Segregation in the Workplace: Trends, Explanations, Remedies. Washington, DC: National Academy Press.

Blechman, Elaine A. 1982. "Are children with one parent at psychological risk? A methodological review." Journal of Marriage and the Family 44: 179-195.

Block, Jeanne H., Jack Block, and Per F. Gjerde. 1986. "The personality of children prior to divorce: A prospective study." Child Development 57: 827-840.

Brenner, Joanna. 1987. "Feminist political discourses: Radical versus liberal approaches to the feminization of poverty and comparable worth." Gender and Society 1: 447–465.

Brown, Carol. 1980. "Mothers, fathers and children: From private to public patriarchy." Pp. 239–267 in Lydia Sargent (ed.), Women and Revolution. Boston: Southwood Press.

Brush, Lisa D. 1988. "Single mothers and 'dependency': Deconstructing a social problem." Unpublished manuscript, Department of Sociology, University of Wisconsin–Madison.

Bumpass, Larry L. 1984. "Children and marital disruption: A replication and update." Demography 21: 71–82.

Cain, Glen G. 1986. "The economic analysis of labor market discrimination: A survey." Pp. 693–785 in O. Ashenfelter and R. Layard (eds.), Handbook of Labor Economics (Vol. 1). Amsterdam: Elsevier.

Cashion, Barbara G. 1982. "Female-headed families: Effects on children and clinical implications." Journal of Marital and Family Therapy 8: 77–85.

Cassetty, Judith (ed.). 1983. The Parental Child Support Obligation: Research, Practice, and Social Policy. Lexington, MA: Lexington Books.

Chase-Lansdale, Lindsay, and E. Mavis Hetherington. 1989. "The impact of divorce on life-span development: Short and long-term effects." In D. Featherman and R. Lerner (eds.), Life Span Development and Behavior (Vol. 10).

Chess, Stella, Alexander Thomas, Mary Mittelman, Sam Korn, and Jacob Cohen. 1984. "Early parental attitudes, divorce and separation, and young adult outcome: Findings of a longitudinal study." Pp. 281–289 in Stella Chess and Alexander Thomas (eds.), Annual Progress in Child Psychiatry and Child Development. New York: Brunner/Mazel.

Cobb, Syndney. 1976. "Social support as a moderator of life stress." Psychosomatic Medicine 38 (September/October): 300–314.

Colletta, Nancy D. 1979. "Support systems after divorce: Incidence and impact." Journal of Marriage and the Family 41: 837–846.

Corcoran, Mary, and Greg J. Duncan. 1979. "Work history, labor force attachment and earnings differences between the races and sexes." Journal of Human Resources 14 (Winter): 3–20.

Corcoran, Mary, R. Gordon, D. Laren, and G. Solon. 1987. "Intergenerational transmission of education, income and earnings." Unpublished manuscript, Institute of Public Policy Studies, University of Michigan, Ann Arbor.

David, Martin H., and Thomas S. Flory. 1988. "Change in marital status and short-term income dynamics." Unpublished manuscript, Institute for Research on Poverty, University of Wisconsin–Madison.

Degler, Carl. 1980. At Odds: Women and the Family in America from Revolution to the Present. Cambridge, MA: Oxford University Press.

Demo, David H., and Alan C. Acock. 1988. "The impact of divorce on children." Journal of Marriage and the Family 50: 619–648. [Reprinted in this volume]

Dornbusch, Sanford M., J. Merrill Carlsmith, Steven J. Bushwall, Philip L. Ritter, Herbert Leiderman, Albert H. Hastorf, and Ruth T. Gross. 1985. "Single parents, extended households, and the control of adolescents." Child Development 56: 326–341.

Duncan, Greg J., and Saul D. Hoffman. 1985. "A reconsideration of the economic consequences of marital disruption." Demography 22: 485–498.

Eisenstein, Zillah. 1983. "The state, the patriarchal family, and working mothers." Pp. 298–309 in Irene Diamond (ed.), Families, Politics, and Public Policy. New York: Longman, Green.

Elder, Glen H., Jr. 1974. Children of the Great Depression. Chicago: University of Chicago Press.

Emery, Robert E. 1982. "Interparental conflict and the children of discord and divorce." Psychological Bulletin 92: 310–330.

Furstenberg, Frank F., S. Philip Morgan, and Paul D. Allison. 1986. "Paternal participation and children's well-being after marital disruption." American Sociological Review 52: 695–701.

Furstenberg, Frank F., and Christine W. Nord. 1985. "Parenting apart: Patterns of childrearing after marital disruption." Journal of Marriage and the Family 47: 893–904.

Garfinkel, Irwin, and Sara S. McLanahan. 1986. Single Mothers and Their Children: A New American Dilemma. Washington, DC: Urban Institute Press.

Garfinkel, Irwin, and Donald Oellerich. 1989. "Noncustodial fathers' ability to pay child support." Demography 26: 219–233.

Gilder, George. 1981. Wealth and Poverty. New York: Basic Books.

Glass, Becky L. 1987. "The 1984 child support enforcement amendments: Impetus, implementation and consequences." Unpublished manuscript, Department of Sociology, State University of New York, Geneseo.

Goetting, Ann. 1981. "Divorce outcome research: Issues and perspectives." Journal of Family Issues 2: 350–378.

Gordon, Linda. 1986. "Feminism and social control: The case of child abuse and neglect." Pp. 63–84 In J. Mitchell and A. Oakley (eds.), What is Feminism? New York: Pantheon.

Gottschalk, Peter. 1988. "A proposal to study intergenerational correlation of welfare dependence." Unpublished manuscript, Institute for Research on Poverty, University of Wisconsin–Madison.

Gove, Walter R. 1972. "The relationship between sex roles, marital status, and mental illness." Social Forces 51: 34–44.

Grief, Geoffrey L. 1985a. "Children and housework in the single father family." Family Relations 34: 353–357.

Grief, Geoffrey L. 1985b. "Single fathers rearing children." Journal of Marriage and the Family 47: 185–191.

Gueron, Judith M. 1986. Work Initiatives for Welfare Recipients: Lessons from a Multi-State Experiment. New York: Manpower Demonstration Research Corp.

Guttentag, Marcia, Susan Salassin, and Deborah Belle. 1981. The Mental Health of Women. New York: Academic Press.

Hartmann, Heidi L. 1985. "The political economy of comparable worth." Paper presented at the Conference on Alternative Approaches to Labor Markets, University of Utah, Salt Lake City (October).

Herzog, Elizabeth, and Cecilia E. Sudia. 1973. "Children in fatherless families." Pp. 141–232 in B. Caldwell and H. N. Ricciuti (eds.), Review of Child Development Research (Vol. 3). Chicago: University of Chicago Press.

Hess, Robert D., and Kathleen A. Camara. 1979. "Post-divorce family relationships as mediating factors in the consequences of divorce for children." Journal of Social Issues 35: 79–96.

Hetherington, E. Mavis. 1980. "Divorce, a child's perspective." Pp. 277–291 in S. Chess and A. Thomas (eds.), Annual Progress in Child Psychiatry and Child Development. New York: Brunner/Mazel.

Hetherington, E. Mavis, and Kathleen A. Camara. 1988. "The effects of family dissolution and reconstitution on children." Pp. 420–431 in Norval D. Glenn and Marion T. Coleman (eds.), Family Relations: A Reader. Chicago: Dorsey Press.

Hetherington, E. Mavis, Kathleen A. Camara, and David L. Featherman. 1983. "Achievement and intellectual functioning of children in one-parent households." Pp. 205–284 in Jack Spence (ed.), Achievement and Achievement Motives. San Francisco: W. H. Freeman.

Hetherington, E. Mavis, Martha Cox, and Roger Cox. 1978. "The aftermath of divorce." In J. H. Stevens, Jr., and M. Matthews (eds.), Mother-Child, Father-Child Relations. Washington, DC: National Association for the Education of Young Children.

Hewlett, Sylvia A. 1986. A Lesser Life: The Myth of Women's Liberation in America. New York: William Morrow.

Heyns, Barbara. 1985. "The influence of parental work on children's school achievement." Pp. 229–267 in Sheila B. Kamerman and C. D. Hayes (eds.), Families That Work: Children in a Changing World. Washington, DC: National Academy Press.

Hill, Martha S., Sue Augustyniak, and Michael Ponza. 1987. "Effects of parental divorce on children's attainments: An empirical comparison of five hypotheses." Unpublished manuscript, Survey Research Institute, University of Michigan, Ann Arbor.

Hoffman, Saul D., and Greg J. Duncan. 1988. "What *are* the economic consequences of divorce?" Demography 25: 641–645.

Hogan, Dennis P. 1985. "Structural and normative factors in single parenthood among black adolescents." Unpublished manuscript, Department of Sociology, University of Chicago.

Hogan, Dennis P., and Evelyn M. Kitagawa. 1985. "The impact of social status, family structure and neighborhood on the fertility of black adolescents." American Journal of Sociology 90: 825–855.

House, James S., and Robert L. Kahn. 1985. "Meas-

ures and concepts of social support." Pp. 83–105 in S. Cohen and L. Syme (eds.), Social Support and Health. New York: Academic Press.

House, James S., Debra Umberson, and K. R. Landis. 1988. "Structures and processes of social support." Annual Review of Sociology 14: 293–318.

Kamerman, Sheila, and Alfred Kahn (eds.). 1978. Family Policy: Government and Families in Fourteen Countries. New York: Columbia University Press.

Kamerman, Sheila, and Alfred Kahn. 1988. Mothers Alone: Strategies for a Time of Change. Dover, MA: Auburn House.

Kellam, Sheppard G., Margaret E. Ensminger, and R. Jay Turner. 1977. "Family structure and the mental health of children." Archives of General Psychiatry 34: 1012–1022.

Kessler, Ron C., and James McRae, Jr. 1981. "Trends in sex and psychological distress." American Sociological Review 47: 216–227.

Krein, Sheila F., and Andrea H. Beller. 1988. "Educational attainment of children from single-parent families: Differences by exposure, gender and race." Demography 25: 221–224.

Leslie, Leigh A., and Katherine Grady. 1985. "Changes in mothers' social networks and social support following divorce." Journal of Marriage and the Family 47: 663–673.

Malvaux, Julianne. 1985. "The economic interests of black and white women: Are they similar? Review of Black Political Economy 14: 5–27.

Matsueda, Ross L., and Karen Heimer. 1987. "Race, family structure and delinquency: A test of differential association and social control theories." American Sociological Review 52: 826–840.

McIntosh, Mary. 1978. "The state and the oppression of women." Pp. 254–289 in Annette Kuhn and Anne Marie Wolpe (eds.), Feminism and Materialism. London: Routledge and Kegan Paul.

McLanahan, Sara S. 1983. "Family structure and stress: A longitudinal comparison of two-parent and female-headed families." Journal of Marriage and the Family 45: 347–357.

McLanahan, Sara S. 1985. "The reproduction of poverty." American Journal of Sociology 90: 873–901.

McLanahan, Sara S. 1988. "Family structure and dependency: Early transitions to female household headship." Demography 25: 1–16.

McLanahan, Sara S., and Julia Adams. 1987. "Parenthood and psychological well-being." Pp. 237–257 in R. Turner and J. Short (eds.), Annual Review of Sociology (Vol. 13). Palo Alto, CA: Annual Reviews, Inc.

McLanahan, Sara S., and Julia Adams. 1989. "The effects of children on adults' psychological well-being: 1957–1976." Social Forces 68: 79–91.

McLanahan, Sara S., Nan M. Astone, and Nadine Marks. 1988. "The role of mother-only families in reproducing poverty." Paper presented to the Conference on Poverty and Children, Lawrence, Kansas (20–22 June).

McLanahan, Sara S., and Larry Bumpass. 1988. "Intergenerational consequences of family disruption."

American Journal of Sociology 94: 130–152.

McLanahan, Sara S., and Irwin Garfinkel. 1989. "Single mothers, the underclass and social policy." Annals of the American Academy of Political and Social Science 501: 92–104.

McLanahan, Sara S., and Jennifer L. Glass. 1985. "A note on the trend in sex differences in psychological distress." Journal of Health and Social Behavior 26: 328–336.

McLanahan, Sara S., Nancy Wedemeyer, and Tina Adelberg. 1981. "Network structure, social support and psychological well-being in the single-parent family." Journal of Marriage and the Family 43: 601–612.

Menaghan, Elizabeth G. 1983. "Individual coping efforts: Moderators of the relationship between life stress and mental health outcomes." Pp. 157–191 in Howard Kaplan (ed.), Psychosocial Stress. New York: Academic Press.

Michael, Robert T., and Nancy B. Tuma. 1985. "Entry into marriage and parenthood by young men and women: The influence of family background." Demography 22: 515–544.

Milardo, Robert M. 1987. "Changes in social networks of women and men following divorce: A review." Journal of Family Issues 8: 78–96.

Morgan, William R., Duane F. Alwin, and Larry J. Griffin. 1979. "Social origins, parental values and the transmission of inequality." American Journal of Sociology 85: 156–166.

Mott, Frank L., and R. Jean Haurin. 1987. "The interrelatedness of age at first intercourse, early childbearing, alcohol and drug use among young American women." Paper presented at the annual meetings of the Population Association of America, Chicago.

Moynihan, Daniel P. 1965. The Negro Family: The Case for National Action. Washington, DC: Office of Policy Planning and Research, U.S. Department of Labor.

Murray, Charles. 1984. Losing Ground: American Social Policy, 1950–1980. New York: Basic Books.

O'Farrell, Brigid, and Sharon L. Harlan. 1984. "Job integration strategies: Today's programs and tomorrow's needs." Pp. 267–291 in Barbara Reskin (ed.), Sex Segregation in the Workplace: Trends, Explanations, Remedies. Washington, DC: National Academy Press.

Peterson, James L., and Nicholas Zill. 1986. "Marital disruption, parent-child relationships, and behavior problems in children." Journal of Marriage and the Family 48: 295–307.

Pichitino, John P. 1983. "Profile of the single father: A thematic integration of the literature." Personnel and Guidance Journal 61: 295–299.

Piven, Frances F. 1985. "Women and the state: Ideology, power, and the welfare state." Pp. 265–287 in A. S. Rossi (ed.), Gender and the Life Course. New York: Aldine.

Piven, Frances F., and Richard A. Cloward. 1971. Regulating the Poor: The Functions of Public Welfare. New York: Pantheon.

Rainwater, Lee, and William Yancy. 1967. "The Moy-

nihan Report and the Politics of Controversy. Cambridge, MA: M.I.T. Press.

Raschke, Helen J., and Vernon J. Raschke. 1979. "Family conflict and children's self-concepts: A comparison of intact and single-parent families." Journal of Marriage and the Family 41: 367–374.

Remick, Helen. 1984. Comparable Worth and Wage Discrimination. Philadelphia: Temple University Press.

Reskin, Barbara (ed.). 1984. Sex Segregation in the Workplace: Trends, Explanations, Remedies. Washington, DC: National Academy Press.

Reskin, Barbara, and Heidi I. Hartmann. 1986. Women's Work, Men's Work. Washington, DC: National Academy Press.

Risman, Barbara J. 1986. "Can men 'mother'? Life as a single father." Family Relations 35: 95–102.

Rossi, Alice S. 1977. "A biosocial perspective on parenting." Daedalus 106: 1–32.

Rubin, Lillian B. 1976. Worlds of Pain: Life in the Working-Class Family. New York: Basic Books.

Rutter, Michael. 1980. "Maternal deprivation, 1972–1978: New findings, new concepts, new approaches." Pp. 44–81 in Stella Chess and Alexander Thomas (eds.), Annual Progress in Child Psychiatry and Child Development. New York: Brunner/Mazel.

Sampson, Robert J. 1987. "Urban black violence: The effect of male joblessness and family disruption." American Journal of Sociology 93: 348–382.

Sandefur, Gary D., Sara S. McLanahan, and Roger A. Wojtkiewicz. 1989. "Race, family structure, and high school graduation." Paper presented at the annual meeting of the Population Association of America, Baltimore (March).

Sarvasy, Wendy, and Judith Van Allen. 1984. "Fighting the feminization of poverty: Socialist-feminist analysis and strategy." Review of Radical Political Economics 16 (4): 89–110.

Shaw, Lois B. 1982. "High school completion for young women: Effects of low income and living with a single parent." Journal of Family Issues 3: 147–163.

Shinn, Marybeth. 1978. "Father absence and children's cognitive development." Psychological Bulletin 85: 295–324.

Smith, Richard M., and Craig W. Smith., 1981. "Child rearing and single-parent fathers." Family Relations 30: 411–417.

Stacey, Judith. 1986. "Are feminists afraid to leave home? The challenge of conservative pro-family feminism." Pp. 208–237 in J. Mitchell and A. Oakley (eds.), What is Feminism? New York: Pantheon.

Stack, Carol. 1974. All Our Kin: Strategies for Survival in a Black Community. New York: Harper and Row.

Starr, Paul. 1988. "The meaning of privatization." Unpublished manuscript, Department of Sociology, Princeton University.

Steinberg, Laurence. 1987. "Single parent, stepparents, and the susceptibility of adolescents to antisocial peer pressure." Child Development 58: 269–275.

Thorne, Barrie. 1982. "Feminist rethinking of the family: An overview." Pp. 1–24 in B. Thorne and M. Yalom (eds.), Rethinking the Family. New York: Longman.

Thornton, Arland, Duane Alwin, and Donald Camburn. 1983. "Causes and consequences of sex-role attitudes and attitude change." American Sociological Review 48: 211–227.

Thornton, Arland, and Donald Camburn. 1983. "The influence of the family on premarital sexual attitudes and behavior." Unpublished manuscript, Institute for Survey Research, University of Michigan, Ann Arbor.

Thornton, Arland, and Donald Camburn. 1987. "The influence of the family on premarital sexual attitudes and behavior." Demography 24: 323–340.

Tietjen, Anne Marie. 1985. "The social networks and social support of married and single mothers in Sweden." Journal of Marriage and the Family 47: 489–496.

U.S. Bureau of the Census. 1960. Marital Status and Family Status: March 1960. Current Population Reports, Series P-20, No. 105. Washington, DC: Government Printing Office.

U.S. Bureau of the Census. 1961. Household and Family Characteristics: March 1960. Current Population Reports, Series P-20, No. 106. Washington, DC: Government Printing Office.

U.S. Bureau of the Census. 1987. Money Income and Poverty Status of Families and Persons in the United States: 1986 (Advance Data from the 1987 Current Population Survey). Current Population Reports, Series P-60, No. 157. Washington, DC: Government Printing Office.

U.S. Bureau of the Census. 1988. Household and Family Characteristics, 1987. Current Population Reports, Series P-20, No. 423. Washington, DC: Government Printing Office.

Waite, Linda J., and Frances K. Goldscheider. 1986. "Nonfamily living and the erosion of traditional family orientations among young adults." American Sociological Review 51: 541–554.

Wallerstein, Judith S. 1986. "Children of divorce: Preliminary report of a ten-year follow-up of older children and adolescents." Pp. 430–477 in S. Chess and A. Thomas (eds.), Annual Progress in Child Psychiatry and Child Development. New York: Brunner/Mazel.

Wallerstein, Judith S., and Joan B. Kelly. 1979. Surviving the Breakup: How Children and Parents Cope with Divorce. New York: Basic Books.

Weiss, Robert. 1969. "The fund of sociability." Trans-Action 6: 36–43.

Weiss, Robert, 1979. "Growing up a little faster: The experience of growing up in a single-parent household." Journal of Social Issues 35: 97–111.

Weitzman, Lenore J. 1985. The Divorce Revolution. New York: Free Press.

White, Lynn K., David B. Brinkerhoff, and Alan Booth. 1985. "The effect of marital disruption on child's attachment to parents." Journal of Family Issues 6: 5–22.

Wilson, Elizabeth. 1977. Women and the Welfare State. London: Tavistock.

Wilson, William Julius. 1987. The Truly Disadvantaged: The Inner City, the Underclass, and Public Policy. Chicago: University of Chicago Press.

Zaslow, Martha J. 1987. "Sex differences in children's response to parental divorce." Paper presented to the Symposium on Sex Differences in Children's Response to Psychosocial Stress, National Research Council, Woods Hole, MA (September).

Zigler, Edward F., and Edmund Gordon (eds.). 1982. Day Care: Scientific and Social Policy Studies. Boston, MA: Auburn House.

Patricia Voydanoff   *University of Dayton*

Economic Distress and Family Relations:

A Review of the Eighties

Research reviewed in this essay documents a complex process in which macroeconomic and family demographic factors are associated with economic distress among individuals and families. Four components of economic distress—employment instability, employment uncertainty, economic deprivation, and economic strain—are shown to be negatively related to individual adjustment and family relations. Several individual and family coping resources and behaviors mediate relationships between economic distress and individual adjustment and family relations. The review closes with suggestions for future research and theory development.

Economic distress is a new addition to topics covered in *Journal of Marriage and Family* decade reviews. As presently formulated, the topic has not been included in recent compehensive review handbooks, an omission that seems particularly striking when one considers the basic relationship between the econony and the structure and quality of family life.

The development of separate research traditions dealing with aspects of economic distress and family life may account for its not being included as a topic for review. Research on men's unemployment and family life began during the Depression of the 1930s and has continued sporadically since that time, mainly during recessionary periods. However, research studies on

structural inequality and families in poverty have generally developed independently of studies of unemployment and of each other. This may be due in part to the qualitative methods and micro level of analysis used in early studies of unemployment and poverty as contrasted with the quantitative structural approach usually taken in studies of inequality. In addition, studies of unemployment tend to examine effects on the families of working- and middle-class men with previously stable work histories, while research on family life among the poor looks at those who are not in the labor force or who experience chronic unemployment or unstable work histories.

However, during the late 1980s various aspects of economic distress have become recognized as important interrelated consequences of the restructuring of the American economy. This article reviews and assesses empirical research on relationships between several components of economic distress and family life. The review is comprehensive in that it brings together research from previously disparate traditions. This makes it necessary, however, to be selective within traditions. The review focuses on U.S. research and emphasizes studies that consolidate previous work or break new ground.

The review begins with a discussion of family responsibility for obtaining economic resources and major societal trends affecting the ability of families to secure these resources. The following section presents four dimensions of economic distress through which structural factors affect the economic well-being of families. The next two sections address relationships among economic distress, adjustment and marital relations, and

Center for the Study of Family Development, University of Dayton, OH 45469-1445.

strategies for coping with economic distress. This is followed by an examination of economic distress and children's health and adjustment. The article concludes with a discussion of research issues for the next decade.

FAMILIES AS ECONOMIC UNITS

Providing the basic means of subsistence to its members is one of the major functions of the family. In addition, a family's standard of living is dependent on the economic activities of its members. Family economic well-being is tied to (a) the number of earners and amount of income brought into the family, (b) unpaid contributions to the family economy, and (c) the needs of the family as determined by family size and composition.

The Worker-Earner Role of Men and Women

Family members generally provide economic resources to their families by earning income through employment, that is, through performance of the worker-earner role. An individual participates in the economy as a worker producing goods and services and as an earner providing income to meet family needs. Traditionally, this responsibility has fallen mainly to men; however, it is shared by most women. Although a majority of married women are employed outside the home, they are in the early stages of developing attachments to long-term careers and making major contributions to family income (see Voydanoff, 1987, for a review). In addition, both husbands and wives view men as holding major responsibility for family economic support (Haas, 1986; Hiller and Philliber, 1986; Hood, 1986).

Unpaid Contributions to Family Economic Well-Being

Men's major contribution to their family's economic well-being has been in the realm of paid employment. Their participation in unpaid family work generally has consisted of helping their wives with household chores and child care and performing traditionally male tasks such as car repair and outside maintenance. Women's economic contributions have been more broadly based, including a mix of paid employment and diverse types of unpaid family work. Several types of unpaid family work make direct or indirect

contributions to family economic well-being. These include housework and the care of dependents such as children, ill and disabled family members, and elderly parents; wives' participation in their husbands' work; and the management of limited resources.

Housework and care of dependents. Women's most universal unpaid contribution to family economic well-being is family work, that is, housework and caring for dependents. The economic value of family work is difficult to assess, since it is not included in traditional measures of economic production. Two measurement approaches include (a) replacement costs, the amount it would cost to hire someone to do the work, and (b) opportunity costs, the amount of income women would earn if they did not stay home to do family work. One study estimates that the replacement costs of housework total more than $750 billion per year in 1976 dollars and that opportunity costs are over one-half trillion dollars per year (Peskin, 1982). Although these figures are estimates based on somewhat artificial assumptions, they illustrate the significance of family work to family economic well-being.

Wives' participation in their husbands' work. Many wives of professionals and managers participate in their husbands' careers by entertaining business associates, assuming responsibility for household and childrearing tasks, attending work-related social functions, and making business contacts through volunteer work in the community. This participation, which is most common among business executives, politicians, ministers, the self-employed, the military, and diplomats, provides career advantages to husbands and creates status and prestige for the family. However, women experience opportunity costs in this situation, since many do not work outside the home (Finch, 1983; Fowlkes, 1980; Papanek, 1979).

The management of financial resources. Many women manage their family's financial resources. Recent qualitative studies from England (Morris, 1984; Wilson, 1987) indicate that women's responsibility for financial management varies with income. Lower-income respondents are more actively engaged in managing money and paying bills than upper-income women. Sharing is most common among middle-income families. Many lower-income women receive a portion of their husbands' income from which they are expected to pay all household expenses. However, when incomes are high enough to allow some flexibility in spending, men often assume greater responsibility for managing the family finances. In addition, low-income women with sole responsibility for children manage extremely limited resources through strategies such as kin-based exchange networks (Richards, 1989).

Family Size and Composition

Family size and composition also influence the level of family economic well-being by determining the number of dependents in relation to the number of potential earners available to the family. The number of dependents is a crucial determinant of the amount of income needed to attain an adequate standard of living. The life-cycle stage of the family also is important. For example, families with young children must support dependents with relatively few earning resources. Families with older children are more likely to have a mother and/or adolescents working to supplement family income (Hayghe, 1986).

SOCIETAL CHANGES ASSOCIATED WITH ECONOMIC DISTRESS

Obviously, not all families are equally successful in providing a stable and secure economic base for their members. Economic difficulties encountered by families derive from two sources: (*a*) constraints imposed by the structure of the labor force and earnings patterns and (*b*) characteristics of the family and its members, such as family size and composition and the number of earners.

The Changing Structure of the Economy

Recent structural shifts in the American economy are having a major impact on the structure of the labor force and patterns of earnings. Although there is some dispute regarding the extent of change and implications for the economy and workers, considerable evidence indicates that the past three decades have seen important shifts in employment. Manufacturing as a percentage of nonagricultural employment decreased from 30% in 1961 to 18% in 1988 while services increased from 14% to 24% (Howe and Parks, 1989). In ad-

dition, although employment in some manufacturing industries has increased, important losses occurred in others between 1969 and 1984, including radio and TV receivers, footwear, motor vehicles, household appliances, textile mill products, tires, containers, and primary metals and steel. These industries vary in average wage rates, with metals and motor vehicles being relatively high and textiles and footwear relatively low. This trend is associated with foreign competition and a shift of capital and manufacturing jobs to foreign countries with lower labor and materials costs (Bluestone, 1984; Harrison and Bluestone, 1988; Kutscher and Personick, 1986).

The greatest growth in employment has been in service-producing industries, especially services and retail trade. These two industries accounted for 84% of all employment growth between 1979 and 1987. However, in 1987, median weekly earnings were $327 for services, $258 for retail trade, and $398 for manufacturing. More generally, in 1985, average weekly wages in expanding industries were $258 compared with $402 in shrinking industries (Mishel and Simon, 1988).

Analysts disagree as to whether these employment trends are contributing to a shift in the distribution of earnings. Some argue that the earnings distribution is changing, with increases in the upper and/or lower thirds and decreases in the middle third. Others suggest that various employment trends counterbalance each other such that the earnings distribution has not changed in recent years (Kosters and Ross, 1988; see Lerman and Salzman, 1988, for a summary of these arguments).

Other employment-related problems during the 1980s have implications for earnings: (*a*) cyclical unemployment and permanent job displacement due to layoffs and closings, (*b*) increases in involuntary part-time and part-year work, (*c*) wage concessions in several unionized industries, and (*d*) the initiation of two-tier wage systems in which new employees are hired for lower pay that increases at a slower rate than that of employees hired previously (Harrison and Bluestone, 1988).

Changing Family Structure

In addition to recent changes in the economy, changes in family structure also have occurred that are relevant to an understanding of economic distress among families. Over the past several decades patterns of marriage and childbearing have changed significantly. Women are marrying and bearing children at later ages and some believe that the percentage who will never marry or have children is increasing. These trends have complex relationships with economic distress. Among men, high current wages and high projected earnings are associated with being married and early first-birth timing. However, later family formation is associated with high wages among women (Teachman and Schollaert, 1989).

Recent estimates suggest that about two-thirds of all first marriages will end in separation or divorce (Martin and Bumpass, 1989). Economic distress is related to both the likelihood and consequences of divorce. Women with high earnings and men experiencing unstable employment and earnings are more likely to divorce (see Teachman, Polonko, and Scanzoni, 1987, for a review), and women's income declines substantially following divorce—30% on average in the first year (Hoffman and Duncan, 1988). In addition, the rate of childbirth among unmarried women has more than doubled since 1950 (Select Committee on Children, Youth, and Families, 1987).

The combined effects of divorce and children born out-of-wedlock have created a large increase in families maintained by women. In 1988, 24% of families with children under 18 years old were one-parent families headed by women. Their numbers more than doubled between 1960 and 1988. The major source of mother-child families is divorce; in 1988, 38% of mother-child families were a result of divorce. Never-married mothers comprised 33% and widows 6% (Rawlings, 1989). Families maintained by women have high rates of poverty. In 1987, 46% of female-householder families with children under 18 were living below the poverty line. The comparable figure for married-couple families with children under 18 is 8% (U.S. Bureau of the Census, 1989b).

ECONOMIC DISTRESS IN FAMILIES

The large-scale changes just discussed become sources of economic distress on the individual and family level by creating problems in the performance of the worker-earner role. Components of economic distress reflect both dimensions of the

worker-earner role: employment and income. Economic distress is a concept referring to aspects of economic life that are potential stressors for individuals and families. Major components include employment instability, employment uncertainty, economic deprivation, and economic strain (Voydanoff, 1984). Employment instability and economic deprivation are relatively objective factors indicating patterns of employment and changes in income over time. Employment uncertainty and economic strain are subjective indicators of an individual's perceived employment and financial situation.

Employment Instability

Changes in the structure of the labor force and frequent recessions have led to wide fluctuations in the level of unemployment in recent years. Since the fall of 1982, the unemployment rate has decreased from 10.7%, the peak during the past recession, to just over 5%. These unemployment figures are underestimates in two ways. First, discouraged and involuntary part-time workers are omitted. The number of discouraged workers, those wanting employment who have given up looking for work, has declined substantially since the 1981–82 recession but the decline has slowed during the past two years. The figure for the second quarter of 1989 is approximately 870,000. The number of involuntary part-time workers has decreased from 6.7 million in 1981–82 to 5 million in 1989; however, it remains relatively high for a period of economic recovery (Haugen, 1989). Second, monthly figures provide a one-time snapshot of the incidence of unemployment. The percentage of individuals reporting some unemployment during 1986 was more than twice the average monthly unemployment rate, 16% versus 7% (Mellor and Parks, 1988).

Employment instability includes several other important dimensions: duration of periods of unemployment, number of periods of employment and unemployment, extent of underemployment and downward mobility, inability of youth to gain entry-level positions, and forced early retirement. The average duration of unemployment varies with economic conditions. In the second quarter of 1989, the average length of unemployment was 11.9 weeks. However, those unemployed for more than six months made up only 10% of the unemployed in 1989, compared with 15% in 1983 (Haughen, 1989; Howe and Parks, 1989).

Structural changes in the economy are associated with permanent job displacement due to plant closings and employment cutbacks. Between 1981 and 1985 approximately 10.8 million workers over 19 years of age were permanently displaced. Of the 5.1 million workers who had worked at least three years on their jobs, about two-thirds had become reemployed by January 1986. However, more than half were working in different occupations and 44% were earning less than they had previously. Over one-third of the employed had held two or more jobs since being displaced, while about the same percentage of the unemployed had been employed once or more since being displaced (Horvath, 1987).

Data on unemployment among individuals conceal patterns of unemployment within families and across family types. On average in the second quarter of 1987, one or more members of 9% of American households were unemployed. Among these families, 29% reported no members employed, while the remaining 71% had at least one member employed. Eight percent of unemployed wives reported no other members working, compared with 38% of married men and 86% of unemployed women maintaining families (U.S. Bureau of Labor Statistics, 1987). In 1986 unemployment was twice as high among women maintaining families than among married women with children (Select Committee on Children, Youth, and Families, 1987).

Thus, despite a long period of economic recovery, significant numbers of individuals and families are experiencing employment instability.

Employment Uncertainty

Employment uncertainty refers to an individual's assessment of prospects for the future regarding the onset of, duration of, and recovery from unemployment. Changes in the structure of the labor force and recession-related unemployment are related to high levels of employment uncertainty among both the employed and unemployed. Many unemployed are discouraged about their prospects for reemployment; many employed are concerned about possible layoffs and cuts in income (Buss, Redburn, and Waldrun, 1983; Kaufman, 1982; Leventman, 1981).

Economic Deprivation

The third component of economic distress, economic deprivation, incorporates two aspects: (*a*) the inability to meet current financial needs and (*b*) the loss of financial resources and income over a period of time.

Although alternative measurement techniques yield different numbers, in general, family income has experienced relatively slow growth since 1970. Despite yearly increases since 1983, census data indicate no overall growth in median family income or earnings since 1973 (U.S. Bureau of the Census, 1989a; see Levy, 1987, for a comprehensive analysis of these trends). Using a measure that accounts for family size, the Congressional Budget Office concludes that adjusted family income increased 11% between 1973 and 1986 and 20% since 1970. Most of this gain is attributed to increased numbers of workers per family. In addition, gains were distributed unevenly among subgroups of the American population. Young families and low-income families with children, especially those maintained by women, had substantially lower adjusted family income in 1986 than in 1970 (Congressional Budget Office, 1988).

These trends are related to shifts in the composition of the poor over the past 15 years. As the median earnings of family heads under 30 with children fell 39% from 1973 to 1986, the poverty rate for these families increased from 16% to 30%. The percentage of young families maintained by women who were poor increased from 57 in 1973 to 63 in 1986 (Johnson, Sum, and Weill, 1988). Another analysis indicates that approximately one-third of the poor were working or looking for work during at least half of 1987. Large numbers of the working poor were characterized as low-wage workers, unmarried women maintaining families, or members of one-earner families (Klein and Rones, 1989).

Research on poverty spells indicates two major components of beginning and ending spells of poverty: changes in income and family composition. Bane and Ellwood's (1986) analysis of the Panel Study of Income Dynamics indicates that 38% of poverty spells among the nonelderly began with a decline in earnings among family heads. Other important sources include declining earnings of other household members (11%), transition to a female-headed family (11%), child born into poverty (9%), and movement of youth to an independent household (15%). Poverty spells are shorter when they begin with earning declines or movement to independent households than when they begin with a transition to a female-headed family or birth into poverty. Over 50% of poverty spells end with earnings increases among household heads, with another 23% ending with earnings changes of wives or other household members. Ten percent of spells end when a woman maintaining a family marries; another 15% end because of increases in transfer payments. Women maintaining families are slightly more likely to end a poverty spell through earnings than through marriage (Bane and Ellwood, 1986; see Duncan and Rodgers, 1987, 1988, and Smith, 1989, for other analyses of these data).

Economic deprivation also is associated with the loss of income because of employment instability. Recession-related and structural unemployment creates economic deprivation for many who previously worked at seemingly secure jobs. The extent of economic deprivation associated with unemployment varies according to prior income level, eligibility for unemployment insurance and other benefits, and the duration of unemployment. The median income of married-couple families in which one or more members had experienced unemployment during 1984 was 24% lower than that of families with no unemployment. Twelve percent of married-couple families with some unemployment during 1984 had incomes below the poverty level, compared with 4% of families with no unemployment. Earnings in families maintained by women were decreased 39% by unemployment. Eighteen percent of families maintained by women were below the poverty line when no unemployment occurred; the comparable figure when a member was unemployed is 42% (Smith, 1986).

The concept of the life-cycle squeeze provides additional insight into the interaction between income, family size, and family life-cycle stage in determining income adequacy. A life-cycle squeeze is a period in which a family's economic needs and aspirations are relatively greater than its resources. Oppenheimer (1982) has documented two life-cycle squeezes during which husbands' earnings are likely to fall short in satisfying the life-style aspirations of the family. These periods are early adulthood when couples are establishing households and bearing children while husbands' earnings are still low and later adulthood when peak childrearing expenses associated with adolescents are not matched by sufficient increases in earnings. The early life-cycle squeeze is more severe among professionals, since their incomes are relatively low in early adulthood; the later squeeze has greater impact on those in blue-collar occupations because their incomes level off relatively early.

Economic Strain

Economic strain is an evaluation of current financial status such as perceived financial adequacy, financial concerns and worries, adjustments to changes in one's financial situation, and one's projected financial situation. Although conceptually distinct, this dimension of economic distress often serves empirically as a global indicator of economic distress.

ECONOMIC DISTRESS, ADJUSTMENT, AND MARITAL AND FAMILY RELATIONS

The remainder of this article assesses linkages between macroeconomic changes as reflected in components of economic distress and individual adjustment, family relations, and children's adjustment. The extent to which these relationships are contingent upon coping strategies also is discussed.

Individual Adjustment

Research on the effects of life events on individual adjustment and mental health often consider economic distress, especially employment instability, as a major stressor. Relatively extensive research shows that unemployment is associated with depression, anxiety, psychophysiological distress, and state mental hospital admissions (Brenner, 1984; Dooley, Catalano, and Rook, 1988; Ensminger and Celentano, 1988; Kessler, House, and Turner, 1987; Kessler, Turner, and House, 1989; McLanahan and Glass, 1985; Shamir, 1986; also see Warr, Jackson, and Banks, 1988, for a review of British research). In addition, there is some evidence that men's unemployment is associated with psychological distress among their wives (Dew, Bromet, and Schulberg, 1987; Liem and Liem, 1988; Penkower, Bromet, and Dew, 1988; Voydanoff and Donnelly, 1989).

Findings for reemployment are inconsistent. Some studies indicate that psychological distress is reduced among the reemployed (Ensminger and Celentano, 1988; Kessler et al., 1989; Liem and Liem, 1988). Others report that reemployment is associated with psychological distress, especially for those who become reemployed at lower skill levels or lower pay or who become unemployed a second time following a layoff (Dooley et al., 1988; Gordus, Jarley, and Ferman, 1981; Leventman, 1981).

While most research on unemployment and mental health is conducted with samples of men, studies including women suggest either that the mental health of women is affected similarly to men's or that men's mental health is more negatively affected than women's. Three explanations have been given for situations in which women have less severe psychological reactions to unemployment: less financial hardship, lower commitment to work, and satisfactions from alternative roles in the family (Jahoda, 1982; Perrucci, Perrucci, Targ, and Targ, 1988; Shamir, 1985). Husband's unemployment is more strongly related to anxiety and depression among women than is their own unemployment (Voydanoff and Donnelly, 1989).

Research on the other components of economic distress is more limited. Some have suggested that employment uncertainty is associated with psychological distress (Buss et al., 1983; Kaufman, 1982: Leventman, 1981); however, Voydanoff and Donnelly (1989) found no relationship between uncertainty and depression or anxiety among married men and women, with the exception of spouse's employment uncertainty for women. Low income is related to several indicators of psychological distress (see Horwitz, 1984, for a review). Low personal earnings are associated with depression and psychophysiological distress among men (Kessler, 1982; Ross and Huber, 1985; Ulbrich, 1988), while low family income is related to anxiety and depression among married women (Voydanoff and Donnelly, 1989). Economic strain is related to depression and anxiety among men and women (Ensminger and Celentano, 1988; Pearlin, Lieberman, Menaghan, and Mullan, 1981; Ross and Huber, 1985; Voydanoff and Donnelly, 1989). Several studies indicate that economic strain mediates relationships between other components of economic distress and depression and anxiety (Conger, Lasley, Lorenz, and Conger, 1987; Ensminger and Celentano, 1988; Kessler, Turner, and Honse, 1987; Pearlin et al., 1981; Ross and Huber, 1985; Voydanoff and Donnelly, 1989).

Marital and Family Relations

The effect of economic distress on families are extensive and wide-ranging. Both aspects of the worker-earner role, employment and income, are crucial determinants of the nature and quality of family life. A minimum level of income and employment stability is necessary for family stability and cohesion. Without it many are unable to form families through marriage and others find themselves subject to separation and divorce. In addition, those experiencing unemployment or income loss make other adjustments in family composition such as postponing childbearing, moving in with relatives, and having relatives or boarders join the household (Fox, Kelly, and Sheldon, 1982).

Several studies indicate that unemployment is not strongly related to marital stability or global indicators of marital and family satisfaction (Atkinson, Liem, and Liem, 1986; Larson, 1984; Perrucci and Targ, 1988; Voydanoff, Donnelly, and Fine, 1988). However, unemployment is associated with separation and divorce among a sample of white- and blue-collar workers (Liem and Liem, 1988) and is negatively related to marital and family satisfaction among a sample of married men (Voydanoff and Donnelly, 1988) and to changes in marital happiness eight months after a plant closing (Perrucci and Targ, 1988).

In general, relationships between employment instability, especially unemployment, and marital and family relations are stronger for specific indicators of marital and family adjustment than for measures of global satisfaction with marriage and family life. Compared with employed blue-collar workers, unemployed workers report lower levels of consensus, communication, and harmony in family relations (Larson, 1984) and more stressful relations with their spouses (Broman, Hamilton, and Hoffman, 1989). In addition, unemployed blue-collar and white-collar husbands report less spouse support, more frequent arguments, and lower family cohesion than those in the control families (Atkinson et al., 1986). These findings are supported by interviewer ratings of lower supportiveness and greater conflict among unemployed couples (Liem and Liem, 1988). Liem and Liem (1988) also find that husbands' psychological reaction to unemployment mediates the relationship between unemployment and family cohesion.

Limited research on relationships between employment uncertainty and marital and family relations yields conflicting results. Broman et al. (1989) report that anticipating unemployment is strongly related to stressful relationships with spouses among autoworkers. However, a study of a national sample reports no association between employment uncertainty and family satisfaction (Voydanoff et al., 1988). A third study finds no relationship between employment uncertainty and marital and family satisfaction except for women reporting uncertainty regarding their spouse's employment (Voydanoff and Donnelly, 1988). These differences may be attributable to the certainty of layoff for the autoworkers in the plant closing study.

Income-related components of economic distress also are related to marital and family relationships. Much research documents that higher levels of income, with the exception of the highest levels, are modestly associated with greater marital happiness, adjustment, and satisfaction (see Piotrkowski, Rapoport, and Rapoport, 1987, for a review) and lower rates of marital disruption and divorce (see Teachman et al., 1987, for a review).

Several studies indicate that relationships between income and income loss and marital and family relations are mediated by either economic strain or types of marital interaction. Recent studies document that the negative relationship between family income and marital and family satisfaction is reduced when economic strain is taken into account (Conger et al., 1990; Voydanoff and Donnelly, 1988; Voydanoff et al., 1988). Other studies document that income loss and a low income-to-needs ratio are negatively associated with marital quality. These relationships operate through financial conflicts, husband's psychological instability, marital tensions and hostility, and lack of warmth and support (Conger et al., 1990; Liker and Elder, 1983). Similar findings are reported in a study of emotional distress among farmers (Conger, Lasley, Lorenz, and Conger, 1987).

Economic strain is strongly related to low levels of marital and family satisfaction. In addition, as with psychological distress, economic strain mediates relationships between other components of economic distress and marital and family satisfaction (Pittman and Lloyd, 1988; Voydanoff and Donnelly, 1988; Voydanoff et al., 1988).

Families Maintained by Women

We know little about the effects of economic distress on adjustment and family life among families maintained by women. Extensive research compares adjustment, supportive relationships, and child outcomes in one-parent and two-parent families (see McLanahan and Booth, 1989, for a review). Another literature examines the effects of divorce on men, women, and children (see Demo and Acock, 1988, and Kitson, Babri, Roach, and Placidi, 1989, for reviews). This work generally does not consider the mediating or moderating effects of economic distress or socioeconomic status (Demo and Acock, 1988). However, those studies that take into account income and other socioeconomic characteristics report that these variables reduce relationships between family structure and child outcomes (see Demo and Acock, 1988, and McLanahan and Booth, 1989, for reviews). A recent study finds negative relationships between several indicators of economic distress and social and emotional adjustment among divorced mothers (Pett and Vaughan-Cole, 1986).

COPING WITH ECONOMIC DISTRESS

Individuals and families vary in their responses to stressors such as economic distress. Stress theory attempts to account for differential responses to stressors by examining the processes and factors intervening between a stressor and individual and family outcomes. Research on relationships between life events and chronic strains and mental and physical health examines the extent to which these relationships are contingent on coping resources and behaviors, including social support (Kessler and McLeod, 1985; Menaghan, 1983; Pearlin, 1989). Family stress theory spells out the conditions under which stressors, such as unemployment, serious illness, and other life events, are associated with family crisis or disrupted family functioning (McCubbin and McCubbin, 1987; McCubbin and Patterson, 1983; Menaghan, 1983;

Walker, 1985). Contingent factors—family definition of the situation and family resources and support—are similar to those analyzed with reference to life events and mental and physical health. Life course analysis uses a similar approach in the analysis of linkages between macroeconomic changes and individual development (Elder and Caspi, 1988; Moen, Kain, and Elder, 1983).

Coping is a major contingency in relationships between stressors, including economic distress, and individual health and family functioning. Coping is a multidimensional concept consisting of two major components: coping resources and coping behaviors. Coping resources include psychological dispositions, family system characteristics, and social networks available to an individual or family to respond to stressors. Coping behaviors involve the use of coping resources in an active process of dealing with stressors and their effects. Such behaviors include direct action to solve problems and the regulation of emotions and meanings associated with economic distress (Menaghan, 1983; Pearlin, 1989).

COPING RESOURCES

Personal coping resources. Personal coping resources are relatively stable personality characteristics that affect an individual's ability to deal effectively with stressors. Despite this stability, personal disruption associated with economic distress is often sufficient to undermine personal coping resources. Research on personal coping resources in relation to economic distress has focused on self-esteem and mastery. Findings on the direct effects of unemployment on self-esteem are mixed; some studies report that unemployment is associated with low self-esteem (Pearlin et al., 1981; Warr, 1984), while others find no significant differences (Larson, 1984; Linn, Sandifer, and Stein, 1985; Shamir, 1986). However, Shamir (1986) reports that self-esteem is negatively related to depression. In addition, self-esteem reduces the relationship between unemployment and psychological distress (Kessler, Turner, and Honse, 1988; Linn et al., 1985; Shamir, 1986). Unemployment and economic strain are directly related to low mastery, which is related to depression (Pearlin et al., 1981; Perrucci et al., 1988).

Family coping resources. Family coping resources

are family system characteristics such as adaptability, cohesion, and nontraditional family roles that facilitate effective problem-solving within families. Research during and since the Depression of the 1930s indicates that the presence of these family system characteristics prior to unemployment is associated with the quality of family relationships during unemployment. For example, Liker and Elder (1983) report that initially strong marital bonds reduced the impact of financial conflicts on the quality of marital relationships during the Depression.

A recent study shows that economic distress is associated with lower levels of family pride and accord, which in turn are positively related to marital and family satisfaction. In addition, family pride and accord partially mediate relationships between economic distress and quality of family life (Voydanoff and Donnelly, 1988).

Liem and Liem (1988) report a more egalitarian division of labor among the unemployed despite a lack of change in norms regarding division of labor. A few studies suggest that shared family work and nontraditional role expectations among the unemployed are associated with better family adjustment (Kaufman, 1982; Larson, 1984; Leventman, 1981). However, family problems result from role reversal when the wives of unemployed professionals become employed following their husbands' job loss (Kaufman, 1982; Leventman, 1981; May, Brown-Standridge, and Jorgensen, 1989).

Coping Behaviors

Individuals and families also use several types of coping behaviors to deal with the stressors they encounter. Coping resources are mobilized and used in the development of cognitive, behavioral, and help-seeking strategies to address problems such as economic distress. Major types of coping behaviors include (*a*) appraisal-focused coping, which defines the meaning of the situation; (*b*) problem-focused coping, which modifies or eliminates the source of the problem, deals with its consequences, or improves the situation; and (*c*) emotion-focused coping, which involves the management of emotions (Moos and Billings, 1982).

Personal coping behaviors. The limited research on coping with economic distress has examined appraisal-focused coping behaviors. Pearlin et al. (1981) report that positive comparisons and the devaluation of economic achievements reduce the effects of job disruption on depression. In addition, these coping behaviors mediate the process through which job disruption affects depression by influencing conditions antecedent to stress such as changes in economic strain, self-esteem, and mastery. A second study reported that the lack of intrusive thoughts had limited buffering effects on relationships between unemployment and mental and physical health (Kessler et al., 1988).

However, avoidance coping, such as denial, keeping feelings to oneself, and eating, drinking, and smoking to relieve tension, is positively related to stress among husbands and wives affected by a mine closing. Avoidance strategies also mediate relationships between financial arguments and stress and reduce the negative association between saving money and stress for husbands (Wilhelm and Ridley, 1988a).

Social supports. The use of social supports to cope with economic distress is a complex process involving several important dimensions: supports must be available, available supports must be used, and the support provided must meet the needs of those receiving it. Major types of support include instrumental aid such as money, goods, and services; emotional support; and information such as advice and feedback. Support can come from several sources: friends, relatives, coworkers, neighbors, self-help groups, and human service professionals.

Findings on the availability of social support to those experiencing economic distress are mixed. Some studies indicate that relatives and friends are generally responsive to requests for assistance (Perrucci and Targ, 1988; Retherford, Hildreth, and Goldsmith, 1989), while others indicate decreases in the size of and contact with nonfamily social networks among the unemployed (Atkinson et al., 1986; Jackson, 1988). Informal supports, especially family members, are considered more desirable and are used more often than support from professionals and agencies (Buss and Redburn, 1983; Rayman, 1983). Women use a relatively wide range of supports, including friends and coworkers, while men depend more exclusively on support from spouses (Rayman, 1983). The use of family members as the major source of sup-

port may be related to a belief in self-reliance and the stigma associated with some formal programs.

However, when support is available and used, it generally is associated with psychological well-being and quality of family life among those experiencing economic distress (see Warr et al., 1988, for a review of British studies). In addition, access to a confidant and integration in a social network reduce relationships between economic distress and psychological distress and quality of family life (Kessler et al., 1988; Voydanoff et al., 1988).

However, recent work indicates several constraints on the effectiveness of social support, including the reciprocity involved in supportive relationships, stressors limiting the ability of others to provide support, and a mixture of supportive and conflict-ridden interactions with sources of support (see Coyne and DeLongis, 1986, and Shinn, Lehmann, and Wong, 1984, for reviews).

Family coping behaviors. Research has documented the use of several problem-focused family coping behaviors designed to improve the financial situation of families experiencing economic distress. These include realigning the family work effort, participating in the informal economy, and cutting back on expenditures.

Family work effort is the extent of participation of family members in paid employment. When one family member becomes unemployed, others, especially spouses and teenage children, may increase their work effort. Studies of plant closings indicate that about 20% of the time other family members, usually spouses, go to work following a closing (Rayman, 1983; Root, 1984). A recent study reports that several types of economic distress are associated with shifts in family work effort; however, these shifts are associated with lower levels of marital and family satisfaction among men (Voydanoff and Donnelly, 1988).

The informal economy consists of the exchange of goods and services for cash or by barter. Skills developed through a hobby or on the job, such as sewing or carpentry, are used to save money or earn additional income. In some cases these activities lead to employment in a new occupation. Individuals and families also exchange goods and services such as household items, child care, and transportation. As with family work effort, economic distress is related to the use of the informal economy, which in turn is associated with lower marital and family satisfaction among men (Voydanoff and Donnelly, 1988).

In addition, economic distress often requires changes in spending patterns. These behaviors include cutting expenditures, increasing home production, comparing prices and value when shopping, spending savings, and going into debt (Larson, 1984; Perrucci, Perrucci, Targ, and Targ, 1985; Rayman, 1983; Root, 1984; Wilhelm and Ridley, 1988b). Although these cuts are effective in improving a family's financial situation, they are not necessarily associated with other positive individual and family outcomes. According to a recent study (Perrucci et al., 1985), workers affected by a plant closing who report a high number of cutbacks in spending are more likely to be depressed than those reporting fewer cutbacks. A second study (Nowak and Snyder, 1986; Snyder and Nowak, 1984) finds that making cutbacks is related to low marital satisfaction and high family tensions among both men and women. However, Wilhelm and Ridley (1988b) report that financial management changes are not significant predictors of depression following a mine closing.

ECONOMIC DISTRESS AND CHILDREN'S HEALTH AND ADJUSTMENT

Relationships between economic distress and children's health and adjustment also are influenced by mediating factors. These include economic strain, parental adjustment and behavior, and the gender of the child. Research has focused on child outcomes such as physical health, psychological well-being, behavior problems, and aspirations and achievements (see McLoyd, 1989, and Targ and Perrucci, in press, for reviews).

Physical Health

Findings on direct relationships between economic distress and children's health are mixed. In a small-sample study, Margolis and Farran (1981) report that fathers' job loss is associated with a greater risk of illness episodes, infectious diseases, and illnesses of longer duration. In a second study, paternal employment status was not related to children's health; however, children whose fathers were insecure in their jobs had a higher risk of illness than those whose fathers felt secure (Margolis and Farran, 1984). A third study finds that the relationship between unemployment and children's health is indirect, that is, unemployment leads to economic strain, which in turn leads to parental health problems and then to children's health difficulties (Kelly, Sheldon, and Fox, 1985).

Psychological Well-Being

Recent research has documented that relationships between economic distress and children's psychological well-being are contingent upon characteristics and behaviors of fathers, mothers, and the children themselves. Although unemployed fathers report greater availability and involvement in child care than employed fathers, a lower proportion of their behavior is classified as nurturing. Fathers experiencing economic strain also report fewer nurturing behaviors than other fathers (Harold-Goldsmith, Radin, and Eccles, 1988). Perceived economic hardship is directly related to psychological distress for a large sample of adolescents. This relationship is partially mediated by low parental nurturance and inconsistent discipline (Lempers, Clark-Lempers, and Simon, 1989).

Similar findings are reported for children during the Depression of the 1930s. Fathers experiencing income loss tended to exhibit inconsistent and arbitrary discipline, which in turn was associated with difficult behavior and temper tantrums (Elder, Liker, and Cross, 1984). Among girls, especially those considered less attractive, income loss was negatively related to psychosocial well-being through the rejecting behavior of fathers (Elder, Van Nguyen, and Caspi, 1985).

Relationships between mothers and children also conditioned associations between income loss and children's well-being during the Depression. In families where the mother was undemonstrative toward the children before the loss of income, fathers were more likely to use arbitrary discipline and children were more likely to exhibit temper tantrums following the loss (Elder and Caspi, 1988; Elder, Caspi, and Van Nguyen, 1986).

In addition, Elder et al. (1984, 1986) document that several characteristics of the children influenced parental behavior. These include age, gender, physical attractiveness, and temperamental characteristics. For example, fathers tended to be somewhat more rejecting of daughters than of sons, especially if the daughters were considered less physically attractive (Elder et al., 1985). Young children perceived as problematic before the Depression also were more likely to receive arbitrary discipline during the Depression than other children (Elder et al., 1986).

Behavior Problems

Parental economic distress also shows some association with behavior problems among children. In a recent study, perceived economic hardship does not show a direct relationship with delinquency and drug use; however, an indirect relationship is found that operates through inconsistent parental discipline (Lempers et al., 1989). Another recent study reports that father's unemployment, employment uncertainty, low income, and economic strain are positively related to the number of children's problems perceived by mothers (Voydanoff and Donnelly, 1986).

Aspirations and Achievement

Little work has examined relationships between parental economic distress and children's aspirations and achievements. A recent study in West Germany finds that income loss is related to a pessimistic life outlook among parents. Fathers' pessimism is associated with low expectancies for job success among adolescent daughters (Galambos and Silbereisen, 1987). However, Isralowitz and Singer (1986) find no relationship between parental unemployment and work values.

Income loss during the Depression had different effects on boys and girls. Girls assumed more household activities and boys worked at paid jobs. This difference carried over into later achievements as young men from families experiencing income loss tended to establish their work roles earlier and move less frequently from one job to another (Elder and Caspi, 1988). However, young men who had high levels of temper tantrums during childhood were relatively likely to experience erratic work histories in adulthood (Elder et al., 1984). Young women from economically deprived families tended to value homemaking and form families relatively early (Elder and Caspi, 1988). In addition, the daughters of rejecting fathers were more likely to have low aspirations than were other girls (Elder et al., 1985).

RESEARCH DIRECTIONS FOR THE 1990s

This review draws on diverse literatures to document processes through which economic and demographic changes are translated into economic distress among individuals and families, which in turn affects individual adjustment and quality of family relations. In addition, these processes incorporate influences from several individual and family coping resources and behaviors.

The review illuminates several strengths and weaknesses of theory and research in this area. Studies cited in the article reflect a range of methodological approaches and vary greatly in sophistication. Information for some areas, such as the mediating role of gender roles in families experiencing distress, is limited to a few studies based on small nonrepresentative samples. As in other areas of family research, longitudinal studies are the exception rather than the rule.

A gap exists between large-scale demographic studies and small-scale qualitative studies. For example, research on poverty and inequality based on data from sources such as the U.S. Census and the Panel Study of Income Dynamics is able to trace patterns of unemployment and economic deprivation. However, these data sources do not include information on how these patterns are actualized in the structure and texture of the family economy or family relations. On the other hand, qualitative research has explored individual adjustment and family relations with regard to a single aspect of economic distress, for example, unemployment of the male breadwinner. However, the small samples used in most qualitative studies do not permit comparisons across type or severity of economic distress. Within the past five years a few studies have begun to establish linkages between these major elements of the process. This is an encouraging trend that should be expanded in the coming decade.

Several substantive aspects of this process have been fairly well researched and explicated. However, our understanding of several important linkages remains weak. Additional work is needed to understand how various economic changes affect specific types of families. For example, we know little about the effects of recent changes in earnings distributions on young workers' families and patterns of family formation, especially among minorities. Little research examines the extent to which economic distress and its consequences vary by race or ethnic group membership.

Most research on societal changes with regard to economic distress focuses on economic change. However, changes in family structure also need to be be considered. These two types of change operate together in relation to economic distress among families. Thus, we need to move beyond the analysis of changes in manufacturing employment for male blue-collar workers and also look at the relevance of earnings in the service industry for families maintained by women.

Research on the four components of economic distress still tends to focus on unemployment among men. This focus needs to be expanded to include other aspects of economic distress, especially employment uncertainty. For example, recent changes in American corporate policy, such as mergers, acquisitions, moving jobs to other countries, and forced early retirement, have created substantial employment uncertainty. The effects of this uncertainty on individual adjustment and family relations have yet to be explored.

In addition, we need to examine economic distress in the context of the family economy. How do the employment and income patterns of family members combine to create economic distress? To what extent do different patterns show similar relationships to adjustment and quality of family life? These questions need to be joined with other issues associated with the family economy such as the mix of paid and unpaid work and gender-based family role structures. In this context the meaning of the provider role for men and women is crucial.

Finally, research in the 1990s must continue to elaborate linkages between economic distress, individual adjustment, and family relations. Significant progress has been made in this area during the past five years. Several studies have demonstrated linkages between individual adjustment and family relationships. For example, Elder and associates (1984) report that father's irritability is related to the use of arbitrary discipline techniques with children. However, reciprocal relationships between individual adjustment and family relations need further investigation.

On a theoretical level, most research has been based on one of three complementary approaches: life events, family stress, and life course analysis. These approaches need to be integrated more completely. For example, life events other than economic distress have been included as a contingent factor in the conceptual model proposed by McLoyd (1989). The role of social support, so prevalent in studies of life events, needs to be incorporated into the analysis of family stress and studies of the effects of macroeconomic changes on individual development over the life course.

Additional work also is needed to establish linkages between the consequences of economic distress for families and public policy issues. These issues include the movement of capital and jobs; differential access to employment according to age, gender, and racial and ethnic group membership; wage levels and pay equity; and the allocation of public and private support resources to alleviate the effects of economic distress on individuals and families.

REFERENCES

Atkinson, Thomas, Ramsay Liem, and Joan H. Liem. 1986. "The social costs of unemployment: Implications for social support." Journal of Health and Social Behavior 27: 317–331.

Bane, Mary Jo, and David T. Ellwood. 1986. "Slipping into and out of poverty: The dynamics of spells." Journal of Human Resources 21: 1–24.

Bluestone, Barry. 1984. "Is deindustrialization a myth? Capital mobility versus absorptive capacity in the U.S. economy." Annals of the American Academy of Political and Social Science 475: 39–51.

Brenner, M. Harvey. 1984. Estimating the Effects of Economic Change on National Health and Social Well-Being. Washington, DC: U.S. Government Printing Office.

Broman, Clifford L., V. Lee Hamilton, and William S. Hoffman. 1989. "Unemployment and family stress: Evidence from a plant closing study." Paper presented at the annual meeting of the North Central Sociological Association (April).

Buss, Terry F., and F. Stevens Redburn. 1983. Shutdown at Youngstown. Albany: State University of New York Press.

Buss, Terry F., and F. Stevens Redburn, with Joseph Waldrun. 1983. Mass Unemployment: Plant Closings and Community Mental Health. Beverly Hills, CA: Sage.

Conger, Rand D., Glen H. Elder, Jr., Frederick O. Lorenz, Katherine J. Conger, Ronald L. Simons, Les B. Whitbeck, Shirley Huck, and Janet N. Melby. 1990. "Linking economic hardship to marital quality and instability." Journal of Marriage and the Family 52: 643–656.

Conger, Rand D., Paul Lasley, Frederick O. Lorenz, and Katherine J. Conger. 1987. "Personal and family processes linking rural economic hardship to men's emotional distress." Paper presented at the annual meeting of the National Council on Family Relations.

Congressional Budget Office. 1988. Trends in Family

Income: 1970–1986. Washington, DC: U.S. Government Printing Office.

Coyne, James C., and Anita DeLongis. 1986. "Going beyond social support: The role of social relationships in adaptation." Journal of Consulting and Clinical Psychology 54: 454–460.

Demo, David H., and Alan C. Acock. 1988. "The impact of divorce on children." Journal of Marriage and the Family 50: 619–648. [Reprinted in this volume]

Dew, Mary Amanda, Evelyn J. Bromet, and Herbert C. Schulberg. 1987. "A comparative analysis of two community stressors' long-term mental health effects." American Journal of Community Psychology 15: 167–184.

Dooley, David, Ralph Catalano, and Karen S. Rook. 1988. "Personal and aggregate unemployment and psychological symptoms." Journal of Social Issues 44: 107–123.

Duncan, Greg J., and Willard Rodgers. 1987. "Single-parent families: Are their economic problems transitory or persistent?" Family Planning Perspectives 19: 171–178.

Duncan, Greg J., and Willard L. Rodgers. 1988. "Longitudinal aspects of childhood poverty." Journal of Marriage and the Family 50: 1007–1021.

Elder, Glen H., Jr., and Avshalom Caspi. 1988. "Economic stress in lives: Developmental perspectives." Journal of Social Issues 44: 25–45.

Elder, Glen H., Jr., Avshalom Caspi, and Tri Van Nguyen. 1986. "Resourceful and vulnerable children: Family influences in stressful times." Pp. 167–186 in R. K. Silbereisen, K. Eyforth, and G. Rudinger (eds.), Development as Action in Context. New York: Springer-Verlag.

Elder, Glen H., Jr., Jeffrey K. Liker, and Catherine E. Cross. 1984. "Parent-child behavior in the Great Depression: Life course and intergenerational influences." Pp. 109–158 in P. B. Baltes and O. G. Brim, Jr. (eds.), Life-Span Development and Behavior (Vol. 6). New York: Academic Press.

Elder, Glen H., Jr., Tri Van Nguyen, and Avshalom Caspi. 1985. "Linking family hardship to children's lives." Child Development 56: 361–375.

Ensminger, Margaret E., and David D. Celentano. 1988. "Unemployment and psychiatric distress." Social Science Medicine 27: 239–247.

Finch, Janet. 1983. Married to the Job: Wife's Incorporation in Men's Work. London: George Allen and Unwin.

Fowlkes, Martha R. 1980. Behind Every Successful Man: Wives of Medicine and Academe. New York: Columbia Univerity Press.

Fox, Greer L., Robert F. Kelly, and Ann W. Sheldon. 1982. "Family responses to economic distress in the Detroit metropolitan area." Paper presented at the annual meeting of the North Central Sociological Association.

Galambos, Nancy L., and Rainer K. Silbereisen. 1987. "Income change, parental life outlook, and adolescent expectations for job success." Journal of Marriage and the Family 49: 141–149.

Gordus, Jeanne P., Paul Jarley, and Louis A. Ferman. 1981. Plant Closings and Economic Dislocation. Kalamazoo: W. E. Upjohn Institute.

Haas, Linda. 1986. "Wives' orientation toward breadwinning: Sweden and the United States." Journal of Family Issues 7: 358–381.

Harold-Goldsmith, Rena, Norma Radin, and Jacquelynne S. Eccles. 1988. "Objective and subjective reality: The effects of job loss and financial stress on fathering behaviors." Family Perspective 22: 309–325.

Harrison, Bennett, and Barry Bluestone. 1988. The Great U-Turn. New York: Basic Books.

Haugen, Steven E. 1989. "Employment gains slow in the first half of 1989." Monthly Labor Review 102: 3–9.

Hayghe, Howard. 1986. "Rise in mother's labor force activity includes those with infants." Monthly Labor Review 109: 43–45.

Hiller, Dana V., and William W. Philliber. 1986. "The division of labor in contemporary marriage: Expectations, perceptions, and performance." Social Problems 33: 191–201.

Hoffman, Saul D., and Greg J. Duncan. 1988. "What are the economic consequences of divorce?" Demography 25: 641–645.

Hood, Jane C. 1986. "The provider role: Its meaning and measurement." Journal of Marriage and the Family 48: 349–359.

Horvath, Francis W. 1987. "The pulse of economic change: Displaced workers of 1981–85." Monthly Labor Review 110: 3–12.

Horwitz, Allan V. 1984. "The economy and social pathology." Annual Review of Sociology 10: 95–119.

Howe, Wayne J., and William Parks II. 1989. "Labor market completes sixth year of expansion in 1988." Monthly Labor Review 112: 3–14.

Isralowitz, R., and M. Singer. 1986. "Unemployment and its impact on adolescent work values." Adolescence 21: 145–158.

Jackson, Paul R. 1988. "Personal networks, support mobilization, and unemployment." Psychological Medicine 18: 397–404.

Jahoda, Marie. 1982. Employment and Unemployment. New York: Cambridge University Press.

Johnson, Clifford M., Andrew M. Sum, and James D. Weill. 1988. Vanishing Dreams: The Growing Plight of America's Young Families. Washington, DC: Children's Defense Fund.

Kaufman, H. G. 1982. Professionals in Search of Work: Coping with the Stress of Job Loss and Underemployment. New York: Wiley.

Kelly, Robert F., Ann W. Sheldon, and Greer L. Fox. 1985. "The impact of economic dislocation on the health of children." Pp. 94–111 in J. Boulet, A. M. Debritto, and S. A. Ray (eds.), Understanding the Economic Crisis. Ann Arbor: University of Michigan.

Kessler, Ronald C. 1982. "A disaggregation of the relationship between socioeconomic status and psychological distress." American Sociological Review 47: 752–764.

Kessler, Ronald C., and Jane D. McLeod. 1985. "Social support and mental health in community samples." Pp. 219–240 in S. Cohen and S. L. Syme (eds.), Social Support and Health. New York: Academic Press.

Kessler, Ronald C., James S. House, and J. Blake Turner. 1987. "Unemployment and health in a community sample." Journal of Health and Social Behavior 28: 51–59.

Kessler, Ronald C., J. Blake Turner, and James House. 1987. "Intervening processes in the relationship between unemployment and health." Psychological Medicine 17: 949–961.

Kessler, Ronald C., J. Blake Turner, and James S. House. 1988. "Effects of unemployment on health in a community survey." Journal of Social Issues 44: 69–85.

Kessler, Ronald C., J. Blake Turner, and James S. House. 1989. "Unemployment, reemployment, and emotional functioning in a community sample." American Sociological Review 54: 648–657.

Kitson, Gay C., Karen Benson Babri, Mary Joan Roach, and Kathleen S. Placidi. 1989. "Adjustment to widowhood and divorce." Journal of Family Issues 10: 5–32.

Klein, Bruce W., and Philip L. Rones. 1989. "A profile of the working poor." Monthly Labor Review 102: 3–13.

Kosters, Marvin H., and Murray N. Ross. 1988. "A shrinking middle class?" Public Interest 92: 3–27.

Kutscher, Ronald E., and Valerie A. Personick. 1986. "Deindustrialization and the shift to services." Monthly Labor Review 109: 3–13.

Larson, Jeffry H. 1984. "The effect of husband's unemployment on marital and family relations in blue-collar families." Family Relations 33: 503–511.

Lempers, Jacques, Dania Clark-Lempers, and Ronald L. Simons. 1989. "Economic hardship, parenting, and distress in adolescence." Child Development 60: 25–39.

Lerman, Robert I., and Harold Salzman. 1988. "Deskilling and declassing: Wither the middle stratum?" Society 25: 60–66.

Leventman, Paula. 1981. Professionals Out of Work. New York: Free Press.

Levy, Frank. 1987. Dollars and Dreams. New York: Russell Sage Foundation.

Liem, Ramsay, and Joan H. Liem. 1988. "Psychological effects of unemployment on workers and their families." Journal of Social Issues 44: 87–105.

Liker, Jeffrey K., and Glen H. Elder, Jr. 1983. "Economic hardship and marital relations in the 1930s." American Sociological Review 48: 343–359.

Linn, Margaret W., Richard Sandifer, and Shayna Stein. 1985. "Effects of unemployment on mental and physical health." American Journal of Physical Health 75: 502–506.

Margolis, Lewis H., and Dale C. Farran. 1981. "Unemployment: The health consequences in children." North Carolina Medical Journal 42: 849–850.

Margolis, Lewis H., and Dale C. Farran. 1984. "Unemployment and children." International Journal of Mental Health 13: 107–124.

Martin, Teresa Castro, and Larry L. Bumpass. 1989. "Recent trends in marital disruption." Demography 26: 37–51.

May, James L., Marcia Brown-Standridge, and Stephen R. Jorgensen. 1989. "Unemployed and underemployed professional males: Stress and sexual difficulties." Paper presented at the annual meeting of the National Council on Family Relations, New Orleans.

McCubbin, Hamilton I., and Joan M. Patterson. 1983. "The family stress process: The double ABCX model of adjustment and adaptation." Marriage and Family Review 6: 7–37.

McCubbin, Marilyn A., and Hamilton I. McCubbin. 1987. "Family stress theory and assessment." Pp. 3–32 in H. I. McCubbin and A. I. Thompson (eds.), Family Assessment Inventories for Research and Practice. Madison: University of Wisconsin-Madison.

McLanahan, Sara S., and Karen Booth. 1989. "Mother-only families; Problems, prospects, and politics." Journal of Marriage and the Family 51: 557–580. [Reprinted in this volume]

McLanahan, Sara S., and Jennifer L. Glass. 1985. "A note on the trend in sex differences in psychological distress." Journal of Health and Social Behavior 26: 328–336.

McLoyd, Vonnie C. 1989. "Socialization and development in a changing economy." American Psychologist 44: 293–302.

Mellor, Earl R., and William Parks II. 1988. "A year's work: Labor force activity from a different perspective." Monthly Labor Review 111: 13–18.

Menaghan, Elizabeth G. 1983. "Individual coping efforts and family studies: Conceptual and methodological issues." Marriage and Family Review 6: 113–135.

Mishel, Lawrence, and Jacqueline Simon. 1988. The State of Working America. Washington, DC: Economic Policy Institute.

Moen, Phyllis, Edward L. Kain, and Glen H. Elder, Jr. 1983. "Economic conditions and family life: Contemporary and historical perspectives." Pp. 213–259 in Richard R. Nelson and Felicity Skidmore (eds.), American Families and the Economy: The High Costs of Living. Washington, DC: National Academy Press.

Moos, Rudolph H., and Andrew G. Billings. 1982. "Conceptualizing and measuring coping resources and processes." Pp. 212–230 in L. Goldberger and S. Breznitz (ed.), Handbook of Stress: Theoretical and Clinical Aspects. New York: Free Press.

Morris, Lydia D. 1984. "Redundancy and patterns of household finance." Sociological Review 32: 492–523.

Nowak, Thomas C., and Kay A. Snyder. 1986. "Sex differences in the long-term consequences of job loss." Paper presented at the annual meeting of the American Sociological Association, New York.

Oppenheimer, Valerie. 1982. Work and the Family: A Study in Social Demography. New York: Academic Press.

Papanek, Hanna. 1979. "Family status production." Signs 4: 775–781.

Pearlin, Leonard I. 1989. "The sociological study of stress." Journal of Health and Social Behavior 30: 241–256.

Pearlin, Leonard I., Mortin A. Lieberman, Elizabeth

Menaghan, and Joseph T. Mullan. 1981. "The stress process." Journal of Health and Social Behavior 22: 337–356.

Penkower, Lili, Evelyn J. Bromet, and Mary Amanda Dew. 1988. "Husbands' layoffs and wives' mental health." Archives of General Psychiatry 45: 994–1000.

Perrucci, Carolyn C., Robert Perrucci, Dena B. Targ, and Harry R. Targ. 1985. "Impact of a plant closing on workers and the community." Pp. 231–260 in I. H. Simpson and R. L. Simpson (eds.), Research in the Sociology of Work: A Research Annual (Vol. 3). Greenwich, CT: JAI.

Perrucci, Carolyn C., Robert Perrucci, Dena B. Targ, and Harry R. Targ. 1988. Plant Closings. New York: Aldine DeGruyter.

Perrucci, Carolyn C., and Dena B. Targ. 1988. "Effects of a plant closing on marriage and family life." Pp. 55–71 in P. Voydanoff and L. C. Majka (eds.), Families and Economic Distress: Coping Strategies and Social Policy. Beverly Hills, CA: Sage.

Peskin, Janice. 1982. "Measuring household production for the GNP." Family Economics Review 3: 16–25.

Pett, Marjorie A., and Beth Vaughan-Cole. 1986. "The impact of income issues and social status on post-divorce adjustment of custodial parents." Family Relations 35: 103–111.

Piotrkowski, Chaya S., Robert N. Rapoport, and Rhona Rapoport. 1987. "Families and work." Pp. 251–283 in Marvin B. Sussman and Suzanne K. Steinmetz (eds.), Handbook of Marriage and the Family. New York: Plenum Press.

Pittman, Joe F., and Sally A. Lloyd. 1988. "Quality of family life, social support, and stress." Journal of Marriage and the Family 50: 53–67.

Rawlings, Steve W. 1989. "Single parents and their children." Pp. 13–25 in U.S. Bureau of the Census, Studies in Marriage and the Family. Current Population Reports, Series P-23, No. 162. Washington, DC: Government Printing Office.

Rayman, Paul. 1983. "Out of work: The effects of urban unemployment." Unpublished paper, Brandeis University.

Retherford, Patricia S., Gladys J. Hildreth, and Elizabeth B. Goldsmith. 1988. "Social support and resource management of unemployed women." E. Goldsmith (ed.), Work and Family: Theory, Research, and Applications. Journal of Social Behavior and Personality 3: 191–204.

Richards, Leslie N. 1989. "The precarious survival and hard-won satisfactions of white single-parent families." Family Relations 38: 396–403.

Root, Kenneth. 1984. "The human response to plant closures." Annals of the American Academy of Political and Social Science 475: 52–65.

Ross, Catherine E., and Joan Huber. 1985. "Hardship and depression." Journal of Health and Social Behavior 26: 312–327.

Select Committee on Children, Youth, and Families. 1987. U.S. Children and Their Families: Current Conditions and Recent Trends, 1987. Washington, DC: Government Printing Office.

Shamir, Boas. 1985. "Sex differences in psychological adjustment to unemployment and reemployment: A question of commitment, alternatives, or finance?" Social Problems 33: 67–79.

Shamir, Boas. 1986. "Self-esteem and the psychological impact of unemployment." Social Psychology Quarterly 49: 61–72.

Shinn, Marybeth, Stanley Lehmann, and Nora W. Wong. 1984. "Social interaction and social support." Journal of Social Issues 40: 55–76.

Smith, James P. 1989. "Children among the poor." Demography 26: 235–248.

Smith, Shirley J. 1986. "Work experience profile, 1984: The effects of recovery continue." Monthly Labor Review 99: 37–45.

Snyder, Kay A., and Thomas C. Nowak. 1984. "Job loss and demoralization." International Journal of Mental Health 13: 92–106.

Targ, Dena, and Carolyn Perrucci. In press. "Plant closings, unemployment, and families." Marriage and Family Review.

Teachman, Jay D., Karen A. Polonko, and John Scanzoni. 1987. "Demography of the family." Pp. 3–36 in M. B. Sussman and S. K. Steinmetz (eds.), Handbook of Marriage and the Family. New York: Plenum Press.

Teachman, Jay D., and Paul T. Schollaert. 1989. "Economic conditions, marital status, and the timing of first births." Sociological Forum 4: 27–45.

Ulbrich, Patricia M. 1988. "The determinants of depression in two-income marriages." Journal of Marriage and the Family 50: 121–131.

U.S. Bureau of the Census. 1989a. Money Income of Households, Families, and Persons in the United States: 1987. Current Population Reports, Series P-60, No. 162. Washington, DC: Government Printing Office.

U.S. Bureau of the Census. 1989b. Poverty in the United States: 1987. Current Population Reports, Series P-60, No. 163. Washington, DC: Government Printing Office.

U.S. Bureau of Labor Statistics. 1987. News. Washington, DC: U.S. Department of Labor.

Voydanoff, Patricia. 1984. "Economic distress and families: Policy issues." Journal of Family Issues 5: 273–288.

Voydanoff, Patricia. 1987. Work and Family Life. Newbury Park, CA: Sage.

Voydanoff, Patricia, and Brenda W. Donnelly. 1986. "Economic distress and mental health: Coping strategies and social supports." Report submitted to the Office of Program Evaluation and Research, Ohio Department of Mental Health.

Voydanoff, Patricia, and Brenda W. Donnelly. 1988. "Economic distress, family coping, and quality of family life." Pp. 97–116 in P. Voydanoff and L. C. Majka (eds.), Families and Economic Distress: Coping Strategies and Social Policy. Beverly Hills, CA: Sage.

Voydanoff, Patricia, and Brenda W. Donnelly. 1989. "Economic distress and mental health." Lifestyles 10: 139–162.

Voydanoff, Patricia, Brenda W. Donnelly, and Mark

A. Fine. 1988. "Economic distress, social integration, and family satisfaction." Journal of Family Issues 9: 545–564.

Walker, Alexis J. 1985. "Reconceptualizing family stress." Journal of Marriage and the Family 47: 827–837.

Warr, Peter. 1984. "Job loss, unemployment and psychological well-being." Pp. 263–285 in V. L. Allen and E. van de Vliert (eds.), Role Transitions. New York: Plenum Press.

Warr, Peter, Paul Jackson, and Michael Banks. 1988. "Unemployment and mental health: Some British studies." Journal of Social Issues 44: 47–68.

Wilhelm, Mari S., and Carl A. Ridley. 1988a. "Stress and unemployment in rural nonfarm couples: A study of hardships and coping resources." Family Relations 37: 50–54.

Wilhelm, Mari S., and Carl A. Ridley. 1988b. "Unemployment induced adaptations." Lifestyles 9: 5–20.

Wilson, Gail. 1987. Money in the Family: Financial Organization and Women's Responsibility. Brookfield, VT: Avebury.

FRED P. PIERCY AND DOUGLAS H. SPRENKLE
Purdue University

Marriage and Family Therapy:

A Decade Review

This review summarizes trends in theory and research on marriage and family therapy over the past decade. Particularly noteworthy are the debates over the "new epistemology" and the feminist critique of family therapy. Research in the field, while underdeveloped in some areas, appears to be maturing in certain methodologically and conceptually appropriate directions. On the basis of these trends, recommendations are offered for research in the '90s.

Family therapy continued to mature as a profession (Everett, 1990) in the 1980s, and as in the previous decade, the literature on family therapy theory, research, and practice increased dramatically. Traditional family therapy models have evolved, new models have emerged, and "family systems thinking" has broadened to allow a greater appreciation of individual and societal influences. Lively debates have also characterized the decade. In this review, we will survey some of what is new in the theory, research, and practice of family therapy since 1980 and consider what it means for the future of this multifaceted field.

THEORETICAL DEVELOPMENTS

Significant theoretical advances were evident in psychoeducational, structural, transgenerational, behavioral, and experiential family therapies. Integrative therapies such as emotion-focused

Department of Child Development and Family Studies, Purdue University, West Lafayette, IN 47907.

therapy (Greenberg and Johnson, 1988) have also emerged. Perhaps the most noteworthy theoretical developments of the decade, however, are those that involve strategic and systemic family therapies.

Strategic Family Therapies

It would be difficult to pick up a family therapy journal published in the 1980s and not find several articles on one of the increasing variants of strategic family therapy. Strategic family therapy is generally characterized by its use of specific strategies for addressing family problems (Madanes and Haley, 1977). In its most generic sense, strategic therapy attempts to change the presenting problem. Typically, the therapist first assesses the cycle of family interaction, then breaks that cycle through straightforward or paradoxical directives (Piercy, Sprenkle, et al., 1986).

Strategic family therapy is practiced quite differently by various groups. The work of Cloe Madanes and Jay Haley (e.g., Haley, 1987; Madanes, 1981) and the Brief Therapy Model developed at the Mental Research Institute (MRI) in Palo Alto, California, are the two primary strategic therapy approaches (Stone Fish and Piercy, 1987). In addition, Milton Erickson's approach to hypnosis has been actively incorporated into the strategic therapy of others (Gordon and Meyers-Anderson, 1981; O'Hanlon, 1987; Zeig, 1985).

Steve deShazer and his colleagues have evolved what they call solution-focused therapy (deShazer, 1985; deShazer et al., 1986; Molnar and deShazer, 1987). This therapy employs many of the indirect features of the MRI approach but focuses on family strengths and "exceptions" to problems rather than the problems themselves. DeShazer offers a variety of "keys," or standard interventions, that he believes are applicable to a wide range of presenting problems. A similar approach is described by O'Hanlon and Weiner-Davis (1989).

The explosion of articles, books, and even a journal (*Journal of Strategic and Systemic Therapies*) on strategic family therapy may be understood by considering what makes this therapy attractive. Strategic therapy mirrors the pragmatic, result-centered technological spirit of the decade. At the same time, it emphasizes inventiveness and creativity. Proponents address symptom relief in a manner that is both challenging and intriguing to the family therapist. Clearly, strategic therapy has lost little of the lure that it had in the early '80s.

Milan Systemic Therapy

The systemic therapy of Mara Selvini Palazzoli, Luigi Boscolo, Gianfranco Cecchin, and Guiliana Prata gained prominence in 1978 with the publication of *Paradox and Counterparadox*. Milan systemic therapy was built on Batesonian tenets, influenced by consultations with Paul Watzlawick of MRI, and enriched by the creativity of Selvini and her colleagues. The Milan group has influenced countless family therapists; their emphasis on such concepts as neutrality, circular questioning, and positive connotation can be seen in the work of Karl Tomm (1987), Michael White (1986), Lynn Hoffman (1985, 1988), Peggy Papp (1983), Peggy Penn (1985) and others. In recent years Selvini Palazzoli and Prata have diverted their attention to an "invariable prescription," an intervention they use with all families with a schizophrenic member (Selvini Palazzoli, 1986).

Selvini Palazzoli's research methods and enthusiastic claims, although embraced by a growing number of therapists, have also been criticized (Anderson, 1986). So has Selvini Palazzoli's thinking which, like that of Bateson and the other authors mentioned above, embraces the notion of circular causality. It is such systems thinking, once a benchmark of family therapy, that is today seen by an increasing number of family therapists

as denying the volition and individual responsibility of family members.

The Family System in Context

Marriage and family therapy is less dependent on the unit of treatment (individual, couple, family) than it is on a way of thinking that emphasizes the interrelatedness of the individual, the family, and the social context. This decade has seen an increase in the acknowledgement of the family system in context. Concepts regarding the individual are beginning to be integrated into family therapy theories (Brighton-Cleghorn, 1987; Gustafson, 1987; Nichols, 1987; Pinsof, 1983). Wachtel (1987), for example, presents tools for working with the individual child while maintaining a systemic perspective. Similarly, Grunebaum and Belfer (1986) review a decade of individual child therapy literature that is relevant to family therapy.

Authors also are increasingly discussing the effects of larger systems, such as psychiatric hospitals, school systems, social networks, and even entire communities and cultures, on families (Imber-Black, 1988; Schwartzman, 1984). McGoldrick, Pearce, and Giordano (1982) have provided perhaps the most comprehensive selection of family therapy articles on specific cultural experiences in this country. Other works on family therapy and culture are also noteworthy (e.g., Domokos-Cheng Ham, 1989; Ho, 1987).

The next decade should see heightened attention to cultural, individual, and "other systems" issues, as family therapy continues to become more aware of the societal context on both macro and micro levels. For example, with increased interest in family therapy in other countries, the development and evaluation of culturally appropriate interventions should become important issues in the '90s.

WAVES OF THEORETICAL DEBATE: THE NEW EPISTEMOLOGY AND THE FEMINIST CRITIQUE

The New Epistemology

One of the most far-reaching critiques of family therapy began with a 1982 issue of *Family Process* in which Allman (1982), Dell (1982), and Keeney and Sprenkle (1982) questioned some of the basic theoretical tenets of family therapy. These and other "new epistemology" writings that followed reflect a logical extension of systems thinking and represent a challenge to established ideas about science. In its most extreme form, the new epistemology questioned such concepts as individual responsibility (Taggart, 1982, 1985), homeostasis and resistance (Dell, 1982), pathology (Dell, 1983), and objectivity (Tomm, 1984). Each can be seen as an illusion within an epistemology that considers behaviors as interconnected, mutually recursive, and part of a larger, ecologically coherent system. For example, although one person may *appear* to cause harm to another, or to be resistant, or dysfunctional, such linear attributions may simply be flawed notions—false dualism—when viewed from a holistic, mutually interactive philosophical framework.

The new epistemologists have also raised important questions about traditional family therapy research. They criticize reductionistic models of research that ignore context and tend to trivialize what they study. Moreover, they contend that the researcher cannot be separated from his or her research findings. Empiricism, they assert, is neither value-free nor theory-free. While the new epistemologists offer few concrete research alternatives, they support more intuition, creativity, and description in family therapy research, and more attention to context and relatedness.

Writers such as Hoffman (1981, 1985), Dell (1986a, 1986b), Golann (1987, 1988), and Anderson and Goolishian (1988) have tried to take the tenets of epistemology and constructivism and apply them to clinical work. Concepts such as collaboration (Hoffman, 1988) and "languaging" (Anderson and Goolishian, 1988) are replacing those of power, hierarchy, and influence. Techniques that are said to be consistent with systemic and constructivist thinking include reframing and positive connotation (Efran, Lukens, and Lukens, 1988), circular questioning (Penn, 1982; Selvini Palazzoli et al., 1978), and the use of the reflecting team (Andersen, 1987), where the reactions of an observing team are shared directly with the family.

The new epistemologists and constructivists have forced the field to examine the logical implications of some cherished systemic assumptions. The result is an enrichment and expansion of theory and an initial effort to develop interventions consistent with that theory. Moreover, the world view that the new epistemologists offered has provided a vivid target for a simultaneous feminist critique.

Feminist Critique of Family Therapy

The '80s saw a sustained feminist critique of some traditional bastions of family therapy theory. Feminists challenged such familiar family therapy tenets as circularity and neutrality, and questioned family therapy's emphasis on the family system at the expense of the individual, usually the woman (Avis, 1986). Old family therapy videotapes and books were examined anew, through eyes that found male therapists blaming women and ignoring the political implications of both therapy and marriage. Hare-Mustin (1987), Goldner (1985), Luepnitz (1988), and others were articulate spokespersons for another way of conceptualizing family therapy, one in which the therapist becomes an active vehicle for changing gender imbalances. The feminist voice could also be heard through debates (e.g., Avis, 1985), books (Goodrich, Rampage, Ellman, and Halstead, 1988; McGoldrick, Anderson, and Walsh, 1989), a new journal (*Journal of Feminist Family Therapy*), and countless workshops. The '90s promise a refining of the feminist voice that should continue to serve as a constructive challenge to the field of family therapy.

APPLICATION OF FAMILY THERAPY TO SPECIFIC PRESENTING PROBLEMS

It is a tribute to the vitality and utility of family therapy that it has been applied in the 1980s not only to traditional marital, sexual, and child concerns but also to such diverse problems as delinquency, anxiety disorders, schizophrenia, mood disorders, family violence and abuse, and a variety of addictive behaviors. The best (but not complete) single review of these applications is by Gurman, Kniskern, and Pinsof (1986). Here we will focus briefly on one presenting problem, schizophrenia, about which some of the most pioneering family therapy research has been conducted this decade. Also, we will note several pressing areas where more attention is needed.

Schizophrenia

Four major controlled studies (Goldstein, Rodnick, Evans, May, and Steinberg, 1978; Leff, Kuipers, Berkowitz, and Sturgeon, 1985; Falloon et al., 1985; Hogarty et al., 1986) on the family management of schizophrenia were conducted in the 1980s. These studies were based on a stress-vulnerability model of etiology in which schizophrenia is seen as the result of an interaction between a genetically based biological vulnerability and exposure to environmental stress (which includes a disturbed family emotional climate called high expressed emotion, or EE). Family management programs address both the environmental stress and the biological vulnerability, and utilize neuroleptic medication to bring psychotic symptoms under control. The family is used as a resource to reduce posthospitalization stress and to facilitate reentry into the community. The family therapy approach has been behavioral, with an emphasis on problem-solving and crisis management skills. Families are also educated to modify their expectations and emotional reactions to patients (Goldstein and Strachan, 1987).

The study by Falloon et al. (1985) was exceptionally strong methodologically and achieved results that corroborated the other investigations. Major conclusions were that (a) psychosocial interventions appear to add significantly to the therapeutic effect of antipsychotic medication; (b) family management may be superior to individual management in the after-care phase of schizophrenia; (c) family management appears to contribute to and enhance social functioning of patients and to ease the burden of family caregivers; and (d) the way in which family members convey emotionally toned remarks is related to the probability of posthospitalization relapse. Conversely, there was very little solid evidence of the efficacy of more traditional family therapy approaches to schizophrenia (Anderson, 1986; Stein, 1989).

Topical Areas in Need of Research

For all of the clinical and media attention given to family violence in the 1980s, there were only a few published studies that examined the effectiveness of treatment for batterers and the abused (e.g., Hamberger and Hastings, 1988). This research is in its infancy. The most effective treatment variables have not been isolated.

Another topic of current interest has been intrafamily sexual abuse of children. Here, too, in spite of excellent treatment manuals (e.g., Trepper and Barrett, 1989), there has been virtually no well-designed and controlled research on treatment.

Similarly, little is known about family treatment in relation to AIDS. Research is needed to determine the best ways to mobilize the strength and support of families of AIDS victims. Also, family therapy could be one possible means of reducing the likelihood that adolescents would turn to intravenous use of drugs and thus heighten their risk of AIDS infection. Obviously, research is needed on family therapy both as potential prevention and in treatment of AIDS.

Finally, with changing demographics, much more attention needs to be paid to family therapy among aging populations. Flori (1989) has argued that elders in marriage and family relationships constitute a new frontier for the extension and elaboration of family therapy.

RESEARCH IN THE 1980s

Shortly before the 1980s decade began, Gurman and Kniskern (1978) published the first comprehensive overview of research in the field. The paper was widely cited because of its comprehensiveness and because it painted an essentially optimistic picture of conjoint marital and family therapy as the treatment of choice for family-related concerns.

These same authors presented an updated version of their review at the start of this decade (Gurman and Kniskern, 1981) and another major review five years later (Gurman et al., 1986). Other significant and comprehensive research reviews in the eighties were written by Todd and Stanton (1983), Beach and O'Leary (1985), Jacobson, Follette, and Elwood (1984), Baucom and Hoffman (1986), Bednar, Burlingame, and Masters (1988), and Hazelrigg, Cooper, and Borduin (1987). Reviews of more specialized topics within marriage and family therapy are legion and are listed in Gurman et al. (1986).

In our judgment, based on a critical examination of these reviews, a reasonable amount of evidence has been amassed to support the *general* efficacy of family therapy. Gurman and associates (1986) list a variety of conclusions that are shared by other reviewers and do not seem to be contradicted by recent data. Among these conclusions are the following:

1. Nonbehavioral marital and family therapies produce beneficial outcomes in about two-thirds of cases, and their effects are superior to no treatment.

2. When both spouses are involved in therapy conjointly for marital problems, there is a greater chance of positive outcome than when only one spouse is treated.

3. Positive results of both nonbehavioral and behavioral marital and family therapies typically occur in treatment of short duration; that is, from 1 to 20 sessions.

4. Family therapy is probably as effective and possibly more effective than many commonly offered individual treatments for problems attributed to family conflict (Gurman et al., 1986: 572).

An interesting countertrend that has emerged over the decade, perhaps because of the maturing of the discipline, is an increased modesty about the *specifics* of efficacy (Paul, 1967). That is, we know much less about what treatment works best for what problem under what set of circumstances.

In fact, most of the influential "schools" of family therapy offer little empirical evidence for their potency, let alone any compelling evidence that they are superior to any other approach. In the Gurman et al. (1986) summary analysis of the effectiveness of the major schools of family therapy, 15 approaches were cross-tabulated with 10 clinical disorders or problems. Outcome research of any sort has been conducted on only 35 of the 150 method-by-problem combinations (23%). It is also true that some of the most influential and clinically useful concepts associated with these "schools" (e.g., enmeshment, triangulation) have never been adequately operationalized or empirically tested.

The excellent progress in establishing the general efficacy of the discipline, therefore, must be viewed against a backdrop that contains gaping holes. With some notable exceptions, marriage and family therapy research offers disappointingly little guidance to the clinician who must choose among competing treatment options.

Trends in Family Therapy Research: Variations on a Theme of "Smaller Is Better"

Family therapy researchers have begun to address specificity issues. A foundation is being laid for the 1990s that has as its cornerstone, "Smaller is better" (Gurman et al., 1986). This trend is being manifested in six ways:

1. From global comparative questions to specificity questions. Although few specificity questions were answered in the decade, at least they were beginning to be asked. Gurman and Kniskern's 1978 review contained global (and somewhat polemical) comparisons of the general efficacy of nonbehavioral and behavioral family therapies. By 1986, Gurman and his associates were much more concerned with the application of family therapy to *specific* presenting problems, and the contrasts between behavioral and nonbehavioral approaches seemed less sharply drawn. This later review highlighted the concrete successes of particular approaches with particular presenting problems (e.g., structural family therapy with psychosomatic disorders, functional therapy with "soft" delinquency, etc.).

By mid-decade, Neil Jacobson, Gurman and Kniskern's friendly antagonist in the nonbehavioral/behavioral debate, was calling for an end to global competition among the various therapies. Jacobson (1985) noted that significant main effects are rarely found in nature, let alone between two psychotherapies, mainly because treatments typically share a number of overlapping features. Instead, investigators should be looking for interaction effects; that is, that a particular approach is more effective with a particular problem or a particular type of client.

Another fruitful alternative to pitting one approach against another is to conduct intraschool component analyses. The comparison by Jacobson et al. (1987) between a complete behavioral marital therapy treatment package and two of its major components, behavior exchange and communication/problem solving, is an excellent example of such dismantling within a treatment school.

2. From hubris to "mellowing." Some family therapists in the '70s became system "purists" and assumed that almost all human problems were a direct result of current interactional dynamics. For example, some downplayed or denied any possible biological component to the etiology of schizophrenia. (Some maintained this position even toward the end of this decade; e.g., Haley, 1989.) The general trend of the decade, however, was more conciliatory. In the previously mentioned research on schizophrenia, family therapy is not considered to be a "cure" nor are family dynamics assumed to "cause" this malady. Rather, the etiological question is bypassed and family therapy is assumed to be a method by which the disease can be "managed." This trend also has led to research in the family management of depression and affective disorders (Coyne, Kahn, and Gotlib, 1987).

3. From outcome to both process and outcome.

One of the more exciting developments of the decade has been the emergence of the "new process perspective" (Gurman et al., 1986). Historically, outcome research has been concerned mainly with what happens after the course of therapy ceases. Process research focuses on what happens within the session itself. The primary task of process research is the identification of relationships between process and outcome variables. Previously, process researchers have employed some kind of "average" process measurement over treatment and related it to final outcome indices (e.g., relating the average degree of therapist relationship skills to change in the presenting problem over ten sessions). This approach is flawed, since process variables often vary significantly over the course of treatment and even within single treatment sessions. The new process perspective looks at "outcome" as a series of "episodes" of therapy in which some kind of theoretically significant change occurs. The researcher then examines what proceeds and/or follows the change in order to develop causal or at least correlational hypotheses about events that may be related (Gurman et al., 1986). (For example, the researcher might examine the degree to which empathetic statements by the therapist are followed by nonresistant responses by the client.)

This approach, however, represents more promise than accomplishment. Because of their complexity and expense, very few high-quality process research studies have been completed. Also, not many reliable and valid instruments are

specific enough to tap processes that can be related to outcome. Finally, the sequential analysis procedures necessary to conduct process research are not well understood by most family therapy researchers (Gottman, 1987).

Perhaps the most impressive example of the new process perspective has been the work of Patterson and his colleagues at the Oregon Social Learning Center (Patterson and Chamberlain, 1988). Specifically, these researchers have been investigating the relationship between therapist behaviors and client resistance, and relating these relationships to outcome. They have developed a highly specific nominal coding system that allows for a microanalytic examination of the process. Another example is William Pinsof's (1985) work at the Family Institute of Chicago.

4. From design weakness to design strength.

In their 1978 research review, Gurman and Kniskern had to reply, in part, on a large body of methodologically inadequate studies to reach their conclusions about the general efficacy of family therapy. Fortunately, the ensuing decade has seen a number of truly outstanding studies that not only confirmed Gurman and Kniskern's (1978) optimistic conclusions but would be given superior design quality ratings by even the most conservative positivists. While any list of model family therapy research studies is bound to be controversial, our honor roll includes Falloon and associates' (1985) outstanding work on the family management of schizophrenia and Jacobson, Schmaling, and Holtzworth-Munroe's (1987) component analysis of behavioral marital therapy. Patterson and Chamberlain (1988) offer perhaps the best example of research with a process perspective. Also exemplary is Russell, Szmukler, Dave, and Eisler's (1987) evaluation of family therapy with anorexia nervosa and bulimia nervosa.

What is particularly impressive about all of these studies, beyond their rigorous controls and careful execution, is the investigators' use of a variety of reliable and valid measures from a number of perspectives. Most also incorporate nonreactive dependent variables such as recidivism and rehospitalization. Furthermore, the authors make diligent attempts to raise and eliminate the possibility of alternative explanations for their findings. This research also provides excellent models of long-term follow-up and attention to attrition and relapse.

5. From statistical to clinical significance. What happens in therapy is often disguised when statistical significance is the only criterion. For example, weight loss from 250 pounds to 247 pounds would be statistically significant with a large enough sample size. Such statistical significance does not reflect either the meaningfulness of the change or the percentage of people who actually improved to a functional level.

One step taken in the past decade has been the application of meta-analysis to marriage and family therapy (Giblin, Sprenkle, and Sheehan, 1985; Hazelrigg, Cooper, and Borduin, 1987; Wampler, 1982). Meta-analysis refers to the statistical analysis of the standardized results of a large collection of studies. The unit of analysis is the effect size, a standard score representing the magnitude of the effect of treatment compared to control group scores.

An even more useful approach, in our judgment, is the concept of clinical significance developed by Neil Jacobson and colleagues (e.g., Jacobson and Revenstorf, 1988). These authors note that although differences between two treatments may be statistically significant (or reflect a large effect size), families in the "improved" condition may remain dysfunctional after therapy. Conversely, there may be major clinical differences between treatment groups but these differences fail to reach statistical significance because of a small sample or heterogeneity within the subject population. Jacobson and colleagues devised the Reliable Change Index (or RC), which converts the degree of change into a standard score that enables one to determine whether change is beyond chance (i.e., beyond 1.96 RC units). They also devised methods to determine clinical significance; that is, the degree to which clients move from a dysfunctional to a functional range on a particular instrument during the course of therapy and remain there at follow-up.

6. From quantitative to both qualitative and quantitative emphases. The decade has seen a growing recognition that quantitative research, however valuable, has limits. For one thing, theories (and clinicians' beliefs about theories) are seldom changed by empirical data. Theories wax and wane for reasons that have more to do with where one was trained, the charisma of the proponent of the theory, the match with one's particular personality, and marketplace considerations (Mahrer, 1988). More important, there has been a growing awareness that while the quantitative paradigm is suitable for testing hypotheses (verification), it is not of much value in the area of the "discovery" of relationships among variables. Qualitative researchers attempt to understand the significance of complex events and interactions in their natural context from the point of view of the participants involved (Moon, Dillon, and Sprenkle, in press). As such, this approach to research mirrors the concerns of the new epistemologists mentioned before. While purists believe that qualitative and quantitative paradigms are incompatible because they make different assumptions about the nature of reality, others (the present authors included) believe that both approaches are useful for answering different types of research questions.

Qualitative research also seems to be theoretically compatible with the new process perspective, which calls for the use of intensive analysis, detailed descriptions and observations, and the smaller-is-better philosophy. Moreover, qualitative methods can provide contextual data that can enrich the interpretation of quantitative outcome studies. For example, Jacobson and associates (1987) two-year follow-up of a component analysis of behavioral marital therapy (BMT) contained not only a traditionally controlled experiment but also qualitative structured interviews.

Research Recommendations

The following are some suggestions for family therapy research in the 1990s. Most build upon the theme of specificity.

1. Treatment variables. Even some of the best research in the 1980s did not adequately describe the treatments being tested. Treatment manuals should be written. Moreover, too few studies provide adequate safeguards to ensure that the treatment described is actually the treatment delivered. Hence, therapists' adherence to treatment protocols needs to be documented. As previously noted, we believe some of the most credible research will be "within-school" component analyses to determine what factors and in what combinations contribute to outcome.

2. Client variables. Family therapy researchers

need to do a better job of discussing what is unique about their client population and how this distinctiveness limits external validity. Perhaps the greatest challenge of the decade will be to continue attempts to find reliable and valid means of describing and classifying couple and family systems. Without this ability, it would be impossible to address the question of what treatment works best for what type of couple or family. Although there have been noteworthy attempts at such classifications—for example, Olson's Circumplex Model (Olson, Bell, and Portner, 1985), and the Beavers System Model (Beavers, Hampton, and Hulgus, 1985), these typologies have not been validated sufficiently to engender widespread acceptance. A major irony of research in family therapy is that after four decades there are no typologies of couples or families with substantial empirical support.

3. Therapist variables. Investigators need to ensure therapist equivalency when treatments are compared. Since meta-analysis has shown that one's degree of allegiance to a therapeutic approach is a significant factor in outcome (Bednar et al., 1988), comparison studies with therapists of differing degrees of allegiance are problematic. That is, considerable bias is injected into studies when such therapists perform operations they do not personally believe in. It is best to use the same therapist to perform competing treatments only when their allegiance to differing treatments is similar (as in "within-school" dismantling comparisons). Usually different therapists of equal experience, competence, and allegiance should be used in comparative studies. Discussion sections of research papers should address specifically this issue of therapist bias.

4. Outcome variables. The present authors join others (e.g., Gurman and Kniskern, 1981; Todd and Stanton, 1983) in calling for the operationalization of the many family therapy constructs that remain fuzzy and elusive. While we agree with Todd and Stanton (1983) that the resolution of the client's presenting problem is the sine qua non of therapy, it is inadequate as a sole criterion. Whenever possible, there should be measures that tap constructs at the individual, couple, and family system levels. As the classic articles in individual psychotherapy have demonstrated, outcome differs substantially depending on who is asked (therapists, clients, relatives) and how data are collected (structural interview, behavioral checklist, global judgment about improvement, etc.; Todd and Stanton, 1983). The possible effects of these choices should be noted and discussed. Some difficulties can be eliminated or minimized by using, when possible, "nonreactive" dependent variables such as recidivism, weight loss, arrests, or divorce. Finally, there is a compelling need to address the issue of the cost-effectiveness of marriage and family therapy (Pike and Piercy, in press). The viability of family therapy in the mental health marketplace will depend upon such endeavors.

5. Qualitative research. There have been only a few good examples of qualitative research as applied to family therapy. The field needs standards by which to evaluate qualitative investigations. Fortunately, a substantial body of qualitative research has been done in the ancillary fields of education and sociology, and family therapists are urged to draw upon this literature.

6. Programmatic research. Perhaps because of the demands of funding sources or tenure committees, family therapy researchers too often jump from one research subject to another. Particularly in the area of process research, investigators often develop a promising typology or coding system, conduct one study using it, and then move on to other projects. Research has not been accretive. The family therapy field offers few examples of researchers who have developed a program of research and have stuck with it long enough to build on what they learn from initial studies and to conduct the dismantling studies we have been advocating. Exceptions include the relationship enhancement (RE) research centered on the work of Guerney and associates (e.g., Hardley and Guerney, 1989), the Oregon work on aggressive children, led by Gerald Patterson (Patterson and Chamberlain, 1988), the behavioral marital research originally spearheaded by Robert Weiss and now under the leadership of Neil Jacobson (Jacobson et al., 1987), James Alexander's behavioral systems approach, now called functional family therapy (Alexander and Parsons, 1982) and the research of Susan Johnson and Leslie Greenberg (Greenberg and Johnson, 1988) on emotionally focused therapy for couples. The field should reward and encourage such programmatic efforts.

CONCLUSION

The growth of family therapy theory and research in this decade serves as testament to the enthusiasm and potential viability of this maturing field. The outcome data that exists are encouraging, as are the trends in research methodology. Although certain research areas are largely underdeveloped, we are reminded of the words of the German philosopher Goethe, who once said, "I find the great thing in this world is, not so much where we stand, as in what direction we are moving."

NOTE

Fred P. Piercy and Douglas H. Sprenkle are equal coauthors. They acknowledge the aid of Connee Pike, Tammy Mitten, James Langford, and Sidney Moon in the development of this review.

REFERENCES

Alexander, James J., and B. Parsons. 1982. Functional Family Therapy. Monterey, CA: Brooks-Cole.

Allman, Lawrence R. 1982. "The aesthetic preference: Overcoming the pragmatic error." Family Process 21: 43–56.

Andersen, Thomas. 1987. "The reflecting team: Dialogue and meta-dialogue in clinical work." Family Process 26: 415–429.

Anderson, Carol M. 1986. "The all-too-short trip from positive to negative connotation." Journal of Marital and Family Therapy 12: 351–354.

Anderson, Harlene, and H. Goolishian. 1988. "Human systems as linguistic systems: Preliminary and evolving ideas about the implications for clinical theory." Family Process 27: 371–394.

Avis, Judith M. 1985. "The politics of functional family therapy: A feminist critique." Journal of Marital and Family Therapy 11: 127–138.

Avis, Judith M. 1986. "Feminist issues in family therapy." Pp. 214–232 in F. Piercy and D. Sprenkle and associates (eds.), Family Therapy Sourcebook. New York: Guilford.

Baucom, D. H., and J. A. Hoffman. 1986. "The effectiveness of marital therapy: Current status and application to the clinical setting." Pp. 597–620 in N. Jacobson and A. Gurman (eds.), Clinical Handbook of Marital Therapy. New York: Guilford.

Beach, S. R., and K. D. O'Leary. 1985. "The current status of outcome research in marital therapy." In L. L'Abate (ed.), Handbook of Family Psychology and Psychotherapy. Homewood, IL: Dorsey.

Beavers, William R., R. B. Hampton, and Y. F. Hulgus. 1985. "Commentary: The Beavers System approach to family assessment." Family Process 24: 398–405.

Bednar, R. L., G. M. Burlingame, and K. S. Masters. 1988. "Systems of family treatment: Substance or semantics?" Annual Review of Psychology 39: 401–413.

Brighton-Cleghorn, J. 1987. "Formulations of self and family systems." Family Process 26: 185–201.

Coyne, James C., J. Kahn, and I. H. Gotlib. 1987. "Depression." In T. Jacob (ed.), Family Interaction and Psychopathology. New York: Plenum Press.

Dell, Paul F. 1982. Beyond homeostasis: Toward a concept of coherence." Family Process 21: 21–41.

Dell, Paul. 1983. "From pathology to ethics." Family Therapy Networker 7: 29–31.

Dell, Paul F. 1986a. "In defense of 'lineal causality'." Family Process 25: 513–521.

Dell, Paul F. 1986b. "Toward a foundation for addressing violence." Family Process 25: 527–529.

deShazer, Steve. 1985. Keys to Solution in Brief Therapy. New York: Norton.

deShazer, Steve, I. Berg, E. Lipchik, E. Nunnally, A. Molnar, W. Gingerich, and M. Weiner-Davis. 1986. "Brief therapy: Focused solution development." Family Process 25: 207–222.

Domokols-Cheng Ham, M. A. 1989. "Family therapy with immigrant families: Constructing a bridge between different world views." Special issue, Journal of Strategies and Systemic Therapies 8.

Efran, Jay S., R. Lukens, and M. D. Lukens. 1988. "Constructivism: What's in it for you?" Family Therapy Networker 12: 27–35.

Everett, Craig. 1990. "The field of marital and family therapy." Journal of Counseling and Development 68: 498–502.

Falloon, Ian R. H., J. L. Boyd, C. W. McGill, M. Williamson, J. Razani, H. B. Moss, A. M. Gilderman, and G. M. Simpson. 1985. "Family management in the prevention of morbidity of schizophrenia: Clinical outcome of a two-year longitudinal study." Archives of General Psychiatry 42: 887–896.

Flori, Denise. 1989. "The prevalence of later life family concerns in the marriage and family therapy journal literature (1976–1985): A content analysis." Journal of Marital and Family Therapy 15: 289–297.

Giblin, Paul, D. Sprenkle, and R. Sheehan. 1985. "Enrichment outcome research: A meta-analysis of premarital, marital, and family interventions." Journal of Marital and Family Therapy 11: 257–271.

Golann, Stuart. 1987. "On description of family therapy." Family Process 26: 331–340.

Golann, Stuart. 1988. "On second-order family therapy." Family Process 27: 51–64.

Goldner, Virginia. 1985. "Feminism and family therapy." Family Process 24: 31–48.

Goldstein, Michael J., E. H. Rodnick, J. R. Evans, P. R. May, and M. Steinberg. 1978. "Drug and family therapy in the aftercare treatment of acute schizophrenia." Archives of General Psychiatry 35: 1169–1177.

Goldstein, Michael J., and A. Strachan. 1987. "The family and schizophrenia." In T. Jacob (ed.), Family Interaction and Psychopathology. New York: Plenum Press.

Goodrich, Thelma J., C. Rampage, B. Ellman, and K. Halstead. 1988. Feminist Family Therapy: A Casebook. New York: Norton.

Gordon, D., and M. Meyers-Anderson. 1981. Phoenix: Therapeutic Patterns of Milton H. Erickson. Cupertino, CA: Meta.

Gottman, John M. 1987. "The sequential analysis of family interaction." In T. Jacob (ed.), Family Interaction and Psychopathology. New York: Plenum Press.

Greenberg, Leslie S., and S. M. Johnson. 1988. Emotionally Focused Therapy for Couples. New York: Guilford.

Grunebaum, Harold, and M. L. Belfer. 1986. "What family therapists might learn from child psychiatry." Journal of Marital and Family Therapy 2: 415–423.

Gurman, Alan S., and D. P. Kniskern. 1978. "Research on marital and family therapy: Progress, perspective, and prospect." In S. Garfield and A. Bergin (eds.), Handbook of Psychotherapy and Behavior Change (2nd ed.). New York: Wiley.

Gurman, Alan S., and D. P. Kniskern. 1981. "Family therapy outcome research: Knowns and unknowns." In A. Gurman and D. Kniskern (eds.), Handbook of Family Therapy. New York: Brunner/Mazel.

Gurman, Alan S., D. P. Kniskern, and W. M. Pinsof. 1986. "Research on the process and outcome of marital and family therapy." In S. Garfield and A. Bergin (eds.), Handbook of Psychotherapy and Behavior Change (3rd ed.). New York: Wiley.

Gustafson, J. 1987. "The neighboring field of brief individual psychotherapy." Journal of Marital and Family Therapy 13: 409–422.

Haley, Jay. 1987. Problem-Solving Therapy (2nd ed.). San Francisco: Jossey-Bass.

Haley, Jay. 1989. "The effect of long-term outcome studies on the therapy of schizophrenia." Journal of Marital and Family Therapy 15: 127–132.

Hamberger, L. K., and J. E. Hastings. 1988. "Skills training for treatments of spouse abusers: An outcome study." Journal of Family Violence 3: 121–130.

Hardley, Gary, and B. Guerney, Jr. 1989. "A psychoeducational approach." Pp. 158–181 in C. R. Figley (ed.), Treating Stress in Families. New York: Brunner/Mazel.

Hare-Mustin, Rachel T. 1987. "The problem of gender in family therapy theory." Family Process 26: 15–28.

Hazelrigg, M. D., H. M. Cooper, and C. M. Borduin. 1987. "Evaluating the effectiveness of family therapies: An integrative review and analysis." Psychological Bulletin 101: 428–442.

Ho, M. K. 1987. Family Therapy with Ethnic Minorities. Newbury Park, CA: Sage.

Hoffman, Lynn. 1981. Foundations of Family Therapy. New York: Basic Books.

Hoffman, Lynn. 1985. "Beyond power and control: Toward a second-order family systems therapy." Family Systems Medicine 3: 381–396.

Hoffman, Lynn. 1988. "Reply to Stuart Golann." Family Process 27: 65–67.

Hogarty, G. E., C. M. Anderson, D. J. Reiss, S. J. Kornblith, D. P. Greenwald, C. D. Javna, M. J. Madonia, and the EPICS Schizophrenia Research Group. 1986. "Family psychoeducation, social skills training, and maintenance chemotherapy in the aftercare treatment of schizophrenia: I. One year effects of a controlled study on relapse and expressed emotion." Archives of General Psychiatry 43: 633–642.

Imber-Black, Evan. 1988. Families and Larger Systems: A Therapists' Guide through the Labyrinth. New York: Guilford.

Jacobson, Neil S. 1985. "Family therapy outcome research: Potential pitfalls and prospects." Journal of Marital and Family Therapy 11: 149–158.

Jacobson, Neil S., W. C. Follette, and R. W. Elwood. 1984. "Outcome research on behavioral marital therapy: A methodological and conceptual reappraisal." In K. Hahlweg and N. Jacobson (eds.), Marital Interaction: Analysis and Modification. New York: Guilford.

Jacobson, Neil S., and D. Revenstorf. 1988. "Statistics for assessing the clinical significance of psychotherapy techniques: Issues, problems, and new developments." Behavioral Assessment 10: 133–145.

Jacobson, Neil S., K. B. Schmaling, and A. Holtzworth-Munroe. 1987. "Component analysis of behavioral marital therapy: Two-year follow-up and prediction of relapse." Journal of Marital and Family Therapy 13: 187–195.

Keeney, Bradford P., and D. Sprenkle. 1982. "Ecosystemic epistemology: Critical implications for the aesthetics and pragmatics of family therapy." Family Process 21: 1–19.

Leff, J. P., L. Kuipers, R. Berkowitz, and D. Sturgeon. 1985. "A controlled trial of social intervention in the families of schizophrenic patients: Two year follow-up." British Journal of Psychiatry 146: 594–600.

Luepnitz, Deborah A. 1988. Family Therapy Interpreted. New York: Basic Books.

Madanes, Cloe. 1981. Strategic Family Therapy. San Francisco: Jossey-Bass.

Madanes, Cloe, and J. Haley. 1977. "Dimensions of family therapy." Journal of Nervous and Mental Disease 165: 88–98.

Mahrer, Alivia R. 1988. "Discovery-oriented psychotherapy research: Rationale, aims and methods." American Psychologist 43: 694–702.

McGoldrick, Monica, C. M. Anderson, and F. Walsh (eds.). 1989. Women in Families. New York: Norton.

McGoldrick, Monica, J. Pearce, and J. Giordano (eds.). 1982. Ethnicity and Family Therapy. New York: Guilford Press.

Molnar, Alex, and S. deShazer. 1987. "Solution-focused therapy: Toward the identification of therapeutic tasks." Journal of Marital and Family Therapy 13: 349–358.

Moon, Sidney M., D. R. Dillon, and D. H. Sprenkle. In press. "Family therapy and qualitative research." Journal of Marital and Family Therapy.

Nichols, Michael P. 1987. The Self in the System. New

York: Brunner/Mazel.

O'Hanlon, William H. 1987. Taproots: Underlying Principles of Milton Erickson's Therapy and Hypothesis. New York: W. W. Norton.

O'Hanlon, William, and M. Weiner-Davis. 1989. In Search of Solutions. New York: Norton.

Olson, David H., R. Bell, J. Portner. 1985. FACES III Manual. Department of Family Social Science, University of Minnesota.

Papp, Peggy. 1983. The Process of Change. New York: Guilford.

Patterson, Gerald R., and P. Chamberlain. 1988. "Treatment process: A problem at three levels." In L. C. Wynne (ed.), The State of the Art in Family Therapy Research: Controversies and Recommendations. New York: Family Process Press.

Paul, G. 1967. "Strategy of outcome research in psychotherapy." Journal of Consulting Psychotherapy 31: 109–118.

Penn, Peggy. 1982. "Circular questioning." Family Process 21: 267–280.

Penn, Peggy. 1985. "Feed-forward: Future questions, future maps." Family Process 24: 299–310.

Piercy, Fred, D. Sprenkle, and associates. 1986. Family Therapy Sourcebook. New York: Guilford.

Pike, Connee, and F. Piercy. In press. "Cost effectiveness research in family therapy." Journal of Marital and Family Therapy.

Pinsof, William M. 1983. "Integrative problem-centered therapy: Toward the synthesis of family and individual psychotherapies." Journal of Marital and Family Therapy 9: 19–36.

Pinsof, William M. 1985. "The process of family therapy: The development of the Family Therapy Coding System." In L. Greenberg and W. Pinsof (eds.), The Psychotherapeutic Process: A Research Handbook. New York: Guilford.

Russell, G. F. M., G. I. Szmukler, C. Dave, and I. Eisler. 1987. "An evaluation of family therapy in anorexia nervosa and bulimia nervosa." Archives of General Psychiatry 44: 1047–1056.

Schwartzman, John. 1984. Families and Other Systems: The Macrosystemic Context of Family Therapy. New York: Guilford.

Selvini Palazzoli, Mara. 1986. "Towards a general model of psychotic family games." Journal of Marital and Family Therapy 12: 339–350.

Selvini Palazzoli, Mara, L. Boscolo, G. Cecchin, and G. Prata. 1978. Paradox and Counterparadox. New York: Aronson.

Stein, L. I. 1989. "The effect of long-term outcome studies on the therapy of schizophrenia: A critique." Journal of Marital and Family Therapy 15: 133–138.

Stone Fish, Linda, and F. Piercy. 1987. "The theory and practice of structural and strategic family therapies: A Delphi study." Journal of Marital and Family Therapy 13: 113–126.

Taggart, Morris. 1982. "Linear versus systemic values: Implications for family therapy." In J. C. Hansen and L. L'Abate (eds.), Values, Ethics, Legalities, and the Family Therapist. Rockville, MD: Aspen.

Taggart, Morris. 1985. "The feminist critique in epistemological perspective: Questions of context in family therapy." Journal of Marital and Family Therapy 11: 113–126.

Todd, Thomas, and M. D. Stanton. 1983. "Research on marital and family therapy: Answers, issues, and recommendations for the future." In B. Wolman and G. Striker (eds.), Handbook of Family and Marital Therapy. New York: Plenum Press.

Tomm, Karl. 1984. "One perspective on the Milan systemic approach: Part I. Overview of development, theory, and practice." Journal of Marital and Family Therapy 12: 113–126.

Tomm, Karl. 1987. "Interventive interviewing: Part I. Strategizing as a fourth guideline for the therapist." Family Process 26: 3–14.

Trepper, Terry S., and M. J. Barrett. 1989. Systemic Treatment of Incest: A Therapeutic Handbook. New York: Brunner/Mazel.

Wachtel, Ellen. 1987. "Family systems and the individual child." Journal of Marital and Family Therapy 13: 15–25.

Wampler, Karen S. 1982. "Bringing the review of literature into the age of quantification: Meta-analysis as a strategy for integrating research findings in family studies." Journal of Marriage and the Family 44: 1009–1023.

White, Michael. 1986. "Negative explanation, restraint, and double description: A template for family therapy." Family Process 25: 169–184.

Zeig, Jeffery K. 1985. Ericksonian Approaches to Hypnosis and Psychotherapy. New York: Brunner/Mazel.

BERNARD GUERNEY, JR., AND PAMELA MAXSON
Pennsylvania State University

Marital and Family Enrichment Research:
A Decade Review and Look Ahead

An initial definition of marital and family enrichment sets the boundaries for the review. The subareas reviewed include methodology and interpretation; subject characteristics and populations; format, composition, process, and leadership; component effectiveness comparisons; and program effectiveness comparisons. For each area, the major research contributions of the decade are briefly summarized and recommendations are offered for research in the 1990s.

It has been argued (Guerney, 1977) that sharp demarcations between problem prevention, enrichment, and therapy have not, and perhaps cannot and should not, be made. However, to limit the scope of this review, we propose the following definition of enrichment: Marital and family enrichment comprises psychoeducational programs designed to strengthen couples or families so as to promote a high level of present and future family harmony and strength, and hence the long-term psychological, emotional, and social well-being of family members. The programs are sufficiently structured, programmatic, replicable, and economical to serve a large segment of the general public. They usually are conducted in a time-limited, group format.

In this review, the major enrichment research accomplishments of the decade—and they have been very significant—will be summarized in the

Department of Human Development and Family Studies, Pennsylvania State University, University Park, PA 16802.

areas of methodology and interpretation; subject characteristics and populations; format composition, process, and leadership; component effectiveness comparisons; and program effectiveness comparisons. In each of these areas, research recommendations for the '90s also will be offered.

METHODOLOGY AND INTERPRETATION

Accomplishments of the '80s

The major methodological accomplishment of the past decade in the enrichment field has been the introduction of meta-analysis, an empirical study-of-studies, by Giblin, Sprenkle, and Sheehan (1985). A meta-analytic study allows one to make overview observations and judgments not possible with the traditional summary-table approach as used, for example, by Zimpfer (1988) in his excellent review of marital enrichment outcome research. (Three other valuable surveys that appeared during the decade were Hof and Miller's 1981 review of marital enrichment outcome, Wampler's 1982 review of Couples Communication Program research, and DeMarsh and Kumpfer's 1985 review of family prevention and enrichment programs in relation to drug-abuse prevention.)

Because we will refer to the findings of the meta-analytic study by Giblin and associates (1985) in almost every section of this review, we first provide some detailed information about its basic methodology. To be included in the meta-analysis, a study had to be experimental or quasi-experimental. Studies with clinical subjects were

457

included along with studies of nonclinical subjects if the goal of the method employed "was greater than symptom removal" (which matches our definition's requirement of promoting high levels of strength) and if "enrichment processes were employed," which we take to mean those programmatic features that make a program applicable to a large segment of the public (also a part of our definition). The number of studies included was 85, and the number of couples and families represented was 3,886.

The major statistic of meta-analysis is effect size (ES). In meta-analysis, a standardized measure of ES is calculated for each outcome measure. A wide array of variables and interactions may then be studied as each relates to ES. In the present context, the magnitude of the ES reflects degree of treatment gains compared to control or alternate-treatment groups. There are three ways of giving relative meaning to the magnitude of ES. One is comparison with psychotherapy, for which Giblin and associates cite an average ES of .85. Another way is to compare the ESs within the study itself, where the average ES of .44 was found. This figure indicates that the mean of the distribution of enriched groups was .44 of a standard deviation above the mean of the control groups; another way of putting this is that after receiving enrichment, the average participant was better off than 67% of nonparticipants. The third way is to recognize that in developmental, social, personality, and clinical research, positive ESs range from .01 to $+1$, and to categorize .33 or less as "small," from .34 to .66 as "moderate," and above .66 as "large."

Giblin et al. (1985) found that it was much harder to show treatment effectiveness with self-report measures (ES = .35) than with behavioral measures (ES = .76). Also, the credibility of a measure—reference citations, citations of reliability or validity data, its use by other investigators—was significantly, but only slightly, related (r = .12) to outcome. With respect to the content of the 89 measures involved, relationship skills yielded significantly higher ESs than measures of (in order of their ES) satisfaction, unspecified "other" variables, and personality variables. Giblin et al. hypothesized that there may be an interaction between choice of variable (e.g., satisfaction vs. relationship) and type of measure chosen (e.g., behavioral vs. self-report) and that

such possible interactions should be taken into account in interpreting results.

Among other methodological accomplishments of the past decade is the work of Stinnett, DeFrain, and colleagues (e.g., Stinnett, Sanders, and DeFrain, 1981), who pioneered the systematic empirical exploration of strong, healthy families. Their research has begun to provide researchers with more specific targets for evaluating enrichment programs. Another significant development is that some carefully designed, theory-based, and scientifically constructed measures appropriate for enrichment research have emerged and/or have been scientifically evaluated during the past decade. Prominent examples are the multilevel, multiperspective couple and family measures developed by Olson (1989). Also, the '80s brought more and better control groups and sophisticated statistical analyses than were seen in the '70s. Finally, more studies have included alternate treatment comparisons and follow-up assessments.

Recommendations for the '90s

A number of recommendations can be made regarding enrichment research *interpretation*. One applies to behavioral research in general but is especially important for establishing a young field such as enrichment because it will help positive findings get their due. The recommendation is that researchers and reviewers should stop assigning the same weight to nonsignificant findings as to significant findings. We refer to the practice of labeling results as "mixed" or "uncertain" when one measure or investigation reports a significant finding and another does not. This miscarriage of the scientific method is commonplace in discussion sections and summaries or reviews of the literature. Aside from replications (which unfortunately are hardly ever done in psychosocial research), for a negative result to counter a positive one, the measures involved in the negative finding must be unquestionably valid, and the number of subjects must be very large and unquestionably representative of the pertinent population—conditions almost never met. True, positive results in any study cannot be regarded with complete confidence until replicated or at least corroborated by similar studies. And of course, well-designed studies with sufficient power, as supported by a power analysis, should be published. But the fact remains that a negative finding, or even several, that are not true replications do not seriously call into question or "mix" positive results of a well-designed and executed study. In such instances, scholars should seek to explain the seeming inconsistencies by analyzing the differing characteristics of the studies. A table of pluses and minuses and a verdict of "mixed" or its equivalent is not an adequate substitute for such analytic spadework.

Another change we recommend in the area of interpretation is to treat certain kinds of therapy studies as also being studies of enrichment, as Giblin and colleagues have done, or at least to treat them as analogs of enrichment. We refer to studies in which the therapy methods are identical to, or very similar to, enrichment methods, with the major differences being format and/or the more clear-cut selection of distressed couples or families (e.g., Baucom, 1982; Mittl and Robin, 1987). Of course, it would be appropriate to do likewise in the reverse direction when findings of studies using methods that are common in enrichment programs seem applicable also to therapy. The same recommendation would hold for studies of prevention pertinent to enrichment and vice versa (see Markman, Floyd, Stanley, and Storaasli, 1988; Markman and Kadushin, 1986; Wolfe and Manion, 1983).

We turn now to recommendations about *methodology*. One great contribution to enrichment research in the '90s would be an update of the meta-analytic study by Giblin et al. (1985). Another suggestion deals with what perhaps is the major challenge of the next decade for all intervention outcome research, enrichment or otherwise—the challenge of diligently extending experimental controls for generic factors. Enrichment researchers should seek to control for positive effects stemming from suggestion, attention from and gratitude toward the investigator, the time that family members share together, the time they talk together (especially about their relationships), and the tendency of people to reduce cognitive dissonance ("If we put this much time into this program, we certainly must have gotten something out of it"), and so forth. All enrichment programs claim to offer positive factors that are specific to the particular program package: the gestalt that comprises particular subject matter taught, the special experiences set up, the par-

ticular attitudes they wish to inculcate, the skills they seek to impart, and/or the instructional methods. A major obligation of the intervention researcher is to demonstrate that the positive effects found in an evaluation stem from such specific factors rather than merely from generic ones.

To control for generic factors by using a placebo program, even aside from the practical and ethical problems it presents, is not really a viable choice today. A placebo control is one in which the specific ingredients have been demonstrated to be (*a*) without meaningful impact on clients yet and (*b*) credible to them as reasonable and promising. Public sophistication being what it is, we think it is almost a practical impossibility to devise a placebo program of a length comparable to most actual programs that meets these criteria. Therefore, when it comes to evaluating the effectiveness of full-length enrichment programs, we strongly recommend that alternate treatment comparisons be a part of the advanced stages of enrichment program evaluation during the coming decade. A multiple baseline design—which we believe appeared in the enrichment evaluation field for the first time during the '80s—is not a substitute for placebo or alternate treatment comparisons, but it can be useful in the early stages of evaluating a program (e.g., Rabin, Blechman, and Milton, 1984).

We foresee an expansion in the '90s of process research and of attempts to study participant characteristics in relation to process and outcome. Such investigations are facilitated by the use of a variety of research methods of analysis hitherto rarely, if ever, used in enrichment research. Pioneers in the use of such new statistical methods are the '80s investigators who have used partial correlation (Barnes, Schumm, and Jurich, 1984) and factor analysis (Gingras, Adam, and Chagnon, 1983).

Also advocated for the '90s is something new to the enrichment field: the deliberate use of *analog research*. In our view, it is an ideal strategy for exploring many important enrichment research questions. Just as animals are used instead of people in certain stages of testing new drugs, so, in enrichment research, stand-ins can be used for couples (e.g., roommates) and families (e.g., volunteers who play the roles of family members) for early testing of marital and family enrichment hypotheses. Through analog studies, it often

would be much easier to get large numbers of subjects in a reasonable period of time. In the early
stages of exploring a set of variables—for example, the effects of different techniques, methods,
processes, and personality variables—one could
conduct an analog study instead of running an actual enrichment program. Also, variables that one
might not be able to manipulate with actual
enrichment groups because of practical or ethical
restrictions (e.g., critical vs. nonjudgmental
leadership), could be assessed experimentally by
analog research.

SUBJECT VARIABLES AND SCOPE

Accomplishments of the '80s

Subject characteristics showed notably negative
results in the meta-analytic study by Giblin et al.
(1985). Unlike Strickland (1982), who found that
older, longer-married couples benefited more
from an enrichment program, Giblin et al. found
no relationship between outcome and years of
marriage. Nor were relationships found between
outcome and life stage, income, religion, or
previous enrichment experience. Men had a
higher ES than women on measures of satisfaction. One surprising finding, although the relationship was weak, was that level of education
was negatively related to ES ($r = -.13; p < .003$).
(However, it should be kept in mind that the level
of education for enrichment participants in the
study was 15 years, well above the U.S. average.)
A further result, which doubtless has much to do
with ceiling effects, is that ES was about twice as
high for distressed (.51) as for nondistressed participants (.27).

The *scope* of enrichment programs has continued to expand in the '80s. Enrichment or
enrichment-like therapy or prevention programs
have been conducted with alcoholics (Matter,
McAllister, and Guerney, 1984); wife-batterers
(Waldo, 1986); distressed families of the
psychiatrically hospitalized members (Daugherty,
1982; Vogelsong, Guerney, and Guerney, 1983);
dual-career couples (e.g., Amatea and Clark,
1984; Avis, 1986); remarried couples (Ellis, 1984);
stepparents and families (Cuddeby, 1984; Hoskins, 1985; Howell, 1982); dating couples (e.g.,
Heitland, 1986; Nix-Early, 1984); singles (Preston
and Guerney, 1982); families attempting to cope
with a member's life-altering disease (Brennan,
1982; Evenson, Evenson, and Fish, 1986; Oshea,

1985); and nicotine addiction (see Guerney, 1986).
Family enrichment training has also extended into
the realm of what Guerney and Guerney (1988)
have labeled "para-families," such as may be
found in homes for the retarded (Sywulak, 1984)
and drug rehabilitation centers (Cadigan, 1981),
where personnel and other residents are, or can
become, family-like in their enriching and healing
capacities.

Recommendations for the '90s

The expansion of the scope of enrichment studies
in the '90s could reach inward to explore effects
on personality dimensions beyond what Busick
(1982), Greene (1985) and, in the prior decade,
Ginsberg (1977) have already done with self-
concept and self-esteem. Other studies could expand outward into ecosystem variables, such as
the effects of enrichment on family isolation and
family support networks. Such ecosystem research would be difficult but hardly impossible.
Two particularly valuable programs to study on
the ecosystem level are the Family Cluster program (Sawin, 1986) and, because of its format,
the Survival Skills for Healthy Families program
(Daub and Scott, 1987).

Just as support groups multiplied from a few
basic types, with Alcoholics Anonymous at the
center, it can be expected that target populations
for enrichment programs will extend further over
the next decade to include single-parent families,
families of prisoners, gay couples, adult children
of alcoholics and their parents, and so on. It
would be desirable for research to keep pace with
such expansion. Also desirable would be expansion of research into new settings such as the
workplace (e.g., as part of stress-reduction efforts
in employee assistance programs). Still another
example of expansion would be to evaluate the effectiveness of enrichment videotape and computer
programs as they are developed. Finally, the
almost nonexistent area of enrichment marketing
research (Blaisure, 1985) seems to cry out for
development.

FORMAT, COMPOSITION, PROCESS, AND LEADERSHIP

Accomplishments of the '80s

With respect to *process* in enrichment programs, a
study by Hammonds and Worthington (1985) on

the focus, action, intent, function, content, and style of the leaders' responses has shown that these factors can have predictable effects on the participants' later statements. The meta-analytic study by Giblin et al. (1985) found that highly structured programs were significantly better than those somewhat less structured. The relationship was weak ($r = -.10$), but since all programs were at least moderately structured, variability and, therefore, the size of the correlation might be artificially low.

With respect to *composition*, Coufal (1982) found that adapting L. Guerney's (1988) Parenting Skills Training Program to include young children along with their parents (Coufal and Brock, 1983) yielded better results. Yet, in the meta-analytic study by Giblin et al. (1985), the inclusion of additional family members tended to reduce ES. This finding could not be attributed to the ages of the family members per se, because parent-adolescent dyad programs yielded higher ESs than programs with adults only. As the investigators pointed out, not many studies included more than two participants from the same family; hence, the finding of lower ESs with the inclusion of more family members may be due to the interaction effects of such inclusion with the particular types of treatments involved rather than to any presumed extra problems or demands created in dealing with entire families.

With respect to *format*, longer programs (over 12 hours) in the meta-analysis tended to yield somewhat better results ($r = .16$) than shorter programs. With respect to *leadership*, Most and Guerney (1983) found that it was possible in two weekends to train lay married couples experienced in the Engaged Encounter program (see Demarest, Sexton, and Sexton, 1977) to reach fairly high levels of leadership skills for conducting premarital Relationship Enhancement (RE) (Guerney, 1977) weekend enrichment programs.

Recommendations for the '90s

In the coming decade, we hope to see research into such process variables as the interpersonal climate created by leaders (warmth, nonjudgmentalness, genuineness, etc.) and into different ways of structuring interactions among participants (e.g., permissibility vs. impermissibility of advice-giving among participants).

COMPONENT EFFECTIVENESS COMPARISONS

Accomplishments of the '80s

With respect to the relative effectiveness of various components and characteristics of programs, the pattern of ES among different programs caused Giblin, Sprenkle, and Sheehan (1985) to conclude that programs which emphasized skills and behavioral practice yielded much better outcomes than those which did not. Cleaver (1987) found that videotaped skill instruction helped marital couples maintain communication skills. Warmbrod (1982) found support for the hypothesis that the generation of alternatives in problem solving came from specific training more than from a generic communication skills approach. Guerney, Vogelsong, and Coufal (1983) demonstrated that mothers and daughters randomly assigned to an RE no-booster condition maintained their gains at six months very well, but those who were assigned to a booster condition did even better.

Recommendations for the '90s

The relative importance of various enrichment components, including the types mentioned above, deserve a good deal of attention in the next decade. Examples of additional areas for study are the effects of using self-selected versus program-selected topics, and the use or nonuse of home assignments as they affect process and outcome.

PROGRAM EFFECTIVENESS COMPARISONS

Accomplishments of the '80s

Three types of programs were distinguished in the meta-analysis by Giblin et al. (1985). Each showed a significant and moderately large ES: premarital, .53; marital, .42; and family, .54. Clearly, on average, persons attending enrichment programs report and show behaviors that indicate positive changes. Moreover, follow-up testing showed that the gains held up well, with an average drop of only .09 in ES from posttesting. Compared to pretesting, follow-up scores remained significantly improved. However, the small drop from posttesting to follow-up was statistically significant and thus provides empirical support for advocates of booster programs.

Giblin and associates obtained ESs for 14 specific types of marital programs (some of which were simply modifications of major programs), in addition to "other" and "placebo" categories. Two types of marital programs—rational-emotive and behavioral exchange—did not do as well as the "placebo" category (ES = .22). Also, with one exception, none of the programs identified by name fared better than programs in a "marital-other" category (ES = .58). These findings suggest that, as a group, specialized and relatively unknown programs showed better gains than the widely known programs. The one exception was the RE program (Guerney, 1977), with an ES of .96. In the family area, the RE program again stood out (ES = .96 here, too). (There was no specific-program breakdown for the premarital area.)

As indicated in the section on methodology, the best way to ascertain that positive results are due to the specific experiences provided by the program, rather than to generic factors, is to compare a program with an alternate program. Hence, the only research we cover here involves such alternate treatment comparisons.

In addition to supporting the meta-analytic finding that, on average, enrichment programs were effective, many of the studies comparing alternative treatment in the '80s support the meta-analytic finding that Relationship Enhancement is a powerful program. With a mixed sample of distressed and nondistressed marital couples, RE was shown to be more effective than Jessee's Gestalt Relationship Facilitation Program (Jessee and Guerney, 1981), and more effective than the Couples Communication Program (CCP) (Brock and Joanning, 1983). In the latter study, RE's comparative effectiveness was especially strong for the more distressed couples. In the family area, RE was effective relative to an eclectic discussion-based program (Guerney, Coufal, and Vogelsong, 1981). With premarital couples, RE was found to be more effective than a relationship discussion program and a problem-solving program (Avery, Ridley, Leslie, and Milholland, 1980; Ridley, Avery, Dent, and Harrell, 1981; Ridley, Avery, Harrell, Haynes-Clements, and McCunney, 1981; Ridley, Avery, Harrell, Leslie, and Dent, 1981), and to the Engaged Encounter program (Sams, 1984). In the large majority of these studies, the non-RE programs themselves proved to be effective in comparison to the control groups. Some of the other programs of lesser effectiveness in the comparisons cited also were found to be effective in other studies. For example, CCP was superior to a communication problem-solving workshop (Witkin, Edelson, Rose, and Hall, 1983).

Another alternate treatment comparison study showed that the Knowledge Increasing Sexual Satisfaction (KISS) program was superior to CCP (Cooper and Stoltenberg, 1987). Robin (1981), studying a parent-adolescent problem-solving training therapy program so similar in many respects to an enrichment program that it may be considered an analog enrichment study, found that approach to be superior to a more traditional eclectic family therapy approach. Similarly, RE marital therapy in a dyadic format, which also may be considered an analog to an enrichment program, was more effective than the therapists' preferred eclectic approaches (Ross, Baker, and Guerney, 1985).

Recommendations for the '90s

The findings that, in general, distressed married couples gain even more from some enrichment programs than do nondistressed couples, and that certain programs seem to be especially helpful to distressed couples, deserve follow-up; that is, what are the ingredients of a program that tends to facilitate versus retard the improvement of distressed couples?

The range of program effectiveness shown in the meta-analytic and individual studies suggests that we should not think about enrichment as if it were a unitary entity nor as if enrichment programs were interchangeable. Rather, the findings suggest that researchers should be very careful about describing and labeling the particular methods they use in their studies. They should also limit their conclusions to their particular methods, instead of drawing generic conclusions about "enrichment" or "communication training" or "problem solving" as if different approaches to group process, teaching, materials, and so forth made little or no difference.

CONCLUSION

The meta-analytic study by Giblin, Sprenkle, and Sheehan (1985) showed that, on average, enrichment programs led to significant improvements in premarital, marital, and family capabilities, and that these gains often were sustained for many months. Many individual studies in the '80s found the same thing. While they may not always be without negative effects (Doherty, Lester, and Leigh, 1986), there is no doubt that, on the whole, enrichment programs work and the field is an entirely legitimate one. No more research or interpretive energy needs to be devoted to that basic concern. Moreover, the meta-analytic study by Giblin et al. has provided bench marks against which new programs can and should be compared. The major questions for future exploration are which programs work best for what populations, what makes them best, and how they—and new programs—can be made more efficient and less costly and be better marketed. That is a formidable task, but a more satisfying one than having to prove the basic worth of marital and family enrichment.

REFERENCES

Amatea, Ellen, and Jack Clark. 1984. "A dual career workshop for college couples: Effects of an intervention program." Journal of College Student Personnel 26: 271–272.

Avery, Arthur W., Carl A. Ridley, Leigh Ann Leslie, and T. Milholland. 1980. "Relationship Enhancement with premarital dyads: A six-month follow-up." American Journal of Family Therapy 8: 23–30.

Avis, Judith M. 1986. "'Working together': An enrichment program for dual-career couples." Journal of Psychotherapy and the Family 2: 29–45.

Barnes, Howard L., Walter R. Schumm, Anthony P. Jurich. 1984. "Marital satisfaction: Positive regard versus effective communications as explanatory variables." Journal of Social Psychology 123: 71–78.

Baucom, Donald H. 1982. "A comparison of behavioral contracting and problem-solving/communications training in behavioral marital therapy." Behavior Therapy 13: 162–174.

Blaisure, Karen R. 1985. "Marital Relationship Enhancement skills workshop: Perceptions of and recruitment for a marriage enrichment program." Unpublished master's thesis, Pennsylvania State University.

Brennan, Anne F. 1982. "Brief skills enhancement counseling with renal dialysis patients." Dissertation Abstracts International 42(11-B): 4569.

Brock, Gregory W., and Harvey Joanning. 1983. "A comparison of the Relationship Enhancement program and the Minnesota Couple Communication Program." Journal of Marital and Family Therapy 9: 413–421.

Busick, Carole A. 1982. "The effects of communication training on marital communication, marital satisfaction and self-concept." Dissertation Abstracts International 43(3-A): 725.

Cadigan, J. Dennis. 1981. "RETEACH program and project: Relationship Enhancement in a therapeutic environment as clients head out." Dissertation Abstracts International 41(10-B): 3881-B.

Cleaver, Glenda. 1987. "Marriage enrichment by means of a structured communication programme." Family Relations 36: 49–54.

Cooper, Alvin, and C. D. Stoltenberg. 1987. "Comparison of a sexual enhancement and a communication training program on sexual and marital satisfaction." Journal of Counseling Psychology 34: 309–314.

Coufal, Jeanette D. 1982. "An experimental evaluation of two approaches to parent skills training: Parent-child participation versus parents only." Paper presented at the annual meeting of the National Council on Family Relations, Washington, DC.

Coufal, Jeanette D., and Gregory W. Brock. 1983. Parent-Child Relationship Enhancement: A Ten-Week Education Program. Lexington, KY: Skills Training Press.

Cuddeby, Gordon W. 1984. "The effects of stepparent education on perceived family cohesion, organization, and conflict." Dissertation Abstracts International 45(4-A): 1072.

Daub, Georg T., and Virginia M. Scott. 1987. Survival Skills for Healthy Families. (Available from Family Wellness Association, Box 3303, San Jose, CA 95156)

Daugherty, Monica E. 1982. "Social skills training with psychiatric patients and their spouses." Dissertation Abstracts International 43(6-B): 1973.

Demarest, D., J. Sexton, and M. Sexton. 1977. Marriage Encounter: A Guide for Sharing. St. Paul, MN: Carillon.

DeMarsh, Joseph, and Karol L. Kumpfer. 1985. "Family-oriented interventions for the prevention of chemical dependency in children and adolescents." Special issue, "Childhood and chemical abuse: Prevention and intervention." Journal of Children in Contemporary Society 18: 117–151.

Doherty, William J., Mary E. Lester, and Geoffery Leigh. 1986. "Marriage encounter weekends: Couples who win and couples who lose." Journal of Marital and Family Therapy 12: 49–61.

Ellis, Amanda J. 1984. "Second time around: A preventive intervention for remarried couples." Australian Journal of Sex, Marriage, and Family 5: 139–146.

Evenson, Thomas L., Merry L. Evenson, and Dale E. Fish. 1986. "Family enrichment: A rehabilitation opportunity." Rehabilitation Literature 47: 274–280.

Giblin, Paul, Douglas H. Sprenkle, and Robert Sheehan. 1985. "Enrichment outcome research: A meta-analysis of premarital, marital, and family interventions." Journal of Marital and Family Therapy 11: 257–271.

Gingras, Marie, Dyane Adam, and Gilles J. Chagnon. 1983. "Marital enrichment: The contribution of sixteen process variables to the effectiveness of a program." Journal of Sex and Marital Therapy 9: 121–136.

Ginsberg, Barry G. 1977. "Parent-adolescent relationship development program." In B. G. Guerney, Jr., Relationship Enhancement: Skill-training programs for therapy, problem prevention, and enrichment. San Francisco: Jossey-Bass.

Greene, Gilbert J. 1985. "The effect of the Relationship Enhancement program on marital communication and self-esteem." Journal of Applied Social Sciences 10: 78–94.

Guerney, Bernard G., Jr. 1977. Relationship Enhancement: Skill-Training Programs for Therapy, Problem Prevention, and Enrichment. San Francisco: Jossey-Bass.

Guerney, Bernard G., Jr. 1986. How to Stop Smoking and Help Others to Stop. (Available from Department of Human Development and Family Studies, Catharine Beecher House, Pennsylvania State University, University Park, PA 16802)

Guerney, Bernard G., Jr., Jeanette Coufal, and Edward Vogelsong. 1981. "Relationship Enhancement versus a traditional approach to therapeutic/preventative/enrichment parent-adolescent programs." Journal of Consulting and Clinical Psychology 49: 927–939.

Guerney, Bernard G., Jr., and Louise F. Guerney. 1988. "Building relationship skills in families and para-family teams." Pp. 49–65 in D. H. Olson (ed.), Family Perspectives in Child and Youth Services. New York: Haworth Press.

Guerney, Bernard G., Jr., Edward Vogelsong, and Jeanette Coufal. 1983. "Relationship Enhancement versus a traditional treatment." Pp. 738–756 in D. H. Olson and B. C. Miller (eds.), Family Studies Review Yearbook (Vol. 1). Beverly Hills, CA: Sage.

Guerney, Louise F. 1988. Parenting: A Skills Training Manual (3rd ed.). (Available from IDEALS, P.O. Box 391, State College, PA 16804)

Hammonds, T. Michael, and Everett L. Worthington. 1985. "The effect of facilitator utterances on participant responses in a brief ACME-type marriage enrichment group." American Journal of Family Therapy 13: 39–49.

Heitland, William. 1986. "An experimental communication program for premarital dating couples." School Counselor, pp. 57–61.

Hof, L., and W. R. Miller. 1981. Marriage Enrichment: Philosophy, Process, and Program. Bowie, MD: Brady.

Hoskins, Joanna T. 1985. "A comparison of skill-enhancement interventions with step-parenting couples." Dissertation Abstracts International 45(12-A): 3549.

Howell, Elizabeth L. 1982. "Evaluation of a communications skills program with stepfather-adolescent-mother triads." Dissertation Abstracts International 43(6-A): 1837.

Jessee, Randall, and Bernard G. Guerney, Jr. 1981. "A comparison of Gestalt and Relationship Enhancement treatments with married couples." American Journal of Family Therapy 9: 31–41.

Markman, Howard J., Frank J. Floyd, Scott M. Stanley, and R. D. Storaasli. 1988. "Prevention of marital distress: A longitudinal investigation." Journal of Consulting and Clinical Psychology 56: 210–217.

Markman, Howard J., and Frederick S. Kadushin. 1986. "Preventive effects of Lamaze training for first-time parents: A short-term longitudinal study." Journal of Consulting and Clinical Psychology 54: 872–874.

Matter, Margaret, William McAllister, and Bernard G. Guerney, Jr. 1984. "Relationship Enhancement for the recovering couple: Working with the intangible." Focus on Family and Chemical Dependency 7: 21–23.

Mittl, Valerie F., and Arthur Robin. 1987. "Acceptability of alternative interventions for parent-adolescent conflict." Behavioral Assessment 9: 417–428.

Most, Robert, and Bernard G. Guerney, Jr. 1983. "An empirical evaluation of the training of lay volunteer leaders for premarital Relationship Enhancement." Family Relations 32: 239–251.

Nix-Early, V. 1984. "A couples' workshop for college students." Journal of College Student Personnel 25: 479–480.

Olson, David H. 1989. "Circumplex model of family systems: VIII. Family assessment and intervention." In D. Olson, C. S. Russell, and D. H. Sprenkle (eds.), Circumplex Model: Systemic Assessment and Treatment of Families. New York: Haworth Press.

Oshea, Michael D. 1985. "An evaluation of marriage enrichment and relationship skills training program for couples coping with heart disease." Dissertation Abstracts International 45(12-B, Pt. 1): 3954.

Preston, Joanne D., and Bernard G. Guerney, Jr. 1982. Relationship Enhancement Skill Training. (Available from Department of Human Development and Family Studies, Catharine Beecher House, Pennsylvania State University, University Park, PA 16802)

Rabin, Clarie, Elaine A. Blechman, and Marianne C. Milton. 1984. "A multiple baseline study of the marriage contract game's effects on problem solving and affective behavior." Child and Family Behavior Therapy 6: 45–60.

Ridley, Carl A., Arthur W. Avery, Judy Dent, and Janet E. Harrell. 1981. "The effects of Relationship Enhancement and problem solving programs on perceived heterosexual competence." Family Therapy 8: 59–66.

Ridley, Carl A., Arthur W. Avery, Janet E. Harrell, Lynda A. Haynes-Clements, and N. McCunney. 1981. "Mutual problem-solving skills training for premarital couples: A six-month follow-up." Journal of Applied Developmental Psychology 2: 179–188.

Ridley Carl A., Arthur W. Avery, Janet E. Harrell, L. A. Leslie, and Judy Dent. 1981. "Conflict management: A premarital training program in mutual problem solving." American Journal of Family Therapy 9: 23–32.

Robin, Arthur L. 1981. "A controlled evaluation of

problem-solving communication training with parent-adolescent conflict.'' Behavior Therapy 12: 593–609.

Ross, Edward R., Stanley B. Baker, and Bernard G. Guerney, Jr. 1985. ''Effectiveness of Relationship Enhancement therapy versus therapist's preferred therapy.'' American Journal of Family Therapy 13: 11–21.

Sams, Weldon P. 1984. ''Marriage preparation: An experimental comparison of the Premarital Relationship Enhancement (PRE) and the Engaged Encounter (EE) programs.'' Dissertation Abstracts International 44(10-B): 3207.

Sawin, Margaret M. 1986. ''The Family Cluster approach to family enrichment.'' Journal of Psychotherapy & the Family 2: 47–57.

Stinnett, Nick, George Sanders, and John DeFrain. 1981. ''Strong Families: A national study.'' In N. Stinnett, J. DeFrain, K. King, P. Knaub, and G. Rowe (eds.), Family Strengths III: Roots of Well-Being. Lincoln: University of Nebraska Press.

Strickland, James H. 1982. ''The effects of two marriage enrichment retreat models on marital satisfaction.'' Dissertation Abstracts International 42(10-A): 4305.

Sywulak, Andrea A. 1984. ''Creating a whole atmosphere in a group home for retarded adolescents.'' Academic Psychology Bulletin 6: 325–327.

Vogelsong, Edward, Bernard G. Guerney Jr., and Louise F. Guerney. 1983. ''Relationship Enhancement therapy with inpatients and their families.'' Pp. 48–68 in R. Luber and C. Anderson (eds.), Family Intervention with Psychiatric Patients. New York: Human Sciences Press.

Waldo, Michael. 1986. ''Group counseling for military personnel who battered their wives.'' Journal for Specialists in Group Work 2: 132–138.

Wampler, Karen. 1982. ''The effectiveness of the Minnesota Couple Communication program: A review of research.'' Journal of Marital and Family Therapy 8: 345–355.

Warmbrod, Mary T. 1982. ''Alternative generation in marital problem solving.'' Family Relations 31: 503–511.

Witkin, Stanley L., Jeffrey L. Edelson, Sheldon D. Rose, and James A. Hall. 1983. ''Group training in marital communication: A comparative study.'' Journal of Marriage and the Family 45: 661–669.

Wolfe, David A., and Ian E. Manion. 1983. ''Impediments of child abuse prevention: Issues and directions.'' Advances in Behaviour Research and Therapy 6: 47–62.

Zimpfer, David G. 1988. ''Marriage enrichment program: A review.'' Journal for Specialists in Group Work 13: 44–53.

Joan Aldous   *University of Notre Dame*

Wilfried Dumon   *Catholic University Leuven, Belgium**

Family Policy in the 1980s:
Controversy and Consensus

The article examines the controversy concerning the efficacy of federal family policy that occurred during Ronald Reagan's early years in the presidency and its effects on family programs. The growing value consensus on what ought to be done about welfare that culminated in the Family Support Act of 1988 is then discussed. Value and morality issues also appear in the analysis of family planning and abortion policies. A comparison of the programs devoted to the elderly and to children follows. A consideration of the role of social scientists in the policy process and the social context of future family legislation conclude the article.

The 1980s were a decade of extremes with regard to family policy in the United States. It began with the coming to office of the first president whose political agenda included dismantling existing family welfare programs that had been initiated during the New Deal era a half century before. It concluded in a time of fiscal constraint with modest attempts at welfare reform based on a growing consensus concerning the elements of family policy. A number of publications summarized issues in the field of family policy over the decade (Aldous and Dumon, 1980; Moen and Schorr, 1987; Wallach, 1981; Zigler, Kagan, and Klugman, 1983; Zimmerman, 1989).

Department of Sociology, University of Notre Dame, 431 Decio, Notre Dame, IN 46556.

*Department of Sociology, Catholic University Leuven, E. van Evenstraat 2c, B-3000 Leuven, Belgium.

This article provides a selective review of the family policy literature in social science publications of the decade just ended. The focus is on continuing issues in the United States. Works concerning such topics as the political implications of divorce and family violence are left to other review articles. The presentation begins with a discussion of what is included in the term *family policy*. The next section covers the continuing controversy over welfare and the agreement that has developed between liberals and conservatives on what should be done. A consideration of family planning policy indicates how morality issues are caught up in family matters and create deep divisions. The comparative well-being of the often dependent populations at the beginning and end of the life cycle introduces an analysis of existing welfare measures. A section on child-care policy suggests an area that is due to receive increased attention in the new decade. After these discussions of particular policies comes an analysis of the roles played by social scientists in policy formation. A final summing up attempts to give some perspective on the family policy scene in the near future.

Defining Family Policy

Family policy is a common term whose users appear to know its meaning while having difficulty articulating a specific definition. Some writers, such as Mary Jo Bane (1980: 155–156), argue that it does not exist in the United States. There is no body of legislation or category of administrative orders clearly labeled "family policy," and high-level offices for family matters are absent in federal and state governments. However, if one includes all aspects of government that affect families, even if the laws themselves in our individualistic society do not mention them, then family policy encompasses most governmental actions.

One escape from the all-or-nothing dilemma of family policy definitions is to define it implicitly through a discussion of specific programs (Cherlin, 1988). A second approach, used by child advocate Marian Wright Edelman (1987: viii), is to contrast "formulating something called family policy" with actually working to feed, clothe, heal, house, and educate children. Family policy becomes a passive element, providing at most a rationale for activists who engage in helping families. Still others restrict it to programs concerning particular types of families. An example would be defining family policy as governmental goals and activities directed toward the well-being of families with children (Aldous and Dumon, 1980: 255; Lynn, 1980: 205). While it may ease the task of the analyst, this perspective eliminates some issues that concern legislators with regard to families at other stages of the life cycle, such as the elderly (Steiner, 1980: 236).

Another definition emphasizes the state's deliberate shaping of programs and policies to realize widely agreed-upon family objectives (Moen and Schorr, 1987: 795). Such a definition cuts down the area to be covered in a review. But much of the controversy surrounding family policy lies in the lack of agreement on family objectives, which discourages the conscious design of programs to fulfill them. In fact, one British observer points to the ambiguous nature of the term due to the "highly complex and often confusing domains of social and political controversy" that family policy incorporates (Bernardes, 1987: 685). And nowhere in this or other definitions does a delineation of the term *family* appear. Given the difficulties in delimiting the family policy concept, it is wise to have a fairly general definition with respect to policies and to families.

In this article, therefore, *family policy* refers to *objectives concerning family well-being and the specific measures taken by governmental bodies to achieve them.* By incorporating the word "specific," the definition limits family policy to programs consciously undertaken to affect families in a positive way. Our definition of

families is a broad one. It includes *cohabiting groups of some duration composed of persons in intimate relations based on biology, law, custom, or choice and usually economically interdependent.*

THE CONSERVATIVE IMPETUS TO FAMILY POLICY

The argument concerning family policy, regardless of how defined, came to a head in the late 1970s and early 1980s with the coming to the presidency of Ronald Reagan. Backed by the New Christian Right and other advocates of a so-called pro-family program, his view of how government could encourage family well-being was different from that of his predecessors. Social scientists have looked at the characteristics, composition, and ideologies of these vocal interest groups (Cherlin, 1983; Goettsch, 1986; Hadden, 1983; McNamara, 1985; Pankhurst and Houseknecht, 1983), but here we restrict our discussion to the program issues the newly empowered conservatives raised.

The controversy centered on the effectiveness of government intervention to promote family well-being and in which areas it should intervene. Both the conservatives and their opponents turned to history, specifically the War on Poverty years of the Johnson administration and their aftermath in the 1970s, to draw their quite different conclusions. The publication voicing the conservative perspective that caught the most attention from scholars and the popular press alike was Charles Murray's (1984) book, *Losing Ground: American Social Policy, 1950–1980.* Unlike liberals who saw government programs as helping the poor, he and other conservatives saw the programs as causing poverty. His argument was that these programs made their recipients dependent upon state aid. He cited statistics on previous decreases in poverty rates and then their rise in the late 1970s. Also to document his point, he described rising rates of unemployment among black males under 25 in the same period.

According to Murray, the reason for the connection between governmental aid and poverty was a failure of policy makers to recognize the factors that motivate individuals to work in a market economy. Without incentives, they avoid work, they become dependent, and families suffer. His solutions were straightforward. Do away with federal welfare programs for families and in-dividuals, such as Aid to Families with Dependent Children (AFDC), Medicaid, food stamps, and housing subsidies. For the truly needy, private charity and local governments would provide suc-cor. Those able but unwilling to take available jobs faced the choice of turning to the illicit economy or not surviving.

Murray's interpretations of the War on Pover-ty outcomes were contested both in earlier policy work (Schwartz, 1983) and in later analyses. The criticisms have centered on the character of the War on Poverty, demographic changes in the population receiving government aid, and the general state of the economy in the last two decades. Daniel Patrick Moynihan (1986), whose family policy credentials go back to the Johnson administration, believed that the War on Poverty was never more than a mock skirmish. It had the character of a demonstration project, handi-capped by limited funds and overblown rhetoric that promised more than could be delivered.

Moreover, economists Danziger and Plotnick (1986), along with Moynihan, pointed out that, because of the growing number of elderly persons, two-thirds of the increases in federal income transfer programs in the years from 1965 to 1982 appeared in the Old Age and Survivors Insurance and Medicare programs, not the Great Society programs. With respect to Murray's argument that government payments discourage work ef-forts, they concluded that these payments had on-ly small negative effects. Poverty in the years Murray pointed to resulted from poor economic conditions along with an increase in the numbers of the elderly and female-headed families, who are more likely to be in poverty. The poverty rate of the nonelderly who were ineligible for Social Security payments went down over the 1970s (Dolbeare and Lidman, 1985: 589, Table 1). Other investigators looked at the worsening employment rate of black males 16 to 19 years of age in the years from 1955 to 1980 and found little evidence that social welfare policies increased the unemployment rate by reducing work incentives (Ellwood and Summers, 1986). Youths 18 years old or over who are not in school, but living in families, have never been counted as a part of the family unit eligible for AFDC benefits.

The findings of these policy-oriented research-es are consistent with the view that fundamental shifts in marriage, divorce, and childbearing out-side marriage, along with mothers' labor force participation—shifts related to poverty in families—have little to do with governmental welfare policies. Instead, broader economic and cultural trends are the primary influences (Cherlin, 1988: 26).

Ronald Reagan had not waited for the ra-tionale supplied by Murray to ask for and to receive cuts in AFDC for poor families. Several investigators have documented the overall threats to health and nutrition resulting from the welfare cuts in the 1981 Omnibus Budget Reconciliation Act (OBRA) (Aldous, 1986; Edelman, 1987). Other policy-oriented researchers focused on whether the consequences of the decreased spend-ing supported Murray's arguments. One study showed that reducing funding for AFDC did not increase their former recipients' work force par-ticipation significantly, as Murray would argue (Joe and Rogers, 1985). Other studies found that the changes in AFDC eligibility did not lessen the work effort of former recipients to any great ex-tent. They did not stop working or decrease their hours to regain benefits (Moscovice, Craig, and Pitt, 1987).

That hardy perennial, the belief that AFDC payments fostered the upsurge in the number of single female heads of families, has also received researchers' attention. Contrary to the argument of Murray and others that such programs en-courage illegitimacy and poverty, states with the most liberal payments do not have the highest rates of single female parents. In addition, 1972 saw the end of the growth in the value of AFDC benefits, and since then, the proportion of children in female-headed families on AFDC has been constant or fallen. During this same period, however, the proportion of children in such households has continued to expand (Ellwood, 1988: 59–61).

After considering studies of the effect of welfare benefits on divorce, out-of-wedlock births, and remarriage rates, as well as the effects of alternative opportunities, Garfinkel and Mc-Clanahan (1986: 63) estimate that within the bot-tom half of the income distribution, welfare benefits might possibly account for 30% of the total growth in single-mother heads of families between 1960 and 1976. They attribute the large rise primarily to economic market conditions. Over the last quarter of a century, there has been a lack of employment opportunities for black males. Fewer black women are marrying as a consequence. In contrast, increased employment opportunities for white women and their greater economic independence account for their higher divorce rates and the sharp rise in their rates of single parenthood (Ellwood, 1988: 66–70).

Consensus and Reform

Despite the heated controversy in the early and mid-1980s concerning the efficacy of governmental intervention to aid families, a consensus on what policy initiatives needed to be taken had emerged by the end of the decade. The major concern expressed by liberals and conservatives alike was that existing programs were not doing enough to provide ladders for able-bodied family heads to climb out of poverty (Osborne, 1988). Discussions calling for policy changes often included appeals to so-called basic American values. Persons at opposite poles in their beliefs about the efficacy of governmental welfare programs could agree that the values of individual autonomy and obligation, the importance of work, and the centrality of the family should underlie welfare policy (Ellwood, 1988: 16; Novak et al., 1987: 3–17). These shared values translated into agreed-upon proposals tying family payments to individual job training or work obligations and requiring absent fathers to provide child support. The goal was to make families eventually more economically independent (Ellwood, 1988; Novak et al., 1987).

There has been criticism of the proposals and the values they embody (Freeman, 1988). Previous experience with job-training programs has indicated that the jobs available to family heads with limited skills are largely determined by general economic conditions and not by their job training. And there are questions about the wisdom of forcing mothers of young children into the labor force (Chilman, 1988). Critics have also pointed out that requiring child support from noncustodial parents could impoverish the families they have later formed. But one thing liberals and conservatives, supporters and critics agreed upon was that there is no "quick fix" for taking families out of poverty. Only long-term efforts would enable the country to achieve this goal.

A welfare reform bill reflecting widely shared values and building upon existing programs mustered enough congressional support in 1988 to pass. Linking aid to becoming independent, the

Family Support Act required single parents on AFDC whose children are older than age 3 to get jobs or to enroll in job-training courses at state and federal expense. Persons under age 20 without a high school diploma were to be encouraged to finish high school. There were also to be transitional child-care, transportation, and Medicaid benefits for persons in the various skills-upgrading programs to enable their participation. But recipients incurred an obligation for receiving these services. States were allowed to charge on a sliding scale for them. To encourage couples to stay together, all states had to pay welfare benefits to two-parent families in which both parents are unemployed. However, to maintain the aid-job linkage, one adult in these families would have to look for a job or to work at least 16 hours a week in some state-organized job. Finally, to improve child support collection so noncustodial parents are responsible for family support, the bill called for a better monitoring procedure of child support payments enforcement and automatic wage withholding for awards. Beginning in November 1990, awards to children on AFDC and other cases handled by child support enforcement agencies will be subject to automatic wage withholding, and all child support orders will be covered by 1994 ("Family Support Act," 1988–1989).

The 1988 Family Support Act's success largely depends upon the strength of the economy, continuing federal funding and the commitment and creativity of the states in their job-training programs ("Family Support Act," 1988–1989). Its relatively low cost strategies are also unlikely to have much effect on the entrenched poverty found in such areas as the urban ghettos and among long-term welfare recipients (Reischauer, 1989). By early 1990, the act's goal of getting families off welfare was already facing budget difficulties. Some states were finding that the costs of providing subsidized child care and medical benefits to welfare clients with outside jobs or in training programs forced them to cut other social service programs. For example, to obtain the necessary funds, Massachusetts and Minnesota were limiting child-care subsidies to other working poor. As a result, these persons could not afford to work and were returning to the welfare rolls at great public expense (Hinds, 1990).

In a similar vein, policy analysts expressed concern that restricting transitional child-care and medical benefits to one year would push clients in the job programs back onto welfare after this period. There was also the question as to whether persons in job-training programs will be able to find affordable child care even with state aid. In Michigan, a relatively generous state, where the state will provide up to $350 a month in child care for two children, depending upon the parents' income, a survey of licensed day care providers showed costs ranging from $260 a month in family care contexts to $1,375 a month in child-care centers (Hinds, 1990).

The Government and Family Planning Policy

The argument over the consequences of governmental welfare payments on families and the research it engendered demonstrate how values and morals are necessarily involved in family policy (Steiner, 1980). Family planning and abortion policies are particularly good examples of how such conflicting values can create bitter divisions. Conservatives who are against governmental intervention in family affairs when it takes the form of income transfers to the less well off are often much in favor of it with respect to sexual matters. In contrast, liberals who press for governmental aid to disadvantaged families insist that the state keep its distance when it comes to these same issues.

It is sometimes forgotten that as recently as 1968, couples' freedom to determine the number and timing of births was restricted within certain governmental jurisdictions. In that year, the Supreme Court in *Griswold v. Connecticut* ruled that a state statute making married couples' possession and use of contraceptives a criminal offense was unconstitutional. The basis for their judgment was the Bill of Rights and the Fourteenth Amendment, which supported the right to privacy of individuals in decisions concerning personal matters. This constitutional right was expanded five years later by the Court in *Roe v. Wade* to include a woman's right to terminate a pregnancy as well as to prevent one (Melton and Pliner, 1986: 3). The legal scene was thereby returned to the situation that existed prior to the 1850s. At that time, the newly organized American Medical Association, in an attempt to legitimate medicine as a profession, began a campaign to forbid abortions by unlicensed practi-

tioners. By the turn of the century, all states had antiabortion legislation on the books, although the laws were not always enforced (Mohr, 1978).

At present, the federal government, along with most of the states (41 in 1987), funds family planning services, with the former providing over five-sixths of the monies. These pay for counseling and patient education and the provision of medically approved methods and devices to prevent contraception (Gold and Guardado, 1988: 229, Table 1). Funds for sterilization are also included. The Reagan years saw cuts in appropriations of some 16% for Title X of the Public Health Service Act, the only federal program specifically targeted for the provision of family planning services (Danielson, McNally, Swanson, Pleinkett, and Klausmeier, 1988). These governmental funds to subsidize family planning clinics are especially important for poor women without health insurance who use such facilities disproportionately ("Poor LA women," 1989). Monies for research on development of contraceptives and educational programs on their correct usage also dropped by about half in the 1980s ("More on Koop's study," 1990).

Federal financing of abortions virtually ended in the late 1970s, a cutoff reflecting the bitter controversy the issue evokes. Caught up in it are moral issues concerning women's family roles, views on sex, and when life begins. For example, the AMA's 1871 committee on criminal abortion expressed an attitude still held on women's marital responsibilities and what sexual intercourse should mean to them. A committee statement warned that a woman seeking an abortion was ignoring "her destiny as established by Providence." According to the statement, she was shirking the duties "imposed" on her by the marriage contract. "She yields to the pleasures but shrinks from the pains and responsibilities of maternity" (Hevesi, 1989).

The original *Roe v. Wade* Supreme Court decision legalizing abortions established a trimester framework for regulating a woman's right to an abortion. During the first trimester, the state was not to interfere, leaving the decision to her in consultation with her physician. Only when the fetus becomes viable at the 22nd week of pregnancy was the state permitted to forbid abortion to guard the potential life unless the pregnancy would threaten the mother's health or life (Melton and Pliner, 1986: 4). The 1989 Supreme Court decision in

Webster v. Reproductive Services nullified this approach by approving state-required fetal viability tests at 20 weeks. As is true of much of the argument over abortion rights, there was little scientific basis for this judgment. No fetus is viable at 20 weeks or can be made viable at that time by any foreseeable development (Rosoff, 1989). The 1989 decision, however, opened the way for states to restrict women's access to abortion.

People's interpretation of the condition of American families affects their reactions to abortion legislation, especially that requiring adolescents who are seeking abortions to obtain parental consent. The Supreme Court has held that parental notification laws must contain a judicial-bypass provision (Greenhouse, 1990). It permits an adolescent to obtain a confidential court ruling permitting an abortion without parental involvement. Although research indicates that a majority of pregnant teenagers do tell at least one parent, their failure to do so is generally the result of fear of parental retaliation (Adler and Dolcine, 1986).

The Bush administration's brief in support of the state of Minnesota's attempt to have the Supreme Court strike down the judicial-bypass doctrine presents an optimistic view of family life. It declares that "a minor's parents, in the typical situation, will have known and cared for their daughter from her birth, and they will be deeply, lovingly concerned about her well-being." The brief of the American Civil Liberties Union that challenges Minnesota's attempt gives a contrasting view of family life. While applauding the situation where the teenager lives with two supportive and loving parents who are ready to assist her in a crisis, it points out that this is not the family in which many adolescents live. Instead, the brief cites testimony from young women who are afraid to inform their parents, as well as from pregnant teenagers' mothers who wish to avoid the two-parent notification requirement because they fear violence from former husbands. The family reality in Minnesota is that although the state law requires that both parents be notified of an impending abortion, "barely" a majority of Minnesota adolescents live with two parents (Greenhouse, 1989). Thus, abortion policy continues to excite controversy among partisans who have different perceptions of family reality.

THE ELDERLY AND THE PERILS OF SUCCESS

One of the most interesting areas of family policy has to do with the elderly. This group's past success in obtaining funds to improve the quality of their lives has left them open to the charge that in a time of fiscal austerity, they have benefited at the expense of other deserving groups. The group most often mentioned as losing out in the zero-sum game of the federal government's welfare allocations is composed of children. Thus, there is controversy concerning the scope of governmental programs that benefit family dependents at both the beginning and ending of life.

Government figures indicate that the lot of the elderly as a whole has improved considerably in the last two decades. After taking into account the effects of inflation, Congressional Budget Office figures show that the average cash income of families with members over 65 years of age rose by almost 18% from 1969 to 1984. For unrelated elderly individuals, the rise was even greater—34%. With adjustment for the smaller numbers in older families, the ratio of the before-taxes family income per capita of the elderly compared to the nonelderly was 0.99 in 1984 as compared with 0.87 in 1969 (Gordon, 1986: 12, Table 1). At the same time, the poverty rates among the elderly were reduced by more than half, from 25% in 1969 to 12.2% in 1987 (Gilford, 1988; U.S. Bureau of the Census, 1989). Much of the greater general affluence among the elderly stems from government programs instituted in the 1960s and 1970s such as Medicare and cost-of-living adjustments in Old Age and Survivors Insurance payments. Even Medicaid, supposedly directed to the poor of all ages, concentrates its funding on hospital and nursing home care rather than the primary and preventive services that are more often used by mothers and children on AFDC (Chilman, 1988). As a consequence of these policies, the federal government in the 1980s spent as much on old-age benefits as it did on defense. Each area accounted for about 30% of the total budget (Binstock, 1985). If defense expenditures were to fall, the proportion of the budget devoted to old-age benefits would be larger. Most of the funding for old-age programs (84% in 1986) comes from special payroll taxes rather than from general revenues (Clark, Pelham, and Clark, 1988: 196).

Demographic trends are related to the rising cost of old-age benefits. The increase in the elderly from 1950 to 1980 was 108% compared with 62% in the general population. Moreover, the so-called oldest-old, those 85 years and older, who are most likely to need costly medical care and other services, have increased by 281% from 577,000 to 2.2. million in the same period (Gilford, 1988: 52, 53). Such figures gave rise to concern that benefits to the elderly will absorb an ever larger share of the federal budget, and ultimately these expenditures cannot be sustained (Binstock, 1983).

Because of the worsening condition of children and the demographic changes detailed above, the picture painted by advocacy groups that the elderly are "poor, frail, socially dependent, objects of discrimination, and above all deserving" of special treatment in public policy was coming into question as a basis for public policy. Binstock (1985: 429), for one, has argued that need rather than assistance based on age alone should characterize eligibility. The subtle ageism in current programs in which persons categorized on the basis of age are treated alike ignores the diversity among the elderly as well as the fact that the non-aged suffer some of the same problems.

Another difficulty with the current age-based public policies is their dependence on biological and psychological models of aging. These emphasize the individual. Aging is seen as a personal problem that results from physiological decline and is apolitical. Whether the elderly person is in need depends upon her or his lifetime work patterns, with financial rewards determined by impersonal market forces. In contrast, a political economy model locates the problems of aging in economic and political structures that have affected the social placement of persons over their life course and the earnings that determine their pensions. Policy initiatives, according to this perspective, would focus on changing institutions, especially the labor market, rather than on individual adjustment (Estes, Swan, and Gerard, 1984; Walker, 1980).

Analysts have shown the effects of this individualist bias to be particularly marked with respect to those elderly and their families who are most likely to be poor. Poverty is concentrated within the categories of older women and among nonwhites (Clark et al., 1988; Dressel, 1988; Hess, 1986; Zones, Estes, and Binney, 1987). Presently,

many aging females are dependent upon their husbands for financial support. Widowhood for them means a decrease in Social Security benefits and poverty, especially when resources run out because of illnesses. When women and nonwhite men are employed, they tend to be limited by labor market structures to poorly paid jobs. Their disadvantaged location within the economy leads to low pensions and poverty in old age.

These issues of categorical age-based and individualistic public policies and their costs come together in the concern over long-term care programs. Groups other than the elderly are subject to lengthy disabilities and chronic health problems, but with the growth in numbers of the oldest-old, the problem becomes especially salient for the elderly and their families, especially women relatives. With increasing numbers of women in the labor force or becoming aged themselves, the normative expectation that they will care for frail parents can prove stressful to them and to their families (Brody, 1985; Kleban, Brody, Schoonover, and Hoffman, 1989).

National survey data indicated that in the early 1980s, there were twice as many bedfast elderly persons in their homes than in institutions of all types (Shanas, 1982). Both families and the disabled elderly resist institutionalization. Financial considerations do not appear to affect these decisions (Doty, 1986). The failing health of the old person is the major reason for the caregiver to seek nursing home care (Arling and McAuley, 1983). Yet, even with spouses and daughters doing the major share of caregiving (Zimmerman, 1988), 1985 estimates placed the costs of nursing home care at almost one percent of the gross national product, or $35.2 billion. Patients and their families paid for $18.1 billion of this total, with Medicare covering $0.6 billion of the amount and Medicaid, $14.7 billion (Waldo, Levitt, and Lazenby, 1986). There has been support, therefore, for a policy that would provide some financial relief to elderly persons who need long-term care (Crystal, 1982). One major policy question concerns who should bear the increasing costs of long-term care that are due to the growing numbers of elderly people subject to disability (Arling and McAuley, 1983; Doty, 1986; Rivlin and Wiener, 1988).

The Catastrophic Illness Act passed by the Congress in 1988 was an attempt to deal with the problem of lengthy illness among the elderly. Its financing provisions took into account the criticism that the elderly have been receiving a disproportionate amount of federal resources. It also recognized the financial diversity within the group. The program's cost was to be borne entirely by the elderly themselves through a surtax with a limit on its amount, to be paid only by the more affluent, and a monthly premium levied on all Medicare beneficiaries. Yet, only a little over a year later, pressure from the better-off elderly, who were angry over having to pay the tax from which poorer beneficiaries were exempted, and already covered through private plans for the benefits specified in the program, led to congressional repealing of the surtax and the program it was to finance (Tolchin, 1989). Given the growing number of the oldest-old and the political power of the elderly, however, the issue of long-term care will continue to be high on lawmakers' policy agendas.

FAMILY POLICY AS CHILDREN'S POLICY

While the elderly were benefiting from increased governmental attention, children were not faring so well (Palmer, Smeeding, and Torrey, 1988). In 1987, for example, 20.6% of them were living below the poverty level (U.S. Bureau of the Census, 1989). The net impact of federal and state welfare programs was differentiated according to the age of the recipient. In 1981, for example, these programs reduced poverty by 48.4 percentage points among the aged, compared with a reduction of 4.2% among the young (Axinn and Stern, 1985: 665). Two advocates of generation equity put the situation this way: "For the first time in our history, an increasing proportion of American children are growing up in poverty, are graduating from high school less well educated than their parents, are not learning entry-level job skills, and are paying for exploding college tuition fees out of their own pockets" (Hewitt and Howe, 1988: 12).

Paradoxically, at a time when federal and state programs for children have experienced cutbacks, and children have become relatively more dependent on their families for support, changes in family composition are threatening their protection in the home. The family has begun to divest itself of the responsibility for the young, just as it earlier abandoned much of its responsibility for the elderly (Preston, 1984). Two main changes in family formation are responsible. Higher illegitimacy and divorce rates result in diminished financial resources for children from fathers. In 1986, almost one out of every four children in the United States was born to an unmarried mother. This proportion amounted to 61% for blacks and 20% for whites (Bumpass and McLanahan, 1989). The second factor contributing to the large number of one-parent families was continuing high divorce rates and falling rates of remarriage. Consequently, the number of children living with a single parent has increased from about 9% in 1960 to 24% in 1986 (Glick, 1988). Presently, it is estimated that approximately 60% of the nation's children will spend some part of their childhood in single-parent families (Stipek and McCroskey, 1989). These children are more likely to be poor than those in two-parent families. Ellwood has estimated the poverty rate for children in all single-parent families to exceed 50%. Moreover, poverty in single-parent families lasts much longer than it does in two-parent families (Ellwood, 1988: 128).

Yet, as with the causes for the increase in general poverty over the last 20 years, Easterlin (1987) contends that increased poverty among children is due to economic factors and not to governmental programs aiding the elderly at the younger generation's expense. The decline in real family income among two-parent and female-headed families, due to higher unemployment and lower wage rates, is a factor in children's poverty, as is the increasing proportion of them in the more hard-pressed, mother-only households. Becker and Murphy (1988: 9), in a more abstract analysis, present an exchange model of intergenerational relations. Parents take care of children as investments in human capital for society, and when old they receive societal support in exchange for these earlier childrearing services. Therefore, Becker and Murphy see the expenditures for the elderly as part of a social compact between the generations.

Regardless of how policy scholars stand with respect to the fairness of the distribution of public welfare monies to the young and the old, there is agreement that public transfer payments affect all children. For the more advantaged, these transfers take the form of tax reductions for parents. Between 1945 and 1985, inflation eroded the real value of tax exemptions for dependents. This is the amount that parents can exclude from their taxable income for each dependent family member, for federal tax purposes. The failure to index these exemptions for inflation put an increasing share of the tax burden on taxpayers with families. As a consequence, the real costs of having children increased. The 1986 tax reform act, which almost doubled the personal exemption for the taxpayer and each dependent, was an attempt to remedy this situation.

As far as poor children are concerned, AFDC remains the major public assistance program. In March 1988, approximately 3.8 million families received income from AFDC. A high rate of turnover makes it likely that AFDC benefits from 16 to 17 million individuals in approximately 6 million different households over a year's time. Dear (1989: 26) estimates that about 15% of all 34 million families with children receive AFDC over the course of a year.

The rising numbers of single-parent families in the last 30 years has made child support payments from noncustodial parents an important family policy issue. Public concern for "equitable" support and enforcement of payments from the absent parent (Robins and Dickinson, 1985), along with the desire to reduce the costs of welfare, explain the increased attention. Policy-oriented research on child support has covered the issues of equity, effectiveness, and feasibility. As to the first issue, Robins and Dickinson (1984) found that only 46% of their sample of single mothers had a formal child support award. The factors related to these awards included ethnicity and marital status. Whites were more likely to receive such awards, as were divorced mothers, followed by separated mothers, with unwed mothers having the least probability. Timing of the awards was important. The longer the period since the marital dissolution, the less likely they were to be made and to be received. Two conclusions can be made. There are a large number of absent fathers who do not contribute to the support of their children, and much of the problem of welfare dependence and lack of child support rests with the never-married group.

In another study based on data from the Current Population Survey of 1979, Robins and Dickinson (1985) found that child support alone has a fairly limited impact on welfare dependence. Part of the reason for this relatively small effectiveness in reducing welfare costs was the low level of child support. However, although enforced payments are not reducing welfare dependence to any great extent, they do generate an overall increase in the economic well-being of single-parent families (Garfinkel and McClanahan, 1986; Robins and Dickinson, 1985).

The third issue of the feasibility of child support payments has been addressed by Garfinkel and Oellerich (1989: 231). They assessed the noncustodial father's ability to pay child support. Their conclusion was that the noncustodial fathers could pay "about two and one-half times their current legal obligations and more than three times what they actually are paying." Mandated withholding of child support from noncustodial parents' wages was part of the 1988 Family Support Act discussed above. The provision was a response to the long-term public concern, fueled by such findings, that absent parents be financially responsible for their offspring.

In the latter part of the 1980s, family policy scholars Edelman (1987) and Ellwood (1988) stressed that, regardless of public and private transfers, at bottom, the basic means for supporting families lies in their wages from jobs. However, wages have declined in real value in the last decade. Between 1973 and 1985, weekly wages (adjusted for inflation) declined by 14.5% and hourly wages declined by 10.1%. In 1985, nearly one in three full-time jobs could not keep a family of four above the poverty line (Stipek and Mc-Croskey, 1989: 416). As a result, poverty occurs among the working poor. The passage of legislation by Congress in 1989 to raise the minimum wage in two stages was an attempt to make more income available to disadvantaged families who work at low wages. Because the increase did not keep up with the rate of inflation since 1981 when the minimum wage was last raised, it will have only minimal effect on improving the lot of the poor (Rosenbaum, 1989).

Child Care and Parental Leave Policies

The responsibility for the care of young children historically has belonged to the family. However, as nations have industrialized and urbanized, some form of extrafamilial child care has emerged (Bridgeland, Smith, and Duane, 1985: 35). The crucial indicator of need for child-care facilities is the number of working mothers. In 1986, more than 70% of mothers with school-age children and more than 55% of mothers of children under six were in the work force (Stipek and Mc-Croskey, 1989). By 1995, these figures were projected to rise to 77% and 65%, respectively (Hofferth and Phillips, 1987: 560, Table 1). The growing number of households that are dependent on the wages of mothers presents women with the alternative of having some place to leave young children or having to turn to some form of welfare. Child care represents the single largest work-related expense among working mothers (Wodarski, Parham, Lindsey, and Blackburn, 1986: 276).

Direct governmental funding for day care centers remains, despite cuts in the early 1980s. By 1986, in real dollar terms, such grants were only three-quarters of what they had been in the 1970s. The majority of the states, as well as the federal government, spent less on child care in 1985 than in 1981, despite the growing number of mothers in the paid labor force. The major federal support for day care consists of the dependent-care tax credit, estimated to cost 4 billion dollars in 1988, which allows a family to deduct a portion of their annual child care expenses from their federal income tax. This tax credit benefits middle- and upper-class families but not poor families, who do not earn enough to take advantage of it. Less than half of all working mother pay enough taxes to claim the deduction (Becharov and Tramontozzi, 1989).

In addition to differences in government aid, class differences also appear in the kind of care mothers can afford. Middle-class women are able to choose higher-quality facilities that emphasize child development and learning opportunities. In contrast, the less well off have had to be content with child care alone, whether provided by relatives or unlicensed family home care or child care centers. One federal program directed to poor children and designed to combine day care with school readiness preparation, along with nutritious meals and medical and dental services, is Head Start. It has proven to be a popular policy with legislators and the public. Research has shown that poor and minority children in model programs did better in school and were less likely when adolescents to become delinquents or become pregnant (Scarr and Weinberg, 1986; Washington and Oyemade, 1987). Because of lack of funding, at the end of the 1980s Head Start served some 450,000 low-income three- and four-year-olds, less than a fifth of the estimated 2.5 million who were potentially eligible ("Partisan bidding war," 1989), and most of the programs did not provide all-day care, a necessity for working mothers (Chilman, 1988: 216).

Despite occasional articles in the popular press describing corporate day care programs, there is little evidence that employers will fill the gap between what is available and what is needed in the way of care for children of working parents. In 1987, only about 2% of establishments with 10 or more employees provided day care facilities. An additional 3% of these companies gave some assistance with child-care expenses (Hayghe, 1988: 41, Table 2).

Government legislation in the area was hampered by disagreements over women's roles. One such issue concerned whether families where the mother stays home full-time should subsidize through their taxes the child care of employed mothers (Bane and Jargowsky, 1989). However, by 1988, confronted by the increasing numbers of mothers in the labor force, both political parties were committed to doing more about child care. By early 1990, both houses of Congress had passed such bills. The legislation expanded earned income tax credits. Dependent-care tax credits were made refundable to working families with incomes too low to pay taxes. There were increased funds for Head Start, and higher-quality child-care standards were set (Holmes, 1990a; Rovner, 1989). Such provisions could ease some of the child-care problems the working poor face, whether covered by the Family Support Act or on their own. However, the bill faced the threat of a presidential veto.

In addition to passing child-care legislation, lawmakers have been showing more interest in maternity or family leave benefits and for the same reason—the increasing number of employed mothers. The increasing number of elderly who require care has added this group at the other extreme of the age range to the dependents benefiting from these policies. By 1990, 26 states and Puerto Rico required leaves extending from four weeks to six months. With the exception of 7 states, the leaves covered newborns but not other family members, such as the ailing elderly. Much of the legislation was gender neutral as to the persons eligible for leave. However, state measures varied in the number of weeks and the size and type of establishment specified. In 7 states, only state agencies were covered (Rector, 1989). More important, the state and proposed federal measures called for unpaid leaves. The opposition of business lobbies such as the Chamber of Commerce and the National Federation of Independent Businesses to a new employee benefit accounts for the restricted coverage and the "unpaid" limitation (Wisensale and Allison, 1989). Because the leaves are unpaid, low-income working women cannot afford to take them. Because their wages are so essential to the physical well-being of their families, even brief work respites are impossible. In 1990, President Bush vetoed a congressional bill that would have required employers of 50 or more workers to grant them 12 weeks of unpaid parental leave. He argued that it constituted unwarranted governmental interference in business. In his view, corporations should be left to institute such policies voluntarily (Holmes, 1990b). As we have seen, this outcome is unlikely.

SOCIAL SCIENTISTS AND FAMILY POLICY

One of the interesting features in the development of family policy over the decade is the part social scientists are playing. This includes evaluation of the achievements of particular policy initiatives, a consideration of the legislative process out of which policy is made, and a shaping of issues that become a matter of public concern. As a consequence of these activities, social scientists have been in a position to debunk popular beliefs such as the supposed relation between welfare and the growing numbers of single mothers.

Their evaluation role is consistent with the increasing trend in federal government circles to provide funding that permits states and local areas to experiment with various types of programs to attain federal goals. State initiatives are serving as laboratories to try out different programs in such areas as job-skills upgrading—Massachusetts and California—and child support payments from absent parents—Wisconsin (Garfinkel and McClanahan, 1986; Osborne, 1988). By evaluating the effectiveness of these state initiatives, social scientists indicate what elements other states might well want to copy. Results of the evaluations of job-training programs support the wisdom of this flexible approach, which is incorporated in the 1988 Family Support Act. Diverse programs in San Diego, Arkansas, and Maryland show no one successful approach that should be

inaugurated on a national basis (Gueron, 1986), although women and the poor appear to have benefited most from the early employment and training programs. There is a danger of overselling the results of job training. Gains in employment and earnings attributable to them are "fairly modest," but so are the funds appropriated for the programs. Moreover, the difficulties inherent in preparing the entrenched poor to hold jobs make these relatively minor successes noteworthy (Bassi and Ashenfelter, 1986: 149; Gueron, 1987).

The evaluation role was highlighted by social experiments carried out in the late 1960s and early 1970s to determine the effect on labor force activity of the so-called negative income tax, a guaranteed income payment for the poor to be decreased in amount as earnings in the families increased. A recent reassessment of the experiments indicated the lessons they held for present family policy (Munnell, 1987). One was the value of the experimental design procedure whereby individuals are randomly assigned to treatment and to control groups, an approach found in studies evaluating the effectiveness of policies. When used to evaluate the job-training portions of the 1988 Family Support Act, this procedure helps to avoid biased results of test programs by discouraging the selection of persons most likely to succeed in the programs. Random assignment of family heads to treatment and control groups in different areas also gives policy makers some idea of the effects of various strategies of job training and other programs for getting families out of poverty.

Research on policy process has moved forward along several lines, including a consideration of the factors associated with the passage of legislation, as well as the process whereby issues become defined as policy and receive legislative attention. One such study compared the 4 states where family leave legislation passed in 1987 with the 24 where it was introduced and did not succeed. It covered the provisions of the bills and the state politics as they affected the votes in the legislatures (Wisensale and Allison, 1988). Not surprisingly, one of its findings was that family policies to be enacted into law must attract the support of the party in power while appealing to broad intergenerational constituencies.

Research on the legislative process shows the difficulties involved in building such coalitions. Torres-Gil and Pynoos (1986) investigated the struggles of groups representing the elderly and the disabled in the passage of long-term care bills and their implementation in California. They conclude that establishing new coalitions to reduce interest-group competition for scarce resources and targeting the needy rather than specific age categories may not be realistic, or at best, harder to achieve than people expect. In another sobering conclusion for family policy practitioners, the investigators point out that the legislative process did not take advantage of the experience of other states. It turned into a trial-and-error procedure favoring the lobbying groups of the elderly, who were widely known among legislators and their staff people.

The discrepancy between a rational model of family policy development and the actual legislative process also stands out in contrasting articles, one from a social work journal, *Social Service Review* (Pine, 1986), and the other from one of the more thoughtful popular magazines, the *Atlantic Monthly* (Lemann, 1988, 1989). The first article deals with the evolution and eventual passage in 1980 of a federal law affecting state child welfare services in foster care and adoption. It is organized around key phases in the policy process, beginning with defining the problem, then publicizing it, placing it on the political calendar, creating a piece of legislation, and examining changes initiated in the bill. In contrast to this rational process of policy creation, the *Atlantic* piece presents a blow-by-blow account of the haphazard, unsystematic, contentious, and subjective way in which the War on Poverty in the Johnson Administration was fashioned. Controversy concerning the Great Society programs dogged the programs from the beginning. Although academicians were called upon for ideas, their implementation and the eventual fate of the policies were largely determined by how well they fit in with existing local political structures.

Besides commenting on the policy process and its outcomes, researchers bring up issues that may foster or discourage policy development; supply rationales used to support proposals; and provide a policy framework for bills. Interviews with congressional staff persons and academics whose research has affected policy indicate the value of this supporting function of policy researchers (Aldous, 1987). If their research is used as a rationale for a particular policy, their input as experts rather than as advocates gives them credibility and lessens misinterpretations of their research findings. But they are dependent upon the willingness of legislators, administrators, and their staffs to draw upon their policy-related work (Munnell, 1987). As we have seen, legislators can overlook not only relevant research in their policy deliberations but also the experience from salient programs that are already in place and functioning elsewhere.

FAMILY POLICY IN FUTURE PERSPECTIVE

The 1980s may well be remembered as a profligate period in which citizens and the federal government alike lived beyond their means, supported by large infusions of foreign capital. Personal savings were down and the government's deficit up (Aldous, 1989). Consequently, there was little money available to handle the nagging problems arising from the ongoing changes in families. Astounding shifts in the international scene in 1989, however, appeared to present the opportunity for a reassessment of national priorities, with a possible expansion of programs to ameliorate the condition of society's weaker members.

If this should prove to be the case, there will be mounting pressure to do more for families with children. There is a ferment in policy initiatives, and their outcomes are recent enough to be reflected more in the popular press than in scholarly publications. Legislation providing additional funding for child care, particularly facilities serving low-income and working-class families, has been passed by Congress. Although rational decision making does not generally characterize the legislative process, subsidizing child care represents an attractive and logical means for attaining the goals that underlie the attempts to get families off welfare. If the poor are to become more self-reliant, the sizable proportion of disadvantaged mothers must have some place to leave their children if they are to join the labor force. At the same time, society at large has a stake in ensuring its future by seeing that its youngest citizens are in relatively benign settings while their mothers are out earning their keep.

If the current crisis in the Middle East does not become a financial quagmire for the U.S., the availability of somewhat more funding for quality-of-life purposes may ease the competition for scarce monies between families of the aged and the young. The record, whether at home or abroad, does not suggest that the interests of the elderly will be overlooked (Palmer et al., 1988). However, the alarming state of the nation's children has not received as much attention. A more favorable fiscal situation may provide their advocates with a larger audience.

One thing that has become clear in the 1980s is that looking to European countries, particularly the Scandinavian nations, for measures to borrow for our own family programs is a flawed strategy. These societies, with their smaller, less diverse populations, face fewer conflicting values concerning policy goals. Moreover, they have a longer history of implementing welfare programs on a national scale. For many of the participant countries, the aftermath of World War II brought Christian-Democratic, Socialist, or Labor party politicians to power who instituted sweeping family services from birth to death. In contrast, the United States entered a period of economic boom in the 1950s that rendered peripheral our collective concerns about family problems. As a consequence, the major components of U.S. policy remain programs such as AFDC and Social Security that were initiated as part of Franklin Roosevelt's New Deal in the 1930s.

Federal money and greater public awareness of family poverty will not address the basic threat to sound family policy—its emotional nature. In attempting to deal with the consequences of family change, policy makers become embroiled in morality issues. Highly vocal pressure groups, usually billing themselves as pro-family, are apt to urge a return to a time that never was, when all mothers stayed home to care for their children, secure in the knowledge that husbands would support them. Under these fanciful conditions, welfare provisions for employed mothers and subsidized child care for their offspring would not be needed. These traditionalists are unwilling to accept a world in which divorced families, families with unwed mothers, and families with women in the labor force exist in overwhelming numbers. Their simplistic solution to this situation is to do as little as possible to assist these families. Presumably, neglect would cause people to desist from the behaviors that lead to their need for assistance. As long as this group continues its noisy nay-saying, policy students as well as lawmakers will find their attempts to create programs for U.S. families as they now exist a source

of controversy.

But the political decision makers of the 1990s will have the advantage of the experience of the past decade, which demonstrated that cutting back on services for hard-pressed families, coupled with rigid ideological stands and a prejudice against government action, have not made their problems go away. Although few proven solutions have issued from the policy community, there is some consensus as to the broad outlines of what is needed. Observers in the next century will be able to pass judgment on how correct those diagnoses were.

NOTE

The authors thank Catherine Chilman, who was particularly generous in her suggestions on an earlier version of this article. It could not have been completed without the transcribing skills of Linda Williams and the bibliographic searches of Volker Frank and Cindy Wise.

REFERENCES

Adler, Nancy E., and Peggy Dolcine. 1986. "Psychological issues in abortion for adolescents." Pp. 74–96 in Gary B. Melton (ed.), Adolescent Abortion: Psychological and Legal Issues. Lincoln: University of Nebraska Press.

Aldous, Joan. 1986. "Cuts in selected welfare programs: The effects on U.S. families." Journal of Family Issues 7: 161–177.

Aldous, Joan. 1987. "Family sociologists and policy-making: A supporting role perspective." American Sociologist 18: 134–140.

Aldous, Joan. 1989. "If inflation returns: Hard lessons from the past." In Ray Rist (ed.), Policy Issues for the 1990's. Policy Studios Review Annual 9. New Brunswick, NJ: Transaction Books.

Aldous, Joan, and Wilfried Dumon with Katrina Johnson (eds.). 1980. The Politics and Programs of Family Policy: United States and European Perspectives. Notre Dame, IN: University of Notre Dame and Leuven University Press.

Arling, Greg, and William J. McAuley. 1983. "The feasibility of public payments for family caregiving." Gerontologist 23: 300–306.

Axinn, June, and Mark J. Stern. 1985. "Age and dependency: Children and the aged in American social policy." Milbank Memorial Fund Quarterly: Health and Society 63: 648–671.

Bane, Mary Jo. 1980. "Toward a description and evaluation of United States family policy." Pp. 155–191 in Joan Aldous and Wilfried Dumon with Katrina Johnson (eds.), The Politics and Programs of Family Policy. Notre Dame, IN: University of Notre Dame and Leuven University Press.

Bane, Mary Jo and Paula Jargowsky. 1989. "The links between government policy and family structure: What matters and what doesn't." Pp. 219–262 in Andrew J. Cherlin (ed.), The Changing American Family and Public Policy. Washington, DC: Urban Institute Press.

Bassi, Laura J., and Orley Ashenfelter. 1986. "The effect of direct job creation and training programs on low-skilled workers." Pp. 133–152 in Sheldon Danziger and Daniel H. Weinberg (eds.), Fighting Poverty: What Works and What Doesn't. Cambridge, MA: Harvard University Press.

Becharov, Douglas J., and Paul N. Tramontozzi. 1989. "Federal child care assistance: A growing middle-class entitlement." Journal of Policy Analysis and Management 8: 313–318.

Becker, Gary S., and Kevin M. Murphy. 1988. "The family and the state." Journal of Law and Economics 31: 1–18.

Bernardes, Jon. 1987. "Doing things with words: Sociology and family policy debates." Sociological Review 35: 679–702.

Binstock, Robert H. 1983. "The aged as scapegoat." Gerontologist 23: 136–143.

Binstock, Robert H. 1985. "The oldest old: A fresh perspective or compassionate ageism revisited?" Milbank Memorial Fund Quarterly: Health and Society 63: 420–451.

Bridgeland, William M., Philip R. Smith, and Edward A. Duane. 1985. "Child-care policy arenas: A comparison between Sweden and the United States." International Journal of Comparative Sociology 26: 35–44.

Brody, Elaine M. 1985. "Parent care as a normative family stress." Gerontologist 25: 19–29.

Bumpass, Larry, and Sara McLanahan. 1989. "Unmarried motherhood: Recent trends, composition, and black-white differences." Demography 26: 279–286.

Cherlin, Andrew J. 1983. "Family policy: The conservative challenge and the progressive response." Journal of Family Issues 4: 427–439.

Cherlin, Andrew J. 1988. "The changing American family and public policy." Pp. 1–31 in Andrew J. Cherlin (ed.), The Changing American Family and Public Policy. Washington, DC: Urban Institute Press.

Chilman, Catherine S. 1988. "Public policies and families in financial trouble." Pp. 183–237 in Catherine S. Chilman, Fred M. Cox, and Elam W. Nunnally (eds.), Employment and Economic Problems. Newbury Park, CA: Sage.

Clark, William F., Anabel O. Pelham, and Marleen L. Clark. 1988. Old and Poor: A Critical Assessment of the Low-Income Elderly. Lexington, MA: Lexington Books.

Crystal, Stephen. 1982. America's Old Age Crisis: Public Policy and the Two Worlds of Aging. New York: Basic Books.

Danielson, Ross, Kevin McNally, Janice Swanson, Anne Pleinkett, and Walter Klausmeier. 1988. "Title X and family planning services for men." Family Planning Perspectives 20: 234–237.

Danziger, Sheldon, and Robert D. Plotnick. 1986. "Poverty and policy: Lessons of the last two decades." Social Service Review 60: 34–51.

Dear, Ronald B. 1989. "What's right with welfare?" Journal of Sociology and Social Welfare 16: 5–43.

Dolbeare, Kenneth M., and Russell M. Lidman. 1985. "Ideology and policy research: The case of Murray's Losing Ground." Policy Studies Review 4: 587–594.

Doty, Pamela. 1986. "Family care of the elderly: The role of public policy." Milbank Memorial Fund Quarterly: Health and Society 64: 34–76.

Dressel, Paula L. 1988. "Gender, race, and class: Beyond the feminization of poverty in later life." Gerontologist 28: 177–180.

Easterlin, Richard A. 1987. "The new age structure of poverty in America: Permanent or transient?" Population and Development Review 13: 195–208.

Edelman, Marion Wright. 1987. Families in Peril: An Agenda for Social Change. Cambridge, MA: Harvard University Press.

Ellwood, David T. 1988. Poor Support: Poverty in the American Family. New York: Basic Books.

Ellwood, David T., and Lawrence H. Summers. 1986. "Is welfare really the problem?" Public Interest 83: 57–79.

Estes, Carroll L., James H. Swan, and Lenore E. Gerard. 1984. "Dominant and competing paradigms in gerontology: Towards a political economy of aging." Pp. 25–36 in Meredith Minkler and Carroll L. Estes (eds.), Readings in the Political Economy of Aging. Farmingdale, NY: Baywood.

"The Family Support Act of 1988." 1988–1989. Focus 11: 15–18.

Freeman, Howard E. 1988. "Dwarf steps for the poor." Contemporary Sociology 17: 805–808.

Garfinkel, Irwin, and Sara S. McLanahan. 1986. Single Mothers and Their Children: A New American Dilemma. Washington, DC: Urban Institute Press.

Garfinkel, Irwin, and Donald Oellerich. 1989. "Noncustodial fathers' ability to pay child support." Demography 26: 219–233.

Gilford, Dorothy M. (ed.). 1988. The Aging Population in the 21st Century: Statistics for Health Policy. Washington, DC: National Academy Press.

Glick, Paul C. 1988. "Fifty years of family demography: A record of social change." Journal of Marriage and the Family 49: 559–571.

Goettsch, Stephen L. 1986. "The New Christian Right and the social sciences: A response to McNamara." Journal of Marriage and the Family 48: 447–453.

Gold, Rachel B., and Sandra Guardado. 1988. "Public funding of family planning, sterilization, and abortion services, 1987." Family Planning Perspectives 20: 228–233.

Gordon, Nancy M. 1986. Statement: Health Care for the Elderly. Wednesday, March 26, 1986, House of Representatives, Committee on Energy and Commerce, Subcommittee on Health and the Environment. U.S. House of Representatives, 99th Congress, 2nd Session. Serial 99-139.

Greenhouse, Linda. 1989. "Abortion: A new round." New York Times, November 24, pp. A1, 11, and 24.

Greenhouse, Linda. 1990. "States may require girl to

notify parents before having abortion." New York Times, June 26, p. A1.

Gueron, Judith. 1986. Work Initiatives for Welfare Recipients: Lessons from a Multi-state Experiment. New York: Manpower Demonstration Research Corporation.

Gueron, Judith. 1987. Reforming Welfare with Work. New York: Ford Foundation.

Hadden, Jeffrey K. 1983. "Televangelism and the mobilization of a New Christian Right family policy." Pp. 247–266 in William D'Antonio and Joan Aldous (eds.), Families and Religions: Conflict and Change in Modern Society. Beverly Hills, CA: Sage.

Hayghe, Howard. 1988. "Employers and child care: What roles do they play?" Monthly Labor Review 111: 38–44.

Hess, Beth B. 1986. "Antidiscrimination policies today and the life changes of older women tomorrow." Gerontologist 26: 132–135.

Hevesi, Dennis. 1989. "How debates over abortion evolved with changing science and society." New York Times, July 4, p. 11.

Hewitt, Paul S., and Neil Howe. 1988. Generational equity and the future of generational politics." Generations Public Policy 7: 10–14.

Hinds, Michael de Courcy. 1990. "Pulling families out of welfare is proving to be an elusive goal." New York Times, April 2, pp. A1, A9.

Hofferth, Sandra L., and Deborah A. Phillips. 1987. "Child care in the United States: 1970 to 1995." Journal of Marriage and the Family 49: 559–571.

Holmes, Steven A. 1990a. "Bush vetoes a bill to give workers family leave." New York Times, June 30, p. A9.

Holmes, Steven A. 1990b. "House, 265–145, votes to widen day care programs in the nation." New York Times, March 30, pp. A1, A14.

Joe, Tom, and Cheryl Rogers. 1985. By the Few for the Few: The Reagan Welfare Legacy. Lexington, MA: Lexington Books.

Kleban, Morton H., Elaine M. Brody, Claire B. Schoonover, and Christine Hoffman. 1989. "Family help to the elderly: Perceptions of sons-in-law regarding parent care." Journal of Marriage and the Family 51: 303–313.

Lemann, Nicholas. 1988. "The unfinished war, I." Atlantic Monthly 262: 37–56.

Lemann, Nicholas. 1989. "The unfinished war, II." Atlantic Monthly 263: 53–68.

Lynn, Laurence E., Jr. 1980. "Fiscal and organizational constraints on United States family policy." Pp. 199–231 in Joan Aldous and Wilfried Dumon with Katrina Johnson (eds.), The Politics and Programs of Family Policy. Notre Dame, IN: University of Notre Dame and Leuven University Press.

McNamara, Patrick H. 1985. "The New Christian Right's view of the family and its social science critics: A study in differing presuppositions." Journal of Marriage and the Family 47: 449–458.

Melton, Gary B., and Anita J. Pliner. 1986. "Adolescent abortion: A psycholegal analysis." Pp. 1–39 in Gary B. Melton (ed.), Adolescent Abortion: Psy-

chological and Legal Issues. Lincoln: University of Nebraska Press.

Moen, Phyllis, and Alvin L. Schorr. 1987. "Families and social policy." Pp. 795–813 in Marvin B. Sussman and Suzanne K. Steinmetz (eds.), Handbook of Marriage and the Family. New York: Plenum Press.

Mohr, James C. 1978. Abortion in America: The Origins and Evolution of National Policy, 1800–1900. New York: Oxford University Press.

"More on Koop's study of abortion." 1990. Family Planning Perspectives 22: 36–40.

Moscovice, Ira, William Craig, and Laura Pitt. 1987. "Meeting the basic needs of the working poor." Social Service Review 61: 420–431.

Moynihan, Daniel P. 1986. Family and Nation. San Diego: Harcourt Brace Jovanovich.

Munnell, Alicia H. 1987. "Lessons from the income maintenance experiments: An overview." Pp. 1–21 in Alicia H. Munnell (ed.), Lessons from the Income Maintenance Experiments. Boston: Federal Reserve Bank.

Murray, Charles. 1984. Losing Ground: American Social Policy, 1950–1980. New York: Basic Books.

Novak, Michael et al. 1987. The New Consensus on Family and Welfare: A Community of Self-Reliance. Washington, DC: American Enterprise Institute for Public Policy.

Osborne, David. 1988. Laboratories of Democracy. Boston: Harvard Business School Press.

Palmer, John L., Timothy Smeeding, and Barbara Boyle Torrey. 1988. The Vulnerable. Washington, DC: Urban Institute Press.

Pankhurst, Jerry G., and Sharon Houseknecht. 1983. "The family, politics, and religion in the 1980s: In fear of the new individualism." Journal of Family Issues 4: 5–34.

"Partisan bidding war erupts over aid to poor children." 1989. Congressional Quarterly Weekly Report 47 (March 25): 653.

Pine, Barbara A. 1986. "Child welfare reform and the political process." Social Service Review 60: 338–359.

"Poor LA women prefer private family planning providers over subsidized clinics." 1989. Family Planning Perspectives 21: 228–233.

Preston, Samuel H. 1984. "Children and the elderly: Divergent paths for America's dependents." Demography 21: 435–457.

Rector, Robert. 1989. "Fourteen myths about families and child care." Harvard Journal on Legislation 26: 517–547.

Reischauer, Robert D. 1989. "The welfare reform legislation: Directions for the future." Pp. 10–41 in Phoebe H. Cottingham and David T. Ellwood (eds.), Welfare Policy for the 1990's. Cambridge, MA: Harvard University Press.

Rivlin, Alice, and Joshua M. Wiener. 1988. Caring for the Disabled Elderly: Who Will Pay? Washington, DC: Brookings Institution.

Robins, Philip K., and Katherine P. Dickinson. 1984. "Receipt of child support by single-parent families." Social Service Review 58: 622–641.

Robins, Philip K., and Katherine P. Dickinson. 1985. "Child support and welfare dependence: A multinominal logit analysis." Demography 22: 367–380.

Rosenbaum, David E. 1989. "Bush and Congress reach accord on raising wage to $4.25." New York Times, November 1, pp. A1, A22.

Rosoff, Jeannie I. 1989. "The Webster Decision: A giant step backwards." Family Planning Perspectives 21: 148–149.

Rovner, Julie. 1989. "Senate approves tax credits, subsidies for child care." Congressional Quarterly Weekly Report 47 (July 8): 1725–1730.

Scarr, Sandra, and Richard A. Weinberg. 1986. "The early childhood enterprise: Care and education of the young." American Psychologist 41: 1140–1146.

Schwartz, John E. 1983. America's Hidden Success: A Reassessment of 20 Years of Public Policy. New York: Norton.

Shanas, Ethel. 1982. National Survey of the Aged. DHHS Pub. No. (OHDS) 83-2045. Washington, DC: U.S. Department of Health and Human Services.

Steiner, Gilbert Y. 1980. "Looking for family policy—big tickets or moral judgments: A comment on papers by Mary Jo Bane and Laurence E. Lynn, Jr." Pp. 231–239 in Joan Aldous and Wilfried Dumon with Katrina Johnson (eds.), The Politics and Programs of Family Policy. Notre Dame, IN: University of Notre Dame and Leuven University Press.

Stipek, Deborah, and Jacquelyn McCroskey. 1989. "Investing in children: Government and workplace policies for parents." American Psychologist 44: 416–423.

Tolchin, Martin. 1989. "How the new Medicare law fell on hard times in a hurry." New York Times, October 9, p. 1.

Torres-Gil, Fernando, and Jon Pynoos. 1986. "Long-term care policy and interest group struggles." Gerontologist 26: 488–495.

U.S. Bureau of the Census. 1989. Poverty in the United States: 1987. Current Population Reports, Series P-60, No. 163. Washington, DC: Government Printing Office.

Waldo, D. R., K. R. Levitt, and H. Lazenby. 1986. "National health expenditures, 1985." Health Care Financing Review 8: 1–28.

Walker, Alan. 1980. "The social creation of poverty and dependency in old age." Journal of Social Policy 9: 49–75.

Wallach, H. C. (ed.). 1981. Approaches to Child and Family Policy. Boulder, CO: Westview Press.

Washington, Valora, and Ura Jean Oyemade. 1987. Project Head Start: Past, Present, and Future Trends in the Context of Family Needs. New York: Garland Publishing.

Wisensale, Steven K., and Michael D. Allison. 1988. "An analysis of 1987 state family leave legislation: Implications for caregivers of the elderly." Gerontologist 28: 779–785.

Wisensale, Steven K., and Michael D. Allison. 1989. "Family leave legislation: State and federal initiatives." Family Relations 33: 182–190.

Wodarski, John S., T. M. Jim Parham, Elizabeth W. Lindsey, and Barry W. Blackburn. 1986. "Reagan's AFDC policy changes: The Georgia experience." Social Work 31: 273–279.

Zigler, Edward, Sharon L. Kagan, and Edgar Klugman (eds.). 1983. Children, Families, and Government: A Perspective on American Social Policy. Cambridge, MA: Cambridge University Press.

Zimmerman, Shirley L. 1988. Understanding Family Policy: Theoretical Approaches. Newbury Park, CA: Sage.

Zimmerman, Shirley L. 1989. Comparing the family policies of three states: A content analysis." Family Relations 38: 190–195.

Zones, Jane Sprague, Carroll L. Estes, and Elizabeth A. Binney. 1987. "Gender, public policy, and the oldest-old." Aging and Society 7: 275–302.